LAROUSSE

MINI DIZIONARIO

ITALIANO
INGLESE

INGLESE
ITALIANO

For this edition / Per la presente edizione

Marc Chabrier Delia Prosperi
Francesca Logi Pat Bulhosen

For the first edition / Per la prima edizione

Francesca Logi Peter Blanchard
Rita Gava Wendy Lee Delia Prosperi Leslie Ray
Callum Brines Carmela Celino

ISBN 2-03-540361-8
Larousse/VUEF, Paris
Diffusion/Sales : Houghton Mifflin Company, Boston.
Library of Congress CIP Data
has been applied for

ISBN 88-525-0021-9
Rcs Libri Spa, Via Mecenate 91, 20138 Milano

LAROUSSE

MINI DICTIONARY

ITALIAN ENGLISH

ENGLISH ITALIAN

Notizie Culturali e Pratiche

Agriturismo
Aperitivo
Befana
Biennale
Caffè
Campidoglio
Carnevale
Carta d'identità
Cinecittà
Il Colosseo
Costituzione
Elezioni
Ferragosto
Festa delle donne
Festival di Spoleto
I laghi
La Liberazione
Il Mercato
Mezzogiorno
Montecitorio
Mostra del Cinema di Venezia
Onomastico
Palazzo Madama
Il Palio di Siena
Pane
Parchi nazionali
Pasquetta
Passeggiata
Pasta
Pompei
Il Ponte Vecchio
Quirinale
Quotidiani
Regione
La Riviera Adriatica
Sagra
San Marino
Santo
La Scala
La Schedina
Spumante
Stabilimenti balneari
Televisione
Terme
La Torre di Pisa
Trattoria
Vaticano
Vigile Urbano
Viminale
Vino

Cultural Notes

Bed & Breakfast
Beer
Best Man
Broadsheet/ Broadside
Buckingham Palace
Cajun
Devolution
Downing Street
Education System
Election
Fish & Chips
Fourth of July
Garage Sale
Graduate School
Great Britain
Green Card
Greyhound Bus
Guy Fawkes Night
Halloween
Houses of Parliament
Ivy League
Mall
Manhattan
Medicaid/Medicare
Mount Rushmore
National Park
Native American
Open University
Pantomime
Pub
Scouts
Silicon Valley
Stars & Stripes
Statue of Liberty
Super Bowl
Tabloid
Thanksgiving
Tipping
Tower Bridge
Tower of London
VAT
Wall Street
Westminster
Westminster Abbey
The White House
World Series
Yankee
Yellow Lines

This MINI dictionnary was developed to meet the needs of both the traveller and the beginner.

With over 30,000 words and phrases and 40,000 translations, this dictionary provides not only general vocabulary but also the language used in everyday life.

Clear sense markers are provided to guide the reader to the correct translation, while special emphasis has been placed on many basic words, with helpful examples of usage and a particularly user-friendly layout.

Cultural notes and practical information can be found throughout which allow an interesting insight into life in another country.

We hope you enjoy using this dictionary, and don't hesitate to send us your comments.

The editor

Il dizionario MINI è stato realizzato per rispondere alle esigenze di chi viaggia o comincia a studiare l'inglese.

Con più di 30 000 parole ed espressioni e oltre 40 000 traduzioni, questo dizionario comprende non solo la terminologia di base, ma anche le espressioni della lingua quotidiana.

Le divisioni semantiche sono accuratamente indicate e la consultazione delle voci complesse è facilitata dai numerosi esempi e dalla presentazione chiara ed efficace.

Potrete inoltre scoprire numerose informazioni di tipo culturale e pratico, che vi daranno un'idea degli aspetti tipici di un altro paese.

Completo e allo stesso tempo praticissimo, questo dizionario si rivelerà un indispensabile compagno di studio e di viaggio. Contiamo sul vostro apprezzamento, e vi preghiamo di inviarci i vostri suggerimenti.

L'editore

Abbreviations		**Abbreviazioni**
abbreviation	*abbr*	abbreviazione
adjective	*adj*	aggettivo
adverb	*adv*	avverbio
adjective	*agg*	aggettivo
American English	*Am*	inglese americano
anatomy	*ANAT*	anatomia
article	*art*	articolo
auxiliary	*aus*	ausiliare
automobile, cars	*AUT(O)*	automobile
auxiliary	*aux*	ausiliare
adverb	*avv*	avverbio
British English	*Br*	inglese britannico
commerce, business	*COMM*	commercio
comparative	*compar*	comparativo
computers	*COMPUT*	informatica
conjunction	*conj/cong*	congiunzione
continuous	*cont*	forma progressiva
culinary, cooking	*CULIN*	cucina, culinaria
before	*dav*	davanti a
juridical, legal	*DIR*	diritto
exclamation	*excl/esclam*	esclamazione
feminine	*f*	femminile
informal	*fam*	familiare
figurative	*fig*	figurato
finance, financial	*FIN*	finanza
formal	*fml/form*	formale
inseparable	*fus*	non separabile
generally	*gen*	generalmente
geography	*GEOG*	geografia
gerund	*ger*	gerundio
grammar	*GRAMM*	grammatica
informal	*inf*	familiare
computers	*INFORM*	informatica
interrogative	*interr*	interrogativo

invariable	*inv*	invariabile
juridical, legal	*JUR*	diritto
masculine	*m*	maschile
mathematics	*MAT(H)*	matematica
medicine	*MED*	medicina
military	*MIL*	militare
music	*MUS*	musica
noun	*n*	sostantivo
nautical, maritime	*NAUT*	nautica
numeral	*num*	numerale
oneself	*o.s.*	
pejorative	*pej*	spregiativo
plural	*pl*	plurale
politics	*POL*	politica
past participle	*pp*	participio passato
preposition	*prep*	preposizione
pronoun	*pron*	pronome
past tense	*pt*	passato
something	*qc*	qualcosa
somebody	*qn*	qualcuno
registered trademark	®	marchio registrato
religion	*RELIG*	religione
noun	*s*	sostantivo
someone, somebody	*sb*	qualcuno
school	*SCH/SCOL*	scuola
Scottish English	*Scot*	scozzese
separable	*sep*	separabile
singular	*sg*	singolare
subject	*sog*	soggetto
pejorative	*spreg*	spregiativo
something	*sthg*	qualcosa
subject	*subj*	soggetto
superlative	*superl*	superlativo
technology	*TECH/TECNOL*	tecnica, tecnologia
verb	*v, vb*	verbo
intransitive verb	*vi*	verbo intransitivo

impersonal verb	*v impers*	verbo impersonale
vulgar	*volg*	volgare
reflexive verb	*vr*	verbo riflessivo
transitive verb	*vt*	verbo transitivo
vulgar	*vulg*	volgare
cultural equivalent	≃	equivalenza culturale
Notes on life and culture	ⓘ	Notizie culturali e pratiche
Core words	☞	Termini importanti

TRADEMARKS

Words considered to be trademarks have been designated in this dictionary by the symbol ®. However, neither the presence nor the absence of such designation should be regarded as affecting the legal status of any trademark.

MARCHI REGISTRATI

Le parole considerate marchi registrati sono contrassegnate in questo dizionario con il simbolo ®. In ogni caso, né la presenza né l'assenza di tale simbolo implica alcuna valutazione del reale stato giuridico di un marchio.

ENGLISH COMPOUNDS

A compound is a word or expression which has a single meaning but is made up of more than one word, e.g. **point of view, kiss of life, virtual reality** and **West Indies**. It is a feature of this dictionary that English compounds appear in the A–Z list in strict alphabetical order. The compound **blood test** will therefore come after **bloodshot** which itself follows **blood pressure**.

COMPOSTI INGLESI

In inglese si definiscono composti quelle espressioni che, pur essendo formate da più di una parola, costituiscono un'unica unità di significato, come ad es. **point of view, kiss of life, virtual reality** e **West Indies**. In questo dizionario i composti inglesi seguono l'ordine alfabetico generale. Il composto **blood test** figura perciò dopo **bloodshot** che, a sua volta, segue **blood pressure**.

ITALIANO-INGLESE
ITALIAN-ENGLISH

a (ad + *vocale*) *prep* - 1. *(complemento di termine)* to ; **dare qc a qn** to give sthg to sb, to give sb sthg ; **chiedere qc a qn** to ask sb sthg.
- 2. *(stato in luogo)* at ; **abito a Torino** I live in Turin ; **stiamo a casa** let's stay (at) home ; **la piscina è a due chilometri da qui** the swimming pool is two kilometres from here.
- 3. *(moto a luogo)* to ; **andiamo a letto** let's go to bed ; **torno a Roma** I'm going back to Rome ; **mi porti allo stadio?** can you take me to the stadium?
- 4. *(temporale)* at ; **c'è un volo alle 8.30** there's a flight at 8.30 ; **a domani!** see you tomorrow! ; **al mattino** in the morning ; **alla sera** in the evening.
- 5. *(modo, mezzo)* : **alla milanese** in the Milanese style, the Milanese way ; **riscaldamento a gas** gas heating ; **a piedi** on foot ; **vestire alla moda** to dress fashionably ; **scrivere a matita** to write in pencil.
- 6. *(con prezzi)* at ; **comprare qc a metà prezzo** to buy sthg half-price.
- 7. *(per caratteristica)* : **camicia a maniche corte** short-sleeved shirt ; **finestra a doppi vetri** double-glazed window.
- 8. *(per rapporto)* per, a ; **50 chilometri all'ora** 50 kilometres per ○ an hour ; **pagato a ore** paid by the hour.

A *abbr* = **autostrada.**

abbacchio *sm* spring lamb ; ~ **alla romana** *lamb cooked slowly with white wine or vinegar, rosemary, anchovies and garlic.*

abbaglianti *smpl* : **accendere gli** ~ to put one's headlights on full beam *(Br)* ○ high beam *(Am)*.

abbagliare *vt (accecare)* to dazzle.

abbaiare *vi* to bark.

abbandonare *vt (persona, luogo)* to abandon ; *(ricerche)* to abandon, to give up.

abbandono *sm (di persona, luogo)* neglect ; *(rinuncia)* abandonment.

abbassare *vt* to lower ; *(volume, radio, tv)* to turn down. ❑ **abbassarsi** *vr (persona)* to bend down ; *(livello)* to drop ; **abbassarsi a fare qc** to lower o.s. by doing sthg.

abbasso *esclam* : ~ **la scuola!** down with school!

abbastanza *avv (a sufficienza)* enough ; *(piuttosto)* rather, quite ; **averne ~ di** to have had enough of.

abbattere *vt (muro)* to knock down ; *(albero)* to cut down ;

(cavallo) to destroy ; *(aereo)* to shoot down ; *(sconfiggere)* to defeat. ❑ **abbattersi** *vr* to lose heart.
abbattuto, a *agg (depresso)* depressed.
abbazia *sf* abbey.
abbeverare *vt (animali)* to water. ❑ **abbeverarsi** *vr* to drink.
abbia → avere.
abbiente *agg* well-off.
abbigliamento *sm* clothes *(pl)* ; ' ~ donna' 'women's wear' ; ~ sportivo sportswear ; ' ~ uomo' 'menswear'.
abbinare *vt* : ~ qc (a qc) to link sthg (to sthg).
abboccare *vi* to bite.
abboccato, a *agg* sweetish.
abbonamento *sm (a giornale)* subscription ; *(a autobus, teatro)* season ticket ; fare l' ~ (a qc) *(a giornale)* to take out a subscription (to sthg) ; *(a autobus, teatro)* to buy a season ticket (for sthg).
abbonarsi *vr* : ~ (a qc) *(a autobus, teatro)* to buy a season ticket (for sthg) ; *(a giornale)* to subscribe (to sthg).
abbonato, a *sm, f (a giornale)* subscriber ; *(a autobus, teatro)* season ticket holder ; *(a telefono)* subscriber ; *(TV)* licence holder.
abbondante *agg* abundant.
abbondanza *sf* abundance.
abbordabile *agg (prezzo)* reasonable.
abbottonare *vt* to button up. ❑ **abbottonarsi** *vr* : abbottonarsi il cappotto to button up one's coat.
abbottonatura *sf* buttons *(pl)*.
abbozzare *vt (disegno)* to sketch ; ~ un sorriso to smile faintly.
abbozzo *sm* sketch.
abbracciare *vt* to embrace, to hug ; *(fede)* to embrace ; *(professione)* to take up. ❑ **abbracciarsi** *vr* to embrace, to hug one another.
abbraccio *sm* embrace, hug.
abbreviare *vt* to shorten.
abbreviazione *sf* abbreviation.
abbronzante *agg* suntan *(dav s)*. ◆ *sm* suntan cream.
abbronzare *vt* to tan. ❑ **abbronzarsi** *vr* to get a tan.
abbronzato, a *agg* tanned.
abbronzatura *sf* suntan.
abbrustolire *vt (pane)* to toast ; *(caffè)* to roast.
abdicare *vi* to abdicate.
abete *sm* fir tree.
abile *agg (bravo)* capable ; *(mossa, manovra)* skilful ; *(idoneo)* : ~ (a qc) fit (for sthg).
abilità *sf (bravura)* ability ; *(astuzia)* cleverness.
abilmente *avv (con bravura)* skilfully ; *(con astuzia)* cleverly.
abisso *sm* abyss.
abitacolo *sm (di auto)* inside ; *(di aereo)* cockpit, cabin ; *(di camion)* cab.
abitante *smf (di paese)* inhabitant ; *(di casa)* occupant.
abitare *vi* to live. ◆ *vt* to live in ; dove abita? where do you live? ; abito a Roma I live in Rome ; abito in Italia I live in Italy.
abitato, a *agg (casa)* occupied ; *(paese)* inhabited. ◆ *sm* built-up area.

Phonetic Transcription

English vowels

[ɪ] pit, big, rid
[e] pet, tend
[æ] pat, bag, mad
[ʌ] run, cut
[ɒ] pot, log
[ʊ] put, full
[ə] mother, suppose
[i:] bean, weed
[ɑ:] barn, car, laugh
[ɔ:] born, lawn
[u:] loop, loose
[ɜ:] burn, learn, bird

English diphthongs

[e] bay, late, great
[a] buy, light, aisle
[ɔ] boy, foil
[əʊ] no, road, blow
[aʊ] now, shout, town
[ɪə] peer, fierce, idea
[eə] pair, bear, share
[ʊə] poor, sure, tour

Trascrizione Fonetica

Vocali italiane

[a] pane, casa
[e] verde, entrare
[ɛ] letto, pezzo
[i] vino, isola
[o] monte, pozzo
[ɔ] corpo, sciocco
[u] una, cultura

Semi-vowels		Semivocali
you, spaniel	[j]	ieri, viola
wet, why, twin	[w]	fuori, guasto

Consonants		Consonanti
pop, people	[p]	porta, sapore
bottle, bib	[b]	barca, libro
train, tip	[t]	torre, patata
dog, did	[d]	dare,odore
come, kitchen	[k]	cane, chiesa
gag, great	[g]	gara, ghiro
chain, wretched	[tʃ]	cena, ciao
jet, fridge	[dʒ]	gente, gioco

fib, **ph**ysical	[f]	**f**ine, a**f**a
vine, li**v**id	[v]	**v**ero, o**vv**io
think, fif**th**	[θ]	
this, wi**th**	[ð]	
seal, pea**c**e	[s]	**s**tella, ca**s**a
zip, hi**s**	[z]	**s**draio, ro**s**a
sheep, ma**ch**ine	[ʃ]	**sc**immia, a**sci**a
u**s**ual, mea**s**ure	[ʒ]	
how, per**h**aps	[h]	
metal, co**mb**	[m]	**mamm**a, a**m**ico
night, di**nn**er	[n]	**n**otte, a**nn**o
su**ng**, parki**ng**	[ŋ]	
	[ɲ]	**gn**occhi, o**gn**i
litt**le**, he**l**p	[l]	**l**ana, po**ll**o
	[ʎ]	**gli**, fi**gli**o
right, ca**rr**y	[r]	**r**e, do**r**ato

The symbol ['] precedes a syllable carrying primary stress and the symbol [ˌ] precedes a syllable carrying secondary stress.

I simboli ['] e [ˌ] indicano rispettivamente un accento primario e uno secondario nella sillaba seguente.

The position of the tonic stress in Italian is indicated by a dot immediately beneath the accented vowel on Italian headwords (**cạmera, valịgia**). No dot is given on those words which end in an accented vowel, as Italian spelling allows for a written accent in these cases (**città, perché**). Full phonetics have been provided for words of foreign origin which do not follow Italian pronunciation rules (**cracker** ['krɛker], **brioche** [bri'ɔʃ]).

L'accento nelle voci italiane è segnalato da un punto sotto la vocale accentata (**cạmera, valịgia**), ad eccezione delle parole con l'accento sull'ultima sillaba, per le quali l'ortografia italiana prevede l'accento grafico (**città, perché**). Le parole di origine straniera sono seguite dalla trascrizione fonetica nei casi in cui la pronuncia generalmente adottata non rispetti le regole fonetiche dell'italiano (**cracker** ['krɛker], **brioche** [bri'ɔʃ]).

abitazione *sf* house.
abito *sm (da donna)* dress ; *(da uomo)* suit ; ~ **da sera** evening dress. ❑ **abiti** *smpl* clothes.
abituale *agg* usual.
abitualmente *avv* usually.
abituare *vt* to accustom ; ~ **qn a fare qc** to accustom sb to doing sthg. ❑ **abituarsi** *vr (adattarsi)* : **abituarsi a qc** to get used to sthg ; **abituarsi a fare qc** to get used to doing sthg.
abitudine *sf* habit ; **aver l' ~ di fare qc** to be in the habit of doing sthg ; **per ~** out of habit.
abolire *vt (tassa)* to abolish ; *(legge)* to repeal ; *(eliminare)* to eliminate.
aborigeno, a *sm, f* aborigine.
abortire *vi (accidentalmente)* to miscarry ; *(volontariamente)* to have an abortion.
aborto *sm (volontario)* abortion ; ~ **(spontaneo)** miscarriage.
abrogare *vt (legge)* to repeal.
Abruzzo *sm* : **l'** ~ the Abruzzo *(region of central Italy)*.
abside *sf* apse.
abusare : **abusare di** *(posizione, potere)* to take advantage of ; *(persona)* to rape ; ~ **dell'alcool** to drink too much.
abusivo, a *agg* unauthorized, unlawful.
abuso *sm (eccesso)* overindulgence ; *(uso illecito)* abuse.
a.C. *(abbr di avanti Cristo)* BC.
accademia *sf* academy, school ; ~ **di belle arti** fine arts academy.
accadere *vi* to happen.
accaduto *sm* : **raccontare l'** ~ to describe what happened.
accalcarsi *vr* to crowd.
accampamento *sm* camp.
accampare *vt (truppe)* to encamp ; *(richieste)* to make ; *(diritti)* to assert. ❑ **accamparsi** *vr (in tende)* to camp ; *fig (in alloggio)* to camp (out).
accanimento *sm (tenacia)* tenacity ; *(odio)* fury.
accanito, a *agg (odio)* fierce ; *(lavoratore)* assiduous ; **fumatore ~** chain smoker.
accanto *avv* nearby. ◆ *agg inv* next door. ◆ *prep* : ~ **a** beside.
accaparrare *vt (fare incetta)* to buy up ; *(voti, favore)* to secure, to gain ; **accaparrarsi qc** to secure sthg for o.s.
accappatoio *sm* bathrobe.
accarezzare *vt (persona, animale)* to caress, to stroke ; *fig (idea)* to toy with.
accattone, a *sm, f* beggar.
accavallare *vt (gambe)* to cross. ❑ **accavallarsi** *vr (eventi)* to overlap.
accecare *vt (rendere cieco)* to blind ; *(abbagliare)* to dazzle.
accedere *vi* : ~ **a qc** to gain access to sthg.
accelerare *vi* to accelerate. ◆ *vt* to speed up.
accelerato, a *agg* quick. ◆ *sm* stopping train.
acceleratore *sm* accelerator.
accendere *vt (fuoco, sigaretta)* to light ; *(radio, luce, fornello, motore)* to turn on ; *(speranza, odio)* to arouse ; **scusi, ha da ~?** excuse me,

have you got a light? ❑ **accendersi** *vr (prendere fuoco)* to catch fire ; *(entrare in funzione)* to start up.

accendigas *sm inv lighter for gas ring.*

accendino *sm* (cigarette) lighter.

accennare *vt (menzionare)* to mention ; *(indicare)* to point to ; ~ **un sorriso** to half-smile. ❑ **accennare a** *v + prep (menzionare)* to mention ; *(alludere a)* to hint at ; *(dare segno di)* to show signs of.

accensione *sf* ignition.

accentare *vt (parola, sillaba)* to stress.

accento *sm* accent ; **mettere l' ~ su qc** to stress sthg.

accentuare *vt (differenze, difetto, pregio)* to emphasize. ❑ **accentuarsi** *vr* to become more marked.

accerchiare *vt* to encircle, to surround.

accertamento *sm* check.

accertare *vt* to check. ❑ **accertarsi di** *vr + prep* to make sure of.

acceso, a *pp* → **accendere**. ◆ *agg (fuoco, sigaretta)* lighted ; *(radio, luce, motore)* on ; *(colore)* bright.

accessibile *agg (luogo)* accessible ; *(prezzo)* affordable.

accesso *sm (entrata)* access ; *MED* fit ; *fig (impeto)* outburst.

accessori *smpl* accessories.

accettare *vt* to accept ; *(proposta)* to agree to ; ~ **di fare qc** to agree to do sthg ; **'si accettano carte di credito'** 'credit cards welcome'.

accettazione *sf (locale)* reception ; **' ~ bagagli'** 'check-in'.

acchiappare *vt* to catch.

acciacco, chi *sm* ailment.

acciaio *sm* steel ; ~ **inossidabile** stainless steel.

accidentale *agg* accidental.

accidentalmente *avv* accidentally.

accidentato, a *agg* uneven.

accidenti *esclam (con rabbia)* blast!, damn! ; *(con stupore)* good heavens!

acciuffare *vt* to catch.

acciuga, ghe *sf* anchovy ; **acciughe al limone** *fresh anchovies marinated in lemon juice and dressed with oil.*

acclamare *vt (applaudire)* to cheer, to applaud ; *(eleggere)* to acclaim.

accludere *vt* to enclose.

accogliente *agg* cosy.

accoglienza *sf* welcome.

accogliere *vt* to receive ; *(dare il benvenuto)* to welcome.

accoltellare *vt* to knife.

accomodare *vt* to repair. ❑ **accomodarsi** *vr (sedersi)* to sit down ; *(venire avanti)* to come in ; **s'accomodi!** *(si sieda)* take a seat! ; *(venga avanti)* come in!

accompagnamento *sm* accompaniment.

accompagnare *vt (persona)* to go/come with, to accompany ; *(piatto, abito)* to go with ; *(con musica)* to accompany.

accompagnatore, trice *sm, f* companion ; ~ **turistico** tourist guide.

acconsentire *vi* : ~ **(a qc)** to agree (to sthg).

accontentare *vt* to satisfy. ❑ **accontentarsi : accontentarsi di** to be satisfied with.

acconto *sm* down payment ; **dare un ~** to pay a deposit ; **in ~** on account.

accorciare *vt* to shorten.

accordare *vt (strumento)* to tune ; *(concedere)* to grant ; *(colori)* to match. ❑ **accordarsi** *vr (mettersi d'accordo)* to agree.

accordo *sm (patto)* agreement ; *(armonia)* harmony ; **d' ~!** all right! ; **andare d' ~ con qn** to get on well with sb ; **essere d' ~ con** to agree with ; **mettersi d' ~ con qn** *(trovare un accordo)* to reach an agreement with sb ; *(per appuntamento)* to make an arrangement with sb.

accorgersi : accorgersi di *v + prep* to notice.

accorrere *vi (in aiuto)* to rush up ; *(verso un luogo)* to rush.

accorto, a *pp* → **accorgersi**. ◆ *agg* shrewd.

accostare *vt (persona)* to approach ; *(porta)* to leave ajar ; *(avvicinare)* : **~ qc a qc** to move sthg near sthg, to pull in ; *(nave)* to come alongside ; *(cambiare rotta)* to change course ; *(in auto)* to draw up.

accreditare *vt (fatto, notizia)* to confirm ; *(denaro)* to credit.

accrescere *vt* to increase. ❑ **accrescersi** *vr* to grow.

accucciarsi *vr (cane)* to lie down.

accudire *vt (malato, bambino)* to look after. ❑ **accudire a** *v + prep (casa, faccende)* to attend to.

accumulare *vt* to accumulate ; *(denaro)* to save ; *(accatastare)* to pile up.

accurato, a *agg (lavoro)* careful ; *(persona)* thorough.

accusa *sf (di una colpa)* accusation ; DIR charge.

accusare *vt* : **~ qn (di qc)** *(incolpare)* to accuse sb of sthg ; DIR to charge.

acerbo, a *agg* unripe.

acero *sm* maple.

aceto *sm* vinegar.

acetone *sm (per unghie)* nail varnish remover.

ACI *sm (abbr di Automobile Club d'Italia)* ≃ AA *(Br)*, ≃ AAA *(Am)*.

acidità *sf* : **~ di stomaco** heartburn.

acido, a *agg (sapore)* sour ; *(commento, persona)* sharp. ◆ *sm* acid.

acino *sm* grape.

acne *sf* acne.

acqua *sf* water ; **sott' ~** underwater ; **~ corrente** running water ; **~ cotta** *Tuscan soup made from stale bread, onions and tomatoes* ; **~ dolce** fresh water ; **~ minerale (gassata/naturale)** (carbonated/still) mineral water ; **~ ossigenata** hydrogen peroxide ; **~ del rubinetto** tap water ; **~ salata** salt water ; **~ tonica** tonic water ; **acque termali** hot springs ; **~ in bocca!** keep it to yourself! ; **' ~ non potabile'** 'not drinking water'.

acquaforte (*pl* **acqueforti**) *sf* etching.

acquaio *sm* sink.

acquamarina (*pl* **acquemarine**) *sf* aquamarine.

acquaragia *sf* turpentine.
acquario *sm* aquarium. ❑ **Acquario** *sm* Aquarius.
acquasanta *sf* holy water.
acquatico, a, ci, che *agg (pianta, animale)* aquatic ; *(sport)* water *(dav s)*.
acquavite *sf* brandy.
acquazzone *sm* cloudburst.
acquedotto *sm* aqueduct.
acqueo *agg m* → **vapore**.
acquerello *sm* watercolour.
acquirente *smf* buyer.
acquisire *vt (ottenere)* to acquire.
acquistare *vt (comperare)* to buy ; *(ottenere)* to acquire.
acquisto *sm* purchase ; **fare acquisti** to shop.
acquolina *sf*: **far venire l' ~ in bocca a qn** to make sb's mouth water.
acquoso, a *agg* watery.
acrilico, a, ci, che *agg* & *sm* acrylic.
acrobata, i, e *smf* acrobat.
acrobazia *sf (di acrobata)* acrobatic feat ; *(di aereo)* stunt.
acropoli *sf inv* acropolis.
aculeo *sm (di vespa)* sting ; *(di riccio)* spine ; *(di pianta)* prickle.
acume *sm* acumen.
acustico, a, ci, che *agg* acoustic.
acuto, a *agg (voce, suono)* high-pitched ; *(intenso)* intense ; *(appuntito)* pointed ; *(intelligente)* sharp ; *MAT* acute.
ad → **a**.
adagio *avv* slowly ; **'entrare/uscire ~'** *sign warning drivers to enter or leave side roads etc slowly*.
adattamento *sm (adeguamento, di opera)* adaptation ; *(modifica)* adjustment.
adattare *vt* to adapt. ❑ **adattarsi** *vr* : **adattarsi (a qc)** *(adeguarsi)* to adapt (to sthg).
adatto, a *agg* : **~ (a)** suitable (for) ; **~ a fare qc** suitable to do sthg.
addebitare *vt* to debit.
addestramento *sm* training.
addestrare *vt* to train.
addetto, a *agg (persona)* responsible. ◆ *sm, f* person responsible ; **~ stampa** press attaché ; **gli addetti ai lavori** *fig* the experts.
addio *esclam* goodbye!
addirittura *avv (perfino)* even ; *(direttamente)* directly. ◆ *esclam* really?
addirsi : **addirsi a** *vr + prep* to be suitable for.
additivo *sm* additive.
addizionale *agg* additional.
addizione *sf* addition.
addobbo *sm* decoration ; **addobbi natalizi** Christmas decorations.
addolcire *vt* to sweeten.
addolorare *vt* to sadden. ❑ **addolorarsi** *vr* to upset o.s.
addome *sm* abdomen.
addomesticare *vt* to house-train.
addormentare *vt* to send to sleep. ❑ **addormentarsi** *vr* to fall asleep.
addossare *vt (al muro)* to lean ; *(attribuire)* to lay.

addosso *avv (sulla persona)* on. ◆ *prep*: ~ **a** *(su)* on; *(contro)* against; **mettersi qc ~** to put sthg on; **dare ~ a** *(criticare)* to attack; **eravamo uno ~ all'altro** we were right next to each other.

adeguare *vt*: **~ qc a qc** to adjust sthg to sthg. ❑ **adeguarsi** *vr*: **adeguarsi a qc** to adapt to sthg.

adeguato, a *agg* adequate.

adempiere *vt (compiere)* to carry out; *(esaudire)* to grant.

adenoidi *sfpl* adenoids.

aderente *agg (attillato)* close-fitting; *(adesivo)* adhesive.

aderire *vi*: **~ a qc** *(attaccarsi)* to stick to sthg; *(partito)* to join sthg; *(proposta)* to support sthg; *(richiesta)* to agree to sthg.

adesivo, a *agg* adhesive. ◆ *sm (etichetta)* sticky label.

adesso *avv (ora)* now; *(tra poco)* any moment now; *(poco fa)* just now.

adiacente *agg* adjacent.

adibire *vt*: **~ qc a qc** to use sthg as sthg.

Adige *sm*: **l' ~** the River Adige.

adirarsi *vr* to get angry.

adocchiare *vt (scorgere)* to glimpse; *(guardare)* to eye.

adolescente *smf* adolescent.

adolescenza *sf* adolescence.

adoperare *vt* to use.

adorabile *agg* adorable.

adorare *vt (persona, cosa)* to adore; *(divinità)* to worship.

adottare *vt (bambino)* to adopt; *(misure, decisione)* to take.

adottivo, a *agg (figlio, patria)* adopted; *(genitori)* adoptive.

adozione *sf* adoption.

adriatico, a, ci, che *agg* Adriatic. ❑ **Adriatico** *sm*: **l'Adriatico** the Adriatic (Sea).

adulterio *sm* adultery.

adulto, a *agg* & *sm, f (di età)* adult.

aerare *vt* to air.

aereo, a *agg* air *(dav s)*. ◆ *sm* (aero)plane, aircraft; **~ da turismo** light aircraft.

aerobica *sf* aerobics *(sg)*.

aeronautica *sf (aviazione)* air-force.

aeroplano *sm* (aero)plane *(Br)*, airplane *(Am)*.

aeroporto *sm* airport.

aerosol *sm* aerosol.

A.F. *(abbr di alta frequenza)* HF.

afa *sf* closeness.

affabile *agg* affable.

affacciarsi *vr (mostrarsi)* to show o.s. ❑ **affacciarsi su** *vr + prep* to show o.s. at.

affamato, a *agg* starving.

affannarsi *vr (stancarsi)* to tire o.s.; *(agitarsi)* to worry.

affanno *sm (di respiro)* breathlessness; *(ansia)* worry.

affare *sm* business; *(faccenda)* business, affair; *(occasione)* bargain; *fam (cosa)* thing; **è un ~!** it's a bargain!; **affari** business *(sg)*; **per affari** on business; **fare affari con** to do business with; **Affari Esteri** Foreign Affairs.

affascinante *agg* charming.

affascinare *vt* to charm, to fascinate.

affaticarsi *vr* to get tired.

affatto *avv* completely; **non ... ~** not ... at all; **niente ~** not at all.

affermare *vt* to affirm. ❑ **affermarsi** *vr* to make a name for o.s.
affermativo, a *agg* affirmative.
affermazione *sf (dichiarazione)* affirmation ; *(successo)* success.
afferrare *vt (prendere)* to seize ; *(capire)* to grasp. ❑ **afferrarsi a** *vr + prep* to grasp at.
affettare *vt* to slice.
affettato, a *agg (a fette)* sliced ; *(artificioso)* affected. ◆ *sm* sliced cold meat.
affetto, a *sm (attaccamento)* affection. ◆ *agg* : **essere ~ da** *(malattia)* to suffer from.
affettuoso, a *agg* affectionate.
affezionarsi *vr* : **~ a** to become fond of.
affezionato, a *agg* fond.
affidamento *sm* DIR custody ; *(fiducia)* : **fare ~ su** to rely on.
affidare *vt* to entrust ; **~ qn/qc a qn** to entrust sb/sthg to sb.
affiggere *vt (cartello, poster)* to stick up.
affilare *vt* to sharpen.
affilato, a *agg (lama, punta)* sharp.
affinché *cong* in order that, so that.
affinità *sf inv* affinity.
affissione *sf* : **'divieto di ~'** 'post no bills'.
affisso, a *pp* → **affiggere**. ◆ *sm* poster.
affittare *vt (dare in affitto)* to let, to rent (out) ; *(prendere in affitto)* to rent ; **'affittasi'** 'to let'.
affitto *sm* rent ; **dare in ~** to let, to rent (out) ; **prendere in ~** to rent.
affliggere *vt* to torment. ❑ **affliggersi** *vr* to torment o.s.
afflitto, a *pp* → **affliggere**. ◆ *agg* afflicted.
affluente *sm* tributary.
affluire *vi (fiume)* to flow ; *(gente, merce)* to pour in.
affogare *vi* & *vt* to drown.
affogato *sm (gelato) ice cream or 'semifreddo' with coffee, whisky or a liqueur poured over it.*
affollato, a *agg* crowded.
affondare *vi* & *vt* to sink.
affrancare *vt* to stamp.
affrancatura *sf* postage.
affresco, schi *sm* fresco.
affrettare *vt* to hurry. ❑ **affrettarsi** *vr* to hurry.
affrontare *vt (nemico)* to confront ; *(spesa)* to meet ; *(argomento)* to tackle.
affronto *sm* insult.
affumicato, a *agg (cibo)* smoked ; *(vetro)* tinted ; *(annerito)* blackened.
afoso, a *agg* close.
Africa *sf* : **l' ~** Africa.
africano, a *agg* & *sm, f* African.
afta *sf* mouth ulcer.
agenda *sf* diary.
agente *sm* agent ; **~ di polizia** policeman (*f* policewoman) ; **gli agenti atmosferici** the elements.
agenzia *sf (impresa)* agency ; *(succursale)* branch ; **~ di cambio** bureau de change ; **~ immobiliare** estate agent's *(Br)*, real-estate office *(Am)* ; **~ di viaggi** travel agency.

agevolare *vt (facilitare)* to facilitate ; *(aiutare)* to help.

agevolazione *sf* : **~ di pagamento** easy (payment) terms *(pl)*.

aggeggio *sm* thing.

aggettivo *sm* adjective.

agghiacciante *agg* terrible.

aggiornare *vt (persona, opera)* to bring up-to-date ; *(seduta)* to postpone. ❑ **aggiornarsi** *vr* to bring o.s. up-to-date.

aggiornato, a *agg* up-to-date.

aggirare *vt* to get round. ❑ **aggirarsi** *vr* to wander. ❑ **aggirarsi su** *vr + prep* to be about.

aggiudicare *vt* to award. ❑ **aggiudicarsi** *vr* to gain.

aggiungere *vt* to add.

aggiunta *sf* : **in ~** in addition.

aggiunto, a *pp* → **aggiungere**.

aggiustare *vt* to mend. ❑ **aggiustarsi** *vr* to come to an agreement.

agglomerato *sm* : **~ urbano** built-up area.

aggrapparsi *vr* to cling on ; **~ a** to cling to.

aggravare *vt* to make worse. ❑ **aggravarsi** *vr* to get worse.

aggredire *vt* to attack.

aggressione *sf* attack.

aggressivo, a *agg* aggressive.

agguato *sm* ambush.

agiato, a *agg (persona)* well-off ; *(vita)* comfortable.

agile *agg* agile, nimble.

agio *sm* : **essere a proprio ~** to feel at ease ; **mettersi a proprio ~** to make o.s. at home.

agire *vi (comportarsi)* to act ; **~ da** *(fare da)* to act as.

agitare *vt* to shake ; *(mano)* to wave ; *(coda)* to wag ; *(turbare)* to upset ; **'~ prima dell'uso'** 'shake before use'.

❑ **agitarsi** *vr (turbarsi)* to get worked up ; *(muoversi)* to writhe ; *(mare)* to get rough ; **agitarsi nel letto** to toss and turn in bed.

agitato, a *agg (inquieto)* worried ; *(mare)* rough.

agitazione *sf (inquietudine)* agitation ; *(subbuglio)* turmoil.

agli = **a** + **gli, a**.

aglio *sm* garlic.

agnello *sm* lamb ; **~ alla norcina** *leg of lamb larded with ham, garlic, parsley and marjoram.*

agnolotti *smpl ravioli stuffed with pork, salami, Parmesan cheese and spinach.*

ago (*pl* **aghi**) *sm* needle.

agonia *sf* agony.

agopuntura *sf* acupuncture.

agosto *sm* August → **settembre**.

agricolo, a *agg* agricultural.

agricoltore *sm (contadino)* farm worker ; *(imprenditore)* farmer.

agricoltura *sf* agriculture.

agriturismo *sm* farm holidays *(pl)*.

AGRITURISMO

A form of tourism popular in Italy, *agriturismo* offers people the opportunity to spend their summer holiday on traditional farms in the Italian countryside. This type of holiday is particularly popular with those who enjoy the outdoor lifestyle, good home cooking and healthy exercise in beautiful rural surroundings. As well as participating in a range of sports such as horseriding, walking, tennis and bowls, holidaymakers also have the opportunity to help on the farm.

---

agrodolce *sm* : **in ~** in a sweet and sour sauce.

agrume *sm* citrus fruit.

aguzzare *vt* to sharpen ; **~ le orecchie** to prick up one's ears.

aguzzo, a *agg* sharp.

ahi *esclam* ouch!

ai = **a + i**, **a**.

Aia *sf* : **l' ~** the Hague.

AIDS *sm o sf* AIDS.

A.I.G. *(abbr di Associazione Italiana Alberghi per la Gioventù)* ≃ YHA.

air-terminal ['ɜr'terminal] *sm inv* air terminal.

aiuola *sf* flower bed.

aiutante *smf* assistant.

aiutare *vt* to help ; **~ qn (a fare qc)** to help sb (to do sthg).

aiuto *sm* help, assistance ; *(assistente)* assistant ; **aiuto!** help! ; **chiedere ~** to ask for help ; **essere di ~ a qn** to be of help to sb ; **venire in ~ di qn** to come to sb's aid.

al = **a + il**, **a**.

ala *(pl* **ali**) *sf* wing ; *(giocatore)* winger.

alano *sm* Great Dane.

alba *sf* dawn ; **all' ~** at dawn.

albanese *agg* & *smf* Albanian.

Albania *sf* : **l' ~** Albania.

albergatore, trice *sm, f* hotelier.

albergo, ghi *sm* hotel ; **~ diurno** *public toilets where people can also wash, have a haircut, get their clothes ironed etc.* ; **~ per la gioventù** youth hostel.

albero *sm* tree ; *(di nave)* mast ; *(di macchina)* shaft ; **~ genealogico** family tree ; **~ di Natale** Christmas tree.

albese *sf thin slices of raw beef served with oil, lemon and mushrooms or Parmesan cheese.*

albicocca, che *sf* apricot.

albino, a *agg* & *sm, f* albino.

album *sm inv* album ; **~ da disegno** sketch book.

albume *sm* egg white.

alcol = **alcool**.

alcolico, a, ci, che *agg* alcoholic. ◆ *sm* alcoholic drink.

alcolizzato, a *sm, f* alcoholic.

alcool *sm* alcohol.

alcuno, a *agg s* : **non ... ~** *(nessuno)* no, not any ; **alcuni, alcune** some, a few ; **alcuni di** some of, a few of.

aldilà *sm* : **l' ~** the next life.

alfabeto *sm* alphabet.

alfiere *sm (portabandiera)* standard bearer ; *(negli scacchi)* bishop.

alga, ghe *sf (di mare)* seaweed.

algebra *sf* algebra.

Algeria *sf* : **l' ~** Algeria.

aliante *sm* glider.

alibi *sm inv* alibi.

alice *sf* anchovy ; **alici areganate** *anchovies cooked in oil, vinegar, garlic, parsley and oregano.*

alienazione *sf (pazzia)* insanity ; *DIR* transfer.
alieno, a *sm, f* alien.
alimentare *agg* food *(dav s)*. ◆ *vt (nutrire)* to feed ; *fig (rafforzare)* to strengthen ; *(rifornire)* to supply. ❑ **alimentari** *smpl (cibi)* foodstuffs ; **negozio di alimentari** grocer's.
alimentazione *sf (nutrimento)* nutrition ; *(rifornimento)* supply.
alimento *sm* food. ❑ **alimenti** *smpl* alimony *(sg)*.
aliscafo *sm* hydrofoil.
alito *sm* breath.
all' = a + l', a.
alla = a + la, a.
allacciare *vt (scarpe)* to tie up ; *(cintura, vestito)* to fasten ; *(telefono, gas)* to connect. ❑ **allacciarsi** *vr* to fasten.
allagare *vt* to flood. ❑ **allagarsi** *vr* to flood.
allargare *vt (ampliare)* to widen ; *(aprire)* to open. ❑ **allargarsi** *vr* to widen.
allarmare *vt* to alarm.
allarme *sm* alarm ; **~ antincendio** fire alarm ; **dare l' ~** to give the alarm.
allattare *vt (al seno)* to breastfeed ; *(artificialmente)* to bottlefeed.
alle = a + le, a.
alleanza *sf* alliance.
allearsi *vr* to form an alliance.
allegare *vt* to enclose.
alleggerire *vt* to lighten.
allegria *sf* cheerfulness.
allegro, a *agg (contento)* cheerful ; *(colore)* bright ; *(vivace)* lively. ◆ *sm MUS* allegro.
allenamento *sm* training ; **tenersi in ~** to keep in training.
allenare *vt* to train. ❑ **allenarsi** *vr* to train.
allenatore, trice *sm, f* trainer, coach.
allentare *vt (vite, nodo)* to loosen ; *(sorveglianza, disciplina)* to relax. ❑ **allentarsi** *vr* to work loose.
allergia *sf* allergy.
allergico, a, ci, che *agg* allergic ; **essere ~ a qc** to be allergic to sthg.
allestire *vt (mostra, spettacolo)* to get ready.
allevamento *sm (attività)* breeding, rearing ; *(animali)* stock.
allevare *vt (animale)* to breed ; *(bambino)* to bring up.
allibratore *sm* bookmaker.
allievo, a *sm, f* pupil, student.
alligatore *sm* alligator.
allineare *vt* to align. ❑ **allinearsi** *vr (mettersi in fila)* to line up.
allo = a + lo, a.
allodola *sf* skylark.
alloggiare *vi* to stay.
alloggio *sm* accommodation.
allontanare *vt (mandare via)* to send away ; *(pericolo)* to avert. ❑ **allontanarsi** *vr* to go away.
allora *avv* then. ◆ *cong (in tal caso)* then ; *(ebbene)* well ; **da ~** since then.
alloro *sm* laurel.
alluce *sm* big toe.
allucinante *agg (spaventoso)* terrifying ; *(incredibile)* incredible.

allucinazione *sf* hallucination.
alludere : **alludere a** *v + prep* to allude to.
alluminio *sm* aluminium.
allungare *vt (accrescere)* to lengthen ; *(gambe)* to stretch ; *(diluire)* to water down. ❑ **allungarsi** *vr (accrescersi)* to lengthen ; *(distendersi)* to stretch out.
allusione *sf* allusion ; **fare allusioni** to drop hints.
alluso, a *pp* → **alludere**.
alluvione *sf* flood.
almeno *avv* at least.
Alpi *sfpl* : **le ~** the Alps.
alpinismo *sm* climbing.
alpinista, i, e *smf* climber.
alpino, a *agg* alpine.
alquanto *avv* somewhat.
alt *esclam* halt!
altalena *sf (con funi)* swing ; *(su asse)* see-saw *(Br)*, teeter-totter *(Am)*.
altare *sm* altar.
alterare *vt* to affect. ❑ **alterarsi** *vr (merce)* to be affected ; *(irritarsi)* to get angry.
alternare *vt* : **~ qn/qc a** to alternate sb/sthg with. ❑ **alternarsi** *vr* to alternate.
alternativa *sf* alternative.
alternato, a *agg* alternate ; *(corrente)* alternating.
alterno, a *agg* alternate.
altezza *sf (statura, di cosa)* height ; *(di acqua)* depth ; *(altitudine)* altitude.
altezzoso, a *agg* haughty.
altipiano = **altopiano**.
altitudine *sf* altitude.
alto, a *agg* high ; *(persona, edificio, albero)* tall ; *(profondo)* deep ; *(suono, voce)* loud. ◆ *sm* top. ◆ *avv* high ; *(parlare)* loud ; **è ~ due metri** he's two metres tall ; **ad alta voce** out loud, aloud ; **alta moda** haute couture ; **dall' ~ in basso** from top to bottom ; **alti e bassi** ups and downs ; **in ~** upwards.
altoparlante *sm* loudspeaker.
altopiano (*pl* **altipiani**) *sm* plateau.
altrettanto, a *agg (tempo, latte)* as much ; *(persone, libri)* as many. ◆ *pron* the same. ◆ *avv* equally ; **auguri! - grazie, ~!** all the best! - thank you, the same to you!
altrimenti *avv (se no)* otherwise ; *(diversamente)* differently.

---

altro, a *agg* - 1. *(diverso)* other ; **ha un ~ modello?** have you got another ○ a different model?.
- 2. *(supplementare)* other ; **un ~ caffè?** another coffee?
- 3. *(rimanente)* other ; **gli altri passeggeri sono pregati di restare al loro posto** would all remaining passengers please stay in their seats.
- 4. *(nel tempo)* : **l' ~ giorno** the other day ; **l'altr'anno** last year ; **l' ~ ieri** the day before yesterday ; **domani l' ~** the day after tomorrow.
- 5. *(in espressioni)* : **è tutt' ~ che bello** it's far from being beautiful ; **d'altra parte** on the other hand.
◆ *pron* : **l' ~** the other (one) ; **un ~** another (one) ; **gli altri** *(il prossimo)* others, other people ; **l'uno o l' ~** one or the other ; **se non ~** at least ; **senz' ~** of course ; **tra l' ~** among other things.

---

altroché *esclam* and how!
altronde : d'altronde *avv* on the other hand.
altrove *avv* elsewhere.
altrui *agg inv* other people's.
altruista, i, e *agg* altruistic.
altura *sf* high ground.
alunno, a *sm, f* pupil.
alveare *sm* beehive.
alzare *vt (oggetto)* to lift ; *(prezzi, volume, voce)* to raise. ❑ **alzarsi** *vr (dal letto, dalla sedia)* to get up ; *(aumentare)* to rise ; *(vento)* to get up.
amaca, che *sf* hammock.
amalgamare *vt* to combine. ❑ **amalgamarsi** *vr* to combine.
amante *smf* lover. ◆ *agg* : **~ di qc** fond of sthg.
amare *vt (persona)* to love ; *(cosa)* to be fond of.
amareggiato, a *agg* embittered.
amarena *sf sour black cherry.*
amaretto *sm (biscotto)* macaroon ; *(liquore) a liqueur made with almonds.*
amarezza *sf* bitterness.
amaro, a *agg (sapore)* bitter ; *(spiacevole)* nasty.
ambasciata *sf* embassy.
ambasciatore, trice *sm, f* ambassador.
ambedue *agg inv & pron* both.
ambientare *vt (film)* to set. ❑ **ambientarsi** *vr* to get used to a place.
ambiente *sm (natura)* environment ; *(cerchia)* surroundings *(pl)*.
ambiguo, a *agg (parola, testo)* ambiguous ; *(comportamento, persona)* dubious.
ambizione *sf* ambition.
ambizioso, a *agg* ambitious.
ambra *sf* amber.
ambulante *agg* itinerant.
ambulanza *sf* ambulance.
ambulatorio *sm* surgery.
America *sf* : **l' ~** America ; **l' ~ latina** Latin America.
americano, a *agg & sm, f* American.
amianto *sm* asbestos.
amichevole *agg* friendly.
amicizia *sf* friendship ; **fare ~ (con qn)** to make friends (with sb).
amico, a, ci, che *sm, f* friend ; **~ del cuore** best friend.
amido *sm* starch.
ammaccare *vt* to dent.
ammaccatura *sf (su metallo)* dent ; *(su gamba)* bruise.
ammaestrare *vt* to train.
ammainare *vt* to lower.
ammalarsi *vr* to fall ill.
ammalato, a *agg* ill. ◆ *sm, f* patient.
ammassare *vt* to amass, to pile up.
ammazzare *vt* to kill. ❑ **ammazzarsi** *vr* to kill o.s.
ammenda *sf* fine.
ammesso, a *pp* → **ammettere**.
ammettere *vt (riconoscere)* to admit ; *(permettere)* to allow ; *(a esame, scuola)* to accept ; *(supporre)* to suppose, to assume.
amministrare *vt* to run, to manage.

amministratore *sm (di condominio)* manager ; ~ **delegato** managing director.
ammirare *vt* to admire.
ammiratore, trice *sm, f* admirer.
ammirazione *sf* admiration.
ammissione *sf (a esame)* admittance.
ammobiliato, a *agg* furnished ; **non** ~ unfurnished.
ammollo *sm* soaking ; **lasciare qc in** ~ to leave sthg to soak.
ammoniaca *sf* ammonia.
ammonire *vt (rimproverare)* to warn ; *SPORT* to book.
ammonizione *sf (rimprovero)* warning ; *SPORT* booking.
ammontare : ammontare a *v + prep* to amount to.
ammorbidente *sm* fabric softener.
ammorbidire *vt (rendere morbido)* to soften.
ammortizzatore *sm* shock absorber.
ammucchiare *vt* to pile up.
ammuffito, a *agg* mouldy.
ammutinamento *sm* mutiny.
amnistia *sf* amnesty.
amo *sm* bait.
amore *sm* love ; **fare l'** ~ **(con qn)** to make love (with sb) ; **amor proprio** self-esteem.
ampio, a *agg (vasto)* wide ; *(spazioso)* spacious ; *(abbondante)* abundant.
ampliare *vt* to widen.
amplificatore *sm* amplifier.
amputare *vt* to amputate.
amuleto *sm* amulet.
anabbaglianti *smpl* dipped headlights *(Br)*, dimmed headlights *(Am)*.
anagrafe *sf (ufficio)* registry office *(Br)*, office of vital statistics *(Am)*.
analcolico, a, ci, che *agg* nonalcoholic. ◆ *sm* soft drink.
analfabeta, i, e *agg* & *smf* illiterate.
analisi *sf inv (studio)* analysis ; *MED* test ; ~ **del sangue** blood test.
analista, i, e *smf* analyst.
analizzare *vt* to analyse.
analogo, a, ghi, ghe *agg* similar.
ananas *sm inv* pineapple.
anarchia *sf* anarchy.
ANAS *sf (abbr di Azienda Nazionale Autonoma delle Strade) national road board.*
anatomia *sf* anatomy.
anatomico, a, ci, che *agg (sedile)* contoured.
anatra *sf* duck.
anca, che *sf* hip.
anche *cong (pure)* too ; *(persino)* even.
ancora[1] *sf* anchor.
ancora[2] *avv (tuttora)* still ; *(persino)* even ; *(di nuovo)* again ; *(di più)* more, still ; ~ **più bello** even more beautiful ; ~ **un po'** a bit more ; ~ **una volta** once more ; **non** ~ not yet.

andare *vi* - 1. *(muoversi)* to go ; **scusi, per** ~ **alla stazione?** could you tell me the way to the station,

please? ; ~ **a Napoli** to go to Naples ; ~ **avanti/indietro** to go forwards/backwards ; ~ **in vacanza** to go on holiday *(Br)*, to go on vacation *(Am)*.
- 2. *(strada)* to go.
- 3. *(indica uno stato)* : **come va?** how are you? ; ~ **bene/male** *(persona)* to be well/unwell ; *(situazione)* to go well/badly.
- 4. *(piacere)* : **il suo modo di fare non mi va** I don't like the way he behaves ; **non mi va di mangiare** I don't feel like eating.
- 5. *(funzionare)* to work.
- 6. *(con participio passato)* : **dove va messa la chiave?** where does the key go? ; ~ **perso** *(essere smarrito)* to get lost.
- 7. *(in espressioni)* : ~ **bene a qn** *(come misura)* to fit sb ; **queste scarpe mi vanno bene** these shoes fit (me) ; **ti va bene andare al cinema?** do you feel like going to the cinema? ; ~ **via** *(partire)* to leave ; *(macchia)* to come out.
◆ *sm* : **a lungo** ~ in time.
❑ **andarsene** *vr* to go away.

---

andata *sf*: **all'** ~ on the way there ; ~ **e ritorno** return (ticket) *(Br)*.
andatura *sf* walk.
andirivieni *sm inv* coming and going.
anello *sm (da dito)* ring ; *(di catena)* link ; ~ **di fidanzamento** engagement ring.
anemia *sf* anaemia.
anestesia *sf* anaesthesia.
anestetico *sm* anaesthetic.
anfiteatro *sm* amphitheatre.
anfora *sf* amphora.
angelo *sm* angel.
angina *sf* tonsillitis ; ~ **pectoris** angina.
anglicano, a *agg* Anglican.
angolo *sm* corner ; ~ **cottura** kitchen area ; **all'** ~ on the corner.
angora *sf*: **d'** ~ angora *(dav s)*.
angoscia *sf* anguish.
anguilla *sf* eel.
anguria *sf* watermelon.
anice *sm* aniseed.
anidride *sf*: ~ **carbonica** carbon dioxide.
anima *sf* soul.
animale *agg* & *sm* animal ; ~ **domestico** pet.
animatore, trice *sm, f*: ~ **turistico** entertainment organizer *(in holiday village)*.
animo *sm (mente)* mind ; *(cuore)* heart ; *(coraggio)* : **perdersi d'** ~ to lose heart.
anitra = **anatra**.
annaffiare *vt* to water.
annaffiatoio *sm* watering can.
annata *sf* year ; *(di vino)* vintage.
annegare *vt* & *vi* to drown.
❑ **annegarsi** *vr* to drown o.s.
anniversario *sm* anniversary.
anno *sm* year ; **buon ~!** Happy New Year! ; **quanti anni hai?** how old are you? ; **ho 21 anni** I'm 21 ; **un bambino di tre anni** a three-year-old ; ~ **accademico** academic year ; ~ **bisestile** leap year ; ~ **scolastico** school year.
annodare *vt* to tie.
annoiare *vt* to bore. ❑ **annoiarsi** *vr* to get bored.

annotare *vt (prendere nota)* to note down; *(commentare)* to annotate.

annuale *agg* annual.

annuario *sm* yearbook.

annuire *vi (con la testa)* to nod.

annullare *vt (partita, riunione, francobollo)* to cancel; *(matrimonio)* to annul; *(rendere vano)* to destroy.

annunciare *vt* to announce; *(indicare)* to indicate.

annunciatore, trice *sm, f* announcer.

Annunciazione *sf*: **l' ~** the Annunciation.

annuncio *sm* announcement; **~ pubblicitario** advertisement; **annunci economici** classified ads.

annuo, a *agg* annual, yearly.

annusare *vt* to smell.

annuvolamento *sm* clouding over.

ano *sm* anus.

anomalo, a *agg* anomalous.

anonimo, a *agg* anonymous.

anoressia *sf* anorexia.

anormale *agg* abnormal. ◆ *smf* abnormal person.

ANSA *sf (abbr di Agenzia Nazionale Stampa Associata) national press agency.*

ansia *sf* anxiety.

ansimare *vi* to pant.

ansioso, a *agg (inquieto)* anxious; *(impaziente)*: **~ di fare qc** eager to do sthg.

anta *sf (di finestra)* shutter; *(di armadio)* door.

antagonista, i, e *smf* rival.

antartico, a, ci, che *agg* Antarctic.

Antartide *sf*: **l' ~** Antarctica.

anteguerra *sm* prewar period.

antenato, a *sm, f* ancestor.

antenna *sf* aerial.

anteprima *sf* preview; **presentare qc in ~** to preview sthg.

anteriore *agg (sedili, ruote)* front *(dav s)*; *(nel tempo)* previous.

antiabbaglianti = **anabbaglianti**.

antibiotico *sm* antibiotic.

anticamera *sf* anteroom.

antichità *sf inv (passato)* antiquity; *(oggetto)* antique.

anticipare *vt (partenza)* to bring forward; *(denaro)* to pay in advance.

anticipo *sm (di denaro)* advance; *(di tempo)*: **il treno ha 10 minuti d' ~** the train is 10 minutes early; **essere/arrivare in ~** to be/arrive early.

antico, a, chi, che *agg (mobilio)* antique; *(dell'antichità)* ancient.

anticoncezionale *agg* & *sm* contraceptive.

anticonformista, i, e *agg* & *smf* nonconformist.

anticorpo *sm* antibody.

antidoto *sm* antidote.

antifascista, i, e *agg* & *smf* antifascist.

antifurto *agg inv* antitheft *(dav s)*. ◆ *sm* antitheft device.

antigelo *sm inv* antifreeze.

Antille *sfpl*: **le ~** the West Indies.

antimafia *agg inv* anti-Mafia.

antincendio *agg inv* fire *(dav s).*
antinebbia *agg inv* fog *(dav s).* ◆ *sm inv* fog lamp.
antiorario *agg m* → **senso.**
antipasto *sm* hors d'œuvre ; ~ **di mare** *mixed seafood hors d'œuvre* ; ~ **a scelta** *hors d'œuvres chosen from a buffet of grilled or baked vegetables, pickled foods, cold meats etc.*
antipatia *sf* antipathy.
antipatico, a, ci, che *agg* unpleasant.
antiquariato *sm (commercio)* antique trade ; **oggetti d'** ~ antiques.
antiquario, a *sm, f* antique dealer.
antiquato, a *agg* old-fashioned.
antiruggine *agg inv* rustproof.
antirughe *agg inv* antiwrinkle *(dav s).*
antisettico, a, ci, che *agg* & *sm* antiseptic.
antitetanica *sf* antitetanus injection.
antivipera *sm inv* antiviper serum.
antivirus *sm inv* INFORM antivirus.
antologia *sf* anthology.
anulare *agg* ring *(dav s).* ◆ *sm* ring finger.
anzi *cong (al contrario)* on the contrary ; *(o meglio)* or rather.
anziano, a *agg (di età)* elderly ; *(di carica)* senior. ◆ *sm, f (vecchio)* senior citizen.
anziché *cong* rather than.
anzitutto *avv* first of all.
apatia *sf* apathy.
apatico, a, ci, che *agg* apathetic.
ape *sf* bee.
aperitivo *sm* aperitif.

APERITIVO

The tradition of taking an alcoholic or non-alcoholic drink before lunch or dinner is common throughout Italy. Italians are especially fond of having an aperitif at some point during their Sunday stroll or *passeggiata.* Although an aperitif is sometimes served at home, it is more usual to go out to a bar where, in addition to the usual range of drinks, there may be local or house specialities on offer. Drinks are generally accompanied by olives, crisps or other savoury snacks.

---

aperto, a *pp* → **aprire.** ◆ *agg* open. ◆ *sm* : **all'** ~ in the open air.
apertura *sf* opening.
apice *sm* peak ; **essere all'** ~ **di qc** to be at the height of sthg.
apicoltura *sf* beekeeping.
apnea *sf* : **in** ~ *(subacqueo)* without breathing apparatus.
apolide *agg* stateless. ◆ *smf* stateless person.
apostolo *sm* apostle.
apostrofare *vt (interpellare)* to address ; *(rimproverare)* to reproach.
apostrofo *sm* apostrophe.
appagare *vt* to satisfy.
appannare *vt (vetro)* to mist ; *fig (mente)* to dim. ❑ **appannarsi** *vr*

(vetro) to mist up ; *fig (vista, mente)* to grow dim.
apparato *sm* ANAT system ; *(impianto)* apparatus.
apparecchiare *vt* : ~ la tavola to lay the table.
apparecchio *sm (congegno)* device ; *(aereo)* aircraft ; *(per i denti)* brace ; ~ acustico hearing aid.
apparente *agg* apparent.
apparentemente *avv* apparently.
apparenza *sf* : in o all' ~ apparently.
apparire *vi (mostrarsi)* to appear ; *(sembrare)* to seem.
appariscente *agg* striking.
apparso, a *pp* → apparire.
appartamento *sm* flat *(Br)*, apartment *(Am)*.
appartenere : **appartenere a** *v + prep* to belong to.
appassionato, a *agg* passionate. ◆ *sm, f* fan ; essere ~ di qc to be keen on sthg.
appello *sm (chiamata)* rollcall ; DIR appeal ; fare ~ a to appeal to ; fare l' ~ to call the roll.
appena *avv (a fatica)* hardly ; *(da poco)* just ; *(solo)* only, just. ◆ *cong* as soon as ; non ~ as soon as.
appendere *vt* to hang up.
appendice *sf* appendix.
appendicite *sf* appendicitis.
Appennini *smpl* : gli ~ the Apennines.
appeso, a *pp* → appendere.
appetito *sm* appetite ; buon ~! enjoy your meal!
appetitoso, a *agg* appetizing.
appezzamento *sm* plot.
appiattire *vt* to flatten. ❑ **appiattirsi** *vr (al suolo, contro il muro)* to flatten o.s. ; *(diventare piatto)* to become flatter.
appiccare *vt* : ~ il fuoco a qc to set fire to sthg.
appiccicare *vt* to stick. ❑ **appiccicarsi** *vr* : appiccicarsi (a) to stick (to) ; *fig (persona)* to cling (to).
appiccicoso, a *agg (attaccaticcio)* sticky ; *fig (persona)* clingy.
appieno *avv* fully.
appigliarsi : **appigliarsi a** *vr + prep (afferrarsi)* to hold on to ; *fig (pretesto)* to cling to.
appiglio *sm (appoggio)* hold ; *fig (pretesto)* pretext.
appisolarsi *vr* to doze off.
applaudire *vt* to applaud.
applauso *sm* applause ; fare un ~ to give a round of applause.
applicare *vt* to apply. ❑ **applicarsi** *vr* to apply o.s.
applicazione *sf (di cerotto, pomata)* application ; *(attuazione)* enforcement.
appoggiare *vt (per terra, sul tavolo)* to put (down) ; *(sostenere)* to support ; *(al muro)* : ~ qc a o contro qc to lean sthg against sthg. ❑ **appoggiarsi a** *vr + prep* to lean against.
appoggiatesta *sm inv* headrest.
apporre *vt form* to add.
appositamente *avv* on purpose ; ~ per te specially for you.
apposito, a *agg* appropriate.
apposta *avv* deliberately ; fare qc ~ to do sthg on purpose.
apposto, a *pp* → apporre.

apprendere *vt* to learn.

apprendista, i, e *smf* apprentice.

apprensivo, a *agg* apprehensive.

appreso, a *pp* → **apprendere**.

appretto *sm* starch.

apprezzamento *sm* appreciation.

apprezzare *vt* to appreciate.

approccio *sm* approach.

approdare *vi* to land ; **non ~ a niente** to come to nothing.

approdo *sm (atto)* landing ; *(luogo)* landing-place.

approfittare : approfittare di *v + prep* to take advantage of.

approfondire *vt (accentuare)* to deepen ; *(studiare)* to study in depth.

appropriarsi : appropriarsi di *vr + prep* to appropriate.

approssimativo, a *agg (calcolo)* approximate ; *(conoscenza)* superficial.

approvare *vt (legge, proposta)* to pass ; *(comportamento)* to approve of.

approvazione *sf* approval.

appuntamento *sm* appointment ; *(amoroso)* date ; **dare (un) ~ a qn** to arrange to meet sb ; **prendere un ~ con** o **da qn** to make an appointment with sb.

appuntare *vt (matita)* to sharpen ; *(fissare)* to pin ; *(annotare)* to note.

appunto *sm (annotazione)* note ; *(rimprovero)* reprimand. ◆ *avv* exactly.

apribottiglie *sm inv* bottle opener.

aprile *sm* April → **settembre**.

aprire *vt* to open ; *(gas, acqua)* to turn on. ◆ *vi* to open ; **vai tu ad ~?** can you answer the door? ; **'non ~ prima che il treno sia fermo'** 'do not open before the train has stopped'.

❑ **aprirsi** *vr (porta)* to open ; *(inchiesta)* to start up ; *(confidarsi)* : **aprirsi con qc** to open one's heart to sb.

apriscatole *sm inv* can opener.

aquila *sf* eagle.

aquilone *sm* kite.

Arabia Saudita *sf*: **l' ~** Saudi Arabia.

arabo, a *agg* & *sm, f* Arab. ◆ *sm (lingua)* Arabic.

arachide *sf* peanut.

aragosta *sf* lobster.

arancia, ce *sf* orange.

aranciata *sf* orange juice.

arancini *smpl rice balls with a filling of tomatoes and mozzarella cheese (a Sicilian speciality).*

arancio *sm* orange tree.

arancione *agg* & *sm* orange.

arare *vt* to plough.

aratro *sm* plough.

arazzo *sm* tapestry.

arbitrario, a *agg* arbitrary.

arbitro *sm* referee.

arbusto *sm* shrub.

archeologia *sf* archaeology.

archeologico, a, ci, che *agg* archaeological.

architetto *sm* architect.

architettura *sf* architecture.

archivio *sm (luogo)* archives *(pl)* ; *(raccolta)* files *(pl)* ; *INFORM* file.
arcipelago, ghi *sm* archipelago.
arcivescovo *sm* archbishop.
arco, chi *sm (volta)* arch ; *(arma)* bow ; *(durata)* : **nell' ~ di due mesi** in the space of two months.
arcobaleno *sm* rainbow.
ardere *vt* & *vi* to burn.
ardesia *sf (pietra)* slate.
ardire *vi* to dare. ◆ *sm* daring.
ardore *sm* ardour.
area *sf* area ; **' ~ pedonale'** 'pedestrian precinct' ; **~ di servizio** services *(pl)*.
arena *sf* arena.
arenarsi *vr* to run aground.
argenteria *sf* silverware.
Argentina *sf* : **l' ~** Argentina.
argentino, a *agg* & *sm, f* Argentinian.
argento *sm* silver ; **d' ~** silver.
argilla *sf* clay.
argine *sm* bank.
argomento *sm (tema)* subject ; *(ragionamento)* argument.
arguto, a *agg (persona)* quick-witted ; *(discorso, battuta)* witty.
aria *sf* air ; *(aspetto)* appearance ; **ha l' ~ familiare** he looks familiar ; **mandare all' ~ qc** to ruin sthg ; **all' ~ aperta** in the open air ; **~ condizionata** air-conditioning ; **darsi delle arie** to fancy o.s.
arido, a *agg (secco)* arid ; *fig (persona, cuore)* cold.
ariete *sm (animale)* ram. ❑ **Ariete** *sm* Aries.
aringa, ghe *sf* herring.
arista *sf* saddle of pork.
aristocratico, a, ci, che *agg* aristocratic. ◆ *sm, f* aristocrat.
aritmetica *sf* arithmetic.
Arlecchino *sm* Harlequin.
arma, i *sf (strumento)* weapon ; *(di esercito)* division ; **~ da fuoco** firearm.
armadio *sm* cupboard ; **~ a muro** built-in cupboard.
armato, a *agg* armed.
armatura *sf* armour.
Armenia *sf* : **l'~** Armenia.
apostrofare *vt (interpellare)* to address ; *(rimproverare)* to reproach.
armonia *sf* harmony.
arnese *sm (attrezzo)* tool ; *fam (oggetto)* thing.
arnia *sf* beehive.
Arno *sm* : **l' ~** the Arno.
aroma, i *sm (odore)* aroma ; *(essenza)* flavouring. ❑ **aromi** *mpl* spices.
arpa *sf* harp.
arpione *sm* harpoon.
arrabbiarsi *vr* to get angry.
arrabbiato, a *agg* angry ; **all'arrabbiata → penne**.
arrampicarsi *vr* to climb.
arrangiarsi *vr* to get by.
arredamento *sm* furnishings *(pl)*.
arredare *vt* to furnish.
arrendersi *vr* to surrender.
arrestare *vt (catturare)* to arrest ; *(emorragia, flusso)* to stop.
arresto *sm (cattura)* arrest ; *(fermata)* stop ; **~ cardiaco** cardiac arrest.

arretrato, a *agg (pagamento, giornale)* back *(dav s)* ; *(sottosviluppato)* backward ; *(sorpassato)* old-fashioned. ❑ **arretrati** *smpl* arrears.
arricchire *vt* to enrich. ❑ **arricchirsi** *vr* to get rich.
arricciacapelli *sm inv* curling tongs *(pl)*.
arricciare *vt (capelli, nastro)* to curl ; ~ **il naso** to wrinkle one's nose.
arrivare *vi* to arrive ; **arriverò a Firenze alle due** I'll get to Florence at two. ❑ **arrivare a** *v + prep (grado, livello)* to reach ; ~ **a fare qc** *(riuscire)* to manage to do sthg ; *(giungere al punto di, osare)* to go so far as to do sthg.
arrivederci *esclam* goodbye!
arrivederla *esclam* goodbye!
arrivista, i, e *smf* social climber.
arrivo *sm* arrival ; *(nello sport)* finishing line ; **essere in** ~ to be arriving ; **'arrivi (nazionali/internazionali)'** '(domestic/international) arrivals'.
arrogante *agg* arrogant.
arrossire *vi* to blush.
arrostire *vt* to roast.
arrosto *sm* roast.
arrotolare *vt* to roll up.
arrotondare *vt (render tondo)* to round ; *(numero)* to round off ; *(stipendio)* to add to.
arrugginito, a *agg* rusty.
arruolarsi *vr* to enlist.
arsenale *sm (di armi)* arsenal ; *(cantiere)* dockyard.
arte *sf* art ; *(abilità)* skill.
arteria *sf* artery.
artico, a, ci, che *agg* Arctic.
articolazione *sf* joint.
articolo *sm* article ; *(merce)* article, item ; **articoli da regalo** gifts.
Artide *sf* : **l'** ~ the Arctic.
artificiale *agg* artificial.
artigianato *sm* craftsmanship ; **di** ~ handcrafted.
artigiano, a *agg* craft *(dav s)*. ◆ *sm, f* craftsman *(f* craftswoman).
artiglio *sm* claw.
artista, i, e *smf* artist.
artistico, a, ci, che *agg* artistic.
arto *sm* limb.
artrite *sf* arthritis.
artrosi *sf* osteoarthritis.
ascella *sf* armpit.
ascendente *sm (influsso)* ascendancy ; *(astrologico)* ascendant.
Ascensione *sf* : **l'** ~ the Ascension.
ascensore *sm* lift *(Br)*, elevator *(Am)*.
ascesso *sm* abscess.
ascia *(pl* asce) *sf* axe.
asciugacapelli *sm inv* hair-dryer.
asciugamano *sm* towel.
asciugare *vt* to dry. ❑ **asciugarsi** *vr (persona)* to dry o.s. ; *(tinta, vestiti)* to dry.
asciutto, a *agg (secco)* dry ; *(magro)* thin.
ascoltare *vt* to listen to.
ascoltatore, trice *sm, f* listener.
ascolto *sm* : **dare** o **prestare** ~ **a**

to pay attention to ; **essere in ~** to be listening.

asfaltato, a *agg* asphalt *(dav s)*.

asfalto *sm* asphalt.

asfissia *sf* asphyxia.

asfissiare *vt* & *vi* to suffocate.

Asia *sf*: **l' ~** Asia.

asiatico, a, ci, che *agg* & *sm, f* Asian.

asilo *sm (scuola)* nursery ; **~ nido** crèche ; **~ politico** political asylum.

asino *sm* donkey.

asma *sf* asthma.

asola *sf* buttonhole.

asparago *sm* asparagus.

aspettare *vt* to wait for ; **mi aspetto una risposta** I expect an answer ; **~ un bambino** to be expecting a child.

aspettativa *sf (previsione)* expectation ; *(congedo)* leave.

aspetto *sm (apparenza)* appearance ; *(punto di vista)* point of view ; *(elemento)* aspect.

aspirapolvere *sm inv* vacuum cleaner.

aspirare *vt (inalare)* to breathe in ; *(risucchiare)* to suck up. ❑ **aspirare a** *v + prep* to aspire to.

aspiratore *sm* extractor.

aspirina® *sf* aspirin.

aspro, a *agg (sapore)* sour.

assaggiare *vt* to taste.

assai *avv (molto)* very ; *(abbastanza)* enough.

assalire *vt* to attack.

assassinare *vt* to murder.

assassinio *sm* murder.

assassino, a *sm, f* murderer.

asse *sf* board. ◆ *sm (di auto)* axle ; *(retta)* axis.

assedio *sm* siege.

assegnare *vt* : **~ qc (a qn)** *(casa, rendita)* to allocate sthg (to sb) ; *(incarico, compiti)* to assign sthg (to sb) ; *(premio)* to award sthg (to sb).

assegno *sm (bancario)* cheque ; *(sussidio)* benefit ; **~ a vuoto** bounced cheque ; **~ circolare** bank draft ; **~ di studio** study grant ; **~ di viaggio** o **turistico** traveller's cheque ; **contro ~** cash on delivery.

assemblea *sf* meeting.

assente *agg (da luogo)* absent ; *(distratto)* vacant. ◆ *smf* absentee.

assenza *sf (lontananza)* absence ; *(mancanza)* lack.

assetato, a *agg* thirsty.

assicurare *vt (auto, casa)* to insure ; *(garantire)* to ensure ; *(fissare)* to secure. ❑ **assicurarsi** *vr* to insure o.s. ; **assicurarsi di fare qc** to be sure to do sthg ; **assicurarsi che** to make sure that.

assicurata *sf* registered letter.

assicurato, a *agg* insured.

assicurazione *sf (contratto)* insurance ; *(garanzia)* assurance ; **~ sulla vita** life assurance.

assillare *vt (infastidire)* to pester ; *(sog : pensiero)* to torment.

Assisi *sf* Assisi.

assistente *smf* assistant ; **~ sociale** social worker ; **~ di volo** steward (*f* stewardess).

assistenza *sf* aid.

assistere *vt* to assist ; *(malato)* to care for. ◆ *vi* : **~ (a qc)** *(a lezioni)* to attend (sthg) ; *(a scena)* to be present (at sthg).

assistito, a *pp* → assistere.

asso *sm* ace.

associare *vt* to associate. ❑ **associarsi** *vr* : associarsi (a ○ con) *(ditta)* to enter into a partnership (with) ; associarsi a qc *(club)* to join sthg.

associazione *sf* association.

assolto, a *pp* → assolvere.

assolutamente *avv* absolutely.

assoluto, a *agg* absolute.

assoluzione *sf (accusato)* acquittal ; RELIG absolution.

assolvere *vt (accusato)* to acquit ; RELIG to absolve ; *(compito)* to carry out.

assomigliare : **assomigliare a** *v + prep* to resemble, to look like.

assonnato, a *agg* sleepy.

assorbente *agg (tampone)* absorbent. ◆ *sm* : ~ (igienico) (sanitary) towel ; ~ interno tampon.

assorbire *vt* to absorb.

assordante *agg* deafening.

assortimento *sm* assortment.

assortito, a *agg (vario)* assorted ; *(accordato)* matching.

assumere *vt (personale)* to take on ; *(impegno)* to accept ; *(atteggiamento)* to assume.

assunto, a *pp* → assumere.

assurdità *sf inv* absurdity.

assurdo, a *agg* absurd.

asta *sf (bastone)* pole ; *(vendita)* auction.

astemio, a *agg* teetotal.

astenersi : **astenersi da** *vr + prep* to abstain from.

asterisco, schi *sm* asterisk.

astigmatico, a, ci, che *agg* astigmatic.

astratto, a *agg* abstract.

astrologia *sf* astrology.

astronauta, i, e *smf* astronaut.

astronomia *sf* astronomy.

astuccio *sm* case.

astuto, a *agg (persona)* cunning ; *(idea, azione)* shrewd.

astuzia *sf (furbizia)* shrewdness ; *(stratagemma)* trick.

A.T. *abbr* = alta tensione.

ateo, a *sm, f* atheist.

ATI *(abbr di Aerotrasporti Italiani) Italian domestic airline.*

atlante *sm (geografico)* atlas.

atlantico, a, ci, che *agg* Atlantic.

Atlantico *sm* : l'(Oceano) ~ the Atlantic (Ocean).

atleta, i, e *smf* athlete.

atletica *sf* athletics *(sg)*.

atletico, a, ci, che *agg* athletic.

atmosfera *sf* atmosphere.

atmosferico, a, ci, che *agg* atmospheric.

atomico, a, ci, che *agg* atomic.

atomo *sm* atom.

atroce *agg* atrocious.

attaccante *sm* forward.

attaccapanni *sm inv* clothes stand.

attaccare *vt (unire)* to attach ; *(appendere)* to hang up ; *(assalire)* to attack ; *(trasmettere)* to give. ❑ **attaccarsi** *vr* to stick.

attacco, chi *sm* attack ; *(presa)* socket.

atteggiamento *sm* attitude.

attendere *vt* to wait for.
attentato *sm* attack.
attento, a *agg (che presta attenzione)* attentive ; *(prudente)* careful ; **stai ~!** *(non distrarti)* pay attention! ; *(stai in guardia)* be careful! ; **'attenti al cane'** 'beware of the dog' ; **'attenti al gradino'** 'mind the step'.
attenzione *sf* attention ; **attenzione!** be careful! ; **fare ~** *(concentrarsi)* to pay attention ; *(essere prudente)* to be careful.
atterraggio *sm* landing.
atterrare *vi* to land.
attesa *sf* wait ; **essere in ~ di** to be waiting for.
atteso, a *pp* → **attendere**.
attestato *sm* certificate.
attico *sm* penthouse.
attillato, a *agg* close-fitting.
attimo *sm* moment.
attirare *vt* to attract.
attitudine *sf* aptitude.
attività *sf inv* activity ; *(occupazione)* occupation ; COMM assets *(pl)*.
attivo, a *agg* active. ◆ *sm* assets *(pl)*.
atto *sm (azione, gesto)* act, deed ; *(documento)* document ; *(di dramma)* act ; **mettere in ~** to put into action.
attonito, a *agg* astonished.
attorcigliare *vt* to twist.
attore, trice *sm, f* actor *(f* actress).
attorno *avv* around.
attracco, chi *sm (manovra)* docking ; *(luogo)* mooring.
attraente *agg* attractive.
attrarre *vt (affascinare)* to attract ; *(richiamare)* to draw.
attrattiva *sf (richiamo)* attraction ; *(qualità)* attractiveness.
attratto, a *pp* → **attrarre**.
attraversamento *sm* crossing ; **~ pedonale** pedestrian crossing.
attraversare *vt (strada, città)* to cross ; *(periodo)* to go through.
attraverso *prep (da parte a parte)* across ; *(per mezzo di)* through.
attrazione *sf* attraction.
attrezzatura *sf* equipment.
attrezzo *sm* tool.
attribuire : attribuire a *v + prep (opera)* to attribute to ; **~ il merito a qn** to give sb the credit.
attrice → **attore**.
attrito *sm* friction.
attuale *agg (presente)* present ; *(moderno)* topical.
attualità *sf inv* current events *(pl)* ; **d' ~** topical.
attualmente *avv* at present.
attuare *vt* to carry out.
attutire *vt (colpo, rumore)* to reduce.
audace *agg* bold.
audacia *sf* audacity.
audiovisivo, a *agg* audiovisual.
auditorio *sm* auditorium.
audizione *sf* audition.
augurare *vt* : **~ qc a qn** to wish sb sthg ; **augurarsi di fare qc** to hope to do sthg ; **mi auguro che tutto vada bene** I hope that all goes well.
augurio *sm* wish ; **auguri** greet-

ings ; (tanti) auguri! all the best! ; *(per compleanno)* happy birthday! ; fare gli auguri a qn to give sb one's best wishes.

aula *sf* classroom.

aumentare *vt* & *vi* to increase.

aumento *sm* increase.

aureola *sf* halo.

auricolare *sm* earphone.

aurora *sf* dawn.

ausiliare *agg* & *sm* auxiliary.

austero, a *agg* austere.

Australia *sf*: l' ~ Australia.

australiano, a *agg* & *sm, f* Australian.

Austria *sf*: l' ~ Austria.

austriaco, a, ci, che *agg* & *sm, f* Austrian.

autenticare *vt* to authenticate.

autentico, a, ci, che *agg (firma, quadro)* authentic ; *(fatto)* true ; è un ~ cretino he's a real cretin.

autista, i, e *smf* driver.

auto *sf inv* car.

autoabbronzante *agg* self-tanning. ◆ *sm* fake tanning cream.

autoadesivo, a *agg* self-adhesive. ◆ *sm* sticker.

autoambulanza *sf* ambulance.

autobiografia *sf* autobiography.

autobus *sm inv* bus.

autocarro *sm* truck.

autocisterna *sf* tanker.

autocontrollo *sm* self-control.

autodidatta, i, e *smf* self-taught person.

autodromo *sm* racing track.

autogol *sm inv* own goal.

autografo *sm* autograph.

autogrill® *sm inv* motorway restaurant.

autolinea *sf* bus service.

automa, i *sm* automaton.

automatico, a, ci, che *agg* automatic.

automazione *sf* automation.

automezzo *sm* motor vehicle.

automobile *sf* car *(Br)*, automobile *(Am)*.

automobilismo *sm* *(sport)* motor racing ; *(industria)* car industry *(Br)*, auto industry *(Am)*.

automobilista, i, e *smf* motorist.

autonoleggio *sm* car hire.

autonomia *sf (indipendenza)* autonomy ; *(di veicolo)* range.

autonomo, a *agg* independent, autonomous.

autopsia *sf* autopsy.

autoradio *sf inv* car radio.

autore, trice *sm, f (di libro)* author ; *(di quadro)* painter ; l' ~ del delitto the person who committed the crime.

autorevole *agg* authoritative.

autorimessa *sf* garage.

autorità *sf inv* authority.

autoritario, a *agg* authoritarian.

autorizzare *vt* to authorize.

autorizzazione *sf* authorization.

autoscatto *sm* timer.

autoscontro *sm* Dodgem® car.

autoscuola *sf* driving school.

autoservizio *sm* bus service.

autoservizi *smpl* bus services.

autostop *sm* hitchhiking ; **fare l' ~** to hitchhike.

autostoppista, i, e *smf* hitchhiker.

autostrada *sf* motorway *(Br)*, freeway *(Am)*.

autostradale *agg* motorway *(dav s) (Br)*, freeway *(dav s) (Am)*.

autoveicolo *sm* motor vehicle.

autovettura *sf* motorcar.

autunno *sm* autumn *(Br)*, fall *(Am)*.

avambraccio *sm* forearm.

avanguardia *sf*: **d' ~** avant-garde ; **essere all' ~** to be in the vanguard.

avanti *avv (stato in luogo)* in front ; *(moto)* forward. ◆ *prep* : **~ a** *(stato in luogo)* ahead of ; *(moto)* ahead of, in front of ; **~!** *(invito a entrare)* come in! ; *(esortazione)* come on! ; **'avanti!'** *(al semaforo)* 'cross now' 'walk' *(Am)* ; *(in banca)* 'enter' ; **~ e indietro** backwards and forwards ; **andare ~** to go on ; **essere ~** *(nel lavoro, studio)* to be well ahead ; **essere ~ negli anni** to be getting on (in years) ; **farsi ~** to come forward ; **passare ~ a qn** to go in front of sb.

avanzare *vt (spostare avanti)* to move forward ; *(proposta)* to put forward. ◆ *vi (procedere)* to advance ; *(restare)* to be left (over).

avanzo *sm (di cibo)* leftovers *(pl)* ; *(di stoffa)* remnant.

avaria *sf (meccanico)* breakdown.

avariato, a *agg (cibo)* off.

avaro, a *agg* mean. ◆ *sm, f* miser.

avena *sf* oats *(pl)*.

☞

avere *vt* - 1. *(possedere)* to have ; **ha due fratelli** he's got two brothers ; **non ho più soldi** I haven't got any money left.
- 2. *(come caratteristica)* to have ; **~ occhi e capelli scuri** to have dark eyes and hair ; **~ molta immaginazione** to have a lot of imagination.
- 3. *(età)* : **quanti anni hai?** how old are you? ; **ho 18 anni** I'm 18 (years old).
- 4. *(portare addosso)* to have on, to wear ; **ha un cappotto grigio** she's wearing a grey coat, she's got a grey coat on.
- 5. *(sentire)* : **~ caldo/freddo** to be hot/cold ; **~ sonno** to be sleepy ; **~ fame** to be hungry ; **ho mal di testa** I've got a headache.
- 6. *(ottenere, ricevere)* to get.
- 7. *(in espressioni)* : **non ha niente a che fare** ○ **vedere con lui** that's got nothing to do with him ; **non ne ho per molto** it won't take me long ; **~ da fare** to have things to do ; **avercela con qn** to be angry with sb ; **quanti ne abbiamo oggi?** what's the date today?
◆ *v aus* to have ; **non ho finito** I haven't finished ; **gli ho parlato ieri** I spoke to him yesterday.
❑ **averi** *smpl (beni)* wealth *(sg)*.

avi *smpl* ancestors.

aviazione *sf* aviation.

avido, a *agg* greedy.

AVIS *sf (abbr di Associazione*

Volontari Italiani del Sangue) blood donors' association.
avocado *sm inv* avocado.
avorio *sm* ivory.
avvallamento *sm* depression.
avvantaggiare *vt* to favour. ❑ **avvantaggiarsi** *vr* : **avvantaggiarsi negli studi** to get ahead with one's studies ; **avvantaggiarsi sui concorrenti** to get ahead of one's competitors. ❑ **avvantaggiarsi di** *vr + prep* to take advantage of.
avvelenamento *sm* poisoning.
avvelenare *vt* to poison ; *(aria)* to pollute.
avvenente *agg* attractive.
avvenimento *sm* event.
avvenire *sm* future. ◆ *vi* to happen.
avventarsi *vr* : **~ su** o **contro** to rush at.
avventato, a *agg* rash.
avventura *sf* adventure ; *(amorosa)* affair.
avventurarsi *vr* to venture.
avventuroso, a *agg* adventurous.
avvenuto, a *pp* → **avvenire.**
avverarsi *vr* to come true.
avverbio *sm* adverb.
avversario, a *agg* opposing. ◆ *sm, f* opponent.
avvertenza *sf (avviso)* notice. ❑ **avvertenze** *sfpl* instructions.
avvertimento *sm* warning.
avvertire *vt (avvisare)* to warn ; *(dolore, fastidio)* to feel.
avviamento *sm (di motore)* starting ; *COMM* goodwill.
avviare *vt (cominciare)* to start ; *(indirizzare)* to introduce. ❑ **avviarsi** *vr* to set off.
avvicinare *vt* to move closer. ❑ **avvicinarsi** *vr* : **avvicinarsi (a)** to move close (to).
avvilirsi *vr* to lose heart.
avvincente *agg* enthralling.
avvisare *vt (informare)* to inform ; *(ammonire)* to warn.
avviso *sm (scritto)* notice ; *(annuncio)* announcement ; *(avvertimento)* warning ; **a mio ~** in my opinion.
avvistare *vt* to sight.
avvitare *vt (lampadina)* to screw in ; *(con viti)* to screw.
avvizzire *vi* to wither.
avvocato *sm* lawyer.
avvolgere *vt (fascia)* to wrap round ; *(tappeto)* to roll up ; *(avviluppare)* to wrap up. ❑ **avvolgersi** *vr (aggrovigliarsi)* to become tangled ; *(avvilupparsi)* to wrap o.s. up.
avvolgibile *sm* roller blind.
avvolto, a *pp* → **avvolgere.**
avvoltoio *sm* vulture.
azalea *sf* azalea.
azienda *sf* business, firm ; **~ agricola** farm.
azionare *vt* to operate.
azione *sf* action ; *COMM* share.
azionista, i, e *smf* shareholder.
azoto *sm* nitrogen.
azzannare *vt* to sink one's teeth into.
azzardare *vt* to venture. ❑ **azzardarsi** *vr* : **azzardarsi a fare qc** to dare to do sthg.

azzardo *sm* risk ; **giocare d' ~** to gamble.
azzeccare *vt* to get right.
azzuffarsi *vr* to scuffle.
azzurro, a *agg* & *sm* blue. ❑ **Azzurri** *smpl* : **gli Azzurri** the Italian national team.

B

babà *sm inv* rum baba.
babbo *sm fam* dad, daddy ; **Babbo Natale** Father Christmas.
baby-sitter [bebi'sitter] *smf inv* babysitter.
bacca, che *sf (frutto)* berry.
baccalà *sm inv* dried salt cod ; **~ alla fiorentina** *dried salt cod cooked with garlic and tomato sauce* ; **~ alla vicentina** *dried salt cod poached in milk with onions, anchovies and parsley*.
bacheca, che *sf (pannello)* notice board ; *(cassetta)* display case.
baciare *vt* to kiss. ❑ **baciarsi** *vr* to kiss (each other).
bacinella *sf* bowl.
bacino *sm (in geografia, catino)* basin ; ANAT pelvis.
bacio *sm* kiss ; **baci di dama** *sweet pastries sandwiched together with chocolate cream*.
badare *vi* : **~ a** *(prendersi cura di)* to look after ; *(fare attenzione a)* to pay attention to ; **~ a** ○ **di fare qc** to take care to do sthg ; **mio fratello non bada a spese** money's no object where my brother's concerned.
badia *sf* abbey.
baffi *smpl* moustache *(sg)*.
bagagliaio *sm (di macchina)* boot *(Br)*, trunk *(Am)* ; *(di treno)* luggage van *(Br)*, baggage car *(Am)*.
bagaglio *sm* luggage, baggage ; **~ a mano** hand luggage ; **ho un solo ~** I have only one piece of luggage. ❑ **bagagli** *smpl* luggage *(sg)* ; **fare i bagagli** to pack.
bagliore *sm (di lampi)* flash ; *(di fari)* glare.
bagna cauda *sf oil, garlic and anchovy dip from Piedmont kept warm at the table and served with vegetables*.
bagnare *vt* to wet ; *(tovaglia, vestiti)* to get wet ; *(annaffiare)* to water ; *(sog : fiume)* to flow through ; *(sog : mare)* to wash. ❑ **bagnarsi** *vr (in mare)* to bathe ; *(di pioggia, spruzzi)* to get wet.
bagnato, a *agg* wet ; **~ fradicio** soaked through.
bagnino, a *sm, f* lifeguard.
bagno *sm (nella vasca)* bath ; *(in piscina, mare)* swim ; *(stanza)* bathroom ; **fare il ~** *(nella vasca)* to have a bath ; *(in mare)* to have a swim ; **~ pubblico** public baths *(pl)*. ❑ **bagni** *smpl (stabilimento)* bathing establishment.
bagnomaria *sm* : **cuocere a ~** to cook in a double saucepan.
bagnoschiuma *sm inv* bath foam.
baia *sf* bay.
baita *sf* chalet.
balaustra *sf* balustrade.
balbettare *vi* to stammer.

balcone *sm* balcony.
balena *sf* whale.
balla *sf fam (frottola)* fib ; *(di merci)* bale.
ballare *vi* & *vt* to dance.
ballerina *sf (scarpa)* pump → ballerino.
ballerino, a *sm, f* dancer ; *(classico)* ballet-dancer (*f* ballerina).
balletto *sm* ballet.
ballo *sm* dance ; *(festa)* dance, ball ; **essere in ~** to be at stake ; **tirare in ~** *(coinvolgere)* to involve ; *(menzionare)* to mention.
balneare *agg* bathing *(dav s)*.
balneazione *sf* bathing ; **'divieto di balneazione'** 'no bathing'.
balsamo *sm (per capelli)* conditioner ; *(pomata)* ointment.
Baltico *sm* : **il (Mar) ~** the Baltic (Sea).
balzare *vi* to leap.
bambinaia *sf* nanny.
bambino, a *sm, f* child ; *(neonato)* baby.
bambola *sf* doll.
banale *agg* banal.
banana *sf* banana.
banca, che *sf* bank ; **~ dati** data bank.
bancarella *sf* stall.
bancario, a *agg* bank *(dav s)*. ◆ *sm, f* bank employee.
bancarotta *sf* bankruptcy.
banchina *sf (di porto)* quay ; *(di stazione)* platform ; **' ~ non transitabile'** 'soft verges'.
banco, chi *sm (di scuola)* desk ; *(di negozio, bar)* counter ; *(di mercato)* stall ; *(banca)* bank ; **~ di corallo** coral reef ; **~ di nebbia** fog bank.
bancomat® *sm inv (sportello)* cash dispenser ; *(tessera)* cash card ; *(sistema)* automated banking.
bancone *sm* counter.
banconota *sf* bank note.
banda *sf (musicale)* band ; *(striscia)* band, strip ; *(di malviventi)* gang ; *(di amici)* group.
bandiera *sf* flag.
bandito *sm* bandit.
bando *sm* announcement ; **~ alle chiacchiere!** that's enough talking!
bar *sm inv* bar ; **~-tabacchi** *bar that also sells cigarettes and stamps*.
bara *sf* coffin.
baracca, che *sf* hut ; *spreg (casa)* dump ; **mandare avanti la ~** *fam* to keep things going.
baraccone *sm* booth.
baratro *sm* barter.
barattolo *sm* jar ; *(di latta)* can.
barba *sf* beard ; **farsi la ~** to shave ; **che ~!** what a bore!
barbaro, a *agg* barbaric. ◆ *sm, f* barbarian.
barbecue [barbe'kju] *sm inv* barbecue.
barbiere *sm* barber.
barbone, a *sm, f* tramp.
barca, che *sf* boat ; **~ a remi** rowing boat *(Br)*, rowboat *(Am)* ; **~ a vela** sailing boat *(Br)*, sailboat *(Am)*.
barcollare *vi* to stagger.
barella *sf* stretcher.
barista, i, e *smf* barman (*f* barmaid).

barman *sm inv* barman.
Barolo *sm* Barolo *(full-bodied red wine from Piedmont)*.
barra *sf* rod, bar; *(lineetta)* stroke; *(di barca)* tiller.
barricare *vt* to barricade. ❑ **barricarsi** *vr*: **barricarsi in/dietro** to barricade o.s. in/behind.
barriera *sf* barrier.
basare *vt* to base. ❑ **basarsi su** *vr + prep (persona)* to base o.s. on.
base *sf* base; *(fondamento)* basis; **a ~ di whisky** whisky-based; **in ~ a qc** on the basis of sthg.
baseball ['beizbol] *sm* baseball.
basette *sfpl* sideboards.
basilica, che *sf* basilica.
basilico *sm* basil.
basso, a *agg* low; *(persona)* short; *(acqua)* shallow. ◆ *sm (fondo)* bottom; *(strumento, cantante)* bass; **in ~** at the bottom.
basta *esclam* that's enough!
bastare *vi* & *v impers* to be enough; **~ a qn** to be enough for sb; **basta che** so long as; **basta così!** that's enough!
bastone *sm* stick; **~ da passeggio** walking stick.
battaglia *sf* battle.
battello *sm* boat.
battere *vt* to beat; *(testa)* to hit; *(ore)* to strike; *(zona)* to scour. ◆ *vi (cuore)* to beat; *(sole, pioggia)* to beat down; *(urtare)*: **~ contro o in qc** to hit sthg; **si battevano i denti dal freddo** our teeth were chattering with the cold; **~ a macchina** to type; **~ le mani** to clap; **in un batter d'occhio** in the twinkling of an eye. ❑ **battersi** *vr* to fight.
batteria *sf (elettrica)* battery; *(strumento)* drums *(pl)*.
battesimo *sm* baptism.
battezzare *vt* to baptize.
battigia *sf* water's edge.
battistrada *sm inv* tread.
battito *sm* beat, beating; *(di orologio)* ticking; **~ cardiaco** heartbeat.
battuta *sf (spiritosaggine)* witty remark; *(teatrale)* cue; *(di tennis)* service.
baule *sm (da viaggio)* trunk; *(di auto)* boot *(Br)*, trunk *(Am)*.
bavaglino *sm* bib.
bavaglio *sm* gag.
bavarese *sf (dolce) cold dessert made with eggs, milk and cream*.
bavero *sm* collar.
bazzecola *sf (cosa poco importante)* trifle; *(cosa facile)*: **è una ~** it's no problem.
beato, a *agg (felice)* happy; RELIG blessed; **~ te!** lucky you!.
beauty-case ['bju:ti'keis] *sm inv* beauty case.
beccare *vt* to peck; *fam (sorprendere)* to catch; **beccarsi qc** *fam (raffreddore)* to catch sthg; *(ceffone)* to get sthg.
becco, chi *sm* beak.
Befana *sf (festa)* Epiphany; *(personaggio) legendary old woman who brings children their presents at the Epiphany*.

i BEFANA

According to legend, the *Befana* is a kindly old hag who delivers presents to children on the night before the Epiphany. Children leave out a stocking before going to bed, and the *Befana* comes down the chimney in the night, bringing sweets and other gifts to good boys and girls and lumps of coal to those who have been naughty.

---

beffa *sf* joke.
beffarsi : **beffarsi di** to make fun of.
begli → **bello.**
bei → **bello.**
beige [bɛʒ] *agg inv* & *sm inv* beige.
bel → **bello.**
belga, gi, ghe *agg* & *smf* Belgian.
Belgio *sm* : **il ~** Belgium.
bella *sf* SPORT decider.
bellezza *sf* beauty ; **che ~!** fantastic!.

☞

bello, a (*dav sm* **bel** (*pl* **bei**) + *consonante ;* **bello** (*pl* **begli**) + *s+consonante, gn, ps, z ;* **bell'** (*pl* **begli**) + *vocale*) *agg* - **1.** (*donna, cosa*) beautiful ; (*uomo*) handsome ; **farsi ~** to make o.s. beautiful ; **le belle arti** fine arts.
- **2.** (*piacevole*) pleasant, lovely.
- **3.** (*tempo*) fine, beautiful ; **la bella stagione** the summer months (*pl*) ; **fa ~** it's lovely weather.
- **4.** (*buono*) good.
- **5.** (*lodevole*) good, kind.
- **6.** (*grande*) : **un bel piatto di spaghetti** a nice big plate of spaghetti ; **una bella dormita** a good sleep ; **è una bella cifra** it's a considerable sum of money.
- **7.** (*rafforzativo*) : **è bell'e (che) andato** he's already gone ; **è una bugia bell'e buona** it's an absolute lie ; **alla bell'e meglio** somehow or other ; **un bel niente** absolutely nothing.
◆ *sm* - **1.** (*bellezza*) beauty.
- **2.** (*punto culminante*) : **sul più ~** at that very moment ; **il ~ è che ...** the best bit is that ...

---

belva *sf* wild beast.
belvedere *sm inv* scenic viewpoint.
benché *cong* although, though.
benda *sf* (*fasciatura*) bandage ; (*per occhi*) blindfold.
bendare *vt* (*ferita*) to bandage ; (*occhi*) to blindfold.

☞

bene (*compar* & *superl* **meglio**) *avv* - **1.** (*in modo soddisfacente*) well ; **avete mangiato ~?** did you enjoy your meal?
- **2.** (*nel modo giusto*) well ; **hai fatto ~** you did the right thing.
- **3.** (*in buona salute*) : **stare/sentirsi ~** to be/feel well.
- **4.** (*a proprio agio*) : **stare ~** to be ○ feel comfortable.
- **5.** (*esteticamente*) : **stare ~** to look good.
- **6.** (*rafforzativo*) : **è ben difficile** it's very difficult ; **è ben più difficile del previsto** it's much more difficult than we thought ; **lo credo ~** I can well believe it ; **spero ~ che** I very much hope that.
- **7.** (*in espressioni*) : **è ~ che lo sappiate** it's as well that you know ; **sarebbe ~ aspettare** it would be better to wait ; **dire ~ di qn** to

speak well of sb ; **ti sta ~!** it serves you right! ; **va ~** all right, OK.
◆ *esclam* fine!, OK!
◆ *sm* good ; **è per il tuo ~** it's for your own good ; **è un ~ per tutti** it is a good thing for everyone.
❑ **beni** *smpl (proprietà)* property *(sg)*.

---

benedire *vt* to bless.
benedizione *sf* blessing.
beneducato, a *agg* well-mannered.
beneficenza *sf* charity.
benessere *sm* wellbeing.
benestante *agg* well-to-do.
benevolo, a *agg* benevolent.
beninteso *avv* certainly, of course.
benvenuto, a *agg* & *sm* welcome ; **benvenuti a Roma!** welcome to Rome! ; **dare il ~ a qn** to welcome sb.
benzina *sf* petrol *(Br)*, gas *(Am)* ; **fare ~** to get petrol *(Br)*, to get gas *(Am)*.
benzinaio, a *sm, f* forecourt attendant.
bere *vt* to drink ; **bevi qualcosa?** would you like something to drink? ; **offrire da ~ a qn** to offer sb a drink.
bermuda *smpl* bermuda shorts.
bernoccolo *sm* bump.
bersaglio *sm* target.
besciamella *sf* béchamel sauce.
bestemmiare *vi* to curse, to swear.
bestia *sf* animal ; **andare in ~** to fly into a rage.
bestiame *sm* livestock.
bevanda *sf* drink.
bevuto, a *pp* → **bere**.
biancheria *sf* linen ; **~ intima** underwear.
bianchetto *sm* correcting fluid.
bianco, a, chi, che *agg* & *sm* white. ◆ *sm, f (persona)* white man (*f* white woman) ; **riso in ~** plain rice ; **pesce in ~** boiled fish ; **in ~ e nero** black and white.
biasimare *vt* to blame.
bibbia *sf* bible.
biberon *sm inv* baby's bottle.
bibita *sf* drink.
biblioteca, che *sf* library.
bicarbonato *sm* : **~ (di sodio)** bicarbonate (of soda).
bicchiere *sm* glass.
bici *sf inv fam* bike.
bicicletta *sf* bicycle ; **andare in ~** to cycle.
bidè *sm inv* bidet.
bidone *sm* bin ; *fam (imbroglio)* swindle ; **fare un ~ a qn** *fam (mancare a un appuntamento)* to stand sb up ; *(imbrogliare)* to cheat sb.
biennale *agg (ogni due anni)* two-yearly ; *(per due anni)* two-year *(dav s)*. ❑ **Biennale** *sf* : **la Biennale** the Venice Arts Festival.

BIENNALE

Established in 1895, this international art festival takes place every two years in the gardens of the International Gallery of Modern Art in Venice. The selection of paintings and sculptures on view reflects the avant-garde emphasis of the festival, a trend which has become more pronounced in recent years and is not without its critics. Alongside the art festival, there are festivals of music, theatre and architecture, as well as an annual film festival.

---

biforcarsi *vr* to fork.

BIGE *sm reduced-price train ticket for people under 26.*

bigiotteria *sf* costume jewellery ; *(negozio)* costume jeweller's.

biglia = **bilia**.

bigliardo = **biliardo**.

bigliettaio, a *sm, f* ticket inspector.

biglietteria *sf* ticket office ; *(al teatro)* box office ; ~ **automatica** ticket machine.

biglietto *sm (scontrino)* ticket ; *(messaggio)* note ; *(banconota)* (bank) note ; **fare il ~** to buy one's ticket ; ~ **d'andata e ritorno** return (ticket) ; ~ **di (sola) andata** single (ticket) ; ~ **collettivo** party ticket ; ~ **cumulativo** group ticket ; ~ **gratuito** complimentary ticket ; ~ **intero** full-price ticket ; ~ **ridotto** reduced-price ticket ; ~ **d'auguri** greetings card ; ~ **da visita** visiting card.

bignè *sm inv choux bun filled with custard or chocolate.*

bigodino *sm* curler.

bigoli : bigoli *smpl* : ~ **coi rovinazzi** *large spaghetti from Veneto in a sauce made with chicken giblets.*

bikini® *sm inv* bikini.

bilancia, ce *sf* scales *(pl)*. ❑ **Bilancia** *sf* Libra.

bilancio *sm COMM* balance sheet ; ~ **preventivo** budget.

bilia *sf (di vetro)* marble ; *(da biliardo)* billiard ball.

biliardo *sm (gioco)* billiards *(sg)* ; *(tavolo)* billiard table.

bilico : in bilico *avv* balanced.

bilingue *agg* bilingual.

bimbo, a *sm, f* little boy (*f* little girl).

binario *sm (rotaie)* railway track ; *(marciapiede)* platform ; **'ai binari'** 'to the trains'.

binocolo *sm* binoculars *(pl)*.

biologia *sf* biology.

biondo, a *agg* blond (*f* blonde).

birichino, a *agg* cheeky. ◆ *sm, f* little rascal.

birillo *sm* skittle.

biro® *sf inv* Biro®.

birra *sf* beer ; ~ **chiara** lager ; ~ **scura** stout ; ~ **alla spina** draught beer.

birreria *sf* pub.

bis *esclam* encore!

bisbigliare *vi* & *vt* to whisper.

biscotto *sm* biscuit.

bisessuale *agg* bisexual.

bisestile *agg* → **anno**.

bisnonno, a *sm, f* great-grandfather (*f* great-grandmother).

bisognare *v impers* : **bisogna stare attenti** we/I must be careful ; **bisogna che tu venga subito** you have to come at once.

bisogno *sm* need, necessity ; **aver ~ di** to need.

bistecca, che *sf* steak ; ~ **al sangue** rare steak ; ~ **alla fiorentina**

T-bone steak grilled or cooked over charcoal.

bisticciare *vi* to bicker.

bitter *sm inv* bitters *(pl).*

bivio *sm* fork, junction.

bizza *sf* tantrum.

bizzarro, a *agg* odd, eccentric.

bloccare *vt* to block; *(città)* to cut off; *(meccanismo)* to jam; *(prezzi)* to freeze. ❑ **bloccarsi** *vr (ascensore)* to get stuck; *(porta)* to jam.

blocchetto *sm (quaderno)* notebook.

blocco, chi *sm* block; *(quaderno)* notebook; *(di meccanismo)* blockage; *(di attività)* stoppage; **~ stradale** roadblock; **in ~** en bloc.

blu *agg inv* & *sm inv* blue.

blue-jeans [blu'dʒins] *smpl* jeans.

blusa *sf* blouse.

boa *sm inv (serpente)* boa. ◆ *sf (galleggiante)* buoy.

bobina *sf (di auto)* coil; *(di pellicola)* reel.

bocca, che *sf* mouth; **in ~ al lupo!** good luck!

boccaccia, ce *sf*: **fare le boccacce** to pull faces.

boccale *sm* jug.

boccia, ce *sf* bowl.

bocciare *vt (studente)* to fail; *(proposta, progetto)* to reject.

boccone *sm* mouthful; **mangiare un ~** to have a bite to eat.

bocconi *avv* face downwards.

boicottare *vt* to boycott.

bolla *sf* bubble; *(vescica)* blister; COMM bill.

bollente *agg* boiling.

bolletta *sf* bill; *(ricevuta)* receipt.

bollettino *sm* bulletin; **~ meteorologico** weather forecast.

bollire *vt* & *vi* to boil.

bollito, a *agg* boiled. ◆ *sm beef, veal or chicken, served with a parsley sauce.*

bollitore *sm* kettle.

bollo *sm (marchio)* stamp.

Bologna *sf* Bologna.

bolognese *agg* of/from Bologna; **alla ~** with meat and tomato sauce.

bomba *sf* bomb.

bombardare *vt* to bomb.

bombola *sf* cylinder.

bombolone *sm* doughnut.

bonaccia *sf* (dead) calm.

bonario, a *agg* good-natured.

bonet *sm inv chocolate-flavoured egg custard.*

bontà *sf* goodness.

borbottare *vi* to grumble. ◆ *vt* to mutter.

bordeaux [bor'do] *agg inv* maroon.

bordo *sm (orlo)* edge; *(guarnizione)* trim, border; *(di nave)* (ship's) side; **a ~ di** *(nave, aereo)* on board; *(auto)* in; *(moto)* on.

borghese *agg* middle-class; **in ~** in plain clothes.

borghesia *sf* middle classes *(pl).*

borgo, ghi *sm (paesino)* hamlet; *(quartiere)* district.

borotalco® *sm* talcum powder.

borraccia, ce *sf* flask.

borsa *sf* bag; **~ dell'acqua calda**

hot-water bottle ; ~ **del ghiaccio** ice bag ; ~ **della spesa** shopping bag ; ~ **di studio** grant. ❏ **Borsa** *sf* Stock Exchange.

borsaiolo *sm* pickpocket.

borsellino *sm* purse.

borsetta *sf* handbag.

bosco, schi *sm* wood.

botanico, a, ci, che *agg* botanic. ◆ *sm, f* botanist.

botta *sf* blow ; *(rumore)* bang ; **fare a botte** to come to blows.

botte *sf* barrel.

bottega, ghe *sf* shop ; *(laboratorio)* workshop.

bottegaio, a *sm, f* shopkeeper.

bottiglia *sf* bottle.

bottiglione *sm* large bottle.

botto *sm (rumore)* bang.

bottone *sm* button ; **attaccare un ~ a qn** to buttonhole sb.

boutique [bu'tik] *sf inv* boutique.

box *sm inv (garage)* lock-up (garage) ; *(per bambini)* playpen ; *(per animali)* pen.

boxe [bɔks] *sf* boxing.

boy-scout [bɔi'skaut] *sm inv* boy scout.

braccetto : **a braccetto** *avv* arm in arm.

bracciale *sm* bracelet.

braccialetto *sm* bracelet.

braccio *sm (arto : pl f braccia)* arm ; *(di edificio : pl m bracci)* wing ; *(di gru, fiume)* arm ; ~ **di ferro** arm wrestling ; **sotto ~** arm in arm.

bracciolo *sm* arm.

brace *sf* embers *(pl)* ; **alla ~** charcoal-grilled.

braciola *sf* steak ; *(con osso)* chop.

braille ['braj] *sm* braille.

branco, chi *sm (di animali)* herd ; *spreg (di persone)* gang, bunch.

branda *sf* camp bed.

brasato *sm* braised beef.

Brasile *sm* : **il ~** Brazil.

bravo *agg* good ; **bravo!** well done! ; ~ **a fare qc** good at doing sthg ; ~ **in qc** good at sthg.

bresaola *sf dried salt beef served thinly sliced.*

bretelle *sfpl (per pantaloni)* braces ; *(spalline)* straps.

breve *agg* short, brief ; **in ~** briefly ; **tra ~** shortly.

brevetto *sm (di invenzione)* patent ; *(patente)* licence.

brezza *sf* breeze.

bricco, chi *sm* jug.

briciola *sf* crumb.

briciolo *sm* : **un ~ di qc** a bit of sthg.

brillante *agg* brilliant ; *(lucente)* bright. ◆ *sm* diamond.

brillare *vi* to shine.

brillo, a *agg* tipsy.

brindisi *sm inv* toast ; **fare un ~ a** to toast.

brioche [bri'ɔʃ] *sf inv round, sweet bread roll made with butter and eaten for breakfast.*

britannico, a, ci, che *agg* British.

brivido *sm* shiver, shudder.

brocca, che *sf* jug.

brodo *sm* broth ; **pasta in ~** noodle soup ; **riso in ~** rice soup.
bronchite *sf* bronchitis.
brontolare *vi* to grumble ; *(stomaco, tuono)* to rumble.
bronzo *sm* bronze.
bruciapelo : abruciapelo *avv* point-blank.
bruciare *vt* to burn ; *(distruggere)* to burn down. ◆ *vi* to burn ; *(produrre bruciore)* to sting. ❑ **bruciarsi** *vr (persona)* to burn o.s. ; *(oggetto)* to burn.
bruciato, a *agg* burnt.
bruciatura *sf* burn.
bruno, a *agg* dark.
bruschetta *sf bread toasted with garlic and olive oil.*
brusio *sm* buzz.
brutale *agg* brutal.
brutto, a *agg (di aspetto)* ugly ; *(tempo, giornata, strada)* bad ; *(situazione, sorpresa, malattia)* nasty ; *(rafforzativo)* : **~ imbroglione!** you rotten cheat! ; **brutti ma buoni** *almond and hazelnut meringues.*
Bruxelles [bru'ksɛl] *sf* Brussels.
buca, che *sf* hole ; **~ delle lettere** letterbox.
bucare *vt* to make a hole o holes in ; **~ una gomma** to puncture a tyre. ❑ **bucarsi** *vr (forarsi)* to have a puncture ; *(pungersi)* to prick o.s. ; *fam (drogarsi)* to mainline.
bucatini *smpl* : **~ all'amatriciana** *dish from Lazio consisting of long, thin pasta tubes in a sauce of tomatoes, bacon, chillies and pecorino cheese.*
bucato *sm* washing.
buccellato *sm light, ring-shaped sponge cake from Sarzana and Lucca.*
buccia, ce *sf* skin.
buco, chi *sm* hole.
budino *sm type of egg custard baked in a mould* ; **~ di riso** *egg custard made with rice, sultanas and sometimes rum.*
bufera *sf* storm.
buffet [by'fɛ] *sm inv* buffet.
buffo, a *agg* funny.
bugia *sf* lie ; *(candeliere)* candleholder.
bugiardo, a *agg* lying. ◆ *sm, f* liar.
buio, a *agg* dark. ◆ *sm* darkness ; **far ~** to get dark.
Bulgaria *sf* : **la ~** Bulgaria.
bulgaro, a *agg* Bulgarian.
bullone *sm* bolt.
buonanotte *esclam* good night!
buonasera *esclam* good evening!
buongiorno *esclam (in mattinata)* good morning! ; *(nel pomeriggio)* good afternoon!.
buongustaio, a *sm, f* gourmet.

☞

buono *(dav sm* **buon** *+ consonante o vocale ;* **buono** *+ s + consonante, gn, ps, z) agg*
- **1.** *(di qualità)* good.
- **2.** *(gradevole)* good.
- **3.** *(generoso)* : **~ (con)** good (to), kind (to).
- **4.** *(bravo, efficiente)* good ; **non essere ~ a nulla** to be no good at anything ; **è ~ solo a criticare** all he can do is criticize.

- 5. *(valido : biglietto, passaporto)* valid.
- 6. *(temperamento)* good ; **avere un buon carattere** to be good-natured ; **essere di buon umore** to be in a good mood.
- 7. *(occasione, momento)* right.
- 8. *(negli auguri)* : **buon appetito!** enjoy your meal! ; **buon compleanno!** Happy Birthday! ; **buona fortuna!** good luck! ; **fate buon viaggio!** have a good journey!
- 9. *(rafforzativo)* : **ci vuole un'ora buona** it takes a good hour.
- 10. *(in espressioni)* : **~ a sapersi** that's nice to know ; **a buon mercato** cheap ; **di buon'ora** early ; **alla buona** *(cena)* simple ; *(vestirsi)* simply ; **farai i compiti, con le buone o con le cattive** like it or not, you'll do your homework.
◆ *sm* - 1. *(aspetto positivo)* good ; **il ~ è che ...** the good thing is that ...
- 2. *(tagliando)* voucher ; *(invece di rimborso)* credit note ; **~ sconto** voucher ; **~ del tesoro** treasury bill.

buonsenso *sm* common sense.
buonumore *sm* good humour.
burattino *sm* puppet.
burla *sf* prank, trick.
burocrazia *sf* bureaucracy.
burrasca, sche *sf* storm.
burrida *sf Sardinian dish made from dogfish cooked with garlic, vinegar, pine kernels and walnuts and served cold.*
burro *sm* butter ; **~ di cacao** cocoa butter.
burrone *sm* ravine.
bus [bʊs] *sm inv (abbr di autobus)* bus.
bussare *vi* to knock.
bussola *sf* compass.
busta *sf (per lettera)* envelope ; *(di plastica, carta)* bag ; **~ paga** pay packet.
bustarella *sf* bribe.
busto *sm* bust ; *(indumento)* corset.
butano *sm* butane.
buttafuori *sm inv* bouncer.
buttare *vt (gettare)* to throw ; **~ all'aria qc** to turn sthg upside down ; **~ fuori qn** to throw sb out ; **~ giù** *(abbattere)* to knock down ; *(inghiottire)* to gulp down ; **~ (via)** *(gettare)* to throw away ; *(sprecare)* to waste. ❑ **buttarsi** *vr (gettarsi)* to jump ; *fig (tentare)* to have a go.
by-pass [bai'pas] *sm inv* bypass.

C

cabina *sf (di nave)* cabin ; *(in spiaggia)* beach hut ; *(in piscina)* cubicle ; *(di camion)* cab ; **~ telefonica** telephone box.
cacao *sm* cocoa.
cacca *sf fam* poo.
caccia, ce *sf (di animali)* hunting ; *(inseguimento)* chase ; **~ al tesoro** treasure hunt.
cacciare *vt (animale)* to hunt ; *(mandar via)* to get rid of ; **~ fuori qn** to throw sb out. ❑ **cacciarsi** *vr* : **dove si sarà cacciato?** where has he got to? ; **cacciarsi nei guai** to get into trouble.
cacciatora *sf* → **pollo**.

cacciavite *sm inv* screwdriver.
cacciucco, chi *sm fish soup from Livorno, served with toast rubbed with garlic.*
cachemire ['kaʃmir] *sm* cashmere.
caciocavallo *sm hard pear-shaped cheese from southern Italy.*
cadavere *sm* corpse, dead body.
cadere *vi* to fall ; *(capelli)* to fall out ; *(abito)* to hang ; **far ~** to knock over.
caduta *sf* fall ; **la ~ dei capelli** hair loss ; ' **~ massi**' 'beware falling rocks'.
caffè *sm inv* coffee ; *(locale)* cafe ; **prendere un ~** to have a coffee ; **~ corretto** coffee with a dash of spirits ; **~ macchiato** coffee with a dash of milk.

CAFFÈ

Drunk at any time of day, *caffè* (coffee) or *espresso*, served in the traditional *tazzina* (little cup) is the typical Italian drink. In bars and restaurants, you can choose from a number of different versions : *normale* (normal), *ristretto* (concentrated), *lungo*, (more diluted), *macchiato caldo* or *macchiato freddo* (with a drop of hot or cold milk), or *corretto* (with a drop of your chosen spirit). If you prefer coffee without caffeine, you can order a *hag*®, a *decaffeinato* or, a recent addition, *caffè d'orzo* (made with barley).

---

caffeina *sf* caffeine.
caffellatte *sm inv* hot milk with coffee.
caffettiera *sf* coffeepot.
cagna *sf* bitch.
CAI *(abbr di Club Alpino Italiano) Italian mountaineering association.*
cala *sf* bay.
calabrone *sm* hornet.
calamaretti *smpl* squid *(sg)*.
calamaro *sm* squid ; **calamari ripieni** *squid stuffed with anchovies, capers, breadcrumbs and parsley, and cooked in white wine.*
calamita *sf* magnet.
calare *vt* to lower. ◆ *vi (prezzo, peso)* to go down ; *(vento)* to drop ; *(sole)* to set.
calca, che *sf* throng.
calcagno *sm* heel.
calce *sf* lime.
calciatore, trice *sm, f* footballer.
calcio *sm (pedata)* kick ; *(sport)* football *(Br)*, soccer ; *(elemento chimico)* calcium ; *(di arma)* butt ; **dare un ~ a** to kick ; **prendere a calci** to kick.
calcolare *vt* to calculate ; *(prevedere)* to reckon on, to take into account.
calcolatrice *sf* calculator.
calcolo *sm (conteggio)* calculation ; *MED* stone ; **fare i calcoli** to do one's calculations ; **è andato tutto secondo i calcoli** everything went according to plan.
caldaia *sf* boiler.
caldo, a *agg* warm ; *(a temperatura elevata)* hot. ◆ *sm (calore)* heat ; **avere ~** to be hot ; **è** o **fa ~** it's hot.
calendario *sm* calendar.

calma *sf* calm. ◆ *esclam* calm down!
calmante *sm* tranquillizer.
calmare *vt* to calm ; *(dolore)* to soothe. ❑ **calmarsi** *vr (persona)* to calm down ; *(mare)* to become calm ; *(vento)* to drop.
calmo, a *agg (tranquillo)* peaceful, calm ; *(mare)* calm.
calore *sm* warmth.
caloria *sf (di cibo)* calorie.
calorifero *sm* radiator.
caloroso, a *agg* warm.
calpestare *vt* to tread on.
calunnia *sf* slander.
calvizie *sf* baldness.
calvo, a *agg* bald.
calza *sf (da donna)* stocking ; *(da uomo)* sock ; **fare la ~** to knit.
calzagatto *sm dish from Emilia Romagna consisting of polenta with beans, onions and bacon.*
calzamaglia (*pl* **calzamaglie**) *sf* tights *(pl) (Br)*, pantyhose *(pl) (Am)*.
calzante *sm* shoehorn.
calzare *vt* to put on. ◆ *vi* to fit.
calzature *sfpl* footwear *(sg)*.
calzettone *sm* knee(-length) sock.
calzino *sm* (short) sock.
calzolaio *sm (riparatore)* cobbler ; *(fabbricante)* shoemaker.
calzoleria *sf* shoe shop.
calzoncini *smpl* shorts.
calzone *sm (cibo) pasty made from pizza dough stuffed with cheese, tomato, ham and egg.* ❑ **calzoni** *smpl* trousers.
camaleonte *sm* chameleon.
cambiale *sf* bill.
cambiamento *sm* change.
cambiare *vt* & *vi* to change ; **~ gli euro in sterline** to change euros into sterling ; **~ un biglietto da cento** to change a hundred euros note. ❑ **cambiarsi** *vr* to change (one's clothes).
cambio *sm (sostituzione)* change ; *(di denaro)* exchange ; *(di automobile)* gears *(pl)* ; **dare il ~ a qn** to take over from sb ; **fare a ~ (con qn)** to swap (with sb) ; **in ~ di qc** in exchange for sthg ; **~ automatico** automatic gearbox.
camera *sf* room ; **~ (da letto)** bedroom ; **~ d'aria** inner tube ; **~ con bagno** room with a bath ; **~ blindata** vault ; **Camera di Commercio** Chamber of Commerce ; **Camera dei Deputati** ≃ House of Commons *(Br)*, House of Representatives *(Am)* ; **~ con doccia** room with a shower ; **~ doppia** double room ; **~ a due letti** twin-bedded room ; **~ matrimoniale** room with a double bed ; **~ degli ospiti** guestroom, spare room ; **~ singola** single room.
cameriere, a *sm, f* waiter *(f* waitress*)*.
camice *sm* white coat.
camicetta *sf* blouse.
camicia *sf (da uomo)* shirt ; *(da donna)* blouse, shirt ; **~ da notte** *(da donna)* nightdress ; *(da uomo)* nightshirt.
caminetto *sm* fireplace, hearth.
camino *sm (focolare)* fireplace, hearth ; *(comignolo)* chimney.
camion *sm inv* truck.
camioncino *sm* van.

cammello *sm* camel; *(tessuto)* camelhair.
cammeo *sm* cameo.
camminare *vi* to walk.
camminata *sf* walk.
cammino *sm* way; **mettersi in ~** to set off.
camomilla *sf* camomile.
camorra *sf* Camorra.
camoscio *sm* chamois; **giacca di ~** suede jacket.
campagna *sf* country; *(propaganda, guerra)* campaign; **in ~** in the country; **andare in ~** to go to the country.
campana *sf* bell; **a ~** bell-shaped.
campanello *sm* bell; **suonare il ~** to ring the bell.
campanile *sm* bell-tower.
campare *vi* to get by.
campato, a *agg*: **~ in aria** unfounded.
campeggiare *vi* to camp.
campeggiatore, trice *sm, f* camper.
campeggio *sm* *(luogo)* campsite; *(attività)* camping.
camper *sm inv* camper van.
Campidoglio *sm*: **il ~** the Capitol.

IL CAMPIDOGLIO

Situated on the Capitoline Hill, one of the seven hills of Rome, and a symbol of power since ancient times when the Senate was located there, it is now the seat of the city council. The square and its surrounding buildings were constructed to Michelangelo's design in the 16th century, and are an important tourist attraction because of their magnificent architecture and the cultural treasures its museums hold.

---

camping *sm inv* campsite.
campionario *sm* (collection of) samples *(pl)*.
campionato *sm* championship.
campione, essa *sm, f* champion. ◆ *sm (esemplare)* sample.
capitone *sm (anguilla) large eel.*
campo *sm* field; *(accampamento)* camp; **~ da tennis** tennis court; **~ di golf** golf course; **~ profughi** refugee camp.
camposanto (*pl* **campisanti**) *sm* cemetery.
Canada *sm*: **il ~** Canada.
canadese *agg* & *smf* Canadian. ◆ *sf (tenda)* ridge tent.
canaglia *sf* rogue.
canale *sm* channel; *(artificiale)* canal; **~ navigabile** ship canal.
canapa *sf* hemp.
canarino *sm* canary.
canasta *sf* canasta.
cancellare *vt (con gomma)* to rub out; *(con penna)* to cross out; *(annullare)* to cancel.
cancelleria *sf (materiale)* stationery.
cancello *sm* gate.
cancerogeno, a *agg* carcinogenic.
cancrena *sf MED* gangrene.

cancro *sm* cancer. ❑ **Cancro** *sm* Cancer.
candeggina *sf* bleach.
candela *sf* candle ; ~ **(di accensione)** spark plug.
candelabro *sm* candelabra.
candeliere *sm* candlestick.
candidato, a *sm, f* candidate.
candido, a *agg (bianco)* (pure) white ; *(puro)* pure, innocent.
candito, a *agg* candied. ◆ *sm* candied fruit.
cane *sm* dog ; ~ **da guardia** guard dog ; ~ **guida** guide dog ; ~ **lupo** Alsatian ; ~ **poliziotto** police dog ; **non c'era un** ~ there wasn't a soul there ; **solo come un** ~ all alone ; **tempo da cani** lousy weather ; **una vita da cani** a dog's life ; **'cani al guinzaglio'** 'dogs must be kept on a lead'.
canestro *sm* basket.
cangiante *agg* iridescent.
canguro *sm* kangaroo.
canicola *sf* heat.
canile *sm (cuccia)* kennel ; *(allevamento)* kennels *(pl)* ; ~ **municipale** dog pound.
canino *sm* canine.
canna *sf (pianta)* reed ; *(di bicicletta)* crossbar ; *(di fucile)* barrel ; ~ **fumaria** chimney flue ; ~ **da pesca** fishing rod ; ~ **da zucchero** sugar cane.
cannariculi *smpl thin curved pastry covered in honey.*
cannella *sf (spezia)* cinnamon ; *(rubinetto)* tap.
cannello *sm* blowlamp.
cannelloni *smpl* cannelloni *(sg)*.
cannibale *smf* cannibal.
cannocchiale *sm* telescope.
cannolo *sm* : ~ **alla crema** *pastry tube filled with custard* ; ~ **siciliano** *'cannolo' filled with sweetened ricotta cheese, candied fuit and chocolate.*
cannone *sm* gun.
cannuccia, ce *sf* straw.
canoa *sf* canoe.
canone *sm (quota)* rent ; *(regola)* rule.
canottaggio *sm* rowing.
canottiera *sf (biancheria)* vest *(Br)*, undershirt *(Am)* ; *(per esterno)* sleeveless T-shirt.
canotto *sm* rubber dinghy ; ~ **di salvataggio** lifeboat.
cantante *smf* singer.
cantare *vt* & *vi* to sing.
cantautore, trice *sm, f* singer-songwriter.
cantiere *sm (edile)* building site ; *(navale)* shipyard.
cantina *sf (seminterrato)* cellar ; *(per il vino)* wine cellar ; *(negozio)* wine shop.
canto *sm (arte)* singing ; *(canzone)* song ; *(di uccello)* chirping ; **d'altro** ~ on the other hand.
cantonata *sf* : **prendere una** ~ to make a blunder.
cantone *sm (in Svizzera)* canton.
Canton Ticino *sm* : **il** ~ the canton of Ticino.
cantucci *smpl wedge-shaped almond biscuits.*
canzonare *vt* to tease.
canzone *sf* song.
caos *sm* chaos.
CAP *abbr* = **codice di avviamento postale.**

capace *agg (esperto)* able, capable ; *(ampio)* capacious ; **essere ~ di fare qc** to be able to do sthg ; **essere ~ di tutto** to be capable of anything.

capacità *sf inv (abilità)* ability ; *(capienza)* capacity.

capanna *sf* hut.

capannone *sm (industriale)* shed ; *(agricolo)* barn.

caparbio, a *agg* stubborn.

caparra *sf* deposit.

capello *sm* hair. ❑ **capelli** *smpl* hair *(sg)* ; **averne fin sopra i capelli** to be fed up to the back teeth.

capezzolo *sm* nipple.

capillare *sm* capillary.

capire *vt* & *vi* to understand ; **non capisco** I don't understand ; **scusi, non ho capito** I'm sorry, I don't understand ; **si capisce!** certainly!. ❑ **capirsi** *vr* to understand each other.

capitale *sf* & *sm* capital. ◆ *agg (pena, peccato)* capital ; *(fondamentale)* fundamental.

capitaneria *sf* : **~ di porto** port authorities *(pl)*.

capitano *sm* captain.

capitare *vi (accadere)* to happen ; *(giungere)* to turn up. ◆ *v impers* to happen ; **~ a qn** to happen to sb ; **~ a proposito** to come at the right time.

capitello *sm* capital.

capitolino, a *agg* Capitoline.

capitolo *sm* chapter.

capitombolo *sm* tumble.

capo *sm (principale)* boss ; *(testa, estremità)* head ; *(di gruppo)* leader ; *(di tribù)* chief ; **~ di vestiario** item of clothing ; **andare a ~** to start a new paragraph ; **venire a ~ di qc** to get through sthg ; **da ~** over again ; **da un ~ all'altro (di qc)** from end to end (of sthg) ; **in ~ a un mese** within a month.

Capodanno *sm* New Year.

capofitto : a capofitto *avv* headfirst.

capolavoro *sm* masterpiece.

capolinea (*pl* **capilinea**) *sm* terminus.

capolino *sm* : **fare ~** to peep in/out.

capoluogo, ghi *sm* : **~ di provincia** provincial capital, county town *(Br)* ; **~ di regione** regional capital.

capostazione (*pl* **capistazione**) *smf* station master.

capotavola (*mpl* **capitavola**, *fpl inv*) *smf* head of the table ; **a ~** at the head of the table.

capoufficio (*mfpl* **capiufficio**) *smf* office manager (*f* manageress).

capoverso *sm* paragraph.

capovolgere *vt (barca, oggetto)* to overturn ; *fig (situazione)* to reverse. ❑ **capovolgersi** *vr (barca)* to capsize ; *(macchina)* to overturn ; *fig (situazione)* to be reversed.

capovolto, a *pp* → **capovolgere**.

cappa *sf (di camino)* hood ; *(mantello)* cape.

cappella *sf* chapel.

cappello *sm* hat ; **~ di paglia** straw hat.

cappero *sm* caper.

cappone *sm* capon ; **~ ripieno al**

forno *capon stuffed with beef, Parmesan cheese and breadcrumbs.*

cappotto *sm* coat.

cappuccino *sm* cappuccino.

cappuccio *sm* hood ; *(di penna)* cap.

capra *sf* goat.

Capri *sf* Capri.

capriccio *sm* tantrum ; *(voglia)* whim ; **fare i capricci** to be naughty.

capriccioso, a *agg* naughty.

Capricorno *sm* Capricorn.

capriola *sf* somersault.

capriolo *sm* roe deer.

capro *sm* : ~ **espiatorio** scapegoat.

capsula *sf (di farmaco)* capsule ; *(di bottiglia)* cap.

carabiniere *sm member of the Italian police force responsible for civil and military matters.*

caraffa *sf* carafe, jug.

Caraibi *smpl* : **i** ~ the Caribbean.

caramella *sf* sweet.

carato *sm* carat.

carattere *sm* character.

caratteristica, che *sf* characteristic.

caratteristico, a, ci, che *agg* characteristic.

caratterizzare *vt* to characterize.

carboidrato *sm* carbohydrate.

carbone *sm* coal.

carburante *sm* fuel.

carburatore *sm* carburettor.

carcerato, a *sm, f* prisoner.

carcere (*pl f* **carceri**) *sm* prison.

carciofo *sm* artichoke ; **carciofi alla romana** *sautéed or baked artichokes with parsley, mint and garlic.*

cardiaco, a, ci, che *agg* cardiac, heart *(dav s)*.

cardigan *sm inv* cardigan.

cardinale *agg* → **numero, punto.** ◆ *sm* cardinal.

cardine *sm* hinge.

cardo *sm* thistle.

carenza *sf* lack, deficiency.

carestia *sf* famine.

carezza *sf* caress ; *(a animale)* stroke.

carezzare *vt* to caress ; *(animale)* to stroke.

carica, che *sf (incarico)* position, office ; *(elettrica, di arma)* charge ; **in** ~ in office.

caricare *vt (mettere su)* to load ; *(sveglia)* to wind up ; ~ **qc di qc** to load sthg with sthg ; ~ **qn di qc** to weigh sb down with sthg.

carico, a, chi, che *agg (arma, macchina fotografica)* loaded ; *(batteria)* charged ; *(orologio)* wound up. ◆ *sm* load ; ~ **(di qc)** weighed down (with sthg) ; **a** ~ **di** *(spesa)* charged to.

carie *sf inv (dei denti)* decay.

carino, a *agg (grazioso)* pretty, lovely ; *(gentile)* nice.

carnagione *sf* complexion.

carne *sf* meat ; *ANAT* flesh ; ~ **di maiale/vitello** pork/veal ; ~ **macinata o tritata** mince.

carneficina *sf* massacre.

carnevale *sm* carnival.

CARNEVALE

The period before Lent, from the Epiphany to Ash Wednesday, is carnival time in Italy. Most festivities take place during the last week of this period, Shrovetide. Both children and adults don masks, go to parties, play tricks on each other, and throw confetti (*coriandoli*) and streamers. In some cities special organized events are held : *Viareggio* is particulary famous for its carnival procession, whilst in Venice the city gives itself over to open-air parties, theatre and concerts.

---

caro, a *agg* expensive, dear ; *(amato)* dear ; **costare ~** to be expensive ; **Caro Luca** Dear Luca.

carogna *sm (di animale)* carrion ; *fig (persona)* swine.

carota *sf* carrot.

carovita *sm* high cost of living.

carpaccio *sm thin slices of raw beef served with oil, lemon and shavings of Parmesan cheese.*

carpire *vt* : **~ qc a qn** *(segreto)* to get sthg out of sb.

carponi *avv* on all fours.

carrabile *agg* → **passo.**

carraio *agg m* → **passo.**

carreggiata *sf* carriageway.

carrello *sm* trolley.

carriera *sf* career ; **far ~** to get on.

carro *sm* cart, wagon ; **~ armato** tank ; **~ attrezzi** breakdown truck *(Br)*, tow truck *(Am)*.

carrozza *sf (cocchio)* coach, carriage ; *(vagone)* carriage *(Br)*, car *(Am)* ; **' ~ letto'** sleeping car ; **' ~ ristorante'** restaurant car.

carrozzeria *sf* bodywork.

carrozziere *sm* coachbuilder.

carrozzina *sf* pram *(Br)*, baby carriage *(Am)*.

carta *sf* paper ; *(tessera)* card ; **alla ~** à la carte ; **~ d'argento** *senior citizens' railcard* ; **~ automobilistica** o **stradale** road map ; **~ da bollo** *paper carrying a government duty stamp* ; **~ di credito** credit card ; **~ geografica** map ; **~ d'identità** identity card ; **~ igienica** toilet paper ; **~ d'imbarco** boarding pass ; **~ da lettere** notepaper ; **~ da pacchi** brown paper, wrapping paper ; **~ da parati** wallpaper ; **~ stagnola** silver foil ; **~ verde** green card ; **~ dei vini** wine list ; **carte da gioco** playing cards.

CARTA D'IDENTITÀ

Every Italian citizen is issued with an identity card, an official document listing details such as place and date of birth, home address, profession, colour of eyes and hair, and marital status. It also contains a photograph of the bearer. By law, Italians must show their identity card when asked to do so by the police, and when booking in at hotels. The card can be used instead of a passport for travel inside the European Union.

---

cartacarbone *sf* carbon paper.

cartaccia, ce *sf* waste paper.

cartapesta *sf* papier-mâché.

cartella *sf (di scolaro)* schoolbag ;

(di professionista) briefcase ; *(per fogli)* folder ; *(scheda)* file ; **~ clinica** case history.

cartello *sm (avviso)* notice ; *(in dimostrazioni)* placard ; **~ stradale** road sign.

cartellone *sm (teatrale)* playbill ; **~ (pubblicitario)** poster.

cartina *sf* : **~ (geografica)** map.

cartoccio *sm* paper bag ; **al ~** in tin foil.

cartoleria *sf* stationer's.

cartolibreria *sf* stationer's and bookseller's.

cartolina *sf (illustrata)* (picture) postcard ; **~ postale** postcard.

cartone *sm* cardboard. ❑ **cartoni animati** *smpl* cartoons.

casa *sf (costruzione)* house ; *(dimora)* house, home ; *(ditta)* firm ; **andare a ~** to go home ; **essere a** o **in ~** to be at home ; **fatto in ~** homemade ; **~ di cura** nursing home.

casalinga, ghe *sf* housewife.

casalingo, a, ghi, ghe *agg* homemade ; *(amante della casa)* home-loving. ❑ **casalinghi** *smpl* household articles.

cascare *vi* to fall down.

cascata *sf* waterfall.

cascina *sf* farmstead.

casco, schi *sm (protettivo)* helmet ; *(per capelli)* dryer ; *(di banane)* bunch.

casella *sf (riquadro)* square ; *(scomparto)* compartment ; **~ postale** post office box.

casello *sm* tollbooth.

caserma *sf* barracks *(pl)*.

casino *sm fam (confusione)* mess.

casinò *sm inv* casino.

caso *sm* chance ; *(eventualità)* event ; *(poliziesco, medico)* case ; **fare ~ a** to pay attention to ; **non è il ~ di offendersi** you shouldn't take offence ; **a ~** at random ; **in ~ contrario** otherwise ; **in ogni ~** in any case ; **nel ~ venisse** should he come ; **per ~** by chance ; **in tutti i casi** at any rate ; **'in ~ d'emergenza rompere il vetro'** 'in case of emergency break glass'.

casomai *cong* if by any chance.

cassa *sf (contenitore)* case, box ; *(di negozio)* cash register ; *(di supermercato)* checkout ; *(di banca)* counter ; *(amplificatore)* speaker ; *(di orologio)* case ; **~ automatica prelievi** cash dispenser ; **~ continua** night safe ; **~ toracica** chest.

cassaforte *(pl* **casseforti***)* *sf* safe.

cassata *sf ice cream dessert containing candied fruit, served in slices like a cake* ; **~ siciliana** *Sicilian dessert made with sponge, ricotta cheese, candied fruit and liqueur*.

casseruola *sf* saucepan.

cassetta *sf (contenitore)* box ; *(di musica, film)* tape ; **~ delle lettere** letterbox *(Br)*, mailbox *(Am)* ; **~ di sicurezza** strongbox.

cassetto *sm* drawer.

cassettone *sm* chest of drawers.

cassiere, a *sm, f (di negozio)* cashier ; *(di banca)* teller.

cassoela *sf pork ribs with salami and savoy cabbage (a speciality of Lombardy)*.

cassonetto *sm large dustbin on wheels*.

castagna *sf* chestnut.

castagnaccio *sm Tuscan cake made from chestnut flour, pine kernels and sometimes sultanas and rosemary.*
castagno *sm* chestnut.
castano, a *agg* chestnut.
castello *sm* castle.
castigo, ghi *sm* punishment ; **mettere qn in ~** to punish sb.
castoro *sm* beaver.
castrare *vt* to castrate.
casual ['kɜʃwal] *agg inv* casual.
casuale *agg* chance *(dav s)*.
catacomba *sf* catacomb.
catalogare *vt* to catalogue.
catalogo, ghi *sm* catalogue.
catamarano *sm* catamaran.
catarifrangente *sm* reflector.
catarro *sm* catarrh.
catasta *sf* stack.
catastrofe *sf* catastrophe.
categoria *sf (gruppo)* category ; *(di albergo)* class.
catena *sf* chain ; **~ di montaggio** assembly line ; **a ~** chain *(dav s)* ; **catene (da neve)** (snow) chains.
catinella *sf* basin ; **piovere a catinelle** to pour down.
catino *sm* basin.
catrame *sm* tar.
cattedra *sf* teacher's desk.
cattedrale *sf* cathedral.
cattiveria *sf (qualità)* wickedness ; *(commento)* spiteful remark ; *(atto)* spiteful act.
cattività *sf* captivity.
cattivo, a *agg* bad ; *(bambino)* naughty; *(sapore, odore)* bad, nasty; *(incapace)* poor.
cattolico, a, ci, che *agg* & *sm, f* Catholic.
cattura *sf* capture.
catturare *vt* to capture.
caucciù *sm* rubber.
causa *sf* cause ; DIR case ; **a o per ~ di** because of.
causare *vt* to cause.
cautela *sf* caution, prudence.
cautelare *vt* to protect. ❑ **cautelarsi da** *vr + prep* to take precautions against.
cauto, a *agg* cautious, prudent.
cauzione *sf* security ; DIR bail.
cava *sf* quarry.
cavalcare *vt* to ride.
cavalcavia *sm inv* flyover.
cavalcioni *avv* : **a ~ di** astride.
cavaliere *sm (chi cavalca)* rider ; *(medioevale, titolo)* knight ; *(in balli)* partner.
cavalleria *sf* MIL cavalry ; *(cortesia)* chivalry.
cavallerizzo, a *sm, f (istruttore)* riding instructor ; *(di circo)* bareback rider.
cavalletta *sf* grasshopper.
cavalletto *sm* easel.
cavallo *sm* horse ; *(di pantaloni)* crotch ; *(negli scacchi)* knight ; **andare a ~** to ride ; **~ (vapore)** horsepower.
cavallone *sm (ondata)* breaker.
cavare *vt* to extract ; **cavarsela** to manage, to cope.
cavatappi *sm inv* corkscrew.
cavatelli *smpl* : **~ alla foggiana** *flat 'gnocchi' in a vegetable, cheese or meat sauce.*
caverna *sf* cave.

cavia *sf* guinea pig ; **fare da ~** to be a guinea pig.

caviale *sm* caviar.

caviglia *sf* ankle.

cavità *sf inv (buca)* hollow ; ANAT chamber.

cavo, a *agg* hollow. ◆ *sm* cable ; *(corda)* rope.

cavolfiore *sm* cauliflower.

cavolo *sm* cabbage ; **che ~ vuole?** *fam* what the hell does he want?

cazzotto *sm fam* punch.

cc *(abbr di centimetro cubico)* cc.

c/c *(abbr di conto corrente)* a/c.

C.C. *abbr* = **Carabinieri**.

C.D. *sm inv* CD.

CD-ROM *sm inv* CD-ROM.

ce → **ci**.

cece *sm* chickpea.

Cecoslovacchia *sf*: **la ~** Czechoslovakia.

cedere *vt* : **~ qc (a qn)** to give sthg up (to sb) ; *(soffitto, pavimento)* to give way ; **~ (a qc)** *fig (persona)* to give in (to sthg), to yield (to sthg).

cedola *sf* coupon.

cedro *sm* lime.

CEE *sf (abbr di Comunità Economica Europea)* EEC.

ceffone *sm* slap.

celebrare *vt* to celebrate.

celebre *agg* famous.

celebrità *sf inv* fame.

celeste *agg* & *sm* sky-blue.

celibe *agg* single. ◆ *sm* bachelor.

cella *sf* cell.

cellophane® ['tʃɛlofan] *sm* Cellophane®.

cellula *sf* cell ; **~ fotoelettrica** photoelectric cell.

cellulare *sm (telefono)* mobile phone ; *(furgone)* Black Maria.

cemento *sm* cement ; **~ armato** reinforced concrete.

cena *sf* dinner.

cenare *vi* to have dinner.

cencio *sm (straccio)* rag. ❑ **cenci** *smpl* CULIN *Tuscan speciality of deep-fried sticks of dough sprinkled with sugar*.

cenere *sf* ash.

cenno *sm (con la mano)* gesture ; *(col capo)* nod ; *(allusione)* hint ; *(sintomo)* sign ; **fare ~ a qn** to beckon to sb ; **fare ~ di sì/no** to nod/shake one's head.

cenone *sm* New Year's Eve dinner.

censimento *sm* census.

censura *sf (controllo)* censorship.

centenario, a *agg (di età)* hundred-year-old ; *(ogni cento anni)* centenary *(dav s)*. ◆ *sm* centenary.

centerbe *sm inv type of liqueur made from herbs*.

centesimo, a *num* hundredth → **sesto**.

centigrado *agg m* → **grado**.

centimetro *sm* centimetre.

centinaio *(pl f* **centinaia**) *sm* : **un ~ (di)** a hundred.

cento *num* a ○ one hundred ; **~ per ~** 100 per cent → **sei**.

centomila *num* a ○ one hundred thousand → **sei**.

centotredici *sm (numero telefonico)* ≃ 999 *(Br)*, ≃ 911 *(Am)* ; *(polizia)* police *(pl)*.

centrale *agg (nel centro)* central ; *(principale)* main. ◆ *sf* head office ; ~ **elettrica** electric power station.

centralinista, i, e *smf* operator.

centralino *sm* telephone exchange ; *(di albergo, ditta)* switchboard.

centrare *vt* to hit the centre of.

centrifuga, ghe *sf* spin-dryer.

centro *sm* centre ; **fare ~** *(colpire)* to hit the bull's eye ; *fig (risolvere)* to hit the nail on the head ; **~ abitato** built-up area ; **~ commerciale** shopping centre ; **~ storico** old town.

ceppo *sm (di albero)* stump ; *(ciocco)* log.

cera *sf* wax.

ceramica *sf* pottery.

cerbiatto *sm* fawn.

cerca *sf* : **essere in ~ di qc** to be in search of sthg.

cercare *vt* to look for. ❑ **cercare di** *v + prep* : **~ di fare qc** to try to do sthg.

cerchio *sm* circle ; **mettersi in ~ (intorno a)** to form a circle (around).

cereale *sm* cereal.

cerimonia *sf* ceremony.

cerino *sm* match.

cernia *sf* grouper.

cerniera *sf (di porte, finestre)* hinge ; **~ (lampo)** zip.

cerotto *sm* plaster.

certamente *avv* certainly.

certezza *sf* certainty ; **sapere qc con ~** to know sthg for sure.

certificato *sm* certificate ; **~ medico** medical certificate ; **~ di nascita** birth certificate.

certo, a *agg* - 1. *(convinto)* certain ; **essere ~ di qc** to be certain of sthg ; **sono ~ di aver prenotato** I'm positive I booked ; **siete certi che sia lui?** are you sure it's him?
- 2. *(assicurato, evidente)* certain ; **la vittoria è data per certa** victory is certain.
- 3. *(non specificato)* certain ; **un ~ signor Rossi** a (certain) Mr Rossi ; **c'è un ~ Paolo al telefono** there's someone called Paolo on the phone ; **ho certe cose da fare** I have some things I need to do ; **in certi casi** in some ○ certain cases.
- 4. *(qualche)* : **certi(-e)** some.
- 5. *(limitativo)* some ; **avere un ~ intuito** to have some insight.
- 6. *(rafforzativo)* some ; **ha certe idee!** he has some strange ideas! ; **ha certi occhi azzurri!** he's got really blue eyes! ; **avere una certa età** to be getting on.
◆ *avv* : **vieni anche tu? - ~!** are you coming too? - of course! ; **di ~** certainly.
❑ **certi, e** *pron (persone)* some (people) ; **certi dicono che ...** some people say that ...

certosa *sf* charterhouse.

cervello *sm* brain.

Cervino *sm* : **il ~** the Cervino.

cervo *sm* deer ; **~ volante** stag beetle.

cesoie *sfpl* shears.

cespuglio *sm* bush.

cessare *vt* to stop.

cesso *sm volg* loo.

cesta *sf* basket.

cestino *sm (cesto)* basket ; *(per*

cartacce) wastepaper basket ; ~ **da viaggio** packed lunch.

cesto *sm* basket.

ceto *sm* class.

cetriolo *sm* cucumber.

champagne [ʃam'paɲ] *sm inv* champagne.

charter ['tʃarter] *sm inv* charter.

che *pron relativo* - 1. *(soggetto : persona)* who, that ; **il dottore ~ mi ha visitato** the doctor who examined me.

- 2. *(complemento oggetto : persona)* whom, that ; **la ragazza ~ hai conosciuto** the girl (whom ○ that) you met.

- 3. *(cosa, animale)* that, which ; **la macchina ~ è in garage** the car which ○ that is in the garage ; **il treno ~ abbiamo perso** the train (which ○ that) we missed.

- 4. *fam (in cui)* : **la sera ~ siamo usciti** the evening we went out.

◆ *pron interr* & *esclam* what ; **~ ne pensi?** what do you think? ; **~ ti succede?** what's the matter? ; **non so ~ fare** I don't know what to do ; **grazie! - non c'è di ~!** thank you! - don't mention it! ; **ma ~ dici!** what are you saying!

◆ *agg interr* - 1. *(tra molti)* what ; *(tra pochi)* which ; **~ libro vuoi, questo ○ quello?** which book do you want, this one or that one? ; **~ tipo è il tuo amico?** what's your friend like?

- 2. *(in esclamazioni)* : **~ strana idea!** what a strange idea! ; **~ bello!** how lovely!

◆ *cong* - 1. *(introduce una subordinata)* that ; **è difficile ~ venga** he's unlikely to come ; **sai ~ non è vero** you know (that) it's not true ; **sono così stanca ~ non mi reggo in piedi** I'm so tired (that) I can hardly stand up ; **sono contenta ~ sia partito** I'm pleased (that) he left.

- 2. *(temporale)* : **è già un anno ~ è partito** it's already a year since he left ; **è un po' ~ non lo vedo** I haven't seen him for a while.

- 3. *(comparativa)* than ; **è più furbo ~ intelligente** he's cunning rather than intelligent ; **è più bello ~ mai** he's more handsome than ever.

- 4. *(introduce alternativa)* whether ; **~ tu venga o no, io ci vado** I'm going, whether you come or not.

---

check-in [tʃɛ'kin] *sm inv* check-in.

chewing-gum ['tʃwingam] *sm* chewing-gum.

chi *pron relativo* - 1. *(colui che)* the person who.

- 2. *(qualcuno che)* : **c'è ancora ~ crede alle sue storie** there are still people who believe his tales.

- 3. *(chiunque)* whoever, anyone who ; **entra ~ vuole** anyone can come in.

◆ *pron interr* - 1. *(soggetto)* who ; **~ è?** who is it? ; **~ è stato?** who was it?

- 2. *(complemento diretto)* who ; **non so ~** I don't know who ; **~ si vede!** look who's here!

- 3. *(complemento indiretto)* who, whom ; **a ~ devo chiedere?** who should I ask? ; **con ~ parti?** who are you leaving with? ; **di ~ è questo**

ombrello? whose umbrella is this? ; **a ~ lo dici!** you're telling me!

chiacchierare *vi (conversare)* to chat ; *(spettegolare)* to gossip.

chiacchiere *sfpl (pettegolezzi)* rumours, gossip *(sg)* ; **fare due** o **quattro ~** to have a chat.

chiacchierone, a *agg (loquace)* talkative ; *(pettegolo)* gossipy.

chiamare *vt* to call. ❑ **chiamarsi** *vr* to be called ; **come ti chiami?** what's your name? ; **mi chiamo ...** my name is ...

chiamata *sf* call.

Chianti *sm* Chianti.

chiarezza *sf* clarity.

chiarire *vt (mettere in chiaro)* to make clear ; *(spiegare)* to clarify ; *(problema)* to clear up. ❑ **chiarirsi** *vr* to be cleared up.

chiaro, a *agg* clear ; *(colore)* light.

chiasso *sm* noise.

chiassoso, a *agg* noisy.

chiave *sf* key ; **chiudere a ~** to lock ; **~ d'accensione** ignition key ; **~ inglese** monkey wrench.

chiavetta *sf (dell'acqua, del gas)* tap ; *(d'accensione)* key.

chic [ʃik] *agg inv* chic.

chicco, chi *sm (di grano)* grain ; *(di caffè)* bean ; **~ d'uva** grape.

chiedere *vt (per sapere)* to ask ; *(per avere)* to ask for ; **~ qc a qn** to ask sb sthg. ❑ **chiedere di** *v + prep (per notizie)* to ask after ; *(al telefono)* to ask for.

chiesa *sf* church.

chiesto, a *pp* → **chiedere**.

chiglia *sf* keel.

chilo *sm (chilogrammo)* kilo ; **mezzo ~ di** half a kilo of.

chilogrammo *sm* kilogram.

chilometro *sm* kilometre.

chimica *sf (disciplina)* chemistry → **chimico**.

chimico, a, ci, che *agg* chemical. ◆ *sm, f* chemist.

chinarsi *vr* to bend.

chinotto *sm (bibita) a type of soft drink.*

chiocciola *sf* snail.

chiodo *sm* nail ; **~ fisso** fixed idea ; **chiodi di garofano** cloves.

chioma *sf (di albero)* foliage ; *(capigliatura)* (head of) hair.

chiosco, schi *sm* kiosk.

chiostro *sm* cloister.

chiromante *smf* fortune-teller.

chirurgia *sf* surgery ; **~ estetica** plastic surgery.

chissà *avv* who knows?

chitarra *sf* guitar.

chiudere *vt* to close, to shut ; *(acqua, gas)* to turn off ; *(strada)* to close ; *(definitivamente)* to close down, to shut down ; *(concludere)* to end. ◆ *vi* to close, to shut ; *(definitivamente)* to close down, to shut down ; **~ a chiave** to lock. ❑ **chiudersi** *vr* to close, to shut ; **chiudersi in casa** to lock o.s. in ; **'si chiude da sé'** 'automatic door'.

chiunque *pron (indefinito)* anyone ; *(relativo)* whoever ; **~ sia** whoever it may be.

chiuso, a *pp* → **chiudere**. ◆ *agg* closed ; *(persona)* reserved ; **'~ per ferie'** 'closed for holidays' ; **'~ per riposo settimanale'** 'weekly closing day'.

chiusura *sf (di negozio, ufficio, scuole)* closing ; *(definitiva)* closure ; *(termine)* end ; *(dispositivo)* fastener.

☞

ci *(diventa* **ce** *se precede lo, la, li, le, ne) pron personale*
- 1. *(complemento oggetto)* us ; **~ vedono** they can see us ; **ascoltaci** listen to us.
- 2. *(complemento di termine)* (to) us ; **~ può fare un favore?** can you do us a favour? ; **non ce lo ha detto** he didn't tell us.
- 3. *(riflessivo)* ourselves ; **~ laviamo** we wash ourselves.
- 4. *(reciproco)* each other ; **~ vediamo stasera** see you tonight.
◆ *pron dimostrativo (a ciò, in ciò, su ciò)* : **~ penso io** I'll take care of it ; **mettici un po' d'impegno!** put a bit of effort into it! ; **quella sedia è vuota : posso appoggiarci la borsa?** that seat is empty : can I put my bag on it? ; **~ puoi scommettere** you can bet on it.
◆ *avv* - 1. *(stato in luogo : qui)* here ; *(stato in luogo : lì)* there ; **~ fermiamo una sola notte** we are staying (here/there) for just one night.
- 2. *(moto a luogo : qui)* here ; *(moto a luogo : lì)* there ; **~ si può andare a piedi** you can walk there ; **~ vengono spesso** they come here often.
- 3. *(moto per luogo)* : **~ passa l'autostrada** the motorway runs through it ; **non ~ passa mai nessuno** nobody ever goes this/that way.
- 4. *(in espressioni)* : **c'è** there is ; **~ sono** there are ; **~ vuole un po'(di tempo)** it takes a bit of time ; **io ~ sto** I agree ; **non ~ sento/vedo** I can't hear/see.

---

ciabatta *sf (pantofola)* slipper ; *(pane) type of long, flat bread.*

cialda *sf* wafer.

ciambella *sf (dolce) ring-shaped cake* ; *(salvagente)* rubber ring ; **~ di salvataggio** life buoy, life belt.

ciao *esclam (all'incontro)* hello! ; *(di commiato)* bye!

ciascuno, a *agg* & *pron* each ; **~ di noi** each of us.

cibo *sm* food.

cicala *sf* cicada.

cicatrice *sf* scar.

cicca, che *sf* cigarette end.

ciccione, a *sm, f fam* fatty.

cicerone *sm* guide.

ciclabile *agg* → **pista**.

ciclamino *sm* cyclamen.

ciclismo *sm* cycling.

ciclista, i, e *smf* cyclist.

ciclo *sm* cycle.

ciclomotore *sm* moped.

ciclone *sm* cyclone.

cicogna *sf* stork.

cieco, a, chi, che *agg* blind. ◆ *sm, f* blind man (*f* woman).

cielo *sm* sky ; *(paradiso)* heaven.

cifra *sf (numero)* figure ; *(di denaro)* sum, figure.

ciglio *sm (di palpebra : pl f ciglia)* eyelash ; *(di strada : pl m cigli)* edge.

cigno *sm* swan.

cigolare *vi* to squeak, to creak.

Cile *sm* : **il ~** Chile.

cilecca *sf* : **fare ~** to fail.

ciliegia, gie ○ **ge** *sf* cherry.

cilindro *sm (di motore)* cylinder ; *(cappello)* top hat.
cima *sf* top ; *(estremità)* end ; **in ~ (a qc)** at the top (of sthg) ; **da ~ a fondo** from top to bottom, from beginning to end ; **~ alla genovese** *veal stuffed with bacon, sweetbreads, brains, mushrooms, peas and grated cheese, served cold in slices.*
cimice *sf (insetto)* bug ; *(puntina)* drawing pin *(Br)*, thumbtack *(Am)*.
ciminiera *sf* chimney ; *(di nave)* funnel.
cimitero *sm* cemetery.
Cina *sf*: **la ~** China.
cin cin *esclam* cheers!
Cinecittà *sf film studios in Rome.*

CINECITTÀ

Meaning 'city of cinema', the name *Cinecittà* has been given to the film complex built in the suburbs of Rome in 1937. *Cinecittà* was most productive in the 1950's, when films like Fellini's *La Dolce Vita* were shot there, and it continues to be widely used by the Italian film industry.

---

cinema *sm inv* cinema.
cinepresa *sf* cine-camera.
cinese *agg, smf* & *sm* Chinese.
cingere *vt* to surround.
cinghia *sf* belt.
cinghiale *sm* wild boar.
cinguettare *vi* to chirp.
cinico, a, ci, che *agg* cynical.
ciniglia *sf* chenille.
cinquanta *num* fifty → **sei.**
cinquantesimo, a *agg* fiftieth → **sesto.**
cinquantina *sf (di età)* : **essere sulla ~** to be about 50 ; **una ~ (di)** about 50.
cinque *num* five → **sei.**
cinquecento *num* five hundred → **sei.** ❑ **Cinquecento** *sm* : **il Cinquecento** the sixteenth century.
cinto, a *pp* → **cingere.**
cintura *sf* belt; *(punto vita)* waist ; **~ di sicurezza** safety ○ seat belt ; **'allacciare le cinture di sicurezza'** 'fasten your seat belts'.
ciò *pron* this, that ; **~ che** what ; **~ nonostante** nevertheless.
cioccolata *sf* chocolate ; *(bevanda)* hot chocolate.
cioccolatino *sm* chocolate.
cioccolato *sm* chocolate.
cioè *avv* that is. ◆ *cong (vale a dire)* that is ; *(anzi)* or rather.
ciondolo *sm* pendant.
ciotola *sf* bowl.
ciottolo *sm* pebble.
cipolla *sf* onion.
cipresso *sm* cypress.
cipria *sf* face powder.
circa *avv* & *prep* about.
circo, chi *sm* circus.
circolare *agg* & *sf* circular. ◆ *vi* to circulate ; *(veicoli)* to drive ; *(persone)* to move along ; *(notizia)* to go round.
circolazione *sf (di merce, moneta, giornali)* circulation ; **mettere in ~** *(notizia)* to spread ; *(merce, moneta)* to put into circulation ; **~ sanguigna** circulation ; **~ stradale** traffic.
circolo *sm* circle.

circondare *vt* to surround.
circonferenza *sf* circumference.
circonvallazione *sf* ring road.
circoscrizione *sf* district.
circostante *agg* surrounding.
circostanza *sf* circumstance ; date le circostanze in ○ under the circumstances.
circuito *sm* circuit.
ciste = cisti.
cisterna *sf* tank.
cisti *sf inv* cyst.
citare *vt* DIR to summon ; *(menzionare)* to cite ; *(opera, autore)* to quote.
citofono *sm* entry phone.
città *sf inv* town ; *(importante)* city ; ~ universitaria (university) campus. ❑ **Città del Vaticano** *sf* Vatican City.
cittadinanza *sf* citizenship ; *(abitanti)* citizens *(pl)*.
cittadino, a *sm, f* citizen. ◆ *agg* town, city *(dav s)*.
ciuco, chi *sm* ass, donkey.
ciuffo *sm* tuft.
civetta *sf* owl ; *fig (donna)* flirt.
civico, a, ci, che *agg* civic.
civile *agg* civil ; *(civilizzato)* civilized. ◆ *sm* civilian.
civiltà *sf inv* civilization.
clacson *sm inv* horn.
clamoroso, a *agg* sensational.
clandestino, a *agg (illegale)* illegal ; *(segreto)* clandestine. ◆ *sm, f* stowaway.
classe *sf* class ; *(aula)* classroom ; ~ turistica tourist class ; prima/seconda ~ first/second class ; che ~ fai? what year are you in?
classico, a, ci, che *agg (letteratura, arte, musica)* classical ; *(moda, esempio)* classic.
classifica, che *sf (sportiva)* league table ; *(d'esame)* results *(pl)* ; *(musicale)* charts *(pl)*.
classificare *vt (ordinare)* to classify ; *(valutare)* to mark. ❑ **classificarsi** *vr* : classificarsi primo to come first.
claudicante *agg (zoppicante)* limping.
clausola *sf* DIR clause.
clavicola *sf* clavicle.
claxon = clacson.
clero *sm* clergy.
cliccare *vi* INFORM to click.
cliente *smf (di negozio, bar)* customer ; *(di professionista)* client.
clientela *sf (di negozio, bar)* clientele ; *(di professionista)* clients *(pl)*.
clima, i *sm* climate.
clinica, che *sf* clinic.
cloro *sm* chlorine.
club [klab] *sm inv* club.
cm *(abbr di centimetro)* cm.
coagulare *vt (sangue)* to coagulate ; *(latte)* to curdle. ❑ **coagularsi** *vr (sangue)* to clot ; *(latte)* to curdle.
coca *sf fam (bibita)* Coke®.
Coca-Cola® *sf* Coca-Cola®.
cocaina *sf* cocaine.
coccinella *sf* ladybird.
coccio *sm (terracotta)* earthenware ; *(frammento)* shard.
cocciuto, a *agg* stubborn.

cocco, chi *sm (albero)* coconut palm ; *(frutto)* coconut.

coccodrillo *sm* crocodile.

coccolare *vt* to cuddle.

cocomero *sm* watermelon.

coda *sf (fila)* queue *(Br)*, line *(Am)* ; *(di animale)* tail ; **fare la ~** to queue *(Br)*, to stand in line *(Am)* ; **mettersi in ~** to join the queue *(Br)*, o line *(Am)* ; **~ (di cavallo)** ponytail.

codardo, a *agg* cowardly.

codesto, a *agg* & *pron* this.

codice *sm* code ; **~ (di avviamento) postale** postcode ; **~ fiscale** tax code ; **~ della strada** highway code.

coerente *agg* consistent.

coetaneo, a *agg* : **siamo coetanei** we are the same age.

cofano *sm* bonnet *(Br)*, hood *(Am)*.

cogliere *vt* to pick ; *fig (occasione, momento)* to seize ; **~ qn sul fatto** to catch sb redhanded.

cognac *sm inv* cognac.

cognato, a *sm, f* brother-in-law (*f* sister-in-law).

cognome *sm* surname.

coi = **con + i, con.**

coincidenza *sf (caso)* coincidence ; *(aereo, treno)* connection.

coincidere *vi* : **~ (con qc)** *(oggetti)* to coincide (with sthg) ; *(versione dei fatti)* to agree (with sthg) ; *(date, eventi)* to clash (with sthg).

coinciso, a *pp* → **coincidere.**

coinvolgere *vt* : **~ qn (in qc)** to involve sb (in sthg).

coinvolto, a *pp* → **coinvolgere.**

col = **con + il, con.**

colapasta = **scolapasta.**

colare *vt (filtrare)* to filter ; *(pasta)* to drain. ◆ *vi (liquido)* to drip ; *(contenitore)* to leak ; *(cera, burro)* to melt ; **~ a picco** to sink.

colazione *sf (pranzo)* lunch ; **(prima) ~** breakfast ; **fare ~** *(al mattino)* to have breakfast.

colera *sm* cholera.

colica, che *sf* colic.

colino *sm* colander.

colla *sf* glue.

collaborare *vi* to cooperate.

collaboratore, trice *sm, f* collaborator.

collana *sf* necklace ; *(serie)* series.

collant [kol'lan] *smpl* tights.

collare *sm* collar.

collasso *sm* collapse.

collaudo *sm* test.

colle *sm* hill.

collega, ghi, ghe *smf* colleague.

collegare *vt* to connect. ❑ **collegarsi** *vr* to link up. ❑ **collegarsi con** *vr + prep (per telefono, radio, TV)* to link up with.

collegio *sm* boarding school.

collera *sf* anger ; **essere in ~ (con qn)** to be angry (with sb).

colletta *sf* collection.

collettivo, a *agg (comune)* common ; *(di gruppo)* group *(dav s)*.

colletto *sm* collar.

collezionare *vt* to collect.

collezione *sf* collection ; **fare (la) ~ di qc** to collect sthg.

collina *sf* hill.

collirio *sm* eyewash.

collisione *sf* impact.
collo *sm* neck ; *(di abito)* collar, neck ; *(pacco)* package.
collocamento *sm* employment.
collocare *vt (disporre)* to place.
colloquio *sm (conversazione)* talk ; *(esame)* oral exam ; ~ **di lavoro** interview.
colmo, a *agg* full. ◆ *sm* : **è il ~!** it's the last straw!
colomba *sf* dove ; *(dolce)* Easter cake.
Colombia *sf* : **la ~** Colombia.
colonia *sf* colony ; *(per bambini)* summer camp ; **(acqua di) ~** (eau de) cologne.
colonna *sf* column ; ~ **vertebrale** spine, spinal column.
colorante *sm (per alimenti)* food colouring ; *(per tessuti)* dye.
colorare *vt* to colour.
colore *sm* colour ; **di che ~?** what colour? ; **di ~** coloured ; **a colori** colour *(dav s)*.
coloro *pron mpl* : ~ **che ...** those who ...
colosseo *sm* : **il Colosseo** the Colosseum.

IL COLOSSEO

One of Rome's most visited monuments, the Colosseum was built between 75 and 80 AD. In its arena spectators watched gladiatorial contests, fights between men and animals, chariot races and simulated naval battles. Pillaged over the centuries, and attacked more recently by pollution, the amphitheatre nevertheless still retains some of its outer walls.

---

colpa *sf (responsabilità)* fault ; *(reato)* offence ; **dare la ~ (di qc) a qn/qc** to blame sb/sthg (for sthg) ; **per ~ di** through, owing to.
colpire *vt* to hit ; *(impressionare, sog : malattia)* to strike.
colpo *sm* blow ; *(sparo)* shot ; *(alla porta)* knock ; *fam (infarto)* stroke ; *fam (rapina)* raid ; **di ~** suddenly ; **fare ~** to make a strong impression ; **un ~ di fulmine** love at first sight ; ~ **di sole** sunstroke ; ~ **di stato** coup (d'état) ; ~ **di telefono** phone call ; ~ **di testa** impulse ; ~ **di vento** gust of wind.
coltello *sm* knife.
coltivare *vt* to cultivate.
colto, a *pp* → **cogliere**. ◆ *agg* cultured.
coma *sm inv* coma.
comandante *sm (di nave)* captain ; *(di esercito)* commanding officer.
comandare *vi* to be in command.
comando *sm* command ; *(congegno)* control.
combaciare *vi* to fit together.
combattere *vt* & *vi* to fight.
combinare *vt (accordare)* to combine ; *(organizzare)* to arrange ; *fam (fare)* to do.
combinazione *sf* combination ; *(caso)* coincidence ; **per ~** by chance.
combustibile *agg* combustible. ◆ *sm* fuel.

☞

come *avv* - 1. *(comparativo)* like ; **ho dormito ~ un ghiro** I slept like a log ; **~ me** like me ; **~ sempre** as always ; **~ se niente fosse** as if nothing had happened.
- 2. *(interrogativo)* how ; **non so ~ fare** I don't know what to do ; **~ sarebbe?** what do you mean? ; **~ stai?** how are you? ; **~ mai?** how come?.
- 3. *(in qualità di)* as ; **viaggiare ~ turista** to travel as a tourist.
- 4. *(in esclamazioni)* how ; **~ mi dispiace!** I'm so sorry!
- 5. *(per esempio)* like ; **mi piacciono i colori accesi ~ il rosso** I like bright colours like red.
◆ *cong* - 1. *(nel modo in cui)* how ; **mi ha spiegato ~ lo ha conosciuto** she told me how she met him ; **fai ~ ti dico** do as I tell you ; **~ vuole** as you like.
- 2. *(comparativa)* as ; **non è caldo ~ pensavo** it's not as hot as I thought.
- 3. *(quanto)* how ; **sai ~ mi piace il cioccolato** you know how much I like chocolate.

---

cometa *sf* comet.
comfort *sm inv* comfort ; **l'hotel dispone di tutti i ~** the hotel offers a wide range of amenities.
comico, a, ci, che *agg* funny ; *(genere)* comic. ◆ *sm (attore)* comedian.
cominciare *vt* & *vi* to begin, to start ; **~ a fare qc** to begin to do sthg, to begin doing sthg ; **~ col fare qc** to begin by doing sthg.
comitiva *sf* group.
comizio *sm* meeting.
commedia *sf* play.
commemorare *vt* to commemorate.
commentare *vt* to comment on.
commento *sm* comment ; *(a un testo, programma)* commentary.
commerciale *agg* commercial.
commerciante *smf (mercante)* trader ; *(negoziante)* shopkeeper.
commerciare : commerciare in *v + prep* to deal in.
commercio *sm (vendita)* trade ; **essere fuori ~** not to be for sale ; **essere in ~** to be on the market.
commesso, a *pp* → **commettere**. ◆ *sm, f* shop assistant.
commestibile *agg* edible. ❑ **commestibili** *smpl* foodstuffs.
commettere *vt (crimine)* to commit ; *(errore)* to make.
commissario *sm (di polizia)* superintendent ; *(d'esami)* member of an examining board ; **~ tecnico** national coach.
commissione *sf* commission. ❑ **commissioni** *sfpl* errands.
commosso, a *pp* → **commuovere**. ◆ *agg* moved.
commovente *agg* touching.
commozione *sf (emozione)* emotion ; **~ cerebrale** concussion.
commuovere *vt* to move, to touch. ❑ **commuoversi** *vr* to be moved, to be touched.
comò *sm inv* chest of drawers.
comodino *sm* bedside table.
comodità *sf inv* comfort.
comodo, a *agg* comfortable ; *(conveniente)* convenient ; *(utile)*

handy. ◆ *sm* : **fare ~ a qn** to be handy for sb ; **fare il proprio ~** to do as one pleases ; **con ~** at one's convenience.

compact disc ['kɔmpat'disk] *sm inv* compact disc.

compagnia *sf* company ; *(di amici)* group ; **fare ~ a qn** to keep sb company ; **~ aerea** airline ; **~ d'assicurazione** insurance company.

compagno, a *sm, f* companion ; *(convivente)* partner ; **~ di scuola** school friend ; **~ di squadra** team mate.

comparire *vi* to appear.

compartimento *sm (di locale, spazio)* section ; *(di treno)* compartment.

compasso *sm* pair of compasses.

compatibile *agg* compatible ; **un comportamento non ~** inexcusable behaviour.

compatire *vt (aver compassione di)* to feel sorry for ; *(scusare)* to make allowances for.

compatto, a *agg (ben unito)* compact ; *(folla)* dense ; *fig (solidale)* united.

compensare *vt* to compensate ; **~ qn di qc** to compensate sb for sthg.

compenso *sm (paga)* payment ; *(risarcimento)* compensation ; *(ricompensa)* recompense ; **in ~** on the other hand.

comperare = **comprare**.

compere *sfpl* : **far ~** to do the shopping.

competente *agg* competent.

competere *vi* to compete.

❑ **competere a** *v + prep* to be due to.

competizione *sf* competition.

compiacere *vt* to please. ❑ **compiacersi** *vr* : **compiacersi di ○ per qc** to be delighted at sthg ; **compiacersi con qn** to congratulate sb.

compiaciuto, a *pp* → **compiacere**.

compiere *vt (eseguire)* to fulfil ; *(concludere)* to complete ; **quando compi gli anni?** when is your birthday? ; **compie 15 anni a maggio** he'll be 15 in May.

compilare *vt* to fill in.

compito *sm (incarico)* task ; *(dovere)* duty ; *(in classe)* test. ❑ **compiti** *smpl* homework *(sg)* ; **fare i compiti** to do one's homework.

compleanno *sm* birthday ; **buon ~!** Happy Birthday!

complessivo, a *agg* overall.

complesso, a *agg* complex. ◆ *sm* complex ; *(musicale)* band, group ; **in ○ nel ~** on the whole.

completamente *avv* completely.

completare *vt* to complete.

completo, a *agg* complete ; *(pieno)* full. ◆ *sm (vestiario)* suit ; *(di oggetti)* set ; **al ~** *(hotel, aereo)* fully booked ; **c'era la famiglia al ~** the whole family was there.

complicare *vt* to complicate. ❑ **complicarsi** *vr* to become complicated.

complicato, a *agg* complicated.

complicazione *sf (difficoltà)* snag ; *(di malattia)* complication.

complice *smf* accomplice.
complimentarsi *vr* : ~ **con qn** to congratulate sb.
complimento *sm* compliment ; **complimenti!** congratulations! ; **non fare complimenti** don't stand on ceremony.
componente *smf (membro)* member. ◆ *sf (aspetto)* element.
componibile *agg* fitted.
comporre *vt (musica, poesia)* to compose ; *(parola)* to make up ; *(numero di telefono)* to dial.
comportamento *sm* behaviour.
comportare *vt* to involve. ❑ **comportarsi** *vr* to behave.
compositore, trice *sm, f* composer.
composizione *sf* composition ; **' ~ principali treni'** *board showing the position of compartments, restaurant car etc making up main line trains.*
composto, a *pp* → **comporre**. ◆ *agg (persona, contegno)* composed ; *(sostanza, parola)* compound. ◆ *sm* compound ; ~ **da** composed of.
comprare *vt* to buy.
comprendere *vt (includere)* to include ; *(capire)* to understand.
comprensione *sf* understanding.
comprensivo, a *agg (tollerante)* understanding ; *(inclusivo)* inclusive.
compreso, a *pp* → **comprendere**. ◆ *agg* inclusive ; ~ **nel prezzo** included in the price.
compressa *sf* tablet.
compromesso *sm* compromise.
compromettere *vt* to compromise.
computer [kom'pjuter] *sm inv* computer.
comunale *agg* municipal.
comune *agg* common ; *(a più persone)* shared ; *(ordinario)* ordinary. ◆ *sm (edificio)* town hall ; *(ente)* town council ; *(area)* ≃ borough ; **avere qc in ~ (con qn)** to have sthg in common (with sb) ; **mettere qc in ~** to share sthg ; **fuori del ~** out of the ordinary.
comunicare *vt* to communicate. ◆ *vi (parlare, corrispondere)* to communicate ; *(porta)* : ~ **con** to lead to.
comunicazione *sf (atto)* communication ; *(annuncio)* announcement ; *(telefonica)* call ; **dare la ~ a qn** to put a call through to sb.
comunione *sf (eucaristia)* Communion ; ~ **dei beni** DIR joint ownership of property.
comunismo *sm* communism.
comunista, i, e *agg* & *smf* communist.
comunità *sf inv* community ; **la Comunità (Economica) Europea** the European (Economic) Community.
comunque *avv* anyway. ◆ *cong (tuttavia)* however ; *(in qualsiasi modo)* no matter how.
con *prep* with ; ~ **piacere!** with pleasure! ; **viaggiare ~ il treno/la macchina** to travel by train/car.
concavo, a *agg* concave.

concedere *vt (dare, accordare)* to grant ; *(ammettere)* to concede ; **~ a qn di fare qc** to allow sb to do sthg ; **concedersi qc** to treat o.s. to sthg.

concentrare *vt* to concentrate ; *(riassumere)* to condense. ❑ **concentrarsi** *vr* to concentrate.

concentrato, a *agg* concentrated, concentrating. ◆ *sm* concentrate.

concentrazione *sf* concentration.

concepimento *sm* conception.

concepire *vt (figlio)* to conceive ; *(idea)* to devise.

concerto *sm* concert.

concessionario *sm* agent.

concesso, a *pp* → **concedere**.

concetto *sm* concept ; *(opinione)* opinion.

conchiglia *sf* shell.

conciliare *vt (impegni, attività)* to reconcile ; *(sonno)* to be conducive to ; *(contravvenzione)* to settle on the spot.

concime *sm* fertilizer.

concludere *vt* to conclude. ❑ **concludersi** *vr* to conclude.

conclusione *sf* conclusion ; **in ~** in conclusion.

concluso, a *pp* → **concludere**.

concordare *vt (stabilire)* to agree on ; GRAMM to make agree. ◆ *vi* to agree.

concorde *agg* in agreement.

concorrente *smf (in gara, affari)* competitor ; *(ad un concorso)* contestant.

concorrenza *sf* competition.

concorso, a *pp* → **concorrere**. ◆ *sm* competition ; *(esame)* competitive examination ; **~ di bellezza** beauty contest.

concreto, a *agg* concrete.

condanna *sf (sentenza)* sentence ; *(pena)* conviction ; *(disapprovazione)* condemnation.

condannare *vt* DIR to sentence ; *(disapprovare)* to condemn.

condimento *sm (per insalata)* dressing ; *(per carne)* seasoning.

condire *vt (insalata)* to dress ; *(carne)* to season.

condividere *vt* to share.

condizionale *agg* & *sm* conditional. ◆ *sf* DIR suspended sentence.

condizionatore *sm* air-conditioner.

condizione *sf* condition ; **a ~ che** on condition that.

condoglianze *sfpl* condolences.

condominio *sm (edificio)* block of flats *(jointly owned)* ; *(persone)* joint owners *(pl)*.

condotta *sf* conduct.

condotto, a *pp* → **condurre**. ◆ *sm* conduit ; ANAT duct.

conducente *sm* driver ; **'non parlare al ~'** 'please do not speak to the driver whilst the vehicle is in motion'.

condurre *vt (affare, azienda)* to run ; *(bambino, prigioniero)* to take ; *(vita)* to lead ; *(gas, acqua)* to carry.

conduttore, trice *sm, f* driver. ◆ *sm (di calore, elettricità)* conductor.

confarsi : **confarsi a** *vr + prep* to suit.
confederazione *sf* confederation.
conferenza *sf (riunione)* conference ; *(discorso)* lecture ; **~ stampa** press conference.
conferire *vt form* : **~ qc a qn** to confer sthg on sb.
conferma *sf* confirmation.
confermare *vt* to confirm.
confessare *vt* to confess. ❑ **confessarsi** *vr RELIG* to confess ; *(dichiararsi)* : **confessarsi colpevole** to plead guilty.
confessione *sf* confession.
confetto *sm (dolciume)* sugared almond ; *(pastiglia)* pill.
confezionare *vt (merce)* to package ; *(pacco)* to make up ; *(vestiario)* to make.
confezione *sf (involucro)* packaging ; *(di vestiario)* tailoring ; **~ regalo** gift pack.
confidare *vt* : **~ qc a qn** to confide sthg to sb. ❑ **confidare in** *v + prep* to have confidence in. ❑ **confidarsi** *vr* : **confidarsi con qn** to open one's heart to sb.
confidenziale *agg* confidential.
confinare : **confinare con** *v + prep* to border on. ❑ **confinarsi in** *vr + prep* to shut o.s. away in.
confine *sm (frontiera)* border ; *(limite)* boundary.
confiscare *vt* to confiscate.
conflitto *sm (guerra)* conflict ; *(contrasto)* clash.
confondere *vt* to confuse, to mix up ; **~ le idee a qn** to confuse sb. ❑ **confondersi** *vr (mescolarsi)* to merge ; *(sbagliarsi)* to get mixed up ; *(turbarsi)* to become confused.
conformità *sf* conformity ; **in ~ con** in accordance with.
confortare *vt* to comfort.
confortevole *agg* comfortable.
confrontare *vt* to compare.
confronto *sm* comparison ; **in ~ (a)** in comparison (with) ; **nei miei confronti** towards me.
confusione *sf (caos)* confusion ; *(disordine)* mess ; *(chiasso)* racket, noise ; **far ~** *(confondersi)* to get mixed up ; *(far rumore)* to make a racket.
confuso, a *pp* → **confondere.** ◆ *agg* confused.
congedare *vt (lasciar andare)* to dismiss ; *MIL* to demobilize. ❑ **congedarsi** *vr (andar via)* to take one's leave ; *MIL* to be demobilized.
congedo *sm* leave ; *MIL* discharge.
congegno *sm* device.
congelare *vt* to freeze. ❑ **congelarsi** *vr* to freeze ; *fig (persona, mani)* to be frozen.
congelato, a *agg* frozen.
congelatore *sm* freezer.
congeniale *agg* congenial.
congenito, a *agg* congenital.
congestione *sf* congestion.
congettura *sf* conjecture.
congiungere *vt* to join (together). ❑ **congiungersi** *vr (strade)* to meet.
congiuntivo *sm* subjunctive.

congiunto, a *pp* → congiungere. ◆ *sm, f* relative.
congiunzione *sf* conjunction.
congiura *sf* conspiracy.
congratularsi *vr* : ~ con qn per qc to congratulate sb on sthg.
congratulazioni *sfpl* congratulations.
congresso *sm* congress.
coniglio *sm* rabbit.
coniugato, a *agg* married.
coniuge *smf* spouse.
connazionale *smf* fellow countryman (*f* fellow countrywoman).
connettere *vt* to connect.
connotati *smpl* description *(sg)*.
cono *sm* cone ; ~ gelato ice-cream cone.
conoscente *smf* acquaintance.
conoscenza *sf* knowledge ; *(persona)* acquaintance ; perdere ~ to lose consciousness.
conoscere *vt* to know ; *(incontrare)* to meet.
conosciuto, a *pp* → conoscere. ◆ *agg* well-known.
conquista *sf (azione)* conquest ; *(risultato, cosa ottenuta)* achievement.
conquistare *vt (impadronirsi di)* to conquer ; *(ottenere)* to gain ; *(persona)* to win over.
consanguineo, a *sm, f* blood relation.
consapevole *agg* : ~ di qc aware of sthg.
conscio, a, sci, sce *agg* : ~ di qc conscious of sthg.
consegna *sf (recapito)* delivery ; *(custodia)* : dare qc in ~ a qn to entrust sb with sthg.
consegnare *vt (recapitare)* to deliver ; *(affidare)* to entrust.
conseguenza *sf* consequence ; di ~ consequently.
conseguire *vt* to obtain. ◆ *vi* : ne ~ che ... it follows that ...
consenso *sm* consent.
consentire *vt* to allow. ❑ **consentire a** *v + prep* to agree to.
conserva *sf* preserve ; ~ di frutta jam ; ~ di pomodoro tomato sauce.
conservante *sm* preservative.
conservare *vt (tenere)* to keep ; *(monumento, resti)* to preserve ; '~ in frigo' 'keep refrigerated'. ❑ **conservarsi** *vr (cibo)* to keep ; *(monumento, resti)* to be preserved.
conservatore, trice *sm, f* conservative.
considerare *vt* to consider. ❑ **considerarsi** *vr* to consider o.s.
considerazione *sf*: prendere in ~ to take into consideration.
considerevole *agg* considerable.
consigliare *vt (persona)* to advise ; *(locale, metodo)* to recommend ; ~ a qn di fare qc to advise sb to do sthg. ❑ **consigliarsi con** *vr + prep* : consigliarsi con qn to ask sb's advice.
consigliere *sm (funzionario)* adviser ; *(politico)* councillor.
consiglio *sm (suggerimento)* piece of advice ; *(riunione)* meeting ; *(organo)* council ; dare un ~ a qn to give sb some advice ; ~ d'amministrazione board ; il Consiglio dei Ministri ≃ the Cabinet.

consistere : **consistere di** *v + prep* to consist of ; **consistere in** to consist in.

consistito, a *pp* → consistere.

consolare *vt (confortare)* to console ; *(sollevare)* to cheer up. ❑ **consolarsi** *vr* to console o.s.

consolato *sm* consulate.

console *sm* consul.

consonante *sf* consonant.

constatare *vt* to notice.

consueto, a *agg* usual.

consulente *smf* consultant.

consultare *vt* to consult. ❑ **consultarsi** *vr* to confer. ❑ **consultarsi con** *vr + prep* to consult with.

consultorio *sm* advice bureau.

consumare *vt* to consume ; *(logorare)* to wear out. ❑ **consumarsi** *vr* to wear out.

consumatore *sm* consumer.

consumazione *sf (bibita)* drink ; *(spuntino)* snack ; **la ~ al tavolo è più cara** it's more expensive to eat/drink sitting at a table ; '**~ obbligatoria**' 'minimum charge'.

consumismo *sm* consumerism.

consumo *sm* consumption.

contabile *smf* accountant.

contabilità *sf inv (operazioni)* accountancy ; *(libri)* accounts *(pl)* ; *(ufficio)* accounts department.

contachilometri *sm inv* ≃ mileometer.

contadino, a *sm, f* farmer.

contagiare *vt* to infect.

contagio *vt (trasmissione)* infection.

contagocce *sm inv* dropper.

contante *agg* → **denaro.** ◆ *sm* cash ; **pagare in contanti** to pay in cash.

contare *vt* & *vi* to count ; **avere soldi contati** not to have a penny to spare. ❑ **contare di** *v + prep* : **~ di fare qc** to intend to do sthg. ❑ **contare su** *vr + prep* to count on.

contatore *sm* meter.

contattare *vt* to contact.

contatto *sm* contact.

conte, essa *sm, f* count *(f* countess).

contegno *sm* attitude.

contemporaneamente *avv* simultaneously.

contemporaneo, a *agg (dello stesso tempo)* contemporaneous ; *(attuale)* contemporary.

contendere *vt* : **~ qc a qn** to compete with sb for sthg.

contenere *vt* to contain. ❑ **contenersi** *vr* to contain o.s.

contenitore *sm* container.

contento, a *agg (lieto)* happy, glad ; *(soddisfatto)* : **~ (di)** pleased (with).

contenuto *sm (cosa racchiusa)* contents *(pl)* ; *(argomento)* content.

contestare *vt* to object to.

contestazione *sf (obiezione)* objection ; *(protesta)* protest.

contesto *sm* context.

contiguo, a *agg* : **~ (a qc)** adjacent (to sthg).

continentale *agg* continental.

continente *sm (geografico)* continent ; *(terraferma)* mainland.

contingente *sm* contingent.

continuamente *avv (senza interruzioni)* continuously ; *(di frequente)* continually.

continuare *vt* & *vi* to continue. ◆ *v impers* : **continua a piovere** it's still raining ; **~ a fare qc** to continue doing sthg.

continuazione *sf* continuation.

continuo, a *agg (incessante)* continuous ; *(serie, fila)* continual ; **di ~** continually.

conto *sm (calcolo)* calculation ; *(di ristorante, albergo)* bill ; *(bancario)* account ; **mi porta il ~, per favore?** could you bring me the bill, please? ; **fare ~ su** to rely on ; **rendersi ~ di qc** to realize sthg ; **tenere ~ di qc** to take account of sthg ; **~ corrente** current account ; **~ alla rovescia** countdown ; **per ~ di qn** on behalf of sb ; **fare i conti con qn** *fam* to sort sb out ; **in fin dei conti** all things considered.

contorno *sm (di pietanza)* vegetables *(pl)* ; *(linea)* outline.

contrabbando *sm* smuggling.

contrabbasso *sm* double bass.

contraccambiare *vt* to return.

contraccettivo, a *agg* contraceptive. ◆ *sm* contraceptive.

contraccolpo *sm* rebound.

contraddire *vt* to contradict. ❑ **contraddirsi** *vr* to contradict o.s.

contraddizione *sf* contradiction.

contraffare *vt* to falsify ; *(firma)* to forge.

contrapporre *vt* to set against.

contrariamente *avv* : **~ a** contrary to.

contrario, a *agg (opposto)* opposite ; *(sfavorevole)* unfavourable. ◆ *sm* opposite ; **essere ~ a qc** to be against sthg ; **avere qualcosa in ~** to have an objection ; **al ~** on the contrary.

contrarre *vt* to contract. ❑ **contrarsi** *vr (muscolo)* to contract.

contrassegno *sm (marchio)* mark ; **spedire qc (in) ~** to send sthg cash on delivery.

contrastare *vt* to hinder. ◆ *vi* : **~ (con)** to clash (with).

contrasto *sm* contrast ; **essere in ~ con qc** *(opinione, esigenza)* to be in contrast with sthg.

contrattare *vt* to negotiate.

contrattempo *sm* hitch.

contratto, a *pp* → **contrarre.** ◆ *sm* contract.

contravvenzione *sf* fine.

contribuire : contribuire a *v + prep* to contribute to.

contributo *sm (partecipazione)* contribution ; *(tassa)* levy.

contro *prep* against ; **~ di me** against me ; **prendere qc ~ il mal di gola** to take sthg for one's sore throat.

controfigura *sf* stuntman *(f* stuntwoman).

controllare *vt* to control ; *(verificare)* to check ; '**~ il resto**' 'please check your change'. ❑ **controllarsi** *vr* to control o.s.

controllo *sm (verifica)* check ; *(sorveglianza)* supervision ; *(dominio)* control ; **perdere il ~** to lose control ; **~ doganale** customs

inspection ; '~ **elettronico della velocità'** 'speed checks' ; '~ **passaporti'** 'passport control'.
controllore *sm (di autobus, treni)* (ticket) inspector ; ~ **di volo** air-traffic controller.
contromano *avv* in the wrong direction.
controproducente *agg* counterproductive.
controsenso *sm* contradiction in terms.
controvoglia *avv* reluctantly.
contusione *sf* bruise.
convalescenza *sf* convalescence.
convalidare *vt (biglietto)* to validate ; *(dubbio, sospetto)* to confirm ; '~ **all'inizio del viaggio'** 'stamp your ticket at the start of your journey'.
convegno *sm* conference.
convenevoli *smpl* civilities.
conveniente *agg* favourable ; *(prezzo)* cheap ; *(affare)* advantageous.
convenire *vi (riunirsi)* to gather ; *(concordare)* to agree ; *(tornare utile)* to be worthwhile. ◆ *v impers (essere consigliabile)* : **conviene avvertirli** it is advisable to inform them ; **ti conviene aspettare** you'd better wait.
convento *sm* convent.
convenuto *pp* → **convenire**.
convenzionale *agg* conventional.
convenzioni *sfpl* conventions.
conversazione *sf (chiacchierata)* conversation.
convertire *vt* to convert. ❑ **convertirsi** *vr* : **convertirsi (a qc)** to convert (to sthg).
convincere *vt* : ~ **qn di qc** to convince sb of sthg ; ~ **qn a fare qc** to persuade sb to do sthg.
convinto, a *pp* → **convincere**. ◆ *agg* convinced.
convivenza *sf (di coppia)* living together.
convivere *vi* to live together.
convocare *vt* to convene.
convoglio *sm* convoy.
convulsioni *sfpl* convulsions.
cooperativa *sf* cooperative.
coordinare *vt* to coordinate.
coperchio *sm* lid.
coperta *sf (da letto)* blanket ; *(di nave)* deck.
copertina *sf* cover.
coperto, a *pp* → **coprire**. ◆ *agg (piscina, campo)* indoor *(dav s)* ; *(persona)* wrapped up ; *(cielo)* overcast. ◆ *sm (a tavola)* place ; *(al ristorante)* cover charge ; ~ **di qc** covered with sthg ; **al** ~ under cover.
copertone *sm (pneumatico)* tyre.
copia *sf* copy ; **bella** ~ final draft ; **brutta** ~ rough draft.
copiare *vt* to copy.
copione *sm* script.
coppa *sf (bicchiere)* goblet ; *(di gelato)* tub ; *(ciotola)* bowl ; *(di reggiseno, trofeo)* cup ; ~ **dell'olio** oil sump.
coppia *sf (paio)* pair ; *(di sposi, amanti)* couple ; **a coppie** in pairs.
copricostume *sm inv* beach robe.
coprifuoco, chi *sm* curfew.
copriletto *sm inv* bedspread.

coprire *vt* to cover ; ~ **qn di qc** to shower sb with sthg ; *(insulti)* to cover sb with sthg. ❑ **coprirsi** *vr (con indumenti)* to cover o.s. ; **coprirsi di qc** *(muffa, fango)* to be covered in sthg.

coraggio *sm (forza d'animo)* courage ; *(faccia tosta)* cheek. ◆ *esclam* cheer up! ; *(forza)* come on! ; **avere il ~ di fare qc** *(avere l'animo)* to have the nerve to do sthg ; *(avere faccia tosta)* to have the cheek to do sthg.

coraggioso, a *agg* courageous, brave.

corallo *sm* coral.

Corano *sm* : **il ~** the Koran.

corazza *sf (armatura)* armour ; *(di animale)* shell.

corazzieri *smpl the President's guard.*

corda *sf (fune)* rope ; *(spago, di strumento)* string ; **tagliare la ~** *fig* to sneak off ; **corde vocali** vocal cords.

cordiale *agg* warm.

cordialmente *avv* warmly.

cordone *sm* cord ; *(di persone)* cordon ; ~ **ombelicale** umbilical cord.

coreografia *sf* choreography.

coriandolo *sm (spezia, pianta)* coriander. ❑ **coriandoli** *smpl* confetti *(sg)*.

coricarsi *vr* to go to bed.

cornamusa *sf* bagpipes *(pl)*.

cornetta *sf* receiver.

cornetto *sm (pasta)* croissant ; *(gelato)* cone.

cornice *sf* frame.

cornicione *sm* cornice.

corno *(pl f* **corna**) *sm* horn ; **facciamo le corna!** *fam* ≃ touch wood! ; **fare** ○ **mettere le corna a qn** *fam* to cheat on sb.

Cornovaglia *sf* : **la ~** Cornwall.

coro *sm* chorus ; *(di chiesa)* choir.

corona *sf (reale)* crown ; *(di fiori)* wreath.

corpo *sm* body ; *(militare)* corps *(sg)* ; ~ **insegnante** teaching staff ; **(a) ~ a ~** hand to hand.

corporatura *sf* build.

corporeo, a *agg* bodily.

corredare *vt* : ~ **qc di qc** to equip sthg with sthg.

corredo *sm (da sposa)* trousseau ; *(attrezzatura)* kit.

correggere *vt* to correct.

corrente *agg (moneta)* valid ; *(mese, anno)* current ; *(comune)* everyday. ◆ *sf* current ; *(tendenza)* trend. ◆ *sm* : **essere al ~ (di qc)** to be informed (about sthg) ; **mettere qn al ~ (di qc)** to inform sb (about sthg) ; ~ **alternata** alternating current ; ~ **continua** direct current.

correntemente *avv (speditamente)* fluently ; *(comunemente)* commonly.

correre *vi* to run ; *(affrettarsi)* to rush. ◆ *vt* to run ; ~ **dietro a qn** to run after sb.

corretto, a *pp* → **correggere.** ◆ *agg (esatto)* correct ; *(onesto)* proper.

correzione *sf* correction ; *(di compiti)* marking.

corridoio *sm* corridor.

corridore *sm (atleta)* runner ; *(pilota)* racer.

corriera *sf* coach, bus.

corriere *sm* courier.
corrimano *sm* handrail.
corrispondente *agg* corresponding. ◆ *smf* correspondent.
corrispondenza *sf* correspondence.
corrispondere *vt* to return. ❑ **corrispondere a** *v* + *prep* to correspond to.
corrisposto, a *pp* → **corrispondere.**
corrodere *vt* to corrode.
corrompere *vt* *(comprare)* to bribe ; *(traviare)* to corrupt.
corroso, a *pp* → **corrodere.**
corrotto, a *pp* → **corrompere.** ◆ *agg (disonesto)* corrupt.
corruzione *sf (disonestà)* corruption ; *(con denaro)* bribery.
corsa *sf (a piedi)* running ; *(gara)* race ; *(di mezzo pubblico)* journey ; **fare una ~** *(correre)* to run ; *(sbrigarsi)* to dash ; **di ~** in a rush ; **corse dei cavalli** horse races.
corsia *sf (di strada)* lane ; *(di ospedale)* ward ; **~ preferenziale** bus and taxi lane ; **~ di sorpasso** overtaking lane ; **' ~ chiusa'** 'lane closed'.
Corsica *sf*: **la ~** Corsica.
corso, a *pp* → **correre.** ◆ *sm* course ; *(strada)* main street ; **fare un ~ (di qc)** to take a course (in sthg) ; **~ accelerato** crash course ; **~ d'acqua** watercourse ; **corsi estivi** summer courses ; **corsi serali** evening classes ; **in ~** *(denaro)* in circulation ; *(riunione, lavori)* in progress ; **fuori ~** out of circulation.
corte *sf (reale)* court ; **fare la ~ a qn** to court sb.
corteccia, ce *sf* bark.
corteggiare *vt* to court.
corteo *sm (manifestazione)* demonstration ; *(processione)* procession.
cortese *agg* polite.
cortesia *sf (qualità)* politeness ; *(atto)* favour ; **per ~** please.
cortile *sm* courtyard.
corto, a *agg* short ; **essere a ~ di qc** to be short of sthg.
cortocircuito *sm* short circuit.
corvo *sm* raven.
cosa *sf* thing ; *(faccenda)* matter ; **è una ~ da niente** it's nothing ; **cosa?** what? ; **~ c'è?** what's the matter? ; **per prima ~** firstly.
coscia, sce *sf (di uomo)* thigh ; *(di pollo, agnello)* leg.
cosciente *agg (sveglio)* conscious ; *(consapevole)* : **~ di qc** aware ○ conscious of sthg.
coscienza *sf* conscience ; **avere qc sulla ~** to have sthg on one's conscience.
coscio *sm* leg.
cosciotto *sm* leg.

così *avv* - 1. *(in questo modo)* like this/like that ; **fai ~** do it this way ; **~ ~** so-so ; **per ~ dire** so to speak ; **meglio ~** it's better like this ; **proprio ~!** just like that! ; **e ~ via** and so on.
- 2. *(per descrivere misure)* so ; **una scatola larga ~ e lunga ~** a box so wide and so long.
- 3. *(talmente)* so ; **è ancora ~ presto** it's still so early! ; **~ poco/tanto** so little/much ; **una ragazza ~ bella** such a beautiful girl.
- 4. *(conclusivo)* so ; **~, non ha**

ancora deciso so you haven't decided yet.
◆ *cong* - 1. *(perciò)* so, therefore. - 2. *(a tal punto)* : ~ ... che so ... (that) ; **sono ~ stanco che non sto in piedi** I'm so tired I can hardly stand up ; ~ ... **da** enough ... to ; **è ~ sciocco da dire di no** he's silly enough to say no.
◆ *agg inv* : **non ho mai visto una macchina ~** I've never seen a car like that.
❑ **cosicché** *cong (affinché)* so (that).

cosicché *cong* so that.
cosiddetto, a *agg* so-called.
cosmetici *smpl* cosmetics.
coso *sm fam* thing.
cospargere *vt* : ~ **qc di qc** to sprinkle sthg with sthg.
cosparso, a *pp* → **cospargere**.
cospicuo, a *agg* sizeable.
cospirare *vi* to conspire.
costa *sf* coast.
costante *agg (stabile, durevole)* constant ; *(persona)* steadfast.
costare *vi* to cost ; **quanto costa?** how much does it cost? ; ~ **caro** to be expensive.
costata *sf* chop.
costatare = **constatare**.
costeggiare *vt (fiancheggiare)* to go alongside ; *(navigare)* to hug the coast of.
costellazione *sf* constellation.
costernato, a *agg* dismayed.
costì *avv* there.
costiero, a *agg* coastal.
costituire *vt (formare)* to constitute ; *(fondare)* to set up. ❑ **costituirsi** *vr* to give o.s. up.
costituzione *sf* constitution ; *(formazione)* setting-up.

LA COSTITUZIONE

On 2nd June 1946 the Italian people voted by referendum to be governed as a Republic. King Umberto II left Italy and his power was handed over to the Constituent Assembly which elected as provisional head of state the Liberal Enrico De Nicola. The drawing up of the new Constitution (which came into force on 1st January 1948) was entrusted to a commission made up of 75 members. The Italian Constitution is composed of 139 articles and 18 provisional regulations ; it is a 'rigid' document can be changed only by passing a constitutional law. The Constitution is not only a document of foundation, drawn up at the same time as the Republic itself, but also a document of liberation, from the dictatorial laws of facism and the negative experiences of the counry's monarchical past.

costo *sm* cost ; **a tutti i costi** at all costs.
costola *sf* rib.
costoletta *sf* cutlet.
costoso, a *agg* expensive.
costretto, a *pp* → **costringere**.
costringere *vt* : ~ **qn (a fare qc)** to force sb (to do sthg).
costruire *vt (fabbricare)* to build.
costruzione *sf* construction.
costume *sm (uso)* custom ; *(abito)* costume ; ~ **da bagno** swimsuit.
cotechino *sm* pork sausage.

cotoletta *sf* chop ; *(di vitello)* cutlet ; ~ **alla milanese** escalope of veal.
cotone *sm* cotton ; ~ **idrofilo** cotton wool.
cotta *sf* : **prendersi una ~ per qn** *fam* to have a crush on sb.
cotto, a *pp* → **cuocere.** ◆ *agg* cooked ; *fam (innamorato)* head over heels in love ; **ben ~** well-done.
cottura *sf* cooking.
coupon [ku'pɔn] *sm inv* coupon.
cozza *sf* mussel.
C.P. *(abbr di casella postale)* P.O. Box.
cracker ['krɛker] *sm inv* cracker.
crampo *sm* cramp.
cranio *sm* skull.
cratere *sm* crater.
crauti *smpl sauerkraut flavoured with cumin and juniper, a speciality of Trento.*
cravatta *sf* tie.
creare *vt* to create.
creativo, a *agg* creative.
creatore, trice *sm, f* creator ; **il Creatore** the Creator.
creatura *sf* creature.
credente *smf* believer.
credenza *sf (convinzione)* belief ; *(mobile)* sideboard.
credere *vt* to believe ; **credo di sì/no** I think/don't think so ; **credo (che) sia vero** I think that's true ; **credo di fare la cosa giusta** I think I'm doing the right thing. ❑ **credere a** *v + prep* to believe ; **non ci credo!** I don't believe it! ❑ **credere in** *v + prep* to believe in. ❑ **credersi** *vr* to consider o.s.
credito *sm* COMM credit ; *(fiducia)* trust.
crema *sf* cream ; *(liquida)* custard ; ~ **di asparagi** cream of asparagus soup ; ~ **depilatoria** hair-removing cream ; ~ **pasticcera** confectioner's custard ; ~ **solare** suntan cream ; **gelato alla ~** vanilla ice-cream.
crematorio *sm* crematorium.
cremazione *sf* cremation.
crème caramel ['krɛm'karamɛl] *sm inv o sf inv* crème caramel.
cremisi *agg inv* crimson.
cremoso, a *agg* creamy.
crepaccio *sm* crevice.
crepapelle : **a crepapelle** *avv* : **ridere a ~** to split one's sides laughing.
crepare *vi fam (morire)* to snuff it ; ~ **dal ridere** to die laughing.
crêpe [krɛp] *sf inv* pancake.
crepuscolo *sm (tramonto)* twilight.
crescere *vi* to grow ; *(diventare adulto)* to grow up. ◆ *vt* to bring up.
crescita *sf* growth.
cresima *sf* confirmation.
crespo, a *agg* frizzy.
cresta *sf* crest.
creta *sf* clay.
cretino, a *agg* idiot.
C.R.I. *sf (abbr di) abbr di* **Croce Rossa Italiana.**
cric *sm inv (attrezzo)* jack.
criminale *agg* & *smf (criminoso)* criminal.
crimine *sm* crime.
criniera *sf* mane.
cripta *sf* crypt.

crisi *sf inv (fase difficile)* crisis ; *(attacco)* fit ; **in ~** in a state of crisis.
cristallo *sm* crystal.
cristianesimo *sm* Christianity.
cristiano, a *agg* & *sm, f* Christian.
Cristo *sm* Christ ; **avanti ~** BC ; **dopo ~** AD.
criterio *sm (regola)* criterion ; *(buon senso)* common sense.
critica, che *sf (biasimo)* criticism ; *(i critici)* critics *(pl)* → **critico**.
criticare *vt* to criticize.
critico, a, ci, che *agg* critical. ◆ *sm, f (persona)* critic.
croccante *agg* crisp. ◆ *sm* almond crunch.
crocchetta *sf* croquette.
croce *sf* cross ; **la Croce Rossa** the Red Cross.
crocevia *sm inv* crossroads *(sg)*.
crociera *sf* cruise.
crocifisso *sm* crucifix.
crollare *vi (edificio, ponte)* to collapse ; *fig (per stanchezza, dolore)* to break down.
crollo *sm (di edificio, ponte)* collapse ; *(di prezzi)* slump.
cronaca, che *sf (attualità)* news *(sg)* ; *(di partita)* commentary ; **~ nera** crime news *(sg)*.
cronico, a, ci, che *agg* chronic.
cronista, i, e *smf* reporter.
cronologico, a, ci, che *agg* chronological.
crosta *sf (di pane)* crust ; *(di formaggio)* rind ; *(di ferita)* scab.
crostaceo *sm* shellfish.
crostacei *smpl* shellfish.
crostata *sf fruit or jam tart with a pastry lattice topping.*
crostino *sm (per minestra)* crouton ; *(tartina)* canapé ; **crostini di fegato** *small pieces of toast spread with chicken liver pâté.*
croupier [kru'pje] *sm inv* croupier.
cruciale *agg* crucial.
cruciverba *sm inv* crossword.
crudele *agg* cruel.
crudo, a *agg* raw.
crusca *sf* bran.
cruscotto *sm* dashboard.
cubo *sm* cube.
cuccetta *sf (di treno)* couchette ; *(di nave)* berth.
cucchiaiata *sf* spoonful.
cucchiaino *sm* teaspoon.
cucchiaio *sm* spoon.
cuccia, ce *sf* dog's bed ; **a ~!** down!.
cucciolo *sm* cub ; *(di cane)* puppy.
cucina *sf (stanza)* kitchen ; *(attività, cibi)* cooking ; *(elettrodomestico)* cooker ; **~ casalinga** home cooking ; **~ a gas** gas cooker.
cucinare *vt* to cook.
cucire *vt* to sew.
cucitura *sf* stitching.
cuculo *sm* cuckoo.
cuffia *sf* cap ; *(per l'ascolto)* headphones *(pl)* ; **'è obbligatorio l'uso della ~'** 'swimming caps must be worn'.
cugino, a *sm, f* cousin.

☞

cui *pron relativo* - **1.** *(in complemento indiretto : persona)* who, whom ; **l'amico a ~ ho prestato il libro** the friend I lent the book to, the friend to whom I lent the book ;

l'amico di ~ ti ho parlato the friend I told you about ; **la ragazza con ~ esco** the girl I'm going out with.
- 2. *(in complemento indiretto : cosa)* which ; **il film a ~ mi riferisco** the film (which) I'm referring to ; **l'appartamento in ~ vivo** the flat (which) I live in ; **il motivo per ~ ti chiamo** the reason (that) I'm calling you.
- 3. *(tra articolo e sostantivo)* : **la città il ~ nome mi sfugge** the town whose name escapes me ; **la persona alla ~ domanda rispondo** the person whose question I'm answering.
❑ **per cui** *cong (perciò)* so ; **sono stanco, per ~ vado a letto** I'm tired, so I'm going to bed.

---

culla *sf* cradle.
culmine *sm* peak.
culo *sm volg* arse *(Br)*, ass *(Am)*.
culto *sm* cult ; *(adorazione)* worship.
cultura *sf* culture.
culturismo *sm* body-building.
cumulativo *agg m* → **biglietto**.
cumulo *sm (mucchio)* heap, pile.
cunetta *sf (avvallamento)* bump.
cuocere *vt* & *vi* to cook.
cuoco, a, chi, che *sm, f* cook.
cuoio *sm* leather ; **~ capelluto** scalp.
cuore *sm* heart ; **avere a ~ qc** to care about sthg ; **nel ~ della notte** in the middle of the night.
cupo, a *agg (scuro)* dark ; *(voce)* deep.
cupola *sf* dome.
cura *sf* care ; *(trattamento, terapia)* treatment ; **avere ~ di** to take care of ; **prendersi ~ di** to look after **~ dimagrante** diet.
curare *vt (trattare)* to treat ; *(guarire)* to cure.
curcuma *sf* turmeric.
curiosare *vi* to look around.
curiosità *sf inv* curiosity.
curioso, a *agg (insolito)* curious *(indiscreto)* inquisitive.
curva *sf* bend ; **in ~** on a bend ; **~ pericolosa'** 'dangerous bend'.
curvare *vi (veicolo, autista)* to turn ; *(strada)* to bend. ◆ *vt* to bend.
curvo, a *agg (linea)* curved ; *(persona, spalle)* bent.
cuscinetto *sm* TECNOL bearing *(per timbri)* pad.
cuscino *sm (da divano)* cushion *(guanciale)* pillow.
custode *smf* attendant ; *(di scuola)* janitor.
custodia *sf (cura, controllo)* custody ; *(astuccio)* case.
custodire *vt (assistere)* to look after ; *(conservare)* to keep.
cute *sf* skin.

D

☞

da *prep* - 1. *(con verbo passivo)* by **il viaggio è pagato dalla ditta** the trip is paid for by the company.
- 2. *(stato in luogo)* at ; **abito ~ una zia** I'm living at an aunt's.
- 3. *(moto a luogo)* to ; **andare da**

medico/dal parrucchiere to go to the doctor's/the hairdresser's.
- 4. *(moto per luogo)* through ; **è entrato dall'ingresso principale** he came in through the main entrance ; **il treno passa ~ Roma** the train goes via Rome.
- 5. *(indica l'origine, la provenienza)* from ; **venire ~ Roma** to come from Rome ; **ricevere una lettera ~ un amico** to get a letter from a friend.
- 6. *(indica tempo)* for ; **aspetto ~ ore** I've been waiting for hours ; **lavoro dalle 9 alle 5** I work from 9 to 5 ; **non lo vedo ~ ieri** I haven't seen him since yesterday; **comincerò ~ domani** I'll start from tomorrow.
- 7. *(indica condizione, funzione)* as ; **~ grande voglio fare il pompiere** when I grow up I want to be a fireman ; **fare ~ guida** to act as a guide.
- 8. *(indica la causa)* with ; **tremare dal freddo** to shiver ; **piangere dalla felicità** to cry for joy.
- 9. *(indica una caratteristica)* with ; **una ragazza dagli occhi verdi** a girl with green eyes, a green-eyed girl ; **una stanza ~ 100 euro a notte** a 100 euros a night room ; **una bottiglia ~ un litro** a litre bottle.
- 10. *(indica il fine)* : **occhiali ~ sole** sunglasses ; **qualcosa ~ mangiare** something to eat.
- 11. *(indica separazione)* from ; **vedere ~ lontano/vicino** to see from a distance/close up ; **essere lontano ~ casa** to be far from home ; **la piscina è a 3 chilometri ~ qui** the swimming pool is 3 kilometres from here ; **isolarsi ~ tutti** to cut o.s. off from everyone ; **mettere qc ~ parte** to save sthg.
- 12. *(indica modo)* like ; **trattare qn ~ amico** to treat sb like ○ as a friend ; **puoi farlo ~ te** you can do it (for) yourself ; **non è cosa ~ te!** it's not like you!
- 13. *(indica la conseguenza)* : **essere stanco ~ morire** to be dead tired.

---

daccapo *avv* from the beginning.
dado *sm (per gioco)* dice ; *(estratto)* stock cube ; *(per vite)* nut.
dagli = **da + gli, da.**
dai[1] = **da + i, da.**
dai[2] *esclam* go on!
daino *sm (animale)* deer.
dal = **da + il, da.**
dall' = **da + l', da.**
dalla = **da + la, da.**
dalle = **da + le, da.**
dallo = **da + lo, da.**
daltonico, a, ci, che *agg* colour-blind.
dama *sf (gioco)* draughts *(sg)* ; *(nel ballo)* partner.
damigiana *sf* demijohn.
danaro = **denaro.**
dancing ['dɛnsin] *sm inv* dance hall.
danese *agg* & *sm* Danish. ◆ *smf* Dane.
Danimarca *sf* : **la ~** Denmark.
danneggiare *vt (rovinare)* to damage ; *(nuocere a)* to harm.
danno *sm (materiale)* damage ; *(morale)* harm ; **i danni** *DIR* damages.
dannoso, a *agg* harmful.
danza *sf* dance.
dappertutto *avv* everywhere.

dappoco *agg inv (persona)* inept ; *(questione)* insignificant.

dapprima *avv* at first.

dare *vt* to give ; *(risultati)* to produce ; *(film)* : **cosa danno all'Odeon?** what's on at the Odeon? ; **~ qc a qn** to give sthg to sb, to give sb sthg ; **~ la mano a qn** to shake hands with sb ; **~ la nausea a qn** to make sb feel sick ; **~ la buonanotte a qn** to say goodnight to sb ; **~ da bere a qn** to give sb something to drink ; **~ una festa** to throw a party ; **~ del lei a qn** to address sb as 'lei' ; **~ del tu a qn** to address sb as 'tu' ; **~ qn per morto** to give sb up for dead ; **~ qc per scontato** to take sthg for granted ; **darsi il cambio** to take it in turns ; **~ alla testa a qn** *(sog : alcol, successo)* to go to sb's head.
❑ **dare su** *v + prep (finestra)* to look out onto ; *(porta)* to lead to.
❑ **darsi a** *vr + prep (dedicarsi a)* to devote o.s. to ; **darsi al bere** to take to drink.

data *sf* date ; **~ di nascita** date of birth.

dato, a *pp* → **dare.** ◆ *agg* particular. ◆ *sm* datum ; **~ che** given that ; **un ~ di fatto** a fact ; **i dati** the data.

datore, trice *sm, f* : **~ di lavoro** employer.

dattero *sm* date.

davanti *avv* in front ; *(avanti)* ahead ; *(nella parte anteriore)* at the front. ◆ *agg inv* front *(dav s)*. ◆ *sm* front. ◆ *prep* : **~ a** in front of ; *(dirimpetto)* opposite.

davanzale *sm* windowsill.

davvero *avv* really.

d.C. *(abbr di dopo Cristo)* A.D.

dea *sf* goddess.

debito *sm* debt.

debole *agg* weak. ◆ *sm* : **avere un ~ per** to have a weakness for.

debolezza *sf* weakness.

debuttare *vi* to make one's debut.

decaffeinato, a *agg* decaffeinated.

decapitare *vt* to decapitate.

decappottabile *agg & sf* convertible.

deceduto, a *agg* deceased.

decennio *sm* decade.

decente *agg* decent.

decesso *sm form* death.

decidere *vt* to decide on. ◆ *vi* to decide ; **~ di fare qc** to decide to do sthg. ❑ **decidersi** *vr* : **decidersi (a fare qc)** to make up one's mind (to do sthg).

decimale *agg* decimal.

decimo, a *num* tenth → **sesto.**

decina *sf* ten ; *(circa dieci)* about ten ; **decine di** dozens of.

decisione *sf* decision ; **prendere una ~** to make a decision.

deciso, a *pp* → **decidere.** ◆ *agg* decisive ; **~ a fare qc** determined to do sthg.

decollare *vi* to take off.

decollo *sm* takeoff.

decorare *vt* to decorate.

decotto *sm* decoction.

decreto *sm* decree.

dedica, che *sf* dedication.

dedicare *vt* : **~ qc a qn** *(poesia, canzone)* to dedicate sthg to sb ; *fig* *(consacrare)* to devote sthg to sb. ❑ **dedicarsi a** *vr + prep* to devote o.s. to.

dedito, a *agg* : ~ **a qc** *(studio)* devoted to sthg ; *(droga, alcool)* addicted to sthg.

dedotto, a *pp* → **dedurre**.

dedurre *vt (concludere)* to deduce ; *(detrarre)* to deduct.

deduzione *sf* deduction.

deficiente *agg spreg* idiotic.

deficit *sm inv* deficit.

definire *vt* to define.

definitivo, a *agg* definitive.

definizione *sf* definition.

deformare *vt* to deform ; *fig (travisare)* to distort. ❑ **deformarsi** *vr* to become deformed.

defunto, a *sm, f* deceased.

degenerare *vi* to degenerate.

degli = **di + gli, di.**

degnarsi *vr* : ~ **di fare qc** to condescend to do sthg.

degno, a *agg* : ~ **di** worthy of.

degradare *vt (peggiorare)* to degrade ; MIL to demote.

degustazione *sf (assaggio)* tasting ; *(negozio) specialist shop where beverages, especially wine or coffee, are tasted.*

dei = **di + i, di.**

delegare *vt* : ~ **qn (a fare qc)** to delegate sb (to do sthg) ; ~ **qc a qn** to delegate sthg to sb.

delegazione *sf* delegation.

delfino *sm* dolphin.

delicatezza *sf (l'essere delicato)* delicacy ; *(gentilezza)* consideration ; *(atto gentile)* considerate act.

delicato, a *agg* delicate ; *(gentile)* considerate.

delineare *vt* to outline. ❑ **delinearsi** *vr (essere visibile)* to be outlined ; *fig (presentarsi)* to take shape.

delinquente *smf* delinquent.

delirio *sm* MED delirium ; *(esaltazione)* frenzy.

delitto *sm* crime.

delizioso, a *agg (cibo)* delicious ; *(gradevole)* delightful.

dell' = **di + l', di.**

della = **di + la, di.**

delle = **di + le, di.**

dello = **di + lo, di.**

delta *sm inv* delta.

deltaplano *sm* hang glider.

deludere *vt* to disappoint.

delusione *sf* disappointment.

deluso, a *pp* → **deludere.** ◆ *agg* disappointed.

democratico, a, ci, che *agg* democratic.

democrazia *sf* democracy.

demolire *vt* to demolish.

demonio *sm* devil.

demoralizzare *vt* to demoralize. ❑ **demoralizzarsi** *vr* to become demoralized.

denaro *sm* money ; ~ **contante** cash.

denigrare *vt* to denigrate.

denominare *vt* to name.

denominazione *sf* name, denomination ; ~ **d'origine controllata** *a mark guaranteeing that the product, especially wine, is of a good quality.*

densità *sf* density.

denso, a *agg* thick.
dente *sm* tooth ; ~ **da latte** milk tooth ; ~ **del giudizio** wisdom tooth ; **al** ~ al dente *(cooked enough to be still firm when bitten)* ; **mettere qc sotto i denti** to have a bite to eat ; **armato fino ai denti** armed to the teeth.
dentiera *sf (denti finti)* dentures *(pl)*.
dentifricio *sm* toothpaste.
dentista, i, e *smf* dentist.
dentro *avv* & *prep* inside ; **darci** ~ *fam* to put one's back into it ; ~ **di sé** inwardly, inside ; **qui/là** ~ in here/there ; **dal di** ~ from the inside ; **in** ~ inwards.
denuncia, ce o **cie** *sf* : **fare la** ~ to make a statement to the police ; ~ **dei redditi** income tax return.
denunciare *vt (sporgere denuncia contro)* to report ; *(rendere noto)* to declare.
deodorante *sm (per il corpo)* deodorant ; *(per ambiente)* air freshener.
deperibile *agg* perishable.
depilazione *sf* hair removal.
dépliant [depli'an] *sm inv* brochure.
deplorevole *agg* deplorable.
depositare *vt* to deposit ; *(persona)* to leave. ❑ **depositarsi** *vr* to settle.
deposito *sm* deposit ; *(per autobus)* depot ; *(per merci)* warehouse ; *(di liquido)* sediment ; ~ **bagagli** left luggage office.
depravato, a *sm, f* degenerate.
depressione *sf* depression.
depresso, a *pp* → **deprimere**. ◆ *agg* depressed.
deprimente *agg* depressing.
deprimere *vt* to depress. ❑ **deprimersi** *vr* to become depressed.
deputato, a *sm, f* ≃ Member of Parliament *(Br)*, ≃ Representative *(Am)*.
derattizzazione *sf* rodent control.
deriva *sf* : **andare alla** ~ to drift.
derivare : **derivare da** *v + prep* to derive from.
dermatologo, a, gi o **-ghi, ghe** *sm, f* dermatologist.
derubare *vt* to rob.
descritto, a *pp* → **descrivere**.
descrivere *vt* to describe.
descrizione *sf* description.
deserto, a *agg (disabitato)* deserted ; *(senza vegetazione)* barren. ◆ *sm* desert.
desiderare *vt* to want, to desire ; *(sessualmente)* to desire ; **desidera?** can I help you? ; ~ **fare qc** to wish to do sthg ; **lasciare a** ~ to leave much to be desired.
desiderio *sm* wish.
desideroso, a *agg* : ~ **di fare qc** eager to do sthg.
designare *vt* to designate.
desistere : **desistere da** *v + prep form* to give up.
desistito *pp* → **desistere**.
destinare *vt (assegnare, riservare)* to assign ; *(indirizzare)* to address.
destinatario, a *sm, f* addressee.
destinazione *sf* destination ;

arrivare a ~ to reach one's destination.
destino *sm* destiny, fate.
destra *sf (mano)* right hand ; *(lato)* right ; la ~ *POL* the right wing ; tenere la ~ to keep to the right ; a ~ *(stato in luogo)* on the right ; *(moto a luogo)* right ; di ~ *(dal lato destro)* right-hand.
destreggiarsi *vr (nel traffico)* to manoeuvre ; *fig (tra difficoltà)* to manage.
destro, a *agg (opposto a sinistra)* right.
detenuto, a *sm, f* prisoner.
detenzione *sf* detention.
detergente *agg* cleansing. ◆ *sm (cosmetico)* cleansing cream ; *(detersivo)* detergent.
deteriorare *vt* to impair. ❑ **deteriorarsi** *vr* to deteriorate.
determinante *agg* decisive.
determinare *vt (stabilire)* to determine.
determinazione *sf* determination.
detersivo *sm* detergent.
detestare *vt* to detest.
detrarre *vt* to deduct.
detratto, a *pp* → detrarre.
dettagliato, a *agg* detailed.
dettaglio *sm* detail ; al ~ *COMM* retail.
dettare *vt* to dictate ; ~ legge to lay down the law.
dettato *sm* dictation.
detto, a *pp* → dire. ◆ *agg (soprannominato)* known as. ◆ *sm* saying.
devastare *vt* to devastate.
deviare *vt* to divert. ◆ *vi (di direzione)* : ~ da qc to turn off sthg.
deviazione *sf (del traffico)* detour ; *(di fiume)* deviation.
devoto, a *agg* devoted.

di *prep* - 1. *(indica appartenenza)* of ; il libro ~ Marco Marco's book ; la porta della camera the bedroom door.
- 2. *(indica l'autore)* by ; un quadro ~ Giotto a painting by Giotto.
- 3. *(partitivo)* of ; alcuni ~ noi some of us.
- 4. *(nei paragoni)* : sono più alto ~ te I'm taller than you ; il migliore ~ tutti the best of all.
- 5. *(indica argomento)* about, of ; un libro ~ storia a history book ; parlare ~ to talk about.
- 6. *(temporale)* in ; d'estate in (the) summer ; ~ mattina in the morning ; ~ notte at/by night ; ~ sabato on Saturdays.
- 7. *(indica provenienza)* from ; ~ dove sei? where are you from? ; sono ~ Messina I'm from Messina.
- 8. *(indica una caratteristica)* : un bambino ~ due anni a two-year-old child, a child of two ; una statua ~ marmo a marble statue ; una torre ~ 40 metri a 40-metre tower ; un film ~ due ore a two-hour film.
- 9. *(indica la causa)* : urlare ~ dolore to scream with pain ; sto morendo ~ fame! I'm starving! ; soffrire ~ mal di testa to suffer from headaches ; morire ~ vecchiaia to die of old age.
- 10. *(indica contenuto)* of ; una bottiglia ~ vino a bottle of wine.
- 11. *(seguito da infinito)* : mi ha

detto ~ non aspettare he told me not to wait ; **pensavo ~ uscire** I was thinking of going out ; **capita ~ sbagliare** anyone can make a mistake ; **mi sembra ~ conoscerlo** I think I know him.
- 12. *(in espressioni)* : **a causa ~** because of ; **~ modo che** so as to ; **dare del bugiardo a qn** to call sb a liar.
◆ *art* some ; *(in negative)* any ; **vorrei del pane** I'd like some bread ; **ha degli spiccioli?** have you got any change?

---

diabete *sm* diabetes.
diabetico, a, ci, che *agg* diabetic.
diaframma, i *sm* diaphragm.
diagnosi *sf inv* diagnosis.
diagonale *agg* & *sf* diagonal.
diagramma, i *sm* diagram.
dialetto *sm* dialect.
dialisi *sf* MED dialysis.
dialogo, ghi *sm* dialogue.
diamante *sm* diamond.
diametro *sm* diameter.
diamine *esclam (certo)* absolutely! ; **che ~ stai facendo?** what on earth are you doing?
diapositiva *sf* slide.
diario *sm* diary ; *(a scuola)* homework book ; *(calendario)* timetable.
diarrea *sf* diarrhoea.
diavolo *sm* devil ; **che ~ vuole?** *fam* what the hell does he want? ; **va al ~!** *fam* go to hell!
dibattito *sm* debate.
dica → **dire**.
dicembre *sm* December → **settembre**.
diceria *sf* piece of gossip, rumour.
dichiarare *vt* to declare.
dichiarazione *sf* declaration.
diciannove *num* nineteen → **sei**.
diciannovesimo, a *num* nineteenth → **sesto**.
diciassette *num* seventeen → **sei**.
diciassettesimo, a *num* seventeenth → **sesto**.
diciottesimo, a *num* eighteenth → **sesto**.
diciotto *num* eighteen → **sei**.
dieci *num* ten → **sei**.
diecina = **decina**.
diesel ['dizel] *agg inv* & *sm inv* diesel.
dieta *sf* diet ; **essere a ~** to be on a diet.
dietetico, a, ci, che *agg* diet *(dav s)*.
dietro *avv (nella parte posteriore)* at/in the back ; *(indietro)* behind.
◆ *sm* back. ◆ *prep* : **~ (a)** *(dopo)* after ; *(di là da)* behind ; **~ di me** behind me ; **di ~** back *(dav s)* ; **qui/lì ~** behind here/there ; **~ pagamento** on payment.
difatti *cong* in fact.
difendere *vt* to defend. ❑ **difendersi** *vr* to defend o.s.
difensore *sm* defender.
difesa *sf* defence.
difeso, a *pp* → **difendere**.
difetto *sm* defect ; *(morale)* fault ; **~ di fabbricazione** manufacturing defect.
difettoso, a *agg (meccanismo)* faulty ; *(vista, abito)* defective.

diffamare *vt (a parole)* to slander ; *(per iscritto)* to libel.
differente *agg* different.
differenza *sf* difference ; **non fa ~** it doesn't make any difference ; **a ~ di** unlike.
difficile *agg* difficult ; **è ~ che esca** *(poco probabile)* it's unlikely that he'll go out.
difficoltà *sf inv* difficulty.
diffidare : diffidare di *v + prep* to mistrust.
diffidente *agg* mistrustful.
diffondere *vt* to spread. ❑ **diffondersi** *vr* to spread.
diffusione *sf* diffusion.
diffuso, a *pp* → **diffondere**. ◆ *agg* widespread.
diga, ghe *sf* dam.
digeribile *agg* digestible.
digerire *vt* to digest.
digestione *sf* digestion.
digestivo, a *agg* digestive. ◆ *sm liqueur drunk to aid digestion, after meals.*
digitale *agg* digital.
digitare *vt INFORM* to key in.
digiunare *vi* to fast.
digiuno, a *sm* fasting. ◆ *agg* : **essere ~** not to have eaten ; **a ~** on an empty stomach.
dignità *sf* dignity.
dignitoso, a *agg (atteggiamento)* dignified ; *(abito)* respectable.
dilagante *agg (fenomeno)* rampant.
dilagare *vi* to be rampant.
dilaniare *vt* to tear to pieces.
dilapidare *vt* to squander.
dilatare *vt (pupille)* to dilate ; *(gas, metallo, corpo)* to expand. ❑ **dilatarsi** *vr (pupille)* to dilate ; *(gas, metallo, corpo)* to expand.
dilazionare *vt* to defer.
dilemma, i *sm* dilemma.
dilettante *smf* amateur.
diligente *agg* diligent.
diluire *vt (allungare)* to dilute ; *(sciogliere)* to dissolve.
dilungarsi *vr* : **~ su** *(argomento)* to dwell upon ; **~ in spiegazioni** to give a longwinded explanation.
diluvio *sm* downpour.
dimagrire *vi* to lose weight.
dimenare *vt (fianchi)* to swing ; *(corpo)* to shake ; *(coda)* to wag. ❑ **dimenarsi** *vr* to fling o.s. about.
dimensione *sf* dimension.
dimenticanza *sf* oversight.
dimenticare *vt* to forget ; *(lasciare)* to leave ; **dimenticarsi qc** to leave sthg. ❑ **dimenticarsi di** *vr + prep* to forget about ; **dimenticarsi di fare qc** to forget to do sthg.
dimesso, a *pp* → **dimettere**. ◆ *agg* humble.
dimestichezza *sf* familiarity.
dimettere *vt* to discharge. ❑ **dimettersi** *vr* to resign.
dimezzare *vt* to halve.
diminuire *vt* to reduce. ◆ *vi* to decrease ; *(prezzi)* to drop.
diminuzione *sf* fall ; *(di prezzi)* drop.
dimissioni *sfpl* resignation *(sg)* ; **dare le ~** to hand in one's resignation.
dimostrare *vt (manifestare)* to show ; *(provare)* to prove ; **dimostra meno di vent'anni** he doesn't

look twenty. ❑ **dimostrarsi** *vr* to prove to be.
dimostrazione *sf (d'affetto, simpatia)* show ; *(di teoria)* proof ; *(protesta, per prodotto)* demonstration.
dinamico, a, ci, che *agg* dynamic.
dinamite *sf* dynamite.
dinamo *sf inv* dynamo.
dinanzi *prep* : ~ **a** *(davanti a)* in front of ; *(alla presenza di)* before.
dinosauro *sm* dinosaur.
dintorni *smpl* outskirts ; **nei ~ di** in the vicinity of.
dio (*pl* **dei**) *sm* god. ❑ **Dio** *sm* God ; **mio Dio!** my God!.
diocesi *sf inv* diocese.
dipartimento *sm* department.
dipendente *agg* subordinate. ◆ *smf* employee.
dipendenza *sf (subordinazione)* dependence ; *(assuefazione)* addiction ; **essere alle dipendenze di qn** to be employed by sb.
dipendere *vi* : ~ **da** to depend on ; *(derivare)* to be due to ; **dipende** it depends.
dipeso, a *pp* → **dipendere.**
dipingere *vt* to paint.
dipinto, a *pp* → **dipingere.** ◆ *sm* painting.
diploma, i *sm* diploma.
diplomarsi *vr* to obtain a diploma.
diplomatico, a, ci, che *agg* diplomatic. ◆ *sm (funzionario)* diplomat ; *(pasta) pastry made of layers of liqueur-soaked sponge, puff pastry and confectioner's custard, topped with icing sugar.*
diplomazia *sf* diplomacy.
diradare *vt* to cut down on. ❑ **diradarsi** *vr (nebbia, nubi)* to clear ; *(vegetazione)* to thin out.

☞

dire *vt* - 1. *(pronunciare)* to say ; ~ **di sì/no** to say yes/no.
- 2. *(esprimere, raccontare)* to say ; ~ **qc a qn** to tell sb sthg ; ~ **a qn che/perché** to tell sb that/why ; ~ **la verità** to tell the truth ; **dimmi tutto** tell me everything ; **dica pure** *(in un negozio)* can I help you?
- 3. *(ordinare)* : ~ **a qn di fare qc** to tell sb to do sthg.
- 4. *(sostenere)* to say ; **dice che non è vero** he says it isn't true.
- 5. *(tradurre)* : **come si dice 'scusi' in inglese?** what's the English for 'scusi'?
- 6. *(pensare)* to think ; **che ne dite di ...?** how about ...? ; **e ~ che ...!** to think that ...!
- 7. *(in espressioni)* : **diciamo che ...** let's say that ... ; **a ~ il vero ...** to tell the truth ... ; **vuol ~ che ...** it means (that) ... ; **non c'è che ~** there's no doubt about it ; **il nome non mi dice niente** the name doesn't mean much to me ; **dico davvero** o **sul serio!** I'm serious! ; **a dir poco** at least ; **a dir tanto** at most ; **volevo ben ~!** I thought so!
◆ *v impers* : **si dice che ...** they say (that) ... ; **si direbbe che ...** it seems (that) ...

---

direttamente *avv (per via diretta)* straight ; *(senza intermediari)* directly.
direttissimo *sm* express train.
diretto, a *pp* → **dirigere.** ◆ *agg*

direct. ◆ *sm (treno)* through train ; **essere ~ a** *(aereo, passeggero)* to be bound for ; *(indirizzato)* to be intended for.

direttore, trice *sm, f* manager (*f* manageress) ; *(di scuola elementare)* head (teacher) *(Br)*, principal *(Am)* ; **~ d'orchestra** conductor.

direzione *sf* direction ; *(di azienda)* management.

dirigente *smf* executive.

dirigere *vt (attenzione, sguardo)* to direct ; *(scuola, azienda)* to run ; *(orchestra)* to conduct. ❑ **dirigersi** *vr* to head.

dirimpetto *avv* opposite.

diritto, a *agg & avv* straight. ◆ *sm* right ; *(leggi)* law ; *(di abito, stoffa)* right side ; *(nel tennis)* forehand ; *(nella maglia)* plain stitch ; **andare ~** *(in linea retta)* to go straight on ; **vai ~ a casa** go straight home ; **sempre ~** straight on ; **avere ~ a qc** to be entitled to sthg.

dirittura *sf* : **~ d'arrivo** home straight.

diroccato, a *agg* in ruins.

dirottare *vt* to hijack ; *(traffico)* to divert.

dirotto, a *agg* : **piovere a ~** to pour.

dirupo *sm* precipice.

disabitato, a *agg* uninhabited.

disaccordo *sm* disagreement.

disadattato, a *agg* maladjusted.

disagio *sm (scomodità)* discomfort ; *(imbarazzo)* uneasiness ; **essere a ~** to be ill at ease.

disapprovare *vt* to disapprove.

disarmare *vt* to disarm.

disarmo *sm* disarmament.

disastro *sm* disaster ; *(danno)* damage.

disastroso, a *agg* disastrous.

disattento, a *agg* inattentive.

disavanzo *sm* deficit.

disavventura *sf* mishap.

discapito *sm* : **a ~ di** to the detriment of.

discarica, che *sf* dump.

discendente *smf* descendant.

discepolo, a *sm, f* disciple.

discesa *sf* slope ; *(movimento)* descent ; **in ~** downhill ; **~ libera** downhill race ; **' ~ a mare'** 'this way down to the sea'.

dischetto *sm* diskette.

disciplina *sf (ubbidienza)* discipline ; *(materia)* subject.

disciplinato, a *agg* disciplined.

disc-jockey [disk'dʒɔkei] *smf inv* disc jockey.

disco, schi *sm (musicale)* record ; *(per computer)* disk ; **~ orario** parking disc ; **~ volante** flying saucer.

discolpare *vt* to clear.

discorde *agg* conflicting.

discorrere : **discorrere di** *v + prep* to talk about.

discorso *pp* → **discorrere.** ◆ *sm* speech ; *(conversazione)* conversation, talk.

discoteca, che *sf* disco.

discretamente *avv (abbastanza bene)* fairly well ; *(con tatto)* discreetly.

discreto, a *agg (persona)* discreet ; *(abbastanza buono)* reasonably good.

discrezione *sf (tatto)* discretion ; *(moderazione)* moderation.
discriminare *vt* to discriminate.
discussione *sf (dibattito)* discussion ; *(litigio)* argument.
discusso, a *pp* → **discutere**.
discutere *vt (parlare di)* to discuss ; *(contestare)* to question. ◆ *vi* to argue ; ~ **di** o **su** *(dibattere)* to discuss.
disdetto, a *pp* → **disdire**.
disdire *vt* to cancel.
disegnare *vt* to draw ; *(progettare)* to design. ◆ *vi* to draw.
disegno *sm* drawing ; *(motivo)* design ; *(progetto)* project ; ~ **di legge** bill.
diseredare *vt* to disinherit.
disertare *vt* & *vi* to desert.
disertore *sm* deserter.
disfare *vt* to undo ; *(valigia)* to unpack ; *(maglia)* to unravel ; *(sciogliere)* to melt.
disfatto, a *pp* → **disfare**.
disgelo *sm* thaw.
disgrazia *sf (incidente)* accident.
disgraziato, a *agg (persona)* wretched ; *(viaggio)* ill-fated ; *(anno)* unlucky. ◆ *sm, f (sfortunato)* poor wretch ; *(canaglia)* rogue.
disguido *sm* error.
disgustare *vt* to disgust.
disgusto *sm* disgust.
disgustoso, a *agg* disgusting.
disidratare *vt* to dehydrate.
disinfestare *vt* to disinfest.
disinfettante *agg* & *sm* disinfectant.
disinfettare *vt* to disinfect.
disinibito, a *agg* uninhibited.
disintegrare *vt* to cause to disintegrate.
disinteressarsi : disinteressarsi di *vr + prep* to take no interest in.
disinteresse *sm (indifferenza)* indifference ; *(generosità)* unselfishness.
disintossicare *vt* to detoxify ; ~ **l'organismo** to clear out one's system. ❑ **disintossicarsi** *vr (da droga)* to be treated for drug addiction.
disintossicazione *sf (da droga)* treatment for drug addiction.
disinvolto, a *agg* free and easy.
disinvoltura *sf* ease.
dislivello *sm (di quota)* difference in height ; *fig (differenza)* gap.
disoccupato, a *agg* unemployed. ◆ *sm, f* unemployed person.
disoccupazione *sf* unemployment.
disonesto, a *agg* dishonest.
disopra *avv* above ; *(al piano superiore)* upstairs. ◆ *agg inv* above.
disordinato, a *agg* untidy ; *(vita)* disorderly.
disordine *sm (materiale)* untidiness ; *(mentale)* confusion ; **in** ~ in a mess.
disorganizzazione *sf* disorganization.
disorientato, a *agg* disorientated.
disossare *vt* to bone.
disotto *avv* below ; *(al piano inferiore)* downstairs. ◆ *agg inv* below.

dispari *agg inv* odd.

disparte *avv* : **tenersi** ○ **starsene in ~** to keep to o.s.

dispendioso, a *agg* expensive.

dispensa *sf (stanza)* larder ; *(mobile)* sideboard ; *(fascicolo)* instalment.

disperarsi *vr* to despair.

disperatamente *avv* desperately.

disperato, a *agg* desperate.

disperazione *sf* desperation.

disperdere *vt* to disperse.

disperso, a *pp* → **disperdere.** ◆ *sm, f* missing person.

dispetto *sm (atto)* spiteful trick ; *(stizza)* vexation ; **fare un ~ a qn** to play a spiteful trick on sb ; **fare qc per ~** to do sthg out of spite ; **a ~ di** despite.

dispiacere *sm (dolore)* grief ; *(rammarico)* regret. ◆ *v impers* : **le dispiace se aspetto qui?** do you mind if I wait here? ; **mi dispiace che sia andata così** I'm sorry it worked out that way ; **mi dispiace di non potermi trattenere** I'm afraid I can't stop.

dispiaciuto, a *pp* → **dispiacere.** ◆ *agg* sorry.

disponibile *agg* available ; *(persona)* willing to help.

disponibilità *sf (di posto, camere)* availability ; *(di persona)* willingness to help ; *(di denaro)* liquid assets *(pl)*.

disporre *vt* to arrange. ❑ **disporre di** *v + prep (poter usare)* to have at one's disposal ; *(avere)* to have.

dispositivo *sm* device.

disposizione *sf (di mobili, oggetti)* arrangement ; *(comando)* order ; *(attitudine)* disposition ; DIR provision ; **essere a ~ di qn** to be at sb's disposal ; **mettere qc a ~ di qn** to make sthg available to sb.

disposto, a *pp* → **disporre.** ◆ *agg* : **~ a fare qc** prepared to do sthg.

disprezzare *vt* to despise.

disprezzo *sm* contempt.

disputa *sf* argument.

dissanguare *vt fig (persona)* to bleed white.

disseminare *vt* to spread.

dissenso *sm (disapprovazione)* dissent ; *(contrasto)* disagreement.

dissenteria *sf* dysentery.

disservizio *sm* inefficiency.

dissestato, a *agg* uneven.

dissidente *smf* dissident.

dissidio *sm* disagreement.

dissimulare *vt* to conceal.

dissoluto, a *pp* → **dissolvere.** ◆ *agg* dissolute.

dissolvere *vt (sciogliere)* to dissolve ; *(nebbia, fumo)* to disperse.

dissuadere *vt* : **~ qn dal fare qc** to dissuade sb from doing sthg.

dissuaso, a *pp* → **dissuadere.**

distaccare *vt (oggetti)* to remove ; *(dipendente)* to transfer ; SPORT to outdistance. ❑ **distaccarsi da** *vr + prep fig (allontanarsi)* to withdraw from.

distacco, chi *sm* separation ; *(indifferenza)* detachment.

distante *agg & avv* far away ; **~ da** far from.

distanza *sf* distance ; *(temporale)* : **a ~ di due mesi** after two months ; **tenere le distanze** to keep one's distance.

distanziare *vt (separare)* to space out ; SPORT to outdistance.

distare *vi* : **quanto dista da qui?** how far is it from here?

distendere *vt (gamba, mano)* to stretch out ; *(telo, coperta)* to spread ; *(rilassare)* to relax. ❑ **distendersi** *vr (sdraiarsi)* to lie down ; *(rilassarsi)* to relax.

distesa *sf* expanse.

disteso, a *pp* → **distendere**.

distillare *vt* to distil.

distillato, a *agg* distilled. ◆ *sm (liquore)* distillate.

distilleria *sf* distillery.

distinguere *vt* to distinguish.

distinta *sf (in banca,* COMM & FIN*)* slip, note.

distintivo, a *agg* distinctive. ◆ *sm* badge.

distinto, a *pp* → **distinguere**. ◆ *agg (diverso)* different ; *(immagine)* distinct ; *(persona)* distinguished ; **distinti saluti** *(in lettera)* Yours faithfully.

distinzione *sf* distinction.

distogliere *vt* : **~ qc da qn** to take sthg away from sb ; **~ qn da qc** to deter sb from sthg.

distolto, a *pp* → **distogliere**.

distorsione *sf* MED sprain ; *(di suono, immagine)* distortion.

distrarre *vt* to distract ; *(divertire)* to amuse. ❑ **distrarsi** *vr* to be distracted ; *(divertirsi)* to amuse o.s..

distratto, a *pp* → **distrarre**. ◆ *agg (sbadato)* absent-minded ; *(disattento)* inattentive.

distrazione *sf* distraction ; *(svago)* amusement.

distretto *sm* district.

distribuire *vt (assegnare compiti)* to allocate ; *(posta, giornali)* to distribute.

distributore *sm* : **~ automatico** vending machine ; **~ (di benzina)** petrol pump *(Br)*, gasoline pump *(Am)*.

distribuzione *sf* distribution ; *(ripartizione)* allocation.

distruggere *vt* to destroy.

distrutto, a *pp* → **distruggere**. ◆ *agg* shattered.

distruzione *sf* destruction.

disturbare *vt* to disturb ; **'non ~ il conducente'** 'do not distract the driver'. ❑ **disturbarsi** *vr* to bother.

disturbo *sm (fastidio)* bother ; *(malessere)* disorder ; *(di comunicazione)* interference.

disubbidiente *agg* disobedient.

disubbidire *vi* : **~ (a qn)** to disobey (sb).

disumano, a *agg* inhuman.

disuso *sm* : **in ~** obsolete.

ditale *sm* thimble.

dito *(pl f* **dita**) *sm* finger ; *(misura)* drop ; **~ (del piede)** toe.

ditta *sf* company, firm.

dittatura *sf* dictatorship.

dittongo, ghi *sm* diphthong.

diurno, a *agg* daytime *(dav s)*.

diva → **divo**.

divampare *vi* to flare up.

divano *sm* sofa ; ~ **letto** sofa-bed.
divaricare *vt* to open wide.
divenire *vi* to become.
diventare *vi* to become ; ~ **rosso** *(persona)* to go red.
diversificare *vt* to diversify.
diversità *sf inv* diversity ; *(l'esser diverso)* difference.
diversivo *sm* diversion.
diverso, a *agg* different ; ~ **da** different from ; **diversi, diverse** various, several. ❑ **diversi** *pron pl* several ; *(varie persone)* several (people).
divertente *agg* amusing.
divertimento *sm* amusement.
divertire *vt* to amuse. ❑ **divertirsi** *vr* to enjoy o.s.
dividere *vt* to divide ; *(spartire)* to share out ; *(separare)* to separate ; *(condividere)* to share. ❑ **dividersi** *vr (ripartirsi)* to split up ; *(coppia)* to separate.
divieto *sm* prohibition ; '~ **di sosta**' 'no waiting' ; '~ **di transito**' 'no thoroughfare'.
divinità *sf inv* divinity.
divino, a *agg* divine.
divisa *sf* uniform.
divisione *sf* division.
diviso, a *pp* → **dividere**.
divisorio, a *agg* dividing.
divo, a *sm, f* star.
divorare *vt* to devour.
divorziare *vi* to divorce.
divorziato, a *agg* divorced. ◆ *sm, f* divorced person.
divorzio *sm* divorce.
divulgare *vt (notizia)* to divulge ; *(scienza, dottrina)* to popularize. ❑ **divulgarsi** *vr* to spread.
dizionario *sm* dictionary.
D.J. [diːˈdʒeɪ] *smf (abbr di disc-jockey)* DJ.
D.N.A *sm* DNA.
do *sm inv (nota musicale)* C.
DOC *(abbr di Denominazione di Origine Controllata)* label guaranteeing the quality of an Italian wine.
doccia, ce *sf* shower ; **fare la** ~ to take o to have a shower.
docente *agg* teaching. ◆ *smf* teacher ; *(di università)* lecturer.
docile *agg (animale)* docile.
documentare *vt* to document. ❑ **documentarsi** *vr* to gather information.
documentario *sm* documentary.
documento *sm* document. ❑ **documenti** *smpl* documents.
dodicesimo, a *num* twelfth → **sesto**.
dodici *num* twelve → **sei**.
dogana *sf* customs *(pl)* ; **passare la** ~ to go through customs.
doganale *agg* customs *(dav s)*.
doganiere *sm* customs officer.
dolce *agg* sweet ; *(persona, carattere)* gentle ; *(suono, musica, voce)* soft. ◆ *sm (torta)* cake ; *(portata)* dessert.
dolcezza *sf* sweetness.
dolcificante *sm* sweetener.
dolciumi *smpl* confectionery *(sg)*.
dolere *vi* to hurt. ❑ **dolersi di** *vr + prep (essere spiacente di)* to regret ; *(lamentarsi di)* to complain of.
dollaro *sm* dollar.

dolo *sm DIR* malice.

Dolomiti *sfpl*: **le ~** the Dolomites.

dolore *sm (fisico)* pain ; *(morale)* sorrow.

doloroso, a *agg (intervento)* painful ; *(situazione)* distressing.

domanda *sf (per sapere)* question ; *(per ottenere)* request ; *COMM* demand ; **fare una ~ a qn** to ask sb a question ; **fare ~** to apply.

domandare *vt (per sapere)* to ask ; *(per ottenere)* to ask for ; **~ qc a qn** to ask sb sthg. ❑ **domandarsi** *vr* to wonder.

domani *avv* tomorrow. ◆ *sm (giorno seguente)* tomorrow ; **a ~!** see you tomorrow! ; **~ l'altro** the day after tomorrow ; **il ~** the future ; **~ mattina** tomorrow morning ; **~ sera** tomorrow evening.

domare *vt (animale)* to tame ; *(rivolta)* to put down ; *(incendio)* to control.

domattina *avv* tomorrow morning.

domenica, che *sf* Sunday → **sabato.**

domestico, a, ci, che *agg & sm, f* domestic.

domicilio *sm* domicile ; **a ~** home *(dav s)*.

dominante *agg* dominant.

dominare *vt* to dominate ; *(paese, popolo)* to rule ; *(situazione, impulso)* to control. ❑ **dominarsi** *vr* to control o.s.

dominio *sm (potere)* power ; *(controllo)* control ; *(territorio)* dominion ; **essere di ~ pubblico** to be common knowledge.

domino *sm* dominoes *(pl)*.

donare *vt* to give. ◆ *vi* : **questo colore ti dona** this colour suits you ; **~ il sangue** to give blood.

donatore, trice *sm, f* giver ; *(di sangue, organi)* donor.

dondolare *vt* to rock. ◆ *vi* to sway. ❑ **dondolarsi** *vr* to sway.

dondolo *sm* swing hammock ; **cavallo/sedia a ~** rocking horse/chair.

donna *sf* woman ; *(nelle carte)* queen ; **~ di servizio** maid.

dono *sm* gift.

doping *sm* doping.

dopo *avv* afterwards ; *(più tardi)* later ; *(nello spazio)* after. ◆ *prep (di tempo)* after ; *(di luogo)* past, after. ◆ *agg inv* after. ◆ *cong* : **~ aver fatto qc** after doing sthg ; **il giorno ~** the following day ; **un giorno ~** a day later ; **a ~!** see you later! ; **~ di me** after me.

dopobarba *sm inv* aftershave.

dopodiché *avv* after which.

dopodomani *avv* the day after tomorrow.

dopoguerra *sm* post-war period.

dopolavoro *sm workers' recreational club.*

dopopranzo *avv* in the early afternoon.

doposci *sm inv* après-ski.

doposcuola *sm inv supervised after-school activities.*

dopotutto *avv* after all.

doppiaggio *sm* dubbing.

doppiare *vt (film)* to dub ; *SPORT* to lap ; *NAUT* to round.

doppiato, a *agg* dubbed.

doppio, a *agg* & *avv* double. ◆ *sm SPORT* doubles ; **ne ha il ~ di me** *(quantità)* he has twice as much as me ; *(numero)* he has twice as many as me.

doppione *sm* duplicate.

doppiopetto *sm* double-breasted jacket.

dorato, a *agg (di colore)* golden ; *(ricoperto d'oro)* gilt.

dormiglione, a *sm, f* sleepyhead.

dormire *vi* to sleep.

dormitorio *sm* dormitory.

dorso *sm* back ; *(di libro)* spine.

dosaggio *sm* dosage.

dosare *vt* to measure out ; *MED* to dose.

dose *sf* amount ; *MED* dose.

dosso *sm* bump ; **togliersi** o **levarsi qc di ~** to take sthg off.

dotare *vt* : **~ qc di qc** to equip sthg with sthg.

dotato, a *agg* gifted.

dote *sf (qualità)* gift ; *(di sposa)* dowry.

Dott. *(abbr di dottore)* Dr.

dottorato *sm* doctorate.

dottore, essa *sm, f (medico)* doctor ; *(laureato)* graduate.

dottrina *sf* doctrine.

Dott.ssa *(abbr di dottoressa)* Dr.

dove *avv* where ; **da ~ vieni?** where do you come from? ; **di ~ sei?** where are you from? ; **dov'è?** where is it? ; **~ vai?** where are you going? ; **siediti ~ vuoi** sit wherever you like.

☞

dovere *vt* - 1. *(essere debitore di)* : **~ qc a qn** to owe sb sthg ; **gli devo dei soldi/un favore** I owe him some money/a favour ; **quanto le devo?** *(in negozio)* how much does it come to?
- 2. *(aver l'obbligo di)* : **~ fare qc** to have to do sthg ; **comportarsi come si deve** to behave o.s. properly ; **ora devo andare** I have to o must go now.
- 3. *(aver bisogno di)* : **~ fare qc** to have to do sthg ; **devo dormire almeno otto ore** I need at least eight hours' sleep ; **devi sapere che ...** you should know that ...
- 4. *(esprime un rimprovero)* : **avreste dovuto pensarci prima** you should have thought of it earlier ; **avrei dovuto saperlo** I should have known.
- 5. *(per suggerire)* : **dovrebbe prendersi delle vacanze** he should o ought to take a holiday.
- 6. *(esprime probabilità)* : **devono essere già le sette** it must be seven o'clock already ; **il tempo dovrebbe rimettersi** the weather should improve.
- 7. *(esprime intenzione)* : **dovevamo partire ieri, ma ...** we were due to leave yesterday, but ...
◆ *sm* duty ; **avere dei doveri verso qn** to have a duty to sb.

dovunque *avv (in qualunque luogo)* wherever ; *(dappertutto)* everywhere.

dovuto, a *agg* : **~ a** due to.

dozzina *sf* dozen ; **una ~ di rose** a dozen roses.

drago, ghi *sm* dragon.

dramma, i *sm* drama.

drammatico, a, ci, che *agg* dramatic.

drastico, a, ci, che *agg* drastic.
drenaggio *sm (di terreno)* drainage ; *MED* drain.
drenare *vt* to drain.
dritto, a *agg* & *avv* = **diritto.**
drizzare *vt (raddrizzare)* to straighten ; ~ **le orecchie** to prick up one's ears. ❑ **drizzarsi** *vr* : **drizzarsi (in piedi)** to stand up.
droga, ghe *sf* drug.
drogare *vt* to drug. ❑ **drogarsi** *vr* to take drugs.
drogato, a *sm, f* drug addict.
drogheria *sf* grocer's.
droghiere *sm* grocer.
dromedario *sm* dromedary.
dubbio, a *agg (incerto)* doubtful ; *(equivoco)* questionable. ◆ *sm* doubt ; **ho il ~ che menta** I suspect that he's lying ; **essere in ~** to be in doubt ; **mettere in ~ qc** to question sthg ; **senza ~** without a doubt.
dubbioso, a *agg* uncertain.
dubitare : **dubitare di** *v + prep* to doubt ; *(mettere in discussione)* to question ; **dubito che venga** I doubt whether he'll come.
duca, chi *sm* duke.
duchessa *sf* duchess.
due *num* two → **sei.**
duecento *num* two hundred → **sei.** ❑ **Duecento** *sm* : **il Duecento** the thirteenth century.
duemila *num* two thousand. ❑ **il Duemila** *sm* the year two thousand → **sei.**
duepezzi *sm inv (bikini)* bikini ; *(abito)* two-piece suit.
duna *sf* dune.
dunque *cong (perciò)* so ; *(allora)* well. ◆ *sm* : **venire al ~** to get to the point.
duo *sm inv MUS* duet, duo ; *(comici, attori)* duo.
duomo *sm* cathedral.
duplex *sm inv* party line.
duplicato *sm* duplicate.
duplice *agg* double ; **in ~ copia** in duplicate.
durante *prep* during.
durare *vi* to last. ◆ *vt* : ~ **fatica (a fare qc)** to tire o.s. out (doing sthg).
durata *sf (periodo)* duration.
durezza *sf (di materiale)* hardness ; *(insensibilità)* severity.
duro, a *agg* hard ; *(carne)* tough ; *(ostinato)* stubborn ; *(severo)* harsh. ◆ *sm, f* tough person ; **tieni ~!** don't give in!
durone *sm* callus.

E

e *cong* and ; ~ **io?** what about me? ; ~ **vacci!** well then, go!
E *(abbr di est)* E.
è → **essere.**
ebano *sm* ebony.
ebbene *cong (allora)* well.
ebbrezza *sf (ubriachezza)* : **in stato di ~** drunk.
ebete *agg* idiotic.
ebollizione *sf* boiling.
ebraico, a, ci, che *agg* & *sm* Hebrew.
ebreo, a *agg* Jewish. ◆ *sm, f* Jew.

Ebridi *sfpl* : le (isole) ~ the Hebrides.
ecc. *(abbr di eccetera)* etc.
eccedenza *sf* excess.
eccedere *vt* to exceed. ❑ **eccedere in** *v + prep* : ~ nel bere/mangiare to drink/eat too much.
eccellente *agg* excellent.
eccellenza *sf* excellence ; *(titolo)* Excellency.
eccellere *vi* : ~ (in qc) to excel (at sthg).
eccelso *pp* → eccellere.
eccentrico, a, ci, che *agg* eccentric.
eccessivo, a *agg* excessive.
eccesso *sm* excess ; ~ di velocità speeding ; all' ~ excessively ; bagaglio in ~ excess baggage.
eccetera *avv* etcetera.
eccetto *prep* except. ◆ *cong* : ~ che unless.
eccettuare *vt* to except.
eccezionale *agg* exceptional.
eccezione *sf* exception ; a ~ di with the exception of ; d' ~ exceptional ; senza ~ without exception.
eccidio *sm* massacre.
eccitante *agg (stimolante)* stimulating ; *(provocante)* exciting.
eccitare *vt (curiosità)* to arouse. ❑ **eccitarsi** *vr* to get excited ; *(sessualmente)* to become aroused.
eccitazione *sf* excitement.
ecclesiastico, a, ci, che *agg* ecclesiastical. ◆ *sm* ecclesiastic.
ecco *avv* here is ; ~ a lei here you are ; ~ fatto! there, that's that! ; eccolo! there he is! ; eccone uno! there's one!
eccome *avv* you bet!
ECG *abbr di* ElettroCardioGramma.
eclissi *sf inv* eclipse.
eco *(pl m* echi) *sf* echo.
ecologia *sf* ecology.
ecologico, a, ci, che *agg* ecological.
economia *sf* economy ; *(scienza)* economics *(sg)* ; fare ~ to economize.
economico, a, ci, che *agg (dell'economia)* economic ; *(poco costoso)* economical.
economista, i, e *smf* economist.
ecosistema, i *sm* ecosystem.
eczema *sm* eczema.
ed → e.
edera *sf* ivy.
edicola *sf* newsstand.
edificare *vt* to build.
edificio *sm* building.
edile *agg* building *(dav s)*.
Edimburgo *sf* Edinburgh.
editore, trice *agg* publishing *(dav s)*. ◆ *sm* publisher.
editoria *sf* publishing (industry).
editoriale *agg* editorial. ◆ *sm* editorial.
edizione *sf* edition ; ~ speciale special edition.
educare *vt (formare)* to educate ; *(bambino)* to bring up.
educato, a *agg* polite.
educazione *sf (maniere)* (good) manners *(pl)* ; *(formazione)* training ; ~ fisica physical education.
effeminato *agg* effeminate.

effervescente *agg* effervescent.
effettivamente *avv* in fact.
effettivo, a *agg* actual, real.
effetto *sm* effect ; **in effetti** in fact, actually.
effettuare *vt* to carry out.
efficace *agg* effective.
efficacia *sf* effectiveness.
efficiente *agg* efficient.
efficienza *sf* efficiency.
effimero, a *agg (gioia, successo)* short-lived.
egemonia *sf (supremazia)* hegemony.
Egitto *sm* : **l' ~** Egypt.
egiziano, a *agg* Egyptian. ◆ *sm, f (abitante)* Egyptian.
egli *pron* he ; **~ stesso** he himself.
egocentrico, a, ci, che *agg* egocentric.
egoismo *sm* selfishness.
egoista, i, e *agg* selfish.
egr. (*abbr di egregio*) ≃ Dear *(in formal letters)*.
egregio, a, gi, gie *agg (nelle lettere)* : **Egregio Signore** Dear Sir.
eguagliare = **uguagliare**.
ehi *esclam* hey!
E.I. *abbr* = **Esercito Italiano**.
elaborare *vt (progetto, piano)* to work out ; *(con computer)* to process.
elaborato, a *agg* elaborate.
elaborazione *sf* : **~ dei dati** data processing.
elasticità *sf* elasticity ; *(di mente)* flexibility.
elasticizzato, a *agg* stretch *(dav s)*.
elastico, a, ci, che *agg* elastic ; *(mente)* flexible. ◆ *sm (gommino)* rubber band ; *(da cucito)* elastic.
Elba *sf* : **l'(isola d') ~** Elba.
elefante *sm* elephant.
elegante *agg* elegant.
eleganza *sf* elegance.
eleggere *vt* to elect.
elementare *agg* elementary.
❑ **elementari** *sfpl* : **le (scuole) elementari** primary school *(sg) (Br)*, grade school *(sg) (Am)*.
elemento *sm (fattore)* element ; *(di cucina)* unit ; *(persona)* individual.
elemosina *sf* alms *(pl)* ; **chiedere l' ~** to beg.
elencare *vt* to list.
elenco, chi *sm* list ; **~ telefonico** telephone directory.
eletto, a *pp* → **eleggere**.
elettorale *agg* electoral.
elettore, trice *sm, f* voter.
elettrauto *sm inv (officina) workshop for electrical repairs on cars* ; *(persona)* car electrician.
elettricista, i *sm* electrician.
elettricità *sf* electricity.
elettrico, a, ci, che *agg* electric.
elettrocardiogramma, i *sm* MED electrocardiogram.
elettrodomestico, ci *sm* electrical household appliance.
elettroencefalogramma, i *sm* MED electroencephalogram.
elettronico, a, ci, che *agg* electronic.
elezione *sf* election.

ELEZIONI

All Italian citizens over the age of eighteen (twenty-five for the Senate) are called upon to vote in political and administrative elections and in popular referenda. Political elections of deputies and senators are held every five years, or less if there is a political crisis. Administrative elections are called every five years for the direct election of the mayor and the nomination of members (Councillors) of the various Councils (local, provinicial and regional). The President of the Republic is elected every seven years by the Parliament in ordinary session and by the regional delegates.

elica, che *sf* propeller.
elicottero *sm* helicopter.
eliminare *vt* to eliminate.
eliminatoria *sf* qualifying round.
ella *pron* she.
elmetto *sm* helmet.
elogio *sm* praise.
eloquente *agg* eloquent.
eludere *vt* to evade.
elusivo, a *agg* elusive.
elvetico, a, ci, che *agg* Swiss.
emaciato, a *agg* emaciated.
emanare *vt (luce)* to send out; *(calore)* to give off; *(legge)* to issue.
emancipato, a *agg* emancipated.
emarginato, a *sm, f* social outcast.
emarginazione *sf (esclusione)* marginalization.
ematoma, i *sm* haematoma.
embolia *sf MED* embolism.
embrione *sm* embryo.
emergenza *sf* emergency.
emergere *vi* to emerge.
emerso, a *pp* → **emergere**.
emicrania *sf* migraine.
emigrante *smf* emigrant.
emigrare *vi (persona)* to emigrate; *(animale)* to migrate.
emiliano, a *agg* Emilian. ◆ *sm, f (abitante)* Emilian; *(dialetto)* Emilian.
Emilia Romagna *sf*: **l'** ~ Emilia Romagna *(region in eastern central Italy)*.
emisfero *sm* hemisphere.
emittente *sf* broadcasting station.
emorragia *sf* hemorrhage.
emozionante *agg* thrilling.
emozione *sf* emotion.
emulsione *sf* emulsion.
enciclopedia *sf* encyclopedia.
ENEL *abbr Italian national electricity company*.
energia *sf* energy; ~ **elettrica** electrical energy.
energico, a, ci, che *agg* energetic.
enfasi *sf inv* emphasis.
enigma, i *sm* enigma.
ennesimo, a *agg* umpteenth.
enorme *agg* enormous.
enoteca, che *sf (negozio)* vintage wine store; *(bar)* wine bar.

ente *sm* body, organization.
entrambi, e *pron pl* both (of them). ◆ *agg pl* : **entrambe le città** both towns.
entrare *vi* to enter, to go in ; ~ **in qc** *(trovar posto)* to fit into sthg ; *(essere ammesso)* to join sthg ; **entra!** come in! ; **questo non c'entra niente** that has nothing to do with it ; ~ **in una stanza** to enter a room ; ~ **in guerra** to go to war ; **far ~ qn** to let sb in.
entrata *sf* entrance ; '~ **libera**' *(in museo)* 'admission free' ; *(in negozio)* 'browsers welcome'. ❑ **entrate** *sfpl (incasso)* takings ; *(guadagno)* income *(sg)*.
entro *prep (periodo)* in, within ; *(scadenza)* by.
entusiasmare *vt* to enthral. ❑ **entusiasmarsi** *vr* : **entusiasmarsi (per)** to get excited (about).
entusiasmo *sm* enthusiasm.
entusiasta, i, e *agg* enthusiastic.
enunciare *vt* to enunciate.
Eolie *sfpl* : **le (isole) ~** the Aeolian Islands.
epatite *sf* hepatitis.
epidemia *sf* epidemic.
epidermide *sf* epidermis.
Epifania *sf* : **l' ~** the Epiphany.
epilessia *sf* epilepsy.
episodio *sm* episode.
epoca, che *sf (era, età)* age ; *(tempo)* time ; **d' ~** *(mobile, costume)* period *(dav s)*.
eppure *cong* and yet, nevertheless.
equatore *sm* equator.
equazione *sf* equation.
equestre *agg* equestrian.
equilibrare *vt* to balance.
equilibrato, a *agg (proporzionato)* balanced ; *(persona)* well-balanced.
equilibrio *sm (stabilità)* balance ; *(posizione, stato)* equilibrium ; **perdere l' ~** to lose one's balance.
equino, a *agg* equine, horse *(dav s)*.
equipaggiamento *sm (di nave, aereo)* fitting out ; *(sportivo)* equipment.
equipaggio *sm* crew.
equitazione *sf* horse riding.
equivalente *agg* & *sm* equivalent.
equivalere : equivalere a *v + prep* to be equivalent to.
equivalso, a *pp* → **equivalere.**
equivoco, a, ci, che *agg (ambiguo)* equivocal ; *(poco onesto)* dubious. ◆ *sm* misunderstanding.
era *sf* age.
erba *sf (prato)* grass ; *(pianta)* herb ; **erbe aromatiche** herbs.
erbazzone *sm spinach and Parmesan cheese tart topped with bacon and parsley (a speciality of Emilia Romagna).*
erboristeria *sf* herbalist's.
erede *smf* heir (*f* heiress).
eredità *sf inv* inheritance ; *(biologica)* heredity ; **lasciare qc in ~ (a qn)** to bequeath sthg (to sb).
ereditare *vt* to inherit.
ereditario, a *agg* hereditary.
eremo *sm (luogo isolato)* retreat.
eresia *sf* heresy.

eretico, a, ci, che *sm, f* heretic.
eretto, a *pp* → **erigere.** ◆ *agg* erect.
ergastolo *sm* life imprisonment.
erigere *vt* to erect.
ernia *sf* hernia.
ero → **essere.**
eroe, eroina *sm, f* hero (*f* heroine).
erogare *vt* to supply.
eroico, a, ci, che *agg* heroic.
eroina *sf (droga)* heroin → **eroe.**
erosione *sf* erosion.
erotico, a, ci, che *agg* erotic.
errare *vi (vagare)* to wander; *(sbagliare)* to be mistaken.
errore *sm (di ortografia, calcolo)* mistake; *(colpa)* error; **per ~** by mistake.
erta *sf*: **stare all' ~** to be on the alert.
eruzione *sf (di vulcano)* eruption; *MED* rash.
esagerare *vt* & *vi* to exaggerate.
esagerato, a *agg* excessive.
esalazione *sf* exhalation.
esaltare *vt (lodare)* to extol; *(entusiasmare)* to excite.
esame *sm* examination; **fare o dare un ~** to take an exam; **~ del sangue** blood test.
esaminare *vt (analizzare)* to examine; *(candidato)* to interview.
esattamente *avv* & *esclam* exactly.
esattezza *sf* accuracy.
esatto, a *agg (giusto)* correct; *(preciso)* exact. ◆ *esclam* exactly!
esattore *sm* collector.
esauriente *agg* exhaustive.
esaurimento *sm* exhaustion; **~ (nervoso)** nervous breakdown.
esaurire *vt* to exhaust. ❑ **esaurirsi** *vr (merce)* to run out; *(persona)* to wear o.s. out.
esaurito, a *agg (provviste, pozzo)* exhausted; *(merce)* sold out; *(persona)* worn out; **'tutto ~'** 'sold out'.
esausto, a *agg* worn out.
esca (*pl* **esche**) *sf* bait.
escandescenza *sf*: **dare in escandescenze** to lose one's temper.
eschimese *smf* Eskimo.
esclamare *vi* to exclaim.
esclamazione *sf* exclamation.
escludere *vt* to exclude.
esclusiva *sf (di notizia)* scoop; *DIR* exclusive rights *(pl)*.
esclusivo, a *agg* exclusive.
escluso, a *pp* → **escludere.**
esco → **uscire.**
escogitare *vt* to come up with.
escursione *sf* excursion; **~ termica** temperature range.
esecutivo, a *agg* & *sm* executive.
esecuzione *sf* execution; *(di concerto)* performance.
eseguire *vt* to carry out; *(in musica)* to perform.
esempio *sm* example; **ad o per ~** for example; **fare un ~** to give an example.
esentare *vt*: **~ qn/qc da qc** to exempt sb/sthg from sthg.
esente *agg*: **~ da** *(esonerato da)*

exempt from; *(libero da)* free from.

esequie *sfpl* funeral rites.

esercitare *vt* to exercise; *(professione)* to practise. ❑ **esercitarsi** *vr* to practise.

esercito *sm* army.

esercizio *sm* exercise; *(di professione)* practice; *(azienda, negozio)* business; **essere fuori ~** to be out of practice.

esibire *vt* to show. ❑ **esibirsi** *vr* to perform.

esigente *agg* demanding.

esigenza *sf (bisogno)* requirement; *(pretesa)* demand.

esigere *vt (pretendere)* to demand; *(richiedere)* to require; *(riscuotere)* to collect.

esile *agg (sottile)* thin; *(persona)* slim.

esilio *sm* exile.

esistente *agg* existing.

esistenza *sf* existence.

esistere *vi* to exist.

esitare *vi* to hesitate.

esitazione *sf* hesitation.

esito *sm* outcome.

esorbitante *agg* exorbitant.

esorcismo *sm* exorcism.

esordio *sm* debut.

esortare *vt*: **~ qn a fare qc** to urge sb to do sthg.

esotico, a, ci, che *agg* exotic.

espandere *vt* to expand. ❑ **espandersi** *vr (ingrandirsi)* to expand; *(odori, liquidi)* to spread.

espansione *sf (allargamento)* expansion; *(di attività)* growth.

espansivo, a *agg* expansive.

espanso, a *pp* → **espandere**.

espediente *sm* expedient.

espellere *vt (da scuola)* to expel; *MED* to excrete.

esperienza *sf* experience.

esperimento *sm (prova)* test; *(scientifico)* experiment.

esperto, a *agg (con esperienza)* experienced; *(bravo)* skilful. ◆ *sm* expert.

espiare *vt* to expiate.

esplicito, a *agg* explicit.

esplodere *vi* to explode. ◆ *vt* to fire.

esplorare *vt* to explore.

esploratore, trice *sm, f* explorer.

esplosione *sf* explosion; *(di gioia, ira)* outburst.

esplosivo, a *agg* & *sm* explosive.

esploso, a *pp* → **esplodere**.

esporre *vt (merce)* to display; *(opera d'arte)* to show; *(pellicola)* to expose; *(idea, fatto)* to explain.

esportare *vt* to export.

esportazione *sf (spedizione)* exportation; *(merce)* exports *(pl)*.

esposizione *sf (di merce)* display; *(mostra)* exhibition; *(di pellicola)* exposure; *(resoconto)* account.

esposto, a *pp* → **esporre**. ◆ *sm* petition. ◆ *agg*: **~ a sud** facing south.

espressione *sf* expression.

espressivo, a *agg* expressive.

espresso, a *pp* → **esprimere**. ◆ *sm (treno)* express; *(caffè)* espresso; *(lettera)* express letter.

esprimere *vt (pensiero, sentimento)* to express. ❑ **esprimersi** *vr (spiegarsi)* to express o.s. ; *(parlare)* to speak.

espulso, a *pp* → **espellere**.

essenziale *agg* essential.

---

essere *vi* - 1. *(per descrivere)* to be ; **sono italiano** I'm Italian ; **sei solo?** are you alone? ; **siamo di Torino** we're from Turin ; **Franco è (un) medico** Franco is a doctor.
- 2. *(trovarsi)* to be ; **dove siete?** where are you? ; **il museo è in centro** the museum is in the town centre ; **sono a casa** I'm at home ; **sono stato in Scozia tre volte** I've been to Scotland three times.
- 3. *(esistere)* : **c'è** there is ; **c'è un'altra possibilità** there's another possibility ; **ci sono** there are ; **ci sono vari alberghi** there are various hotels.
- 4. *(con data, ora)* to be ; **oggi è martedì** today is Tuesday ; **è l'una** it's one o'clock ; **sono le due** it's two o'clock.
- 5. *(con prezzo, peso)* : **quant'è?** - **(sono) 10 euro** how much is it? - (that's) 10 euros ; **sono due chili e mezzo** that's two and a half kilos.
- 6. *(indica appartenenza)* : ~ **di qn** to belong to sb ; **questa macchina è di Paolo** this car is Paolo's.
- 7. *(indica bisogno, obbligo)* : **è da fare** it's still to be done ; **la camera è da prenotare** the room is to be booked.
◆ *v impers* to be ; **è tardi** it's late ; **è vero che ...** it's true that ... ; **oggi è freddo** it's cold today ; **è meglio telefonare** it's better to phone.
◆ *v aus* - 1. *(in tempi passati)* to have, to be ; **sono tornato ieri** I came back yesterday ; **erano già usciti** they'd already gone out ; **sono nata a Roma** I was born in Rome ; **ti sei lavato?** did you wash yourself?
- 2. *(in passivi)* to be ; **questo oggetto è fatto a mano** this object is handmade ; **sono stato pagato ieri** I was paid yesterday.
◆ *sm (creatura)* being ; ~ **umano** human being ; **gli esseri viventi** the living.

---

essi, e → **esso**.

esso, a *pron* it. ❑ **essi, e** *pron pl (soggetto)* they ; *(con preposizione)* them.

est *sm* east ; **a ~ di Milano** east of Milan.

estate *sf* summer.

estendere *vt* to extend.

esteriore *agg (esterno)* external, outward ; *(apparente)* superficial.

esterno, a *agg* exterior ; *(muro)* outer ; *(pericolo)* external. ◆ *sm* outside ; **all' ~** on the outside.

estero, a *agg* foreign. ◆ *sm* : **l' ~** foreign countries *(pl)* ; **all' ~** abroad.

esteso, a *pp* → **estendere**. ◆ *agg* extensive.

estetista, i, e *smf* beautician.

estinguere *vt (fuoco)* to extinguish ; *(debito)* to settle. ❑ **estinguersi** *vr (fuoco)* to go out ; *(specie)* to become extinct.

estinto, a *pp* → **estinguere**.

estintore *sm* (fire) extinguisher.

estivo, a *agg* summer *(dav s)*.

Estonia *sf* : **l'~** Estonia.

estorcere *vt* to extort.
estraneo, a *agg* unconnected. ◆ *sm, f* stranger.
estrarre *vt* to extract ; *(sorteggiare)* to draw.
estratto, a *pp* → estrarre. ◆ *sm (di sostanza)* essence ; *(di libro)* extract ; ~ conto bank statement.
estrazione *sf* extraction ; ~ a sorte draw ; ~ sociale social class.
estremità *sf inv* end. ◆ *sfpl* extremities.
estremo, a *agg (grande)* extreme ; *(drastico)* drastic ; *(ultimo)* final, last. ◆ *sm (punto)* extreme ; *fig (limite)* limit. ❑ **estremi** *smpl* details.
estroverso, a *agg* extrovert.
estuario *sm* estuary.
esuberante *agg* exuberant.
età *sf inv* age ; abbiamo la stessa ~ we are the same age ; la maggiore ~ the legal age ; di mezza ~ middle-aged ; la terza ~ old age.
etere *sm* ether.
eternità *sf* eternity.
eterno, a *agg* eternal.
eterogeneo, a *agg* heterogeneous.
eterosessuale *agg* & *smf* heterosexual.
etica *sf* ethics.
etichetta *sf (di prodotto)* label ; *(cerimoniale)* etiquette.
Etna *sm* : l' ~ Mount Etna.
etrusco, a, schi, sche *agg* Etruscan. ❑ **Etruschi** *smpl* : gli Etruschi the Etruscans.
ettaro *sm* hectare.
etto *sm* 100 grams.
ettogrammo *sm* hectogram.
eucaristia *sf* : l' ~ the Eucharist.
euforia *sf* euphoria.
EUR *sm residential area of Rome built on the site of the Rome Exhibition.*
euro *sm inv* euro.
Europa *sf* : l' ~ Europe.
europeo, a *agg* & *sm, f* European.
eurovisione *sf* : in ~ Eurovision *(dav s)*.
eutanasia *sf* euthanasia.
evacuare *vt* to evacuate.
evacuazione *sf* evacuation.
evadere *vt (tasse, fisco)* to evade ; *(corrispondenza)* to deal with. ◆ *vi* : ~ (da qc) to escape (from sthg).
evaporare *vi* to evaporate.
evasione *sf* escape ; ~ fiscale tax evasion ; d' ~ escapist.
evasivo, a *agg* evasive.
evaso, a *pp* → evadere. ◆ *sm, f* escapee.
evenienza *sf* : in ogni ~ should the need arise.
evento *sm* event.
eventuale *agg* possible.
eventualità *sf inv* possibility.
eventualmente *avv* if necessary.
evidente *agg (chiaro)* clear ; *(ovvio)* obvious.
evidenza *sf* evidence ; mettere in ~ to highlight.
evitare *vt* to avoid ; ~ di fare qc to avoid doing sthg ; ~ qc a qn to spare sb sthg.

evocare *vt (ricordare)* to recall ; *(spiriti)* to evoke.
evoluto, a *agg (tecnica, paese)* advanced ; *(persona)* broad-minded.
evoluzione *sf (biologica)* evolution ; *(progresso)* progress.
evviva *esclam* hurrah!
ex *prep* : **l' ~ presidente** the former president ; **la sua ~ moglie** his ex-wife.
extra *agg inv* & *sm inv* extra.
extracomunitario, a *agg* from outside the EU. ◆ *sm, f immigrant from a non-EU country.*
extraconiugale *agg* extramarital.
extraterrestre *smf* alien.

F

fa[1] → **fare.**
fa[2] *avv* : **un anno ~** a year ago ; **tempo ~** some time ago.
fabbisogno *sm* needs *(pl)*.
fabbrica, che *sf* factory.
fabbricare *vt (costruire)* to build ; *(produrre)* to make.
faccenda *sf (questione)* affair, matter. ❑ **faccende** *sfpl* : **faccende domestiche)** housework *(sg)*.
facchino *sm* porter.
faccia, ce *sf* face ; **di ~ a** opposite ; **~ a ~** face to face ; **che ~ tosta!** what a nerve!
facciata *sf (di edificio)* facade ; *(di pagina)* side.
faccio → **fare.**
facile *agg* easy ; **è ~ che il treno sia in ritardo** the train is likely to be late.
facilità *sf (caratteristica)* easiness ; *(attitudine)* ease.
facilitare *vt* to make easier.
facoltà *sf inv* faculty ; *(potere)* power.
facoltativo, a *agg* optional.
facsimile *sm inv* facsimile.
fagiano *sm* pheasant.
fagiolino *sm* French bean *(Br)*, string bean *(Am)*.
fagiolo *sm* bean ; **fagioli all'uccelletto** *white beans cooked with tomatoes and pepper (a Tuscan speciality)*.
fagotto *sm* bundle ; *(strumento)* bassoon ; **far ~** to pack one's bags and leave.
fai da te *sm inv* do-it-yourself.
falange *sf* finger bone.
falciare *vt* to mow.
falda *sf (di cappello)* brim ; *(d'acqua)* water table ; *(di monte)* slope.
falegname *sm* carpenter.
falla *sf* leak.
fallimento *sm* failure ; DIR bankruptcy.
fallire *vi* DIR to go bankrupt ; *(non riuscire)* : **~ (in qc)** to fail (in sthg), to miss.
fallo *sm* foul.
falò *sm inv* bonfire.
falsificare *vt* to forge.
falso, a *agg* false ; *(gioiello)* fake ; *(banconota, quadro)* forged. ◆ *sm* forgery.
fama *sf* fame ; *(reputazione)* reputation.

fame *sf* hunger ; **aver ~** to be hungry.
famiglia *sf* family.
familiare *agg (della famiglia)* family *(dav s)* ; *(noto)* familiar ; *(atmosfera)* friendly ; *(informale)* informal. ❑ **familiari** *smpl* relations.
famoso, a *agg* famous.
fanale *sm* light.
fanatico, a, ci, che *agg* fanatical.
fango, ghi *sm* mud.
fanno → fare.
fannullone, a *sm, f* loafer.
fantascienza *sf* science fiction.
fantasia *sf (immaginazione)* imagination. ◆ *agg inv* patterned.
fantasma, i *sm* ghost.
fantastico, a, ci, che *agg* fantastic ; *(immaginario)* fantasy *(dav s)*.
fantino *sm* jockey.
fantoccio *sm* puppet.
farabutto *sm* crook.
faraglione *sm* stack.
faraona *sf* guinea fowl.
farcito, a *agg (pollo)* stuffed ; *(torta)* filled.
fard *sm inv* blusher.

☞

fare *vt* - 1. *(fabbricare, preparare)* to make ; **~ progetti** to make plans ; **~ da mangiare** to cook.
- 2. *(attuare)* to make ; **~ un viaggio** to go on a trip ; **~ un sogno** to dream.
- 3. *(essere occupato in)* to do ; **cosa fai stasera?** what are you doing tonight? ; **fa il meccanico** he's a mechanic ; **~ l'università** to go to university ; **faccio tennis** I play tennis.
- 4. *(percorrere)* to do ; **che percorso facciamo per rientrare?** which route shall we take to go back?
- 5. *(suscitare)* to make ; **mi fa pena** I feel sorry for him ; **farsi male** to hurt o.s. ; **~ paura** to be frightening ; **~ chiasso** to be noisy.
- 6. *(atteggiarsi a)* to play, to act ; **~ lo scemo** to behave like an idiot.
- 7. *(indica il risultato)* : **2 più 2 fa 4** 2 and 2 makes 4 ; **quanto fa?** what's the total?
- 8. *(credere)* : **ti facevo più furbo** I thought you were smarter than that.
- 9. *(acquisire)* : **farsi degli amici** to make friends ; **farsi la macchina nuova** *fam* to get a new car.
- 10. *(con infinito)* to make ; **far credere qc a qn** to make sb believe sthg ; **far vedere qc a qn** to show sb sthg ; **far costruire qc** to have sthg built.
- 11. *(in espressioni)* : **non ~ caso a** not to pay attention to ; **non fa niente** *(non importa)* it doesn't matter ; **farcela** to manage ; **non ce la faccio più** I can't go on ; **far bene/male a (qn)** to be good/bad (for sb).
◆ *vi* - 1. *(agire)* to do ; **come si fa a uscire?** how do you get out? ; **fai come ti pare** do as you like ; **non fa che ripetere le stesse cose** all he does is repeat the same things ; **darsi da ~** to get busy.
- 2. *fam (dire)* to say.
◆ *v impers* to be ; **fa bello/brutto** it's lovely/awful weather ; **fa caldo/freddo** it's hot/cold.
❑ **farsi** *vr (diventare)* : **farsi grande** to grow up ; **farsi furbo** *fam* to get

smart ; **farsi vivo** to get in touch ; **farsi avanti/indietro** *(spostarsi)* to move forward/back.

---

farfalla *sf* butterfly ; **cravatta a ~** bow tie.
farina *sf* flour ; **~ gialla** maize flour.
farinata *sf type of bread similar to a very thin 'focaccia' but made from chickpea flour (a speciality of Liguria).*
faringite *sf* pharyngitis.
farmacia *sf (negozio)* chemist's *(Br)*, drugstore *(Am)* ; *(scienza)* pharmacy ; **'farmacie di turno'** 'duty chemists'.
farmacista, i, e *smf* pharmacist.
farmaco, ci *sm* medicine.
faro *sm (per navi)* lighthouse ; *(di veicoli)* headlight ; *(per aerei)* beacon.
farsa *sf* farce.
farsumagru *sm inv beef roll stuffed with mince, pecorino cheese, sausage and boiled eggs, cooked in Marsala and tomato puree (a Sicilian speciality).*
fascia, sce *sf (striscia)* strip, band ; *(medica)* bandage ; *(di territorio)* strip ; *(di popolazione)* band ; **~ elastica** elastic bandage ; **~ oraria** time band.
fasciare *vt* to bandage.
fasciatura *sf* bandage.
fascicolo *sm (di rivista)* issue ; *(di documenti)* file.
fascino *sm* charm.
fascio *sm (d'erba, di fibre)* bunch ; *(di legna)* bundle ; *(di luce)* beam.
fascismo *sm* Fascism.
fascista, i, e *agg* & *smf* Fascist.
fase *sf* phase ; *(di motore)* stroke.
fast food [fast'fud] *sm inv* fast-food restaurant.
fastidio *sm* bother, trouble ; **dare ~ a qn** to annoy sb ; **le dà ~ se fumo?** do you mind if I smoke?
fastidioso, a *agg* inconvenient.
fastoso, a *agg* sumptuous.
fasullo, a *agg (falso)* fake.
fata *sf* fairy.
fatale *agg (mortale)* fatal ; *(inevitabile)* inevitable ; *(sguardo)* irresistible.
fatalità *sf inv (inevitabilità)* inevitability ; *(destino)* fate ; *(disgrazia)* misfortune.
fatica *sf* hard work ; *(stanchezza)* fatigue ; **fare ~ a fare qc** to have difficulty doing sthg ; **a ~** hardly.
faticoso, a *agg (stancante)* exhausting ; *(difficile)* hard.
fatidico, a, ci, che *agg* fateful.
fato *sm* fate.
fatto, a *pp* → **fare**. ◆ *sm (cosa concreta)* fact ; *(avvenimento)* event. ◆ *agg* : **~ a mano** hand-made ; **~ in casa** home-made ; **il ~ è che ...** the fact is that ... ; **cogliere qn sul ~** t[o] catch sb in the act ; **in ~ di vini** when it comes to wine ... ; **s[ono]** **fatti miei** that's my business.
fattoria *sf* farm.
fattorino *sm (per consegn[e])* [de]livery man ; *(d'albergo)* m[essen]ger.
fattura *sf* invoice ; *(mag[ia])*
fauna *sf* fauna.
favola *sf* fairy tale ; *(*...
dream.
favoloso, a *agg* fab[ulous]

favore *sm* favour ; **per ~** please.
favorevole *agg* favourable ; *(voto)* in favour.
favorire *vt (promuovere)* to promote ; *(aiutare)* to favour ; **vuoi ~?** would you like some?
favorito, a *agg* favourite.
fax *sm inv* fax.
faxare *vt* to fax.
fazzoletto *sm (da naso)* handkerchief ; *(per la testa)* headscarf.
febbraio *sm* February → **settembre**.
febbre *sf* fever ; **avere la ~** to have a temperature.
feci *sfpl* excrement *(sg)*.
fecondazione *sf* fertilization.
fede *sf* faith ; *(anello)* wedding ring ; **aver ~ in** to have faith in ; **essere in buona/cattiva ~** to act in good/bad faith.
fedele *agg* faithful ; *(cliente)* loyal ; *(preciso)* accurate. ◆ *smf* believer.
fedeltà *sf (lealtà)* faithfulness, loyalty ; *(precisione)* accuracy.
federa *sf* pillowcase.
federazione *sf* federation.
fegato *sm* liver ; *fig (coraggio)* guts *(pl)* ; **~ alla veneziana** *thinly sliced calves' liver and onions.*
felice *agg* happy.
'elicità *sf* happiness.
elicitarsi *vr* : **~ con qn per qc** to ›ngratulate sb on sthg.
›lino, a *agg* & *sm* feline.
!pa *sf (maglia)* sweatshirt ; *(tes-›)* plush.
nmina *sf (animale)* female ; *'a, ragazza)* girl.
femminile *agg* female ; *(rivista, modi)* women's *(dav s)* ; GRAMM feminine. ◆ *sm* feminine.
femminismo *sm* feminism.
fenomenale *agg* phenomenal.
fenomeno *sm* phenomenon.
feriale *agg* working *(dav s)*.
ferie *sfpl* holidays *(Br)*, vacation *(sg) (Am)* ; **andare in ~** to go on holiday *(Br)*, to go on vacation *(Am)* ; **essere in ~** to be on holiday *(Br)*, to be on vacation *(Am)*.
ferire *vt (colpire)* to injure ; *(addolorare)* to hurt. ❑ **ferirsi** *vr* to injure o.s.
ferita *sf* wound.
ferito, a *agg* injured. ◆ *sm, f* injured person.
fermaglio *sm* clip.
fermare *vt* to stop ; *(bottone)* to fasten ; *(sospetto)* to detain. ◆ *vi* to stop. ❑ **fermarsi** *vr* to stop ; *(sostare)* to stay ; **fermarsi a fare qc** to stop to do sthg.
fermata *sf* stop ; **~ dell'autobus** bus stop ; **'~ prenotata'** 'bus stopping' ; **'~ a richiesta'** 'request stop'.
fermento *sm* ferment.
fermo, a *agg (persona)* still ; *(veicolo)* stationary ; *(mano, voce)* steady ; *(orologio)* stopped ; *(saldo)* firm ; **stare ~** to keep still.
fermoposta *avv* & *sm inv* poste restante *(Br)*, general delivery *(Am)*.
feroce *agg (animale)* ferocious ; *(dolore)* terrible.
ferragosto *sm (giorno) Italian public holiday which falls on 15*

August ; *(periodo)* August holidays *(pl)*.

FERRAGOSTO

August 15, the feast of the Assumption, is a national holiday in Italy and marks the peak of the holiday season. The Italian name, *Ferragosto*, comes from the Latin *feriae augustae*, meaning *August holidays*. Cities become ghost towns, as families and groups of friends flock to the coast, the mountains and the lakes, and most factories and businesses close down.

ferramenta *sf inv* ironmonger's *(Br)*, hardware store *(Am)*.
ferro *sm* iron ; **toccare ~** to touch wood ; **~ battuto** wrought iron ; **~ da calza** knitting needle ; **~ da stiro** iron ; **carne ai ferri** grilled meat.
ferrovia *sf* railway *(Br)*, railroad *(Am)* ; **Ferrovie dello Stato** *Italian railway system, British Rail (Br), Amtrak (Am)*.
ferroviario, a *agg* railway *(Br) (dav s)*, railroad *(Am) (dav s)*.
fertile *agg* fertile.
fervido, a *agg* fervent, ardent.
fesso, a *agg fam* stupid.
fessura *sf* crack ; *(per gettone, moneta)* slot.
festa *sf (religiosa)* feast ; *(giorno festivo)* holiday ; *(ricevimento)* party ; *(ricorrenza)* : **la ~ della mamma** Mother's Day ; **far ~** to have a holiday ; **far ~ a qn** to give sb a warm welcome ; **buone feste!** *(a Natale)* Merry Christmas!

FESTA DELLE DONNE

Since the 1970's, March 8 has been celebrated as National Women's Day in Italy. Meetings, debates and conferences on women's issues are held, and there is now a tradition of presenting women with the gift of a bunch of mimosa.

festeggiare *vt (ricorrenza)* to celebrate ; *(persona)* to throw a party for.
festival *sm inv* festival.

FESTIVAL DI SPOLETO

Also known as the *Festival dei Due Mondi* (Festival of the Two Worlds), the Festival of Spoleto has been held every June and July since 1958. It hosts top-class performances of opera, theatre, music and ballet, attracting internationally renowned artists and a cosmopolitan audience.

festivo, a *agg* festive ; **giorno ~** holiday ; **orario ~** *timetable for Sundays and public holidays*.
festone *sm* festoon.
festoso, a *agg* merry.
feto *sm* foetus.
fetta *sf* slice.
fettuccine *sfpl ribbons of* [illegible] *pasta*.
fettunta *sf toast flavoured* [illegible] *garlic and olive oil (a Tuscan s*[illegible]*ity)*.
FF.SS *abbr* ≃ BR *(Br)*, ≃ [illegible] *(Am)*.
fiaba *sf* fairy tale.

fiaccola *sf* torch.
fiamma *sf* flame ; **dare alle fiamme** to set on fire.
fiammifero *sm* match.
fiancheggiare *vt* to border.
fianco, chi *sm (di persona)* hip ; *(di edificio, collina)* side ; **di ~ a** next to.
fiasco, schi *sm* flask ; **fare ~** to flop.
fiato *sm (respiro)* breath ; *(resistenza)* stamina ; **avere il ~ grosso** to be out of breath.
fibbia *sf* buckle.
fibra *sf* fibre.
ficcanaso (*pl m* **ficcanasi**, *pl f inv*) *smf* busybody.
ficcare *vt* to put. ❑ **ficcarsi** *vr* : **dove ti eri ficcato?** where did you get to?
fico, chi *sm* fig ; **~ d'India** prickly pear.
fidanzamento *sm* engagement.
fidanzarsi *vr* to get engaged.
fidanzato, a *agg* engaged. ◆ *sm, f* fiancé (*f* fiancée).
fidarsi *vr* : **~ di** to trust.
fidato, a *agg* trustworthy.
fiducia *sf* confidence.
fiducioso, a *agg* confident.
fieno *sm* hay.
fiera *sf* fair.
fiero, a *agg* proud.
fifa *sf fam* fright.
fifone, a *sm, f fam (vigliacco)* chicken.
figlio, a *sm, f* son (*f* daughter), child ; **~ unico** only child.
figura *sf* figure ; *(illustrazione)* illustration, picture ; **fare bella/brutta ~** to create a good/bad impression.
figurare *vi* to appear. ◆ *vt* : **figurarsi qc** to imagine sthg. ❑ **figurarsi** *vr* : **figurati!** of course not!
figurina *sf* picture card.
fila *sf (coda)* queue *(Br)*, line *(Am)* ; *(di macchine)* line ; *(di posti)* row ; *(serie)* series ; **fare la ~** to queue *(Br)*, to stand in line *(Am)* ; **di ~** in succession.
filare *vt (lana)* to spin. ◆ *vi (ragno, baco)* to spin ; *(formaggio)* to go stringy ; *(discorso)* to be coherent ; *fam (andarsene)* to split ; **fila!** off you go! ; **~ diritto** to toe the line.
filastrocca, che *sf* nursery rhyme.
filatelia *sf* philately, stamp-collecting.
filatelli *smpl thin strips of egg pasta served with a sauce made from pork, tomatoes, chillis and pecorino cheese (a speciality of Calabria).*
filatieddi = **filatelli**.
file *sm inv* INFORM file.
filetto *sm* fillet ; **~ al pepe verde** fillet steak with green peppercorns.
film *sm inv* film *(Br)*, movie *(Am)*.
filo *sm* thread ; *(cavo)* wire ; *(di lama, rasoio)* edge ; *(di pane)* stick ; **~ d'erba** blade of grass ; **~ spinato** barbed wire ; **fil di ferro** wire ; **per ~ e per segno** word for word.
filobus *sm inv* trolleybus.
filone *sm (di minerale)* vein ; *(di pane)* French loaf.
filosofia *sf* philosophy.

filtrare *vt* & *vi* to filter.
filtro *sm (apparecchio)* filter ; *(di sigarette)* filter tip.
fin → **fino.**
finale *agg* & *sf* final. ◆ *sm* end, ending.
finalmente *avv* at (long) last.
finanza *sf* finance ; *(di frontiera)* ≃ Customs and Excise. ❑ **finanze** *sfpl* finances.
finanziere *sm (banchiere)* financier ; *(di frontiera)* customs officer ; *(per tasse)* ≃ Inland Revenue officer *(Br)*, ≃ Internal Revenue officer *(Am)*.
finché *cong (per tutto il tempo)* as long as ; *(fino a quando)* until.
fine *agg (sottile)* thin ; *(polvere)* fine ; *(elegante)* refined ; *(vista, udito)* keen, sharp. ◆ *sf (conclusione)* end. ◆ *sm (scopo)* aim ; **lieto ~** happy ending ; **~ settimana** weekend ; **alla ~** in the end.
finestra *sf* window.
finestrino *sm* window.
fingere *vt (simulare)* to feign ; **~ di fare qc** to pretend to do sthg. ❑ **fingersi** *vr* : **fingersi malato** to pretend to be ill.
finimondo *sm* pandemonium.
finire *vt* to finish. ◆ *vi* to finish ; *(avere esito)* to end ; *(cacciarsi)* to get to ; **~ col fare qc** to end up doing sthg ; **~ di fare qc** to finish doing sthg.
finlandese *agg* & *sm* Finnish. ◆ *smf* Finn.
Finlandia *sf* : **la ~** Finland.
fino, a *agg (sottile)* thin ; *(oro, argento)* pure ; *(udito, vista)* keen, sharp. ◆ *avv* even. ◆ *prep* : **~ a** *(di tempo)* until ; *(di luogo)* as far as ; **~ da** *(luogo)* as far as ; **fin da domani** from tomorrow ; **fin da ieri** since yesterday ; **~ qui/lì** as far as here/there.
finocchio *sm* fennel.
finora *avv* so far.
finta *sf (finzione)* pretence ; *(nel pugilato)* feint ; *(nel calcio)* dummy ; **fare ~ di fare qc** to pretend to do sthg.
finto, a *pp* → **fingere.** ◆ *agg* false.
fiocco, chi *sm (di nastro)* bow ; *(di neve)* flake ; **coi fiocchi** *(ottimo)* excellent, first-rate.
fiocina *sf* harpoon.
fioco, a, chi, che *agg (voce)* faint ; *(luce)* dim.
fioraio, a *sm, f* florist.
fiore *sm* flower ; **a fior d'acqua** on the surface of the water ; **a fiori** *(stoffa)* with a floral pattern ; **fiori di zucca ripieni** *fried courgette flowers stuffed with breadcrumbs, parsley and anchovies.* ❑ **fiori** *smpl (nelle carte)* clubs.
fiorentino, a *agg* & *sm, f* Florentine.
fiorire *vi (albero)* to blossom ; *(fiore)* to bloom.
fiorista, e, i *smf* florist = fior[illegible]
Firenze *sf* Florence.
firma *sf (sottoscrizione)* s[illegible]ture ; *(marca)* designer bran[illegible]
firmare *vt* to sign.
fiscale *agg* tax *(dav s)*.
fischiare *vi* to whistl[illegible] whistle ; *(disapprovare)* [illegible]
fischio *sm* whistle.

fisco *sm* ≃ Inland Revenue *(Br)*, ≃ Internal Revenue *(Am)*.

fisica *sf (materia)* physics *(sg)* → **fisico**.

fisico, a, ci, che *agg* physical. ◆ *sm (corpo)* physique. ◆ *sm, f* physicist.

fisionomia *sf* face.

fissare *vt (guardare)* to stare at ; *(rendere fisso)* to fix ; *(appuntamento)* to arrange ; *(camera, volo)* to book. ❑ **fissarsi** *vr* : **fissarsi di fare qc** to set one's heart on doing sthg.

fisso, a *agg (fissato)* fixed ; *(impiego)* permanent ; *(reddito)* regular. ◆ *avv* : **guardare ~** to stare.

fitta *sf* sharp pain.

fitto, a *agg* thick. ◆ *sm (affitto)* rent.

fiume *sm* river.

fiutare *vt sog (cane)* to smell ; *fig (accorgersi di)* to get wind of.

flacone *sm* bottle.

flagrante *agg* : **cogliere qc in ~** to catch sb in the act.

flash [flɛʃ] *sm inv* flash.

flessibile *agg* flexible.

flessione *sf (sulle gambe)* knee-bend ; *(a terra)* sit-up ; *(calo)* dip.

flesso, a *pp* → **flettere**.

flettere *vt* to bend.

flipper *sm inv* pinball machine.

.lli *abbr* Bros.

lora *sf* flora.

otta *sf* fleet.

uido, a *agg* & *sm* fluid.

ire *vi* to flow.

so *sm* flow ; *(in fisica)* flux.

fluttuare *vi (ondeggiare)* to rise and fall ; FIN to fluctuate.

F.M. *(abbr di Modulazione di frequenza)* FM.

foca *sf* seal.

focaccia, ce *sf (dolce)* bun ; *(pane) type of flat salted bread made with olive oil* ; **~ alla valdostana** *'focaccia' filled with fontina cheese*.

foce *sf* mouth.

focolare *sm* hearth.

fodera *sf (interna)* lining ; *(esterna)* cover.

foglia *sf* leaf.

foglio *sm (di carta, di metallo)* sheet ; *(documento)* document ; *(banconota)* note ; **~ rosa** provisional driving licence ; **~ di via** expulsion order.

fogna *sf* sewer.

fognature *sfpl* sewers.

föhn = **fon**.

folclore *sm* folklore.

folcloristico, a, ci, che *agg* folk *(dav s)*.

folder *sm inv* INFORM folder.

folgorare *vt sog (fulmine)* to strike ; *sog (alta tensione)* to electrocute.

folla *sf* crowd.

folle *agg (pazzo)* mad ; TECNOL idle ; **in ~** *(di auto)* in neutral.

folletto *sm (spirito)* elf.

follia *sf (pazzia)* madness ; *(atto)* act of madness.

folto, a *agg* thick.

fon *sm inv* hairdryer.

fondale *sm* bottom (of the sea).

fondamentale *agg* fundamental, basic.

fondamento *sm* foundation. ❑ **fondamenta** *sfpl* foundations.

fondare *vt* to found ; *(basare)* : ~ **qc su qc** to base sthg on sthg. ❑ **fondarsi su** *vr + prep* to be based on.

fondazione *sf* foundation.

fondere *vt* to melt ; *(aziende)* to merge. ◆ *vi* to melt. ❑ **fondersi** *vr* to melt.

fondo, a *agg (profondo)* deep. ◆ *sm* bottom ; *(di strada)* surface ; *(di liquido)* dregs *(pl)* ; *(sfondo)* background ; *(sport)* long distance race ; *(proprietà)* property ; **andare a ~** *(affondare)* to sink ; **conoscere a ~** to know very well ; **in ~** *fig (tutto sommato)* after all ; **andare fino in ~ a qc** *(approfondire)* to get to the bottom of sthg ; **in ~ (a qc)** at the bottom (of sthg) ; *(stanza)* at the back (of sthg) ; *(libro, mese)* at the end (of sthg). ❑ **fondi** *smpl (denaro)* funds.

fonduta *sf* fondue.

fonetica *sf* phonetics *(sg)*.

fontana *sf* fountain.

fonte *sf (sorgente)* spring ; *(origine)* source. ◆ *sm* : ~ **battesimale** font.

fontina *sf a hard cheese made from cow's milk (a speciality of the Valle d'Aosta)*.

foraggio *sm* fodder.

forare *vt (praticare un foro in)* to pierce ; *(gomma)* to puncture ; *(biglietto)* to punch ; *(pallone)* to burst.

forbici *sfpl* scissors.

forca, che *sf (attrezzo)* pitchfork ; *(patibolo)* gallows *(pl)*.

forchetta *sf* fork.

forcina *sf* hairpin.

foresta *sf* forest.

forestiero, a *agg* foreign. ◆ *sm, f* foreigner.

forfora *sf* dandruff.

forma *sf* shape ; *(tipo)* form ; *(stampo)* mould ; **essere in ~** to be fit ; **a ~ di** in the shape of. ❑ **forme** *sfpl (del corpo)* figure *(sg)*.

formaggino *sm* processed cheese.

formaggio *sm* cheese.

formale *agg* formal.

formalità *sf inv* formality.

formare *vt* to form ; *(comporre)* to make up ; *(persona)* to train. ❑ **formarsi** *vr* to form.

formattare *vt* INFORM to format.

formato *sm* size.

formazione *sf* formation ; *(istruzione)* education ; ~ **professionale** professional training.

formica[1], che *sf* ant.

formica[2] *sf* Formica®.

formicolio *sm (intorpidimento)* pins and needles *(pl)*.

formidabile *agg* fantastic, amazing.

formula *sf (chimica)* formula ; *(frase rituale)* set phrase ; ~ **uno** formula one.

fornaio, a *sm, f* baker.

fornello *sm (di elettrodomestico)* ring ; ~ **elettrico** hotplate.

fornire *vt* : ~ **qc a qn** to supply sb with sthg ; ~ **qn/qc di qc** to supply sb/sthg with sthg.

fornitore, trice *sm, f* supplier.

forno *sm* oven ; ~ a legna wood-burning stove ; ~ a microonde microwave (oven).

foro *sm (buco)* hole ; *(romano)* forum.

forse *avv* perhaps, maybe ; *(circa)* about.

forte *agg* strong ; *(suono)* loud ; *(luce, colore)* bright. ◆ *avv (vigorosamente)* hard ; *(ad alta voce)* loudly ; *(velocemente)* fast. ◆ *sm (fortezza)* fort ; *(specialità)* strong point.

fortezza *sf* fortress.

fortuito, a *agg* chance *(dav s)*, fortuitous.

fortuna *sf* luck ; *(patrimonio)* fortune ; buona ~! good luck! ; portare ~ to bring luck ; per ~ luckily, fortunately.

fortunatamente *avv* luckily, fortunately.

fortunato, a *agg (persona)* lucky ; *(evento)* successful.

forviare = fuorviare.

forza *sf* strength ; *(in fisica, violenza)* force ; a ~ di by dint of ; per ~ *(naturalmente)* of course ; *(contro la volontà)* against one's will ; le forze armate the armed forces.

forzare *vt (porta, finestra)* to force open ; *(obbligare)* : ~ qn a fare qc to force sb to do sthg.

foschia *sf* haze.

fossa *sf (buca)* pit, hole ; *(tomba)* grave.

fossato *sm* ditch ; *(di castello)* moat.

fossile *sm* fossil.

fosso *sm* ditch.

foto *sf inv* photo.

fotocopia *sf* photocopy.

fotocopiare *vt* to photocopy.

fotogenico, a, ci, che *agg* photogenic.

fotografare *vt* to photograph.

fotografia *sf (arte)* photography ; *(immagine)* photograph ; ~ a colori colour photograph ; ~ in bianco e nero black and white photograph.

fotografo, a *sm, f* photographer.

fototessera *sf* passport-size photograph.

fra = tra.

fracassare *vt* to smash.

fracasso *sm* crash.

fradicio, a, ci, ce *agg* soaked.

fragile *agg* fragile ; *(persona)* delicate.

fragola *sf* strawberry.

fragore *sm* loud noise.

fraintendere *vt* to misunderstand.

frammento *sm* fragment.

frana *sf* landslide ; *fig (persona)* : essere una ~ to be useless.

francese *agg* & *sm* French. ◆ *smf (abitante)* Frenchman *(f* Frenchwoman) ; i francesi the French.

Francia *sf* : la ~ France.

franco, a, chi, che *agg (sincero)* frank ; COMM free. ◆ *sm* franc ; farla franca to get away with it.

francobollo *sm* stamp.

frangia, ge *sf* fringe.

frantumare *vt* to smash. ❑ **frantumarsi** *vr* to smash.

frantumi *smpl* : andare in ~ to smash ; *(sogno)* to be shattered.

frappé *sm inv* (milk) shake.

frase *sf* GRAMM sentence ; *(espressione)* expression.
frastuono *sm* din.
frate *sm (monaco)* friar ; *(pasta)* ring doughnut.
fratellastro *sm* stepbrother.
fratello *sm* brother.
frattempo *sm* : **nel ~** in the meantime, meanwhile.
frattura *sf* fracture.
frazione *sf (parte)* fraction ; *(di comune)* village.
freccia, ce *sf* arrow ; **~ di direzione** indicator ; **mettere la ~** to put the indicator on.
freddo, a *agg* & *sm* cold ; **aver ~** to be cold ; **è** ○ **fa ~** it's cold.
freddoloso, a *agg* : **essere ~** to feel the cold.
freezer ['fridzer] *sm inv* freezer.
fregare *vt (strofinare)* to rub ; *fam (imbrogliare)* to trick ; **~ qc a qn** *fam (rubare)* to nick sthg from sb ; **fregarsene (di qc)** *volg* not to give a damn (about sthg).
frenare *vi* to brake. ◆ *vt (rabbia, entusiasmo)* to curb ; *(lacrime)* to hold back ; *(avanzata, progresso)* to hold up.
frenata *sf* braking ; **fare una ~** to brake.
frenetico, a, ci, che *agg* hectic.
freno *sm (di veicolo)* brake ; *(per cavallo)* bit ; **~ a mano** handbrake.
frequentare *vt (corso, scuola)* to attend ; *(locale)* to go to ; *(persona)* to mix with.
frequente *agg* frequent.
fresco, a, schi, sche *agg* fresh ; *(temperatura)* cool ; *(notizie)* recent. ◆ *sm (temperatura)* cool ; **è** ○ **fa ~** it's cool ; **mettere al ~** to put in a cool place ; **stare ~** to be way out.
fretta *sf (urgenza)* hurry ; *(rapidità)* haste ; **avere ~** to be in a hurry ; **in ~ e furia** in a hurry.
fricassea *sf stewed meat and vegetables in an egg and lemon sauce.*
friggere *vt* to fry. ◆ *vi* to sizzle.
frigo *sm inv* fridge.
frigobar *sm inv* minibar.
frigorifero *sm* refrigerator.
frittata *sf* omelette.
frittella *sf* fritter ; **frittelle di mele** apple fritters.
fritto, a *pp* → **friggere**. ◆ *agg* fried. ◆ *sm* : **~ misto** *mixed deep-fried fish and seafood.*
frittura *sf* : **~ di pesce** *deep-fried fish and seafood.*
frivolo, a *agg* frivolous.
frizione *sf (di auto)* clutch ; *(massaggio)* massage.
frizzante *agg* fizzy ; *(vino)* sparkling.
frode *sf* fraud.
frontale *agg* frontal ; *(scontro)* head-on.
fronte *sf* forehead. ◆ *sm* front ; **di ~** opposite ; **di ~ a** *(faccia a faccia)* opposite ; *(in una fila)* in front of ; *(in confronto a)* compared with.
frontiera *sf* frontier.
frottola *sf (bugia)* lie.
frugare *vi* & *vt* to search.
frullare *vt* to whisk.
frullato *sm* milk shake.
frullatore *sm* blender, liquidizer.

frullino *sm* whisker.
frusta *sf (per animali)* whip.
frustino *sm* (riding) crop.
frutta *sf* fruit ; **~ secca** dried fruit and nuts.
fruttivendolo *sm (negozio)* greengrocer's.
frutto *sm* fruit ; *(profitto)* profit ; **frutti di mare** seafood *(sg)*.
FS = **FF.SS.**
fu → **essere.**
fucile *sm* rifle.
fuga, ghe *sf* escape ; **~ di gas** gas leak.
fuggire *vi (allontanarsi)* to escape ; *(rifugiarsi)* to run away.
fulmine *sm* bolt of lightning.
fumare *vt* to smoke. ◆ *vi* to smoke ; *(emettere vapore)* to steam ; **'vietato ~'** 'no smoking'.
fumatore, trice *sm, f* smoker ; **fumatori o non fumatori?** smoking or non-smoking?
fumetti *smpl (vignette)* cartoon strip *(sg)* ; *(giornalino)* comics.
fumo *sm* smoke ; *(vapore)* steam.
fune *sf* rope.
funebre *agg* funeral *(dav s)* ; *(lugubre)* funereal.
funerale *sm* funeral.
fungo, ghi *sm* mushroom ; *MED* fungus ; **~ mangereccio** edible mushroom.
funicolare *sf* funicular railway.
funivia *sf* cable way.
funzionamento *sm* functioning.
funzionare *vi* to work. ❑ **funzionare da** *v + prep* to act as.
funzione *sf* function ; *(compito)* duty ; *(religiosa)* service ; **essere in ~** to be working ; **in ~ di** *(secondo)* according to.
fuoco, chi *sm* fire ; *(fornello)* ring ; *(in ottica)* focus ; **al ~!** fire! ; **dar ~ a qc** to set fire to sthg ; **fare ~** to fire ; **prender ~** to catch fire ; **fuochi d'artificio** fireworks.
fuorché *cong* except.
fuori *avv* out, outside ; *(fuori di casa)* out ; *(all'aperto)* outdoors, outside. ◆ *prep* : **~ (di)** out of, outside ; **far ~ qn** *fam* to kill sb ; **essere ~ di sé** to be beside oneself ; **lasciare ~** to leave out ; **tirare ~** to get out ; **~ luogo** uncalled for ; **~ mano** out of the way ; **andare ~ strada** to leave the road ; **' ~ servizio'** 'out of order'.
fuoribordo *sm inv* outboard.
fuorilegge *smf inv* outlaw.
fuoristrada *sm inv* Jeep® ◆ *agg inv* : **moto ~** trail bike.
fuorviare *vt* to mislead.
furbo, a *agg* clever, smart ; *(spreg)* cunning.
furgone *sm* van.
furia *sf (ira)* fury ; *(impeto)* violence ; **a ~ di fare qc** by (means of) doing sthg ; **andare su tutte le furie** to get into a towering rage.
furioso, a *agg* furious.
furore *sm* fury ; **far ~** to be all the rage.
furto *sm* theft ; **~ con scasso** burglary.
fusa *sfpl* : **fare le ~** to purr.
fusibile *sm* fuse.
fusione *sf (di cera, metallo)* melting ; *(unione)* fusion.

fuso, a *pp* → fondere. ◆ *sm* : ~ orario time zone.
fustino *sm* tub.
fusto *sm (di pianta)* stem ; *(contenitore)* drum ; *fam (ragazzo)* hunk.
futile *agg* futile.
futuro, a *agg* & *sm* future.

G

gabbia *sf* cage.
gabbiano *sm* seagull.
gabinetto *sm (bagno)* toilet ; *(ministero)* cabinet ; *(di dentista)* surgery.
gaffe [gaf] *sf inv* blunder.
gala *sf (sfarzo)* pomp ; *(festa)* gala.
galassia *sf* galaxy.
galateo *sm* etiquette.
galera *sf* prison.
galla *sf* : stare a ~ to float ; venire a ~ *fig* to come out.
galleggiante *agg* floating. ◆ *sm (boa)* buoy ; *(per la pesca)* float.
galleria *sf (traforo)* tunnel ; *(museo)* gallery ; *(di teatro)* circle ; *(di cinema)* balcony ; *(strada coperta)* arcade.
galletta *sf* cracker.
gallina *sf* hen.
gallo *sm* cock.
gamba *sf* leg ; essere in ~ to be smart.
gamberetto *sm* shrimp.
gambero *sm* prawn.
gamberoni *smpl* : ~ alla griglia grilled crayfish.
gambo *sm* stem.
gancio *sm* hook.
gangheri *smpl* : essere fuori dai ~ to fly off the handle.
gara *sf (nello sport)* race ; *(concorso)* competitive bidding ; fare a ~ to compete.
garage [ga'raʒ] *sm inv* garage.
garantire *vt* to guarantee.
garanzia *sf (di merce)* guarantee ; *(di debito)* guarantee, security.
gareggiare *vi* to compete.
gargarismo *sm* : fare i gargarismi to gargle.
garza *sf* gauze.
garzone : **garzone** *sm* boy.
gas *sm inv* gas ; dare ~ to step on the gas ; ~ lacrimogeno tear gas.
gasato, a = gassato.
gasolio *sm* diesel oil.
gassato, a *agg (bevanda)* fizzy.
gassosa *sf* fizzy drink.
gastronomia *sf* gastronomy ; *(negozio)* delicatessen.
gastronomico, a, ci, che *agg* gastronomic.
gattino, a *sm, f* kitten.
gatto, a *sm, f* cat ; ~ delle nevi snow cat ; eravamo in quattro gatti there were only a few of us.
gazzetta *sf* gazette.
G.d.F. *abbr* = Guardia di Finanza.
gel *sm inv* gel.
gelare *vi, vt* & *v impers* to freeze.
gelateria *sf* ice-cream shop *(Br)*, ice-cream parlour *(Am)*.

gelatina *sf* gelatine ; ~ **di frutta** fruit jelly.
gelato, a *agg* frozen. ◆ *sm* ice cream.
gelido, a *agg* freezing, icy.
gelo *sm (freddo)* intense cold ; *(ghiaccio)* ice.
gelosia *sf* jealousy.
geloso, a *agg* jealous.
gemello, a *agg* twin. ❑ **gemelli** *smpl (di camicia)* cuff links. ❑ **Gemelli** *smpl* Gemini *(sg)*.
gemere *vi* to moan.
gemma *sf (pietra)* gem ; *(di pianta)* bud.
generale *agg* & *sm* general ; **in ~** in general.
generalità *sfpl* particulars.
generalmente *avv* generally.
generare *vt (produrre)* to generate, to produce.
generatore *sm* generator.
generazione *sf* generation.
genere *sm (tipo)* kind, type ; *(di arte)* genre ; GRAMM gender ; *(di animali, vegetali)* genus ; **il ~ umano** mankind ; **in ~** generally. ❑ **generi** *smpl* : **generi alimentari** foodstuffs.
generico, a, ci, che *agg (generale)* generic ; *(vago)* vague ; **medico ~** general practitioner.
genero *sm* son-in-law.
generoso, a *agg* generous.
gengiva *sf* gum.
geniale *agg* brilliant.
genio *sm* genius ; **andare a ~ a qn** to be liked by sb.
genitali *smpl* genitals.
genitore *sm* parent ; **i nostri genitori** our parents.
gennaio *sm* January → **settembre**.
Genova *sf* Genoa.
gente *sf* people *(pl)*.
gentile *agg* kind, nice ; **Gentile Signore** Dear Sir ; **Gentile Signor G. Paoli** Mr G. Paoli.
gentilezza *sf* kindness ; **per ~** please.
gentiluomo (*pl* **gentiluomini**) *sm* gentleman.
genuino, a *agg* genuine.
geografia *sf* geography.
geologia *sf* geology.
geometria *sf* geometry.
Georgia *sf* : **la ~** Georgia.
geranio *sm* geranium.
gerarchia *sf* hierarchy.
gergo, ghi *sm (di giovani)* slang ; *(specialistico)* jargon.
Germania *sf* : **la ~** Germany.
germe *sm* germ.
gerundio *sm* gerund.
gesso *sm* chalk ; *(per frattura)* plaster.
gestione *sf* management.
gestire *vt* to run.
gesto *sm* gesture.
gestore *sm* manager.
Gesù *sm* Jesus.
gettare *vt (lanciare)* to throw ; *(buttar via)* to throw away ; *(grido)* to utter ; *(acqua)* to spout ; *(scultura)* to cast ; **'non ~ alcun oggetto dal finestrino'** 'do not throw objects out of the window'. ❑ **gettarsi** *vr* : **gettarsi da/in** to throw o.s.

from/into ; **gettarsi in** *(fiume)* to flow into.

getto *sm (d'acqua, gas)* jet ; *(vapore)* puff ; **di ~** *(scrivere)* in one go.

gettone *sm* token ; **~ telefonico** telephone token.

ghiacciaio *sm* glacier.

ghiacciato, a *agg* frozen ; *(freddo)* ice-cold.

ghiaccio *sm* ice.

ghiacciolo *sm (gelato)* ice lolly *(Br)*, Popsicle® *(Am)* ; *(di fontana)* icicle.

ghiaia *sf* gravel.

ghiandola *sf* gland.

ghiotto, a *agg (persona)* greedy ; *(cibo)* appetizing.

già *avv* already ; *(precedentemente)* already, before. ◆ *esclam* of course!, yes! ; **di ~?** already?.

giacca, che *sf* jacket ; **~ a vento** windcheater.

giacché *cong* as, since.

giaccone *sm* heavy jacket.

giacere *vi* to lie.

giallo, a *agg (colore)* yellow ; *(carnagione)* sallow. ◆ *sm (colore)* yellow ; *(romanzo)* detective story ; **film ~** thriller.

gianduiotto *sm* hazelnut chocolate.

Giappone *sm* : **il ~** Japan.

giapponese *agg, smf & sm* Japanese.

giardinaggio *sm* gardening.

giardiniera *sf (verdure) starter of mixed pickled vegetables* → **giardiniere.**

giardiniere, a *sm, f* gardener.

giardino *sm* garden ; **~ botanico** botanical gardens *(pl)* ; **~ d'infanzia** nursery, kindergarten ; **~ pubblico** park ; **~ zoologico** zoo.

gigante *agg (enorme)* gigantic. ◆ *sm* giant.

gigantesco, a, schi, sche *agg* gigantic.

gilè *sm inv* waistcoat.

gin [dʒin] *sm inv* gin.

ginecologo, a, gi, ghe *sm, f* gynaecologist.

ginestra *sf* broom.

Ginevra *sf* Geneva.

ginnastica *sf* gymnastics *(sg)* ; **fare ~** to do exercises.

ginocchio (*pl m* **ginocchi** ○, *pl f* **ginocchia**) *sm* knee ; **stare in ~** to be on one's knees, to kneel.

giocare *vi* to play ; *(scommettere)* to gamble. ◆ *vt* to play ; *(scommettere)* to gamble ; *(ingannare)* to take in ; **sai ~ a tennis?** can you play tennis? ; **giocarsi il posto** to lose one's job.

giocatore, trice *sm, f* player ; **~ d'azzardo** gambler.

giocattolo *sm* toy.

gioco, chi *sm* game ; *(divertimento)* play ; **mettere in ~ qc** to risk sthg ; **~ d'azzardo** game of chance ; **~ di parole** pun ; **per ~** as a joke.

giocoliere *sm* juggler.

gioia *sf* joy ; *(gioiello)* jewel ; **darsi alla pazza ~** to live it up.

gioielleria *sf* jeweller's shop.

gioiello *sm* jewel, piece of jewellery.

giornalaio, a *sm, f* newsagent *(Br)*, newsdealer *(Am)*.

giornale *sm (quotidiano)* newspaper ; *(rivista)* magazine ; **~ radio** news bulletin.

giornaliero, a *agg* daily.

giornalista, i, e *smf* journalist.

giornata *sf* day ; **oggi è una bella ~** it's lovely today ; **~ lavorativa** working day ; **vivere alla ~** to live for the day.

giorno *sm (ventiquattro ore)* day ; *(opposto alla notte)* day, daytime ; *(periodo di luce)* daylight ; **a giorni alterni** on alternate days ; **l'altro ~** the other day ; **~ feriale** working day ; **~ festivo** holiday ; **~ libero** day off ; **al ~** by the day, per day ; **di ~** by day , during the day.

giostra *sf* merry-go-round.

giovane *agg* young ; **da ~** as a young man/woman ; **i giovani** young people.

giovanile *agg* youthful.

giovanotto *sm* young man.

giovare a : giovare a *v + prep* to be good for. ❑ **giovarsi di** *vr + prep* to make use of.

giovedì *sm inv* Thursday ; **~ grasso** *last Thursday of Carnival, before Lent, sabato.*

gioventù *sf (età)* youth ; *(giovani)* young people *(pl)*.

giovinezza *sf* youth.

giraffa *sf* giraffe.

giramento *sm* : **~ di testa** dizziness.

girare *vt* to turn ; *(visitare)* to go round ; *(filmare)* to shoot ; *(assegno, cambiale)* to endorse. ◆ *vi* to turn ; *(velocemente)* to spin ; *(terra)* to revolve ; *(andare in giro)* to go around. ❑ **girarsi** *vr* to turn around.

girarrosto *sm* spit.

girasole *sm* sunflower.

girata *sf (passeggiata)* stroll ; *(in macchina)* drive ; FIN endorsement.

girello *sm (di carne)* topside ; *(per bambini)* baby-walker.

girevole *agg* turning, revolving.

giro *sm (viaggio)* tour ; *(rotazione)* turn ; *(di amici, colleghi)* circle ; *(di pista)* lap ; **fare un ~** *(a piedi)* to go for a walk ; *(in macchina)* to go for a drive ; *(in bicicletta)* to go for a ride ; **fare il ~ di** *(città, negozi)* to go round ; **~ d'affari** turnover ; **~ di parole** circumlocution ; **~ di prova** test drive ; **in ~** around ; **nel ~ di un anno** in the space of a year ; **prendere in ~ qn** to tease sb, to pull sb's leg ; **essere su di giri** to be excited.

girotondo *sm* ring-a-ring-o'-roses.

gita *sf* trip ; **andare in ~ a Roma** to go on a trip to Rome.

giù *avv* down ; *(al piano di sotto)* downstairs ; **in ~** down , downwards ; **~ di lì** thereabouts ; **~ per le scale** down the stairs ; **essere ~** *fig (essere depresso)* to be low.

giubbotto *sm* jacket.

giudicare *vt (valutare)* to judge ; *(reputare)* to consider ; DIR to find. ◆ *vi* to judge.

giudice *sm* judge ; *(nello sport)* umpire.

giudizio *sm* judgment ; *(opinione)* opinion ; *(a scuola)* report ; **a mio ~** in my opinion.

giugno *sm* June → **settembre**.

giungere *vi* : ~ **a/in** to reach.
giungla *sf* jungle.
giunta *sf* committee ; **per ~** in addition.
giunto, a *pp* → **giungere**.
giuramento *sm* oath.
giurare *vt* to swear. ◆ *vi* to take an oath.
giuria *sf (di gare, concorsi)* judges *(pl)* ; *(di tribunale)* jury.
giustificare *vt* to justify.
giustificazione *sf (scusa)* excuse ; SCOL note (of absence).
giustizia *sf* justice.
giusto, a *agg (equo)* fair, just ; *(vero, adeguato)* right ; *(esatto)* correct. ◆ *avv (esattamente)* correctly ; *(proprio)* just ; **cercavo ~ te!** you're just the person I was looking for!
gli *(dav s + consonante, gn, ps, z, vocale e h) art mpl* the → **il**. ◆ *pron (a lui)* (to) him ; *(a esso)* (to) it ; *(a loro)* (to) them ; **glielo hai detto?** have you told him/her? ; **gliene devo due** I owe him/her two (of them).
gliela → **gli**.
gliele → **gli**.
glieli → **gli**.
globale *agg* global.
globo *sm* globe.
globulo *sm* : ~ **rosso/bianco** red/white corpuscle.
gloria *sf* glory.
gnocchi *smpl* gnocchi, *small dumplings made from potatoes and flour or from semolina.*
goal [gɔl] *sm inv* goal.
gobba *sf (su schiena)* hump ; *(rigonfiamento)* bump.
gobbo, a *agg* hunchbacked ; *(curvo)* round-shouldered. ◆ *sm* hunchback.
goccia, ce *sf* drop.
gocciolare *vi* & *vt* to drip.
godere *vt* : **godersi qc** to enjoy sthg. ❑ **godere di** *v + prep (avere)* to enjoy ; ~ **di una riduzione** to benefit from a reduction.
goffo, a *agg* clumsy.
gola *sf* throat ; *(golosità)* greed ; *(di monte)* gorge.
golf *sm inv (maglia)* sweater, jumper ; *(sport)* golf.
golfo *sm* gulf.
goloso, a *agg* greedy.
gomito *sm* elbow.
gomma *sf* rubber ; *(per cancellare)* rubber *(Br)*, eraser *(Am)* ; *(pneumatico)* tyre ; **bucare** o **forare una ~** to have a puncture ; **~ a terra** flat tyre ; **~ (da masticare)** chewing gum.
gommapiuma® *sf* foam rubber.
gommista *sm* tyre centre.
gommone *sm* rubber dinghy.
gondola *sf* gondola.
gondoliere *sm* gondolier.
gonfiare *vt (pallone, gomme)* to inflate ; *(dilatare, ingrossare)* to swell ; *(notizia, impresa)* to exaggerate. ❑ **gonfiarsi** *vr* to swell ; *(fiume)* to rise.
gonfio, a *agg (piede, occhi)* swollen ; *(stomaco)* bloated.
gonna *sf* skirt ; **~ a pieghe** pleated skirt ; **~ pantalone** culottes *(pl)*.
gorgogliare *vi* to gurgle.
gorgonzola *sm* Gorgonzola *(a*

strong green-veined cheese made from cow's milk).

gorilla *sm inv (animale)* gorilla ; *(guardia del corpo)* bodyguard.

goulash ['gulaʃ] *sm* goulash.

governante *sf (per bambini)* governess ; *(di casa)* housekeeper.

governare *vt* to govern ; *(animale)* to look after.

governatore *sm* governor.

governo *sm* government.

gracile *agg* delicate.

gradazione *sf (di colori)* scale ; *(sfumatura)* shade ; ~ **alcolica** alcoholic strength.

gradevole *agg* pleasant.

gradinata *sf (scalinata)* (flight of) steps ; *(in stadi, teatri)* tiers *(pl)*.

gradino *sm* step.

gradire *vt (regalo)* to like, to appreciate ; *(desiderare)* to like ; **gradisce un caffè?** would you like a coffee?

grado *sm* degree ; *(sociale)* level ; *MIL* rank ; **quanti gradi ha questo vino?** how strong is this wine? ; **essere in ~ di fare qc** to be able to do sthg ; ~ **centigrado** centigrade.

graduale *agg* gradual.

graduatoria *sf* (ranked) list.

graffetta *sf (fermaglio)* clip ; *(di pinzatrice)* staple.

graffiare *vt* to scratch.

graffio *sm* scratch.

grafica *sf* graphics *(pl)*.

grafico, a, ci, che *agg (rappresentazione, arti)* graphic. ◆ *sm, f (pubblicitario)* designer. ◆ *sm* graph.

grammatica, che *sf (disciplina)* grammar ; *(libro)* grammar book.

grammo *sm* gram.

grana *sf fam (soldi)* cash ; *(seccatura)* trouble. ◆ *sm inv a hard cheese similar to Parmesan.*

granaio *sm* granary, barn.

Gran Bretagna *sf*: **la** ~ Great Britain.

granché *pron* : **non ne so (un)** ~ I don't know much about it ; **non è (un)** ~ it's nothing special.

granchio *sm* crab ; **prendere un** ~ *fig* to blunder.

grande *(a volte* **gran***) agg (gen)* big ; *(albero)* tall ; *(rumore)* loud ; *(scrittore, affetto, capacità)* great. ◆ *sm (adulto)* grown-up, adult ; ~ **magazzino** department store ; **cosa farai da ~?** what will you do when you grow up? ; **fare le cose in ~** to do things on a grand scale ; **è un gran bugiardo** he's such a liar ; **fa un gran caldo** it's very hot.

grandezza *sf (dimensioni)* size ; *(eccellenza)* greatness.

grandinare *v impers* to hail.

grandine *sf* hail.

granello *sm (di sale, sabbia, polvere)* grain.

granita *sf* granita *(crushed ice with syrup, fruit juice or coffee poured over)*.

grano *sm* wheat.

granoturco *sm* maize.

grappa *sf (acquavite)* grappa *(spirit distilled from grape marc)*.

grappolo *sm* bunch.

grasso, a *agg (persona)* fat ; *(cibo)* fatty ; *(pelle, capelli)* greasy. ◆ *sm* fat ; *(unto)* grease.

grassoccio, a, ci, ce *agg* plump.

grata *sf* grating.
gratis *avv* free.
gratitudine *sf* gratitude.
grato, a *agg* grateful.
grattacielo *sm* skyscraper.
grattare *vt* to scratch ; *(formaggio)* to grate ; *fam (rubare)* to pinch ; **grattarsi il naso/la gamba** to scratch one's nose/leg. ❑ **grattarsi** *vr* to scratch o.s.
grattugia *sf* grater.
grattugiare *vt* to grate.
gratuito, a *agg* free.
grave *agg (malattia, ferita)* serious ; *(danno, perdite)* serious, great ; *(responsabilità)* heavy ; *(sacrificio)* great ; *(voce, suono)* deep ; *(contegno)* solemn.
gravemente *avv* seriously.
gravidanza *sf* pregnancy.
gravità *sf (in fisica)* gravity ; *(serietà)* seriousness.
grazia *sf* grace ; *DIR* pardon.
grazie *esclam* thank you! ; **~ tante** o **mille!** thank you so much! ; **~ dei** o **per i fiori** thank you for the flowers ; **~ a** thanks to.
grazioso, a *agg* pretty, charming.
Grecia *sf* : **la ~** Greece.
greco, a, ci, che *agg & sm, f* Greek.
gregge (*pl f* **greggi**) *sm* flock.
greggio, a, gi, ge *agg* raw, unrefined ; *(tessuto)* unbleached ; *(diamante)* rough, uncut. ◆ *sm* crude oil.
grembiule *sm (da cucina)* apron ; *(per bambini)* smock.
grezzo = **greggio**.
gridare *vi* to shout ; *(di dolore)* to yell, to cry out. ◆ *vt* to shout.
grido (*pl f* **grida**) *sm (di persona)* shout, cry ; **di ~** famous.
grigio, a, gi, gie *agg & sm* grey.
griglia *sf* grill ; **alla ~** grilled.
grigliata *sf* mixed grill *(of meat or fish)*.
grill *sm* = **griglia**.
grilletto *sm* trigger.
grillo *sm* cricket.
grinta *sf* determination.
grinzoso, a *agg (tessuto)* creased ; *(pelle)* wrinkled.
grissini *smpl* bread-sticks.
grolla *sf wooden goblet or bowl, typical of the Valle d'Aosta*.
grondare *vi* to stream. ❑ **grondare di** *v + prep* to drip with.
groppa *sf* rump.
groppo *sm* tangle ; **avere un ~ alla gola** to have a lump in one's throat.
grossista, i, e *smf* wholesaler.
grosso, a *agg* big, large ; *(spesso)* thick ; *(importante)* important ; *(grave)* great. ◆ *sm* majority ; **dirla grossa** to tell a whopping lie ; **questa volta l'hai fatta grossa!** you've really done it this time! ; **sbagliarsi di ~** to make a big mistake ; **mare ~** rough sea ; **pezzo ~** big shot ; **sale ~** coarse salt.
grossolano, a *agg (persona)* coarse ; *(lavoro)* crude ; *(errore)* gross.
grossomodo *avv* roughly, approximately.
grotta *sf* cave.
grottesco, a, schi, sche *agg* grotesque.

groviera *sm o sf* Gruyère cheese.
groviglio *sm* tangle.
gru *sf inv (macchina)* crane.
gruccia, ce *sf (stampella)* crutch ; *(per abiti)* coat hanger.
grugnire *vi* to grunt.
grumo *sm (di sangue)* clot ; *(di farina)* lump.
gruppo *sm* group ; **~ sanguigno** blood group.
gruviera = **groviera**.
guadagnare *vt (soldi)* to earn ; *(ottenere)* to gain ; **guadagnarsi da vivere** to earn one's living.
guadagno *sm (denaro)* earnings *(pl)* ; *(tornaconto)* profit.
guado *sm* ford.
guai *esclam* : **~ a te!** you'll be for it!
guaio *sm (pasticcio)* trouble ; *(inconveniente)* problem ; **essere nei guai** to be in trouble ; **mettere qn nei guai** to get sb into trouble.
guancia, ce *sf* cheek.
guanciale *sm* pillow.
guanto *sm* glove.
guardaboschi *sm inv* forest ranger.
guardacoste *sm inv (persona)* coastguard ; *(nave)* (coastguard's) patrol boat.
guardalinee *sm inv* linesman.
guardamacchine *sm inv* car park attendant.
guardare *vt (osservare)* to look at, to watch ; *(televisione, film)* to watch ; *(bambini, borsa)* to look after. ◆ *vi (edificio)* to look, to face ; *(badare)* : **non ~ a spese** to spare no expense ; **guarda!** look!
❑ **guardarsi** *vr* to look at o.s.
❑ **guardarsi da** *vr + prep* to be wary of ; **guardarsi dal fare qc** to be careful not to do sthg.
guardaroba *sm inv* wardrobe ; *(di locale)* cloakroom.
guardia *sf* guard ; *(attività)* watch, guard duty ; **fare la ~ a** to guard ; **mettere qn in ~ contro qc** to warn sb about sthg ; **~ del corpo** bodyguard ; **Guardia di Finanza** *military body responsible for customs and fiscal matters* ; **~ forestale** forest ranger ; **~ medica** first-aid station ; **di ~** on duty.
guardiano *sm* caretaker ; **~ notturno** night watchman.
guardrail [gar'dreɪl] *sm inv* crash barrier.
guarire *vi* to recover ; *(ferita)* to heal. ◆ *vt* to cure ; *(ferita)* to heal.
guarnizione *sf (ornamento)* trim ; *(contorno)* accompaniment, garnish ; *(per recipienti)* seal ; *(di auto)* gasket.
guastafeste *smf inv* spoilsport.
guastare *vt* to spoil. ❑ **guastarsi** *vr (meccanismo)* to break down ; *(cibo)* to go bad ; *(tempo)* to change for the worse.
guasto, a *agg (radio)* broken ; *(ascensore, telefono)* out of order ; *(cibo)* bad. ◆ *sm* breakdown ; **un ~ al motore** engine trouble.
guerra *sf* war ; **essere in ~** to be at war ; **~ mondiale** World War.
guerriglia *sf* guerrilla warfare.
gufo *sm* owl.
guglia *sf* spire.
guida *sf* guide ; *(di veicolo)*

driving ; ~ **a destra** right-hand drive ; ~ **a sinistra** left-hand drive.
guidare *vt (veicolo)* to drive ; *(accompagnare)* to guide ; **sai ~?** can you drive?
guidatore, trice *sm, f* driver.
guinzaglio *sm* lead.
guscio *sm (di lumaca)* shell.
gustare *vt (cibo)* to taste ; *(godersi)* to enjoy.
gusto *sm* taste ; **al ~ di banana** banana-flavoured ; **mangiare di ~** to enjoy one's food ; **ridere di ~** to laugh heartily ; **ci ha preso ~** he's come to like it.
gustoso, a *agg* tasty.

ha → avere.
habitat *sm inv* habitat.
hai → avere.
hall [ol] *sf inv* hall, foyer.
hamburger [am'burger] *sm inv* hamburger.
handicap ['andikap] *sm inv* handicap.
handicappato, a *agg* handicapped. ◆ *sm, f* handicapped person, disabled person.
hanno → avere.
hardware ['ard'warɛ] *sm inv* INFORM hardware.
henné *sm inv* henna.
hg *(abbr di ettogrammo)* hg.
hi-fi [ai'fai] *sm inv* hi-fi.
hippy ['ippi] *agg inv* & *smf inv* hippy.
hi-tech ['ai'tɛk] *sm inv* hi-tech.
ho → avere.
hobby *sm inv* hobby.
hockey *sm inv* hockey *(Br)*, field hockey *(Am)* ; ~ **su ghiaccio** ice hockey.
hostess *sf inv (di volo)* airhostess.
hotel *sm inv* hotel.

I

i *art mpl* **→ il.**
iceberg ['aizberg] *sm inv* iceberg.
icona *sf* INFORM icona ; *(immagine religiosa)* icon.
Iddio *sm* God.
idea *sf* idea ; *(opinione, impressione)* impression ; *(progetto)* : **avere ~ di fare qc** to think of doing sthg ; **neanche per ~!** don't even think about it! ; **non avere la più pallida ~ di qc** not to have the slightest idea of sthg ; **non ne ho ~** I've no idea ; **cambiare ~** to change one's mind.
ideale *agg* & *sm* ideal.
ideare *vt (metodo, sistema)* to devise ; *(viaggio)* to plan.
idem *avv fam (lo stesso)* the same.
identico, a, ci, che *agg* identical.
identità *sf inv* identity.
ideologia, gie *sf* ideology.
idiota, i, e *agg* idiotic, stupid. ◆ *smf* idiot.
idolo *sm* idol.
idoneo, a *agg (adatto)* : ~ **a** suitable for ; MIL fit for.
idrante *sm* hydrant.
idratante *agg* moisturizing.

idratare *vt* to moisturize.

idraulico, a, ci, che *agg* hydraulic. ◆ *sm* plumber ; **impianto ~** plumbing.

idrofilo *agg m* → **cotone**.

idrogeno *sm* hydrogen.

idroscalo *sm* seaplane base.

idrosolubile *agg* soluble (in water).

iella *sf fam* bad luck.

iena *sf (animale)* hyena ; *fig (persona)* monster.

ieri *avv* yesterday ; **~ mattina** yesterday morning ; **~ notte** last night ; **l'altro ~, ~ l'altro** the day before yesterday ; **la posta di ~** yesterday's mail.

igiene *sf* hygiene.

igienico, a, ci, che *agg* hygienic.

ignorante *agg* ignorant.

ignorare *vt (non sapere)* not to know ; *(trascurare)* to ignore.

ignoto, a *agg* unknown.

---

il *(mpl* **i** *; dav sm* **lo** *(pl* **gli***) + s+consonante, gn, ps, z ; f* **la**, *fpl* **le** *; dav sm o sf* **l'** *+ vocale e h) art* - 1. *gen* the.
- 2. *(con nome comune)* the ; **~ lago** the lake ; **la finestra** the window ; **lo studente** the student ; **l'isola** the island.
- 3. *(con nome astratto)* : **~ tempo** time ; **la vita** life.
- 4. *(con titolo)* : **~ signor Pollini** Mr Pollini ; **la regina Elisabetta** Queen Elizabeth.
- 5. *(con nomi geografici)* : **~ Po** the Po ; **le Dolomiti** the Dolomites.
- 6. *(indica possesso)* : **si è rotto ~ naso** he broke his nose ; **ha i capelli biondi** she has fair hair.
- 7. *(indica il tempo)* : **~ sabato** *(tutti i sabati)* on Saturdays ; *(quel sabato)* on Saturday ; **la sera** in the evening ; **è ~ 29 dicembre** it's the 29th of December ; **dopo le tre** after three o'clock.
- 8. *(ciascuno)* : **2 euro l'uno** 2 euros each.

---

illazione *sf* inference.

illecito, a *agg* illicit.

illegale *agg* illegal.

illegittimo, a *agg* illegitimate.

illeso, a *agg* unhurt.

illimitato, a *agg (spazio, tempo)* unlimited ; *(fiducia)* absolute.

illudere *vt* to deceive. ❑ **illudersi** *vr* to deceive o.s.

illuminare *vt* to light up, to illuminate.

illuminazione *sf* lighting ; *fig (intuizione)* enlightenment.

illusione *sf (falsa apparenza)* illusion ; *(falsa speranza)* delusion.

illusionista, i, e *smf* conjurer.

illuso, a *pp* → **illudere**. ◆ *sm, f* : **essere un ~** to be fooling o.s.

illustrare *vt* to illustrate.

illustrazione *sf* illustration, picture.

imballaggio *sm* packaging.

imballare *vt* to pack (up).

imbalsamare *vt* to embalm.

imbarazzante *agg* embarrassing.

imbarazzare *vt* to embarrass.

imbarazzato, a *agg* embarrassed.

imbarcadero *sm* landing stage.

imbarcare *vt (passeggero)* to board ; *(merce)* to load. ❑ **imbarcarsi** *vr* to board.

imbarcazione *sf* boat ; **imbarcazioni da diporto** pleasure boats.

imbarco, chi *sm (salita a bordo)* boarding ; *(carico)* loading ; *(luogo)* point of departure.

imbattersi in : imbattersi in *vr + prep* to run into.

imbecille *agg* stupid, idiotic. ◆ *smf* imbecile, idiot.

imbellire *vt* to embellish. ◆ *vi* to become more beautiful.

imbiancare *vt* to whitewash. ◆ *vi (diventare bianco)* to turn white.

imbianchino *sm* decorator.

imboccare *vt (bambino)* to feed ; *(strada)* to turn into.

imboccatura *sf (di condotto)* mouth ; *(di strada)* entrance ; *(di strumento musicale)* mouthpiece.

imbocco, chi *sm* entrance.

imbottigliare *vt (liquido)* to bottle ; *(nave)* to blockade ; **è rimasto imbottigliato** he got stuck in a traffic jam.

imbottire *vt (cuscino)* to stuff ; *(giacca)* to pad.

imbottito, a *agg* stuffed ; *(indumento)* padded, quilted ; **panino ~** filled roll.

imbranato, a *agg fam* clumsy.

imbrattare *vt* to dirty.

imbrogliare *vt (ingannare)* to deceive ; *(ingarbugliare)* to entangle.

imbroglio *sm* swindle.

imbroglione, a *sm, f* swindler.

imbronciato, a *agg* sulky.

imbucare *vt* to post *(Br)*, to mail *(Am)*.

imburrare *vt* to butter.

imbuto *sm* funnel.

imitare *vt* to imitate.

imitazione *sf* imitation.

immacolato, a *agg (bianco)* pure white ; *(puro)* immaculate, pure.

immaginare *vt (rappresentarsi)* to imagine ; *(supporre)* to suppose ; **si immagini!** don't mention it! ; **~ di fare qc** to imagine doing sthg.

immaginazione *sf* imagination.

immagine *sf* image.

immatricolare *vt (auto)* to register ; *(studente)* to enrol.

immaturo, a *agg* immature.

immedesimarsi : immedesimarsi in *vr + prep* to identify with.

immediatamente *avv* immediately.

immediato, a *agg* immediate.

immenso, a *agg* immense, enormous.

immergere *vt* to immerse. ❑ **immergersi** *vr* to dive. ❑ **immergersi in** *vr + prep (dedicarsi a)* to immerse o.s. in.

immersione *sf* dive.

immerso, a *pp* → **immergere**.

immesso, a *pp* → **immettere**.

immettere *vt* to introduce.

immigrante *smf* immigrant.

immigrato, a *sm, f* immigrant.

imminente *agg* imminent.

immobile *agg* immobile. ◆ *sm* property *(Br)*, real estate *(Am)*.
immobiliare *agg* property *(dav s) (Br)*, real estate *(dav s) (Am)*.
immodesto, a *agg* immodest.
immondizia *sf* rubbish.
immorale *agg* immoral.
immortale *agg* immortal.
immunità *sf* immunity.
immunizzare *vt* to immunize.
impacchettare *vt* to wrap.
impacciato, a *agg (goffo)* awkward ; *(imbarazzato)* embarrassed.
impacco, chi *sm* compress.
impadronirsi di : impadronirsi di *vr + prep (città, beni)* to take possession of ; *(lingua)* to master.
impalcatura *sf* scaffolding.
impallidire *vi* to go pale.
impalpabile *agg* impalpable.
impappinarsi *vr* to stumble.
imparare *vt* to learn ; **~ a fare qc** to learn to do sthg.
imparziale *agg* impartial, unbiased.
impassibile *agg* impassive.
impastare *vt (pane)* to knead ; *(mescolare)* to mix.
impasto *sm (di farina)* dough ; *(amalgama)* mixture.
impatto *sm* impact.
impaurire *vt* to frighten. ❑ **impaurirsi** *vr* to get frightened.
impaziente *agg* impatient ; **essere ~ di fare qc** to be impatient to do sthg.
impazzire *vi* to go mad.
impedimento *sm* obstacle.
impedire *vt (ostacolare)* to obstruct ; *(vietare)* : **~ a qn di fare qc** to prevent sb from doing sthg.
impegnare *vt (occupare)* to keep busy ; *(dare in pegno)* to pawn. ❑ **impegnarsi** *vr* to commit o.s. ; **impegnarsi a fare qc** to undertake to do sthg ; **impegnarsi in qc** to commit o.s. to sthg.
impegnativo, a *agg (lavoro)* demanding, exacting ; *(promessa)* binding.
impegnato, a *agg (occupato)* busy ; *(militante)* committed.
impegno *sm* commitment ; *(incombenza)* engagement, appointment.
impellente *agg* pressing, urgent.
impenetrabile *agg* impenetrable.
impennarsi *vr (cavallo)* to rear (up) ; *(moto)* to do a wheelie ; *(aereo)* to climb.
impennata *sf (di cavallo)* rearing ; *(di moto)* wheelie ; *(di aereo)* climb.
impensabile *agg* unthinkable, inconceivable.
impepata *sf* : **~ di cozze** *mussels cooked with lots of pepper or chilli (a speciality of Naples)*.
imperativo *sm* imperative.
imperatore, trice *sm, f* emperor (*f* empress).
imperfezione *sf* imperfection.
impermeabile *agg* waterproof. ◆ *sm* raincoat.
impero *sm* empire.
impersonale *agg* impersonal.
impersonare *vt* to play.

impertinente *agg* impertinent.

imperturbabile *agg* imperturbable.

imperversare *vi (calamità)* to rage ; *fam (moda)* to be all the rage.

impervio, a *agg* passable with difficulty.

impeto *sm (forza)* force ; *(slancio)* surge.

impianto *sm (installazione)* installation ; *(elettrico, del gas, antifurto)* system ; *(macchinario)* plant ; **~ di riscaldamento** heating system ; **~ sportivo** sports complex ; **impianti di risalita** ski lifts.

impiccare *vt* to hang. ❑ **impiccarsi** *vr* to hang o.s.

impiccione, a *sm, f* busybody.

impiegare *vt (tempo)* to take ; *(utilizzare)* to use ; *(assumere)* to employ. ❑ **impiegarsi** *vr* to get a job.

impiegato, a *sm, f* employee ; **~ di banca** bank clerk.

impiego, ghi *sm (lavoro)* work, employment ; *(uso)* use.

impigliare *vt* to entangle. ❑ **impigliarsi** *vr* : **impigliarsi in qc** to get entangled in sthg.

impigrire *vt* to make lazy. ◆ *vi* to become lazy. ❑ **impigrirsi** *vr* to become lazy.

implacabile *agg* implacable, relentless.

implicare *vt (comportare)* to imply, to entail ; *(coinvolgere)* to involve.

implicato, a *agg* : **essere ~ in qc** to be implicated in sthg.

implicazione *sf* implication.

implicito, a *agg* implicit.

implorare *vt* to implore.

impolverare *vt* to cover with dust. ❑ **impolverarsi** *vr* to get dusty.

imponente *agg* imposing.

impopolare *agg* unpopular.

imporre *vt (volontà, silenzio)* to impose ; *(costringere)* : **~ a qn di fare qc** to make sb do sthg. ❑ **imporsi** *vr (farsi ubbidire)* to impose o.s., to assert o.s. ; *(avere successo)* to be successful ; **imporsi di fare qc** to make o.s. do sthg.

importante *agg* important.

importanza *sf* importance ; **avere ~** to be important, to matter ; **dare ~ a qc** to give weight to sthg.

importare *vt* to import. ◆ *vi* to matter, to be important. ◆ *v impers* to matter ; **non importa!** it doesn't matter! ; **non mi importa** I don't care.

importato, a *agg* imported.

importazione *sf* importation ; *(prodotto)* import.

importo *sm* amount.

importunare *vt* to bother.

impossessarsi : **impossessarsi di** *vr + prep* to take possession of.

impossibile *agg* impossible. ◆ *sm* : **fare l' ~** to do all one can.

impostare *vt (lettera)* to post *(Br)*, to mail *(Am)* ; *(lavoro)* to plan ; *(domanda)* to formulate.

imposto, a *pp* → **imporre**.

impostore, a *sm, f* impostor.

impotente *agg* powerless ; MED impotent.

impraticabile *agg* impassable.

imprecare *vi* to curse.
imprecazione *sf* curse.
impregnare *vt* : ~ **qc (di qc)** *(inzuppare)* to soak sthg (with sthg) ; *(di fumo, odore)* to impregnate sthg (with sthg).
imprenditore, trice *sm, f (industriale)* entrepreneur ; *(appaltatore)* contractor.
impreparato, a *agg* unprepared.
impresa *sf (azione)* undertaking ; *(ditta)* business.
impresario, a *sm, f (teatrale)* impresario ; ~ **edile** building constructor.
impressionante *agg* impressive.
impressionare *vt (turbare)* to disturb ; *(colpire)* to impress. ❑ **impressionarsi** *vr* to get upset.
impressione *sf* impression ; *(sensazione)* impression, feeling ; **ho l' ~ di conoscerlo** I have the impression ○ feeling I know him ; **fare ~** *(colpire)* to impress ; *(turbare)* to upset ; **fare buona/cattiva ~** to make a good/bad impression.
impresso, a *pp* → **imprimere**.
imprestare *vt* : ~ **qc a qn** to lend sthg to sb.
imprevisto, a *agg* unexpected. ◆ *sm* unexpected event ; **salvo imprevisti** circumstances permitting.
imprigionare *vt (incarcerare)* to imprison ; *(tenere chiuso)* to confine.
imprimere *vt* to print ; *(movimento)* to transmit.
improbabile *agg* improbable, unlikely.
impronta *sf (di piede, mano, zampa)* print ; ~ **digitale** fingerprint.
improvvisamente *avv* suddenly, unexpectedly.
improvvisare *vt* to improvise. ❑ **improvvisarsi** *vr* : **si è improvvisato cuoco** he acted as cook.
improvvisata *sf* surprise.
improvviso, a *agg (inatteso)* sudden, unexpected ; *(istantaneo)* sudden ; **all' ~** suddenly.
imprudente *agg (persona)* unwise, imprudent ; *(azione)* rash.
imprudenza *sf* rash action.
impudente *agg* impudent.
impugnare *vt (stringere)* to grasp ; DIR to contest.
impugnatura *sf* handle.
impulsivo, a *agg* impulsive.
impulso *sm* impulse ; **d' ~** on impulse.
impuntarsi *vr (bambino)* to stop dead ; *(cavallo)* to jib ; *(ostinarsi)* to dig one's heels in.
imputare *vt* : ~ **qc a qn** to attribute sthg to sb ; ~ **qn di qc** to accuse sb of sthg.
imputato, a *sm, f* defendant.

in *prep* - 1. *(stato in luogo)* in ; **abitare ~ campagna** to live in the country ; **essere ~ casa** to be at home ; **l'ho lasciato ~ macchina/nella borsa** I left it in the car/in the bag ; **vivo ~ Italia** I live in Italy ; **avere qc ~ mente** to have sthg in mind.
- 2. *(moto a luogo)* to ; **andare ~ Italia** to go to Italy ; **andare ~ montagna** to go to the mountains ; **mettersi qc ~ testa** to get sthg into one's

head ; **entrare ~ macchina** to get into the car ; **entrare nella stanza** to go into the room.
- 3. *(indica un momento)* in ; **~ primavera** in spring ; **nel 1995** in 1995.
- 4. *(indica durata)* in ; **l'ho fatto ~ cinque minuti** I did it in five minutes ; **~ giornata** within the day.
- 5. *(indica modo)* : **parlare ~ italiano** to speak in Italian ; **~ silenzio** in silence ; **sono ancora ~ pigiama** I'm still in my pyjamas ; **quant'è ~ euro?** how much is that in euros? ; **~ vacanza** on holiday *(Br)*, on vacation *(Am)*.
- 6. *(indica mezzo)* by ; **pagare ~ contanti** to pay cash ; **viaggiare ~ macchina** to travel by car.
- 7. *(indica materia)* made of ; **statua ~ bronzo** bronze statue.
- 8. *(indica fine)* : **ha speso un capitale ~ libri** he spent a fortune on books ; **dare ~ omaggio** to give as a free gift ; **~ onore di** in honour of.
- 9. *(con valore distributivo)* : **siamo partiti ~ tre** three of us left ; **~ tutto sono 5 euro** it's 5 euros in total.

---

inabile *agg* : **~ (a qc)** unfit (for sthg).

inaccessibile *agg (luogo)* inaccessible ; *(persona)* unapproachable.

inaccettabile *agg* unacceptable.

inadatto, a *agg* unsuitable.

inadeguato, a *agg (insufficiente)* inadequate ; *(non idoneo)* unsuitable.

inagibile *agg* unfit for use.

inalare *vt* to inhale.

inalberarsi *vr* to get angry.

inalterato, a *agg* unchanged.

inamidare *vt* to starch.

inammissibile *agg* inadmissible.

inappetenza *sf* lack of appetite.

inappuntabile *agg (persona)* faultless, irreproachable ; *(lavoro, vestito)* impeccable.

inarcare *vt (schiena)* to arch ; **~ le sopracciglia** to raise one's eyebrows. ❑ **inarcarsi** *vr* to arch.

inaridire *vt* to dry (up). ❑ **inaridirsi** *vr* to dry up.

inaspettato, a *agg* unexpected.

inasprire *vt* to make worse. ❑ **inasprirsi** *vr* to become bitter.

inattendibile *agg* unbelievable, unreliable.

inatteso, a *agg* unexpected.

inattività *sf* inactivity.

inattuabile *agg* impractical, unfeasible.

inaudito, a *agg* unheard-of, unprecedented.

inaugurare *vt (luogo, mostra)* to open ; *(monumento)* to unveil.

inavvertenza *sf* carelessness.

inavvertitamente *avv* inadvertently.

incagliarsi *vr (nave)* to run aground ; *fig (trattative)* to break down.

incalcolabile *agg* incalculable.

incallito, a *agg (mani, piedi)* calloused ; *fig (fumatore, giocatore)* inveterate.

incalzare *vt (inseguire)* to pursue ; *fig (premere)* to press. ◆ *vi* to be imminent.

incamminarsi *vr* to set out.
incantevole *agg* enchanting.
incanto *sm (incantesimo)* enchantment ; *(asta)* auction ; **come per ~** as if by magic.
incapace *agg* incapable.
incapacità *sf (inettitudine)* incapacity ; *DIR* incompetence.
incappare : incappare in *v + prep* to run into.
incaricare *vt* to entrust ; **~ qn di qc** to entrust sb with sthg ; **~ qn di fare qc** to ask sb to do sthg. ❑ **incaricarsi di** *vr + prep* to undertake to.
incaricato, a *agg* : **~ di qc** entrusted with sthg, representative.
incarico, chi *sm* task.
incarnare *vt* to embody.
incarnirsi *vr* to become ingrown.
incartare *vt* to wrap up ; **me lo può ~?** can you wrap it up for me?
incassare *vt (denaro)* to receive ; *(assegno)* to cash ; *(colpo, offesa)* to take ; *(mobile)* to build in.
incasso *sm* takings *(pl)*.
incastrare : incastrare *vt (connettere)* to join ; *fam (intrappolare)* to catch. ❑ **incastrarsi** *vr (rimanere bloccato)* to get stuck ; *(combaciare)* to fit together.
incastro *sm* joint ; **a ~** interlocking.
incatenare *vt (legare)* to chain.
incauto, a *agg* imprudent, rash.
incavato, a *agg* hollow ; *(occhi)* sunken.
incavo *sm* hollow.
incavolarsi *vr fam* to lose one's temper.
incendiare *vt (dare fuoco a)* to set fire to. ❑ **incendiarsi** *vr* to catch fire.
incendio *sm* fire.
incenerire *vt* to incinerate.
incenso *sm* incense.
incensurato, a *agg* : **essere ~** to have no previous convictions.
incentivo *sm* incentive.
inceppare *vt* to block, to obstruct. ❑ **incepparsi** *vr* to jam.
incerata *sf (tela)* oilcloth ; *(giaccone)* oilskin.
incertezza *sf* uncertainty.
incerto, a *agg* uncertain ; *(tempo)* variable.
incetta *sf* : **fare ~ di qc** to buy sthg up.
inchiesta *sf* enquiry.
inchinarsi *vr (uomo)* to bow ; *(donna)* to curtsy.
inchino *sm (di uomo)* bow ; *(di donna)* curtsy.
inchiodare *vt* to nail.
inchiostro *sm* ink.
inciampare *vi* to trip ; **~ in qc** to trip over sthg.
incidente *sm* accident ; **~ stradale** road accident.
incidere *vt (intagliare)* to engrave ; *(canzone)* to record ; *(ascesso)* to lance. ❑ **incidere su** *v + prep* to affect.
incinta *agg f* pregnant.
incirca *avv* : **all' ~** approximately, about.
incisione *sf (taglio)* cut ; *(in arte)* engraving ; *(di disco, canzone)* recording ; *MED* incision.

incisivo, a *agg* incisive. ◆ *sm* incisor.
inciso, a *pp* → **incidere**. ◆ *sm* : **per** ~ incidentally.
incitare *vt* to incite.
incivile *agg (non civilizzato)* uncivilized ; *(maleducato)* rude.
inclinazione *sf* inclination.
includere *vt (accludere)* to enclose ; *(comprendere)* to include.
incluso, a *pp* → **includere**. ◆ *agg (accluso)* enclosed ; *(compreso)* included ; ~ **nel prezzo** included in the price.
incognito *sm* : **in** ~ incognito.
incollare *vt (sovrapporre)* to stick ; *(unire)* to stick, to glue. ❑ **incollarsi** *vr (stare vicino)* : **incollarsi a qn** to stick close to sb.
incolpare *vt* : ~ **qn (di qc)** to blame sb (for sthg).
incolume *agg* unhurt.
incominciare *vt* & *vi* to begin, to start ; ~ **a fare qc** to begin to do sthg o doing sthg, to start to do sthg o doing sthg.
incompatibile *agg* incompatible.
incompetente *agg* incompetent.
incompiuto, a *agg* unfinished, incomplete.
incompleto, a *agg* incomplete.
incomprensibile *agg* incomprehensible.
inconcepibile *agg* inconceivable.
inconcludente *agg (persona)* ineffectual ; *(discorsi)* inconclusive.
incondizionato, a *agg* unconditional.
inconfondibile *agg* unmistakable.
inconsapevole *agg* unaware.
inconscio, a, sci, sce *agg* unconscious.
incontaminato, a *agg* uncontaminated.
incontentabile *agg* impossible to please.
incontinenza *sf* incontinence.
incontrare *vt* to meet ; *(difficoltà, favore)* to meet with. ❑ **incontrarsi** *vr* to meet.
incontrario : all'incontrario *avv fam (alla rovescia)* back to front ; *(all'indietro)* backwards.
incontro *sm* meeting ; *(casuale)* encounter ; *(sportivo)* match. ◆ *avv* towards ; **andare/venire** ~ **a qn** *(avanzare verso)* to go/to come towards sb ; *(incontrare)* to go/to come to meet sb ; *fig (con compromesso)* to meet sb halfway ; **andare** ~ **a qc** *(spese)* to incur ; *(difficoltà)* to encounter.
inconveniente *sm* setback, problem.
incoraggiare *vt* to encourage.
incosciente *agg (privo di coscienza)* unconscious ; *(irresponsabile)* irresponsible.
incredibile *agg* incredible.
incrementare *vt* to increase.
incremento *sm* increase.
incrociare *vt* to cross ; *(persona, veicolo)* to pass ; ~ **le gambe/braccia** to cross one's legs/arms ; ~ **le dita** to cross one's fingers. ❑ **incrociarsi** *vr (strade, linee)* to cross ;

(persone, veicoli) to pass each other.
incrocio *sm (crocevia)* crossroads *(sg)* ; *(combinazione)* cross-breed.
incubatrice *sf* incubator.
incubo *sm* nightmare.
incurabile *agg* incurable.
incurante *agg* : ~ **di** careless of, indifferent to.
incuriosire *vt* to make curious. ❑ **incuriosirsi** *vr* to become curious.
incustodito, a *agg* unattended.
indaco *sm* indigo.
indaffarato, a *agg* busy.
indagine *sf (di polizia)* investigation ; *(studio)* research.
indebolire *vt* to weaken. ❑ **indebolirsi** *vr* to weaken, to become weak.
indecente *agg* indecent.
indecifrabile *agg* indecipherable.
indeciso, a *agg* uncertain.
indefinito, a *agg* indefinite.
indegno, a *agg* disgraceful.
indelebile *agg* indelible.
indenne *agg* unhurt.
indennità *sf inv (rimborso)* payment ; *(risarcimento)* compensation.
indescrivibile *agg* indescribable.
indeterminativo, a *agg* indefinite.
indeterminato, a *agg* indeterminate, vague.
India *sf* : **l'** ~ India.
indiano, a *agg* & *sm, f* Indian.
indicare *vt (mostrare)* to show ; *(col dito)* to point to ; *(suggerire)* to recommend.
indicatore *sm* TECNOL gauge ; ~ **della benzina** petrol gauge ; ~ **di direzione** indicator ; ~ **di velocità** speedometer.
indicazione *sf (segnalazione)* indication ; *(informazione)* piece of information ; *(prescrizione)* direction.
indice *sm (dito)* index finger ; *(di libro)* index ; *(lancetta)* needle ; *(indizio)* rating.
indietro *avv* back ; *(moto a luogo)* backwards ; **essere** ~ *(col lavoro)* to be behind ; *(orologio)* to be slow ; **rimandare** ~ to send back ; **tornare** ~ to go back ; **all'** ~ backwards.
indifeso, a *agg* defenceless.
indifferente *agg (insensibile)* indifferent ; *(irrilevante)* insignificant ; **mi è** ~ it's all the same to me.
indigeno, a *sm, f* native.
indigente *agg* destitute.
indigestione *sf* indigestion.
indigesto, a *agg* indigestible.
indimenticabile *agg* unforgettable.
indipendente *agg* independent.
indipendenza *sf* independence.
indire *vt (concorso)* to announce ; *(elezioni)* to call.
indiretto, a *agg* indirect.
indirizzare *vt (lettera, discorso)* to address ; *(mandare)* to refer.
indirizzo *sm* address ; **scuola a ~ tecnico** ≃ technical college.

indisciplinato, a *agg* undisciplined.
indiscreto, a *agg* indiscreet.
indiscrezione *sf (invadenza)* indiscretion ; *(notizia)* unconfirmed report.
indiscusso, a *agg* undisputed.
indiscutibile *agg* unquestionable.
indispensabile *agg* indispensable.
indispettire *vt* to annoy. ❑ **indispettirsi** *vr* to become annoyed.
indisponente *agg* annoying.
indistruttibile *agg* indestructible.
individuale *agg* individual.
individuare *vt* to identify.
individuo *sm* individual.
indiziato, a *agg* suspected. ◆ *sm, f* suspect.
indizio *sm (segno)* sign ; *(per polizia)* clue ; DIR piece of evidence.
indole *sf* nature.
indolenzito, a *agg* aching, stiff.
indolore *agg* painless.
indomani *sm* : **l' ~** the next day.
indossare *vt (mettere addosso)* to put on ; *(avere addosso)* to wear.
indossatore, trice *sm, f* model.
indotto, a *pp* → **indurre**.
indovinare *vt* to guess ; *(prevedere)* to predict ; *(azzeccare)* to get right.
indovinello *sm* riddle.
indovino, a *sm, f* fortune-teller.
indubbiamente *avv* undoubtedly.
indugiare *vi (temporeggiare)* to take one's time.
indugio *sm* delay ; **senza ~** without delay.
indulgente *agg* indulgent.
indumento : indumento *sm* garment ; **indumenti** *(abiti)* clothes. ◆ *(abiti)* clothes.
indurire *vt* to harden. ❑ **indurirsi** *vr* to harden.
indurre *vt* : **~ qn a fare qc** to induce sb to do sthg.
industria *sf* industry ; *(stabilimento)* industrial plant.
industriale *agg* industrial. ◆ *sm* industrialist.
inebetito, a *agg* stunned.
inebriante *agg* intoxicating.
ineccepibile *agg* unexceptionable.
inedito, a *agg* unpublished.
inefficiente *agg* inefficient.
ineluttabile *agg* inescapable.
inerente *agg* : **~ a** concerning.
inerme *agg* unarmed, defenceless.
inerzia *sf* inactivity.
inesatto, a *agg* inaccurate.
inesauribile *agg* inexhaustible.
inesistente *agg* nonexistent.
inesperienza *sf* inexperience.
inesperto, a *agg* inexperienced.
inestimabile *agg* inestimable.
inevaso, a *agg* outstanding.
inevitabile *agg* inevitable.
inevitabilmente *avv* inevitably.
in extremis *avv* in extremis.
infallibile *agg* infallible.

infantile *agg (di, per bambini)* child *(dav s)* ; *(immaturo)* infantile.
infanzia *sf (periodo)* childhood ; *(bambini)* children *(pl)* ; **prima ~** infancy.
infarinare *vt (di farina)* to cover with flour ; *(cospargere)* to sprinkle.
infarto *sm* heart attack.
infastidire *vt* to annoy. ❑ **infastidirsi** *vr* to get annoyed.
infatti *cong* in fact.
infatuarsi di : infatuarsi di *vr + prep* to become infatuated with.
infatuazione *sf* infatuation.
infedele *agg* unfaithful.
infedeltà *sf inv* infidelity.
infelice *agg* unhappy ; *(sfavorevole)* unsuccessful ; *(mal riuscito)* poor ; *(inopportuno)* unfortunate.
infelicità *sf* unhappiness.
inferiore *agg (sottostante)* lower ; *(per qualità)* inferior. ◆ *smf* inferior ; **~ a** *(minore)* below ; *(peggiore)* inferior to.
infermeria *sf* infirmary ; *(di scuola)* sickbay.
infermiere, a *sm, f* nurse.
infermo, a *agg* infirm.
infernale *agg fam (terribile)* terrible ; *(diabolico)* diabolical.
inferno *sm* hell.
inferriata *sf* grating.
infestare *vt* to infest.
infettare *vt* to infect. ❑ **infettarsi** *vr* to become infected.
infettivo, a *agg* infectious ; **malattie infettive** infectious diseases.
infezione *sf* infection.
infiammabile *agg* flammable.
infiammare *vt (incendiare)* to set alight ; MED to inflame. ❑ **infiammarsi** *vr (incendiarsi)* to catch fire ; MED to become inflamed.
infiammazione *sf* inflammation.
infilare *vt (introdurre)* to insert ; *(ago)* to thread ; *(anello, vestito)* to slip on. ❑ **infilarsi in** *vr + prep* to slip into.
infine *avv (alla fine)* finally ; *(insomma)* in short.
infinità *sf* infinity ; **un' ~ di** countless.
infinito, a *agg (illimitato)* infinite ; *(enorme, innumerevole)* countless. ◆ *sm (spazio, tempo)* infinite ; GRAMM infinitive.
infischiarsi : infischiarsene di *vr + prep* not to care about.
inflazione *sf* inflation.
inflessibile *agg* inflexible.
infliggere *vt* to inflict.
inflitto, a *pp* → **infliggere**.
influente *agg* influential.
influenza *sf* influence ; *(malattia)* flu ; **avere ~ su** to have an influence on ; **avere l' ~** to have flu.
influenzare *vt* to influence.
influire : influire su *v + prep* to have an effect on.
influsso *sm* influence.
infondato, a *agg* unfounded.
infondere *vt* to instil.
inforcare *vt (fieno)* to fork up ; *(bicicletta, moto)* to get onto ; *(occhiali)* to put on.
informale *agg* informal.
informare *vt* : **~ qn (di qc)** to inform sb (of sthg). ❑ **informarsi**

vr : **informarsi di** o **su** to find out about.
informatica *sf* information technology.
informativo, a *agg* informative.
informatore *sm* informer.
informazione *sf* piece of information ; **chiedere informazioni (a qn)** to ask (sb) for information ; **'informazioni'** 'information'.
informicolirsi *vr* : **mi si è informicolita una gamba** I've got pins and needles in my leg.
infortunio *sm* accident.
infossarsi *vr* *(terreno)* to sink ; *(guance)* to become hollow.
infradito *sm inv o sf inv* flip-flop.
infrangere *vt* to break. ❑ **infrangersi** *vr* to break.
infrangibile *agg* unbreakable.
infranto, a *pp* → **infrangere.** ◆ *agg* broken.
infrazione *sf* infringement.
infreddolito, a *agg* chilled.
infuori *avv* : **all' ~** outwards ; **all' ~ di** apart from.
infusione *sf* infusion.
infuso, a *pp* → **infondere.** ◆ *sm* herb tea.
ingannare *vt (imbrogliare)* to deceive ; *(tempo)* to while away. ❑ **ingannarsi** *vr* to be mistaken.
inganno *sm* deception.
ingarbugliare *vt* to tangle ; *(situazione, conti)* to muddle. ❑ **ingarbugliarsi** *vr* to become tangled ; *(situazione)* to become muddled ; *(impappinarsi)* to falter.
ingegnere *sm* engineer.
ingegneria *sf* engineering.
ingegno *sm (intelligenza)* intelligence ; *(creatività)* ingenuity.
ingegnoso, a *agg* ingenious.
ingelosire *vt* to make jealous. ❑ **ingelosirsi** *vr* to become jealous.
ingente *agg* huge.
ingenuo, a *agg* naive.
ingerire *vt* to ingest.
ingessare *vt* to put in plaster.
Inghilterra *sf* : **l' ~** England.
inghiottire *vt* to swallow ; *(sopportare)* to put up with.
ingiallire *vi* to yellow.
ingigantire *vt (foto)* to enlarge ; *fig (problema)* to exaggerate.
inginocchiarsi *vr* to kneel down.
ingiù *avv* : **(all') ~** downwards.
ingiustizia *sf (qualità)* injustice ; *(atto)* unjust act.
ingiusto, a *agg* unfair.
inglese *agg* English. ◆ *smf* Englishman (*f* Englishwoman). ◆ *sm (lingua)* English.
ingoiare *vt (inghiottire)* to swallow ; *fig (sopportare)* to put up with.
ingolfare *vt* to flood. ❑ **ingolfarsi** *vr* to flood.
ingombrante *agg* cumbersome.
ingombrare *vt (passaggio, strada)* to obstruct ; *(tavolo, stanza)* to clutter up.
ingombro, a *agg* obstructed. ◆ *sm* : **essere d' ~** to be in the way.
ingordo, a *agg* greedy.
ingorgo, ghi *sm* traffic jam.

ingranaggio *sm (meccanismo)* gear ; *fig (operazioni, attività)* machinery.
ingranare *vt* to engage. ◆ *vi (ingranaggio)* to engage ; *fam (prendere avvio)* to get going.
ingrandimento *sm* enlargement ; *(ottico)* magnification.
ingrandire *vt* to enlarge ; *(con microscopio, lente)* to magnify. ❑ **ingrandirsi** *vr (di misura)* to get bigger ; *(d'importanza)* to become more important.
ingrassare *vi* to put on weight. ◆ *vt (animali)* to fatten up ; *(motore)* to grease.
ingrediente *sm* ingredient.
ingresso *sm (porta)* entrance ; *(stanza)* hall ; *(permesso di entrare)* admission ; '~ **gratuito**' 'admission free' ; '~ **libero**' 'admission free'.
ingrossare *vt (gambe, fegato)* to cause to swell. ❑ **ingrossarsi** *vr (gambe, fegato)* to swell.
ingrosso *avv* : **all' ~** *(vendita)* wholesale ; *(grossomodo)* about, roughly.
inguine *sm* groin.
inibire *vt* to inhibit.
iniettare *vt* to inject.
iniezione *sf* injection.
inimicare *vt* : **inimicarsi qn** to make an enemy of sb.
inimitabile *agg* inimitable.
ininterrottamente *avv* nonstop.
ininterrotto, a *agg* continuous, unbroken.
iniziale *agg* & *sf* initial.
inizialmente *avv* initially.
iniziare *vt* & *vi* to begin, to start ; ~ **qn a qc** to introduce sb to sthg ; ~ **a fare qc** to begin ○ start to do sthg.
iniziativa *sf* initiative ; **prendere l'** ~ to take the initiative.
inizio *sm* start, beginning ; **all'** ~ at the start, at the beginning ; **dare** ~ **a qc** to start ○ begin sthg ; **avere** ~ to start , to begin.
innaffiare = **annaffiare.**
innalzare *vt* to erect.
innamorarsi *vr* : ~ **(di qn)** to fall in love (with sb).
innamorato, a *agg* : ~ **(di qn)** in love (with sb).
innanzi *avv* in front. ◆ *prep (davanti a)* in front of ; *(prima di)* before.
innanzitutto *avv* first of all.
innato, a *agg* innate.
innervosire *vt* to make nervous. ❑ **innervosirsi** *vr* to get nervous.
innescare *vt (bomba)* to prime ; *fig (fenomeno, meccanismo)* to trigger.
innestare *vt (pianta)* to graft ; *(meccanismo, marcia)* to engage.
inno *sm* hymn ; ~ **nazionale** national anthem.
innocente *agg* innocent.
innocuo, a *agg* harmless.
innovazione *sf* innovation.
innumerevole *agg* countless.
inodore *agg* odourless.
inoffensivo, a *agg* inoffensive.
inoltrare *vt* to forward. ❑ **inoltrarsi** *vr* to advance.
inoltrato, a *agg* late.

inoltre *avv* besides.
inondazione *sf* flood.
inopportuno, a *agg* inappropriate.
inorridire *vt* to horrify. ◆ *vi* to be horrified.
inosservato, a *agg* : **passare ~** to go unnoticed.
inquadrare *vt (personaggio, avvenimento)* to place ; *(con telecamera)* : **~ qn/qc** to get sb/sthg in the shot.
inquadratura *sf* shot.
inqualificabile *agg* contemptible.
inquietante *agg* disturbing.
inquilino, a *sm, f* tenant.
inquinamento *sm* pollution.
inquinare *vt (contaminare)* to pollute ; *fig (prove)* to corrupt.
inquinato, a *agg* polluted.
insabbiare *vt* to shelve. ❑ **insabbiarsi** *vr (nave)* to run aground ; *(pratica, progetto)* to be shelved.
insaccato *sm* sausage.
insalata *sf (di verdure)* salad ; *(lattuga)* lettuce ; **~ mista** mixed salad ; **~ di mare** seafood salad ; **~ di riso** rice salad ; **~ russa** Russian salad *(cold diced cooked vegetables mixed with mayonnaise)*.
insalatiera *sf* salad bowl.
insaponare *vt* to soap. ❑ **insaponarsi** *vr* to soap o.s.
insapore *agg* tasteless.
insaporire *vt* to flavour.
insaputa *sf* : **all' ~ di qn** without sb's knowledge.
inscenare *vt* to stage.
insegna *sf* sign.
insegnamento *sm* teaching.
insegnante *smf* teacher.
insegnare *vt* & *vi* to teach ; **~ qc a qn** to teach sb sthg ; **~ a qn a fare qc** to teach sb to do sthg.
inseguire *vt* to pursue.
insenatura *sf* inlet, creek.
insensato, a *agg (persona)* foolish ; *(discorso, idea)* senseless.
insensibile *agg* insensitive.
inseparabile *agg* inseparable.
inserire *vt (introdurre)* to insert ; *(includere)* to put in. ❑ **inserirsi** *vr* : **inserirsi in qc** *(entrare a far parte di)* to become part of sthg.
inserto *sm* insert.
inserviente *smf* attendant.
inserzione *sf* advertisement.
insetticida, i *sm* insecticide.
insetto *sm* insect.
insicurezza *sf* insecurity.
insicuro, a *agg* insecure.
insidia *sf* hidden danger.
insieme *avv* together. ◆ *sm (totalità)* whole ; *MAT* set. ◆ *prep* : **~ a** o **con** with ; **mettere ~** *(raccogliere)* to put together ; **tutto ~** all together ; **tutti ~** all together ; **nell' ~** taken as a whole.
insignificante *agg* insignificant.
insinuare *vt* to insinuate.
insinuazione *sf* insinuation.
insipido, a *agg* insipid.
insistente *agg (persona, richieste)* insistent ; *(pioggia, dolore)* persistent.
insistere *vi* to insist ; **~ a** o **col fare qc** to persist in doing sthg.

insoddisfacente *agg* unsatisfactory.
insoddisfatto, a *agg* : ~ di dissatisfied with.
insolazione *sf* sunstroke.
insolente *agg* insolent.
insolito, a *agg* unusual.
insoluto, a *agg* *(non risolto)* unsolved ; *(non pagato)* outstanding.
insomma *avv* well. ◆ *esclam* for Heaven's sake!
insonne *agg* *(persona)* unable to sleep ; *(notte)* sleepless.
insonnia *sf* insomnia.
insonnolito, a *agg* sleepy.
insopportabile *agg* unbearable.
insorgere *vi* *(popolo)* to rise up ; *(difficoltà)* to arise.
insospettire *vt* to arouse suspicions in. ❑ **insospettirsi** *vr* to become suspicious.
insozzare *vt* to dirty.
insperato, a *agg* unhoped-for.
inspiegabile *agg* inexplicable.
inspirare *vt* to breathe in.
installare *vt* to install.
instaurare *vt* to establish.
insù *avv* : (all') ~ upwards.
insuccesso *sm* failure.
insudiciare *vt* to dirty. ❑ **insudiciarsi** *vr* to get dirty.
insufficiente *agg* insufficient.
insulina *sf* insulin.
insultare *vt* to insult.
insulto *sm* insult.
intaccare *vt* to attack ; *(fare tacche in)* to cut into ; *(risparmi)* to break into.
intanto *avv* *(nel frattempo)* meanwhile.
intarsio *sm* inlay.
intasare *vt* to block. ❑ **intasarsi** *vr* to become blocked.
intatto, a *agg* *(intero)* intact ; *(mai toccato)* untouched.
integrale *agg* *(totale)* complete ; *(pane, farina)* wholemeal.
integrare *vt* to integrate. ❑ **integrarsi** *vr* to integrate.
integrità *sf* integrity.
integro, a *agg* *(intero)* intact ; *(onesto)* honest.
intelaiatura *sf* framework.
intelletto *sm* intellect.
intellettuale *agg* & *smf* intellectual.
intelligente *agg* intelligent.
intelligenza *sf* intelligence.
intemperie *sfpl* bad weather *(sg)*.
intendere *vt* *(capire)* to understand ; *(udire)* to hear ; *(avere intenzione di)* : ~ fare qc to intend to do sthg ; non intende ragioni he won't listen to reason ; intendersela con qn to have an affair with sb. ❑ **intendersi di** *vr + prep* to know about.
intenditore, trice *sm, f* expert.
intensificare *vt* to intensify. ❑ **intensificarsi** *vr* to intensify.
intensità *sf* intensity.
intensivo, a *agg* intensive.
intenso, a *agg* intense.
intento, a *sm* intention. ◆ *agg* : ~ (a fare qc) intent (on doing sthg).
intenzione *sf* intention ; aver ~ di fare qc to intend to do sthg.

interamente *avv* completely.
intercalare *sm* catchphrase. ◆ *vt* to insert.
intercettare *vt* to intercept.
intercity [inter'siti] *sm inv fast train connecting major Italian cities.*
interdetto, a *agg* taken aback.
interessamento *sm (interesse)* interest ; *(intervento)* intervention.
interessante *agg* interesting ; **in stato ~** *(incinta)* expecting.
interessare *vt (destare l'interesse di)* to interest ; *(riguardare)* to concern. ◆ *vi* : **~ a qn** to interest sb ; **ciò non mi interessa** I'm not interested in it. ❑ **interessarsi a** *vr + prep* to be interested in ; **interessarsi di** *(per informazioni)* to find out about ; *(per lavoro, hobby)* to be interested in.
interessato, a *agg (partecipe)* interested ; *(calcolatore)* self-interested.
interesse *sm* interest ; *(tornaconto)* self-interest. ❑ **interessi** *smpl* interests.
interferire *vi* to interfere.
interiezione *sf* interjection.
interiora *sfpl* entrails.
interiore *agg (lato, parte)* interior.
interlocutore, trice *sm, f* interlocutor.
intermezzo *sm* interval.
interminabile *agg* endless.
intermittente *agg* intermittent.
internazionale *agg* international.
interno, a *agg (di dentro)* interior, internal ; *(nazionale)* domestic. ◆ *sm* interior ; *(telefono)* extension ; *(in indirizzo)* : **~ 20** flat 20 ; **all' ~** inside. ❑ **interni** *smpl* : **ministero degli Interni** ≃ Home Office *(Br)*, Department of the Interior *(Am)*.
intero, a *agg* whole ; *(prezzo)* full ; *(latte)* full-cream ; **per ~** in full.
interpretare *vt* to interpret ; *(recitare)* to perform.
interprete *smf (traduttore)* interpreter ; *(attore, musicista)* performer.
interrogare *vt (studente)* to examine ; *(sospetto)* to question.
interrogativo, a *agg (sguardo)* enquiring ; *GRAMM* interrogative. ◆ *sm* question.
interrogazione *sf* oral examination.
interrompere *vt* to interrupt ; *(linea telefonica, strada)* to cut off. ❑ **interrompersi** *vr* to stop.
interrotto, a *pp* → **interrompere**. ◆ *agg* cut off.
interruttore *sm* switch.
intersecare *vt* to intersect.
interurbana *sf* long-distance call.
interurbano, a *agg (trasporti)* intercity ; *(chiamata)* long-distance.
intervallo *sm* interval.
intervenire *vi* to intervene ; *(partecipare)* to take part ; *MED* to operate.
intervento *sm (intromissione)* intervention ; *(partecipazione)*

participation ; *(discorso)* speech ; *MED* operation.
intervenuto, a *pp* → intervenire.
intervista *sf* interview.
intesa *sf (tra persone)* understanding ; *(tra stati)* agreement.
inteso, a *pp* → intendere. ◆ *agg* : resta ~ che it is understood that ; siamo intesi? are we agreed?
intestare *vt (lettera)* to address ; ~ qc a qn *(casa, auto)* to register sthg in sb's name ; *(assegno)* to make sthg out to sb.
intestino *sm* intestine.
Internet *sm inv* Internet.
intimare *vt* to order.
intimidire *vt* to intimidate.
intimità *sf (spazio privato)* privacy ; *(familiarità)* intimacy.
intimo, a *agg* intimate ; *(cerimonia, parti)* private ; *(interiore)* innermost ; *(igiene)* personal. ◆ *sm (persona)* close friend.
intimorire *vt* to frighten.
intingolo *sm* sauce.
intitolare *vt (libro, film)* to entitle ; *(via, piazza)* : ~ a to name after. ❑ **intitolarsi** *vr* to be entitled.
intollerabile *agg* unbearable.
intollerante *agg* intolerant.
intolleranza *sf* intolerance.
intonaco, ci o **chi** *sm* plaster.
intonare *vt (canto)* to intone ; *(vestiti)* : ~ qc a qc to match sthg with sthg. ❑ **intonarsi** *vr* to go together.
intontire *vt* to stun.
intorno *avv* around, round. ◆ *prep* : ~ a around.
intossicare *vt* to poison.
intossicato, a *agg* poisoned.
intossicazione *sf* poisoning.
intraducibile *agg* untranslatable.
intralciare *vt* to hamper.
intramontabile *agg* timeless.
intramuscolare *agg* → iniezione.
intransigente *agg* intransigent.
intransitivo, a *agg* intransitive.
intraprendente *agg* enterprising.
intraprendere *vt* to undertake.
intrapreso, a *pp* → intraprendere.
intrattabile *agg (persona)* intractable ; *(prezzo)* non-negotiable.
intrattenere *vt (persona)* to entertain ; *(relazioni, rapporti)* to maintain. ❑ **intrattenersi** *vr* : intrattenersi su qc to dwell on sthg.
intrecciare *vt (capelli)* to plait, to braid ; *(nastri)* to intertwine. ❑ **intrecciarsi** *vr (fili)* to intertwine.
intrigante *agg* scheming.
intrigo, ghi *sm (macchinazione)* intrigue.
introdurre *vt* to introduce ; *(moneta)* to insert ; 'vietato ~ cani' 'dogs not allowed'. ❑ **introdursi** *vr (uso, tecnica)* to be introduced ; *(entrare)* to enter.
introduzione *sf* introduction.
introito *sm (incasso)* income.
intromettersi *vr (immischiarsi)*

to interfere ; *(interporsi)* to intervene.

introvabile *agg* not to be found.

introverso, a *agg* introverted.

intruso, a *sm, f* intruder.

intuire *vt (cogliere)* to grasp ; *(accorgersi)* to realize.

intuito *sm* intuition.

intuizione *sf* intuition.

inumidire *vt* to dampen. ❑ **inumidirsi** *vr* to become damp.

inutile *agg* useless ; *(superfluo)* pointless.

inutilmente *avv* in vain.

invadente *agg* intrusive.

invadere *vt* to invade.

invaghirsi di : invaghirsi di *vr + prep* to take a fancy to.

invalido, a *agg* disabled. ◆ *sm, f* disabled person.

invano *avv* in vain.

invasione *sf* invasion.

invasore *sm* invader.

invecchiare *vi (persona)* to grow old ; *(vino)* to age. ◆ *vt (vino, formaggio)* to age ; *(persona)* to make look older.

invece *avv* but. ◆ *prep* : ~ **di** instead of.

inveire *vi* : ~ **(contro)** to rail (against).

inventare *vt* to invent ; **si è inventato tutto** he made it all up.

inventario *sm (registrazione)* stocktaking ; *(lista)* inventory.

inventore, trice *sm, f* inventor.

invenzione *sf* invention.

invernale *agg* winter *(dav s)*.

inverno *sm* winter ; **in** ○ **d'** ~ in (the) winter.

inverosimile *agg* unbelievable.

inversione *sf (di ordine, tendenza)* inversion ; *(di marcia)* U-turn.

inverso, a *agg* & *sm* opposite ; **fare qc all'** ~ to do sthg the wrong way round.

invertire *vt (ordine)* to invert ; ~ **la marcia** to do a U-turn.

invertito, a *agg (rovesciato)* inverted. ◆ *sm (omosessuale)* homosexual.

investimento *sm* investment.

investire *vt (denaro)* to invest ; *(persona, animale)* to knock down.

inviare *vt* to send.

inviato, a *sm, f (incaricato)* envoy ; *(giornalista)* correspondent.

invidia *sf* envy.

invidiare *vt* to envy ; ~ **qc a qn** to envy sb sthg.

invidioso, a *agg* envious.

invincibile *agg (imbattibile)* invincible.

invio *sm (spedizione)* dispatching ; *(merci)* consignment.

inviperito, a *agg* furious.

invischiarsi in : invischiarsi in *vr + prep* to get involved in.

invisibile *agg* invisible.

invitare *vt* to invite ; ~ **qn a fare qc** *(proporre di)* to invite sb to do sthg ; *(sollecitare)* to request sb to do sthg.

invitato, a *sm, f* guest.

invito *sm* invitation.

invocare *vt (Dio)* to invoke ; *(chiedere)* to beg for ; *(legge, diritto)* to cite.

invogliare *vt* to tempt.
involontario, a *agg* involuntary.
involtino *sm thin slice of meat, rolled up and sometimes stuffed*; ~ **primavera** spring roll.
involucro *sm* covering.
inzaccherare *vt* to splash with mud.
inzuppare *vt* to soak; *(biscotto)* to dip.
io *pron* I; **sono** ~ it's me; ~ **stesso** I myself.
iodio *sm* iodine.
iogurt = **yogurt**.
Ionio *sm*: **lo** ~, **il mar** ~ the Ionian (Sea).
ipertensione *sf* hypertension.
ipnosi *sf* hypnosis.
ipnotizzare *vt* to hypnotize.
ipocrisia *sf* hypocrisy.
ipocrita, i, e *agg* hypocritical. ◆ *smf* hypocrite.
ipoteca, che *sf* mortgage.
ipotesi *sf inv* hypothesis.
ippica *sf* horse racing.
ippico, a, ci, che *agg* horse *(dav s)*.
ippodromo *sm* racecourse.
ippopotamo *sm* hippopotamus.
Iran *sm*: **l'** ~ Iran.
Iraq *sm*: **l'** ~ Iraq.
iride *sf (di occhio)* iris; *(arcobaleno)* rainbow.
iris *sf inv* iris.
Irlanda *sf*: **l'** ~ Ireland; **l'** ~ **del Nord** Northern Ireland.
irlandese *agg* Irish. ◆ *smf* Irishman (*f* Irishwoman).
ironia *sf* irony.
ironico, a, ci, che *agg* ironic.
irradiare *vt* to light up. ◆ *vi* to radiate.
irraggiungibile *agg* unreachable.
irragionevole *agg* unreasonable.
irrazionale *agg* irrational.
irreale *agg* unreal.
irrecuperabile *agg (oggetto)* irretrievable; *fig (persona)* irredeemable.
irregolare *agg* irregular; *(discontinuo)* uneven.
irregolarità *sf inv* irregularity; *(discontinuità)* unevenness.
irremovibile *agg* inflexible.
irreparabile *agg* irreparable.
irrequieto, a *agg* restless.
irresponsabile *agg* irresponsible.
irreversibile *agg* irreversible.
irriducibile *agg* unyielding.
irrigare *vt* to irrigate.
irrigidirsi *vr* to stiffen.
irrilevante *agg* insignificant.
irrisorio, a *agg* ridiculous.
irritabile *agg* irritable.
irritante *agg* irritating.
irritare *vt* to irritate. ❑ **irritarsi** *vr* to become irritated.
irrompere : irrompere in *v + prep* to burst into.
irrotto, a → **irrompere**.
irruente *agg* impetuous.
irruzione *sf* raid.

iscritto, a *pp* → iscrivere. ◆ *agg* : essere ~ a qc *(ad un circolo, partito)* to be a member of sthg ; *(all'università)* to be enrolled in sthg ; *(ad un esame)* to be entered for sthg ; per ~ in writing.

iscrivere *vt* : ~ qn (a qc) *(scuola)* to register sb (at sthg), to enrol sb (at sthg) ; *(corso)* to register sb (for sthg) , to enrol sb (for sthg). ❑ **iscriversi** *vr + prep* : iscriversi (a) *(circolo, partito)* to become a member (of) ; *(university)* to enrol (in) ; *(esame)* to enter.

iscrizione *sf (a università)* enrolment ; *(a esame)* entry ; *(a partito)* membership ; *(funeraria)* inscription.

Islanda *sf* : l' ~ Iceland.

islandese *agg* Icelandic. ◆ *smf* Icelander.

isola *sf* island ; ~ pedonale pedestrian precinct.

isolamento *sm (solitudine)* isolation ; *(elettrico, termico)* insulation ; *(acustico)* soundproofing.

isolante *agg* insulating. ◆ *sm* insulator.

isolare *vt (tenere lontano)* to isolate ; *(da freddo, corrente elettrica)* to insulate ; *(da rumore)* to soundproof. ❑ **isolarsi** *vr* to cut o.s. off.

isolato, a *agg* isolated. ◆ *sm* block.

ispettore *sm* inspector.

ispezionare *vt* to inspect.

ispezione *sf* inspection.

ispirare *vt* to inspire. ❑ **ispirarsi a** *vr + prep* to draw one's inspiration from.

Israele *sm* Israel.

issare *vt* to hoist.

istantanea *sf* snapshot.

istantaneo, a *agg* instantaneous, instant.

istante *sm* instant ; all' ~ instantly, at once.

isterico, a, ci, che *agg* hysterical.

istigare *vt* : ~ qn a fare qc to incite sb to do sthg.

istinto *sm* instinct.

istituire *vt* to institute.

istituto *sm (organismo)* institute ; *(universitario)* department ; ~ di bellezza beauty salon.

istituzione *sf* institution ; le istituzioni *(le autorità)* the Establishment.

istmo *sm (GEOG)* isthmus.

istrice *sm (animale)* porcupine.

istruire *vt (insegnare a)* to teach ; *(informare)* to instruct.

istruito, a *agg* educated.

istruttore, trice *sm, f* instructor.

istruzione *sf (insegnamento)* education ; *(cultura)* learning. ❑ **istruzioni** *sfpl* : istruzioni (per l'uso) instructions (for use).

Italia *sf* : l' ~ Italy.

italiano, a *agg* & *sm, f* Italian.

itinerario *sm (percorso)* route ; *(descrizione)* itinerary ; ~ turistico *(percorso)* tourist route.

Iugoslavia *sf* : la ~ Yugoslavia.

IVA *sf (abbr di Imposta sul Valore Aggiunto)* VAT.

J

jazz [dʒɛts] *sm* jazz.
jeans [dʒins] *smpl* jeans. ◆ *sm (tessuto)* denim.
jeep® [dʒip] *sf inv* Jeep®.
jolly ['dʒɔlli] *sm inv* joker.
Jonio = Ionio.
jota *sf bean soup with onions and turnips marinated in wine (a speciality of Friuli).*
joystick ['dʒɔi'stik] *sm inv INFORM* joystick.
Jugoslavia = Iugoslavia.
juke-box [dʒu'bɔks] *sm inv* juke-box.

K

karaoke *sm inv (gioco)* karaoke ; *(locale)* karaoke bar.
karatè *sm* karate.
Kenia *sm* : il ~ Kenya.
kg *(abbr di chilogrammo)* kg.
killer *smf inv* killer.
kit *sm inv (insieme)* kit ; *INFORM* kit, package.
kitsch [kitʃ] *agg inv* kitsch.
kiwi ['kiwi] *sm inv* kiwi fruit.
km *(abbr di chilometro)* km.
k.o. *avv* : mettere qn ~ to knock sb out.
koala *sm inv* koala.
Kosovo *sm* : le ~ Kosovo.
K-way® [ki'wei] *sm inv* cagoule.

L

l' → la, lo.
la (l' *dav vocale e h) art f* the → il. ◆ *pron (persona)* her ; *(animale, cosa)* it ; *(forma di cortesia)* you.
là *avv* there ; di ~ *(nella stanza accanto)* in there ; *(moto da luogo)* from there ; *(nei paraggi)* over there ; al di ~ di beyond.
labbro (*pl f* labbra) *sm ANAT* lip.
labirinto *sm (di strade, corridoi)* labyrinth ; *(giardino)* maze.
laboratorio *sm (scientifico)* laboratory ; *(artigianale)* workshop ; ~ linguistico language laboratory.
lacca, che *sf (per capelli)* lacquer, hair spray ; *(vernice)* lacquer.
laccio *sm* lace.
lacerare *vt* to tear, to rip. ❑ **lacerarsi** *vr* to tear.
lacero, a *agg* torn.
lacrima *sf* tear ; in lacrime in tears.
lacrimogeno *agg m* → gas.
lacuna *sf* gap.
ladro, a *sm, f* thief.
laggiù *avv (in basso)* down there ; *(lontano)* over there.
lagnarsi *vr (piagnucolare)* to moan, to groan ; *(protestare)* : ~ (di) to complain (about).
lago, ghi *sm* lake.

I LAGHI

The most famous of the many Italian lakes are undoubtedly those in northern Italy: Lake

Garda (the largest), Lake Maggiore and Lake Como. Millions of Italian and foreign tourists alike visit them every year, attracted by their scenic splendour and pleasant climate, the grand villas and lush gardens lining their shores, and the many varieties of wild flower to be found in the area. In summer the lakes attract swimmers, sunbathers and watersports enthusiasts looking for an alternative to the coastal resorts.

---

laguna *sf* lagoon.
laico, a, ci, che *agg* lay *(dav s)*.
lama *sf* blade.
lamentarsi *vr (emettere lamenti)* to groan, to moan ; ~ **(di)** *(dimostrarsi insoddisfatto)* to complain (about).
lamentela *sf* complaint, complaining *(sg)*.
lametta *sf* razor blade.
lamiera *sf* sheet metal.
lampada *sf* lamp ; **fare la ~** to use a sunlamp ; **~ da tavolo** table lamp.
lampadario *sm* chandelier.
lampadina *sf* light bulb ; **~ tascabile** torch *(Br)*, flashlight *(Am)*.
lampeggiare *vi* to flash.
lampeggiatore *sm (freccia)* indicator ; *(di ambulanza)* flashing light.
lampione *sm* streetlight.
lampo *sm (fulmine)* flash of lightning ; *(bagliore)* flash. ◆ *sf inv (cerniera)* zip *(Br)*, zipper *(Am)*.
lampone *sm* raspberry.
lana *sf* wool ; **pura ~ vergine** pure new wool.
lancetta *sf* hand.
lancia, ce *sf (arma)* lance ; *(imbarcazione)* launch.
lanciare *vt (pietra, palla)* to throw ; *(missile)* to launch ; *(grido)* to give ; *(insulto)* to hurl ; *fig (appello, moda, prodotto)* to launch. ❑ **lanciarsi** *vr* to throw o.s. ; **lanciarsi in qc** *(mare)* to throw o.s. into sthg ; *(impresa)* to embark on sthg.
lancinante *agg* piercing, shooting.
lancio *sm (tiro)* throw ; *(di prodotti, missile)* launch.
languido, a *agg* languid.
languore *sm (di stomaco)* hunger pangs *(pl)*.
lapide *sf (funeraria)* tombstone ; *(commemorativa)* plaque.
lapis *sm inv* pencil.
lapsus *sm inv* slip.
lardo *sm* lard, bacon fat.
larghezza *sf (dimensione)* width, breadth ; *(abbondanza)* generosity.
largo, a, ghi, ghe *agg* wide, broad ; *(indumento)* loose ; *(percentuale, parte)* large. ◆ *sm* width ; *(piazza)* square ; *(alto mare)* : **andare al ~** to take to the open sea ; **è ~ 10 metri** it's 10 metres wide ; **stare** ○ **tenersi alla larga (da)** to keep one's distance (from) ; **farsi ~** to push one's way.
larva *sf (insetto)* larva.
lasagne *sfpl* lasagne *(sg)*.
lasciare *vt* to leave ; *(cessare di tenere)* to let go of ; **posso ~ i**

bagagli in camera? can I leave the luggage in the room? ; ~ la porta aperta to leave the door open ; ~ qn in pace to leave sb in peace ; lasciar detto a qn che ... to leave sb word that ... ; ~ a desiderare to leave a lot to be desired ; prendere o ~ take it or leave it ; ~ la presa to let go.

◆ *vb aus* : lasciami vedere let me see ; lascia che faccia come vuole let him do as he wants ; lascia perdere! forget it! ; lasciar credere qc a qn to let sb believe sthg ; lascialo stare! leave him alone!

❑ **lasciarsi** *vr (separarsi)* to leave each other ; lasciarsi andare to let o.s. go ; lasciarsi convincere to allow o.s. to be persuaded.

laser *sm inv* & *agg inv* laser.

lassativo *sm* laxative.

lassù *avv* up there.

lastra *sf (di ghiaccio, vetro)* sheet ; *(di pietra)* slab ; *(radiografia)* plate.

laterale *agg* lateral, side *(dav s)*.

latino, a *agg* & *sm* Latin.

latinoamericano, a *agg* Latin-American.

latitante *smf* fugitive.

latitudine *sf* latitude.

lato *sm* side ; a ~ (di qc) beside (sthg) ; da un ~ ... dall'altro ... on the one hand ... on the other hand ...

latta *sf* tin.

lattaio, a *sm, f* milkman (*f* milkwoman).

lattante *smf* baby.

latte *sm* milk ; ~ detergente cleansing milk ; ~ intero full cream milk ; ~ magro o scremato skimmed milk ; ~ in polvere powdered milk ; ~ di soia soya milk.

latteria *sf* dairy.

latticini *smpl* dairy products.

lattina *sf* can.

lattuga, ghe *sf* lettuce.

laurea *sf* degree.

laurearsi *vr* to graduate ; ~ in qc to graduate in sthg.

laureato, a *agg* & *sm, f* graduate ; è ~ in legge he has a law degree.

lava *sf* lava.

lavaggio *sm* washing ; ~ automatico *(per auto)* car wash.

lavagna *sf* blackboard.

lavanda *sf* lavender ; fare una ~ gastrica a qn to pump sb's stomach.

lavanderia *sf* laundry ; ~ automatica launderette ; ~ a secco dry cleaner's.

lavandino *sm* sink.

lavapiatti *sf inv* dishwasher.

lavare *vt* to wash ; ~ a secco qc to dry-clean sthg ; lavarsi le mani to wash one's hands ; lavarsi i denti to clean one's teeth. ❑ **lavarsi** *vr* to wash o.s.

lavasecco *sm inv o sf inv* dry cleaner's.

lavastoviglie *sf inv* dishwasher.

lavatrice *sf* washing machine.

lavorare *vi* & *vt* to work ; ~ a maglia to knit.

lavorativo, a *agg* working *(dav s)*.

lavorato, a *agg (mobile, tessuto)* elaborate ; *(terreno)* cultivated.

lavoratore, trice *sm, f* worker.

lavorazione *sf (di legno)* carving ; *(di cotone)* manufacture.
lavoro *sm* work ; *(occupazione)* work, job ; **'lavori in corso'** 'men at work' ; **lavori stradali** road works.
le *art fpl* the → **il.** ◆ *pron (complemento oggetto)* them ; *(a lei)* (to) her ; *(forma di cortesia)* (to) you.
leader ['lider] *smf inv* leader.
leale *agg* loyal.
lecca lecca *sm inv* lollipop.
leccare *vt* to lick.
lecito, a *agg* permitted.
lega, ghe *sf (associazione)* league ; *(alleanza politica)* alliance ; *(di metalli)* alloy.
legale *agg* legal. ◆ *smf (avvocato)* lawyer.
legalizzare *vt* to legalize.
legame *sm (sentimentale)* tie ; *(nesso)* link.
legare *vt (con catena, laccio)* to tie (up) ; *(sog : sentimento, interesse)* to bind.
legge *sf* law.
leggenda *sf (favola)* legend ; *(didascalia)* key.
leggendario, a *agg* legendary.
leggere *vt & vi* to read.
leggerezza *sf (di materiale, corpo)* lightness ; *fig (sconsideratezza)* thoughtlessness.
leggero, a *agg* light ; *(caffè, tè)* weak ; *(di poca importanza)* slight.
legittimo, a *agg* legitimate ; **legittima difesa** self-defence.
legna *sf* firewood.
legname *sm* wood.
legno *sm (materia)* wood ; *(pezzo)* piece of wood, stick.
legumi *smpl* pulses.
lei *pron (soggetto)* she ; *(complemento oggetto, con preposizione)* her ; *(forma di cortesia)* you ; **è ~** it's her ; **io sto bene, e ~?** I'm fine, and you? ; **~ stessa** she herself/you yourself.
lentamente *avv* slowly.
lente *sf* lens ; **~ di ingrandimento** magnifying glass ; **lenti a contatto** contact lenses.
lentezza *sf* slowness.
lenticchie *sfpl* lentils.
lento, a *agg* slow ; *(allentato)* loose. ◆ *sm* slow dance.
lenza *sf* fishing line.
lenzuolo *(pl f* **lenzuola***) sm* sheet.
leone *sm* lion. ❑ **Leone** *sm* Leo.
leopardo *sm* leopard.
lepre *sf* hare ; **~ in salmì** *marinated hare in a sauce made from its offal.*
lesbica, che *sf* lesbian.
lesione *sf* lesion.
lesso, a *agg* boiled. ◆ *sm* boiled beef.
letale *agg* lethal.
letame *sm* manure.
lettera *sf* letter ; **alla ~** literally. ❑ **lettere** *sfpl (facoltà)* ≃ arts.
letteratura *sf* literature.
lettino *sm (del medico)* couch ; *(per bambini)* cot.
letto, a *pp* → **leggere.** ◆ *sm* bed ; **andare a ~** to go to bed ; **~ matrimoniale** ○ **a due piazze** double bed ; **~ a una piazza** single bed ; **letti a castello** bunk beds ; **letti gemelli** twin beds.
Lettonia *sf* : **la ~** Latvia.
lettore, trice *sm, f (di libro, giornale)* reader ; *(di università)* foreign

language assistant. ◆ *sm* : ~ **di compact** CD player.

lettura *sf* reading.

leva *sf* lever ; *(militare)* conscription ; **fare ~ su qc** *fig* to play on sthg ; **~ del cambio** gear lever *(Br)*, gear shift *(Am)*.

levante *sm* east.

levare *vt (togliere)* to remove ; *(alzare)* to raise. ❑ **levarsi** *vr (vento)* to get up, to rise.

levata *sf* collection.

levatoio *agg m* → **ponte**.

levigare *vt* to smooth.

lezione *sf* lesson ; *(all'università)* lecture.

lezioso, a *agg* affected.

lezzo *sm* stink.

li *pron mpl* them.

lì *avv* there ; **essere ~ (~) per fare qc** to be on the point of doing sthg ; **da ~ in poi** *(tempo)* from then on ; *(spazio)* from that point onwards.

Libano *sm* : **il ~** Lebanon.

libeccio *sm* southwest wind.

libellula *sf* dragonfly.

liberale *agg* liberal.

liberamente *avv* freely.

liberare *vt (prigioniero)* to free, to release ; *(camera, posto)* to vacate. ❑ **liberarsi** *vr (annullare un impegno)* to free o.s. ; **liberarsi di** to get rid of.

libero, a *agg* free ; **essere ~ di fare qc** to be free to do sthg ; **~ professionista** self-employed professional ; **'libero'** *(su taxi)* 'for hire' ; *(in toilette)* 'vacant'.

libertà *sf inv* freedom ; *(permesso)* liberty ; **mettere in ~ qn** to free sb.

liberazione *sf* : **la Liberazione** the Liberation.

LA LIBERAZIONE

On 25th April 1945 the *Comitato di Liberazione Nazionale Alta Italia* ordered a general revolt against the German occupying forces. The general strike started in Milan and Mussolini fled the Lombard capital. These events, which within the space of a few days led to the country's liberation from nazi-facism, dictatorship and war, are remembered every year with political and cultural events. The day of the 'Liberation' is an Italian national holiday, as is the anniversary of the end of the Second World War.

Libia *sf* : **la ~** Libya.

libreria *sf (negozio)* bookshop ; *(mobile)* bookcase.

libretto *sm* MUS libretto ; **~ degli assegni** cheque book ; **~ di circolazione** log book ; **~ di risparmio** savings book ; **~ universitario** university report card.

libro *sm* book ; **~ giallo** thriller.

licenza *sf (autorizzazione)* licence ; *(militare)* leave ; **~ media** school-leaving certificate.

licenziamento *sm* dismissal.

licenziare *vt* to dismiss. ❑ **licenziarsi** *vr* to resign.

liceo *sm* secondary school *(Br)*, high school *(Am)*.

lido *sm* beach ; **il Lido di Venezia** the Venice Lido.
lieto, a *agg (contento)* : **~ di conoscerla!** pleased to meet you! ; **molto ~!** pleased to meet you!
lievitare *vi* to rise.
lievito *sm* yeast ; **~ di birra** brewer's yeast.
Liguria *sf* : **la ~** Liguria.
lillà *agg inv* & *sm inv* lilac.
lima *sf* file.
limetta *sf* : **~ per unghie** nail file.
limitare *vt* to limit, to restrict. ❑ **limitarsi** *vr* : **limitarsi a fare qc** to limit o.s. to do sthg ; **limitarsi nel bere** to restrict one's drinking.
limitato, a *agg* limited.
limite *sm (confine)* border ; *(punto estremo)* limit ; **~ di velocità** speed limit ; **entro certi limiti** within certain limits ; **al ~** if the worst comes to the worst.
limitrofo, a *agg* neighbouring.
limonata *sf* lemonade.
limone *sm* lemon.
limpido, a *agg* clear.
linea *sf* line ; *(itinerario)* route ; **mantenere la ~** to look after one's figure ; **avere qualche ~ di febbre** to have a slight temperature ; **linee urbane** local buses ; **in ~ d'aria** as the crow flies ; **in ~ di massima** as a general rule ; **a grandi linee** in broad outline ; **è caduta la ~** we have been cut off.
lineare *agg* linear.
lineetta *sf* dash.
lingua *sf* ANAT & CULIN tongue ; *(linguaggio)* language ; **~ madre** mother tongue ; **~ straniera** foreign language.
linguaggio *sm* language ; **~ dei segni** sign language.
linguetta *sf* tongue.
linguistico, a, ci, che *agg* linguistic.
lino *sm* linen.
linoleum *sm inv* linoleum.
liofilizzato, a *agg* freeze-dried.
liquefare *vt* to melt. ❑ **liquefarsi** *vr* to melt.
liquefatto, a *pp* → **liquefare**.
liquidare *vt (società, beni)* to liquidate ; *(merce)* to sell off ; *(sbarazzarsi di)* to get rid of ; *fig (questione, problema)* to solve.
liquidazione *sf (di merci)* selling off, clearance ; *(indennità)* severance pay.
liquido, a *agg* liquid. ◆ *sm* liquid ; *(denaro)* cash.
liquirizia *sf* liquorice.
liquore *sm* liqueur.
lira *sf* lira ; **non avere una ~** not to have a penny *(Br)*, not to have a dime *(Am)*.
lirica *sf* opera.
lirico, a, ci, che *agg (musica)* lyric.
lisca, sche *sf* fishbone.
liscio, a, sci, sce *agg (pietra, pelle)* smooth ; *(capelli)* straight ; *(whisky)* neat. ◆ *sm (ballo)* ballroom dance ; **andar ~** to go smoothly.
lista *sf* list ; **essere in ~ d'attesa** to be on a waiting list ; **~ dei vini** wine list.
listino *sm* : **~ (dei) prezzi** price list ; **~ dei cambi** exchange rate.
Lit *abbr* = **lira**.
lite *sf* quarrel.

litigare *vi* to quarrel.
litigio *sm* quarrel.
litorale *sm* coast.
litoraneo, a *agg* coastal.
litro *sm* litre.
livello *sm (altezza, piano)* level ; ~ **del mare** sea level.
livido, a *agg (per percosse)* black and blue. ◆ *sm* bruise ; ~ **per il freddo** blue with cold.
Livorno *sm* Livorno.
lo *art* the → **il**. ◆ *pron (persona)* him ; *(animale, cosa)* it ; ~ **so** I know.
locale *agg* local. ◆ *sm (stanza)* room ; *(luogo pubblico)* premises *(pl)* ; ~ **notturno** night club.
località *sf inv* locality.
locanda *sf* inn.
locandina *sf* theatre poster.
locomotiva *sf* locomotive.
lodare *vt* to praise.
lode *sf (elogio)* praise ; **laurearsi con 110 e** ~ to graduate with first-class honours *(Br)*, to graduate summa cum laude *(Am)*.
loggia, ge *sf* loggia.
loggione *sm* : **il** ~ the gods *(pl)*.
logica *sf* logic.
logico, a, ci, che *agg* logical.
logorare *vt* to wear out. ❑ **logorarsi** *vr* to wear out.
logorio *sm* wear and tear.
Lombardia *sf* : **la** ~ Lombardy.
lombardo, a *agg* Lombard.
lombata *sf* loin.
lombrico, chi *sm* earthworm.
Londra *sf* London.
longitudine *sf* longitude.
lontananza *sf (distanza)* distance ; *(di persona)* absence ; **in** ~ in the distance.
lontano, a *agg (luogo)* distant, faraway ; *(nel tempo)* far off ; *(assente)* absent ; *(parente)* distant. ◆ *avv* far ; **è ~?** is it far? ; **è ~ 3 chilometri** it's 3 kilometres from here ; ~ **da** far (away) from ; **da** ~ from far away ; **più** ~ farther.
loquace *agg* talkative.
lordo, a *agg* gross.
loro *pron (soggetto)* they ; *(complemento oggetto, con preposizione)* them ; *form (complemento di termine)* (to) them ; ~ **stessi** they themselves. ❑ **il loro** (*f* **la loro**, *mpl* **i loro**, *fpl* **le loro**) *agg* their. ◆ *pron* theirs.
losco, a, schi, sche *agg* suspicious, shady.
lotta *sf* struggle, fight.
lottare *vi* to fight.
lotteria *sf* lottery.
lotto *sm (gioco)* lottery ; *(di terreno)* lot.
lozione *sf* lotion.
lubrificante *sm* lubricant.
lucchetto *sm* padlock.
luccicare *vi* to sparkle.
lucciola *sf* glow-worm, firefly.
luce *sf* light ; *(elettricità)* electricity ; **dare alla** ~ to give birth to ; **mettere in ~ qc** to highlight sthg ; ~ **del sole** sunlight ; **luci d'arresto** brake lights ; **luci di direzione** indicators ; **luci di posizione** parking lights ; **film a luci rosse** porno film.
lucernario *sm* skylight.
lucertola *sf* lizard.
lucidare *vt* to polish.

lucidatrice *sf* floor polisher.
lucido, a *agg (pavimento, tessuto)* shiny ; *fig (mente, persona)* lucid. ◆ *sm (da proiettore)* acetate ; ~ **da scarpe** shoe polish.
lucro *sm* profit.
luganega, ghe *sf type of sausage (a speciality of Veneto and Lombardy).*
luglio *sm* July → **settembre**.
lugubre *agg* gloomy.
lui *pron (soggetto)* he ; *(complemento oggetto, con preposizione)* him ; **è ~** it's him ; ~ **stesso** he himself.
lumaca, che *sf* snail.
lume *sm* lamp ; **a ~ di candela** by candlelight.
luminaria *sf* illuminations *(pl)*.
luminoso, a *agg* luminous, bright.
luna *sf* moon ; ~ **di miele** honeymoon ; ~ **park** funfair ; ~ **piena** full moon.
lunario *sm* : **sbarcare il ~** to make ends meet.
lunedì *sm inv* Monday → **sabato**.
lungarno *sm (a Firenze) the embankment along the Arno.*
lunghezza *sf* length ; ~ **d'onda** wavelength.
lungo, a, ghi, ghe *agg* long ; *(caffè)* weak ; **è ~ 3 metri** it's 3 metres long ; **saperla lunga** to know what's what ; **a ~** for a long time ; **di gran lunga** by far ; **in ~ e in largo** far and wide ; **andare per le lunghe** to drag on.
lungofiume *sm* embankment.
lungolago, ghi *sm road around a lake.*
lungomare *sm* promenade.
lungotevere *sm (a Roma)* the embankment along the Tiber.
lunotto *sm* rear window.
luogo, ghi *sm* place ; *(di delitto, incidente)* scene ; **aver ~** to take place ; **dare ~ a qc** to give rise to sthg ; ~ **comune** commonplace ; ~ **di culto** place of worship ; ~ **di nascita** place of birth ; **del ~** local ; **in primo ~** in the first place.
lupino *sm* lupin.
lupini *smpl* lupins.
lupo *sm* wolf.
lurido, a *agg* filthy.
lusinga, ghe *sf* flattery.
lusingare *vt* to flatter.
lussare *vt* to dislocate.
Lussemburgo *sm* : **il ~** Luxembourg.
lusso *sm* luxury ; **di ~** de luxe, luxury.
lussuoso, a *agg* luxurious.
lussureggiante *agg* luxuriant.
lussuria *sf* lust.
lustrare *vt* to polish.
lustrino *sm* sequin.
lustro, a *agg* shiny.
lutto *sm* mourning ; **essere in ~** to be in mourning.

M

ma *cong* but.
macabro, a *agg* macabre.
macché *esclam* of course not!
maccheroni *smpl* macaroni *(sg)* ; ~ **alla chitarra** *flat ribbons of egg pasta in a sauce of either*

tomatoes and chillis, or lamb (a speciality of Abruzzo).

macchia *sf (chiazza)* spot, stain ; *(di colore)* spot ; *(bosco)* scrub.

macchiare *vt* to stain, to mark. ❑ **macchiarsi** *vr (persona)* to get stains O marks on one's clothes ; *(abiti, tappeto)* to become stained OR marked.

macchiato, a *agg* stained.

macchina *sf (automobile)* car ; *(apparecchio)* machine ; **andare in ~** to go by car, to drive ; **~ fotografica** camera ; **~ da scrivere** typewriter.

macchinario *sm* machinery.

macchinetta *sf (caffettiera)* percolator ; **~ mangiasoldi** slot machine.

macchinista, i *sm (di treno)* driver ; *(di nave)* engineer.

macedonia *sf* fruit salad.

Macedonia *sf (stato balcanico)* : **la ~** Macedonia.

macellaio, a *sm, f* butcher.

macelleria *sf* butcher's.

macerie *sfpl* rubble *(sg)*.

macigno *sm* rock, boulder.

macinacaffè *sm inv* coffee grinder.

macinapepe *sm inv* pepper grinder.

macinare *vt (grano)* to mill, to grind ; *(caffè, pepe)* to grind ; *(carne)* to mince *(Br)*, to grind *(Am)*.

macinato, a *agg* minced *(Br)*, ground *(Am)*. ◆ *sm* mince *(Br)*, ground beef *(Am)*.

macrobiotico, a, ci, che *agg* macrobiotic.

Madonna *sf* Madonna.

madre *sf* mother.

madrelingua *agg inv* mother tongue *(dav s)*. ◆ *sf* mother tongue.

madreperla *sf* mother-of-pearl.

madrina *sf* godmother.

maestrale *sm* northwest wind.

maestro, a *sm, f* teacher. ◆ *sm* MUS maestro ; *(artigiano, artista)* master ; **~ di tennis** tennis coach.

mafia *sf* Mafia.

mafioso, a *agg* of the Mafia, Mafia *(dav s)*. ◆ *sm, f* member of the Mafia.

magari *esclam* if only! ◆ *avv* maybe.

magazzino *sm* warehouse.

maggio *sm* May ; **il primo ~** May Day → **settembre**.

maggioranza *sf* majority ; **nella ~ dei casi** in the majority of cases.

maggiorana *sf (erba)* marjoram.

---

maggiore *agg* - 1. *(comparativo : più grande, più numeroso)* larger, bigger ; *(di quantità)* greater ; *(più importante)* major, more important ; *(più vecchio)* elder, older. - 2. *(superlativo : più grande, più numeroso)* largest, biggest ; *(di quantità)* greatest ; *(più importante)* most important ; *(più vecchio)* eldest, oldest. ◆ *sm* MIL major ; **andare per la ~** to be very popular ; **la ~ età** the age of majority ; **la maggior parte (di)** the majority (of).

---

maggiorenne *agg* of age. ◆ *smf* person who has come of age.

maggiormente *avv* much more.
magia *sf* magic.
magico, a, ci, che *agg* magic.
magistratura *sf* magistracy.
maglia *sf (indumento)* sweater, jersey ; *(di sportivo, tessuto)* jersey ; *(di catena)* link ; **lavorare a ~** to knit.
maglieria *sf* knitwear.
maglietta *sf* T-shirt ; *(canottiera)* vest *(Br)*, undershirt *(Am)*.
maglione *sm* sweater, jumper.
magnate *sm* magnate.
magnetico, a, ci, che *agg* magnetic.
magnifico, a, ci, che *agg* magnificent.
mago, a, ghi, ghe *sm, f (stregone)* sorcerer (*f* sorceress) ; *(illusionista)* magician.
magro, a *agg (persona)* thin ; *(formaggio, yogurt)* low-fat ; *(carne)* lean ; *fig (scarso)* meagre.
mai *avv* never ; *(qualche volta)* : **l'hai ~ visto?** have you ever seen him? ; **non ... ~** never ; **~ più** never again.
maiale *sm (animale)* pig ; *(carne)* pork ; **~ alle mele** *pork with brandy-flavoured apple sauce.*
maiolica *sf* majolica.
maionese *sf* mayonnaise.
mais *sm* maize.
maiuscola *sf* capital letter.
maiuscolo, a *agg* capital.
mal = **male.**
malafede *sf* bad faith.
malaga *sm* : **gelato al ~** *rum and raisin ice cream.*
malandato, a *agg (persona)* in poor shape ; *(oggetto)* shabby.
malanno *sm* ailment.
malapena : **a malapena** *avv* hardly, scarcely.
malato, a *agg* ill, sick. ◆ *sm, f* sick person, patient ; **essere ~ di cuore** to have a bad heart.
malattia *sf* illness, disease ; **essere in ~** to be on sick leave.
malavita *sf* underworld.
malconcio, a, ci, ce *agg* in a sorry state.
maldestro, a *agg (poco abile)* inept ; *(impacciato, goffo)* clumsy.
maldicenza *sf* malicious gossip.
male *sm (ingiustizia)* evil ; *(dolore)* pain ; *(malattia)* complaint. ◆ *avv* badly ; **ti fa ~?** does it hurt? ; **mi fanno ~ i piedi** my feet hurt ; **fare del ~ a qn** to hurt sb ; **non c'è ~!** not bad! ; **mal d'aereo** airsickness ; **mal d'auto** carsickness ; **mal di gola** sore throat ; **mal di mare** seasickness ; **mal di stomaco** stomachache ; **mal di testa** headache ; **andare a ~** to go off ; **restarci** o **rimanerci ~** to be disappointed ; **sentirsi ~** to feel ill ; **di ~ in peggio** from bad to worse.
maledetto, a *pp* → **maledire.** ◆ *agg* damned.
maledire *vt* to curse.
maledizione *sf* curse.
maleducato, a *agg* rude.
maleducazione *sf* rudeness.
maleodorante *agg* smelly.
malessere *sm (fisico)* ailment ; *(mentale)* uneasiness.
malfamato, a *agg* notorious.

malfattore, trice *sm, f* wrongdoer.
malfermo, a *agg* unsteady.
malformazione *sf* malformation, deformity.
malgrado *prep* in spite of. ◆ *cong* although ; **mio ~** against my will.
malignità *sf inv (d'animo)* malice ; *(insinuazione)* spiteful remark.
maligno, a *agg (persona, commento)* malicious ; *MED* malignant.
malinconia *sf* melancholy.
malinconico, a, ci, che *agg* gloomy.
malincuore : a malincuore *avv* reluctantly.
malintenzionato, a *agg* ill-intentioned.
malinteso *sm* misunderstanding.
malizia *sf* cunning, malice.
malizioso, a *agg* malicious.
malleabile *agg* malleable.
malmenare *vt* to beat up.
malnutrizione *sf* malnutrition.
malore *sm* : **ho avuto un ~** I suddenly felt ill.
malridotto, a *agg* in a bad state.
malsano, a *agg* unhealthy.
Malta *sf* Malta.
maltagliati *smpl soup pasta, cut into irregular shapes.*
maltempo *sm* bad weather.
malto *sm* malt.
maltrattare *vt* to ill-treat.
malumore *sm* bad temper ; **essere di ~** to be in a bad mood.
malvagio, a, gi, gie *agg* wicked.
malvolentieri *avv* unwillingly.
mamma *sf* mum *(Br)*, mom *(Am)* ; **~ mia!** my goodness!
mammella *sf (di donna)* breast ; *(di animale)* udder.
mammifero *sm* mammal.
manager ['menadʒer] *smf inv* manager (*f* manageress).
manata *sf* slap.
mancanza *sf (scarsità, assenza)* lack ; *(colpa)* fault ; **sentire la ~ di qn** to miss sb ; **in ~ di** for lack of.
mancare *vi (non esserci)* to be missing ; *(essere lontano)* to be away ; *form (morire)* to pass away. ◆ *vt (colpo, bersaglio)* to miss ; **è mancata la luce per due ore** the electricity was off for two hours ; **mi manchi molto** I miss you a lot ; **manca il latte** there's no milk ; **mi manca il tempo** I haven't got the time ; **mi mancano cinque euro** I still need a five euros ; **ci è mancato poco che cadesse** it nearly fell ; **manca un quarto alle quattro** it's quarter to four. ❑ **mancare a** *v + prep (promessa)* to fail to keep. ❑ **mancare di** *v + prep* to lack.
mancia, ce *sf* tip ; **dare la ~ (a qn)** to tip (sb).
manciata *sf* handful.
mancino, a *agg* left-handed.
manco *avv fam* not even ; **~ per sogno** o **per idea** I wouldn't dream of it.
mandarancio *sm* clementine.
mandare *vt* to send ; *(grido)* to give ; **~ a chiamare qn** to send for sb ; **~ via qn** to send sb away ;

~ **avanti qn** to send sb on ahead ; ~ **avanti qc** to provide for sthg ; ~ **giù** to swallow.

mandarino *sm* mandarin (orange), tangerine.

mandata *sf (di chiave)* turn ; **chiudere a doppia** ~ to double-lock.

mandato *sm* DIR warrant ; ~ **d'arresto** arrest warrant.

mandibola *sf* jaw.

mandolino *sm* mandolin.

mandorla *sf* almond.

maneggiare *vt (strumenti, attrezzi)* to handle ; *(denaro)* to manage, to deal with.

maneggio *sm* riding school.

manetta *sf* handle. ❑ **manette** *sfpl* handcuffs.

mangiare *vt (cibo)* to eat ; *fig (patrimonio)* to squander ; *(negli scacchi)* to take. ◆ *vi* to eat ; **far da** ~ to do the cooking ; **mangiarsi le parole** to mumble.

mangiasoldi *agg inv* → **macchinetta.**

mangime *sm* fodder.

mangione, a *sm, f* glutton.

mania *sf (fissazione)* obsession ; **avere la** ~ **di fare qc** to have a habit of doing sthg.

maniaco, a, ci, che *agg* manic. ◆ *sm, f* maniac.

manica, che *sf* sleeve ; **a maniche corte** ○ **a mezze maniche** short-sleeved. ❑ **Manica** *sf*: **la Manica, il Canale della Manica** the (English) Channel.

manicaretto *sm* delicacy.

manichino *sm (di negozio)* dummy ; *(per artisti)* model.

manico, ci *sm* handle.

manicomio *sm (ospedale)* mental hospital ; *fig (confusione)* madhouse.

manicure *sf inv (persona)* manicurist ; *(trattamento)* manicure.

maniera *sf* way ; **in** ~ **che** so that ; **in** ~ **da fare qc** so as to do sthg ; **in tutte le maniere** at all costs.

manifestare *vt* to show. ◆ *vi* to demonstrate. ❑ **manifestarsi** *vr* to appear.

manifestazione *sf (corteo)* demonstration ; *(di sentimento)* show ; *(di malattia)* symptom ; *(spettacolo)* event.

manifesto *sm (cartellone)* poster.

maniglia *sf (di porta)* handle ; *(di autobus)* strap.

manipolare *vt (con le mani)* to handle ; *fig (alterare)* to manipulate.

mano, i *sf* hand ; *(di vernice)* coat ; **dare una** ~ **a qn** to give sb a hand ; **darsi la** ~ to shake hands ; **fatto a** ~ handmade ; **di seconda** ~ second-hand ; **man** ~ gradually ; **andare contro** ~ to drive on the wrong side of the road ; **essere alla** ~ to be easygoing ; **fare man bassa** to take everything ; **fuori** ~ out of the way ; **stare con le mani in** ~ to twiddle one's thumbs.

manodopera *sf (lavoratori)* workforce ; *(costo)* labour.

manomesso, a *pp* → **manomettere.**

manomettere *vt (serratura)* to force.

manopola *sf* knob, control.

manovale *sm* labourer.

manovella *sf* handle.
manovra *sf* manoeuvre.
manovrare *vt (congegno)* to operate ; *fig (persona)* to manipulate. ◆ *vi MIL* to manoeuvre ; *fig (tramare)* to plot.
manrovescio *sm* slap.
mansarda *sf* attic.
mansione *sf* task, job.
mantella *sf* cape.
mantello *sm (di animale)* coat ; *(indumento)* cloak.
mantenere *vt* to keep ; *(sostentare)* to support. ❑ **mantenersi** *vr (pagarsi da vivere)* to support o.s. ; *(conservarsi)* to stay, to keep.
mantenimento *sm* maintenance.
manuale *agg* & *sm* manual.
manubrio *sm (di bicicletta, moto)* handlebars *(pl)* ; *(di congegno)* handle.
manutenzione *sf* maintenance.
manzo *sm (carne)* beef.
mappa *sf* map.
mappamondo *sm (globo)* globe ; *(su carta)* map of the world.
maraschino *sm* maraschino *(cherry liqueur)*.
maratona *sf* marathon.
marca, che *sf (di prodotto)* brand ; *(scontrino)* ticket ; **~ da bollo** revenue stamp ; **prodotto di ~** quality product.
marcare *vt* to mark ; *(goal)* to score.
marchio *sm* mark ; *(di bestiame)* brand ; **~ di fabbrica** trademark ; **~ registrato** registered trademark.
marcia, ce *sf* march ; *(di auto)* gear ; *SPORT* walking ; **fare ~ indietro** to reverse ; **mettersi in ~** to start off.
marciapiede *sm* pavement *(Br)*, sidewalk *(Am)* ; *(di stazione)* platform.
marciare *vi* to march.
marcio, a, ci, ce *agg* rotten.
marcire *vi (cibo)* to rot ; *(ferita)* to fester.
marco, chi *sm* mark.
mare *sm* sea ; **andare al ~** to go to the seaside ; **il Mare del Nord** the North Sea.
marea *sf* tide ; **alta ~** high tide ; **bassa ~** low tide.
mareggiata *sf* stormy sea.
maresciallo *sm* ≃ warrant officer.
margarina *sf* margarine.
margherita *sf* daisy.
margine *sm (di pagina)* margin ; *(di strada, bosco)* edge.
marina *sf* navy.
marinaio *sm* sailor.
marinare *vt* to marinate ; **~ la scuola** to play truant.
marinaro, a *agg (popoli, tradizioni)* seafaring ; **alla marinara** cooked with seafood.
marinata *sf* marinade.
marino, a *agg* sea *(dav s)*.
marionetta *sf* marionette.
marito *sm* husband.
maritozzo *sm type of sweet bread containing sultanas, pine kernels and candied peel (a speciality of Lazio)*.
marittimo, a *agg (clima)*

maritime ; *(scalo)* coastal ; **località marittima** seaside resort.

marmellata *sf* jam ; *(di arance)* marmalade.

marmitta *sf (di auto, moto)* silencer ; *(pentola)* large cooking pot.

marmo *sm* marble.

marocchino, a *agg* & *sm, f* Moroccan.

Marocco *sm* : **il ~** Morocco.

marrone *agg inv* brown. ◆ *sm (colore)* brown ; *(frutto)* chestnut.

marron glacé [marron'gla'se] *sm inv* marron glacé *(crystallized chestnut)*.

marsala *sm inv* Marsala *(sweet fortified wine)*.

marsupio *sm (borsello)* bum bag *(Br)*, fanny pack *(Am)* ; *(di animale)* pouch.

martedì *sm inv* Tuesday → **sabato**.

martellare *vt* to hammer. ◆ *vi* to throb.

martello *sm* hammer.

martini® *sm inv (vermut)* Martini ; *(cocktail)* Martini cocktail.

martire *smf* martyr.

marzapane *sm* marzipan.

marziale *agg* martial.

marziano, a *sm, f* Martian.

marzo *sm* March → **settembre**.

mascalzone *sm* scoundrel.

mascara *sm inv* mascara.

mascarpone *sm* mascarpone *(type of cream cheese)*.

mascella *sf* jaw.

maschera *sf* mask ; *(costume)* fancy dress ; *(di bellezza)* face pack ; *(di cinema, teatro)* usher *(f* usherette).

mascherare *vt (volto)* to mask ; *(emozioni)* to conceal. ❑ **mascherarsi** *vr* : **mascherarsi (da)** to dress up (as).

maschile *agg* GRAMM masculine ; *(sesso, anatomia)* male ; *(abiti)* men's *(dav s)* ; *(per ragazzi)* boy's *(dav s)*.

maschio, a *agg* male. ◆ *sm (animale, individuo)* male ; *(ragazzo, figlio, neonato)* boy ; **figlio ~** son.

mascolino, a *agg* masculine.

mascotte [ma'skɔt] *sf inv* mascot.

masochista, i, e *smf* masochist.

massa *sf* mass ; **una ~ di** *(errori, gente)* loads of ; *(mattoni, legna)* a pile of ; **la ~** the masses *(pl)* ; **di ~** mass *(dav s)* ; **in ~** en masse.

massacro *sm* massacre.

massaggiare *vt* to massage.

massaggiatore, trice *sm, f* masseur *(f* masseuse).

massaggio *sm* massage.

massaia *sf* housewife.

massiccio, a, ci, ce *agg (corporatura)* stout, big ; *(edificio)* solid ; **oro ~** solid gold , massif.

massima *sf (detto)* maxim ; *(temperatura)* maximum temperature ; **in linea di ~** generally speaking.

massimo, a *agg* & *sm* maximum ; **al ~** at most.

mass media *smpl* mass media.

masso *sm* rock.

masticare *vt* to chew.

mastice *sm* putty.

mastino *sm* mastiff.
matassa *sf* skein.
matematica *sf* mathematics *(sg)*.
matematico, a, ci, che *agg* mathematical ; *(sicuro)* certain.
materassino *sm* air bed ; *(da ginnastica)* mat.
materasso *sm* mattress.
materia *sf (in fisica)* matter ; *(materiale)* material ; *(disciplina, argomento)* subject ; **materie prime** raw materials.
materiale *agg* material. ◆ *sm* material ; *(attrezzatura)* equipment ; **beni ~** worldly goods ; **~ sintetico** man-made material.
maternità *sf inv (condizione)* motherhood ; *(di ospedale)* maternity ward ; **essere in ~** to be on maternity leave.
materno, a *agg* maternal ; *(paese, lingua)* mother *(dav s)*.
matita *sf* pencil.
matrigna *sf* stepmother.
matrimoniale *agg* matrimonial.
matrimonio *sm* marriage ; *(cerimonia)* wedding.
mattatoio *sm* slaughterhouse.
mattina *sf* morning ; **di ~** in the morning.
mattinata *sf* morning.
mattiniero, a *agg* : **essere ~** to be an early riser.
mattino *sm* morning.
matto, a *agg* mad. ◆ *sm, f* madman (*f* madwoman) ; **andare ~ per** to be crazy about.
mattone *sm* brick.
mattonella *sf* tile.
maturare *vi* & *vt (frutta, grano)* to ripen ; *(persona)* to mature.
maturità *sf (diploma, esame)* ≃ A levels *(pl) (Br)*, ≃ SATs *(pl) (Am)*.
maturo, a *agg (frutto)* ripe ; *(persona)* mature.
mazza *sf (bastone)* club ; *(da baseball, cricket)* bat ; **~ da golf** golf club.
mazzo *sm (di fiori, chiavi)* bunch ; *(di carte)* pack.
me *pron* me → **mi**.
MEC *abbr* = **Mercato Comune**.
meccanica *sf (scienza)* mechanics *(sg)* → **meccanico**.
meccanico, a, ci, che *agg* mechanical. ◆ *sm* mechanic.
meccanismo *sm* mechanism.
mèche [mɛʃ] *sfpl* streaks.
medaglia *sf* medal.
medaglione *sm (gioiello)* locket ; **~ di vitello** veal medallion.
medesimo, a *agg* same.
media *sf (valore intermedio)* average ; *(di voti)* average mark *(Br)*, average grade *(Am)* ; **in ~** on average ; **le (scuole) medie** ≃ secondary school *(sg) (Br)*, junior high school *(sg) (Am)*.
mediante *prep* by means of.
mediatore, trice *sm, f* mediator ; COMM middleman.
medicare *vt* to dress.
medicina *sf* medicine.
medicinale *sm* medicine, drug.
medico, a, ci, che *agg* medical. ◆ *sm* doctor ; **~ di guardia** doctor on call.

medievạle *agg* medieval.

mẹdio, a *agg* average ; *(di mezzo)* middle. ◆ *sm* : (dito) ~ middle finger.

mediọcre *agg* mediocre.

medioevạle = medievale.

medioẹvo *sm* Middle Ages *(pl)*.

meditạre *vt* to plan. ◆ *vi* to meditate.

meditaziọne *sf (riflessione)* reflection ; *(disciplina orientale)* meditation.

mediterrạneo, a *agg* Mediterranean. ❑ **Mediterraneo** *sm* : il (mar) Mediterraneo the Mediterranean (Sea).

medụsa *sf* jellyfish.

megạfono *sm* megaphone.

---

mẹglio *avv* - 1. *(comparativo)* better ; mi sento ~ di ieri I feel better than I did yesterday ; andare ~ to get better ; così va ~ that's better ; per ~ dire or rather.
- 2. *(superlativo)* best ; è la cosa che mi riesce ~ It's the thing I do best ; le persone ~ vestite the best-dressed people.
◆ *agg inv* - 1. *(migliore)* better ; la tua macchina è ~ della mia your car is better than mine.
- 2. *(in costruzioni impersonali)* better ; è ~ rimanere qui it would be better to stay here ; è ~ che te lo dica I'd better tell you.
◆ *sm* : fare del proprio ~ to do one's best ; agire per il ~ to do the right thing.
◆ *sf* : avere la ~ su qn to get the better of sb.

---

mẹla *sf* apple.

melagrạna *sf* pomegranate.

melanzạna *sf* aubergine *(Br)*, eggplant *(Am)* ; melanzane alla parmigiana *fried aubergine slices covered in tomato and Parmesan cheese.*

melẹnso, a *agg* dull.

mẹlma *sf* mud.

mẹlo *sm* apple tree.

melodịa *sf* melody.

melodrạmma, i *sm* melodrama.

melọne *sm* melon.

mẹmbro, i *sm (di club, associazione)* member.

memorạbile *agg* memorable.

memọria *sf* memory ; sapere qc a ~ to know sthg by heart.

mendicạnte *smf* beggar.

mẹno *avv* - 1. *(in comparativi)* less ; ~ di less than ; ~ vecchio (di) younger (than) ; camminate ~ in fretta don't walk so fast ; ne voglio (di) ~ I want less ; ~ lo vedo meglio sto the less I see him, the better I feel.
- 2. *(in superlativi)* least ; la camera ~ cara the cheapest room ; il ~ interessante the least interesting ; fare il ~ possibile to do as little as possible ; la macchina che costa ~ (di tutte) the least expensive car (of all) ; è Luca che mi preoccupa ~ Luca worries me the least.
- 3. *(no)* : non so se accettare o ~ I don't know whether to accept or not.
- 4. *(nelle ore)* : le nove ~ un quarto a

quarter to nine *(Br)*, a quarter of nine *(Am)*.
- 5. *(nelle sottrazioni, nelle temperature)* minus.
- 6. *(in espressioni)* : **non essere da ~ (di qn)** to be just as good (as sb) ; **fare a ~ di** to do without ; **~ male (che) c'eri tu!** thank goodness you were there! ; **venir ~ a** *(promessa)* to break ; *(impegno)* not to fulfil ; **non poteva fare a ~ di urlare** he couldn't help screaming.
◆ *prep* except (for) ; **c'erano tutti ~ (che) lei** they were all there except (for) her ; **pensa a tutto ~ che a divertirsi** enjoying himself is the last thing on his mind.
◆ *agg inv* less ; **oggi c'è ~ gente** there are fewer people today.
❑ **a meno che** *cong* unless ; **vengo a ~ che non piova** I'm coming unless it rains.

---

menopausa *sf* menopause.

mensa *sf* canteen.

mensile *agg* & *sm* monthly.

mensola *sf* shelf.

menta *sf* mint ; *(bibita)* peppermint cordial.

mentale *agg* mental.

mentalmente *avv* mentally.

mente *sf* mind ; **avere in ~ di fare qc** to be thinking of doing sthg ; **imparare/sapere qc a ~** to learn/know sthg by heart ; **sfuggire** o **passare di ~ a qn** to slip sb's mind ; **tenere a ~ qc** to bear sthg in mind.

mentire *vi* to lie.

mento *sm* chin.

mentre *cong (temporale)* while ; *(avversativa)* while, whereas.

menù *sm inv (lista)* menu ; *INFORM* menu.

menzionare *vt* to mention.

menzogna *sf* lie.

meraviglia *sf (stupore)* amazement ; *(cosa, persona)* marvel ; **a ~** perfectly.

meravigliare *vt* to amaze.
❑ **meravigliarsi di** *vr + prep* to be amazed at.

meraviglioso, a *agg* wonderful.

mercante *sm* trader.

mercantile *agg* merchant *(dav s)*. ◆ *sm (nave)* merchant ship.

mercanzia *sf* goods *(pl)*, merchandise.

mercatino *sm* local market.

mercato *sm* market ; **~ dei cambi** foreign exchange market ; **~ nero** black market ; **a buon ~** cheap ; **Mercato Comune Europeo** Common Market.

MERCATO

Almost every Italian town has an indoor or outdoor market selling food, flowers and plants. Once or twice a week there will also be a general market with stalls selling clothes, shoes and household items among other things. Prices are generally lower than in shops, and shoppers and stallholders often haggle.

---

merce *sf* goods *(pl)*, merchandise.

merceria *sf* haberdasher's *(Br)*, notions store *(Am)*.

mercoledì *sm inv* Wednesday → sabato.

mercurio *sm* mercury.

merda *sf* & *esclam volg* shit!

merenda *sf* afternoon snack.

meridionale *agg* southern. ◆ *smf* southerner.

Meridione *sm* : il ~ the South of Italy.

meringa, ghe *sf* meringue.

meritare *vt* to deserve. ◆ *vi* to be good ; meritarsi qc to deserve sthg.

merito *sm (qualità)* merit ; *(riconoscimento)* credit ; per ~ di qn thanks to sb ; finire a pari ~ to tie.

merletto *sm (pizzo)* lace.

merlo *sm (uccello)* blackbird ; *(di mura)* battlement.

merluzzo *sm* cod.

meschino, a *agg (spregevole)* mean.

mescolare *vt (mischiare)* to mix ; *(insalata)* to toss ; *(caffè)* to stir ; *(mettere in disordine)* to mix up. ❑ **mescolarsi** *vr (confondersi)* to mingle.

mese *sm* month.

messa *sf* mass.

messaggio *sm* message.

messicano, a *agg* Mexican. ◆ *sm, f (abitante)* Mexican ; messicani di vitello *(involtini) Stuffed veal escalopes.*

Messico *sm* : il ~ Mexico.

messinscena *sf (teatrale)* production ; *(finzione)* act.

messo, a *pp* → mettere.

mestiere *sm (professione)* job ; *(artigianale)* craft ; *(manuale)* trade.

mestolo *sm* ladle.

mestruazioni *sfpl* period *(sg)*.

meta *sf (destinazione)* destination ; *(scopo)* aim, goal.

metà *sf inv (parte)* half ; *(punto di mezzo)* middle ; dividere qc a ~ to divide sthg in half ; essere a ~ strada to be halfway ; fare a ~ (con qn) to go halves (with sb).

metabolismo *sm* metabolism.

metafora *sf* metaphor.

metallico, a, ci, che *agg (di metallo)* metal *(dav s)* ; *(rumore, voce)* metallic.

metallo *sm* metal.

metallurgico, a *agg* metallurgical.

metano *sm* methane.

meteo *sm (alla TV o radio)* weather report.

meteorologico, a, ci, che *agg* meteorological, weather *(dav s)*.

meticoloso, a *agg* meticulous.

metodico, a, ci, che *agg* methodical.

metodo *sm* method.

metrico, a, ci, che *agg* metric.

metro *sm (unità di misura)* metre ; *(nastro)* tape measure ; *(a stecche)* rule ; ~ cubo cubic metre ; ~ quadrato square metre.

metronotte *sm inv* night security guard.

metropoli *sf inv* metropolis.

metropolitana *sf* underground *(Br)*, subway *(Am)*.

☞

mettere *vt* - 1. *(collocare)* to put ; ~ **un annuncio** to place an advert ; ~ **i piatti in tavola** to set the table ; ~ **qn alla prova** to put sb to the test ; ~ **i libri in ordine** to tidy (up) the books ; ~ **l'antenna dritta** to put the aerial straight.
- 2. *(indossare)* : **mettersi qc** to put sthg on ; **mettersi una sciarpa** to put a scarf on, to wear a scarf ; **cosa mi metto oggi?** what shall I wear today?
- 3. *(tempo)* : **metterci** : **ci si mette un'ora per andare** it takes an hour to get there.
- 4. *(dedicare)* : ~ **attenzione in qc** to do sthg with care ; **mettercela tutta** to do one's best.
- 5. *(far funzionare)* to put on ; ~ **gli abbaglianti** to put one's headlights on full beam.
- 6. *(suscitare)* : ~ **appetito a qn** to make sb hungry ; ~ **paura a qn** to scare sb.
- 7. *(supporre)* : **mettiamo che non venga** let's suppose he doesn't come.
- 8. *(in espressioni)* : ~ **avanti/indietro l'orologio** to put the clock forward/back ; ~ **in chiaro qc** to clear sthg up ; ~ **in dubbio qc** to cast doubt on sthg ; **mettersi in testa di fare qc** to get it into one's head to do sthg ; ~ **insieme** to put together. ❑ **mettersi** *vr* - 1. *(porsi)* : **mettiti a sedere qui** sit here ; **mettersi a tavola** to sit down to eat ; **mettersi nei guai** to get into trouble.
- 2. *(vestirsi)* : **mettersi in pigiama** to put one's pyjamas on.
- 3. *(cominciare)* : **mettersi a fare qc** to start doing sthg ; **s'è messo a gridare** he started screaming ; **mettersi in viaggio** to set off.
- 4. *(in espressioni)* : **mettersi d'accordo** to agree ; **mettersi bene/male** to turn out well/badly ; **mettersi con qn** *(in società)* to go into partnership with sb ; *(in coppia)* to go out with sb.

---

mezza *sf*: **la** ~ *(mezzogiorno e mezzo)* half-past twelve.

mezzaluna (*pl* **mezzelune**) *sf* *(parte di luna)* half moon ; *(coltello)* chopping blade ; *(islamica)* crescent.

mezzanino *sm* mezzanine floor.

mezzanotte *sf* midnight.

mezzo, a *agg* half. ◆ *sm* *(metà)* half ; *(parte centrale)* middle ; *(strumento, procedimento)* means ; *(veicolo)* vehicle. ◆ *avv* : ~ **pieno** half-full ; ~ **chilo** half a kilo ; ~ **litro** half a litre ; **mezza pensione** half board ; **abiti di mezza stagione** spring/autumn clothes ; **a mezze maniche** short-sleeved ; **di mezza età** middle-aged ; **quello di** ~ the one in the middle, the middle one ; **per** ~ **di** by means of ; **le cinque e mezza** ○ ~ half-past five ; **non vuole andarci di** ~ he doesn't want to get involved ; **fare a** ~ **(con qn)** to share (with sb) ; **levarsi** ○ **togliersi di** ~ to get out of the way ; **mezzi di comunicazione (di massa)** (mass) media ; **mezzi pubblici** public transport *(sg)* ; **mezzi di trasporto** means of transport. ❑ **mezzi** *smpl (economici)* means.

mezzogiorno *sm (ora)* midday, noon. ❑ **Mezzogiorno** *sm* : **il Mezzogiorno** Southern Italy.

MEZZOGIORNO

The south of Italy, including Sicily and Sardinia, is called *il Mezzogiorno*. This area is less industrial than the rest of the country, but is rich in art and culture and is blessed with spectacular scenery.

---

mezzora *sf* half an hour.
mi *(diventa* **me** *se precede lo, la, li, le, ne) pron (complemento oggetto)* me ; *(complemento di termine)* (to) me ; *(riflessivo)* myself ; **me li dai?** will you give them to me?
miagolare *vi* to miaow.
mica *avv fam* : **non ci avrai ~ creduto?** you didn't believe it, did you? ; **non sono ~ scemo!** I'm not stupid, am I! ; **~ male** not bad (at all).
michetta *sf region (pane)* bread roll.
miccia, e *sf* fuse.
micidiale *agg (mortale)* deadly ; *(dannoso)* murderous ; *(insopportabile)* unbearable.
micosi *sf inv* MED fungus.
microfono *sm* microphone.
microscopio *sm* microscope.
midolla *sf (mollica)* crumb.
midollo (*pl f* **midolla**) *sm* marrow.
mie → **mio.**
miei → **mio.**
miele *sm* honey.
migliaio (*pl f* **migliaia**) *sm* thousand ; **un ~ (di persone)** about a thousand (people) ; **a migliaia** by the thousand.
miglio *sm (unità di misura pl f* **miglia***)* mile ; *(pianta)* millet.
miglioramento *sm* improvement.
migliorare *vt* to improve. ◆ *vi (tempo, situazione)* to improve ; *(malato)* to get better.
migliore *agg (comparativo)* better ; **il/la ~** *(superlativo)* the best.
mignolo *sm* little finger *(Br)*, pinkie *(Am)* ; *(del piede)* little toe.
mila *pl* → **mille.**
milanese *agg* Milanese. ◆ *smf* person from Milan.
Milano *sf* Milan.
miliardo *sm* thousand million *(Br)*, billion *(Am)*.
milione *sm* million.
militare *agg* military. ◆ *sm* serviceman ; **fare il ~** to do one's military service.
mille (*pl* **mila**) *num* a ○ one thousand → **sei.**
millefoglie *sm inv* millefeuille *(Br)*, napoleon *(Am)*.
millennio *sm* millennium.
millepiedi *sm inv* millipede.
millesimo, a *num* thousandth → **sesto.**
millimetro *sm* millimetre.
milza *sf* spleen.
mimare *vt* to mime.
mimetizzare *vt* to camouflage. ❑ **mimetizzarsi** *vr (animali, piante)* to camouflage o.s.
mimo *sm* mime.
mimosa *sf* mimosa.
min. *(abbr di minimo, di minuto)* min.

mina *sf (esplosiva)* mine ; *(di matita)* lead.
minaccia, ce *sf* threat.
minacciare *vt* to threaten ; ~ **di fare qc** to threaten to do sthg.
minaccioso, a *agg* threatening, menacing.
minatore *sm* miner.
minerale *agg* & *sm* mineral.
minerva *smf* MED orthopaedic collar ; *(fiammiferi)* safety match.
minestra *sf* soup ; ~ **in brodo** noodle broth ; ~ **di verdure** vegetable soup.
minestrone *sm minestrone.*
miniatura *sf* miniature.
miniera *sf* mine.
minigolf *sm* minigolf.
minigonna *sf* miniskirt.
minima *sf* minimum temperature.
minimizzare *vt* to minimize.
minimo, a *agg (il più piccolo)* slightest, least ; *(il più basso)* lowest ; *(molto piccolo)* very small, slight. ◆ *sm (parte più piccola)* minimum ; *(di motore)* idling speed ; **come** ~ at the very least.
ministero *sm (settore amministrativo)* ministry.
ministro *sm* minister ; ~ **degli Esteri** Foreign Secretary *(Br)*, Secretary of State *(Am)*.
minoranza *sf* minority ; **essere in** ~ to be in a minority.
minorato, a *agg* disabled. ◆ *sm, f* disabled person.
minore *agg comparativo (di età)* younger ; *(di grandezza)* smaller ; *(di importanza)* minor ; *(numero)* lower ; *(grado)* lesser. ◆ *agg superlativo (di età)* youngest ; *(di grandezza)* smallest ; *(di importanza)* least important ; *(di numero)* lowest. ◆ *smf (minorenne)* minor.
minorenne *smf* minor.
minuscola *sf* small letter.
minuscolo, a *agg (scrittura)* small ; *(molto piccolo)* tiny.
minuto, a *agg (persona, corpo)* small ; *(piccolo)* tiny, minute ; *(fine)* fine. ◆ *sm (unità)* minute.
mio (*f* **mia**, *mpl* **miei**, *f pl* **mie**) *agg* : **il** ~ **(la mia)** my.
◆ *pron* : **il** ~ **(la mia)** mine ; ~ **padre** my father ; **un** ~ **amico** a friend of mine ; **questa bici** ~ **è mia** this bike is mine.
miope *agg* short-sighted.
mira *sf* aim ; **prendere la** ~ to take aim ; **prendere di** ~ **qc** *fig* to pick on sb.
miracolo *sm* miracle.
miraggio *sm* mirage.
mirare *vi* : ~ **a** to aim at.
miriade *sf* multitude ; **una** ~ **di** a multitude of.
mirtillo *sm* blueberry.
miscela *sf (miscuglio)* mixture ; *(di caffè)* blend ; *(benzina)* petrol and oil mixture.
mischia *sf* brawl ; *(nel rugby)* scrum.
mischiare *vt* to mix ; ~ **le carte** to shuffle the cards. ❑ **mischiarsi** *vr* to mix.
miseria *sf* (extreme) poverty ; *(quantità insufficiente)* : **è costato una** ~ it cost next to nothing ; **porca** ~! *fam (accidenti)* damn! , bloody hell!
misericordia *sf* mercy.

misero, a *agg (povero)* poor, poverty-stricken ; *(infelice)* wretched, miserable ; *(insufficiente)* miserable.
missile *sm* missile.
missionario, a *sm, f* missionary.
missione *sf* mission.
misterioso, a *agg* mysterious.
mistero *sm* mystery.
misto, a *agg* mixed. ◆ *sm* mixture ; **insalata mista** mixed salad ; ~ **lana** wool blend ; ~ **cotone** cotton blend.
misura *sf (unità, provvedimento)* measure ; *(dimensione)* measurement ; *(taglia)* size ; *(moderazione)* moderation ; **prendere le misure di qc** to measure sthg ; **su ~** made-to-measure.
misurare *vt* to measure ; *(abito)* to try on ; *(vista)* to test. ◆ *vi* to measure. ❑ **misurarsi con** *vr + prep* to compete with.
misurino *sm* measure.
mite *agg* mild.
mito *sm* myth.
mitra *sm inv* submachine gun.
mitragliatrice *sf* machine gun.
mittente *smf* sender.
mobile *agg* movable. ◆ *sm* piece of furniture ; **mobili** *(mobilia)* furniture *(sg)*.
mobilia *sf* furniture.
mobilitare *vt* to mobilize.
moca *sf inv* coffee machine.
mocassino *sm* mocassin.
moda *sf* fashion ; **essere** o **andare di ~** to be in fashion ; **passare di ~** to go out of fashion ; **alla ~** fashionable ; **di ~** fashionable.
modellare *vt* to model.
modellino *sm* model.
modello, a *sm, f* model. ◆ *sm* model ; *(per sarta)* pattern ; *(modulo)* form.
modem *sm inv* INFORM modem.
moderare *vt* to moderate.
moderato, a *agg* moderate.
moderno, a *agg* modern.
modestia *sf* modesty.
modesto, a *agg* modest.
modico, a, ci, che *agg* low.
modifica, che *sf* alteration.
modo *sm* way ; *(opportunità)* chance ; GRAMM *(verbale)* mood ; **a ~ mio** in my way ; **in ~ da fare qc** so as to do sthg ; **~ di dire** expression ; **di ~ che** so that ; **in nessun ~** in no way ; **in ogni ~** anyway ; **in qualche ~** in some way ; **in tutti i modi** in every way.
modulazione *sf* : **~ di frequenza** frequency modulation.
modulo *sm* form.
moglie, gli *sf* wife.
mole *sf (dimensione)* massive shape ; *(quantità)* : **una ~ di lavoro** masses of work.
molestare *vt* to annoy.
molesto, a *agg* annoying.
molla *sf (meccanica)* spring. ❑ **molle** *sfpl (per camino, ghiaccio)* tongs.
mollare *vt (allentare)* to slacken ; *(lasciar andare)* to let go ; *fam (fidanzato)* to ditch ; **~ un ceffone a qn** *fam (dare uno schiaffo)* to slap sb.
molle *agg (morbido)* soft ; *fig (persona)* weak.
molletta *sf (per capelli)* hair grip ; *(per panni)* clothes peg.

mollica, che *sf* crumb.
molo *sm (di porto)* jetty.
molteplice *agg (complesso)* complex. ❑ **molteplici** *agg pl (numerosi)* various, numerous.
moltiplicare *vt* to multiply.
moltiplicazione *sf* MAT multiplication ; *(accrescimento)* increase.
moltitudine *sf* multitude.

molto, a *agg* - 1. *(in grande quantità)* a lot of, much ; **non ho ~ tempo** I don't have (very) much time ; **hai molta fame?** are you very hungry? - 2. *(di numero elevato)* : **molti** a lot of, many ; **ci sono molti turisti** there are a lot of tourists.
◆ *pron* a lot, much ; **molti** *(molta gente)* many (people) ; **molti di noi** many of us.
◆ *avv* - 1. *(con verbi)* a lot, (very) much ; **mi piace ~** I like it a lot ○ very much.
- 2. *(con aggettivi, avverbi)* very ; *(con participio passato)* much ; **è ~ simpatica** she's very nice ; **è ~ meglio così** it's much better like this ; **è ~ presto/tardi** it's very early/late ; **~ volentieri!** certainly!

---

momentaneamente *avv* at the moment.
momentaneo, a *agg* momentary.
momento *sm* moment ; *(circostanza)* time ; **all'ultimo ~** at the last moment ; **da un ~ all'altro (tra poco)** (at) any moment ; **dal ~ che** since ; **per il ~** for the time being ; **a momenti** *(tra poco)* soon ; *(quasi)* nearly.
monaca, che *sf* nun.
monaco, ci *sm* monk.
monarchia *sf* monarchy.
monastero *sm (di monaci)* monastery ; *(di monache)* convent.
mondano, a *agg (di società)* society *(dav s)* ; *(terreno)* earthly.
mondiale *agg* world *(dav s)*.
mondo *sm* world.
moneta *sf (di metallo)* coin ; *(valuta)* currency ; **~ spicciola** change.
monetario, a *agg* monetary.
monitor *sm inv (schermo)* monitor ; INFORM monitor.
monolocale *sm* studio flat *(Br)*, studio apartment *(Am)*.
monopattino *sm* scooter.
monopolio *sm* monopoly.
monosci *sm inv* monoski.
monotono, a *agg (ripetitivo)* monotonous ; *(noioso)* dull.
montacarichi *sm inv* goods lift.
montagna *sf* mountain ; *(zona)* the mountains *(pl)* ; **andare in ~** to go to the mountains ; **montagne russe** roller coaster *(sg)*.
montanaro, a *sm, f* mountain dweller.
montano, a *agg* mountain *(dav s)*.
montare *vi (salire)* to go up ; *(cavalcare)* to ride. ◆ *vt (congegno)* to assemble ; *(cavallo, pietra preziosa)* to mount ; *(panna)* to whip ; *(albumi)* to whisk ; *(fecondare)* to cover ; **~ in macchina** to get into a car ; **~ in treno** to get on a train ; **montarsi la testa** to become bigheaded.
montatura *sf (di occhiali)* frames *(pl)* ; *(di gioiello)* setting.
monte *sm* mountain ; **andare a ~**

to come to nothing ; **mandare a ~ qc** to upset sthg ; **~ premi** prize money ; **il Monte Bianco** Mont Blanc.

Montecitorio *sm* : **il ~** *the House of Parliament.*

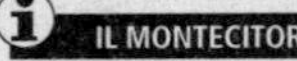

IL MONTECITORIO

Built in the 17th Century and designed by Bernini, the *Montecitorio* was the center of papal governement, housing the Apostolic Curia. After the unification of Italy, the Palace was adapted and became the house of Parlement in 1871.

Montenegro *sm (stato balcanico)* Montenegro ; **il ~** Montenegro.

montone *sm (animale)* ram ; *(carne)* mutton ; *(giaccone)* sheepskin jacket.

montuoso, a *agg* mountainous.

monumento *sm* monument.

mora *sf (commestibile)* blackberry ; *(del gelso)* mulberry ; DIR default.

morale *agg* moral. ◆ *sf* morals *(pl)* ; *(insegnamento)* moral. ◆ *sm* morale ; **essere giù di ~** to be feeling down.

morbido, a *agg* soft.

morbillo *sm* measles *(sg)*.

morbo *sm* disease.

morboso, a *agg* morbid.

mordere *vt* to bite.

morfina *sf* morphine.

moribondo, a *agg* dying.

morire *vi* to die ; *(estinguersi)* to die out ; **~ di fame** to die of hunger ; **~ di noia** to die of boredom ; **~ dal ridere** to kill o.s. laughing ; **bello da ~** stunning.

mormorare *vi (bisbigliare)* to whisper ; *(sparlare)* to gossip. ◆ *vt* to murmur.

moro, a *agg* dark.

morso, a *pp* → **mordere**. ◆ *sm* bite ; *(di briglia)* bit.

mortadella *sf* Mortadella *(large pork sausage served cold in thin slices)*.

mortaio *sm (per alimenti)* mortar ; *(arma)* mortar.

mortale *agg* mortal ; *(letale)* deadly. ◆ *sm* mortal.

mortalità *sf* mortality.

morte *sf* death ; **avercela a ~ con qn** to have it in for sb.

mortificare *vt* to mortify.

morto, a *pp* → **morire**. ◆ *agg* dead. ◆ *sm, f* dead man *(f* dead woman) ; **fare il ~** *(nell'acqua)* to float on one's back.

mosaico, ci *sm* mosaic.

Mosca *sf* Moscow.

mosca, sche *sf* fly ; **~ cieca** blind man's buff.

moscato *sm* muscatel *(sweet wine)*.

moscerino *sm* gnat.

moschettone *sm* spring clip.

moscone *sm (insetto)* bluebottle ; *(imbarcazione)* pedalo.

mossa *sf* movement ; *(negli scacchi)* move.

mosso, a *pp* → **muovere**. ◆ *agg (mare)* rough ; *(capelli)* wavy ; *(fotografia)* blurred.

mostarda *sf* mustard.
mostra *sf* exhibition ; **mettersi in ~** to draw attention to o.s. ; **in ~** on show ; **la Mostra del cinema di Venezia** Venice Film Festival.

LA MOSTRA DEL CINEMA DI VENEZIA

The Venice Film Festival, or the *Mostra internazionale d'arte cinematografica di Venezia*, has been held every year since 1938 during the last week in August and the first week in September. Film fans flock to the *Palazzo del Cinema in Lido di Venezia* to see the celebrities, to watch important new films and retrospectives, and to attend premières. The festival concludes with the awarding of prizes, including the prestigious *Leone d'oro* (golden lion).

---

mostrare *vt* to show. ❑ **mostrarsi** *vr* to look ; **mostrarsi in pubblico** to appear in public.
mostro *sm* monster.
mostruoso, a *agg (orrendo)* monstrous ; *(feroce)* ferocious ; *(smisurato)* incredible.
motel *sm inv* motel.
motivo *sm (causa)* reason ; *(di stoffa)* pattern ; *(musicale)* tune ; **per quale ~?** for what reason? ; **senza ~** without a reason.
moto *sm (in fisica)* motion ; *(movimento)* movement ; *(esercizio fisico)* exercise. ◆ *sf inv* motorbike ; **mettere in ~** *(auto)* to start.
motocicletta *sf* motorcycle.
motocross *sm* motocross.
motore *sm* motor, engine ; **a ~** motor *(dav s)*.
motorino *sm* moped ; **~ d'avviamento** starter.
motoscafo *sm* motorboat.
motto *sm* maxim.
mousse [mus] *sf inv* mousse.
mouse [maus] *sm inv INFORM* mouse.
movimentare *vt* to liven up.
movimento *sm (attività)* activity.
mozzafiato *agg inv* breathtaking.
mozzare *vt* to cut off ; **~ il fiato a qn** to take sb's breath away.
mozzarella *sf* mozzarella *(a round fresh cheese from Naples made from cow's or buffalo's milk)* ; **~ in carrozza** *mozzarella sandwiched between two slices of bread, then dipped in egg and fried.*
mozzicone *sm* stub.
mozzo, a *agg* cut off. ◆ *sm* ship's boy.
mucca, che *sf* cow.
mucchio *sm (cumulo)* heap ; **un ~ di** *fig (grande quantità)* loads of.
muffa *sf* mould.
muffole *sfpl* mittens.
muflone *sm (animale)* mouflon.
mughetto *sm (fiore)* lily of the valley.
mugolare *vi* to whine.
mulattiera *sf* mule track.
mulatto, a *agg* & *sm, f* mulatto.
mulinello *sm (vortice)* whirl ; *(da pesca)* reel.
mulino *sm* mill ; **~ a vento** windmill.
mulo *sm* mule.

multa *sf* fine.
multare *vt* to fine.
multiplo, a *agg* & *sm* multiple.
multiproprietà *sf inv* time-share.
mungere *vt* to milk.
municipale *agg* municipal.
municipio *sm* town hall.
munire *vt* : ~ **qn/qc di qc** to equip sb/sthg with sthg. ❑ **munirsi di** *vr + prep* to equip o.s. with.
muovere *vt* to move ; *(critica, accusa)* to make. ❑ **muoversi** *vr* to move ; *fam (sbrigarsi)* to hurry up, to get a move on.
mura *sfpl* walls.
murale *agg* mural. ◆ *sm (affresco)* mural ; **i murali di Orgosolo** *the Orgosolo murals.*
murare *vt* to wall up.
muratore *sm* bricklayer.
murena *sf* moray eel.
muro *sm* wall.
muscolare *agg* muscular, muscle *(dav s)*.
muscolo *sm* muscle ; **muscoli** *(forza)* brawn *(sg)*.
muscoloso, a *agg* muscular.
museo *sm* museum.
museruola *sf* muzzle.
musica *sf* music ; ~ **classica** classical music ; ~ **leggera** light music.
musicale *agg* musical.
musicista, , e *smf* musician.
muso *sm (di animale)* muzzle ; *fam spreg> ; (di persona)* mug ; *(di auto)* front end ; *(aereo)* nose ; **tenere il ~** to sulk.
muta *sf (da sub)* wet suit ; *(di cani)* pack.
mutamento *sm* change.
mutande *sfpl* pants.
mutandine *sfpl* knickers.
mutare *vt* & *vi* to change.
mutazione *sf* change ; *(genetica)* mutation.
mutilato, a *sm, f* person who has lost a limb ; ~ **di guerra** disabled ex-serviceman *(Br)*, disabled war veteran *(Am)*.
muto, a *agg* dumb ; *(silenzioso)* silent ; *(cinema, consonante)* silent.
mutua *sf* ≃ National Health Service.
mutuo, a *agg* mutual. ◆ *sm* loan.

N

N *(abbr di nord)* N.
nafta *sf (olio combustibile)* fuel oil ; *(gasolio)* diesel oil.
naftalina *sf* mothballs *(pl)*.
nailon® *sm* nylon.
nanna *sf fam* : **andare a ~** to go to beddy-byes.
nano, a *agg* & *sm, f* dwarf.
napoletana *sf a type of coffee percolator.*
napoletano, a *agg* & *sm, f* Neapolitan.
Napoli *sf* Naples.
narice *sf* nostril.
narrare *vt* to tell.
narrativa *sf* fiction.
nasale *agg* nasal.
nascere *vi* to be born ; *(pianta)* to come up ; *(sole)* to rise ; *(fiume)*

to have its source ; *(dente)* to come through ; *(attività, impresa)* to start up ; **sono nata il 31 luglio del 1965** I was born on the 31st of July 1965. ❑ **nascere da** *v + prep* to arise from.

nascita *sf (di bambino, animale)* birth ; *(di attività, movimento)* start ; **data di ~** date of birth ; **luogo di ~** place of birth.

nascondere *vt* to hide ; *(dissimulare)* to hide, to conceal. ❑ **nascondersi** *vr* to hide.

nascondino *sm* hide and seek.

nascosto, a *pp* → **nascondere**. ◆ *agg* hidden ; **di ~** secretly.

naso *sm* nose ; **ficcare il ~ in qc** to poke one's nose into sthg.

nastro *sm* ribbon ; **~ adesivo** adhesive tape ; **~ trasportatore** conveyor belt.

Natale *sm* Christmas.

natalità *sf* birth rate.

natante *sm* craft.

nato, a *pp* → **nascere**. ◆ *agg fig (per natura)* born ; **nata Mattei** *(da nubile)* née Mattei.

NATO *sf* NATO.

natura *sf* nature ; **~ morta** still life.

naturale *agg* natural.

naturalmente *avv* naturally ; *(certamente sì)* naturally, of course.

naufragare *vi (nave)* to be wrecked ; *(persona)* to be shipwrecked.

naufragio *sm* shipwreck.

naufrago, a, ghi, ghe *sm, f* shipwrecked person.

nausea *sf* nausea.

nauseante *agg* nauseating.

nauseare *vt* to make sick.

nautico, a, ci, che *agg* nautical.

navale *agg* naval.

navata *sf* nave.

nave *sf* ship ; **~ passeggeri** passenger ship ; **~ traghetto** ferry.

navetta *sf* shuttle ; **~ (spaziale)** space shuttle.

navigabile *agg* navigable.

navigare *vi (nave)* to sail ; *(persona)* to navigate.

navigazione *sf* navigation.

naviglio *sm (nave)* vessel ; *(canale)* canal.

nazionale *agg* national. ◆ *sf (squadra)* national team.

nazionalità *sf inv* nationality.

nazione *sf* nation.

---

ne *pron* - **1.** *(di lui)* of/about him ; *(di lei)* of/about her ; *(di loro)* of/about them ; **~ apprezzo l'onestà** I value his honesty.
- **2.** *(di un insieme)* of it, of them ; **ha dei panini? - ~ vorrei due** have you got any rolls? - I'd like two (of them).
- **3.** *(di ciò)* about it ; **non parliamone più** let's not talk about it any more ; **non ~ ho idea** I've no idea.
- **4.** *(da ciò)* : **~ deriva che ...** it follows that ...
◆ *avv (di là)* from there ; **~ veniamo proprio ora** we've just come from there.

---

né *cong* : **né ... né** neither ... nor ; **~ l'uno ~ l'altro sono italiani** neither of them are Italian ; **non si è fatto ~ sentire ~ vedere** I haven't heard from him or seen him ; **non voglio ~ il primo ~ il secondo** I don't want either the first one or the second.

neanche *cong* & *avv* not even ; **non ... ~** not even ; **~ io lo conosco** I don't know him either ; **non ho mangiato - ~ io** I haven't eaten - neither have I ○ I haven't either ; **~ per sogno** ○ **per idea!** not on your life!

nebbia *sf* fog.

nebulizzatore *sm* spray.

nebuloso, a *agg (poco chiaro)* nebulous. ◆ *sf (costellazione)* nebula.

necessariamente *avv* necessarily.

necessario, a *agg* necessary. ◆ *sm* necessities *(pl)* ; **è ~ farlo** it must be done ; **~ per toeletta** toiletries *(pl)*.

necessità *sf inv (bisogno)* necessity.

necessitare di : necessitare di *v + prep* to need, to require.

necrologio *sm (annuncio)* obituary.

negare *vt* to deny ; *(rifiutare)* : **~ qc (a qn)** to refuse (sb) sthg ; **~ di aver fatto qc** to deny having done sthg.

negativo, a *agg* & *sm* negative.

negato, a *agg* : **essere ~ per qc** to be hopeless at sthg.

negli = **in + gli, in.**

negligente *agg* negligent.

negoziante *smf* shopkeeper.

negozio *sm* shop ; **~ di giocattoli** toy shop.

negro, a *agg* & *sm, f* black.

nei = **in + i, in.**

nel = **in + il, in.**

nell' = **in + l' → in.**

nella = **in + la, in.**

nelle = **in + le, in.**

nello = **in + lo, in.**

nemico, a, ci, che *agg (esercito, stato)* enemy *(dav s)* ; *(ostile)* hostile. ◆ *sm, f* enemy.

nemmeno = **neanche.**

neo *sm* mole.

neofascismo *sm* neofascism.

neon *sm* neon.

neonato, a *sm, f* newborn baby.

neozelandese *agg* New Zealand *(dav s)*. ◆ *smf* New Zealander.

neppure = **neanche.**

nero, a *agg (colore)* black ; *(scuro)* dark ; *(pane)* wholemeal. ◆ *sm* black.

nervo *sm* nerve ; **dare ai** ○ **sui nervi a qc** to get on sb's nerves.

nervosismo *sm* nervousness.

nervoso, a *agg* nervous. ◆ *sm* : **avere il ~** to be on edge.

nespola *sf* medlar.

nessuno, a *agg* no. ◆ *pron (non una persona)* nobody, no one ; *(non una cosa)* none ; *(qualcuno)* : **c'è ~?** is anybody in? ; **nessuna città è bella quanto Roma** there's no city more beautiful than Rome ; **non c'è nessun posto libero** there aren't any free seats ; **da nessuna parte** nowhere ; **~ lo sa** nobody knows ; **non ho visto ~** I didn't see anybody ; **~ di noi** none of us ; **~ dei due** neither of them ; **non me ne piace ~** I don't like any of them.

net *sm inv INFORM* net ; *SPORT (tennis, ping pong)* net.

nettezza *sf* : ~ **urbana** refuse department.

netto, a *agg (preciso)* clear ; *(deciso)* definite ; *(peso, stipendio)* net.

netturbino *sm* dustman.

neutrale *agg* neutral.

neutralizzare *vt* to neutralize.

neutro, a *agg* neutral ; **essere** ~ *(imparziale)* to be neutral ; *(in linguistica)* neuter.

neve *sf* snow.

nevicare *v impers* to snow ; **nevica** it's snowing.

nevicata *sf* snowfall.

nevischio *sm* sleet.

nevralgia *sf* neuralgia.

nevrotico, a, ci, che *agg* neurotic.

nicchia *sf* niche.

nicotina *sf* nicotine.

nido *sm* nest.

☞

niente *pron* - 1. *(nessuna cosa)* nothing ; **non ... ~** nothing ; **non faccio ~ la domenica** I do nothing on Sundays, I don't do anything on Sundays ; **~ di ~** nothing at all ; **grazie! - di ~!** thank you - not at all. - 2. *(qualcosa)* anything ; **le serve~?** do you need anything? ; **non per ~, ma ...** not that it matters, but ... - 3. *(poco)* : **da ~** *(cosa)* not important ; *(persona)* worthless. ◆ *agg inv fam (nessuno)* : **non ha ~ buon senso** he has no common sense ; **~ paura!** never fear! ◆ *avv* : **non ... ~** not ... at all ; **non me ne importa ~** I couldn't care less ; **questo non c'entra ~** this doesn't come into it at all ; **non fa ~** it doesn't matter ; **ti piace? - per ~!** do you like it? - not at all! ◆ *sm* : **basta un ~ per farlo contento** the slightest thing makes him happy ; **un bel ~** nothing at all.

nientemeno *avv* no less, actually. ◆ *esclam* you don't say!

night(-club) ['nait(kleb)] *sm inv* nightclub.

Nilo *sm* : **il ~** the Nile.

ninnananna *sf* lullaby.

ninnolo *sm* knick-knack.

nipote *smf (di zii)* nephew (*f* niece) ; *(di nonni)* grandson (*f* granddaughter).

nitido, a *agg* well-defined.

nitrire *vi* to neigh.

no *avv* no ; **c'eri anche tu, ~?** you were there too, weren't you? ; **lo sai, ~, com'è fatto** you know, don't you, what he's like? ; **lo vuoi o ~?** do you want it or not? ; **~ di certo** certainly not ; **perché ~?** why not?

nobile *agg* & *smf* noble.

nobiltà *sf (aristocrazia)* nobility ; *(di animo, azione)* nobleness.

nocciola *sf* hazelnut. ◆ *agg inv* hazel.

nocciolina *sf* : **~ (americana)** peanut.

nocciolo[1] *sm (di frutto)* stone.

nocciolo[2] *sm (albero)* hazel.

noce *sf* & *sm* walnut ; **~ di cocco** coconut ; **~ moscata** nutmeg.

nocivo, a *agg* harmful.

nodo *sm* knot ; **avere un ~ alla gola** to have a lump in one's throat.

noi *pron (soggetto)* we ; *(complemento oggetto, con preposizione)* us ; da ~ *(nel nostro paese)* in our country ; ~ stessi we ourselves.
noia *sf (tedio)* boredom ; *(fastidio)* nuisance ; gli è venuto a ~ he's tired of it ; dar ~ a qn to annoy sb ; avere delle noie con to have trouble with.
noioso, a *agg (monotono)* boring ; *(fastidioso)* annoying.
noleggiare *vt (prendere a nolo)* to hire ; *(dare a nolo)* to hire out.
noleggio *sm* hire *(Br)*, rental ; prendere qc a ~ to hire sthg.
nolo = noleggio.
nome *sm* name ; GRAMM noun ; conoscere qn di ~ to know sb by name ; a ~ di qn on behalf of sb ; ~ di battesimo Christian name ; ~ da ragazza maiden name.
nominare *vt (menzionare)* to mention ; *(eleggere)* to appoint.
non *avv* not → affatto, ancora *(ecc)*.
nonché *cong (e anche)* as well as ; *(tanto meno)* let alone.
noncurante *agg* : ~ (di) indifferent (to).
nondimeno *cong* nevertheless, however.
nonno, a *sm, f* grandfather (*f* grandmother).
nonnulla *sm inv* : un ~ a trifle.
nono, a *num* ninth → sesto.
nonostante *prep* in spite of. ◆ *cong* although.
non vedente *smf* blind person.
nord *sm* north. ◆ *agg inv* north, northern ; a ~ (di) north (of) ; nel ~ in the north.
nordest *sm* northeast.
nordico, a, ci, che *agg* Nordic.
nordovest *sm* northwest.
norma *sf* rule ; di ~ as a rule ; a ~ di legge according to the law.
normale *agg* normal.
normalità *sf* normality.
normanno, a *agg* Norman.
norvegese *agg, smf* & *sm* Norwegian.
Norvegia *sf* : la ~ Norway.
nostalgia *sf* nostalgia ; avere ~ di casa o del paese to be homesick.
nostro, a *agg* : il ~ (la nostra) our. ◆ *pron* : il ~ (la nostra) ours ; ~ padre our father ; un ~ amico a friend of ours ; questa casa è nostra it's our house.
nota *sf* note ; *(conto)* bill ; *(elenco)* list ; prendere ~ (di qc) to make a note (of sthg).
notaio *sm* notary public.
notare *vt (osservare, accorgersi di)* to notice ; *(annotare)* to note down ; farsi ~ to get o.s. noticed.
notevole *agg (differenza, prezzo)* considerable ; *(persona)* remarkable.
notificare *vt (form)* to notify.
notizia *sf (informazione)* news *(sg)*, piece of news ; le ultime notizie the latest news ; avere notizie di qn to hear from sb.
notiziario *sm* news *(sg)*.
noto, a *agg* well-known ; rendere ~ qc a qn to make sthg known to sb.
nottambulo, a *sm, f* night bird.
notte *sf* night ; di ~ at night ; una ~ in bianco a sleepless night.

notturno, a *agg* night *(dav s)* ; animale ~ nocturnal animal.
novanta *num* ninety → sei.
novantesimo, a *num* ninetieth → sesto.
nove *num* nine → sei.
novecento *num* nine hundred → sei. ❑ **Novecento** *sm* : il Novecento the twentieth century.
novella *sf* short story.
novellino, a *agg (principiante)* inexperienced.
novembre *sm* November → settembre.
novità *sf inv (cosa nuova)* something new ; *(fatto, notizia recente)* (piece of) news *(sg)* ; le ~ musicali the latest releases.
novizio, a *sm, f* RELIG novice.
nozione *sf* notion, idea ; nozioni *(di matematica, francese)* rudiments.
nozze *sfpl* wedding *(sg)* ; ~ d'oro golden wedding.
nube *sf* cloud.
nubifragio *sm* rainstorm.
nubile *agg* single.
nuca, che *sf* nape of the neck.
nucleare *agg* nuclear.
nucleo *sm (di cellula, atomo)* nucleus ; *(di persone)* group ; *(di soldati, polizia)* squad ; ~ familiare family unit.
nudismo *sm* nudism.
nudista, i, e *smf* nudist.
nudo, a *agg (persona)* naked ; *(parete)* bare ; mettere a ~ qc to lay sthg bare ; ARTE nude.
nugolo *sm* : un ~ di a host of.
nulla = niente.
nullità *sf inv (di ragionamento, documento)* nullity ; *(persona)* nobody.
nullo, a *agg (non valido)* (null and) void ; SPORT drawn.
numerale *agg* & *sm* numeral.
numerare *vt* to number.
numerico, a *agg* TECNOL numerical ; INFORM digital.
numero *sm* MAT *(quantità)* number ; *(segno, cifra)* numeral ; *(di scarpe)* size ; *(di rivista)* issue ; ~ civico house number ; ~ chiuso selective entry system ; ~ di conto account number ; ~ di targa numberplate ; ~ di telefono telephone number ; ~ verde ≃ freefone number *(Br)*, toll-free number *(Am)* ; dare i numeri *fig* to be off one's head.
numeroso, a *agg (molteplice)* numerous ; *(grande)* large.
numismatica *sf* numismatics *(sg)*.
nuocere a : nuocere a *v + prep* to harm.
nuora *sf* daughter-in-law.
nuotare *vi* to swim.
nuoto *sm* swimming.
nuovamente *avv* again.
Nuova Zelanda *sf* : la ~ New Zealand.
nuovo, a *agg* new ; di ~ again ; ~ di zecca brand-new.
nuraghe, ghi *sm prehistoric stone monument in Sardinia.*
nutriente *agg* nutritious.
nutrimento *sm* nourishment.
nutrire *vt (con cibo)* to feed ; *fig*

(sentimento) to feel. ❑ **nutrirsi di** *vr + prep* to feed on.
nuvola *sf* cloud ; **cascare dalle nuvole** to be flabbergasted.
nuvoloso, a *agg* cloudy.

o *cong* or ; ~ ... ~ either ... or.
O *(abbr di ovest)* W.
oasi *sf inv* oasis.
obbediente = **ubbidiente**.
obbedire = **ubbidire**.
obbligare *vt* : ~ **qn a fare qc** to force sb to do sthg.
obbligato, a *agg (percorso, passaggio)* fixed ; *(costretto)* : ~ **a fare qc** obliged to do sthg.
obbligatorio, a *agg* compulsory.
obbligo, ghi *sm* obligation ; **avere l' ~ di fare qc** to be obliged to do sthg.
obelisco, schi *sm* obelisk.
obeso, a *agg* obese.
obiettare *vt* to object.
obiettivo, a *agg* objective. ◆ *sm (fotografico)* lens ; *(bersaglio, scopo)* objective.
obiettore *sm* objector ; ~ **di coscienza** conscientious objector.
obiezione *sf* objection.
obitorio *sm* mortuary.
obliquo, a *agg* slanting.
obliterare *vt* to stamp.
oblò *sm inv* porthole.
obsoleto, a *agg* obsolete.
oca *(pl* **oche**) *sf* goose.
occasione *sf (momento favorevole)* opportunity ; *(affare)* bargain ; *(causa, circostanza)* occasion ; **avere ~ di fare qc** to have the chance to do sthg ; **cogliere l' ~ per fare qc** to take the opportunity to do sthg ; **d' ~** second-hand.
occhiaia *sf (contorno degli occhi)* bag ; **avere le occhiaie** to have bags under your eyes.
occhiali *smpl* : ~ **(da vista)** glasses ; ~ **da sole** sunglasses.
occhiata *sf* : **dare un' ~ a** to have a look at.
occhiello *sm* buttonhole.
occhio *sm* eye ; **a ~ nudo** with the naked eye ; **tenere** ○ **non perdere d' ~ qn/qc** to keep an eye on sb/sthg ; **a ~ e croce** roughly ; **costare un ~ della testa** to cost a fortune ; **saltare** ○ **balzare all' ~** to be obvious ; **a quattr'occhi** in private ; **sognare a occhi aperti** to daydream.
occhiolino *sm* : **fare l' ~ (a qn)** to wink (at sb).
occidentale *agg (zona)* west, western ; *(cultura, società)* Western.
occidente *sm* west. ❑ **Occidente** *sm* : **l'Occidente** the West.
occorrente *sm* everything necessary.
occorrenza *sf* : **all' ~** if need be.
occorrere *vi* to be necessary ; **occorre aspettare** you/we have to wait ; **mi occorre tempo** I need time.
occorso, a *pp* → **occorrere**.
occulto, a *agg* occult.

occupare *vt (ingombrare)* to take up ; *(paese, università)* to occupy ; *(impegnare)* to keep busy. ❑ **occuparsi di** *vr + prep (prendersi cura di)* to take care of, to look after ; *(impicciarsi in)* to interfere in ; *(interessarsi di)* : **si occupa di politica** he's in politics ; **occupati dei fatti tuoi!** mind your own business!

occupato, a *agg (sedia, posto)* taken ; *(telefono, bagno)* engaged ; *(impegnato)* busy.

occupazione *sf (impiego)* occupation ; *(in economia)* employment.

Oceania *sf* : **l'** ~ Oceania.

oceano *sm* ocean.

oculista, i, e *smf* eye specialist.

odiare *vt* to hate.

odio *sm* hatred.

odioso, a *agg* hateful, odious.

odorare *vt* to smell. ❑ **odorare di** *v + prep* to smell of.

odorato *sm* (sense of) smell.

odore *sm* smell. ❑ **odori** *smpl (da cucina)* herbs.

offendere *vt* to offend. ❑ **offendersi** *vr* to take offence.

offensivo, a *agg* offensive.

offerto, a *pp* → **offrire.** ◆ *sf (proposta)* offer ; *(donazione)* donation ; FIN supply ; ~ **speciale** special offer.

offesa *sf* offence.

offeso, a *pp* → **offendere.** ◆ *agg* offended.

officina *sf (di fabbrica)* workshop ; *(per auto)* garage.

offrire *vt* to offer ; *(cena, caffè)* to pay for ; ~ **da bere a qn** to buy sb a drink. ❑ **offrirsi di** *vr + prep* : **offrirsi di fare qc** to offer to do sthg.

offuscare *vt (luce)* to darken ; *(vista, mente, memoria)* to dim. ❑ **offuscarsi** *vr (vista)* to dim.

oggettivo, a *agg* objective.

oggetto *sm* object ; **(ufficio) oggetti smarriti** lost property (office) *(Br)*, lost-and-found office *(Am)*.

oggi *avv* today ; *(attualmente)* nowadays ; ~ **pomeriggio** this afternoon ; **il giornale di ~** today's newspaper ; **dall' ~ al domani** from one day to the next.

oggigiorno *avv* nowadays.

OGN *sf (abbr di Organismo Geneticamente Modificato)* GMO.

ogni *agg inv (tutti)* every, each ; *(distributivo)* every ; **gente di ~ tipo** all sorts of people ; ~ **giorno/mese/anno** every day/month/year ; ~ **tre giorni** every three days ; **in ~ caso** in any case ; **ad ~ modo** anyway ; ~ **tanto** every so often ; ~ **volta che** whenever.

Ognissanti *sm* All Saints' Day.

ognuno, a *pron* everyone, everybody ; ~ **di voi** each of you.

Olanda *sf* : **l'** ~ Holland.

olandese *agg & sm* Dutch. ◆ *smf* Dutchman *(f* Dutchwoman) ; **gli olandesi** the Dutch.

oleoso, a *agg* oily.

olfatto *sm* sense of smell.

oliare *vt* to oil.

oliera *sf* oil and vinegar cruet.

olimpiadi *sfpl* : **le** ~ the Olympic Games.

olio *sm* oil ; ~ **(extra-vergine) d'oliva** (extra-virgin) olive oil ; ~ **di semi** vegetable oil ; **sott'** ~ in oil.

oliva *sf* olive ; **olive farcite all'anconetana** *olives stuffed with meat* *and vegetables, then covered in breadcrumbs and fried.*

olivastro, a *agg (carnagione)* sallow.

olivo *sm* olive tree.

olmo *sm* elm.

ologramma *sm* hologram.

oltraggio *sm* DIR offence.

oltralpe : d'oltralpe *agg* on the other side of the Alps.

oltralpe *avv* on the outside of the Alps.

oltranza : aoltranza *avv* to the (bitter) end.

oltre *prep (di là da)* beyond ; *(più di)* over, more than ; *(in aggiunta a)* as well as, besides. ◆ *avv (più in là)* further ; **~ a** *(all'infuori di)* apart from ; *(in aggiunta a)* as well as ; **non ~ le cinque** no later than five o'clock.

oltrepassare *vt* to go beyond.

omaggio *sm (tributo)* homage ; *(regalo)* gift ; **in ~** *(con prodotto)* free.

ombelico, chi *sm* navel.

ombra *sf (zona)* shade ; *(figura)* shadow ; **all' ~** in the shade.

ombrello *sm* umbrella.

ombrellone *sm* beach umbrella.

ombretto *sm* eye shadow.

omeopatia *sf* homeopathy.

omeopatico, a *agg (medico)* homeopathic ; *(sostanza)* homeopathic.

omesso, a *pp* → **omettere**.

omettere *vt* to omit ; **~ di fare qc** to omit to do sthg.

omicidio *sm* murder.

omissione *sf* omission.

omogeneizzato *sm* baby food.

omogeneo, a *agg (uniforme)* homogeneous ; *(armonico)* harmonious.

omonimo, a *sm, f (persona)* namesake.

omosessuale *smf* homosexual.

On. *(abbr di onorevole)* Hon.

onda *sf* wave ; **andare in ~** to go on the air ; **mandare in ~ qc** to broadcast sthg ; **onde lunghe/ medie / corte** long / medium / short wave *(sg)* ; **'onde pericolose'** *sign warning swimmers to take care.*

ondulato, a *agg (terreno)* undulating ; *(capelli)* wavy ; *(lamiera, carta)* corrugated.

onere *sm (form)* burden. ❑ **oneri fiscali** DIR taxes.

onestà *sf* honesty.

onesto, a *agg* honest.

onnipotente *agg* omnipotent.

onomastico *sm* name day.

ONOMASTICO

Along with their birthdays, Italians also celebrate their *onomastico*, or name day, albeit in a minor way. This is the day when the saint after whom they are named is honoured. Relatives and friends send cards, small gifts or simply their best wishes.

---

onorare *vt (celebrare)* to honour ; *(fare onore a)* to do credit to.

onorario, a *agg (cittadinanza, console)* honorary. ◆ *sm* fee.

onore *sm* honour ; **fare ~ a qc** *(pranzo)* to do justice to sthg ; *(scuola, famiglia)* to be a credit to sthg ; **in ~ di** in honour of ; **fare gli onori di casa** to be the host (*f* Ü hostess) ; **farsi ~** to distinguish o.s.

onorevole *agg (parlamentare)* Honourable. ◆ *smf* ≃ Member of Parliament *(Br)*, ≃ Congressman (*f* Congresswoman) *(Am)*.

ONU *(abbr di Organizzazione delle Nazioni Unite)* UN.

opaco, a, chi, che *agg (vetro)* opaque ; *(colore, metallo)* dull.

opera *sf* work ; *(in musica)* opera ; **è tutta ~ sua!** it's all his doing! ; **mettersi all' ~** to get down to work ; **~ d'arte** work of art ; **opere pubbliche** public works.

operaio, a *agg* working-class. ◆ *sm, f* worker.

operare *vt (realizzare)* to carry out ; *MED* to operate on. ◆ *vi (agire)* to act. ❑ **operarsi** *vr (compiersi)* to take place ; *(subire un'operazione)* to have an operation.

operatore, trice *sm, f (di televisione, cinema)* cameraman (*f* camerawoman) ; **~ turistico** tour operator.

operazione *sf* operation ; *FIN* transaction.

opinione *sf* opinion ; **l' ~ pubblica** public opinion.

opporre *vt (argomenti, ragioni)* to put forward ; **~ resistenza** to put up some resistance ; **~ un rifiuto** to refuse. ❑ **opporsi** *vr* : **opporsi (a)** to oppose.

opportunità *sf inv* opportunity.

opportuno, a *agg* opportune.

opposizione *sf* opposition.

opposto, a *pp* → **opporre.** ◆ *agg (lato, senso)* opposite ; *(idee)* opposing. ◆ *sm* opposite.

oppressione *sf* oppression.

oppresso, a *pp* → **opprimere.**

opprimente *agg* oppressive.

opprimere *vt (popolo)* to oppress ; *(angosciare)* to weigh down.

oppure *cong (o invece)* or ; *(se no)* or else, otherwise.

optare : **optare per** *v + prep* to opt for.

opuscolo *sm* brochure.

opzione *sf (scelta)* option ; *INFORM* option ; **questa gita è in ~** this trip is optional.

ora *sf* hour ; *(momento)* time. ◆ *avv* now ; **a che ~ parte il treno?** what time does the train leave? ; **è ~ di partire** it's time to leave ; **che ~ è?, che ore sono?** what's the time? ; **e ~?** now what? ; **~ come ~** right now ; **~ legale** summertime ; **~ locale** local time ; **~ di punta** rush hour ; **50 km all' ~** 50 km an hour ; **di buon' ~** early ; **d' ~ in poi** ○ **in avanti** from now on ; **fare le ore piccole** to stay up till the small hours.

orale *agg* & *sm* oral.

oramai → **ormai.**

orario, a *agg (segnale)* time *(dav s)* ; *(velocità)* per hour ; *(tariffa)* hourly. ◆ *sm (di lavoro, visite)* hours *(pl)* ; *(tabella)* timetable ; **fuori ~** after hours ; **in ~** on time ; **~ di arrivo** arrival time ; **~ di partenza** departure time ; **~ di apertura** opening hours *(pl)* ; **~ di chiusura** closing time ; **~ d'ufficio** office hours *(pl)*.

orata *sf* sea bream.

orbita *sf (di satellite)* orbit ; *(di occhio)* eye socket.
orchestra *sf* orchestra.
ordigno *sm* device.
ordinare *vt (al ristorante, bar)* to order ; *(disporre in ordine)* to put in order ; *(comandare)* : **~ a qn di fare qc** to order sb to do sthg.
ordinario, a *agg (normale)* ordinary ; *(mediocre, scadente)* poor.
ordinato, a *agg* tidy.
ordinazione *sf* order.
ordine *sm* order ; **essere in ~** *(stanza)* to be tidy ; *(documenti)* to be in order ; **mettere in ~ qc** *(stanza)* to tidy sthg ; *(documenti)* to put sthg in order ; **~ pubblico** public order.
orecchiabile *agg* catchy.
orecchiette *sfpl tiny ear-shaped pasta from Puglia.*
orecchino *sm* earring.
orecchio (*pl f* **orecchie**) *sm* ear ; **avere ~** to have a good ear (for music).
orecchioni *smpl* mumps *(sg)*.
oreficeria *sf (negozio)* jeweller's.
orfano, a *agg* & *sm, f* orphan.
organico, a, ci, che *agg* organic. ◆ *sm* staff.
organismo *sm (essere vivente)* organism ; *(ente)* body.
organizzare *vt* to organize. ❑ **organizzarsi** *vr* to organize o.s.
organizzato, a *agg* organized.
organizzatore, trice *sm, f* organizer.
organizzazione *sf* organization.
organo *sm* organ.
orgasmo *sm* orgasm.
orgoglio *sm* pride.
orgoglioso, a *agg* proud.
orientale *agg (paese, prodotto)* eastern ; *(persona)* oriental. ◆ *smf* Oriental.
orientamento *sm (posizione)* orientation ; *fig (indirizzo)* leanings *(pl)* ; **perdere l' ~** to lose one's bearings ; **~ professionale** careers guidance.
orientare *vt (carta)* to orientate. ❑ **orientarsi** *vr* to find one's bearings.
oriente *sm* east. ❑ **Oriente** *sm* : **l'Oriente** the East.
origano *sm* oregano.
originale *agg* original ; *(stravagante)* eccentric. ◆ *sm* original.
originario, a *agg (iniziale)* original ; *(paese, lingua)* native.
origine *sf* origin ; *(causa)* origin, cause ; **avere ~ da qc** to originate from sthg ; **dare ~ a qc** to cause sthg ; **di ~ italiana** of Italian origin.
origliare *vi* to eavesdrop.
orina = **urina**.
oriundo, a *sm, f* : **essere ~ italiano** to be of Italian extraction.
orizzontale *agg* horizontal.
orizzonte *sm* horizon.
orlo *sm (di fosso)* edge ; *(di bicchiere)* rim ; *(di gonna, pantaloni)* hem.
orma *sf* footprint.
ormai *avv (a questo punto)* by now ; *(a quel punto)* by then ; *(quasi)* almost ; **~ è tardi** it's too late now.
ormeggiare *vt* & *vi* to moor.
ormeggio *sm* mooring.
ormone *sm* hormone.

ornamento *sm* ornament.
ornare *vt* to decorate.
oro *sm* gold ; **d' ~** gold.
orologio *sm* clock ; *(da polso)* watch.
oroscopo *sm* horoscope.
orrendo, a *agg (spaventoso, atroce)* horrendous ; *(brutto)* horrible, awful.
orribile *agg* horrible.
orrore *sm* horror.
orsacchiotto *sm* teddy bear.
orso *sm* bear.
ortaggio *sm* vegetable.
ortica, che *sf* nettle.
orticaria *sf* hives *(pl)*.
orto *sm* vegetable garden.
ortodosso, a *agg* orthodox.
ortografia *sf* spelling.
orzaiolo *sm* stye.
orzo *sm* barley.
osare *vt* : **~ (fare qc)** to dare (to do sthg).
osceno, a *agg* obscene.
oscillare *vi (dondolare)* to swing ; *fig (variare)* to vary.
oscillazione *sf (di pendolo)* swing ; *(di prezzi)* fluctuation ; *(di temperatura)* variation.
oscurità *sf* darkness.
oscuro, a *agg* dark. ◆ *sm* : **essere all' ~ di qc** to be in the dark about sthg.
ospedale *sm* hospital.
ospitale *agg (persona)* hospitable ; *(paese)* friendly.
ospitalità *sf* hospitality ; **mi ha dato ~ per una notte** he put me up for a night.
ospitare *vt* to put up.
ospite *smf (chi ospita)* host (*f* hostess) ; *(ospitato)* guest.
ospizio *sm* old people's home.
ossa *pl* → **osso**.
osseo, a *agg* bone *(dav s)*.
osservare *vt (guardare)* to observe, to watch ; *(rilevare)* to notice ; *(rispettare, mantenere)* to observe ; **far ~ qc a qn** to point sthg out to sb.
osservatorio *sm* observatory.
osservazione *sf (esame)* observation ; *(commento)* observation, remark ; *(rimprovero)* criticism.
ossessionare *vt* to obsess.
ossessione *sf* obsession.
ossia *cong* that is.
ossidare *vt* to oxidize. ❑ **ossidarsi** *vr* to oxidize.
ossido *sm* oxide ; **~ di carbonio** carbon monoxide.
ossigenare *vt* to oxygenate ; *(capelli)* to bleach.
ossigeno *sm* oxygen.
osso *sm (umano : pl f ossa)* bone ; *(di carne : pl m ossi)* bone.
ossobuco (*pl* **ossibuchi**) *sm veal knuckle cooked on the bone in tomatoes and white wine (a speciality of Milan)*.
ostacolare *vt* to obstruct.
ostacolo *sm* obstacle ; *(in atletica)* hurdle ; *(in equitazione)* fence.
ostaggio *sm* hostage.
ostello *sm* : **~ (della gioventù)** (youth) hostel.
ostentare *vt* to flaunt.
osteria *sf* inn.
ostetrica, che *sf* midwife.
ostia *sf* RELIG host.

ostile *agg* hostile.
ostilità *sf* hostility. ◆ *sfpl* MIL hostilities.
ostinarsi *vr* : ~ a fare qc to persist in doing sthg.
ostinato, a *agg* obstinate.
ostinazione *sf* persistence.
ostrica, che *sf* oyster.
ostruire *vt* to obstruct, to block.
ottanta *num* eighty → sei.
ottantesimo, a *num* eightieth → sesto.
ottantina *sf*: una ~ (di) about eighty ; essere sull' ~ to be in one's eighties.
ottavo, a *num* eighth → sesto.
ottenere *vt* to get.
ottico, a, ci, che *agg (nervo)* optic ; *(strumento)* optical. ◆ *sm* optician.
ottimale *agg* optimum.
ottimismo *sm* optimism.
ottimista, i, e *smf* optimist.
ottimo, a *agg* excellent, very good.
otto *num* eight → sei. ◆ *sm* : ~ volante roller coaster.
ottobre *sm* October → settembre.
ottocento *num* eight hundred → sei. ❏ **Ottocento** *sm* : l'Ottocento the nineteenth century.
ottone *sm* brass.
otturare *vt* to fill.
otturazione *sf* filling.
ottuso, a *agg* obtuse.
ovale *agg* oval.
ovatta *sf* cotton wool.
overdose *sf inv* overdose.
ovest *sm* & *agg inv* west ; a ~ (di qc) west (of sthg).
ovile *sm* sheepfold.
ovino, a *agg* sheep *(dav s)*.
ovovia *sf* ski lift *(with oval cabins)*.
ovunque = dovunque.
ovvero *cong* or, in other words.
ovviare *vi* : ~ a qc to avoid sthg.
ovvio, a *agg* obvious.
ozio *sm* idleness.
ozono *sm* ozone.

P

pacato, a *agg* calm.
pacca, che *sf* pat.
pacchetto *sm (di sigarette, caramelle)* packet ; *(pacco)* parcel.
pacchiano, a *agg* garish.
pacco, chi *sm* parcel.
pace *sf* peace ; in ~ in peace ; fare (la) ~ to make it up.
pacemaker [pei'smɛker] *sm inv* pacemaker.
pacifico, a, ci, che *agg* peaceful. ❏ **Pacifico** *sm* : il Pacifico the Pacific.
pacifista, i, e *agg* & *smf* pacifist.
padella *sf (da cucina)* frying pan ; *(per malati)* bedpan.
padiglione *sm (di ospedale, fiera)* pavilion ; *(di giardino)* marquee.
Padova *sf* Padua.
padre *sm* father.
padrino *sm* godfather.

padrone, a *sm, f* owner ; **essere ~ di fare qc** to be free to do sthg ; **~ di casa** landlord (*f* landlady).

paesaggio *sm* landscape ; *(panorama)* scenery.

paese *sm (nazione)* country ; *(villaggio)* village ; **~ di provenienza** country of origin ; **mandare qn a quel ~** *volg* to tell sb to get lost. ❑ **Paesi Bassi** *smpl* : **i Paesi Bassi** the Netherlands.

paffuto, a *agg* plump, chubby.

paga, ghe *sf* pay.

pagamento *sm* payment ; '**~ pedaggio**' 'toll to be paid here'.

pagano, a *agg* & *sm, f* pagan.

pagare *vt* to pay ; *(offrire)* to buy ; **quanto l'hai pagato?** how much did you pay for it? ; **~ con assegno** to pay by cheque ; **~ con carta di credito** to pay by credit card ; **~ in contanti** to pay cash.

pagella *sf* (school) report.

pagina *sf* page.

paglia *sf* straw.

pagliaccio *sm* clown.

pagnotta *sf* round loaf.

paio (*pl f* **paia**) *sm* pair ; **un ~ di** *(alcuni)* a couple of ; **un ~ di scarpe** a pair of shoes.

Pakistan *sm* : **il ~** Pakistan.

pala *sf (vanga)* shovel ; *(di mulino, elica)* blade.

palato *sm* palate.

palazzo *sm (signorile)* palace ; *(edificio)* building ; *(condominio)* block of flats *(Br)*, apartment building *(Am)* ; **~ di giustizia** law courts *(pl)* ; **~ dello sport** indoor stadium.

PALAZZO MADAMA

The *Palazzo Madama* in Rome was built in the XVIth century for the Medici family. In 1538, it became the residence of Margaret of Austria the widow of Alessandro de' Medici, so – called the *'Madama'*, and from hence was named after her. Since 1871 the Palace houses the Senate of the Italian Republic.

palco, chi *sm (palcoscenico)* stage ; *(pedana)* stand ; *(a teatro)* box.

palcoscenico, ci *sm* stage.

Palermo *sf* Palermo.

Palestina *sf* : **la ~** Palestine.

palestra *sf* gymnasium.

paletta *sf (giocattolo, per giardiniere)* spade ; *(per lo sporco)* dustpan ; *(di polizia, capostazione)* signalling disc.

paletto *sm* stake.

palio *sm* : **mettere qc in ~** to offer sthg as a prize. ❑ **Palio** *sm* : **il Palio (di Siena)** the Palio *(traditional horse race held in the centre of Siena)*.

IL PALIO DI SIENA

Siena's famous horse race attracts thousands of tourists to Tuscany on July 2 and August 16 every year. Representatives of Siena's 17 *contrade* (districts) parade in Renaissance costumes, and 10 districts enter a horse and rider in the race which follows. The race is very rough, and the walls of the *Piazza del Campo* are padded to protect the contestants. The winner is awarded a *palio* (painted banner), and is paraded through the town.

palla *sf* ball ; **che palle!** *volg* what a drag!
pallacanestro *sf* basketball.
pallanuoto *sf* water polo.
pallavolo *sf* volleyball.
pallido, a *agg* pale.
palloncino *sm* balloon.
pallone *sm (palla)* ball ; *(da calcio)* football ; **~ aerostatico** hot air balloon.
pallottola *sf* bullet.
palma *sf* palm tree.
palmo *sm* palm.
palo *sm (di legno)* post ; *(di telefono)* pole ; **~ della luce** lamppost.
palombaro *sm* (deep sea) diver.
palpebra *sf* eyelid.
palude *sf* marsh, swamp.
panca, che *sf* bench.
pancarrè *sm* sliced bread.
pancetta *sf* bacon.
panchina *sf (di parco)* bench ; *(di giardino)* garden seat.
pancia, ce *sf fam* belly.
panciotto *sm* waistcoat.
panda *sm inv* panda.
pandoro *sm conical sponge cake eaten at Christmas.*
pane *sm* bread ; *(pagnotta)* loaf ; *(di burro)* block ; **~ a o in cassetta** sliced bread ; **~ integrale** wholemeal bread ; **~ tostato** toast ; **pandolce** *Christmas cake with candied fruit (a speciality of Genoa)* ; **pan di Spagna** sponge cake.

PANE

A staple of the Mediterranean diet, bread is eaten with all Italian meals and waiters bring it automatically to the restaurant table. The main varieties are *pane bianco* (white bread), which is either *speciale* (made with oil) or *comune*, and *pane integrale* (wholemeal bread). It is sold in loaves or sticks or as rolls, and its shapes and names differ from region to region and city to city.

panetteria *sf* bakery.
panettone *sm traditional dome-shaped Christmas cake containing raisins and candied fruit.*
panforte *sm very rich round, flat cake made with almonds, hazelnuts, candied fruit and spices (a speciality of Siena).*
pangrattato *sm* breadcrumbs *(pl)*.
panico *sm* panic.
panificio *sm* baker's.
panino *sm* roll ; **~ imbottito o ripieno** filled roll ; **~ al prosciutto** ham roll.
paninoteca, che *sf* sandwich bar.
panna *sf* : **~ (montata)** whipped cream ; **~ cotta** *cold dessert made from cream and sugar, eaten with chocolate or fruit sauce* ; **~ da cucina** cream.
panne *agg inv* : **ho l'auto in ~** my car has broken down.
pannello *sm* panel.
panno *sm* cloth ; **mettersi nei panni di qn** to put o.s. in sb's shoes.

pannocchia *sf* cob.
pannolino *sm* nappy *(Br)*, diaper *(Am)*.
panorama, i *sm* panorama.
panoramico, a, ci, che panoramic.
panpepato *sm* ≃ gingerbread.
pantaloni *smpl* trousers *(Br)*, pants *(Am)*.
pantera *sf* panther.
pantofole *sfpl* slippers.
panzanella *sf Tuscan salad of tomatoes, anchovies, tuna, onion and herbs, whose special ingredient is moistened bread.*
panzerotti *smpl large ravioli stuffed with cheese and tomato, and fried in oil.*
paonazzo, a *agg* purple.
papà *sm inv fam* daddy, dad.
papavero *sm* poppy.
papera *sf (errore)* : **fare una ~** to make a slip of the tongue, papero.
papero, a *sm, f* gosling.
papillon [papi'jɔn] *sm inv* bow tie.
pappa *sf fam* baby food.
pappagallo *sm (animale)* parrot ; *(per malati)* bedpan.
pappardelle *sfpl* large noodles ; **~ alla lepre** *'pappardelle' served with hare sauce.*
paprica *sf* paprika.
para *sf* crepe rubber.
parabola *sf MAT* parabola ; *RELIG* parable.
parabrezza *sm inv* windscreen.
paracadute *sm inv* parachute.
paracarro *sm* post.
paradiso *sm RELIG* paradise, heaven.
paradossale *agg* paradoxical.
paradosso *sm* paradox.
parafango, ghi *sm* mudguard.
parafulmine *sm* lightning conductor.
paraggi *smpl* : **nei ~** in the neighbourhood.
paragonare *vt* : **~ con** to compare with.
paragone *sm* comparison.
paragrafo *sm* paragraph.
paralisi *sf inv* paralysis.
paralizzare *vt* to paralyse.
parallela *sf* parallel. ❑ **parallele** *sfpl (attrezzo)* parallel bars.
parallelo, a *agg* & *sm* parallel.
paralume *sm* lampshade.
parapetto *sm* parapet.
parare *vt (colpi)* to parry ; *(occhi)* to shield ; *(nel calcio)* to save.
parassita, i *sm* parasite.
parata *sf (militare)* parade ; *(nel calcio)* save.
paraurti *sm inv* bumper.
paravento *sm* screen.
parcella *sf* fee.
parcheggiare *vt* to park.
parcheggio *sm (area)* car park *(Br)*, parking lot *(Am)* ; *(manovra)* parking ; **~ a pagamento** *car park where drivers must pay to park* ; **~ riservato** private car park.
parchimetro *sm* parking meter.
parco, chi *sm* park ; **~ giochi o dei divertimenti** swing park.

PARCHI NAZIONALI

Five Italian national parks have been created by the government to protect the environment and preserve the balance of nature in these designated areas. They are areas of great natural beauty and are well equipped to welcome visitors. In the Alps the *Parco del Gran Paradiso* shelters the ibex, and the *Parco dello Stelvio*, the chamois. In the central Appenines are the *Parco Nazionale d'Abruzzo* and the *Parco del Circeo*, and in the south is the *Parco Nazionale della Calabria*.

---

parecchio, a *agg* quite a lot of. ◆ *pron* quite a lot. ◆ *avv (con agg)* quite ; *(con verbo)* quite a lot ; **è ~ (tempo) che aspetto** I've been waiting for quite a while.

pareggiare *vt (capelli, orlo)* to make even ; *(terreno)* to level ; *(bilancio, conti)* to balance. ◆ *vi* to draw.

pareggio *sm (in partite)* draw ; *(del bilancio)* balance.

parente *smf* relative.

parentela *sf (vincolo)* relationship ; *(famiglia)* relatives *(pl)*.

parentesi *sf inv (segno)* bracket ; *(commento)* digression ; **tra ~** in brackets.

pareo *sm* pareo.

parere *sm (opinione)* opinion. ◆ *vi (sembrare)* to seem ; *(apparire)* to look. ◆ *v impers* : **pare che** it seems that ; **che te ne pare?** what do you think? ; **fate come vi pare** do as you like ; **mi pare di no** I don't think so ; **mi pare di sì** I think so ; **mi pare (che) vada bene** it seems (to be) all right ; **pare (che) sia vero** it seems (to be) true.

parete *sf (di stanza)* wall ; *(di montagna)* face.

pari *agg inv (in partite, giochi, superficie)* level ; *(numero)* even. ◆ *sm inv* equal ; **alla ~** *(ragazza)* au pair ; **ora siamo ~** now we're even ; **essere ~ a** *(uguale)* to be the same as , to be equal to ; **essere alla ~** to be even ; **mettersi in ~ con qc** to catch up with sthg ; **~ ~** word for word.

Parigi *sf* Paris.

parlamentare *agg* parliamentary. ◆ *smf* ≃ Member of Parliament *(Br)*, ≃ Congressman *(f* Congresswoman) *(Am)*.

parlamento *sm* parliament.

parlantina *sf fam* : **avere una bella ~** to have the gift of the gab.

parlare *vi* to talk, to speak. ◆ *vt (lingua)* to speak ; **~ (a qn) di** to talk o to speak (to sb) about ; **parla italiano?** do you speak Italian?

Parma *sf* Parma.

parmigiano *sm* Parmesan (cheese).

parola *sf* word ; **prendere la ~** to (begin to) speak ; **rivolgere la ~ a qn** to talk to sb ; **rimangiarsi la ~** to go back on one's word ; **~ d'onore** word of honour ; **~ d'ordine** password ; **parole crociate** crossword (puzzle) *(sg)* ; **è una ~!** it's not easy!

parolaccia, ce *sf* swearword.

parrocchia *sf (chiesa)* parish church ; *(zona)* parish.

parroco, ci *sm* parish priest.
parrucca, che *sf* wig.
parrucchiere, a *sm, f (per signora)* hairdresser.
parso, a *pp* → **parere.**
parte *sf* part ; *(lato)* side ; *(direzione)* way ; *(quota)* share ; DIR party ; **fare ~ di qc** to be part of sthg ; **mettere da ~ qc** *(risparmiare)* to put sthg aside ; **prendere ~ a qc** to take part in sthg ; **stare dalla ~ di** to be on the side of ; **la maggior ~ di** most ; **la maggior ~ degli italiani** most Italians ; **a ~ questo** apart from that ; **a ~** *(spese, pacco)* separate ; *(pagare, incartare)* separately ; **da ~ di qn** from ; *(ringraziare)* on sb's behalf ; **d'altra ~** on the other hand ; **dall'altra ~** the other way ; **da nessuna ~** nowhere ; **da ogni ~** everywhere ; **da qualche ~** somewhere ; **da questa ~** this way ; **in ~** partly.
partecipare a : partecipare a *v + prep (intervenire)* to take part in ; *(spese)* to contribute to ; *(gioia, dolore)* to share in.
partecipazione *sf (di nozze)* invitation ; *(a qc)* participation (in sth).
partenza *sf* departure ; *(nello sport)* start ; **essere in ~ (per Roma)** to be about to leave (for Rome) ; **'partenze nazionali/internazionali'** 'domestic/international departures'.
participio *sm* participle.
particolare *agg* particular ; *(caratteristico)* distinctive. ◆ *sm* detail ; **niente di ~** nothing special ; **in ~** in particular.
particolareggiato, a *agg* detailed.
partigiano, a *sm, f* partisan.
partire *vi (persona)* to leave ; *(treno, aereo)* to depart ; *(nello sport)* to start ; *(colpo)* to go off ; **a ~ da** from ; **parto da Milano alle cinque** I leave Milan at five.
partita *sf (competizione)* match ; *(a carte, a tennis)* game ; *(di merce)* consignment ; **~ IVA** VAT registration number.
partito *sm* party.
parto *sm* birth.
partorire *vt* to give birth to.
parziale *agg (limitato)* partial ; *(ingiusto)* biased.
pascolo *sm* pasture.
Pasqua *sf* Easter.
pasquale *agg* Easter *(dav s)*.
Pasquetta *sf* Easter Monday.

PASQUETTA

In Italy, Easter still retains its religious significance. Holy Week culminates in a mass celebrated by the Pope from the balcony of St Peter's, and on Easter Sunday families have a special lunch and exchange Easter eggs. In many regions Easter Monday, a national holiday, is called *Pasquetta*. It is traditionally celebrated with a picnic in the country or by the sea.

passabile *agg* passable.
passaggio *sm (transito)* passage ; *(varco)* thoroughfare ; *(in macchina)* lift ; *(cambiamento)* change ; **essere di ~** to be passing through ; **~ a livello** level crossing *(Br)*, grade

crossing *(Am)* ; ~ **pedonale** pedestrian crossing.

passamontagna *sm inv* balaclava.

passante *smf (persona)* passer-by. ◆ *sm (per cintura)* loop.

passaporto *sm* passport.

passare *vi* to go by ; *(da un'apertura)* to go through ; *(fare una visita)* to call in ; *(cessare)* to go away ; *(proposta)* to be passed. ◆ *vt (attraversare)* to cross ; *(trascorrere)* to spend ; *(cera, vernice)* to apply ; *(esame)* to pass ; *(oltrepassare)* to go beyond ; *(verdure)* to puree ; *(porgere)* to pass ; **mi è passato di mente!** it slipped my mind! ; **ti passo Matteo** *(al telefono)* here's Matteo ; **il treno passa da Firenze** the train goes via Florence ; ~ **l'aspirapolvere** to vacuum ; ~ **qc a qn** to pass o to give sb sthg ; ~ **avanti a qn** to push infront of sb ; ~ **da** o **per scemo** to be taken for a fool ; ~ **sopra qc** *fig (tollerare)* to overlook ; **passarsela bene** to get on well ; **come te la passi?** how are you getting on?

passatempo *sm* pastime.

passato, a *agg (trascorso)* over. ◆ *sm* past ; ~ **di verdure** thin vegetable soup.

passaverdura *sm inv* vegetable mill.

passeggero, a *agg* passing. ◆ *sm, f* passenger.

passeggiare *vi* to walk.

passeggiata *sf (camminata)* walk ; *(strada)* promenade ; **fare una** ~ to take a walk.

PASSEGGIATA

The Italian custom of taking a stroll with friends or family has survived many changes in fashion and still brings different generations together. Courting couples, families and teenagers alike meet up on Sunday morning or in the late afternoon and stroll slowly round the main square or the park, or along the main street or the promenade. They may stop to say hello to friends and acquaintances, to have an aperitif or to buy cakes and pastries for dessert.

---

passeggino *sm* pushchair.

passeggio *sm* : **andare a** ~ to go for a walk.

passerella *sf (passaggio)* footbridge ; *(di aereo, nave)* gangway ; *(di sfilata)* catwalk.

passerotto *sm* sparrow.

passione *sf* passion.

passivo, a *agg* passive. ◆ *sm* GRAMM passive ; COMM liabilities *(pl)*.

passo *sm (movimento)* step ; *(andatura)* pace ; *(rumore)* footstep ; *(valico)* pass ; **allungare il** ~ to quicken one's pace ; **fare il primo** ~ *fig* to make the first move ; **a** ~ **d'uomo** dead slow ; '~ **carraio** o **carrabile**' 'keep clear' ; **fare due** o **quattro passi** to go for a short walk ; **a due passi** a stone's throw away ; **di questo** ~ at this rate.

password ['pasword] *sf inv* INFORM password.

pasta *sf* pasta ; *(impasto)* dough ; *(pasticcino)* pastry ; *(di colla)* paste ;

~ **in brodo** *soup with pasta in it* ; ~ **frolla** shortcrust pastry ; ~ **sfoglia** puff pastry.

PASTA

Most Italians eat pasta at least once a day, and an infinite variety of types can be found : *spaghetti, bucatini* and *tagliatelle* are just a few examples of *pasta lunga* (long pasta) ; *penne, rigatoni* and *fusilli* are common types of *pasta corta* (short pasta). The basic dough is just flour and water, but it can be varied by using a different type of flour and by adding different ingredients and flavourings. *Pasta integrale* is wholemeal pasta, *pasta all'uovo* is enriched with egg, and *pasta verde* is flavoured with spinach. The tradition of making one's own pasta (*pasta fatta in casa*) still survives in many families.

---

pastasciutta *sf* pasta.

pastella *sf* batter.

pasticca, che = pastiglia.

pasticceria *sf* ≃ cake shop.

pasticcino *sm* pastry.

pasticcio *sm (vivanda)* pie ; *(disordine)* mess ; *(guaio)* trouble ; **essere nei pasticci** to be in trouble.

pasticcione, a *sm, f* bungler.

pastiera *sf Neapolitan Easter tart with a filling of ricotta cheese and candied fruit.*

pastiglia *sf* pastille.

pastizzada *sf horse meat or beef and vegetables marinated in wine, generally serves with polenta (a speciality of Veneto).*

pasto *sm* meal.

pastore *sm (di greggi)* shepherd ; *(sacerdote)* minister ; ~ **tedesco** German shepherd, Alsatian *(Br)*.

pastorizzato, a *agg* pasteurized.

patata *sf* potato ; **patate fritte** chips *(Br)*, French fries *(Am)*.

patatine *sfpl* crisps *(Br)*, chips *(Am)*.

paté *sm inv* pâté.

patente *sf* licence ; ~ **(di guida)** driving licence *(Br)*, driver's license *(Am)*.

paternità *sf* paternity.

paterno, a *agg* paternal.

patetico, a, ci, che *agg* pathetic.

patire *vt* & *vi* to suffer.

patria *sf* homeland.

patrigno *sm* stepfather.

patrimonio *sm (beni)* property ; *(culturale, spirituale)* heritage.

patrono *sm* patron saint.

pattinaggio *sm* skating ; ~ **su ghiaccio** ice skating.

pattinare *vi* to skate ; ~ **su ghiaccio** to ice-skate.

pattini *smpl* : ~ **a rotelle** roller skates ; ~ **da ghiaccio** ice skates.

pattino *sm pedalo with oars.*

patto *sm (accordo)* pact ; **a ~ che** on condition that.

pattuglia *sf* patrol.

pattumiera *sf* dustbin.

paura *sf* fear ; **avere ~ (di)** to be afraid (of) ; **avere ~ di fare qc** to be afraid of doing sthg ; **fare ~ a qn** to frighten sb ; **per ~ di fare qc** for fear of doing sthg ; **per ~ che** for fear that.

pauroso, a *agg (spaventoso)* frightening ; *(timoroso)* fearful.

pausa *sf (intervallo)* break ; *MUS* pause ; **fare una ~** to take a break.

pavesini® *smpl (biscotti) sweet finger biscuits.*

pavimento *sm* floor.

pavone *sm* peacock.

paziente *agg & smf* patient.

pazienza *sf* patience ; **perdere la ~** to lose one's patience ; **pazienza!** never mind!.

pazzamente *avv* madly.

pazzesco, a, schi, sche *agg* crazy.

pazzia *sf* madness ; *(azione)* crazy thing.

pazzo, a *agg (malato)* mad. ◆ *sm, f* madman (*f* madwoman) ; **andare ~ per qc** to be crazy about sthg ; **essere ~ di qn** to be crazy about sb ; **darsi alla pazza gioia** to live it up.

PC *sm* (*abbr di Personal Computer*) PC.

peccare *vi* to sin ; **~ di qc** to be guilty of sthg.

peccato *sm* sin ; **è un ~ che ...** it's a pity that ... ; **(che) ~!** what a pity!

peccatore, trice *sm, f* sinner.

pecora *sf* sheep.

pecorino *sm a cheese made from ewe's milk.*

pedaggio *sm* toll.

pedalare *vi* to pedal.

pedale *sm* pedal ; **a pedali** pedal *(dav s)*.

pedana *sf (poggiapiedi)* footboard ; *(in atletica)* springboard ; *(nella scherma)* piste.

pedata *sf (impronta)* footmark ; *(calcio)* kick.

pediatra, i, e *smf* paediatrician.

pedicure *sm* pedicure.

pedina *sf* piece.

pedonale *agg* pedestrian *(dav s)*.

pedone *sm* pedestrian ; *(negli scacchi)* pawn.

peggio *avv & agg inv* worse. ◆ *smf* : **il/la ~** the worst ; **~ per te!** so much the worse for you! ; **temere il ~** to fear the worst ; **alla ~** if the worst comes to the worst ; **~ che mai** worse than ever.

peggioramento *sm* deterioration.

peggiorare *vt & vi* to worsen.

peggiore *agg (comparativo)* worse ; *(superlativo)* worst. ◆ *smf* : **il/la ~** the worst.

pelare *vt* to peel.

pelato, a *agg* bald. ❑ **pelati** *smpl* peeled tomatoes.

pelle *sf* skin ; *(conciata)* leather ; **avere la ~ d'oca** to have goose pimples.

pellegrinaggio *sm* pilgrimage.

pelletteria *sf (prodotti)* leather goods *(pl)* ; *(negozio)* leather goods shop.

pelliccia, ce *sf (di animale)* fur ; *(indumento)* fur coat.

pellicola *sf* film ; **~ a colori** colour film.

pelo *sm (del corpo, di tessuto)* hair ; *(di animale)* fur ; **ce l'ho fatta per un ~** I made it by the skin of my teeth ; **c'è mancato un ~ che lo**

investissero they narrowly missed hitting him.

peloso, a *agg* hairy.

peltro *sm* pewter.

peluche [pe'luʃ] *sm inv (tessuto)* plush ; *(pupazzo)* cuddly toy.

pena *sf (condanna)* sentence ; *(cruccio)* anxiety ; *(pietà)* pity ; *RELIG* torment ; **mi fanno ~** I feel sorry for them ; **(non) vale la ~ di andarci** it's (not) worth going ; **~ di morte** death penalty ; **a mala ~** hardly.

penalità *sf inv* penalty.

pendente *agg (appeso)* hanging ; *(conto)* pending. ◆ *sm (ciondolo)* pendant ; *(orecchino)* drop earring.

pendenza *sf (inclinazione)* slope ; *(di conto)* outstanding account.

pendere *vi (essere appeso)* to hang ; *(essere inclinato)* to slope.

pendici *sfpl* slopes.

pendio *sm* slope.

pendola *sf* pendulum clock.

pendolare *smf* commuter.

pene *sm* penis.

penetrare *vi* : **~ in qc** *(entrare in)* to enter sthg ; *sog (chiodo, liquido)* to penetrate sthg.

penicillina *sf* penicillin.

penisola *sf* peninsula.

penitenza *sf (religiosa)* penitence ; *(nei giochi)* forfeit.

penitenziario *sm* prison.

penna *sf* pen ; *(di uccello)* feather ; **~ a sfera** ballpoint pen ; **~ stilografica** fountain pen. ❑ **penne** *sfpl* pasta quills ; **penne all'arrabbiata** *'penne' in a spicy sauce of tomatoes and chillies.*

pennarello *sm* felt-tip pen.

pennello *sm (da pittore)* brush ; *(per vernici, tinte)* paintbrush ; **~ da barba** shaving brush ; **a ~** like a glove.

penombra *sf* half-light.

penoso, a *agg* painful.

pensare *vi* to think. ◆ *vt (immaginare)* to think ; *(escogitare)* to think up ; **cosa ne pensi?** what do you think (of it)? ; **~ a** *(riflettere su, ricordare)* to think about ; *(occuparsi di)* to see to ; **pensa a un numero** think of a number ; **~ di fare qc** to be thinking of doing sthg ; **penso di no** I don't think so ; **penso di sì** I think so ; **pensarci su** to think it over.

pensiero *sm* thought ; *(preoccupazione)* worry ; **stare in ~ per qn** to be worried about sb.

pensile *agg* hanging. ◆ *sm* wall cupboard.

pensilina *sf (di stazione)* platform roof ; *(per autobus)* bus shelter.

pensionante *smf* lodger.

pensionato, a *sm, f (persona)* pensioner. ◆ *sm (per studenti)* hostel.

pensione *sf (somma)* pension ; *(albergo)* boardinghouse ; *(vitto e alloggio)* board and lodging ; **andare in ~** to retire ; **essere in ~** to be retired ; **~ completa** full board ; **mezza ~** half board.

Pentecoste *sf* Whitsun.

pentirsi *vr* : **~ di qc** to regret sthg ; **~ di aver fatto qc** to regret doing sthg.

pentola *sf* pot ; ~ **a pressione** pressure cooker.

penultimo, a *agg* penultimate.

pepare *vt* to pepper.

pepato, a *agg* peppery.

pepe *sm* pepper.

peperonata *sf stewed sliced peppers, tomatoes and onions.*

peperoncino *sm* chilli pepper ; ~ **rosso** red chilli pepper.

peperone *sm* (capsicum) pepper.

---

per *prep* - 1. *(indica lo scopo, la destinazione)* for ; **è ~ te** it's for you ; **fare qc ~ i soldi** to do sthg for money ; **equipaggiarsi ~ la montagna** to kit o.s. out for the mountains ; ~ **fare qc** (in order) to do sthg ; **sono venuto ~ vederti** I've come to see you ; **è abbastanza grande ~ capire certe cose** he's old enough to understand these things.
- 2. *(attraverso)* through ; **ti ho cercato ~ tutta la città** I've been looking for you all over town.
- 3. *(moto a luogo)* for, to ; **il treno ~ Genova** the Genoa train ; **partire ~ Napoli** to leave for Naples.
- 4. *(indica una durata, una scadenza)* for ; ~ **tutta la vita** for one's whole life ; **sarò di ritorno ~ le cinque** I'll be back by five ; **l'ho vista ~ Pasqua** I saw her at Easter ; **fare qc ~ tempo** to do sthg in time ; ~ **sempre** forever.
- 5. *(indica il mezzo, il modo)* by ; **gli ho parlato ~ telefono** I talked to him over the phone ; **viaggiare ~ mare** to travel by sea ; **fare qc ~ scherzo** to do sthg for a joke ; ~ **caso** by chance.
- 6. *(indica la causa)* for ; **piangere ~ la rabbia** to cry with rage ; **viaggiare ~ lavoro** to travel on business ; ~ **aver fatto qc** for doing sthg.
- 7. *(con valore distributivo)* per ; **entrare uno ~ volta** to go in one at a time ; **uno ~ uno** one by one.
- 8. *(come)* as ; **tenere qc ~ certo** to take sthg for granted.
- 9. *(indica il prezzo)* : **lo ha venduto ~ un milione** he sold it for a million euros.
- 10. MAT : **2 ~ 3 fa 6** 2 times 3 makes 6.
- 11. *(indica la conseguenza)* : **è troppo bello ~ essere vero** it's too good to be true.
- 12. *(indica limitazione)* for ; ~ **me, vi sbagliate** as far as I'm concerned, you are wrong ; ~ **questa volta** this time.

---

pera *sf* pear.

peraltro *avv* what is more.

perbene *agg inv* decent. ◆ *avv* properly.

percentuale *sf* percentage.

percepire *vt (sentire)* to perceive ; *(ricevere)* to receive.

---

perché *avv* why ; ~ **corri?** why are you running? ; ~ **non ci andiamo?** why don't we go? ; **spiegami ~ lo hai fatto** tell me why you did it ; ~ **no?** why not? ; **chissà ~** who knows why ; **ecco ~** that's why.
◆ *cong* - 1. *(per il fatto che)* because ; **vado ~ ho fretta** I'm going

because I'm in a hurry; **~ sì/no!** (just) because!
- 2. *(affinché)* so that; **telefona ~ non stiano in pensiero** phone so that (they) don't worry.
- 3. *(cosicché)* : **è troppo complicato ~ si possa capire** it's too complicated for anyone to understand.
◆ *sm inv (ragione)* reason; **senza un ~** for no reason.

---

perciò *cong* therefore.
percorrere *vt (regione)* to travel over; *(distanza)* to cover.
percorso, a *pp* → **percorrere.** ◆ *sm* journey.
percosse *sfpl* blows.
percosso, a *pp* → **percuotere.**
percuotere *vt form* to beat.
perdere *vt* to lose; *(treno, lezione, film)* to miss; *(tempo, denaro)* to waste; *(liquido, gas)* to leak; **~ sangue** to lose blood; **lasciare ~** not to bother; **non avere nulla da ~** to have nothing to lose; **~ la testa** to lose one's head. ❑ **perdersi** *vr* to get lost.
perdita *sf* loss; *(di acqua, gas)* leak; **una ~ di tempo** a waste of time; **a ~ d'occhio** as far as the eye can see.
perdonare *vt* to forgive.
perdono *sm (di colpa, peccato)* pardon; *(scusa)* forgiveness.
perdutamente *avv* desperately.
perfettamente *avv* perfectly.
perfetto, a *agg* perfect.
perfezionare *vt* to perfect.
perfezione *sf* perfection; **alla ~** perfectly.
perfido, a *agg* treacherous.
perfino *avv* even.
perforare *vt* to pierce.
pergola *sf* pergola.
pericolante *agg* unsafe.
pericolo *sm* danger; **essere fuori ~** to be out of danger; **essere in ~** to be in danger; **'~ (di morte)'** 'danger of death'.
pericoloso, a *agg* dangerous.
periferia *sf* outskirts *(pl)*.
perimetro *sm* perimeter.
periodico, a, ci, che *agg* periodic. ◆ *sm* periodical.
periodo *sm* period.
perito *sm (esperto)* expert; **~ chimico** qualified chemist.
perla *sf* pearl.
perlustrare *vt* to patrol.
permaloso, a *agg* touchy.
permanente *agg* permanent. ◆ *sf* perm; **'permanente'** 'at all times'.
permanenza *sf* continued stay.
permesso, a *pp* → **permettere.** ◆ *sm (autorizzazione)* permission; *(congedo)* leave; *(documento)* permit; **(è) ~?** *(per entrare)* may I come in?; **~!** *(per passare)* excuse me!; **~ di soggiorno** residence permit.
permettere *vt* to allow; **~ a qn di fare qc** to allow sb to do sthg; **potersi ~ qc** *(spesa, acquisto)* to be able to afford sthg; **permettersi di fare qc** *(prendersi la libertà)* to take the liberty of doing sthg; **potersi ~ di fare qc** *(finanziariamente)* to be able to afford to do sthg.
perno *sm* hinge.
pernottamento *sm* overnight stay.

però *cong (ma)* but ; *(tuttavia)* however.
perpendicolare *agg* perpendicular.
perplesso, a *agg* puzzled.
perquisire *vt* to search.
perquisizione *sf* search.
perseguitare *vt* to persecute.
perseverare *vi* to persevere.
persiana *sf* shutter.
persiano, a *agg* Persian. ◆ *sm (pelliccia)* Persian lamb.
persino = **perfino**.
persistente *agg* persistent.
perso, a *pp* → **perdere**.
persona *sf* person ; **c'è una ~ che ti aspetta** there's somebody waiting for you ; **conoscere qn di ~** to know sb personally ; **in ~** in person.
personaggio *sm (di libro, film)* character ; *(pubblico, politico)* figure.
personale *agg* personal. ◆ *sm (dipendenti)* personnel, staff ; *(fisico)* build.
personalità *sf inv* personality.
personalmente *avv* personally.
persuadere *vt* to persuade ; **~ qn a fare qc** to persuade sb to do sthg ; **~ qn di qc** to convince sb of sthg.
persuaso *pp* → **persuadere**.
pertanto *cong (perciò)* therefore.
perturbare *vt* to upset.
perturbazione *sf* disturbance.
Perugia *sf* Perugia.
pesante *agg* heavy ; *fig (persona, film)* boring ; *(scherzo)* in bad taste.
pesare *vt* to weigh. ◆ *vi* to weigh ; *(essere pesante)* to be heavy ; *(essere spiacevole)* to be hard. ❑ **pesarsi** *vr* to weigh o.s.
pesca, sche *sf (frutto)* peach ; *(attività)* fishing ; **pesche ripiene** *peaches stuffed with macaroons and baked in white wine* ; **andare a ~** to go fishing ; **~ di beneficenza** lucky dip ; **~ subacquea** underwater fishing.
pescare *vt (pesce)* to catch ; *(carta)* to draw ; *(trovare)* to find out ; **mi piace ~** I like fishing.
pescatore *sm* fisherman.
pesce *sm* fish ; **~ d'aprile!** April Fool! ❑ **Pesci** *smpl* Pisces *(sg)*.
pescheria *sf* fishmonger's.
pescivendolo, a *sm, f* fishmonger.
peso *sm* weight ; **lancio del ~** shotput ; **~ lordo** gross weight ; **~ netto** net weight ; **essere di ~ a qn** to be a burden on sb.
pessimismo *sm* pessimism.
pessimista, i, e *smf* pessimist.
pessimo, a *agg* dreadful.
pestare *vt (calpestare)* to tread on ; *(uva, aglio)* to crush ; *(picchiare)* to beat up.
peste *sf (malattia)* plague ; *fig (bambino, persona)* pest.
pesto, a *agg* : **buio ~** pitch-black ; **occhio ~** black eye. ◆ *sm* : **~ (alla genovese)** pesto *(sauce made from basil, pine kernels, garlic, olive oil and cheese ; a speciality of Genova)*.
petalo *sm* petal.
petardo *sm* firecracker.
petroliera *sf* oil tanker.

petrolio *sm* oil.
pettegolezzi *smpl* gossip *(sg)*.
pettinare *vt* to comb. ❑ **pettinarsi** *vr* to comb one's hair.
pettine *sm* comb.
petto *sm (torace)* chest ; *(seno)* breast ; **~ di pollo** chicken breast ; **a doppio ~** double-breasted.
pezzo *sm* piece ; *(di spazio, tempo)* bit ; **è un bel ~ che ti cerco** I've been looking for you for quite a while ; **andare in (mille) pezzi** to be smashed (to smithereens) ; **cadere a pezzi** to fall to pieces ; **~ di ricambio** spare part ; **~ grosso** *fig* big shot.
phon ['fɔn] *sm inv (asciugacapelli)* hair-dryer.
piacere *sm* pleasure ; *(favore)* favour. ◆ *vi* : **mi piace** I like it ; **mi piacciono i tulipani** I like tulips ; **mi ha fatto molto ~ vederla** I was delighted to see her ; **per ~** please ; **~ (di conoscerla)!** pleased to meet you! ; **~ mio!** the pleasure is mine!
piacevole *agg* pleasant.
piaga, ghe *sf (lesione)* sore ; *fig (flagello)* plague.
pianerottolo *sm* landing.
pianeta, i *sm* planet.
piangere *vi* to cry, to weep.
pianista, i, e *smf* pianist.
piano, a *agg (piatto)* flat ; MAT plane. ◆ *avv (lentamente)* slowly ; *(a bassa voce)* softly. ◆ *sm (di edificio)* floor, storey ; GEOG & MAT plane ; *(livello)* level ; *(programma, disegno)* plan ; *(pianoforte)* piano ; **andarci ~** to act with caution ; **piano piano** *(poco a poco)* little by little ; *(lentamente)* very slowly ; **abitano al primo ~** they live on the first floor *(Br)*, they live on the second floor *(Am)* ; **il ~ di sopra/di sotto** the floor above/below ; **in primo ~** in the foreground.
piano-bar *sm inv bar with music provided by pianist.*
pianoforte *sm* piano.
pianoterra = **pianterreno**.
pianta *sf* plant ; *(di piede)* sole ; *(di città)* map ; *(di casa)* plan ; **~ grassa** succulent.
piantare *vt (semi)* to plant ; *(conficcare)* to knock in ; *fam (abbandonare)* to leave ; **piantala!** stop it!.
pianterreno *sm* ground floor *(Br)*, first floor *(Am)* ; **al ~** on the ground floor *(Br)*, on the first floor *(Am)*.
pianto *pp* → **piangere**. ◆ *sm* crying, weeping.
pianura *sf* plain ; **la ~ padana** the Paduan Plain.
piastrella *sf* tile.
piattaforma *sf (superficie piana)* platform ; *(galleggiante)* rig.
piattino *sm* saucer.
piatto, a *agg (piano)* flat ; *(monotono)* dreary. ◆ *sm (recipiente)* plate, dish ; *(vivanda)* dish ; *(portata)* course ; **~ freddo** cold dish ; **~ del giorno** today's special ; **~ tipico** typical dish ; **primo ~** first course ; **secondo ~** second course ; **lavare i piatti** to wash the dishes ; **piatti pronti** ready meals.
piazza *sf* square ; **fare ~ pulita di** to make a clean sweep of.
piazzale *sm* large square.
piazzare *vt (collocare)* to place ;

(vendere) to sell. ❑ **piazzarsi** *vr (in gara)* to be placed.
piccante *agg* spicy.
picchetto *sm (di tenda)* peg ; *(di scioperanti, soldati)* picket.
picchiare *vt (dar botte)* to beat (up) ; *(testa, pugni)* to bang. ◆ *vi (alla porta, sul tavolo)* to thump ; *(sole)* to beat down ; ~ **conto il muro** *(urtare)* to hit the wall. ❑ **picchiarsi** *vr* to fight.
piccino, a *agg* small.
piccione *sm* pigeon.
picco, chi *sm (vetta)* peak ; **a ~** vertically ; **colare a ~** to sink.
piccolo, a *agg* small ; *(breve)* short ; *(di poco conto)* slight.
piccozza *sf* ice-axe.
picnic [pik'nik] *sm inv* picnic.
pidocchio *sm* louse.
piede *sm* foot ; *(di mobile)* leg ; **andare a piedi** to go on foot ; **essere a piedi** to be on foot ; **in piedi** standing ; **prendere ~** to gain ground.
piedistallo *sm* pedestal.
piega, ghe *sf* fold ; *(di gonna)* pleat ; *(di pantaloni, grinza)* crease ; **prendere una brutta ~** to take a turn for the worse.
piegare *vt* to bend ; *(foglio, tovaglia)* to fold ; *(letto, sedia)* to fold up. ❑ **piegarsi** *vr (curvarsi)* to bend ; *(letto, sedia)* to fold up. ❑ **piegarsi a** *vr + prep* to give in to.
pieghevole *agg (flessibile)* pliable ; *(sedia, tavolo)* folding.
Piemonte *sm* : **il ~** Piedmont.
piena *sf* flood.
pieno, a *agg* full. ◆ *sm (di carburante)* full tank ; *(culmine)* peak ; **~ di** full of ; **~ di sé** full of oneself ; **a stomaco ~** on a full stomach ; **in ~ inverno** in the middle of winter ; **il ~ per favore** fill her up, please.
pietà *sf (compassione)* pity ; **avere ~ di qn** to take pity on sb ; **come attore fa ~** as an actor he's useless.
pietanza *sf* dish, course.
pietoso, a *agg (che sente pietà)* compassionate ; *(che ispira pietà)* pitiful.
pietra *sf* stone ; **~ dura** semiprecious stone ; **~ preziosa** precious stone.
pigiama, i *sm* pyjamas *(pl)*.
pigiare *vt* to press.
pigliare *vt (prendere)* to take ; *(afferrare)* to grab.
pigna *sf* pine cone.
pignolo, a *agg* fussy, meticulous.
pignorare *vt DIR* to distrain.
pigrizia *sf* laziness.
pigro, a *agg* lazy.
pila *sf (cumulo)* pile ; *(batteria)* battery.
pilastro *sm* pillar.
pile ['pajl] *sm inv (fibra tessile)* fleece.
pillola *sf* pill.
pilone *sm* pylon ; *(di ponte)* pier.
pilota, i, e *smf (di aereo, nave)* pilot ; *(di auto)* driver.
pinacoteca, che *sf* art gallery.
pineta *sf* pinewood.
ping-pong *sm* table tennis.
pinguino *sm (animale)* penguin ; *(gelato)* chocolate-coated ice cream on a stick.

pinna *sf (di pesce)* fin ; *(per nuotare)* flipper.

pino *sm (albero)* pine tree ; *(legno)* pine.

pinoccate *sfpl* : ~ **alla perugina** *almond and pine kernel sweets.*

pinolo *sm* pine kernel.

pinza *sf (utensile)* pliers, tongs ; *(di gambero, granchio)* pincer.

pinzare *vt (con graffette)* to staple ; *sog (granchio)* to nip.

pinze *sfpl (utensile)* pliers.

pinzette *sfpl* tweezers.

pinzimonio *sm dip of seasoned oil.*

pioggia, ge *sf* rain.

piolo *sm* rung.

piombare *vi (giungere)* to arrive unexpectedly ; *fig (nella disperazione)* to plunge ; *(gettarsi)* : ~ **su** to fall upon.

piombino *sm (per pacchi)* lead seal ; *(da pesca)* sinker.

piombo *sm* lead ; **senza ~** unleaded.

piovere *v impers* to rain ; *(proteste)* to pour in. ◆ *vi (pietre, proiettili, insulti)* to rain down ; **piove** it's raining.

piovigginare *v impers* to drizzle.

piovoso, a *agg* rainy.

pipa *sf* pipe.

pipì *sf fam* : **fare (la) ~** to have a wee.

pipistrello *sm* bat.

pirata, i *agg & sm* pirate ; ~ **della strada** road hog.

Pirenei *smpl* : **i ~** the Pyrenees.

pirofila *sf* Pyrex® dish.

piromane *smf* pyromaniac.

piroscafo *sm* steamer.

Pisa *sf* Pisa.

pisarei *smpl* : ~ **e fasò piacentini** *'gnocchi' in a sauce of beans, tomatoes and other vegetables.*

pisciare *vi volg* to piss.

piscina *sf* swimming pool.

pisello *sm* pea.

pisolino *sm* : **fare un ~** to take a nap.

pista *sf (traccia)* trail ; *(per corse)* track ; *(da sci)* run ; *(di aeroporto)* runway ; ~ **da ballo** dance floor ; ~ **ciclabile** cycle lane.

pistacchio *sm* pistachio.

pistola *sf* pistol, gun.

pitta *sf tart made with a yeasted dough and filled with tomatoes, anchovies, tuna and capers or ricotta cheese and boiled eggs.*

pittore, trice *sm, f* painter.

pittoresco, a, schi, sche *agg* picturesque.

pittura *sf* painting ; ' ~ **fresca**' 'wet paint'.

pitturare *vt* to paint.

☞

più *avv* - 1. *(in comparativi)* : ~ **(di)** more (than) ; **ho fatto ~ tardi del solito** I was later than usual ; ~ **triste che mai** sadder than ever ; **poco ~ di** just over ; **di ~** *(in maggior quantità)* more ; **l'ho pagato di ~** I paid more for it.

- 2. *(in superlativi)* : **la ~ bella città** the most beautiful city ; **la collina ~ alta** the highest hill ; **il ~ grande** the biggest ; **il ~ velocemente possibile** as quickly as possible.

- 3. *(oltre)* any more ; **non parlo ~** I'm not saying any more ; **mai ~** never again.
- 4. *(in espressioni)* : **~ o meno** more or less ; **per di ~** what's more ; **tre di** ○ **in ~** three more ; **~ ci pensi, peggio è** the more you think about it, the worse it seems.
◆ *prep* - 1. *(con l'aggiunta di)* plus ; **siamo in sei ~ gli ospiti** there are six of us plus guests.
- 2. *MAT* : **3 ~ 3 fa 6** 3 plus 3 makes 6.
◆ *agg inv* - 1. *(in quantità, numero maggiore)* more ; **ho ~ lavoro del solito** I've got more work than usual ; **ho fatto ~ punti di te** I got more points than you ; **~ siamo, meglio è** the more of us there are, the better.
- 2. *(diversi)* several ; **l'ho ripetuto ~ volte** I repeated it several times.
◆ *sm inv* - 1. *(la maggior parte)* most ; **il ~ delle volte** more often than not ; **parlare del ~ e del meno** to talk about this and that.
- 2. *(la maggioranza)* : **i ~** the majority.

---

piuma *sf* feather.
piumino *sm (trapunta)* duvet ; *(giaccone)* quilted jacket.
piumone® *sm (trapunta)* duvet.
piuttosto *avv* rather ; **~ che** rather than.
pizza *sf* pizza ; **~ capricciosa** *pizza with cheese, tomato, artichokes and capers* ; **~ margherita** *pizza with cheese and tomato* ; **~ napoletana** *pizza with cheese, tomato, anchovies and capers* ; **~ quattro stagioni** *pizza with a different topping on each quarter.*
pizzaiola *sf* : **alla ~** *in a tomato, garlic and oregano sauce.*
pizzeria *sf* pizzeria, pizza restaurant.
pizzetta *sf small pizza eaten as a snack.*
pizzicagnolo, a *sm, f* delicatessen owner.
pizzicare *vt (con le dita)* to pinch ; *(pungere)* to sting. ◆ *vi (prudere)* to itch ; *(cibo)* to be spicy.
pizzicheria *sf* delicatessen.
pizzico, chi *sm* dash ; **un ~ di sale** a pinch of salt.
pizzicotto *sm* pinch.
pizzo *sm (merletto)* lace ; *(barba)* goatee.
placare *vt (ira)* to pacify ; *(fame, sete)* to satisfy. ❑ **placarsi** *vr (vento)* to die down ; *(mare)* to become calmer.
placca, che *sf (targa)* plate ; *(dentaria)* plaque.
placcare *vt (rivestire)* to plate ; **placcato d'oro** gold-plated.
plagiare *vt (libro, canzone)* to plagiarize ; *(persona)* to coerce.
plagio *sm (imitazione)* plagiarism ; *(di persona)* coercion.
plancia, ce *sf* bridge.
planetario, a *agg* planetary. ◆ *sm* planetarium.
plasmare *vt* to mould.
plastica, che *sf (sostanza)* plastic ; *MED* plastic surgery.
plastico, a, ci, che *agg* plastic. ◆ *sm (modello)* model ; *(esplosivo)* plastic explosive.
plastilina® *sf* Plasticine®.
platano *sm* plane tree.

platẹa *sf (settore)* stalls *(pl)* ; *(pubblico)* audience.

plausịbile *agg* plausible.

plịco, chi *sm* parcel.

plurạle *agg* & *sm* plural.

pneumạtico, ci *sm* tyre.

po' = poco.

Po *sm* : il ~ the Po.

☞

pọco, a, chi, che *agg* - 1. *(in piccola quantità)* little, not much ; **ha poca fantasia** he doesn't have much imagination ; **a ~ prezzo** cheap.
- 2. *(in piccolo numero)* : **pochi** few, not many ; **in poche parole** in few words.
◆ *sm* little.
◆ *pron* - 1. *(una piccola quantità)* (a) little ; *(un piccolo numero)* few, not many ; **pochi** *(non molta gente)* few (people) ; **pochi di noi** few of us.
- 2. *(in espressioni)* : **aver ~ da fare** to have little to do ; **ci vuole ~ a capire che ...** it doesn't take much to understand that ... ; **siamo tornati da ~** we've just got back ; **è una cosa da ~** it's nothing ; **per ~** nearly ; **tra ~** soon , shortly ; **(a) ~ a poco** little by little.
◆ *avv* - 1. *(con verbo)* little, not much ; **mangia ~** he doesn't eat much.
- 2. *(con aggettivo, avverbio)* not very ; **~ lontano da qui** not very far from here ; **è ~ simpatica** she's not very nice ; **sta poco bene** he's not very well.
- 3. *(indica tempo)* : **durare ~** not to last long ; **~ dopo/prima** shortly afterwards/before.
❑ **un po'** *avv* a bit, a little ; **restiamo ancora un po'** we'll stay a bit longer ; **un po' di** a bit of, a little ; **compra un po' di pane** buy some bread.

---

podẹre *sm* farm.

poderọso, a *agg* powerful.

pọdio *sm* podium.

poesịa *sf (arte)* poetry ; *(componimento)* poem.

poẹta, ẹssa, i, ẹssa *sm, f* poet.

poẹtico, a, ci, che *agg* poetic.

poggiạre *vt* to rest. ◆ *vi* : **~ su qc** to rest on sthg.

poggiatẹsta *sm inv* headrest.

pọi *avv* then ; *(dopo)* later.

poiché *cong* as, since.

polạcco, a, chi, che *agg* Polish. ◆ *sm, f (abitante)* Pole. ◆ *sm (lingua)* Polish.

polạre *agg* polar.

polarọid® *sf inv* Polaroid®.

polẹmica, che *sf* controversy.

polẹmico, a, ci, che *agg (persona, tono)* argumentative ; *(discorso)* controversial.

polẹnta *sf* polenta *(type of savoury porridge made with maize flour)* ; **~ concia valdostana** *'polenta' cooked with soft cheeses and served with parmesan cheese* ; **~ e osei** *'polenta' served with small birds wrapped in pork loin and flavoured with sage (a speciality of Lombardy)* ; **~ pasticciata alla veneta** *'polenta' baked in a meat, tomato and sausage sauce.*

poliambulatọrio *sm* ≃ health centre.

poliẹstere *sm* polyester.

polipo *sm (mollusco & MED)* polyp.
polistirolo *sm* polystyrene.
politica, che *sf (scienza)* politics *(sg)* ; *(linea di condotta)* policy → politico.
politico, a, ci, che *agg* political. ◆ *sm, f* politician.
polizia *sf* police ; ~ **stradale** traffic police.
poliziesco, a, schi, sche *agg* police *(dav s)* ; *(romanzo, film)* detective *(dav s)*.
poliziotto, a *sm, f* policeman *(f* policewoman).
polizza *sf* policy ; ~ **di assicurazione** insurance policy.
pollaio *sm* hen house.
pollame *sm* poultry.
pollice *sm* thumb ; *(unità di misura)* inch.
polline *sm* pollen.
pollo *sm* chicken ; ~ **arrosto** roast chicken ; ~ **alla cacciatora** *chicken in a sauce of mushrooms, tomatoes, olives, herbs and wine* ; ~ **alla diavola** *chicken cut open and flattened out, marinated in lemon juice.*
polmone *sm* lung.
polmonite *sf* pneumonia.
polo *sm* pole. ◆ *sf inv* polo shirt ; **il** ~ **Nord/Sud** the North/South Pole.
Polonia *sf*: **la** ~ Poland.
polpaccio *sm* calf.
polpastrello *sm* fingertip.
polpetta *sf* meatball.
polpettone *sm* meat loaf.
polpo *sm* octopus.
polsino *sm* cuff.
polso *sm* wrist ; *MED* pulse.
poltiglia *sf* paste.
poltrona *sf* armchair ; *(di teatro)* seat in the stalls.
poltrone, a *sm, f* lazy person.
polvere *sf* dust ; **latte in** ~ powdered milk ; **sapone in** ~ soap powder.
polveroso, a *agg* dusty.
pomata *sf* ointment.
pomeridiano, a *agg* afternoon *(dav s)*.
pomeriggio *sm* afternoon ; **di** ~ in the afternoon.
pomice *sf* pumice.
pomo *sm* knob ; ~ **d'Adamo** Adam's apple.
pomodoro *sm* tomato ; **pomodori ripieni** *tomatoes stuffed with breadcrumbs, parsley, garlic and egg.*
pompa *sf* pump ; *(sfarzo)* pomp ; **pompe funebri** undertaker's *(sg)*.
pompare *vt* to pump.
Pompei *n* Pompei.

POMPEI

One of the world's most famous archeological sites, the ancient town of Pompei, not far from Naples, was totally buried in 79 AD when Mount Vesuvius erupted. Today it is open to the public, and offers a unique insight into the ancient Roman way of life.

---

pompelmo *sm* grapefruit.
pompiere *sm* fireman.

pompọso, a *agg (sfarzoso)* full of pomp ; *(ostentato)* pompous.
ponderạre *vt* & *vi* to ponder.
ponẹnte *sm* west.
pọnte *sm* bridge ; *(di nave)* deck ; *(impalcatura)* scaffolding ; **~ levatoio** drawbridge ; **fare il ~** *to have the day off between a national holiday and a weekend* ; **il Ponte Vecchio** the Ponte Vecchio.

IL PONTE VECCHIO

One of Italy's most picturesque bridges, the *Ponte Vecchio* has come to be the symbol of Florence. Built in 1345 and so the oldest bridge in the city (hence its name), it stands at the narrowest point of the Arno and is connected to the Uffizi Gallery and the Pitti Palace by an arcade. The *Ponte Vecchio* is famous for the goldsmiths and silversmiths which line it on both sides.

---

pontẹfice *sm* pontiff.
pọny *sm inv* pony ; **~ express** express courier service.
pọpcorn *sm* popcorn.
popolạre *agg* popular ; *(popolano)* working-class *(dav s)*. ◆ *vt* to populate.
popolarità *sf* popularity.
popolaziọne *sf* population.
pọpolo *sm* people *(pl)*.
popọne *sm* melon.
pọppa *sf NAUT* stern.
poppạre *vt* to suck (from the breast).
porcellạna *sf* porcelain.
porcellịno *sm (maialino)* piglet ; **~ d'India** guinea pig.
porcịno *sm* cep *(edible brown mushroom with nutty flavour)*.
pọrco, ci *sm (animale)* pig ; *(carne)* pork.
porcospịno *sm* porcupine.
pọrgere *vt (tendere)* to hold out ; *(dare)* to give ; **porgo distinti saluti** *(in lettera)* yours sincerely.
pornografico, a, ci, che *agg* pornographic.
pọro *sm* pore.
pọrpora *agg inv* crimson.
pọrre *vt* to put ; *(condizioni, limiti)* to set ; *(riporre)* to place ; *(supporre)* : **poniamo che ...** let us suppose that ... ; **~ una domanda** to ask a question ; **~ fine a qc** to put an end to sthg.
pọrro *sm (verdura)* leek ; *MED* wart.
pọrta *sf* door ; *(di città)* gate ; *(nel calcio)* goal.
portabagạgli *sm inv (bagagliaio)* boot *(Br)*, trunk *(Am)* ; *(sul tetto)* roof rack.
portacẹnere *sm inv* ashtray.
portachiạvi *sm inv* key ring.
portacịpria *sm inv* compact.
portaẹrei *sf inv* aircraft carrier.
portafinẹstra (*pl* **portefinestre**) *sf* French window.
portafọglio *sm (per denaro)* wallet ; *FIN* & *POL* portfolio.
portafortụna *sm inv* lucky charm.
portagiọie *sm inv* jewel box.
portalẹttere = **postino**.
portamẹnto *sm* bearing.
portamonẹte *sm inv* purse.

portapacchi *sm inv* luggage rack.
portare *vt (trasportare)* to carry ; *(condurre, prendere)* to take ; *(abiti, occhiali)* to wear ; *(barba, capelli, lunghi)* to have ; *fig (spingere)* to drive ; **~ qc a qn** *(consegnare)* to take sthg to sb ; **portar via** to take ; **~ avanti** to carry on ; **~ fortuna** to bring luck.
portasapone *sm inv* soap dish.
portasigarette *sm inv* cigarette case.
portata *sf (piatto)* course ; *(di veicolo)* capacity ; *(di fiume)* flow ; *(importanza)* importance ; **essere a ~ di mano** to be within reach ; **alla ~ di tutti** within everybody's grasp.
portatile *agg* portable.
portatore, trice *sm, f (di assegno)* bearer; **~ di handicap** disabled.
portatovagliolo *sm* napkin ring.
portauovo *sm inv* eggcup.
portico *sm* portico.
portiera *sf* door.
portiere, a *sm, f (portinaio)* concierge, caretaker ; *(di albergo)* porter ; *(nel calcio)* goalkeeper.
portineria *sf (di palazzo)* caretaker's lodge ; *(di albergo)* reception.
porto, a *pp* → **porgere**. ◆ *sm* port ; **~ d'armi** licence to carry firearms.
Portogallo *sm* : **il ~** Portugal.
portoghese *agg, sm & sf* Portuguese.
portone *sm* main entrance.
porzione *sf* portion ; *(di cibo)* helping.
posa *sf* pose ; **mettersi in ~** to pose.
posacenere *sm inv* ashtray.
posare *vt* to put down. ◆ *vi* to pose. ❑ **posarsi** *vr (uccello)* to perch.
posate *sfpl* cutlery *(sg)*.
positivo, a *agg* positive.
posizione *sf* position.
posologia *sf* dosage.
possedere *vt (cose)* to own, to possess ; *(qualità)* to have, to possess.
possessivo, a *agg* possessive.
possesso *sm* possession, ownership ; **essere in ~ di qc** to be in possession of sthg.
possibile *agg* possible. ◆ *sm* : **fare (tutto) il ~ (per fare qc)** to do everything possible (to do sthg) ; **ma non è ~!** it can't be true! ; **il più presto ~** as soon as possible ; **se ~** if possible ; **il più ~** *(quantità)* as much as possible ; *(numero)* as many as possible.
possibilità *sf inv (eventualità)* possibility ; *(occasione)* chance ; *(capacità)* : **avere la ~ di fare qc** to be able to do sthg.
posta *sf (negozio)* post office ; *(lettere, servizio)* post, mail ; **per ~** by post ○ mail ; **~ aerea** air mail.
postale *agg* postal, post *(dav s)*.
posteggiare *vt* to park.
posteggiatore, trice *sm, f* car park attendant *(Br)*, parking lot attendant *(Am)*.
posteggio *sm* car park *(Br)*, parking lot *(Am)* ; **~ a pagamento**

car park where drivers must pay to park.

poster *sm inv* poster.

posteriore *agg (nello spazio)* rear, back ; *(nel tempo)* later.

posticipare *vt* to postpone.

postino, a *sm, f* postman (*f* postwoman).

posto, a *pp* → **porre**. ◆ *sm* place ; *(spazio)* room ; *(per persona)* place, seat ; *(impiego)* job ; **mettere a ~** to tidy (up) ; **~ di blocco** roadblock ; **~ letto** bed ; **~ di polizia** police station ; **al ~ di** in (the) place of.

potabile *agg* → **acqua**.

potare *vt* to prune.

potente *agg* powerful.

☞

potere *vi* - 1. *(essere in grado di)* can, to be able ; **non ci posso andare** I can't go, I'm not able to go ; **puoi farmi un favore?** can you do me a favour? ; **non posso farci niente** I can't do anything about it.
- 2. *(avere il permesso di)* can, to be able ; **non potete parcheggiare qui** you can't park here ; **posso entrare?** can ○ may I come in?
- 3. *(esprime eventualità)* : **può far freddo** it can get cold ; **possono aver perso il treno** they might ○ could have missed the train ; **potrei sbagliarmi** I could be wrong ; **può darsi** perhaps ; **può darsi che sia partito** he may ○ might have left.
- 4. *(esprime suggerimento)* : **puoi provare** you can try.
- 5. *(in espressioni)* : **non ne posso più!** *(sono stufo)* I can't take any more! ; *(sono stanco)* I'm exhausted! ; **a più non posso** *(correre)* really fast ; *(lavorare)* really hard ; **si può fare** it can be done.
◆ *sm* - 1. *(comando)* power ; **essere al ~** to be in power.
- 2. *(facoltà)* power, ability.

povero, a *agg* poor. ◆ *sm, f* poor man (*f* woman) ; **i poveri** the poor ; **~ di qc** lacking in sthg.

pozza *sf* pool.

pozzanghera *sf* puddle.

pozzo *sm* well ; **~ petrolifero** oil well.

pranzare *vi* to have lunch.

pranzo *sm (di mezzogiorno)* lunch ; *(banchetto)* dinner.

prassi *sf* usual procedure.

pratica, che *sf* practice ; *(esperienza)* practical experience ; *(documenti)* paperwork ; **mettere in ~ qc** to put sthg into practice ; **in ~** in practice.

praticamente *avv (quasi)* practically ; *(concretamente)* in a practical way.

pratico, a, ci, che *agg* practical.

prato *sm (distesa d'erba)* meadow ; *(di giardino)* lawn.

preavviso *sm* notice.

precario, a *agg* precarious.

precauzione *sf* precaution.

precedente *agg* preceding, previous. ◆ *sm* precedent ; **senza precedenti** unprecedented ; **precedenti penali** criminal record *(sg)*.

precedenza *sf (in auto)* right of way ; *(priorità)* priority ; **dare la ~ (a)** *(in auto)* to give way (to).

precedere *vt (nello spazio)* to be ahead of ; *(nel tempo)* to precede.

precipitare *vi (cadere)* to fall; *fig (situazione)* to come to a head. ❑ **precipitarsi** *vr* to rush.

precipitazione *sf (atmosferica)* precipitation; *(fretta)* haste.

precipizio *sm* precipice.

precisare *vt* to specify.

precisione *sf (esattezza)* precision; *(accuratezza)* accuracy.

preciso, a *agg* precise; **sono le due precise** it's exactly two o'clock.

precoce *agg (bambino)* precocious; *(vecchiaia)* premature.

preda *sf* prey; **essere in ~ a qc** to be prey to sthg.

predetto, a *pp* → **predire**.

predica, che *sf* RELIG sermon; *fam (ramanzina)* telling-off.

predire *vt* to foretell.

predisporre *vt* to prepare; **~ qn/qc a qc** to predispose sb/sthg to sthg.

predisposizione *sf* tendency.

predominare *vi* to predominate.

prefabbricato, a *agg* prefabricated.

preferenza *sf* preference.

preferire *vt* to prefer; **~ qn/qc a** to prefer sb/sthg to.

preferito, a *agg* favourite.

prefiggersi *vr*: **~ uno scopo** to set o.s. a goal.

prefisso, a *pp* → **prefiggersi**. ◆ *sm* code.

pregare *vi* to pray. ◆ *vt (Dio)* to pray to; **~ qn di fare qc** *(supplicare)* to beg sb to do sthg; *(chiedere a)* to ask sb to do sthg; **i passeggeri sono gentilmente pregati di non fumare** passengers are kindly requested not to smoke.

preghiera *sf* prayer.

pregiato, a *agg* precious.

pregio *sm (qualità)* good quality; *(valore)* value.

pregiudicare *vt* to prejudice.

pregiudicato, a *sm, f* previous offender.

pregiudizio *sm* prejudice.

prego *esclam (risposta a ringraziamento)* don't mention it!; *(invito a sedersi)* take a seat!; *(invito ad entrare prima)* after you!.

preistorico, a, ci, che *agg* prehistoric.

prelavaggio *sm* prewash.

prelevare *vt (soldi)* to withdraw; *(campione, sangue)* to take.

prelievo *sm (in banca)* withdrawal; MED sample.

preliminare *agg* & *sm* preliminary.

premaman *agg inv* maternity *(dav s)*.

prematuro, a *agg* premature.

premere *vt* to press. ◆ *vi*: **~ su** to press on. ❑ **premere a** *v + prep*: **~ a qn** to matter to sb.

premiare *vt (dare un premio)* to give a prize to; *(merito, onestà)* to reward.

premiazione *sf* prize-giving.

premio *sm (vincita)* prize; *(ricompensa)* reward; **~ (di assicurazione)** *(insurance)* premium.

premunirsi *vr*: **~ contro qc** to protect o.s. against sthg.

premuroso, a *agg* thoughtful.

☞

prendere *vt* - 1. *(afferrare)* to take.
- 2. *(portare con sé)* to take ; **prendi l'ombrello** take the umbrella.
- 3. *(mezzi di trasporto, strada)* to take ; **~ il treno** to take the train ; **prenda la prima a destra** take the first on the right.
- 4. *(mangiare, bere)* to have ; **andiamo a ~ un caffè** let's go for a coffee ; **~ qualcosa da bere** to have something to drink ; **che cosa prendete?** *(da bere)* what would you like to drink?
- 5. *(lezioni, voto, stipendio)* to get ; **~ qc in affitto** to rent sthg.
- 6. *(interpretare)* to take ; **prenderla bene/male** to take it well/badly.
- 7. *(catturare, sorprendere)* to catch ; **quanti pesci hai preso?** how many fish have you caught? ; **~ qn con le mani nel sacco** to catch sb redhanded.
- 8. *(malattia, stato fisico)* : **~ freddo** to catch cold ; **~ il sole** to sunbathe ; **prendersi un raffreddore** to catch a cold.
- 9. *(sottrarre)* : **~ qc a qn** to take sthg (away) from sb.
- 10. *(scambiare)* : **~ qn per** to take sb for.
- 11. *(in espressioni)* : **andare a ~** *(persona)* to meet ; *(cosa)* to go to get ; **prendersi cura di** to look after ; **~ fuoco** to catch fire ; **~ un impegno** to take on a commitment ; **~ le misure di** *(oggetto, persona)* to measure ; **che ti prende?** what's the matter with you? ; **prendersela** *(offendersi)* to get annoyed ; *(preoccupare)* to worry ; **prendersela con qn** *(arrabiarsi)* to get angry with sb.
◆ *vi* - 1. *(colla, cemento)* to set ; *(fuoco)* to catch.
- 2. *(cominciare)* : **~ a fare qc** to start doing sthg.

---

prendisole *sm inv* sundress.

prenotare *vt* to book ; **ho prenotato una camera** I've booked a room.

prenotazione *sf* booking.

preoccupare *vt* to worry. ❏ **preoccuparsi** *vr* : **preoccuparsi (per)** to worry (about). ❏ **preoccuparsi di** *vr + prep (occuparsi di)* to think about.

preoccupato, a *agg* worried.

preoccupazione *sf* worry.

preparare *vt* to prepare ; *(documenti, cose)* to get ready ; *(esame, concorso)* to prepare for ; **~ da mangiare** to cook. ❏ **prepararsi** *vr (vestirsi)* to get ready ; **~ a fare qc** to get ready to do sthg.

preparativi *smpl* preparations.

preposizione *sf* preposition.

prepotente *agg* domineering. ◆ *smf* bully.

presa *sf (il prendere)* grip ; *(nello sport, appiglio)* hold ; *(di acqua, gas)* supply point ; *(di sale, pepe)* pinch ; *(di colla, cemento)* setting ; *(di città)* capture ; *(per spina)* : **~ (di corrente)** socket ; **far ~** to set ; **far ~ su qn** to captivate sb ; **~ d'aria** air intake ; **essere alle prese con** to be up against.

presbite *agg* longsighted.

prescindere : prescindere da *v + prep* to leave aside ; **a ~ da** apart from.

prescritto, a *pp* → prescrivere.
prescrivere *vt* to prescribe.
presentare *vt* to present ; *(domanda, dimissioni)* to submit ; *(persona)* : ~ **qn a qn** to introduce sb to sb ; **le presento mia moglie** this is my wife. ❑ **presentarsi** *vr (farsi conoscere)* to introduce o.s. ; *(recarsi)* to present o.s. ; *(capitare)* to arise ; *(mostrarsi)* to look.
presentatore, trice *sm, f* presenter.
presentazione *sf* presentation ; **fare le presentazioni** to make the introductions.
presente *agg* present. ◆ *smf* : **i presenti** those present ; **tener ~ che** to bear in mind that ; **aver ~** to remember.
presentimento *sm* presentiment.
presenza *sf* presence ; **in ~ di tutti** in front of everybody.
presepe = **presepio.**
presepio *sm* Nativity scene, crib.
preservativo *sm* condom.
preside *smf* headteacher *(Br)*, principal *(Am)*.
presidente *smf* president ; ~ **del Consiglio** ≃ Prime Minister ; **il ~ della Repubblica** the Italian President.
preso, a *pp* → prendere.
pressappoco *avv* more or less.
pressare *vt* to press.
pressione *sf* pressure ; **far ~ su qn** to put pressure on sb ; **essere sotto ~** to be under pressure.
presso *prep (sulle lettere)* c/o ; *(vicino a)* near ; *(alle dipendenze di)* for, with ; ~ **qn** *(a casa di)* at sb's home. ❑ **pressi** *smpl* : **nei pressi di Siena** in the vicinity of Siena.
prestare *vt* to lend ; ~ **qc (a qn)** *(denaro, oggetti)* to lend (sb) sthg, to lend sthg (to sb) ; ~ **aiuto a qn** to lend sb a hand ; ~ **attenzione a** to pay attention to. ❑ **prestarsi a** *vr + prep* : **prestarsi a fare qc** to offer to do sthg.
prestazione *sf* performance ; **prestazioni** services.
prestigiatore, trice *sm, f* conjurer.
prestito *sm* loan ; **dare in ~ qc (a qn)** to lend sthg (to sb) ; **prendere qc in ~ (da qn)** to borrow sthg (from sb).
presto *avv (fra poco)* soon ; *(in fretta)* quickly ; *(nella giornata, nel tempo)* early ; **fai ~!** hurry up! ; **a ~!** see you soon! ; **al più ~** as soon as possible.
presumere *vt* to presume.
presunto, a *pp* → presumere.
presuntuoso, a *agg* conceited.
prete *sm* priest.
pretendere *vt* to claim ; *(a torto)* to pretend ; **pretende che tutti lo ascoltino** he expects everyone to listen to him ; **pretende di essere il migliore** he thinks he's the best.
preteso, a *pp* → pretendere.
pretesto *sm (scusa)* excuse, pretext ; *(occasione)* opportunity.
prevalente *agg* prevalent.
prevalere *vi* to prevail.
prevedere *vt* to foresee. ❑ **prevedere di** *v + prep* to expect.
prevenire *vt (anticipare)* to forestall ; *(evitare)* to prevent.

preventivo, a *agg* preventive. ◆ *sm* estimate.

prevenzione *sf* prevention.

previdenza *sf* foresight ; **~ sociale** social security *(Br)*, welfare *(Am)*.

previo, a *agg* : **~ pagamento** upon payment.

previsione *sf (valutazione)* prediction ; *(aspettativa)* expectation ; **in ~ di** in anticipation of ; **previsioni del tempo** ○ **meteorologiche** weather forecast.

previsto, a *pp* → **prevedere**. ◆ *agg* expected. ◆ *sm* : **più/meno del ~** more/less than expected.

prezioso, a *agg* precious, valuable.

prezzemolo *sm* parsley.

prezzo *sm* price ; **~ comprensivo del servizio** price including service charge ; **a buon ~** cheap.

prigione *sf* prison.

prigioniero, a *agg (rinchiuso)* imprisoned ; *(catturato)* captive. ◆ *sm, f* prisoner.

prima *avv (in precedenza)* before ; *(più presto)* earlier ; *(per prima cosa, nello spazio)* first ; *(un tempo)* once. ◆ *sf (di teatro)* first night ; *(marcia)* first gear ; *(in treno, aereo)* first class. ◆ *cong* before. ◆ *prep* : **~ di** before ; **fai ~ di qua** it's quicker this way ; **~ che arrivi** before he arrives ; **~ di fare qc** before doing sthg ; **~ o poi** sooner or later ; **~ d'ora** before now ; **~ di tutto** first of all ; **l'anno ~** the year before.

primario, a *agg* primary. ◆ *sm* MED chief physician.

primato *sm (supremazia)* primacy ; SPORT record.

primavera *sf* spring.

primitivo, a *agg (uomo, civiltà)* primitive ; *(originario)* original.

primo, a *agg* first ; *(nel tempo)* early. ◆ *sm (portata)* first course ; *(giorno)* first ; **il ~ (di) marzo** the first of March ; **di prima qualità** first-class ; **ai primi d'ottobre** in early October ; **sulle prime** at first, in the beginning.

primogenito, a *agg & sm, f* firstborn.

principale *agg* main, principal. ◆ *smf* manager, boss.

principe *sm* prince.

principessa *sf* princess.

principiante *smf* beginner.

principio *sm (inizio, origine)* beginning ; *(concetto, norma)* principle ; **in** ○ **al ~** at first ; **per ~** on principle.

priorità *sf inv (precedenza)* priority.

privare *vt* : **~ qn di qc** to deprive sb of sthg. ❑ **privarsi di** *vr + prep* : **privarsi di qc** to go without sthg.

privato, a *agg* private. ◆ *sm, f (cittadino)* private citizen. ◆ *sm* : **in ~** in private.

privilegiare *vt* to favour.

privo, a *agg* : **~ di qc** without sthg, lacking in sthg.

pro *sm inv* : **a che ~?** for what purpose? ; **i ~ e i contro** the pros and cons.

probabile *agg* probable ; **è ~ che piova** it will probably rain.

probabilità *sf inv* probability.

probabilmente *avv* probably.

problema, i *sm* problem.

proboscide *sf* trunk.

procedere *vi (avanzare, progredire)* to proceed ; *(agire)* to behave.
procedimento *sm* procedure.
processare *vt* to try.
processione *sf* procession.
processo *sm* DIR trial ; *(operazione, metodo)* process.
processore *sm* INFORM process.
procinto *sm* : **essere in ~ di fare qc** to be about to do sthg.
proclamare *vt* to proclaim.
procurare *vt* : **~ qc a qn** to obtain sthg for sb, to get sthg for sb ; **procurarsi qc** to get sthg.
prodotto, a *pp* → **produrre**. ◆ *sm* product.
produrre *vt* to produce ; *(provocare)* to cause.
produttore, trice *sm, f* producer.
produzione *sf* production.
Prof. *(abbr di professore)* Prof.
profano, a *agg* profane. ◆ *sm* layman.
professionale *agg* professional.
professione *sf* profession.
professionista, i, e *smf (avvocato, medico)* professional person ; *(non dilettante)* professional.
professore, essa *sm, f* teacher ; *(all'università)* professor.
profilo *sm* profile ; **di ~** in profile.
profiterole [profite'rɔl] *sm inv* profiteroles *(pl)*.
profitto *sm* profit ; **trarre ~ da qc** to take advantage of sthg.
profondità *sf inv* depth.
profondo, a *agg* deep.
Prof.ssa *(abbr di professoressa)* Prof..
profugo, a, ghi, ghe *sm, f* refugee.
profumare *vt* to perfume. ◆ *vi* to smell good ; **~ di** to smell of.
profumato, a *agg* scented.
profumeria *sf* perfumery.
profumo *sm (odore)* scent, fragrance ; *(cosmetico)* perfume.
progettare *vt* to plan.
progetto *sm* plan.
programma, i *sm* programme ; *(per vacanze, serata)* plan ; SCOL syllabus ; INFORM program.
programmare *vt (pianificare)* to plan ; INFORM to program.
progredire *vi (avanzare)* to advance ; *(migliorare)* to progress.
progressivo, a *agg* progressive.
progresso *sm* progress ; **fare progressi** to make progress.
proibire *vt* to forbid ; **~ a qn di fare qc** to forbid sb to do sthg ; **è proibito fumare** smoking is prohibited.
proiettare *vt (film)* to show ; *(luce, ombra)* to cast.
proiettile *sm* bullet.
proiezione *sf (di film)* projection, showing.
proletariato *sm* proletariat.
proletario *agg* proletarian. ◆ *sm, f* proletarian.
prolunga, ghe *sf* extension.
prolungare *vt* to prolong. ❑ **prolungarsi** *vr* to go on.
promessa *sf* promise ; **mantenere una ~** to keep a promise.
promesso, a *pp* → **promettere**.

promettere *vt*: ~ **qc (a qn)** to promise (sb) sthg ; ~ **(a qn) di fare qc** to promise (sb) to do sthg ; **promette bene!** that's a good start.
promontorio *sm* promontory.
promosso, a *pp* → **promuovere**.
promotore, trice *sm, f* promoter.
promozione *sf* promotion ; *SCOL* : **avere la ~** to go up a class.
promulgare *vt* to promulgate.
promuovere *vt SCOL* to pass ; *(impiegato, iniziativa)* to promote.
pronome *sm* pronoun.
pronto, a *agg* ready. ◆ *esclam* hello! *(on the phone)* ; **essere ~ a fare qc** to be ready to do sthg ; **~ soccorso** first aid ; **~, chi parla?** hello, who's speaking?
pronuncia, ce *sf* pronunciation.
pronunciare *vt (parola, lettera)* to pronounce ; *(dire)* to say. ❑ **pronunciarsi** *vr (parola, lettera)* to be pronounced ; *(dichiararsi)* to declare o.s..
pronunzia = **pronuncia**.
proporre *vt*: ~ **qc (a qn)** to propose sthg (to sb) ; ~ **di fare qc** to suggest doing sthg. ❑ **proporsi di** *vr + prep* : **proporsi di fare qc** to decide to do sthg.
proporzionato, a *agg* well proportioned.
proporzione *sf MAT* ratio ; **in ~ a** in proportion to.
proposito *sm (progetto)* intention ; **fare qc di ~** to do sthg on purpose ; **a ~, ...** by the way, ... ; **capitare a ~** *(avvenimento)* to happen at the right time.
proposta *sf* proposal.
proposto, a *pp* → **proporre**.
proprietà *sf inv* property ; '**~ privata**' 'private property'.
proprietario, a *sm, f* owner.
proprio, a *agg (possessivo)* own ; *(senso)* literal, exact ; *(tipico)* characteristic. ◆ *avv (veramente)* really ; *(precisamente)* just ; *(affatto)* at all ; **non ne ho ~ idea** I really have no idea ; **~ così** that's just it ; **non ~** not exactly ; **mettersi in ~** to set up on one's own.
prora *sf (di nave)* prow ; *(di aereo)* nose.
prosa *sf* prose.
prosciutto *sm* ham ; **~ cotto** (cooked) ham ; **~ crudo** Parma ham.
proseguire *vt* to carry on with, to continue. ◆ *vi* to carry on, to continue.
prospettiva *sf (di disegno, punto di vista)* perspective ; *(possibilità)* prospect.
prossimità *sf*: **in ~ di qc** near sthg.
prossimo, a *agg* next. ◆ *sm* neighbour.
prostituta *sf* prostitute.
protagonista, i, e *smf* protagonist.
proteggere *vt*: ~ **qn/qc (da)** to protect sb/sthg (from).
protesta *sf* protest.
protestante *agg* & *smf* Protestant.
protestare *vi* & *vt* to protest.
protetto, a *pp* → **proteggere**.
protezione *sf* protection.
prototipo *sm* prototype.
prova *sf (dimostrazione, conferma)*

proof ; *(esperimento)* test, trial ; *DIR* proof, evidence ; *(di spettacolo)* rehearsal ; *(esame)* exam ; **dar ~ di abilità** to prove to be skilful ; **mettere qn alla ~** to put sb to the test ; **fino a ~ contraria** until (it's) proved otherwise ; **in ~** on trial ; **fare le prove** to rehearse.

provare *vt (cibo)* to try ; *(vestito)* to try on ; *(sentire)* to feel, to experience ; *(dimostrare)* to show ; *(tentare)* : **~ a fare qc** to try to do sthg ; **provarsi qc** to try sthg on. ❑ **provarsi a** *vr + prep* : **provarsi a fare qc** to try to do sthg.

provenienza *sf* origin ; **in ~ da** *(treno, aereo)* from.

provenire : provenire da *v + prep* to come from ; **proveniente da** *(treno, aereo)* from.

provenuto *pp* → **provenire**.

proverbio *sm* proverb.

provetta *sf* test tube.

provincia, ce *sf (ente)* province ; *(opposta a grandi città)* provinces *(pl)*.

provinciale *agg* provincial. ◆ *sf* main road.

provino *sm (audizione)* audition ; *(fotografico)* screen test.

provocante *agg* provocative.

provocare *vt (causare)* to cause ; *(sfidare)* to provoke.

provocazione *sf* provocation.

provolone *sm a hard cheese made from cow's milk.*

provvedere *vi (prendere provvedimenti)* to take measures ; *(occuparsi di)* : **~ (a qc)** to provide (for sthg).

provvedimento *sm* measure.

provvisorio, a *agg* temporary, provisional.

provviste *sfpl* supplies.

prua *sf* prow.

prudente *agg* cautious, prudent.

prudenza *sf* caution, prudence ; **'prudenza'** 'caution'.

prudere *vi* to itch ; **mi prude una gamba** my leg is itchy.

prugna *sf* plum ; **~ secca** prune.

pruno *sm* prickle, thorn.

prurito *sm* itch.

P.S. *(abbr di Post Scriptum)* PS. ◆ *abbr* = **Pubblica Sicurezza**.

pseudonimo *sm* pseudonym.

psicanalisi *sf* psychoanalysis.

psiche *sf* psyche.

psichiatra, i, e *smf* psychiatrist.

psicologia *sf* psychology.

psicologo, a, gi, ghe *sm, f* psychologist.

P.T. *(abbr di Poste e Telecomunicazioni)* PO.

P.T.P. *(abbr di Posto Telefonico Pubblico)* payphone.

pubblicare *vt* to publish.

Pubblica Sicurezza *sf (polizia)* Public Safety Police.

pubblicazione *sf* publication. ❑ **pubblicazioni** *sfpl* : **~ (matrimoniali)** (marriage) banns.

pubblicità *sf inv (annuncio)* advertisement ; *(divulgazione)* publicity ; *(attività)* advertising.

pubblico, a, ci, che *agg* public ; *(statale)* state *(dav s)*. ◆ *sm (utenti)* public ; *(spettatori)* audience ; **in ~** in public ; **la Pubblica Sicurezza** the police.

pube *sm* pubis.

pubertà *sf inv* puberty.
pudore *sm* modesty.
puerile *agg (bambinesco)* puerile.
pugilato *sm* boxing.
pugile *sm* boxer.
Puglia *sf*: **la ~** Apulia.
pugnalare *vt* to stab.
pugno *sm (mano)* fist; *(colpo)* punch; *(quantità)* handful.
pulce *sf* flea.
Pulcinella *sm* Punch.
pulcino *sm* chick.
puledro, a *sm, f* colt (*f* filly).
pulire *vt* to clean; **pulirsi il viso/le scarpe** to clean one's face/shoes.
pulita *sf*: **dare una ~** to clean up.
pulito, a *agg* clean; *(coscienza)* clear.
pulizia *sf (stato)* cleanliness; *(atto)* cleaning; **fare le pulizie** to do the cleaning.
pullman *sm inv* coach.
pullover *sm inv* pullover.
pulmino *sm* minibus.
pulsante *sm* button.
pulsare *vi* to beat.
puma *sm inv* puma.
pungere *vt* to sting.
pungiglione *sm* sting.
punire *vt* to punish.
punizione *sf (castigo)* punishment; *(nel calcio)* free kick.
punta *sf (di matita, spillo, coltello)* point; *(di continente, dita)* tip; **in ~ dei piedi** *(camminare)* on tiptoe.
puntare *vt (arma)* to aim; *(scommettere)* to bet; **~ i piedi** to dig one's heels in.
puntata *sf (episodio)* episode; *(scommessa)* bet; **teleromanzo a puntate** serial.
punteggiatura *sf* punctuation.
punteggio *sm* score.
puntina *sf*: **~ (da disegno)** drawing pin.
puntino *sm* dot; **fare qc a ~** to do sthg properly; **puntini di sospensione** suspension points.
punto, a *pp* → **pungere**. ◆ *sm* point; *(segno grafico)* full stop *(Br)*, period *(Am)*; *MED (di cucito)* stitch; **~ esclamativo** exclamation mark; **~ interrogativo** question mark; **~ di riferimento** point of reference, landmark; **~ di ritrovo** meeting point; **~ vendita** point of sale; **~ e virgola** semi-colon; **~ di vista** point of view; **due punti** colon; **punti cardinali** points of the compass; **essere sul ~ di fare qc** to be about to do sthg; **essere a buon ~** to be at a good point; **fare il ~ della situazione** to take stock; **mettere a ~ qc** to adjust sthg; **di ~ in bianco** all of a sudden; **a tal ~ che** to such an extent that; **le tre in ~** three o'clock sharp.
puntuale *agg* punctual.
puntualità *sf* punctuality.
puntura *sf (di insetto)* sting; *(di spillo)* prick; *fam (iniezione)* injection.
punzecchiare *vt (pungere)* to prick; *fig (infastidire)* to tease.
pupazzo *sm* puppet.
pupilla *sf* pupil.
purché *cong* provided that.
pure *avv (anche)* also, too. ◆ *cong* even if; **pur di fare qc** just to do

sthg; faccia ~! please do!, go ahead!

purè *sm (di patate) mashed potatoes with milk, butter and Parmesan cheese.*

purezza *sf* purity.

purga, ghe *sf* laxative.

purgatorio *sm* Purgatory.

puro, a *agg* pure; *(verità)* simple.

purosangue *agg inv* thoroughbred.

purtroppo *avv* unfortunately.

pustola *sf* pimple.

putiferio *sm* row.

putrefare *vi* to putrefy, to rot.

putrefatto, a *pp* → putrefare. ◆ *agg* rotten.

putrido, a *agg* putrid.

puttana *sf volg* whore.

puzza *sf* = puzzo.

puzzare *vi* to stink.

puzzo *sm* stink.

puzzola *sf* polecat.

puzzolente *agg* stinking.

Q

qua *avv* here; al di ~ di on this side of; di ~ e di là here and there; per di ~ this way.

quaderno *sm* exercise book.

quadrante *sm (di orologio)* face; *(di bussola)* quarter.

quadrare *vi (bilancio)* to balance; *(coincidere)* to correspond; non mi quadra *fam* there's something not quite right about it.

quadrato, a *agg* & *sm* square; 2 al ~ 2 squared.

quadretto *sm*: a quadretti *(tessuto)* checked; *(foglio)* squared.

quadrifoglio *sm* four-leaf clover.

quadrimestre *sm* SCOL term; *(periodo)* period of four months.

quadro *sm (pittura)* painting; *fig (situazione)* picture; TECNOL board, panel; *(in azienda)* executive. ❑ **quadri** *smpl (nelle carte)* diamonds.

quadruplo, a *agg* & *sm* quadruple.

quaggiù *avv* down here.

quaglia *sf* quail.

---

qualche *agg* - 1. *(alcuni)* a few, some; restiamo solo ~ giorno we are only staying a few days; ~ volta a few times; c'è ~ novità? is there any news?

- 2. *(indeterminato)* some; l'ho letto in ~ articolo I read it in some article; hai ~ libro da prestarmi? have you any books to lend me?; in ~ modo somehow; da ~ parte somewhere.

- 3. *(un certo)* some; ci siamo frequentati per ~ tempo we've been seeing each other for some time; ~ cosa = qualcosa.

---

qualcheduno, a = qualcuno.

qualcosa *pron* something; *(nelle interrogative)* anything; ~ di nuovo something new; ~ da bere something to drink; qualcos'altro something else.

qualcuno, a *pron (uno)* someone, somebody; *(nelle interrogative)* anyone, anybody ; *(alcuni)* some ; *(alcuni : nelle interrogative)* any ; **qualcun altro** *(persona)* someone else ; **qualcuno di voi** some of you ; *(nelle interrogative)* any of you.

☞

quale *agg interr* - 1. *(persona)* which ; **qual è il tuo scrittore preferito?** who is your favourite writer? ; **da ~ dentista sei stato?** which dentist have you been to?
- 2. *(cosa)* which, what ; **non so ~ libro scegliere** I don't know which book to choose ; **in ~ albergo hai prenotato?** which hotel have you booked? ◆ *agg relativo* such as, like ; **alcuni animali quali il cane** some animals such as the dog.
◆ *pron interr* which (one) ; **~ vuole di questi cappelli?** which of these hats do you want? ; **non so ~ scegliere** I don't know which (one) to choose. ◆ *pron relativo* - 1. *(soggetto)* : **il/la ~** *(persona)* who ; *(cosa)* which, that ; **suo fratello, il ~ è un mio amico** his brother, who is a friend of mine.
- 3. *(con preposizioni : persona)* who(m) ; *(cosa)* which, that ; **l'albergo nel ~ alloggio** the hotel (that) I'm staying in ; **la persona con la ~ parlavo** the person (whom) I was talking to ; **l'uomo del ~ conosco il figlio** the man whose son I know.
- 4. *(in qualità di)* as ; **vengo ~ accompagnatore** I'm coming as a tour guide.

qualifica, che *sf* qualification.
qualificare *vt* to describe, to define. ❑ **qualificarsi** *vr* to qualify.
qualificativo, a *agg* qualifying.
qualità *sf inv* quality ; *(varietà)* type ; **in ~ di** in one's capacity as.
qualsiasi = **qualunque.**
qualunque *agg* any ; *(quale che)* whatever ; **~ cosa** anything ; **~ cosa succeda** whatever happens ; **~ persona** anyone ; **prendine uno ~** take whichever you want.
quando *avv* & *cong* when ; **da ~ sono qui** from when I got here ; **da ~ sei qui?** how long have you been here? ; **da ~ in qua** since when ; **di ~ sono queste foto?** when were these photos taken?
quantità *sf inv* quantity, amount ; **una ~ di** a lot ○ lots of.

☞

quanto, a *agg interr* - 1. *(quantità)* how much ; *(numero)* how many ; **~ tempo ci vuole?** how long does it take? ; **quanti anni hai?** how old are you?
- 2. *(in frasi esclamative)* what ; **quanta fatica sprecata!** what a waste of energy!
◆ *agg relativo (quantità)* as much as ; *(numero)* as many as ; **puoi restare quanti giorni vuoi** you can stay for as many days as you like.
◆ *pron interr (quantità)* how much ; *(numero)* how many ; **prima di comprare il pane guarda ~ ce n'è** before buying the bread see how much there is ; **quanti ne vuoi?** how many do you want? ; **quanti ne abbiamo oggi?** what's the date today?
◆ *pron relativo (quello che : quantità)* as much as ; *(numero)* as many as ; **dammene ~ ti pare** give me as

much as you want ; **per ~ ne so** as far as I know.

◆ *avv* - 1. *(interrogativo : quantità)* how much ; *(numero)* how many ; **quant'è?** how much is it? ; **~ ti fermi?** how long are you staying? ; **~ è alta questa montagna?** how high is this mountain? ; **~ mi dispiace!** I'm so sorry! ; **~ costa/costano?** how much is it/are they?
- 2. *(relativo)* as much as ; **mi sforzo ~ posso** I try as hard as I can ; **~ prima** as soon as possible.
- 3. *(in espressioni)* : **in ~** *(perché)* as ; **per ~** however.

---

quaranta *num* forty → **sei**.

quarantena *sf* quarantine.

quarantesimo, a *num* fortieth → **sesto**.

quarantina *sf* : **una ~ (di)** about forty ; **essere sulla ~** to be in one's forties.

quaresima *sf* RELIG : **la ~** Lent.

quarta *sf (marcia)* fourth gear.

quartetto *sm* quartet.

quartiere *sm* area, district ; **quartier generale** headquarters *(pl)*.

quarto, a *num* fourth. ◆ *sm (parte)* quarter ; **un ~ d'ora** a quarter of an hour ; **le tre e un ~** quarter past three *(Br)*, quarter after three *(Am)* ; **le tre meno un ~** quarter to three *(Br)*, quarter of three *(Am)* ; **un ~ di vino** a quarter litre of wine, sesto.

quarzo *sm* quartz.

quasi *avv* nearly. ◆ *cong* as if ; **~ mai** hardly ever ; **~ sempre** almost always ; **~ ~ vengo anch'io** I might just come too.

quassù *avv* up here.

quattordicesimo, a *num* fourteenth → **sesto**.

quattordici *num* fourteen → **sei**.

quattrini *smpl fam* money *(sg)*.

quattro *num* four ; **farsi in ~ (per fare qc)** to go out of one's way (to do sthg) ; **eravamo ~ gatti** *fam* there were only a few of us there ; **in ~ e quattr'otto** in less than no time, **sei**.

quattrocento *num* four hundred → **sei**. ❑ **Quattrocento** *sm* : **il Quattrocento** the fifteenth century.

quegli quello.

quei → **quello**.

---

quello, a *(dav sm* **quel** *(pl* **quei***) + consonante ;* **quello** *(pl* **quegli***) + s+consonante, gn, ps, x, z ;* **quell'** *(pl* **quegli***) + vocale) agg* - 1. *(indica lontananza)* that, those *(pl)* ; **quella casa** that house ; **quegli alberi** those trees ; **quei bambini** those children.
- 2. *(per sottolineare)* : **spegni quella tv!** switch that TV off!
- 3. *(per cosa, persona già nota)* that, those *(pl)* ; **non mi piace quella gente** I don't like those people.

◆ *pron* - 1. *(indica lontananza)* that (one), those (ones) *(pl)* ; **quella è la mia macchina** that one's my car ; **prendo ~ in offerta** I'll take the one on special offer ; **~ lì** that one (there).
- 2. *(con pronome relativo)* : **faccio ~ che posso** I'll do what I can ; **quelli che potevano si sono fermati** those who could, stopped.

quercia, ce *sf* oak.

querelare *vt* to bring a legal action against.

quesito *sm* query.

questionario *sm* questionnaire.

questione *sf* question ; **è ~ di giorni** it's a matter of days ; **in ~** in question.

☞

questo, a *agg* - 1. *(indica prossimità)* this, these *(pl)* ; **questa finestra è aperta** this window is open ; **partiamo ~ giovedì** we're leaving this Thursday.
- 2. *(simile)* such ; **non uscire con questa pioggia** don't go out in rain like this.
- 3. *(il seguente/precedente)* this, these *(pl)* ; **~ è il mio consiglio** this is my advice.
◆ *pron* - 1. *(indica prossimità)* this (one), these (ones) *(pl)* ; **~ è Franco** this is Franco ; **~ qui** ○ **qua** this one (here).
- 2. *(per riassumere)* that ; **~ è tutto** that's all ; **questa è bella!** that's rich!

---

questura *sf (organo)* police headquarters *(pl)*.

qui *avv* here ; **da ~ in avanti** from now on ; **di** ○ **da ~** from here ; **di ~ a un anno** in a year's time ; **di ~ a poco** in a little while.

quiete *sf* quiet.

quindi *cong* so, therefore.

quindicesimo, a *num* fifteenth → **sesto**.

quindici *num* fifteen ; **~ giorni** a fortnight, sei.

quindicina *sf* about fifteen ; **una ~ di giorni** about a fortnight.

quinta *sf (marcia)* fifth gear. ❑ **quinte** *sfpl (di teatro)* wings.

quintale *sm* = 100 kilograms.

quinto, a *num* fifth → **sesto**.

quintuplo *sm* : **il ~ del prezzo normale** five times the normal price.

Quirinale *nm* : **il ~** official residence of the President of Italy.

IL QUIRINALE

The *Palazzo del Quirinale* has been the official residence of the president of the Italian republic since 1947. It overlooks the square of the same name in Rome and is guarded by armed policemen in full dress uniform. It is here that the president receives foreign heads of state on official business.

---

quota *sf (altitudine)* altitude ; *(di denaro, bene)* share ; **perdere ~** to lose height ; **prendere ~** to climb ; **~ d'iscrizione** *(a circolo)* membership fee.

quotato, a *agg* valued.

quotidianamente *avv* daily.

quotidiano, a *agg* daily. ◆ *sm* daily (newspaper).

I QUOTIDIANI

Daily newspapers are sold by newsagents, supermarkets and booksellers, and by subscription. Many can also be accessed on the Internet. The major dailies contain political stories from at home and abroad, news, finance and sport, while cultural items feature on the so-called 'third page'. The most important titles are the *Corriere della Sera*, first printed in Milan in 1876, the Roman *La Repubblica* (1976), and *La Stampa* (1895) which is printed in Turin. No less than three daily papers are dedicated exclusively to sport: *La Gazzetta dello Sport*, *Tuttosport* and *Il Corriere dello Sport*. Milan's *Il Sole 24 Ore*, on the other hand, deals with economics and finance. On a local level there are a number of newspapers which concentrate on regional, provincial and local news with a summary of the major national and foreign stories.

---

quoziente *sm* quotient; **~ d'intelligenza** IQ.

R

rabarbaro *sm* rhubarb.

rabbia *sf (collera)* anger, rage; *(malattia)* rabies; **far ~ a qn** to drive sb mad.

rabbino *sm* rabbi.

rabbioso, a *agg* angry; *MED* rabid.

rabbonire *vt* to calm down. ❑ **rabbonirsi** *vr* to calm down.

rabbrividire *vi (di freddo)* to shiver; *(di paura)* to shudder.

rabbuiarsi *vr (oscurarsi)* to darken; *fig (incupirsi)* to darken.

raccapezzarsi *vr*: **non mi ci raccapezzo** I can't make it out.

raccapricciante *agg* horrifying.

raccattapalle *smf inv* ball-boy (*f* ball-girl).

raccattare *vt* to pick up.

racchetta *sf (da tennis)* racket; *(da ping-pong)* bat *(Br)*, paddle *(Am)*; *(da sci)* ski pole.

raccogliere *vt (da terra)* to pick up; *(frutti, fiori)* to pick; *(mettere insieme)* to collect; *(voti)* to win. ❑ **raccogliersi** *vr (radunarsi)* to meet, to gather; *(in meditazione, preghiera)* to gather one's thoughts.

raccolta *sf* collection; *(agricola)* harvest; **fare la ~ di qc** to collect sthg.

raccolto, a *pp* → **raccogliere.** ◆ *sm* harvest, crop.

raccomandare *vt* to recommend; *(affidare)* to entrust; **~ a qn di fare qc** to urge sb to do sthg. ❑ **raccomandarsi** *vr*: **raccomandarsi a** to appeal to; **mi raccomando, non fare tardi!** don't be late now, will you?

raccomandata *sf* registered letter.

raccomandato, a *agg (lettera)* registered; *(candidato)* recommended.

raccomandazione *sf (consiglio)* recommendation.

raccontare *vt* to tell.

racconto *sm (esposizione)* account; *(romanzo)* short story.

raccordo *sm* connection, link; *(di autostrada)* slip road *(Br)*,

entrance/exit ramp *(Am)* ; ~ **anulare** ring road *(Br)*, beltway *(Am)*.
racimolare *vt* to scrape together.
racket *sm inv* racket.
rada *sf* harbour.
radar *sm inv* radar.
raddoppiare *vt (rendere doppio)* to double ; *(aumentare)* to redouble. ◆ *vi* to double.
radente *agg (tiro, volo)* very low.
radere *vt* to shave ; ~ **qc al suolo** to raze sthg to the ground. ❑ **radersi** *vr* to shave.
radiare *vt* to strike off.
radiatore *sm* radiator.
radiazione *sf* radiation.
radicale *agg* radical.
radicalmente *avv* radically, completely.
radicchio *sm* chicory.
radice *sf* root ; ~ **quadrata** square root.
radio *sf inv* radio ; *(stazione)* radio station ; **alla** ~ on the radio.
radioamatore, trice *sm, f* radio ham.
radioascoltatore, trice *sm, f* listener.
radioattivo, a *agg* radioactive.
radiocomandato, a *agg* remote-controlled.
radiografia *sf* X-ray.
radioso, a *agg* bright.
radiotaxi *sm inv* minicab.
rado, a *agg* sparse ; **di** ~ rarely.
radunare *vt (persone)* to gather ; *(cose)* to assemble. ❑ **radunarsi** *vr* to gather.
raduno *sm* meeting.
rafano *sm* radish.
raffermo, a *agg* stale.
raffica, che *sf (di vento)* gust ; *(di mitra)* burst.
raffigurare *vt* to portray.
raffinato, a *agg* refined ; *(stile)* sophisticated.
raffineria *sf* refinery.
rafforzare *vt* to strengthen.
raffreddare *vt* to cool ; *fig (rapporti, interesse)* to cool, to dampen. ❑ **raffreddarsi** *vr (bevanda, cibo)* to get cold ; *fig (persona, amicizia)* to cool down ; *(ammalarsi)* to catch a cold.
raffreddato, a *agg* : **essere** ~ to have a cold.
raffreddore *sm* cold.
rafia *sf* raffia.
ragazza *sf (giovane donna)* girl ; *(fidanzata)* girlfriend ; ~ **madre** single mother.
ragazzata *sf* childish trick.
ragazzo *sm (giovane)* boy ; *(fidanzato)* boyfriend.
raggiante *agg* radiant, beaming.
raggio *sm (di sole, infrarosso)* ray ; *(area)* range ; MAT radius ; *(di ruota)* spoke.
raggirare *vt* to trick, to cheat.
raggiungere *vt (persona)* to catch up ; *(luogo)* to reach ; *fig (fine)* to achieve.
raggiunto, a *pp* → **raggiungere**.
raggomitolarsi *vr* to curl up.
raggranellare *vt* to scrape together.
raggrinzire *vt & vi* to shrivel up. ❑ **raggrinzirsi** *vr* to shrivel.

raggruppare *vt (mettere insieme)* to assemble ; *(a gruppi)* to group together. ❑ **raggrupparsi** *vr* to assemble.
ragguagli *smpl*: **dare ~** to give details.
ragionamento *sm (riflessione)* reasoning ; *(discorso)* argument.
ragionare *vi* to reason. ❑ **ragionare di** *v + prep (parlare di)* to argue about.
ragione *sf* reason ; **avere ~** to be right ; **dare ~ a qn** to side with sb ; **a maggior ~** even more so.
ragioneria *sf (materia)* accountancy ; *(scuola)* commercial school ; *(reparto)* accounts *(pl)*.
ragionevole *agg* reasonable.
ragioniere, a *sm, f* accountant.
ragliare *vi* to bray.
ragnatela *sf* cobweb, spider's web.
ragno *sm* spider.
ragù *sm inv sauce of minced beef, tomatoes and onions.*
RAI *sf Italian broadcasting corporation.*
rallegramenti *smpl* congratulations.
rallentare *vt* to slow down.
rally ['rɛlli] *sm inv* rally.
ramaiolo *sm* ladle.
ramanzina *sf* telling-off.
rame *sm* copper.
ramino *sm* rummy.
rammaricarsi : rammaricarsi di *vr + prep* to regret.
rammendare *vt (stoffa)* to mend ; *(lana)* to darn.
rammentare *vt* to remember ; **~ qc a qn** to remind sb of sthg. ❑ **rammentarsi di** *vr + prep* to remember.
rammollito, a *agg* soft.
ramo *sm* branch.
ramoscello *sm* twig.
rampa *sf* flight *(of stairs)* ; **~ di lancio** launch pad.
rampicante *agg* climbing.
rampone *sm (fiocina)* harpoon ; *(in alpinismo)* crampon.
rana *sf* frog.
rancido, a *agg* rancid.
rancore *sm* rancour.
randagio, a *agg* stray.
randello *sm* club.
rango, ghi *sm* rank.
rannicchiarsi *vr* to huddle up.
rannuvolarsi *vr* to cloud over.
ranocchio *sm* frog.
rantolo *sm* death rattle.
rapa *sf* turnip.
rapace *agg* predatory. ◆ *sm* bird of prey.
rapanello *sm* radish = **ravanello**.
rapare *vt* to crop.
rapida *sf* rapids *(pl)*.
rapidamente *avv* rapidly, fast.
rapidità *sf* rapidity.
rapido, a *agg (svelto)* fast ; *(breve)* quick, rapid. ◆ *sm* express (train).
rapimento *sm* kidnapping.
rapina *sf* robbery ; **~ a mano armata** armed robbery.
rapinare *vt* to rob.
rapinatore, trice *sm, f* robber.
rapire *vt* to kidnap.
rapitore, trice *sm, f* kidnapper.

rapporto *sm (resoconto)* report ; *(tra persone)* relationship ; *(connessione)* connection, relation ; *MAT* ratio ; **rapporti sessuali** sexual intercourse *(sg)*.
rapprendersi *vr* to curdle.
rappresentante *smf* representative.
rappresentare *vt* to represent ; *(raffigurare)* to depict ; *(mettere in scena)* to stage, to perform.
rappresentazione *sf (spettacolo)* performance ; *(raffigurazione)* representation.
rappreso, a *pp* → **rapprendersi**.
raramente *avv* rarely.
rarità *sf inv (scarsità)* rarity ; *(oggetto)* rare thing.
raro, a *agg* rare.
rasare *vt* to shave. ❑ **rasarsi** *vr* to shave.
rasato, a *agg* shaven.
raschiamento *sm MED* curettage.
raschiare *vt* to scrape.
rasentare *vt (sfiorare)* to graze ; *(muro)* to hug, to keep close to ; *fig (avvicinarsi a)* to border on.
rasente *prep* close to.
raso, a *pp* → **radere**. ◆ *agg (cucchiaio)* level ; **~ terra** close to the ground.
rasoio *sm* razor ; **~ elettrico** electric razor.
rassegna *sf* review ; *(cinematografica, teatrale)* season ; **passare in ~** *MIL* to review.
rassegnare *vt* : **~ le dimissioni** to hand in one's resignation. ❑ **rassegnarsi** *vr* to resign o.s.
rasserenarsi *vr* to clear up.
rassettare *vt (stanza, capelli)* to tidy (up) ; *(vestito)* to mend.
rassicurare *vt* to reassure.
rassodare *vt (terreno)* to harden ; *(muscoli)* to tone.
rassomigliare : **rassomigliare a** *v + prep* to resemble.
rastrellare *vt (foglie)* to rake ; *fig (zona)* to comb.
rastrello *sm* rake.
rata *sf* instalment ; **pagare qc a rate** to pay for sthg in instalments.
rateale *agg* by ○ in instalments.
ratificare *vt DIR* to ratify.
ratto *sm* rat.
rattoppare *vt* to patch.
rattrappire *vt* to numb. ❑ **rattrappirsi** *vr* to go numb.
rattristare *vt* to make sad. ❑ **rattristarsi** *vr* to become sad.
rauco, a, chi, che *agg* raucous.
ravanello *sm* radish.
ravioli *smpl* ravioli.
ravvicinare *vt (avvicinare)* to bring closer ; *(rappacificare)* to reconcile. ❑ **ravvicinarsi** *vr* to be reconciled.
ravvivare *vt* to brighten up.
razionale *agg* rational.
razionalità *sf* rationality.
razionare *vt* to ration.
razione *sf* ration.
razza *sf (di persone)* race ; *(di animali)* breed ; *(pesce)* ray ; **che ~ di domanda è questa?** *fam* what sort of question is that?
razzia *sf* raid.
razziale *agg* racial.
razzismo *sm* racism.
razzista, i, e *agg* & *smf* racist.

razzo *sm* rocket.
razzolare *vi* to scratch about.
re *sm inv* king.
reagire *vi* : ~ (a qc) to react (to sthg).
reale *agg (vero)* real ; *(di re)* royal.
realista, i, e *smf* realist.
realizzare *vt (progetto)* to carry out ; *(sogno)* to fulfil ; *(film)* to produce ; *(rendersi conto di)* to realize ; COMM to realize. ❑ **realizzarsi** *vr (persona)* to be fulfilled ; *(progetto)* to be carried out ; *(sogno)* to come true.
realizzazione *sf (attuazione)* carrying-out.
realmente *avv* really.
realtà *sf inv* reality ; in ~ in reality.
reato *sm* offence, crime.
reattore *sm (aereo)* jet ; *(motore)* jet engine ; *(in fisica)* reactor.
reazionario, a *agg* reactionary.
reazione *sf* reaction.
rebus *sm inv game in which pictures represent the syllables of words.*
recapitare *vt* to deliver.
recapito *sm (luogo)* address ; *(consegna)* delivery ; ~ telefonico (tele)phone number.
recare *vt* : ~ disturbo a qn to disturb sb. ❑ **recarsi** *vr* to go.
recensione *sf* review.
recente *agg* recent ; di ~ recently.
recentemente *avv* recently.
recessione *sf* recession.
recidere *vt* to cut off.
recintare *vt* to fence in.
recinto *sm (spazio)* enclosure ; *(recinzione)* fence.
recipiente *sm* container.
reciproco, a, ci, che *agg* reciprocal.
reciso, a *pp* → recidere.
recita *sf* play.
recitare *vt (poesia)* to recite ; *(ruolo)* to play. ◆ *vi* to act.
reclamare *vi* to complain. ◆ *vt* to claim.
réclame [re'klam] *sf inv* advertising.
reclamo *sm (protesta)* complaint.
reclinabile *agg* reclining.
reclusione *sf* DIR imprisonment.
reclutare *vt* to recruit.
record *sm inv* record.
recuperare *vt (riprendere)* to recover, to get back ; *(svantaggio, tempo)* to mske up ; *(rottami)* to salvage.
redatto, a *pp* → redigere.
redattore, trice *sm, f* editor.
redazione *sf (stesura)* writing ; *(ufficio)* editorial department ; *(personale)* editorial staff.
redditizio, a *agg* profitable.
reddito *sm* income.
redigere *vt (articolo, lettera)* to write ; *(documento, contratto)* to draw up.
redini *sfpl* reins.
referendum *sm inv* referendum.
referenze *sfpl* references.
referto *sm* medical report.

refettorio *sm* refectory, dining hall.
refrigerare *vt* to refrigerate.
refurtiva *sf* stolen goods *(pl)*.
regalare *vt (dono)* to give (as a present) ; *(dare gratis)* to give away.
regale *agg (da re)* regal.
regalo *sm (dono)* present, gift.
regata *sf* regatta.
reggere *vt (tenere)* to hold ; *(sostenere)* to bear, to support ; *(sopportare)* to bear ; *(governare)* to govern ; GRAMM to take, to be followed by. ◆ *vi (durare)* to last ; *(essere logico)* to stand up, to hold good ; *(resistere)* : **~ a qc** to withstand sthg. ❑ **reggersi** *vr* : **non mi reggo in piedi** I can't stand up.
reggia, ge *sf* palace.
reggicalze *sm inv* suspender belt.
reggimento *sm* regiment.
reggipetto = **reggiseno**.
reggiseno *sm* bra.
regia *sf (di film)* direction ; *(di dramma)* production.
regime *sm (politico)* regime ; *(alimentare)* diet.
regina *sf* queen.
regionale *agg* regional.
regione *sf* region.

REGIONE

For administrative purposes Italy is divided up into 20 regions. Each region is made up of different provinces (*province*), and each province is made up of municipalities known as *comuni*. Five of the regions have a special statute granting them a greater degree of autonomy than the others : they are *Valle d'Aosta, Friuli-Venezia Giulia, Trentino-Alto Adige, Sicilia* and *Sardegna*.

---

regista, i, e *smf* director.
registrare *vt* to register ; *(su cassetta)* to record ; COMM to enter.
registratore *sm* tape recorder ; **~ di cassa** cash register.
registrazione *sf (di nascita, morte)* registration ; *(di musica, programma)* recording ; COMM entry.
registro *sm* register ; **~ di classe** attendance register.
regnare *vi* to reign.
regno *sm* kingdom ; *fig (ambito)* realm. ❑ **Regno Unito** *sm* : **il Regno Unito** the United Kingdom.
regola *sf* rule ; **essere in ~** to be (all) in order ; **fare qc a ~ d'arte** to do sthg perfectly.
regolabile *agg* adjustable.
regolamento *sm* regulations *(pl)*.
regolare *agg* regular. ◆ *vt* to regulate ; *(apparecchio, macchina)* to adjust ; *(questione, conto)* to settle. ❑ **regolarsi** *vr (comportarsi)* to behave ; *(moderarsi)* to control o.s. ; **regolarsi nel bere/mangiare** to watch what one drinks/eats.
regolarmente *avv* regularly.
regolo *sm* ruler ; **~ calcolatore** slide rule.
regredire *vi* to regress.
reintegrare *vt* to reinstate.
relativamente *avv* relatively,

comparatively ; ~ a in relation to, as regards.

relativo, a *agg* relative ; ~ a relating to.

relax *sm inv* relaxation.

relazione *sf* relationship ; *(amorosa)* affair ; *(resoconto)* report.

relegare *vt* to relegate.

religione *sf* religion.

religioso, a *agg* religious. ◆ *sm, f* monk (*f* nun).

reliquia *sf* relic.

relitto *sm* wreck, piece of wreckage.

remare *vi* to row.

remo *sm* oar.

rendere *vt (restituire)* to give back, to return ; *(far diventare)* to make ; *(produrre)* to yield. ◆ *vi (persona, azienda)* to do well ; *(lavoro)* to pay well ; ~ **possibile qc** to make sthg possible ; ~ **l'idea** *(persona)* to make o.s. clear. ❑ **rendersi** *vr (diventare)* to become ; **rendersi utile** to make o.s. useful.

rendiconto *sm (relazione)* report ; COMM statement of accounts.

rendimento *sm (efficienza)* efficiency ; *(di scolaro, macchina)* performance.

rendita *sf* unearned income ; **vivere di** ~ *fig (studente)* to get by on one's past performance.

rene *sm* kidney.

renitente *agg* reluctant ; **è ~ ai consigli** he won't listen to advice ; **essere ~ alla leva** *to fail to report for military service.*

renna *sf* reindeer.

Reno *sm* : **il ~** the Rhine.

reparto *sm (di negozio)* department ; *(d'ospedale)* ward ; MIL unit.

repentaglio *sm* : **mettere a ~ qc** to put sthg at risk.

reperibile *agg (merce, persona)* available ; *(al lavoro)* on call.

reperto *sm (resto)* find ; *(resoconto)* report.

repertorio *sm (teatrale)* repertoire ; *(elenco)* index.

replica, che *sf (in televisione)* repeat ; *(a teatro)* repeat performance.

replicare *vt* to reply.

repressione *sf* repression.

represso, a *pp* → **reprimere**.

reprimere *vt* to repress. ❑ **reprimersi** *vr* to restrain o.s.

repubblica, che *sf* republic.

Repubblica Ceca *sf* Czech Republic.

repubblicano, a *agg* republican.

repulsione *sf* repulsion.

reputare *vt* to consider.

reputazione *sf* reputation.

requisire *vt* to requisition.

requisito *sm* requisite.

resa *sf (l'arrendersi)* surrender ; *(restituzione)* return ; *(rendimento)* yield ; ~ **dei conti** *fig* day of reckoning.

residence ['rɛzidens] *sm inv* residential hotel.

residente *agg* resident.

residenza *sf* residence.

residenziale *agg* residential.

residuo, a *agg* residual, remaining. ◆ *sm (avanzo)* remainder ; *(scoria)* waste.
resina *sf* resin.
resistente *agg (robusto)* strong ; *(durevole)* durable ; ~ **al calore** heat proof, heat-resistant.
resistenza *sf* resistance ; *(di materiale)* strength ; *(a fatica, dolore)* endurance ; ~ **(elettrica)** (electrical) resistance.
resistere *vi (tener duro)* to hold put. ❑ **resistere a** *v + prep (opporsi)* to resist ; *(sopportare)* to withstand.
resistito, a *pp* → **resistere.**
reso, a *pp* → **rendere.**
resoconto *sm* account.
respingere *vt* to reject ; *(attacco, aggressore)* to repel ; SCOL to fail.
respinto, a *pp* → **respingere.**
respirare *vi* & *vt* to breathe.
respiratore *sm (per immersione)* aqualung ; MED respirator.
respirazione *sf* breathing ; ~ **artificiale** artificial respiration.
respiro *sm (respirazione)* breathing ; *(movimento)* breath ; **tirare un ~ di sollievo** to heave a sigh of relief.
responsabile *agg* responsible. ◆ *smf (in azienda, negozio)* person in charge ; *(colpevole)* culprit ; **essere ~ di qc** *(incaricato di)* to be in charge of sthg ; *(colpevole di)* to be responsible for sthg.
responsabilità *sf inv* responsibility ; *(colpa)* responsibility, liability.
ressa *sf* crowd.
restare *vi* to stay, to remain ; *(avanzare)* to be left, to remain ; *(trovarsi)* to be ; ~ **a piedi** to remain standing ; **mi restano pochi giorni** I only have a few days left.
restaurare *vt* to restore.
restauro *sm* restoration.
restituire *vt* to give back, to return.
resto *sm* rest, remainder ; *(di denaro)* change ; MAT remainder ; **del ~** moreover, besides. ❑ **resti** *smpl (ruderi)* ruins ; *(di cibo)* leftovers ; *(di persona, animale)* remains.
restringere *vt (dimensioni)* to reduce ; *(tessuto)* to shrink ; *(limitare)* to limit, to restrict. ❑ **restringersi** *vr (strada)* to (become) narrow ; *(stoffa)* to shrink ; *(per numero, estensione)* to reduce.
resurrezione *sf* resurrection.
resuscitare = **risuscitare.**
rete *sf* net ; *(recinzione)* wire fence ; *(radiotelevisiva, stradale)* network ; *(del letto)* bedsprings *(pl)* ; *(nel calcio : punto)* goal.
reticente *agg* reticent.
reticolato *sm (intreccio di linee)* network ; *(recinzione)* fencing, wire netting.
retina *sf* ANAT retina.
retino *sm* net.
retorico, a, ci, che *agg spreg* pompous.
retribuire *vt* to remunerate, to pay.
retribuzione *sf* remuneration, pay.
retro *sm inv* back ; **sul ~** at the back ; **vedi ~** see over.
retrocedere *vi* to recede ; SPORT to be relegated.
retrocesso, a *pp* → **retrocedere.**

retrogrado, a *agg* retrograde.
retromarcia *sf* reverse.
retroscena *sm inv (antefatti)* background.
retrospettivo, a *agg* retrospective.
retrovisore *sm* rear-view mirror.
retta *sf (linea)* straight line ; *(di pensionato)* charge ; **dar ~ a** to pay attention to.
rettangolare *agg* rectangular.
rettangolo *sm* rectangle.
rettificare *vt form* to rectify.
rettile *sm* reptile.
rettilineo, a *agg* & *sm* straight.
retto, a *pp* → **reggere**. ◆ *agg (diritto)* straight ; *(persona, comportamento)* honest ; **angolo ~** right angle.
rettore *sm* rector.
reumatismi *smpl* rheumatism *(sg)*.
reversibile *agg* reversible.
revisionare *vt (apparecchio, macchina)* to service, to overhaul ; *(testo)* to revise.
revisione *sf (di apparecchio)* service ; *(di conti)* audit(ing) ; *(di scritto)* revision.
revocare *vt* to revoke.
revolver *sm inv* revolver.
riabilitare *vt* to rehabilitate.
riacquistare *vt* to regain.
riaggiustare *vt* to readjust.
rialzare *vt* to raise. ❑ **rialzarsi** *vr* to get up.
rialzo *sm* rise.
rianimazione *sf (reparto)* intensive care.
riaperto, a *pp* → **riaprire**.
riapertura *sf* reopening ; **~ delle scuole** beginning of the school term.
riaprire *vt* & *vi* to reopen. ❑ **riaprirsi** *vr* to reopen.
riarmo *sm* rearming.
riassetto *sm* reorganization.
riassumere *vt (ricapitolare)* to summarize ; *(impiegato)* to re-employ ; *(riprendere)* to resume.
riassunto, a *pp* → **riassumere**. ◆ *sm* summary.
riattaccare *vt (attaccare di nuovo)* to re-attach ; *(bottone)* to sew back on ; *(ricominciare)* to start again ; *(al telefono)* to hang up.
riavere *vt (avere di nuovo)* to have again ; *(avere indietro)* to get back ; *(riacquistare)* to regain, to recover. ❑ **riaversi da** *vr + prep* to recover from.
ribadire *vt* to confirm.
ribaltabile *agg* folding.
ribaltare *vt* to overturn.
ribassare *vt* to lower. ◆ *vi* to fall.
ribasso *sm* fall, reduction.
ribattere *vt (palla)* to return. ◆ *vi (replicare)* to answer back.
ribellarsi *vr* to rebel ; **~ a qn** to rebel against sb.
ribelle *agg* rebellious.
ribellione *sf* rebellion.
ribes *sm inv* : **~ nero** blackcurrant ; **~ rosso** redcurrant.
ribollire *vi fig* to seethe.
ribrezzo *sm* horror ; **far ~ a qn** to revolt sb.
ricadere *vi (cadere di nuovo)* to fall again ; *(in errore, vizio)* to

relapse ; *(capelli, vestiti)* to hang down. ❑ **ricadere su** *v + prep* to fall on.
ricalcare *vt* to trace.
ricamare *vt* to embroider.
ricambiare *vt (sentimento, favore)* to return ; *(cambiare di nuovo)* to change again.
ricambio *sm (sostituzione)* exchange, replacement ; **in ~** in return. ❑ **ricambi** *smpl* spare parts.
ricamo *sm* embroidery.
ricapitolare *vt* to summarize.
ricaricare *vt (macchina fotografica, arma)* to reload ; *(batteria)* to recharge ; *(orologio)* to wind up.
ricattare *vt* to blackmail.
ricatto *sm* blackmail.
ricavare *vt (estrarre)* to extract ; *(ottenere)* to obtain.
ricavato *sm (guadagno)* proceeds *(pl)*.
ricchezza *sf* wealth. ❑ **ricchezze** *sfpl* wealth *(sg)* ; **~ naturali** natural resources.
ricciarelli *smpl diamond-shaped sweets made from marzipan (a speciality of Siena).*
riccio, a, ci, ce *agg* curly. ◆ *sm (di capelli)* curl ; *(animale)* hedgehog ; **~ di mare** sea urchin.
ricciolo *sm* curl.
ricciuto, a *agg* curly.
ricco, a, chi, che *agg* rich, wealthy ; **~ di qc** rich in sthg.
ricerca, a, che *sf* research ; *(di persona, di cosa)* search ; **essere alla ~ di** to be in search of.
ricercare *vt (cercare di nuovo)* to look for (again) ; *(ladro)* to look for, to search for.
ricercatezza *sf* refinement.
ricercato, a *agg (elegante)* refined ; *(apprezzato)* in demand, sought-after ; **essere ~ dalla polizia** to be wanted by the police.
ricercatore, trice *sm, f* researcher.
ricetta *sf* recipe ; **~ medica** prescription.
ricettazione *sf* receiving (stolen goods).
ricevere *vt (lettera, regalo)* to receive, to get ; *(schiaffo, palla)* to get ; *(accogliere)* to welcome ; *(ospite)* to entertain ; *(cliente, paziente)* to receive.
ricevimento *sm* reception.
ricevitore *sm* receiver.
ricevuta *sf* receipt ; **mi può fare una ~?** may I have a receipt?
ricezione *sf* reception.
richiamare *vt (ritelefonare, per far tornare)* to call back ; *(attirare)* to attract ; *(rimproverare)* to reprimand ; **~ alla mente qc a qn** to remind sb of sthg.
richiamo *sm (per far tornare)* call ; *(attrazione)* appeal, attraction ; *(di vaccinazione)* booster.
richiedere *vt (ridomandare)* to ask again ; *(aiuto, spiegazioni)* to ask for ; *(necessitare di)* to require ; **gli ho richiesto le chiavi** *(indietro)* I asked him for my keys back.
richiesta *sf (domanda)* request ; *(esigenza)* demand ; **a ~** on request.
richiesto, a *pp* → **richiedere.** ◆ *agg* in demand, sought-after.
richiudere *vt* to close again.
riciclare *vt* to recycle.

ricollegare *vt (centri isolati)* to reconnect ; *(fatti discorsi)* to connect, to relate. ❑ **ricollegarsi** *vr* : **ricollegarsi a** *(riferirsi)* to refer to ; *(fatto)* to be connected with.

ricominciare *vt* & *vi* to begin again, to start again ; **~ a fare qc** to begin again, to resume doing sthg.

ricompensa *sf* reward.

ricompensare *vt* to reward.

ricomporre *vt* to reconstruct. ❑ **ricomporsi** *vr* to regain one's composure.

ricomposto, a *pp* → **ricomporre**.

riconciliare *vt* to reconcile. ❑ **riconciliarsi** *vr* to be reconciled.

ricondotto, a *pp* → **ricondurre**.

ricondurre *vt (in luogo)* to take back, to bring back.

riconferma *sf (conferma ulteriore)* reconfirmation ; *(dimostrazione)* proof.

riconfermare *vt* to reconfirm.

riconoscente *agg* grateful.

riconoscenza *sf (gratitudine)* grattitude.

riconoscere *vt* to recognize ; *(ammettere)* to admit.

riconquistare *vt (territorio)* to reconquer ; *(stima, rispetto)* to regain.

riconsegnare *vt* to give back.

ricoperto, a *pp* → **ricoprire**.

ricopiare *vt* to copy.

ricoprire *vt (poltrona, dolce)* to cover ; *(carica)* to hold ; **~ qn/qc di qc** to cover sb/sthg with sthg.

ricordare *vt* to remember, to recall ; **~ qc a qn** to remind sb of sthg ; **non mi ricordo l'indirizzo** I don't remember the address. ❑ **ricordarsi di** *vr + prep* to remember ; **ricordarsi di aver fatto qc** to remember doing o having done sthg ; **ricordarsi di fare qc** to remember to do sthg.

ricordo *sm (memoria)* memory ; *(oggetto)* souvenir.

ricorrente *agg* recurrent.

ricorrenza *sf* anniversary.

ricorrere *vi (ripetersi)* to recur. ❑ **ricorrere a** *v + prep (rivolgersi a)* to turn to ; *(utilizzare)* to resort to.

ricorso, a *pp* → **ricorrere**. ◆ *sm* DIR appeal ; **far ~ a qc** *(utilizzare)* to resort to sthg.

ricostruire *vt (edificio)* to rebuild ; *(fatto)* to reconstruct.

ricotta *sf* ricotta *(soft cheese made from milk whey)*.

ricoverare *vt* : **~ qn in ospedale** to admit sb to hospital.

ricreare *vt (creare di nuovo)* to recreate.

ricreazione *sf (a scuola)* break.

ricredersi *vr* to change one's mind.

ricucire *vt* to mend.

ricuperare = **recuperare**.

ridacchiare *vi* to snigger.

ridare *vt (dare di nuovo)* to give again ; *(restituire)* to give back.

ridere *vi* to laugh ; **morire dal ~** to die laughing. ❑ **ridere di** *v + prep* to laugh at.

ridetto, a *pp* → **ridire**.

ridicolo, a *agg* ridiculous.

ridimensionare *vt* : **~ un problema** to get a problem into perspective.

ridire *vt (ripetere)* to repeat ; **avere qualcosa da ~** to find fault.
ridondante *agg* redundant.
ridosso *sm* : **a ~ (di qc)** behind (sthg).
ridotto, a *pp* → **ridurre.** ◆ *agg (prezzo)* reduced ; *(formato)* smaller ; **~ male** in a bad state.
ridurre *vt* to reduce. ❑ **ridursi** *vr (diminuire)* to shrink. ❑ **ridursi a** *vr + prep* to be reduced to.
riduzione *sf* reduction.
rielaborare *vt* to redesign.
riempire *vt* to fill ; *(modulo)* to fill in ; **~ di** to fill with. ❑ **riempirsi di** *vr + prep (stadio, cinema)* to fill with ; *fam (mangiare)* to stuff o.s. with.
rientrare *vi (entrare di nuovo)* to go/come back in ; *(a casa, in patria)* to return ; *(essere compreso)* to be included ; *(avere una rientranza)* to curve inwards.
riepilogo, ghi *sm* summary.
rievocare *vt (ricordare)* to recall ; *(far ricordare)* to commemorate.
rifare *vt (fare di nuovo)* to do again ; *(ricostruire)* to rebuild ; **~ il letto** to make the bed. ❑ **rifarsi di** *vr + prep (perdita)* to recover ; **rifarsi di qc su qn** to get one's own back on sb for sthg.
rifatto, a *pp* → **rifare.**
riferimento *sm* reference ; **fare ~ a** to refer to.
riferire *vt* : **~ qc (a qn)** to report sthg (to sb). ❑ **riferirsi a** *vr + prep* to refer to.
rifilare *vt* : **~ qc a qn** *(merce) fam* to palm sthg off on sb ; *fam (compito)* to saddle sb with sthg.
rifiniture *sfpl* finishing touches.
rifiorire *vi* to flower again.
rifiutare *vt* to refuse ; **~ di fare qc** to refuse to do sthg.
rifiuto *sm* refusal. ❑ **rifiuti** *smpl (spazzatura)* rubbish *(sg) (Br)*, trash *(sg) (Am)*.
riflessione *sf* reflection.
riflessivo, a *agg* reflexive.
riflesso, a *pp* → **riflettere.** ◆ *sm (luce)* reflection ; *(conseguenza)* repercussion ; *MED* reflex.
riflettere *vt* & *vi* to reflect ; **~ su** to reflect on, to think about. ❑ **riflettersi** *vr* to be reflected. ❑ **riflettersi su** *vr + prep (influire)* to influence, to have repercussions on.
riflettore *sm (di teatro)* spotlight ; *(di stadio)* floodlight.
riflusso *sm (flusso contrario)* flow ; *(di marea)* ebb.
riforma *sf* reform.
riformare *vt* to reform ; *MIL* to invalid out.
rifornimento *sm* : **fare ~ di qc** to stock up with sthg. ❑ **rifornimenti** *smpl* supplies.
rifornire *vt* : **~ qn/qc di** to supply sb/sthg with. ❑ **rifornirsi di** *vr + prep* to stock up with.
rifrangere *vt* to refract.
rifratto, a *pp* → **rifrangere.**
rifugiarsi *vr* to take refuge.
rifugiato, a *sm, f* refugee.
rifugio *sm (riparo)* shelter, refuge ; **~ alpino** mountain hut.
riga, ghe *sf* line ; *(di capelli)* parting ; *(righello)* ruler ; **mettersi in ~** to get into line ; **a righe** *(tessuto)* striped ; *(foglio)* lined.

rigare *vt* to scratch. ◆ *vi* : ~ **diritto** to toe the line.
rigattiere *sm* junk dealer.
rigettare *vt (gettare indietro)* to throw back ; *(respingere)* to reject ; *fam (vomitare)* to throw up.
rigetto *sm MED* rejection.
rigidità *sf (di oggetto)* rigidity ; *(del corpo)* stiffness ; *(di clima)* harshness ; *(di regolamento, persona)* strictness.
rigido, a *agg (non elastico)* rigid ; *(membra)* stiff ; *(clima)* harsh ; *(severo)* strict.
rigirare *vt (voltare)* to turn (round) ; ~ **il discorso** to change the subject. ❑ **rigirarsi** *vr (voltarsi)* to turn round ; *(nel letto)* to turn over.
rigo, ghi *sm* line.
rigoglioso, a *agg* luxuriant.
rigore *sm* rigour ; *SPORT* penalty ; **essere di** ~ to be compulsory.
rigoroso, a *agg* rigorous.
rigovernare *vt* to wash up.
riguardare *vt (guardare di nuovo)* to look at again ; *(controllare)* to check ; *(concernere)* to concern. ❑ **riguardarsi** *vr* to look after o.s. ; **riguardati!** look after yourself!, take care! ; **questo non ti riguarda** this has nothing to do with you.
riguardo *sm (attenzione)* care ; *(stima)* regard, respect ; ~ **a** with regard to.
rilanciare *vt* to relaunch.
rilancio *sm* relaunch ; *(economico)* recovery.
rilasciare *vt (intervista)* to give ; *(ostaggio)* to release ; *(documento, diploma)* to issue.
rilassare *vt* to relax. ❑ **rilassarsi** *vr* to relax.
rilegare *vt* to bind.
rilento *avv* : **a** ~ slowly.
rilevante *agg* relevant.
rilevare *vt (notare)* to notice ; *(mettere in evidenza)* to point out ; *(dati)* to collect ; *COMM* to take over.
rilievo *sm* relief ; **mettere in** ~ **qc** to emphasize sthg.
riluttante *agg* reluctant.
rima *sf* rhyme.
rimandare *vt (mandare di nuovo)* to send again ; *(mandare indietro)* to send back ; *(riunione, esame)* to postpone ; ~ **qn a qc** *(in testo)* to refer sb to sthg ; ~ **qn in italiano** *SCOL* to make sb resit their Italian exam.
rimando *sm* cross-reference.
rimanente *agg* remaining. ◆ *sm* remainder.
rimanenza *sf* remainder.
rimanere *vi (in luogo)* to stay, to remain ; *(nel tempo)* to last, to remain ; *(avanzare)* to be left ; *(essere)* to be ; **mi sono rimasti dieci euro** I have ten euro left ; **siamo rimasti in due** there are (only) two of us left ; **sono rimasto solo** I was left on my own ; ~ **indietro** *(di luogo)* to be left behind ; *(nel lavoro)* to fall behind.
rimarginare *vt* to heal. ❑ **rimarginarsi** *vr* to heal.
rimasto, a *pp* → **rimanere**.
rimasuglio *sm* scrap.

rimbalzare *vi (palla)* bounce ; *(proiettile)* to ricochet.
rimbalzo *sm (di palla)* bounce ; *(di proiettile)* ricochet.
rimbambito, a *agg* daft.
rimboccare *vt (lenzuola, coperta)* to tuck in ; *(maniche, pantaloni)* to turn up ; **rimboccarsi le maniche** to roll up one's sleeves.
rimbombare *vi* to rumble.
rimborsare *vt* to reimburse, to refund.
rimborso *sm* refund ; **~ spese** refund of expenses.
rimediare *vt fam (procurarsi)* to find. ◆ *vi* : **~ a qc** *(sbaglio, danno)* to make amends for sthg.
rimedio *sm* remedy ; **porre ~ a qc** to remedy sthg.
rimescolare *vt (liquido)* to mix well ; *(carte)* to shuffle.
rimessa *sf (per veicoli)* garage ; *(per aerei)* hangar ; *(nel calcio)* throw-in.
rimesso, a *pp* → **rimettere**.
rimettere *vt (mettere di nuovo)* to put back ; *(indossare di nuovo)* to put back on ; *(perdonare)* to forgive, to pardon ; *(vomitare)* to vomit ; **~ a posto** to tidy up ; **rimetterci (qc)** to lose (sthg). ❑ **rimettersi** *vr (guarire)* to get better, to recover ; *(tempo)* to clear up ; **rimettersi a fare qc** to start doing sthg again.
rimmel® *sm inv* mascara.
rimodernare *vt* to modernize.
rimontare *vt* to reassemble. ◆ *vi* to catch up.
rimorchiare *vt (veicolo)* to tow ; *fam (ragazza)* to pick up.
rimorchiatore *sm* tug.
rimorchio *sm (operazione)* towing ; *(di veicolo)* trailer.
rimorso *sm* remorse.
rimosso, a *pp* → **rimuovere**.
rimozione *sf (spostamento)* removal ; *(da carica, impiego)* dismissal ; **'~ forzata o coatta'** tow-away zone.
rimpatriare *vt* to repatriate. ◆ *vi* to go home.
rimpiangere *vt* : **~ di aver fatto qc** to regret doing sthg.
rimpianto, a *pp* → **rimpiangere**. ◆ *sm* regret.
rimpiattino *sm* hide-and-seek.
rimpiazzare *vt* to replace.
rimpicciolire *vt* to make smaller. ◆ *vi* to become smaller.
rimpinzarsi : **rimpinzarsi di** *vr + prep* to stuff o.s. with.
rimproverare *vt* to scold.
rimprovero *sm* scolding.
rimuginare *vt* to brood over. ◆ *vi* : **~ (su qc)** to ponder (sthg).
rimuovere *vt (spostare)* to remove ; *(da carica)* to dismiss.
Rinascimento *sm* : **il ~** the Renaissance.
rinascita *sf (di foglie, capelli)* regrowth ; *(economica, sociale)* revival.
rincalzare *vt (lenzuola)* to tuck in ; *(muro, scala)* to prop up.
rincarare *vi* to increase in price.
rincasare *vi* to return home.
rinchiudere *vt* to confine. ❑ **rinchiudersi in** *vr + prep* to shut o.s. up in.
rinchiuso, a *pp* → **rinchiudere**.

rincorrere *vt* to chase.
rincorsa *sf* run-up.
rincorso, a *pp* → rincorrere.
rincrescere *vi*: **mi rincresce che tu parta** I'm sorry you're leaving; **mi rincresce di non poterti aiutare** I'm sorry I can't help you.
rinculo *sm* recoil.
rinfacciare *vt*: ~ **qc a qn** *(colpa, difetto)* to reproach sb with ○ for sthg; *(favore)* to throw sthg in sb's face.
rinforzare *vt (muscoli, capelli)* to strengthen; *(rendere più solido)* to reinforce.
rinforzo *sm* reinforcement.
rinfrescante *agg* refreshing.
rinfrescare *vt (atmosfera)* to cool. ◆ *v impers*: **è rinfrescato** it's got cooler; ~ **la memoria a qn** to refresh sb's memory. ❑ **rinfrescarsi** *vr (ristorarsi)* to refresh o.s.; *(lavarsi)* to freshen up.
rinfresco, schi *sm* reception.
rinfusa : **alla rinfusa** *avv* higgledy-piggledy.
ringhiare *vi* to snarl.
ringhiera *sf (di balcone)* railings *(pl)*; *(di scala)* banisters *(pl)*.
ringiovanire : **ringiovanire** *vt*: ~ **qn** to make sb look younger. ◆ *vi* to look young again, to be rejuvenated.
ringraziamento *sm* thanks *(pl)*.
ringraziare *vt* to thank; ~ **qn di qc** to thank sb for sthg.
rinnegare *vt (persona)* to disown; *(fede)* to renounce.
rinnovamento *sm (cambiamento)* updating; *(di impianti, locale)* renovation.
rinnovare *vt* to renew; *(locale)* to renovate; *(ripetere)* to repeat.
rinnovo *sm (di contratto, guardaroba)* renewal; *(di casa)* renovation.
rinoceronte *sm* rhinoceros.
rinomato, a *agg* famous.
rinsaldare *vt* to strengthen.
rintocco, chi *sm (di campana)* toll; *(di orologio)* chime.
rintracciare *vt* to track down.
rintronare *vt* to deafen. ◆ *vi* to boom.
rinuncia, ce *sf* renunciation.
rinunciare : **rinunciare a** *v + prep (rifiutare)* to renounce; *(privarsi di)* to give up; ~ **a fare qc** to give up doing sthg.
rinunzia = rinuncia.
rinunziare = renunciare.
rinvenire *vt (trovare)* to find; *(scoprire)* to find out. ◆ *vi* to come round/to, to revive.
rinvenuto, a *pp* → rinvenire.
rinviare *vt* to return; ~ **qc (a)** *(posporre)* to postpone sthg (until).
rinvio *sm (di lettera, palla)* return; *(di appuntamento, riunione)* postponement; *(a pagina, capitolo)* cross-reference.
rione *sm* quarter.
riordinare *vt (mettere in ordine)* to tidy up; *(cambiare ordine)* to reorganize.
riorganizzare *vt* to reorganize.
riparare *vt (aggiustare)* to repair; *(proteggere)* to protect; *(rimediare)* to make up for. ❑ **ripa-**

rarsi *vr* to shelter ; **ripararsi da qc** to shelter/protect o.s. from sthg.

riparazione *sf* repair.

riparo *sm (protezione)* protection ; *(rifugio)* shelter.

ripartire *vt (eredità, guadagno)* to share out ; *(compiti, responsabilità)* to allocate. ◆ *vi* to leave again.

ripassare *vt* to go over. ◆ *vi* to go/come back.

ripensare : **ripensare a** *v + prep (riflettere su)* to think over ; *(cambiare idea)* to change one's mind about ; *(ricordare)* to recall.

ripercosso, a *pp* → **ripercuotersi.**

ripercuotersi : **ripercuotersi su** *vr + prep* to influence.

ripercussione *sf* repercussion.

ripescare *vt (dall'acqua)* to fish out ; *(ritrovare)* to find.

ripetere *vt* to repeat. ❑ **ripetersi** *vr (persona)* to repeat o.s. ; *(avvenimento)* to happen again.

ripetitivo, a *agg* repetitive.

ripetizione *sf (replica)* repetition. ❑ **ripetizioni** *sfpl* private lessons.

ripiano *sm* shelf.

ripicca, che *sf*: **per ~** out of spite.

ripido, a *agg* steep.

ripiegare *vt (lenzuola)* to fold (up) ; *(piegare di nuovo)* to refold. ◆ *vi (indietreggiare)* to retreat. ❑ **ripiegare su** *v + prep (rassegnarsi a)* to make do with.

ripiego, ghi *sm* expedient ; **per ~** as a makeshift.

ripieno, a *agg* : **~ (di qc)** *(casa, cassetto)* full (of sthg) ; *(panino)* filled (with sthg) ; *(tacchino)* stuffed (with sthg) ; *(di panino)* filling.

riporre *vt (mettere al suo posto)* to put back ; *(mettere via)* to put away ; **~ la propria fiducia in qn** to place one's trust in sb.

riportare *vt (restituire, ricondurre)* to take/bring back ; *(riferire)* to report, to tell ; *(ottenere)* to obtain.

riposare *vi (rilassarsi)* to rest ; *(dormire)* to sleep. ◆ *vt* to rest. ❑ **riposarsi** *vr (rilassarsi)* to rest ; *(dormire)* to sleep.

riposo *sm* rest ; *(sonno)* sleep ; **a ~** retired.

ripostiglio *sm* store room.

riposto, a *pp* → **riporre.**

riprendere *vt (prendere di nuovo)* to take again ; *(ritirare)* to take back ; *(ricominciare)* to resume ; *(rimproverare)* to reproach ; *(filmare)* to shoot, to film. ◆ *vi* : **~ a fare qc** to start doing sthg again. ❑ **riprendersi da** *vr + prep* to recover from.

ripresa *sf (di attività)* resumption ; *(da malattia)* recovery ; *(di motore)* acceleration ; *(cinematografica)* shot ; **a più riprese** several times.

ripreso, a *pp* → **riprendere.**

riprodotto, a *pp* → **riprodurre.**

riprodurre *vt* to reproduce. ❑ **riprodursi** *vr* to reproduce.

riproduzione *sf* reproduction.

ripromettersi *vr* : **~ di fare qc** to intende to do sth.

riprova *sf* confirmation.

riprovevole *agg* reprehensible.

ripudiare *vt (moglie, figli)* to reject, disown.

ripugnante *agg* disgusting.
ripugnare *vi* : ~ a qn *(disgustare qn)* to repel ○ disgust sb.
ripulire *vt (pulire)* to clean up ; *(rubare)* to clean out.
riquadro *sm* square ; *(di parete, soffitto)* panel.
risalire *vt* to go back up. ❑ **risalire a** *v + prep* to go back to.
risaltare *vi* to stand out.
risalto *sm* prominence ; **mettere in ~ qc** to make sthg stand out.
risaputo, a *agg* : **è ~ che ...** it is common knowledge that ...
risarcimento *sm* compensation.
risarcire *vt* : **~ qn (di qc)** to compensate sb (for sthg).
risata *sf* laugh.
riscaldamento *sm* heating ; **~ centrale** central heating.
riscaldare *vt (stanza)* to heat ; *(mani)* to warm ; *(cibo)* to heat up. ❑ **riscaldarsi** *vr (persona)* to warm up ; *(diventare caldo)* to get warmer.
riscatto *sm* ransom.
rischiarare *vt* to light up. ❑ **rischiararsi** *vr* to clear.
rischiare *vt* to risk. ◆ *vi* : **rischio di arrivare in ritardo** I'm likely to be late ; **ha rischiato di essere investito** he nearly got run over.
rischio *sm* risk ; **correre il ~ di fare qc** to run the risk of doing sthg.
rischioso, a *agg* risky.
risciacquare *vt* to rinse.
riscontrare *vt* to find.
riscontro *sm (conferma)* confirmation.
riscosso, a *pp* → **riscuotere**.
riscuotere *vt (somma)* to collect ; *(stipendio, pensione)* to receive ; *(assegno)* to cash ; *(successo, consenso)* to win, to earn.
risentire : **risentire di** *v + prep* to be affected by. ❑ **risentirsi** *vr* : **risentirsi di** ○ **per qc** to take offence at sthg.
riserva *sf (provvista, giocatore)* reserve ; *(di caccia, pesca)* preserve ; *(restrizione)* reservation ; **essere in ~** *(auto)* to be low on petrol *(Br)* ○ gas *(Am)* ; **di ~** in reserve.
riservare *vt* to save ; *(prenotare)* to book, to reserve.
riservato, a *agg (posto, carattere)* reserved ; *(informazione, lettera)* confidential.
risi e bisi *smpl* rice and pea soup *(a speciality of Veneto)*.
risiedere *vi* to reside.
riso *pp* → **ridere**. ◆ *sm (cereale)* rice ; *(il ridere : pl f risa)* laughter.
risolto, a *pp* → **risolvere**.
risoluto, a *agg (deciso)* determined.
risoluzione *sf (decisione)* resolution.
risolvere *vt (problema, caso)* to solve ; *(questione)* to resolve. ❑ **risolversi** *vr (problema)* to resolve itself. ❑ **risolversi a** *vr + prep* : **risolversi a fare qc** to make up one's mind to do sthg. ❑ **risolversi in** *vr + prep (andare a finire)* to turn out.
risonanza *sf* resonance ; **avere grande ~** *(fatto, notizia)* to arouse a great deal of interest.
risorgere *vi (risuscitare)* to revive ; *(problema)* to recur.

Risorgimento *sm* : il ~ Risorgimento.
risorsa *sf* resort. ❑ **risorse** *sfpl* resources.
risorto, a *pp* → risorgere.
risotto *sm* risotto ; ~ alla boscaiola *risotto with tomatoes, mushrooms and parsley* ; ~ di mare seafood risotto ; ~ alla milanese *risotto with saffron and lots of Parmesan cheese* ; ~ ai tartufi *risotto with truffles.*
risparmiare *vi* to save. ◆ *vt (non consumare)* to save ; *(non uccidere)* to spare ; *(evitare)* : ~ qc a qn to spare sb sthg.
risparmio *sm (somma)* savings *(pl)* ; *(di tempo, soldi, fatica)* saving.
rispecchiare *vt* to reflect.
rispettabile *agg* respectable.
rispettare *vt* to respect ; farsi ~ to command respect.
rispettivamente *avv* respectively.
rispettivo, a *agg* respective.
rispetto *sm* respect ; mancare di ~ (a qn) to be disrespectful (to sb) ; ~ a *(a paragone di)* compared to ; *(in relazione a)* as for.
rispettoso, a *agg* respectful.
risplendere *vi* to shine.
rispondere *vi* to answer, to reply ; *(freni)* to respond. ❑ **rispondere a** *v + prep (corrispondere)* to meet ; ~ a qn to answer sb. ❑ **rispondere di** *v + prep* to be responsible for.
risposta *sf* answer ; *(azione)* response ; in ~ a qc in reply to sthg.
risposto *pp* → rispondere.
rissa *sf* brawl.
ristabilire *vt* to restore. ❑ **ristabilirsi** *vr* to recover.
ristagnare *vi (acqua)* to become stagnant ; *fig (industria)* to stagnate.
ristampa *sf (opera)* reprint.
ristorante *sm* restaurant.
ristoro *sm* refreshment.
ristretto, a *pp* → restringere. ◆ *agg (numero)* limited ; *(brodo)* thick ; *(uso)* restricted.
ristrutturare *vt (azienda)* to reorganize ; *(casa)* to alter.
risucchiare *vt* to suck in.
risultare *vi* to turn out to be ; mi risulta che ... I understand that ... ; non mi risulta not as far as I know. ❑ **risultare da** *v + prep* to result from.
risultato *sm* result.
risuolare *vt* to resole.
risuscitare *vt* to resuscitate.
risvegliare *vt (dal sonno)* to wake up ; *(memoria, appetito)* to awaken.
risvolto *sm (di pantaloni)* turn-up *(Br)*, cuff *(Am)* ; *(di giacca)* lapel ; *fig (conseguenza)* implication.
ritagliare *vt* to cut out.
ritaglio *sm (di giornale)* cutting ; *(di stoffa)* scrap ; nei ritagli di tempo in one's spare time.
ritardare *vi* to be late. ◆ *vt (rimandare)* to delay ; *(rallentare)* to slow down.
ritardatario, a *sm, f* latecomer.
ritardo *sm (di treno, pagamento)* delay ; in ~ late.
ritenere *vt (giudicare)* to believe ; *(somma)* to deduct.
ritentare *vt* to try again.

ritirare *vt* to withdraw ; *(pacco, da lavanderia)* to collect ; *(insulto, promessa)* to take back. ❑ **ritirarsi** *vr (da attività)* to retire ; *(restringersi)* to shrink.

ritirata *sf* retreat.

ritiro *sm (di pacco)* collection ; *(di patente, passaporto)* confiscation ; *(sportivo, spirituale)* retreat ; *(da attività)* retirement.

ritmo *sm MUS* rhythm ; *(di pulsazioni)* beat ; *(di vita, lavoro)* pace.

rito *sm* rite.

ritornare *vi (andare, venire di nuovo)* to return, to go/come back ; *(ricomparire)* to recur ; *(ridiventare)* : ~ **pulito** to be clean again.

ritornello *sm* chorus.

ritorno *sm* return ; **essere di ~** to be back.

ritrarre *vt (ritirare)* to withdraw ; *(rappresentare)* to portray.

ritratto, a *pp* → **ritrarre.** ◆ *sm* portrait.

ritrovare *vt (cosa persa)* to find ; *(riacquistare)* to regain. ❑ **ritrovarsi** *vr (incontrarsi)* to meet ; *(in situazione)* to find o.s..

ritrovo *sm* meeting place.

ritto, a *agg* upright.

rituale *agg* ritual. ◆ *sm* ritual.

riunione *sf (incontro)* meeting ; *(riconciliazione)* reconciliation.

riunire *vt* to bring together. ❑ **riunirsi** *vr* to meet.

riuscire *vi (avere esito)* to turn out ; *(aver successo)* to succeed ; **~ a fare qc** to manage to do sthg ; **~ in qc** to succeed in sthg.

riva *sf (di fiume)* bank ; *(di lago, mare)* shore.

rivale *agg* & *smf* rival.

rivalutare *vt* to revalue.

rivedere *vt (vedere di nuovo)* to see again ; *(riesaminare)* to review ; *(ripassare)* to revise. ❑ **rivedersi** *vr* to meet again.

rivelare *vt* to reveal.

rivelazione *sf (di notizie)* revelation ; *REL* revelation.

rivendicare *vt (diritto, bene)* to claim ; *(attentato)* to claim responsibility for.

rivendita *sf (negozio)* dealer.

rivenditore, trice *sm, f* retailer ; **~ autorizzato** authorized dealer.

riversare *vt fig (affetto)* to lavish ; *(colpa)* to heap. ❑ **riversarsi** *vr* to pour.

rivestimento *sm* covering.

rivestire *vt (poltrona)* to cover ; *(carica)* to hold ; *(ruolo)* to play. ❑ **rivestirsi** *vr* to get dressed again.

riviera *sf* coast.

LA RIVIERA ADRIATICA

The bathing resorts which line the winding Adriatic coast are collectively known as *Riviera Adriatica*. Tourists from the rest of Italy and from abroad flock to famous resorts like Jesolo near Venice and Rimini on the Romagna coast. Renowned for its beautiful beaches and its first-rate amenities, Rimini is the quintessential Italian seaside town, teeming with life 24 hours a day.

rivincita sf *(di partita)* return match ; *(rivalsa)* revenge.
rivisto, a pp → **rivedere.** ◆ sf *(giornale)* magazine.
rivolgere vt *(parola)* to address ; *(attenzione, occhiata)* to direct. ❑ **rivolgersi a** vr + prep to go and speak to.
rivoltante agg revolting.
rivoltare vt *(rigirare)* to turn over ; *(disgustare)* to disgust. ❑ **rivoltarsi** vr to rebel.
rivoltella sf revolver.
rivolto, a pp → **rivolgere.** ◆ sf revolt.
rivoluzionario, a agg & sm, f revolutionary.
rivoluzione sf revolution.
rizoma, i sm rhizome.
rizzare vt to stand on end. ❑ **rizzarsi** vr to stand up.
roastbeef ['rɔzbif] sm inv *joint of beef braised or grilled, then served sliced.*
roba sf *(cose)* stuff, things *(pl)* ; **~ da mangiare** things to eat ; **~ da matti!** (well I) never!
robiola sf *a type of soft rindless cheese.*
robot sm inv *(automa)* robot ; *(da cucina)* food processor.
robotica sf TECNOL robotics.
robusto, a agg robust, sturdy.
rocca, che sf fortress.
roccaforte sf stronghold.
rocchetto sm reel, spool.
roccia, ce sf rock.
rocciatore, trice sm, f *(alpinista)* rock-climber.
roccioso, a agg rocky.
roco, a, chi, che agg hoarse.
rodaggio sm running-in.
rodere vt to gnaw. ❑ **rodersi di** vr + prep to be consumed with.
rogna sf *(malattia)* scabies ; fam *(guaio)* nuisance.
rognone sm kidney ; **rognoni alla romana** *kidneys fried with garlic, parsley and white wine.*
rogo, ghi sm *(supplizio)* stake ; *(incendio)* balze.
Roma sf Rome.
romanesco sm *(dialetto)* Roman.
Romania sf: **la ~** Romania.
romanico, a, ci, che agg Romanesque.
romano, a agg & sm, f Roman.
romanticismo sm romanticism.
romantico, a, ci, che agg romantic.
romanza sf MUS aria.
romanzo sm *(libro)* novel.
rombo sm *(rumore)* roar ; *(pesce)* turbot ; **a rombi** *(disegno)* diamond patterned.
rompere vt to break ; *(fidanzamento)* to break off ; *(strappare)* to tear. ◆ vi *(coppia)* to break up ; **rompersi una gamba** to break one's leg ; **smettila di ~!** fam lay off! ❑ **rompersi** vr to break.
rompicapo sm puzzle.
rompiscatole smf inv fam pest, pain in the neck.
rondine sf swallow.
ronzare vi to buzz.
ronzio sm *(di insetti)* buzzing ; *(rumore)* drone.

rosa *agg inv (di colore)* pink ; *(sentimentale)* sentimental. ◆ *sf* rose. ◆ *sm* pink.
rosé *sm inv* rosé.
rosicchiare *vt* to gnaw, to nibble.
rosmarino *sm* rosemary.
roso, a *pp* → **rodere**.
rosolare *vt* to brown.
rosolia *sf* German measles *(sg)*.
rosone *sm (di soffitti)* ceiling rose ; *(vetrata)* rose window.
rospo *sm* toad.
rossetto *sm* lipstick.
rosso, a *agg* & *sm* red ; **~ d'uovo** egg yolk.
rosticceria *sf shop selling cooked food such as roast chicken, lasagne etc.*
rosticciana *sf grilled or fried pork.*
rotaie *sfpl* rails.
rotazione *sf* rotation.
rotella *sf* cog.
rotolare *vi (palla, valanga)* to roll. ❑ **rotolarsi** *vr* to roll.
rotolo *sm* roll ; **andare a rotoli** to go to rack and ruin.
rotonda *sf* circular terrace.
rotondo, a *agg* round.
rotta *sf* route.
rottame *sm* scrap.
rotto, a *pp* → **rompere**. ◆ *agg (spezzato, guasto)* broken ; *(strappato)* torn.
rottura *sf (azione)* breaking ; *(interruzione)* breaking-off ; *fam (seccatura)* nuisance.
roulette [ru'lɛt] *sf* roulette.
roulotte [ru'lɔt] *sf inv* caravan.
routine [ru'tin] *sf inv* routine.
rovente *agg* red-hot.
rovescia *sf* : **alla ~** upside down ; *(sottosopra)* inside out.
rovesciare *vt (liquido)* to spill ; *(tavolo, sedia)* to overturn ; *(situazione)* to turn upside down. ❑ **rovesciarsi** *vr (versarsi)* to spill ; *(capovolgersi)* to overturn ; *(barca)* to capsize.
rovescio *sm (di vestito, stoffa)* wrong side ; *(pioggia)* downpour ; *(nel tennis)* backhand ; **al ~** *(con l'interno all'esterno)* inside out ; *(con il davanti di dietro)* back to front.
rovina *sf* ruin ; **andare in ~** to collapse. ❑ **rovine** *sfpl* ruins.
rovinare *vt* to ruin. ❑ **rovinarsi** *vr (cosa)* to be ruined ; *(persona)* to be ruined.
rovo *sm* bramble bush.
rozzo, a *agg* rough.
ruba *sf* : **andare a ~** to sell like hot cakes.
rubare *vt* to steal. ◆ *vi* : **hanno rubato in casa mia** my house has been burgled ; **~ qc a qn** to steal sthg from sb.
rubinetto *sm* tap.
rubino *sm* ruby.
rubrica, che *sf (di indirizzi)* address book ; *(di giornale)* column.
ruderi *smpl* ruins.
rudimentale *agg* rudimentary, basic.
ruffiano, a *sm, f* creep.
ruga, ghe *sf* wrinkle.
rugby ['rɛgbi] *sm* rugby.
ruggine *sf* rust.
ruggire *vi* to roar.

rugiada *sf* dew.
rullino *sm* roll of film ; **un ~ da 24** a 24-exposure film.
rullo *sm (rotolo, arnese)* roller ; *(di tamburo)* roll.
rum *sm inv* rum.
rumeno, a *agg (della Romania)* Romanian. ◆ *sm, f (persona)* Romanian. ◆ *sm (lingua)* Romanian.
rumore *sm* noise.
rumoroso, a *agg* noisy.
ruolo *sm* role.
ruota *sf* wheel ; **~ di scorta** spare wheel.
ruotare *vi* & *vt* to rotate.
rupe *sf* cliff.
ruscello *sm* stream.
ruspa *sf* excavator.
Russia *sf* : **la ~** Russia.
russo, a *agg, sm* & *sf* Russian.
rustico, a, ci, che *agg* rustic.
ruttare *vi* to belch.
rutto *sm* belch.
ruvido, a *agg* rough.
ruzzolare *vi* to tumble down.
ruzzolone *sm* tumble.

S

sabato *sm* Saturday ; **torniamo ~** we'll be back on Saturday ; **oggi è ~** it's Saturday today ; **~ 6 maggio** Saturday 6 May ; **~ pomeriggio** Saturday afternoon ; **~ prossimo** next Saturday ; **~ scorso** last Saturday ; **di ~** on Saturdays ; **a ~!** see you Saturday!
sabbia *sf* sand.
sabotare *vt* to sabotage.
sacca, che *sf (borsa)* bag.
saccarina *sf* saccharin.
saccente *agg* conceited.
saccheggiare *vt (case, villaggi)* to loot ; *fig (con acquisti)* to buy up.
sacchetto *sm* bag.
sacco, chi *sm (di carta, nylon)* bag ; *(di iuta)* sack ; **un ~ di** a lot of ; **~ a pelo** sleeping bag.
sacerdote *sm* priest.
sacrificare *vt* to sacrifice. ❑ **sacrificarsi** *vr* to make sacrifices.
sacrificio *sm* sacrifice.
sacro, a *agg* sacred.
sadico, a, ci, che *agg* sadistic. ◆ *sm, f* sadist.
safari *sm inv* safari.
saggezza *sf* wisdom.
saggio, a, gi, ge *agg* wise. ◆ *sm (persona)* wise man, sage ; *(campione)* sample ; *(libro, ricerca)* essay.
Sagittario *sm* Sagittarius.
sagoma *sf (profilo, forma)* outline ; *fam (persona)* character.
sagra *sf* festival, feast.

i SAGRA

A *sagra* is a local festival held in celebration of the agricultural produce typical of a particular town or village (wine, truffles, cherries and so on). As well as sampling and buying the local produce, you can eat and drink in the open air and sometimes dance to the music of the local brass band.

---

sagrestano, a *sm, f* sacristan.
sai → **sapere**.

saint-honoré [sɛntɔnɔ're] *sm inv dessert consisting of a puff pastry base topped with cream and surrounded by choux buns.*
sala *sf (salotto)* living room ; *(di palazzo)* hall ; **~ d'aspetto** ○ **d'attesa** waiting room ; **~ da gioco** gaming room ; **~ operatoria** operating theatre ; **~ da pranzo** dining room.
salame *sm* salami.
salare *vt* to salt.
salario *sm* wage.
salatini *smpl* salted crackers.
salato, a *agg (con sale)* salted ; *(con troppo sale)* salty ; *fam (caro)* expensive.
saldare *vt (metalli)* to weld ; *(debito, conto)* to settle.
saldo, a *agg (resistente, stabile)* firm. ◆ *sm* balance. ❑ **saldi** *mpl* sales.
sale *sm* salt ; **~ grosso** cooking salt.
salice *sm* willow ; **~ piangente** weeping willow.
saliente *agg* salient.
saliera *sf* saltcellar *(Br)*, salt shaker *(Am)*.
salire *vt (scale)* to go up. ◆ *vi* to go up ; *(aereo)* to climb ; **~ in** ○ **su** *(treno, moto)* to get onto ; *(auto)* to get into ; **~ su** *(tetto, podio)* to climb onto ; **~ a bordo** to board.
salita *sf* climb ; **in ~** uphill.
saliva *sf* saliva.
salma *sf form (cadavere)* corpse.
salmì *sm* → **lepre**.
salmone *sm* salmon.
salone *sm (sala)* sitting room ; *(mostra)* show.
salotto *sm* lounge.
salpare *vi (partire)* to set sail. ◆ *vt* : **~ l'ancora** to weigh anchor.
salsa *sf* sauce ; **~ di pomodoro** tomato sauce.
salsiccia, ce *sf* sausage.
saltare *vt (scavalcare)* to jump (over) ; *(omettere)* to skip. ◆ *vi* to jump ; **fare ~ qc** to blow sthg up ; **~ fuori (da qc)** to jump out (from sthg) ; **~ giù da qc** to jump down from sthg ; **~ su (qc)** to jump on (sthg).
saltimbocca *sm inv thin slices of veal rolled up with ham and sage.*
salto *sm (balzo)* jump ; *(visita)* : **fare un ~ in città** to pop into town ; **~ in alto/lungo** high/long jump ; **~ con l'asta** pole vault.
salumeria *sf* delicatessen.
salumi *smpl* cold meats and salami.
salutare *vt (incontrandosi)* to greet, to say hello to ; *(andando via)* to say goodbye to. ❑ **salutarsi** *vr (incontrandosi)* to say hello ; *(andando via)* to say goodbye ; **salutamelo!** say hello to him from me!
salute *sf* health ; **bere alla ~ di qn** to drink to sb's health.
saluto *sm (incontrandosi)* greeting ; *(andando via)* goodbye ; *(col capo)* nod ; *(con la mano)* wave.
salvadanaio *sm* moneybox.
salvagente *sm (giubbotto)* life jacket ; *(ciambella)* life buoy ; *(spartitraffico)* traffic island.
salvaguardare *vt* to safeguard.
salvare *vt (vita, persona)* to survive ; *(onore)* to protect. ❑ **salvarsi** *vr* to save o.s.

salvataggio *sm* rescue.
salvavita® *sm inv* fuse box.
salve *esclam fam* hello!
salvezza *sf* safety.
salvia *sf* sage.
salvietta *sf* wet wipe.
salvo, a *agg* safe. ◆ *prep* except for ; **essere in ~** to be safe ; **~ imprevisti** barring accidents.
san → **santo.**
sandali *smpl* sandals.
San Daniele *sm (prosciutto)* san Daniele ham (type of prosciuto).
sangue *sm* blood ; **a ~ freddo** in cold blood.
sanguinare *vi* to bleed.
sanità *sf* health service.
sanitario, a *agg (sistema, servizio)* health *(dav s)* ; *(condizioni)* sanitary. ❑ **sanitari** *smpl* bathroom fittings.
San Marino *sf* San Marino.

SAN MARINO

In central northern Italy, not far from the Adriatic coast, sits *San Marino*, one of the world's smallest countries. Although it is only 60 kilometres square, it is a fully independent sovereign state, and has its own currency and stamps.

---

sano, a *agg* healthy ; **~ e salvo** safe and sound ; **~ come un pesce** as fit as a fiddle.
San Silvestro *sf*: **la notte di ~** New Year's Eve.
santità *sf (condizione)* sancity ; **Sua Santità** *(Papa)* His Holiness.
santo, a *agg* holy. ◆ *sm, f* saint ; **Santo Stefano** ≃ Boxing Day ; **tutto il ~ giorno** all day long.

SANTO

Every village, town and city in Italy has its own patron saint, honoured once a year with a festival combining religious processions and ceremonies with other more secular events. The streets are decorated with illuminations and there is often a funfair and sweet stalls. Schools and businesses are closed for the day.

---

santuario *sm* sanctuary.
sanzione *sf* sanction.
sapere *vt* to know ; **mi sa che non viene** I don't think he's coming ; **~ fare qc** to know how to do sthg ; **sai sciare?** can you ski? ; **far ~ qc a qn** to let sb know sthg. ❑ **sapere di** *v + prep* to taste of.
sapone *sm* soap ; **~ da bucato** ≃ household.
saponetta *sf* bar of soap.
sapore *sm* taste, flavour.
saporito, a *agg* tasty.
saracinesca, sche *sf* rolling shutter.
sarcastico, a, ci, che *agg* sarcastic.
sarde *sfpl* : **~ a beccaficu** *fried sardines stuffed with breadcrumbs, pecorino cheese and tomatoes.*
Sardegna *sf* : **la ~** Sardinia.
sardina *sf* sardine.
sardo, a *agg* & *sm, f* Sardinian.

sarto, a *sm, f* dressmaker; *(per azienda)* tailor.

sartù *sm inv*: ~ **di riso** *rice mould filled with liver, mushrooms, peas, meatballs, mozzarella cheese and boiled eggs (a speciality of Naples).*

sasso *sm* stone.

sassofono *sm* saxophone.

satellite *sm (naturale, artificiale)* satellite; *TV* satellite TV.

satira *sf* satire.

saturo, a *agg (soluzione)* saturated; *(mercato)* saturated.

sauna *sf* sauna.

savoiardi *smpl* sponge fingers.

saziare *vt* to satisfy.

sazietà *sf*: **mangiare a** ~ to eat one's fill.

sazio, a *agg* full.

sbadato, a *agg* careless.

sbadigliare *vi* to yawn.

sbadiglio *sm* yawn.

sbafo *sm*: **a** ~ at somebody else's expense.

sbagliare *vt* to get wrong; *(indirizzo, persona)* to get wrong. ◆ *vi (fare un errore)* to make a mistake; *(avere torto)* to be wrong; ~ **mira** to miss one's aim; ~ **strada** to take the wrong road; **ho sbagliato a** ~ I counted wrong. ❑ **sbagliarsi** *vr (fare un errore)* to make a mistake; *(avere torto)* to be wrong; **sbagliarsi di grosso** to be completely wrong.

sbagliato, a *agg* wrong.

sbaglio *sm* mistake; **fare uno** ~ to make a mistake; **fare qc per** ~ to do sthg by mistake.

sballottare *vt* to toss about.

sbalzare *vt* to throw.

sbalzo *sm (di temperatura)* change.

sbandare *vi* to skid.

sbandata *sf* skid; **prendersi una** ~ **per qn** to fall for sb.

sbandato, a *sm, f (delinquente)* drop-out.

sbandierare *vt (sventolare)* to wave; *(ostentare)* to show off.

sbando *sm*: **allo** ~ adrift.

sbaraglio *sm*: **andare allo** ~ to risk everything.

sbarazzare *vt* to clear up. ❑ **sbarazzarsi di** *vr + prep* to get rid of.

sbarazzino, a *agg* cheeky.

sbarcare *vt (merce)* to unload; *(passeggeri)* to disembark. ◆ *vi (da nave)* to disembark.

sbarco *sm (di merci)* unloading; *(di passeggeri)* disembarkation.

sbarra *sf (spranga)* bar; *(segno grafico)* stroke; *(di passaggio a livello)* barrier.

sbarrare *vt (porta, finestra)* to bar; *(passaggio)* to block; ~ **gli occhi** to open one's eyes wide.

sbarrato, a *agg (strada)* blocked; *(porta)* barred; *(casella)* crossed; *(parola)* crossed; *(occhi)* wide open.

sbatacchiare *vt* to bang, to slam.

sbattere *vt* to beat; *(porta)* to bang, to slam. ◆ *vi* to bang; ~ **contro** *(muro)* to bang against, to knock against; ~ **fuori qn** to throw sb out. ❑ **sbattersene** *vr fam* not to give a damn.

sbattuto, a *agg* downcast.

sbavare *vi* to dribble.

sbellicarsi *vr*: ~ **dal ridere** to split one's sides laughing.

sbiadire *vt* to fade. ❑ **sbiadirsi** *vr* to fade.

sbiadito, a *agg* faded.

sbiancare *vi* to grow pale. ◆ *vt* to bleach.

sbieco, a, chi, che *agg*: **di ~** *(obliquamente)* at an angle.

sbigottire *vt* to dismay. ❑ **sbigottirsi** *vr* to be dismayed.

sbigottito, a *agg* dismayed, aghast.

sbilanciare *vt* to unbalance. ❑ **sbilanciarsi** *vr (perdere l'equilibrio)* to lose one's balance; *fig (compromettersi)* to compromise o.s.

sbirciare *vt (con curiosità)* to eye; *(di sfuggita)* to peep at.

sbizzarrirsi *vr* to satisfy one's whims.

sbloccare *vt* to unblock; **~ la situazione** to get things moving. ❑ **sbloccarsi** *vr (meccanismo)* to become unblocked; *(situazione)* to return to normal.

sboccare : **sboccare in** *v + prep (fiume)* to flow into; *(strada)* to lead into; *(concludersi con)* to end in.

sboccato, a *agg* foul-mouthed.

sbocciare *vi* to bloom.

sbocco, chi *sm (di strada)* end; *(di fiume)* mouth; *fig (esito)* way out.

sbornia *sf fam* : **prendersi una ~** to get plastered.

sborsare *vt (pagare)* to pay out.

sbottare *vi (in risata)* to burst out; *(di rabbia)* to explode.

sbottonare *vt* to unbutton; **sbottonarsi la giacca** to undo one's jacket. ❑ **sbottonarsi** *vr fam (confidarsi)* to open up.

sbracciarsi *vr* to wave one's arms about.

sbracciato, a *agg (vestito)* sleeveless; *(persona)* with bare arms.

sbraitare *vi* to shout.

sbranare *vt* to tear to pieces.

sbriciolare *vt* to crumble. ❑ **sbriciolarsi** *vr (pane, muro)* to crumble.

sbrigare *vt (faccenda)* to deal with. ❑ **sbrigarsi** *vr* to hurry; **sbrigarsi a fare qc** to hurry up and do sthg.

sbrisolona *sf (torta) crumbly almond cake.*

sbrodolare *vt* to stain.

sbronza *sf fam* : **prendersi una ~** to get plastered.

sbronzo, a *agg fam* plastered.

sbucare *vi (uscire)* to come out; *(saltar fuori)* to spring out.

sbucciare *vt* to peel; **sbucciarsi un ginocchio** to graze one's knee.

sbuffare *vi (per fastidio, noia)* to snort; *(per caldo)* to pant.

scabroso, a *agg* indecent.

scacchi *smpl* chess *(sg)*; **a ~** *(tessuto)* checked.

scacciare *vt (persona, animale)* to drive away; *(preoccupazioni)* to dispel.

scadente *agg (prodotto)* poor-quality; *(qualità)* poor.

scadenza *sf (di cibo)* sell-by

date ; *(di documento, contratto)* expiry date ; *(di medicinali)* 'use-by' date ; *(per iscrizione, consegna)* deadline.

scadere *vi* to expire ; *(cibo)* to pass it's sell by date.

scaffale *sm* shelf.

scafo *sm* hull.

scagionare *vt* to exonerate, excuse.

scaglia *sf (frammento)* flake, chip ; *(di pesce)* scale.

scagliare *vt* to throw. ❑ **scagliarsi contro** *vr + prep (assalire)* to hurl o.s. against ; *fig (insultare)* to hurl abuse at.

scaglionare *vt (persona)* to group ; *(pagamento)* stagger.

scaglione *sm* echelon ; **a scaglioni** in groups.

scala *sf (gradini)* stairs *(pl)*, staircase ; *(a pioli)* ladder ; *(di valori)* scale ; **su larga ~** on a large scale ; **~ mobile** escalator ; **le scale** the stairs.

LA SCALA

The new *Teatro alla Scala* was inaugurated on 3rd August 1778 in the presence of the Archduke Ferdinand. The opera presented on that occasion was A. Salieri's *L'Europa riconosciuta*. From the outset *La Scala*'s dual role as a temple of opera and of dance was therefore evident. In 1813 the *Imperial Regia Accademia di ballo alla Scala* was born, the second professional school after the *San Carlo* in Naples. Bombed in 1943, it was reopened in 1946 with a concert by A. Toscanini. Since then, this theatre has been host to the best-known ballets, the most famous operas, world stars of dance, musical virtuosi and great conductors. Still today, the beginning of the season at *La Scala* is an important artistic and cultural event and its first nights are reserved for the elite.

---

scalare *vt (mura, montagna)* to climb ; *(somma)* to knock off ; *(capelli)* to layer.

scalata *sf* climb.

scalatore, trice *sm, f* climber.

scalcinato, a *agg fig (casa)* shabby.

scaldabagno *sm* water heater.

scaldare *vt* to heat. ❑ **scaldarsi** *vr (al fuoco, al sole)* to warm o.s. ; *fig (accalorarsi)* to get excited.

scaleo *sm* stepladder.

scalfire *vt* to scratch.

scalinata *sf* flight of steps.

scalino *sm* step.

scalmanarsi *vr* to get worked up.

scalo *sm* call ; **fare ~ a** *(in aereo)* to make a stopover at ; *(in nave)* to call at ; **~ merci** goods yard *(Br)*, freight yard *(Am)*.

scaloppina *sf* escalope.

scalpore *sm (risonanza)* stir ; **fare o destare ~** to cause a stir.

scaltro, a *agg* shrewd.

scalzo, a *agg* barefooted.

scambiare *vt* to exchange, to

swap ; ~ **qn/qc per** *(confondere)* to mistake sb/sthg for ; **scambiarsi qc** to exchange sthg.

scambio *sm (di regali, opinioni)* exchange ; *(confusione)* mistake ; COMM trade ; **fare a ~ con qn** to swap with sb.

scampagnata *sf* trip to the country.

scampare *vt* to escape ; **scamparla (bella)** to have a narrow escape. ❑ **scampare a** *v + prep* to escape.

scampo *sm* : **non c'è (via di) ~** there is no way out ; **trovare ~ in qc** to find safety in sthg. ❑ **scampi** *smpl* scampi *(sg)*.

scampolo *sm* remnant.

scandagliare *vt (mare)* to sound.

scandalizzare *vt* to scandalize. ❑ **scandalizzarsi** *vr* to be scandalized.

scandalo *sm* scandal ; **dare ~** to make a spectacle of o.s. ; **fare ~** to cause a scandal.

scandaloso, a *agg* scandalous.

Scandinavia *sf* : **la ~** Scandinavia.

scandire *vt* to articulate.

scannare *vt (animale)* to butcher ; *(persona)* to cut the throat of.

scanner *sm* INFORM scanner.

scansafatiche *smf inv* idler, waster.

scansare *vt (spostare)* to shift ; *(colpo)* to ward off ; *(difficoltà, fatica)* to avoid ; *(persona)* to shun. ❑ **scansarsi** *vr* to step aside.

scanso *sm* : **a ~ di equivoci** *(in order)* to avoid any misunderstandings.

scantinato *sm* basement.

scanzonato, a *agg* easygoing.

scapaccione *sm* slap.

scapestrato, a *agg* dissolute.

scapito *sm* : **a ~ di** to the detriment of.

scapolo *sm* bachelor.

scappamento *sm* → **tubo**.

scappare *vi (fuggire)* to escape ; *(da casa)* to run away ; *(andare)* to rush ; **mi è scappato detto** I let it slip ; **mi è scappato di mano** it slipped out of my hands ; **mi è scappato di mente** it slipped my mind ; **mi è scappato da ridere** I couldn't help laughing ; **lasciarsi ~ l'occasione** to miss an opportunity.

scappatella *sf* casual affair.

scappatoia *sf* way out.

scarabocchiare *vt* to scrawl. ◆ *vi* to scribble.

scarafaggio *sm* cockroach.

scaramanzia *sf* : **per ~** for luck.

scaraventare *vt* to hurl. ❑ **scaraventarsi** *vr* to fling o.s.

scarcerare *vt* to release.

scarica, che *sf (di pugni)* hail ; *(di pistola)* volley ; **~ elettrica** electrical discharge.

scaricare *vt (merci, camion, arma)* to unload ; *(passeggeri)* to let off ; *(batteria)* to run down ; *fig (colpa)* to shift. ❑ **scaricarsi** *vr (batteria)* to go flat ; *fig (rilassarsi)* to unwind.

scarico, a, chi, che *agg (camion, arma)* unloaded ; *(batteria)* flat. ◆ *sm (di merci)* unloading ;

(discarica) dump ; **'divieto di ~'** 'no dumping'.

scarlatto, a *agg* scarlet.

scarpa *sf* shoe ; **che numero di scarpe porta?** what size shoe do you take? ; **scarpe da ginnastica** plimsolls *(Br)*, sneakers *(Am)*.

scarpata *sf* slope.

scarponi *smpl* boots ; **~ da sci** ski boots.

scarseggiare *vi* to be scarce. ❑ **scarseggiare di** *v + prep* to be short of.

scarsità *sf inv* scarcity, shortage.

scarso, a *agg* scarce ; **un chilo ~** just under a kilo.

scartare *vt (regalo)* to unwrap ; *(eliminare)* to reject ; *(nelle carte)* to discard.

scarto *sm (scelta)* discarding ; *(cosa scartata)* reject ; *(differenza)* gap, difference.

scassare *vt fam (rompere, rovinare)* to annoy.

scassato *agg fam (rovinato, rotto)* smashed.

scassinare *vt* to break open.

scasso *sm* → **furto**.

scatenare *vt* to provoke, to stir up. ❑ **scatenarsi** *vr (temporale)* to break ; *(persona)* to go wild.

scatenato, a *agg (persona, ballo)* wild.

scatola *sf* box ; *(di latta)* tin, can ; **in ~** *(cibo)* tinned, canned ; **rompere le scatole a qn** *fam* to get up sb's nose.

scattante *agg* agile.

scattare *vt (foto)* to take. ◆ *vi (balzare)* to jump ; *(molla, congegno)* to be released ; *(allarme)* to go off ; *(manifestare ira)* to fly into a rage ; **far ~** *(molla, congegno)* to release sthg ; *(allarme)* to set off.

scatto *sm (di congegno)* release ; *(rumore)* click ; *(di foto)* shot ; *(balzo)* fit ; **di ~** suddenly.

scaturire : scaturire da *v + prep (sgorgare)* to gush from ; *fig (derivare)* to come from.

scavalcare *vt (muro, ostacolo)* to climb over ; *fig (concorrenti)* to overtake.

scavare *vt (fossa, terreno)* to dig ; *(render cavo)* to hollow out.

scavo *sm* excavation.

scegliere *vt* to choose.

scelta *sf* choice ; *(raccolta)* selection ; **non avere ~** to have no choice ; **'frutta o formaggio a ~'** 'choice of fruit or cheese'.

scelto, a *pp* → **scegliere**. ◆ *agg (gruppo)* select ; *(frutta)* choice.

scemo, a *agg fam* stupid, silly.

scena *sf* scene.

scenata *sf* row, scene.

scendere *vi (venir giù)* to go/come down ; *(da treno)* to get off ; *(diminuire)* to go down. ◆ *vt* to go/come down ; **~ dal treno** to get off the train ; **~ dalla macchina** to get out of the car.

sceneggiata *sf (messinscena)* performance ; **~ napoletana** *Napolitain melodrama.*

sceneggiato *sm* serial.

sceneggiatura *sf* screenplay.

scervellarsi *vr* to rack one's brains.

sceso, a *pp* → **scendere**.

scettico, a, ci, che *agg* sceptical.

scheda *sf (cartoncino)* card ; *(modulo)* form ; ~ **magnetica** magnetic card.
schedare *vt (libro)* to catalogue ; **è stato schedato dalla polizia** he has a police record.
schedario *sm (raccolta)* file ; *(mobile)* filing cabinet.
schedina *sf* ≃ pools coupon.

SCHEDINA

The coupon you fill in to play *totocalcio* (the football pools) is called a *schedina*; it can be bought at tobacconists and bars. Players must predict the results of 13 games, marking the coupon with 1 for a home win, 2 for an away win and X for a draw. Winners receive prizes ranging from a few hundred to several million euros.

---

scheggia, ge *sf* splinter.
scheletro *sm* skeleton.
schema, i *sm* plan.
scherma *sf* fencing.
schermare *vt (nascondere)* to shield ; *(da raggi, radiazioni)* to screen.
schermo *sm* screen.
scherno *sm* derision.
scherzare *vi* to joke.
scherzo *sm (battuta, gesto)* joke ; *(brutto tiro)* trick ; **fare qc per ~** to do sthg for a laugh ; **è uno ~** *(cosa facile)* it's child's play.
scherzoso, a *agg* playful.
schiaccianoci *sm inv* nutcrackers *(pl)*.
schiacciare *vt (comprimere)* to crush ; *(noce)* to crack ; *(pulsante)* to press ; *fig (avversario)* to overwhelm ; SPORT to smash. ❑ **schiacciarsi** *vr* to get squashed.
schiacciata *sf (focaccia) type of flat salted bread made with olive oil.*
schiacciato, a *agg (appiattito)* flat ; *(deformato)* squashed.
schiaffo *sm* slap.
schiamazzi *smpl* screams.
schiantare *vt* to break. ❑ **schiantarsi** *vr* to break up.
schianto *sm (rumore)* crash ; **è uno ~!** *fam* she's/it's a knockout!
schiarire *vt* to lighten. ❑ **schiarirsi** *vr (cielo)* to clear up ; *(colore)* to become lighter ; **schiarirsi la voce** to clear one's throat.
schiavitù *sf* slavery.
schiavo, a *sm, f* slave. ◆ *agg* : **~ di** a slave to.
schiena *sf* back.
schienale *sm* back.
schiera *sf* group.
schierare *vt (esercito, squadra)* to draw up ; *(libri, oggetti)* to line up. ❑ **schierarsi** *vr (mettersi in fila)* to line up ; **schierarsi con/contro qn** to side with/oppose sb.
schietto, a *agg (persona)* frank ; *(vino)* not watered-down.
schifezza *sf* : **essere una ~** *(cibo)* to be disgusting ; *(film)* to be awful.
schifo *sm* disgust ; **mi fa ~** it makes me sick ; **fare ~** *(cibo, insetto)* to be disgusting ; *(film)* to be awful.
schifoso, a *agg (disgustoso)* disgusting ; *(pessimo, brutto)* awful.
schioccare *vt (dita)* to snap ; *(lingua)* to click.
schioppo *sm (fucile)* shotgun.

schiuma *sf (marina)* foam ; *(di sapone)* lather ; ~ **da barba** shaving foam.

schivare *vt* to dodge, to avoid.

schivo, a *agg* reserved, shy.

schizzare *vt* to splash. ◆ *vi (acqua, getto)* to spurt ; *fig (saltar via)* to dart away.

schizzo *sm (spruzzo)* stain, splash ; *(disegno)* sketch.

sci *sm inv (attrezzo)* ski ; *(attività)* skiing ; ~ **d'acqua** water skiing ; ~ **di fondo** cross-country skiing.

scia *sf (di nave)* wake ; *(di profumo, fumo)* trail.

sciabola *sf (spada)* sabre.

sciacquare *vt* to rinse ; **sciacquarsi la bocca** to rinse out one's mouth.

sciacquone *sm* flush ; **tirare lo ~** to flush the toilet.

sciagura *sf* disaster.

sciagurato, a *agg (sfortunato)* unlucky ; *(cattivo)* wicked.

scialacquare *vt* to squander.

scialbo, a *agg (colore)* pale ; *(sapore)* bland ; *(persona)* dull.

scialle *sm* shawl.

scialuppa *sf* sloop ; ~ **di salvataggio** lifeboat.

sciame *sm* swarm.

sciangai *sm (gioco)* pick-up-sticks.

sciare *vi* to ski.

sciarpa *sf* scarf.

sciatica *sf (nevralgia)* sciatica.

sciatore, trice *sm, f* skier.

sciatto, a *agg* untidy.

scientifico, a, ci, che *agg* scientific.

scienza *sf (studio della realtà)* science ; *(sapere)* knowledge. ❑ **scienze** *sfpl* science *(sg)*.

scienziato, a *sm, f* scientist.

scimmia *sf* monkey.

scimmiottare *vt* to ape.

scindere *vt (dividere)* to divide.

scintilla *sf* spark.

scintillare *vi* to sparkle.

scioccare *vt* to shock.

sciocchezza *sf (cosa stupida)* silly thing ; *(cosa poco importante)* trifle.

sciocco, a, chi, che *agg* silly.

sciogliere *vt (nodo)* to untie ; *(capelli)* to loosen ; *(animale)* to let loose ; *(ghiaccio, burro)* to melt ; *(pastiglia, società)* to dissolve ; *(mistero)* to solve ; *(assemblea)* to close. ❑ **sciogliersi** *vr (nodo)* to come untied ; *(neve, burro)* to melt.

scioglilingua *sm inv* tongue twister.

sciolina *sf (per sci di fondo)* ski wax.

sciolto, a *pp* → **sciogliere**. ◆ *agg (disinvolto)* easy ; *(agile)* agile.

sciopero *sm* strike ; **essere in ~** to be on strike.

sciovia *sf* ski lift.

scippare *vt* : ~ **qn** to snatch sb's bag.

scippo *sm* bagsnatching.

sciroppo *sm (medicina)* cough mixture ; *(di frutta)* syrup.

scissione *sf (separazione)* split.

scisso, a *pp* → **scindere**.

sciupare *vt (vestito, libro)* to spoil, to ruin. ❑ **sciuparsi** *vr*

(rovinarsi) to get spoiled ; *(deperire)* to become run down.
scivolare *vi (scorrere)* to glide ; *(perdere l'equilibrio)* to slip, to slide.
scivolo *sm (gioco)* slide.
scivoloso, a *agg* slippery.
scoccare *vt (freccia)* to shoot. ◆ *vi (ore)* to strike.
scocciare *vt fam* to annoy. ❑ **scocciarsi** *vr fam* to be annoyed.
scodella *sf* bowl.
scodinzolare *vi* to wag its tail.
scogliera *sf* rocks *(pl)*.
scoglio *sm (roccia)* rock ; *fig* stumbling block.
scoiattolo *sm* squirrel.
scolapasta *sm inv* colander.
scolapiatti *sm inv* draining rack.
scolare *vt* to drain.
scolaro, a *sm, f* schoolboy (*f* schoolgirl).
scolastico, a, ci, che *agg* school *(dav s)*.
scollare *vt (staccare)* to unstick. ❑ **scollarsi** *vr* to come unstuck.
scollato, a *agg (abito)* low-cut.
scollatura *sf* neckline.
scolorire *vt* to fade. ❑ **scolorirsi** *vr* to fade.
scolpire *vt* to sculpt ; *(legno)* to carve ; *(iscrizione)* to engrave.
scombussolare *vt* to upset.
scommessa *sf* bet.
scommesso, a → **scommettere**.
scommettere *vt* to bet.
scomodare *vt* to bother. ❑ **scomodarsi** *vr* to put o.s. out ; **scomodarsi a fare qc** to go to the bother of doing sthg.
scomodo, a *agg (poltrona)* uncomfortable ; *(orario)* inconvenient.
scompagnato, a *agg (calzini)* odd.
scomparire *vi (sparire)* to disappear.
scomparso, a *pp* → **scomparire**.
scompartimento *sm (di treno)* compartment.
scomparto *sm* compartment.
scompigliare *vt (capelli)* to ruffle, to mess up.
scompiglio *sm* confusion.
scomporre *vt (mobile, armadio)* to take to pieces. ❑ **scomporsi** *vr (perdere il controllo)* to lose one's composure.
scomposto, a *pp* → **scomporre**.
sconcertare *vt* to disconcert.
sconcio, a, ci, ce *agg (osceno)* obscene.
sconfiggere *vt* to defeat.
sconfinare *vi (uscire dai confini)* to cross the border ; *fig* : ~ **da** to stray from.
sconfinato, a *agg* boundless.
sconfitta *sf* defeat.
sconfitto, a *pp* → **sconfiggere**.
sconforto *sm* dejection.
scongelare *vt* to defrost.
scongiurare *vt (supplicare)* to implore ; *(pericolo, minaccia)* to ward off.
sconnesso, a *agg (ragionamento)* incoherent.
sconosciuto, a *agg* unknown. ◆ *sm, f* stranger.

sconsiderato, a *agg* thoughtless.
sconsigliare *vt* to advise against ; ~ **qc a qn** to advise sb against sthg ; ~ **a qn di fare qc** to advise sb against doing sthg.
scontare *vt (detrarre)* to deduct ; *(pena)* to serve ; *(colpa, errore)* to pay for.
scontato, a *agg (prezzo)* discounted ; *(previsto)* taken for granted ; **dare qc per ~** to take sthg for granted.
scontento, a *agg* : ~ **(di)** dissatisfied (with).
sconto *sm* discount ; **fare uno ~** to give a discount.
scontrarsi *vr (urtarsi)* to collide ; *(combattere, discordare)* to clash.
scontrino *sm* receipt ; **'munirsi dello scontrino alla cassa'** 'pay at the till and obtain a receipt'.
scontro *sm (urto)* collision ; *(combattimento, fig)* clash.
scontroso, a *agg* surly.
sconveniente *agg (indecente)* improper.
sconvolgente *agg* disturbing.
sconvolgere *vt (persona)* to disturb, to shake ; *(ordine, piani)* to upset.
sconvolto, a *pp* → **sconvolgere.**
scopa *sf (arnese)* broom.
scoperta *sf* discovery.
scoperto, a *pp* → **scoprire.** ◆ *agg* uncovered ; *(capo, braccia)* bare.
scopo *sm* purpose, aim ; **allo ~ di fare qc** in order to do sthg ; **a che ~?** for what purpose?
scoppiare *vi (spaccarsi)* to burst ; *(esplodere)* to explode ; ~ **dal caldo** *fam* to be boiling (hot) ; ~ **a piangere** to burst into tears ; ~ **a ridere** to burst out laughing.
scoppio *sm (rumore, di pneumatico)* bang ; *(esplosione)* explosion ; *(di risa)* burst ; *(di guerra)* outbreak ; **a ~ ritardato** delayed-action.
scoprire *vt* to discover ; *(liberare da copertura)* to uncover. ❑ **scoprirsi** *vr (svestirsi)* to dress less warmly ; *(rivelarsi)* to give o.s. away.
scoraggiare *vt* to discourage. ❑ **scoraggiarsi** *vr* to become discouraged.
scorbutico, a, ci, che *agg (scontroso)* cantankerous.
scorciatoia *sf* short cut ; **prendere una ~** to take a short cut.
scordare *vt* to forget. ❑ **scordarsi di** *vr + prep* to forget ; **scordarsi di fare qc** to forget to do sthg.
scorgere *vt* to see, to make out.
scoria *sf (residuo)* slag.
scorpacciata *sf* : **fare una ~ (di qc)** to stuff o.s. (with sthg).
scorpione *sm* scorpion. ❑ **Scorpione** *sm* Scorpio.
scorrazzare *vi* to run around.
scorrere *vi (liquido, fiume, traffico)* to flow ; *(fune)* to run ; *(tempo)* to pass. ◆ *vt (giornale, libro)* to glance through.
scorretto, a *agg (errato)* incorrect ; *(sleale)* unfair.
scorrevole *agg (porta)* sliding ; *(traffico, stile)* flowing.
scorrimento *sm (di traffico)* flow.

scorsa *sf*: **dare una ~ a qc** to glance through sthg.
scorso, a *pp* → **scorrere**. ◆ *agg* last.
scorta *sf*: **fare ~ di qc** to stock up with sthg ; **di ~** spare.
scortare *vt* to escort.
scortese *agg* impolite.
scorticare *vt (pelle)* to graze ; *(animale)* to skin.
scorto, a *pp* → **scorgere**.
scorza *sf (di albero)* bark ; *(di frutto)* peel.
scorzonera *sf type of bitter-tasting root vegetable.*
scosceso, a *agg* steep.
scossa *sf (movimento)* jolt ; *(elettrica)* shock.
scosso, a *pp* → **scuotere**. ◆ *agg* shaken.
scossone *sm* jolt.
scostare *vt* to move aside. ❑ **scostarsi** *vr* to move aside.
scotch[1] [skɔtʃ] *sm inv (nastro adesivo)* ≃ Sellotape® *(Br)* Scotch® tape *(Am)*.
scotch[2] [skɔtʃ] *sm inv (whisky)* Scotch.
scottadito : **a scottadito** *avv* piping hot.
scottare *vt (ustionare)* to burn ; *(cuocere)* to scald. ◆ *vi (bevanda, pietanza)* to be too hot. ❑ **scottarsi** *vr* to burn o.s.
scottatura *sf* burn.
scotto, a *agg* overcooked.
scout ['skaut] *smf inv* scout.
scovare *vt (negozio, ristorante)* to discover.
Scozia *sf*: **la ~** Scotland.
scozzese *agg* Scottish. ◆ *smf* Scotsman *(f* Scotswoman) ; **gli scozzesi** the Scots.
screditare *vt* to discredit.
screpolare *vt* to crack. ❑ **screpolarsi** *vr* to crack.
screziato, a *agg* streaked.
screzio *sm* disagreement.
scricchiolare *vi* to creak.
scricchiolio *sm* creaking.
scriminatura *sf* parting.
scritta *sf* inscription.
scritto, a *pp* → **scrivere**. ◆ *agg* written. ◆ *sm (opera)* work ; *(cosa scritta)* letter.
scrittore, trice *sm, f* writer.
scrittura *sf* writing.
scrivania *sf* writing desk.
scrivere *vt* & *vi* to write ; **~ a qn** to write to sb. ❑ **scriversi** *vr (parola)* : **come si scrive 'cuore'?** how do you write ○ spell 'cuore'?
scroccare *vt fam* to scrounge.
scrollare *vt (agitare)* to shake ; *(spalle)* to shrug ; **scrollarsi qc di dosso** to shake sthg off.
scrosciare *vi (pioggia)* to pelt down ; *(applausi)* to thunder.
scroscio *sm (d'acqua)* pelting ; *(d'applausi)* thunder.
scrostare *vt (intonaco)* to strip off. ❑ **scrostarsi** *vr (pareti, tegame)* to peel.
scrupolo *sm (timore)* scruple ; *(diligenza)* conscientiousness ; **senza scrupoli** unscrupulous.
scrupoloso, a *agg (persona)* scrupulous ; *(resoconto, lavoro)* meticulous.
scrutare *vt* to scrutinize ; *(orizzonte)* to search.

scucire *vt (cucitura)* to unpick. ❑ **scucirsi** *vr* to come unstitched.

scuderia *sf* stable.

scudetto *sm* SPORT championship shield.

scudo *sm* shield.

sculacciare *vt* to spank.

scultore, trice *sm, f* sculptor.

scultura *sf* sculpture.

scuola *sf* school ; **andare a ~** to go to school ; **~ elementare** ≃ primary school *(Br)*, grade school *(Am)(for children aged from 6 to 11)* ; **~ guida** driving school ; **~ materna** nursery school *(for children aged from 3 to 5)* ; **~ media** *first three years of secondary school for children aged from 11 to 14* ; **~ dell'obbligo** compulsory education ; **scuole tecniche** *schools which prepare their students for practical professions* ; **scuole serali** evening classes.

scuotere *vt* to shake ; *(spalle)* to shrug. ❑ **scuotersi** *vr* to shake o.s.

scurire *vt* to darken. ◆ *vi* to grow dark. ❑ **scurirsi** *vr* to grow dark.

scuro, a *agg* dark. ◆ *sm (buio)* darkness.

scusa *sf* excuse ; **chiedere ~ (a qn)** to apologize (to sb).

scusare *vt (perdonare)* to forgive ; *(giustificare)* to excuse. ❑ **scusarsi** *vr* to apologize ; **(mi) scusi, dov'è la stazione?** excuse me, where is the station? ; **scusi!** sorry!

sdebitarsi *vr* : **~ con qn di qc** to repay sb for sthg.

sdentato, a *agg* toothless.

sdolcinato, a *agg* over-sentimental.

sdraia *sf* deckchair.

sdraiarsi *vr* to lie down.

sdraio *sm* : **(sedia a) ~** deckchair.

sdrammatizzare *vt* to play down.

sdrucciolare *vi* to slip.

☞ ———

se *cong* - 1. *(nel caso in cui)* if ; **rimani ~ vuoi** stay if you want ; **~ è possibile** if it's possible ; **~ fossi in te** if I were you ; **~ non sbaglio ...** if I'm not wrong ...
- 2. *(dato che)* if ; **~ lo dici, sarà vero** if you say so, it must be true.
- 3. *(con frasi dubitative) (indirette)* whether, if ; **vedi ~ puoi venire** see whether ○ if you can come ; **chiedile ~ le piace** ask her if she likes it.
- 4. *(esprime un suggerimento)* : **e ~ andassimo al cinema?** how about going to the cinema?
- 5. *(esprime un augurio)* if ; **~ solo potessi!** if only I could!
- 6. *(in espressioni)* : **anche ~** even if ; **~ mai** if ; **neanche ~** even if ; **~ non altro** if nothing else ; **~ no** otherwise.
◆ *pron* → **si**.

---

sé *pron (per cosa)* itself ; *(per persona)* himself/herself/themselves ; **tenere qc per ~** to keep sthg for oneself ; **pensa solo a se stesso** he only thinks of himself.

sebbene *cong* although.

sec. *(abbr di secolo)* c.

secca, che *sf (di mare, fiume)* shallows *(pl)*.

seccare *vt* to dry ; *(prosciugare)* to dry up ; *(infastidire)* to annoy. ❑ **seccarsi** *vr* to dry ; *(prosciugarsi)* to dry up ; *(infastidirsi)* to get annoyed.

seccato, a *agg (infastidito)* annoyed.

seccatore, trice *sm, f* nuisance.

seccatura *sf (fastidio)* nuisance.

secchiello *sm (contenitore)* bucket.

secchio *sm* bucket.

secchione, a *sm, f fam* swot.

secco, a, chi, che *agg* dry ; *(funghi, prugne)* dried ; *(brusco)* curt. ◆ *sm* : **essere a ~ di qc** *(non avere) fig* to be without sthg ; **tirare in ~ una barca** to beach a boat ; **lavare a ~** to dry-clean.

secolare *agg (vecchio di secoli)* age-old.

secolo *sm* century ; *(periodo lungo)* : **non lo vedo da secoli** I haven't seen him for ages.

seconda *sf (marcia)* second gear ; **viaggiare in ~** to travel second-class ; **a ~ di** according to.

secondario, a *agg* secondary ; **scuola secondaria** secondary school.

secondo, a *num* second. ◆ *agg (altro)* second. ◆ *sm (tempo)* second ; *(portata)* main course. ◆ *prep* according to ; **~ me** in my opinion ; **di seconda mano** second-hand, sesto.

sedano *sm* celery.

sedativo *sm* sedative.

sede *sf (di organizzazione)* headquarters *(pl)* ; *(di azienda)* head office.

sedentario, a *agg* sedentary.

sedere *sm (parte del corpo)* bottom. ◆ *vi* : **mettersi a ~** to sit down. ❑ **sedersi** *vr* to sit down.

sedia *sf* chair.

sedicesimo, a *num* sixteenth → sesto.

sedici *num* sixteen → **sei**.

sedile *sm (di veicolo)* seat.

sedotto, a *pp* → **sedurre**.

seducente *agg* seductive.

sedurre *vt (uomo, donna)* to seduce ; *(sog : idea, proposta)* to appeal to.

seduta *sf* session.

seduttore, trice *sm, f* seducer.

sega, ghe *sf* saw.

segale *sf* rye.

segare *vt* to saw.

seggio *sm* seat ; **~ elettorale** polling station.

seggiola *sf* chair.

seggiolino *sm (sedia pieghevole)* folding chair.

seggiolone *sm (per bambini)* high chair.

seggiovia *sf* chair lift.

segnalare *vt (comunicare)* to point out ; *(indicare)* to indicate.

segnalazione *sf (indicazione)* indication ; *(raccomandazione)* recommendation.

segnale *sm (indicazione)* signal ; *(stradale)* sign ; **~ acustico** sound signal ; **~ d'allarme** alarm ; **~ orario** time signal.

segnaletica *sf (stradale)* road signs *(pl)*.

segnalibro *sm* bookmark.

segnaposto *sm* place card.

segnare *vt (mettere un segno)* to mark ; *(indicare)* to indicate ;

SPORT to score; **segnarsi qc** to make a note of sthg.

segno *sm* sign; *(lettera, numero)* symbol; *(contrassegno, traccia)* mark; **fare ~ a qn di fare qc** to signal sb to do sthg; **fare ~ di no** to shake one's head; **fare ~ di sì** to nod one's head; **perdere il ~** to lose one's place; **cogliere** o **colpire nel ~** *fig* to hit the mark.

segretario, a *sm, f* secretary.

segreteria *sf (di azienda, scuola)* secretary's office; *(di partito)* position of Secretary. ❑ **segreteria telefonica** *sf* answering machine.

segreto, a *agg* & *sm* secret.

seguente *agg* following, next.

seguire *vt* to follow. ◆ *vi* to follow; *(continuare)*: **segue a pag. 70** continued on page 70.

seguito *sm (proseguimento)* continuation; *(risultato)* result; *(scorta)* retinue; *(favore)* following; **in ~ a** following; **di ~** at a stretch, on end; **in ~** subsequently.

sei[1] → **essere**.

sei[2] *agg num* six; **ha ~ anni** he/she is six (years old); **sono le ~** it's six o'clock; **il ~ gennaio** the sixth of January; **pagina ~** page six; **il ~ di picche** the six of spades; **erano in ~** there were six of them.

seicento *num* six hundred. ❑ **Seicento** *sm*: **il Seicento** the seventeenth century → **sei**.

selciato *sm* cobbles *(pl)*, cobbled surface.

selettivo, a *agg* selective.

selezionare *vt* to select.

selezione *sf* selection.

self-service ['sɛl'sɛrvis] *agg inv* & *sm inv* self-service.

sella *sf* saddle.

selvaggina *sf* game.

selvaggio, a, gi, ge *agg* wild; *(tribù)* savage; *(delitto)* brutal. ◆ *sm, f* savage.

selvatico, a, ci, che *agg* wild.

semaforo *sm (apparecchio)* traffic lights *(pl)*.

sembrare *vi* to seem. ◆ *v impers*: **sembra che** it seems that; **mi sembra di conoscerlo** I think I know him; **sembra che stia per piovere** it looks like it's going to rain.

seme *sm* seed; *(nocciolo)* stone; *(di carte da gioco)* suit.

semestre *sm* six-month period; SCOL semester.

semifinale *sf* semifinal.

semifreddo *sm dessert similar to ice cream.*

seminare *vt* to sow.

seminario *sm* seminar; RELIG seminary.

seminterrato *sm* basement.

semmai *cong* if (ever). ◆ *avv* if anything.

semolino *sm* semolina.

semplice *agg* simple; *(filo, consonante)* single; **è una ~ proposta** it's just a suggestion.

semplicemente *avv* simply.

semplicità *sf* simplicity.

semplificare *vt* to simplify.

sempre *avv* always; *(ancora)* still; **va ~ meglio/peggio** things are getting better and better/worse and worse; **~ che ci riesca** provided he manages it; **da ~** always; **di ~** usual; **per ~** forever.

senape *sf* mustard.
senato *sm* senate.
senatore, trice *sm, f* senator.
sennò *avv (altrimenti)* otherwise.
seno *sm (petto)* breast.
sensazionale *agg* sensational.
sensazione *sf* sensation, feeling ; **fare ~** to cause a sensation.
sensibile *agg* sensitive ; *(notevole)* noticeable ; **~ a** *(caldo, freddo)* sensitive to ; *(complimenti)* susceptible to.
sensibilità *sf* sensitivity.
senso *sm (facoltà, coscienza)* sense ; *(sentimento, impressione)* feeling ; *(significato)* meaning, sense ; *(direzione)* direction ; **non avere ~** to make no sense ; **a ~ unico** one-way ; **in ~ orario** clockwise ; **perdere i sensi** to lose consciousness.
sentenza *sf (di processo)* sentence ; *(massima)* maxim.
sentiero *sm* path.
sentimentale *agg* sentimental.
sentimento *sm* feeling.
sentire *vt (udire)* to hear ; *(percepire, con il tatto)* to feel ; *(odore)* to smell ; *(sapore)* to taste ; **senti!** listen! ❑ **sentirsi** *vr (bene, stanco, allegro)* to feel ; **sentirsi di fare qc** to feel like doing sthg ; **sentirsi bene/male** to feel well/ill ; *(telefonarsi)* : **ci sentiamo domani** speak to you tomorrow.
senza *prep & cong* without ; **~ di me** without me ; **senz'altro** certainly, of course ; **~ dubbio** undoubtedly ; **~ che tu te ne accorga** without you noticing it.
senzatetto *smf inv* homeless person.
separare *vt* to separate. ❑ **separarsi** *vr (coniugi)* to separate ; *(gruppo)* to split up ; **separarsi da** *(coniuge)* to separate from.
separato, a *agg (disgiunto)* separate ; *(coniuge)* separated.
separazione *sf* separation.
sepolto, a *pp* → **seppellire**.
seppellire *vt* to bury.
seppia *sf* cuttlefish.
sequenza *sf* sequence.
sequestrare *vt* DIR to sequestrate ; *(persona)* to kidnap.
sequestro *sm* DIR sequestration ; *(rapimento)* kidnapping.
sera *sf* evening ; **di ~** in the evening.
serale *agg* evening *(dav s)*.
serata *sf* evening ; *(ricevimento)* party.
serbare *vt* to put aside, to keep ; **~ rancore a qn** to bear sb a grudge.
serbatoio *sm (di veicolo)* tank.
Serbia *sf* Serbia.
serbo *sm* : **avere qc in ~** to have sthg in store ; **tenere qc in ~** to put sthg aside.
serenata *sf* serenade.
sereno, a *agg (tempo, cielo)* clear ; *(persona)* calm. ◆ *sm (bel tempo)* fine weather.
serie *sf inv (successione)* series *(inv)* ; *(insieme)* set ; SPORT division ; **produzione in ~** mass production.
serietà *sf* seriousness ; *(coscienziosità)* reliability.
serio, a *agg* serious ; *(coscienzioso)* reliable. ◆ *sm* : **sul ~** *(davvero)*

seriously ; **prendere qn/qc sul ~** to take sb/sthg seriously.
serpente *sm* snake ; *(pelle)* snakeskin.
serra *sf (per piante)* greenhouse.
serranda *sf* rolling shutter.
serrare *vt (chiudere)* to close ; *(stringere)* to shut tightly.
serratura *sf* lock.
servire *vt* to serve. ◆ *vi (in tennis, pallavolo)* to serve ; *(essere utile)* to be of use ; **~ a fare qc** to be used for doing sthg ; **~ a qn** to be of use to sb ; **mi serve un martello** I need a hammer ; **~ da** to be used as. ❑ **servirsi** *vr (prendere da mangiare/bere)* to help o.s. ❑ **servirsi da** to shop at. ❑ **servirsi di** *vr + prep (utilizzare)* to use.
servitù *sf (condizione)* slavery ; *(personale)* domestic staff.
servizio *sm* service ; *(di piatti, bicchieri)* set ; *(giornalistico)* report ; **essere di ~** to be on duty ; **'~ compreso'** 'service included' ; **~ militare** military service. ❑ **servizi** *smpl (di abitazione)* kitchen and bathroom.
sesamo *sm* sesame.
sessanta *num* sixty → **sei**.
sessantesimo, a *num* sixtieth → **sesto**.
sessantina *sf*: **una ~ (di)** about sixty ; **essere sulla ~** to be in one's sixties.
sesso *sm* sex.
sessuale *agg* sexual.
sesto, a *agg num & pron num* sixth. ◆ *sm (frazione)* sixth ; **rimettersi in ~** to recover.
seta *sf* silk.
setacciare *vt (separare)* to sieve.
sete *sf* thirst ; **avere ~** to be thirsty.
settanta *num* seventy → **sei**.
settantesimo, a *num* seventieth → **sesto**.
settantina *sf*: **una ~ (di)** about seventy ; **essere sulla ~** to be in one's seventies.
sette *num* seven → **sei**.
settecento *num* seven hundred. ❑ **Settecento** *sm* : **il Settecento** the eighteenth century → **sei**.
settembre *sm* September ; **a** o **in ~** in September ; **lo scorso ~** last September ; **il prossimo ~** next September ; **all'inizio di ~** at the beginning of September ; **alla fine di ~** at the end of September ; **il due ~** the second of September.
settentrionale *agg* northern.
settentrione *sm* north.
setter *sm inv* setter.
settimana *sf* week.
settimanale *agg* weekly. ◆ *sm* weekly publication.
settimo, a *num* seventh → **sesto**.
settore *sm* sector.
severamente *avv* : **'è ~ vietato attraversare i binari'** 'crossing the track is strictly forbidden'.
severo, a *agg* strict, severe.
sevizie *sfpl* torture *(sg)*.
sexy *agg inv* sexy.
sezione *sf* section ; *MED* dissection.
sfaccendato, a *agg* lazy.
sfacchinata *sf* hard work.

sfacciato, a *agg (persona)* cheeky.
sfacelo *sm (rovina)* ruin.
sfamare *vt* to feed. ❑ **sfamarsi** *vr* to satisfy one's hunger.
sfare *vt* to undo.
sfarzo *sm* pomp, magnificence.
sfasciare *vt (sbendare)* to unbandage; *(rompere)* to smash. ❑ **sfasciarsi** *vr (rompersi)* to fall to pieces.
sfaticato, a *agg* lazy.
sfatto, a *pp* → **sfare**.
sfavorevole *agg* unfavourable.
sfera *sf* sphere.
sferrare *vt (attacco)* to launch; **~ un colpo contro qn** to lash out at sb.
sfibrare *vt* to exhaust.
sfida *sf* challenge.
sfidare *vt* to challenge; *(pericolo, morte)* to defy; **~ qn a fare qc** to challenge sb to do sthg.
sfiducia *sf* distrust.
sfigurare *vt* to disfigure. ◆ *vi* to make a bad impression.
sfilare *vt (togliere)* to take off. ◆ *vi (marciare)* to parade; **sfilarsi le scarpe** to slip off one's shoes. ❑ **sfilarsi** *vr (calze)* to ladder.
sfilata *sf (corteo)* march; *(di moda)* fashion show.
sfinire *vt* to exhaust.
sfiorare *vt* to skim (over).
sfiorire *vi* to wither.
sfitto, a *agg* vacant.
sfizioso, a *agg* enticing.
sfocato, a = **sfuocato**.
sfociare : sfociare in *v + prep (fiume)* to flow into.
sfoderare *vt (giacca)* to remove the lining from; *(spada)* to draw; *fig* to show off.
sfoderato, a *agg* unlined.
sfogare *vt* to give vent to. ❑ **sfogarsi** *vr (aprirsi)* to pour out one's feelings; **sfogarsi su qn** *(scaricare la collera)* to vent one's anger on sb.
sfoggiare *vt* to show off.
sfogliare *vt (giornale)* to leaf through.
sfogliatelle *sfpl puff pastries filled with spiced ricotta cheese and candied fruit.*
sfogo, ghi *sm (passaggio)* outlet; *(di sentimenti)* outburst; *(eruzione cutanea)* rash; **dare ~ a qc** to give vent to sthg.
sfoltire *vt* to thin.
sfondare *vt (contenitore)* to break the bottom of; *(porta)* to break down. ❑ **sfondarsi** *vr (contenitore)* to burst at the bottom.
sfondo *sm* background.
sformato *sm savoury pudding made with vegetables and cheese or sometimes with meat, baked in a mould and then turned out.*
sfornare *vt (pane, dolci)* to take out of the oven.
sfortuna *sf* misfortune; **portare ~** to bring bad luck.
sfortunatamente *avv* unfortunately.
sfortunato, a *agg* unlucky.
sforzare *vt* to force; *(occhi, voce, motore)* to strain. ❑ **sforzarsi** *vr* to make an effort.
sforzo *sm* effort; **fare uno ~** to make an effort.
sfottere *vt fam* to tease.

sfratto *sm* eviction.
sfrecciare *vi* to shoot past.
sfregare *vt (strofinare)* to rub.
sfregio *sm (taglio)* gash.
sfrenato, a *agg* unrestrained.
sfrontato, a *agg* impudent.
sfruttamento *sm* exploitation.
sfruttare *vt* to exploit.
sfuggire *vi (scappare)* to escape. ❑ **sfuggire a** *v + prep (sottrarsi a)* to escape from ; ~ **di mano a qn** to slip out of sb's hands ; ~ **di mente a qn** to slip sb's mind ; **non gli sfugge nulla** he misses nothing.
sfuggita : di sfuggita *avv* in passing.
sfumare *vt (colore)* to shade off ; *(capelli)* to taper. ◆ *vi (colore)* to shade off ; *(svanire)* to vanish.
sfumato, a *agg (colore)* soft.
sfumatura *sf (tonalità)* shade ; *fig (piccola differenza)* touch, hint ; *(di capelli)* tapering.
sfuocato, a *agg* blurred, out of focus.
sfuriata *sf (sfogo violento)* outburst of anger ; *(rimprovero)* telling off.
sgabello *sm* stool.
sgabuzzino *sm* storage room.
sgambetto *sm* : **fare lo ~ a qn** to trip sb up.
sganciare *vt (vestito, allacciatura)* to unfasten ; *(rimorchio, vagone)* to uncouple ; *(bombe)* to drop ; *fam (soldi)* to fork out. ❑ **sganciarsi** *vr (staccarsi)* to come undone.
sgarbato, a *agg* impolite.
sghignazzare *vi* to laugh scornfully.
sgobbare *vi fam* to slog.
sgocciolare *vt (bottiglia)* to drain. ◆ *vi* to drip.
sgolarsi *vr* to make o.s. hoarse.
sgomb(e)rare *vt (strada, soffitta)* to clear.
sgombero, a = **sgombro**.
sgombro, a *agg* clear. ◆ *sm (evacuazione)* evacuation ; *(pesce)* mackerel.
sgomentare *vt* to dismay. ❑ **sgomentarsi** *vr* to be dismayed.
sgominare *vt* to rout.
sgonfiare *vt* to deflate. ❑ **sgonfiarsi** *vr (canotto)* to deflate ; *(caviglia)* to go down.
sgorbio *sm (scarabocchio)* scribble ; *fig (persona)* fright.
sgradevole *agg* unpleasant.
sgradito, a *agg* unwelcome.
sgranare *vt (fagioli)* to shell.
sgranchirsi *vr* : ~ **le gambe** to stretch one's legs.
sgranocchiare *vt* to munch.
sgraziato, a *agg* graceless.
sgretolare *vt (frantumare)* to cause to crumble. ❑ **sgretolarsi** *vr* to crumble.
sgridare *vt* to scold.
sguaiato, a *agg* coarse.
sgualcire *vt* to crumple. ❑ **sgualcirsi** *vr* to become crumpled.
sguardo *sm (occhiata)* look ; *(espressione)* expression.
sguinzagliare *vt (cane)* to take off the lead.
sgusciare *vt (fagioli)* to shell. ◆ *vi (sfuggire)* to slip away.

shampo ['ʃampo] *sm inv* shampoo.
shock [ʃɔk] *sm inv* shock.

---

si *(diventa* **se** *quando precede lo, la, li, le, ne) pron* - 1. *(riflessivo : persona)* himself (*f* herself), themselves *(pl)* ; *(impersonale)* oneself ; *(cosa, animale)* itself, themselves *(pl)* ; **lavarsi** to wash (onself) ; **~ stanno preparando** they are getting ready.
- 2. *(con verbo transitivo)* : **lavarsi i denti** to brush one's teeth ; **~ è comprato un vestito** he bought himself a suit.
- 3. *(reciproco)* each other, one another ; **~ sono conosciuti a Roma** they met in Rome.
- 4. *(impersonale)* : **~ può sempre provare** one ○ you can always try ; **~ dice che ...** they say that ..., it is said that ... ; **~ vede che è stanco** one ○ you can see he's tired ; '**~ prega di non fumare**' 'please do not smoke' ; **non ~ sa mai** you never know.
- 5. *(passivo)* : **questi prodotti ~ trovano dappertutto** these products are found everywhere.

---

sì *avv & sm inv* yes ; **dire di ~** to say yes ; **uno ~ e uno no** every other one.
sia[1] → **essere.**
sia[2] *cong* : **~ ... che, ~ ... ~** both ... and ; **~ che ... ~ che** whether ... or ; **~ che tu venga, ~ che tu non venga** whether you come or not.
siamo → **essere.**
sicché *cong (e quindi)* and so.
siccità *sf inv* drought.
siccome *cong* as, since.
Sicilia *sf* : **la ~** Sicily.
siciliano, a *agg & sm, f* Sicilian.
sicura *sf (di auto)* safety lock ; *(di arma)* safety catch.
sicurezza *sf (mancanza di pericolo)* safety, security ; *(certezza)* certainty ; **di ~** safety *(dav s)*, security *(dav s)*.
sicuro, a *agg* safe ; *(amico, informazione)* reliable ; *(fiducioso)* confident ; *(certo)* certain. ◆ *avv* certainly ; **di ~** certainly ; **andare sul ~** to play safe ; **essere ~ di sè** to be sure of o.s. ; **al ~** in a safe place.
Siena *sf* Siena.
siepe *sf* hedge.
sieropositivo, a *agg* HIV-positive.
siete → **essere.**
Sig. *(abbr di signor)* Mr.
Sig.a *(abbr di signora)* Ms.
sigaretta *sf* cigarette.
sigaro *sm* cigar.
Sigg. *abbr* Messrs.
sigla *sf (abbreviazione)* acronym ; *(musicale)* signature tune ; **~ automobilistica** *two-letter abbreviation of province on a vehicle's number plate.*
Sig.na *(abbr di signorina)* Miss.
significare *vt* to mean ; **che cosa significa?** what does it mean?
significativo, a *agg (discorso)* significant ; *(sguardo)* meaningful.
significato *sm* meaning.
signor *sm* → **signore.**
signora *sf (donna)* lady ; *(moglie)* wife ; **buon giorno ~** good morning (Madam) ; **Gentile Signora** *(in una lettera)* Dear Madam ; **la ~ Poli** Mrs

Poli ; **signore e signori** ladies and gentlemen.
signore *sm (uomo)* gentleman ; **buon giorno ~** good morning (Sir) ; **il ~ desidera?** what can I do for you, sir? ; **Gentile Signore** *(in una lettera)* Dear Sir ; **i signori Rossi** *(marito e moglie)* Mr and Mrs Rossi ; **il signor Martini** Mr Martini.
signorina *sf (ragazza)* young lady ; **buon giorno ~** good morning (Madam) ; **la ~ Logi** Miss Logi.
Sig.ra *abbr* Mrs.
silenzio *sm* silence ; **fare ~** to be quiet.
silenzioso, a *agg* quiet, silent.
sillaba *sf* syllable.
simbolico, a, ci, che *agg* symbolic.
simbolo *sm* symbol.
simile *agg (analogo)* similar ; *(tale)* : **una persona ~** such a person ; **~ a** similar to.
simmetrico, a, ci, che *agg* symmetric(al).
simpatia *sf (inclinazione)* liking ; *(qualità)* pleasantness.
simpatico, a, ci, che *agg* nice.
simulare *vt (fingere)* to feign ; *(imitare)* to simulate.
simultaneo, a *agg* simultaneous.
sin = sino.
sinagoga, ghe *sf* synagogue.
sincero, a *agg (persona)* sincere ; *(dolore, gioia)* genuine, heart-felt.
sindacalista, i, e *smf* trade unionist.
sindacato *sm (di lavoratori)* trade union.
sindaco, ci *sm* mayor.
sinfonia *sf* symphony.
singhiozzo *sm* hiccups *(pl)*. ❑ **i singhiozzi** *smpl* sobs ; **a singhiozzi** *fig* by fits and starts.
single *smf inv* single person.
singolare *agg (originale)* unusual ; GRAMM singular. ◆ *sm* GRAMM singular.
singolo, a *agg* single.
sinistra *sf*: **la ~** the left ; POL the left (wing) ; **scrivere con la ~** to write with one's left hand ; **a ~** left ; **a ~ di** to the left of.
sinistro, a *agg* left ; *(minaccioso)* sinister. ◆ *sm* accident.
sino = fino.
sinonimo *sm* synonym.
sintesi *sf inv (riassunto)* summary.
sintetico, a, ci, che *agg (artificiale)* synthetic ; *(succinto)* brief.
sintetizzare *vt (riassumere)* to summarize.
sintomo *sm* symptom.
sintonizzare *vt* to tune in. ❑ **sintonizzarsi su** *vr + prep* to tune in to.
sipario *sm* curtain.
sirena *sf (apparecchio)* siren ; *(nella mitologia)* mermaid.
Siria *sf*: **la ~** Syria.
siringa, ghe *sf (per iniezioni)* syringe ; *(da cucina)* ≃ piping bag.
sistema, i *sm* system.
sistemare *vt (ordinare)* to tidy up ; *(risolvere)* to sort out, to settle ; *(alloggiare)* to find accommodation *(Br)*, ○ accomodations *(Am)* for ; *(procurare un lavoro a)* to find a job for ; *(maritare)* to marry off. ❑ **sistemarsi** *vr (risolversi)* to be

settled ; *(trovare alloggio)* to find accommodation *(Br)*, ○ accomodations *(Am)* ; *(trovare lavoro)* to find work ; *(sposarsi)* to marry.
sistematico, a, ci, che *agg* systematic.
sistemazione *sf (disposizione)* arrangement ; *(alloggio)* accommodation *(Br)*, accommodations *(Am)* ; *(lavoro)* employment.
situare *vt* to situate, to locate.
situazione *sf* situation.
skate-board ['skeit'bord] *sm inv* skateboard.
skinhead [ski'ned] *sm inv speg* skinhead.
ski-lift [ski'lift] *sm inv* ski lift.
ski-pass [ski'pas] *sm inv* ski pass.
slacciare *vt* to undo.
slanciato, a *agg* slender.
slancio *sm (balzo)* dash ; *fig* burst.
slavina *sf* snowslide.
slavo, a *agg* Slavonic, Slav.
sleale *agg (persona)* disloyal ; *(azione)* treacherous.
slegare *vt* to untie.
slip *sm inv* briefs *(pl)*.
slitta *sf* sledge.
slittare *vi* to slide ; *(automobile)* to skid.
slogan *sm inv* slogan.
slogare *vt* to dislocate.
slogatura *sf* dislocation.
smacchiatore *sm* stain remover.
smagliante *agg* dazzling.
smagliare *vt (collant, calze)* to ladder.
smagliatura *sf (di calze)* ladder ; *(della pelle)* stretch mark.
smaltire *vt (merce)* to sell off ; *(rifiuti)* to discharge ; *(cibo)* to digest ; **~ la sbornia** to get over one's hangover.
smalto *sm (per metalli, di denti)* enamel ; *(per ceramica)* glaze ; *(per unghie)* nail varnish.
smania *sf (agitazione)* restlessness ; *(desiderio)* craving ; **aver la ~ di qc** to have a craving for sthg.
smarrire *vt* to lose. ❑ **smarrirsi** *vr* to get lost.
smarrito, a *agg* lost ; *(sbigottito)* bewildered.
smascherare *vt* to unmask.
smemorato, a *agg* absent-minded.
smentire *vt (notizia)* to deny ; *(testimonianza)* to refute.
smentita *sf (di notizia)* denial.
smeraldo *sm* emerald.
smesso, a *pp* → **smettere**.
smettere *vt* to stop ; *(abito)* to stop wearing ; **smettere di fare qc** to stop doing sthg ; **smettila!** stop it!.
smidollato, a *agg* spineless.
sminuire *vt* to belittle.
sminuzzare *vt* to crumble.
smistamento *sm (di posta, pacchi)* sorting ; *(di treni)* shunting.
smistare *vt (posta)* to sort ; *(treni)* to shunt.
smisurato, a *agg* enormous, huge.
smodato, a *agg* excessive.
smog *sm inv* smog.
smoking *sm inv* dinner jacket *(Br)*, tuxedo *(Am)*.

smontabile *agg* that can be dismantled.
smontare *vt (macchina, libreria)* to take to pieces ; *fig (far perdere l'entusiasmo a)* to discourage. ◆ *vi (da cavallo)* to dismount ; *(da turno di lavoro)* to finish (work).
smorfia *sf* grimace.
smorfioso, a *agg* simpering.
smorzare *vt (suoni)* to muffle ; *(colore)* to tone down ; *(entusiasmo)* to dampen.
smosso, a *pp* → **smuovere**.
smottamento *sm* landslide.
smunto, a *agg* pinched.
smuovere *vt (spostare)* to shift ; *(da proposito, intenzione)* to deter.
smussare *vt (spigolo)* to round off.
snack-bar ['snɛk'bar] *sm inv* snack bar.
snaturato, a *agg* inhuman.
snello, a *agg* slim, slender.
snervante *agg* exhausting.
snidare *vt* to flush out.
snobismo *sm* snobbery.
snodare *vt (slegare)* to untie ; *(arti)* to loosen up. ❑ **snodarsi** *vr (slegarsi)* to come loose.
soccombere *vi (cedere)* to give in ; *(essere sconfitto)* to be overcome.
sobbalzare *vi (balzare)* to jolt ; *(trasalire)* to jump.
sobborgo, ghi *sm* suburb.
sobrio, a *agg* sober.
socchiudere *vt (porta)* to leave ajar ; *(occhi)* to half-close.
socchiuso, a *pp* → **socchiudere**.
soccorrere *vt* to help.
soccorso, a *pp* → **soccorrere**. ◆ *sm* help, aid ; ~ **stradale** breakdown service.
sociale *agg* social.
socialista, i, e *agg* socialist.
socializzare *vi* to socialize.
società *sf inv (gruppo umano)* society ; *(associazione)* association, club ; *COMM* company ; ~ **per azioni** limited company *(Br)*, incorporated company *(Am)*.
socievole *agg* sociable.
socio, a, ci, cie *sm, f (di circolo)* member ; *COMM* partner.
soda®[1] *sf* soda.
soda[2] *sf (bevanda)* soda water.
soddisfacente *agg* satisfactory.
soddisfare *vt* to satisfy.
soddisfatto, a *agg* satisfied ; **essere ~ di** *(contento)* to be satisfied with.
soddisfazione *sf* satisfaction.
sodo, a *agg* hard, firm.
sofà *sm inv* sofa.
sofferente *agg* suffering.
sofferto, a *pp* → **soffrire**.
soffiare *vi* to blow. ◆ *vt* to blow ; ~ **qn/qc a qn** to pinch sb/sthg from sb ; **soffiarsi il naso** to blow one's nose.
soffiata *sf fam* tip-off.
soffice *agg* soft.
soffio *sm (di fiato, vento)* breath ; ~ **al cuore** heart murmur.
soffitta *sf* attic.
soffitto *sm* ceiling.
soffocante *agg* suffocating, stifling.
soffocare *vt* to suffocate. ◆ *vi* to suffocate.

soffriggere *vt & vi* to fry lightly.
soffrire *vt (patire)* to suffer ; *(sopportare)* to bear. ◆ *vi* to suffer. ❑ **soffrire di** *v + prep* to suffer from.
soffritto *sm lightly fried onions and herbs.*
sofisticato, a *agg* sophisticated.
software ['sɔftwɛr] *sm inv* software.
soggetto, a *agg* : **essere ~ a** to be subject to, subject.
soggezione *sf (sottomissione)* subjection ; *(imbarazzo)* uneasiness ; **dare ~ a qn** to make sb ill at ease.
soggiorno *sm (permanenza)* stay ; *(stanza)* living room.
soglia *sf* threshold.
sogliola *sf* sole.
sognare *vt* to dream of o about. ◆ *vi* to dream ; **~ ad occhi aperti** to daydream.
sogno *sm* dream ; **fare un brutto ~** to have a bad dream.
soia *sf* soya.
solaio *sm* attic.
solamente *avv* only, just.
solare *agg* solar, sun *(dav s)*.
solarium *sm inv* solarium.
solco, chi *sm (in terreno)* furrow ; *(incisione)* groove ; *(scia)* wake.
soldato *sm* soldier ; **~ semplice** private.
soldo *sm* : **non avere un ~** to be penniless. ❑ **soldi** *smpl (denaro)* money *(sg)*.
sole *sm* sun ; **prendere il ~** to sunbathe.
soleggiato, a *agg* sunny.
solenne *agg* solemn.
solere *v impers* : **come si suol dire** as they say.
soletta *sf (suola)* insole.
solfo = **zolfo.**
solidale *agg* : **essere ~ con qn** to be in agreement with sb.
solidarietà *sf* solidarity.
solido, a *agg & sm* solid.
solista, i, e *smf* soloist.
solitario, a *agg (persona)* lonely, solitary ; *(luogo)* lonely. ◆ *sm (di carte)* patience *(Br)*, solitaire *(Am)* ; *(brillante)* solitaire.
solito, a *agg* usual ; **essere ~ fare qc** to be in the habit of doing sthg ; **(come) al ~** as usual ; **di ~** usually.
solitudine *sf* solitude.
sollecitare *vt (risposta, pagamento)* to press for.
solleone *sm (caldo)* summer heat ; *(periodo)* dog days *(pl)*.
solletico *sm* tickling ; **soffrire il ~** to be ticklish.
sollevamento *sm* lifting ; **~ pesi** *SPORT* weight-lifting.
sollevare *vt (tirare su)* to lift, to raise ; *(problema, questione)* to raise ; *(fare insorgere)* to stir up. ❑ **sollevarsi** *vr (da terra)* to get up ; *(insorgere)* to rise up.
sollevato, a *agg (confortato)* relieved.
sollievo *sm* relief.
solo, a *agg (senza compagnia)* alone ; *(isolato)* lonely ; *(unico)* only. ◆ *avv (soltanto)* only, just ; **c'è un ~ posto a sedere** there's only one seat ; **da ~** by oneself ; **ho ~ 5 euro** I only have 5 euros ; **non ~ ...**

ma anche not only ... but also ; a ~ *MUS* solo.

soltanto *avv* only.

solubile *agg* soluble ; caffè ~ instant coffee.

soluzione *sf* solution.

Somalia *sf* : la ~ Somalia.

somaro, a *sm, f (asino)* donkey, ass ; *fig (a scuola)* dunce.

somiglianza *sf* resemblance.

somigliare : somigliare a *v + prep (nell'aspetto)* to look like ; *(nel modo di essere)* to be like. ❑ somigliarsi *vr* to be alike.

somma *sf* sum.

sommare *vt MAT* to add up.

sommario, a *agg* brief. ◆ *sm (di libro)* index.

sommergere *vt* to submerge ; ~ di *fig* to overwhelm with.

sommergibile *sm* submarine.

sommerso, a *pp* → sommergere. ◆ *agg (isola, città)* underwater.

somministrare *vt* to administer.

sommità *sf inv (cima)* summit.

sommo, a *agg* highest ; *(eccellente)* outstanding, excellent ; per sommi capi in short , in brief.

sommossa *sf* uprising.

sommozzatore, trice *sm, f* (deep-sea) diver.

sonda *sf (spaziale, MED)* probe.

sondaggio *sm (indagine)* survey.

sondare *vt (fondo marino)* to sound ; *(intenzioni, opinioni)* to sound out.

sonnambulo, a *agg* : essere ~ to sleepwalk.

sonnellino *sm* nap.

sonnifero *sm* sleeping pill.

sonno *sm* sleep ; avere ~ to be sleepy ; prendere ~ to fall asleep.

sono → essere.

sonoro, a *agg (onde, di film)* sound *(dav s)* ; *(voce, risata, schiaffo)* ringing. ◆ *sm (di film)* soundtrack.

sontuoso, a *agg* sumptuous.

soppiatto : di soppiatto *avv* secretly.

sopportare *vt (peso)* to support, to bear ; *(umiliazione, dolore)* to bear ; *(tollerare)* to put up with.

soppresso, a *pp* → sopprimere.

sopprimere *vt (legge)* to abolish ; *(servizio, treno)* to withdraw, to do away with ; *(parola)* to delete.

sopra *prep (su)* on ; *(al di sopra di)* above ; *(al di là di)* over ; *(riguardo a)* about, on. ◆ *avv (in alto)* above ; *(in lettera, scritto)* : come precisato ~ as detailed above ; al di ~ di above ; di ~ upstairs.

soprabito *sm* overcoat.

sopracciglio *(pl f* sopracciglia) *sm* eyebrow.

sopraffare *vt* to overcome.

sopraffatto, a *pp* → sopraffare.

sopraggiungere *vi (giungere all'improvviso)* to arrive (unexpectedly) ; *(accadere)* to occur (unexpectedly).

sopraggiunto, a *pp* → sopraggiungere.

sopralluogo, ghi *sm (di polizia)* on-the-spot investigation ; *(visita)* inspection.

soprammobile *sm* ornament.

soprannaturale *agg* supernatural.
soprannome *sm* nickname.
soprano *sm* soprano.
soprassalto : **disoprassalto** *avv* with a start.
soprattutto *avv* above all, especially.
sopravvalutare *vt* to overestimate.
sopravvento *sm* : **avere il ~ su** to have the upper hand over.
sopravvissuto, a *pp* → **sopravvivere.** ◆ *sm, f* survivor.
sopravvivere *vi* to survive. ❑ **sopravvivere a** *v + prep* to survive.
soprelevata *sf* elevated section.
soprintendente *smf (a attività, lavoro)* superintendent, supervisor.
soprintendenza *sf (attività)* supervision ; *(ufficio)* superintendency.
sopruso *sm* abuse of power.
soqquadro *sm* : **mettere qc a ~** to turn sthg upside down.
sorbetto *sm* sorbet.
sorbire *vt* to sip ; **sorbirsi qn/qc** *fig* to put up with sb/sthg.
sorcio *sm* mouse.
sordido, a *agg* sordid, squalid.
sordina *sf* : **in ~** softly.
sordo, a *agg (non udente)* deaf ; *(rumore, tonfo)* muffled, dull. ◆ *sm, f* deaf person.
sordomuto, a *agg* deaf and dumb. ◆ *sm, f* deaf and dumb person.
sorella *sf* sister.
sorellastra *sf* stepsister.
sorgente *sf (d'acqua)* spring ; *(di fiume, elettricità, calore)* source.
sorgere *vi* to rise ; *(sospetto, dubbio)* to arise.
sorpassare *vt* AUTO to overtake ; *(superare)* to exceed.
sorpassato, a *agg* old-fashioned.
sorpasso *sm (di veicolo)* overtaking ; **fare un ~** to overtake.
sorprendere *vt (cogliere)* to catch ; *(stupire)* to surprise. ❑ **sorprendersi di** *vr + prep* to be surprised at.
sorpresa *sf* surprise ; **fare una ~ a qn** to give sb a surprise ; **di ~** by surprise.
sorpreso, a *pp* → **sorprendere.**
sorreggere *vt* to support.
sorretto, a *pp* → **sorreggere.**
sorridente *agg* smiling.
sorridere *vi* to smile.
sorriso, a *pp* → **sorridere.** ◆ *sm* smile.
sorsata *sf* gulp.
sorso *sm (sorsata)* gulp ; *(piccola quantità)* sip.
sorta *sf* kind, sort.
sorte *sf* fate ; **tirare a ~** to draw lots.
sorteggio *sm* draw.
sortilegio *sm* spell.
sorveglianza *sf* supervision ; *(polizia)* surveillance.
sorvegliare *vt* to watch.
sorvolare *vt (territorio)* to fly over. ◆ *vi* : **~ su** *(territorio)* to fly over ; *fig* to pass over.

S.O.S. [ɛsɛ'ɔ'ɛsɛ] *sm inv* SOS ; **lanciare un ~** to send out an SOS.

sosia *smf inv* double.

sospendere *vt (attaccare)* to hang ; *(attività, pagamenti, funzionario)* to suspend.

sospensione *sf* suspension.

sospeso, a *pp* → **sospendere**. ◆ *agg (interrotto)* suspended ; **lasciare qc in ~** to leave sthg unfinished ; **tenere qn in ~** to keep sb in suspense.

sospettare *vt* to suspect. ◆ *vi* : **~ di qn** *(avere sospetti su)* to suspect sb ; *(diffidare di)* to be suspicious of sb.

sospetto, a *agg* suspicious. ◆ *sm, f* suspect. ◆ *sm* suspicion.

sospirare *vi* to sigh ; **farsi ~** to keep sb waiting.

sospiro *sm* sigh ; **tirare un ~ di sollievo** to heave a sigh of relief.

sosta *sf (in luogo)* stop ; *(pausa)* break ; **fare ~ a/in** to make a stop at/in ; **'divieto di ~'** 'no waiting' ; **senza ~** nonstop ; **' ~ consentita solo per carico e scarico'** 'no waiting except for loading and unloading'.

sostantivo *sm* noun.

sostanza *sf* substance.

sostanzioso, a *agg (cibo)* nourishing ; *(notevole)* substantial.

sostare *vi (fermarsi)* to stop.

sostegno *sm* support.

sostenere *vt* to support ; **~ che** to maintain (that) ; **~ gli esami** to sit exams. ❑ **sostenersi** *vr (tenersi dritto)* to hold o.s. up.

sostenitore, trice *sm, f* supporter.

sostentamento *sm* maintenance.

sostenuto, a *agg (tono, stile)* elevated ; *(ritmo, passo)* sustained.

sostituire *vt (rimpiazzare)* to replace ; *(prendere il posto di)* to take over from ; **~ qn/qc con** to substitute sb/sthg with ; **~ qn/qc a** to substitute sb/sthg for.

sostituto, a *sm, f* substitute.

sostituzione *sf* substitution.

sottaceti *smpl* pickles.

sottana *sf (gonna)* skirt ; *(di prete)* cassock.

sotterfugio *sm* subterfuge.

sotterraneo, a *agg* underground ; *fig* clandestine, secret. ◆ *sm* cellar.

sottigliezza *sf (di spessore)* thinness ; *fig* subtlety ; *(dettaglio)* quibble.

sottile *agg (non spesso)* thin ; *(capelli)* fine ; *(slanciato)* slim ; *(vista, odorato, ingegno)* sharp, keen ; **non andare per il ~** not to mince matters.

sottintendere *vt* to imply.

sottinteso, a *pp* → **sottintendere**. ◆ *sm* allusion.

sotto *prep* under ; *(più in basso di)* below. ◆ *avv (in posizione inferiore)* underneath ; *(più in basso, in scritto)* below ; **al di ~ di** under, below ; **sott'olio** in oil ; **di ~** *(al piano inferiore)* downstairs.

sottobanco *avv (comprare)* under the counter.

sottobicchiere *sm* coaster.

sottobosco *sm* undergrowth.

sottobraccio *avv (prendere)* by the arm ; *(camminare)* arm in arm.

sottofondo *sm MUS* background music.
sottolineare *vt* to underline; *(dare risalto a)* to emphasize.
sottolio → sotto.
sottomarino, a *agg* underwater *(dav s)*. ◆ *sm* submarine.
sottomesso, a *pp* → sottomettere. ◆ *agg* submissive.
sottomettere *vt (al proprio dominio)* to subdue. ❑ **sottomettersi a** *vr + prep* to submit to.
sottopassaggio *sm (per auto)* underpass; *(per pedoni, in stazione)* subway, underpass; 'servirsi del ~' 'please use the subway'.
sottoporre *vt*: ~ qn a qc to subject sb to sthg; ~ qc a qn to submit sthg to sb. ❑ **sottoporsi a** *vr + prep (subire)* to undergo.
sottoposto, a *pp* → sottoporre.
sottoscala *sm inv* cupboard under the stairs.
sottoscritto, a *pp* → sottoscrivere. ◆ *sm, f* the undersigned.
sottoscrivere *vt* to sign. ❑ **sottoscrivere a** *v + prep* to subscribe to.
sottosopra *avv* upside down.
sottostante *agg* lower.
sottosuolo *sm (di terreno)* subsoil; *(locale)* basement.
sottosviluppato, a *agg* underdeveloped.
sottoterra *avv* underground.
sottotitolo *sm (di TV, cinema)* subtile.
sottotitoli *smpl* subtitles.
sottovalutare *vt* to underestimate.
sottoveste *sf* underskirt.
sottovoce *avv* in a low voice.
sottovuoto *avv* vacuum-packed.
sottrarre *vt MAT* to subtract; *(fondi)* to take away, to remove; ~ qc a qn *(rubare)* to steal sthg from sb. ❑ **sottrarsi a** *vr + prep* to escape, to avoid.
sottratto, a *pp* → sottrarre.
sottrazione *sf MAT* subtraction; *(furto)* removal.
souvenir [suve'nir] *sm inv* souvenir.
sovietico, a, ci, che *agg* soviet.
sovraccaricare *vt* to overload.
sovrano, a *agg* & *sm, f* sovereign.
sovrapporre *vt* to put on top of.
sovrapposto, a *pp* → sovrapporre.
sovrastare *vt (valle, paese)* to overhang.
sovrumano, a *agg* superhuman.
sovvenzionare *vt* to subsidize.
sovversivo, a *agg* subversive.
sozzo, a *agg* filthy.
S.p.A. *(abbr di Società per Azioni)* ≃ Ltd *(Br)*, ≃ Inc. *(Am)*.
spaccare *vt* to break, to split. ❑ **spaccarsi** *vr* to break, to split.
spaccatura *sf* split.
spacciare *vt (droga)* to push. ❑ **spacciarsi per** *vr + prep* to pass o.s. off as.
spacciatore, trice *sm, f (di droga)* pusher.
spaccio *sm (bottega)* shop; *(di droga)* trafficking.

spacco, chi *sm* split ; *(di gonna)* slit.
spaccone, a *sm, f* boaster.
spada *sf* sword.
spaesato, a *agg* disorientated.
spaghetteria *sf restaurant specializing in pasta dishes.*
spaghetti *smpl* spaghetti *(sg)* ; ~ **aglio, olio e peperoncino** *spaghetti with garlic, chilli and olive oil* ; ~ **alla carbonara** *spaghetti in an egg, bacon and cheese sauce* ; ~ **pomodoro e basilico** *spaghetti in a fresh tomato and basil sauce* ; ~ **alla puttanesca** *spaghetti in a sauce of tomatoes, anchovies, olives and capers* ; ~ **alle vongole** *spaghetti in a clam sauce.*
Spagna *sf* : **la** ~ Spain.
spagnolo, a *agg* Spanish. ◆ *sm, f* Spaniard. ◆ *sm (lingua)* Spanish.
spago, ghi *sm* string.
spaiato, a *agg* odd.
spalancare *vt* to open wide.
spalla *sf* shoulder ; **voltare le spalle a qn** to turn one's back on sb ; **di spalle** from behind.
spalliera *sf (di letto)* head ; SPORT wall bars *(pl)*.
spallina *sf (di reggiseno, sottoveste)* strap ; *(imbottitura)* shoulder pad.
spalmare *vt* to spread.
spalti *smpl (di stadio)* terraces.
spandere *vt (versare)* to pour ; *(spargere)* to spread. ❑ **spandersi** *vr* to spread.
spappolare *vt* to pulp. ❑ **spappolarsi** *vr* to get mushy.
sparare *vi* to fire. ◆ *vt (colpo, fucilata)* to fire.
sparecchiare *vi* to clear the table. ◆ *vt* : ~ **la tavola** to clear the table.
spareggio *sm* SPORT play-off.
spargere *vt (sparpagliare)* to scatter ; *(versare)* to spill ; *(divulgare)* to spread. ❑ **spargersi** *vr (sparpagliarsi)* to scatter ; *(divulgarsi)* to spread.
sparire *vi* to disappear.
sparlare : **sparlare di** *v + prep* to run down.
sparo *sm* shot.
sparpagliare *vt* to scatter. ❑ **sparpagliarsi** *vr* to scatter.
sparso, a *pp* → **spargere.** ◆ *agg* scattered.
spartire *vt (dividere)* to share out.
spartitraffico *sm inv* central reservation *(Br)*, median strip *(Am)*.
spasmo *sm* spasm.
spassarsela *vr* to have a good time.
spasso *sm (film, scena)* amusement, fun ; *(persona)* laugh, scream ; *(passeggiata)* : **andare a** ~ to go for a walk ; **essere a** ~ *fig* to be out of work.
spauracchio *sm* scarecrow.
spaventapasseri *sm inv* scarecrow.
spaventare *vt* to frighten. ❑ **spaventarsi** *vr* to become frightened.
spavento *sm (paura)* fear, fright ; **far ~ a qn** to give sb a fright.
spaventoso, a *agg* frightening.
spazientirsi *vr* to lose one's patience.
spazio *sm* space.

spazioso, a *agg* spacious.
spazzaneve *sm inv* snowplough.
spazzare *vt (pavimento)* to sweep ; *(sporco, foglie)* to sweep up.
spazzatura *sf (rifiuti)* rubbish.
spazzino, a *sm, f* road sweeper.
spazzola *sf (per capelli)* hairbrush ; *(per abiti)* clothes brush ; ~ **da scarpe** shoe brush.
spazzolare *vt* to brush.
spazzolino *sm* : ~ **(da denti)** toothbrush.
spazzolone *sm* scrubbing brush.
specchiarsi *vr* to look at o.s. (in a mirror).
specchietto *sm (da borsetta)* pocket mirror ; *(prospetto)* scheme, table ; ~ **(retrovisore)** rear-view mirror.
specchio *sm* mirror.
speciale *agg* special.
specialista, i, e *sm, f* specialist.
specialità *sf inv* speciality ; ~ **della casa** speciality of the house.
specialmente *avv* especially.
specie *sf inv (di piante, animali)* species *(inv)* ; *(sorta)* kind. ◆ *avv* especially ; **una ~ di** a kind of.
specificare *vt* to specify.
specifico, a, ci, che *agg* specific.
speculare *vi* to speculate.
speculazione *sf* speculation.
spedire *vt* to send.
spedizione *sf (di lettera, merci)* sending ; *(viaggio)* expedition.
spegnere *vt (fuoco, sigaretta)* to put out ; *(luce, TV, gas)* to turn off.
spellare *vt (coniglio)* to skin. ❑ **spellarsi** *vr* to peel.
spendere *vt* & *vi* to spend.
spensierato, a *agg* carefree.
spento, a *pp* → **spegnere**. ◆ *agg (colore)* dull ; *(sguardo)* lifeless.
speranza *sf* hope.
sperare *vt* to hope for ; **spero che venga** I hope he'll come ; **spero di sì** I hope so ; ~ **di fare qc** to hope to do sthg. ❑ **sperare in** *v + prep* to trust in.
sperduto, a *agg (luogo)* out-of-the-way ; *(persona)* lost.
spericolato, a *agg* fearless.
sperimentale *agg* experimental.
sperimentare *vt (sottoporre a esperimento, fig)* to test ; *(fare esperienza di)* to experience.
sperma, i *sm* sperm.
sperperare *vt* to squander.
spesa *sf (somma)* expense ; *(acquisti)* shopping ; **fare la ~** to do the shopping ; **fare spese** *(acquisti)* to go shopping. ❑ **spese** *sfpl (uscite)* expenses ; **spese postali** postage *(sg)* ; **spese di viaggio** travel expenses ; **a spese di** at the expense of.
spesso, a *agg* thick. ◆ *avv* often.
spessore *sm* thickness.
Spett. *abbr* = **spettabile**.
spettabile *agg (nelle lettere)* : ~ **ditta** Messrs ... & Co.
spettacolo *sm (rappresentazione)* show ; *(vista)* sight.
spettare : **spettare a** *v + prep* to be up to ; **spetta a te dirglielo** it's up to you to tell him.

spettatore, trice *sm, f (di spettacolo)* member of the audience ; *(di avvenimento)* onlooker.
spettinare *vt* : ~ **qn** to ruffle sb's hair. ❑ **spettinarsi** *vr* to get one's hair messed up.
spettro *sm (fantasma)* spectre.
spezia *sf* spice.
spezzare *vt (rompere)* to break ; *(viaggio, giornata)* to break (up). ❑ **spezzarsi** *vr* to break.
spezzatino *sm* stew.
spezzato, a *agg (diviso)* broken. ◆ *sm (vestito)* jacket and trousers.
spezzettare *vt* to break into small pieces.
spia *sf (di polizia)* informer ; *(agente)* spy ; *(luminosa)* warning light ; *(indizio)* indication, sign ; **fare la** ~ to be a sneak.
spiacente *agg* : **essere** ~ **(di fare qc)** to be sorry (for doing sthg).
spiacevole *agg* unpleasant.
spiaggia, ge *sf* beach ; ~ **privata** private beach.
spianare *vt (terreno)* to level ; *(pasta)* to roll out ; ~ **il terreno** *fig* to prepare the ground.
spiare *vt* to spy on.
spiazzo *sm* open space.
spiccare *vi (risaltare)* to stand out. ◆ *vt* : ~ **un balzo** to jump ; ~ **il volo** to fly off.
spiccato, a *agg* marked, strong.
spicchio *sm (d'arancia)* segment ; *(di mela, pera)* slice ; ~ **d'aglio** clove of garlic.
spicciarsi *vr* to hurry up.
spicciolo, a *agg* : **moneta spicciola** small change. ❑ **spiccioli** *smpl* small change.
spiedino *sm (pietanza)* kebab.
spiedo *sm* spit ; **allo** ~ spit-roasted.
spiegare *vt (far capire)* to explain ; *(vele)* to unfurl ; *(lenzuola)* to unfold ; ~ **qc a qn** to explain sthg to sb. ❑ **spiegarsi** *vr (farsi capire)* to make o.s. clear ; *(diventare chiaro)* to become clear ; **spieghiamoci!** let's get things straight!
spiegazione *sf* explanation.
spietato, a *agg* ruthless.
spiga, ghe *sf (di grano)* ear.
spigolo *sm (di mobile, muro)* corner.
spilla *sf* brooch ; ~ **da balia** safety pin.
spillare *vt (soldi)* : ~ **qc a qn** to tap sb for sthg.
spillo *sm (da sarto)* pin.
spilorcio, a, ci, ce *agg* mean, stingy.
spina *sf (di pianta)* thorn ; *(di riccio)* spine ; *(lisca)* bone ; *(elettrica)* plug ; **birra alla** ~ draught beer ; ~ **dorsale** backbone.
spinaci *smpl* spinach *(sg)*.
spinello *sm fam (sigaretta)* joint.
spingere *vt & vi* to push ; ~ **qn a fare qc** to press sb to do sthg. ❑ **spingersi** *vr* to push on.
spinoso, a *agg* prickly, thorny.
spinta *sf (pressione, urto)* push ; *(incoraggiamento)* incentive, spur ; *(raccomandazione)* : **dare una** ~ **a qn** to pull strings for sb.
spinto, a *pp* → **spingere**. ◆ *agg (scabroso)* risqué.
spintone *sm* push, shove.
spionaggio *sm* espionage.

spioncino *sm* peephole, spy hole.
spiraglio *sm (fessura)* chink ; *(di luce)* gleam, glimmer.
spirale *sf* spiral ; *(anticoncezionale)* coil.
spirito *sm (intelletto)* mind ; *(fantasma, disposizione d'animo* & RELIG) spirit ; *(vivacità d'ingegno)* wit ; *(senso dell'umorismo)* humour ; *(alcol)* : **ciliegie sotto ~** cherries preserved in alcohol.
spiritoso, a *agg* witty.
spirituale *agg* spiritual.
splendente *agg* shining.
splendere *vi* to shine.
splendido, a *agg (bellissimo)* magnificent.
splendore *sm* splendour ; *(luce)* brilliance.
spogliare *vt (svestire)* to undress ; **~ qn di qc** *(derubare, privare)* to strip sb of sthg. ❑ **spogliarsi** *vr* to undress.
spogliarello *sm* striptease.
spogliatoio *sm (di palestra, piscina)* changing room ; *(di abitazione)* dressing room.
spoglio *sm (di schede elettorali)* counting.
spola *sf (bobina)* spool ; **fare la ~ (tra)** to go to and fro (between).
spolpare *vt* to strip the flesh off.
spolverare *vt* & *vi* to dust.
sponda *sf (di fiume)* bank ; *(di lago)* shore ; *(di letto)* edge ; *(di biliardo)* cushion.
sponsorizzare *vt* sponsor.
spontaneo, a *agg* spontaneous ; *(non artificioso)* natural.
spopolare *vt* to depopulate. ◆ *vi* to draw the crowds. ❑ **spopolarsi** *vr* to become depopulated.
sporadico, a, ci, che *agg* sporadic.
sporcare *vt* to dirty ; **sporcarsi le mani** to get one's hands dirty. ❑ **sporcarsi** *vr* to get dirty.
sporcizia *sf (l'esser sporco)* dirtiness ; *(cosa sporca)* dirt.
sporco, a, chi, che *agg* dirty. ◆ *sm* dirt.
sporgente *agg* protruding ; *(occhi)* bulging.
sporgere *vt* to put out. ◆ *vi* to stick out. ❑ **sporgersi** *vr* to lean out.
sport *sm inv* sport.
sporta *sf* shopping bag.
sportello *sm (di mobile, treno)* door ; *(di banca, posta)* window, counter ; **~ automatico** cash dispenser.
sportivo, a *agg (programma, campo)* sports *(dav s)* ; *(persona)* sporty ; *(abbigliamento)* casual ; *(comportamento, spirito)* sporting. ◆ *sm, f* sportsman *(f* sportswoman).
sporto, a *pp* → **sporgere**.
sposare *vt* to marry. ❑ **sposarsi** *vr* to get married. ❑ **sposarsi con** *vr + prep* to marry.
sposato, a *agg* married.
sposo, a *sm, f* bridegroom *(f* bride) ; **gli sposi** the newlyweds.
spossante *agg* exhausting.
spostare *vt* to move ; *(cambiare)* to change. ❑ **spostarsi** *vr* to move.

spot *sm inv (faretto)* spotlight; *(pubblicità)* advert.
spranga, ghe *sf* bar.
spray *sm inv* spray.
sprecare *vt* to waste.
spreco, chi *sm* waste.
spregiudicato, a *agg (senza scrupoli)* unscrupulous.
spremere *vt (arancia, limone)* to squeeze.
spremiagrumi *sm inv* lemon squeezer.
spremuta *sf* fresh fruit juice; ~ **di arancia** freshly-squeezed orange juice.
sprezzante *agg* scornful.
sprigionare *vt* to emit. ❑ **sprigionarsi** *vr* to emanate.
sprizzare *vi* to spurt.
sprofondare *vi (crollare)* to collapse; *(affondare)* to sink.
sproporzionato, a *agg* out of all proportion.
sproposito *sm* blunder; *(somma esagerata)* : **costa uno ~** it costs a fortune; **parlare a ~** to talk out of turn.
sprovveduto, a *agg* inexperienced.
sprovvisto, a *agg* : ~ **di** lacking in; **cogliere qn alla sprovvista** to catch sb unawares.
spruzzare *vt (profumo)* to spray; *(acqua)* to sprinkle; *(persona)* to splash.
spruzzatore *sm* spray.
spruzzo *sm* spray.
spugna *sf (da bagno)* sponge; *(tessuto)* towelling.
spuma *sf (schiuma)* foam, froth.
spumante *sm* sparkling wine.

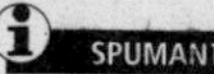

SPUMANTE

The sparkling wine called *spumante* can be drunk as an aperitif or as a dessert wine, and comes in sweet, dry or muscat versions, the latter being named after the grape variety. This Italian answer to champagne gets its name from the fact that it releases lots of bubbles, or foam (*spuma*), when uncorked. No birthday or wedding is complete without *spumante*, and it is also traditional to open a bottle at midnight on New Year's Eve.

spumone *sm (dolce) a foamy dessert made from whisked egg white, milk and sugar.*
spuntare *vi (apparire)* to appear. ◆ *vt (tagliare la punta di)* to break the point of; **spuntarsi i capelli** to trim one's hair; **spuntarla** *fig* to make it.
spuntino *sm* snack.
spunto *sm (punto di partenza)* starting point.
sputare *vt* to spit out. ◆ *vi* to spit.
sputo *sm* spit.
squadra *sf (di operai, SPORT)* squad, team; *(strumento)* set square.
squadrare *vt (scrutare)* to look at closely; *(foglio, blocco)* to square.
squagliare *vt* to melt; **squagliarsela** *fam* to clear off. ❑ **squagliarsi** *vr* to melt.
squalificare *vt* to disqualify.
squallido, a *agg* wretched, miserable.

squallore *sm* wretchedness, misery.
squalo *sm* shark.
squama *sf* scale.
squamare *vt (pesce)* to scale. ❑ **squamarsi** *vr (pelle)* to flake.
squamarsi *vr* to flake off.
squarciagola : asquarciagola *avv* at the top of one's voice.
squarciare *vt* to rip.
squartare *vt* to quarter.
squattrinato, a *agg* penniless.
squilibrato, a *agg* unbalanced.
squilibrio *sm (fisico)* disequilibrium ; *(psichico)* derangement ; *(disparità)* imbalance.
squillo *sm (di telefono, campanello)* ring ; *(di tromba)* blare.
squisito, a *agg (cibo)* delicious ; *(raffinato)* exquisite ; *(persona)* delightful.
sradicare *vt (albero)* to uproot.
srotolare *vt* to unroll.
stabile *agg* stable ; *(lavoro, occupazione)* steady. ◆ *sm (edificio)* building.
stabilimento *sm (complesso)* factory, plant ; ~ **balneare** bathing establishment.

STABILIMENTI BALNEARI

Many Italian seaside resorts have their *stabilimenti balneari*, bathing clubs on the beach which provide a bar, showers and changing huts, and hire out beach umbrellas, deckchairs and pedalos. Some even organize volleyball tournaments, treasure hunts and dances.

stabilire *vt* to establish ; *(fissare)* to fix ; ~ **che** *(decidere)* to decide (that). ❑ **stabilirsi** *vr* to settle.
stabilità *sf* stability.
staccare *vt (separare)* to detach, to separate ; SPORT to leave behind. ◆ *vi (risaltare)* to stand out ; *fam (finire il lavoro)* to knock off. ❑ **staccarsi** *vr (bottone, cerotto)* to come off ; **staccarsi da** *(venir via da)* to come off ; *fig (allontanarsi)* to move away from.
staccionata *sf (recinzione)* fence ; SPORT hurdle.
stadio *sm* SPORT stadium ; *(fase)* stage.
staffa *sf (di sella, pantaloni)* stirrup ; **perdere le staffe** *fig* to fly off the handle.
staffetta *sf* SPORT relay race.
stagionale *agg* seasonal. ◆ *smf* seasonal worker.
stagionato, a *agg* seasoned.
stagione *sf* season ; **alta/bassa ~** high/low season ; **vestiti di mezza ~** clothes for spring and autumn.
stagno, a *agg (a tenuta d'acqua)* watertight ; *(a tenuta d'aria)* airtight. ◆ *sm (laghetto)* pond ; *(metallo)* tin.
stagnola *sf* tinfoil.
stalla *sf (per cavalli)* stable ; *(per bovini)* cowshed.
stamattina *avv* this morning.
stambecco, chi *sm* ibex.
stampa *sf (tecnica)* printing ; *(con stampante, opera)* print ; *(giornalisti)* : **la ~** the press ; **'stampe'** 'printed matter'.
stampante *sf* INFORM printer.
stampare *vt* to print ; *(pubblicare)*

to publish ; *(nella memoria)* to impress.

stampatello *sm* block letters *(pl)*.

stampella *sf* crutch.

stampo *sm* mould ; *fig (sorta)* type.

stancare *vt (affaticare)* to tire ; *(stufare)* to bore. ❑ **stancarsi** *vr* to get tired ; **stancarsi di** *(stufarsi di)* to grow tired of.

stanchezza *sf* tiredness.

stanco, a, chi, che *agg* tired ; *(stufo)* : **~ di** fed up with ; **~ morto** dead tired.

stanghetta *sf (di occhiali)* leg.

stanotte *avv* tonight ; *(nella notte appena passata)* last night.

stante *agg* : **a sé ~** separate, independent.

stantio, a *agg (cibo)* stale.

stanza *sf (camera)* room ; **~ da bagno** bathroom ; **~ da letto** bedroom.

stanziare *vt* to allocate.

stare *vi (rimanere)* to stay ; *(abitare)* to live ; *(con gerundio)* : **sto leggendo** I'm reading ; **come sta?** how are you? ; **ti sta bene!** it serves you right! ; **ci stai?** is that OK with you? ; **sta a voi decidere** it's up to you to decide ; **queste scarpe mi stanno strette** these shoes are tight ; **~ per fare qc** to be about to do sthg ; **~ bene/male** to be well/ not very well ; **~ a guardare** to watch ; **~ in piedi** to stand (up) ; **~ seduto** to sit , to be sitting ; **~ simpatico a qn** to like sb ; **~ zitto** to shut up ; **starci** to fit.

starnutire *vi* to sneeze.

starnuto *sm* sneeze.

stasera *avv* this evening, tonight.

statale *agg* state *(dav s)*, government *(dav s)*. ◆ *smf* civil servant. ◆ *sf* main road.

statistica, che *sf (disciplina)* statistics *(pl)* ; *(dati)* statistic.

stato, a → **essere, stare.** ◆ *sm (condizione)* state, condition ; *(nazione)* state ; **essere in ~ interessante** to be pregnant ; **~ d'animo** state of mind ; **~ civile** marital status ; **gli Stati Uniti (d'America)** the United States (of America).

statua *sf* statue.

statunitense *agg* United States *(dav s)*, of the United States.

statura *sf (fisica)* height.

statuto *sm* statute.

stazionario, a *agg (immutato)* unchanged.

stazione *sf* station ; **~ degli autobus** bus station ; **~ balneare** seaside resort ; **~ centrale** central station ; **~ ferroviaria** railway station *(Br)*, railroad station *(Am)* ; **~ di polizia** police station ; **~ sciistica** ski resort ; **~ di servizio** petrol station *(Br)*, gas station *(Am)* ; **~ termale** spa.

stecca, che *sf (asticella)* stick ; *(di sigarette)* carton ; *(da biliardo)* cue.

steccato *sm* fence.

stella *sf* star ; **stelle filanti** shooting stars ; **albergo a tre stelle** three-star hotel.

stellato, a *agg* starry.

stelo *sm (di fiore)* stem.

stemma, i *sm* coat of arms.

stendere *vt (allungare)* to stretch (out) ; *(panni, vele)* to spread (out) ; *(bucato)* to hang out. ❑ **stendersi** *vr (sdraiarsi)* to lie down.

stenografare *vt* to take down in shorthand.

stentare *vi* : ~ **a fare qc** to find it hard to do sthg.

stento *sm* : **a** ~ with difficulty. ❑ **stenti** *smpl (privazioni)* hardship *(sg)*.

sterco, chi *sm* dung.

stereo *sm inv* stereo.

stereotipo *sm* stereotype.

sterile *agg (uomo, donna)* sterile.

sterilizzare *vt* to sterilize.

sterlina *sf* pound (sterling).

sterminare *vt* to exterminate.

sterminato, a *agg* immense.

sterminio *sm* extermination.

sterzare *vi* to steer.

sterzo *sm* steering.

steso, a *pp* → **stendere**.

stesso, a *agg* same ; *(in persona, proprio)* : **il presidente** ~ the president himself ○ in person ; **lo ~/la stessa** the same (one) ; **io** ~ I myself ; **lei stessa** she herself ; **lo faccio per me** ~ I'm doing it for myself ; **fare qc lo** ~ *to do sthg* just the same ; **fa** ○ **è lo** ~ it doesn't matter ; **per me è lo** ~ it's all the same to me.

stesura *sf (atto)* drafting ; *(documento)* draft.

stile *sm* style ; ~ **libero** freestyle.

stilista, i, e *smf* designer.

stilografica, che *sf* fountain pen.

stima *sf (valutazione)* valuation ; *(apprezzamento)* esteem ; **fare la ~ di qc** to estimate the value of sthg ; **avere ~ di qn** to have a high opinion of sb.

stimare *vt (valutare)* to value ; *(ritenere)* to consider ; *(apprezzare)* to respect.

stimolare *vt* to stimulate ; ~ **qn a fare qc** to spur sb on to do sthg.

stimolo *sm* stimulus.

stingere *vi* to fade. ❑ **stingersi** *vr* to fade.

stinto, a *pp* → **stingere**.

stipendio *sm* salary.

stipite *sm (di porta, finestra)* jamb.

stipulare *vt* to draw up.

stirare *vt (con il ferro)* to iron.

stiro *sm* → **asse, ferro**.

stirpe *sf* stock, birth.

stitichezza *sf* constipation.

stivale *sm* boot.

stivaletto *sm* ankle boot.

stizza *sf* anger.

stizzirsi *vr* to get irritated.

stoccafisso *sm* wind-dried cod, stockfish.

stoffa *sf* material, fabric ; **avere la ~ di** to have the makings of.

stola *sf* stole.

stolto, a *agg* stupid.

stomaco, chi ○ **ci** *sm* stomach.

stonato, a *agg* MUS off key.

stop *sm inv* AUTO *(segnale)* stop sign ; AUTO *(luce)* brake light *(Br)*, stoplight. ◆ *esclam* stop! ; **'stop con segnale rosso'** 'stop when light is on red'.

storcere *vt* to twist ; ~ **il naso** to turn up one's nose ; **storcersi una**

caviglia to twist one's ankle. ❑ **storcersi** *vr* to twist.

stordire *vt* to stun.

stordito, a *agg* stunned.

storia *sf (avvenimenti umani, materia, opera)* history ; *(vicenda, invenzione)* story ; *(faccenda)* business *(no pl)* ; *(scusa)* excuse.

storico, a, ci, che *agg* historic(al). ◆ *sm, f* historian.

stormo *sm (di uccelli)* flock.

storpiare *vt (rendere storpio)* to cripple ; *(parola)* to mangle ; *(concetto)* to twist.

storta *sf* : **prendere una ~ alla caviglia** to sprain one's foot.

storto, a *pp* → **storcere.** ◆ *agg (chiodo)* twisted, bent ; *(gambe, quadro)* crooked ; **andare ~** to go wrong.

stoviglie *sfpl* dishes.

strabico, a, ci, che *agg (persona)* squint-eyed ; *(occhi)* squint.

straccadenti *smpl type of very hard biscuit.*

stracchino *sm a creamy cow's milk cheese from Lombardy.*

stracciare *vt (vestito, foglio)* to tear.

stracciatella *sf (gelato) chocolate-chip ice cream ; (minestra) broth enriched with eggs, semolina and Parmesan cheese.*

straccio *sm* rag ; *(per pulizie)* duster, cloth.

straccione, a *sm, f* ragamuffin.

strada *sf* road ; *(urbana)* street ; *(percorso)* way ; **~ facendo** on the way ; **tagliare la ~ a qn** to cut across sb ; **~ panoramica** scenic route ; **~ senza uscita** dead end ; **' ~ deformata'** 'uneven road surface' ; **' ~ privata'** 'private road' ; **' ~ transitabile con catene'** 'road negotiable with chains'.

stradale *agg* road *(dav s).* ◆ *sf* traffic police.

strafalcione *sm (sproposito)* howler.

straforo : **di straforo** *avv* on the sly.

strafottente *agg* arrogant.

strage *sf* massacre.

stralunato, a *agg (occhi)* rolling ; *(persona)* dazed.

stramazzare *vi* to fall heavily.

strangolare *vt* to strangle.

straniero, a *agg* foreign. ◆ *sm, f* foreigner.

strano, a *agg* strange.

straordinario, a *agg* extraordinary ; *(treno)* special. ◆ *sm (lavoro)* overtime.

strapazzare *vt* to ill-treat. ❑ **strapazzarsi** *vr* to tire o.s. out.

strappo *sm (in tessuto, MED)* tear ; *fam (passaggio)* lift *(Br)*, ride *(Am)* ; **fare uno ~ alla regola** to make an exception to the rule.

straripare *vi* to overflow.

strascico, chi *sm (di abito)* train ; *fig (conseguenza)* aftereffect.

strascinati *smpl squares of pasta in a tomato and minced meat sauce (a speciality of Calabria).*

stratagemma, i *sm* stratagem.

strategia *sf* strategy.

strato *sm (di polvere, di crema)* layer ; *(di vernice, smalto)* coat.

stravagante *agg* eccentric.

stravedere : stravedere per *v + prep* to be crazy about.

stravisto, a *pp* → stravedere.
stravolgere *vt* to distort.
stravolto, a *pp* → stravolgere.
strazio *sm* : essere uno ~ *(libro, film)* to be awful ; *(persona)* to be a pain.
strega, ghe *sf* witch.
stregone *sm (mago)* sorcerer ; *(di tribù)* witchdoctor.
stremare *vt* to exhaust.
stremo *sm* : essere allo ~ delle forze to be at the end of one's tether.
strepitare *vi (gridare)* to shout.
strepitoso, a *agg* resounding.
stress *sm* stress.
stressante *agg* stressful.
stretta *sf* grip ; ~ di mano handshake ; mettere alle strette qn to put sb in a tight corner.
strettamente *avv (serratamente)* tightly ; *(rigorosamente)* strictly.
stretto, a *pp* → stringere. ◆ *agg (strada, stanza)* narrow ; *(vestito, scarpe)* tight ; *(rigoroso, preciso)* strict. ◆ *sm* strait ; parenti stretti close family *(sg)*.
strettoia *sf* bottleneck.
striato, a *agg* streaked.
stridere *vi (freni)* to creak ; *(cicale, grilli)* to chirr ; *(colori)* to clash.
strillare *vi* & *vt* to scream.
strillo *sm* scream.
striminzito, a *agg (vestito)* shabby ; *(persona)* skinny.
stringa, ghe *sf* lace.
stringato, a *agg* concise.
stringere *vt (vite, nodo)* to tighten ; *(denti, pugno)* to clench ; *(labbra)* to press ; *(tenere stretto)* to grip ; *(abito)* to take in ; *(patto, accordo)* to conclude. ◆ *vi* to be tight ; ~ qn tra le braccia to hug sb ; ~ la mano a qn to shake hands with sb ; ~ i tempi to get a move on ; il tempo stringe time is short. ❑ **stringersi** *vr* to squeeze up.
striscia, sce *sf (nastro)* strip ; *(riga)* stripe ; strisce (pedonali) zebra crossing *(sg)*.
strisciare *vi (serpente)* to slither ; *(passare rasente)* to scrape. ◆ *vt (macchina)* to scrape ; *(piedi)* to drag.
striscione *sm* banner.
stritolare *vt* to crush.
strizzare *vt* to wring out ; ~ l'occhio to wink.
strofinaccio *sm* cloth.
strofinare *vt* to rub.
stroncare *vt* to break off ; *(rivolta)* to put down ; *(libro, film)* to pan.
stropicciare *vt (braccio, occhi)* to rub ; *(vestito)* to crease.
strozzapreti *smpl 'gnocchi' either in a meat sauce, or made with eggs and spinach and served with butter and cheese.*
strozzare *vt (strangolare)* to strangle ; *(sog : cibo)* to choke. ❑ **strozzarsi** *vr* to choke.
strudel *sm inv* apple strudel.
strumento *sm (musicale, di precisione)* instrument ; *(di fabbro, meccanico)* tool.
strusciare *vt* to rub. ❑ **strusciarsi** *vr* to rub o.s.
strutto *sm* lard.
struttura *sf* structure.
struzzo *sm* ostrich.

stuccare *vt (buco)* to plaster ; *(vetro)* to putty.
stucco, chi *sm (malta)* plaster ; *(decorazione)* stucco ; **rimanere di ~** to be dumbfounded.
studente, essa *sm, f* student ; *(di liceo)* pupil.
studentesco, a, schi, sche *agg* student *(dav s)*.
studentessa → **studente**.
studiare *vt & vi* to study.
studio *sm (attività)* studying ; *(ricerca, stanza)* study ; *(di professionista)* office ; *(di televisione, radio)* studio ; **~ medico** surgery *(Br)*, office *(Am)* ; **gli studi** *(scuola, università)* studies.
studioso, a *agg* studious. ◆ *sm, f* scholar.
stufa *sf* stove ; **~ elettrica** heater.
stufare *vt (seccare)* : **mi hai stufato con le tue chiacchiere!** I'm sick and tired of you talking! ❑ **stufarsi** *vr* : **stufarsi (di)** *fam* to get fed up (with).
stufato *sm* stew.
stufo, a *agg fam* : **essere ~ (di)** to be fed up (with).
stuoia *sf* straw mat.
stupefacente *agg* amazing. ◆ *sm* drug.
stupendo, a *agg* marvellous.
stupidaggine *sf* stupid thing.
stupido, a *agg* stupid.
stupire *vt* to amaze. ❑ **stupirsi di** *vr + prep* to be amazed by.
stupore *sm* astonishment.
stupro *sm* rape.
sturare *vt* to unblock.
stuzzicadenti *sm inv* toothpick.
stuzzicare *vt (irritare)* to tease ; **~ l'appetito** to whet one's appetite.

su *prep* - 1. *(stato in luogo)* on ; **le chiavi sono sul tavolo** the keys are on the desk ; **a 2 000 metri sul livello del mare** at 2, 000 metres above sea level ; **una casa sul mare** a house by the sea.
- 2. *(moto a luogo)* on, onto ; **venite sulla terrazza** come onto the terrace.
- 3. *(argomento)* about, on ; **un libro sulla vita di Napoleone** a book about Napoleon's life.
- 4. *(tempo)* around ; **vengo sul tardo pomeriggio** I'll come in the late afternoon ; **sul momento** at that moment ; **sul presto** fairly early.
- 5. *(prezzo e misura)* about ; **costerà sui 200 euro** it will cost about 200 euros ; **peserà sui tre chili** he weighs about three kilos ; **un uomo sulla quarantina** a man about forty years old.
- 6. *(modo)* : **facciamo dolci solo ~ ordinazione** we only make cakes to order ; **~ appuntamento** by appointment ; **vestito ~ misura** made-to-measure suit ; **parlare sul serio** to be serious ; **nove volte ~ dieci** nine times out of ten.
◆ *avv* - 1. *(in alto)* up ; *(al piano di sopra)* upstairs ; **in ~** *(verso l'alto)* up(wards) ; *(in poi)* onwards ; **dai 18 anni in ~** from the age of 18 onwards.
- 2. *(per esortare)* come on ; **~, sbrigatevi!** come on, hurry up! ; **~ con la vita!** cheer up!

sub *smf inv* diver.

subacqueo, a *agg* underwater. ◆ *sm, f* diver.

subbuglio *sm* turmoil ; **essere in ~** to be in a turmoil.

subdolo, a *agg* sly.

subentrare *vi* : **~ a qn** to take sb's place.

subire *vt (ingiustizia, conseguenze)* to suffer ; *(operazione)* to undergo ; **~ un torto** to be wronged.

subissare *vt* : **~ qn di qc** to shower sb with sthg.

subito *avv (immediatamente)* straightaway, immediately, at once ; **torno ~** I'll be right back.

sublime *agg* sublime.

subordinato, a *agg* : **~ a** *(dipendente da)* dependent on.

suburbano, a *agg* suburban.

succedere *vi (accadere)* to happen ; **~ a qn** *(subentrare)* to succeed sb ; **che cos'è successo?** what happened? ❑ **succedersi** *vr* to follow one another.

successivamente *avv* afterwards.

successivo, a *agg* following.

successo, a *pp* → **succedere**. ◆ *sm* success ; **di ~** successful.

successore *sm* successor.

succhiare *vt* to suck.

succhiotto *sm* dummy.

succinto, a *agg (conciso)* succinct ; *(abito)* scanty.

succo, chi *sm* juice ; **~ di frutta** fruit juice ; **~ di pomodoro** tomato juice.

sud *sm* south. ◆ *agg inv* south ; **a ~ (di qc)** south (of sthg) ; **nel ~** in the south.

Sudafrica *sm* : **il ~** South Africa.

Sudamerica *sm* : **il ~** South America.

sudare *vi* to sweat.

suddetto, a *agg* abovementioned.

suddividere *vt* to subdivide.

sudest *sm* southeast.

sudicio, a, ci, ce o **cie** *agg* dirty.

sudore *sm* sweat.

sudovest *sm* southwest.

sue → **suo**.

sufficiente *agg (che basta)* enough, sufficient ; *(tono, atteggiamento)* arrogant. ◆ *sm* SCOL pass.

sufficienza *sf* : **a ~** enough.

suffragio *sm (voto)* vote ; **~ universale** universal suffrage.

suggerimento *sm* suggestion.

suggerire *vt (consigliare)* to suggest ; *(risposta)* to tell.

suggestionare *vt* to influence.

suggestivo, a *agg* evocative.

sughero *sm* cork.

sugli = **su** + **gli**, **su**.

sugo, ghi *sm (condimento)* sauce ; *(di arrosto)* juices *(pl)* ; *(succo)* juice ; **~ di pomodoro** tomato sauce.

sui = **su** + **i**, **su**.

suicidarsi *vr* to commit suicide.

suicidio *sm* suicide.

suino, a *agg* pork *(dav s)*. ◆ *sm* pig.

sul = **su** + **il**, **su**.

sull' = **su** + **l'**, **su**.

sulla = **su** + **la**, **su**.

sulle = **su** + **le**, **su**.

sullo = su + lo, su.

suo (*f* sua, *mpl* suoi, *fpl* sue) *agg (di lui)* his ; *(di lei)* her ; *(di esso, essa)* its ; *(forma di cortesia)* your ; *(proprio)* one's.
◆ *pron (di lui)* his ; *(di lei)* hers ; *(di esso, essa)* its ; *(forma di cortesia)* yours ; *(proprio)* one's ; **i suoi** *(di lui)* his family ; *(di lei)* her family.

suocero, a *sm, f* father-in-law (*f* mother-in-law). ❑ **suoceri** *smpl* in-laws.

suoi → suo.

suola *sf* sole.

suolo *sm (terra)* ground ; *(terreno)* soil.

suonare *vt (strumento)* to play ; *(campanello)* to ring ; *(clacson)* to sound ; *(allarme)* to set off ; *(ore)* to strike. ◆ *vi (musicista)* to play ; *(telefono, campana)* to ring ; *(allarme, sveglia)* to go off ; *fig (parole)* to sound.

suono *sm* sound.

suora *sf* nun.

super *sf inv* four-star (petrol) *(Br)*, premium *(Am)*.

superare *vt (confine, traguardo, fiume)* to cross ; *(limite)* to exceed ; *(veicolo)* to overtake ; *(esame, concorso, prova)* to pass ; *(ostacolo)* to overcome ; *(essere migliore di)* to beat ; **ha superato la trentina** he is over 30.

superbo, a *agg (arrogante)* haughty ; *(grandioso)* superb.

superficiale *agg* superficial.

superficie, ci *sf* surface ; MAT area.

superfluo, a *agg* superfluous.

superiore *sm, f* superior. ◆ *agg (di sopra)* upper ; *(quantità, numero)* larger, greater ; *(prezzo)* higher ; *(qualità)* superior ; **di età ~ ai 26 anni** above 26.

superlativo *sm* superlative.

supermercato *sm* supermarket.

superstrada *sf* ≃ (toll-free) motorway *(Br)*, ≃ (toll-free) expressway *(Am)*.

suppergiù *avv* more or less.

supplementare *agg* extra.

supplemento *sm* supplement ; *(di prezzo)* extra charge ; **~ rapido** additional charge for fast train.

supplente *smf* SCOL supply teacher.

supporre *vt* to suppose.

supposta *sf* suppository.

supposto, a *pp* → supporre.

surriscaldare *vt* to overheat.

suscitare *vt* to arouse.

susina *sf* plum.

susseguire *vt* to follow. ❑ **susseguirsi** *vr* to follow one another.

sussidio *sm* subsidy.

sussulto *sm (sobbalzo)* start.

sussurrare *vt* to whisper.

svagarsi *vr (divertirsi)* to enjoy o.s. ; *(distrarsi)* to take one's mind off things.

svago, ghi *sm (divertimento)* fun ; *(passatempo)* pastime.

svaligiare *vt* to burgle.

svalutare *vt* to devalue.

svanire *vi* to disappear, to vanish.

svantaggio *sm (aspetto negativo)* disadvantage ; **essere in ~** SPORT to be behind.

svariato, a *agg (vario)* varied ; *(numeroso)* various.
svedese *agg* & *sm* Swedish. ◆ *smf* Swede.
sveglia *sf (orologio)* alarm clock ; **la ~ è alle sei** we have to get up at six.
svegliare *vt* to wake (up). ❑ **svegliarsi** *vr* to wake up.
sveglio, a *agg (desto)* awake ; *(intelligente)* smart.
svelare *vt* to reveal.
svelto, a *agg* quick ; **alla svelta** quickly.
svendita *sf* sale.
svenire *vi* to faint.
sventare *vt* to foil.
sventolare *vt* to wave. ◆ *vi* to flutter.
sventura *sf (sfortuna)* bad luck, misfortune ; *(disgrazia)* disaster.
svestire *vt* to undress. ❑ **svestirsi** *vr* to get undressed.
Svezia *sf*: **la ~** Sweden.
sviare *vt* to distract ; **~ il discorso** to change the subject.
svignarsela *vr fam* to sneak off.
sviluppare *vt* to develop. ❑ **svilupparsi** *vr (ragazzo)* to grow ; *(industria, attività)* to expand, to grow ; *(incendio, infezione)* to spread.
sviluppo *sm* development ; **età dello ~** puberty.
svincolo *sm (stradale)* motorway junction.
svitare *vt* to unscrew.
Svizzera *sf*: **la ~** Switzerland.
svizzero, a *agg* & *sm, f* Swiss.
svogliato, a *agg* listless.
svolgere *vt (attività, lavoro)* to carry out ; *(srotolare)* to unroll, to unwind ; *(tema)* to write. ❑ **svolgersi** *vr (fatto, film)* to take place ; *(srotolarsi)* to unwind.
svolta *sf* turn ; *(mutamento)* turning point.
svoltare *vi* to turn ; **~ a sinistra** to turn left.
svolto, a *pp* → **svolgere**.
svuotare *vt* to empty.

T

T *(abbr di tabaccheria) sign for Tobacconist's shop.*
tabaccaio, a *sm, f* tobacconist.
tabaccheria *sf* tobacconist's.
tabacco, chi *sm* tobacco.
TAC *sm inv (abbr di Tomografia Assiale Computerizzata)* CAT.
tabella *sf (cartellone)* board ; *(prospetto)* table ; **~ oraria** timetable.
tabellone *sm (con orari)* timetable (board) ; *(per affissioni)* billboard.
tabù *sm inv* taboo.
tacca, che *sf* notch.
taccagno, a *agg* mean.
tacchino *sm* turkey.
tacciare *vt*: **~ qn di qc** to accuse sb of sthg.
tacco, chi *sm* heel ; **tacchi a spillo** stilettos.
taccuino *sm* notebook.
tacere *vi* to be quiet. ◆ *vt* to keep quiet about.

taciturno, a *agg* taciturn.
tafano *sm* horsefly.
tafferuglio *sm* brawl.
taglia *sf (misura)* size ; *(corporatura)* build ; ~ **unica** one size.
tagliacarte *sm inv* paper knife.
taglialegna *sm inv* woodcutter.
tagliando *sm* coupon.
tagliare *vt* to cut ; *(affettare)* to slice ; *(carne)* to carve ; *(legna)* to chop ; *(recidere)* to cut off ; *(ritagliare)* to cut out ; *(intersecare)* to cut across ; *(vino)* to mix ; ~ **corto** to cut short ; ~ **la strada a qn** to cut in front of sb ; **tagliarsi i capelli** to have one's hair cut. ❑ **tagliarsi** *vr* to cut o.s.
tagliatelle *sfpl* tagliatelle *(sg)*.
tagliaunghie *sm inv* nail clippers *(pl)*.
tagliente *agg* sharp.
tagliere *sm* chopping board.
taglio *sm* cut ; *(di stoffa)* length ; *(parte tagliente)* edge ; ~ **cesareo** *MED* caesarean section ; **banconote di piccolo/grosso** ~ small/large denomination bank notes.
tagliuzzare *vt* to cut into small pieces.
tailleur [ta'jœr] *sm inv* suit *(for women)*.
Taiwan *sm* : **il** ~ Taiwan.
talco *sm* talcum powder.

☞

tale *agg dimostrativo* - 1. *(di questo tipo)* such ; **non ammetto tali atteggiamenti** I won't allow such behaviour.
- 2. *(così grande)* : **mi hai fatto una** ~ **paura!** you gave me such a fright! ; **è un** ~ **disordinato!** he's so untidy! ; **fa un** ~ **freddo!** it's so cold! ; **è di una gentilezza** ~ **che non si può dirgli di no** he's so nice (that) you can't say no to him ; **fa un rumore** ~ **da farti venire il mal di testa** it makes so much noise (that) it gives you a headache.
- 3. *(in paragoni)* : ~ ... ~ like ... like ; ~ **madre** ~ **figlia** like mother like daughter ; ~ **quale** just like ; **è** ~ **quale lo ricordavo** he's just like I remembered.
◆ *agg indefinito (non precisato)* : **ti cerca un tal signor Marchi** someone called Mr Marchi is looking for you ; **il giorno** ~ **all'ora** ~ on such and such a day at such and such a time.
◆ *pron indefinito (persona non precisata)* : **un** ~ **mi ha chiesto di te** some man asked me about you ; **quel** ~ that person.

---

taleggio *sm a type of soft cheese from Lombardy.*
talento *sm* talent.
talloncino *sm* counterfoil.
tallone *sm* heel.
talmente *avv* so.
talora *avv* sometimes.
talpa *sf* mole.
talvolta *avv* sometimes.
tamburellare *vi* to drum.
tamburello *sm (strumento)* tambourine ; *(gioco) ball game played with a round bat.*
tamburo *sm* drum.
Tamigi *sm* : **il** ~ the Thames.
tamponamento *sm* collision ; ~ **a catena** pileup.
tamponare *vt AUTO* to bump into ; *(ferita)* to plug.

tampone *sm MED* wad ; *(assorbente interno)* tampon.
tana *sf* den.
tandem *sm inv* tandem.
tanfo *sm* stench.
tanga *sm inv* tanga.
tangente *sf MAT* tangent ; *(quota)* share.
tangenziale *sf* bypass.
tango, ghi *sm* tango.
tanica, che *sf (recipiente)* (jerry) can.
tantino : un tantino *avv* a little, a bit.

tanto, a *agg* - 1. *(in grande quantità)* a lot of, much ; *(così tanto)* such a lot of, so much ; **abbiamo ancora ~ tempo** we've still got a lot of time ; **lo conosco da ~ tempo** I've known him for a long time.
- 2. *(in numero elevato)* : **tanti, tante** a lot of , many ; *(così tanti)* such a lot of, so many ; **ho tanti amici** I've got a lot of o many friends ; **tanti auguri!** all the best! ; *(di compleanno)* happy birthday!
- 3. *(in paragoni)* : **~ ... quanto** *(quantità)* as much ... as ; *(numero)* as many ... as ; **non ho tanta immaginazione quanta ne hai tu** I haven't got as much imagination as you ; **ha tanti fratelli quante sorelle** he's got as many brothers as sisters.
◆ *pron* - 1. *(una grande quantità)* a lot, much ; *(così tanto)* such a lot, so much ; **mi piace il cioccolato e ne mangio ~** I like chocolate and eat a lot of it ; **c'è ~ da fare** there's a lot o plenty to do.
- 2. *(un grande numero)* : **tanti, tante** many , a lot ; *(così tanti)* so many, such a lot ; **è una ragazza come tante** she's just an ordinary girl ; **l'hanno visto in tanti** many people saw it.
- 3. *(una quantità indeterminata)* : **di questi soldi tanti sono per la casa, tanti per le tue spese** so much of this money is for the house and so much for your expenses ; **pago un ~ al mese** I pay so much per month.
- 4. *(in paragoni)* : **~ quanto** as much as ; **tanti quanti** as many as.
- 5. *(in espressioni)* : **~ vale che tu stia a casa** you may as well stay at home ; **di ~ in ~** from time to time.
◆ *avv* - 1. *(molto)* very ; **ti ringrazio ~** thank you very much ; **non ~** *(poco)* not much ; **~ meglio!** so much the better!
- 2. *(così)* so ; **è ~ sciocco da crederci** he's silly enough to believe it ; **è ~ grasso che non ci passa** he's so fat that he can't get through ; **non pensavo piovesse ~** I didn't think it rained so much.
- 3. *(in paragoni)* : **~ ... quanto** as ... as ; **non studia ~ quanto potrebbe** he doesn't study as much as he could.
- 4. *(soltanto)* : **~ per divertirsi/parlare** just for enjoyment/for the sake of talking ; **~ per cambiare** just for a change ; **una volta ~** for once.
◆ *cong* after all.

tappa *sf (fermata)* stop ; *(parte di tragitto, nel ciclismo)* stage.
tappare *vt (buco, falla)* to plug ; *(bottiglia)* to cork ; **tapparsi le orecchie** to turn a deaf ear.
tapparella *sf* store.
tappeto *sm (da pavimento)*

carpet ; *(più piccolo)* rug ; **mandare qn al ~** *SPORT* to floor sb.

tappezzare *vt (pareti)* to paper ; *(poltrona)* to cover.

tappezzeria *sf (tessuto)* soft furnishings *(pl)* ; *(carta da parati)* wallpaper.

tappo *sm (di plastica, metallo)* top ; *(di sughero)* cork ; *fam (spreg : persona bassa)* shorty.

taralli *smpl ring-shaped biscuits flavoured with aniseed and pepper (a speciality of southern Italy)*.

tarantella *sf* tarantella *(a folk dance from the South of Italy)*.

tarantola *sf* tarantula.

tarchiato, a *agg* stocky.

tardare *vi (arrivare tardi)* to be late. ◆ *vt (ritardare)* to delay ; **~ a fare qc** to be late in doing sthg.

tardi *avv* late ; **fare ~** to be late ; **più ~** later ; **al più ~** at the latest ; **sul ~** late in the day.

targa, ghe *sf (di auto)* number-plate ; *(con indicazione)* plate.

targhetta *sf (su campanello)* nameplate ; *(piccola targa)* tag.

tariffa *sf* rate ; *(di trasporti)* fare ; **~ ridotta** reduced fare ; **~ unica** flat rate.

tarlo *sm* woodworm.

tarma *sf* moth.

tarocchi *smpl* tarot cards.

tartagliare *vi* to stammer, to stutter.

tartaro *sm* tartar.

tartaruga, ghe *sf (di terra)* tortoise ; *(di mare)* turtle ; *(materiale)* tortoiseshell.

tartina *sf* canapé.

tartufo *sm (fungo)* truffle ; *(gelato) type of chocolate ice cream*.

tasca, sche *sf (di giacca, pantaloni)* pocket.

tascabile *agg* pocket *(dav s)*. ◆ *sm* paperback.

taschino *sm* breast pocket.

tassa *sf (imposta)* tax ; *(per servizio)* fee ; **~ di iscrizione** membership fee.

tassametro *sm* taximeter.

tassare *vt* to tax.

tassativo, a *agg* peremptory.

tassello *sm* plug.

tassì = **taxi**.

tassista, i, e *smf* taxi driver.

tasso *sm (indice)* rate ; *(percentuale)* percentage ; *(animale)* badger ; **~ di cambio** exchange rate.

tastare *vt (polso)* to take ; **~ il terreno** *fig* to see how the land lies.

tastiera *sf* keyboard.

tasto *sm (di pianoforte, computer)* key ; *(di TV, radio)* button.

tastoni *avv* : **procedere (a) ~** to feel one's way.

tattico, a, ci, che *agg* tactical.

tatto *sm (senso)* touch ; *fig (accortezza)* tact.

tatuaggio *sm* tattoo.

tatuare *vt* to tattoo.

tavola *sf MAT (mobile)* table ; *(asse)* plank ; **mettersi o andare a ~** to sit down to eat ; **~ calda** snack bar.

tavoletta *sf* bar.

tavolino *sm (da salotto)* small table ; *(di bar)* table ; *(scrivania)* writing desk.

tavolo *sm* table.

taxi *sm inv* taxi.

tazza *sf* cup ; *(del water)* toilet bowl ; **una ~ di caffè** a cup of coffee.

tazzina *sf* coffee cup.

T.C.I. *(abbr di Touring Club Italiano)* ≃ AA, ≃ RAC.

te *pron* you → **ti**.

tè *sm inv* tea.

teatrale *agg* theatrical.

teatrino *sm* puppet theatre.

teatro *sm* theatre ; **~ tenda** *marquee used for public performances.*

tecnica, che *sf* technique ; *(tecnologia)* technology → **tecnico**.

tecnico, a, ci, che *agg* technical. ◆ *sm, f* technician.

tecno *agg* techno. ◆ *sf* techno.

tecnologia *sf* technology.

tecnologico, a, ci, che *agg* technological.

tedesco, a, schi, sche *agg, sm* & *sf* German.

tegame *sm* pan.

teglia *sf* baking tin.

tegola *sf* tile.

teiera *sf* teapot.

tel. *(abbr di telefono)* tel.

tela *sf (tessuto)* cloth ; *(quadro)* canvas ; **~ cerata** oilcloth.

telaio *sm (per tessere)* loom ; *(di macchina)* chassis ; *(di finestra, letto)* frame.

telecamera *sf* television camera.

telecomando *sm* remote control.

telecronaca, che *sf* television report.

teleferica, che *sf* cableway.

telefilm *sm inv* TV film *(Br)*, TV movie *(Am)*.

telefonare *vi* & *vt* to (tele)phone ; **~ a qn** to (tele)phone sb.

telefonata *sf* (tele)phone call ; **~ a carico (del destinatario)** reverse charge call.

telefonico, a, ci, che *agg* (tele)phone *(dav s)*.

telefonino *sm* mobile phone.

telefonista, i, e *smf* switchboard operator.

telefono *sm* telephone ; **~ cellulare** mobile phone ; **~ pubblico** public phone ; *(cabina)* call box ; **~ a scatti** metered phone ; **~ a scheda (magnetica)** cardphone ; **al ~** on the phone ; **per ~** by phone.

telegiornale *sm* television news *(sg)*.

telegrafare *vt* & *vi* to cable, to telegraph.

telegramma, i *sm* telegram.

teleobiettivo *sm* telephoto lens.

Telepass® *sm inv* motorway toll card.

teleromanzo *sm* serial.

teleschermo *sm* television screen.

telescopio *sm* telescope.

teleselezione *sf* direct dialling.

televideo *sm teletex service on RAI channels.*

televisione *sf* television ; **alla ~** on television.

TELEVISIONE

State television, which is paid for by an annual fee, is broadcast throughout Italy on three channels : RAI 1, RAI 2 and RAI 3. Competition comes from Canale 5, Rete 4 and Italia 1, the three commercial television stations owned by MEDIASET, the powerful private group owned by Silvio Berlusconi, and a multitude of small private channels which are mainly local or regional. There are also private networks that can be viewed only on payment of a subscription (TELE+1 ; TELE +2), which broadcast mostly films and sport.

---

televisịvo, a *agg* television *(dav s)*.

televisọre *sm* television (set) ; **~ a colori** colour television.

tẹlex *sm inv* telex.

tẹlo *sm* cloth.

tẹma, i *sm (argomento, soggetto)* topic, subject ; *SCOL* essay ; *MUS* theme.

temẹre *vt* to fear, to be afraid of. ◆ *vi* to be afraid ; **temo che non venga** I'm afraid he won't come ; **temo di no** I'm afraid not ; **temo di sì** I'm afraid so ; **temo di non farcela** I'm afraid I can't make it. ❑ **temere per** *v + prep* to fear for.

tẹmpera *sf* tempera.

temperamatịte *sm inv* pencil sharpener.

temperamẹnto *sm (carattere)* temperament ; *(carattere forte)* strong character.

temperạto, a *agg (clima, stagione)* temperate.

temperatụra *sf* temperature.

temperịno *sm (coltello)* penknife ; *(temperamatite)* pencil sharpener.

tempẹsta *sf* storm ; **~ di neve** blizzard.

tempestạre *vt* : **~ qn di domande** to bombard sb with questions.

tempestịvo, a *agg* timely.

tempestọso, a *agg* stormy.

tẹmpia *sf* temple *(building)*.

tẹmpio *sm* temple *(ANAT)*.

tẹmpo *sm (cronologico, ritmo)* time ; *(meteorologico)* weather ; *GRAMM* tense ; *(di partita)* half ; *(di film)* part ; **quanto ~ ci vuole?** how long does it take? ; **avere il ~ di** o **per fare qc** to have the time to do sthg ; **fare qc per ~** to do sthg in time ; **perdere ~** to waste time ; **~ di cottura** cooking time ; **~ libero** free time ; **~ fa** some time ago ; **in ~** in time ; **allo stesso ~** at the same time.

temporạle *agg GRAMM* of time. ◆ *sm* (thunder)storm.

temporạneo, a *agg* temporary.

temporeggiạre *vi* to play for time.

tenạce *agg (persona, carattere)* tenacious.

tenạcia *sf* tenacity.

tenạglie *sfpl* pliers.

tẹnda *sf (di finestra)* curtain ; *(da*

campeggio) tent ; ~ **canadese** ridge tent.

tendenza *sf* tendency.

tendere *vt (elastico, muscoli)* to stretch ; *(corda)* to tighten ; *(mano)* to hold out. ❑ **tendere a** *v + prep* : ~ **a qc** *(propendere per)* to be inclined to sthg ; *(essere simile a)* to verge on sthg ; ~ **a fare qc** to tend to do sthg.

tendine *sm* tendon.

tenebre *sfpl* darkness *(sg)*.

tenente *sm* lieutenant.

☞

tenere *vt* - 1. *(reggere)* to hold ; ~ **qc in mano** to hold sthg (in one's hand) ; ~ **qn per mano** to hold sb by the hand.
- 2. *(mantenere)* to keep ; ~ **la finestra aperta** to keep the window open ; ~ **le mani in tasca** to keep one's hands in one's pockets ; ~ **qc a mente** to remember sthg ; ~ **il posto a qn** to keep a seat for sb ; ~ **qn occupato** to keep sb busy ; **tenga pure il resto** keep the change.
- 3. *(promessa, segreto)* to keep.
- 4. *(conferenza, riunione)* to hold ; ~ **un discorso** to make a speech.
- 5. *(non allontanarsi da)* : ~ **la destra/sinistra** to keep right/left ; ~ **la strada** to hold the road.
- 6. *(in espressioni)* : **tieni!** *(dando qc)* here! ; **la lana tiene caldo** wool is warm ; ~ **compagnia a qn** to keep sb company ; ~ **conto di qc** to take sthg into account ; ~ **d'occhio qn** to keep an eye on sb.
◆ *vi (corda, diga)* to hold ; **questa colla non tiene** this glue isn't sticking ; ~ **duro** to hold out.
❑ **tenere a** *v + prep (dare importanza a)* to care about ; ~ **a fare qc** to be keen to do sthg.
❑ **tenere per** *v + prep (fare il tifo per)* to support ; **per che squadra tieni?** which team do you support?
❑ **tenersi** *vr* - 1. *(reggersi)* : **tenersi (a)** to hold on (to) ; **tienti forte!** hold on!.
- 2. *(restare)* : **tieniti pronto** be ready ; **tenersi in disparte** to stand apart ; **tenersi a disposizione di qn** to be at sb's disposal ; **tenersi a distanza** to keep one's distance.
- 3. *(aver luogo)* to be held.

tenerezza *sf* tenderness.

tenero, a *agg (cibo)* tender ; *(materia)* soft.

tenia *sf* tapeworm.

tennis *sm* tennis ; ~ **da tavolo** table tennis.

tennista, i, e *smf* tennis player.

tenore *sm (tono)* tone ; MUS tenor ; ~ **di vita** standard of living.

tensione *sf* tension ; **alta** ~ high voltage.

tentacolo *sm* tentacle.

tentare *vt (sperimentare)* to try ; *(allettare)* to tempt ; ~ **di fare qc** to try o to attempt to do sthg.

tentativo *sm* attempt.

tentazione *sf* temptation.

tentennare *vi (oscillare)* to wobble ; *(esitare)* to hesitate.

tentoni *avv* : **andare (a)** ~ to feel one's way.

tenuta *sf (abbigliamento)* clothes *(pl)* ; *(di liquidi, gas)* capacity ; *(podere)* estate ; **a** ~ **d'aria** airtight ; ~ **di strada** roadholding.

teoria *sf* theory ; **in** ~ in theory.

teoricamente *avv* theoretically.

teorico, a, ci, che *agg* theoretical.

tepore *sm* warmth.

teppista, i, e *smf* hooligan.

tequila [te'kila] *sf inv* tequila.

terapeutico, a, ci, che *agg* therapeutic.

terapia *sf* therapy.

tergicristallo *sm* windscreen wiper.

tergiversare *vi* to avoid the issue.

tergo *sm* : **a ~** overleaf.

terital® *sm* Terylene®.

termale *agg* thermal.

terme *sfpl (stabilimento)* spa *(sg)* ; *(nell'antica Roma)* baths.

TERME

Thermal spas abound in Italy because of its wealth of mineral springs and its temperate climate, especially in central and northern Italy. The best-known are at Abano (Veneto), Salsomaggiore (Emilia Romagna), Chianciano and Montecatini (Toscana), Fiuggi (Lazio) and Ischia (Campania). Most of the Italian spas have rich sources of mineral salts as well as hot springs.

---

termico, a, ci, che *agg (di temperatura)* thermal.

terminal *sm inv* (air) terminal.

terminale *agg* final. ◆ *sm* terminal.

terminare *vt* to finish. ◆ *vi* to end.

termine *sm (fine)* end ; *(scadenza)* deadline ; *(parola)* term ; **portare ○ condurre a ~ qc** to bring sthg to a conclusion ; **a breve/lungo ~** short-/long-term ; **senza mezzi termini** without beating about the bush. ❑ **termini** *smpl* terms.

termite *sf* termite.

termometro *sm* thermometer.

termos = **thermos**.

termosifone *sm* radiator.

termostato *sm* thermostat.

terra *sf (pianeta)* Earth ; *(terraferma, territorio)* land ; *(suolo)* ground ; *(sostanza)* soil ; **~ battuta** SPORT clay ; **a ○ per ~** *(sedere)* on the ground ; *(cadere)* to the ground ; **essere a ~** to feel low ; **essere ~ ~** to be down to earth.

terracotta *sf* terracotta.

terraferma *sf* dry land.

terrapieno *sm* embankment.

terrazza *sf* terrace.

terrazzo *sm (balcone)* balcony ; *(di terreno)* terrace.

terremoto *sm* earthquake.

terreno, a *agg (vita)* earthly ; *(beni)* worldly. ◆ *sm (suolo)* land ; *(appezzamento)* plot of land.

terreo, a *agg* wan.

terrestre *agg (del pianeta)* of the Earth ; *(di terraferma)* land *(dav s)*.

terribile *agg* terrible ; *(irrequieto)* wild.

terrificante *agg* terrifying.

terrina *sf* tureen.

territoriale *agg* territorial.

territorio *sm (nazionale, straniero)* territory ; *(montuoso, desertico)* region.
terrore *sm* terror.
terrorismo *sm* terrorism.
terrorista, i, e *smf* terrorist.
terrorizzare *vt* to terrorize.
terso, a *agg* clear.
terza *sf (marcia)* third gear.
terzetto *sm* trio.
terzino *sm* fullback.
terzo, a *num* third ; **la terza età** old age. ❑ **terzi** *smpl (altri)* others → **sesto.**
terzultimo, a *sm, f* third from last.
tesa *sf* brim.
teschio *sm* skull.
tesi *sf inv* theory ; **~ (di laurea)** thesis.
teso, a *pp* → **tendere.** ◆ *agg (corda)* taut ; *(faccia, situazione)* tense ; *(rapporti)* strained.
tesoreria *sf* treasury.
tesoro *sm (oggetti preziosi, denaro)* treasure ; *(naturale)* resources *(pl)* ; *fam (appellativo)* darling ; **ministro del Tesoro** Chancellor of the Exchequer *(Br)*, Secretary of the Treasury *(Am)*.
tessera *sf* membership card ; **~ magnetica** magnetic card.
tessere *vt* to weave.
tessile *agg* textile *(dav s)*.
tessitura *sf* weaving.
tessuto *sm (stoffa)* material ; *(muscolare, osseo)* tissue.
test *sm inv* test ; **~ di gravidanza** pregnancy test.
testa *sf* head ; **di ~** *(vagone)* front ; **mettersi in ~ di fare qc** to set one's mind on doing sthg ; **dalla ~ ai piedi** from head to foot ; **essere in ~ (a qc)** to be in the lead (in sthg) ; **fare qc di ~ propria** to do sthg off one's own bat ; **montarsi la ~** to become bigheaded ; **perdere la ~** to lose one's head ; **dare alla ~ a qn** to go to sb's head ; **essere fuori di ~** to be out of one's mind ; **fare a ~ o croce** to toss up ; **a ~** each.
testamento *sm* will.
testardo, a *agg* stubborn.
testaroli *smpl broad pasta in a pesto' sauce (a speciality of La Spezia)*.
teste *smf* witness.
testicolo *sm* testicle.
testimone *smf* witness.
testimoniare *vt (il vero, falso)* to testify ; *(provare)* to prove. ◆ *vi* to testify.
testina *sf* head.
testo *sm* text.
testone, a *sm, f* stubborn person.
testuggine *sf* tortoise.
tetano *sm* tetanus.
tetro, a *agg* gloomy.
tetta *sf fam* tit.
tettarella *sf* teat.
tette *sfpl fam* boobs.
tetto *sm* roof ; **i senza ~** the homeless.
tettoia *sf* canopy.
Tevere *sm* : **il ~** the Tiber.
TG *sm inv* TV news *(sg)*.
thermos® *sm inv* Thermos flask®.
thriller *sm inv* thriller.

ti *pron (complemento oggetto)* you ; *(complemento di termine)* (to) you ; *(riflessivo)* yourself.

tibia *sf* tibia.

tic *sm inv (nervoso)* tic ; *(rumore)* tick.

ticchettio *sm* ticking.

ticket *sm inv MED* prescription charge.

tiepido, a *agg* lukewarm.

tifare : **tifare per** *v + prep* to support.

tifo *sm SPORT* : **fare il ~ per** to be a fan of.

tifone *sm* typhoon.

tifoso, a *sm, f* supporter, fan.

tiglio *sm* lime.

tigrato, a *agg* striped.

tigre *sm o f* tiger.

tilt *sm* : **andare in ~** to stop functioning.

timballo *sm* pie.

timbrare *vt* to stamp.

timbro *sm (arnese, marchio)* stamp ; *(di voce)* timbre.

timer ['taimer] *sm inv* timer.

timidezza *sf* shyness.

timido, a *agg (persona, sguardo)* shy, timid ; *(tentativo, accenno)* bashful.

timo *sm* thyme.

timone *sm* rudder.

timore *sm* fear.

timpano *sm* eardrum.

tinello *sm* small dining room.

tingere *vt* to dye ; **tingersi i capelli** to dye one's hair.

tinozza *sf* tub.

tinta *sf (materiale)* paint ; *(colore)* colour ; **farsi la ~** *(dal parrucchiere)* to have one's hair dyed ; **in ~ unita** in one colour.

tintarella *sf fam* suntan.

tintinnare *vi* to tinkle.

tinto, a *pp* → **tingere**. ◆ *agg* dyed.

tintoria *sf* dry cleaner's.

tintura *sf* : **~ di iodio** iodine.

tipa *sf fam (donna)* woman ; *(ragazza)* girl.

tipico, a, ci, che *agg* typical.

tipo *sm (specie)* type, kind ; *(modello)* type ; *fam (individuo)* bloke *(Br)*, guy *(Am)*.

tipografia *sf (stabilimento)* printing works *(sg)*.

tipografo, a *sm, f* printer.

TIR *sm inv (abbr di Transports Internationaux Routiers)* HGV.

tiramisù *sm inv dessert made from sponge soaked in coffee and covered with sweetened cream cheese and cocoa.*

tiranno, a *sm, f* tyrant.

tirare *vt* to pull ; *(lanciare)* to throw ; *(riga, tende)* to draw ; *(sparare)* to fire. ◆ *vi* to be tight ; **tira vento** it's windy ; **~ calci contro qc** to kick sthg ; **~ diritto** to go straight on ; **~ fuori** to pull out ; **~ a indovinare** to guess ; **~ a sorte** to draw lots ; **~ su** to lift ; **tirarsi indietro** *(rinunciare)* to draw back ; **'tirare'** *(su porta)* 'pull'.

tiratore *sm* shot.

tiratura *sf (di giornale)* circulation.

tirchio, a *agg fam* mean.

tiro *sm (d'arma)* shooting ; *SPORT* shot ; *(traino)* draught ; **~ con l'arco**

archery ; **giocare un brutto ~ a qn** to play a nasty trick on sb.

tirocinio *sm* apprenticeship.

tiroide *sf* thyroid.

tirrenico, a, ci, che *agg* Tyrrhenian.

Tirreno *sm* : **il (mar) ~** the Tyrrhenian Sea.

tisana *sf* herb tea.

titolare *smf* owner.

titolo *sm* title ; **~ di studio** academic qualification ; **titoli di credito** instruments of credit.

titubante *agg* hesitant.

tivù *sf inv fam* TV, telly *(Br)*.

tizio, a *sm, f* person.

tizzone *sm* ember.

toast [tɔst] *sm inv* toasted sandwich.

toccare *vt* to touch ; *(tastare)* to feel ; *(argomento)* to touch on ; *(riguardare)* to concern. ◆ *vi* to touch the bottom ; **'vietato ~'** 'do not touch'.

❑ **toccare a** *v + prep (spettare)* to be up to ; *(capitare)* to happen to ; **a chi tocca?** whose turn is it? ; **mi tocca ricomprarlo** I have to buy it back.

tocco, chi *sm* touch.

tofu *sm (formaggio di soia)* tofu.

toga, ghe *sf (di magistrato)* robe.

togliere *vt (rimuovere)* to take off ; *(privare di)* to take away ; *(liberare)* to get out ; **~ qc a qn** to take sthg (away) from sb ; **ciò non toglie che ...** this doesn't mean that ... ; **togliersi gli occhiali** to take one's glasses off ; **~ l'appetito a qn** to put sb off his food.

toilette [twa'lɛt] *sf inv* toilet.

tollerabile *agg* tolerable.

tollerante *agg* tolerant.

tollerare *vt* to tolerate.

tolto, a *pp* → **togliere.**

tomba *sf* grave.

tombino *sm* manhole.

tombola *sf* ≃ bingo.

tonaca, che *sf* habit.

tonalità *sf inv (di colore)* shade ; *MUS* key.

tondo, a *agg (circolare)* round.

tonfo *sm (rumore)* thud ; *(caduta)* fall.

tonico, a, ci, che *agg* & *sm* tonic.

tonificare *vt* to tone up.

tonnellata *sf* ton.

tonno *sm* tuna fish ; **~ in scatola** tinned tuna fish.

tono *sm* tone ; **essere giù di ~** to be under the weather.

tonsille *sfpl* tonsils.

tonto, a *agg* stupid ; **fare il finto ~** to pretend not to understand.

top *sm inv* top.

topaia *sf* dump.

topazio *sm* topaz.

topless : topless *sm inv* : **essere in ~** to be topless.

topo *sm* mouse.

toppa *sf (di stoffa)* patch ; *(di serratura)* keyhole.

torace *sm* thorax, chest.

torbido, a *agg* cloudy.

torcere *vt (panni)* to wring ; *(piegare)* to twist. ❑ **torcersi** *vr* to double up.

torchio *sm* press.

torcia, ce *sf* torch.

torcicollo *sm* stiff neck.

torero *sm* bullfighter.
Torino *sf* Turin.
tormenta *sf* blizzard.
tormentare *vt (procurare fastidio)* to annoy. ❑ **tormentarsi** *vr* to fret.
tormento *sm (angoscia)* torment ; *(fastidio)* nuisance.
tornaconto *sm* advantage.
tornante *sm* hairpin bend.
tornare *vi* to go/come back ; *(ridiventare)* to become again ; *(riuscire giusto)* to be correct ; ~ **utile** to come in handy ; ~ **a casa** to go/ come home.
torneo *sm* tournament.
toro *sm* bull. ❑ **Toro** *sm* Taurus.
torre *sf (edificio)* tower ; *(negli scacchi)* rook ; ~ **di controllo** control tower ; **la ~ di Pisa** the Leaning Tower of Pisa.

LA TORRE DI PISA

The famous bell tower of Pisa cathedral, known as the *Torre Pendente,* (Leaning Tower), stands in the magnificent *Campo dei Miracoli.* The building dates back to the late XIIth century but is now closed to the public. A total of 294 steps lead up the spiral staircase to the bell chamber above. It was from here that Galileo conducted his famous experiments regarding the laws of gravity.

---

torrefazione *sf (negozio) shop where coffee is roasted and sold.*
torrente *sm* torrent.
torrido, a *agg* torrid.
torrione *sm* keep.
torrone *sm* nougat.
torsione *sf* twisting.
torso *sm* torso ; **a ~ nudo** bare-chested.
torsolo *sm* core.
torta *sf (dolce)* cake ; ~ **gelato** ice-cream gâteau ; ~ **di mele** apple tart ; ~ **pasqualina** *puff-pastry tart filled with spinach, ricotta cheese, Parmesan cheese and eggs (a speciality of Genoa)* ; ~ **salata** flan.
tortellini *smpl* tortellini ; ~ **all'emiliana** *'tortellini' filled with pork, ham, Parmesan cheese and spices, generally served in broth.*
tortiera *sf* cake tin.
tortino *sm* pie.
torto, a *pp* → **torcere**. ◆ *sm (ingiustizia)* wrong ; *(colpa)* : **avere ~** to be wrong ; **a ~** wrongly.
tortora *sf* turtledove.
tortuoso, a *agg* winding.
tortura *sf* torture.
torturare *vt* to torture.
tosaerba *sm inv o sf inv* lawn-mower.
tosare *vt (pecora)* to shear ; *(siepe)* to clip.
Toscana *sf* : **la ~** Tuscany.
toscano, a *agg* Tuscan.
tosse *sf* cough.
tossico, a, ci, che *agg* toxic.
tossicomane *smf* drug addict.
tossire *vi* to cough.
tosta *agg f* → **faccia**.
tostapane *sm inv* toaster.
tostare *vt* to toast.
tosto, a *sm, f* toast ; *fam* : **faccia tosta** cheek.
tot *agg inv & pron inv (quantità)* so much ; *(numero)* so many *(pl)*.

totale *agg* & *sm* total ; **in ~** in total.
totalità *sf* : **la ~ di** all of.
totalizzare *vt* to score.
totano *sm* squid.
totip *sm betting game based on horse racing similar to the pools.*
totocalcio *sm* pools *(pl)*.
toupet [tu'pe] *sm inv* toupee.
tournée [tur'ne] *sf inv* tour.
tovaglia *sf* tablecloth.
tovagliolo *sm* napkin.
tozzo, a *agg* squat. ◆ *sm* : **un ~ di pane** a crust of bread.
tra *prep (in mezzo a due)* between ; *(in mezzo a molti)* among(st) ; *(di tempo, distanza)* in ; **tenere qn ~ le braccia** to hold sb in one's arms ; **quale preferisci ~ questi?** which one of these do you like best? ; **detto ~ (di) noi** between me and you ; **~ sé e sé** to oneself.
traballare *vi* to stagger.
trabiccolo *sm fam* car.
traboccare *vi* to overflow.
trabocchetto *sm* trap.
tracannare *vt* to gulp down.
traccia, ce *sf (segno)* mark ; *(indizio)* trace.
tracciare *vt (solco)* to trace ; *(disegnare)* to draw.
tracciato *sm (percorso)* route ; *(grafico)* graph.
trachea *sf* windpipe.
tracolla *sf* shoulder bag ; **a ~** over one's shoulder.
tradimento *sm (slealtà)* treachery ; *(adulterio)* infidelity ; **a ~** by surprise.
tradire *vt* to betray ; *(coniuge)* to be unfaithful to. ❑ **tradirsi** *vr* to give o.s. away.
traditore, trice *sm, f* traitor.
tradizionale *agg* traditional.
tradizione *sf* tradition.
tradotto, a *pp* → **tradurre**.
tradurre *vt* to translate.
traduttore, trice *sm, f* translator.
traduzione *sf* translation.
trafelato, a *agg* breathless.
trafficante *smf (di droga, armi)* dealer.
trafficare *vt* to deal in. ◆ *vi* to busy o.s.
traffico, ci *sm (di veicoli)* traffic ; *(di droga, armi)* dealing.
trafiggere *vt* to pierce.
trafiletto *sm* short article.
trafitto, a *pp* → **trafiggere**.
traforo *sm* tunnel.
tragedia *sf* tragedy.
traghetto *sm* ferry.
tragico, a, ci, che *agg* tragic.
tragitto *sm* journey.
traguardo *sm* finishing line.
traiettoria *sf* trajectory.
trainare *vt (tirare)* to tow.
traino *sm (operazione)* pulling ; *(di auto)* towing.
tralasciare *vt* to leave out.
traliccio *sm (per elettricità)* pylon.
tram *sm inv* tram.
trama *sf* plot.
tramandare *vt* to pass on.
tramare *vt fig (macchinare)* to plot.
trambusto *sm* turmoil.
tramestio *sm* hubbub.

tramezzino *sm* sandwich.
tramite *prep* through.
tramontana *sf* north wind.
tramonto *sm* sunset.
tramortire *vt* to stun.
trampoli *sm (bastoni)* stilts.
trampolino *sm (per tuffi)* springboard, divingboard ; *(sci)* ski jump.
tramutare *vt* : ~ **qn/qc in** to change sb/sthg into. ❑ **tramutarsi in** *vr + prep* to turn into.
trancio *sm* slice.
tranello *sm* trap.
trangugiare *vt* to gulp down.
tranne *prep* except (for) ; ~ **che** unless.
tranquillante *sm* tranquillizer.
tranquillità *sf (stato d'animo)* calm ; *(di luogo)* peacefulness ; *(sicurezza)* peace of mind.
tranquillizzare *vt* to reassure. ❑ **tranquillizzarsi** *vr* to calm down.
tranquillo, a *agg* quiet ; *(non preoccupato)* calm ; **stai ~** don't worry.
transalpino, a *agg* transalpine.
transatlantico, a, ci, che *agg* transatlantic. ◆ *sm* ocean liner.
transatto *pp* → **transigere.**
transazione *sf* transaction.
transenna *sf* barrier.
transigere *vi* : **in fatto di puntualità non transige** she won't stand for people being late.
transistor *sm inv* transistor.
transitabile *agg* passable.
transitare *vi* to pass.
transitivo, a *agg* GRAMM transitive.
transito *sm* transit ; **'divieto di ~'** 'no entry'.
transizione *sf* transition.
trapanare *vt (muro, dente)* to drill.
trapano *sm* drill.
trapassare *vt* to pierce.
trapelare *vi* to leak out.
trapezio *sm (di circo)* trapeze.
trapezista, i, e *smf* trapeze artist.
trapiantare *vt* to transplant.
trapianto *sm* transplant.
trappola *sf* trap.
trapunta *sf* quilt.
trarre *vt* : ~ **in inganno qn** to deceive sb ; ~ **origine da qc** to come from sthg ; ~ **in salvo qn** to rescue sb ; ~ **vantaggio da qc** to gain benefit from sthg.
trasalire *vi* to jump.
trasandato, a *agg* shabby.
trasbordare *vt* to transfer. ◆ *vi* to change ship/plane/train.
trascinare *vt* to drag. ❑ **trascinarsi** *vr (strisciare)* to drag o.s. along ; *(nel tempo)* to drag on.
trascorrere *vt* to spend. ◆ *vi* to pass.
trascorso, a *pp* → **trascorrere.**
trascritto, a *pp* → **trascrivere.**
trascrivere *vt* to transcribe.
trascurabile *agg* negligible.
trascurare *vt (lavoro, persona)* to neglect ; *(dettagli)* to disregard.
trascurato, a *agg* neglected.
trasecolare *vi* to be amazed.
trasferibile *agg (biglietto)* transferable. ◆ *sm* transfer.
trasferimento *sm* transfer.
trasferire *vt (impiegato)* to

transfer ; *(negozio, sede)* to move. ❑ **trasferirsi** *vr* to move.

trasferta *sf (viaggio)* transfer ; *(indennità)* travelling expenses *(pl)* ; SPORT away game.

trasformare *vt* to transform ; ~ qc in qc to turn sthg into sthg ; *(edificio, stanza)* to convert sthg into sthg. ❑ **trasformarsi** *vr* to change completely ; trasformarsi in to turn into.

trasformatore *sm* transformer.

trasformazione *sf* transformation.

trasformista, i, e *smf (artista)* quick-change artist ; *spreg (politica, società) transformist (absorbing different political groups in order to achieve a majority).*

trasfusione *sf* transfusion.

trasgredire *vt* to disobey.

trasgressore *sm* trespasser ; 'i trasgressori saranno puniti' 'trespassers will be prosecuted'.

traslocare *vi* to move.

trasloco, chi *sm (di mobili)* removal ; *(trasferimento)* move.

trasmesso, a *pp* → trasmettere.

trasmettere *vt* RADIO & TV to broadcast ; *(malattia)* to pass on ; *(far pervenire)* to send.

trasmissione *sf (programma)* programme ; TECNOL transmission.

trasparente *agg (acqua)* transparent ; *(vestito)* see-through.

trasparenza *sf* transparency.

trasparire *vi (essere visibile)* to shine through.

traspirazione *sf* perspiration.

trasportare *vt* to transport.

trasporto *sm* transport.

trastullarsi *vr (divertirsi)* to amuse o.s. ; *(perdere tempo)* to waste time.

trasversale *agg (obliquo)* cross *(dav s)* ; *(via)* side *(dav s)*.

trattamento *sm* treatment.

trattare *vt (persona)* to treat ; *(argomento)* to discuss ; *(negoziare)* to negotiate ; *(commerciare)* to deal in. ❑ **trattare di** *v + prep* to deal with. ❑ **trattarsi** *vr* : di cosa si tratta? what is it about?

trattative *sfpl* negotiations.

trattato *sm (patto)* treaty ; *(testo)* treatise.

trattenere *vt (far rimanere)* to detain ; *(lacrime, risa)* to hold back ; *(somma)* to deduct ; ~ qn dal fare qc to stop sb doing sthg. ❑ **trattenersi** *vr* to stay ; quanto si trattiene? how long are you staying? ; trattenersi dal fare qc to stop o.s. doing sthg.

trattenuta *sf* deduction.

trattino *sm (tra parole)* hyphen ; *(per discorso diretto)* dash.

tratto, a *pp* → trarre. ◆ *sm (di penna)* stroke ; *(di strada, mare)* stretch ; ad un ~, d'un ~ suddenly. ❑ **tratti** *smpl* features.

trattore *sm* tractor.

trattoria *sf restaurant specializing in local cuisine.*

TRATTORIA

In the past the term *trattoria* was used to describe an inexpensive family-run restaurant, but today trattorie can be very expensive.

They serve traditional Italian food typical of the region in rustic-looking but often upmarket surroundings.

---

trauma, i *sm (shock)* shock ; *MED* trauma.
traumatizzare *vt (perturbare)* to shock ; *MED* to traumatize.
travagliato, a *agg* troubled.
travaglio *sm* labour.
travasare *vt* to decant.
trave *sf* beam.
traveggole *sfpl* : **avere le ~** to be seeing things.
traveller's cheque ['traveler'tʃɛk] *sm inv* traveller's cheque.
traversa *sf (via)* side street ; *SPORT* crossbar.
traversare *vt* to cross.
traversata *sf (marittima)* crossing ; *(aerea)* flight.
traverso, a *agg* side *(dav s)*. ◆ *avv* : **di ~** crosswise.
travestimento *sm* disguise.
travestire *vt* to dress up. ❑ **travestirsi da** *vr + prep* to dress up as.
travestito, a *sm (mascherato)* *someone in disguise* ; *(omosessuale)* travestite ; **~ da** disguised as.
travisare *vt* to misinterpret.
travolgente *agg (impetuoso)* overpowering ; *fig (irresistibile)* overwhelming.
travolgere *vt* to sweep away.
travolto, a *pp* → **travolgere**.
tre *num* three → **sei**.
treccia, ce *sf* plait.
trecento *num* three hundred → **sei**. ❑ **Trecento** *sm* : **il ~** the fourteenth century.
tredicesima *sf* Christmas bonus.
tredicesimo, a *num* thirteenth → **sesto**.
tredici *num* thirteen → **sei**.
tregua *sf (armistizio)* truce ; *(sosta)* rest.
trekking *sm inv* trekking.
tremare *vi* : **~ (di)** *(paura)* to shake ○ tremble (with) ; *(freddo)* to shiver ○ tremble (with).
tremarella *sf fam* shivers *(pl)*.
tremendo, a *agg* terrible, awful.
trementina *sf* turpentine.
tremila *num* three thousand → **sei**.
Tremiti *sfpl* : **le (isole) ~** the Tremiti Islands.
tremito *sm* shudder.
trenino *sm* toy train.
treno *sm* train ; **~ diretto** fast train ; **~ espresso** express train ; **~ intercity** Intercity train® ; **~ interregionale** long-distance train ; **~ merci** goods train *(Br)*, freight train *(Am)* ; **~ regionale** local train ; **'treni in arrivo'** 'arrivals' ; **'treni in partenza'** 'departures'.
trenta *num* thirty → **sei**.
trentesimo, a *num* thirtieth → **sesto**.
trentina *sf* : **una ~ (di)** about thirty ; **essere sulla ~** to be in one's thirties.
Trentino *sm* : **il ~-Alto Adige** Trentino-Alto Adige.
tresca, sche *sf* intrigue.
triangolare *agg* triangular.
triangolo *sm* triangle.
tribolare *vi* to suffer.

tribù *sf inv* tribe.
tribuna *sf* stand.
tribunale *sm* court.
tributo *sm* tax.
tricheco, chi *sm* walrus.
triciclo *sm* tricycle.
tricolore *agg* three-coloured.
tridimensionale *agg* three-dimensional.
trielina *sf* trichloethylene.
triennio *sm* three-year period.
Trieste *sf* Trieste.
trifoglio *sm* clover.
trifolato, a *agg (verdura, carne) cooked in oil, garlic and parsley.*
triglia *sf* red mullet.
trimestre *sm (tre mesi)* quarter ; SCOL term.
trina *sf* lace.
trincea *sf* trench.
trinciapollo *sm inv* poultry shears *(pl)*.
trio *sm* trio.
trionfale *agg* triumphal.
trionfare *vi (vincere)* to triumph.
trionfo *sm* triumph.
triplicare *vt* to triple.
triplice *agg* triple.
triplo, a *agg* triple. ◆ *sm* : **il ~** three times as much.
trippa *sf* tripe.
tris *sm inv* three.
triste *agg* sad ; *(luogo)* gloomy.
tristezza *sf (afflizione)* sadness ; *(squallore)* dreariness.
tritacarne *sm inv* mincer *(Br)*, grinder *(Am)*.
tritaghiaccio *sm inv* ice crusher.
tritare *vt* to chop ; *(carne)* to mince *(Br)*, to grind *(Am)*.
trito, a *agg* chopped. ◆ *sm* chopped ingredients *(pl)* ; **~ e ritrito** *fig* trite.
triturare *vt* to mince *(Br)*, to grind *(Am)*.
trivellare *vt* to drill.
triviale *agg* crude.
trofeo *sm* trophy.
tromba *sf* trumpet ; **~ d'aria** whirlwind ; **~ delle scale** stairwell.
trombone *sm* trombone.
troncare *vt* to cut off.
tronco, chi *sm* trunk.
trono *sm* throne.
tropicale *agg* tropical.
tropico *sm* tropic ; **i tropici** the tropics.

☞

troppo, a *agg* - 1. *(in quantità eccessiva)* too much ; **c'è troppa acqua** there's too much water.
- 2. *(in numero eccessivo)* : **troppi, troppe** too many ; **ho mangiato troppi biscotti** I've eaten too many biscuits.
◆ *pron* - 1. *(una quantità eccessiva)* too much ; **ho poco tempo libero, tu ~** I have little free time, you have too much.
- 2. *(un numero eccessivo)* : **troppi** too many ; **non voglio altri problemi, ne ho fin troppi** I don't want any more problems, I've got too many already ; **lo sanno in troppi** too many people know.
◆ *avv* - 1. *(in misura eccessiva)* too ; **sei ~ stanco** you are too tired ; **parla ~ velocemente** he speaks too quickly ; **spendo ~** I spend too

much ; **ho bevuto un bicchiere di ~** I've had one drink too many; **essere di ~** to be in the way.
- 2. *(molto)* : **non mi sento ~ bene** I'm not feeling too good.

---

trota *sf* trout.
trottare *vi* to trot.
trotto *sm* trot.
trottola *sf* spinning top.
troupe [trup] *sf inv* troupe.
trovare *vt* to find ; *(per caso)* to come across ; **andare a ~ qn** to go and see sb. ❑ **trovarsi** *vr (essere, stare)* to be ; *(incontrarsi)* to meet.
trovata *sf* good idea.
truccare *vt (attore)* to make up ; *(motore)* to soup up ; *(risultato, partita)* to fix. ❑ **truccarsi** *vr* to make o.s. up.
trucco, chi *sm (artificio, inganno)* trick ; *(cosmetico)* make-up ; *(operazione)* making-up.
truce *agg* fierce.
trucidare *vt* to slaughter.
truciolo *sm* shaving.
truffa *sf* fraud.
truffare *vt* to swindle.
truffatore, trice *sm, f* swindler.
truppa *sf* troop.
tu *pron* you. ◆ *sm* : **a ~ per ~** face to face ; **~ stesso** you yourself ; **se lo dici ~!** if you say so!
tua → **tuo.**
tubare *vi* to coo.
tubatura *sf* piping, pipes *(pl)*.
tubercolosi *sf* tuberculosis.
tubero *sm* tuber.
tubetto *sm* tube.
tubo *sm* pipe ; **~ di scappamento** exhaust (pipe).
tue → **tuo.**
tuffare : tuffare *vt (immergere)* to dive. ❑ **tuffarsi** *vr (immergersi)* to immerse oneself ; *(gettarsi giù)* to dive.
tuffarsi *vr (in acqua)* to dive.
tuffo *sm* dive.
tugurio *sm* hovel.
tulipano *sm* tulip.
tumbada *sf baked egg custard with crushed macaroons.*
tumore *sm* tumour.
tunica, che *sf* tunic.
Tunisia *sf* : **la ~** Tunisia.
tunnel *sm inv* tunnel.
tuo (*f* **tua**, *mpl* **tuoi**, *fpl* **tue**) *agg* your. ◆ *pron* : **il ~ (la tua)** yours ; **~ padre** your father ; **un ~ amico** a friend of yours ; **questi soldi sono tuoi** this is your money.
tuoi → **tuo.**
tuonare *v impers* : **tuona** it's thundering.
tuono *sm (di lampo)* thunder.
tuorlo *sm* : **~ (d'uovo)** yolk.
turacciolo *sm (di sughero)* cork ; *(di plastica)* top.
turare *vt (buco)* to plug ; *(orecchie, naso)* to block. ❑ **turarsi** *vr* : **~ il naso** to hold one's nose.
turbamento *sm (sconcerto)* anxiety.
turbante *sm (copricapo)* turban.
turbare *vt (sconcertare)* to trouble.
turbolento, a *agg (persona)* boisterous.
turchese *agg & sm* turquoise.
Turchia *sf* : **la ~** Turkey.

turchino, a *agg* deep blue.
turismo *sm* tourism.
turista, i, e *smf* tourist.
turistico, a, ci, che *agg* tourist *(dav s)*.
turno *sm (di lavoro)* shift ; *(di gioco)* turn ; **è il tuo ~** it's your turn ; **fare a ~ (a fare qc)** to take turns (to do sthg) ; **essere di ~** to be on duty.
turpiloquio *sm* dab language.
tuta *sf (da lavoro)* overalls *(pl)* ; *(sportiva)* tracksuit.
tutela *sf* protection.
tutelare *vt* to protect. ❑ **tutelarsi** *vr* to protect o.s.
tutina *sf* romper suit.
tuttavia *cong* yet, nevertheless.

---

tutto, a *agg* - 1. *(la totalità di)* all (of), the whole (of) ; **~ il vino** all the wine ; **~ il giorno** all day, the whole day ; **in tutta Europa** all over Europe ; **tutti i presenti** everyone present ; **tutte le piante** all the plants ; **tutti e cinque** all five of us/you/them ; **tutti e due** both of us/you/them ; **tutta una pizza** a whole pizza.
- 2. *(ogni)* : **tutti, tutte** every ; **telefona tutti i giorni** he phones every day ; **in tutti i casi** in every case ; **tutte le volte che** every time (that).
- 3. *(esclusivamente)* all ; **è tutta colpa tua** it's all your fault ; **è ~ casa e chiesa** he's a family man and a regular churchgoer.
- 4. *(molto)* very ; **è tutta contenta** she's very happy ; **sei ~ sporco** you're all dirty.
◆ *pron* - 1. *(la totalità)* all ; **bevilo ~** drink all of it ; **li ho visti tutti** I've seen all of them ; **in ~** *(nel complesso)* in all ; **in ~ fanno 300 euro** that's 300 euros in all.
- 2. *(la totalità della gente)* : **tutti** everyone , all ; **verremo tutti (quanti)** we will all come, everybody will come ; **tutti voi** all of you.
- 3. *(ogni cosa)* everything ; **mi ha raccontato ~** he told me everything ; **non è ~** that's not everything ; **vende di ~** it sells all sorts of things ; **mangio un po' di ~** I eat a bit of everything ; **in ~ e per ~** completely ; **~ compreso** all in ; **~ esaurito** sold out ; **~ sommato** all things considered.
- 4. *(qualunque cosa)* anything ; **è capace di ~** he's capable of anything.
◆ *avv (interamente)* completely ; **tutt'altro** anything but ; **~ il contrario** quite the opposite ; **del ~** completely ; **tutt'al più** at the most.
◆ *sm* : **il ~** the lot ; **il ~ per ~** everything.

---

tuttora *avv* still.
tutù *sm inv* tutu.
T.V. [ti'vu] *sf inv* TV.
tweed [twid] *sm inv* tweed.

U

ubbidiente *agg* obedient.
ubbidire *vi* to obey.
ubriacare *vt* : **~ qn** to get sb drunk. ❑ **ubriacarsi** *vr* to get drunk.
ubriaco, a, chi, che *agg & sm, f* drunk.

uccello *sm* bird.
uccidere *vt* to kill. ❑ **uccidersi** *vr* to kill o.s.
udienza *sf (colloquio)* audience ; DIR hearing.
udire *vt* to hear.
udito *sm* hearing.
U.E. *sf* (*abbr di Unione Europea*) E.U.
uffa *esclam* tut!
ufficiale *agg* official. ◆ *sm* MIL officer ; *(funzionario)* : ~ **giudiziario** clerk of the court.
ufficialmente *avv* officially.
ufficio *sm* office ; ~ **cambi** bureau de change ; ~ **di collocamento** employment office ; ~ **informazioni** information bureau ; ~ **oggetti smarriti** lost property office *(Br)*, lost-and-found office *(Am)* ; ~ **postale** post office ; ~ **turistico** tourist office.
Uffizi *mpl* : **gli** ~ the Uffizi *(art gallery in Florence)*.
ufo *sm inv* UFO. ❑ **a ufo** *avv* free.
uggioso, a *agg* dull.
uguaglianza *sf* equality ; MAT XXX.
uguagliare *vt* to equal.
uguale *agg (identico)* same ; MAT *(pari)* equal. ◆ *avv* : **costano** ~ they cost the same ; **essere** ~ **a** *(identico)* to be the same as ; *(pari)* to be equal to.
ugualmente *avv (in modo uguale)* equally ; *(lo stesso)* all the same.
ulcera *sf* ulcer.
uliva = **oliva**.
ulivo = **olivo**.
ulteriore *agg* further.
ultimare *vt* to finish.
ultimatum *sm inv* ultimatum.
ultimo, a *agg* last ; *(più recente)* latest. ◆ *sm, f* last (one) ; **da** ~ in the end ; **fino all'** ~ till the end ; **per** ~ last ; **l'** ~ **piano** the top floor.
ultras *smf inv (tifosi di calcio) fanatical football fans*.
ultravioletto, a *agg* ultraviolet.
ululare *vi (lupo, cane)* to howl.
umanità *sf* humanity.
umano, a *agg* human ; *(benevolo)* humane.
Umbria *sf* : **l'**~ Umbria.
umidità *sf (di clima)* humidity ; *(di stanza, muro)* dampness.
umido, a *agg (bagnato)* damp ; *(clima)* humid. ◆ *sm* : **in** ~ stewed.
umile *agg* humble.
umiliante *agg* humiliating.
umiliare *vt* to humiliate. ❑ **umiliarsi** *vr* to humble o.s.
umiliazione *sf* humiliation.
umore *sm* mood ; **essere di buon/cattivo** ~ to be in a good/bad mood.
umorismo *sm* humour.
umoristico, a, ci, che *agg* humorous.
un → **uno**.
un' → **uno**.
una → **uno**.
unanime *agg* unanimous.
unanimità *sf* unanimity ; **all'** ~ unanimously.
uncinetto *sm* crochet hook.
undicesimo, a *num* eleventh → **sesto**.
undici *num* eleven → **sei**.

ungere *vt (padella, teglia)* to grease ; *(macchiare)* to get greasy. ❑ **ungersi** *vr (macchiarsi)* to get covered in grease ; **ungersi di crema solare** to put suntan lotion on.

Ungheria *sf* : **l'** ~ Hungary.

unghia *sf* nail.

unicamente *avv* only.

unico, a, ci, che *agg (singolo)* only ; *(incomparabile)* unique.

unifamiliare *agg* one-family *(dav s)*.

unificare *vt (unire)* to unify ; *(uniformare)* to standardize.

uniformare *vt (adeguare)* to adapt ; *(superficie)* to level. ❑ **uniformarsi a** *vr + prep* to comply with.

uniforme *agg* & *sf* uniform.

unione *sf* union.

unire *vt (mettere insieme)* to join ; *(persone)* to unite ; *(collegare)* to link ; *(mescolare)* to combine. ❑ **unirsi** *vr (associarsi)* to join together ; *(strade)* to meet.

unità *sf inv* unit ; *(unione)* unity ; ~ **di misura** unit of measurement.

unito, a *agg (amici, parenti)* close ; *(da uno scopo)* united ; *(oggetti)* joined.

universale *agg* universal.

università *sf inv* university.

universitario, a *agg* university *(dav s)*.

universo *sm* universe.

uno, a *(dav sm* **un**, *+ consonante o vocale inv, + s+consonante, gn, ps, x, z ; dav sf* **un'**, *+ vocale* **una**, *+ consonante) art indeterminativo* a, an ; ~ **studente** a student ; **una donna** a woman ; **un albero** a tree ; **un'arancia** an orange ; **un giorno ci andrò** one day I'll go ; **ho avuto una fortuna!** it was such a stroke of luck!
◆ *pron* - **1.** *(uno qualunque)* one ; **me ne dai ~?** can you give me one (of them)? ; ~ **dei miei libri/dei migliori** one of my books/of the best ; **l'un l'altro** each other , one another ; **sanno tutto l'** ~ **dell'altro** they know everything about each other ; **l'** ~ **o l'altro** either (of you/ them/us) ; **né l'** ~ **né l'altro** neither (of you/them/us) ; **l'** ~ **e l'altro** both (of you/them/us).
- **2.** *(un tale)* someone, somebody ; **sta parlando con una** he's talking to some woman.
- **3.** *(uso impersonale)* one, you ; **se ~ può** if one ○ you can.
◆ *num* one → **sei**.

---

unto, a *pp* → **ungere**. ◆ *sm* grease.

untuoso, a *agg* greasy.

uomo *(pl* **uomini***) sm* man ; ~ **d'affari** businessman ; **da ~** men's.

uovo *(pl f* **uova***) sm* egg ; ~ **in camicia** poached egg ; ~ **alla coque** boiled egg ; ~ **di Pasqua** Easter egg ; ~ **sodo** hard-boiled egg ; ~ **al tegamino** fried egg ; **uova strapazzate** scrambled eggs.

uragano *sm* hurricane.

urbano, a *agg* urban.

urgente *agg* urgent.

urgenza *sf (necessità)* urgency ; MED emergency ; **essere operato d'** ~ to have emergency surgery.

urgere *vi* to be needed urgently.

urina *sf* urine.

urlare *vi (persona)* to scream; *(animale)* to howl. ◆ *vt* to yell.
urlo *sm (di persona: pl f urla)* scream; *(di animale: pl m urli)* howl.
urna *sf*: **andare alle urne** to go to the polls.
urrà *esclam* hurrah!
URSS *sf*: **l'(ex) ~** the former USSR.
urtare *vt (scontrare)* to bump into; *(irritare)* to annoy. ◆ *vi*: **~ contro** o **in qc** to bump into sthg. ❑ **urtarsi** *vr (scontrarsi)* to collide; *(irritarsi)* to get annoyed.
urto *sm* crash.
USA *smpl*: **gli ~** the USA *(sg)*.
usanza *sf* custom.
usare *vt* to use; **~ fare qc** to be in the habit of doing sthg; **qui usa così** it's the custom here.
usato, a *agg (consumato)* worn; *(di seconda mano)* used. ◆ *sm* second-hand goods *(pl)*.
usciere, a *sm, f* usher.
uscio *sm* door.
uscire *vi* to go out; *(libro, numero)* to come out; **~ di strada** to go off the road.
uscita *sf (porta)* exit, way out; *(al cinema, ristorante)* evening out; *(di autostrada)* junction; *(di libro)* publication; *(di film)* release; COMM expenditure; **ci vediamo all' ~ da scuola** I'll meet you after school; **~ di sicurezza** o **emergenza** emergency exit.
usignolo *sm* nightingale.
uso *sm (impiego)* use; *(abitudine)* custom; **fuori ~** out of use; **'per ~ esterno'** 'for external use'.
USSL *(abbr di Unità Socio-Sanitaria Locale) local health and social centre.*
ustionare *vt* to burn; **ustionarsi un braccio** to burn one's arm.
ustione *sf* burn.
usuale *agg* common.
usufruire : **usufruire di** *v + prep* to make use of.
usuraio, a *sm, f* moneylender.
utensile *sm* tool; **utensili da cucina** kitchen utensils.
utente *smf* user.
utero *sm* uterus.
utile *agg* useful. ◆ *sm* COMM profit; **rendersi ~** to be helpful; **posso esserle ~?** can I help you?
utilità *sf* usefulness; **essere di grande ~** to be of great use.
utilitaria *sf* economy car.
utilizzare *vt* to use, to make use of.
uva *sf* grapes *(pl)*.
uvetta *sf* raisins *(pl)*.

V

va → **andare**.
vacanza *sf* holiday *(Br)*, vacation *(Am)*; **andare/essere in ~** to go/be on holiday *(Br)*, to go/be on vacation *(Am)*.
vacca, che *sf* cow.
vaccinare *vt* to vaccinate.
vaccinazione *sf* vaccination.
vacillare *vi (barcollare)* to sway; *fig (memoria, coraggio)* to be failing.

vado → andare.
vagabondo, a *sm, f (senza dimora fissa)* tramp ; *(fannullone)* loafer.
vagare *vi* to wander.
vagina *sf* vagina.
vagito *sm* wailing.
vaglia *sm inv* money order ; ~ postale postal order.
vagliare *vt (valutare)* to weigh up.
vago, a, ghi, ghe *agg* vague.
vagone *sm* carriage *(Br)*, car *(Am)* ; ~ letto sleeper ; ~ ristorante restaurant car.
vai → andare.
valanga, ghe *sf* avalanche.
Val d'Aosta = Valle d'Aosta.
valere *vi (biglietto)* to be valid ; *(regola)* to apply ; *(avere valore)* to be worth. ◆ *vt (avere un valore di)* to be worth ; *(equivalere a)* to be equal to ; ~ la pena di fare qc to be worth doing sthg ; far ~ qc to assert sthg ; vale a dire that is to say. ❑ **valersi di** *vr + prep* to take advantage of.
valevole *agg* valid.
valico, chi *sm* pass.
validità *sf* validity.
valido, a *agg (valevole)* valid ; *(efficace)* effective ; *(abile)* capable.
valigia, gie ○ **ge** *sf* suitcase ; fare le valigie to pack.
vallata *sf* valley.
valle *sf* valley. ❑ **Valle d'Aosta** *sf* : la Valle d'Aosta Valle d'Aosta.
valore *sm* value ; *(validità)* validity ; *(talento)* merit. ❑ **valori** *smpl (gioielli)* valuables ; *(ideali)* values.
valorizzare *vt* to bring out.
valoroso, a *agg* courageous.
valso, a *pp* → valere.
valuta *sf* currency.
valutare *vt (quadro, persona)* to value ; *(valore, peso)* to estimate.
valutazione *sf (di un bene)* valuation ; *(calcolo sommario)* estimate ; *SCOL* assessment.
valvola *sf (in meccanica)* valve ; *(in elettrotecnica)* fuse.
vampata *sf* blaze.
vampiro *sm* vampire.
vandalismo *sm* vandalism.
vandalo, a *sm, f* vandal.
vanga, ghe *sf* spade.
vangelo *sm* gospel.
vanificare *vt* to nullify.
vaniglia *sf* vanilla.
vanità *sf* vanity.
vanitoso, a *agg* vain.
vanno → andare.
vano, a *agg* vain. ◆ *sm (stanza)* room ; *(apertura)* opening.
vantaggio *sm* advantage ; *(in competizioni)* lead ; trarre ~ da qc to benefit from sthg ; essere in ~ to be in the lead.
vantaggioso, a *agg* favourable.
vantarsi *vr* to boast ; ~ di fare qc to boast about doing sthg.
vanvera *sf* : parlare a ~ to talk nonsense.
vapore *sm* : ~ (acqueo) steam ; cuocere a ~ to steam.
vaporetto *sm* steamer.
vaporizzatore *sm* spray.
vaporoso, a *agg (abito)* floaty.
varare *vt (legge)* to pass ; *(nave)* to launch.

varcare *vt* to cross.
varco, chi *sm* passage.
variabile *agg* variable.
variante *sf* variation.
variare *vt* to vary. ◆ *vi (modificarsi)* to vary; *(essere diverso)* to fluctuate.
variazione *sf* variation.
varice *sf* varicose vein.
varicella *sf* chickenpox.
variegato, a *agg* variegated.
varietà *sf inv* variety. ◆ *sm inv* variety show.
vario, a *agg (svariato)* varied; *(numeroso, diverso)* various.
variopinto, a *agg* multicoloured.
vasca, sche *sf (contenitore)* tank; *(di fontana)* basin; *(nel nuoto)* length; ~ **(da bagno)** bath.
vaschetta *sf* basin.
vasellame *sm* crockery.
vasetto *sm (di yogurt)* pot; *(di marmellata)* jar.
vaso *sm* vase; *(per piante)* pot.
vassoio *sm* tray.
vasto, a *agg (superficie)* vast.
Vaticano *sm*: **il ~** the Vatican.

IL VATICANO

The Vatican City, situated on the right bank of the Tiber in Rome, is the Pope's official residence. The Basilica of Saint Peter, one of the most magnificent Catholic churches in the world, stands here. The Vatican is an independent country, with its own currency and stamps, and the Pope is the head of state. The vast number of works of art concentrated here make it one of Italy's most important cultural centres.

---

ve → **vi**.
vecchiaia *sf* old age.
vecchio, a *agg* old; *(sorpassato)* old-fashioned. ◆ *sm, f* old man (*f* old woman).
vece *sf*: **fare le veci di qn** to take sb's place.
vedere *vt* & *vi* to see; **vedrò di fare qualcosa** I'll see what I can do; **questo non ha niente a che ~ con me** this has nothing to do with me; **non la posso ~** *fig* I can't stand her; **non vedo l'ora di arrivare** I can't wait to get there; **farsi ~ da uno specialista** to see a specialist; **da qui si vede il mare** you can see the sea from there. ❑ **vedersi** *vr (guardarsi)* to see o.s.; *(incontrarsi)* to meet; **ci vediamo!** see you!.
vedovo, a *sm, f* widower (*f* widow).
veduta *sf* view.
vegetale *agg* vegetable *(dav s)*. ◆ *sm* plant.
vegetariano, a *agg* vegetarian.
vegetazione *sf* vegetation.
veglia *sf* wakefulness.
veglione *sm* ball.
veicolo *sm* vehicle; **'veicoli lenti'** 'slow lane'.
vela *sf (tela)* sail; *(sport)* sailing.
velare *vt* to veil.
veleno *sm* poison.
velenoso, a *agg (sostanza)* poisonous.
velina *sf* tissue paper.

velivolo *sm* aircraft.
vellutato, a *agg* velvety.
velluto *sm* velvet; ~ **a coste** cord.
velo *sm (indumento)* veil.
veloce *agg* fast.
velocemente *avv* quickly.
velocità *sf* speed; **' ~ max 15 kmh'** ≃ 'maximum speed 10 kph'.
vena *sf* vein; **non essere in ~ di qc** not to be in the mood for sthg.
vendemmia *sf* grape harvest.
vendemmiare *vi* to harvest the grapes.
vendere *vt* to sell; **'vendesi'** 'for sale'.
vendetta *sf* revenge.
vendicare *vt* to avenge. ❑ **vendicarsi** *vr* to avenge o.s.; **vendicarsi di** to take one's revenge for; **vendicarsi su qn** to take one's revenge on sb.
vendita *sf* sale; **essere in ~** to be on sale; **'in ~ qui'** 'on sale here'.
venditore, trice *sm, f* seller; ~ **ambulante** pedlar.
venerdì *sm inv* Friday → **sabato**.
venereo, a *agg (malattia)* venereal.
Venezia *sf* Venice.
veneziana *sf* venetian blind → **veneziano**.
veneziano, a *agg* & *sm, f* Venetian.
venire *vi* to come; **mi viene da piangere** I feel like crying; **quanto vengono le mele?** how much are the apples?; **~ bene/male** to turn out well/badly; **~ giù** to come down; **~ via** *(persona)* to leave; *(macchia)* to come out; *(etichetta)* to come off; **~ a sapere qc** to learn sthg.
ventata *sf* gust.
ventesimo, a *num* twentieth → **sesto**.
venti *num* twenty → **sei**.
ventilare *vt* to ventilate.
ventilatore *sm* ventilator.
ventina *sf*: **una ~ (di)** about twenty; **essere sulla ~** to be in one's twenties.
vento *sm* wind; **'forte ~ laterale'** 'strong side wind'.
ventosa *sf (di gomma)* suction pad.
ventoso, a *agg* windy.
ventre *sm* stomach.
venturo, a *agg* next.
venuto, a *pp* → **venire**.
veramente *avv* really.
veranda *sf* veranda.
verbale *sm* minutes *(pl)*.
verbo *sm* verb.
verde *agg* green. ◆ *sm (colore)* green; *(vegetazione)* greenery.
verdetto *sm* verdict.
verdura *sf* vegetables *(pl)*.
verduraio, a *sm, f* greengrocer.
vergine *agg* virgin; *(cassetta)* blank. ❑ **Vergine** *sf* Virgo.
vergogna *sf (pentimento, scandalo)* shame; *(timidezza)* shyness; *(imbarazzo)* embarrassment.
vergognarsi *vr*: **~ (di)** *(per disonore)* to be ashamed (of); *(per timidezza)* to be embarrassed (about).
vergognoso, a *agg (scandaloso)* shameful; *(timido)* shy.
verifica, che *sf* check.

verificare *vt* to check. ❑ **verificarsi** *vr* to happen.
verità *sf* truth ; **dire la ~** to tell the truth.
verme *sm* worm.
vermicelli *smpl* vermicelli *(sg)*.
vermut *sm inv* vermouth.
vernice *sf (sostanza)* paint ; *(pelle)* patent leather ; '**~ fresca**' 'wet paint'.
verniciare *vt* to paint.
vero, a *agg (reale)* true ; *(autentico)* real, genuine. ◆ *sm* truth.
verosimile *agg* likely, probable.
verruca, che *sf* wart.
versamento *sm* deposit.
versante *sm* slopes *(pl)*.
versare *vt (in recipiente)* to pour ; *(rovesciare)* to spill ; *(pagare)* to pay ; *(depositare)* to deposit. ❑ **versarsi** *vr* to spill.
versatile *agg* versatile.
versione *sf* version ; *(traduzione)* translation.
verso *sm (di poesia)* line ; *(di animale)* cry ; *(direzione)* direction. ◆ *prep (in direzione di, nei confronti di)* towards ; *(in prossimità di)* near ; *(di tempo, età)* around, about ; **non c'è ~ di convincerlo** there's no way of convincing him ; **fare il ~ a qn** to mimic sb.
vertebra *sf* vertebra.
verticale *agg* & *sf* vertical.
vertice *sm* peak ; *MAT* vertex.
vertigine *sf* dizziness ; **soffrire di vertigini** to be afraid of heights.
vescovo *sm* bishop.
vespa *sf* wasp.
vestaglia *sf* dressing gown.
veste *sf* : **in ~ di** as.
vestiario *sm* wardrobe, clothes *(pl)*.
vestire *vt* & *vi* to dress. ❑ **vestirsi** *vr* to get dressed.
vestito *sm (da uomo)* suit ; *(da donna)* dress. ❑ **vestiti** *smpl (indumenti)* clothes.
Vesuvio *sm* : **il ~** Vesuvius.
veterinario, a *sm, f* vet(erinary surgeon) *(Br)*, veterinarian *(Am)*.
vetrata *sf (di casa)* glass door/window ; *(di chiesa)* stained glass window.
vetrina *sf (di negozio)* shop window.
vetro *sm (materiale)* glass ; *(frammento)* piece of glass ; *(di finestra)* windowpane ; *(di auto)* window.
vetta *sf* top.
vettovaglie *sfpl* supplies.
vettura *sf (automobile)* car ; *(di treno)* carriage *(Br)*, car *(Am)*.
vezzeggiativo *sm* term of endearment.
vezzo *sm* habit.
vi *(diventa* **ve** *se precede lo, la, li, le, ne) pron (complemento oggetto)* you ; *(complemento di termine)* (to) you ; *(riflessivo)* yourselves ; *(reciproco)* each other. ◆ *avv* = **ci** ; **ve li do** I'll give them to you.
via *sf* way ; *(strada)* street, road. ◆ *avv* away. ◆ *prep* via. ◆ *esclam (per scacciare)* go away! ; *(in gara, gioco)* go! ◆ *sm inv* : **dare il ~** *SPORT* to give the starting signal ; **dare il ~ a qc** *(progetto)* to give the green light to sthg ; **~ aerea** *(posta)* by

airmail ; ~ **mare** by sea ; ~ **terra** overland ; **in ~ eccezionale** as an exception ; **per ~ di** *(a causa di)* because of ; **in ~ di guarigione** on the road to recovery ; **una ~ di mezzo** a middle course ; **e così ~** and so on.

viabilità *sf* practicability.

Viacard® *sf inv credit card for motorway tolls.*

viaggiare *vi* to travel.

viaggiatore, trice *sm, f* passenger.

viaggio *sm* travel ; *(tragitto)* journey ; *(gita)* trip ; **buon ~!** have a good trip! ; **essere in ~** to be away ; **fare un ~** to go on a trip ; **~ d'affari** business trip ; **~ di nozze** honeymoon ; **~ organizzato** package tour.

viale *sm (corso)* avenue ; *(in un parco)* path.

viavai *sm* coming and going.

vibrare *vi* to vibrate.

vibrazione *sf* vibration.

vice *smf inv* deputy.

vicenda *sf* event. ❑ **a vicenda** *avv* in turn.

viceversa *avv* vice versa.

vicinanza *sf* proximity ; **nelle vicinanze (di qc)** in the vicinity (of sthg).

vicinato *sm (zona)* neighbourhood ; *(vicini)* neighbours *(pl)*.

vicino, a *agg (nello spazio)* near, nearby ; *(nel tempo)* close at hand. ◆ *sm, f* neighbour. ◆ *avv* nearby. ◆ *prep* : **~ a** *(accanto a)* next to ; *(nei pressi di)* near ; **~ di casa** neighbour ; **da ~** close up.

vicolo *sm* alley ; **~ cieco** blind alley.

video *sm inv (musicale)* video ; *(schermo)* screen.

videocassetta *sf* video(cassette).

videocitofono *sm entryphone with closed circuit TV.*

videogame = **videogioco.**

videogioco, chi *sm* video game.

videoregistratore *sm* video (recorder) *(Br)*, VCR *(Am)*.

Videotel® *sm* ≃ Viewdata®.

vietare *vt* to forbid ; **~ a qn di fare qc** to forbid sb to do sthg ; **~ qc a qn** to forbid sthg to sb.

vietato, a *agg* forbidden ; '**~ l'accesso**' 'no entry' ; '**~ l'accesso ai mezzi non autorizzati**' 'no entry for unauthorized vehicles' ; '**è ~ fare il bagno nelle ore notturne**' 'no swimming at night' ; '**~ fumare**' 'no smoking' ; '**~ ai minori**' 'adults only'.

Vietnam *sm* : **il ~** Vietnam.

vigilare *vt* to watch over.

vigile *agg* watchful. ◆ *smf* : **~ (urbano)** *local police officer who deals mainly with traffic offences* ; **i vigili del fuoco** the fire brigade.

VIGILE URBANO

Some people think that the municipal police only control the traffic, and for many the municipal policeman is synonymous with parking tickets, but that is not the case. The Municipal Police have many other functions, for example relating to the control of businesses (times, prices, advertising posters), buildings (respect for urban laws), the environment and the quality of urban life. Thanks to the constitution of the *Nucleo Assistenza Emarginati*, the Municipal Police also take action where there are social problems (the abandonment of minors, security of travellers' camps, issues connected with immigration).

---

vigilia *sf* eve ; **~ di Natale** Christmas Eve.
vigliacco, a, chi, che *agg* cowardly. ◆ *sm, f* coward.
vigna *sf* vines *(pl)*.
vigore *sm* vigour ; **in ~** *DIR* in force.
vile *agg* cowardly.
villa *sf* villa.
villaggio *sm* village ; **~ turistico** holiday village.
villano, a *agg* rude. ◆ *sm, f* boor.
villeggiatura *sf* holiday *(Br)*, vacation *(Am)*.
villetta *sf* cottage.
Viminale *sm* : **il ~** The Viminal.

IL VIMINALE

The *Viminale*, on the hill of the same name, was inaugurated on 9th July 1925, after being forcefully promoted by Giovanni Giolitti as a symbol of the prestige of executive power, and is now the seat of the Ministry of the Interior. It has a famous library of about 110,000 volumes, the most prestigious being those published in Italy and Europe between 1500 and 1800. The other seats of political power in Italy are the *Quirinale (President of the Republic) ; Palazzo Madama (Senate) ; Palazzo Chigi (Foreign Ministry)*.

---

vimini *smpl* wicker *(sg)*.
vinavil® *sm* glue.
vincere *vt (gioco, partita, battaglia)* to win ; *(avversario)* to beat. ◆ *vi* to win.
vincita *sf (vittoria)* win ; *(premio)* winnings *(pl)*.
vincitore, trice *sm, f* winner.
vincolo *sm (legame)* tie ; *(obbligo)* obligation.
vino *sm* wine ; **~ bianco** white wine ; **~ rosso** red wine.

VINO

Wines are produced in every Italian region, and their names reflect either the area where they are produced (like *Chianti*) or the grape variety they are made from *moscato*. *Vino da tavola* on a label indicates an inexpensive table wine, while DOC (*denominazione d'origine controllata*, DOCG (*denominazione d'origine controllata e garantita*), and VQPRD (*vino di qualità prodotto in regioni delimitate*) all indicate that the wine is of superior quality.

---

vinto, a *pp* → **vincere**. ◆ *agg (partita)* won ; *(concorrente)* beaten ; **darla vinta a qn** to let sb have their way ; **non darsi per ~** not to give up.
viola *agg inv* & *sm inv* purple. ◆ *sf (fiore)* violet.

violare *vt* to violate.
violentare *vt* to rape.
violento, a *agg* violent.
violenza *sf* violence.
violino *sm* violin.
viottolo *sm* track.
vipera *sf* viper.
virare *vi NAUT* to come about ; *(aereo)* to turn.
virgola *sf GRAMM* comma ; *MAT* point.
virgolette *sfpl* quotation marks.
virile *agg* manly.
virtù *sf inv* virtue.
virtuale *agg* virtual.
virus *sm inv* virus.
viscere *sfpl* entrails.
viscido, a *agg* slimy.
viscosa *sf* viscose.
visibile *agg (che si vede)* visible ; *(chiaro)* evident.
visibilità *sf* visibility.
visiera *sf* peak.
visionare *vt* to examine.
visione *sf (vista)* sight ; *(modo di vedere)* view ; *(apparizione)* vision ; **prendere ~ di qc** to look over sthg ; **prima ~** TV premiere.
visita *sf (di amico)* visit ; *(di medico)* examination ; **fare ~ a qn** to pay sb a visit ; **~ medica** medical examination.
visitare *vt* to visit ; *(sog : medico)* to examine.
viso *sm* face.
vispo, a *agg* lively.
vissuto, a *pp* → **vivere**.
vista *sf (facoltà)* (eye)sight ; *(possibilità di vedere)* sight ; *(panorama)* view ; **conoscere qn di ~** to know sb by sight ; **a prima ~** at first sight.
visto, a *pp* → **vedere**. ◆ *sm* visa.
vistoso, a *agg* gaudy.
vita *sf* life ; *ANAT* waist.
vitale *agg* vital.
vitamina *sf* vitamin.
vite *sf (pianta)* vine ; *(utensile)* screw.
vitello *sm (animale)* calf ; *(carne)* veal ; *(pelle)* calfskin ; **~ tonnato** *boiled veal served cold with tuna mayonnaise.*
vittima *sf* victim.
vitto *sm* food ; **~ e alloggio** board and lodging.
vittoria *sf* victory.
viva *esclam* : **~ le vacanze!** hurray for the holidays!
vivace *agg (persona)* lively ; *(colore)* bright.
vivacità *sf* vivacity.
vivaio *sm (di piante)* nursery ; *(di pesci)* hatchery.
vivanda *sf* food.
vivente *agg* → **essere**.
vivere *vi* to live. ◆ *vt (vita)* to live ; *(passare)* to live through.
viveri *smpl* food *(sg)*.
vivido, a *agg (colore)* vivid.
vivo, a *agg (vivente)* alive, living ; *(persona)* lively ; *(colore)* bright ; **dal ~** from life ; **farsi ~ (con qn)** to get in touch (with sb).
viziare *vt* to spoil.
viziato, a *agg (bambino)* spoilt ; *(aria)* stale.
vizio *sm (cattiva abitudine)* bad habit ; *(morale)* vice ; *(difetto)* defect.

V.le *(abbr di viale)* Ave.
vocabolario *sm (dizionario)* dictionary ; *(lessico)* vocabulary.
vocabolo *sm* word.
vocale *agg* vocal. ◆ *sf* vowel.
vocazione *sf (inclinazione)* natural bent.
voce *sf (suono)* voice ; *(diceria)* rumour ; *(di elenco)* entry ; **a bassa/alta ~** in a low/loud voice ; **sotto ~** in a whisper.
voga *sf* : **essere in ~** to be in fashion.
vogatore, trice *sm, f* oarsman (*f* oarswoman). ◆ *sm* rowing machine.
voglia *sf (desiderio)* desire ; *(sulla pelle)* birthmark ; **avere ~ di fare qc** to feel like doing sthg ; **avere ~ di qc** to feel like sthg ; **levarsi la ~ di qc** to satisfy one's desire for sthg ; **contro ~** unwillingly.
voi *pron* you ; **~ stessi** you yourselves.
volano *sm* shuttlecock.
volante *agg* flying. ◆ *sm (di veicolo)* steering wheel. ◆ *sf (polizia)* flying squad.
volantino *sm* leaflet.
volare *vi* to fly.
volata *sf (corsa)* rush.
volontariato *sm (civile)* voluntary service.
volatile *sm* bird.
vol-au-vent [volo'van] *sm inv* vol-au-vent.
volenteroso, a *agg* willing.
volentieri *avv (con piacere)* willingly ; *(come risposta)* with pleasure.

---

volere *vt* - 1. *(desiderare, esigere)* to want ; **cosa vuoi?** what do you want? ; **voglio delle spiegazioni** I want some explanations ; **~ fare qc** to want to do sthg ; **voglio che tu venga** I want you to come ; **cosa volete fare stasera?** what do you want to do tonight? ; **ti vogliono al telefono** you're wanted on the phone ; **come vuoi** as you like ; **vorrei un cappuccino** I'd like a cappuccino ; **vorrei andare** I'd like to go ; **senza volerlo** unintentionally ; **se si vuole accomodare** if you would care to take a seat?
- 2. *(consentire a)* : **se tua madre vuole, ti porto al cinema** if your mother agrees, I'll take you to the cinema ; **vogliamo andare?** shall we go?
- 3. *(soldi)* : **quanto vuole per questo orologio?** how much do you want for this watch?
- 4. *(credere)* to think ; **la leggenda vuole che ...** legend has it that ...
- 5. *(decidersi a)* : **la macchina non vuole partire** the car won't start.
- 6. *(necessitare di)* to need ; **volerci** *(coraggio, materiale)* to need ; *(tempo)* to take ; **ci vuole pazienza** you must be patient ; **ci vogliono ancora dieci minuti per finire** it'll take another ten minutes to finish.
- 7. *(in espressioni)* : **voler bene a qn** *(affetto)* to be fond of sb ; *(amare)* to love sb ; **voler dire** to mean ; **volerne a qn** to have a grudge against sb.
◆ *sm* will, wish ; **contro il ~ di qn** against sb's wishes.

---

volgare *agg* vulgar.
volgere *vt* to turn ; **il tempo volge**

al bello the weather's getting better ; ~ al termine to draw to an end.
volo *sm* flight ; ~ charter charter flight ; ~ di linea scheduled flight ; capire qc al ~ to understand sthg straightaway.
volontà *sf inv* will ; buona ~ goodwill ; a ~ as much as one likes.
volontario, a *agg* voluntary. ◆ *sm, f* volunteer.
volpe *sf* fox.
volt *sm inv* volt.
volta *sf (circostanza)* time ; *(di edificio)* vault ; a sua ~ in his/her turn ; di ~ in ~ from time to time ; una ~ once ; due volte twice ; tre volte three times ; una ~ che once ; una ~ tanto just for once ; uno per ○ alla ~ one at a time ; a volte sometimes.
voltafaccia *sm inv* about-turn.
voltare *vt & vi* to turn ; ~ l'angolo to turn the corner ; ~ pagina to turn over a new leaf. ❑ **voltarsi** *vr* to turn.
voltastomaco *sm* nausea ; dare il ~ a qn to make sb feel sick.
volto, a *pp* → volgere. ◆ *sm* face.
volubile *agg* fickle.
volume *sm* volume.
voluminoso, a *agg* voluminous, bulky.
vomitare *vt & vi* to vomit, to throw up.
vomito *sm* vomit.
vongola *sf* clam.
vorace *agg (animale)* voracious ; *(persona)* greedy.
voragine *sf* abyss.
vortice *sm* whirl.
vostro, a *agg* : il ~ (la vostra) your.
◆ *pron* : il ~ (la vostra) yours ; ~ padre your father ; un ~ amico a friend of yours ; sono vostri questi bagagli? is this your luggage?
votare *vt* to vote on. ◆ *vi* to vote.
votazione *sf (procedimento)* vote ; SCOL marks *(pl)*.
voto *sm* DIR vote ; SCOL marks *(pl)*.
vulcanico, a, ci, che *agg* volcanic.
vulcano *sm* volcano.
vulnerabile *agg* vulnerable.
vuotare *vt* to empty. ❑ **vuotarsi** *vr* to empty.
vuoto, a *agg* empty ; *(pagina)* blank. ◆ *sm (spazio vuoto)* empty space ; *(bottiglia)* empty (bottle) ; *(in fisica)* vacuum ; andare a ~ to fail ; parlare a ~ to waste one's breath.

W

wafer ['vafer] *sm inv* wafer.
Walkman® [wolk'men] *sm inv* Walkman®, personal stereo.
water (closet) ['vater ('kloz)] *sm inv* toilet.
watt [vat] *sm inv* watt.
wc *(abbr di water closet)* WC.
week-end [wi'kend] *sm inv* weekend.
western ['western] *agg inv* : film ~ western.

whisky ['wiski] *sm inv* whisky.
windsurf ['windsərf] *sm inv (tavola)* windsurf board ; *(sport)* windsurfing.
word processor [wərd'proce'sor] *sm inv* INFORM word processor.
würstel ['vurstel] *sm inv* frankfurter.

X

xenofobia *sf* xenophobia.
xilofono *sm* xylophone.

Y

yacht [jɔt] *sm inv* yacht.
yoga *sm* yoga.
yogurt *sm inv* yoghurt.

Z

zabaglione *sm* = **zabaione**.
zabaione *sm cream dessert made from egg yolks whipped with sugar and Marsala.*
zafferano *sm* saffron.
zaino *sm* rucksack.
zampa *sf* paw ; **a quattro zampe** on all fours.
zampillo *sm* spurt.
zampirone *sm* mosquito repellent.
zampone *sm boiled pig's trotter stuffed with minced meat and spices.*
zanna *sf (di elefante)* tusk ; *(di carnivori)* fang.
zanzara *sf* mosquito.
zanzariera *sf* mosquito net.
zappa *sf* hoe.
zappare *vt* to hoe.
zattera *sf* raft.
zavorra *sf* ballast.
zazzera *sf* fringe.
zebra *sf* zebra. ❑ **zebre** *sfpl fam* zebra crossing *(sg) (Br)*, crosswalk *(sg) (Am)*.
zecca, che *sf (insetto)* tick ; *(officina di monete)* mint.
zelante *agg* zealous.
zelo *sm* zeal.
zenzero *sm* ginger.
zeppo, a *agg* crammed.
zeppole *sfpl type of ring doughnut eaten at carnival time in the south of Italy.*
zerbino *sm* doormat.
zero *sm* zero ; SPORT nil ; **sotto ~** subzero.
zigomo *sm* cheekbone.
zigzag *sm inv* zigzag.
zimbello *sm* laughingstock.
zingaro, a *sm, f* gipsy.
zio, a *sm, f* uncle (*f* aunt).
zip *sm inv* zip.
zitella *sf spreg* spinster.
zittire *vt* to hiss, hush.
zitto, a *agg* silent ; **state zitti!** be quiet!.
zoccolo *sm (calzatura)* clog ; *(di cavallo)* hoof.
zodiaco *sm* zodiac.
zolfo *sm* sulphur.

zolla *sf* clod.
zolletta *sf* lump.
zona *sf* area ; ~ **blu** o **verde** *zone where traffic is restricted* ; ~ **disco** parking meter zone ; ~ **industriale** industrial estate ; '~ **militare**' army property ; ~ **pedonale** pedestrian precinct *(Br)*, pedestrian zone *(Am)*.
zonzo : **a zonzo** *avv* : **andare a** ~ to wander about.
zoo *sm inv* zoo.
zoom [dzum] *sm inv* zoom.
zoppicare *vi* to limp.
zoppo, a *agg* lame.
zucca, che *sf* pumpkin.
zuccherato, a *agg* sweetened.
zuccheriera *sf* sugar bowl.
zucchero *sm* sugar ; ~ **filato** candyfloss ; ~ **vanigliato** vanilla sugar ; ~ **a velo** icing sugar *(Br)*, confectioner's sugar *(Am)*.
zuccheroso, a *agg* sugary.
zucchina *sf* courgette ; **zucchine ripiene** *courgettes stuffed with minced meat, breadcrumbs, eggs and spices.*
zucchino = **zucchina**.
zuccone, a *sm, f (sciocco)* blockhead ; *(testardo)* stubborn person.
zuccotto *sm* ice-cream sponge.
zuffa *sf* brawl.
zuppa *sf* soup ; ~ **inglese** ≃ trifle *(Br), dessert made from sponge soaked in liqueur, with custard and chocolate.*
zuppiera *sf* tureen.
zuppo, a *agg* : ~ **(di)** soaked (with).
Zurigo *sf* Zurich.

Verbi Italiani

Key: *pr ind* = presente indicativo, *imperf* = imperfetto, *fut* = futuro, *cond* = condizionale, *pr cong* = presente congiuntivo, *imperat* = imperativo, *ger* = gerundio, *pp* = participio passato

AMARE: *pr ind* amo, ami, ama, amiamo, amate, amano, *imperf* amavo, amavi, amava, amavamo, amavate, amavano, *fut* amerò, amerai, amerà, ameremo, amerete, ameranno, *cond* amerei, ameresti, amerebbe, ameremmo, amereste, amerebbero, *pr cong* ami, ami, ami, amiamo, amiate, amino, *imperat* ama, ami, amate, *ger* amando, *pp* amato

andare: *pr ind* vado, vai, va, andiamo, andate, vanno, *fut* andrò, *cond* andrei, *pr cong* vada, vada, vada, andiamo, andiate, vadano, *imperat* va', vada, andate, *ger* andando, *pp* andato

aprire: *pr ind* apro, *pr cong* apra, *pp* aperto

avere: *pr ind* ho, hai, ha, abbiamo, avete, hanno, *imperf* avevo, *fut* avrò, *cond* avrei, *pr cong* abbia, *imperat* abbi, abbia, abbiate, *ger* avendo, *pp* avuto

bere: *pr ind* bevo, *imperf* bevevo, *fut* berrò, *cond* berrei, *pr cong* beva, *imperat* bevi, beva, bevete, *ger* bevendo, *pp* bevuto

cadere: *fut* cadrò

correre: *pp* corso

cuocere: *pr ind* cuocio, cuoci, cuoce, cuociamo, cuocete, cuociono, *pp* cotto

dare: *pr ind* do, dai, dà, diamo, date, danno, *fut* darò, *pr cong* dia, *imperat* da', dia, date

dire: *pr ind* dico, dici, dice, diciamo, dite, dicono, *imperf* dicevo, *fut* dirò, *pr cong* dica, dica, dica, diciamo, diciate, dicano, *imperat* di', dica, dite, *ger* dicendo, *pp* detto

dovere: *pr ind* devo, devi, deve, dobbiamo, dovete, devono, *fut* dovrò, *cond* dovrei, *pr cong* deva, deva, deva, dobbiamo, dobbiate, devano

essere: *pr ind* sono, sei, è, siamo, siete, sono, *imperf* ero, eri, era, eravamo, eravate, erano, *fut* sarò, *cond* sarei, *pr cong* sia, *imperat* sii, sia, siate, *ger* essendo, *pp* stato

fare: *pr ind* faccio, fai, fa, facciamo, fate, fanno, *imperf* facevo, *pr cong* faccia, *imperat* fai, faccia, fate, *ger* facendo, *pp* fatto

FINIRE: *pr ind* finisco, finisci, finisce, finiamo, finite, finiscono, *imperf* finivo, finivi, finiva, finivamo, finivate, finivano, *fut* finirò, finirai, finirà, finiremo, finirete, finiranno, *cond* finirei, finiresti, finirebbe, finiremmo, finireste, finirebbero, *pr cong* finisca, finisca, finisca, finiamo, finiate, finiscano, *imperat* finisci, finisca, finite, *ger* finendo, *pp* finito
giungere: *pp* giunto
leggere: *pp* letto
mettere: *pp* messo
morire: *pr ind* muoio, muori, muore, moriamo, morite, muoiono, *fut* morirò, *pr cong* muoia, *imperat* muori, muoia, morite, *pp* morto
muovere: *pp* mosso
nascere: *pp* nato
piacere: *pr ind* piaccio, piaci, piace, piacciamo, piacete, piacciono, *pr cong* piaccia, *pp* piaciuto
porre: *pr ind* pongo, poni, pone, poniamo, ponete, pongono, *imperf* ponevo, *fut* porrò, *cond* porrei, *pr cong* ponga, *imperat* poni, ponga, ponete, *ger* ponendo, *pp* posto
potere: *pr ind* posso, puoi, può, possiamo, potete, possono, *fut* potrò, *pr cong* possa
prendere: *pp* preso
ridurre: *pr ind* riduco, *imperf* riducevo, *fut* ridurrò, *pr cong* riduca, *ger* riducendo, *pp* ridotto
riempire: *pr ind* riempio, riempi, riempie, riempiamo, riempite, riempiono, *ger* riempiendo
rimanere: *pr ind* rimango, rimani, rimane, rimaniamo, rimanete, rimangono, *fut* rimarrò, *pr cong* rimanga, *pp* rimasto
rispondere: *pp* risposto
salire: *pr ind* salgo, sali, sale, saliamo, salite, salgono, *pr cong* salga
sapere: *pr ind* so, sai, sa, sappiamo, sapete, sanno, *fut* saprò, *pr cong* sappia, *imperat* sappi, sappia, sappiate
scegliere: *pr ind* scelgo, scegli, sceglie, scegliamo, scegliete, scelgono, *pr cong* scelga, *imperat* scegli, scelga, scegliete, *pp* scelto
sciogliere: *pr ind* sciolgo, sciogli, scioglie, sciogliamo, sciogliete, sciolgono, *pr cong* sciolga, *imperat* sciogli, sciolga, sciogliete, *pp* sciolto
scrivere: *pp* scritto
sedere: *pr ind* siedo, siedi, siede, sediamo, sedete, siedono, *pr cong* sieda

SERVIRE: *pr ind* servo, servi, serve, serviamo, servite, servono, *imperf* servivo, servivi, serviva, servivamo, servivate, servivano, *fut* servirò, servirai, servirà, serviremo, servirete, serviranno, *cond* servirei, serviresti, servirebbe, serviremmo, servireste, servirebbero, *pr cong* serva, serva, serva, serviamo, serviate, servano, *imperat* servi, serva, servite, *ger* servendo, *pp* servito

spegnere: *pr ind* spengo, spegni, spegne, spegniamo, spegnete, spengono, *pr cong* spenga, *pp* spento

stare: *pr ind* sto, stai, sta, stiamo, state, stanno, *fut* starò, *pr cong* stia, *imperat* sta, stia, state, *pp* stato

tacere: *pr ind* taccio, taci, tace, tacciamo, tacete, tacciono, *pr cong* taccia, *pp* taciuto

TEMERE: *pr ind* temo, temi, teme, temiamo, temete, temono, *imperf* temevo, temevi, temeva, temevamo, temevate, temevano, *fut* temerò, temerai, temerà, temeremo, temerete, temeranno, *cond* temerei, temeresti, temerebbe, temeremmo, temereste, temerebbero, *pr cong* tema, tema, tema, temiamo, temiate, temano, *imperat* temi, tema, temete, *ger* temendo, *pp* temuto

tenere: *pr ind* tengo, tieni, tiene, teniamo, tenete, tengono, *fut* terrò, *pr cong* tenga

togliere: *pr ind* tolgo, togli, toglie, togliamo, togliete, tolgono, *pr cong* tolga, *imperat* togli, tolga, togliete, *pp* tolto

trarre: *pr ind* traggo, trai, trae, traiamo, traete, traggono, *fut* trarrò, *pr cong* tragga, *imperat* trai, tragga, traete, *ger* traendo, *pp* tratto

uscire: *pr ind* esco, esci, esce, usciamo, uscite, escono, *pr cong* esca

vedere: *fut* vedrò, *pp* visto

venire: *pr ind* vengo, vieni, viene, veniamo, venite, vengono, *fut* verrò, *pr cong* venga, *pp* venuto

vivere: *pp* vissuto

volere: *pr ind* voglio, vuoi, vuole, vogliamo, volete, vogliono, *fut* vorrò, *cond* vorrei, *pr cong* voglia

English irregular verbs

Infinitive	Past Tense	Past Participle
arise	arose	arisen
awake	awoke	awoken
be	was/ were	been
bear	bore	born(e)
beat	beat	beaten
begin	began	begun
bend	bent	bent
bet	bet /betted	bet /betted
bid	bid	bid
bind	bound	bound
bite	bit	bitten
bleed	bled	bled
blow	blew	blown
break	broke	broken
breed	bred	bred
bring	brought	brought
build	built	built
burn	burnt /burned	burnt /burned
burst	burst	burst
buy	bought	bought
can	could	–
cast	cast	cast
catch	caught	caught
choose	chose	chosen
come	came	come
cost	cost	cost
creep	crept	crept
cut	cut	cut
deal	dealt	dealt
dig	dug	dug
do	did	done
draw	drew	drawn
dream	dreamed /dreamt	dreamed /dreamt
drink	drank	drunk
drive	drove	driven
eat	ate	eaten
fall	fell	fallen
feed	fed	fed
feel	felt	felt
fight	fought	fought
find	found	found
fling	flung	flung
fly	flew	flown
forget	forgot	forgotten
freeze	froze	frozen
get	got	got (*Am* gotten)
give	gave	given
go	went	gone
grind	ground	ground
grow	grew	grown
hang	hung /hanged	hung /hanged
have	had	had

Infinitive	Past Tense	Past Participle
hear	heard	heard
hide	hid	hidden
hit	hit	hit
hold	held	held
hurt	hurt	hurt
keep	kept	kept
kneel	knelt /kneeled	knelt /kneeled
know	knew	known
lay	laid	laid
lead	led	led
lean	leant /leaned	leant /leaned
leap	leapt /leaped	leapt /leaped
learn	learnt /learned	learnt /learned
leave	left	left
lend	lent	lent
let	let	let
lie	lay	lain
light	lit /lighted	lit /lighted
lose	lost	lost
make	made	made
may	might	–
mean	meant	meant
meet	met	met
mow	mowed	mown /mowed

Infinitive	Past Tense	Past Participle
pay	paid	paid
put	put	put
quit	quit /quitted	quit /quitted
read	read	read
rid	rid	rid
ride	rode	ridden
ring	rang	rung
rise	rose	risen
run	ran	run
saw	sawed	sawn
say	said	said
see	saw	seen
seek	sought	sought
sell	sold	sold
send	sent	sent
set	set	set
shake	shook	shaken
shall	should	–
shed	shed	shed
shine	shone	shone
shoot	shot	shot
show	showed	shown
shrink	shrank	shrunk
shut	shut	shut
sing	sang	sung
sink	sank	sunk
sit	sat	sat
sleep	slept	slept

INFINITIVE	PAST TENSE	PAST PARTICIPLE
slide	slid	slid
sling	slung	slung
smell	smelt /smelled	smelt /smelled
sow	sowed	sown /sowed
speak	spoke	spoken
speed	sped /speeded	sped /speeded
spell	spelt /spelled	spelt /spelled
spend	spent	spent
spill	spilt /spilled	spilt /spilled
spin	spun	spun
spit	spat	spat
split	split	split
spoil	spoiled /spoilt	spoiled /spoilt
spread	spread	spread
spring	sprang	sprung
stand	stood	stood
steal	stole	stolen
stick	stuck	stuck
sting	stung	stung
stink	stank	stunk

INFINITIVE	PAST TENSE	PAST PARTICIPLE
strike	struck	struck /stricken
swear	swore	sworn
sweep	swept	swept
swell	swelled	swollen /swelled
swim	swam	swum
swing	swung	swung
take	took	taken
teach	taught	taught
tear	tore	torn
tell	told	told
think	thought	thought
throw	threw	thrown
tread	trod	trodden
wake	woke /waked	woken /waked
wear	wore	worn
weave	wove /weaved	woven /weaved
weep	wept	wept
win	won	won
wind	wound	wound
wring	wrung	wrung
write	wrote	written

ENGLISH-ITALIAN
INGLESE-ITALIANO

A

☞

a [*stressed* eɪ, *unstressed* ə] (an before vowel or silent 'h') *indefinite article* - 1. un/uno (una/un') ; **a restaurant** un ristorante ; **a brush** uno spazzolino ; **a chair** una sedia ; **an island** un'isola ; **a friend** un amico (un'amica) ; **to be a doctor** essere medico, fare il medico.
- 2. *(instead of the number one)* un/uno (una/un') ; **a month ago** un mese fa ; **a hundred and twenty pounds** centoventi sterline ; **a thousand** mille ; **four and a half** quattro e mezzo.
- 3. *(in prices, ratios)* a ; **£2 a kilo** 2 sterline al chilo ; **three times a week** tre volte alla settimana.

AA *n Br* (*abbr of Automobile Association*) ≃ ACI *m*.
aback [ə'bæk] *adv* : **to be taken ~** restare sbalordito(a).
abandon [ə'bændən] *vt* abbandonare.
abattoir ['æbətwaːʳ] *n* mattatoio *m*.
abbey ['æbɪ] *n* abbazia *f*.
abbreviation [əˌbriːvɪ'eɪʃn] *n* abbreviazione *f*.
abdomen ['æbdəmən] *n* addome *m*.
abide [ə'baɪd] *vt* : **I can't ~ him** non lo sopporto. ❑ **abide by** *vt fus* rispettare.
ability [ə'bɪlətɪ] *n* capacità *f inv*.
able ['eɪbl] *adj* capace ; **to be ~ to do sthg** essere capace di fare qc, poter fare qc.
abnormal [æb'nɔːml] *adj* anormale.
aboard [ə'bɔːd] *adv* a bordo. ◆ *prep* a bordo di, su.
abolish [ə'bɒlɪʃ] *vt* abolire.
abort [ə'bɔːt] *vt (call off)* sospendere.
abortion [ə'bɔːʃn] *n* aborto *m* ; **to have an ~** abortire.

☞

about [ə'baut] *adv* - 1. *(approximately)* circa, più o meno ; **~ 50 people** una cinquantina di persone ; **~ a thousand** un migliaio ; **at ~ six o'clock** verso le sei.
- 2. *(referring to place)* qua e là ; **to walk ~** camminare.
- 3. *(on the point of)* : **to be ~ to do sthg** stare per fare qc.
◆ *prep* - 1. *(concerning)* su, a proposito di ; **a book ~ Scotland** un libro sulla Scozia ; **what's it ~?** di che cosa si tratta? ; **I'll talk to you ~ it** te ne parlerò ; **what ~ a coffee?** cosa ne diresti di un caffè?
- 2. *(referring to place)* per, in giro

per ; there are lots of hotels ~ the town ci sono molti alberghi nella città.

---

above [ə'bʌv] *prep* sopra. ◆ *adv (higher)* (di) sopra ; *(more)* oltre ; ~ all soprattutto.

abroad [ə'brɔːd] *adv* all'estero.

abrupt [ə'brʌpt] *adj (sudden)* improvviso(a).

abscess ['æbses] *n* ascesso *m*.

absence ['æbsəns] *n* assenza *f*.

absent ['æbsənt] *adj* assente.

absent-minded [-'maɪndɪd] *adj* distratto(a).

absolute ['æbsəluːt] *adj* assoluto(a).

absolutely [*adv* 'æbsəluːtlɪ, *excl* ˌæbsə'luːtlɪ] *adv (completely)* assolutamente. ◆ *excl* assolutamente!

absorb [əb'sɔːb] *vt* assorbire.

absorbed [əb'sɔːbd] *adj* : to be ~ in sthg essere assorto(a) in qc.

absorbent [əb'sɔːbənt] *adj* assorbente.

abstain [əb'steɪn] *vi* : to ~ (from) astenersi (da).

absurd [əb'sɜːd] *adj* assurdo(a).

abuse [*n* ə'bjuːs, *vb* ə'bjuːz] *n (insults)* insulti *mpl* ; *(wrong use)* abuso *m* ; *(maltreatment)* maltrattamento *m*. ◆ *vt (insult)* insultare ; *(use wrongly)* abusare di ; *(maltreat)* maltrattare.

abusive [ə'bjuːsɪv] *adj* offensivo(a).

academic [ˌækə'demɪk] *adj (educational)* accademico(a). ◆ *n* professore *m* universitario, professoressa universitaria *f*.

academy [ə'kædəmɪ] *n* accademia *f*.

accelerate [ək'seləreɪt] *vi* accelerare.

accelerator [ək'seləreɪtəʳ] *n* acceleratore *m*.

accent ['æksent] *n* accento *m*.

accept [ək'sept] *vt* accettare.

acceptable [ək'septəbl] *adj* accettabile.

access ['ækses] *n* accesso *m*.

accessible [ək'sesəbl] *adj (place)* accessibile.

accessories [ək'sesərɪz] *npl* accessori *mpl*.

accident ['æksɪdənt] *n* incidente *m* ; by ~ per caso.

accidental [ˌæksɪ'dentl] *adj* accidentale.

accident insurance *n* assicurazione *f* contro gli infortuni.

accident-prone *adj* soggetto(a) a frequenti infortuni.

acclimatize [ə'klaɪmətaɪz] *vi* acclimatarsi.

accommodate [ə'kɒmədeɪt] *vt* alloggiare.

accommodation [əˌkɒmə'deɪʃn] *n* alloggio *m*.

accommodations [əˌkɒmə'deɪʃnz] *npl Am* = accommodation.

accompany [ə'kʌmpənɪ] *vt* accompagnare.

accomplish [ə'kʌmplɪʃ] *vt* realizzare.

accord [ə'kɔːd] *n* : of one's own ~ di propria iniziativa.

accordance [ə'kɔːdəns] *n* : in ~ with in conformità a.

according [ə'kɔːdɪŋ] : according to secondo.

account [ə'kaʊnt] *n (at bank, shop)* conto *m* ; *(report)* resoconto *m* ; **to take into ~** tener conto di ; **on no ~** in nessun caso ; **on ~ of** a causa di. ❑ **account for** *vt fus (explain)* spiegare ; *(constitute)* rappresentare.

accountant [ə'kaʊntənt] *n* ragioniere *m*, -a *f*.

account number *n* numero *m* di conto.

accumulate [ə'kju:mjʊleɪt] *vt* accumulare.

accurate ['ækjʊrət] *adj* preciso(a).

accuse [ə'kju:z] *vt* : **to ~ sb of sthg** accusare qn di qc.

accused [ə'kju:zd] *n* : **the ~** l'imputato *m*, -a *f*.

ace [eɪs] *n (card)* asso *m*.

ache [eɪk] *n* dolore *m*. ◆ *vi* : **my head ~s** mi fa male la testa.

achieve [ə'tʃi:v] *vt* ottenere.

acid ['æsɪd] *adj* acido(a). ◆ *n* acido *m*.

acid rain *n* pioggia *f* acida.

acknowledge [ək'nɒlɪdʒ] *vt (accept)* riconoscere ; *(letter)* accusare ricevuta di.

acne ['æknɪ] *n* acne *f*.

acorn ['eɪkɔ:n] *n* ghianda *f*.

acoustic [ə'ku:stɪk] *adj* acustico(a).

acquaintance [ə'kweɪntəns] *n (person)* conoscente *mf*.

acquire [ə'kwaɪə'] *vt* acquisire.

acre ['eɪkə'] *n* = 4 046,9 m², acro *m*.

acrobat ['ækrəbæt] *n* acrobata *mf*.

across [ə'krɒs] *prep (to, on other side of)* dall'altra parte di ; *(from one side to the other of)* attraverso, da una parte all'altra di. ◆ *adv (to other side)* dall'altra parte ; **to walk ~ sthg** attraversare qc (a piedi) ; **to drive ~ sthg** attraversare qc (in macchina) ; **10 miles ~** largo 10 miglia ; **~ from** di fronte a.

acrylic [ə'krɪlɪk] *n* acrilico *m*.

act [ækt] *vi* agire ; *(behave)* comportarsi ; *(in play, film)* recitare. ◆ *n* atto *m* ; POL legge *f* ; *(performance)* numero *m* ; **to ~ as** *(serve as)* fare da.

action ['ækʃn] *n* azione *f* ; **to take ~** agire ; **to put sthg into ~** mettere in pratica qc ; **out of ~** *(machine)* fuori uso ; *(person)* fuori combattimento.

active ['æktɪv] *adj (busy)* attivo(a).

activity [æk'tɪvətɪ] *n* attività *f inv*.

activity holiday *n vacanza organizzata per ragazzi con attività ricreative di vario genere.*

actor ['æktə'] *n* attore *m*.

actress ['æktrɪs] *n* attrice *f*.

actual ['æktʃʊəl] *adj (real)* effettivo(a), reale ; *(itself)* in sé.

actually ['æktʃʊəlɪ] *adv (really)* veramente ; *(in fact)* in effetti.

acupuncture ['ækjʊpʌŋktʃə'] *n* agopuntura *f*.

acute [ə'kju:t] *adj* acuto(a).

ad [æd] *n (inf) inf (for product)* pubblicità *f inv* ; *(for job)* annuncio *m*.

AD (*abbr of Anno Domini*) d.C..

adapt [ə'dæpt] *vt* adattare. ◆ *vi* adattarsi.

adapter [ə'dæptəʳ] *n (for foreign plug)* adattatore *m* ; *(for several plugs)* presa *f* multipla.
add [æd] *vt (put, say in addition)* aggiungere ; *(numbers, prices)* sommare. ❑ **add up** *vt sep* sommare. ❑ **add up to** *vt fus (total)* ammontare a.
adder ['ædəʳ] *n* vipera *f*.
addict ['ædɪkt] *n* tossicodipendente *mf*.
addicted [ə'dɪktɪd] *adj* : **to be ~ to sthg** essere assuefatto(a) a qc.
addiction [ə'dɪkʃn] *n* dipendenza *f*.
addition [ə'dɪʃn] *n (added thing)* aggiunta *f* ; *(in maths)* addizione *f* ; **in ~** inoltre ; **in ~ to** oltre a.
additional [ə'dɪʃənl] *adj* supplementare.
additive ['ædɪtɪv] *n* additivo *m*.
address [ə'dres] *n (on letter)* indirizzo *m*. ◆ *vt (speak to)* rivolgersi a ; *(letter)* indirizzare.
address book *n* rubrica *f*.
addressee [ˌædre'siː] *n* destinatario *m*, -a *f*.
adequate ['ædɪkwət] *adj* adeguato(a).
adhere [əd'hɪəʳ] *vi* : **to ~ to** *(stick to)* aderire a ; *(obey)* rispettare.
adhesive [əd'hiːsɪv] *adj* adesivo(a). ◆ *n* adesivo *m*.
adjacent [ə'dʒeɪsənt] *adj* adiacente.
adjective ['ædʒɪktɪv] *n* aggettivo *m*.
adjoining [ə'dʒɔɪnɪŋ] *adj* contiguo(a).
adjust [ə'dʒʌst] *vt* aggiustare. ◆ *vi* : **to ~ to** adattarsi a.
adjustable [ə'dʒʌstəbl] *adj* regolabile.
adjustment [ə'dʒʌstmənt] *n (of machine)* regolazione *f* ; *(of plan)* modifica *f*.
administration [ədˌmɪnɪ'streɪʃn] *n* amministrazione *f*.
administrator [əd'mɪnɪstreɪtəʳ] *n* amministratore *m*, -trice *f*.
admire [əd'maɪəʳ] *vt* ammirare.
admission [əd'mɪʃn] *n (permission to enter, entrance cost)* ingresso *m*.
admission charge *n* ingresso *m*.
admit [əd'mɪt] *vt (confess)* ammettere ; *(allow to enter)* far entrare ; **to ~ to sthg** ammettere qc ; **' ~s one'** *(on ticket)* 'valido per una sola persona'.
adolescent [ˌædə'lesnt] *n* adolescente *mf*.
adopt [ə'dɒpt] *vt* adottare.
adopted [ə'dɒptɪd] *adj* adottivo(a).
adorable [ə'dɔːrəbl] *adj* adorabile.
adore [ə'dɔːʳ] *vt* adorare.
Adriatic [eidrɪ'ætɪk] *n*.
adult ['ædʌlt] *n* adulto *m*, -a *f*. ◆ *adj (entertainment, films)* per adulti ; *(animal)* adulto(a).
adult education *n* ≃ educazione *f* permanente.
adultery [ə'dʌltərɪ] *n* adulterio *m*.
advance [əd'vaːns] *n (money)* anticipo *m* ; *(movement)* avanzamento *m*. ◆ *adj (payment)* anticipato(a). ◆ *vt* anticipare. ◆ *vi (move*

forward) avanzare ; *(improve)* fare progressi ; **~ warning** preavviso *m*.

advance booking *n* prenotazione *f* anticipata.

advanced [əd'vaːnst] *adj (student)* di livello avanzato ; *(level)* avanzato(a).

advantage [əd'vaːntɪdʒ] *n* vantaggio *m* ; **to take ~ of** approfittare di.

adventure [əd'ventʃəʳ] *n* avventura *f*.

adventurous [əd'ventʃərəs] *adj* avventuroso(a).

adverb ['ædvɜːb] *n* avverbio *m*.

adverse ['ædvɜːs] *adj* avverso(a).

advert ['ædvɜːt] = **advertisement**.

advertise ['ædvətaɪz] *vt (product, event)* fare pubblicità a.

advertisement [əd'vɜːtɪsmənt] *n (for product)* pubblicità *f inv* ; *(for job)* annuncio *m*.

advice [əd'vaɪs] *n* consigli *mpl* ; **a piece of ~** un consiglio ; **to ask for sb's ~** chiedere consiglio a qn.

advisable [əd'vaɪzəbl] *adj* consigliabile.

advise [əd'vaɪz] *vt* consigliare ; **to ~ sb to do sthg** consigliare a qn di fare qc ; **to ~ sb against doing sthg** sconsigliare a qn di fare qc.

advocate [*n* 'ædvəkət, *vb* 'ædvəkeɪt] *n JUR* avvocato *m* (difensore). ◆ *vt* sostenere.

aerial ['eərɪəl] *n* antenna *f*.

aerobics [eə'rəubɪks] *n* aerobica *f*.

aeroplane ['eərəpleɪn] *n* aeroplano *m*.

aerosol ['eərəsɒl] *n* aerosol *m*.

affair [ə'feəʳ] *n (event)* affare *m* ; *(love affair)* relazione *f*.

affect [ə'fekt] *vt (influence)* incidere su.

affection [ə'fekʃn] *n* affetto *m*.

affectionate [ə'fekʃnət] *adj* affettuoso(a).

affluent ['æfluənt] *adj* ricco(a).

afford [ə'fɔːd] *vt* : **to be able to ~ sthg** potersi permettere qc ; **I can't ~ it** non me lo posso permettere ; **I can't ~ the time** non ho tempo.

affordable [ə'fɔːdəbl] *adj* accessibile.

afloat [ə'fləut] *adj* a galla.

afraid [ə'freɪd] *adj* spaventato(a) ; **to be ~ of** aver paura di ; **I'm ~ so/not** temo di sì/di no.

after ['aːftəʳ] *prep* & *adv* dopo. ◆ *conj* dopo che ; **he arrived ~ me** arrivò dopo di me ; **a quarter ~ ten** *Am* le dieci e un quarto ; **to be ~ sb/sthg** *(in search of)* cercare qn/qc ; **~ all** dopo tutto. ❑ **afters** *npl* dessert *m*.

aftercare ['aːftəkeəʳ] *n* assistenza *f* postospedaliera.

aftereffects ['aːftərɪˌfekts] *npl* conseguenze *fpl* ; *(of illness)* postumi *mpl*.

afternoon [ˌaːftə'nuːn] *n* pomeriggio *m* ; **good ~!** buon giorno! *(il pomeriggio)*.

afternoon tea *n spuntino pomeridiano a base di tramezzini, dolci, tè o caffè.*

aftershave ['aːftəʃeɪv] *n* dopobarba *m*.

aftersun ['aːftəsʌn] *n* doposole *m*.

afterwards ['a:ftəwədz] *adv* dopo.

again [ə'gen] *adv* ancora, di nuovo ; ~ **and** ~ più volte ; **never** ... ~ non ... mai più.

against [ə'genst] *prep* contro ; **to lean ~ sthg** appoggiarsi a qc ; ~ **the law** contro la legge.

age [eɪdʒ] *n* età *f*; **under** ~ minorenne ; **I haven't seen him for ~s** *(inf)* non lo vedo da secoli.

aged [eɪdʒd] *adj* : ~ **eight** di otto anni.

age group *n* fascia *f* d'età.

age limit *n* limite *m* d'età.

agency ['eɪdʒənsɪ] *n* agenzia *f*.

agenda [ə'dʒendə] *n* ordine *m* del giorno.

agent ['eɪdʒənt] *n* agente *mf*.

aggression [ə'greʃn] *n* aggressività *f*; **act of ~** aggressione *f*.

aggressive [ə'gresɪv] *adj* aggressivo(a).

agile [*Br* 'ædʒaɪl, *Am* 'ædʒəl] *adj* agile.

agitated ['ædʒɪteɪtɪd] *adj* agitato(a).

ago [ə'gəʊ] *adv* : **a month ~** un mese fa ; **how long ~?** quanto tempo fa?

agonizing ['ægənaɪzɪŋ] *adj* *(pain)* atroce ; *(decision)* straziante.

agony ['ægənɪ] *n* *(physical)* dolore *m* atroce ; *(mental)* agonia *f*.

agree [ə'gri:] *vi* *(be in agreement)* essere d'accordo ; *(consent)* acconsentire ; *(correspond)* concordare ; **it doesn't ~ with me** *(food)* mi fa male ; **to ~ to sthg** accettare qc ; **to ~ to do sthg** accettare di fare qc.

❑ **agree on** *vt fus* *(time, price)* concordare, mettersi d'accordo su.

agreed [ə'gri:d] *adj* stabilito(a) ; **to be ~** *(person)* essere d'accordo.

agreement [ə'gri:mənt] *n* accordo *m* ; **in ~ with** d'accordo con.

agriculture ['ægrɪkʌltʃə^r] *n* agricoltura *f*.

ahead [ə'hed] *adv* *(in front)* davanti ; *(forwards)* avanti ; **the months ~** i prossimi mesi ; **to be ~** *(winning)* condurre ; ~ **of** *(in front of)* davanti a ; *(in better position than)* in vantaggio su ; *(in time)* in anticipo su.

aid [eɪd] *n* aiuto *m*. ◆ *vt* aiutare ; **in ~ of** a favore di ; **with the ~ of** con l'aiuto di.

AIDS [eɪdz] *n* AIDS *m*.

ailment ['eɪlmənt] *n* *fml* acciacco *m*.

aim [eɪm] *n* *(purpose)* scopo *m*. ◆ *vt* *(gun, camera, hose)* puntare. ◆ *vi* : **to ~ (at)** mirare (a) ; **to ~ to do sthg** avere l'intenzione di fare qc.

air [eə^r] *n* aria *f*. ◆ *vt* *(room)* arieggiare. ◆ *adj* aereo(a) ; *(travel)* in aereo ; **by ~** *(travel)* in aereo ; *(send)* via aerea.

airbed ['eəbed] *n* materassino *m*.

airborne ['eəbɔ:n] *adj* in volo.

air-conditioned [-kən'dɪʃnd] *adj* con aria condizionata.

air-conditioning [-kən'dɪʃnɪŋ] *n* aria *f* condizionata.

aircraft ['eəkra:ft] (*pl inv*) *n* aeromobile *m*.

airforce ['eəfɔ:s] *n* aeronautica *f* militare.

air freshener [-,freʃnə^r] *n* deodorante *m* per ambienti.

airhostess ['eəˌhəʊstɪs] *n* hostess *f inv*.
airletter ['eəˌletəʳ] *n* aerogramma *m*.
airline ['eəlaɪn] *n* compagnia *f* aerea.
airliner ['eəˌlaɪnəʳ] *n* aereo *m* di linea.
airmail ['eəmeɪl] *n* posta *f* aerea ; **by ~** per via aerea.
airplane ['eərpleɪn] *n Am* aeroplano *m*.
airport ['eəpɔːt] *n* aeroporto *m*.
airsick ['eəsɪk] *adj* : **to be ~** soffrire di mal d'aria.
air steward *n* assistente *m* di volo.
air stewardess *n* assistente *f* di volo.
air traffic control *n (people)* controllori *mpl* di volo.
aisle [aɪl] *n (in church)* navata *f* ; *(in plane, cinema)* corridoio *m* ; *(in supermarket)* corsia *f*.
aisle seat *n* posto *m* corridoio.
ajar [ə'dʒaːʳ] *adj* socchiuso(a).
alarm [ə'laːm] *n* allarme *m*. ◆ *vt* allarmare.
alarm clock *n* sveglia *f*.
alarmed [ə'laːmd] *adj (door, car)* dotato(a) di allarme.
alarming [ə'laːmɪŋ] *adj* allarmante.
album ['ælbəm] *n* album *m inv*.
alcohol ['ælkəhɒl] *n* alcool *m*.
alcohol-free *adj* analcolico(a).
alcoholic [ˌælkə'hɒlɪk] *adj* alcolico(a). ◆ *n* alcolizzato *m*, -a *f*.
alcoholism ['ælkəhɒlɪzm] *n* alcolismo *m*.
alcove ['ælkəʊv] *n* rientranza *f*.
ale [eɪl] *n* birra *f*.
alert [ə'lɜːt] *adj* vigile. ◆ *vt* allertare.
A levels *npl* ≃ esami *mpl* di maturità.
algebra ['ældʒɪbrə] *n* algebra *f*.
alias ['eɪlɪəs] *adv* alias.
alibi ['ælɪbaɪ] *n* alibi *m inv*.
alien ['eɪlɪən] *n (foreigner)* straniero *m*, -a *f* ; *(from outer space)* alieno *m*, -a *f*.
alight [ə'laɪt] *adj* in fiamme. ◆ *vi fml (from train, bus)* : **to ~ (from)** scendere (da).
align [ə'laɪn] *vt* allineare.
alike [ə'laɪk] *adj* simile. ◆ *adv* allo stesso modo ; **to look ~** assomigliarsi.
alive [ə'laɪv] *adj (living)* vivo(a).

☞

all [ɔːl] *adj* tutto(a) ; **~ the food** tutto il cibo ; **~ the money** tutti i soldi ; **~ the time** sempre ; **~ day** tutto il giorno ; **~ the houses** tutte le case.
◆ *adv* - 1. *(completely)* completamente, interamente ; **~ alone** tutto solo (tutta sola).
- 2. *(in scores)* : **it's two ~** sono due pari.
- 3. *(in phrases)* : **~ but empty** quasi vuoto ; **~ over** *(finished)* finito(a).
◆ *pron* - 1. *(the whole amount)* tutto(a) ; **~ of the work** tutto il lavoro ; **is that ~?** *(in shop)* basta così?
- 2. *(everybody, everything)* tutti(e) ; **~ of the girls/rooms** tutte le ragazze/camere ; **~ of us went** ci siamo andati tutti.

- 3. *(with superlative)* : **the best of ~** il migliore di tutti.
- 4. *(in phrases)* : **in ~** *(in total)* in tutto ; *(in summary)* nel complesso ; **can I help you at ~?** posso esserle di aiuto?

Allah ['ælə] *n* Allah *m*.
allege [ə'ledʒ] *vt* asserire.
allergic [ə'lɜ:dʒɪk] *adj* : **to be ~ to** essere allergico(a) a.
allergy ['ælədʒɪ] *n* allergia *f*.
alleviate [ə'li:vɪeɪt] *vt* alleviare.
alley ['ælɪ] *n (narrow street)* vicolo *m*.
alligator ['ælɪgeɪtə^r] *n* alligatore *m*.
all-in *adj Br (inclusive)* tutto compreso *(inv)*.
all-night *adj (bar, petrol station)* aperto(a) tutta la notte.
allocate ['æləkeɪt] *vt (money, task)* assegnare.
allow [ə'laʊ] *vt (permit)* permettere ; *(time, money)* calcolare ; **to ~ sb to do sthg** permettere a qn di fare qc ; **to be ~ed to do sthg** avere il permesso di fare qc, poter fare qc. ❑ **allow for** *vt fus* tener conto di.
allowance [ə'laʊəns] *n (state benefit)* assegno *m* ; *(for expenses)* indennità *f inv* ; *Am (pocket money)* paghetta *f*.
all right *adv (satisfactorily)* bene ; *(yes, okay)* va bene. ◆ *adj* : **is everything ~?** va tutto bene? ; **is it ~ if I smoke?** Le dispiace se fumo? ; **are you ~?** ti senti bene? ; **how was the film? - it was ~** com'era il film? - niente di speciale ; **how are you? - I'm ~** come stai? - non c'è male.
ally ['ælaɪ] *n* alleato *m*, -a *f*.
almond ['a:mənd] *n* mandorla *f*.
almost ['ɔ:lməʊst] *adv* quasi.
alone [ə'ləʊn] *adj* solo(a). ◆ *adv* da solo(a) ; **to leave sb ~** lasciare qn in pace ; **to leave sthg ~** lasciar stare qc.
along [ə'lɒŋ] *prep* lungo. ◆ *adv* : **to walk ~** camminare ; **to bring sthg ~** portare qc ; **all ~** sempre ; **~ with** insieme a.
alongside [ə,lɒŋ'saɪd] *prep* accanto a. ◆ *adv* : **to come ~** accostare.
aloud [ə'laʊd] *adv* a voce alta.
alphabet ['ælfəbet] *n* alfabeto *m*.
Alps [ælps] *npl* : **the ~** le Alpi.
already [ɔ:l'redɪ] *adv* già.
also ['ɔ:lsəʊ] *adv* anche.
altar ['ɔ:ltə^r] *n* altare *m*.
alter ['ɔ:ltə^r] *vt* cambiare.
alteration [,ɔ:ltə'reɪʃn] *n* modifica *f*.
alternate [*Br* ɔ:l'tɜ:nət, *Am* 'ɔ:ltərnət] *adj* alterni(e).
alternating current ['ɔ:ltəneɪtɪŋ-] *n* corrente *f* alternata.
alternative [ɔ:l'tɜ:nətɪv] *adj* alternativo(a). ◆ *n* alternativa *f*.
alternatively [ɔ:l'tɜ:nətɪvlɪ] *adv* in alternativa.
although [ɔ:l'ðəʊ] *conj* sebbene, benché.
altitude ['æltɪtju:d] *n* altitudine *f*.
altogether [,ɔ:ltə'geðə^r] *adv (completely)* del tutto ; *(in total)* in tutto.
aluminium [,ælju'mɪnɪəm] *n Br* alluminio *m*.
aluminum [ə'lu:mɪnəm] *Am* = **aluminium**.

always ['ɔ:lweɪz] *adv* sempre.
am [æm] → **be**.
a.m. (*abbr of ante meridiem*) : **at two ~** alle due di notte ; **at ten ~** alle dieci di mattina.
amateur ['æmətəʳ] *n* dilettante *mf*.
amazed [ə'meɪzd] *adj* stupito(a).
amazing [ə'meɪzɪŋ] *adj* incredibile.
ambassador [æm'bæsədəʳ] *n* ambasciatore *m*, -trice *f*.
amber ['æmbəʳ] *adj (traffic lights)* giallo(a) ; *(jewellery)* d'ambra.
ambiguous [æm'bɪgjʊəs] *adj* ambiguo(a).
ambition [æm'bɪʃn] *n* ambizione *f*.
ambitious [æm'bɪʃəs] *adj* ambizioso(a).
ambulance ['æmbjʊləns] *n* ambulanza *f*.
ambush ['æmbʊʃ] *n* imboscata *f*.
amenities [ə'mi:nətɪz] *npl (in hotel)* comfort *m inv* ; *(in town)* strutture *fpl (sportive, ricreative ecc.)*.
America [ə'merɪkə] *n* l'America *f*.
American [ə'merɪkən] *adj* americano(a). ◆ *n (person)* americano *m*, -a *f*.
amiable ['eɪmɪəbl] *adj* amabile.
ammunition [ˌæmjʊ'nɪʃn] *n* munizioni *fpl*.
amnesia [æm'ni:zɪə] *n* amnesia *f*.
among(st) [ə'mʌŋ (st)] *prep* tra, fra.
amount [ə'maʊnt] *n (quantity)* quantità *f inv* ; *(sum)* somma *f*. ❑ **amount to** *vt fus (total)* ammontare a.
amp [æmp] *n* ampere *m inv* ; **a 13- ~ plug** una spina con fusibile da 13 ampere.
ample ['æmpl] *adj* più che sufficiente.
amplifier ['æmplɪfaɪəʳ] *n* amplificatore *m*.
amputate ['æmpjʊteɪt] *vt* amputare.
amuse [ə'mju:z] *vt* divertire.
amusement arcade [ə'mju:zmənt-] *n* sala *f* giochi.
amusement park *n* luna park *m inv*.
amusements [ə'mju:zmənts] *npl* giostre e giochi al luna park.
amusing [ə'mju:zɪŋ] *adj* divertente.
an [*stressed* æn, *unstressed* ən] → **a**.
anaemic [ə'ni:mɪk] *adj Br (person)* anemico(a).
anaesthetic [ˌænɪs'θetɪk] *n Br* anestetico *m*.
analgesic [ˌænæl'dʒi:sɪk] *n* analgesico *m*.
analyse ['ænəlaɪz] *vt* analizzare.
analyst ['ænəlɪst] *n* analista *mf*.
analyze ['ænəlaɪz] *Am* = **analyse**.
anarchy ['ænəkɪ] *n* anarchia *f*.
anatomy [ə'nætəmɪ] *n (science)* anatomia *f* ; *(of animal)* struttura *f* ; *(of person)* corpo *m*.
ancestor ['ænsestəʳ] *n* antenato *m*, -a *f*.
anchor ['æŋkəʳ] *n* àncora *f*.
anchovy ['æntʃəvɪ] *n* acciuga *f*.
ancient ['eɪnʃənt] *adj (customs, monument)* antico(a).
and [*strong form* ænd, *weak form* ənd, ən] *conj* e, ed *(before vowel)* ;

... more sempre più ; ~ you? e a hundred ~ one centouno ; to ~ do sthg cercare di fare qc ; to ~ see andare a vedere.

anecdote ['ænɪkdəʊt] *n* aneddoto *m*.

anemic [ə'ni:mɪk] *Am* = anaemic.

anesthetic [ˌænɪs'θetɪk] *Am* = anaesthetic.

angel ['eɪndʒl] *n* angelo *m*.

anger ['æŋgə^r] *n* rabbia *f*.

angina [æn'dʒaɪnə] *n* angina *f* pectoris.

angle ['æŋgl] *n* angolo *m* ; at an ~ storto(a).

angler ['æŋglə^r] *n* pescatore *m*, -trice *f*.

angling ['æŋglɪŋ] *n* pesca *f*.

angry ['æŋgrɪ] *adj (person)* arrabbiato(a) ; *(words)* pieno(a) di rabbia ; to get ~ (with sb) arrabbiarsi (con qn).

animal ['ænɪml] *n* animale *m*.

aniseed ['ænɪsi:d] *n* semi *mpl* d'anice.

ankle ['æŋkl] *n* caviglia *f*.

annex ['æneks] *n (building)* edificio *m* annesso.

anniversary [ˌænɪ'vɜ:sərɪ] *n* anniversario *m*.

announce [ə'naʊns] *vt* annunciare.

announcement [ə'naʊnsmənt] *n* annuncio *m*.

announcer [ə'naʊnsə^r] *n* annunciatore *m*, -trice *f*.

annoy [ə'nɔɪ] *vt* dare fastidio a.

annoyed [ə'nɔɪd] *adj* seccato(a) ; to get ~ (with sb) arrabbiarsi (con qn).

annoying [ə'nɔɪɪŋ] *adj* seccante, irritante.

annual ['ænjʊəl] *adj* annuale.

anonymous [ə'nɒnɪməs] *adj* anonimo(a).

anorak ['ænəræk] *n* giacca *f* a vento.

another [ə'nʌðə^r] *adj* un altro (un'altra). ◆ *pron* un'altro (un'altra) ; can I have ~ (one)? posso prenderne un altro? ; in ~ two weeks fra altre due settimane ; one ~ l'un l'altro (l'un l'altra) ; to help one ~ aiutarsi (l'un l'altro) ; to talk to one ~ parlarsi ; one after ~ uno dopo l'altro (una dopo l'altra).

answer ['ɑ:nsə^r] *n* risposta *f*. ◆ *vt* rispondere a. ◆ *vi* rispondere ; to ~ the door andare ad aprire (la porta) ; to ~ the phone rispondere al telefono. ❑ **answer back** *vi* rispondere male.

answering machine ['ɑ:nsərɪŋ-] = answerphone.

answerphone ['ɑ:nsəfəʊn] *n* segreteria *f* telefonica.

ant [ænt] *n* formica *f*.

Antarctic [æn'tɑ:ktɪk] *n* : the ~ l'Antartide *f*.

antenna [æn'tenə] *n Am (aerial)* antenna *f*.

anthem ['ænθəm] *n* inno *m*.

antibiotics [ˌæntɪbaɪ'ɒtɪks] *npl* antibiotici *mpl*.

anticipate [æn'tɪsɪpeɪt] *vt (expect)* aspettarsi ; *(guess correctly)* prevedere.

anticlimax [æntɪ'klaɪmæks] *n* delusione *f*.

anticlockwise [ˌæntɪ'klɒkwaɪz] *adv Br* in senso antiorario.

antidote ['æntɪdəʊt] *n* antidoto *m*.
antifreeze ['æntɪfriːz] *n* antigelo *m*.
antihistamine [ˌæntɪ'hɪstəmɪn] *n* antistaminico *m*.
antiperspirant [ˌæntɪ'pɜːspərənt] *n* deodorante *m* (ad azione antitraspirante).
antique [æn'tiːk] *n* pezzo *m* d'antiquariato.
antique shop *n* negozio *m* d'antiquariato.
antiseptic [ˌæntɪ'septɪk] *n* antisettico *m*.
antisocial [ˌæntɪ'səʊʃl] *adj (person)* asociale ; *(behaviour)* incivile.
antlers ['æntləz] *npl* palchi *mpl*.
anxiety [æŋ'zaɪətɪ] *n* ansia *f*.
anxious ['æŋkʃəs] *adj (worried)* preoccupato(a) ; *(eager)* ansioso(a).

☞

any ['enɪ] *adj* - 1. *(in questions)* : **have you got ~ money?** hai (dei) soldi? ; **is there ~ coffee left?** c'è ancora del caffè?
- 2. *(in negatives)* : **I haven't got ~ money** non ho soldi ; **I haven't got ~ Italian stamps** non ho nessun francobollo italiano ; **we don't have ~ rooms** non abbiamo camere libere.
- 3. *(no matter which)* qualunque, qualsiasi ; **take ~ one you like** prendi quello che preferisci.
◆ *pron* - 1. *(in questions)* ne ; **I'm looking for a hotel - are there ~ nearby?** sto cercando un albergo - ce ne sono da queste parti?
- 2. *(in negatives)* ne ; **I don't want ~ (of them)** non ne voglio ; *(no matter which one)* : **you can sit at ~ of the tables** potete sedere a qualsiasi tavolo.
◆ *adv* - 1. *(in questions)* : **is that ~ better?** così va un po' meglio? ; **is there ~ more ice cream?** c'è ancora un po' di gelato? ; **~ other questions?** altre domande?
- 2. *(in negatives)* : **he's not ~ better** non c'è nessun miglioramento ; **we can't wait ~ longer** non possiamo più aspettare.

---

anybody ['enɪˌbɒdɪ] = **anyone**.
anyhow ['enɪhaʊ] *adv* comunque ; *(carelessly)* alla rinfusa.
anyone ['enɪwʌn] *pron (someone)* qualcuno ; *(any person)* chiunque ; **is ~ there?** c'è nessuno? ; **there wasn't ~ in** non c'era nessuno.
anything ['enɪθɪŋ] *pron (something)* qualcosa ; *(no matter what)* qualunque cosa, qualsiasi cosa ; **have you ~ bigger?** ha niente di più grande? ; **I don't want ~ to eat** non voglio mangiare niente.
anyway ['enɪweɪ] *adv* comunque.
anywhere ['enɪweə^r] *adv (in questions)* da qualche parte ; *(with negative)* da nessuna parte ; *(any place)* dovunque, da qualunque OR qualsiasi parte ; **did you go ~ else?** siete andati da qualche altra parte? ; **~ you like** dove vuoi.
apart [ə'pɑːt] *adv (separated)* : **the towns are 5 miles ~** le due città distano 8 km l'una dall'altra ; **we live ~** non viviamo insieme ; **to come ~** andare in pezzi ; **~ from** *(except for)* a parte ; *(as well as)* oltre a.

apartheid [ə'pa:theɪt] *n* apartheid *f.*
apartment [ə'pa:tmənt] *n Am* appartamento *m.*
apathetic [ˌæpə'θetɪk] *adj* apatico(a).
ape [eɪp] *n* scimmia *f.*
aperitif [əˌperə'ti:f] *n* aperitivo *m.*
aperture ['æpətʃə^r] *n (of camera)* apertura *f.*
APEX ['eɪpeks] *n (plane ticket)* biglietto *m* APEX ; *Br (train ticket) biglietto ferroviario con data prefissata e dal prezzo ridotto, comprato due settimane prima della partenza.*
apiece [ə'pi:s] *adv (for each item)* l'uno (l'una) ; *(to, for each person)* ciascuno(a).
apologetic [əˌpɒlə'dʒetɪk] *adj* : **to be ~** scusarsi.
apologize [ə'pɒlədʒaɪz] *vi* : **to ~ (to sb for sthg)** scusarsi (con qn per qc).
apology [ə'pɒlədʒɪ] *n* scuse *fpl.*
apostrophe [ə'pɒstrəfɪ] *n* apostrofo *m.*
appal [ə'pɔ:l] *vt Br* sconvolgere.
appall [ə'pɔ:l] *Am* = **appal.**
appalling [ə'pɔ:lɪŋ] *adj* spaventoso(a).
apparatus [ˌæpə'reɪtəs] *n (device)* apparecchio *m* ; *(in gym)* attrezzatura *f.*
apparently [ə'pærəntlɪ] *adv (it seems)* a quanto pare ; *(evidently)* evidentemente.
appeal [ə'pi:l] *n* JUR appello *m* ; *(fundraising campaign)* raccolta *f* di fondi. ◆ *vi* JUR fare appello ; **to ~ to sb for help** chiedere aiuto a qn ; **it doesn't ~ to me** non mi attira.
appear [ə'pɪə^r] *vi* apparire ; *(seem)* sembrare ; *(before court)* comparire ; **it ~s that** sembra che.
appearance [ə'pɪərəns] *n (arrival)* comparsa *f* ; *(look)* aspetto *m.*
appendices [ə'pendɪsi:z] *pl* → **appendix.**
appendicitis [əˌpendɪ'saɪtɪs] *n* appendicite *f.*
appendix [ə'pendɪks] (*pl* **-dices**) *n* appendice *f.*
appetite ['æpɪtaɪt] *n* appetito *m.*
appetizer ['æpɪtaɪzə^r] *n* stuzzichino *m.*
appetizing ['æpɪtaɪzɪŋ] *adj* appetitoso(a).
applaud [ə'plɔ:d] *vt* & *vi* applaudire.
applause [ə'plɔ:z] *n* applauso *m.*
apple ['æpl] *n* mela *f.*
apple crumble *n mele cotte ricoperte da uno strato di pasta frolla sbriciolata.*
apple juice *n* succo *m* di mela.
apple pie *n* torta *f* di mele ricoperta di pasta.
apple sauce *n* mele *fpl* grattugiate.
apple tart *n* crostata *f* di mele.
appliance [ə'plaɪəns] *n* apparecchio *m* ; **electrical/domestic ~** elettrodomestico *m.*
applicable [ə'plɪkəbl] *adj* : **to be ~ (to)** essere applicabile (a) ; **if ~** se pertinente.
applicant ['æplɪkənt] *n* candidato *m*, -a *f.*
application [ˌæplɪ'keɪʃn] *n (for job, membership)* domanda *f.*

application form *n* modulo *m* di domanda.

apply [ə'plaɪ] *vt (lotion, paint)* dare ; *(brakes)* azionare. ◆ *vi* : **to ~ (to sb for sthg)** *(make request)* fare domanda (per qc presso qn) ; **to ~ (to sb)** *(be applicable)* essere valido (per qn) ; **to ~ for a job** fare domanda di lavoro.

appointment [ə'pɔɪntmənt] *n (with doctor, hairdresser, businessman)* appuntamento *m* ; **to have/make an ~ (with)** avere/prendere un appuntamento (con) ; **by ~** per OR su appuntamento.

appreciable [ə'priːʃəbl] *adj* apprezzabile.

appreciate [ə'priːʃɪeɪt] *vt* apprezzare ; *(understand)* rendersi conto di.

apprehensive [ˌæprɪ'hensɪv] *adj* preoccupato(a).

apprentice [ə'prentɪs] *n* apprendista *mf*.

apprenticeship [ə'prentɪsʃɪp] *n* apprendistato *m*.

approach [ə'prəʊtʃ] *n (road)* accesso *m* ; *(to problem, situation)* approccio *m*. ◆ *vt (come nearer to)* avvicinare ; *(problem, situation)* affrontare. ◆ *vi* avvicinarsi.

appropriate [ə'prəʊprɪət] *adj* adatto(a).

approval [ə'pruːvl] *n* approvazione *f*.

approve [ə'pruːv] *vi* : **to ~ (of sb/sthg)** approvare (qn/qc).

approximate [ə'prɒksɪmət] *adj* approssimativo(a).

approximately [ə'prɒksɪmətlɪ] *adv* circa.

Apr. *(abbr of April)* apr.

apricot ['eɪprɪkɒt] *n* albicocca *f*.

April ['eɪprəl] *n* aprile *m* → **September**.

April Fools' Day *n il primo aprile, giorno in cui si fanno i 'pesci d'aprile'.*

apron ['eɪprən] *n* grembiule *m* (da cucina).

apt [æpt] *adj (appropriate)* appropriato(a) ; **to be ~ to do sthg** avere tendenza a fare qc.

aquarium [ə'kweərɪəm] (*pl* **-ria** [-rɪə]) *n* acquario *m*.

Aquarius [ə'kweərɪəs] *n* Acquario *m*.

aqueduct ['ækwɪdʌkt] *n* acquedotto *m*.

arbitrary ['ɑːbɪtrərɪ] *adj* arbitrario(a).

arc [ɑːk] *n* arco *m*.

arcade [ɑː'keɪd] *n (for shopping)* galleria *f* ; *(of video games)* sala *f* giochi.

arch [ɑːtʃ] *n* arco *m*.

archaeology [ˌɑːkɪ'ɒlədʒɪ] *n* archeologia *f*.

archbishop [ˌɑːtʃ'bɪʃəp] *n* arcivescovo *m*.

archery ['ɑːtʃərɪ] *n* tiro *m* con l'arco.

archipelago [ˌɑːkɪ'peləgəʊ] *n* arcipelago *m*.

architect ['ɑːkɪtekt] *n* architetto *mf*.

architecture ['ɑːkɪtektʃə'] *n* architettura *f*.

archives ['ɑːkaɪvz] *npl* archivi *mpl*.

Arctic ['ɑːktɪk] *n* : **the ~** l'Artide *f*.

are [*weak form* əʳ, *strong form* aːʳ] → **be**.
area ['eərɪə] *n (region)* zona *f* ; *(space, zone)* area *f* ; *(surface size)* superficie *f* ; **dining ~** zona pranzo.
area code *n Am* prefisso *m*.
arena [ə'riːnə] *n (at circus)* pista *f* ; *(sports ground)* campo *m*.
aren't = **are not**.
Argentina [ˌaːdʒən'tiːnə] *n* l'Argentina *f*.
argue ['aːgjuː] *vi (quarrel)* : **to ~ (with sb about sthg)** litigare (con qn per qc) ; **to ~ (that)** ... sostenere (che) ...
argument ['aːgjumənt] *n (quarrel)* discussione *f* ; *(reason)* argomento *m*.
arid ['ærɪd] *adj* arido(a).
Aries ['eəriːz] *n* Ariete *m*.
arise [ə'raɪz] (*pt* **arose**, *pp* **arisen** [ə'rɪzn]) *vi (problem, opportunity)* presentarsi ; **to ~ from** derivare da.
aristocracy [ˌærɪ'stɒkrəsɪ] *n* aristocrazia *f*.
arithmetic [ə'rɪθmətɪk] *n* aritmetica *f*.
arm [aːm] *n (of person)* braccio *m* ; *(of chair)* bracciolo *m* ; *(of garment)* manica *f*.
armbands ['aːmbændz] *npl (for swimming)* braccioli *mpl*.
armchair ['aːmtʃeəʳ] *n* poltrona *f*.
armed [aːmd] *adj* armato(a).
armed forces *npl* : **the ~** le forze armate.
armor *Am* = **armour**.
armour ['aːməʳ] *n Br* armatura *f*.
armpit ['aːmpɪt] *n* ascella *f*.
arms [aːmz] *npl (weapons)* armi *fpl*.
army ['aːmɪ] *n* esercito *m*.
A road *n Br* strada *f* statale.
aroma [ə'rəumə] *n* aroma *m*.
aromatic [ˌærə'mætɪk] *adj* aromatico(a).
arose [ə'rəuz] *pt* → **arise**.
around [ə'raund] *adv* in giro. ◆ *prep (surrounding)* intorno a ; *(to the other side of)* dall'altra parte di ; *(near)* vicino a ; *(all over)* per ; *(approximately)* circa ; **~ here** *(in the area)* da queste parti ; **~ the corner** dietro l'angolo ; **to turn ~** girarsi ; **to look ~** *(turn head)* guardarsi intorno ; *(in shop, city)* dare un'occhiata in giro ; **at ~ two o'clock** verso le due ; **is Paul ~?** c'è Paul?
arouse [ə'rauz] *vt* destare.
arrange [ə'reɪndʒ] *vt (flowers, books)* sistemare ; *(meeting, event)* organizzare ; **to ~ to do sthg (with sb)** mettersi d'accordo (con qn) per fare qc.
arrangement [ə'reɪndʒmənt] *n (agreement)* accordo *m* ; *(layout)* disposizione *f* ; **by ~** su richiesta ; **to make ~s (to do sthg)** fare il necessario (per fare qc).
arrest [ə'rest] *n* arresto *m*. ◆ *vt* arrestare ; **under ~** in arresto.
arrival [ə'raɪvl] *n* arrivo *m* ; **on ~** all'arrivo ; **new ~** *(person)* nuovo arrivato *m*, nuova arrivata *f*.
arrive [ə'raɪv] *vi* arrivare ; **to ~ at** *(place)* arrivare in/a.
arrogant ['ærəgənt] *adj* arrogante.
arrow ['ærəu] *n* freccia *f*.

arson ['a:sn] *n* incendio *m* doloso.

art [a:t] *n* arte *f.* ❑ **arts** *npl (humanities)* discipline *fpl* umanistiche ; **the ~s** *(fine arts)* l'arte *f.*

artefact ['a:tɪfækt] *n* manufatto *m.*

artery ['a:tərɪ] *n* arteria *f.*

art gallery *n* galleria *f* d'arte.

arthritis [a:'θraɪtɪs] *n* artrite *f.*

artichoke ['a:tɪtʃəʊk] *n* carciofo *m.*

article ['a:tɪkl] *n* articolo *m.*

articulate [a:'tɪkjʊlət] *adj* chiaro(a).

artificial [ˌa:tɪ'fɪʃl] *adj* artificiale.

artist ['a:tɪst] *n* artista *mf.*

artistic [a:'tɪstɪk] *adj (design)* artistico(a) ; *(person)* dotato(a) di senso artistico.

arts centre *n* centro *m* artistico.

☞

as [*unstressed* əz, *stressed* æz] *adv (in comparisons)* : ~ ... ~ (così) ... come ; **~ white ~ snow** bianco come la neve ; **he's ~ tall ~ I am** è alto quanto me ; **~ many ~** tanti ... quanti, (tante ... quante) ; **~ much ~** tanto ... quanto (tanta ... quanta) ; **twice ~ big** due volte più grande.

◆ *conj* - 1. *(referring to time)* mentre, nel momento in cui ; **~ the plane was coming in to land** nel momento in cui l'aereo si preparava ad atterrare.

- 2. *(referring to manner)* come ; **~ expected** ... come previsto ... ; **do ~ you like** fa' come vuoi.

- 3. *(introducing a statement)* come ; **~ you know** ... come sai ...

- 4. *(because)* poiché, dato che.

- 5. *(in phrases)* : **~ for** quanto a ; **~ from** (a partire) da ; **~ if** come se ; **it looks ~ if it will rain** sembra che stia per piovere.

◆ *prep (referring to function, job)* come ; **to work ~ a teacher** fare l'insegnante.

---

asap (*abbr of as soon as possible*) il più presto possibile.

ascent [ə'sent] *n (climb)* scalata *f.*

ascribe [ə'skraɪb] *vt* : **to ~ sthg to** attribuire qc a.

ash [æʃ] *n (from cigarette, fire)* cenere *f* ; *(tree)* frassino *m.*

ashore [ə'ʃɔ:ʳ] *adv* a riva.

ashtray ['æʃtreɪ] *n* portacenere *m inv.*

aside [ə'saɪd] *adv (to one side)* di lato ; **to move ~** spostarsi.

ask [a:sk] *vt (person)* chiedere a ; *(request)* chiedere ; *(invite)* invitare. ◆ *vi* : **to ~ about sthg** chiedere informazioni su qc ; **to ~ sb sthg** chiedere qc a qn ; **to ~ sb about sthg** chiedere a qn di qc ; **to ~ sb to do sthg** chiedere a qn di fare qc ; **to ~ sb for sthg** chiedere qc a qn ; **to ~ a question** fare una domanda ; **can I ~ you about this translation?** posso farti qualche domanda su questa traduzione?.

❑ **ask for** *vt fus (ask to talk to)* chiedere di ; *(request)* chiedere.

asleep [ə'sli:p] *adj* addormentato(a) ; **to be ~** dormire ; **to fall ~** addormentarsi.

asparagus [ə'spærəgəs] *n* asparagi *mpl.*

aspect ['æspekt] *n* aspetto *m*.
aspirin ['æsprɪn] *n* aspirina® *f*.
ass [æs] *n (animal)* asino *m*.
assassinate [ə'sæsɪneɪt] *vt* assassinare.
assault [ə'sɔ:lt] *n* aggressione *f*. ◆ *vt* aggredire.
assemble [ə'sembl] *vt (bookcase, model)* montare. ◆ *vi* riunirsi.
assembly [ə'semblɪ] *n (at school) riunione quotidiana di alunni e professori.*
assembly hall *n (at school) locale di una scuola dove alunni e professori si riuniscono ogni giorno prima delle lezioni.*
assembly point *n punto di raduno in caso di emergenza.*
assert [ə'sɜ:t] *vt (fact, innocence)* sostenere ; *(authority)* far valere ; **to ~ o.s.** farsi valere.
assess [ə'ses] *vt (person, situation, effect)* valutare ; *(value, damage, cost)* stimare.
assessment [ə'sesmənt] *n (of person, situation, effect)* valutazione *f* ; *(of value, damage, cost)* stima *f*.
asset ['æset] *n (valuable person, thing)* punto *m* di forza.
assign [ə'saɪn] *vt* : **to ~ sthg to sb** *(give)* assegnare qc a qn ; **to ~ sb to do sthg** *(designate)* incaricare qn di fare qc.
assignment [ə'saɪnmənt] *n (task)* incarico *m* ; *SCH* ricerca *f*.
assist [ə'sɪst] *vt* aiutare.
assistance [ə'sɪstəns] *n* aiuto *m* ; **to be of ~ (to sb)** essere d'aiuto (a qn).
assistant [ə'sɪstənt] *n* assistente *mf*.
associate [*n* ə'səʊʃɪət, *vb* ə'səʊʃɪeɪt] *n (partner)* socio *m*, -a *f* ; *(colleague)* collega *mf*. ◆ *vt* : **to ~ sb/sthg with** associare qn/qc a ; **to be ~d with** venire associato a.
association [əˌsəʊsɪ'eɪʃn] *n* associazione *f*.
assorted [ə'sɔ:tɪd] *adj* assortito(a).
assortment [ə'sɔ:tmənt] *n* assortimento *m*.
assume [ə'sju:m] *vt (suppose)* supporre ; *(control)* assumere ; *(responsibility)* assumersi.
assurance [ə'ʃʊərəns] *n (promise)* promessa *f* ; *(insurance)* assicurazione *f*.
assure [ə'ʃʊə^r] *vt* assicurare ; **to ~ sb (that)** ... assicurare a qn che ...
asterisk ['æstərɪsk] *n* asterisco *m*.
asthma ['æsmə] *n* asma *f*.
asthmatic [æs'mætɪk] *adj* asmatico(a).
astonished [ə'stɒnɪʃt] *adj* stupito(a).
astonishing [ə'stɒnɪʃɪŋ] *adj* incredibile.
astound [ə'staʊnd] *vt* sbalordire.
astray [ə'streɪ] *adv* : **to go ~** smarrirsi.
astrology [ə'strɒlədʒɪ] *n* astrologia *f*.
astronomy [ə'strɒnəmɪ] *n* astronomia *f*.

☞

at [*unstressed* ət, *stressed* æt] *prep* - 1. *(indicating place, position)* a ;

~ school a scuola ; **~ the hotel** in OR all'albergo ; **~ home** a casa ; **~ my mother's** da mia madre.
- 2. *(indicating direction)* : **to throw sthg ~** tirare qc contro ; **to look ~ sb/sthg** guardare qn/qc ; **to smile ~ sb** sorridere a qn.
- 3. *(indicating time)* a ; **~ nine o'clock** alle nove ; **~ night** di notte.
- 4. *(indicating rate, level, speed)* a ; **it works out ~ £5 each** viene 5 sterline a testa ; **~ 60 km/h** a 60km/h.
- 5. *(indicating activity)* : **she's ~ lunch** sta pranzando ; **to be good/bad ~ sthg** essere/non essere bravo in qc.
- 6. *(indicating cause)* : **shocked ~ sthg** scioccato da qc ; **angry ~ sb** arrabbiato con qn ; **delighted ~ sthg** contentissimo di qc.

---

ate [*Br* et, *Am* eɪt] *pt* → **eat**.

atheist ['eɪθɪɪst] *n* ateo *m*, -a *f*.

athlete ['æθli:t] *n* atleta *mf*.

athletics [æθ'letɪks] *n* atletica *f*.

Atlantic [ət'læntɪk] *n* : **the ~ (Ocean)** l'Atlantico *m*, l'Oceano Atlantico *m*.

atlas ['ætləs] *n* atlante *m*.

atmosphere ['ætməsfɪə^r] *n* atmosfera *f* ; *(air in room)* aria *f*.

atrocious [ə'trəʊʃəs] *adj (very bad)* orrendo(a).

attach [ə'tætʃ] *vt* attaccare ; **to ~ sthg to sthg** attaccare qc a qc.

attachment [ə'tætʃmənt] *n (device)* accessorio *m*.

attack [ə'tæk] *n* attacco *m*. ◆ *vt* aggredire.

attacker [ə'tækə^r] *n* aggressore *m*.

attain [ə'teɪn] *vt fml* conseguire.

attempt [ə'tempt] *n* tentativo *m*. ◆ *vt* tentare ; **to ~ to do sthg** tentare di fare qc.

attend [ə'tend] *vt (meeting)* partecipare a ; *(school)* frequentare ; *(Mass)* ascoltare. ❑ **attend to** *vt fus (deal with)* occuparsi di.

attendance [ə'tendəns] *n (people at concert, match)* affluenza *f* ; *(at school)* frequenza *f*.

attendant [ə'tendənt] *n (at public toilets, cloakroom)* addetto *m*, -a *f* ; *(at museum)* custode *mf*.

attention [ə'tenʃn] *n* attenzione *f* ; **to pay ~ (to)** fare attenzione (a).

attic ['ætɪk] *n* soffitta *f*.

attitude ['ætɪtju:d] *n* atteggiamento *m*.

attorney [ə'tɜ:nɪ] *n Am* avvocato *m*.

attract [ə'trækt] *vt* attirare.

attraction [ə'trækʃn] *n (liking)* attrazione *f* ; *(attractive feature)* attrattiva *f*.

attractive [ə'træktɪv] *adj* attraente.

attribute [ə'trɪbju:t] *vt* : **to ~ sthg to** attribuire qc a.

aubergine ['əʊbəʒi:n] *n Br* melanzana *f*.

auburn ['ɔ:bən] *adj* castano ramato *(inv)*.

auction ['ɔ:kʃn] *n* asta *f*.

audience ['ɔ:dɪəns] *n (of play, concert, film)* pubblico *m* ; *(of TV)* telespettatori *mpl* ; *(of radio)* ascoltatori *mpl*.

audio ['ɔ:dɪəʊ] *adj* audio *(inv)*.

audio-visual [-'vɪʒʊəl] *adj* audiovisivo(a).

Aug. (*abbr of August*) ago.

August ['ɔːgəst] *n* agosto *m* → September.
aunt [ɑːnt] *n* zia *f*.
au pair [ˌəʊ'peəʳ] *n* ragazza *f* alla pari.
aural ['ɔːrəl] *adj* uditivo(a).
Australia [ɒ'streɪlɪə] *n* l'Australia *f*.
Australian [ɒ'streɪlɪən] *adj* australiano(a). ◆ *n* australiano *m*, -a *f*.
Austria ['ɒstrɪə] *n* l'Austria *f*.
Austrian ['ɒstrɪən] *adj* austriaco(a). ◆ *n* austriaco *m*, -a *f*.
authentic [ɔː'θentɪk] *adj* autentico(a).
author ['ɔːθəʳ] *n (of book, article)* autore *m*, -trice *f*; *(by profession)* scrittore *m*, -trice *f*.
authority [ɔː'θɒrətɪ] *n* autorità *f inv* ; **the authorities** le autorità.
authorization [ˌɔːθəraɪ'zeɪʃn] *n* autorizzazione *f*.
authorize ['ɔːθəraɪz] *vt* autorizzare ; **to ~ sb to do sthg** autorizzare qn a fare qc.
autobiography [ˌɔːtəbaɪ'ɒgrəfɪ] *n* autobiografia *f*.
autograph ['ɔːtəgrɑːf] *n* autografo *m*.
automatic [ˌɔːtə'mætɪk] *adj* automatico(a). ◆ *n (car)* automobile *f* con cambio automatico.
automatically [ˌɔːtə'mætɪklɪ] *adv* automaticamente.
automobile ['ɔːtəməbiːl] *n Am* automobile *f*.
autumn ['ɔːtəm] *n* autunno *m* ; **in (the) ~** d'autunno.
auxiliary (verb) [ɔːg'zɪljərɪ-] *n* ausiliare *m*.
available [ə'veɪləbl] *adj* disponibile.
avalanche ['ævəlɑːnʃ] *n* valanga *f*.
Ave. *(abbr of avenue)* V.le.
avenue ['ævənjuː] *n* viale *m*.
average ['ævərɪdʒ] *adj* medio(a) ; *(not very good)* mediocre. ◆ *n* media *f* ; **on ~** in media.
aversion [ə'vɜːʃn] *n* avversione *f*.
aviation [ˌeɪvɪ'eɪʃn] *n* aviazione *f*.
avid ['ævɪd] *adj* avido(a).
avocado [ˌævə'kɑːdəʊ] (*pl* **-s** OR **-es**) *n* : **~ (pear)** avocado *m inv*.
avoid [ə'vɔɪd] *vt* evitare ; **to ~ doing sthg** evitare di fare qc.
await [ə'weɪt] *vt* attendere.
awake [ə'weɪk] (*pt* **awoke**, *pp* **awoken**) *adj* sveglio(a). ◆ *vi* svegliarsi.
award [ə'wɔːd] *n* premio *m*. ◆ *vt* : **to ~ sb sthg** *(prize)* assegnare qc a qn ; *(damages, compensation)* accordare qc a qn.
aware [ə'weəʳ] *adj* consapevole ; **to be ~ of** rendersi conto di.
away [ə'weɪ] *adv* via ; *(look, turn)* da un'altra parte ; **to drive ~** allontanarsi ; **to walk ~** allontanarsi ; **to go ~ on holiday** partire per le vacanze ; **to put sthg ~** mettere via qc, mettere a posto qc ; **to take sthg ~ (from sb)** portare via qc (a qn), prendere qc (a qn) ; **far ~** molto lontano ; **it's 10 miles ~ (from here)** è a 10 miglia (da qui) ; **the festival is two weeks ~** mancano due settimane al festival.

awesome ['ɔːsəm] *adj (impressive)* imponente ; *inf (excellent)* fantastico(a).
awful ['ɔːfəl] *adj* orribile ; **I feel ~** sto malissimo ; **an ~ lot of** un mucchio di.
awfully ['ɔːflɪ] *adv (very)* molto, terribilmente.
awkward ['ɔːkwəd] *adj (movement)* sgraziato(a) ; *(position)* goffo ; *(shape, size)* poco funzionale ; *(situation, question)* imbarazzante ; *(task, time)* difficile.
awning ['ɔːnɪŋ] *n* tenda *f*.
awoke [ə'wəʊk] *pt* → **awake**.
awoken [ə'wəʊkən] *pp* → **awake**.
axe [æks] *n* scure *f*.
axle ['æksl] *n* asse *m*.

B

BA (*abbr of Bachelor of Arts*) *(degree)* laurea *f* in materie umanistiche ; *(person)* laureato *m*, -a *f* in materie umanistiche.
babble ['bæbl] *vi* balbettare.
baby ['beɪbɪ] *n* bambino *m*, -a *f* ; **to have a ~** avere un bambino.
baby carriage *n Am* carrozzina *f*.
baby food *n* alimenti *mpl* per l'infanzia.
baby-sit *vi* fare da baby-sitter.
baby wipe *n* salvietta *f* umidificata (per bambini).
back [bæk] *adv* indietro. ◆ *n (of person)* schiena *f* ; *(of chair)* schienale *m* ; *(of car, book, bank note)* retro *m* ; *(of room)* fondo *m* ; *(of hand)* dorso *m*. ◆ *adj (seat, wheels)* posteriore. ◆ *vi (car, driver)* fare retromarcia. ◆ *vt (support)* appoggiare ; **to put sthg ~** rimettere qc (a posto) ; **to arrive ~** ritornare ; **to give sthg ~** restituire OR dare indietro qc ; **to write ~ to sb** rispondere a qn ; **at the ~ of** sul retro di, dietro ; **in ~ of** *Am* sul retro di, dietro ; **~ to front** davanti di dietro. ❑ **back up** ◆ *vt sep (support)* appoggiare. ◆ *vi (car, driver)* fare retromarcia.
backache ['bækeɪk] *n* mal *m* di schiena.
backbone ['bækbəʊn] *n* spina *f* dorsale.
back door *n* porta *f* posteriore.
backfire [ˌbæk'faɪəʳ] *vi (car)* fare un'autoaccensione.
background ['bækgraʊnd] *n* sfondo *m* ; *(of person)* background *m inv*.
backlog ['bæklɒg] *n* cumulo *m* ; **a ~ of work** del lavoro arretrato.
backpack ['bækpæk] *n* zaino *m*.
backpacker ['bækpækəʳ] *n persona che viaggia con zaino e sacco a pelo*.
back seat *n* sedile *m* posteriore.
backside [ˌbæk'saɪd] *n inf* sedere *m*.
back street *n* viuzza *f*.
backstroke ['bækstrəʊk] *n* dorso *m (nel nuoto)*.
backwards ['bækwədz] *adv (look)* indietro ; *(fall, move)* all'indietro ; *(wrong way round)* al contrario.
bacon ['beɪkən] *n* pancetta *f*, bacon *m* ; **~ and eggs** uova *fpl* e pancetta.

bacteria [bæk'tɪərɪə] *npl* batteri *mpl*.
bad [bæd] (*compar* **worse**, *superl* **worst**) *adj* cattivo(a) ; *(harmful)* dannoso(a) ; *(accident, wound)* brutto(a) ; *(eyesight, heart)* debole ; *(arm, leg)* malandato(a) ; **drinking is ~ for you** bere ti fa male ; **to go ~** *(milk, yoghurt)* andare a male ; **not ~** *(film, food, journey)* niente male ; **how are you? - not ~** come stai? - non c'è male.
badge [bædʒ] *n* distintivo *m*.
badger ['bædʒəʳ] *n* tasso *m*.
badly ['bædlɪ] (*compar* **worse**, *superl* **worst**) *adv* male ; *(injured)* gravemente ; *(affected)* profondamente ; *(very much)* tanto.
badly paid [-peɪd] *adj* mal pagato(a).
badminton ['bædmɪntən] *n* badminton *m*.
bad-tempered [-'tempəd] *adj* irascibile.
bag [bæg] *n* sacchetto *m* ; *(handbag)* borsa *f* ; *(piece of luggage)* borsone *m* ; **a ~ of crisps** un sacchetto di patatine.
bagel ['beɪgəl] *n panino a forma di ciambella.*
baggage ['bægɪdʒ] *n* bagagli *mpl*.
baggage allowance *n* franchigia *f* bagaglio.
baggage reclaim *n* ritiro *m* bagagli.
baggy ['bægɪ] *adj* largo(a).
bagpipes ['bægpaɪps] *npl* cornamusa *f*.
bail [beɪl] *n* cauzione *f*.
bait [beɪt] *n* esca *f*.
bake [beɪk] *vt* cuocere (al forno). ◆ *n* : **vegetable ~** verdure al forno.
baked [beɪkt] *adj* cotto(a) al forno.
baked beans *npl* fagioli *mpl* al sugo di pomodoro.
baked potato *n* patata *f* cotta al forno con la buccia.
baker ['beɪkəʳ] *n* fornaio *m*, -a *f* ; **~'s** *(shop)* panificio *m*, panetteria *f*.
balance ['bæləns] *n* *(of person)* equilibrio *m* ; *(of bank account, remainder)* saldo *m*. ◆ *vt (object)* tenere in equilibrio.
balcony ['bælkənɪ] *n* balcone *m*.
bald [bɔːld] *adj* calvo.
bale [beɪl] *n* balla *f*.
ball [bɔːl] *n* SPORT palla *f* ; *(in football, rugby)* pallone *m* ; *(in golf, table tennis)* pallina *f* ; *(of wool, string)* gomitolo *m* ; *(dance)* ballo *m* ; **on the ~** *fig* in gamba.
ballerina [ˌbælə'riːnə] *n* ballerina *f*.
ballet ['bæleɪ] *n* balletto *m*.
ballet dancer *n* ballerino *m* classico, (ballerina classica *f*).
balloon [bə'luːn] *n (at party etc)* palloncino *m*.
ballot ['bælət] *n (vote)* votazione *f* a scrutinio segreto.
ballpoint pen ['bɔːlpɔɪnt *n* penna *f* a sfera.
ballroom ['bɔːlrʊm] *n* sala *f* da ballo.
ballroom dancing *n* ballo *m* liscio.
bamboo [bæm'buː] *n* bambù *m*.
ban [bæn] *n* divieto *m*. ◆ *vt* vietare ; **to ~ sb from doing sthg** vietare a qn di fare qc.

banana [bə'nɑːnə] *n* banana *f*.

band [bænd] *n (musical group)* banda *f* ; *(for rock, jazz)* complesso *m*, gruppo *m* ; *(strip of paper, rubber)* striscia *f*.

bandage ['bændɪdʒ] *n* benda *f*. ◆ *vt* fasciare.

B and B *abbr* = **bed and breakfast**.

bandstand ['bændstænd] *n* palco *m* dell'orchestra.

bang [bæŋ] *n (of gun, explosion)* scoppio *m*. ◆ *vt* sbattere.

banger ['bæŋəʳ] *n Br inf (sausage)* salsiccia *f* ; **~s and mash** salsicce e purè di patate.

bangle ['bæŋgl] *n* braccialetto *m*.

bangs [bæŋz] *npl Am* frangia *f*.

banister ['bænɪstəʳ] *n* ringhiera *f*.

banjo ['bændʒəʊ] (*pl* **-s** OR **-es**) *n* banjo *m inv*.

bank [bæŋk] *n (for money)* banca *f* ; *(of river, lake)* riva *f* ; *(slope)* scarpata *f*.

bank account *n* conto *m* bancario.

bank book *n* libretto *m* di banca.

bank charges *npl* commissioni *fpl* bancarie.

bank clerk *n* impiegato *m*, -a *f* di banca.

bank draft *n* assegno *m* circolare.

banker ['bæŋkəʳ] *n* banchiere *m*.

banker's card *n* carta *f* assegni.

bank holiday *n Br* giorno *m* festivo.

bank manager *n* direttore *m*, -trice *f* di banca.

bank note *n* banconota *f*.

bankrupt ['bæŋkrʌpt] *adj* fallito(a).

bank statement *n* estratto *m* conto.

banner ['bænəʳ] *n* striscione *m*.

bannister ['bænɪstəʳ] = **banister**.

banquet ['bæŋkwɪt] *n (formal dinner)* banchetto *m* ; *(at Indian restaurant etc) menu per più persone*.

bap [bæp] *n Br* panino *m*.

baptize [*Br* bæp'taɪz, *Am* 'bæptaɪz] *vt* battezzare.

bar [bɑːʳ] *n (pub, in hotel)* bar *m inv* ; *(counter in pub)* banco *m* ; *(of metal, wood)* sbarra *f* ; *(of chocolate)* tavoletta *f*. ◆ *vt (obstruct)* sbarrare ; **a ~ of soap** una saponetta.

barbecue ['bɑːbɪkjuː] *n* barbecue *m inv*. ◆ *vt* arrostire alla griglia.

barbecue sauce *n salsa piccante usata per condire carne o pesce alla griglia*.

barbed wire [bɑːbd-] *n* filo *m* spinato.

barber ['bɑːbəʳ] *n* barbiere *m* ; **~'s** *(shop)* barbiere *m*.

bar code *n* codice *m* a barre.

bare [beəʳ] *adj (feet, arms)* nudo(a) ; *(head)* scoperto(a) ; *(room, cupboard)* vuoto(a) ; **the ~ minimum** il minimo indispensabile.

barefoot [ˌbeə'fʊt] *adv* a piedi nudi.

barely ['beəlɪ] *adv (hardly)* appena ; *(with difficulty)* a malapena.

bargain ['bɑːgɪn] *n (agreement)* accordo *m* ; *(cheap buy)* occasione *f*. ◆ *vi (haggle)* contrattare sul prezzo. ❑ **bargain for** *vt fus* aspettarsi.

bargain basement *n* reparto *m* occasioni.

barge [ba:dʒ] *n* chiatta *f*. ❑ **barge in** *vi* fare irruzione ; **to ~ in on sb** interrompere qn.

bark [ba:k] *n (of tree)* corteccia *f*. ◆ *vi* abbaiare.

barley ['ba:lɪ] *n* orzo *m*.

barmaid ['ba:meɪd] *n* barista *f*.

barman ['ba:mən] (*pl* **-men** [-mən]) *n* barista *m*.

bar meal *n pasto leggero servito in un bar o un pub*.

barn [ba:n] *n* granaio *m*.

barometer [bə'rɒmɪtəʳ] *n* barometro *m*.

baron ['bærən] *n* barone *m*.

baroque [bə'rɒk] *adj* barocco(a).

barracks ['bærəks] *npl* caserma *f*.

barrage ['bæra:ʒ] *n (of questions)* raffica *f*; *(of criticism)* ondata *f*.

barrel ['bærəl] *n (of beer, wine, oil)* barile *m* ; *(of gun)* canna *f*.

barren ['bærən] *adj (land, soil)* sterile.

barricade [ˌbærɪ'keɪd] *n* barricata *f*.

barrier ['bærɪəʳ] *n* barriera *f*.

barrister ['bærɪstəʳ] *n Br* avvocato *m*.

bartender ['ba:tendəʳ] *n Am* barista *m*.

barter ['ba:təʳ] *vi* barattare.

base [beɪs] *n* base *f*. ◆ *vt*: **to ~ sthg on** basare qc su ; **I'm ~d in London** ho base a Londra.

baseball ['beɪsbɔ:l] *n* baseball *m*.

baseball cap *n* berretto *m* da baseball.

basement ['beɪsmənt] *n* seminterrato *m*.

bases ['beɪsi:z] *pl* → **basis**.

bash [bæʃ] *vt inf* sbattere.

basic ['beɪsɪk] *adj (fundamental)* fondamentale ; *(accommodation, meal)* semplice. ❑ **basics** *npl*: **the ~s** i rudimenti.

basically ['beɪsɪklɪ] *adv (in conversation)* in sostanza ; *(fundamentally)* fondamentalmente.

basil ['bæzl] *n* basilico *m*.

basin ['beɪsn] *n (washbasin)* lavabo *m* ; *(bowl)* terrina *f*.

basis ['beɪsɪs] (*pl* **-ses** ['beɪsi:z]) *n* base *f*; **on a weekly ~** settimanalmente ; **on the ~ of** sulla base di.

basket ['ba:skɪt] *n* cesto *m*.

basketball ['ba:skɪtbɔ:l] *n (game)* pallacanestro *f*.

basmati rice [bəz'mæti-] *n tipo di riso aromatico utilizzato nella cucina indiana*.

bass[1] [beɪs] *n (singer)* basso *m*. ◆ *adj*: **~ guitar** basso *m*.

bass[2] [bæs] *n (freshwater fish)* pesce *m* persico ; *(sea fish)* spigola *f*, branzino *m*.

bassoon [bə'su:n] *n* fagotto *m*.

bastard ['ba:stəd] *n vulg* stronzo *m*, -a *f*.

bat [bæt] *n (in cricket, baseball)* mazza *f*; *(in table tennis)* racchetta *f*; *(animal)* pipistrello *m*.

batch [bætʃ] *n (of goods)* lotto *m* ; *(of people)* scaglione *m*.

bath [ba:θ] *n* bagno *m* ; *(tub)* vasca *f* (da bagno). ◆ *vt* fare il bagno a ; **to have a ~** fare il OR un bagno. ❑ **baths** *npl Br (public swimming pool)* piscina *f*.

bathe [beɪð] *vi* fare il bagno.
bathrobe ['ba:θrəub] *n (for bathroom, swimming pool)* accappatoio *m* ; *(dressing gown)* vestaglia *f*.
bathroom ['ba:θrum] *n* bagno *m*.
bathroom cabinet *n* armadietto *m* del bagno.
bathtub ['ba:θtʌb] *n* vasca *f* da bagno.
baton ['bætən] *n (of conductor)* bacchetta *f*; *(truncheon)* manganello *m*.
batter ['bætəʳ] *n* CULIN pastella *f*. ◆ *vt (wife, child)* picchiare.
battered ['bætəd] *adj* CULIN *ricoperto di pastella e fritto*.
battery ['bætərɪ] *n (for radio)* pila *f* ; *(for car)* batteria *f*.
battery charger [-ˌtʃa:dʒəʳ] *n* caricabatteria *m inv*.
battle ['bætl] *n* battaglia *f*.
bay [beɪ] *n (on coast)* baia *f*; *(for parking)* posto *m* macchina.
bay leaf *n* foglia *f* d'alloro.
bay window *n* bow-window *m inv*.
B & B *abbr* = **bed and breakfast**.
BC (*abbr of before Christ*) a.C..

☞

be [bi:] (*pt* **was, were**, *pp* **been**) *vi* - 1. *(exist)* essere ; **there is** c'è ; **there are** ci sono ; **are there any shops near here?** ci sono dei negozi qui vicino?
- 2. *(referring to location)* essere ; **the hotel is near the airport** l'albergo è OR si trova vicino all'aeroporto.
- 3. *(referring to movement)* : **has the postman been?** è venuto il postino? ; **have you ever been to Ireland?** sei mai stato in Irlanda? ; **I'll ~ there in ten minutes** sarò lì tra dieci minuti.
- 4. *(occur)* essere ; **my birthday is in November** il mio compleanno è in novembre.
- 5. *(identifying, describing)* essere ; **he's a doctor** è medico ; **I'm Italian** sono italiano ; **I'm hot/cold** ho caldo/freddo.
- 6. *(referring to health)* stare ; **how are you?** come sta? ; **I'm fine** sto bene ; **she's ill** è malata.
- 7. *(referring to age)* : **how old are you?** quanti anni hai? ; **I'm 14 (years old)** ho 14 anni.
- 8. *(referring to cost)* costare ; **how much is it?** *(item)* quanto costa? ; *(meal, shopping)* quant'è? ; **it's £10** *(item)* costa 10 sterline ; *(meal, shopping)* sono 10 sterline.
- 9. *(referring to time, dates)* essere ; **what time is it?** che ore sono? ; **it's ten o'clock** sono le dieci ; **it's the 9th of April** è il 9 aprile.
- 10. *(referring to measurement)* essere ; **it's 2 m wide/long** è largo/lungo 2 m ; **I'm 6 feet tall** sono alto 1 metro e 80 ; **I'm 8 stone** peso 50 chili.
- 11. *(referring to weather)* fare ; **it's hot/cold** fa caldo/freddo ; **it's sunny** c'è il sole ; **it's windy** c'è vento ; **it's going to be nice today** oggi farà bello.
◆ *aux vb* - 1. *(forming continuous tense)* : **I'm learning Italian** sto imparando l'italiano ; **what are you reading?** cosa stai leggendo?, cosa leggi? ; **he's arriving tomorrow** arriva domani, arriverà domani ; **we've been visiting the museum** abbiamo visitato il museo.

- 2. *(forming passive)* essere ; **the flight was delayed** il volo è stato ritardato.
- 3. *(with infinitive to express order)* : **all rooms are to ~ vacated by 10 a.m.** tutte le camere devono essere lasciate libere entro le 10.
- 4. *(with infinitive to express future tense)* : **the race is to start at noon** la corsa è prevista per mezzogiorno.
- 5. *(in tag questions)* : **it's cold, isn't it?** fa freddo, (non è) vero?

---

beach [biːtʃ] *n* spiaggia *f*.
bead [biːd] *n (of glass, wood etc)* grano *m*.
beak [biːk] *n* becco *m*.
beaker ['biːkəʳ] *n* bicchiere *m*.
beam [biːm] *n (of light)* raggio *m* ; *(of wood, concrete)* trave *f*. ◆ *vi (smile)* sorridere.
bean [biːn] *n* fagiolo *m* ; *(of coffee)* chicco *m*.
beansprouts ['biːnsprauts] *npl* germogli *mpl* di soia.
bear [beəʳ] (*pt* **bore**, *pp* **borne**) *n (animal)* orso *m*. ◆ *vt (support)* reggere ; *(endure)* sopportare ; **to ~ left/right** tenersi sulla sinistra/destra.
bearable ['beərəbl] *adj* sopportabile.
beard [bɪəd] *n* barba *f*.
bearer ['beərəʳ] *n (of cheque)* portatore *m* ; *(of passport)* titolare *mf*.
bearing ['beərɪŋ] *n (relevance)* attinenza *f* ; **to get one's ~s** orizzontarsi.
beast [biːst] *n* bestia *f*.
beat [biːt] (*pt* **beat**, *pp* **beaten** ['biːtn]) *n (of heart, pulse)* battito *m* ; MUS tempo *m*. ◆ *vt* battere ; *(eggs, cream)* sbattere. ❑ **beat down** ◆ *vi (sun, rain)* battere. ◆ *vt sep* : **I ~ him down to £20** gli ho fatto abbassare il prezzo a 20 sterline. ❑ **beat up** *vt sep* pestare.
beautiful ['bjuːtɪful] *adj* bello(a).
beauty ['bjuːtɪ] *n* bellezza *f*.
beauty parlour *n* istituto *m* di bellezza.
beauty spot *n (place)* bellezza *f* naturale.
beaver ['biːvəʳ] *n* castoro *m*.
became [bɪ'keɪm] *pt* → **become**.
because [bɪ'kɒz] *conj* perché ; **~ of** a causa di.
beckon ['bekən] *vi* : **to ~ (to)** fare cenno (a).
become [bɪ'kʌm] (*pt* **became**, *pp* **become**) *vi* diventare ; **what became of him?** cosa ne è stato di lui?
bed [bed] *n* letto *m* ; *(of sea)* fondo *m* ; CULIN strato *m* ; **in ~** a letto ; **to get out of ~** alzarsi ; **to go to ~** andare a letto ; **to go to ~ with sb** andare a letto con qn ; **to make the ~** fare il letto.
bed and breakfast *n Br* ≃ pensione *f*.

BED AND BREAKFAST

I *B & B.*, detti anche *guest houses.*, sono delle abitazioni private che hanno una o più camere riservate a ospiti paganti. Si trovano in tutte le città e nelle principali località turistiche e sono di solito meno care degli alberghi. Nel prezzo della camera è inclusa la tipica colazione all'inglese, a base di uova e pancetta, salsicce, pane tostato, tè o caffè.

---

bedclothes ['bedkləuðz] *npl* lenzuola *fpl* e coperte *fpl*.

bedding ['bedɪŋ] *n* biancheria *f* da letto.

bed linen *n* lenzuola *fpl* (e federe *fpl*).

bedroom ['bedrum] *n* camera *f* da letto.

bedside table ['bedsaɪd-] *n* comodino *m*.

bedsit ['bed͵sɪt] *n Br* camera *f* ammobiliata.

bedspread ['bedspred] *n* copriletto *m inv*.

bedtime ['bedtaɪm] *n* ora *f* di andare a letto.

bee [bi:] *n* ape *f*.

beech [bi:tʃ] *n* faggio *m*.

beef [bi:f] *n* manzo *m* ; **~ Wellington** pasticcio *m* di manzo.

beefburger ['bi:f͵bɜ:gəʳ] *n* hamburger *m inv*.

beehive ['bi:haɪv] *n* alveare *m*.

been [bi:n] *pp* → **be**.

beer [bɪəʳ] *n* birra *f*.

BEER

La birra è di gran lunga la bevanda alcolica più diffusa in Gran Bretagna. Qui, le birre si dividono in due categorie principali : *bitter* e *lager*. La *bitter*, conosciuta in Scozia come *heavy*, è birra scura e ha un sapore amarognolo, mentre la *lager* è la birra chiara diffusa anche nel resto d'Europa. La *real ale* è un particolare tipo di birra scura, prodotto da piccole birrerie con metodi tradizionali e generalmente è più cara. Negli Stati Uniti la birra è prevalentemente birra chiara.

---

beer garden *n giardino per i clienti di un pub*.

beer mat *n* sottobicchiere *m*.

beetle ['bi:tl] *n* scarabeo *m*.

beetroot ['bi:tru:t] *n* barbabietola *f*.

before [bɪ'fɔ:ʳ] *adv* prima. ◆ *prep* prima di ; *fml (in front of)* davanti a. ◆ *conj* : **~ it gets too late** prima che sia troppo tardi ; **I've been there ~** ci sono già stato ; **~ doing sthg** prima di fare qc ; **~ you leave** prima di partire ; **the day ~** il giorno prima ; **the week ~ last** due settimane fa.

beforehand [bɪ'fɔ:hænd] *adv* in anticipo.

befriend [bɪ'frend] *vt* trattare da amico.

beg [beg] *vi* elemosinare. ◆ *vt* : **to ~ sb to do sthg** supplicare qn di fare qc.

began [bɪ'gæn] *pt* → **begin**.

beggar ['begəʳ] *n* mendicante *mf*.

begin [bɪ'gɪn] (*pt* **began**, *pp* **begun**) *vt* & *vi* cominciare, iniziare ; **to ~ doing** OR **to do sthg** cominciare a fare qc ; **to ~ by doing sthg** cominciare col fare qc ; **to ~ with** *(at the start)* all'inizio ; *(firstly)* per prima cosa.

beginner [bɪ'gɪnəʳ] *n* principiante *mf*.

beginning [bɪ'gɪnɪŋ] *n* inizio *m*.

begun [bɪ'gʌn] *pp* → **begin**.

behalf [bɪ'ha:f] *n* : on ~ of a nome di.
behave [bɪ'heɪv] *vi* comportarsi ; to ~ (o.s.) *(be good)* comportarsi bene.
behavior [bɪ'heɪvjəʳ] *Am* = behaviour.
behaviour [bɪ'heɪvjəʳ] *n* comportamento *m*.
behind [bɪ'haɪnd] *adv (at the back)* dietro ; *(late)* indietro. ◆ *prep (at the back of)* dietro. ◆ *n inf* didietro *m* ; to leave sthg ~ dimenticare qc ; to stay ~ restare indietro ; we're all ~ you *(supporting)* siamo tutti con te.
beige [beɪʒ] *adj* beige *(inv)*.
being ['bi:ɪŋ] *n* essere *m*.
belated [bɪ'leɪtɪd] *adj* tardivo(a).
belch [beltʃ] *vi* ruttare.
Belgian ['beldʒən] *adj* belga. ◆ *n* belga *mf*.
Belgian waffle *n Am cialda dalla caratteristica superficie a quadretti che si mangia con sciroppo d'acero, panna o frutta.*
Belgium ['beldʒəm] *n* il Belgio.
belief [bɪ'li:f] *n (faith)* fede *f*; *(opinion)* convinzione *f*.
believe [bɪ'li:v] *vt* credere. ◆ *vi* : to ~ in *(God)* credere in ; to ~ in doing sthg credere che sia giusto fare qc.
believer [bɪ'li:vəʳ] *n* credente *mf*.
bell [bel] *n (of church)* campana *f*; *(of phone)* suoneria *f*; *(of door)* campanello *m*.
bellboy ['belbɔɪ] *n* fattorino *m* d'albergo.
bellow ['beləʊ] *vi* muggire.
belly ['belɪ] *n inf* pancia *f*.
belly button *n inf* ombelico *m*.
belong [bɪ'lɒŋ] *vi (be in right place)* essere al suo posto ; to ~ to *(property)* appartenere a ; *(to club, party)* far parte di ; where does this ~? dove sta questo?
belongings [bɪ'lɒŋɪŋz] *npl* effetti *mpl* personali.
below [bɪ'ləʊ] *adv* sotto ; *(downstairs)* di sotto ; *(in text)* qui sotto. ◆ *prep* sotto.
belt [belt] *n (for clothes)* cintura *f* ; *TECH* cinghia *f*.
beltway ['beltweɪ] *n Am* raccordo *m* anulare.
bench [bentʃ] *n* panchina *f*.
bend [bend] (*pt* & *pp* **bent**) *n (in road)* curva *f* ; *(in river)* ansa *f* ; *(in pipe)* gomito *m*. ◆ *vt* piegare. ◆ *vi (road, river, pipe)* fare una curva.
❑ **bend down** *vi* abbassarsi.
❑ **bend over** *vi* chinarsi.
beneath [bɪ'ni:θ] *adv* & *prep* sotto.
beneficial [ˌbenɪ'fɪʃl] *adj* benefico(a).
benefit ['benɪfɪt] *n (advantage)* beneficio *m* ; *(money)* indennità *f inv*. ◆ *vt* giovare a. ◆ *vi* : to ~ (from) beneficiare (di) ; for the ~ of per.
benign [bɪ'naɪn] *adj MED* benigno(a).
bent [bent] *pt* & *pp* → **bend**.
bereaved [bɪ'ri:vd] *adj (family)* del defunto.
beret ['bereɪ] *n* basco *m*.
Bermuda shorts [bə'mju:də-] *npl* bermuda *mpl*.
berry ['berɪ] *n* bacca *f*.
berserk [bə'zɜ:k] *adj* : to go ~ andare su tutte le furie.

berth [bɜːθ] *n (for ship)* ormeggio *m* ; *(in ship, train)* cuccetta *f.*

beside [bɪ'saɪd] *prep (next to)* accanto a ; **that's ~ the point** questo non c'entra.

besides [bɪ'saɪdz] *adv* inoltre. ◆ *prep* oltre a.

best [best] *adj* migliore. ◆ *adv* meglio. ◆ *n* : **the ~** il migliore (la migliore) ; **a pint of ~** *(beer)* ≃ un boccale di birra scura ; **I like this one ~** questo mi piace più di tutti ; **she played ~** ha giocato meglio di tutti ; **the ~ thing to do is ...** la miglior cosa da fare è ... ; **to make the ~ of sthg** accontentarsi di qc ; **to do one's ~** fare del proprio meglio ; '**~ before ...**' "da consumarsi preferibilmente entro ... ' ; **at ~** per bene che vada ; **all the ~!** auguri!

best man *n* testimone *m* (di nozze).

BEST MAN

Per tradizione, nei paesi anglosassoni il testimone consegna la fede nuziale allo sposo e, durante il pranzo di nozze, pronuncia un breve discorso che contiene aneddoti divertenti e commenti scherzosi sullo sposo.

---

best-seller [-'seləʳ] *n (book)* best seller *m inv.*

bet [bet] *(pt & pp* **bet**) *n* scommessa *f.* ◆ *vt* scommettere. ◆ *vi* : **to ~ (on)** scommettere (su) ; **I ~ (that) you can't do it** scommetto che non sei capace di farlo.

betray [bɪ'treɪ] *vt* tradire.

better ['betəʳ] *adj* migliore. ◆ *adv* meglio ; **she's ~ at tennis than me** è più brava di me a tennis ; **are you ~ now?** stai meglio adesso? ; **you had ~ ...** faresti meglio a ... ; **to get ~** migliorare.

betting ['betɪŋ] *n* scommesse *fpl.*

betting shop *n Br* ≃ sala *f* scommesse.

between [bɪ'twiːn] *prep* tra, fra. ◆ *adv (in time)* nel frattempo ; **in ~** *(in space)* in mezzo ; *(in time)* nel frattempo.

beverage ['bevərɪdʒ] *n fml* bevanda *f.*

beware [bɪ'weəʳ] *vi* : **to ~ of** stare attento a ; '**~ of the dog**' 'attenti al cane'.

bewildered [bɪ'wɪldəd] *adj* sconcertato(a).

beyond [bɪ'jɒnd] *prep* oltre. ◆ *adv* più avanti ; **~ doubt** senza dubbio ; **~ reach** irraggiungibile.

biased ['baɪəst] *adj* di parte.

bib [bɪb] *n (for baby)* bavaglino *m.*

bible ['baɪbl] *n* bibbia *f.*

biceps ['baɪseps] *n* bicipite *m.*

bicycle ['baɪsɪkl] *n* bicicletta *f.*

bicycle path *n* pista *f* ciclabile.

bicycle pump *n* pompa *f* per la bicicletta.

bid [bɪd] *(pt & pp* **bid**) *n (at auction)* offerta *f* ; *(attempt)* tentativo *m.* ◆ *vt (money)* fare un'offerta di. ◆ *vi* : **to ~ (for)** fare un'offerta (per).

bidet ['biːdeɪ] *n* bidè *m inv.*

big [bɪg] *adj* grande ; *(problem, mistake, risk)* grosso(a) ; **my ~ brother** mio fratello maggiore ; **how ~ is it?** quanto è grande?

bike [baɪk] *n inf (bicycle)* bici *f inv* ; *(motorcycle)* moto *f inv*.

biking ['baɪkɪŋ] *n* : **to go ~** *(on bicycle)* andare in bicicletta ; *(on motorcycle)* andare in moto.

bikini [bɪ'ki:nɪ] *n* bikini *m inv*.

bilingual [baɪ'lɪŋgwəl] *adj* bilingue.

bill [bɪl] *n (for meal, hotel room)* conto *m* ; *(for electricity etc)* bolletta *f* ; *Am (bank note)* banconota *f* ; *(at cinema, theatre)* programma *m* ; POL proposta *f* di legge ; **can I have the ~, please?** il conto, per favore.

billboard ['bɪlbɔ:d] *n* tabellone *m*.

billfold ['bɪlfəʊld] *n Am* portafoglio *m*.

billiards ['bɪljədz] *n* biliardo *m*.

billion ['bɪljən] *n (thousand million)* miliardo *m* ; *Br (million million)* mille miliardi.

bin [bɪn] *n (rubbish bin)* pattumiera *f* ; *(wastepaper bin)* cestino *m* ; *(for flour)* barattolo *m* ; *(on plane)* armadietto *m* in alto ; **bread ~** portapane *m inv*.

bind [baɪnd] (*pt* & *pp* **bound**) *vt (tie up)* legare.

binding ['baɪndɪŋ] *n (of book)* rilegatura *f* ; *(for ski)* attacco *m*.

bingo ['bɪŋgəʊ] *n* ≃ tombola *f*.

binoculars [bɪ'nɒkjʊləz] *npl* binocolo *m*.

biodegradable [ˌbaɪəʊdɪ'greɪdəbl] *adj* biodegradabile.

biography [baɪ'ɒgrəfɪ] *n* biografia *f*.

biological [ˌbaɪə'lɒdʒɪkl] *adj* biologico(a).

biology [baɪ'ɒlədʒɪ] *n* biologia *f*.

birch [bɜ:tʃ] *n* betulla *f*.

bird [bɜ:d] *n* uccello *m* ; *Br inf (woman)* pollastrella *f*.

bird-watching [-ˌwɒtʃɪŋ] *n* osservazione *f* degli uccelli.

Biro® ['baɪərəʊ] (*pl* **-s**) *n* biro® *f inv*.

birth [bɜ:θ] *n* nascita *f* ; **by ~** di nascita ; **to give ~ to** dare alla luce, partorire.

birth certificate *n* certificato *m* di nascita.

birth control *n* controllo *m* delle nascite.

birthday ['bɜ:θdeɪ] *n* compleanno *m* ; **happy ~!** buon compleanno!

birthday card *n* biglietto *m* d'auguri di compleanno.

birthday party *n* festa *f* di compleanno.

birthplace ['bɜ:θpleɪs] *n* luogo *m* di nascita.

biscuit ['bɪskɪt] *n Br* biscotto *m* ; *Am (scone) focaccina di pasta non lievitata da mangiare con burro e marmellata o insieme a piatti salati.*

bishop ['bɪʃəp] *n* RELIG vescovo *m* ; *(in chess)* alfiere *m*.

bistro ['bi:strəʊ] (*pl* **-s**) *n* ristorantino *m*.

bit [bɪt] *pt* → **bite**. ◆ *n (piece)* pezzetto *m* ; *(of drill)* punta *f* ; *(of bridle)* morso *m* ; *(amount)* : **a ~** un po' ; **a ~ of money** un po' di soldi ; **to do a ~ of reading** leggere un po' ; **not a ~** per niente ; **~ by ~** a poco a poco.

bitch [bɪtʃ] *n vulg (woman)* stronza *f* ; *(dog)* cagna *f*.

bite [baɪt] (*pt* **bit**, *pp* **bitten**) *n* morso *m* ; *(from insect)* puntura *f*. ◆ *vt* mordere ; *(subj : insect)* pungere ; **to have a ~ to eat** mangiare un boccone.

bitter ['bɪtəʳ] *adj (taste, food)* amaro(a) ; *(weather, wind)* pungente ; *(person)* amareggiato(a) ; *(argument, conflict)* aspro(a). ◆ *n Br (beer) tipo di birra amarognola.*

bitter lemon *n* limonata *f* amara.

bizarre [bɪ'zɑːʳ] *adj* bizzarro(a).

black [blæk] *adj* nero(a). ◆ *n (colour)* nero *m* ; *(person)* negro *m*, -a *f*. ❑ **black out** *vi* perdere conoscenza.

black and white *adj* in bianco e nero.

blackberry ['blækbrɪ] *n* mora *f*.

blackbird ['blækbɜːd] *n* merlo *m*.

blackboard ['blækbɔːd] *n* lavagna *f*.

black cherry *n* ciliegia *f* nera.

blackcurrant [,blæk'kʌrənt] *n* ribes *m inv* nero.

black eye *n* occhio *m* nero.

Black Forest gâteau *n* torta *f* di cioccolato e panna.

black ice *n* strato *m* di ghiaccio invisibile.

blackmail ['blækmeɪl] *n* ricatto *m*. ◆ *vt* ricattare.

blackout ['blækaʊt] *n (power cut)* black-out *m inv*.

black pepper *n* pepe *m* nero.

black pudding *n Br* sanguinaccio *m*.

blacksmith ['blæksmɪθ] *n* fabbro *m*.

bladder ['blædəʳ] *n* vescica *f*.

blade [bleɪd] *n (of knife, saw)* lama *f* ; *(of propeller, oar)* pala *f* ; *(of grass)* filo *m*.

blame [bleɪm] *n* colpa *f*. ◆ *vt* incolpare ; **to ~ sb for sthg** incolpare qn di qc ; **to ~ sthg on sb** dare a qn la colpa di qc.

bland [blænd] *adj (food)* insipido(a).

blank [blæŋk] *adj (space, cassette)* vuoto(a) ; *(page)* bianco(a) ; *(expression)* assente. ◆ *n (empty space)* spazio *m* (in) bianco.

blank cheque *n* assegno *m* in bianco.

blanket ['blæŋkɪt] *n* coperta *f*.

blast [blɑːst] *n (explosion)* esplosione *f* ; *(of wind)* raffica *f* ; *(of air)* folata *f*. ◆ *excl inf* maledizione! ; **at full ~** a tutto volume.

blaze [bleɪz] *n (fire)* incendio *m*. ◆ *vi (fire)* ardere ; *(sun, light)* risplendere.

blazer ['bleɪzəʳ] *n* blazer *m inv*.

bleach [bliːtʃ] *n* candeggina *f*. ◆ *vt (clothes)* candeggiare ; *(hair)* decolorare.

bleak [bliːk] *adj* triste.

bleed [bliːd] (*pt* & *pp* **bled** [bled]) *vi* sanguinare.

blend [blend] *n (of coffee, whisky)* miscela *f*. ◆ *vt* mescolare.

blender ['blendəʳ] *n* frullatore *m*.

bless [bles] *vt* benedire ; **~ you!** *(said after sneeze)* salute!

blessing ['blesɪŋ] *n* benedizione *f*.

blew [bluː] *pt* → **blow**.

blind [blaɪnd] *adj* cieco(a). ◆ *n (for window)* tendina *f* avvolgibile. ◆ *npl* : **the ~** i non vedenti.

blind corner *n* svolta *f* senza visibilità.
blindfold ['blaındfəʊld] *n* benda *f*. ◆ *vt* bendare.
blind spot *n AUT* punto *m* senza visibilità.
blink [blıŋk] *vi* battere le palpebre.
blinkers ['blıŋkəz] *npl Br* paraocchi *mpl*.
bliss [blıs] *n* estasi *f*.
blister ['blıstəʳ] *n* vescica *f*.
blizzard ['blızəd] *n* bufera *f* di neve.
bloated ['bləʊtıd] *adj (after eating)* strapieno(a).
blob [blɒb] *n (of paint)* chiazza *f*.
block [blɒk] *n (of stone, wood, ice)* blocco *m* ; *(building)* palazzo *m* ; *Am (in town, city)* isolato *m*. ◆ *vt (obstruct)* bloccare ; **to have a ~ed (up) nose** avere il naso chiuso. ❑ **block up** *vt sep* ostruire.
blockage ['blɒkıdʒ] *n* ostruzione *f*.
block capitals *npl* stampatello *m* maiuscolo.
block of flats *n* condominio *m*.
bloke [bləʊk] *n Br inf* tipo *m*, tizio *m*.
blond [blɒnd] *adj* biondo(a). ◆ *n* biondo *m*.
blonde [blɒnd] *adj* biondo(a). ◆ *n* bionda *f*.
blood [blʌd] *n* sangue *m*.
blood donor *n* donatore *m*, -trice *f* di sangue.
blood group *n* gruppo *m* sanguigno.
blood poisoning *n* setticemia *f*.
blood pressure *n* pressione *f* sanguigna ; **to have high ~** avere la pressione alta ; **to have low ~** avere la pressione bassa.
bloodshot ['blʌdʃɒt] *adj* arrossato(a).
blood test *n* analisi *f inv* del sangue.
blood transfusion *n* trasfusione *f* di sangue.
bloody ['blʌdı] *adj (hands, handkerchief)* insanguinato(a) ; *Br vulg (damn)* maledetto(a). ◆ *adv Br vulg* veramente.
bloody mary *n* Bloody Mary *m inv*.
bloom [blu:m] *n* fiore *m*. ◆ *vi* fiorire ; **in ~** in fiore.
blossom ['blɒsəm] *n* fiori *mpl*.
blot [blɒt] *n* macchia *f*.
blotch [blɒtʃ] *n* chiazza *f*.
blotting paper ['blɒtıŋ-] *n* carta *f* assorbente.
blouse [blaʊz] *n* camicetta *f*.
blow [bləʊ] (*pt* **blew**, *pp* **blown**) *vt (subj : wind)* soffiare ; *(whistle, trumpet)* suonare ; *(bubbles)* fare. ◆ *vi* soffiare ; *(fuse)* saltare. ◆ *n* colpo *m* ; **to ~ one's nose** soffiarsi il naso. ❑ **blow up** ◆ *vt sep (cause to explode)* far saltare in aria ; *(inflate)* gonfiare. ◆ *vi (explode)* saltare in aria.
blow-dry *n* piega *f* föhn. ◆ *vt* fonare.
blown [bləʊn] *pp* → **blow**.
BLT *n panino imbottito con pancetta, lattuga e pomodoro*.
blue [blu:] *adj* azzurro(a) ; *(film)* spinto(a). ◆ *n* azzurro *m*. ❑ **blues** *n MUS* blues *m*.

bluebell ['blu:bel] *n* campanula *f*.
blueberry ['blu:bərı] *n* mirtillo *m*.
bluebottle ['blu:ˌbɒtl] *n* moscone *m*.
blue cheese *n formaggio con muffa di stagionatura*.
bluff [blʌf] *n (cliff)* promontorio *m*. ◆ *vi* bluffare.
blunder ['blʌndəʳ] *n* cantonata *f*.
blunt [blʌnt] *adj (pencil)* spuntato(a) ; *(knife)* non affilato(a) ; *fig (person)* brusco(a).
blurred [blɜ:d] *adj (photo)* sfocato(a) ; *(vision)* offuscato(a).
blush [blʌʃ] *vi* arrossire.
blusher ['blʌʃəʳ] *n* fard *m inv*.
blustery ['blʌstərı] *adj* burrascoso(a).
board [bɔ:d] *n (plank)* tavola *f* ; *(notice board, for games)* tabellone *m* ; *(for chess)* scacchiera *f* ; *(blackboard)* lavagna *f* ; *(of company)* consiglio *m* d'amministrazione. ◆ *vt (plane, ship)* imbarcarsi su ; *(bus)* salire su ; ~ **and lodging** vitto e alloggio ; **full** ~ pensione *f* completa ; **half** ~ mezza pensione. ❑ **on board** ◆ *adv* a bordo. ◆ *prep* su.
board game *n* gioco *m* di società.
boarding ['bɔ:dıŋ] *n* imbarco *m*.
boarding card *n* carta *f* d'imbarco.
boardinghouse ['bɔ:dıŋhaus, *pl* -hauzız] *n* pensione *f*.
boarding school *n* collegio *m*.
board of directors *n* consiglio *m* d'amministrazione.
boast [bəust] *vi* : to ~ (about sthg) vantarsi (di qc).
boat [bəut] *n (small)* barca *f* ; *(large)* nave *f* ; **by** ~ in barca.
bob [bɒb] *n (hairstyle)* carré *m inv*.
bobby pin ['bɒbı-] *n Am* forcina *f*.
bodice ['bɒdıs] *n* corpino *m*.
body ['bɒdı] *n* corpo *m* ; *(of car)* carrozzeria *f* ; *(organization)* organismo *m*.
bodyguard ['bɒdıga:d] *n (person)* guardia *f* del corpo.
bodywork ['bɒdıwɜ:k] *n* carrozzeria *f*.
bog [bɒg] *n* pantano *m*.
bogus ['bəugəs] *adj* falso(a).
boil [bɔıl] *vt (water)* bollire, far bollire ; *(kettle)* mettere a bollire ; *(food)* lessare. ◆ *vi* bollire. ◆ *n (on skin)* foruncolo *m*.
boiled egg [bɔıld-] *n* uovo *m* alla coque.
boiled potatoes [bɔıld-] *npl* patate *fpl* lesse.
boiler ['bɔıləʳ] *n* caldaia *f*.
boiling (hot) ['bɔılıŋ-] *adj inf (water)* bollente ; **I'm** ~ sto morendo di caldo ; **it's** ~ si scoppia dal caldo.
bold [bəuld] *adj (brave)* audace.
bollard ['bɒla:d] *n Br (on road)* colonnina *f* spartitraffico.
bolt [bəult] *n (on door, window)* chiavistello *m* ; *(screw)* bullone *m*. ◆ *vt (door, window)* sprangare.
bomb [bɒm] *n* bomba *f*. ◆ *vt* bombardare.
bombard [bɒm'ba:d] *vt* bombardare.

bomb scare *n allarme causato dalla presunta presenza di una bomba.*
bond [bɒnd] *n (tie, connection)* legame *m*.
bone [bəʊn] *n (of person, animal)* osso *m* ; *(of fish)* lisca *f*.
boned [bəʊnd] *adj (chicken)* disossato(a) ; *(fish)* senza lische.
boneless ['bəʊnləs] *adj (chicken, pork)* disossato(a).
bonfire ['bɒn,faɪəʳ] *n* falò *m inv*.
bonnet ['bɒnɪt] *n Br (of car)* cofano *m*.
bonus ['bəʊnəs] (*pl* **-es**) *n (extra money)* gratifica *f*; *(additional advantage)* extra *m inv*.
bony ['bəʊnɪ] *adj (fish)* pieno(a) di lische ; *(chicken)* pieno di ossi.
boo [bu:] *vi* fischiare.
book [bʊk] *n* libro *m* ; *(for writing in)* quaderno *m* ; *(of tickets, stamps)* blocchetto *m* ; *(of matches)* pacchetto *m*. ◆ *vt (reserve)* prenotare. ❑ **book in** *vi (at hotel)* registrarsi.
bookable ['bʊkəbl] *adj (seats, flight)* prenotabile.
bookcase ['bʊkkeɪs] *n* libreria *f*.
booking ['bʊkɪŋ] *n (reservation)* prenotazione *f*.
booking office *n (at theatre)* botteghino *m* ; *(at station)* ufficio *m* prenotazioni.
bookkeeping ['bʊk,ki:pɪŋ] *n* contabilità *f*.
booklet ['bʊklɪt] *n* opuscolo *m*.
bookmaker's ['bʊk,meɪkəz] *n* ≃ sala *f* scommesse.
bookmark ['bʊkma:k] *n* segnalibro *m*.
bookshelf ['bʊkʃelf] (*pl* **-shelves**) *n* scaffale *m*.
bookshop ['bʊkʃɒp] *n* libreria *f*.
bookstall ['bʊkstɔ:l] *n* bancarella *f* di libri.
bookstore ['bʊkstɔ:ʳ] = **bookshop**.
book token *n* buono *m* libri.
boom [bu:m] *n (sudden growth)* boom *m inv*. ◆ *vi (voice, guns)* tuonare.
boost [bu:st] *vt (profits, production)* incrementare ; *(confidence)* aumentare ; *(spirits)* sollevare.
booster ['bu:stəʳ] *n (injection)* richiamo *m*.
boot [bu:t] *n (shoe)* stivale *m* ; *(for walking)* scarpone *m* ; *(for football)* scarpetta *f*; *Br (of car)* bagagliaio *m*.
booth [bu:ð] *n (for telephone)* cabina *f*; *(at fairground)* baraccone *m*.
booze [bu:z] *n inf* alcool *m*. ◆ *vi inf* sbevazzare.
bop [bɒp] *n inf (dance)* : **to have a ~** ballare.
border ['bɔ:dəʳ] *n (of country)* frontiera *f*; *(edge)* orlo *m*.
bore [bɔ:ʳ] *pt* → **bear**. ◆ *n inf* noia *f*. ◆ *vt (person)* annoiare ; *(hole)* praticare.
bored [bɔ:d] *adj* annoiato(a).
boredom ['bɔ:dəm] *n* noia *f*.
boring ['bɔ:rɪŋ] *adj* noioso(a).
born [bɔ:n] *adj* : **to be ~** nascere.
borne [bɔ:n] *pp* → **bear**.
borough ['bʌrə] *n* ≃ comune *m*.
borrow ['bɒrəʊ] *vt* : **to ~ sthg (from sb)** prendere in prestito qc (da qn).
bosom ['bʊzəm] *n* seno *m*.

boss [bɒs] *n* capo *m*. ❑ **boss around** *vt sep* dare ordini a.

bossy ['bɒsɪ] *adj* autoritario(a).

botanical garden [bə'tænɪkl-] *n* giardino *m* botanico.

both [bəʊθ] *adj* & *pron* tutti(e) e due, entrambi(e). ◆ *adv* : **~ ... and** sia ... sia, sia ... che ; **it is ~ stupid and dangerous** è stupido e pericoloso insieme.

bother ['bɒðə^r] *vt (worry)* preoccupare ; *(annoy, pester)* disturbare. ◆ *vi* preoccuparsi. ◆ *n (trouble)* fatica *f* ; **I can't be ~ed** non ne ho voglia ; **don't ~, I'll go!** non ti scomodare, vado io!

bottle ['bɒtl] *n* bottiglia *f* ; *(for baby)* biberon *m inv*.

bottle bank *n* campana *f* per la raccolta del vetro.

bottled ['bɒtld] *adj* imbottigliato(a) ; **~ beer** birra in bottiglia ; **~ water** acqua minerale.

bottle opener [-ˌəʊpnə^r] *n* apribottiglie *m inv*.

bottom ['bɒtəm] *adj (lowest, last)* ultimo(a) ; *(worst)* più basso(a). ◆ *n* fondo *m* ; *(of hill)* piedi *mpl* ; *(buttocks)* sedere *m* ; **the ~ shelf** l'ultimo scaffale in basso ; **~ gear** prima *f*.

bought [bɔːt] *pt* & *pp* → **buy**.

boulder ['bəʊldə^r] *n* masso *m*.

bounce [baʊns] *vi (rebound)* rimbalzare ; *(jump)* saltare ; *(cheque)* essere scoperto.

bouncer ['baʊnsə^r] *n inf* buttafuori *m inv*.

bouncy ['baʊnsɪ] *adj (person)* pimpante.

bound [baʊnd] *pt* & *pp* → **bind**. ◆ *vi* saltellare. ◆ *adj* : **it's ~ to rain** pioverà di sicuro ; **to be ~ for** essere diretto(a) a ; **it's out of ~s** l'accesso è vietato.

boundary ['baʊndrɪ] *n* confine *m*.

bouquet [bʊ'keɪ] *n* bouquet *m inv* ; *(big bunch of flowers)* mazzo *m* di fiori.

bout [baʊt] *n (of illness)* attacco *m* ; *(of activity)* periodo *m*.

boutique [buː'tiːk] *n* boutique *f inv*.

bow[1] [baʊ] *n (of head)* inchino *m* ; *(of ship)* prua *f*. ◆ *vi* inchinarsi.

bow[2] [bəʊ] *n (knot)* fiocco *m* ; *(weapon)* arco *m* ; MUS archetto *m*.

bowels ['baʊəlz] *npl* ANAT intestino *m*.

bowl [bəʊl] *n* ciotola *f* ; *(for washing)* bacinella *f* ; *(of toilet)* tazza *f* ; **fruit ~** fruttiera *f* ; **salad ~** insalatiera *f* ; **sugar ~** zuccheriera *f*. ❑ **bowls** *npl* bocce *fpl*.

bowling alley ['bəʊlɪŋ-] *n (building)* bowling *m inv*.

bow tie [ˌbəʊ-] *n* farfalla *f*.

box [bɒks] *n* scatola *f* ; *(on form)* casella *f* ; *(in theatre)* palco *m*. ◆ *vi* fare del pugilato ; **a ~ of chocolates** una scatola di cioccolatini ; **jewellery ~** portagioie *m inv* ; **tool ~** cassetta *f* degli attrezzi.

boxer ['bɒksə^r] *n (fighter)* pugile *m*.

boxer shorts *npl* boxer *mpl*.

boxing ['bɒksɪŋ] *n* pugilato *m*.

Boxing Day *n* Santo Stefano *m*.

boxing gloves *npl* guantoni *mpl*.

boxing ring *n* ring *m inv*.

box office *n* botteghino *m*.
boy [bɔɪ] *n* ragazzo *m* ; *(son)* figlio *m*. ◆ *excl inf* : **(oh)** ~! accidenti!
boycott ['bɔɪkɒt] *vt* boicottare.
boyfriend ['bɔɪfrend] *n* ragazzo *m*.
boy scout *n* boy-scout *m inv*.
bra [brɑː] *n* reggiseno *m*.
brace [breɪs] *n (for teeth)* apparecchio *m* (per i denti). ❑ **braces** *npl Br* bretelle *fpl*.
bracelet ['breɪslɪt] *n* braccialetto *m*.
bracken ['brækn] *n* felce *f*.
bracket ['brækɪt] *n (written symbol)* parentesi *f inv* ; *(support)* reggimensola *m inv*.
brag [bræg] *vi* vantarsi.
brain [breɪn] *n* cervello *m*.
brainy ['breɪnɪ] *adj inf* sveglio(a).
braised [breɪzd] *adj* brasato(a).
brake [breɪk] *n* freno *m*. ◆ *vi* frenare.
brake light *n* stop *m inv*.
brake pad *n* pastiglia *f* (del freno).
brake pedal *n* (pedale *m* del) freno *m*.
bran [bræn] *n* crusca *f*.
branch [brɑːntʃ] *n* ramo *m* ; *(of bank, company)* filiale *f*. ❑ **branch off** *vi* diramarsi.
branch line *n* diramazione *f*.
brand [brænd] *n* marca *f*. ◆ *vt* : **to ~ sb (as)** bollare qn (come).
brand-new *adj* nuovo(a) di zecca.
brandy ['brændɪ] *n* brandy *m inv*.
brash [bræʃ] *adj pej* sfrontato(a).
brass [brɑːs] *n* ottone *m*.
brass band *n* fanfara *f*.
brasserie ['bræsərɪ] *n* ≃ trattoria *f*.
brassiere [*Br* 'bræsɪəʳ, *Am* brə'zɪr] *n* reggiseno *m*.
brat [bræt] *n inf* discolo *m*, -a *f*.
brave [breɪv] *adj* coraggioso(a).
bravery ['breɪvərɪ] *n* coraggio *m*.
bravo [ˌbrɑː'vəʊ] *excl* bravo(a)!
brawl [brɔːl] *n* rissa *f*.
brazil nut *n* noce *f* del Brasile.
breach [briːtʃ] *vt (contract)* rompere ; *(confidence)* tradire.
bread [bred] *n* pane *m* ; **~ and butter** pane *m* imburrato.
bread bin *n Br* portapane *m inv*.
breadboard ['bredbɔːd] *n* tagliere *m* (per il pane).
bread box *Am* = **bread bin**.
breadcrumbs ['bredkrʌmz] *npl* pangrattato *m*.
breaded ['bredɪd] *adj* impanato(a).
bread knife *n* coltello *m* da pane.
bread roll *n* panino *m*.
breadth [bretθ] *n* larghezza *f*, ampiezza *f*.
break [breɪk] (*pt* **broke**, *pp* **broken**) *n (interruption)* interruzione *f* ; *(rest, pause)* pausa *f* ; SCH ricreazione *f*. ◆ *vt* rompere ; *(law, rule)* infrangere ; *(promise, contract)* non rispettare ; *(a record)* battere. ◆ *vi* rompersi ; *(dawn)* spuntare ; *(voice)* cambiare ; **without a ~** senza sosta ; **a lucky ~** un colpo di fortuna ; **to ~ one's leg** rompersi la gamba ; **to ~ the news to sb** dare una notizia a qn ; **to ~ one's journey** fare una sosta. ❑ **break down**

◆ *vi (car, machine)* guastarsi. ◆ *vt sep (door, barrier)* abbattere. ❑ **break in** *vi (enter by force)* fare irruzione. ❑ **break off** ◆ *vt (detach)* staccare ; *(holiday)* interrompere. ◆ *vi (stop suddenly)* interrompersi. ❑ **break out** *vi (fire, war, panic)* scoppiare ; **he broke out in a rash** gli è venuto uno sfogo. ❑ **break up** *vi (with spouse, partner)* lasciarsi ; *(meeting, marriage, school)* finire.

breakage ['breɪkɪdʒ] *n* danni *mpl.*

breakdown ['breɪkdaʊn] *n (of car)* guasto *m* ; *(in communications, negotiation)* interruzione *f* ; *(mental)* esaurimento *m* nervoso.

breakdown truck *n* carro *m* attrezzi.

breakfast ['brekfəst] *n* colazione *f* ; **to have ~** fare colazione ; **to have sthg for ~** mangiare qc a colazione.

breakfast cereal *n* cereali *mpl.*

break-in *n* scasso *m.*

breakwater ['breɪk,wɔːtəʳ] *n* frangiflutti *m inv.*

breast [brest] *n (of woman)* seno *m* ; *(of chicken, duck)* petto *m.*

breastbone ['brestbəʊn] *n* sterno *m.*

breast-feed *vt* allattare (al seno).

breaststroke ['breststrəʊk] *n* nuoto *m* a rana.

breath [breθ] *n (of person)* alito *m* ; *(air inhaled)* respiro *m* ; **out of ~** senza fiato ; **to go for a ~ of fresh air** andare a prendere una boccata d'aria.

Breathalyser® ['breθəlaɪzəʳ] *n Br* etilometro *m.*

Breathalyzer® ['breθəlaɪzər] *Am* = **Breathalyser**®.

breathe [briːð] *vi* respirare. ❑ **breathe in** *vi* inspirare. ❑ **breathe out** *vi* espirare.

breathtaking ['breθ,teɪkɪŋ] *adj* mozzafiato *(inv).*

breed [briːd] *(pt & pp* **bred** [bred]) *n (of animal)* razza *f* ; *(of plant)* varietà *f inv.* ◆ *vt (animals)* allevare. ◆ *vi* riprodursi.

breeze [briːz] *n* brezza *f.*

breezy ['briːzɪ] *adj (weather, day)* ventilato(a).

brew [bruː] *vt (tea)* fare. ◆ *vi* : **the tea/coffee is ~ed** il tè/caffè è pronto.

brewery ['brʊərɪ] *n* fabbrica *f* di birra.

bribe [braɪb] *n* bustarella *f*, tangente *f.* ◆ *vt* corrompere.

bric-a-brac ['brɪkəbræk] *n* cianfrusaglie *fpl.*

brick [brɪk] *n* mattone *m.*

bricklayer ['brɪk,leɪəʳ] *n* muratore *m.*

brickwork ['brɪkwɜːk] *n* muratura *f* di mattoni.

bride [braɪd] *n* sposa *f.*

bridegroom ['braɪdgrʊm] *n* sposo *m.*

bridesmaid ['braɪdzmeɪd] *n* damigella *f* d'onore.

bridge [brɪdʒ] *n* ponte *m* ; *(card game)* bridge *m.*

brief [briːf] *adj* breve. ◆ *vt* mettere al corrente ; **in ~** in breve. ❑ **briefs** *npl* mutande *fpl.*

briefcase ['briːfkeɪs] *n (hard)*

ventiquattr'ore *f inv* ; *(soft)* cartella *f*.

briefly ['bri:flɪ] *adv* brevemente.

brigade [brɪ'geɪd] *n* brigata *f*.

bright [braɪt] *adj (light, sun)* vivido(a) ; *(weather, room, idea)* luminoso(a) ; *(clever)* sveglio(a) ; *(lively, cheerful, in colour)* vivace.

brilliant ['brɪljənt] *adj* brillante ; *inf (wonderful)* stupendo(a).

brim [brɪm] *n (of hat)* tesa *f* ; **it's full to the ~** è pieno fino all'orlo.

brine [braɪn] *n* salamoia *f*.

bring [brɪŋ] (*pt* & *pp* **brought**) *vt* portare. ❑ **bring along** *vt sep* portare. ❑ **bring back** *vt sep* riportare. ❑ **bring in** *vt sep (introduce)* introdurre ; *(earn)* rendere. ❑ **bring out** *vt sep (new product)* far uscire. ❑ **bring up** *vt sep (child)* allevare ; *(subject)* sollevare ; *(food)* vomitare.

brink [brɪŋk] *n* : **on the ~ of sthg** sull'orlo di qc ; **on the ~ of doing sthg** sul punto di fare qc.

brisk [brɪsk] *adj (quick)* rapido(a) ; *(efficient)* energico(a) ; *(wind)* pungente.

bristle ['brɪsl] *n (of brush)* setola *f* ; *(on chin)* pelo *m* ispido.

Britain ['brɪtn] *n* la Gran Bretagna.

British ['brɪtɪʃ] *adj* britannico(a). ◆ *npl* : **the ~** i Britannici.

British Rail *n* ≃ le Ferrovie dello Stato.

British Telecom [-'telɪkɒm] *n* ≃ la Telecom Italia.

Briton ['brɪtn] *n* britannico *m*, -a *f*.

brittle ['brɪtl] *adj* friabile.

broad [brɔ:d] *adj* ampio(a) ; *(accent)* marcato(a).

B road *n Br* ≃ strada *f* provinciale.

broad bean *n* fava *f*.

broadcast ['brɔ:dkɑ:st] (*pt* & *pp* **broadcast**) *n* trasmissione *f*. ◆ *vt* trasmettere.

broadly ['brɔ:dlɪ] *adv (in general)* grossomodo ; **~ speaking** in linea di massima.

broadsheet ['brɔ:dʃi:t] *n* giornale *m* di qualità.

 **BROADSHEET**

Il termine *Broadsheet* in Gran Bretagna o *Broadside* negli Stati Uniti si usa con riferimento ai cosiddetti quotidiani "di qualità", seri e autorevoli, che si contrappongono ai *tabloids* di formato più piccolo e di stile più semplice, non solo per le dimensioni ma proprio per il modo di presentare le notizie e per le ampie sezioni dedicate alla cultura, allo sport e alla finanza.

broccoli ['brɒkəlɪ] *n* broccoli *mpl*.

brochure ['brəʊʃə'] *n* opuscolo *m*.

broiled [brɔɪld] *adj Am* alla griglia.

broke [brəʊk] *pt* → **break**. ◆ *adj inf* al verde.

broken ['brəʊkn] *pp* → **break**. ◆ *adj* rotto(a) ; *(English, Italian)* stentato(a).

bronchitis [brɒŋ'kaɪtɪs] *n* bronchite *f*.

bronze [brɒnz] *n* bronzo *m*.
brooch [brəʊtʃ] *n* spilla *f*.
brook [brʊk] *n* ruscello *m*.
broom [bru:m] *n* scopa *f*.
broomstick ['bru:mstɪk] *n* manico *m* di scopa.
broth [brɒθ] *n* brodo *m*.
brother ['brʌðəʳ] *n* fratello *m*.
brother-in-law *n* cognato *m*.
brought [brɔ:t] *pt* & *pp* → **bring**.
brow [braʊ] *n (forehead)* fronte *f* ; *(eyebrow)* sopracciglio *m*.
brown [braʊn] *adj (tanned)* abbronzato(a) ; *(eyes, hair)* castano(a). ◆ *n* marrone *m*.
brown bread *n* pane *m* integrale.
brownie ['braʊnɪ] *n* CULIN *biscotto con noci e cioccolato.*
Brownie ['braʊnɪ] *n* giovane esploratrice *f*, coccinella *f*.
brown rice *n* riso *m* integrale.
brown sauce *n Br salsa piccante, usata con la carne e i salumi.*
brown sugar *n* zucchero *m* di canna.
browse [braʊz] *vi (in shop)* dare un'occhiata ; **to ~ through** *(book, paper)* sfogliare.
browser ['braʊzəʳ] *n* : **' ~s welcome'** 'entrata libera'.
bruise [bru:z] *n* livido *m*.
brunch [brʌntʃ] *n* brunch *m inv*.
brunette [bru:'net] *n* bruna *f*.
brush [brʌʃ] *n (for hair)* spazzola *f* ; *(for teeth)* spazzolino *m* ; *(for painting)* pennello *m*. ◆ *vt* spazzolare ; *(clean, tidy)* spazzare ; *(move with hand)* scostare ; **to ~ one's hair** spazzolarsi i capelli ; **to ~ one's teeth** lavarsi i denti.
Brussels ['brʌslz] *n* Bruxelles *f*.
brussels sprouts *npl* cavolini *mpl* di Bruxelles.
brutal ['bru:tl] *adj* brutale.
BSc *n* (*abbr of Bachelor of Science*) *(titolare di una) laurea in discipline scientifiche.*
BT *abbr* = **British Telecom**.
bubble ['bʌbl] *n* bolla *f*.
bubble bath *n* bagnoschiuma *m inv*.
bubble gum *n* gomma *f* da masticare *(con cui si possono fare le bolle)*.
bubbly ['bʌblɪ] *n inf* spumante *m*.
buck [bʌk] *n Am inf (dollar)* dollaro *m* ; *(male animal)* maschio *m*.
bucket ['bʌkɪt] *n* secchio *m*.
Buckingham Palace ['bʌkɪŋəm-] *n* il Palazzo di Buckingham *(residenza della famiglia reale britannica)*.

BUCKINGHAM PALACE

Situato alla fine del Mall, fra Green Park e St James's Park, il Palazzo di Buckingham è la residenza ufficiale del sovrano britannico a Londra. Fu costruito nel 1703 dal Duca di Buckingham. Nel cortile antistante si svolge ogni giorno la cerimonia del cambio della Guardia.

---

buckle ['bʌkl] *n* fibbia *f*. ◆ *vt (fasten)* allacciare. ◆ *vi (warp)* piegarsi.
buck's fizz [ˌbʌks'fɪz] *n bibita a base di champagne e succo d'arancia.*

bud [bʌd] *n* germoglio *m.* ◆ *vi* germogliare.
Buddhist ['budɪst] *n* buddista *mf.*
buddy ['bʌdɪ] *n inf* amico *m.*
budge [bʌdʒ] *vi* spostarsi.
budgerigar ['bʌdʒərɪgaːʳ] *n* pappagallino *m.*
budget ['bʌdʒɪt] *adj (holiday, travel)* a basso prezzo. ◆ *n* bilancio *m* preventivo ; **the Budget** *Br* la Legge finanziaria.
budgie ['bʌdʒɪ] *n Inf* pappagallino *m.*
buff [bʌf] *n inf* patito *m*, -a *f.*
buffalo ['bʌfələu] (*pl* **-s** OR **-es**) *n* bufalo *m.*
buffer ['bʌfəʳ] *n (on train)* respingente *m.*
buffet [*Br* 'bufeɪ, *Am* bə'feɪ] *n* buffet *m inv.*
buffet car *n* vagone *m* ristorante.
bug [bʌg] *n (insect)* insetto *m* ; *inf (mild illness)* virus *m inv.* ; INF bug *m inv* ◆ *vt inf (annoy)* dare fastidio a.
buggy ['bʌgɪ] *n (pushchair)* passeggino *m* ; *Am (pram)* carrozzina *f.*
build [bɪld] (*pt* & *pp* **built**) *n* corporatura *f.* ◆ *vt* costruire. ❑ **build up** ◆ *vt sep* aumentare. ◆ *vi* accumularsi.
builder ['bɪldəʳ] *n* costruttore *m*, -trice *f.*
building ['bɪldɪŋ] *n* edificio *m.*
building site *n* cantiere *m* edile.
building society *n Br* ≃ istituto *m* di credito edilizio.
built [bɪlt] *pt* & *pp* → **build**.
built-in *adj* incorporato(a).
built-up area *n* agglomerato *m* urbano.
bulb [bʌlb] *n (for lamp)* lampadina *f* ; *(of plant)* bulbo *m.*
bulge [bʌldʒ] *vi* essere rigonfio(a).
bulk [bʌlk] *n* : **the ~ of** la maggior parte di ; **in ~** all'ingrosso.
bulky ['bʌlkɪ] *adj* ingombrante.
bull [bul] *n* toro *m.*
bulldog ['buldɒg] *n* bulldog *m inv.*
bulldozer ['buldəuzəʳ] *n* bulldozer *m inv.*
bullet ['bulɪt] *n* proiettile *m*, pallottola *f.*
bulletin ['bulətɪn] *n (on radio, TV)* notiziario *m* ; *(publication)* bollettino *m.*
bullfight ['bulfaɪt] *n* corrida *f.*
bull's-eye *n* centro *m* (del bersaglio).
bully ['bulɪ] *n* prepotente *mf.* ◆ *vt* fare il prepotente con.
bum [bʌm] *n inf (bottom)* sedere *m* ; *Am inf (tramp)* barbone *m*, -a *f.*
bum bag *n Br* marsupio *m.*
bumblebee ['bʌmblbiː] *n* bombo *m.*
bump [bʌmp] *n (on knee, leg)* rigonfiamento *m* ; *(on head)* bernoccolo *m* ; *(on road)* cunetta *f* ; *(sound)* tonfo *m* ; *(minor accident)* scontro *m* leggero. ◆ *vt (head, leg)* sbattere. ❑ **bump into** *vt fus (hit)* sbattere contro ; *(meet)* imbattersi in.
bumper ['bʌmpəʳ] *n (on car)*

paraurti *m inv* ; *Am (on train)* respingente *m*.

bumpy ['bʌmpɪ] *adj (road)* dissestato(a) ; **the flight was ~** c'è stata un po' di turbolenza durante il volo.

bun [bʌn] *n (cake)* focaccina *f* ; *(bread roll)* panino *m* ; *(hairstyle)* crocchia *f*.

bunch [bʌntʃ] *n (of people)* gruppo *m* ; *(of flowers, keys)* mazzo *m* ; *(of grapes)* grappolo *m* ; *(of bananas)* casco *m*.

bundle ['bʌndl] *n* fascio *m*.

bung [bʌŋ] *n* tappo *m*.

bungalow ['bʌŋgələʊ] *n casa a un solo piano.*

bunion ['bʌnjən] *n* rigonfiamento *m* dell'alluce.

bunk [bʌŋk] *n (bed)* cuccetta *f*.

bunk bed *n* letto *m* a castello.

bunker ['bʌŋkəʳ] *n* bunker *m inv* ; *(for coal)* carbonaia *f*.

bunny ['bʌnɪ] *n* coniglietto *m*.

buoy [*Br* bɔɪ, *Am* 'bu:ɪ] *n* boa *f*.

buoyant ['bɔɪənt] *adj* galleggiante.

burden ['bɜ:dn] *n (load)* carico *m* ; *(responsibility)* peso *m*.

bureaucracy [bjʊə'rɒkrəsɪ] *n* burocrazia *f*.

bureau de change [ˌbjʊərəʊdə'ʃɒndʒ] *n* agenzia *f* di cambio.

burger ['bɜ:gəʳ] *n* hamburger *m inv* ; *(made with nuts, vegetables etc)* hamburger vegetariano.

burglar ['bɜ:gləʳ] *n* scassinatore *m*, -trice *f*.

burglar alarm *n* allarme *m* antifurto.

burglarize ['bɜ:gləraɪz] *Am* = **burgle**.

burglary ['bɜ:glərɪ] *n* furto *m* con scasso.

burgle ['bɜ:gl] *vt* scassinare.

burial ['berɪəl] *n* sepoltura *f*.

burn [bɜ:n] (*pt* & *pp* **burnt** OR **burned**) *n* bruciatura *f*. ◆ *vt* & *vi* bruciare. ❑ **burn down** ◆ *vt sep* incendiare. ◆ *vi* : **the building was ~ed down** l'edificio è stato interamente distrutto dalle fiamme.

burning (hot) ['bɜ:nɪŋ-] *adj* rovente.

Burns' Night [bɜ:nz-] *n festa celebrata in onore del poeta scozzese Robert Burns il 25 gennaio.*

burnt [bɜ:nt] *pt* & *pp* → **burn**.

burp [bɜ:p] *vi inf* ruttare.

burrow ['bʌrəʊ] *n* tana *f*.

burst [bɜ:st] (*pt* & *pp* **burst**) *n* scoppio *m*. ◆ *vt* far scoppiare. ◆ *vi* scoppiare ; **he ~ into the room** irruppe nella stanza ; **to ~ into tears** scoppiare in lacrime ; **to ~ open** *(door)* spalancarsi.

bury ['berɪ] *vt* seppellire.

bus [bʌs] *n* autobus *m inv* ; **by ~** in autobus.

bus conductor [-ˌkən'dʌktəʳ] *n* bigliettaio *m*, -a *f*.

bus driver *n* conducente *mf*.

bush [bʊʃ] *n* cespuglio *m*.

business ['bɪznɪs] *n* affari *mpl* ; *(shop, firm)* impresa *f* ; *(affair)* faccenda *f* ; **mind your own ~!** fatti gli affari tuoi! ; **' ~ as usual'** 'aperto (regolarmente)'.

business card *n* biglietto *f* da visita.
business class *n* business class *f inv*.
business hours *npl* orario *m* di apertura.
businessman ['bɪznɪsmæn] (*pl* **-men** [-men]) *n* uomo *m* d'affari.
business studies *npl* ≃ amministrazione *f* aziendale.
businesswoman ['bɪznɪs,wʊmən] (*pl* **-women** [-,wɪmɪn]) *n* donna *f* d'affari.
busker ['bʌskəʳ] *n Br* musicista *mf* ambulante.
bus lane *n* corsia *f* preferenziale (per autobus).
bus pass *n* abbonamento *m* all'autobus.
bus shelter *n* pensilina *f*.
bus station *n* stazione *f* degli autobus.
bus stop *n* fermata *f* dell'autobus.
bust [bʌst] *n (of woman)* seno *m*. ◆ *adj* : **to go ~** *inf* fallire.
bustle ['bʌsl] *n (activity)* trambusto *m*.
bus tour *n* gita *f* in autobus.
busy ['bɪzɪ] *adj* occupato(a) ; *(day, schedule)* pieno(a) ; *(street, office)* affollato(a) ; **to be ~ doing sthg** essere occupato a fare qc.
busy signal *n Am* segnale *m* di occupato.
but [bʌt] *conj* ma, però. ◆ *prep* tranne ; **the last ~ one** il penultimo (la penultima) ; **~ for** a parte.
butcher ['bʊtʃəʳ] *n* macellaio *m*, -a *f* ; **~'s** *(shop)* macelleria *f*.
butt [bʌt] *n (of rifle)* calcio *m* ; *(of cigarette, cigar)* mozzicone *m*.
butter ['bʌtəʳ] *n* burro *m*. ◆ *vt* imburrare.
butter bean *n* fagiolo *m* bianco.
buttercup ['bʌtəkʌp] *n* ranunculo *m*.
butterfly ['bʌtəflaɪ] *n* farfalla *f*.
butterscotch ['bʌtəskɒtʃ] *n caramella dura di zucchero e burro*.
buttocks ['bʌtəks] *npl* natiche *fpl*.
button ['bʌtn] *n* bottone *m* ; *Am (badge)* distintivo *m*.
buttonhole ['bʌtnhəʊl] *n (hole)* occhiello *m*.
button mushroom *n* champignon *m inv*.
buy [baɪ] (*pt* & *pp* **bought**) *vt* comprare. ◆ *n* : **a good ~** un buon acquisto ; **to ~ sthg for sb, to ~ sb sthg** comprare qc per qn, comprare qc a qn.
buzz [bʌz] *vi* ronzare. ◆ *n inf (phone call)* : **to give sb a ~** dare un colpo di telefono a qn.
buzzer ['bʌzəʳ] *n* cicalino *m*.

☞

by [baɪ] *prep* - 1. *(expressing cause, agent)* da ; **he was hit ~ a car** è stato investito da un'automobile ; **funded ~ the government** finanziato dal governo ; **a book ~ Joyce** un libro di Joyce.
- 2. *(expressing method, means)* : **~ car/train/plane** in macchina/treno/aereo ; **~ post/phone** per posta/telefono ; **to pay ~ credit card** pagare con la carta di credito ; **to**

win ~ cheating vincere con l'inganno.

- 3. *(near to, beside)* vicino a, accanto a ; **~ the sea** *(holiday)* al mare ; *(town)* sul mare.

- 4. *(past)* davanti a ; **a car went ~ the house** un'automobile è passata davanti alla casa.

- 5. *(via)* da ; **go out ~ the door on the left** uscite dalla porta sulla sinistra.

- 6. *(with time)* : **be there ~ nine** trovati lì per le nove ; **~ day/night** di giorno/notte ; **~ now** ormai.

- 7. *(expressing quantity)* a ; **sold ~ the dozen/thousand** venduti a dozzine/migliaia ; **prices fell ~ 20%** i prezzi sono diminuiti del 20% ; **we charge ~ the hour** facciamo pagare a ore.

- 8. *(expressing meaning)* : **what do you mean ~ that?** cosa intendi dire con questo?

- 9. *(in sums, measurements)* per ; **two metres ~ five** due metri per cinque.

- 10. *(according to)* per, secondo ; **~ law** per legge ; **it's fine ~ me** per me va bene.

- 11. *(expressing gradual process)* : **bit ~ bit** (a) poco a poco ; **one ~ one** uno per uno ; **year ~ year** di anno in anno.

- 12. *(in phrases)* : **~ mistake** per errore ; **~ oneself** *(alone)* (da) solo ; *(unaided)* da solo ; **he's a lawyer ~ profession** è avvocato di professione.

◆ *adv (past)* : **to go ~** passare.

bye(-bye) [baɪ (baɪ)] *excl inf* ciao!

bypass ['baɪpɑːs] *n (road)* circonvallazione *f.*

C

C *(abbr of Celsius, centigrade)* C.

cab [kæb] *n (taxi)* taxi *m inv* ; *(of lorry)* cabina *f.*

cabaret ['kæbəreɪ] *n* spettacolo *m* di cabaret.

cabbage ['kæbɪdʒ] *n* cavolo *m.*

cabin ['kæbɪn] *n* cabina *f* ; *(wooden house)* capanna *f.*

cabin crew *n* personale *m* di bordo.

cabinet ['kæbɪnɪt] *n (cupboard)* armadietto *m* ; POL consiglio *m* di gabinetto.

cable ['keɪbl] *n* cavo *m.*

cable car *n* funivia *f.*

cable television *n* televisione *f* via cavo.

cactus ['kæktəs] *(pl* **-tuses** OR **-ti** [-taɪ]) *n* cactus *m inv.*

Caesar salad [ˌsiːzə-] *n insalata di lattuga, acciughe, olive, crostini e parmigiano.*

cafe ['kæfeɪ] *n* caffè *m.*

cafeteria [ˌkæfɪ'tɪərɪə] *n* ristorante *m* self-service.

cafetière [kæf'tjeəʳ] *n tipo di caffettiera con pressa, che separa la polvere dal caffè ottenuto.*

caffeine ['kæfiːn] *n* caffeina *f.*

cage [keɪdʒ] *n* gabbia *f.*

cagoule [kə'guːl] *n Br* K-way® *m inv.*

Cajun ['keɪdʒən] *adj tipico della popolazione di origine francese della Louisiana.*

CAJUN

Coloni di origine francese, i *Cajuns.* si stabilirono inizialmente nella Nuova Scozia da dove, nel diciottesimo secolo, furono deportati in Louisiana. Lì svilupparono una lingua e una cultura proprie ed oggi sono conosciuti per la loro cucina, caratterizzata dall'uso di spezie piccanti, e per la loro musica folkloristica, in cui predominano il violino e la fisarmonica.

---

cake ['keɪk] *n (large)* torta *f*; *(small)* pasta *f*; *(of soap)* pezzo *m*.

calculate ['kælkjuleɪt] *vt* calcolare.

calculator ['kælkjuleɪtəʳ] *n* calcolatrice *f*.

calendar ['kælɪndəʳ] *n* calendario *m*.

calf [kaːf] (*pl* **calves**) *n (of cow)* vitello *m*; *(part of leg)* polpaccio *m*.

call [kɔːl] *n (visit)* visita *f*; *(phone call)* telefonata *f*; *(of bird)* richiamo *m*; *(at airport)* chiamata *f*; *(at hotel)* sveglia *f*. ◆ *vt* chiamare; *(meeting)* convocare; *(elections, strike)* indire. ◆ *vi (visit)* passare; *(phone)* chiamare; **on ~** *(nurse, doctor)* reperibile; **to pay sb a ~** fare una visita a qn; **to be ~ed** chiamarsi; **what is he ~ed?** come si chiama?; **to ~ sb a liar** dare del bugiardo a qn; **to ~ sb's name** chiamare qn; **this train ~s at ...** questo treno ferma a ...; **who's ~ing?** chi parla? ❑ **call back** ◆ *vt sep* richiamare. ◆ *vi (phone again)* richiamare; *(visit again)* ripassare. ❑ **call for** *vt fus (come to fetch)* passare a prendere; *(demand)* chiedere; *(require)* richiedere. ❑ **call on** *vt fus (visit)* fare visita a; **to ~ on sb to do sthg** chiedere a qn di fare qc. ❑ **call out** ◆ *vt sep (name, winner)* annunciare; *(doctor, fire brigade)* chiamare. ◆ *vi* gridare.

call box *n* cabina *f* telefonica.

caller ['kɔːləʳ] *n (visitor)* visitatore *m*, -trice *f*; *(on phone)* persona *che chiama*.

calm [kaːm] *adj* calmo(a). ◆ *vt* calmare. ❑ **calm down** ◆ *vt sep* calmare. ◆ *vi* calmarsi.

calorie ['kælərɪ] *n* caloria *f*.

calves [kaːvz] *pl* → **calf**.

camcorder ['kæm,kɔːdəʳ] *n* videocamera *f*.

came [keɪm] *pt* → **come**.

camel ['kæml] *n* cammello *m*.

camera ['kæmərə] *n (for photographs)* macchina *f* fotografica; *(for filming)* macchina da presa.

cameraman ['kæmərəmæn] (*pl* **-men** [-men]) *n* cameraman *m inv*.

camera shop *n* fotografo *m*.

camisole ['kæmɪsəʊl] *n* canottiera *f*.

camp [kæmp] *n (for holidaymakers)* campeggio *m*, camping *m inv*; *(for soldiers, prisoners)* campo *m*. ◆ *vi* accamparsi.

campaign [kæm'peɪn] *n* campagna *f*. ◆ *vi*: **to ~ (for/against)** fare una campagna (per/contro).

camp bed *n* branda *f*.

camper ['kæmpəʳ] *n (person)* campeggiatore *m*, -trice *f*; *(van)* camper *m inv*.

camping ['kæmpɪŋ] *n* : **to go ~** andare in campeggio.

camping stove *n* fornello *m* da campeggio.

campsite ['kæmpsaɪt] *n* campeggio *m*, camping *m inv*.

can[1] [kæn] *n (of food)* scatola *f*; *(of drink)* lattina *f*; *(of paint)* barattolo *m*; *(of oil)* latta *f*.

☞ ———

can[2] [*weak form* kən, *strong form* kæn] (*pt & conditional* **could**) *aux vb* - 1. *(be able to)* potere ; **~ you help me?** puoi aiutarmi? ; **I ~ see you** ti vedo. - 2. *(know how to)* sapere ; **~ you drive?** sai guidare? ; **I ~ speak Italian** parlo (l')italiano. - 3. *(be allowed to)* potere ; **you can't smoke here** è proibito fumare qui. - 4. *(in polite requests)* potere ; **~ you tell me the time?** mi può dire l'ora?, mi sa dire l'ora? ; **~ I speak to the manager?** posso parlare col direttore? - 5. *(expressing occasional occurrence)* : **it ~ get cold at night** può fare freddo la notte. - 6. *(expressing possibility)* potere ; **they could be lost** si potrebbero essere persi.

Canada ['kænədə] *n* il Canada.

Canadian [kə'neɪdɪən] *adj* canadese. ◆ *n* canadese *mf*.

canal [kə'næl] *n* canale *m*.

canapé ['kænəpeɪ] *n* tartina *f*.

cancel ['kænsl] *vt* annullare.

cancellation [ˌkænsə'leɪʃn] *n* annullamento *m*.

cancer ['kænsəʳ] *n* cancro *m*.

candidate ['kændɪdət] *n* candidato *m*, -a *f*.

candle ['kændl] *n* candela *f*.

candlelit dinner ['kændllɪt-] *n* cena *f* a lume di candela.

candy ['kændɪ] *n [Am] (confectionery)* dolciumi *mpl* ; *(sweet)* caramella *f*.

cane [keɪn] *n (for walking)* bastone *m* ; *(for punishment)* bacchetta *f*; *(for furniture, baskets)* vimini *mpl*.

canister ['kænɪstəʳ] *n (for tea)* barattolo *m* ; *(for gas)* bombola *f*.

canned [kænd] *adj (food)* in scatola ; *(drink)* in lattina.

cannot ['kænɒt] = **can not**.

canoe [kə'nuː] *n* canoa *f*.

canoeing [kə'nuːɪŋ] *n* canottaggio *m*.

canopy ['kænəpɪ] *n (over bed etc)* baldacchino *m*.

can't [kɑːnt] = **cannot**.

canteen [kæn'tiːn] *n* mensa *f*.

canvas ['kænvəs] *n (for tent, bag)* tela *f*.

cap [kæp] *n (hat)* berretto *m* ; *(of pen, bottle)* tappo *m* ; *(contraceptive)* diaframma *m*.

capable ['keɪpəbl] *adj (competent)* capace ; **to be ~ of doing sthg** essere capace di fare qc.

capacity [kə'pæsɪtɪ] *n (ability)* capacità *f inv* ; *(of stadium, theatre)* capienza *f*.

cape [keɪp] *n (of land)* capo *m* ; *(cloak)* cappa *f*.

capers ['keɪpəz] *npl* capperi *mpl*.

capital ['kæpɪtl] *n (of country)* capitale *f* ; *(money)* capitale *m* ; *(letter)* maiuscola *f*.

capital punishment *n* pena *f* capitale.

cappuccino [ˌkæpʊ'tʃiːnəʊ] (*pl* -s) *n* cappuccino *m*.

Capricorn *n* Capricorno *m*.

capsicum ['kæpsɪkəm] *n* peperone *m*.
capsize [kæp'saɪz] *vi* rovesciarsi.
capsule ['kæpsju:l] *n (for medicine)* capsula *f*.
captain ['kæptɪn] *n* capitano *m*.
caption ['kæpʃn] *n* didascalia *f*.
capture ['kæptʃəʳ] *vt (person, animal)* catturare ; *(town, castle)* conquistare.
car [ka:ʳ] *n (motorcar)* automobile *f*, macchina *f* ; *(railway wagon)* vagone *m*.
carafe [kə'ræf] *n* caraffa *f*.
caramel ['kærəmel] *n (sweet)* caramella *f* mou® ; *(burnt sugar)* caramello *m*.
carat ['kærət] *n* carato *m* ; **24-~ gold** oro a 24 carati.
caravan ['kærəvæn] *n Br* roulotte *f inv*.
caravanning ['kærəvænɪŋ] *n Br* : **to go ~** andare in vacanza in roulotte.
caravan site *n Br* campeggio *m* per roulotte.
carbohydrate [ˌka:bəʊ'haɪdreɪt] *n (in foods)* carboidrato *m*.
carbon dioxide [-daɪ'ɒksaɪd] *n* anidride *f* carbonica.
car boot sale *n Br mercatino di oggetti usati, esposti nei bagagliai aperti delle automobili dei venditori.*
carburetor [ˌka:bə'retəʳ] *Am* = **carburettor**.
carburettor [ˌka:bə'retəʳ] *n Br* carburatore *m*.
car crash *n* incidente *m* automobilistico.
card [ka:d] *n (for filing, notes)* scheda *f* ; *(for greetings)* biglietto *m* ; *(showing membership)* tessera *f* ; *(of businessperson)* biglietto da visita ; *(postcard)* cartolina *f* ; *(playing card)* carta *f* ; *(cardboard)* cartoncino *m* ; **~s** *(game)* carte *fpl*.
cardboard ['ka:dbɔ:d] *n* cartone *m*.
cardiac arrest [ˌka:dɪæk-] *n* arresto *m* cardiaco.
cardigan ['ka:dɪgən] *n* cardigan *m inv*.
care [keəʳ] *n* cura *f*. ◆ *vi* : **I don't ~** non me ne importa ; **to take ~ of** *(look after)* prendersi cura di ; *(deal with)* occuparsi di ; **would you ~ to ...?** *fml* se vuole ...? ; **take ~!** *(goodbye)* stammi bene! ; **with ~** con cura ; **to ~ about** *(think important)* avere a cuore ; *(person)* voler bene a.
career [kə'rɪəʳ] *n* carriera *f*.
carefree ['keəfri:] *adj* spensierato(a).
careful ['keəfʊl] *adj (cautious)* attento(a) ; *(driver)* prudente ; *(thorough)* accurato(a) ; **be ~!** attento(a)!
carefully ['keəflɪ] *adv (cautiously)* con cautela ; *(thoroughly)* attentamente.
careless ['keələs] *adj (inattentive)* sbadato(a) ; *(unconcerned)* spensierato(a).
caretaker ['keəˌteɪkəʳ] *n Br* custode *mf*.
car ferry *n* traghetto *m*.
cargo ['ka:gəʊ] (*pl* **-es** OR **-s**) *n* carico *m*.
car hire *n Br* autonoleggio *m*.
caring ['keərɪŋ] *adj* premuroso(a).

carnation [kɑːˈneɪʃn] *n* garofano *m*.

carnival [ˈkɑːnɪvl] *n* carnevale *m*.

carousel [ˌkærəˈsel] *n (for luggage)* nastro *m* trasportatore ; *Am (merry-go-round)* giostra *f*.

car park *n Br* parcheggio *m*.

carpenter [ˈkɑːpəntəʳ] *n* falegname *m*.

carpentry [ˈkɑːpəntrɪ] *n* falegnameria *f*.

carpet [ˈkɑːpɪt] *n (rug)* tappeto *m* ; *(wall-to-wall)* moquette *f inv*.

car rental *n Am* autonoleggio *m*.

carriage [ˈkærɪdʒ] *n* carrozza *f*.

carriageway [ˈkærɪdʒweɪ] *n Br* carreggiata *f*.

carrier (bag) [ˈkærɪəʳ-] *n* sacchetto *m*.

carrot [ˈkærət] *n* carota *f*.

carrot cake *n* torta *f* di carote.

carry [ˈkærɪ] *vt* portare ; *(disease)* essere portatore di. ◆ *vi (voice, sound)* arrivare. ❑ **carry on** ◆ *vi* continuare. ◆ *vt fus (continue)* continuare ; *(conduct)* compiere ; **to ~ on doing sthg** continuare a fare qc. ❑ **carry out** *vt sep (work, repairs, investigation)* effettuare ; *(plan)* portare a compimento ; *(order)* eseguire ; *(promise)* adempiere.

carrycot [ˈkærɪkɒt] *n Br* culla *f* portatile.

carryout [ˈkærɪaʊt] *n Am & Scot (meal)* cibo *m* da asporto.

carsick [ˈkɑːˌsɪk] *adj* : **to be ~** soffrire il mal d'auto.

cart [kɑːt] *n (for transport)* carro *m* ; *inf (video game cartridge)* cartuccia *f* ; *Am (in supermarket)* carrello *m*.

carton [ˈkɑːtn] *n (of milk, juice)* cartone *m* ; *(box)* scatola *f*.

cartoon [kɑːˈtuːn] *n (drawing)* vignetta *f* ; *(comic strip)* fumetto *m* ; *(film)* cartone *m* animato.

cartridge [ˈkɑːtrɪdʒ] *n* cartuccia *f*.

carve [kɑːv] *vt (wood, stone)* intagliare ; *(meat)* tagliare.

carvery [ˈkɑːvərɪ] *n ristorante dove si mangia carne arrosto, tagliata appositamente al banco per il cliente.*

car wash *n* autolavaggio *m*.

case [keɪs] *n Br (suitcase)* valigia *f* ; *(container)* custodia *f* ; *(instance, patient)* caso *m* ; JUR *(trial)* causa *f* ; **in any ~** in ogni caso ; **in ~ it rains** nel caso che piova ; **in ~ of** in caso di ; **(just) in ~** in caso di necessità ; **in that ~** allora.

cash [kæʃ] *n (coins, notes)* contanti *mpl* ; *(money in general)* soldi *mpl*. ◆ *vt* : **to ~ a cheque** incassare un assegno ; **to pay ~** pagare in contanti.

cash desk *n* cassa *f*.

cash dispenser [-ˌdɪˈspensəʳ] *n* cassa *f* automatica.

cashew (nut) [ˈkæʃuː-] *n* anacardo *m*.

cashier [kæˈʃɪəʳ] *n* cassiere *m*, -a *f*.

cashmere [kæʃˈmɪəʳ] *n* cachemire *m*.

cashpoint [ˈkæʃpɔɪnt] *n Br* cassa *f* automatica, bancomat®.

cash register *n* registratore *m* di cassa.

casino [kə'si:nəʊ] (*pl* **-s**) *n* casinò *m inv*.
casserole ['kæsərəʊl] *n (stew)* stufato *m* ; ~ **(dish)** casseruola *f*.
cassette [kæ'set] *n* cassetta *f*.
cassette recorder *n* registratore *m* (a cassette).
cast [ka:st] (*pt* & *pp* **cast**) *n (actors)* cast *m inv* ; *(for broken bone)* ingessatura *f*. ◆ *vt (shadow, light, look)* gettare ; **to ~ doubt on** mettere in dubbio ; **to ~ one's vote** votare.
caster sugar *n Br* zucchero *m* semolato.
castle ['ka:sl] *n (building)* castello *m* ; *(in chess)* torre *f*.
casual ['kæʒʊəl] *adj (relaxed)* disinvolto(a) ; *(offhand)* noncurante ; *(clothes)* casual *(inv)* ; **~ work** lavoro occasionale.
casualty ['kæʒjʊəltɪ] *n (injured person)* ferito *m*, -a *f* ; *(dead person)* morto *m*, -a *f* ; **~ (ward)** pronto soccorso *m*.
cat [kæt] *n* gatto *m*.
catalog ['kætəlɒg] *Am* = **catalogue**.
catalogue ['kætəlɒg] *n* catalogo *m*.
catapult ['kætəpʌlt] *n* fionda *f*.
cataract ['kætərækt] *n (in eye)* cataratta *f*.
catarrh [kə'ta:ʳ] *n* catarro *m*.
catastrophe [kə'tæstrəfɪ] *n* catastrofe *f*.
catch [kætʃ] (*pt* & *pp* **caught**) *vt* prendere ; *(surprise, hear)* cogliere ; *(attention)* attirare. ◆ *vi (become hooked)* impigliarsi. ◆ *n (of window, door)* fermo *m* ; *(snag)* intoppo *m*. ❑ **catch up** ◆ *vt sep* raggiungere. ◆ *vi* : **to ~ up (with sthg)** *(sleep, work)* recuperare (qc) ; **to ~ up with sb** raggiungere qn.
catching ['kætʃɪŋ] *adj inf* contagioso(a).
category ['kætəgərɪ] *n* categoria *f*.
cater ['keɪtəʳ] : **cater for** *vt fus Br (needs)* provvedere a ; *(anticipate)* tenere conto di ; *(tastes)* soddisfare.
caterpillar ['kætəpɪləʳ] *n* bruco *m*.
cathedral [kə'θi:drəl] *n* cattedrale *f*, duomo *m*.
Catholic ['kæθlɪk] *adj* cattolico(a). ◆ *n* cattolico *m*, -a *f*.
Catseyes® ['kætsaɪz] *npl Br* catarifrangenti *mpl*.
cattle ['kætl] *npl* bestiame *m*.
cattle grid *n griglia metallica posta sul suolo stradale per impedire il passaggio di pecore, mucche, ecc.*
caught [kɔ:t] *pt* & *pp* → **catch**.
cauliflower ['kɒlɪˌflaʊəʳ] *n* cavolfiore *m*.
cauliflower cheese *n cavolfiore gratinato con besciamella.*
cause [kɔ:z] *n* causa *f* ; *(justification)* ragione *f*. ◆ *vt* causare ; **to ~ sb to make a mistake** far fare un errore a qn.
causeway ['kɔ:zweɪ] *n* strada *f* rialzata.
caution ['kɔ:ʃn] *n (care)* cautela *f* ; *(warning)* avvertimento *m*.
cautious ['kɔ:ʃəs] *adj* cauto(a).
cave [keɪv] *n* grotta *f*. ❑ **cave in** *vi* crollare.
caviar(e) ['kævɪa:ʳ] *n* caviale *m*.

cavity ['kævətɪ] *n (in tooth)* carie *f inv.*

CD *n (abbr of compact disc)* CD *m inv.*

CDI *n (abbr of compact disc interactive)* CDI *m (inv).*

CD player *n* lettore *m* di compact disc.

cease [siːs] *vt & vi fml* cessare.

ceasefire ['siːsˌfaɪəʳ] *n* cessate il fuoco *m inv.*

ceilidh ['keɪlɪ] *n festa scozzese o irlandese con danze folcloristiche.*

ceiling ['siːlɪŋ] *n* soffitto *m.*

celebrate ['selɪbreɪt] *vt (win, birthday)* festeggiare ; *(Mass)* celebrare. ◆ *vi* festeggiare.

celebration [ˌselɪ'breɪʃn] *n (event)* festa *f.* ❏ **celebrations** *npl (festivities)* festeggiamenti *mpl.*

celebrity [sɪ'lebrətɪ] *n (person)* celebrità *f inv.*

celeriac [sɪ'lerɪæk] *n* sedano *m* rapa.

celery ['selərɪ] *n* sedano *m.*

cell [sel] *n (of plant, body)* cellula *f* ; *(in prison)* cella *f.*

cellar ['seləʳ] *n* cantina *f.*

cello ['tʃeləʊ] (*pl* -s) *n* violoncello *m.*

Cellophane® ['seləfeɪn] *n* cellophane® *m.*

Celsius ['selsɪəs] *adj* Celsius *(inv).*

cement [sɪ'ment] *n* cemento *m.*

cemetery ['semɪtrɪ] *n* cimitero *m.*

cent [sent] *n Am* cent *m inv.*

center ['sentəʳ] *Am* = **centre.**

centigrade ['sentɪgreɪd] *adj* centigrado(a).

centimetre ['sentɪˌmiːtəʳ] *n* centimetro *m.*

centipede ['sentɪpiːd] *n* centopiedi *m inv.*

central ['sentrəl] *adj* centrale.

central heating *n* riscaldamento *m* autonomo.

central locking [-'lɒkɪŋ] *n* chiusura *f* delle porte centralizzata.

central reservation *n Br* zona *f* spartitraffico.

centre ['sentəʳ] *n Br* centro *m.* ◆ *adj Br* centrale ; **the ~ of attention** il centro dell'attenzione.

century ['sentʃʊrɪ] *n* secolo *m.*

ceramic [sɪ'ræmɪk] *adj* di ceramica. ❏ **ceramics** *npl* oggetti *mpl* di ceramica.

cereal ['sɪərɪəl] *n (breakfast food)* cereali *mpl.*

ceremony ['serɪmənɪ] *n* cerimonia *f.*

certain ['sɜːtn] *adj* certo(a) ; **she's ~ to be late** farà tardi di sicuro ; **to be ~ of sthg** essere certo di qc ; **to make ~ (that)** assicurarsi che.

certainly ['sɜːtnlɪ] *adv* certamente, certo.

certificate [sə'tɪfɪkət] *n* certificato *m.*

certify ['sɜːtɪfaɪ] *vt (declare true)* attestare.

chain [tʃeɪn] *n* catena *f* ; *(of islands)* arcipelago *m.* ◆ *vt* : **to ~ sthg to sthg** incatenare qc a qc.

chain store *n negozio che fa parte di una catena.*

chair [tʃeəʳ] *n* sedia *f.*

chair lift *n* seggiovia *f.*

chairman ['tʃeəmən] (*pl* **-men** [-mən]) *n* presidente *m*.

chairperson ['tʃeə,pɜːsn] (*pl* **-s**) *n* presidente *m*, -essa *f*.

chairwoman ['tʃeə,wʊmən] (*pl* **-women** [-,wɪmɪn]) *n* presidentessa *f*.

chalet ['ʃæleɪ] *n* chalet *m inv* ; *(at holiday camp)* bungalow *m inv*.

chalk [tʃɔːk] *n* gesso *m* ; **a piece of ~** un gesso.

chalkboard ['tʃɔːkbɔːd] *n Am* lavagna *f*.

challenge ['tʃælɪndʒ] *n* sfida *f*. ◆ *vt (question)* mettere in discussione ; **to ~ sb (to sthg)** sfidare qn (a qc).

chamber ['tʃeɪmbə'] *n (room)* sala *f*.

chambermaid ['tʃeɪmbəmeɪd] *n* cameriera *f* (d'albergo).

champagne [,ʃæm'peɪn] *n* champagne *m inv*.

champion ['tʃæmpjən] *n* campione *m*, -essa *f*.

championship ['tʃæmpjənʃɪp] *n* campionato *m*.

chance [tʃɑːns] *n (luck)* caso *m* ; *(possibility)* probabilità *f inv* ; *(opportunity)* possibilità *f inv*, occasione *f*. ◆ *vt* : **to ~ it** *inf* provarci ; **to take a ~** rischiare ; **by ~** per caso ; **I came on the off ~ you'd be here** sono venuto per vedere se per caso ci fossi.

Chancellor of the Exchequer [,tʃɑːnsələrəvðəɪks'tʃekə'] *n Br* ≃ ministro *m* del Tesoro.

chandelier [,ʃændə'lɪə'] *n* lampadario *m*.

change [tʃeɪndʒ] *n (alteration)* cambiamento *m* ; *(money received back)* resto *m* ; *(coins)* spiccioli *mpl*. ◆ *vt* cambiare. ◆ *vi* cambiare ; *(change clothes)* cambiarsi ; **a ~ of clothes** vestiti *mpl* di ricambio ; **do you have ~ for a pound?** mi può cambiare una sterlina? ; **for a ~** per cambiare ; **to get ~d** cambiarsi ; **to ~ money** cambiare i soldi ; **to ~ a nappy** cambiare un pannolino ; **to ~ a wheel** cambiare una ruota ; **to ~ trains/planes** cambiare treno/aereo ; **all ~!** *(on train)* per tutte le altre stazioni si cambia!

changeable ['tʃeɪndʒəbl] *adj (weather)* variabile.

change machine *n distributore automatico di monete*.

changing room ['tʃeɪndʒɪŋ-] *n (for sport)* spogliatoio *m* ; *(in shop)* camerino *m*.

channel ['tʃænl] *n* canale *m* ; **the (English) Channel** la Manica.

Channel Islands *npl* : **the ~** le Isole della Manica.

Channel Tunnel *n* : **the ~** il tunnel sotto la Manica.

chant [tʃɑːnt] *vt* RELIG cantare ; *(words, slogan)* scandire.

chaos ['keɪɒs] *n* caos *m*.

chaotic [keɪ'ɒtɪk] *adj* caotico(a).

chap [tʃæp] *n Br inf* tipo *m*.

chapatti [tʃə'pætɪ] *n* pane *m* azzimo indiano.

chapel ['tʃæpl] *n* cappella *f*.

chapped [tʃæpt] *adj* screpolato(a).

chapter ['tʃæptə'] *n* capitolo *m*.

character ['kærəktə'] *n* carattere

m ; *(in film, book, play)* personaggio *m* ; *inf (person, individual)* tipo *m*.

characteristic [ˌkærəktəˈrɪstɪk] *adj* caratteristico(a). ◆ *n* caratteristica *f*.

charcoal [ˈtʃɑːkəʊl] *n (for barbecue)* carbone *m* di legna.

charge [tʃɑːdʒ] *n (price)* spesa *f* ; JUR accusa *f*. ◆ *vt (customer)* far pagare ; *(money)* chiedere ; JUR accusare ; *(battery)* ricaricare. ◆ *vi (ask money)* far pagare ; *(rush)* precipitarsi ; **to be in ~ (of)** essere responsabile (di) ; **to take ~ (of)** assumere la responsabilità (di) ; **free of ~** gratis ; **extra ~** supplemento *m* ; **there is no ~ for service** il servizio è gratuito.

char-grilled [ˈtʃɑːgrɪld] *adj* alla brace.

charity [ˈtʃærətɪ] *n (organization)* ente *m* di beneficenza ; **to give to ~** dare soldi in beneficenza.

charity shop *n negozio che vende articoli vari, il cui ricavato è destinato ad un ente di beneficenza.*

charm [tʃɑːm] *n (attractiveness)* fascino *m*. ◆ *vt* affascinare.

charming [ˈtʃɑːmɪŋ] *adj* affascinante.

chart [tʃɑːt] *n (diagram)* grafico *m* ; *(map)* carta *f* ; **the ~s** l'hit-parade *f inv*.

chartered accountant [ˌtʃɑːtəd-] *n* esperto *m*, -a *f* contabile.

charter flight [ˈtʃɑːtə-] *n* volo *m* charter.

chase [tʃeɪs] *n* inseguimento *m*. ◆ *vt* inseguire.

chat [tʃæt] *n* chiacchierata *f*. ◆ *vi* chiacchierare ; **to have a ~ (with)** fare quattro chiacchiere (con). ❑ **chat up** *vt sep Br inf* agganciare.

château [ˈʃætəʊ] *n* castello *m*.

chat show *n Br* talk show *m inv*.

chatty [ˈtʃætɪ] *adj (person)* chiacchierone(a) ; *(letter)* pieno di pettegolezzi.

chauffeur [ˈʃəʊfəʳ] *n* autista *m*.

cheap [tʃiːp] *adj* a buon mercato ; *pej (low-quality)* dozzinale.

cheap day return *n biglietto di andata e ritorno a prezzo ridotto, valido per un solo giorno e soggetto a restrizioni di orario.*

cheaply [ˈtʃiːplɪ] *adv* a basso prezzo.

cheat [tʃiːt] *n* imbroglione *m*, -a *f*. ◆ *vi* imbrogliare. ◆ *vt* : **to ~ sb out of sthg** sottrarre qc a qn con l'inganno.

check [tʃek] *n (inspection)* controllo *m* ; *Am (bill)* conto *m* ; *Am (tick)* segno *m* ; *Am* = **cheque**. ◆ *vt* controllare ; *Am (tick)* spuntare. ◆ *vi* verificare ; **to ~ for sthg** controllare qc ; **to ~ on sthg** controllare qc. ❑ **check in** ◆ *vt sep (luggage)* far passare al check-in. ◆ *vi (at hotel)* farsi registrare ; *(at airport)* fare il check-in. ❑ **check off** *vt sep* spuntare. ❑ **check out** *vi* saldare il conto e andarsene. ❑ **check up** *vi* : **to ~ up (on)** fare delle indagini (su).

checked [tʃekt] *adj* a quadri.

checkers [ˈtʃekəz] *n Am* dama *f*.

check-in desk *n* banco *m* dell'accettazione bagagli OR del check-in.

checkout [ˈtʃekaʊt] *n* cassa *f*.

checkpoint ['tʃekpɔɪnt] *n* posto *m* di blocco.
checkroom ['tʃekrʊm] *n Am* deposito *m* bagagli.
checkup ['tʃekʌp] *n* check-up *m inv.*
cheddar (cheese) ['tʃedəʳ-] *n tipo di formaggio semi-stagionato.*
cheek [tʃi:k] *n* guancia *f*; **what a ~!** che faccia tosta!
cheeky ['tʃi:kɪ] *adj* sfacciato(a).
cheer [tʃɪəʳ] *n* acclamazione *f*. ◆ *vi* acclamare.
cheerful ['tʃɪəfʊl] *adj* allegro(a) ; *(colour)* vivace.
cheerio [ˌtʃɪərɪ'əʊ] *excl Br inf* ciao!
cheers [tʃɪəz] *excl (when drinking)* cin cin! ; *Br inf (thank you)* grazie!
cheese [tʃi:z] *n* formaggio *m*.
cheeseboard ['tʃi:zbɔ:d] *n (cheese and biscuits)* piatto *m* di formaggi.
cheeseburger ['tʃi:zˌbɜ:gəʳ] *n* cheeseburger *m inv (panino con hamburger e formaggio fuso).*
cheesecake ['tʃi:zkeɪk] *n dolce a base di biscotti, formaggio fresco e panna.*
chef [ʃef] *n* chef *m inv.*
chef's special *n* specialità *f inv* della casa.
chemical ['kemɪkl] *adj* chimico(a). ◆ *n* sostanza *f* chimica.
chemist ['kemɪst] *n Br (pharmacist)* farmacista *mf* ; *(scientist)* chimico *m*, -a *f*; **~'s** *Br (shop)* farmacia *f*.
chemistry ['kemɪstrɪ] *n* chimica *f*.
cheque [tʃek] *n Br* assegno *m* ; **to pay by ~** pagare con un assegno.
chequebook ['tʃekbʊk] *n* libretto *m* degli assegni.
cheque card *n* carta *f* assegni.
cherry ['tʃerɪ] *n* ciliegia *f*.
chess [tʃes] *n* scacchi *mpl.*
chest [tʃest] *n (of body)* torace *m* ; *(box)* cassa *f*.
chestnut ['tʃesnʌt] *n* castagna *f*. ◆ *adj (colour)* castano(a).
chest of drawers *n* cassettone *m*.
chew [tʃu:] *vt* masticare. ◆ *n (sweet)* caramella *f* (morbida).
chewing gum ['tʃu:ɪŋ-] *n* gomma *f* da masticare.
chic [ʃi:k] *adj* alla moda, chic *(inv)*.
chicken ['tʃɪkɪn] *n (bird)* gallina *f*; *(meat)* pollo *m*.
chicken pox *n* varicella *f*.
chickpea ['tʃɪkpi:] *n* cece *m*.
chicory ['tʃɪkərɪ] *n* cicoria *f*.
chief [tʃi:f] *adj (highest-ranking)* capo *(inv)* ; *(main)* principale. ◆ *n* capo *m*.
chiefly ['tʃi:flɪ] *adv (mainly)* principalmente ; *(especially)* soprattutto.
child [tʃaɪld] (*pl* **children**) *n (young boy, girl)* bambino *m*, -a *f*; *(son, daughter)* figlio *m*, -a *f*.
child abuse *n* maltrattamento *m* di minori.
child benefit *n Br* ≃ assegno *m* famigliare.
childhood ['tʃaɪldhʊd] *n* infanzia *f*.
childish ['tʃaɪldɪʃ] *adj pej* infantile.

childminder ['tʃaɪld,maɪndəʳ] *n Br* bambinaia *f*.

children ['tʃɪldrən] *pl* → **child**.

child seat *n (in car)* seggiolino *m* per bambini.

Chile ['tʃɪlɪ] *n* il Cile.

chill [tʃɪl] *n (illness)* infreddatura *f*. ◆ *vt* raffreddare ; **there's a ~ in the air** l'aria è fredda.

chilled [tʃɪld] *adj* freddo(a) ; **'serve ~'** 'servire fresco'.

chilli ['tʃɪlɪ] (*pl* **-ies**) *n (vegetable)* peperoncino *m* piccante ; *(dish)* = **chilli con carne**.

chilli con carne ['tʃɪlɪkɒn'kɑːnɪ] *n piatto messicano a base di carne e fagioli rossi cotti con spezie e salsa piccante.*

chilly ['tʃɪlɪ] *adj* freddo(a).

chimney ['tʃɪmnɪ] *n* camino *m*.

chimneypot ['tʃɪmnɪpɒt] *n* comignolo *m*.

chimpanzee [,tʃɪmpən'ziː] *n* scimpanzé *m inv*.

chin [tʃɪn] *n* mento *m*.

china ['tʃaɪnə] *n (material)* porcellana *f*.

China ['tʃaɪnə] *n* la Cina.

Chinese [,tʃaɪ'niːz] *adj* cinese. ◆ *n (language)* cinese *m*. ◆ *npl* : **the ~** i cinesi ; **a ~ restaurant** un ristorante cinese.

chip [tʃɪp] *n (small piece)* scheggia *f* ; *(mark)* scheggiatura *f* ; *(counter)* fiche *f inv* ; COMPUT chip *m inv*. ◆ *vt* scheggiare. ❑ **chips** *npl Br (French fries)* patate *fpl* fritte ; *Am (crisps)* patatine *fpl*.

chiropodist [kɪ'rɒpədɪst] *n* callista *mf*.

chives [tʃaɪvz] *npl* erba *f* cipollina.

chlorine ['klɔːriːn] *n* cloro *m*.

choc-ice ['tʃɒkaɪs] *n Br blocco di gelato ricoperto di cioccolato.*

chocolate ['tʃɒkələt] *n (food)* cioccolato *m*, cioccolata *f* ; *(sweet)* cioccolatino *m* ; *(drink)* cioccolata. ◆ *adj* al cioccolato.

chocolate biscuit *n* biscotto *m* al cioccolato.

choice [tʃɔɪs] *n* scelta *f*. ◆ *adj (meat, ingredients)* di prima qualità ; **the dressing of your ~** il condimento di vostra scelta.

choir ['kwaɪəʳ] *n* coro *m*.

choke [tʃəʊk] *n* AUT (valvola *f* dell')aria *f*. ◆ *vt* soffocare. ◆ *vi (on fishbone etc)* strozzarsi ; *(to death)* soffocare.

cholera ['kɒlərə] *n* colera *m*.

choose [tʃuːz] (*pt* **chose**, *pp* **chosen**) *vt* & *vi* scegliere ; **to ~ to do sthg** scegliere di fare qc.

chop [tʃɒp] *n (of meat)* braciola *f*. ◆ *vt* tagliare. ❑ **chop down** *vt sep* abbattere. ❑ **chop up** *vt sep* tagliare a pezzetti.

chopper ['tʃɒpəʳ] *n inf (helicopter)* elicottero *m*.

chopping board ['tʃɒpɪŋ-] *n* tagliere *m*.

choppy ['tʃɒpɪ] *adj* increspato(a).

chopsticks ['tʃɒpstɪks] *npl* bastoncini *mpl* cinesi.

chop suey [,tʃɒp'suːɪ] *n piatto cinese a base di riso, striscioline di maiale* OR *pollo, verdura e germogli di soia.*

chord [kɔːd] *n* accordo *m*.

chore [tʃɔːʳ] *n* faccenda *f*.
chorus ['kɔːrəs] *n (part of song)* ritornello *m* ; *(group of singers, dancers)* coro *m*.
chose [tʃəuz] *pt* → **choose**.
chosen ['tʃəuzn] *pp* → **choose**.
Christ [kraɪst] *n* Cristo *m*.
christen ['krɪsn] *vt (baby)* battezzare.
Christian ['krɪstʃən] *adj* cristiano(a). ◆ *n* cristiano *m*, -a *f*.
Christian name *n* nome *m* di battesimo.
Christmas ['krɪsməs] *n* Natale *m* ; **Happy ~!** Buon Natale!
Christmas card *n* biglietto *m* d'auguri di Natale.
Christmas carol [-'kærəl] *n* canto *m* di Natale.
Christmas Day *n* il giorno di Natale.
Christmas Eve *n* la vigilia di Natale.
Christmas pudding *n dolce tradizionale natalizio a base di uva passa e frutta candita.*
Christmas tree *n* albero *m* di Natale.
chrome [krəum] *n* cromo *m*.
chuck [tʃʌk] *vt inf (throw)* buttare ; *(boyfriend, girlfriend)* mollare. ❑ **chuck away** *vt sep* buttare via.
chunk [tʃʌŋk] *n* pezzo *m*.
church [tʃɜːtʃ] *n* chiesa *f*; **to go to ~** andare in chiesa.
churchyard ['tʃɜːtʃjaːd] *n* cimitero *m*.
chute [ʃuːt] *n* scivolo *m*.
cider ['saɪdəʳ] *n* sidro *m*.
cigar [sɪ'gaːʳ] *n* sigaro *m*.
cigarette [ˌsɪgə'ret] *n* sigaretta *f*.
cigarette lighter *n* accendino *m*.
cinema ['sɪnəmə] *n* cinema *m inv*.
cinnamon ['sɪnəmən] *n* cannella *f*.
circle ['sɜːkl] *n (shape, ring)* cerchio *m* ; *(in theatre)* galleria *f*. ◆ *vt (draw circle around)* cerchiare ; *(move round)* girare intorno a. ◆ *vi (plane)* girare in circolo.
circuit ['sɜːkɪt] *n (track)* circuito *m* ; *(lap)* giro *m*.
circular ['sɜːkjuləʳ] *adj* circolare. ◆ *n* circolare *f*.
circulation [ˌsɜːkju'leɪʃn] *n (of blood)* circolazione *f*; *(of newspaper, magazine)* tiratura *f*.
circumstances ['sɜːkəmstənsɪz] *npl* circostanze *fpl* ; **in** OR **under the ~** date le circostanze.
circus ['sɜːkəs] *n* circo *m*.
cistern ['sɪstən] *n (of toilet)* serbatoio *m* dell'acqua.
citizen ['sɪtɪzn] *n* cittadino *m*, -a *f*.
city ['sɪtɪ] *n* città *f inv* ; **the City** la City *(il centro finanziario di Londra)*.
city centre *n* centro *m* (della) città.
city hall *n Am* municipio *m*.
civilian [sɪ'vɪljən] *n* civile *m*.
civilized ['sɪvɪlaɪzd] *adj (society)* civilizzato(a) ; *(person, evening)* cortese.
civil rights [ˌsɪvl-] *npl* diritti *mpl* civili.
civil servant [ˌsɪvl-] *n* impiegato *m*, -a *f* statale.
civil service [ˌsɪvl-] *n* amministrazione *f* pubblica.

civil war [ˌsɪvl-] *n* guerra *f* civile.

cl (*abbr of centilitre*) cl.

claim [kleɪm] *n (assertion)* affermazione *f*; *(demand)* richiesta *f*, domanda *f*; *(for insurance)* domanda di indennizzo. ◆ *vt (allege)* affermare, sostenere ; *(demand)* richiedere ; *(credit, responsibility)* rivendicare. ◆ *vi (on insurance)* richiedere l'indennizzo.

claimant ['kleɪmənt] *n (of benefit)* richiedente *mf*.

claim form *n* modulo *m* per il rimborso.

clam [klæm] *n* vongola *f*.

clamp [klæmp] *n (for car)* ganascia *f* (bloccaruota). ◆ *vt (car)* bloccare con ganasce.

clap [klæp] *vi* applaudire.

claret ['klærət] *n vino rosso di Bordeaux*.

clarinet [ˌklærə'net] *n* clarinetto *m*.

clash [klæʃ] *n (noise)* rumore *m* metallico ; *(confrontation)* scontro *m*. ◆ *vi (colours)* stonare ; *(event, date)* coincidere.

clasp [klaːsp] *n (fastener)* fermaglio *m*. ◆ *vt* stringere.

class [klaːs] *n* classe *f*; *(teaching period)* lezione *f*. ◆ *vt* : **to ~ sb/sthg (as)** classificare qn/qc (come).

classic ['klæsɪk] *adj* classico(a). ◆ *n* classico *m*.

classical ['klæsɪkl] *adj* classico(a).

classical music *n* musica *f* classica.

classification [ˌklæsɪfɪ'keɪʃn] *n* classificazione *f*.

classified ads [ˌklæsɪfaɪd-] *npl* piccoli annunci *mpl*.

classroom ['klaːsrum] *n* aula *f*.

claustrophobic [ˌklɔːstrə'fəʊbɪk] *adj (person)* claustrofobo(a) ; *(place, situation)* claustrofobico(a).

claw [klɔː] *n (of bird, cat, dog)* artiglio *m* ; *(of crab, lobster)* pinza *f*.

clay [kleɪ] *n* argilla *f*.

clean [kliːn] *vt* pulire. ◆ *adj* pulito(a) ; **to ~ one's teeth** lavarsi i denti ; **I have a ~ driving licence** non sono mai stato multato per infrazioni gravi.

cleaner ['kliːnə'] *n (person)* addetto *m*, -a *f* alle pulizie ; *(substance)* detergente *m*.

cleanse [klenz] *vt* pulire.

cleanser ['klenzə'] *n* detergente *m*.

clear [klɪə'] *adj* chiaro(a) ; *(transparent)* trasparente ; *(unobstructed)* libero(a) ; *(view)* sgombro(a) ; *(day, sky)* sereno(a). ◆ *vt (road, path)* sgombrare ; *(pond)* ripulire ; *(jump over)* saltare ; *(declare not guilty)* scagionare ; *(authorize)* autorizzare ; *(cheque)* autorizzare l'accreditamento di. ◆ *vi (weather)* schiarirsi ; *(fog)* levarsi ; **to be ~ (about sthg)** avere capito esattamente (qc) ; **to be ~ of sthg** *(not touching)* essere staccato da qc ; **to ~ one's throat** schiarirsi la voce ; **to ~ the table** sparecchiare. ❑ **clear up** ◆ *vt sep (room, toys)* mettere a posto ; *(problem, confusion)* chiarire. ◆ *vi (weather)* schiarirsi ; *(tidy up)* mettere a posto.

clearance ['klɪərəns] *n (authorization)* autorizzazione *f*; *(free*

distance) distanza *f*; *(for takeoff)* autorizzazione (al decollo).
clearance sale *n* liquidazione *f* totale della merce.
clearing ['klɪərɪŋ] *n* radura *f*.
clearly ['klɪəlɪ] *adv* chiaramente.
clementine ['kleməntaɪn] *n* mandarancio *m*.
clerk [*Br* klaːk, *Am* klɜːrk] *n (in office)* impiegato *m*, -a *f*; *Am (in shop)* commesso *m*, -a *f*.
clever ['klevəʳ] *adj (person)* intelligente ; *(idea, device)* ingegnoso(a).
click [klɪk] *n* scatto *m*. ◆ *vi (make sound)* schioccare.
client ['klaɪənt] *n* cliente *mf*.
cliff [klɪf] *n (by the sea)* scoglio *m* ; *(inland)* rupe *f*.
climate ['klaɪmɪt] *n* clima *m*.
climax ['klaɪmæks] *n* culmine *m*.
climb [klaɪm] *vt* salire su ; *(tree)* arrampicarsi su ; *(mountain)* scalare. ◆ *vi* salire ; *(plane)* prendere quota. ❑ **climb down** ◆ *vt fus* scendere da. ◆ *vi* scendere. ❑ **climb up** *vt fus* salire su.
climber ['klaɪməʳ] *n (person)* scalatore *m*, -trice *f*.
climbing ['klaɪmɪŋ] *n* alpinismo *m* ; **to go ~** fare alpinismo.
climbing frame *n Br* castello *m (gioco per bambini)*.
clingfilm ['klɪŋfɪlm] *n Br* pellicola *f* (per alimenti).
clinic ['klɪnɪk] *n* clinica *f*.
clip [klɪp] *n (fastener)* fermaglio *m* ; *(for paper)* graffetta *f* ; *(of film, programme)* sequenza *f*. ◆ *vt (fasten)* fermare insieme ; *(cut)* tagliare ; *(tickets)* forare.
cloak [kləʊk] *n* mantello *m*.
cloakroom ['kləʊkrʊm] *n (for coats)* guardaroba *m inv* ; *Br (toilet)* toilettes *fpl*.
clock [klɒk] *n* orologio *m* ; *(mileometer)* contachilometri *m inv* ; **round the ~** 24 ore su 24.
clockwise ['klɒkwaɪz] *adv* in senso orario.
clog [klɒg] *n* zoccolo *m*. ◆ *vt* intasare.
close[1] [kləʊs] *adj* vicino(a) ; *(relation, contact, resemblance)* stretto(a) ; *(friend)* intimo(a) ; *(examination)* attento(a) ; *(race, contest)* combattuto(a). ◆ *adv* vicino ; **~ by** vicino ; **~ to** *(near)* vicino a ; *(on the verge of)* sull'orlo di.
close[2] [kləʊz] *vt* chiudere. ◆ *vi (door, jar, eyes)* chiudersi ; *(shop, office)* chiudere ; *(deadline, offer, meeting)* finire. ❑ **close down** *vt sep & vi* chiudere (definitivamente).
closed [kləʊzd] *adj* chiuso(a).
closely ['kləʊslɪ] *adv (related, involved)* strettamente ; *(follow, examine)* da vicino, attentamente.
closet ['klɒzɪt] *n Am* armadio *m*.
close-up ['kləʊs-] *n* primo piano *m*.
closing time ['kləʊzɪŋ-] *n* orario *m* di chiusura.
clot [klɒt] *n (of blood)* grumo *m*.
cloth [klɒθ] *n (fabric)* stoffa *f*, tessuto *m* ; *(piece of cloth)* strofinaccio *m*, panno *m*.
clothes [kləʊðz] *npl* vestiti *mpl*, abiti *mpl*.
clothesline ['kləʊðzlaɪn] *n* filo *m* della biancheria.

clothes peg *n Br* molletta *f*.
clothespin ['kləʊðzpɪn] *Am* = clothes peg.
clothes shop *n* negozio *m* di abbigliamento.
clothing ['kləʊðɪŋ] *n* abbigliamento *m*.
clotted cream [ˌklɒtɪd-] *n panna molto densa tipica della Cornovaglia*.
cloud [klaʊd] *n* nuvola *f*.
cloudy ['klaʊdɪ] *adj (sky, day)* nuvoloso(a) ; *(liquid)* torbido(a).
clove [kləʊv] *n (of garlic)* spicchio *m*. ❑ **cloves** *npl (spice)* chiodi *mpl* di garofano.
clown [klaʊn] *n* pagliaccio *m*.
club [klʌb] *n (organization)* club *m inv*, circolo *m* ; *(nightclub)* locale *m* notturno ; *(stick)* mazza *f*. ❑ **clubs** *npl (in cards)* fiori *mpl*.
clubbing ['klʌbɪŋ] *n* : **to go ~** *inf* andare in discoteca.
club class *n* club class *f inv*.
club sandwich *n Am sandwich a due* OR *più strati*.
club soda *n Am acqua f di seltz*.
clue [kluː] *n (information)* indizio *m* ; *(in crossword)* definizione *f*; **I haven't got a ~** non ho la minima idea.
clumsy ['klʌmzɪ] *adj (person)* goffo(a).
clutch [klʌtʃ] *n* frizione *f*. ◆ *vt* tenere stretto, afferrare.
cm (*abbr of centimetre*) cm.
c/o (*abbr of care of*) c/o.
Co. (*abbr of company*) C.ia.
coach [kəʊtʃ] *n (bus)* pullman *m inv*, autobus *m inv* ; *(of train)* carrozza *f* ; SPORT allenatore *m*, -trice *f*.
coach station *n* stazione *f* dei pullman.
coach trip *n Br* escursione *f* in pullman.
coal [kəʊl] *n* carbone *m*.
coal mine *n* miniera *f* di carbone.
coarse [kɔːs] *adj (rough)* ruvido(a) ; *(vulgar)* rozzo(a).
coast [kəʊst] *n* costa *f*.
coaster ['kəʊstəʳ] *n (for glass)* sottobicchiere *m*.
coastguard ['kəʊstgaːd] *n* guardia *f* costiera.
coastline ['kəʊstlaɪn] *n* costa *f*.
coat [kəʊt] *n* cappotto *m* ; *(of animal)* pelo *m*. ◆ *vt* : **to ~ sthg (with)** ricoprire qc (con OR di).
coat hanger *n* gruccia *f* (per abiti).
coating ['kəʊtɪŋ] *n* rivestimento *m*.
cobbles ['kɒblz] *npl* ciottoli *mpl*.
cobweb ['kɒbweb] *n* ragnatela *f*.
Coca-Cola® [ˌkəʊkə'kəʊlə] *n* Coca-Cola® *f*.
cocaine [kəʊ'keɪn] *n* cocaina *f*.
cock [kɒk] *n (male chicken)* gallo *m*.
cockles ['kɒklz] *npl* cardii *mpl*.
cockpit ['kɒkpɪt] *n* cabina *f* di pilotaggio.
cockroach ['kɒkrəʊtʃ] *n* scarafaggio *m*.
cocktail ['kɒkteɪl] *n* cocktail *m inv*.
cocktail party *n* cocktail *m inv*.
cock-up *n Br (vulg)* casino *m*.

cocoa ['kəukəu] *n (drink)* cacao *m*.
coconut ['kəukənʌt] *n* noce *f* di cocco.
cod [kɒd] *(pl inv) n* merluzzo *m*.
code [kəud] *n* codice *m* ; *(dialling code)* prefisso *m*.
coeducational [ˌkəuedjuːˈkeɪʃənl] *adj* misto(a).
coffee ['kɒfɪ] *n* caffè *m inv* ; **black/white ~** caffè nero/macchiato ; **ground/instant ~** caffè macinato/istantaneo.
coffee bar *n Br* caffè *m inv*.
coffee break *n* pausa *f* per il caffè.
coffeepot ['kɒfɪpɒt] *n* caffettiera *f*.
coffee shop *n (cafe)* caffè *m inv*, bar *m inv* ; *(in store etc)* caffetteria *f*.
coffee table *n* tavolino *m* (basso).
coffin ['kɒfɪn] *n* bara *f*.
cog(wheel) ['kɒg (wiːl)] *n* ingranaggio *m*.
coil [kɔɪl] *n (of rope)* rotolo *m* ; *Br (contraceptive)* spirale *f*. ◆ *vt* avvolgere, arrotolare.
coin [kɔɪn] *n* moneta *f*.
coinbox ['kɔɪnbɒks] *n Br* telefono *m* a monete.
coincide [ˌkəuɪn'saɪd] *vi* : **to ~ (with)** coincidere (con).
coincidence [kəu'ɪnsɪdəns] *n* coincidenza *f*.
Coke® [kəuk] *n* coca® *f*.
colander ['kʌləndəʳ] *n* colino *m*.
cold [kəuld] *adj* freddo(a). ◆ *n (illness)* raffreddore *m* ; *(low temperature)* freddo *m* ; **I'm ~** ho freddo ; **it's ~** fa freddo ; **to get ~** *(food, drink)* raffreddarsi ; *(person)* avere freddo ; *(weather)* venire freddo ; **to catch ~** prendere freddo ; **to catch a ~** prendere il raffreddore.
cold cuts *Am* = **cold meats**.
cold meats *npl* affettati *mpl*.
coleslaw ['kəulslɔː] *n insalata di cavolo, carote, cipolle e maionese*.
colic ['kɒlɪk] *n* colica *f*.
collaborate [kə'læbəreɪt] *vi* collaborare.
collapse [kə'læps] *vi (building, tent)* crollare ; *(person)* avere un collasso.
collar ['kɒləʳ] *n (of shirt, coat)* colletto *m* ; *(of dog, cat)* collare *m*.
collarbone ['kɒləbəun] *n* clavicola *f*.
colleague ['kɒliːg] *n* collega *mf*.
collect [kə'lekt] *vt* raccogliere ; *(as a hobby)* collezionare ; *(go and get)* andare a prendere. ◆ *vi (dust, leaves, crowd)* raccogliersi. ◆ *adv Am* : **to call ~** fare una telefonata a carico del destinatario.
collection [kə'lekʃn] *n (of stamps, coins etc)* collezione *f*, raccolta *f* ; *(of stories, poems)* raccolta ; *(of money)* colletta *f* ; *(of mail)* levata *f*.
collector [kə'lektəʳ] *n (as a hobby)* collezionista *mf*.
college ['kɒlɪdʒ] *n (school)* istituto *m* superiore ; *Br (of university)* tipo di organizzazione indipendente di studenti e professori in cui si dividono certe università ; *Am (university)* università *f inv*.
collide [kə'laɪd] *vi* : **to ~ (with)** scontrarsi (con).
collision [kə'lɪʒn] *n* collisione *f*.

cologne [kə'ləʊn] *n* (acqua *f* di) colonia.

colon ['kəʊlən] *n* GRAMM due punti *mpl*.

colony ['kɒlənɪ] *n* colonia *f*.

color ['kʌlər] *Am* = **colour**.

colour ['kʌləʳ] *n* colore *m*. ◆ *adj (photograph, film)* a colori. ◆ *vt (hair)* tingere ; *(food)* colorare.
❑ **colour in** *vt sep* colorare.

colour-blind *adj* daltonico(a).

colourful ['kʌləfʊl] *adj* vivace.

colouring ['kʌlərɪŋ] *n (of food)* colorante *m* ; *(complexion)* colorito *m*.

colouring book *n* album *m inv* da colorare.

colour supplement *n* supplemento *m* a colori.

colour television *n* televisione *f* a colori.

column ['kɒləm] *n* colonna *f*; *(newspaper article)* rubrica *f*.

coma ['kəʊmə] *n* coma *m inv*.

comb [kəʊm] *n* pettine *m*. ◆ *vt* : **to ~ one's hair** pettinarsi.

combination [ˌkɒmbɪ'neɪʃn] *n* combinazione *f*.

combine [kəm'baɪn] *vt* : **to ~ sthg (with)** combinare qc (con).

☞

come [kʌm] (*pt* **came**, *pp* **come**) *vi*
- 1. *(move)* venire ; **we came by taxi** siamo venuti in taxi ; **~ and see!** vieni a vedere! ; **~ here!** vieni qui!
- 2. *(arrive)* arrivare ; **they still haven't ~** non sono ancora arrivati ; **to ~ home** tornare a casa ; **'coming soon'** 'prossimamente'.
- 3. *(in order)* : **to ~ first** *(in sequence)* venire per primo ; *(in competition)* arrivare primo ; **to ~ last** *(in sequence)* venire per ultimo ; *(in competition)* arrivare ultimo.
- 4. *(reach)* : **to ~ up/down to** arrivare a.
- 5. *(become)* : **to ~ undone** slacciarsi ; **to ~ true** realizzarsi.
- 6. *(be sold)* : **they ~ in packs of six** si vendono in confezioni da sei.

❑ **come across** *vt fus (person)* imbattersi in ; *(thing)* trovare (per caso).

❑ **come along** *vi (progress)* procedere ; *(arrive)* arrivare ; **~ along!** *(as encouragement)* forza! ; *(hurry up)* sbrigati!

❑ **come apart** *vi* cadere a pezzi.

❑ **come back** *vi* tornare.

❑ **come down** *vi (price)* calare.

❑ **come down with** *vt fus (illness)* buscarsi.

❑ **come from** *vt fus* venire da.

❑ **come in** *vi (enter)* entrare ; *(arrive)* arrivare ; *(tide)* salire ; **~ in!** avanti!.

❑ **come off** *vi (become detached)* staccarsi, venir via ; *(succeed)* riuscire.

❑ **come on** *vi (project)* procedere ; *(student)* fare progressi ; **~ on!** *(as encouragement)* forza! ; *(hurry up)* sbrigati!

❑ **come out** *vi* uscire ; *(photo)* venire, riuscire ; *(stain)* scomparire ; *(sun, moon)* apparire.

❑ **come over** *vi (visit)* venire.

❑ **come round** *vi (visit)* venire ; *(regain consciousness)* riprendere conoscenza.

❑ **come to** *vt fus (subj : bill)* : **it ~s to £10** viene 10 sterline.

❑ **come up** *vi (go upstairs)* salire ; *(be mentioned)* essere sollevato(a) ;

(happen, arise) presentarsi ; *(sun, moon)* sorgere.
❑ **come up with** *vt fus (idea)* proporre.

comedian [kə'mi:djən] *n* comico *m*, -a *f*.
comedy ['kɒmədɪ] *n* commedia *f*; *(humour)* humour *m*.
comfort ['kʌmfət] *n (ease)* benessere *m* ; *(luxury)* comfort *m inv*, comodità *f inv* ; *(consolation)* conforto *m*. ◆ *vt* confortare, consolare.
comfortable ['kʌmftəbl] *adj* comodo(a) ; *(after operation)* in condizioni stazionarie ; *(financially)* agiato(a) ; **I don't feel ~ here** non mi sento a mio agio qui.
comic ['kɒmɪk] *adj* comico(a). ◆ *n (person)* comico *m*, -a *f* ; *(magazine)* giornalino *m*.
comical ['kɒmɪkl] *adj* comico(a).
comic strip *n* fumetto *m*.
comma ['kɒmə] *n* virgola *f*.
command [kə'ma:nd] *n (order)* comando *m*, ordine *m* ; *(mastery)* padronanza *f*. ◆ *vt (order)* ordinare a ; *(be in charge of)* comandare.
commander [kə'ma:ndə^r] *n* comandante *m*.
commemorate [kə'memәreɪt] *vt* commemorare.
commence [kə'mens] *vi fml* cominciare.
comment ['kɒment] *n* commento *m*. ◆ *vi* commentare.
commentary ['kɒməntrɪ] *n (on TV)* telecronaca *f* ; *(on radio)* radiocronaca *f*.
commentator ['kɒmənteɪtə^r] *n (on TV)* telecronista *mf* ; *(on radio)* radiocronista *mf*.
commerce ['kɒmɜ:s] *n* commercio *m*.
commercial [kə'mɜ:ʃl] *adj* commerciale. ◆ *n* pubblicità *f inv*.
commercial break *n* intervallo *m* pubblicitario.
commission [kə'mɪʃn] *n* commissione *f*.
commit [kə'mɪt] *vt (crime, sin)* commettere ; **to ~ o.s. (to doing sthg)** impegnarsi (a fare qc) ; **to ~ suicide** suicidarsi.
committee [kə'mɪtɪ] *n* comitato *m*.
commodity [kə'mɒdətɪ] *n* merce *f*, articolo *m*.
common ['kɒmən] *adj* comune ; *pej (vulgar)* volgare. ◆ *n Br (land)* prato *m* pubblico ; **in ~** *(shared)* in comune.
commonly ['kɒmənlɪ] *adv (generally)* comunemente.
Common Market *n* Mercato *m* comune.
common sense *n* buonsenso *m*.
Commonwealth ['kɒmənwelθ] *n* : **the ~** il Commonwealth.
communal ['kɒmjʊnl] *adj (bathroom, kitchen)* in comune.
communicate [kə'mju:nɪkeɪt] *vi* : **to ~ (with)** comunicare (con).
communication [kə,mju:nɪ'keɪʃn] *n* comunicazione *f*.
communication cord *n Br* freno *m* di emergenza.
communist ['kɒmjʊnɪst] *n* comunista *mf*.

community [kə'mju:nətɪ] *n* comunità *f inv*.

community centre *n* centro *m* sociale.

commute [kə'mju:t] *vi* fare il pendolare.

commuter [kə'mju:tə^r] *n* pendolare *mf*.

compact [*adj* kəm'pækt, *n* 'kɒmpækt] *adj* compatto(a). ◆ *n (for make-up)* portacipria *m inv*; *Am (car)* utilitaria *f*.

compact disc player *n* lettore *m* di compact disc.

company ['kʌmpənɪ] *n (business)* società *f inv*, compagnia *f*; *(companionship, guests)* compagnia; **to keep sb ~** fare OR tenere compagnia a qn.

company car *n* auto *f* della ditta.

comparatively [kəm'pærətɪvlɪ] *adv* relativamente.

compare [kəm'peə^r] *vt*: **to ~ sthg (with)** confrontare qc (con); **~d with** paragonato a.

comparison [kəm'pærɪsn] *n* confronto *m*, paragone *m*; **in ~ with** in confronto a.

compartment [kəm'pa:tmənt] *n (of train)* scompartimento *m*; *(section)* compartimento *m*.

compass ['kʌmpəs] *n (magnetic)* bussola *f*; **(a pair of) ~es** un compasso.

compatible [kəm'pætəbl] *adj* compatibile.

compensate ['kɒmpenseɪt] *vt* risarcire. ◆ *vi*: **to ~ (for sthg)** compensare (qc); **to ~ sb for sthg** compensare qn di OR per qc.

compensation [ˌkɒmpen'seɪʃn] *n (money)* risarcimento *m*.

compete [kəm'pi:t] *vi (take part)* gareggiare, concorrere; **to ~ with sb for sthg** competere con qn per qc.

competent ['kɒmpɪtənt] *adj* competente.

competition [ˌkɒmpɪ'tɪʃn] *n (race, contest)* gara *f*, competizione *f*; *(rivalry)* concorrenza *f*; **the ~** *(rivals)* la concorrenza.

competitive [kəm'petətɪv] *adj (price)* competitivo(a); *(person)* che ha spirito di competizione.

competitor [kəm'petɪtə^r] *n* concorrente *mf*.

complain [kəm'pleɪn] *vi*: **to ~ (about)** lamentarsi (di).

complaint [kəm'pleɪnt] *n (statement)* lamentela *f*, reclamo *m*; *(illness)* malattia *f*.

complement ['kɒmplɪˌment] *vt* completare.

complete [kəm'pli:t] *adj* completo(a). ◆ *vt* completare; *(a form)* riempire; **~ with** completo di.

completely [kəm'pli:tlɪ] *adv* completamente.

complex ['kɒmpleks] *adj* complesso(a). ◆ *n* complesso *m*.

complexion [kəm'plekʃn] *n (of skin)* carnagione *f*.

complicated ['kɒmplɪkeɪtɪd] *adj* complicato(a).

compliment [*n* 'kɒmplɪmənt, *vb* 'kɒmplɪment] *n* complimento *m*. ◆ *vt* fare i complimenti a.

complimentary [ˌkɒmplɪ'mentərɪ] *adj (seat, ticket)*

(in) omaggio *(inv)* ; *(words, person)* lusinghiero(a).

compose [kəm'pəʊz] *vt* comporre ; **to be ~d of** essere composto da OR di.

composed [kəm'pəʊzd] *adj* composto(a), calmo(a).

composer [kəm'pəʊzəʳ] *n* compositore *m*, -trice *f*.

composition [ˌkɒmpə'zɪʃn] *n* *(essay)* composizione *f*.

compound ['kɒmpaʊnd] *n* *(substance)* composto *m* ; *(word)* parola *f* composta.

comprehensive [ˌkɒmprɪ'hensɪv] *adj* esauriente, completo(a).

comprehensive (school) *n Br* *scuola secondaria ad ammissione non selettiva.*

comprise [kəm'praɪz] *vt* comprendere.

compromise ['kɒmprəmaɪz] *n* compromesso *m*.

compulsory [kəm'pʌlsərɪ] *adj* obbligatorio(a).

computer [kəm'pju:təʳ] *n* computer *m inv*.

computer game *n* gioco *m* su computer.

computerized [kəm'pju:təraɪzd] *adj* computerizzato(a).

computer operator *n* operatore *m*, -trice *f* di computer.

computer programmer [-'prəʊgræməʳ] *n* programmatore *m*, -trice *f*.

computing [kəm'pju:tɪŋ] *n* informatica *f*.

con [kɒn] *n inf (trick)* truffa *f* ; **all mod ~s** tutti i comfort.

conceal [kən'si:l] *vt* nascondere.

conceited [kən'si:tɪd] *adj pej* presuntuoso(a).

concentrate ['kɒnsəntreɪt] *vi* concentrarsi. ◆ *vt* : **to be ~d** *(in one place)* essere concentrato ; **to ~ on sthg** concentrarsi su qc.

concentrated ['kɒnsəntreɪtɪd] *adj (juice, soup, baby food)* concentrato(a).

concentration [ˌkɒnsən'treɪʃn] *n* concentrazione *f*.

concern [kən'sɜ:n] *n* *(worry)* preoccupazione *f* ; *(matter of interest)* affare *m* ; COMM azienda *f*. ◆ *vt* *(be about)* trattare di ; *(worry)* preoccupare ; *(involve)* riguardare ; **to be ~ed about** essere preoccupato per ; **to be ~ed with** riguardare ; **to ~ o.s. with sthg** preoccuparsi di qc ; **as far as I'm ~ed** per quanto mi riguarda.

concerned [kən'sɜ:nd] *adj (worried)* preoccupato(a).

concerning [kən'sɜ:nɪŋ] *prep* riguardo a, circa.

concert ['kɒnsət] *n* concerto *m*.

concession [kən'seʃn] *n* *(reduced price)* riduzione *f*.

concise [kən'saɪs] *adj* conciso(a).

conclude [kən'klu:d] *vt* concludere. ◆ *vi fml (end)* concludersi.

conclusion [kən'klu:ʒn] *n* conclusione *f*.

concrete ['kɒŋkri:t] *adj (building, path)* di cemento ; *(idea, plan)* concreto(a). ◆ *n* calcestruzzo *m*, cemento *m* armato.

concussion [kən'kʌʃn] *n* commozione *f* cerebrale.

condensation [ˌkɒnden'seɪʃn] *n* condensazione *f*.

condition [kən'dɪʃn] *n* condizione *f*; *(illness)* malattia *f*; **on ~ that** a condizione che *(+ subjunctive)*.

conditioner [kən'dɪʃnəʳ] *n (for hair)* balsamo *m*; *(for clothes)* ammorbidente *m*.

condo ['kɒndəʊ] *Am inf* = **condominium**.

condom ['kɒndəm] *n* preservativo *m*.

condominium [ˌkɒndə'mɪnɪəm] *n Am (block of flats)* condominio *m*; *(flat)* appartamento *m* in un condominio.

conduct [*vb* kən'dʌkt, *n* 'kɒndʌkt] *vt (investigation, business)* dirigere, condurre; MUS dirigere. ◆ *n fml (behaviour)* condotta *f*; **to ~ o.s.** *fml* comportarsi.

conductor [kən'dʌktəʳ] *n* MUS direttore *m*, -trice *f* d'orchestra; *(on bus)* bigliettaio *m*, -a *f*; *Am (on train)* capotreno *mf*.

cone [kəʊn] *n* cono *m*; *(on roads)* cono spartitraffico.

confectionery [kən'fekʃnərɪ] *n* dolciumi *mpl*.

conference ['kɒnfərəns] *n* conferenza *f*.

confess [kən'fes] *vi*: **to ~ (to sthg)** confessare (qc).

confession [kən'feʃn] *n* confessione *f*.

confidence ['kɒnfɪdəns] *n (self-assurance)* sicurezza *f* di sé; *(trust)* fiducia *f*; **to have ~ in** avere fiducia in.

confident ['kɒnfɪdənt] *adj (self-assured)* sicuro(a) di sé; *(certain)* sicuro.

confined [kən'faɪnd] *adj* ristretto(a).

confirm [kən'fɜːm] *vt* confermare.

confirmation [ˌkɒnfə'meɪʃn] *n* conferma *f*; RELIG cresima *f*.

conflict [*n* 'kɒnflɪkt, *vb* kən'flɪkt] *n* conflitto *m*. ◆ *vi*: **to ~ (with)** essere in conflitto (con).

conform [kən'fɔːm] *vi*: **to ~ (to)** conformarsi (a).

confuse [kən'fjuːz] *vt* confondere; **to ~ sthg with sthg** confondere qc con qc.

confused [kən'fjuːzd] *adj* confuso(a).

confusing [kən'fjuːzɪŋ] *adj (explanation, plot)* confuso(a).

confusion [kən'fjuːʒn] *n* confusione *f*.

congested [kən'dʒestɪd] *adj (street)* congestionato(a).

congestion [kən'dʒestʃn] *n (traffic)* congestione *f*.

congratulate [kən'grætʃʊleɪt] *vt*: **to ~ sb (on sthg)** congratularsi con qn (per OR di qc).

congratulations [kənˌgrætʃʊ'leɪʃənz] *excl* congratulazioni!

congregate ['kɒŋgrɪgeɪt] *vi* riunirsi.

Congress ['kɒŋgres] *n Am* il Congresso.

conifer ['kɒnɪfəʳ] *n* conifera *f*.

conjunction [kən'dʒʌŋkʃn] *n* GRAMM congiunzione *f*.

conjurer ['kʌndʒərəʳ] *n* prestigiatore *m*, -trice *f*.

connect [kə'nekt] *vt* collegare, connettere ; *(telephone, machine)* collegare ; *(caller on phone)* dare la linea a. ◆ *vi* : **to ~ with** *(train, plane)* avere la coincidenza con ; **to ~ sthg with sthg** *(associate)* collegare qc con OR a qc.

connecting flight [kə'nektɪŋ-] *n* volo *m* di coincidenza.

connection [kə'nekʃn] *n (link)* collegamento *m* ; *(train, plane)* coincidenza *f* ; **it's a bad ~** *(on phone)* la linea è disturbata ; **a loose ~** *(in machine)* un contatto difettoso ; **in ~ with** riguardo a, a proposito di.

conquer ['kɒŋkə^r] *vt (country)* conquistare.

conscience ['kɒnʃəns] *n* coscienza *f*.

conscientious [ˌkɒnʃɪ'enʃəs] *adj* coscienzioso(a).

conscious ['kɒnʃəs] *adj (awake)* cosciente ; *(deliberate)* consapevole ; **to be ~ of** *(aware)* essere consapevole di.

consent [kən'sent] *n* consenso *m*.

consequence ['kɒnsɪkwəns] *n (result)* conseguenza *f*.

consequently ['kɒnsɪkwəntlɪ] *adv* di conseguenza.

conservation [ˌkɒnsə'veɪʃn] *n* tutela *f* dell'ambiente.

conservative [kən'sɜːvətɪv] *adj* conservatore(trice). ❑ **Conservative** *adj* conservatore(trice). ◆ *n* conservatore *m*, -trice *f*.

conservatory [kən'sɜːvətrɪ] *n* veranda *f* vetrata.

consider [kən'sɪdə^r] *vt* considerare ; **to ~ doing sthg** pensare di fare qc.

considerable [kən'sɪdrəbl] *adj* considerevole.

consideration [kənˌsɪdə'reɪʃn] *n* considerazione *f* ; **to take sthg into ~** prendere qc in considerazione.

considering [kən'sɪdərɪŋ] *prep* considerando.

consist [kən'sɪst] ◆**consist in** *vt fus* consistere in ; **to ~ in doing sthg** consistere nel fare qc. ❑ **consist of** *vt fus* essere composto di OR da.

consistent [kən'sɪstənt] *adj (coherent)* coerente ; *(worker, performance)* costante.

consolation [ˌkɒnsə'leɪʃn] *n* consolazione *f*.

console ['kɒnsəʊl] *n* console *f inv*.

consonant ['kɒnsənənt] *n* consonante *f*.

conspicuous [kən'spɪkjʊəs] *adj* cospicuo(a).

constable ['kʌnstəbl] *n Br* agente *m* di polizia.

constant ['kɒnstənt] *adj (unchanging)* costante ; *(continuous)* continuo(a).

constantly ['kɒnstəntlɪ] *adv (all the time)* continuamente.

constipated ['kɒnstɪpeɪtɪd] *adj* stitico(a).

constitution [ˌkɒnstɪ'tjuːʃn] *n* costituzione *f*.

construct [kən'strʌkt] *vt* costruire.

construction [kən'strʌkʃn] *n* costruzione *f* ; **under ~** in costruzione.

consul ['kɒnsəl] *n* console *m*.

consulate ['kɒnsjʊlət] *n* consolato *m*.

consult [kən'sʌlt] *vt* consultare.

consultant [kən'sʌltənt] *n Br (doctor)* specialista *mf*.

consume [kən'sjuːm] *vt* consumare.

consumer [kən'sjuːmər] *n* consumatore *m*, -trice *f*.

contact ['kɒntækt] *n (communication)* contatto *m* ; *(person)* conoscenza *f*. ◆ *vt* mettersi in contatto con ; **in ~ with** *(in communication with)* in contatto con ; *(touching)* a contatto con.

contact lens *n* lente *f* a contatto.

contagious [kən'teɪdʒəs] *adj* contagioso(a).

contain [kən'teɪn] *vt* contenere.

container [kən'teɪnər] *n (box etc)* contenitore *m*, recipiente *m*.

contaminate [kən'tæmɪneɪt] *vt* contaminare.

contemporary [kən'tempərərɪ] *adj* contemporaneo(a). ◆ *n* contemporaneo *m*, -a *f*.

contend [kən'tend] ◆**contend with** *vt fus* affrontare.

content [*adj* kən'tent, *n* 'kɒntent] *adj* contento(a). ◆ *n (of vitamins, fibre etc)* contenuto *m*. ❑ **contents** *npl (things inside)* contenuto *m* ; *(at beginning of book)* indice *m*.

contest [*n* 'kɒntest, *vb* kən'test] *n (competition)* gara *f*, concorso *m* ; *(struggle)* lotta *f*. ◆ *vt (election, seat)* candidarsi per ; *(decision, will)* contestare.

context ['kɒntekst] *n* contesto *m*.

continent ['kɒntɪnənt] *n* continente *m* ; **the Continent** *Br* l'Europa *f* continentale.

continental [ˌkɒntɪ'nentl] *adj Br (European)* (dell'Europa) continentale.

continental breakfast *n* colazione *f* continentale.

continental quilt *n Br* piumone® *m*.

continual [kən'tɪnjʊəl] *adj* continuo(a).

continually [kən'tɪnjʊəlɪ] *adv* continuamente, di continuo.

continue [kən'tɪnjuː] *vt & vi* continuare ; **to ~ doing sthg** continuare a fare qc ; **to ~ with sthg** continuare con qc.

continuous [kən'tɪnjʊəs] *adj* continuo(a).

continuously [kən'tɪnjʊəslɪ] *adv* continuamente, senza interruzione.

contraception [ˌkɒntrə'sepʃn] *n* contraccezione *f*.

contraceptive [ˌkɒntrə'septɪv] *n* contraccettivo *m*.

contract [*n* 'kɒntrækt, *vb* kən'trækt] *n* contratto *m*. ◆ *vt fml (illness)* contrarre.

contradict [ˌkɒntrə'dɪkt] *vt* contraddire.

contrary ['kɒntrərɪ] *n* : **on the ~** al contrario.

contrast [*n* 'kɒntraːst, *vb* kən'traːst] *n* contrasto *m*. ◆ *vt* mettere in contrasto ; **in ~ to** contrariamente a.

contribute [kən'trɪbjuːt] *vt (help,*

money) dare come contributo. ◆ *vi* : **to ~ to** contribuire a.

contribution [ˌkɒntrɪ'bjuːʃn] *n* contributo *m*.

control [kən'trəʊl] *n* controllo *m* ; *(operating device)* comando *m*. ◆ *vt* controllare ; *(machine)* regolare ; **to be in ~** avere la situazione sotto controllo ; **to get out of ~** *(situation)* sfuggire di mano ; **to go out of ~** *(car, plane)* non rispondere ai comandi ; **under ~** sotto controllo. ❑ **controls** *npl* comandi *mpl*.

control tower *n* torre *f* di controllo.

controversial [ˌkɒntrə'vɜːʃl] *adj* controverso(a) ; *(person)* polemico(a).

convenience [kən'viːnjəns] *n* comodità *f inv* ; **at your ~** quando Le è più comodo.

convenient [kən'viːnjənt] *adj* comodo(a) ; **would tomorrow be ~?** domani andrebbe bene?

convent ['kɒnvənt] *n* convento *m*.

conventional [kən'venʃənl] *adj* convenzionale.

conversation [ˌkɒnvə'seɪʃn] *n* conversazione *f*.

conversion [kən'vɜːʃn] *n (change)* trasformazione *f*; *(of currency)* conversione *f* ; *(to building)* ristrutturazione *f*.

convert [kən'vɜːt] *vt (change)* trasformare ; *(currency, person)* convertire ; **to ~ sthg into** trasformare qc in.

converted [kən'vɜːtɪd] *adj (barn, loft)* ristrutturato(a).

convertible [kən'vɜːtəbl] *n* cabriolet *m inv*.

convey [kən'veɪ] *vt fml (transport)* trasportare ; *(idea, impression)* dare.

convict [*n* 'kɒnvɪkt, *vb* kən'vɪkt] *n* carcerato *m*, -a *f*. ◆ *vt* : **to ~ sb (of)** giudicare qn colpevole (di).

convince [kən'vɪns] *vt* : **to ~ sb (of sthg)** convincere qn (di qc) ; **to ~ sb to do sthg** convincere qn a fare qc.

convoy ['kɒnvɔɪ] *n* convoglio *m*.

cook [kʊk] *n* cuoco *m*, -a *f*. ◆ *vt (meal)* cucinare ; *(food)* cuocere. ◆ *vi (person)* cucinare ; *(food)* cuocere.

cookbook ['kʊkˌbʊk] = **cookery book**.

cooker ['kʊkə'] *n* cucina *f (elettrodomestico)*.

cookery ['kʊkərɪ] *n* cucina *f*.

cookery book *n* libro *m* di cucina.

cookie ['kʊkɪ] *n Am* biscotto *m*.

cooking ['kʊkɪŋ] *n* cucina *f*.

cooking apple *n* mela *f* da cuocere.

cooking oil *n* olio *m* per cucinare.

cool [kuːl] *adj (temperature)* fresco(a) ; *(calm)* calmo(a) ; *(unfriendly)* freddo(a) ; *inf (great)* fantastico(a). ◆ *vt* raffreddare. ❑ **cool down** *vi (become colder)* raffreddarsi ; *(become calmer)* calmarsi.

cooperate [kəʊ'ɒpəreɪt] *vi* collaborare, cooperare.

cooperation [kəʊˌɒpə'reɪʃn] *n* collaborazione *f*.

cooperative [kəʊ'ɒpərətɪv] *adj (helpful)* disposto(a) a collaborare.

coordinates [kəʊ'ɔːdɪnəts] *npl (clothes)* coordinati *mpl.*

cope [kəʊp] *vi* : **to ~ with** far fronte a ; **I can't ~!** non ce la faccio!

copilot ['kəʊˌpaɪlət] *n* secondo pilota *m.*

copper ['kɒpəʳ] *n (metal)* rame *m* ; *Br inf (coin) moneta in rame da uno o due penny.*

copy ['kɒpɪ] *n* copia *f.* ◆ *vt* copiare.

cord(uroy) ['kɔːd (ərɔɪ)] *n* velluto *m* a coste.

core [kɔːʳ] *n (of fruit)* torsolo *m.*

coriander [ˌkɒrɪ'ændəʳ] *n* coriandolo *m (spezia).*

cork [kɔːk] *n (in bottle)* tappo *m* (di sughero).

corkscrew ['kɔːkskruː] *n* cavatappi *m inv.*

corn [kɔːn] *n Br (crop)* cereali *mpl* ; *Am (maize)* granoturco *m* ; *(on foot)* callo *m.*

corned beef [ˌkɔːnd-] *n* carne *f* di manzo in scatola.

corner ['kɔːnəʳ] *n* angolo *m* ; *(bend in road)* curva *f* ; *(in football)* calcio *m* d'angolo ; **it's just around the ~** è qui dietro l'angolo.

corner shop *n Br* negozietto *m (di alimentari e prodotti per la casa).*

cornflakes ['kɔːnfleɪks] *npl* cornflakes *mpl.*

corn-on-the-cob *n* pannocchia *f* bollita.

Cornwall ['kɔːnwɔːl] *n* la Cornovaglia.

corporal ['kɔːpərəl] *n* caporale *m.*

corpse [kɔːps] *n* cadavere *m.*

correct [kə'rekt] *adj* giusto(a). ◆ *vt* correggere.

correction [kə'rekʃn] *n* correzione *f.*

correspond [ˌkɒrɪ'spɒnd] *vi* : **to ~ (to)** *(match)* corrispondere (a) ; **to ~ (with)** *(exchange letters)* essere in corrispondenza (con).

corresponding [ˌkɒrɪ'spɒndɪŋ] *adj* corrispondente.

corridor ['kɒrɪdɔːʳ] *n* corridoio *m.*

corrugated iron ['kɒrəgeɪtɪd-] *n* lamiera *f* ondulata.

corrupt [kə'rʌpt] *adj* corrotto(a).

cosmetics [kɒz'metɪks] *npl* cosmetici *mpl.*

cost [kɒst] (*pt* & *pp* **cost**) *n* costo *m* ; *fig (loss)* prezzo *m.* ◆ *vt* costare ; **how much does it ~?** quanto costa?

costly ['kɒstlɪ] *adj (expensive)* costoso(a).

costume ['kɒstjuːm] *n* costume *m.*

cosy ['kəʊzɪ] *adj Br (room, house)* accogliente.

cot [kɒt] *n Br (for baby)* lettino *m (per bambini)* ; *Am (camp bed)* brandina *f.*

cottage ['kɒtɪdʒ] *n* cottage *m inv.*

cottage cheese *n* formaggio *m* magro in fiocchi.

cottage pie *n Br pasticcio a base di carne macinata e purè di patate.*

cotton ['kɒtn] *adj* di cotone. ◆ *n* cotone *m.*

cotton wool *n* cotone *m* idrofilo.

couch [kaʊtʃ] *n* divano *m* ; *(at doctor's)* lettino *m.*

couchette [kuːˈʃet] *n* cuccetta *f*.
cough [kɒf] *n* tosse *f*. ◆ *vi* tossire ; **to have a ~** avere la tosse.
cough mixture *n* sciroppo *m* per la tosse.
could [kʊd] *pt* → **can**.
couldn't [ˈkʊdnt] = **could not**.
could've [ˈkʊdəv] = **could have**.
council [ˈkaʊnsl] *n Br (of town)* comune *m* ; *Br (of county)* ≃ regione *f* ; *(organization)* consiglio *m*.
council house *n Br* casa *f* popolare.
councillor [ˈkaʊnsələʳ] *n Br (of town, county)* consigliere *m*, -a *f*.
council tax *n Br* ≃ tassa *f* comunale.
count [kaʊnt] *vt* & *vi* contare. ◆ *n (nobleman)* conte *m*. ❑ **count on** *vt fus* contare su.
counter [ˈkaʊntəʳ] *n (in shop)* banco *m* ; *(in bank)* sportello *m* ; *(in board game)* fiche *f inv*.
counterclockwise [ˌkaʊntəˈklɒkwaɪz] *adv Am* in senso antiorario.
counterfoil [ˈkaʊntəfɔɪl] *n* matrice *f*.
countess [ˈkaʊntɪs] *n* contessa *f*.
country [ˈkʌntrɪ] *n* paese *m* ; *(countryside)* campagna *f*. ◆ *adj* di campagna.
country and western *n* (musica *f*) country *m*.
country house *n* villa *f* di campagna.
country road *n* strada *f* di campagna.
countryside [ˈkʌntrɪsaɪd] *n* campagna *f*.
county [ˈkaʊntɪ] *n* contea *f*.
couple [ˈkʌpl] *n* coppia *f* ; **a ~ (of)** un paio (di).
coupon [ˈkuːpɒn] *n (for discount etc)* buono *m* ; *(for orders, enquiries)* tagliando *m*.
courage [ˈkʌrɪdʒ] *n* coraggio *m*.
courgette [kɔːˈʒet] *n Br* zucchino *m*.
courier [ˈkʊrɪəʳ] *n (for holidaymakers)* accompagnatore *m*, -trice *f* ; *(for delivering letters)* corriere *m*.
course [kɔːs] *n* corso *m* ; *(of meal)* portata *f* ; *(of treatment, injections)* ciclo *m* ; *(of ship, plane)* rotta *f* ; *(for golf)* campo *m* ; **of ~** *(certainly)* certo ; *(evidently)* naturalmente ; **of ~ not** certo che no ; **in the ~ of** nel corso di, durante.
court [kɔːt] *n* JUR *(building, room)* tribunale *m* ; SPORT campo *m* ; *(of king, queen)* corte *f*.
court shoes *npl* scarpe *fpl* décolleté.
courtyard [ˈkɔːtjaːd] *n* cortile *m*.
cousin [ˈkʌzn] *n* cugino *m*, -a *f*.
cover [ˈkʌvəʳ] *n (covering)* fodera *f* ; *(lid)* coperchio *m* ; *(of book, magazine)* copertina *f* ; *(blanket)* coperta *f* ; *(insurance)* copertura *f*. ◆ *vt* coprire ; *(apply to)* comprendere ; *(discuss)* trattare ; *(report)* fare un servizio su ; **to be ~ed in** essere ricoperto di OR da ; **to ~ sthg with sthg** coprire qc con qc ; **to take ~** mettersi al riparo. ❑ **cover up** *vt sep (put cover on)* coprire ; *(facts, truth)* nascondere.
cover charge *n* coperto *m*.
cover note *n Br* polizza *f* di assicurazione provvisoria.
cow [kaʊ] *n* vacca *f*.

coward ['kauəd] *n* vigliacco *m*, -a *f*.

cowboy ['kaubɔı] *n* cow-boy *m* *inv*.

crab [kræb] *n* granchio *m*.

crack [kræk] *n (in cup, glass)* incrinatura *f*, crepa *f*; *(gap)* fessura *f*. ◆ *vi (cup, glass, wood)* incrinarsi. ◆ *vt (cup, glass, wood)* incrinare ; *(nut)* schiacciare ; *(egg)* rompere ; *(whip)* schioccare ; **to ~ a joke** *inf* fare una battuta.

cracker ['krækər] *n (biscuit)* cracker *m inv* ; *(for Christmas) tubo di cartone rivestito di carta da regalo che quando viene aperto produce uno scoppio e rilascia una sorpresa, tipico delle feste natalizie.*

cradle ['kreıdl] *n* culla *f*.

craft [kra:ft] *n (skill)* arte *f*; *(trade)* artigianato *m* ; *(boat : pl inv)* imbarcazione *f*.

craftsman ['kra:ftsmən] (*pl* **-men** [-mən]) *n* artigiano *m*.

cram [kræm] *vt* : **to ~ sthg into** stipare qc in ; **to be crammed with** essere stipato di.

cramp [kræmp] *n* crampo *m* ; **stomach ~s** crampi allo stomaco.

cranberry ['krænbərı] *n* mirtillo *m*.

cranberry sauce *n* salsa *f* di mirtilli.

crane [kreın] *n (machine)* gru *f inv*.

crap [kræp] *adj vulg* di merda. ◆ *n vulg* merda *f*.

crash [kræʃ] *n (accident)* incidente *m* ; *(noise)* schianto *m*. ◆ *vt (car)* sfasciare. ◆ *vi (car, train)* schiantarsi ; *(plane)* precipitare. ❑ **crash into** *vt fus* schiantarsi contro.

crash helmet *n* casco *m*.

crash landing *n* atterraggio *m* di fortuna.

crate [kreıt] *n* cassa *f*.

crawl [krɔ:l] *vi (baby)* andare carponi ; *(person)* strisciare ; *(insect)* muoversi lentamente ; *(traffic)* andare a passo d'uomo. ◆ *n (swimming stroke)* stile *m* libero.

crawler lane ['krɔ:lər-] *n Br* corsia *f* per veicoli lenti.

crayfish ['kreıfıʃ] (*pl* **inv**) *n* gambero *m* di fiume.

crayon ['kreıɒn] *n* matita *f* colorata.

craze [kreız] *n* mania *f*.

crazy ['kreızı] *adj* matto(a), pazzo(a) ; **to be ~ about** andare matto per.

crazy golf *n* minigolf *m*.

cream [kri:m] *n* crema *f*; *(fresh)* panna *f*. ◆ *adj (in colour)* color crema *(inv)*.

cream cheese *n* formaggio *m* cremoso.

cream sherry *n* sherry *m inv* dolce.

cream tea *n Br merenda a base di tè e 'scones' serviti con marmellata e panna.*

creamy ['kri:mı] *adj (food)* alla panna ; *(texture)* cremoso(a).

crease [kri:s] *n* grinza *f*.

creased [kri:st] *adj* sgualcito(a).

create [kri:'eıt] *vt* creare.

creative [kri:'eıtıv] *adj* creativo(a).

creature ['kri:tʃər] *n* creatura *f*.

crèche [kreʃ] *n Br* nursery *f inv*.

credit ['kredıt] *n (praise)* merito *m* ; *(money)* credito *m* ; *(part of school, university course) sezione* *completata di un corso di studio* ; **to be in ~** essere in attivo. ❑ **credits** *npl (of film)* titoli *mpl*.

credit card *n* carta *f* di credito ; **to pay by ~** pagare con la carta di credito ; **'all major ~s accepted'** 'si accettano tutte le principali carte di credito'.

creek [kri:k] *n (inlet)* insenatura *f* ; *Am (river)* ruscello *m*.

creep [kri:p] (*pt* & *pp* **crept**) *vi (crawl)* strisciare ; *(walk)* muoversi furtivamente. ◆ *n inf (groveller)* leccapiedi *mf inv*.

cremate [krɪ'meɪt] *vt* cremare.

crematorium [ˌkremə'tɔ:rɪəm] *n* crematorio *m*.

crepe [kreip] *n (thin pancake)* crêpe *f inv*.

crept [krept] *pt* & *pp* → **creep**.

cress [kres] *n* crescione *m*.

crest [krest] *n* cresta *f* ; *(emblem)* stemma *m*.

crew [kru:] *n (of ship, plane)* equipaggio *m*.

crew neck *n* girocollo *m*.

crib [krɪb] *n Am (cot)* lettino *m* (per bambini).

cricket ['krɪkɪt] *n (game)* cricket *m* ; *(insect)* grillo *m*.

crime [kraɪm] *n* crimine *m*.

criminal ['krɪmɪnl] *adj* criminale. ◆ *n* criminale *mf*.

cripple ['krɪpl] *n* storpio *m*, -a *f*. ◆ *vt (subj : disease, accident)* storpiare.

crisis ['kraɪsɪs] (*pl* **crises** ['kraɪsi:z]) *n* crisi *f inv*.

crisp [krɪsp] *adj (bacon, pastry)* croccante ; *(fruit, vegetable)* sodo(a). ❑ **crisps** *npl Br* patatine *fpl*.

crispy ['krɪspɪ] *adj* croccante.

critic ['krɪtɪk] *n* critico *m*, -a *f*.

critical ['krɪtɪkl] *adj* critico(a).

criticize ['krɪtɪsaɪz] *vt* criticare.

crockery ['krɒkərɪ] *n* stoviglie *fpl*.

crocodile ['krɒkədaɪl] *n* coccodrillo *m*.

crocus ['krəʊkəs] (*pl* **-es**) *n* croco *m*.

crooked ['krʊkɪd] *adj (bent, twisted)* storto(a).

crop [krɒp] *n (kind of plant)* coltivazione *f* ; *(harvest)* raccolto *m*. ❑ **crop up** *vi* saltare fuori.

cross [krɒs] *adj* arrabbiato(a). ◆ *n* croce *f* ; *(mixture)* incrocio *m*. ◆ *vt (road, river, ocean)* attraversare ; *(arms, legs)* incrociare ; *Br (cheque)* sbarrare. ◆ *vi (intersect)* incrociarsi. ❑ **cross out** *vt sep* sbarrare. ❑ **cross over** *vt fus (road)* attraversare.

crossbar ['krɒsba:ʳ] *n (of goal)* traversa *f* ; *(of bicycle)* canna *f*.

cross-Channel ferry *n* traghetto *m* di servizio sulla Manica.

cross-country (running) *n* corsa *f* campestre.

crossing ['krɒsɪŋ] *n (on road)* attraversamento *m* ; *(sea journey)* traversata *f*.

crossroads ['krɒsrəʊdz] (*pl* **inv**) *n* incrocio *m*.

crosswalk ['krɒswɔ:k] *n Am* passaggio *m* pedonale.

crossword (puzzle) ['krɒswɜ:d-] *n* cruciverba *m inv*.

crotch [krɒtʃ] *n (of person)* inforcatura *f*.

crouton ['kru:tɒn] *n* crostino *m*.

crow [krəʊ] *n* cornacchia *f*.
crowbar ['krəʊbaːʳ] *n* piede *m* di porco.
crowd [kraʊd] *n* folla *f* ; *(at match)* spettatori *mpl*.
crowded ['kraʊdɪd] *adj* affollato(a).
crown [kraʊn] *n (of king, queen, on tooth)* corona *f* ; *(of head)* sommità *f inv*.
Crown Jewels *npl* : the ~ i gioielli della Corona.
crucial ['kruːʃl] *adj* cruciale.
crude [kruːd] *adj (drawing)* abbozzato(a) ; *(estimato)* approssimativo(a) ; *(rude)* rozzo(a).
cruel [krʊəl] *adj* crudele.
cruelty ['krʊəltɪ] *n* crudeltà *f*.
cruet (set) ['kruːɪt-] *n* ampolliera *f*.
cruise [kruːz] *n* crociera *f*. ◆ *vi (car, plane, ship)* andare a velocità di crociera.
cruiser ['kruːzəʳ] *n (pleasure boat)* cabinato *m*.
crumb [krʌm] *n* briciola *f*.
crumble ['krʌmbl] *n frutta cotta ricoperta da uno strato di pasta frolla sbriciolata*. ◆ *vi (building, cliff)* sgretolarsi ; *(pastry, cake, cheese)* sbriciolarsi.
crumpet ['krʌmpɪt] *n tipo di focaccina da mangiarsi calda con burro, marmellata, ecc.*
crunchy ['krʌntʃɪ] *adj* croccante.
crush [krʌʃ] *n (drink)* spremuta *f*. ◆ *vt* schiacciare ; *(ice)* frantumare.
crust [krʌst] *n* crosta *f*.
crusty ['krʌstɪ] *adj* croccante.
crutch [krʌtʃ] *n (stick)* stampella *f* ; *(between legs)* = **crotch**.
cry [kraɪ] *n* urlo *m*, grido *m* ; *(of bird)* verso *m*. ◆ *vi (weep)* piangere ; *(shout)* urlare, gridare. ❑ **cry out** *vi* urlare, gridare.
crystal ['krɪstl] *n (in jewellery etc)* cristallo *m* ; *(glass)* cristallo *m*.
cub [kʌb] *n (animal)* cucciolo *m*.
Cub [kʌb] *n* lupetto *m*.
cube [kjuːb] *n* cubo *m* ; *(of sugar, ice)* cubetto *m*.
cubicle ['kjuːbɪkl] *n* cabina *f*.
Cub Scout = **Cub**.
cuckoo ['kʊkuː] *n* cuculo *m*.
cucumber ['kjuːkʌmbəʳ] *n* cetriolo *m*.
cuddle ['kʌdl] *n* coccola *f*.
cuddly toy ['kʌdlɪ-] *n* pupazzo *m* di peluche.
cue [kjuː] *n (in snooker, pool)* stecca *f*.
cuff [kʌf] *n (of sleeve)* polsino *m* ; *Am (of trousers)* risvolto *m*.
cuff links *npl* gemelli *mpl*.
cuisine [kwɪ'ziːn] *n* cucina *f*.
cul-de-sac ['kʌldəsæk] *n* vicolo *m* cieco.
cult [kʌlt] *n* RELIG culto *m*. ◆ *adj* di culto.
cultivate ['kʌltɪveɪt] *vt (grow)* coltivare.
cultivated ['kʌltɪveɪtɪd] *adj (person)* raffinato(a).
cultural ['kʌltʃərəl] *adj* culturale.
culture ['kʌltʃəʳ] *n* cultura *f*.
cumbersome ['kʌmbəsəm] *adj* ingombrante.
cumin ['kjuːmɪn] *n* cumino *m*.
cunning ['kʌnɪŋ] *adj* furbo(a).
cup [kʌp] *n* tazza *f* ; *(trophy, competition, of bra)* coppa *f*.

cupboard ['kʌbəd] *n (for food, dishes)* credenza *f*; *(for clothes)* armadio *m*.
curator [ˌkjʊə'reɪtəʳ] *n* conservatore *m (di museo)*.
curb [kɜːb] *Am* = **kerb**.
curd cheese [ˌkɜːd-] *n* cagliata *f*.
cure [kjʊəʳ] *n (for illness)* cura *f*. ◆ *vt (illness, person)* curare ; *(food)* trattare.
curious ['kjʊərɪəs] *adj* curioso(a).
curl [kɜːl] *n (of hair)* riccio *m*. ◆ *vt (hair)* arricciare.
curler ['kɜːləʳ] *n* bigodino *m*.
curly ['kɜːlɪ] *adj* riccio(a).
currant ['kʌrənt] *n* uvetta *f*.
currency ['kʌrənsɪ] *n (money)* moneta *f*.
current ['kʌrənt] *adj* attuale. ◆ *n* corrente *f*.
current account *n Br* conto *m* corrente.
current affairs *npl* attualità *f*.
currently ['kʌrəntlɪ] *adv* attualmente.
curriculum [kə'rɪkjələm] *n* curricolo *m*.
curriculum vitae [-'viːtaɪ] *n Br* curriculum vitae *m inv*.
curried ['kʌrɪd] *adj* al curry.
curry ['kʌrɪ] *n* piatto *m* al curry.
curse [kɜːs] *vi* bestemmiare.
cursor ['kɜːsəʳ] *n* cursore *m*.
curtain ['kɜːtn] *n (in house)* tenda *f*; *(in theatre)* sipario *m*.
curve [kɜːv] *n* curva *f*. ◆ *vi* curvare.
curved [kɜːvd] *adj* curvo(a).
cushion ['kʊʃn] *n (for sitting on)* cuscino *m*.
custard ['kʌstəd] *n* crema *f* gialla.
custom ['kʌstəm] *n (tradition)* usanza *f*; **'thank you for your ~'** 'arrivederci e grazie'.
customary ['kʌstəmrɪ] *adj* abituale.
customer ['kʌstəməʳ] *n (of shop)* cliente *mf*.
customer services *n (department)* servizio *m* clienti.
customs ['kʌstəmz] *n* dogana *f*; **to go through ~** passare la dogana.
customs duty *n* dazio *m* doganale.
customs officer *n* doganiere *m*.
cut [kʌt] (*pt* & *pp* **cut**) *n* taglio *m* ; *(in taxes)* riduzione *f*. ◆ *vt* & *vi* tagliare ; **~ and blow-dry** taglio e piega föhn ; **to ~ o.s.** tagliarsi ; **to ~ one's finger** tagliarsi un dito ; **to have one's hair ~** tagliarsi i capelli ; **to ~ the grass** tagliare l'erba ; **to ~ sthg open** aprire qc. ❑ **cut back** *vi* : **to ~ back on sthg** ridurre qc. ❑ **cut down** *vt sep (tree)* tagliare. ❑ **cut down on** *vt fus* ridurre. ❑ **cut off** *vt sep* tagliare ; *(supply)* sospendere ; **I've been ~ off** *(on phone)* è caduta la linea ; **to be ~ off** *(isolated)* rimanere isolato. ❑ **cut out** ◆ *vt sep (newspaper article, photo)* ritagliare. ◆ *vi (engine)* spegnersi ; **to ~ out smoking** smettere di fumare ; **~ it out!** *inf* dacci un taglio! ❑ **cut up** *vt sep* tagliare a pezzetti.
cute [kjuːt] *adj* carino(a).
cut-glass *adj* in vetro intagliato.
cutlery ['kʌtlərɪ] *n* posate *fpl*.
cutlet ['kʌtlɪt] *n (of meat)* costoletta *f*; *(of nuts, vegetables)* crocchetta *f*.

cut-price *adj* a prezzo scontato.
cutting ['kʌtɪŋ] *n (from newspaper)* ritaglio *m*.
CV *n Br (abbr of curriculum vitae)* curriculum *m inv*.
cwt *abbr* = **hundredweight**.
cycle ['saɪkl] *n (bicycle)* bicicletta *f*; *(series)* ciclo *m*. ◆ *vi* andare in bicicletta.
cycle hire *n* noleggio *m* biciclette.
cycle lane *n* pista *f* ciclabile.
cycle path *n* pista *f* ciclabile.
cycling ['saɪklɪŋ] *n* ciclismo *m* ; **to go ~** andare in bicicletta.
cycling shorts *npl* pantaloncini *mpl* da ciclista.
cyclist ['saɪklɪst] *n* ciclista *mf*.
cylinder ['sɪlɪndəʳ] *n (of gas)* bombola *f*; *(in engine)* cilindro *m*.
cynical ['sɪnɪkl] *adj* cinico(a).
Czech [tʃek] *adj* ceco(a). ◆ *n (person)* ceco *m*, -a *f*; *(language)* ceco *m*.
Czech Republic *n* : **the ~** la Repubblica Ceca.

D

dab [dæb] *vt (wound)* tamponare.
dad [dæd] *n inf* papà *m inv*, babbo *m*.
daddy ['dædɪ] *n inf* papà *m inv*, babbo *m*.
daddy longlegs [-'lɒŋlegz] (*pl* **inv**) *n* tipula *f*.
daffodil ['dæfədɪl] *n* giunchiglia *f*.
daft [dɑːft] *adj Br inf* stupido(a).
daily ['deɪlɪ] *adj* quotidiano(a). ◆ *adv* quotidianamente. ◆ *n* : a **~ (newspaper)** un quotidiano.
dairy ['deərɪ] *n (on farm)* caseificio *m* ; *(shop)* latteria *f*.
dairy product *n* latticino *m*.
daisy ['deɪzɪ] *n* margherita *f*.
dam [dæm] *n* diga *f*.
damage ['dæmɪdʒ] *n* danno *m*. ◆ *vt* danneggiare ; *(back, leg)* lesionare.
damn [dæm] *excl inf* accidenti! ◆ *adj inf* maledetto(a) ; **I don't give a ~** non me ne importa un accidente.
damp [dæmp] *adj* umido(a). ◆ *n* umidità *f*.
damson ['dæmzn] *n* susina *f* damaschina.
dance [dɑːns] *n* danza *f*; *(social event)* ballo *m*. ◆ *vi* ballare ; **to have a ~** ballare.
dance floor *n (in club)* pista *f* da ballo.
dancer ['dɑːnsəʳ] *n* ballerino *m*, -a *f*.
dancing ['dɑːnsɪŋ] *n* danza *f*; **to go ~** andare a ballare.
dandelion ['dændɪlaɪən] *n* dente *m* di leone.
dandruff ['dændrʌf] *n* forfora *f*.
danger ['deɪndʒəʳ] *n* pericolo *m* ; **in ~** in pericolo.
dangerous ['deɪndʒərəs] *adj* pericoloso(a).
Danish ['deɪnɪʃ] *adj* danese. ◆ *n (language)* danese *m*.
dare [deəʳ] *vt* : **to ~ to do sthg** osare fare qc ; **to ~ sb to do sthg** sfidare

qn a fare qc ; **how ~ you!** come ti permetti!

daring ['deərɪŋ] *adj* audace.

dark [dɑ:k] *adj (room, night)* buio(a) ; *(colour, skin)* scuro(a) ; *(person)* bruno(a). ◆ *n* : **after ~** col buio ; **the ~** il buio.

dark chocolate *n* cioccolato *f* fondente.

darkness ['dɑ:knɪs] *n* oscurità *f*.

darling ['dɑ:lɪŋ] *n (term of affection)* caro *m*, -a *f*.

dart [dɑ:t] *n* freccia *f*. ❑ **darts** *n (game)* freccette *fpl*.

dartboard ['dɑ:tbɔ:d] *n* bersaglio *m* per freccette.

dash [dæʃ] *n (of liquid)* goccio *m* ; *(in writing)* trattino *m*. ◆ *vi* precipitarsi.

dashboard ['dæʃbɔ:d] *n* cruscotto *m*.

data ['deɪtə] *n* dati *mpl*.

database ['deɪtəbeɪs] *n* data base *m inv*.

date [deɪt] *n (day)* data *f* ; *(meeting)* appuntamento *m* ; *Am (person)* ragazzo *m*, -a *f* ; *(fruit)* dattero *m*. ◆ *vt (cheque, letter)* datare ; *(person)* uscire con. ◆ *vi (become unfashionable)* passare di moda ; **what's the ~?** quanti ne abbiamo oggi? ; **to have a ~ with sb** avere (un) appuntamento con qn.

date of birth *n* data *f* di nascita.

daughter ['dɔ:tə'] *n* figlia *f*.

daughter-in-law *n* nuora *f*.

dawn [dɔ:n] *n* alba *f*.

day [deɪ] *n (of week)* giorno *m* ; *(period, working day)* giornata *f* ; **what ~ is it today?** che giorno è oggi? ; **what a lovely ~!** che bella giornata! ; **to have a ~ off** avere un giorno libero ; **to have a ~ out** trascorrere una giornata fuori ; **by ~** *(travel)* di giorno ; **the ~ after tomorrow** dopodomani ; **the ~ before** il giorno prima ; **the ~ before yesterday** l'altro ieri, ieri l'altro ; **the following ~** il giorno dopo ; **have a nice ~!** buona giornata!

daylight ['deɪlaɪt] *n (light)* luce *f* (del giorno) ; *(dawn)* alba *f*.

day return *n Br (railway ticket)* *biglietto di andata e ritorno valido per un giorno*.

dayshift ['deɪʃɪft] *n* turno *m* di giorno.

daytime ['deɪtaɪm] *n* giorno *m*.

day-to-day *adj (everyday)* quotidiano(a).

day trip *n* gita *f (di un giorno)*.

dazzle ['dæzl] *vt* abbagliare.

dead [ded] *adj* morto(a) ; *(battery)* scarico(a). ◆ *adv* proprio ; **the line has gone ~** è caduta la linea ; **~ on time** in perfetto orario ; **it's ~ ahead** è proprio a diritto ; **'~ slow'** 'a passo d'uomo'.

dead end *n (street)* strada *f* senza uscita.

deadline ['dedlaɪn] *n* termine *m* ultimo, scadenza *f*.

deaf [def] *adj* sordo(a). ◆ *npl* : **the ~** i non udenti.

deal [di:l] (*pt* & *pp* **dealt**) *n (agreement)* accordo *m*. ◆ *vt (cards)* dare ; **a good/bad ~** un buon/cattivo affare ; **a great ~ of** una gran quantità di ; **it's a ~!** affare fatto! ❑ **deal in** *vt fus* commerciare in. ❑ **deal with** *vt fus (handle)* affrontare ; *(be about)* trattare di.

dealer ['diːləʳ] *n COMM* commerciante *mf*; *(in drugs)* spacciatore *m*, -trice *f*.

dealt [delt] *pt* & *pp* → **deal**.

dear [dɪəʳ] *adj* caro(a). ◆ *n* : **my ~** mio caro (mia cara) ; **Dear Sir** Gentile Signore ; **Dear Madam** Gentile Signora ; **Dear John** Caro John ; **oh ~!** oh Dio!

death [deθ] *n* morte *f*.

debate [dɪ'beɪt] *n* dibattito *m*. ◆ *vt (wonder)* riflettere su.

debit ['debɪt] *n* debito *m*. ◆ *vt (account)* addebitare su.

debt [det] *n (money owed)* debito *m* ; **to be in ~** essere indebitato.

Dec. (*abbr of December*) dic.

decaff ['diːkæf] *n inf* caffè *m inv* decaffeinato.

decaffeinated [dɪ'kæfɪneɪtɪd] *adj* decaffeinato(a).

decanter [dɪ'kæntəʳ] *n* bottiglia *f* da liquore.

decay [dɪ'keɪ] *n (of wood)* disfacimento *m* ; *(of building)* rovina *f* ; *(of tooth)* carie *f*. ◆ *vi (rot)* putrefarsi.

deceive [dɪ'siːv] *vt* ingannare.

decelerate [ˌdiː'seləreɪt] *vi* decelerare.

December [dɪ'sembəʳ] *n* dicembre *m* → **September**.

decent ['diːsnt] *adj (adequate, respectable)* decente ; *(kind)* carino(a) ; *(people)* perbene *(inv)*.

decide [dɪ'saɪd] *vt* & *vi* decidere ; **to ~ to do sthg** decidere di fare qc. ❑ **decide on** *vt fus* scegliere.

decimal ['desɪml] *adj* decimale.

decimal point *n* ≃ virgola *f*.

decision [dɪ'sɪʒn] *n* decisione *f* ; **to make a ~** prendere una decisione.

decisive [dɪ'saɪsɪv] *adj (person)* deciso(a) ; *(event, factor)* decisivo(a).

deck [dek] *n (level of ship)* ponte *m* ; *(exposed part of ship)* coperta *f* ; *(of bus)* piano *m* ; *(of cards)* mazzo *m*.

deckchair ['dektʃeəʳ] *n* sedia *f* a sdraio.

declare [dɪ'kleəʳ] *vt* dichiarare ; **to ~ (that)** dichiarare che ; **'goods to ~'** 'articoli da dichiarare' ; **'nothing to ~'** 'nulla da dichiarare'.

decline [dɪ'klaɪn] *n* calo *m* ; *(of country)* declino *m*. ◆ *vi (get worse)* peggiorare ; *(refuse)* declinare.

decorate ['dekəreɪt] *vt (with wallpaper)* tappezzare ; *(with paint)* pitturare ; *(make attractive)* decorare.

decoration [ˌdekə'reɪʃn] *n (decorative object)* decorazione *f*.

decorator ['dekəreɪtəʳ] *n* imbianchino *m*.

decrease [*n* 'diːkriːs, *vb* diː'kriːs] *n* diminuzione *f*. ◆ *vi* diminuire.

dedicated ['dedɪkeɪtɪd] *adj (committed)* devoto(a).

deduce [dɪ'djuːs] *vt* dedurre.

deduct [dɪ'dʌkt] *vt* dedurre.

deduction [dɪ'dʌkʃn] *n* deduzione *f*.

deep [diːp] *adj* profondo(a) ; *(colour)* intenso(a). ◆ *adv* in profondità ; **the pool is 2 metres ~** la piscina è profonda 2 metri.

deep end *n (of swimming pool)* parte dove l'acqua è più profonda.

deep freeze *n* congelatore *m*.

deep-fried [-'fraɪd] *adj* fritto(a).
deep-pan *adj*: ~ **pizza** *pizza a pasta alta e soffice.*
deer [dɪəʳ] (*pl* **inv**) *n* cervo *m.*
defeat [dɪ'fiːt] *n* sconfitta *f.* ◆ *vt (team, army, government)* sconfiggere.
defect ['diːfekt] *n* difetto *m.*
defective [dɪ'fektɪv] *adj* difettoso(a).
defence [dɪ'fens] *n* difesa *f.*
defend [dɪ'fend] *vt* difendere.
defense [dɪ'fens] *Am* = **defence**.
deficiency [dɪ'fɪʃnsɪ] *n (lack)* carenza *f.*
deficit ['defɪsɪt] *n* deficit *m inv.*
define [dɪ'faɪn] *vt* definire.
definite ['defɪnɪt] *adj (clear)* preciso(a) ; *(certain)* sicuro(a) ; *(improvement)* deciso(a).
definite article *n* articolo *m* determinativo.
definitely ['defɪnɪtlɪ] *adv (certainly)* senz'altro.
definition [defɪ'nɪʃn] *n (of word)* definizione *f.*
deflate [dɪ'fleɪt] *vt (tyre)* sgonfiare.
deflect [dɪ'flekt] *vt (ball)* deviare.
defogger [ˌdiː'fɒgər] *n Am* deumidificatore *m.*
deformed [dɪ'fɔːmd] *adj* deformato(a).
defrost [ˌdiː'frɒst] *vt (food)* scongelare ; *(fridge)* sbrinare ; *Am (demist)* disappannare.
degree [dɪ'griː] *n (unit of measurement, amount)* grado *m* ; *(qualification)* ≃ laurea *f* ; **to have a ~ in sthg** avere una laurea in qc.
dehydrated [ˌdiːhaɪ'dreɪtɪd] *adj (food)* liofilizzato(a) ; *(person)* disidratato(a).
de-ice [diː'aɪs] *vt* togliere il ghiaccio da.
de-icer [diː'aɪsəʳ] *n* antighiaccio *m.*
dejected [dɪ'dʒektɪd] *adj* sconsolato(a).
delay [dɪ'leɪ] *n* ritardo *m.* ◆ *vt (flight, departure)* ritardare ; *(person)* trattenere. ◆ *vi* indugiare ; **without ~** senza indugio.
delayed [dɪ'leɪd] *adj (train, flight)* in ritardo.
delegate [*n* 'delɪgət, *vb* 'delɪgeɪt] *n* delegato *m*, -a *f.* ◆ *vt (person)* delegare.
delete [dɪ'liːt] *vt* cancellare.
deli ['delɪ] *n inf (abbr of delicatessen)* negozio *m* di specialità gastronomiche.
deliberate [dɪ'lɪbərət] *adj (intentional)* intenzionale.
deliberately [dɪ'lɪbərətlɪ] *adv (intentionally)* deliberatamente.
delicacy ['delɪkəsɪ] *n (food)* leccornia *f.*
delicate ['delɪkət] *adj* delicato(a).
delicatessen [ˌdelɪkə'tesn] *n* negozio *m* di specialità gastronomiche.
delicious [dɪ'lɪʃəs] *adj* squisito(a).
delight [dɪ'laɪt] *n (feeling)* gioia *f.* ◆ *vt* deliziare ; **to take (a) ~ in doing sthg** provare piacere a fare qc.
delighted [dɪ'laɪtɪd] *adj* felicissimo(a).

delightful [dɪ'laɪtful] *adj* delizioso(a).
deliver [dɪ'lɪvəʳ] *vt (goods, letters, newspaper)* consegnare ; *(speech, lecture)* tenere ; *(baby)* far nascere.
delivery [dɪ'lɪvərɪ] *n (of goods, letters)* consegna *f* ; *(birth)* parto *m*.
delude [dɪ'lu:d] *vt* illudere.
de luxe [də'lʌks] *adj* di lusso.
demand [dɪ'ma:nd] *n (request)* richiesta *f* ; *(claim)* rivendicazione *f* ; COMM domanda *f* ; *(requirement)* esigenza *f*. ◆ *vt (request forcefully)* pretendere ; *(require)* richiedere ; **to ~ to do sthg** esigere di fare qc ; **in ~** richiesto.
demanding [dɪ'ma:ndɪŋ] *adj* esigente.
demerara sugar [demə'reərə-] *n* zucchero *m* di canna.
demist [ˌdi:'mɪst] *vt Br* disappannare.
demister [ˌdi:'mɪstəʳ] *n Br* deumidificatore *m*.
democracy [dɪ'mɒkrəsɪ] *n* democrazia *f*.
Democrat ['deməkræt] *n Am* democratico *m*, -a *f*.
democratic [demə'krætɪk] *adj* democratico(a).
demolish [dɪ'mɒlɪʃ] *vt (building)* demolire.
demonstrate ['demənstreɪt] *vt (prove)* dimostrare ; *(machine, appliance)* mostrare il funzionamento di. ◆ *vi* dimostrare.
demonstration [demən'streɪʃn] *n* dimostrazione *f*.
denial [dɪ'naɪəl] *n (refusal)* rifiuto *m* ; *(statement)* smentita *f*.
denim ['denɪm] *n* denim *m*. ❑ **denims** *npl* jeans *mpl*.
denim jacket *n* giubbotto *m* di jeans.
Denmark ['denma:k] *n* la Danimarca.
dense [dens] *adj (crowd, forest)* fitto(a) ; *(smoke)* denso(a).
dent [dent] *n* ammaccatura *f*.
dental ['dentl] *adj* dentale.
dental floss [-flɒs] *n* filo *m* interdentale.
dental surgeon *n* dentista *mf*.
dental surgery *n (place)* studio *m* dentistico.
dentist ['dentɪst] *n* dentista *mf* ; **to go to the ~'s** andare dal dentista.
dentures ['dentʃəz] *npl* dentiera *f*.
deny [dɪ'naɪ] *vt* negare.
deodorant [di:'əudərənt] *n* deodorante *m*.
depart [dɪ'pa:t] *vi* partire.
department [dɪ'pa:tmənt] *n (of business, shop)* reparto *m* ; *(of government)* ministero *m* ; *(of school, university)* dipartimento *m*.
department store *n* grandi magazzini *mpl*.
departure [dɪ'pa:tʃəʳ] *n* partenza *f* ; '**~s**' *(at airport)* 'partenze'.
departure lounge *n* sala *f* partenze.
depend [dɪ'pend] *vi* : **it ~s** dipende. ❑ **depend on** *vt fus* dipendere da ; **~ing on** a seconda di.
dependable [dɪ'pendəbl] *adj* affidabile.
deplorable [dɪ'plɔ:rəbl] *adj* deplorevole.
deport [dɪ'pɔ:t] *vt* espellere.

deposit [dɪ'pɒzɪt] *n* deposito *m*. ◆ *vt* depositare.

deposit account *n Br* conto *m* vincolato.

depot ['di:pəʊ] *n Am (for buses, trains)* stazione *f*.

depressed [dɪ'prest] *adj* depresso(a).

depressing [dɪ'presɪŋ] *adj* deprimente.

depression [dɪ'preʃn] *n* depressione *f*.

deprive [dɪ'praɪv] *vt*: **to ~ sb of sthg** privare qn di qc.

depth [depθ] *n (distance down)* profondità *f inv* ; **out of one's ~** *(when swimming)* dove non si tocca ; *fig (unable to cope)* non all'altezza ; **~ of field** *(in photography)* profondità di campo.

deputy ['depjʊtɪ] *adj* vice *(inv)*.

derailment [dɪ'reɪlmənt] *n* deragliamento *m*.

derelict ['derəlɪkt] *adj* abbandonato(a).

descend [dɪ'send] *vt & vi* scendere.

descendant [dɪ'sendənt] *n* discendente *mf*.

descent [dɪ'sent] *n* discesa *f*.

describe [dɪ'skraɪb] *vt* descrivere.

description [dɪ'skrɪpʃn] *n* descrizione *f*.

desert [*n* 'dezət, *vb* dɪ'zɜ:t] *n* deserto *m*. ◆ *vt* abbandonare.

deserted [dɪ'zɜ:tɪd] *adj* deserto(a).

deserve [dɪ'zɜ:v] *vt* meritare.

design [dɪ'zaɪn] *n (pattern)* disegno *m* ; *(art)* design *m* ; *(of machine, building)* progetto *m*. ◆ *vt (dress)* disegnare ; *(machine, building)* progettare ; **to be ~ed for** essere concepito per.

designer [dɪ'zaɪnə^r^] *n (of clothes)* stilista *mf* ; *(of building)* architetto *m* ; *(of product)* designer *mf inv*. ◆ *adj (clothes, sunglasses)* firmato(a).

desirable [dɪ'zaɪərəbl] *adj* desiderabile.

desire [dɪ'zaɪə^r^] *n* desiderio *m*. ◆ *vt* desiderare ; **it leaves a lot to be ~d** lascia molto a desiderare.

desk [desk] *n (in home, office)* scrivania *f* ; *(at airport, station, of pupil)* banco *m* ; *(at hotel)* portineria *f*.

desktop publishing ['desk,tɒp-] *n* desktop publishing *m*.

despair [dɪ'speə^r^] *n* disperazione *f*.

despatch [dɪ'spætʃ] = **dispatch**.

desperate ['desprət] *adj* disperato(a) ; **to be ~ for sthg** avere un disperato bisogno di qc.

despicable [dɪ'spɪkəbl] *adj* spregevole.

despise [dɪ'spaɪz] *vt* disprezzare.

despite [dɪ'spaɪt] *prep* nonostante.

dessert [dɪ'zɜ:t] *n* dessert *m inv*.

dessertspoon [dɪ'zɜ:tspu:n] *n* cucchiaino *m*.

destination [,destɪ'neɪʃn] *n* destinazione *f*.

destroy [dɪ'strɔɪ] *vt* distruggere.

destruction [dɪ'strʌkʃn] *n* distruzione *f*.

detach [dɪ'tætʃ] *vt* staccare.

detached house [dɪ'tætʃt-] *n* villetta *f* unifamiliare.

detail ['di:teɪl] *n* dettaglio *m* ; **in ~** dettagliatamente. ❑ **details** *npl (facts)* informazioni *fpl*.

detailed ['di:teɪld] *adj* dettagliato(a).

detect [dɪ'tekt] *vt (sense)* avvertire ; *(find)* scoprire.

detective [dɪ'tektɪv] *n* detective *mf inv* ; **a ~ story** un racconto poliziesco.

detention [dɪ'tenʃn] *n* SCH *punizione che consiste nel trattenere un alunno a scuola oltre l'orario scolastico.*

detergent [dɪ'tɜ:dʒənt] *n* detersivo *m*.

deteriorate [dɪ'tɪərɪəreɪt] *vi* deteriorarsi.

determination [dɪˌtɜ:mɪ'neɪʃn] *n* determinazione *f*.

determine [dɪ'tɜ:mɪn] *vt (control)* determinare ; *(find out)* accertare.

determined [dɪ'tɜ:mɪnd] *adj* risoluto(a) ; **to be ~ to do sthg** essere determinato a fare qc.

deterrent [dɪ'terənt] *n* deterrente *m*.

detest [dɪ'test] *vt* detestare.

detour ['di:ˌtʊə^r] *n* deviazione *f*.

deuce [dju:s] *n (tennis)* parità *f*.

devastate ['devəsteɪt] *vt* devastare.

develop [dɪ'veləp] *vt* sviluppare ; *(machine, method)* perfezionare ; *(illness, habit)* contrarre. ◆ *vi (evolve)* svilupparsi.

developing country [dɪ'veləpɪŋ-] *n* paese *m* in via di sviluppo.

development [dɪ'veləpmənt] *n* sviluppo *m* ; **a housing ~** un complesso residenziale.

device [dɪ'vaɪs] *n* congegno *m*.

devil ['devl] *n* diavolo *m* ; **what the ~ ...?** *inf* che diavolo ...?

devise [dɪ'vaɪz] *vt* escogitare.

devolution [ˌdi:və'lu:ʃn] *n* decentralizzazione *f*.

 **DEVOLUTION**

Nel 1999 il governo laburista ha riconosciuto alla Scozia, al Galles, all'Irlanda del Nord e a Londra una maggiore autonomia su materie specifiche all'interno dei rispettivi ambiti territoriali, ed ha trasferito una serie di competenze e poteri dal governo centrale ad assemblee legislative autonome : il Parlamento scozzese, l'Assemblea Nazionale del Galles, l'Assemblea dell'Irlanda del Nord e l'Assemblea di Londra. Di queste, il Parlamento scozzese è quello che gode di maggiori poteri, con un suo sistema giuridico e autorità in materia di sanità, istruzione e trasporti all'interno della Scozia.

devoted [dɪ'vəʊtɪd] *adj (person)* affezionato(a).

dew [dju:] *n* rugiada *f*.

diabetes [ˌdaɪə'bi:ti:z] *n* diabete *m*.

diabetic [ˌdaɪə'betɪk] *adj (person)* diabetico(a) ; *(chocolate)* per diabetici. ◆ *n* diabetico *m*, -a *f*.

diagnosis [ˌdaɪəg'nəʊsɪs] (*pl* **-oses** [-əʊsi:z]) *n* diagnosi *f inv*.

diagonal [daɪ'ægənl] *adj* diagonale.
diagram ['daɪəgræm] *n* diagramma *m*.
dial ['daɪəl] *n (of telephone)* disco *m* combinatore ; *(of clock)* quadrante *m* ; *(of radio)* scala *f*. ◆ *vt (number)* comporre.
dialling code ['daɪəlɪŋ-] *n Br* prefisso *m* telefonico.
dialling tone ['daɪəlɪŋ-] *n Br* segnale *m* di libero.
dial tone *Am* = **dialling tone**.
diameter [daɪ'æmɪtəʳ] *n* diametro *m*.
diamond ['daɪəmənd] *n (gem)* diamante *m*. ❑ **diamonds** *npl (in cards)* quadri *mpl*.
diaper ['daɪpəʳ] *n Am* pannolino *m*.
diarrhoea [daɪə'rɪə] *n* diarrea *f*.
diary ['daɪərɪ] *n (for appointments)* agenda *f* ; *(journal)* diario *m*.
dice [daɪs] *(pl inv) n* dado *m*.
diced [daɪst] *adj* a dadini.
dictate [dɪk'teɪt] *vt* dettare.
dictation [dɪk'teɪʃn] *n* dettato *m*.
dictator [dɪk'teɪtəʳ] *n* dittatore *m*.
dictionary ['dɪkʃənrɪ] *n* dizionario *m*.
did [dɪd] *pt* → **do**.
die [daɪ] *(pt & pp* **died**, *cont* **dying** ['daɪɪŋ]) *vi* morire ; **to be dying for sthg** *inf* morire dalla voglia di qc ; **to be dying to do sthg** *inf* morire dalla voglia di fare qc. ❑ **die away** *vi* spegnersi. ❑ **die out** *vi* scomparire.
diesel ['di:zl] *n (fuel)* gasolio *m* ; *(car)* diesel *m inv*.
diet ['daɪət] *n (for slimming, health)* dieta *f* ; *(food eaten)* alimentazione *f*. ◆ *vi* essere a dieta. ◆ *adj* dietetico(a).
diet Coke® *n* coca *f* light®.
differ ['dɪfəʳ] *vi* : **to ~ (from)** *(disagree)* non essere d'accordo (con) ; *(be dissimilar)* essere diverso (da).
difference ['dɪfrəns] *n* differenza *f* ; **it makes no ~** è lo stesso ; **a ~ of opinion** una divergenza di opinioni.
different ['dɪfrənt] *adj* diverso(a) ; **to be ~ (from)** essere diverso (da) ; **a ~ route** un'altra strada.
differently ['dɪfrəntlɪ] *adv* in modo diverso.
difficult ['dɪfɪkəlt] *adj* difficile.
difficulty ['dɪfɪkəltɪ] *n* difficoltà *f inv*.
dig [dɪg] *(pt & pp* **dug**) *vt & vi* scavare. ❑ **dig out** *vt sep (rescue)* estrarre ; *(find)* scovare. ❑ **dig up** *vt sep (from ground)* dissotterrare.
digest [dɪ'dʒest] *vt* digerire.
digestion [dɪ'dʒestʃn] *n* digestione *f*.
digestive (biscuit) [dɪ'dʒestɪv-] *n Br biscotto di frumento con farina integrale*.
digit ['dɪdʒɪt] *n (figure)* cifra *f* ; *(finger, toe)* dito *m*.
digital ['dɪdʒɪtl] *adj* digitale.
dill [dɪl] *n* aneto *m*.
dilute [daɪ'lu:t] *vt (liquid)* diluire.
dim [dɪm] *adj (light)* debole ; *(room)* buio(a) ; *inf (stupid)* ottuso(a). ◆ *vt (light)* abbassare.
dime [daɪm] *n Am* moneta *f* da dieci centesimi di dollaro.

dimensions [dɪ'menʃnz] *npl* dimensioni *fpl*.

din [dɪn] *n* baccano *m*.

dine [daɪn] *vi* cenare. ❑ **dine out** *vi* cenare fuori.

diner ['daɪnəʳ] *n Am (restaurant)* ≃ tavola *f* calda ; *(person)* cliente *mf*.

dinghy ['dɪŋgɪ] *n (with sail, oars)* barca *f* ; *(for racing)* dinghy *m inv* ; *(made of rubber)* canotto *m*.

dingy ['dɪndʒɪ] *adj (clothes)* sporco(a) ; *(town, hotel)* squallido(a).

dining car ['daɪnɪŋ-] *n* carrozza *f* ristorante.

dining hall ['daɪnɪŋ-] *n* refettorio *m*.

dining room ['daɪnɪŋ-] *n* sala *f* da pranzo.

dinner ['dɪnəʳ] *n (at lunchtime)* pranzo *m* ; *(in evening)* cena *f* ; **to have ~** *(at lunchtime)* pranzare ; *(in evening)* cenare.

dinner jacket *n* giacca *f* dello smoking.

dinner party *n* cena *f*.

dinner set *n* servizio *m* da tavola.

dinner suit *n* smoking *m inv*.

dinnertime ['dɪnətaɪm] *n (at lunchtime)* ora *f* di pranzo ; *(in evening)* ora di cena.

dinosaur ['daɪnəsɔːʳ] *n* dinosauro *m*.

dip [dɪp] *n (in road, land)* avvallamento *m* ; *(food) salsetta cremosa in cui intingere patatine o verdure crude*. ◆ *vt (into liquid)* immergere. ◆ *vi (road, land)* digradare ; **to have a ~** *(swim)* fare una nuotatina ; **to ~ one's headlights** *Br* spegnere gli abbaglianti.

diploma [dɪ'pləʊmə] *n* diploma *m*.

dipstick ['dɪpstɪk] *n* asta *f* di livello.

direct [dɪ'rekt] *adj* diretto(a). ◆ *adv (go)* direttamente ; *(travel)* senza fermarsi. ◆ *vt* : **can you ~ me to the railway station?** mi può indicare la strada per la stazione?.

direction [dɪ'rekʃn] *n (of movement)* direzione *f* ; **to ask for ~s** chiedere indicazioni. ❑ **directions** *npl (instructions)* istruzioni *fpl*.

directly [dɪ'rektlɪ] *adv (exactly)* proprio ; *(soon)* subito.

director [dɪ'rektəʳ] *n (of company)* amministratore *m*, -trice *f* ; *(of film, play, TV programme)* regista *mf* ; *(organizer)* direttore *m*, -trice *f*.

directory [dɪ'rektərɪ] *n* elenco *m*.

directory enquiries *n Br* informazioni *fpl* elenco abbonati.

dirt [dɜːt] *n* sporcizia *f* ; *(earth)* terra *f*.

dirty ['dɜːtɪ] *adj* sporco(a).

disability [ˌdɪsə'bɪlətɪ] *n* handicap *m inv* ; *(through old age, illness)* invalidità *f inv*.

disabled [dɪs'eɪbld] *adj* disabile. ◆ *npl* : **the ~** i portatori di handicap ; **'~ toilet'** 'toilette per portatori di handicap'.

disadvantage [ˌdɪsəd'vaːntɪdʒ] *n* svantaggio *m*.

disagree [ˌdɪsə'griː] *vi* non essere d'accordo ; **to ~ with sb (about)** non essere d'accordo con qn (su) ;

those mussels ~d with me quelle cozze mi hanno fatto male.
disagreement [ˌdɪsə'gri:mənt] *n (argument)* discussione *f* ; *(dissimilarity)* disaccordo *m*.
disappear [ˌdɪsə'pɪə^r] *vi* sparire.
disappearance [ˌdɪsə'pɪərəns] *n* scomparsa *f*.
disappoint [ˌdɪsə'pɔɪnt] *vt* deludere.
disappointed [ˌdɪsə'pɔɪntɪd] *adj* deluso(a).
disappointing [ˌdɪsə'pɔɪntɪŋ] *adj* deludente.
disappointment [ˌdɪsə'pɔɪntmənt] *n* delusione *f*.
disapprove [ˌdɪsə'pru:v] *vi* : to ~ of disapprovare.
disarmament [dɪs'ɑ:məmənt] *n* disarmo *m*.
disaster [dɪ'zɑ:stə^r] *n* disastro *m*.
disastrous [dɪ'zɑ:strəs] *adj* disastroso(a).
disc [dɪsk] *n Br* disco *m* ; *Br (CD)* compact disc *m inv* ; I slipped a ~ mi è venuta l'ernia del disco.
discard [dɪ'skɑ:d] *vt* scartare.
discharge [dɪs'tʃɑ:dʒ] *vt (prisoner)* rilasciare ; *(patient)* dimettere ; *(soldier)* congedare ; *(smoke, gas)* emettere ; *(liquid)* scaricare.
discipline ['dɪsɪplɪn] *n* disciplina *f*.
disc jockey *n* disc-jockey *mf inv*.
disco ['dɪskəʊ] (*pl* -s) *n (place)* discoteca *f* ; *(event)* festa *f*.
discoloured [dɪs'kʌləd] *adj* scolorito(a).
discomfort [dɪs'kʌmfət] *n* fastidio *m*.
disconnect [ˌdɪskə'nekt] *vt* staccare ; *(gas supply)* chiudere ; *(pipe)* scollegare.
discontinued [ˌdɪskən'tɪnju:d] *adj (product)* di fine serie.
discount ['dɪskaʊnt] *n* sconto *m*.
discover [dɪ'skʌvə^r] *vt* scoprire.
discovery [dɪ'skʌvərɪ] *n* scoperta *f*.
discreet [dɪ'skri:t] *adj* discreto(a).
discrepancy [dɪ'skrepənsɪ] *n* discrepanza *f*.
discriminate [dɪ'skrɪmɪneɪt] *vi* : to ~ against sb discriminare contro qn.
discrimination [dɪˌskrɪmɪ'neɪʃn] *n (unfair treatment)* discriminazione *f*.
discuss [dɪ'skʌs] *vt* discutere.
discussion [dɪ'skʌʃn] *n* discussione *f*.
disease [dɪ'zi:z] *n* malattia *f*.
disembark [ˌdɪsɪm'bɑ:k] *vi* sbarcare.
disgrace [dɪs'greɪs] *n (shame)* vergogna *f* ; it's a ~! è una vergogna!
disgraceful [dɪs'greɪsfʊl] *adj* vergognoso(a).
disguise [dɪs'gaɪz] *n* travestimento *m*. ◆ *vt* travestire ; in ~ mascherato.
disgust [dɪs'gʌst] *n* disgusto *m*. ◆ *vt* disgustare.
disgusting [dɪs'gʌstɪŋ] *adj* disgustoso(a).
dish [dɪʃ] *n* piatto *m* ; to do the ~es lavare i piatti ; '~ of the day' 'piatto del giorno'. ❑ **dish up** *vt sep* servire.

dishcloth ['dɪʃklɒθ] *n* strofinaccio *m*.

disheveled [dɪ'ʃevəld] *Am* = **dishevelled**.

dishevelled [dɪ'ʃevəld] *adj Br (hair)* arruffato(a) ; *(appearance)* trasandato(a).

dishonest [dɪs'ɒnɪst] *adj* disonesto(a).

dish towel *n Am* strofinaccio *m*.

dishwasher ['dɪʃ,wɒʃə'] *n (machine)* lavastoviglie *f inv*.

disinfectant [,dɪsɪn'fektənt] *n* disinfettante *m*.

disintegrate [dɪs'ɪntɪgreɪt] *vi* disintegrarsi.

disk [dɪsk] *n Am* = **disc** ; COMPUT dischetto *m*.

disk drive *n* drive *m inv*.

dislike [dɪs'laɪk] *n (poor opinion)* antipatia *f*. ◆ *vt* : **I ~ them** non mi piacciono ; **to take a ~ to** prendere in antipatia.

dislocate ['dɪsləkeɪt] *vt* : **to ~ one's shoulder** slogarsi la spalla.

dismal ['dɪzml] *adj (weather, place)* deprimente ; *(terrible)* pessimo(a).

dismantle [dɪs'mæntl] *vt* smontare.

dismay [dɪs'meɪ] *n* sgomento *m*.

dismiss [dɪs'mɪs] *vt (not consider)* ignorare ; *(from job)* licenziare ; *(from classroom)* congedare.

disobedient [,dɪsə'bi:djənt] *adj* disubbidiente.

disobey [,dɪsə'beɪ] *vt* disubbidire.

disorder [dɪs'ɔ:də'] *n (confusion)* disordine *m* ; *(illness)* disturbo *m*.

disorganized [dɪs'ɔ:gənaɪzd] *adj* disorganizzato(a).

dispatch [dɪ'spætʃ] *vt* inviare.

dispense [dɪ'spens] ◆**dispense with** *vt fus* fare a meno di.

dispenser [dɪ'spensə'] *n (device)* distributore *m*.

dispensing chemist [dɪ'spensɪŋ-] *n Br (shop)* farmacia *f*.

disperse [dɪ'spɜ:s] *vt* disperdere. ◆ *vi* disperdersi.

display [dɪ'spleɪ] *n (of goods)* esposizione *f* ; *(public event)* spettacolo *m* ; *(readout)* schermo *m*. ◆ *vt (goods, information)* esporre ; *(feeling, quality)* manifestare ; **on ~** in mostra.

displeased [dɪs'pli:zd] *adj* contrariato(a).

disposable [dɪ'spəuzəbl] *adj* usa e getta *(inv)*.

dispute [dɪ'spju:t] *n (argument)* controversia *f* ; *(industrial)* vertenza *f*. ◆ *vt* mettere in discussione.

disqualify [,dɪs'kwɒlɪfaɪ] *vt* squalificare ; **he is disqualified from driving** *Br* gli hanno ritirato la patente.

disregard [,dɪsrɪ'ga:d] *vt* ignorare.

disrupt [dɪs'rʌpt] *vt* disturbare.

disruption [dɪs'rʌpʃn] *n* disordine *m*.

dissatisfied [,dɪs'sætɪsfaɪd] *adj* insoddisfatto(a).

dissolve [dɪ'zɒlv] *vt* sciogliere. ◆ *vi* sciogliersi.

dissuade [dɪ'sweɪd] *vt* : **to ~ sb from doing sthg** dissuadere qn dal fare qc.

distance ['dɪstəns] *n* distanza *f* ;

from a ~ da lontano ; in the ~ in lontananza.

distant ['dɪstənt] *adj* distante ; *(in time)* lontano(a).

distilled water [dɪ'stɪld-] *n* acqua *f* distillata.

distillery [dɪ'stɪlərɪ] *n* distilleria *f*.

distinct [dɪ'stɪŋkt] *adj (separate)* distinto(a) ; *(noticeable)* chiaro(a).

distinction [dɪ'stɪŋkʃn] *n (difference)* distinzione *f* ; *(mark in exam)* lode *f*.

distinctive [dɪ'stɪŋktɪv] *adj* inconfondibile.

distinguish [dɪ'stɪŋgwɪʃ] *vt (perceive)* distinguere ; to ~ sthg from sthg distinguere qc da qc.

distorted [dɪ'stɔ:tɪd] *adj* distorto(a).

distract [dɪ'strækt] *vt* distrarre.

distraction [dɪ'strækʃn] *n* distrazione *f*.

distress [dɪ'stres] *n (pain)* sofferenza *f* ; *(anxiety)* angoscia *f*.

distressing [dɪ'stresɪŋ] *adj* doloroso(a).

distribute [dɪ'strɪbju:t] *vt* distribuire.

distributor [dɪ'strɪbjʊtəʳ] *n* COMM distributore *m* ; AUT spinterogeno *m*.

district ['dɪstrɪkt] *n* regione *f* ; *(of town)* quartiere *m*.

district attorney *n Am* ≃ procuratore *m* della Repubblica.

disturb [dɪ'stɜ:b] *vt (interrupt)* disturbare ; *(worry)* turbare ; *(move)* muovere ; 'do not ~' 'non disturbare'.

disturbance [dɪ'stɜ:bəns] *n (violence)* disordini *mpl*.

ditch [dɪtʃ] *n* fossato *m*.

ditto ['dɪtəʊ] *adv* idem.

divan [dɪ'væn] *n* divano *m*.

dive [daɪv] (*pt Am* **-d** OR **dove**, *pt Br* **-d**) *n (of swimmer)* tuffo *m*. ◆ *vi* tuffarsi ; *(under sea)* immergersi.

diver ['daɪvəʳ] *n (from divingboard, rock)* tuffatore *m*, -trice *f* ; *(under sea)* sommozzatore *m*, -trice *f*.

diversion [daɪ'vɜ:ʃn] *n (of traffic)* deviazione *f* ; *(amusement)* diversivo *m*.

divert [daɪ'vɜ:t] *vt (traffic, river)* deviare ; *(attention)* distrarre.

divide [dɪ'vaɪd] *vt* dividere. ❑ **divide up** *vt sep* dividere.

diving ['daɪvɪŋ] *n (from divingboard, rock)* tuffi *mpl* ; *(under sea)* immersioni *fpl* ; to go ~ fare sub.

divingboard ['daɪvɪŋbɔ:d] *n* trampolino *m*.

division [dɪ'vɪʒn] *n* divisione *f* ; *(in football league)* serie *f*.

divorce [dɪ'vɔ:s] *n* divorzio *m*. ◆ *vt* divorziare da.

divorced [dɪ'vɔ:st] *adj* divorziato(a).

DIY *n* (*abbr of do-it-yourself*) il fai da te.

dizzy ['dɪzɪ] *adj* : I feel ~ mi gira la testa.

DJ *n* (*abbr of disc jockey*) disc-jockey *mf inv*.

☞

do [du:] (*pt* **did**, *pp* **done**, *pl* **dos**) *aux vb* - 1. *(in negatives)* : don't ~ that! non farlo! ; she didn't listen non ha ascoltato.

- 2. *(in questions)* : **~ you like it?** ti piace? ; **how ~ you do it?** come si fa?
- 3. *(referring to previous verb)* : **I eat more than you ~** io mangio più di te ; **you made a mistake - no I didn't!** ti sei sbagliato - non è vero! ; **so ~ I** anch'io.
- 4. *(in question tags)* vero?, non è vero? ; **so, you like Scotland, ~ you?** e così ti piace la Scozia, non è vero?
- 5. *(for emphasis)* : **I ~ like this bedroom** questa camera mi piace proprio ; **~ come in!** si accomodi!
◆ *vt* - 1. *(perform)* fare ; **to ~ one's homework** fare i compiti ; **what is she doing?** cosa sta facendo? ; **what can I ~ for you?** in cosa posso esserle utile?
- 2. *(attend to)* : **to ~ one's hair** pettinarsi ; **to ~ one's make-up** truccarsi ; **to ~ one's teeth** lavarsi i denti.
- 3. *(cause)* fare ; **to ~ damage** danneggiare ; **to ~ sb good** fare bene a qn.
- 4. *(have as job)* : **what do you ~?** che lavoro fai?
- 5. *(provide, offer)* fare ; **we ~ pizzas for under £4** facciamo pizze a meno di 4 sterline.
- 6. *(study)* fare.
- 7. *(subj : vehicle)* fare ; **the car was doing 50 mph** la macchina andava a 80 all'ora.
- 8. *inf (visit)* fare ; **we're doing Scotland next week** la settimana prossima facciamo la Scozia.
◆ *vi* - 1. *(behave, act)* fare ; **~ as I say** fai come ti dico.
- 2. *(progress, get on)* andare ; **to ~ badly** andare male ; **to ~ well** andare bene.
- 3. *(be sufficient)* bastare ; **will £5 ~?** bastano 5 sterline?
- 4. *(in phrases)* : **how do you ~?** piacere! ; **what has that got to ~ with it?** e questo che c'entra?
◆ *n (party)* festa *f* ; **the ~s and don'ts** le cose da fare e da non fare.
❑ **do out of** *vt sep inf* : **to ~ sb out of sthg** fregare qc a qn.
❑ **do up** *vt sep (fasten)* allacciare ; *(decorate)* rinnovare ; *(wrap up)* impacchettare.
❑ **do with** *vt fus (need)* : **I could ~ with a drink** mi ci vuole proprio un bicchierino.
❑ **do without** *vt fus* fare a meno di.

---

dock [dɒk] *n (for ships)* molo *m* ; *JUR* banco *m* degli imputati. ◆ *vi* attraccare.

doctor ['dɒktəʳ] *n* dottore *m*, -essa *f* ; **to go to the ~'s** andare dal dottore.

document ['dɒkjumənt] *n* documento *m*.

documentary [ˌdɒkju'mentərɪ] *n* documentario *m*.

Dodgems® ['dɒdʒəmz] *npl Br* autoscontri *mpl*.

dodgy ['dɒdʒɪ] *adj Br inf (plan)* rischioso(a) ; *(car)* poco sicuro(a).

does [*weak form* dəz, *strong form* dʌz] → **do**.

doesn't ['dʌznt] = **does not**.

dog [dɒg] *n* cane *m*.

dog food *n* cibo *m* per cani.

doggy bag ['dɒgɪ-] *n sacchetto per portar via gli avanzi di un pasto consumato al ristorante.*

do-it-yourself *n* il fai da te.

dole [dəul] *n* : **to be on the ~** *Br*

prendere il sussidio di disoccupazione.

doll [dɒl] *n* bambola *f*.

dollar ['dɒlə'] *n* dollaro *m*.

Dolomites ['dɒləmaɪts] *npl*: the ~ le Dolomiti.

dolphin ['dɒlfɪn] *n* delfino *m*.

dome [dəum] *n* cupola *f*.

domestic [də'mestɪk] *adj (of house, family)* domestico(a) ; *(of country)* nazionale, interno(a).

***domestic* appliance** *n* elettrodomestico *m*.

domestic flight *n* volo *m* nazionale.

domestic science *n* economia *f* domestica.

dominate ['dɒmɪneɪt] *vt* dominare.

dominoes ['dɒmɪnəuz] *n* domino *m*.

donate [də'neɪt] *vt* donare.

donation [də'neɪʃn] *n* donazione *f*.

done [dʌn] *pp* → **do**. ◆ *adj (finished)* finito(a) ; *(cooked)* cotto(a).

donkey ['dɒŋkɪ] *n* asino *m*.

don't [dəunt] = **do not**.

door [dɔː'] *n (of building)* porta *f* ; *(of vehicle, cupboard)* sportello *m*.

doorbell ['dɔːbel] *n* campanello *m*.

doorknob ['dɔːnɒb] *n* pomello *m*.

doorman ['dɔːmən] (*pl* **-men**) *n* portiere *m*.

doormat ['dɔːmæt] *n* zerbino *m*.

doormen ['dɔːmən] *pl* → **doorman**.

doorstep ['dɔːstep] *n* gradino *m* della porta ; *Br inf (piece of bread)* grossa fetta *f* di pane.

doorway ['dɔːweɪ] *n* porta *f*.

dope [dəup] *n inf (any illegal drug)* roba *f* ; *(marijuana)* erba *f*.

dormitory ['dɔːmətrɪ] *n* dormitorio *m*.

Dormobile® ['dɔːmə,biːl] *n* camper *m inv*.

dosage ['dəusɪdʒ] *n* dosaggio *m*.

dose [dəus] *n (amount)* dose *f* ; *(of illness)* attacco *m*.

dot [dɒt] *n* punto *m* ; **on the ~** *fig* in punto.

dotted line ['dɒtɪd-] *n* linea *f* punteggiata.

double ['dʌbl] *adj* doppio(a). ◆ *adv (twice)* due volte. ◆ *n (twice the amount)* doppio *m* ; *(alcohol)* dose *f* doppia. ◆ *vt* & *vi* raddoppiare ; **~ three, two, eight** trentatrè, ventotto ; **a ~ whisky** un doppio whisky ; **to bend sthg ~** piegare qc in due. ❑ **doubles** *n (in tennis)* doppio *m*.

double bed *n* letto *m* matrimoniale.

double-breasted [-'brestɪd] *adj* a doppiopetto.

double cream *n Br panna molto densa ad alto contenuto di grassi.*

double-decker (bus) [-'dekə'-] *n* autobus *m inv* a due piani.

double doors *npl* porte *fpl* a due battenti.

double-glazing [-'gleɪzɪŋ] *n* doppi vetri *mpl*.

double room *n* camera *f* per due.

doubt [daut] *n* dubbio *m*. ◆ *vt* dubitare di ; **I ~ it** ne dubito ;

I ~ she'll be there dubito che ci sarà ; **in ~** in dubbio ; **no ~** *(almost certainly)* senza dubbio.

doubtful ['dautful] *adj (uncertain)* incerto(a) ; **it's ~ that ...** è improbabile che ... *(+ subjunctive)*.

dough [dəu] *n* pasta *f*, impasto *m* *(per pane, dolci)*.

doughnut ['dəunʌt] *n* bombolone *m*.

dove[1] [dʌv] *n (bird)* colomba *f*.

dove[2] [dəuv] *pt Am* → **dive**.

Dover ['dəuvə'] *n* Dover.

down [daun] *adv* - 1. *(towards the bottom)* giù ; **~ here** quaggiù ; **~ there** laggiù ; **to fall ~** cadere.
- 2. *(along)* : **I'm going ~ to the shops** vado ai negozi.
- 3. *(downstairs)* : **I'll come ~ later** scenderò più tardi.
- 4. *(southwards)* : **we're going ~ to London** andiamo a Londra.
- 5. *(in writing)* : **to write sthg ~** scrivere qc.
◆ *prep* - 1. *(towards the bottom of)* : **they ran ~ the hill** corsero giù per la collina.
- 2. *(along)* lungo ; **I was walking ~ the street** camminavo lungo la strada.
◆ *adj inf (depressed)* giù *(inv)*.
◆ *n (feathers)* piumino *m*.

downhill [,daun'hɪl] *adv* in discesa.

Downing Street ['daunɪŋ-] *n* Downing Street *f (strada di Londra dove si trova la residenza del primo ministro)*.

DOWNING STREET

Questa strada di Londra è divenuta famosa in quanto ospita al numero 10 la residenza ufficiale del primo ministro e al numero 11 quella del Cancelliere dello Scacchiere (ministro delle Finanze). L'espressione *Downing Street* designa per estensione il primo ministro stesso e i suoi collaboratori.

downpour ['daunpɔː'] *n* acquazzone *m*.

downstairs [,daun'steəz] *adj* di sotto. ◆ *adv* al piano di sotto ; **to go ~** scendere.

downtown [,daun'taun] *adj (hotel)* del centro ; *(train)* per il centro. ◆ *adv* in centro ; **~ New York** il centro di New York.

down under *adv Br inf (in Australia)* in Australia.

downwards ['daunwədz] *adv* verso il basso.

doz. *abbr* = **dozen**.

doze [dəuz] *vi* fare un pisolino.

dozen ['dʌzn] *n* dozzina *f* ; **a ~ eggs** una dozzina di uova.

Dr (*abbr of doctor*) Dott. *m (Dott.ssa f)*.

drab [dræb] *adj* grigio(a).

draft [drɑːft] *n (early version)* bozza *f* ; *(money order)* tratta *f* ; *Am* = **draught**.

drag [dræg] *vt (pull along)* trascinare. ◆ *vi (along ground)* strascicare ; **what a ~!** *inf* che seccatura!
❑ **drag on** *vi* trascinarsi.

dragonfly ['drægnflaɪ] *n* libellula *f*.

drain [dreɪn] *n (sewer)* fogna *f*; *(grating in street)* tombino *m*. ◆ *vt (tank, radiator)* svuotare. ◆ *vi (vegetables, washing-up)* scolare.
draining board ['dreɪnɪŋ-] *n* scolatoio *m*.
drainpipe ['dreɪnpaɪp] *n* tubo *m* di scarico.
drama ['drɑːmə] *n (play, exciting event)* dramma *m* ; *(art)* teatro *m* ; *(excitement)* emozioni *fpl*.
dramatic [drə'mætɪk] *adj (impressive)* sensazionale.
drank [dræŋk] *pt* → **drink**.
drapes [dreɪps] *npl Am* tende *fpl*.
drastic ['dræstɪk] *adj* drastico(a) ; *(improvement)* netto(a).
drastically ['dræstɪklɪ] *adv* sensibilmente.
draught [drɑːft] *n Br (of air)* corrente *f* d'aria.
draught beer *n* birra *f* alla spina.
draughts [drɑːfts] *n Br* dama *f*.
draughty ['drɑːftɪ] *adj* pieno di correnti d'aria.
draw [drɔː] (*pt* **drew**, *pp* **drawn**) *vt (with pen, pencil)* disegnare ; *(line)* tracciare ; *Pull* tirare ; *(attract)* attirare ; *(conclusion)* trarre ; *(comparison)* fare. ◆ *vi (with pen, pencil)* disegnare ; SPORT pareggiare. ◆ *n* SPORT *(result)* pareggio *m* ; *(lottery)* estrazione *f* ; **to ~ the curtains** tirare le tende. ❑ **draw out** *vt sep (money)* prelevare. ❑ **draw up** ◆ *vt sep (list, plan)* stendere. ◆ *vi (car, bus)* accostarsi.
drawback ['drɔːbæk] *n* inconveniente *m*.
drawer [drɔː^r] *n* cassetto *m*.
drawing ['drɔːɪŋ] *n* disegno *m*.
drawing pin *n Br* puntina *f* da disegno.
drawing room *n* salotto *m*.
drawn [drɔːn] *pp* → **draw**.
dreadful ['dredful] *adj* terribile.
dream [driːm] *n* sogno *m*. ◆ *vt* sognare. ◆ *vi* : **to ~ (of)** sognare (di) ; **a ~ house** una casa di sogno.
dress [dres] *n* vestito *m* ; *(clothes)* abbigliamento *m*. ◆ *vt* vestire ; *(wound)* fasciare ; *(salad)* condire. ◆ *vi (get dressed)* vestirsi ; *(in particular way)* vestire ; **to be ~ed in** essere vestito di ; **to get ~ed** vestirsi. ❑ **dress up** *vi* mettersi in ghingheri.
dress circle *n* prima galleria *f*.
dresser ['dresə^r] *n Br (for crockery)* credenza *f*; *Am (chest of drawers)* comò *m inv*.
dressing ['dresɪŋ] *n (for salad)* condimento *m* ; *(for wound)* fasciatura *f*.
dressing gown *n* vestaglia *f*.
dressing room *n* camerino *m*.
dressing table *n* toilette *f inv*.
dressmaker ['dres,meɪkə^r] *n* sarta *f*.
dress rehearsal *n* prova *f* generale.
drew [druː] *pt* → **draw**.
dribble ['drɪbl] *vi (liquid)* gocciolare ; *(baby)* sbavare.
drier ['draɪə^r] = **dryer**.
drift [drɪft] *n (of snow)* cumulo *m*. ◆ *vi (in wind)* essere spinto dal vento ; *(in water)* essere spinto dalla corrente.
drill [drɪl] *n* trapano *m*. ◆ *vt (hole)* fare.

drink [drɪŋk] (*pt* **drank**, *pp* **drunk**) *n* bevanda *f* ; *(alcoholic)* bicchierino *m.* ◆ *vt* & *vi* bere ; **would you like a ~?** vuoi qualcosa da bere? ; **to have a ~** *(alcoholic)* bere un bicchierino.
drinkable ['drɪŋkəbl] *adj (safe to drink)* potabile ; *(wine)* bevibile.
drinking water ['drɪŋkɪŋ-] *n* acqua *f* potabile.
drip [drɪp] *n (drop)* goccia *f* ; MED flebo *f inv.* ◆ *vi* gocciolare.
drip-dry *adj* che non si stira.
dripping (wet) ['drɪpɪŋ-] *adj* fradicio(a).
drive [draɪv] (*pt* **drove**, *pp* **driven**) *n (journey)* viaggio *m* (in macchina) ; *(in front of house)* viale *m* d'accesso. ◆ *vi (drive car)* guidare ; *(travel in car)* andare in macchina. ◆ *vt (car, bus, train)* guidare ; *(take in car)* portare (in macchina) ; *(operate, power)* : **it's driven by electricity** funziona a elettricità ; **it's two hours' ~ from here** è a due ore di macchina da qui ; **to go for a ~** andare a fare un giro in macchina ; **to ~ sb to do sthg** spingere qn a fare qc ; **to ~ sb mad** far diventare matto qn ; **can you ~ me to the station?** mi accompagni alla stazione?
drivel ['drɪvl] *n* scemenze *fpl.*
driven ['drɪvn] *pp* → **drive.**
driver ['draɪvəʳ] *n (of car, bus)* conducente *mf* ; *(of train)* macchinista *mf* ; *(of taxi)* tassista *mf.*
driver's license *Am* = **driving licence.**
driveway ['draɪvweɪ] *n* vialetto *m* d'accesso.
driving lesson ['draɪvɪŋ-] *n* lezione *f* di guida.
driving licence ['draɪvɪŋ-] *n Br* patente *f* di guida.
driving test ['draɪvɪŋ-] *n* esame *m* di guida.
drizzle ['drɪzl] *n* pioggerellina *f.*
drop [drɒp] *n (drip)* goccia *f* ; *(small amount)* goccio *m* ; *(distance down)* salto *m* ; *(decrease)* calo *m* ; *(in wages)* riduzione *f.* ◆ *vt* lasciar cadere ; *(reduce)* ridurre ; *(from vehicle)* far scendere ; *(omit)* saltare. ◆ *vi (fall)* cadere ; *(decrease)* diminuire ; **to ~ a hint that** far capire che ; **to ~ sb a line** scrivere due righe a qn. ❑ **drop in** *vi inf* fare un salto. ❑ **drop off** ◆ *vt sep (from vehicle)* far scendere. ◆ *vi (fall asleep)* addormentarsi ; *(fall off)* staccarsi. ❑ **drop out** *vi (of college, race)* ritirarsi.
drought [draʊt] *n* siccità *f inv.*
drove [drəʊv] *pt* → **drive.**
drown [draʊn] *vi* annegare.
drug [drʌg] *n* MED farmaco *m* ; *(stimulant)* droga *f.* ◆ *vt* drogare.
drug addict *n* tossicodipendente *mf.*
druggist ['drʌgɪst] *n Am* farmacista *mf.*
drum [drʌm] *n* MUS tamburo *m* ; *(container)* fusto *m.* ❑ **drums** *npl* batteria *f.*
drummer ['drʌməʳ] *n* batterista *mf.*
drumstick ['drʌmstɪk] *n (of chicken)* coscia *f* (di pollo).
drunk [drʌŋk] *pp* → **drink.** ◆ *adj* ubriaco(a). ◆ *n* ubriaco *m* ; **to get ~** ubriacarsi.
dry [draɪ] *adj* secco(a) ; *(weather, day)* asciutto(a). ◆ *vt* asciugare.

◆ *vi* asciugarsi ; **to ~ o.s.** asciugarsi ; **to ~ one's hair** asciugarsi i capelli. ❑ **dry up** *vi (become dry)* seccarsi ; *(dry the dishes)* asciugare i piatti.

dry-clean *vt* pulire a secco.

dry cleaner's *n* lavanderia *f* (a secco).

dryer ['draɪəʳ] *n (for clothes)* asciugabiancheria *m inv* ; *(for hair)* asciugacapelli *m inv*.

dry-roasted peanuts [-'rəʊstɪd-] *npl* arachidi *fpl* tostate.

DSS *n Br ministero britannico per la previdenza sociale.*

DTP *n (abbr of desktop publishing)* desktop publishing *m*.

dual carriageway ['dju:əl-] *n Br* strada *f* a doppia carreggiata.

dubbed [dʌbd] *adj (film)* doppiato(a).

dubious ['dju:bjəs] *adj (suspect)* dubbio(a).

duchess ['dʌtʃɪs] *n* duchessa *f*.

duck [dʌk] *n* anatra *f*. ◆ *vi* abbassarsi.

due [dju:] *adj (expected)* atteso(a) ; *(owed)* dovuto(a) ; **to be ~** *(bill, rent)* scadere ; **in ~ course** a tempo debito ; **~ to** a causa di.

duet [dju:'et] *n* duetto *m*.

duffel bag ['dʌfl-] *n* sacca *f* da viaggio.

duffel coat ['dʌfl-] *n* montgomery *m inv*.

dug [dʌg] *pt & pp* → **dig**.

duke [dju:k] *n* duca *m*.

dull [dʌl] *adj (boring)* noioso(a) ; *(not bright)* spento(a) ; *(weather)* coperto(a) ; *(pain)* sordo(a).

dumb [dʌm] *adj inf (stupid)* stupido(a) ; *(unable to speak)* muto(a).

dummy ['dʌmɪ] *n Br (for baby)* ciuccio *m* ; *(for clothes)* manichino *m*.

dump [dʌmp] *n (for rubbish)* discarica *f* ; *inf (place)* porcile *m*. ◆ *vt (drop carelessly)* gettare ; *(get rid of)* scaricare.

dumpling ['dʌmplɪŋ] *n gnocco di pasta cotto a vapore e servito insieme agli stufati.*

dune [dju:n] *n* duna *f*.

dungarees [ˌdʌŋgə'ri:z] *npl (for work)* tuta *f* ; *Br (fashion item)* salopette *f inv*.

dungeon ['dʌndʒən] *n* segreta *f*.

duplicate ['dju:plɪkət] *n* duplicato *m*.

during ['djʊərɪŋ] *prep* durante.

dusk [dʌsk] *n* crepuscolo *m*.

dust [dʌst] *n* polvere *f*. ◆ *vt* spolverare.

dustbin ['dʌstbɪn] *n Br* pattumiera *f*.

dustcart ['dʌstka:t] *n Br* camion *m inv* delle immondizie.

duster ['dʌstəʳ] *n* straccio *m (per spolverare)*.

dustman ['dʌstmən] *(pl* **-men** [-mən]) *n Br* netturbino *m*.

dustpan ['dʌstpæn] *n* paletta *f (per la spazzatura)*.

dusty ['dʌstɪ] *adj* polveroso(a).

Dutch [dʌtʃ] *adj* olandese. ◆ *n (language)* olandese *m*. ◆ *npl*: **the ~** gli olandesi.

duty ['dju:tɪ] *n (moral obligation)* dovere *m* ; *(tax)* dazio *m*, tassa *f* ; **to be on ~** essere in OR di servizio ; **to be off ~** essere fuori servizio, essere libero. ❑ **duties** *npl (job)* mansioni *fpl*.

duty chemist's *n* farmacia *f* di turno.

duty-free *adj* esente da dazio. ◆ *n* duty free *m inv*.

duvet ['du:veɪ] *n* piumone® *m*.

dwarf [dwɔ:f] (*pl* **dwarves** [dwɔ:vz]) *n* nano *m*, -a *f*.

dwelling ['dwelɪŋ] *n fml* abitazione *f*.

dye [daɪ] *n* tinta *f*. ◆ *vt* tingere.

dynamite ['daɪnəmaɪt] *n* dinamite *f*.

dynamo ['daɪnəməʊ] (*pl* **-s**) *n (on bike)* dinamo *f inv*.

dyslexic [dɪs'leksɪk] *adj* dislessico(a).

E

E (*abbr of east*) E.

E111 *n* E111 *m*.

each [i:tʃ] *adj* ogni *(inv)*, ciascuno(a). ◆ *pron* ciascuno *m*, -a *f*, ognuno *m*, -a *f*; ~ **one** ognuno ; **one** ~ uno ciascuno ; **one of** ~ uno di ognuno ; **they know** ~ **other** si conoscono.

eager ['i:gəʳ] *adj (pupil, expression)* entusiasta ; **to be ~ to do sthg** essere impaziente di fare qc.

eagle ['i:gl] *n (bird)* aquila *f*.

ear [ɪəʳ] *n* orecchio *m* ; *(of corn)* spiga *f*.

earache ['ɪəreɪk] *n* : **to have** ~ avere mal *m* d'orecchi.

earl [ɜ:l] *n* conte *m*.

early ['ɜ:lɪ] *adj (childhood)* primo(a) ; *(train)* di buon'ora ; *(before usual or arranged time)* anticipato(a), precoce. ◆ *adv* presto ; **in the ~ morning** di primo mattino ; **in the ~ 20th century** all'inizio del xx secolo ; **at the earliest** al più presto ; ~ **on** presto ; **to have an ~ night** andare a letto presto.

earn [ɜ:n] *vt (money)* guadagnare ; *(praise, success)* guadagnarsi ; **to ~ a living** guadagnarsi da vivere.

earnings ['ɜ:nɪŋz] *npl* guadagni *mpl*.

earphones ['ɪəfəʊnz] *npl* cuffie *fpl*.

earplugs ['ɪəplʌgz] *npl* tappi *mpl* per le orecchie.

earrings ['ɪərɪŋz] *npl* orecchini *mpl*.

earth [ɜ:θ] *n* terra *f*. ◆ *vt Br (appliance)* mettere a terra ; **how on ~ ...?** come diavolo ...?

earthenware ['ɜ:θnweəʳ] *adj* di terracotta.

earthquake ['ɜ:θkweɪk] *n* terremoto *m*.

ease [i:z] *n (lack of difficulty)* facilità *f*. ◆ *vt (pain, problem)* alleviare ; **at ~** a proprio agio ; **with ~** con facilità. ❑ **ease off** *vi (pain, rain)* attenuarsi.

easily ['i:zɪlɪ] *adv* facilmente ; *(by far)* senza dubbio.

east [i:st] *n* est *m*. ◆ *adj* dell'est. ◆ *adv* a est ; **in the ~ of England** nell'Inghilterra orientale ; **the East** *(Asia)* l'Oriente *m*.

eastbound ['i:stbaʊnd] *adj* diretto(a) a est.

Easter ['i:stəʳ] *n* Pasqua *f*.

eastern ['i:stən] *adj* orientale, dell'est. ❑ **Eastern** *adj (Asian)* orientale.
Eastern Europe *n* l'Europa *f* dell'Est.
eastwards ['i:stwədz] *adv* verso est.
easy ['i:zɪ] *adj* facile ; *(without problems)* tranquillo(a) ; **to take it ~** prendersela con calma.
easygoing [ˌi:zɪ'gəʊɪŋ] *adj* rilassato(a).
eat [i:t] (*pt* **ate**, *pp* **eaten** ['i:tn]) *vt* & *vi* mangiare. ❑ **eat out** *vi* mangiare fuori.
ebony ['ebənɪ] *n* ebano *m*.
EC *n* (*abbr of European Community*) CE *f*.
eccentric [ɪk'sentrɪk] *adj* eccentrico(a).
echo ['ekəʊ] (*pl* **-es**) *n* eco. ◆ *vi* fare eco.
ecology [ɪ'kɒlədʒɪ] *n* ecologia *f*.
economic [ˌi:kə'nɒmɪk] *adj* economico. ❑ **economics** *n* economia *f*.
economical [ˌi:kə'nɒmɪkl] *adj (car, system)* economico(a) ; *(person)* parsimonioso(a).
economize [ɪ'kɒnəmaɪz] *vi* economizzare, risparmiare.
economy [ɪ'kɒnəmɪ] *n* economia *f*.
economy class *n* classe *f* economica.
economy size *adj* in confezione economica.
ecstasy ['ekstəsɪ] *n* estasi *f*.
eczema ['eksɪmə] *n* eczema *m*.
edge [edʒ] *n* bordo *m* ; *(of knife)* taglio *m*.
edible ['edɪbl] *adj* commestibile.
Edinburgh ['edɪnbrə] *n* Edimburgo *f*.
Edinburgh Festival *n* : **the ~** il festival di Edimburgo.
edition [ɪ'dɪʃn] *n* edizione *f* ; *(of TV programme)* puntata *f*.
editor ['edɪtə'] *n (of newspaper, magazine)* direttore *m*, -trice *f* ; *(of book)* curatore *m*, -trice *f* ; *(of film, TV programme)* tecnico *m*, -a *f* del montaggio.
editorial [ˌedɪ'tɔ:rɪəl] *n* editoriale *m*.
educate ['edʒʊkeɪt] *vt* istruire.
education [ˌedʒʊ'keɪʃn] *n* istruzione *f*.

EDUCATION

In Gran Bretagna e negli Stati Uniti il sistema scolastico si divide in due cicli fondamentali : scuola primaria e scuola secondaria. La scuola primaria (chiamata *primary school* in Gran Bretagna e *grade school* negli Stati Uniti) dura sei anni, dalla 1° alla 6°, anche se per i bambini inglesi la scuola comincia in realtà un anno prima nella *Reception class*. In Gran Bretagna la scuola secondaria *(secondary school)* va dagli undici ai sedici anni e a conclusione di questo ciclo si sostengono degli esami chiamati GCSE *(General Certificate of Secondary Education)*. Gli studenti che vogliono continuare gli studi fino ai 18 anni devono superare gli esami in almeno cinque materie e ciò darà loro la possibilità di prepararsi per gli *A levels*, requisito obbligatorio per accedere poi all'Università. Negli Stati Uniti la scuola primaria è seguita da una tappa intermedia *(la middle school o junior high school)* che dura due o tre anni ; la scuola secondaria vera e propria, la high school, comincia intorno ai 14 anni e dura quattro anni (dal 9° al 12°) ; gli studenti generalmente si diplomano a 18 anni.

EEC *n* C.E.E. *f*.

eel [iːl] *n* anguilla *f*.

effect [ɪ'fekt] *n* effetto *m* ; **to put sthg into ~** mettere qc in atto ; **to take ~** *(drug)* fare effetto ; *(law)* entrare in vigore.

effective [ɪ'fektɪv] *adj (successful)* efficace ; *(law, system)* effettivo(a).

effectively [ɪ'fektɪvlɪ] *adv (successfully)* efficacemente ; *(in fact)* effettivamente.

efficient [ɪ'fɪʃənt] *adj* efficiente.

effort ['efət] *n* sforzo *m* ; **to make an ~ to do sthg** fare uno sforzo per fare qc ; **it's not worth the ~** non ne vale la pena.

e.g. *adv* ad es.

egg [eg] *n* uovo *m*.

egg cup *n* portauovo *m inv*.

egg mayonnaise *n* uova *fpl* sode in maionese.

eggplant ['egplaːnt] *n Am* melanzana *f*.

egg white *n* albume *m*.

egg yolk *n* tuorlo *m*.

eiderdown ['aɪdədaun] *n* piumone® *m*.

eight [eɪt] *num* otto → **six**.

eighteen [ˌeɪ'tiːn] *num* diciotto → **six**.

eighteenth [ˌeɪ'tiːnθ] *num* diciottesimo(a) → **sixth**.

eighth [eɪtθ] *num* ottavo(a) → **sixth**.

eightieth ['eɪtɪɪθ] *num* ottantesimo(a) → **sixth**.

eighty ['eɪtɪ] *num* ottanta → **six**.

Eire ['eərə] *n* la Repubblica d'Irlanda.

Eisteddfod [aɪ'stedfəd] *n festival culturale gallese*.

either ['aɪðəʳ, 'iːðəʳ] *adj* : **~ book will do** va bene sia l'uno che l'altro libro. ◆ *pron* : **I'll take ~ (of them)** prendo o l'uno(a) o l'altro(a) ; **I don't like ~ (of them)** non mi piace né l'uno(a) né l'altro(a). ◆ *adv* : **I can't ~** non posso neanch'io ; **~ ... or** o ... o ; **on ~ side** su entrambi i lati.

eject [ɪ'dʒekt] *vt (cassette)* espellere.

elaborate [ɪ'læbrət] *adj (needlework, design)* elaborato(a).

elastic [ɪ'læstɪk] *n* elastico *m*.

elastic band *n Br* elastico *m*.

elbow ['elbəu] *n (of person)* gomito *m*.

elder ['eldəʳ] *adj* più vecchio(a), maggiore.

elderly ['eldəlɪ] *adj* anziano(a). ◆ *npl* : **the ~** gli anziani.

eldest ['eldɪst] *adj* : **the ~ son/daughter** il figlio/la figlia maggiore.

elect [ɪ'lekt] *vt* eleggere ; **to ~ to**

do sthg *fml (choose)* scegliere di fare qc.

election [ɪ'lekʃn] *n* elezione *f*.

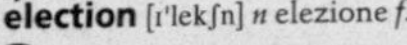

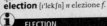

ELECTION

Negli Stati Uniti le elezioni presidenziali si tengono ogni quattro anni. In base alla Costituzione, che fissa anche il giorno delle elezioni, il Presidente non può essere rieletto per più di due volte consecutive. In Gran Bretagna il Primo Ministro ha facoltà di indire un'elezione in qualsiasi momento della legislatura, ma le elezioni devono svolgersi almeno una volta ogni cinque anni.

---

electric [ɪ'lektrɪk] *adj* elettrico(a).

electrical goods [ɪ'lektrɪkl-] *npl* apparecchi *mpl* elettrici.

electric blanket *n* coperta *f* elettrica.

electric drill *n* trapano *m* elettrico.

electric fence *n* recinto *m* elettrificato.

electrician [ˌɪlek'trɪʃn] *n* elettricista *mf*.

electricity [ˌɪlek'trɪsətɪ] *n* elettricità *f*.

electric shock *n* scossa *f* elettrica.

electrocute [ɪ'lektrəkjuːt] *vt* fulminare.

electronic [ˌɪlek'trɒnɪk] *adj* elettronico(a).

elegant ['elɪgənt] *adj* elegante.

element ['elɪmənt] *n* elemento *m*; *(of fire, kettle)* resistenza *f*; **the ~s** *(weather)* gli elementi.

elementary [ˌelɪ'mentərɪ] *adj* elementare.

elephant ['elɪfənt] *n* elefante *m*.

elevator ['elɪveɪtə^r] *n Am* ascensore *m*.

eleven [ɪ'levn] *num* undici → **six**.

eleventh [ɪ'levnθ] *num* undicesimo(a) → **sixth**.

eligible ['elɪdʒəbl] *adj* che ha i requisiti.

eliminate [ɪ'lɪmɪneɪt] *vt* eliminare.

Elizabethan [ɪˌlɪzə'biːθn] *adj* elisabettiano *(seconda metà del XVI sec.)*.

elm [elm] *n* olmo *m*.

else [els] *adv*: **I don't want anything ~** non voglio nient'altro; **anything ~?** altro?; **everyone ~** tutti gli altri; **nobody ~** nessun altro; **nothing ~** nient'altro; **somebody ~** qualcun altro; **something ~** qualcos'altro; **somewhere ~** da qualche altra parte; **what ~?** che altro?; **who ~?** chi altri?; **or ~** altrimenti.

elsewhere [els'weə^r] *adv* altrove.

embankment [ɪm'bæŋkmənt] *n* *(next to river)* argine *m*; *(next to road, railway)* terrapieno *m*.

embark [ɪm'baːk] *vi (board ship)* imbarcarsi.

embarrass [ɪm'bærəs] *vt* imbarazzare.

embarrassed [ɪm'bærəst] *adj* imbarazzato(a).

embarrassing [ɪm'bærəsɪŋ] *adj* imbarazzante.

embarrassment [ɪm'bærəsmənt] *n* imbarazzo *m*.
embassy ['embəsɪ] *n* ambasciata *f*.
emblem ['embləm] *n* emblema *m*.
embrace [ɪm'breɪs] *vt* abbracciare.
embroidered [ɪm'brɔɪdəd] *adj* ricamato(a).
embroidery [ɪm'brɔɪdərɪ] *n* ricamo *m*.
emerald ['emərəld] *n* smeraldo *m*.
emerge [ɪ'mɜːdʒ] *vi* emergere.
emergency [ɪ'mɜːdʒənsɪ] *n* emergenza *f*. ◆ *adj* di emergenza ; **in an ~** in caso di emergenza.
emergency exit *n* uscita *f* di sicurezza.
emergency landing *n* atterraggio *m* di emergenza.
emergency services *npl* servizi *mpl* di pronto intervento.
emigrate ['emɪgreɪt] *vi* emigrare.
emit [ɪ'mɪt] *vt* emettere.
emotion [ɪ'məʊʃn] *n* emozione *f*.
emotional [ɪ'məʊʃənl] *adj* emotivo(a).
emphasis ['emfəsɪs] (*pl* **-ases** [-əsiːz]) *n* enfasi *f*; **to put the ~ on sthg** dare importanza a qc.
emphasize ['emfəsaɪz] *vt* sottolineare.
empire ['empaɪəʳ] *n* impero *m*.
employ [ɪm'plɔɪ] *vt* impiegare.
employed [ɪm'plɔɪd] *adj* impiegato(a).
employee [ɪm'plɔɪiː] *n* dipendente *mf*.
employer [ɪm'plɔɪəʳ] *n* datore *m*, -trice *f* di lavoro.
employment [ɪm'plɔɪmənt] *n* impiego *m*.
employment agency *n* agenzia *f* di collocamento.
empty ['emptɪ] *adj* vuoto(a) ; *(threat, promise)* vano(a). ◆ *vt* vuotare.
EMU *n* (*abbr of Economic Monetary Union*) unione *f* economica e monetaria.
emulsion (paint) [ɪ'mʌlʃn-] *n* pittura *f* a emulsione.
enable [ɪ'neɪbl] *vt* : **to ~ sb to do sthg** permettere a qn di fare qc.
enamel [ɪ'næml] *n* smalto *m*.
enclose [ɪn'kləʊz] *vt* *(surround)* cingere, circondare ; *(with letter)* allegare.
enclosed [ɪn'kləʊzd] *adj* *(space)* contenuto(a), limitato(a).
encounter [ɪn'kaʊntəʳ] *vt* incontrare.
encourage [ɪn'kʌrɪdʒ] *vt* incoraggiare ; **to ~ sb to do sthg** incoraggiare qn a fare qc.
encouragement [ɪn'kʌrɪdʒmənt] *n* incoraggiamento *m*.
encyclopedia [ɪnˌsaɪklə'piːdjə] *n* enciclopedia *f*.
end [end] *n* fine *f*; *(purpose)* fine *m*. ◆ *vt (story, evening, holiday)* finire ; *(war, practice)* finire, mettere fine a. ◆ *vi* finire ; **to come to an ~** finire, giungere alla fine ; **to put an ~ to sthg** mettere fine a qc ; **for days on ~** per giorni e giorni ; **in the ~** alla fine ; **to make ~s meet** sbarcare il lunario. ❑ **end up** *vi* finire.

endangered species [ɪn'deɪn-dʒəd-] *n* specie *f inv* in via d'estinzione.
ending ['endɪŋ] *n (of story, film, book)* fine *f* ; *GRAMM* desinenza *f*.
endive ['endaɪv] *n (curly)* indivia *f* (riccia) ; *(chicory)* cicoria *f*.
endless ['endlɪs] *adj* interminabile, senza fine.
endorsement [ɪn'dɔːsmənt] *n (of driving licence) infrazione registrata sulla patente*.
endurance [ɪn'djʊərəns] *n* resistenza *f*, sopportazione *f*.
endure [ɪn'djʊə'] *vt* sopportare.
enemy ['enɪmɪ] *n* nemico *m*, -a *f*.
energy ['enədʒɪ] *n* energia *f*.
enforce [ɪn'fɔːs] *vt (law)* applicare, far rispettare.
engaged [ɪn'geɪdʒd] *adj (to be married)* fidanzato(a) ; *Br (phone)* occupato(a) ; *(toilet)* occupato(a) ; **to get ~** fidanzarsi.
engaged tone *n Br* segnale *m* di occupato.
engagement [ɪn'geɪdʒmənt] *n (to marry)* fidanzamento *m* ; *(appointment)* appuntamento *m*.
engagement ring *n* anello *m* di fidanzamento.
engine ['endʒɪn] *n (of vehicle)* motore *m* ; *(of train)* locomotiva *f*.
engineer [ˌendʒɪ'nɪə'] *n (of roads, machinery)* ingegnere *m* ; *(to do repairs)* tecnico *m*, -a *f*.
engineering [ˌendʒɪ'nɪərɪŋ] *n* ingegneria *f*.
engineering works *npl (on railway line)* lavori *mpl* in corso.
England ['ɪŋglənd] *n* l'Inghilterra *f*.
English ['ɪŋglɪʃ] *adj* inglese. ◆ *n (language)* inglese *m*. ◆ *npl* : **the ~** gli inglesi.
English breakfast *n* colazione *f* all'inglese.
English Channel *n* : **the ~** la Manica.
Englishman ['ɪŋglɪʃmən] (*pl* **-men** [-mən]) *n* inglese *m*.
Englishwoman ['ɪŋglɪʃˌwʊmən] (*pl* **-women** [-ˌwɪmɪn]) *n* inglese *f*.
engrave [ɪn'greɪv] *vt* incidere.
engraving [ɪn'greɪvɪŋ] *n* incisione *f*.
enjoy [ɪn'dʒɔɪ] *vt* godersi ; **to ~ doing sthg** divertirsi a fare qc ; **I ~ swimming** mi piace nuotare ; **to ~ o.s.** divertirsi ; **~ your meal!** buon appetito!
enjoyable [ɪn'dʒɔɪəbl] *adj* piacevole.
enjoyment [ɪn'dʒɔɪmənt] *n* piacere *m*.
enlargement [ɪn'lɑːdʒmənt] *n (of photo)* ingrandimento *m*.
enormous [ɪ'nɔːməs] *adj* enorme.
enough [ɪ'nʌf] *adj* abbastanza *(inv)*, sufficiente. ◆ *pron* & *adv* abbastanza ; **~ time** abbastanza tempo ; **is that ~?** è abbastanza?, basta? ; **it's not big ~** non è abbastanza grande ; **to have had ~ (of)** averne abbastanza (di).
enquire [ɪn'kwaɪə'] *vi* informarsi.
enquiry [ɪn'kwaɪərɪ] *n (question)* domanda *f* ; *(investigation)* indagine *f*, inchiesta *f* ; **'Enquiries'** 'Informazioni'.

enquiry desk *n* banco *m* informazioni.
enrol [ɪn'rəʊl] *vi Br* iscriversi.
enroll [ɪn'rəʊl] *Am* = **enrol**.
en suite bathroom [ɒn'swiːt-] *n* bagno *m* privato.
ensure [ɪn'ʃʊəʳ] *vt* garantire, assicurare.
entail [ɪn'teɪl] *vt* comportare.
enter ['entəʳ] *vt* entrare in ; *(college, competition)* iscriversi a ; *(on form)* scrivere. ◆ *vi* entrare ; *(in competition)* iscriversi.
enterprise ['entəpraɪz] *n (company)* impresa *f* ; *(plan)* iniziativa *f*.
entertain [ˌentə'teɪn] *vt (amuse)* divertire.
entertainer [ˌentə'teɪnəʳ] *n* intrattenitore *m*, -trice *f*.
entertaining [ˌentə'teɪnɪŋ] *adj* divertente.
entertainment [ˌentə'teɪnmənt] *n (amusement)* divertimento *m* ; *(show)* spettacolo *m*.
enthusiasm [ɪn'θjuːzɪæzm] *n* entusiasmo *m*.
enthusiast [ɪn'θjuːzɪæst] *n* appassionato *m*, -a *f*.
enthusiastic [ɪnˌθjuːzɪ'æstɪk] *adj* entusiasta.
entire [ɪn'taɪəʳ] *adj* intero(a).
entirely [ɪn'taɪəlɪ] *adv* completamente.
entitle [ɪn'taɪtl] *vt* : **to ~ sb to sthg** dare a qn diritto a qc ; **to ~ sb to do sthg** dare diritto a qn di fare qc.
entrance ['entrəns] *n* entrata *f*, ingresso *m*.
entrance fee *n* biglietto *m* d'ingresso.
entry ['entrɪ] *n (door, gate, admission)* entrata *f*, ingresso *m* ; *(in dictionary)* voce *f* ; *(piece in competition)* cosa *f* presentata ; **'no ~'** *(sign on door)* 'ingresso vietato' ; *(road sign)* 'divieto d'accesso'.
envelope ['envələʊp] *n* busta *f*.
envious ['envɪəs] *adj* invidioso(a).
environment [ɪn'vaɪərənmənt] *n* ambiente *m* ; **the ~** l'ambiente (naturale).
environmental [ɪnˌvaɪərən'mentl] *adj* ambientale.
environmentally friendly [ɪnˌvaɪərən'mentəlɪ-] *adj* che rispetta l'ambiente, ecologico(a).
envy ['envɪ] *vt* invidiare.
epic ['epɪk] *n* epopea *f*.
epidemic [ˌepɪ'demɪk] *n* epidemia *f*.
epileptic [ˌepɪ'leptɪk] *adj* epilettico(a).
episode ['epɪsəʊd] *n* episodio *m*.
equal ['iːkwəl] *adj (of same amount)* uguale ; *(with equal rights)* uguale, pari *(inv)*. ◆ *vt (number)* fare ; **to be ~ to** *(number)* essere uguale a.
equality [ɪ'kwɒlətɪ] *n* uguaglianza *f*.
equalize ['iːkwəlaɪz] *vi* pareggiare.
equally ['iːkwəlɪ] *adv (bad, good, matched)* ugualmente ; *(pay, treat, share)* equamente ; *(at the same time)* allo stesso modo.
equation [ɪ'kweɪʒn] *n* equazione *f*.
equator [ɪ'kweɪtəʳ] *n* : **the ~** l'equatore *m*.

equip [ɪ'kwɪp] *vt* : **to ~ sb/sthg with** fornire qn/qc di.
equipment [ɪ'kwɪpmənt] *n* attrezzatura *f*.
equipped [ɪ'kwɪpt] *adj* : **to be ~ with** essere fornito(a) di.
equivalent [ɪ'kwɪvələnt] *adj* equivalente. ◆ *n* equivalente *m*.
erase [ɪ'reɪz] *vt (letter, word)* cancellare.
eraser [ɪ'reɪzə^r] *n* gomma *f*.
erect [ɪ'rekt] *adj (person, posture)* eretto(a). ◆ *vt (tent)* montare ; *(monument)* erigere.
erotic [ɪ'rɒtɪk] *adj* erotico(a).
errand ['erənd] *n* commissione *f*.
erratic [ɪ'rætɪk] *adj* irregolare, incostante.
error ['erə^r] *n* errore *m*.
escalator ['eskəleɪtə^r] *n* scala *f* mobile.
escalope ['eskəlɒp] *n* cotoletta *f* alla milanese.
escape [ɪ'skeɪp] *n* fuga *f*. ◆ *vi* : **to ~ (from)** *(from prison)* evadere (da) ; *(from danger)* fuggire (da) ; *(leak)* fuoriuscire (da).
escort [*n* 'eskɔːt, *vb* ɪ'skɔːt] *n (guard)* scorta *f*. ◆ *vt* accompagnare.
especially [ɪ'speʃəlɪ] *adv (in particular)* specialmente, soprattutto ; *(on purpose)* apposta ; *(very)* particolarmente.
esplanade [ˌesplə'neɪd] *n* passeggiata *f* (a mare).
essay ['eseɪ] *n (at school, university)* composizione *f*, tema *m*.
essential [ɪ'senʃl] *adj (indispensable)* essenziale. ❑ **essentials** *npl* : **the ~s** l'essenziale *m* ; **the bare ~s** il minimo indispensabile.
essentially [ɪ'senʃəlɪ] *adv* essenzialmente.
establish [ɪ'stæblɪʃ] *vt (set up, create)* fondare ; *(fact, truth)* stabilire.
establishment [ɪ'stæblɪʃmənt] *n (business)* azienda *f*.
estate [ɪ'steɪt] *n (land in country)* proprietà *f inv* ; *(for housing)* complesso *m* residenziale ; *Br (car)* = **estate car**.
estate agent *n Br* agente *mf* immobiliare.
estate car *n Br* station wagon *f inv*.
estimate [*n* 'estɪmət, *vb* 'estɪmeɪt] *n (guess)* stima *f* ; *(from builder, plumber)* preventivo *m*. ◆ *vt* stimare, valutare.
estuary ['estjʊərɪ] *n* estuario *m*.
ethnic minority ['eθnɪk-] *n* minoranza *f* etnica.
EU *n (abbr of European Union)* U.E. *f*.
Eurocheque ['jʊərəʊˌtʃek] *n* eurochèque *m inv*.
Europe ['jʊərəp] *n* l'Europa *f*.
European [ˌjʊərə'pɪən] *adj* europeo(a). ◆ *n* europeo *m*, -a *f*.
European Community *n* Comunità *f* Europea.
evacuate [ɪ'vækjʊeɪt] *vt* evacuare.
evade [ɪ'veɪd] *vt (person, issue)* evitare ; *(responsibility)* sottrarsi a.
eve [iːv] *n* : **on the ~ of** alla vigilia di.
even ['iːvn] *adj (uniform, equal)* regolare, uniforme ; *(level, flat)*

liscio(a), piano(a) ; *(contest)* alla pari ; *(number)* pari *(inv)*. ◆ *adv* perfino, anche ; **to break ~** fare pari ; **not ~** nemmeno ; **~ so** ciò nonostante ; **~ though** anche se.

evening ['iːvnɪŋ] *n* sera *f* ; *(event, period)* serata *f* ; **good ~!** buona sera! ; **in the ~** di OR la sera.

evening classes *npl* corsi *mpl* serali.

evening dress *n (formal clothes)* abito *m* da sera ; *(woman's garment)* vestito *m* da sera.

evening meal *n* cena *f*.

event [ɪ'vent] *n (occurrence)* evento *m*, avvenimento *m* ; SPORT prova *f* ; **in the ~ of** *fml* in caso di.

eventual [ɪ'ventʃʊəl] *adj* finale.

eventually [ɪ'ventʃʊəlɪ] *adv* alla fine.

ever ['evəʳ] *adv* mai ; **it's the worst ~** è il peggiore che sia mai esistito ; **he was ~ so angry** era veramente arrabbiato ; **for ~** *(eternally)* per sempre ; **we've been waiting for ~** aspettiamo da tantissimo ; **hardly ~** quasi mai. ❑ **ever since** *adv* fin da allora. ◆ *prep* da ... in poi. ◆ *conj* fin da quando.

every ['evrɪ] *adj* ogni *(inv)* ; **~ day** ogni giorno, tutti i giorni ; **~ other day** ogni due giorni ; **one in ~ ten** uno su dieci ; **we make ~ effort ...** facciamo ogni sforzo ... ; **~ so often** ogni tanto.

everybody ['evrɪˌbɒdɪ] = **everyone**.

everyday ['evrɪdeɪ] *adj* di ogni giorno, quotidiano(a).

everyone ['evrɪwʌn] *pron* ognuno *m*, -a *f*, tutti *mpl*, -e *fpl*.

everyplace ['evrɪˌpleɪs] *Am* = **everywhere**.

everything ['evrɪθɪŋ] *pron* tutto, ogni cosa.

everywhere ['evrɪweəʳ] *adv* dappertutto ; *(wherever)* dovunque.

evidence ['evɪdəns] *n (proof)* prova *f* ; *(legal statement)* testimonianza *f*.

evident ['evɪdənt] *adj* evidente.

evidently ['evɪdəntlɪ] *adv* evidentemente.

evil ['iːvl] *adj* cattivo(a), malvagio(a). ◆ *n* male *m*.

ex [eks] *n inf (wife, husband, partner)* ex *mf*.

exact [ɪg'zækt] *adj* esatto(a) ; '**~ fare ready please**' 'si prega di munirsi dell'esatta somma per il biglietto'.

exactly [ɪg'zæktli] *adv & excl* esattamente.

exaggerate [ɪg'zædʒəreɪt] *vt & vi* esagerare.

exaggeration [ɪgˌzædʒə'reɪʃn] *n* esagerazione *f*.

exam [ɪg'zæm] *n* esame *m* ; **to take an ~** fare un esame.

examination [ɪgˌzæmɪ'neɪʃn] *n* esame *m* ; MED visita *f*.

examine [ɪg'zæmɪn] *vt* esaminare ; MED visitare.

example [ɪg'zaːmpl] *n* esempio *m*.

exceed [ɪk'siːd] *vt (be greater than)* superare ; *(go beyond)* oltrepassare.

excellent ['eksələnt] *adj* eccellente.

except [ɪk'sept] *prep & conj*

eccetto, tranne ; ~ for a parte, all'infuori di ; ' ~ for access' 'escluso residenti' ; ' ~ for loading' 'escluso (per le operazioni di) carico'.

exception [ɪk'sepʃn] *n (thing excepted)* eccezione *f*.

exceptional [ɪk'sepʃnəl] *adj* eccezionale.

excerpt ['eksɜːpt] *n* estratto *m*.

excess [ɪk'ses, *before noun* 'ekses] *adj* in eccesso. ◆ *n* eccesso *m*.

excess baggage *n* bagaglio *m* in eccedenza.

excess fare *n Br* supplemento *m*.

excessive [ɪk'sesɪv] *adj* eccessivo(a).

exchange [ɪks'tʃeɪndʒ] *n (of telephones)* centralino *m* ; *(of students)* scambio *m*. ◆ *vt* scambiare ; to ~ sthg for sthg scambiare qc con qc ; we're here on an ~ siamo qui con uno scambio.

exchange rate *n* tasso *m* di cambio.

excited [ɪk'saɪtɪd] *adj* eccitato(a).

excitement [ɪk'saɪtmənt] *n* eccitazione *f* ; *(exciting thing)* cosa *f* eccitante.

exciting [ɪk'saɪtɪŋ] *adj* eccitante, emozionante.

exclamation mark [ˌekskləˈmeɪʃn-] *n Br* punto *m* esclamativo.

exclamation point [ˌekskləˈmeɪʃn-] *Am* = exclamation mark.

exclude [ɪk'skluːd] *vt* escludere.

excluding [ɪk'skluːdɪŋ] *prep* escluso(a).

exclusive [ɪk'skluːsɪv] *adj* esclusivo(a). ◆ *n* esclusiva *f* ; ~ of escluso(a).

excursion [ɪk'skɜːʃn] *n* escursione *f*.

excuse [*n* ɪk'skjuːs, *vb* ɪk'skjuːz] *n* scusa *f*. ◆ *vt (forgive)* scusare ; *(let off)* dispensare ; ~ me! mi scusi!.

ex-directory *adj Br* fuori elenco.

execute ['eksɪkjuːt] *vt (kill)* giustiziare.

executive [ɪg'zekjʊtɪv] *adj (room)* per dirigenti. ◆ *n (person)* dirigente *mf*.

exempt [ɪg'zempt] *adj* : ~ (from) esente (da).

exemption [ɪg'zempʃn] *n* esenzione *f*.

exercise ['eksəsaɪz] *n* esercizio *m*. ◆ *vi* fare esercizio OR del moto ; to do ~s fare degli esercizi.

exercise book *n* quaderno *m*.

exert [ɪg'zɜːt] *vt* esercitare.

exhaust [ɪg'zɔːst] *vt* esaurire. ◆ *n* : ~ (pipe) tubo *m* di scappamento.

exhausted [ɪg'zɔːstɪd] *adj* esausto(a).

exhibit [ɪg'zɪbɪt] *n (in museum, gallery)* oggetto *m* esposto. ◆ *vt (in exhibition)* esporre.

exhibition [ˌeksɪ'bɪʃn] *n (of art)* esposizione *f*, mostra *f*.

exist [ɪg'zɪst] *vi* esistere.

existence [ɪg'zɪstəns] *n* esistenza *f* ; to be in ~ esistere.

existing [ɪg'zɪstɪŋ] *adj* esistente.

exit ['eksɪt] *n* uscita *f*. ◆ *vi* uscire.

exotic [ɪg'zɒtɪk] *adj* esotico(a).

expand [ɪk'spænd] *vi (in size)* espandersi ; *(in number)* aumentare.

expect [ɪk'spekt] *vt (believe likely)* aspettarsi, prevedere ; *(await)* aspettare ; **to ~ to do sthg** prevedere di fare qc ; **to ~ sb to do sthg** *(require)* aspettarsi che qn faccia qc ; **to be ~ing** *(be pregnant)* aspettare un bambino.

expedition [ˌekspɪ'dɪʃn] *n* spedizione *f* ; *(short outing)* gita *f*.

expel [ɪk'spel] *vt (from school)* espellere.

expense [ɪk'spens] *n* spesa *f*, costo *m* ; **at the ~ of** *fig* a spese di. ❑ **expenses** *npl (of business trip)* spese *fpl*.

expensive [ɪk'spensɪv] *adj* costoso(a), caro(a).

experience [ɪk'spɪərɪəns] *n* esperienza *f*. ◆ *vt* provare.

experienced [ɪk'spɪərɪənst] *adj* esperto(a).

experiment [ɪk'sperɪmənt] *n* esperimento *m*. ◆ *vi* fare esperimenti.

expert ['ekspɜːt] *adj (advice)* esperto(a) ; *(treatment)* apposito(a). ◆ *n* esperto *m*, -a *f*.

expire [ɪk'spaɪəʳ] *vi* scadere.

expiry date [ɪk'spaɪərɪ-] *n* data *f* di scadenza.

explain [ɪk'spleɪn] *vt* spiegare.

explanation [ˌeksplə'neɪʃn] *n* spiegazione *f*.

explode [ɪk'spləʊd] *vi (bomb)* esplodere.

exploit [ɪk'splɔɪt] *vt (person)* sfruttare.

explore [ɪk'splɔːʳ] *vt (place)* esplorare.

explosion [ɪk'spləʊʒn] *n (of bomb etc)* esplosione *f*.

explosive [ɪk'spləʊsɪv] *n* esplosivo *m*.

export [*n* 'ekspɔːt, *vb* ɪk'spɔːt] *n (of goods)* esportazione *f* ; *(goods themselves)* merce *f* d'esportazione. ◆ *vt* esportare.

exposed [ɪk'spəʊzd] *adj (place)* non riparato(a).

exposure [ɪk'spəʊʒəʳ] *n (photograph)* foto *f inv* ; MED assideramento *m* ; *(to heat, radiation)* esposizione *f*.

express [ɪk'spres] *adj (letter, delivery, train)* espresso(a). ◆ *n (train)* espresso *m*. ◆ *vt* esprimere. ◆ *adv* per espresso.

expression [ɪk'spreʃn] *n* espressione *f*.

expresso [ɪk'spresəʊ] (*pl* **-s**) *n* espresso *m*.

expressway [ɪk'spresweɪ] *n Am* autostrada *f* (urbana).

extend [ɪk'stend] *vt* prolungare ; *(hand)* offrire. ◆ *vi* estendersi.

extension [ɪk'stenʃn] *n (of building)* sala *f* annessa ; *(for phone at work)* interno *m* ; *(for phone in private house)* apparecchio *m* supplementare ; *(for permit, essay)* proroga *f*.

extension lead *n* prolunga *f*.

extensive [ɪk'stensɪv] *adj (area)* esteso(a), ampio(a) ; *(damage)* grave ; *(selection)* ampio.

extent [ɪk'stent] *n (of damage, knowledge)* estensione *f* ; **to a certain ~** fino ad un certo punto ; **to what ~ ...?** fino a che punto ...?

exterior [ɪk'stɪərɪəʳ] *adj* esterno(a). ◆ *n (of car, building)* esterno *m*.
external [ɪk'stɜːnl] *adj* esterno(a).
extinct [ɪk'stɪŋkt] *adj* estinto(a).
extinction [ɪk'stɪŋkʃn] *n* estinzione *f*.
extinguish [ɪk'stɪŋgwɪʃ] *vt (fire, cigarette)* spegnere.
extinguisher [ɪk'stɪŋgwɪʃəʳ] *n* estintore *m*.
extortionate [ɪk'stɔːʃnət] *adj* esorbitante.
extra ['ekstrə] *adj (additional)* extra *(inv)*, supplementare ; *(spare)* altro(a), in più. ◆ *n* extra *m inv*. ◆ *adv (especially)* eccezionalmente ; *(more)* di più ; **~ charge** supplemento *m* ; **~ large** extra-large *(inv)*. ❑ **extras** *npl (in price)* spese *fpl* supplementari.
extract [*n* 'ekstrækt, *vb* ɪk'strækt] *n (of yeast, malt etc)* estratto *m* ; *(from book, opera)* brano *m*. ◆ *vt (tooth)* estrarre.
extraordinary [ɪk'strɔːdnrɪ] *adj* straordinario(a).
extravagant [ɪk'strævəgənt] *adj* dispendioso(a).
extreme [ɪk'striːm] *adj* estremo(a). ◆ *n* estremo *m*.
extremely [ɪk'striːmlɪ] *adv* estremamente.
extrovert ['ekstrəvɜːt] *n* estroverso *m*, -a *f*.
eye [aɪ] *n* occhio *m* ; *(of needle)* cruna *f*. ◆ *vt* osservare attentamente ; **to keep an ~ on** tenere d'occhio.
eyebrow ['aɪbraʊ] *n* sopracciglio *m*.
eyeglasses ['aɪglaːsɪz] *npl Am* occhiali *mpl*.
eyelash ['aɪlæʃ] *n* ciglio *m*.
eyelid ['aɪlɪd] *n* palpebra *f*.
eyeliner ['aɪˌlaɪnəʳ] *n* eye-liner *m inv*.
eye shadow *n* ombretto *m*.
eyesight ['aɪsaɪt] *n* vista *f*.
eye test *n* esame *m* oculistico.
eyewitness [ˌaɪ'wɪtnɪs] *n* testimone *mf* oculare.

F

F *(abbr of Fahrenheit)* F.
fabric ['fæbrɪk] *n (cloth)* stoffa *f*, tessuto *m*.
fabulous ['fæbjʊləs] *adj* favoloso(a).
facade [fə'saːd] *n* facciata *f*.
face [feɪs] *n* faccia *f* ; *(of cliff, mountain)* parete *f* ; *(of clock, watch)* quadrante *m*. ◆ *vt* essere di fronte a ; *(accept, cope with)* affrontare ; **to be ~d with** avere di fronte. ❑ **face up to** *vt fus* affrontare.
facecloth ['feɪsklɒθ] *n Br* panno *m* di spugna.
facial ['feɪʃl] *n* trattamento *m* del viso.
facilitate [fə'sɪlɪteɪt] *vt fml* facilitare.
facilities [fə'sɪlɪtɪz] *npl* attrezzature *fpl*.
facsimile [fæk'sɪmɪlɪ] *n* facsimile *m inv*.
fact [fækt] *n* fatto *m* ; **in ~** in effetti.

factor ['fæktəʳ] *n* fattore *m*.

factory ['fæktərɪ] *n* fabbrica *f*.

faculty ['fækltɪ] *n* facoltà *f inv*.

fade [feɪd] *vi (light, sound)* affievolirsi ; *(flower)* appassire ; *(jeans, wallpaper)* sbiadire, sbiadirsi.

faded ['feɪdɪd] *adj (jeans)* sbiadito(a).

fag [fæg] *n Br inf (cigarette)* sigaretta *f*.

fail [feɪl] *vt (exam)* non superare. ◆ *vi* fallire ; *(in exam)* essere bocciato ; *(engine)* guastarsi ; **to ~ to do sthg** *(not do)* non fare qc.

failing ['feɪlɪŋ] *n* difetto *m*. ◆ *prep* : **~ that** se no.

failure ['feɪljəʳ] *n* fallimento *m* ; *(unsuccessful person)* fallito *m*, -a *f* ; *(act of neglecting)* mancanza *f*.

faint [feɪnt] *vi* svenire. ◆ *adj* debole ; *(outline)* indistinto(a) ; **I haven't the ~est idea** non ho la più pallida idea.

fair [feəʳ] *adj (just)* giusto(a), equo(a) ; *(quite large, quite good)* discreto(a) ; *(hair, person)* biondo(a) ; *(skin)* chiaro(a) ; *(weather)* bello(a). ◆ *n (funfair)* luna park *m inv* ; *(trade fair)* fiera *f* ; **~ enough!** mi sembra giusto!

fairground ['feəgraund] *n* luna park *m inv*.

fair-haired [-'heəd] *adj* biondo(a).

fairly ['feəlɪ] *adv (quite)* abbastanza.

fairy ['feərɪ] *n* fata *f*.

fairy tale *n* fiaba *f*.

faith [feɪθ] *n* fede *f*.

faithfully ['feɪθfulɪ] *adv* : **Yours ~** distinti saluti.

fake [feɪk] *n (painting etc)* falso *m*. ◆ *vt (signature, painting)* falsificare.

fall [fɔːl] (*pt* **fell**, *pp* **fallen** ['fɔːln]) *vi* cadere ; *(number, pound, night)* scendere. ◆ *n* caduta *f* ; *(decrease)* abbassamento *m* ; *Am (autumn)* autunno *m* ; **to ~ asleep** addormentarsi ; **to ~ ill** ammalarsi ; **to ~ in love** innamorarsi. ❑ **falls** *npl (waterfall)* cascate *fpl*. ❑ **fall behind** *vi (with work, rent)* rimanere indietro. ❑ **fall down** *vi (lose balance)* cadere. ❑ **fall off** *vi* cadere. ❑ **fall out** *vi (hair, teeth)* cadere ; *(argue)* litigare. ❑ **fall over** *vi* cadere per terra. ❑ **fall through** *vi* fallire.

false [fɔːls] *adj* falso(a).

false alarm *n* falso allarme *m*.

false teeth *npl* dentiera *f*.

fame [feɪm] *n* fama *f*.

familiar [fə'mɪljəʳ] *adj (known)* familiare ; *(informal)* (troppo) confidenziale ; **to be ~ with** *(know)* conoscere.

family ['fæmlɪ] *n* famiglia *f*. ◆ *adj (size)* familiare, da famiglia ; *(film, holiday)* per famiglie.

family planning clinic [-'plænɪŋ-] *n* ≃ consultorio *m* familiare.

family room *n (at hotel)* camera *f* familiare ; *(at pub, airport)* sala *f* per famiglie con bambini.

famine ['fæmɪn] *n* carestia *f*.

famished ['fæmɪʃt] *adj inf* molto affamato(a).

famous ['feɪməs] *adj* famoso(a).

fan [fæn] *n (held in hand)* ventaglio *m* ; *(electric)* ventilatore *m* ;

(enthusiast) ammiratore *m*, -trice *f*; *(supporter)* tifoso *m*, -a *f*.

fan belt *n* cinghia *f* del ventilatore.

fancy ['fænsɪ] *vt inf (feel like)* avere voglia di. ◆ *adj (elaborate)* ricercato(a) ; **I ~ her** *inf* mi piace ; **~ (that)!** pensa un po'!

fancy dress *n* costume *m* (per maschera).

fantastic [fæn'tæstɪk] *adj* fantastico(a).

fantasy ['fæntəsɪ] *n (imagined thing)* fantasia *f*.

far [fa:ʳ] (*compar* **further** OR **farther**, *superl* **furthest** OR **farthest**) *adv* lontano ; *(in degree)* molto, assai. ◆ *adj* : **at the ~ (of)** in fondo (a) ; **how ~ is it (to London)?** quanto è lontano (da Londra)? ; **as ~ as** *(place)* fino a ; **as ~ as I'm concerned** per quanto mi riguarda ; **as ~ as I know** per quel che ne so ; **~ better** assai migliore ; **by ~** di gran lunga ; **so ~** *(until now)* finora ; **to go too ~** *(behave unacceptably)* oltrepassare i limiti.

farce [fa:s] *n (ridiculous situation)* farsa *f*.

fare [feəʳ] *n (on bus, train etc)* tariffa *f* ; *fml (food)* cibo *m*. ◆ *vi* passarsela.

Far East *n* : **the ~** l'Estremo Oriente *m*.

farm [fa:m] *n* fattoria *f*.

farmer ['fa:məʳ] *n* agricoltore *m*.

farmhouse ['fa:mhaʊs, *pl* -haʊzɪz] *n* casa *f* colonica.

farming ['fa:mɪŋ] *n* agricoltura *f* ; *(of animals)* allevamento *m*.

farmland ['fa:mlænd] *n* terreno *m* coltivabile.

farmyard ['fa:mja:d] *n* aia *f*.

farther ['fa:ðəʳ] → **far**.

farthest ['fa:ðəst] → **far**.

fascinating ['fæsɪneɪtɪŋ] *adj* affascinante.

fascination [,fæsɪ'neɪʃn] *n* fascino *m*.

fashion ['fæʃn] *n* moda *f* ; *(manner)* modo *m*, maniera *f* ; **to be in ~** essere di moda.

fashionable ['fæʃnəbl] *adj* di moda, alla moda.

fashion show *n* sfilata *f* di moda.

fast [fa:st] *adv (quickly)* velocemente, rapidamente ; *(securely)* saldamente. ◆ *adj* veloce, rapido(a) ; **to be ~** *(clock)* andare avanti ; **~ asleep** profondamente addormentato ; **a ~ train** un treno diretto.

fasten ['fa:sn] *vt (belt)* allacciare ; *(coat)* abbottonare ; *(two things)* fissare.

fastener ['fa:snəʳ] *n* chiusura *f*, fermaglio *m*.

fast food *n* : **~ outlet** fast food *m inv*.

fat [fæt] *adj* grasso(a). ◆ *n* grasso *m*.

fatal ['feɪtl] *adj (accident, disease)* mortale.

father ['fa:ðəʳ] *n* padre *m*.

Father Christmas *n Br* Babbo *m* Natale.

father-in-law *n* suocero *m*.

fattening ['fætnɪŋ] *adj* che fa ingrassare.

fatty ['fætɪ] *adj* grasso(a).

faucet ['fɔːsɪt] *n Am* rubinetto *m*.

fault ['fɔːlt] *n (responsibility)* colpa *f* ; *(flaw)* difetto *m* ; *(in machine)* guasto *m* ; **it's your ~** è colpa tua.

faulty ['fɔːltɪ] *adj* difettoso(a).

favor ['feɪvər] *Am* = **favour**.

favour ['feɪvəʳ] *n Br (kind act)* favore *m*. ◆ *vt (prefer)* preferire ; **to be in ~ of** essere in favore di ; **to do sb a ~** fare un favore a qn.

favourable ['feɪvrəbl] *adj* favorevole.

favourite ['feɪvrɪt] *adj* favorito(a). ◆ *n* favorito *m*, -a *f*.

fawn [fɔːn] *adj* fulvo chiaro *(inv)*.

fax [fæks] *n* fax *m inv*. ◆ *vt (document)* inviare per fax, faxare ; *(person)* inviare un fax a.

fear [fɪəʳ] *n* paura *f*. ◆ *vt (be afraid of)* avere paura di, temere ; **for ~ of** per paura di.

feast [fiːst] *n (meal)* banchetto *m*.

feather ['feðəʳ] *n* penna *f*, piuma *f*.

feature ['fiːtʃəʳ] *n (characteristic)* caratteristica *f* ; *(in newspaper, on radio, TV)* servizio *m* (speciale). ◆ *vt (subj : film)* avere come protagonista ; **~s** *(of face)* lineamenti *mpl*.

feature film *n* lungometraggio *m*.

Feb. (*abbr of February*) feb..

February ['februərɪ] *n* febbraio *m* → **September**.

fed [fed] *pp* → **feed**.

fed up *adj* stufo(a) ; **to be ~ with** essere stufo di.

fee [fiː] *n* pagamento *m* ; *(of doctor, lawyer)* onorario *m*.

feeble ['fiːbəl] *adj* debole.

feed [fiːd] (*pt* & *pp* **fed**) *vt (person, animal)* dare da mangiare a ; *(baby)* allattare ; *(insert)* immettere.

feel [fiːl] (*pt* & *pp* **felt**) *vt (touch)* tastare, toccare ; *(experience)* sentire ; *(think)* credere, pensare. ◆ *vi* sentirsi ; *(seem)* essere. ◆ *n (of material)* : **I like the ~ of it** è piacevole al tatto ; **to ~ cold/hungry** avere freddo/fame ; **to ~ like** *(fancy)* avere voglia di ; **to ~ up to doing sthg** sentirsela di fare qc.

feeling ['fiːlɪŋ] *n (emotion)* sentimento *m* ; *(sensation)* sensazione *f* ; *(belief)* opinione *f* ; **to hurt sb's ~s** ferire i sentimenti di qn.

feet [fiːt] → **foot**.

fell [fel] *pt* → **fall**. ◆ *vt (tree)* abbattere.

fellow ['feləʊ] *n (man)* tipo *m*, individuo *m*. ◆ *adj* : **my ~ students** i miei compagni di classe.

felt [felt] *pt* & *pp* → **feel**. ◆ *n* feltro *m*.

felt-tip pen *n* pennarello *m*.

female ['fiːmeɪl] *adj* femminile ; *(child, animal)* femmina. ◆ *n (animal)* femmina *f*.

feminine ['femɪnɪn] *adj* femminile.

feminist ['femɪnɪst] *n* femminista *mf*.

fence [fens] *n* recinto *m*.

fencing ['fensɪŋ] *n* SPORT scherma *f*.

fend [fend] *vi* : **to ~ for o.s.** provvedere a se stesso.

fender ['fendəʳ] *n (for fireplace)* parafuoco *m* ; *Am (on car)* parafango *m*.

fennel ['fenl] *n* finocchio *m*.

fern [fɜːn] *n* felce *f*.
ferocious [fəˈrəʊʃəs] *adj* feroce.
ferry [ˈferɪ] *n* traghetto *m*.
fertile [ˈfɜːtaɪl] *adj (land)* fertile.
fertilizer [ˈfɜːtɪlaɪzəʳ] *n* fertilizzante *m*.
festival [ˈfestəvl] *n (of music, arts etc)* festival *m inv* ; *(holiday)* festa *f*.
feta cheese [ˈfetə-] *n formaggio bianco di latte di pecora di origine greca*.
fetch [fetʃ] *vt* andare a prendere ; *(be sold for)* essere venduto per.
fete [feɪt] *n* festa *f* all'aperto *(a scopo di beneficenza)*.
fever [ˈfiːvəʳ] *n* MED febbre *f*; **to have a ~** avere la febbre.
feverish [ˈfiːvərɪʃ] *adj (having a fever)* febbricitante.
few [fjuː] *adj* pochi. ◆ *pron* pochi *mpl*, -e *fpl*. ❑ **a few** ◆ *adj* qualche *(inv)*. ◆ *pron* alcuni(e) ; **quite a ~** parecchi.
fewer [ˈfjuːəʳ] *adj & pron* meno *(inv)*.
fiancé [fɪˈɒnseɪ] *n* fidanzato *m*.
fiancée [fɪˈɒnseɪ] *n* fidanzata *f*.
fib [fɪb] *n inf* (piccola) bugia *f*.
fiber [ˈfaɪbər] *Am* = **fibre**.
fibre [ˈfaɪbəʳ] *n* fibra *f*.
fibreglass [ˈfaɪbəglaːs] *n* fibra *f* di vetro.
fickle [ˈfɪkl] *adj* incostante, volubile.
fiction [ˈfɪkʃn] *n* narrativa *f*.
fiddle [ˈfɪdl] *n (violin)* violino *m*. ◆ *vi* : **to ~ with sthg** giocherellare con qc.
fidget [ˈfɪdʒɪt] *vi* agitarsi.
field [fiːld] *n* campo *m*.
field glasses *npl* binocolo *m*.
fierce [fɪəs] *adj* feroce ; *(storm, heat)* violento(a).
fifteen [fɪfˈtiːn] *num* quindici → **six**.
fifteenth [ˌfɪfˈtiːnθ] *num* quindicesimo(a) → **sixth**.
fifth [fɪfθ] *num* quinto(a) → **sixth**.
fiftieth [ˈfɪftɪəθ] *num* cinquantesimo(a) → **sixth**.
fifty [ˈfɪftɪ] *num* cinquanta → **six**.
fig [fɪg] *n* fico *m*.
fight [faɪt] *(pt & pp* **fought***)* *n* rissa *f* ; *(argument)* lite *f* ; *(struggle)* lotta *f*. ◆ *vt* combattere ; *(person)* azzuffarsi con. ◆ *vi (physically)* combattere ; *(quarrel)* litigare ; *(struggle)* lottare ; **to have a ~ with sb** fare a pugni con qn. ❑ **fight back** *vi* difendersi. ❑ **fight off** *vt sep (attacker)* respingere ; *(illness)* vincere.
fighting [ˈfaɪtɪŋ] *n* combattimento *m*.
figure [*Br* ˈfɪgəʳ, *Am* ˈfɪgjər] *n* figura *f* ; *(number, statistic)* cifra *f*. ❑ **figure out** *vt sep* riuscire a capire.
file [faɪl] *n (folder)* cartella *f* ; *(box)* schedario *m* ; *(information on person)* scheda *f* ; COMPUT file *m inv* ; *(tool)* lima *f*. ◆ *vt (complaint, petition)* presentare ; *(nails)* limare ; **in single ~** in fila indiana.
filing cabinet [ˈfaɪlɪŋ-] *n* schedario *m*.
fill [fɪl] *vt* riempire ; *(role)* ricoprire ; *(tooth)* otturare. ❑ **fill in** *vt sep (form)* riempire. ❑ **fill out** = **fill in**. ❑ **fill up** *vt sep* riempire.
filled roll [ˈfɪld-] *n* panino *m* imbottito.

fillet ['fɪlɪt] *n* filetto *m*.

fillet steak *n* bistecca *f* di filetto.

filling ['fɪlɪŋ] *n (of cake, sandwich)* ripieno *m* ; *(in tooth)* otturazione *f*. ◆ *adj* : **it's very ~** sazia molto.

filling station *n* stazione *f* di servizio.

film [fɪlm] *n (at cinema)* film *m inv* ; *(for camera)* pellicola *f*. ◆ *vt* filmare.

film star *n* divo *m*, -a *f* del cinema.

filter ['fɪltə^r] *n* filtro *m*.

filthy ['fɪlθɪ] *adj* sudicio(a).

fin [fɪn] *n* pinna *f*.

final ['faɪnl] *adj* ultimo(a) ; *(decision)* definitivo(a). ◆ *n* finale *f*.

finalist ['faɪnəlɪst] *n* finalista *mf*.

finally ['faɪnəlɪ] *adv (at last)* finalmente ; *(lastly)* infine.

finance [*n* 'faɪnæns, *vb* faɪ'næns] *n (money)* finanziamento *m* ; *(profession)* finanza *f*. ◆ *vt* finanziare. ❑ **finances** *npl* finanze *fpl*.

financial [fɪ'nænʃl] *adj* finanziario(a).

find [faɪnd] (*pt* & *pp* **found**) *vt* trovare ; *(find out)* scoprire. ◆ *n* scoperta *f* ; **to ~ the time to do sthg** trovare il tempo di fare qc. ❑ **find out** ◆ *vt sep (fact, truth)* scoprire. ◆ *vi* : **to ~ out (about sthg)** *(learn)* scoprire (qc) ; *(get information)* informarsi (su qc).

fine [faɪn] *adv (thinly)* finemente ; *Well* bene. ◆ *n* multa *f*. ◆ *vt* multare. ◆ *adj (good)* buono(a) ; *(weather, day)* bello(a) ; *(thin)* sottile ; **it's ~** *(satisfactory)* va bene ; **I'm ~** *(in health)* sto bene.

fine art *n* belle arti *fpl*.

finger ['fɪŋgə^r] *n* dito *m*.

fingernail ['fɪŋgəneɪl] *n* unghia *f*.

fingertip ['fɪŋgətɪp] *n* polpastrello *m*.

finish ['fɪnɪʃ] *n* fine *f* ; *(on furniture)* finitura *f*. ◆ *vt* & *vi* finire ; **to ~ doing sthg** finire di fare qc. ❑ **finish off** *vt sep* finire. ❑ **finish up** *vi* finire.

Finland ['fɪnlənd] *n* la Finlandia.

Finnan haddock ['fɪnən-] *n Scot* eglefino *m* affumicato *(specialità di pesce tipica della Scozia)*.

Finnish ['fɪnɪʃ] *adj* finlandese. ◆ *n (language)* finlandese *m*.

fir [fɜː^r] *n* abete *m*.

fire ['faɪə^r] *n* fuoco *m* ; *(uncontrolled)* incendio *m* ; *(device)* stufa *f*. ◆ *vt (from job)* licenziare ; **to ~ a gun** sparare ; **on ~** in fiamme ; **to catch ~** prendere fuoco ; **to make a ~** accendere un fuoco.

fire alarm *n* allarme *m* antincendio.

fire brigade *n Br* vigili *mpl* del fuoco.

fire department *Am* = **fire brigade**.

fire engine *n* autopompa *f*.

fire escape *n* scala *f* antincendio.

fire exit *n* uscita *f* di sicurezza.

fire extinguisher *n* estintore *m*.

fire hazard *n* : **it's a ~** rappresenta un pericolo di incendio.

fireman ['faɪəmən] (*pl* **-men** [-mən]) *n* vigile *m* del fuoco.

fireplace ['faɪəpleɪs] *n* caminetto *m*.
fire regulations *npl* norme *fpl* antincendio.
fire station *n* caserma *f* dei vigili del fuoco.
firewood ['faɪəwʊd] *n* legna *f* da ardere.
firework display ['faɪəwɜːk-] *n* fuochi *mpl* d'artificio.
fireworks ['faɪəwɜːks] *npl* *(rockets)* fuochi *mpl* d'artificio.
firm [fɜːm] *adj (fruit)* sodo(a) ; *(mattress)* duro(a) ; *(structure)* solido(a) ; *(grip)* saldo(a) ; *(decision, belief)* fermo(a). ◆ *n* ditta *f*.
first [fɜːst] *adj* primo(a). ◆ *adv* prima ; *(for the first time)* per la prima volta. ◆ *n (event)* novità *f inv*. ◆ *pron* : **the ~** il primo (la prima) ; **~** (gear) prima *f* ; **~ thing (in the morning)** per prima cosa ; **for the ~ time** per la prima volta ; **the ~ of January** il primo gennaio ; **at ~** dapprima ; **~ of all** prima di tutto.
first aid *n* pronto soccorso *m*.
first-aid kit *n* cassetta *f* del pronto soccorso.
first class *n (mail) posta celere, di solito consegnata entro uno o due giorni* ; *(on train, plane, ship)* prima classe *f*.
first-class *adj (stamp) per consegna celere* ; *(ticket)* di prima(classe) ; *(very good)* di prima qualità.
first floor *n Br (floor above ground floor)* primo piano *m* ; *Am (ground floor)* pianterreno *m*.
firstly ['fɜːstlɪ] *adv* in primo luogo.
First World War *n* : **the ~** la prima guerra mondiale.
fish [fɪʃ] (*pl* **inv**) *n* pesce *m*. ◆ *vi* pescare.
fish and chips *n* pesce *m* e patate fritti.

FISH AND CHIPS

È il piatto da asporto inglese per eccellenza. Il pesce viene fritto in una pastella a base di farina, latte e uova e viene servito insieme alle patate fritte, avvolto prima in carta da pacchi e quindi in carta di giornale. Spesso è consumato direttamente per strada. I negozi di *fish and chips*, molto diffusi in tutta la Gran Bretagna, vendono altri cibi fritti, come ad esempio salsicce, pollo, sanguinacci e spesso anche tortine di carne.

---

fishcake ['fɪʃkeɪk] *n* crocchetta *f* di pesce.
fisherman ['fɪʃəmən] (*pl* **-men** [-mən]) *n* pescatore *m*.
fish farm *n* vivaio *m*.
fish fingers *npl Br* bastoncini *mpl* di pesce.
fishing ['fɪʃɪŋ] *n* pesca *f* ; **to go ~** andare a pesca.
fishing boat *n* barca *f* da pesca.
fishing rod *n* canna *f* da pesca.
fishmonger's ['fɪʃˌmʌŋgəz] *n (shop)* pescheria *f*.
fish sticks *Am* = **fish fingers**.
fist [fɪst] *n* pugno *m*.
fit [fɪt] *adj (healthy)* in forma. ◆ *vt (be right size for)* andare (bene) a ;

(kitchen, bath) installare ; *(a lock)* mettere ; *(insert)* inserire. ◆ *vi (be right size)* andare bene. ◆ *n (of coughing, anger)* attacco *m* ; *(epileptic)* crisi *f inv* epilettica ; **they're a good ~** *(clothes, shoes)* sono della misura giusta ; **to be ~ for sthg** *(suitable)* essere adatto a qc ; **~ to eat** buono da mangiare ; **it doesn't ~** *(object)* non c'entra ; **it doesn't ~ me** *(jacket, skirt)* non mi sta OR va ; **to get ~** rimettersi in forma ; **to keep ~** tenersi in forma. ❑ **fit in** ◆ *vt sep (find time to do)* trovare il tempo per. ◆ *vi (belong)* inserirsi.

fitness ['fɪtnɪs] *n (health)* forma *f*.

fitted carpet [ˌfɪtəd-] *n* moquette *f inv*.

fitted sheet [ˌfɪtəd-] *n* lenzuolo *m* con gli angoli.

fitting room ['fɪtɪŋ-] *n* camerino *m*.

five [faɪv] *num* cinque → **six**.

fiver ['faɪvəʳ] *n Br (inf)* cinque sterline *fpl* ; *(note)* banconota *f* da cinque sterline.

fix [fɪks] *vt (attach, decide on)* fissare ; *(mend)* riparare ; *(drink, food)* preparare ; *(arrange)* organizzare. ❑ **fix up** *vt sep* : **to ~ sb up with sthg** procurare qc a qn.

fixture ['fɪkstʃəʳ] *n* SPORT incontro *m* ; **~s and fittings** installazioni *fpl*.

fizzy ['fɪzɪ] *adj* frizzante.

flag [flæg] *n* bandiera *f*.

flake [fleɪk] *n (of snow)* fiocco *m*. ◆ *vi* sfaldarsi.

flame [fleɪm] *n* fiamma *f*.

flammable ['flæməbl] *adj* infiammabile.

flan [flæn] *n* flan *m inv*.

flannel ['flænl] *n (material)* flanella *f* ; *Br (for washing face)* panno *m* di spugna. ❑ **flannels** *npl* pantaloni *mpl* di flanella.

flap [flæp] *n (of envelope)* linguetta *f* ; *(of pocket)* risvolto *m*. ◆ *vt (wings)* battere.

flapjack ['flæpdʒæk] *n Br* biscotto *m* di avena.

flare [fleəʳ] *n (signal)* razzo *m*.

flared [fleəd] *adj (trousers)* a zampa d'elefante ; *(skirt)* scampanato(a).

flash [flæʃ] *n (of light)* lampo *m* ; *(for camera)* flash *m inv*. ◆ *vi (light)* lampeggiare ; **a ~ of lightning** un lampo ; **to ~ one's headlights** lampeggiare.

flashlight ['flæʃlaɪt] *n* torcia *f* elettrica.

flask [flɑːsk] *n (Thermos)* thermos® *m inv* ; *(hip flask)* borraccia *f*.

flat [flæt] *adj* piatto(a) ; *(battery)* scarico(a) ; *(drink)* non gasato(a) ; *(rate, fee)* unico(a). ◆ *adv (level)* in piano. ◆ *n Br (apartment)* appartamento *m* ; **a ~ (tyre)** una gomma a terra ; **~ out** a più non posso.

flatter ['flætəʳ] *vt* adulare.

flavor ['fleɪvər] *Am* = **flavour**.

flavour ['fleɪvəʳ] *n Br (taste)* sapore *m* ; *(of ice cream)* gusto *m*.

flavoured ['fleɪvəd] *adj* : **lemon-~** al gusto di limone.

flavouring ['fleɪvərɪŋ] *n* aroma *m*.

flaw [flɔː] *n* difetto *m*.

flea [fliː] *n* pulce *f*.

flea market *n* mercato *m* delle pulci.

fleece [fli:s] *n (downy material)* vello *m*.

fleet [fli:t] *n (of ships)* flotta *f*.

flesh [fleʃ] *n (of person, animal)* carne *f* ; *(of fruit, vegetable)* polpa *f*.

flew [flu:] *pt* → **fly**.

flex [fleks] *n* cavetto *m*.

flexible ['fleksəbl] *adj* flessibile.

flick [flɪk] *vt (a switch)* premere ; *(with finger)* colpire con il dito. ❑ **flick through** *vt fus* sfogliare.

flies [flaɪz] *npl (of trousers)* patta *f*.

flight [flaɪt] *n* volo *m* ; **a ~ (of stairs)** una rampa (di scale).

flight attendant *n* assistente *mf* di volo.

flimsy ['flɪmzɪ] *adj (object)* poco consistente ; *(clothes)* leggero(a).

fling [flɪŋ] (*pt* & *pp* **flung**) *vt* lanciare.

flint [flɪnt] *n (of lighter)* pietrina *f*.

flip-flop [flɪp-] *n Br (shoe)* infradito *m inv* OR *f inv*.

flirt [flɜ:t] *vi* : **to ~ (with sb)** flirtare (con qn).

float [fləʊt] *n (for swimming)* tavoletta *f*; *(for fishing)* galleggiante *m* ; *(in procession)* carro *m* ; *(drink)* *bevanda con del gelato aggiunto*. ◆ *vi* galleggiare.

flock [flɒk] *n (of birds)* stormo *m* ; *(of sheep)* gregge *m*. ◆ *vi (people)* accalcarsi.

flood [flʌd] *n* alluvione *f*. ◆ *vt* inondare. ◆ *vi* straripare.

floodlight ['flʌdlaɪt] *n* riflettore *m*.

floor [flɔ:ʳ] *n (of room)* pavimento *m* ; *(storey)* piano *m* ; *(of nightclub)* pista *f*.

floorboard ['flɔ:bɔ:d] *n* asse *f* del pavimento.

flop [flɒp] *n inf* fiasco *m*.

floppy disk ['flɒpɪ-] *n* floppy disk *m inv*.

floral ['flɔ:rəl] *adj (pattern)* floreale.

Florence ['flɒrəns] *n* Firenze *f*.

Florida Keys ['flɒrɪdə-] *npl* : **the ~** l'arcipelago *m* Keys.

florist's ['flɒrɪsts] *n (shop)* fioraio *m*.

flour ['flaʊəʳ] *n* farina *f*.

flow [fləʊ] *n (of river, blood)* flusso *m*. ◆ *vi (river, blood)* scorrere.

flower ['flaʊəʳ] *n* fiore *m*.

flowerbed ['flaʊəbed] *n* aiuola *f*.

flowerpot ['flaʊəpɒt] *n* vaso *m* da fiori.

flown [fləʊn] *pp* → **fly**.

flu [flu:] *n* influenza *f*.

fluent ['flu:ənt] *adj* : **to be ~ in Italian, to speak ~ Italian** parlare italiano correntemente.

fluff [flʌf] *n (on clothes)* pelucchi *mpl*.

flume [flu:m] *n* canale *m*.

flung [flʌŋ] *pp* → **fling**.

flunk [flʌŋk] *vt Am inf (exam)* essere bocciato(a) a.

fluorescent [flʊə'resənt] *adj* fluorescente.

flush [flʌʃ] *vi (toilet)* funzionare. ◆ *vt* : **to ~ the toilet** tirare lo sciacquone.

flute [flu:t] *n* flauto *m* traverso.

fly [flaɪ] (*pt* **flew**, *pp* **flown**) *n (insect)* mosca *f* ; *(of trousers)* patta *f*.

◆ *vt (plane, helicopter)* pilotare ; *(airline)* volare con ; *(transport)* trasportare in aereo. ◆ *vi* volare ; *(passenger)* andare in aereo ; *(pilot a plane)* pilotare un aereo ; *(flag)* sventolare.

fly-drive *n* fly and drive *m inv*.

flying ['flaɪɪŋ] *n* : **I'm frightened of ~** ho paura di volare.

flyover ['flaɪˌəʊvəʳ] *n Br* cavalcavia *m inv*.

flysheet ['flaɪʃiːt] *n* telo *m* protettivo.

foal [fəʊl] *n* puledro *m*.

foam [fəʊm] *n (bubbles)* schiuma *f* ; *(foam rubber)* gommapiuma® *f*.

focus ['fəʊkəs] *n (of camera)* fuoco *m*. ◆ *vi (with camera, binoculars)* mettere a fuoco ; **in ~** a fuoco ; **out of ~** sfocato.

fog [fɒg] *n* nebbia *f*.

fogbound ['fɒgbaʊnd] *adj* bloccato(a) dalla nebbia.

foggy ['fɒgɪ] *adj* nebbioso(a).

fog lamp *n* antinebbia *m inv*.

foil [fɔɪl] *n (thin metal)* foglio *m* di alluminio.

fold [fəʊld] *n (in paper, material)* piega *f*. ◆ *vt* piegare ; *(wrap)* avvolgere ; **to ~ one's arms** incrociare le braccia. ❑ **fold up** *vi (chair, bed, bicycle)* piegarsi.

folder ['fəʊldəʳ] *n* cartella *f*.

foliage ['fəʊlɪɪdʒ] *n* fogliame *m*.

folk [fəʊk] *npl (people)* gente *f*. ◆ *n* : **~ (music)** folk *m*. ❑ **folks** *npl inf (relatives)* : **my ~s** i miei.

follow ['fɒləʊ] *vt* seguire ; *(in order, time)* seguire a. ◆ *vi* seguire ; **~ed by** *(in time)* seguito da ; **as ~s** come segue. ❑ **follow on** *vi (come later)* seguire.

following ['fɒləʊɪŋ] *adj (next)* successivo(a) ; *(mentioned below)* seguente. ◆ *prep* dopo.

fond [fɒnd] *adj* : **to be ~ of** amare.

fondue ['fɒnduː] *n* fonduta *f*.

food [fuːd] *n* cibo *m*.

food poisoning [-ˌpɔɪznɪŋ] *n* avvelenamento *m* da cibo.

food processor [-ˌprəʊsesəʳ] *n* tritatutto-frullatore *m inv* elettrico.

foodstuffs ['fuːdstʌfs] *npl* generi *mpl* alimentari.

fool [fuːl] *n (idiot)* stupido *m*, -a *f* ; *(pudding)* mousse *f inv* di frutta. ◆ *vt* ingannare.

foolish ['fuːlɪʃ] *adj* stupido(a).

foot [fʊt] (*pl* **feet**) *n (of person)* piede *m* ; *(of animal)* zampa *f* ; *(measurement)* = 30,48 cm, piede ; *(of hill, cliff, bed)* piedi *mpl* ; *(of wardrobe, tripod, stairs)* base *f* ; **by ~** a piedi ; **on ~** a piedi.

football ['fʊtbɔːl] *n Br (soccer)* calcio *m* ; *Am (American football)* football *m* americano ; *(ball)* pallone *m*.

footballer ['fʊtbɔːləʳ] *n Br* calciatore *m*, -trice *f*.

football pitch *n Br* campo *m* di calcio.

footbridge ['fʊtbrɪdʒ] *n* sovrappassaggio *m*.

footpath ['fʊtpɑːθ, *pl* -pɑːðz] *n* sentiero *m*.

footprint ['fʊtprɪnt] *n* orma *f*.

footstep ['fʊtstep] *n* passo *m*.

footwear ['fʊtweəʳ] *n* calzature *fpl*.

☞

for [fɔːʳ] *prep* - 1. *(expressing intention, purpose, reason)* per ; **this book is ~ you** questo libro è per te ; **what did you do that ~?** perché l'hai fatto? ; **what's it ~?** a cosa serve? ; **a town famous ~ its wine** una città famosa per il suo vino ; **~ this reason** per questo motivo ; **to go ~ a walk** andare a fare una passeggiata ; **' ~ sale'** 'vendesi'.
- 2. *(during)* : **I've lived here ~ ten years** abito qui da dieci anni, sono dieci anni che abito qui ; **we talked ~ hours** abbiamo chiacchierato per ore.
- 3. *(by, before)* per ; **be there ~ eight p.m.** trovati lì per le otto di sera ; **I'll do it ~ tomorrow** lo farò per domani.
- 4. *(on the occasion of)* per ; **I got socks ~ Christmas** ho avuto dei calzini per Natale ; **what's ~ dinner?** cosa c'è per cena?
- 5. *(on behalf of)* per ; **to do sthg ~ sb** fare qc per qn.
- 6. *(with time and space)* per ; **there's no room ~ your suitcase** non c'è posto per la tua valigia ; **have you got time ~ a coffee?** hai tempo per un caffè? ; **it's time ~ dinner** è ora di cena.
- 7. *(expressing distance)* per ; **'road works ~ 20 miles'** 'lavori in corso per 32 chilometri'.
- 8. *(expressing destination)* per ; **a ticket ~ Edinburgh** un biglietto per Edimburgo ; **this train is ~ London only** questo treno ferma solo a Londra.
- 9. *(expressing price)* : **I bought it ~ £5** l'ho comprato per 5 sterline, l'ho pagato 5 sterline.
- 10. *(expressing meaning)* per ; **what's the Italian ~ 'boy'?** come si dice 'boy' in italiano?
- 11. *(with regard to)* per ; **it's warm ~ November** fa caldo per essere novembre ; **it's easy ~ you** è facile per te ; **it's too far ~ us to walk** è troppo lontano per andarci a piedi.

---

forbid [fəˈbɪd] (*pt* **-bade** [-ˈbeɪd], *pp* **-bidden** [-ˈbɪdn]) *vt* proibire, vietare ; **to ~ sb to do sthg** proibire OR vietare a qn di fare qc.

forbidden [fəˈbɪdn] *adj* proibito(a).

force [fɔːs] *n* forza *f*. ◆ *vt* forzare ; **to ~ sb to do sthg** costringere qn a fare qc ; **to ~ one's way through** farsi strada con la forza ; **the ~s** le forze armate.

ford [fɔːd] *n* guado *m*.

forecast [ˈfɔːkaːst] *n* previsione *f*.

forecourt [ˈfɔːkɔːt] *n* spiazzo *m*.

forefinger [ˈfɔːˌfɪŋgəʳ] *n* indice *m*.

foreground [ˈfɔːgraʊnd] *n* primo piano *m*.

forehead [ˈfɔːhed] *n* fronte *f*.

foreign [ˈfɒrən] *adj* straniero(a) ; *(travel)* all'estero.

foreign currency *n* valuta *f* estera.

foreigner [ˈfɒrənəʳ] *n* straniero *m*, -a *f*.

foreign exchange *n* cambio *m*.

Foreign Secretary *n Br* ministro *m* degli Esteri.

foreman [ˈfɔːmən] (*pl* **-men** [-mən]) *n (of workers)* capo operaio *m*.

forename ['fɔːneɪm] *n fml* nome *m* (di battesimo).
foresee [fɔː'siː] (*pt* **-saw** [-'sɔː], *pp* **-seen** [-'siːn]) *vt* prevedere.
forest ['fɒrɪst] *n* foresta *f*.
forever [fə'revəʳ] *adv (eternally)* per sempre ; *(continually)* in continuazione.
forgave [fə'geɪv] *pt* → **forgive**.
forge [fɔːdʒ] *vt (copy)* falsificare.
forgery ['fɔːdʒərɪ] *n (copy)* falso *m*.
forget [fə'get] (*pt* **-got**, *pp* **-gotten**) *vt* dimenticare ; *(give up)* lasciar perdere. ◆ *vi* dimenticarsi ; **to ~ about sthg** dimenticarsi di qc ; **to ~ how to do sthg** dimenticare come si fa qc ; **to ~ to do sthg** dimenticare di fare qc ; **~ it!** lascia perdere!
forgetful [fə'getful] *adj* smemorato(a).
forgive [fə'gɪv] (*pt* **-gave**, *pp* **-given** [-'gɪvn]) *vt* perdonare.
forgot [fə'gɒt] *pt* → **forget**.
forgotten [fə'gɒtn] *pp* → **forget**.
fork [fɔːk] *n (for eating with)* forchetta *f* ; *(for gardening)* forca *f* ; *(of road, path)* bivio *m*.
form [fɔːm] *n (type, shape)* forma *f* ; *(piece of paper)* modulo *m* ; SCH classe *f*. ◆ *vt* formare ; *(constitute)* costituire ; *(produce)* creare. ◆ *vi* formarsi ; **off ~** giù di forma ; **on ~** in forma ; **to ~ part of** fare parte di.
formal ['fɔːml] *adj* formale.
formality [fɔː'mælətɪ] *n* formalità *f inv* ; **it's just a ~** è solo una formalità.
format ['fɔːmæt] *n* formato *m*.
former ['fɔːməʳ] *adj (previous)* precedente ; *(first)* primo(a). ◆ *pron* : **the ~** il primo ; **the ~ President** l'ex Presidente.
formerly ['fɔːməlɪ] *adv* precedentemente.
formula ['fɔːmjʊlə] (*pl* **-as** OR **-ae** [-iː]) *n* formula *f*.
fort [fɔːt] *n* forte *m*.
forthcoming [fɔːθ'kʌmɪŋ] *adj (future)* prossimo(a).
fortieth ['fɔːtɪɪθ] *num* quarantesimo(a) → **sixth**.
fortnight ['fɔːtnaɪt] *n Br* quindici giorni *mpl*.
fortunate ['fɔːtʃnət] *adj* fortunato(a).
fortunately ['fɔːtʃnətlɪ] *adv* fortunatamente.
fortune ['fɔːtʃuːn] *n* fortuna *f* ; **it costs a ~** *inf* costa una fortuna.
forty ['fɔːtɪ] *num* quaranta → **six**.
forward ['fɔːwəd] *adv (move, lean)* in avanti. ◆ *n* SPORT attaccante *mf*. ◆ *vt* spedire ; **to look ~ to doing sthg** non vedere l'ora di fare qc.
forwarding address ['fɔːwədɪŋ-] *n* recapito *m* nuovo.
fought [fɔːt] *pp* → **fight**.
foul [faʊl] *adj (unpleasant)* disgustoso(a). ◆ *n* fallo *m*.
found [faʊnd] *pp* → **find**. ◆ *vt* fondare.
foundation (cream) [faʊn'deɪʃn-] *n* fondotinta *m inv*.
foundations [faʊn'deɪʃnz] *npl* fondamenta *fpl*.
fountain ['faʊntɪn] *n* fontana *f*.
fountain pen *n* penna *f* stilografica.
four [fɔːʳ] *num* quattro → **six**.

fourteen [ˌfɔːˈtiːn] *num* quattordici → **six**.
fourteenth [ˌfɔːˈtiːnθ] *num* quattordicesimo(a) → **sixth**.
fourth [fɔːθ] *num* quarto(a) → **sixth**.

FOURTH OF JULY

Il 4 Luglio, chiamato anche Giorno dell'indipendenza è una delle feste nazionali più importanti degli Stati Uniti e viene festeggiato quasi ovunque con sfilate e con fuochi d'artificio nei quali predominano i colori rosso, bianco e azzurro. Le case vengono addobbate con decorazioni degli stessi colori, alle finestre sventolano bandierine a stelle e strisce e molte famiglie lasciano la città per un picnic a base di hot dog e anguria .

four-wheel drive *n (car)* veicolo *m* a quattro ruote motrici.
fowl [faʊl] (*pl inv*) *n* volatile *m*.
fox [fɒks] *n* volpe *f*.
foyer [ˈfɔɪeɪ] *n (of hotel)* hall *f inv* ; *(of theatre)* foyer *m inv*.
fraction [ˈfrækʃn] *n* frazione *f*.
fracture [ˈfræktʃəʳ] *n* frattura *f*. ◆ *vt* fratturare.
fragile [ˈfrædʒaɪl] *adj* fragile.
fragment [ˈfrægmənt] *n* frammento *m*.
fragrance [ˈfreɪgrəns] *n* profumo *m*.
frail [freɪl] *adj* debole.
frame [freɪm] *n (of window, tent, bicycle)* telaio *m* ; *(of picture, photo)* cornice *f* ; *(of glasses)* montatura *f*. ◆ *vt (photo, picture)* incorniciare.
France [frɑːns] *n* la Francia.
frank [fræŋk] *adj* franco(a).
frankfurter [ˈfræŋkfɜːtəʳ] *n* würstel *m inv*.
frankly [ˈfræŋklɪ] *adv* francamente.
frantic [ˈfræntɪk] *adj* frenetico(a).
fraud [frɔːd] *n (crime)* frode *f*.
freak [friːk] *adj* strano(a). ◆ *n inf (fanatic)* fanatico *m*, -a *f*.
freckles [ˈfreklz] *npl* lentiggini *fpl*.
free [friː] *adj* libero(a) ; *(costing nothing)* gratuito(a). ◆ *vt (prisoner)* liberare. ◆ *adv* gratis ; **~ of charge** gratis ; **to be ~ to do sthg** essere libero di fare qc.
freedom [ˈfriːdəm] *n* libertà *f*.
freefone [ˈfriːfəʊn] *n Br* ≃ numero *m* verde.
free gift *n* omaggio *m*.
free house *n Br* pub *m inv (che può vendere qualsiasi birra, non appartendo a nessuna ditta)*.
free kick *n* calcio *m* di punizione.
freelance [ˈfriːlɑːns] *adj* freelance *(inv)*.
freely [ˈfriːlɪ] *adv* liberamente ; *(available)* facilmente.
free period *n* SCH ora *f* buca.
freepost [ˈfriːpəʊst] *n* affrancatura *f* a carico del destinatario.
free-range *adj (chicken)* ruspante ; *(eggs)* di galline ruspanti.
free time *n* tempo *m* libero.
freeway [ˈfriːweɪ] *n Am* superstrada *f*.
freeze [friːz] (*pt* **froze**, *pp* **frozen**) *vt* congelare. ◆ *vi* gelare. ◆ *v im-*

pers : it's freezing fa un freddo polare.

freezer ['fri:zəʳ] *n (deep freeze)* congelatore *m* ; *(part of fridge)* freezer *m inv*.

freezing ['fri:zɪŋ] *adj* gelato(a) ; *(temperatures)* sotto zero.

freezing point *n* temperatura *f* di congelamento.

freight [freɪt] *n (goods)* carico *m*.

French [frentʃ] *adj* francese. ◆ *n (language)* francese *m*. ◆ *npl* : the ~ i Francesi.

French bean *n* fagiolino *m*.

French bread *n* baguette *f inv*.

French dressing *n (in UK) condimento per insalata a base di olio e aceto* ; *(in US) condimento per insalata a base di maionese e ketchup*.

French fries *npl* patatine *fpl* fritte.

French windows *npl* portafinestra *f*.

frequency ['fri:kwənsɪ] *n* frequenza *f*.

frequent ['fri:kwənt] *adj* frequente.

frequently ['fri:kwəntlɪ] *adv* frequentemente.

fresh [freʃ] *adj* fresco(a) ; *(water)* dolce ; *(new)* nuovo(a) ; to get some ~ air prendere un po' d'aria fresca.

fresh cream *n* panna *f* fresca.

freshen ['freʃn] ◆**freshen up** *vi* rinfrescarsi.

freshly ['freʃlɪ] *adv* appena.

Fri. (*abbr of Friday*) ven..

Friday ['fraɪdɪ] *n* venerdì *m inv* → Saturday.

fridge [frɪdʒ] *n* frigorifero *m*.

fried egg [fraɪd-] *n* uovo *m* al tegame.

fried rice [fraɪd-] *n piatto cinese a base di riso fritto*.

friend [frend] *n* amico *m*, -a *f* ; to be ~s with sb essere amico di qn ; to make ~s with sb fare amicizia con qn.

friendly ['frendlɪ] *adj* cordiale ; to be ~ with sb essere amico di qn.

friendship ['frendʃɪp] *n* amicizia *f*.

fries [fraɪz] = French fries.

fright [fraɪt] *n* spavento *m*, paura *f* ; to give sb a ~ far paura a qn.

frighten ['fraɪtn] *vt* spaventare, far paura a.

frightened ['fraɪtnd] *adj (scared)* spaventato(a) ; to be ~ (that) ... *(worried)* avere paura che ... ; to be ~ of avere paura di.

frightening ['fraɪtnɪŋ] *adj* spaventoso(a).

frightful ['fraɪtfʊl] *adj (very bad, unpleasant)* terribile.

frilly ['frɪlɪ] *adj* arricciato(a).

fringe [frɪndʒ] *n* frangia *f*.

frisk [frɪsk] *vt* perquisire.

fritter ['frɪtəʳ] *n* frittella *f*.

fro [frəʊ] *adv* → to.

frog [frɒg] *n* rana *f*.

☞

from [frɒm] *prep* - 1. *(expressing origin, source)* da ; I'm ~ England sono inglese ; I bought it ~ a supermarket l'ho comprato al supermercato ; the train ~ Manchester il treno (proveniente) da Manchester.

- 2. *(expressing removal, deduction)* da ; **away ~ home** lontano da casa ; **to take sthg (away) ~ sb** prendere qc a qn ; **10% will be deducted ~ the total** dal totale verrà dedotto il 10%.
- 3. *(expressing distance)* da ; **5 miles ~ London** a 5 miglia da Londra ; **it's not far ~ here** non è lontano (da qui).
- 4. *(expressing position)* da ; **~ here you can see the valley** da qui si vede la valle.
- 5. *(expressing starting time)* da ; **open ~ nine to five** aperto dalle nove alle cinque ; **~ next year** dall'anno prossimo.
- 6. *(expressing change)* da ; **the price has gone up ~ £1 to £2** il prezzo è salito da 1 a 2 sterline.
- 7. *(expressing range)* da ; **tickets are ~ £10** i biglietti vanno dalle 10 sterline in su.
- 8. *(as a result of)* : **I'm tired ~ walking all day** sono stanco per aver camminato tutto il giorno.
- 9. *(expressing protection)* da ; **sheltered ~ the wind** al riparo dal vento.
- 10. *(in comparisons)* : **different ~** diverso da.

---

fromage frais [ˌfrɒmaːʒ'freɪ] *n formaggio fresco cremoso.*
front [frʌnt] *adj* anteriore. ◆ *n* parte *f* anteriore ; *(of weather)* fronte *m* ; *(by the sea)* lungomare *m* ; **in ~** *(further forward)* avanti ; *(in the lead)* d'avanti ; **in ~ of** davanti a.
front door *n* porta *f* principale.
frontier [frʌn'tɪəʳ] *n* frontiera *f*.
front page *n* prima pagina *f*.
front seat *n* sedile *m* anteriore.
frost [frɒst] *n* gelo *m*.
frosty ['frɒstɪ] *adj (morning, weather)* gelato(a).
froth [frɒθ] *n* spuma *f*.
frown [fraʊn] *n* fronte *f* aggrottata. ◆ *vi* aggrottare la fronte.
froze [frəʊz] *pt* → **freeze**.
frozen [frəʊzn] *pp* → **freeze**. ◆ *adj* gelato(a) ; *(food)* congelato(a).
fruit [fruːt] *n (food)* frutta *f* ; *(variety, single fruit)* frutto *m* ; **a piece of ~** un frutto ; **~s of the forest** frutti di bosco.
fruit cake *n torta con frutta secca.*
fruit juice *n* succo *m* di frutta.
fruit machine *n Br* slot machine *f inv*.
fruit salad *n* macedonia *f*.
frustrating [frʌ'streɪtɪŋ] *adj* frustrante.
frustration [frʌ'streɪʃn] *n* frustrazione *f*.
fry [fraɪ] *vt* soffriggere ; *(deep-fry)* friggere.
frying pan ['fraɪɪŋ-] *n* padella *f*.
ft *abbr* = **foot, feet**.
fudge [fʌdʒ] *n dolciume gommoso fatto con burro, latte e zucchero.*
fuel [fjʊəl] *n (for engine)* carburante *m* ; *(for heating)* combustibile *m*.
fuel pump *n* pompa *f* del carburante.
fulfil [fʊl'fɪl] *vt [Br] (promise)* mantenere ; *(duty, role, need)* adempiere ; *(conditions, request)* soddisfare ; *(instructions)* eseguire.
fulfill [fʊl'fɪl] *Am* = **fulfil**.
full [fʊl] *adj* pieno(a) ; *(extent, fare)* intero(a) ; *(name)* completo(a). ◆ *adv (directly)* in pieno ; **I'm**

~ (up) sono pieno ; at ~ speed a tutta velocità ; in ~ per esteso.
full board *n* pensione *f* completa.
full-cream milk *n* latte *m* intero.
full-length *adj (skirt, dress)* lungo(a).
full moon *n* luna *f* piena.
full stop *n* punto *m*.
full-time *adj* & *adv* a tempo pieno.
fully ['fʊlɪ] *adv (completely)* completamente.
fully-licensed *adj autorizzato a vendere alcolici.*
fumble ['fʌmbl] *vi (search clumsily)* rovistare.
fun [fʌn] *n* divertimento *m* ; it's good ~ è divertente ; for ~ per divertimento ; to have ~ divertirsi ; to make ~ of prendere in giro.
function ['fʌŋkʃn] *n (role)* funzione *f* ; *(formal event)* ricevimento *m*. ◆ *vi* funzionare.
fund [fʌnd] *n (of money)* fondo *m*. ◆ *vt* finanziare. ❑ **funds** *npl* fondi *mpl*.
fundamental [ˌfʌndə'mentl] *adj* fondamentale.
funeral ['fjuːnərəl] *n* funerale *m*.
funfair ['fʌnfeəʳ] *n* luna park *m inv*.
funky ['fʌŋkɪ] *adj inf (music)* funky *(inv)*.
funnel ['fʌnl] *n (for pouring)* imbuto *m* ; *(on ship)* fumaiolo *m*.
funny ['fʌnɪ] *adj (amusing)* divertente ; *(strange)* strano(a) ; to feel ~ *(ill)* sentirsi strano.
fur [fɜːʳ] *n* pelliccia *f*.
furious ['fjʊərɪəs] *adj (angry)* furioso(a).
furnished ['fɜːnɪʃt] *adj* ammobiliato(a).
furnishings ['fɜːnɪʃɪŋz] *npl* arredamento *m*.
furniture ['fɜːnɪtʃəʳ] *n* mobilia *f* ; a piece of ~ un mobile.
furry ['fɜːrɪ] *adj* peloso(a).
further ['fɜːðəʳ] → far. ◆ *adv (in distance)* più lontano ; *(more)* di più. ◆ *adj (additional)* ulteriore ; until ~ notice fino a nuovo avviso.
furthermore [ˌfɜːðə'mɔːʳ] *adv* inoltre.
furthest ['fɜːðɪst] → far. ◆ *adj (most distant)* il più lontano (la più lontana). ◆ *adv (in distance)* il più lontano (possibile).
fuse [fjuːz] *n (of plug)* fusibile *m* ; *(on bomb)* detonatore *m*. ◆ *vi (plug, device)* saltare.
fuse box *n* scatola *f* dei fusibili.
fuss [fʌs] *n (agitation)* confusione *f* ; *(complaints)* storie *fpl*.
fussy ['fʌsɪ] *adj (person)* difficile.
future ['fjuːtʃəʳ] *n* futuro *m*. ◆ *adj* futuro(a) ; in ~ in futuro.

G

g *(abbr of gram)* g.
gable ['geɪbl] *n* timpano *m*.
gadget ['gædʒɪt] *n* aggeggio *m*.
Gaelic ['geɪlɪk] *n* gaelico *m*.
gag [gæg] *n inf (joke)* gag *f inv*.
gain [geɪn] *n (improvement)* avanzamento *m* ; *(profit)* guadagno *m*. ◆ *vt* guadagnare ; *(weight)* aumen-

tare di ; *(confidence, speed, popularity)* acquistare ; *(achieve)* ottenere ; *subj (clock, watch)* andare avanti di. ◆ *vi (get benefit)* : **to ~ from sthg** trarre vantaggio da qc.

gale [geɪl] *n* burrasca *f*.

gallery ['gælərɪ] *n* galleria *f*.

gallon ['gælən] *n Br* = 4,546 l, gallone *m* ; *Am* = 3,791 l, gallone.

gallop ['gæləp] *vi* galoppare.

gamble ['gæmbl] *n* azzardo *m*. ◆ *vi (bet money)* giocare d'azzardo.

gambling ['gæmblɪŋ] *n* gioco *m* d'azzardo.

game [geɪm] *n gen (in tennis)* gioco *m* ; *(of football, squash, cards)* partita *f* ; *(wild animals, meat)* cacciagione *f*. ❑ **games** *n SCH* ≃ attività *fpl* sportive. ◆ *npl (sporting event)* gare *fpl*.

gammon ['gæmən] *n coscia di maiale da cuocere*.

gang [gæŋ] *n (of criminals)* banda *f* ; *(of friends)* gruppo *m*.

gangster ['gæŋstəʳ] *n* gangster *m inv*.

gaol [dʒeɪl] *Br* = **jail**.

gap [gæp] *n (space)* buco *m* ; *(of time)* intervallo *m* ; *(difference)* divario *m*.

garage ['gærɑːʒ, 'gærɪdʒ] *n (for keeping car)* garage *m inv* ; *Br (for petrol)* stazione *f* di servizio ; *(for repairs)* autofficina *f* ; *Br (for selling cars)* concessionaria *f*.

GARAGE SALE

Le *Garage sales* sono molto popolari negli Stati Uniti. Chiunque voglia disfarsi di vecchie cianfrusaglie, o anche di libri, mobili, abiti e attrezzi vari, monta una bancarella in giardino, in garage o davanti a casa e poi pubblicizza la vendita sulla stampa locale o con dei cartelloni affissi in punti strategici del quartiere.

---

garbage ['gɑːbɪdʒ] *n Am (refuse)* spazzatura *f*.

garbage can *n Am* pattumiera *f*.

garbage truck *n Am* camion *m inv* della nettezza urbana.

garden ['gɑːdn] *n* giardino *m*. ◆ *vi* fare giardinaggio. ❑ **gardens** *npl (public park)* giardini *mpl* pubblici.

garden centre *n* vivaio *m*.

gardener ['gɑːdnəʳ] *n* giardiniere *m*, -a *f*.

gardening ['gɑːdnɪŋ] *n* giardinaggio *m*.

garden peas *npl* piselli *mpl*.

garlic ['gɑːlɪk] *n* aglio *m*.

garlic bread *n* ≃ bruschetta *f*.

garlic butter *n* burro *m* all'aglio.

garment ['gɑːmənt] *n* indumento *m*.

garnish ['gɑːnɪʃ] *n* guarnizione *f*. ◆ *vt* guarnire.

gas [gæs] *n* gas *m inv* ; *Am (petrol)* benzina *f*.

gas cooker *n Br* cucina *f* a gas.

gas cylinder *n* bombola *f* del gas.

gas fire *n Br* stufa *f* a gas.

gasket ['gæskɪt] *n* guarnizione *f*.

gas mask *n* maschera *f* antigas.

gasoline ['gæsəli:n] *n Am* benzina *f*.
gasp [ga:sp] *vi (in shock)* rimanere senza fiato.
gas pedal *n Am* acceleratore *m*.
gas station *n Am* stazione *f* di servizio.
gas stove *Br* = **gas cooker**.
gas tank *n Am* serbatoio *m* della benzina.
gasworks ['gæswɜ:ks] (*pl inv*) *n* officina *f* del gas.
gate [geɪt] *n (to garden, field)* cancello *m* ; *(at airport)* uscita *f*.
gâteau ['gætəʊ] (*pl* **-x** [-z]) *n Br* torta *f*.
gateway ['geɪtweɪ] *n (entrance)* entrata *f*.
gather ['gæðə^r] *vt (collect)* raccogliere ; *(speed)* acquistare ; *(understand)* dedurre. ◆ *vi (come together)* riunirsi.
gaudy ['gɔ:dɪ] *adj* vistoso(a).
gauge [geɪdʒ] *n (for measuring)* indicatore *m* ; *(of railway track)* scartamento *m*. ◆ *vt (calculate)* misurare.
gauze [gɔ:z] *n* garza *f*.
gave [geɪv] *pt* → **give**.
gay [geɪ] *adj (homosexual)* gay *(inv)*.
gaze [geɪz] *vi* : **to ~ at** fissare.
GB (*abbr of Great Britain*) GB.
GCSE *n esami sostenuti a conclusione della scuola dell'obbligo.*
gear [gɪə^r] *n (wheel)* ingranaggio *m* ; *(speed)* marcia *f* ; *(belongings)* roba *f* ; *(equipment, clothes)* attrezzatura *f* ; **in ~** con la marcia inserita.
gearbox ['gɪəbɒks] *n* cambio *m*.
gear lever *n* leva *f* del cambio.
gear shift *Am* = **gear lever**.
gear stick *Br* = **gear lever**.
geese [gi:s] *pl* → **goose**.
gel [dʒel] *n* gel *m inv*.
gelatine [ˌdʒelə'ti:n] *n* gelatina *f*.
gem [dʒem] *n* gemma *f*.
gender ['dʒendə^r] *n* genere *m*.
general ['dʒenərəl] *adj* generale ; *(idea, statement)* generico(a). ◆ *n* generale *m* ; **in ~** in generale ; *(usually)* in genere.
general anaesthetic *n* anestesia *f* totale.
general election *n* elezioni *fpl* politiche.
generally ['dʒenərəlɪ] *adv* generalmente.
general practitioner [-præk'tɪʃənə^r] *n* medico *m* generico.
general store *n* drogheria *f*.
generate ['dʒenəreɪt] *vt* generare.
generation [ˌdʒenə'reɪʃn] *n* generazione *f*.
generator ['dʒenəreɪtə^r] *n* generatore *m*.
generosity [ˌdʒenə'rɒsətɪ] *n* generosità *f*.
generous ['dʒenərəs] *adj* generoso(a).
genitals ['dʒenɪtlz] *npl* genitali *mpl*.
genius ['dʒi:njəs] *n* genio *m*.
gentle ['dʒentl] *adj (careful)* delicato(a) ; *(kind)* gentile ; *(movement, breeze)* leggero(a).
gentleman ['dʒentlmən] (*pl* **-men** [-mən]) *n* signore *m* ; *(with*

good manners) gentiluomo *m* ; **'gentlemen'** *(men's toilets)* 'uomini'.

gently ['dʒentlɪ] *adv (carefully)* delicatamente.

gents [dʒents] *n Br* toilette *f inv* degli uomini.

genuine ['dʒenjuɪn] *adj (authentic)* autentico(a) ; *(sincere)* sincero(a).

geographical [dʒɪə'græfɪkl] *adj* geografico(a).

geography [dʒɪ'ɒgrəfɪ] *n* geografia *f*.

geology [dʒɪ'ɒlədʒɪ] *n* geologia *f*.

geometry [dʒɪ'ɒmətrɪ] *n* geometria *f*.

Georgian ['dʒɔːdʒən] *adj (architecture etc)* georgiano(a) *(del periodo dei re Giorgio I-IV, 1714-1830)*.

geranium [dʒɪ'reɪnjəm] *n* geranio *m*.

German ['dʒɜːmən] *adj* tedesco(a). ◆ *n (person)* tedesco *m*, -a *f* ; *(language)* tedesco *m*.

German measles *n* rosolia *f*.

Germany ['dʒɜːmənɪ] *n* la Germania.

germs [dʒɜːmz] *npl* germi *mpl*.

gesture ['dʒestʃəʳ] *n (movement)* gesto *m*.

☞

get [get] (*pt & pp* **got**, *Am pp* **gotten**) *vt* - 1. *(obtain)* ottenere ; *(job, house)* trovare ; **I got some crisps from the shop** ho comprato delle patatine al negozio ; **she got a job** ha trovato lavoro.

- 2. *(receive)* ricevere ; **I got a book for Christmas** mi hanno regalato un libro per Natale ; **you ~ a lot of rain here in winter** qui piove molto in inverno.

- 3. *(means of transport)* prendere ; **let's ~ a taxi** prendiamo un taxi.

- 4. *(fetch)* andare a prendere ; **could you ~ me the manager?** *(in shop)* mi può chiamare il direttore? ; *(on phone)* mi può passare il direttore?.

- 5. *(illness)* avere, prendere ; **I've got a headache** ho mal di testa.

- 6. *(cause to become, do)* : **to ~ sthg done** *(do)* fare qc ; *(have done)* far fare qc ; **to ~ sb to do sthg** far fare qc a qn ; **I can't ~ it open** non riesco ad aprirlo ; **can I ~ my car repaired here?** posso far riparare qui la mia macchina?

- 7. *(move)* : **to ~ sthg in/out** far entrare/uscire qc ; **I can't ~ it through the door** non riesco a farlo passare dalla porta.

- 8. *(understand)* capire ; **to ~ a joke** capire una barzelletta.

- 9. *(time, chance)* avere, trovare ; **we didn't ~ the chance to see everything** non siamo riusciti a vedere tutto.

- 10. *(answer)* : **I'll ~ it!** *(phone)* rispondo io! ; *(door)* vado io!.

◆ *vi* - 1. *(become)* diventare ; **it's getting late** si sta facendo tardi ; **to ~ bored** annoiarsi ; **to ~ ready** prepararsi ; **to ~ lost** perdersi ; **~ lost!** *inf* vattene!

- 2. *(arrive)* arrivare ; **when does the train ~ here?** a che ora arriva il treno?

- 3. *(go)* : **to ~ to/from** andare a/da.

- 4. *(manage)* : **to ~ to do sthg** riuscire a fare qc.

◆ *aux vb* : **to ~ delayed** essere trattenuto ; **to ~ killed** essere ucciso.

❑ **get back** *vi (return)* ritornare.
❑ **get in** *vi (arrive)* arrivare ; *(enter)* entrare.
❑ **get into** *vt fus (enter)* entrare in ; **to ~ into the car** salire in macchina ; **to ~ into bed** mettersi a letto ; **to ~ into trouble** mettersi nei guai.
❑ **get off** *vi (leave train, bus)* scendere ; *(depart)* partire.
❑ **get on** *vi (enter train, bus)* salire ; *(in relationship)* andare d'accordo ; **how are you getting on?** come va la vita?
❑ **get out** *vi (of car, bus, train)* scendere.
❑ **get through** *vi (on phone)* ottenere la comunicazione.
❑ **get up** *vi* alzarsi.

---

get-together *n inf* riunione *f.*
ghastly ['ga:stlı] *adj inf* terribile.
gherkin ['gɜ:kın] *n* cetriolino *m.*
ghetto blaster ['getəʊ͵bla:stəʳ] *n inf* stereo *m* portatile.
ghost [gəʊst] *n* fantasma *m.*
giant ['dʒaıənt] *adj* gigantesco(a). ◆ *n (in stories)* gigante *m.*
giblets ['dʒıblıts] *npl* rigaglie *fpl.*
giddy ['gıdı] *adj (dizzy)* : **I feel ~** mi gira la testa.
gift [gıft] *n* regalo *m* ; *(talent)* talento *m.*
gifted ['gıftıd] *adj* dotato(a).
gift shop *n* negozio *m* di articoli da regalo.
gift voucher *n Br* buono *m* acquisto.
gig [gıg] *n inf (concert)* concerto *m.*
gigantic [dʒaı'gæntık] *adj* gigantesco(a).
giggle ['gıgl] *vi* ridacchiare.
gimmick ['gımık] *n* trovata *f.*
gin [dʒın] *n* gin *m inv* ; **~ and tonic** gin tonic.
ginger ['dʒındʒəʳ] *n* zenzero *m.* ◆ *adj (colour)* rosso(a).
ginger ale *n bibita analcolica gassata allo zenzero.*
ginger beer *n bibita analcolica allo zenzero.*
gingerbread ['dʒındʒəbred] *n torta o biscotto allo zenzero.*
gipsy ['dʒıpsı] *n* zingaro *m*, -a *f.*
giraffe [dʒı'ra:f] *n* giraffa *f.*
girl [gɜ:l] *n (child)* bambina *f* ; *(young woman)* ragazza *f* ; *(daughter)* femmina *f.*
girlfriend ['gɜ:lfrend] *n (of boy, man)* ragazza *f* ; *(of girl, woman)* amica *f.*
girl guide *n Br* giovane *f* esploratrice.
girl scout *Am* = **girl guide.**
giro ['dʒaırəʊ] *n (system)* giroconto *m.*
give [gıv] (*pt* **gave**, *pp* **given** ['gıvn]) *vt* dare ; *(a smile, speech)* fare ; *(attention)* prestare ; *(time)* dedicare ; **to ~ sb sthg** dare qc a qn ; *(as present)* regalare qc a qn ; **to ~ sthg a push** dare una spinta a qc ; **to ~ sb a kiss** dare un bacio a qn ; **it took an hour, ~ or take a few minutes** c'è voluta un'ora, minuto più minuto meno. ❑ **give away** *vt sep (get rid of)* dare via ; *(reveal)* rivelare. ❑ **give back** *vt sep* restituire. ❑ **give in** *vi* arrendersi. ❑ **give off** *vt fus* emettere. ❑ **give out** *vt sep (distribute)* distribuire. ❑ **give up** *vt sep (cigarettes, chocolate)* rinunciare a ; *(seat)* cedere. ◆ *vi (admit defeat)* arrendersi ; **to ~ up** *(smoking)* smettere di fumare.

glacier ['glæsjəʳ] *n* ghiacciaio *m*.
glad [glæd] *adj* contento(a) ; **to be ~ to do sthg** essere contento di fare qc.
gladly ['glædlɪ] *adv (willingly)* volentieri.
glamorous ['glæmərəs] *adj* affascinante.
glance [glɑːns] *n* sguardo *m*. ◆ *vi* : **to ~ (at)** dare uno sguardo (a).
gland [glænd] *n* ghiandola *f*.
glandular fever ['glændjʊlə-] *n* mononucleosi *f*.
glare [gleəʳ] *vi (person)* lanciare sguardi truci ; *(sun, light)* abbagliare.
glass [glɑːs] *n (material)* vetro *m* ; *(container, glassful)* bicchiere *m*. ◆ *adj* di vetro. ❑ **glasses** *npl* occhiali *mpl*.
glassware ['glɑːsweəʳ] *n* oggetti *mpl* in vetro.
glen [glen] *n Scot* valle *f*.
glider ['glaɪdəʳ] *n* aliante *m*.
glimpse [glɪmps] *vt* intravedere.
glitter ['glɪtəʳ] *vi* luccicare.
global warming [,gləʊbl'wɔːmɪŋ] *n* effetto *m* serra.
globe [gləʊb] *n* globo *m* ; **the ~** *(Earth)* il globo.
gloomy ['gluːmɪ] *adj* cupo(a).
glorious ['glɔːrɪəs] *adj (weather, sight)* magnifico(a) ; *(victory, history)* glorioso(a).
glory ['glɔːrɪ] *n* gloria *f*.
gloss [glɒs] *n (shine)* lucido *m* ; **~ (paint)** vernice *f* lucida.
glossary ['glɒsərɪ] *n* glossario *m*.
glossy ['glɒsɪ] *adj (magazine)* patinato(a) ; *(photo)* lucido(a).
glove [glʌv] *n* guanto *m*.
glove compartment *n* vano *m* portaoggetti.
glow [gləʊ] *n* barlume *m*. ◆ *vi* brillare.
glucose ['gluːkəʊs] *n* glucosio *m*.
glue [gluː] *n* colla *f*. ◆ *vt* incollare.
gnat [næt] *n* pappataci *m inv*.
gnaw [nɔː] *vt* rosicchiare.

☞

go [gəʊ] (*pt* **went**, *pp* **gone**, *pl* **goes**) *vi* - 1. *(move, travel, attend)* andare ; **to ~ home** andare a casa ; **to ~ to Italy** andare in Italia ; **to ~ by bus** andare con l'autobus ; **to ~ to school** andare a scuola ; **to ~ for a walk** andare a fare una passeggiata ; **to ~ and do sthg** andare a fare qc ; **to ~ shopping** andare a fare spesa.
- 2. *(leave)* andarsene ; *(bus, train)* partire ; **it's time to ~** è ora d'andare ; **~ away!** vattene!.
- 3. *(become)* diventare ; **she went pale** è impallidita ; **the milk has gone sour** il latte è inacidito.
- 4. *(expressing future tense)* : **to be going to do sthg** stare per fare qc ; *(intend to do)* avere intenzione di fare qc ; **I'm going to be sick** sto per vomitare ; **I'm going to phone them tonight** ho intenzione di chiamarli stasera.
- 5. *(function)* funzionare ; **the car won't ~** la macchina non parte.
- 6. *(stop working)* rompersi ; **the fuse has gone** è saltato il fusibile.
- 7. *(time)* passare.
- 8. *(progress)* andare ; **to ~ well** andar bene.
- 9. *(bell, alarm)* suonare.

- 10. *(match, be appropriate)* : **to ~ (with)** andare (con).
- 11. *(be sold)* essere venduto(a) ; **'everything must ~'** 'svendita totale'.
- 12. *(fit)* entrare.
- 13. *(lead)* andare, portare ; **where does this path ~?** dove porta questo sentiero?
- 14. *(belong)* andare.
- 15. *(in phrases)* : **to let ~ of sthg** *(drop)* lasciare (andare) qc ; **to ~** *Am (to take away)* da asportare ; **there are only three weeks to ~** mancano solo tre settimane.
◆ *n* - 1. *(turn)* turno *m* ; **it's your ~** tocca a te.
- 2. *(attempt)* prova *f*, tentativo *m* ; **to have a ~ at sthg** provare qc ; **'50p a ~'** *(in game)* '50 pence a partita'.
❑ **go ahead** *vi (take place)* aver luogo ; **~ ahead!** fai pure!
❑ **go back** *vi (return)* ritornare.
❑ **go down** *vi (decrease)* abbassarsi, scendere ; *(sun)* tramontare ; *(tyre)* sgonfiarsi.
❑ **go down with** *vt fus inf (illness)* prendere.
❑ **go in** *vi (enter)* entrare.
❑ **go off** *vi (alarm, bell)* suonare ; *(go bad)* andare a male ; *(lights, heating)* spegnersi.
❑ **go on** *vi (happen)* succedere ; *(lights, heating)* accendersi ; *(continue)* : **to ~ on doing sthg** continuare a fare qc.
❑ **go out** *vi (leave house)* uscire ; *(light, fire, cigarette)* spegnersi ; *(have relationship)* : **to ~ out (with sb)** stare insieme (a qn) ; **to ~ out for a meal** andare a mangiare fuori.
❑ **go over** *vt fus (check)* controllare.
❑ **go round** *vi (revolve)* girare ; *(be enough)* bastare per tutti.
❑ **go through** *vt fus (experience)* passare ; *(spend)* spendere ; *(search)* esaminare.
❑ **go up** *vi (increase)* aumentare.
❑ **go without** *vt fus* fare a meno di.

---

goal [gəʊl] *n (posts)* porta *f* ; *(point scored)* goal *m inv* ; *(aim)* scopo *m*.

goalkeeper ['gəʊl,kiːpəʳ] *n* portiere *m*.

goalpost ['gəʊlpəʊst] *n* palo *m*.

goat [gəʊt] *n* capra *f*.

gob [gɒb] *n Br inf (mouth)* bocca *f*.

god [gɒd] *n* dio *m*. ❑ **God** *n* Dio *m*.

goddaughter ['gɒd,dɔːtəʳ] *n* figlioccia *f*.

godfather ['gɒd,fɑːðəʳ] *n* padrino *m*.

godmother ['gɒd,mʌðəʳ] *n* madrina *f*.

gods [gɒdz] *npl* : **the ~** *(in theatre) Br inf* il loggione.

godson ['gɒdsʌn] *n* figlioccio *m*.

goes [gəʊz] → **go**.

goggles ['gɒglz] *npl (for swimming)* occhialini *mpl* ; *(for skiing)* occhiali *mpl* da neve.

going ['gəʊɪŋ] *adj (available)* disponibile ; **the ~ rate** la tariffa corrente.

go-kart [-kɑːt] *n* go-kart *m inv*.

gold [gəʊld] *n* oro *m*. ◆ *adj* d'oro.

goldfish ['gəʊldfɪʃ] (*pl inv*) *n* pesce *m* rosso.

gold-plated [-'pleɪtɪd] *adj* placcato(a) d'oro.

golf [gɒlf] *n* golf *m*.
golf ball *n* pallina *f* da golf.
golf club *n (place)* circolo *m* del golf ; *(piece of equipment)* mazza *f* da golf.
golf course *n* campo *m* di golf.
golfer ['gɒlfəʳ] *n* golfista *mf*.
gone [gɒn] *pp* → **go**. ◆ *prep Br (past)* : **it's ~ ten** sono le dieci passate.
good [gʊd] *(compar* **better**, *superl* **best**) *adj* buono(a) ; *(enjoyable)* bello(a) ; *(skilled, well-behaved)* bravo(a) ; *(kind)* gentile. ◆ *n* bene *m* ; **the weather's ~** fa bel tempo ; **to have a ~ time** divertirsi ; **to be ~ at sthg** saper fare qc bene ; **a ~ ten minutes** dieci minuti buoni ; **in ~ time** in anticipo ; **to make ~ sthg** compensare qc ; **for the ~ of** per il bene di ; **to do sb ~** far bene a qn ; **it's no ~** *(there's no point)* è inutile ; **~ afternoon!** buon giorno! ; **~ evening!** buona sera! ; **~ morning!** buon giorno! ; **~ night!** buona notte! ❑ **goods** *npl* merce *f*.
goodbye [,gʊd'baɪ] *excl* arrivederci!
Good Friday *n* venerdì *m* Santo.
good-looking [-'lʊkɪŋ] *adj* attraente.
goose [gu:s] *(pl* **geese**) *n* oca *f*.
gooseberry ['gʊzbərɪ] *n* uva *f* spina.
gorge [gɔ:dʒ] *n* gola *f*.
gorgeous ['gɔ:dʒəs] *adj* stupendo(a).
gorilla [gə'rɪlə] *n* gorilla *m inv*.
gossip ['gɒsɪp] *n (about someone)* pettegolezzi *mpl*. ◆ *vi (about someone)* fare pettegolezzi ; *(chat)* chiacchierare ; **to have a ~** chiacchierare.
gossip column *n* cronaca *f* rosa.
got [gɒt] *pt & pp* → **get**.
gotten ['gɒtn] *pp Am* → **get**.
goujons ['gu:dʒɒnz] *npl (of fish)* frittelle *fpl*.
goulash ['gu:læʃ] *n* gulasch *m inv*.
gourmet ['gʊəmeɪ] *n* buongustaio *m*, -a *f*. ◆ *adj* per intenditori.
govern ['gʌvən] *vt (country, city)* governare.
government ['gʌvnmənt] *n* governo *m*.
gown [gaʊn] *n (dress)* abito *m* lungo.
GP *abbr* = **general practitioner**.
grab [græb] *vt (take hold of)* afferrare.
graceful ['greɪsfʊl] *adj (elegant)* aggraziato(a).
grade [greɪd] *n (quality)* categoria *f* ; *(in exam)* voto *m* ; *Am (year at school)* classe *f*.
gradient ['greɪdjənt] *n* pendenza *f*.
gradual ['grædʒʊəl] *adj* graduale.
gradually ['grædʒʊəlɪ] *adv* gradualmente.
graduate [*n* 'grædʒʊət, *vb* 'grædʒʊeɪt] *n (from university)* laureato *m*, -a *f* ; *Am (from high school)* diplomato *m*, -a *f*. ◆ *vi (from university)* laurearsi ; *Am (from high school)* diplomarsi.

GRADUATE SCHOOL

Negli Stati Uniti molti diplomati continuano gli studi per conseguire un master o un dottorato. Il master dura uno o due anni, dopo i quali è possibile continuare per altri due o tre anni che si concludono con la presentazione di una tesi per il conseguimento del dottorato. Per iscriversi alla *graduate school* bisogna aver superato un esame chiamato GRE. Sebbene i corsi universitari siano molto costosi, oggigiorno un titolo post-diploma è considerato quasi indispensabile per ottenere un buon impiego.

---

graduation [ˌgrædʒʊ'eɪʃn] *n (ceremony at university)* consegna *f* delle lauree ; *Am (ceremony at school)* consegna dei diplomi.

graffiti [grə'fi:tɪ] *n* graffiti *mpl.*

grain [greɪn] *n (seed)* chicco *m* ; *(crop)* cereali *mpl* ; *(of sand, salt)* granello *m.*

gram [græm] *n* grammo *m.*

grammar ['græmə^r] *n* grammatica *f.*

grammar school *n (in UK) scuola secondaria più selettiva e tradizionale delle altre.*

gramme [græm] = **gram.**

gramophone ['græməfəʊn] *n* grammofono *m.*

gran [græn] *n Br inf* nonna *f.*

grand [grænd] *adj (impressive)* grandioso(a). ◆ *n inf (£1,000)* mille sterline *fpl* ; *($1,000)* mille dollari *mpl.*

grandad ['grændæd] *n inf* nonno *m.*

grandchild ['græntʃaɪld] (*pl* **-children** [-ˌtʃɪldrən]) *n* nipote *mf.*

granddaughter ['grænˌdɔ:tə^r] *n* nipote *f.*

grandfather ['grændˌfa:ðə^r] *n* nonno *m.*

grandma ['grænma:] *n inf* nonna *f.*

grandmother ['grænˌmʌðə^r] *n* nonna *f.*

grandpa ['grænpa:] *n inf* nonno *m.*

grandparents ['grænˌpeərənts] *npl* nonni *mpl.*

grandson ['grænsʌn] *n* nipote *m.*

granite ['grænɪt] *n* granito *m.*

granny ['grænɪ] *n inf* nonna *f.*

grant [gra:nt] *n POL* sovvenzione *f* ; *(for university)* borsa *f* di studio. ◆ *vt fml (give)* concedere ; **to take sthg for ~ed** dare qc per scontato ; **to take sb for ~ed** pensare di poter sempre contare su qn.

grapefruit ['greɪpfru:t] *n* pompelmo *m.*

grapefruit juice *n* succo *m* di pompelmo.

grapes [greɪps] *npl* uva *f.*

graph [gra:f] *n* grafico *m.*

graph paper *n* carta *f* millimetrata.

grasp [gra:sp] *vt* afferrare.

grass [gra:s] *n (plant)* erba *f* ; *(lawn)* prato *m* ; **'keep off the ~'** 'non calpestare il prato'.

grasshopper ['gra:sˌhɒpə^r] *n* cavalletta *f.*

grate [greɪt] *n* grata *f.*

grated ['greɪtɪd] *adj* grattugiato(a).

grateful ['greɪtfʊl] *adj (person)* grato(a).

grater ['greɪtə'] *n* grattugia *f*.

gratitude ['grætɪtju:d] *n* gratitudine *f*.

gratuity [grə'tju:ɪtɪ] *n fml* mancia *f*.

grave[1] [greɪv] *adj (mistake, news, concern)* grave. ◆ *n* tomba *f*.

grave[2] [gra:v] *adj (accent)* grave.

gravel ['grævl] *n* ghiaia *f*.

graveyard ['greɪvja:d] *n* cimitero *m*.

gravity ['grævətɪ] *n* gravità *f*.

gravy ['greɪvɪ] *n salsa ottenuta dal sugo di carne arrosto e resa più densa con della farina.*

gray [greɪ] *Am* = **grey**.

graze [greɪz] *vt (injure)* scorticare, escoriare.

grease [gri:s] *n (for machine)* olio *m*, lubrificante *m* ; *(animal fat)* grasso *m*.

greaseproof paper ['gri:spru:f-] *n Br* carta *f* oleata.

greasy ['gri:sɪ] *adj (food, skin, hair)* grasso(a) ; *(tools, clothes)* unto(a).

great [greɪt] *adj* grande ; *(very good)* eccellente, fantastico(a) ; (that's) ~! fantastico!

Great Britain *n* la Gran Bretagna.

GREAT BRITAIN

La Gran Bretagna è un'isola che comprende l'Inghilterra, la Scozia e il Galles. Non va confusa con il Regno Unito, che include l'Irlanda del Nord, o con le Isole Britanniche, di cui fanno parte anche la Repubblica d'Irlanda, l'Isola di Man, le Orcadi, le Shetlands e le Isole della Manica.

great-grandfather *n* bisnonno *m*.

great-grandmother *n* bisnonna *f*.

greatly ['greɪtlɪ] *adv* molto.

Greece [gri:s] *n* la Grecia.

greed [gri:d] *n* avidità *f*.

greedy ['gri:dɪ] *adj* avido(a).

Greek [gri:k] *adj* greco(a). ◆ *n (person)* greco *m*, -a *f* ; *(language)* greco *m*.

green [gri:n] *adj* verde ; *(environmentalist)* ambientalista ; *inf (inexperienced)* inesperto(a). ◆ *n (colour)* verde *m* ; *(in village)* prato *m* pubblico ; *(on golf course)* green *m inv*. ❑ **greens** *npl (vegetables)* verdura *f*.

green beans *npl* fagiolini *mpl*.

green card *n Br (for car)* carta *f* verde ; *Am (work permit)* permesso *m* di soggiorno.

GREEN CARD

Sebbene non sia verde, si chiama così il documento che permette ad un cittadino straniero di vivere e lavorare negli Stati Uniti. L'iter da seguire per ottenere una *green card* è piuttosto lungo e complicato. Per farne richiesta bisogna essere parenti stretti di un cittadino americano o dipendenti di un'impresa americana ; in alternativa, è necessario avere mezzi finanziari tali da poter investire ingenti somme di denaro nell'economia statunitense.

green channel *n uscita di porto o aeroporto riservata ai passeggeri che non hanno niente da dichiarare.*
greengage ['gri:ngeɪdʒ] *n* susina *f* Regina Claudia.
greengrocer's ['gri:nˌgrəʊsəz] *n (shop)* negozio *m* di frutta e verdura.
greenhouse ['gri:nhaʊs, *pl* -haʊzɪz] *n* serra *f*.
greenhouse effect *n* effetto *m* serra.
green light *n (go-ahead)* : **to give sb the ~** dare il via libera a qn.
green pepper *n* peperone *m* verde.
green salad *n* insalata *f* verde.
greet [gri:t] *vt (say hello to)* salutare.
greeting ['gri:tɪŋ] *n* saluto *m*.
grenade [grə'neɪd] *n* granata *f*.
grew [gru:] *pt* → **grow**.
grey [greɪ] *adj* grigio(a). ◆ *n* grigio *m* ; **to go ~** diventar grigio.
greyhound ['greɪhaʊnd] *n* levriero *m*.

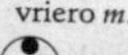
GREYHOUND

L'autobus può talvolta rivelarsi il mezzo più economico per viaggiare negli Stati Uniti. Gli autobus della *Greyhound*, a differenza di quelli di altre compagnie, sono i soli che coprono tutti gli stati e che raggiungono anche alcune zone del Messico e del Canada. I *Greyhound* inoltre, sono importanti perché garantiscono il collegamento con parti del paese che non sono raggiunte dalle linee aeree commerciali.

grid [grɪd] *n (grating)* grata *f* ; *(on map etc)* reticolato *m*.
grief [gri:f] *n* dolore *m* ; **to come to ~** *(plan)* naufragare ; *(person)* finire male.
grieve [gri:v] *vi* affliggersi.
grill [grɪl] *n (on cooker)* grill *m inv* ; *(for open fire)* griglia *f* ; *(part of restaurant) area di un ristorante dove si cucina alla griglia.* ◆ *vt* cuocere ai ferri OR alla griglia.
grille [grɪl] *n* AUT griglia *f*.
grilled [grɪld] *adj* alla griglia, ai ferri.
grim [grɪm] *adj (expression)* severo(a) ; *(place)* lugubre ; *(news)* triste.
grimace ['grɪməs] *n* smorfia *f*.
grimy ['graɪmɪ] *adj* sudicio(a).
grin [grɪn] *n* (gran) sorriso *m*. ◆ *vi* fare un gran sorriso.
grind [graɪnd] (*pt* & *pp* **ground**) *vt (pepper, coffee)* macinare.
grip [grɪp] *n (hold)* presa *f* ; *(of tyres)* tenuta *f* di strada ; *(handle)* impugnatura *f* ; *(bag)* borsa *f* da viaggio. ◆ *vt (hold)* afferrare.
gristle ['grɪsl] *n* cartilagine *f*.
groan [grəʊn] *n* lamento *m*. ◆ *vi* lamentarsi.
groceries ['grəʊsərɪz] *npl* generi *mpl* alimentari.
grocer's ['grəʊsəz] *n (shop)* drogheria *f*.
grocery ['grəʊsərɪ] *n (shop)* drogheria *f*.
groin [grɔɪn] *n* inguine *m*.
groove [gru:v] *n* solco *m*.
grope [grəʊp] *vi* andare a tastoni.
gross [grəʊs] *adj (weight, income)* lordo(a).

grossly ['grəʊslı] *adv (extremely)* estremamente.
grotty ['grɒtı] *adj Br inf* squallido(a).
ground [graʊnd] *pt & pp* → **grind.** ◆ *n (surface of earth)* terra *f* ; *(soil)* terreno *m* ; SPORT campo *m.* ◆ *adj (coffee)* macinato(a). ◆ *vt Am (electrical connection)* mettere a terra ; **to be ~ed** *(plane)* essere trattenuto a terra ; **on the ~** a OR per terra. ❑ **grounds** *npl (of building)* terreni *mpl* ; *(of coffee)* fondi *mpl* ; *(reason)* motivo *m*, ragione *f*.
ground floor *n* pianterreno *m.*
groundsheet ['graʊndʃiːt] *n* telo *m* impermeabile.
group [gruːp] *n* gruppo *m.*
grouse [graʊs] *(pl inv) n (bird)* gallo *m* cedrone.
grovel ['grɒvl] *vi (be humble)* umiliarsi.
grow [grəʊ] *(pt* **grew**, *pp* **grown**) *vi (person, animal, plant)* crescere ; *(fears, traffic)* aumentare ; *(company, city)* espandersi ; *(become)* diventare. ◆ *vt (plant, crop)* coltivare ; *(beard)* farsi crescere ; **to ~ old** invecchiare. ❑ **grow up** *vi* crescere, diventare grande.
growl [graʊl] *vi (dog)* ringhiare.
grown [grəʊn] *pp* → **grow.**
grown-up *adj* adulto(a). ◆ *n* adulto *m*, -a *f*.
growth [grəʊθ] *n (increase)* crescita *f* ; MED tumore *m.*
grub [grʌb] *n inf (food)* cibo *m.*
grubby ['grʌbı] *adj inf* sporco(a).
grudge [grʌdʒ] *n* rancore *m.* ◆ *vt* : **to ~ sb sthg** invidiare qc a qn.
grueling ['grʊəlıŋ] *Am* = **gruelling.**
gruelling ['grʊəlıŋ] *adj Br* estenuante.
gruesome ['gruːsəm] *adj* raccapricciante.
grumble ['grʌmbl] *vi (complain)* lagnarsi.
grumpy ['grʌmpı] *adj inf* scorbutico(a).
grunt [grʌnt] *vi* grugnire.
guarantee [ˌgærən'tiː] *n* garanzia *f*. ◆ *vt* garantire.
guard [gaːd] *n (of prisoner etc)* guardia *f* ; *Br (on train)* capotreno *mf* ; *(protective cover)* schermo *m* di protezione. ◆ *vt (watch over)* sorvegliare ; **to be on one's ~** stare in guardia.
guess [ges] *n* supposizione *f*. ◆ *vt & vi* indovinare ; **I ~ (so)** penso di sì ; **have a ~!** indovina!
guest [gest] *n (in home)* ospite *mf* ; *(in hotel)* cliente *mf*.
guesthouse ['gesthaʊs, *pl* -haʊzız] *n* pensione *f*.
guestroom ['gestrʊm] *n* camera *f* degli ospiti.
guidance ['gaıdəns] *n* guida *f*, direzione *f*.
guide [gaıd] *n* guida *f*. ◆ *vt* guidare. ❑ **Guide** *n Br* giovane esploratrice *f*.
guidebook ['gaıdbʊk] *n* guida *f*.
guide dog *n* cane *m* guida.
guided tour ['gaıdıd-] *n* visita *f* guidata.
guidelines ['gaıdlaınz] *npl* direttive *fpl.*
guilt [gılt] *n* colpa *f*.
guilty ['gıltı] *adj* colpevole ; **to feel ~** sentirsi in colpa.
guinea pig ['gını-] *n* cavia *f*.
guitar [gı'taːʳ] *n* chitarra *f*.

guitarist [gɪ'tɑːrɪst] *n* chitarrista *mf*.

gulf [gʌlf] *n (of sea)* golfo *m*.

Gulf War *n* : the ~ la guerra del Golfo.

gull [gʌl] *n* gabbiano *m*.

gullible ['gʌləbl] *adj* credulone(a).

gulp [gʌlp] *n (of drink)* sorso *m*.

gum [gʌm] *n* gomma *f* da masticare ; *(adhesive)* colla *f*. ❑ **gums** *npl* gengive *fpl*.

gun [gʌn] *n (pistol)* pistola *f*; *(rifle)* fucile *m* ; *(cannon)* cannone *m*.

gunfire ['gʌnfaɪə^r] *n* sparatoria *f*.

gunshot ['gʌnʃɒt] *n* sparo *m*.

gust [gʌst] *n (of wind)* raffica *f*.

gut [gʌt] *n inf (stomach)* stomaco *m*. ❑ **guts** *npl inf (intestines)* budella *fpl* ; *(courage)* : to have ~s avere fegato.

gutter ['gʌtə^r] *n (beside road)* cunetta *f*; *(of house)* grondaia *f*.

guy [gaɪ] *n inf (man)* tipo *m*. ❑ **guys** *npl Am inf (people)* gente *f*.

Guy Fawkes Night [-'fɔːks-] *n festa che si celebra il 5 novembre per ricordare il fallimento della Congiura delle polveri.*

GUY FAWKES NIGHT

Chiamata anche *Bonfire Night*, (la notte dei falò), questa festa viene celebrata il 5 novembre di ogni anno con falò e fuochi d'artificio, e segna l'anniversario della scoperta della Congiura delle polveri, complotto d'ispirazione cattolica il cui obiettivo era l'uccisione di re Giacomo I e la distruzione del Parlamento britannico (1605). Per l'occasione i bambini realizzano dei pupazzi raffiguranti Guy Fawkes, uno dei cospiratori, con i quali girano per le strade chiedendo soldi ai passanti. La sera, poi, i pupazzi vengono messi in cima ai falò e bruciati.

guy rope *n* cavo *m*.

gym [dʒɪm] *n* palestra *f*; *(school lesson)* ginnastica *f*.

gymnast ['dʒɪmnæst] *n* ginnasta *mf*.

gymnastics [dʒɪm'næstɪks] *n* ginnastica *f*.

gym shoes *npl* scarpe *fpl* da ginnastica.

gynaecologist [ˌgaɪnə'kɒlədʒɪst] *n* ginecologo *m*, -a *f*.

gypsy ['dʒɪpsɪ] = **gipsy**.

H

H *(abbr of hospital)* H. ◆ *abbr* = **hot**.

habit ['hæbɪt] *n (custom)* abitudine *f*.

hacksaw ['hæksɔː] *n* seghetto *m*.

had [hæd] *pt* & *pp* → **have**.

haddock ['hædək] *(pl inv) n* eglefino *m (pesce simile al merluzzo)*.

hadn't ['hædnt] = **had not**.

haggis ['hægɪs] *n piatto tipico scozzese a base di avena e frattaglie di pecora.*

haggle ['hægl] *vi* mercanteggiare.

hail [heɪl] *n* grandine *f.* ◆ *v impers* grandinare.

hailstone ['heɪlstəun] *n* chicco *m* di grandine.

hair [heəʳ] *n (on head)* capelli *mpl* ; *(on animal)* pelo *m* ; *(on human skin)* peli *mpl* ; *(individual hair on head)* capello *m* ; *(individual hair on skin)* pelo *m* ; **to have one's ~ cut** tagliarsi i capelli.

hairband ['heəbænd] *n* cerchietto *m* per capelli.

hairbrush ['heəbrʌʃ] *n* spazzola *f* per capelli.

hairclip ['heəklɪp] *n* fermaglio *m* per capelli.

haircut ['heəkʌt] *n (style)* taglio *m* di capelli ; **to have a ~** farsi tagliare i capelli.

hairdo ['heədu:] (*pl* -s) *n* acconciatura *f*, pettinatura *f*.

hairdresser ['heəˌdresəʳ] *n* parrucchiere *m*, -a *f* ; **~'s** *(salon)* negozio *m* di parrucchiere ; **to go to the ~'s** andare dal parrucchiere.

hairdryer ['heəˌdraɪəʳ] *n* asciugacapelli *m inv*, föhn *m inv*.

hair gel *n* gel *m inv* per capelli, gommina *f*.

hairgrip ['heəgrɪp] *n Br* molletta *f (per capelli)*.

hairpin bend ['heəpɪn-] *n* tornante *m*.

hair remover [-rɪˌmu:vəʳ] *n* crema *f* depilatoria.

hair slide *n* fermacapelli *m inv*.

hairspray ['heəspreɪ] *n* lacca *f* per capelli.

hairstyle ['heəstaɪl] *n* acconciatura *f*, pettinatura *f*.

hairy ['heərɪ] *adj (person, chest, legs)* peloso(a).

half [*Br* hɑ:f, *Am* hæf] (*pl* **halves**) *n* metà *f inv* ; *(of match)* tempo *m* ; *(half pint)* mezza pinta *f* ; *(child's ticket)* biglietto *m* ridotto. ◆ *adj* mezzo(a). ◆ *adv* : **~ cooked** cotto a metà ; **~ full** mezzo pieno ; **I'm ~ Scottish** per metà sono scozzese ; **a day and a ~** un giorno e mezzo ; **four and a ~** quattro e mezzo ; **~ past seven** sette e mezza ; **~ as big as** la metà di ; **an hour and a ~** un'ora e mezza ; **~ an hour** mezz'ora ; **~ a dozen** mezza dozzina ; **~ price** a metà prezzo.

half board *n* mezza pensione *f*.

half-day *n* mezza giornata *f*.

half fare *n* mezza tariffa *f*.

half portion *n* mezza porzione *f*.

half-price *adj* a metà prezzo.

half term *n Br vacanza a metà trimestre.*

half time *n* intervallo *m*.

halfway [hɑ:f'weɪ] *adv (in space)* a metà strada ; *(in time)* a metà.

halibut ['hælɪbət] (*pl inv*) *n* halibut *m inv*.

hall [hɔ:l] *n (of house)* ingresso *m* ; *(large room, building)* sala *f*, salone *m* ; *(country house)* maniero *m*.

hallmark ['hɔ:lmɑ:k] *n (on silver, gold)* marchio *m*.

hallo [hə'ləu] = **hello**.

hall of residence *n* casa *f* dello studente.

Halloween [ˌhæləu'i:n] *n vigilia d'Ognissanti*.

HALLOWEEN

Il 31 ottobre, la vigilia d'Ognissanti è, secondo la tradizione popolare, la notte dei fantasmi e delle steghe. In questa occasione i bambini giocano a *trick or treat*, gioco che consiste nel recarsi mascherati a casa dei vicini minacciandoli di far loro uno scherzo (*trick*) se non regalano loro soldi, caramelle o frutta (il *treat*). Altra tradizione associata alla celebrazione di Halloween sia in Gran Bretagna che negli Stati Uniti sono le lanterne di zucca, ottenute svuotando e intagliando un viso in grandi zucche gialle, all'interno delle quali vengono poste delle candele.

---

halt [hɔːlt] *vi* fermarsi. ◆ *n* : **to come to a ~** fermarsi.

halve [*Br* haːv, *Am* hæv] *vt* dimezzare.

halves [*Br* haːvz, *Am* hævz] *pl* → half.

ham [hæm] *n (meat)* prosciutto *m* (cotto).

hamburger ['hæmbɜːgəʳ] *n (beefburger)* hamburger *m inv* ; *Am (mince)* carne *f* macinata.

hamlet ['hæmlɪt] *n* paesino *m*.

hammer ['hæməʳ] *n* martello *m*. ◆ *vt (nail)* piantare.

hammock ['hæmək] *n* amaca *f*.

hamper ['hæmpəʳ] *n* cesta *f*.

hamster ['hæmstəʳ] *n* criceto *m*.

hamstring ['hæmstrɪŋ] *n* tendine *m* del ginocchio.

hand [hænd] *n* mano *f*; *(of clock, watch, dial)* lancetta *f*; **to give sb a ~** dare una mano a qn ; **to get out of ~** sfuggire di mano ; **by ~** a mano ; **in ~** *(time)* a disposizione ; **on the one ~** da una parte ; **on the other ~** d'altra parte. ❑ **hand in** *vt sep* consegnare. ❑ **hand out** *vt sep* distribuire. ❑ **hand over** *vt sep (give)* consegnare.

handbag ['hændbæg] *n* borsetta *f*.

handbasin ['hændbeɪsn] *n* lavabo *m*.

handbook ['hændbʊk] *n* manuale *m*.

handbrake ['hændbreɪk] *n* freno *m* a mano.

hand cream *n* crema *f* per le mani.

handcuffs ['hændkʌfs] *npl* manette *fpl*.

handful ['hændfʊl] *n (amount)* manciata *f*.

handicap ['hændɪkæp] *n* handicap *m inv*.

handicapped ['hændɪkæpt] *adj* handicappato(a). ◆ *npl* : **the ~** i portatori di handicap.

handkerchief ['hæŋkətʃɪf] (*pl* **-chiefs** OR **-chieves** [-tʃiːvz]) *n* fazzoletto *m*.

handle ['hændl] *n (of door, window)* maniglia *f*; *(of knife, pan, suitcase)* manico *m*. ◆ *vt (touch)* toccare ; *(deal with)* occuparsi di ; **'~ with care'** 'fragile'.

handlebars ['hændlbaːz] *npl* manubrio *m*.

hand luggage *n* bagaglio *m* a mano.

handmade [ˌhænd'meɪd] *adj* fatto(a) a mano.

handout ['hændaʊt] *n (leaflet)* volantino *m*.

handrail ['hændreɪl] *n* corrimano *m*.

handset ['hændset] *n* ricevitore *m* ; **'please replace the ~'** 'si prega di riattaccare il ricevitore'.

handshake ['hændʃeɪk] *n* stretta *f* di mano.

handsome ['hænsəm] *adj (man)* bello(a).

handstand ['hændstænd] *n* verticale *f*.

handwriting ['hænd,raɪtɪŋ] *n* calligrafia *f*.

handy ['hændɪ] *adj (useful)* utile ; *(convenient)* comodo(a) ; *(good with one's hands)* abile ; *(near)* vicino(a), a portata di mano ; **to come in ~** *inf* tornare utile.

hang [hæŋ] *(pt & pp* **hung**) *vt* appendere ; *(execute : pt & pp hanged)* impiccare. ◆ *vi (be suspended)* penzolare, pendere. ◆ *n* : **to get the ~ of sthg** fare la mano a qc. ❑ **hang about** *vi Br inf* ciondolare. ❑ **hang around** *inf* = **hang about**. ❑ **hang down** *vi* penzolare. ❑ **hang on** *vi inf (wait)* aspettare. ❑ **hang out** ◆ *vt sep (washing)* stendere. ◆ *vi inf* stare. ❑ **hang up** *vi (on phone)* riagganciare.

hanger ['hæŋəʳ] *n* gruccia *f*, stampella *f*.

hang gliding *n* deltaplano *m*.

hangover ['hæŋ,əʊvəʳ] *n* postumi *mpl* di sbornia.

hankie ['hæŋkɪ] *n inf* fazzoletto *m*.

happen ['hæpən] *vi* succedere, accadere ; **I ~ed to catch sight of him** mi è capitato di vederlo.

happily ['hæpɪlɪ] *adv (luckily)* fortunatamente.

happiness ['hæpɪnɪs] *n* felicità *f*.

happy ['hæpɪ] *adj* felice ; **to be ~ about sthg** essere contento(a) di qc ; **to be ~ to do sthg** *(willing)* fare qc volentieri ; **to be ~ with sthg** essere soddisfatto(a) di qc ; **Happy Birthday!** buon compleanno! ; **Happy Christmas!** buon Natale! ; **Happy New Year!** buon anno!

happy hour *n inf momento della giornata, di solito nel tardo pomeriggio, in cui nei bar le bevande vengono vendute a prezzo ridotto.*

harassment ['hærəsmənt] *n* molestie *fpl*.

harbor ['hɑːbər] *Am* = **harbour**.

harbour ['hɑːbəʳ] *n Br* porto *m*.

hard [hɑːd] *adj* duro(a) ; *(difficult)* difficile ; *(strenuous)* faticoso(a) ; *(forceful)* forte ; *(winter, frost)* rigido(a) ; *(drugs)* pesante. ◆ *adv (work)* duro ; *(listen)* attentamente ; *(hit)* con forza ; *(rain)* a dirotto.

hardback ['hɑːdbæk] *n* edizione *f* rilegata.

hardboard ['hɑːdbɔːd] *n* pannello *m* di legno compresso.

hard-boiled egg [-bɔɪld-] *n* uovo *m* sodo.

hard disk *n* hard disk *m inv*, disco *m* rigido.

hardly ['hɑːdlɪ] *adv* a malapena, appena ; **~ ever** quasi mai.

hardship ['hɑːdʃɪp] *n (difficult conditions)* privazioni *fpl* ; *(difficult circumstance)* avversità *fpl*.

hard shoulder *n Br* corsia *f* d'emergenza.
hard up *adj inf* in bolletta.
hardware ['ha:dweəʳ] *n (tools, equipment)* ferramenta *fpl* ; COMPUT hardware *m*.
hardwearing [ˌha:d'weərɪŋ] *adj Br* resistente.
hardworking [ˌha:d'wɜ:kɪŋ] *adj* instancabile.
hare [heəʳ] *n* lepre *f*.
harm [ha:m] *n (injury)* male *m* ; *(damage)* danno *m*. ◆ *vt (injure)* far male a ; *(damage)* danneggiare.
harmful ['ha:mful] *adj* nocivo(a).
harmless ['ha:mlɪs] *adj* innocuo(a).
harmonica [ha:'mɒnɪkə] *n* armonica *f*.
harmony ['ha:mənɪ] *n* armonia *f*.
harness ['ha:nɪs] *n (for horse)* finimenti *mpl* ; *(for child)* briglie *fpl*.
harp [ha:p] *n* arpa *f*.
harsh [ha:ʃ] *adj (weather)* rigido(a) ; *(conditions)* duro(a) ; *(cruel)* severo(a) ; *(sound)* sgradevole.
harvest ['ha:vɪst] *n (of corn, fruit)* raccolto *m* ; *(of grapes)* vendemmia *f*.
has [*weak form* həz, *strong form* hæz] → **have**.
hash browns [hæʃ-] *npl Am frittelle fpl di patate*.
hasn't ['hæznt] = **has not**.
hassle ['hæsl] *n inf (problem)* seccatura *f*.
hastily ['heɪstɪlɪ] *adv (rashly)* precipitosamente.
hasty ['heɪstɪ] *adj (hurried)* affrettato(a) ; *(rash)* precipitoso(a).
hat [hæt] *n* cappello *m*.
hatch [hætʃ] *n (for food)* passavivande *m inv*. ◆ *vi (egg)* schiudersi.
hatchback ['hætʃˌbæk] *n (car)* tre OR cinque porte *f inv*.
hatchet ['hætʃɪt] *n* accetta *f*.
hate [heɪt] *n* odio *m*. ◆ *vt* odiare, detestare ; **to ~ doing sthg** detestare fare qc.
hatred ['heɪtrɪd] *n* odio *m*.
haul [hɔ:l] *vt* trascinare. ◆ *n* : **a long ~** un percorso lungo e faticoso.
haunted ['hɔ:ntɪd] *adj (house)* abitato(a) da fantasmi.

have [hæv] (*pt & pp* **had**) *aux vb*
- 1. *(to form perfect tenses : gen)* avere ; *(with many intransitive verbs)* essere ; **I ~ finished** ho finito ; **~ you been there? - no, I haven't** ci sei stato? - no ; **the train had already gone** il treno era già partito.
- 2. *(must)* : **to ~ (got) to do sthg** dover fare qc ; **do you ~ to pay?** si deve pagare?
◆ *vt* - 1. *(possess)* : **to ~ (got)** avere ; **do you ~** OR **~you got a double room?** avete una camera doppia? ; **she has (got) brown hair** ha i capelli castani.
- 2. *(experience)* avere ; **to ~ a cold** avere il raffreddore ; **we had a great time** ci siamo divertiti un mondo.
- 3. *(replacing other verbs)* : **to ~ breakfast** fare colazione ; **to ~ dinner** cenare ; **to ~ lunch** pranzare ; **to ~ a drink** bere qualcosa ; **to ~ a shower** fare una doccia ; **to ~ a swim** fare una nuotata ; **to ~ a walk** fare una passeggiata.
- 4. *(cause to be)* : **to ~ sthg done** far

fare qc ; to ~ **one's hair cut** farsi tagliare i capelli.
- 5. *(be treated in a certain way)* : **I've had my wallet stolen** mi hanno rubato il portafoglio.

---

haversack ['hævəsæk] *n* zaino *m*.

havoc ['hævək] *n* caos *m*.

hawk [hɔ:k] *n* falco *m*.

hawker ['hɔ:kə^r] *n* venditore *m*, -trice *f* ambulante.

hay [heɪ] *n* fieno *m*.

hay fever *n* raffreddore *m* da fieno.

haystack ['heɪˌstæk] *n* pagliaio *m*.

hazard ['hæzəd] *n* rischio *m*, pericolo *m*.

hazardous ['hæzədəs] *adj* rischioso(a), pericoloso(a).

hazard warning lights *npl Br* luci *fpl* di emergenza.

haze [heɪz] *n* foschia *f*.

hazel ['heɪzl] *adj* nocciola *(inv)*.

hazelnut ['heɪzlˌnʌt] *n* nocciola *f*.

hazy ['heɪzɪ] *adj (misty)* offuscato(a).

he [hi:] *pron* lui, egli ; ~**'s tall** è alto.

head [hed] *n (of body)* testa *f*, capo *m* ; *(of queue, page, bed)* cima *f* ; *(of company, department, table)* capo ; *(head teacher of primary or lower secondary school)* direttore *m*, -trice *f* di scuola ; *(head teacher of upper secondary school)* preside *mf* ; *(of beer)* schiuma *f*. ◆ *vt (list)* essere in testa a ; *(organization)* dirigere, essere a capo di. ◆ *vi* dirigersi ; **£10 a ~** 10 sterline a testa ; ~**s or tails?** testa o croce? ❑ **head for** *vt fus* dirigersi verso OR a.

headache ['hedeɪk] *n (pain)* mal *m* di testa ; **to have a ~** avere mal di testa.

heading ['hedɪŋ] *n* intestazione *f*.

headlamp ['hedlæmp] *Br* = **headlight**.

headlight ['hedlaɪt] *n* fanale *m* anteriore.

headline ['hedlaɪn] *n (in newspaper)* titolo *m* ; *(on TV, radio)* notizie *fpl* principali.

headmaster [ˌhed'ma:stə^r] *n (of primary or lower secondary school)* direttore *m* di scuola ; *(of upper secondary school)* preside *m*.

headmistress [ˌhed'mɪstrɪs] *n (of primary or lower secondary school)* direttrice *f* di scuola ; *(of upper secondary school)* preside *f*.

head of state *n* capo *m* di Stato.

headphones ['hedfəunz] *npl* cuffie *fpl*.

headquarters [ˌhed'kwɔ:təz] *npl (of company, bank)* sede *f* centrale ; *(of police, army)* quartiere *m* generale.

headrest ['hedrest] *n* poggiatesta *m inv*.

headroom ['hedrum] *n (under bridge)* altezza *f* massima.

headscarf ['hedska:f] (*pl* **-scarves** [-ska:vz]) *n* foulard *m inv*.

head start *n* vantaggio *m*.

head teacher *n (of primary or lower secondary school)* direttore *m*, -trice *f* di scuola ; *(of upper secondary school)* preside *mf*.

headwaiter *n* capocameriere *m*.
heal [hi:l] *vt* curare. ◆ *vi* guarire.
health [helθ] *n* salute *f*; **to be in good ~** essere in buona salute ; **to be in poor ~** essere in cattive condizioni di salute ; **your (very) good ~!** alla tua salute!
health centre *n* centro *m* sanitario.
health food *n* cibo *m* naturale.
health food shop *n* negozio *m* di prodotti naturali.
health insurance *n* assicurazione *f* contro le malattie.
healthy ['helθɪ] *adj* sano(a).
heap [hi:p] *n* mucchio *m* ; **~s of** *inf* un mucchio di.
hear [hɪəʳ] (*pt* & *pp* **heard** [hɜ:d]) *vt* sentire ; *(case, evidence)* esaminare. ◆ *vi* sentire ; **to ~ about sthg** sapere OR sentire di qc ; **to ~ from sb** ricevere notizie da qn ; **to have heard of** aver sentito parlare.
hearing ['hɪərɪŋ] *n* *(sense)* udito *m* ; *(at court)* udienza *f*; **to be hard of ~** esser duro d'orecchi.
hearing aid *n* apparecchio *m* acustico.
heart [ha:t] *n* cuore *m* ; **to know sthg (off) by ~** sapere qc a memoria ; **to lose ~** scoraggiarsi. ❑ **hearts** *npl (in cards)* cuori *mpl*.
heart attack *n* infarto *m*.
heartbeat ['ha:tbi:t] *n* *(rhythm)* battito *m* cardiaco.
heartburn ['ha:tbɜ:n] *n* bruciore *m* di stomaco.
heart condition *n* : **to have a ~** avere un disturbo cardiaco.
hearth [ha:θ] *n* focolare *m*.
hearty ['ha:tɪ] *adj (meal)* abbondante, sostanzioso(a).
heat [hi:t] *n* *(warmth)* calore *m* ; *(warm weather)* caldo *m* ; *(of oven)* temperatura *f*. ❑ **heat up** *vt sep* riscaldare.
heater ['hi:təʳ] *n* *(for room)* stufa *f* ; *(radiator)* radiatore *m* ; *(in car)* riscaldamento *m* ; *(for water)* scaldabagno *m*.
heath [hi:θ] *n* brughiera *f*.
heather ['heðəʳ] *n* erica *f*.
heating ['hi:tɪŋ] *n* riscaldamento *m*.
heat wave *n* ondata *f* di caldo.
heave [hi:v] *vt* *(push)* spingere (con forza) ; *(pull)* tirare (con forza) ; *(lift)* sollevare (con forza).
Heaven ['hevn] *n* paradiso *m*.
heavily ['hevɪlɪ] *adv* *(smoke, drink)* molto ; *(rain)* a dirotto.
heavy ['hevɪ] *adj* pesante ; *(rain, traffic)* intenso(a) ; *(fighting)* violento(a) ; *(losses, defeat)* grave ; **how ~ is it?** quanto pesa? ; **to be a ~ smoker** essere un fumatore accanito.
heavy cream *n Am panna molto densa ad alto contenuto di grassi.*
heavy goods vehicle *n Br* veicolo *m* per trasporti pesanti.
heavy industry *n* industria *f* pesante.
heavy metal *n* heavy metal *m*.
heckle ['hekl] *vt* interrompere di continuo.
hectic ['hektɪk] *adj* frenetico(a).
hedge [hedʒ] *n* siepe *f*.
hedgehog ['hedʒhɒg] *n* riccio *m*.
heel [hi:l] *n* *(of person)* calcagno *m* ; *(of shoe)* tacco *m*.

hefty ['heftɪ] *adj (person)* robusto(a) ; *(fine)* salato.
height [haɪt] *n* altezza *f* ; *(peak period)* apice *m* ; **what ~ is it?** quanto è alto?
heir [eəʳ] *n* erede *m*.
heiress ['eərɪs] *n* erede *f*.
held [held] *pt* & *pp* → **hold**.
helicopter ['helɪkɒptəʳ] *n* elicottero *m*.
he'll [hi:l] = **he will, he shall**.
Hell [hel] *n* inferno *m*.
hello [hə'ləʊ] *excl (as greeting)* ciao! ; *(more formal)* buongiorno! ; *(on phone)* pronto! ; *(to attract attention)* ehi!
helmet ['helmɪt] *n* casco *m*.
help [help] *n* aiuto *m*. ◆ *vt* aiutare ; *(contribute to)* contribuire a. ◆ *vi* aiutare, essere d'aiuto. ◆ *excl* aiuto! ; **I can't ~ it** non ci posso fare niente ; **to ~ sb (to) do sthg** aiutare qn a fare qc ; **to ~ o.s. (to sthg)** servirsi (di qc) ; **can I ~ you?** *(in shop)* desidera?.
❑ **help out** *vi* aiutare, dare una mano.
helper ['helpəʳ] *n (assistant)* aiutante *mf* ; *Am (cleaner)* uomo *m*, donna *f* delle pulizie.
helpful ['helpful] *adj (person)* di grande aiuto ; *(useful)* utile.
helping ['helpɪŋ] *n* porzione *f*.
helpless ['helplɪs] *adj* impotente ; *(child)* indifeso(a).
hem [hem] *n* orlo *m*.
hemophiliac [ˌhi:mə'fɪlɪæk] *n* emofiliaco *m*, -a *f*.
hemorrhage ['hemərɪdʒ] *n* emorragia *f*.
hen [hen] *n* gallina *f*.
hepatitis [ˌhepə'taɪtɪs] *n* epatite *f*.
her [hɜ:ʳ] *adj* il suo, i suoi *(pl)*. ◆ *pron (direct)* la ; *(indirect)* le ; *(after prep, stressed)* lei ; **~ brother** suo fratello ; **I know ~** la conosco ; **it's ~** è lei ; **send it to ~** mandaglielo, mandalo a lei ; **tell ~** diglielo ; **tell ~ that ...** dille che ... ; **he's worse than ~** lui è peggio di lei.
herb [hɜ:b] *n* erba *f*.
herbal tea ['hɜ:bl-] *n* tisana *f*.
herd [hɜ:d] *n (of cattle)* mandria *f*.
here [hɪəʳ] *adv* qui, qua ; **~'s your book** eccoti il libro ; **~ you are** eccoti (qui OR qua).
heritage ['herɪtɪdʒ] *n* eredità *f*, patrimonio *m*.
hernia ['hɜ:njə] *n* ernia *f*.
hero ['hɪərəʊ] (*pl* **-es**) *n* eroe *m*.
heroin ['herəʊɪn] *n* eroina *f (droga)*.
heroine ['herəʊɪn] *n* eroina *f*.
heron ['herən] *n* airone *m*.
herring ['herɪŋ] *n* aringa *f*.
hers [hɜ:z] *pron* il suo, i suoi *(pl)* ; **a friend of ~** un suo amico.
herself [hɜ:'self] *pron (reflexive)* si ; *(after prep)* se stessa, sé ; **she did it ~** l'ha fatto da sola.
hesitant ['hezɪtənt] *adj* esitante.
hesitate ['hezɪteɪt] *vi* esitare.
hesitation [ˌhezɪ'teɪʃn] *n* esitazione *f*.
heterosexual [ˌhetərəʊ'sekʃʊəl] *adj* eterosessuale. ◆ *n* eterosessuale *mf*.
hey [heɪ] *excl inf* ehi!
HGV *abbr* = **heavy goods vehicle**.
hi [haɪ] *excl inf* ciao!

hiccup ['hɪkʌp] *n* : **to have (the) ~s** avere il singhiozzo.

hide [haɪd] (*pt* **hid** [hɪd], *pp* **hidden** [hɪdn]) *vt* nascondere. ◆ *vi* nascondersi. ◆ *n (of animal)* pelle *f*.

hideous ['hɪdɪəs] *adj* raccapricciante.

hi-fi ['haɪfaɪ] *n* hi-fi *m inv*.

high [haɪ] *adj* alto(a) ; *(price, speed, temperature)* alto, elevato(a) ; *(wind)* forte ; *(sound, voice)* acuto(a), alto ; *inf (from drugs)* fatto(a). ◆ *n (weather front)* anticiclone *m*. ◆ *adv* alto, in alto ; **how ~ is it?** quanto è alto? ; **it's 10 metres ~** è alto 10 metri.

high chair *n* seggiolone *m*.

high-class *adj* di lusso.

Higher ['haɪəʳ] *n Scot esame sostenuto alla fine di studi secondari.*

higher education *n* istruzione *f* universitaria.

high heels *npl* tacchi *mpl* alti.

high jump *n* salto *m* in alto.

Highland Games ['haɪlənd-] *npl* : **the ~** *gare sportive disputate all'aperto nelle Highlands scozzesi.*

Highlands ['haɪləndz] *npl* : **the ~** le Highlands *fpl (regione montuosa nel nord della Scozia)*.

highlight ['haɪlaɪt] *n (best part)* clou *m inv*. ◆ *vt (emphasize)* evidenziare. ❑ **highlights** *npl (of football match etc)* sintesi *f inv* ; *(in hair)* colpi *mpl* di sole.

highly ['haɪlɪ] *adv (extremely)* molto ; *(very well)* molto bene ; **to think ~ of sb** avere grande stima di qn.

high-pitched [-'pɪtʃt] *adj* acuto(a).

high-rise *adj* con tanti piani.

high school *n (in UK)* ≃ scuola *f* secondaria inferiore e superiore ; *(in US)* ≃ scuola secondaria superiore.

high season *n* alta stagione *f*.

high-speed train *n* treno *m* ad alta velocità.

high street *n Br* strada *f* principale.

high tide *n* alta marea *f*.

highway ['haɪweɪ] *n Am (between towns)* superstrada *f* ; *Br (any main road)* strada *f* principale.

Highway Code *n Br* codice *m* stradale.

hijack ['haɪdʒæk] *vt* dirottare.

hijacker ['haɪdʒækəʳ] *n* dirottatore *m*, -trice *f*.

hike [haɪk] *n* lunga camminata *f*. ◆ *vi* fare una lunga camminata.

hiking ['haɪkɪŋ] *n* : **to go ~** andare a fare lunghe camminate.

hilarious [hɪ'leərɪəs] *adj* spassoso(a).

hill [hɪl] *n* collina *f*, colle *m*.

hillwalking ['hɪlwɔːkɪŋ] *n* : **to go ~** fare lunghe camminate.

hilly ['hɪlɪ] *adj* collinoso(a).

him [hɪm] *pron (direct)* lo ; *(indirect)* gli ; *(after prep, stressed)* lui ; **I know ~** lo conosco ; **it's ~** è lui ; **send it to ~** mandaglielo, mandalo a lui ; **tell ~** diglielo ; **tell ~ that** digli che … ; **she's worse than ~** lei è peggio di lui.

himself [hɪm'self] *pron (reflexive)* si ; *(after prep)* se stesso, sé ; **he did it ~** l'ha fatto da solo.

hinder ['hɪndəʳ] *vt* ostacolare.

Hindu ['hɪnduː] (*pl* -s) *adj* indù (*inv*). ◆ *n (person)* indù *mf inv*.
hinge [hɪndʒ] *n* cardine *m*.
hint [hɪnt] *n (indirect suggestion)* accenno *m*, allusione *f*; *(piece of advice)* consiglio *m* ; *(slight amount)* accenno, punta *f*. ◆ *vi* : **to ~ at sthg** alludere a qc.
hip [hɪp] *n* fianco *m*.
hippopotamus [ˌhɪpəˈpɒtəməs] *n* ippopotamo *m*.
hippy ['hɪpɪ] *n* hippy *mf inv*.
hire ['haɪəʳ] *vt (car, bicycle, television)* noleggiare ; **'for ~ '** *(boats)* 'a noleggio' ; *(taxi)* 'libero'. ❑ **hire out** *vt sep (car, bicycle, television)* dare a noleggio.
hire car *n Br* vettura *f* a noleggio.
hire purchase *n Br* acquisto *m* rateale.
his [hɪz] *adj* il suo, la sua, i suoi, le sue (*pl*). ◆ *pron* il suo, la sua, i suoi, le sue (*pl*) ; **~ brother** suo fratello ; **a friend of ~** un suo amico.
historical [hɪˈstɒrɪkəl] *adj* storico(a).
history ['hɪstərɪ] *n* storia *f*; *(record)* passato *m*.
hit [hɪt] (*pt* & *pp* **hit**) *vt* colpire ; *(bang)* sbattere, picchiare. ◆ *n (record, play, film)* successo *m*.
hit-and-run *adj* : **~ accident** *incidente in cui l'automobilista colpevole non si ferma a prestare soccorso.*
hitch [hɪtʃ] *n (problem)* contrattempo *m*. ◆ *vt* : **to ~ a lift** farsi dare un passaggio, fare l'autostop.
hitchhike ['hɪtʃhaɪk] *vi* fare l'autostop.
hitchhiker ['hɪtʃhaɪkəʳ] *n* autostoppista *mf*.
hive [haɪv] *n (of bees)* alveare *m*.
HIV-positive *adj* sieropositivo(a).
hoarding ['hɔːdɪŋ] *n Br (for adverts)* tabellone *m* per pubblicità.
hoarse [hɔːs] *adj* rauco(a).
hoax [həʊks] *n* burla *f*.
hob [hɒb] *n* piano *m* di cottura.
hobby ['hɒbɪ] *n* hobby *m inv*, passatempo *m*.
hockey ['hɒkɪ] *n (on grass)* hockey *m* su prato ; *Am (ice hockey)* hockey su ghiaccio.
hoe [həʊ] *n* zappa *f*.
Hogmanay ['hɒgmənei] *n Scot* l'ultimo *m* dell'anno.
hold [həʊld] (*pt* & *pp* **held**) *vt* tenere ; *(contain)* contenere ; *(possess)* avere, possedere. ◆ *vi (weather)* mantenersi ; *(luck, offer)* permanere ; *(on telephone)* restare in linea. ◆ *n (grip)* presa *f* ; *(of ship)* stiva *f* ; *(of aircraft)* bagagliaio *m* ; **to ~ sb prisoner** tenere prigioniero qn ; **~ the line, please** resti in linea, per favore. ❑ **hold back** *vt sep (restrain)* trattenere ; *(keep secret)* tenere segreto. ❑ **hold on** *vi (wait)* aspettare, attendere ; *(on telephone)* restare in linea ; **to ~ on to sthg** *(grip)* tenersi (stretto) a qc. ❑ **hold out** *vt sep (hand)* porgere, tendere. ❑ **hold up** *vt sep (delay)* bloccare.
holdall ['həʊldɔːl] *n Br* borsone *m* da viaggio.
holder ['həʊldəʳ] *n (of passport, licence)* titolare *mf*, proprietario *m*, -a *f* ; *(container)* contenitore *m*.
holdup ['həʊldʌp] *n (delay)* ritardo *m*.

hole [həʊl] *n (in sock, wall)* buco *m* ; *(in ground, golf)* buca *f*.

holiday ['hɒlɪdeɪ] *n Br (period of time)* vacanze *fpl* ; *(time off work)* ferie *fpl* ; *(public holiday)* festa *f*. ◆ *vi Br* trascorrere le vacanze ; **to be on ~** essere in vacanza ; **to go on ~** andare in vacanza.

holidaymaker ['hɒlɪdɪˌmeɪkəʳ] *n Br* villeggiante *mf*.

holiday pay *n Br* retribuzione *f* delle ferie.

Holland ['hɒlənd] *n* l'Olanda *f*.

hollow ['hɒləʊ] *adj* cavo(a).

holly ['hɒlɪ] *n* agrifoglio *m*.

holy ['həʊlɪ] *adj* sacro(a).

home [həʊm] *n* casa *f* ; *(own country)* patria *f* ; *(for old people)* istituto *m*, ricovero *m*. ◆ *adv* a casa. ◆ *adj (not foreign)* interno(a), nazionale ; *(cooking)* casereccio(a) ; **at ~** *(in one's house)* a casa ; **to make o.s. at ~** fare come se si fosse a casa propria ; **to go ~** andare a casa ; **to leave ~** *(for good)* andarsene di casa ; **~ address** indirizzo *m* di casa ; **~ number** numero *m* (telefonico) di casa.

home help *n Br* collaboratore *m* domestico (collaboratrice domestica *f*).

homeless ['həʊmlɪs] *npl* : **the ~** i senzatetto.

homemade [ˌhəʊm'meɪd] *adj (food)* casereccio(a).

homeopathic [ˌhəʊmɪəʊ'pæθɪk] *adj* omeopatico(a).

Home Secretary *n Br* ministro *m* degli Interni.

homesick ['həʊmsɪk] *adj* : **to be ~** avere nostalgia di casa.

homework ['həʊmwɜːk] *n* compiti *mpl* a casa.

homosexual [ˌhɒmə'sekʃʊəl] *adj* omosessuale. ◆ *n* omosessuale *mf*.

honest ['ɒnɪst] *adj (trustworthy)* onesto(a) ; *(frank)* sincero(a), franco(a).

honestly ['ɒnɪstlɪ] *adv (truthfully)* onestamente ; *(frankly)* sinceramente, francamente.

honey ['hʌnɪ] *n* miele *m*.

honeymoon ['hʌnɪmuːn] *n* luna *f* di miele, viaggio *m* di nozze.

honor ['ɒnər] *Am* = **honour**.

honour ['ɒnəʳ] *n Br* onore *m*.

honourable ['ɒnrəbl] *adj* onorevole.

hood [hʊd] *n (of jacket, coat)* cappuccio *m* ; *(on convertible car)* capote *f inv* ; *Am (car bonnet)* cofano *m*.

hoof [huːf] *n* zoccolo *m*.

hook [hʊk] *n* gancio *m* ; *(for fishing)* amo *m* ; **off the ~** *(telephone)* staccato.

hooligan ['huːlɪgən] *n* teppista *mf*, hooligan *mf inv*.

hoop [huːp] *n* cerchio *m*.

hoot [huːt] *vi (driver)* suonare il clacson.

Hoover® ['huːvəʳ] *n Br* aspirapolvere *m inv*.

hop [hɒp] *vi (person)* saltellare su una gamba.

hope [həʊp] *n* speranza *f*. ◆ *vt* sperare ; **to ~ to do sthg** sperare di fare qc ; **I ~ so** spero di sì.

hopeful ['həʊpfʊl] *adj (optimistic)* fiducioso(a).

hopefully ['həʊpfəlɪ] *adv (with luck)* se tutto va bene.

hopeless ['həuplɪs] *adj (without any hope)* disperato(a) ; **he's ~!** *inf* è un disastro!
horizon [hə'raɪzn] *n* orizzonte *m*.
horizontal [ˌhɒrɪ'zɒntl] *adj* orizzontale.
horn [hɔːn] *n (of car)* clacson *m inv* ; *(on animal)* corno *m*.
horoscope ['hɒrəskəup] *n* oroscopo *m*.
horrible ['hɒrəbl] *adj* orribile.
horrid ['hɒrɪd] *adj (very bad)* orrendo(a) ; *(unkind)* odioso(a) ; *(food, drink)* pessimo(a).
horrific [hɒ'rɪfɪk] *adj* orripilante, terrificante.
hors d'oeuvre [hɔː'dɜːvrə] *n* antipasto *m*.
horse [hɔːs] *n* cavallo *m*.
horseback ['hɔːsbæk] *n* : **on ~** a cavallo.
horse chestnut *n* ippocastano *m*.
horsepower ['hɔːsˌpauəʳ] *n* cavallo *m* vapore.
horse racing *n* ippica *f*.
horseradish (sauce) ['hɔːsˌrædɪʃ-] *n* salsa *f* di rafano.
horse riding *n* equitazione *f*.
horseshoe ['hɔːsʃuː] *n* ferro *m* di cavallo.
hose [həuz] *n (hosepipe)* tubo *m* per annaffiare.
hosepipe ['həuzpaɪp] *n* tubo *m* per annaffiare.
hosiery ['həuzɪərɪ] *n* calzetteria *f*.
hospitable [hɒ'spɪtəbl] *adj* ospitale.
hospital ['hɒspɪtl] *n* ospedale *m* ; **in ~** all'ospedale.
hospitality [ˌhɒspɪ'tælətɪ] *n* ospitalità *f*.
host [həust] *n (of party, event)* ospite *m* ; *(of show, TV programme)* conduttore *m*, -trice *f*.
hostage ['hɒstɪdʒ] *n* ostaggio *m*.
hostel ['hɒstl] *n (youth hostel)* ostello *m*.
hostess ['həustes] *n (on aeroplane)* hostess *f inv* ; *(of party, event)* ospite *f*.
hostile [*Br* 'hɒstaɪl, *Am* 'hɒstl] *adj* ostile.
hostility [hɒ'stɪlətɪ] *n* ostilità *f*.
hot [hɒt] *adj* caldo(a) ; *(spicy)* piccante ; **to be ~** *(person)* aver caldo ; **it's ~** fa caldo.
hot chocolate *n* cioccolata *f* calda.
hot-cross bun *n panino dolce con uvetta e spezie tipico del periodo pasquale.*
hot dog *n* hot dog *m inv (panino imbottito con würstel e senape).*
hotel [həu'tel] *n* hotel *m inv*, albergo *m*.
hot line *n* telefono *m* rosso.
hotplate ['hɒtpleɪt] *n* piastra *f*.
hotpot ['hɒtpɒt] *n spezzatino di carne con patate.*
hot-water bottle *n* borsa *f* dell'acqua calda.
hour ['auəʳ] *n* ora *f* ; **I've been waiting for ~s** è un secolo che aspetto.
hourly ['auəlɪ] *adj (per hour)* orario(a) ; *(every hour)* ogni ora. ◆ *adv (per hour)* a ore ; *(every hour)* ogni ora.
house [*n* haus, *pl* 'hauzɪz, *vb* hauz] *n* casa *f* ; SCH *uno dei gruppi in cui sono divisi gli alunni di una scuola*

media o superiore in occasione di competizioni sportive, ecc. ◆ *vt (person)* alloggiare.

household ['haʊshəʊld] *n* famiglia *f*.

housekeeping ['haʊs,ki:pɪŋ] *n* amministrazione *f* della casa.

House of Commons *n Br* Camera *f* dei Comuni.

House of Lords *n Br* Camera *f* dei Lord.

Houses of Parliament *npl Br (building)* palazzo *m* del Parlamento.

HOUSES OF PARLIAMENT

Il Parlamento britannico comprende la Camera dei Comuni *(House of Commons)* e la Camera dei Lord *(House of Lords)*. Ha sede a Londra, nel Palazzo di Westminster, sulla riva del Tamigi. Gli edifici attuali risalgono alla metà del diciannovesimo secolo, quando vennero costruiti sulle macerie del palazzo originario, distrutto da un incendio nel 1934.

housewife ['haʊswaɪf] (*pl* **-wives** [-waɪvz]) *n* casalinga *f*.

house wine *n* vino *m* della casa.

housewives *pl* → **housewife**.

housework ['haʊswɜ:k] *n* lavori *mpl* di casa.

housing ['haʊzɪŋ] *n* alloggi *mpl*.

housing estate *n Br* complesso *m* residenziale.

housing project *Am* = **housing estate**.

hovercraft ['hɒvəkrɑ:ft] *n* hovercraft *m inv*.

hoverport ['hɒvəpɔ:t] *n* porto *m* per hovercraft.

---

how [haʊ] *adv* - **1.** *(asking about way or manner)* come ; ~ **do you get there?** come ci si arriva? ; ~ **does it work?** come funziona? ; **tell me ~ to do it** dimmi come devo fare. - **2.** *(asking about health, quality)* come ; ~ **are you?** come stai? ; ~ **are you doing?** come va? ; ~ **are things?** come vanno le cose? ; ~ **do you do?** piacere! - **3.** *(asking about degree, amount)* : ~ **tall is he?** quanto è alto? ; ~ **far is it?** quanto dista? ; ~ **long will it take?** quanto tempo ci vorrà? ; ~ **many?** quanti(e) ; ~ **much?** quanto(a) ; ~ **much is it?** quant'è? ; ~ **old are you?** quanti anni hai? - **4.** *(in phrases)* : ~ **about some coffee?** cosa ne diresti di un caffè? ; ~ **lovely!** che bello!

---

however [haʊ'evəʳ] *adv (nevertheless)* tuttavia ; ~ **difficult it is** per quanto sia difficile.

howl [haʊl] *vi* ululare.

HP *abbr* = **hire purchase**.

HQ *n (abbr of headquarters)* Q.G. *m*.

hubcap ['hʌbkæp] *n* coprimozzo *m*.

hug [hʌg] *vt* abbracciare. ◆ *n* : **to give sb a ~** abbracciare qn.

huge [hju:dʒ] *adj* enorme.

hum [hʌm] *vi (bee, machine)* ronzare ; *(person)* canterellare.

human ['hju:mən] *adj* umano(a). ◆ *n* : ~ (being) essere *m* umano.
humanities [hju:'mænətɪz] *npl* materie *fpl* umanistiche.
human rights *npl* diritti *mpl* dell'uomo.
humble ['hʌmbl] *adj* umile.
humid ['hju:mɪd] *adj* umido(a).
humidity [hju:'mɪdətɪ] *n* umidità *f*.
humiliating [hju:'mɪlɪeɪtɪŋ] *adj* umiliante.
humiliation [hju:ˌmɪlɪ'eɪʃn] *n* umiliazione *f*.
hummus ['hʊməs] *n salsetta cremosa a base di ceci, aglio e pasta di sesamo.*
humor ['hju:mər] *Am* = humour.
humorous ['hju:mərəs] *adj (story)* umoristico(a) ; *(person)* spiritoso(a).
humour ['hju:məʳ] *n* umorismo *m* ; sense of ~ senso *m* dell'umorismo.
hump [hʌmp] *n (bump)* dosso *m* ; *(of camel)* gobba *f*.
hunch [hʌntʃ] *n* impressione *f*.
hundred ['hʌndrəd] *num* cento ; a ~ cento , six.
hundredth ['hʌndrətθ] *num* centesimo(a) → sixth.
hung [hʌŋ] *pt* & *pp* → hang.
Hungarian [hʌŋ'geərɪən] *adj* ungherese. ◆ *n (person)* ungherese *mf* ; *(language)* ungherese *m*.
Hungary ['hʌŋgərɪ] *n* l'Ungheria *f*.
hunger ['hʌŋgəʳ] *n* fame *f*.
hungry ['hʌŋgrɪ] *adj* affamato(a) ; to be ~ avere fame.
hunt [hʌnt] *n Br (for foxes)* caccia *f*. ◆ *vt* & *vi* cacciare ; to ~ (for sb/sthg) *(search)* cercare (qn/qc).
hunting ['hʌntɪŋ] *n* caccia *f*.
hurl [hɜ:l] *vt (throw)* scaraventare, scagliare.
hurricane ['hʌrɪkən] *n* uragano *m*.
hurry ['hʌrɪ] *vt (person)* mettere fretta a. ◆ *vi* affrettarsi, sbrigarsi. ◆ *n* : to be in a ~ avere fretta ; to do sthg in a ~ fare qc in fretta. ❑ **hurry up** *vi* sbrigarsi.
hurt [hɜ:t] (*pt* & *pp* hurt) *vt (injure)* fare male a ; *(emotionally)* ferire. ◆ *vi* far male ; my arm ~s mi fa male il braccio ; I ~ my arm mi sono fatto male al braccio ; to ~ o.s. farsi male.
husband ['hʌzbənd] *n* marito *m*.
hustle ['hʌsl] *n* : ~ and bustle attività *f* febbrile.
hut [hʌt] *n* capanna *f*.
hyacinth ['haɪəsɪnθ] *n* giacinto *m*.
hydrofoil ['haɪdrəfɔɪl] *n* aliscafo *m*.
hygiene ['haɪdʒi:n] *n* igiene *f*.
hygienic [haɪ'dʒi:nɪk] *adj* igienico(a).
hymn [hɪm] *n* inno *m*.
hypermarket ['haɪpəˌma:kɪt] *n* ipermercato *m*.
hyphen ['haɪfn] *n* trattino *m*.
hypocrite ['hɪpəkrɪt] *n* ipocrita *mf*.
hypodermic needle [ˌhaɪpə'dɜ:mɪk-] *n* ago *m* ipodermico.
hysterical [hɪs'terɪkl] *adj (person)* isterico(a) ; *inf (very funny)* esilarante.

I

I [aɪ] *pron* io ; **I'm tall** sono alto.

ice [aɪs] *n* ghiaccio *m* ; *(ice cream)* gelato *m*.

iceberg ['aɪsbɜːg] *n* iceberg *m inv*.

iceberg lettuce *n* lattuga *f* iceberg.

icebox ['aɪsbɒks] *n Am (fridge)* frigorifero *m*.

ice-cold *adj* ghiacciato(a).

ice cream *n* gelato *m*.

ice cube *n* cubetto *m* di ghiaccio.

ice hockey *n* hockey *m* su ghiaccio.

ice lolly *n Br* ghiacciolo *m*.

ice rink *n* pista *f* di pattinaggio su ghiaccio.

ice skates *npl* pattini *mpl* da ghiaccio.

ice-skating *n* pattinaggio *m* su ghiaccio ; **to go ~** andare a pattinare sul ghiaccio.

icicle ['aɪsɪkl] *n* ghiacciolo *m*.

icing ['aɪsɪŋ] *n* glassa *f*.

icing sugar *n* zucchero *m* a velo.

icy ['aɪsɪ] *adj (covered with ice)* ghiacciato(a) ; *(very cold)* gelido(a), gelato(a).

I'd [aɪd] = **I would, I had**.

ID *n* (*abbr of identification*) documento *m* (d'identità).

ID card *n* carta *f* d'identità.

idea [aɪ'dɪə] *n* idea *f* ; **I've no ~** non ho idea.

ideal [aɪ'dɪəl] *adj* ideale. ◆ *n* ideale *m*.

ideally [aɪ'dɪəlɪ] *adv* idealmente ; *(suited)* perfettamente.

identical [aɪ'dentɪkl] *adj* identico(a).

identification [aɪˌdentɪfɪ'keɪʃn] *n (document)* documento *m* d'identità.

identify [aɪ'dentɪfaɪ] *vt* identificare.

identity [aɪ'dentətɪ] *n* identità *f inv*.

idiom ['ɪdɪəm] *n (phrase)* espressione *f* idiomatica.

idiot ['ɪdɪət] *n* idiota *mf*.

idle ['aɪdl] *adj (lazy)* ozioso(a) ; *(not working)* inattivo(a) ; *(unemployed)* disoccupato(a). ◆ *vi (engine)* girare al minimo.

idol ['aɪdl] *n (person)* idolo *m*.

idyllic [ɪ'dɪlɪk] *adj* idilliaco(a).

i.e. (*abbr of id est*) cioè.

if [ɪf] *conj* se ; **~ I were you** se fossi in te ; **~ not** *(otherwise)* se no.

ignition [ɪg'nɪʃn] *n AUT* accensione *f*.

ignorant ['ɪgnərənt] *adj* ignorante.

ignore [ɪg'nɔːʳ] *vt* ignorare.

ill [ɪl] *adj (in health)* malato(a) ; *(bad)* cattivo(a).

I'll [aɪl] = **I will, I shall**.

illegal [ɪ'liːgl] *adj* illegale.

illegible [ɪ'ledʒəbl] *adj* illeggibile.

illegitimate [ˌɪlɪ'dʒɪtɪmət] *adj* illegittimo(a).

illiterate [ɪ'lɪtərət] *adj* analfabeta.

illness ['ɪlnɪs] *n* malattia *f*.
illuminate [ɪ'lu:mɪneɪt] *vt* illuminare.
illusion [ɪ'lu:ʒn] *n* illusione *f*.
illustration [ˌɪlə'streɪʃn] *n* illustrazione *f*.
I'm [aɪm] = **I am**.
image ['ɪmɪdʒ] *n* immagine *f*.
imaginary [ɪ'mædʒɪnrɪ] *adj* immaginario(a).
imagination [ɪˌmædʒɪ'neɪʃn] *n* immaginazione *f*.
imagine [ɪ'mædʒɪn] *vt* immaginare.
imitate ['ɪmɪteɪt] *vt* imitare.
imitation [ˌɪmɪ'teɪʃn] *n* imitazione *f*. ◆ *a dj* finto(a).
immaculate [ɪ'mækjʊlət] *adj* *(very clean)* immacolato(a), lindo(a) ; *(perfect)* impeccabile.
immature [ˌɪmə'tjʊəʳ] *adj* immaturo(a).
immediate [ɪ'mi:djət] *adj* *(without delay)* immediato(a).
immediately [ɪ'mi:djətlɪ] *adv* *(at once)* immediatamente, subito. ◆ *conj Br* non appena.
immense [ɪ'mens] *adj* immenso(a).
immersion heater [ɪ'mɜ:ʃn-] *n* scaldabagno *m inv* elettrico.
immigrant ['ɪmɪgrənt] *n* immigrato *m*, -a *f*.
immigration [ˌɪmɪ'greɪʃn] *n* *(to country)* immigrazione *f* ; *(section of airport, port)* dogana *f*.
imminent ['ɪmɪnənt] *adj* imminente.
immune [ɪ'mju:n] *adj* : **to be ~ to** *MED* essere immune da.
immunity [ɪ'mju:nətɪ] *n MED* immunità *f*.
immunize ['ɪmju:naɪz] *vt* immunizzare.
impact ['ɪmpækt] *n* impatto *m*.
impair [ɪm'peəʳ] *vt* danneggiare.
impatient [ɪm'peɪʃnt] *adj* impaziente ; **to be ~ to do sthg** essere impaziente di fare qc.
imperative [ɪm'perətɪv] *n GRAMM* imperativo *m*.
imperfect [ɪm'pɜ:fɪkt] *n GRAMM* imperfetto *m*.
impersonate [ɪm'pɜ:səneɪt] *vt* *(for amusement)* imitare.
impertinent [ɪm'pɜ:tɪnənt] *adj* impertinente.
implement [*n* 'ɪmplɪmənt, *vb* 'ɪmplɪment] *n* attrezzo *m* ; *(for cooking)* utensile *m*. ◆ *vt* mettere in atto, realizzare.
implication [ˌɪmplɪ'keɪʃn] *n* *(consequence)* implicazione *f*.
imply [ɪm'plaɪ] *vt* *(suggest)* lasciar intendere, sottintendere.
impolite [ˌɪmpə'laɪt] *adj* scortese.
import [*n* 'ɪmpɔ:t, *vb* ɪm'pɔ:t] *n* merce *f* d'importazione. ◆ *vt* importare.
importance [ɪm'pɔ:tns] *n* importanza *f*.
important [ɪm'pɔ:tnt] *adj* importante.
impose [ɪm'pəʊz] *vt* imporre. ◆ *vi* approfittare ; **to ~ sthg on** imporre qc a.
impossible [ɪm'pɒsəbl] *adj* impossibile.

impractical [ɪm'præktɪkl] *adj* non pratico(a).

impress [ɪm'pres] *vt* fare una buona impressione a.

impression [ɪm'preʃn] *n* impressione *f*.

impressive [ɪm'presɪv] *adj* impressionante.

improbable [ɪm'prɒbəbl] *adj* *(event)* improbabile ; *(story, excuse)* inverosimile.

improper [ɪm'prɒpəʳ] *adj* *(incorrect, illegal)* scorretto(a) ; *(rude)* sconveniente.

improve [ɪm'pruːv] *vt* & *vi* migliorare. ❑ **improve on** *vt fus* migliorare.

improvement [ɪm'pruːvmənt] *n* *(in weather, health)* miglioramento *m* ; *(to home)* miglioria *f*.

improvise ['ɪmprəvaɪz] *vi* improvvisare.

impulse ['ɪmpʌls] *n* impulso *m* ; **on ~** d'impulso.

impulsive [ɪm'pʌlsɪv] *adj* impulsivo(a).

---

in [ɪn] *prep* - 1. *(expressing place, position)* in ; **~ a box** in una scatola ; **~ the bedroom** in camera da letto ; **~ the street** per strada ; **~ Scotland** in Scozia ; **~ Sheffield** a Sheffield ; **~ the United States** negli Stati Uniti ; **~ here/there** qui/là dentro ; **~ the sun** al sole ; **~ the rain** sotto la pioggia ; **~ the middle** al centro ; **an article ~ the paper** un articolo sul giornale.
- 2. *(participating in)* in ; **who's ~ the play?** chi recita nella commedia?
- 3. *(expressing arrangement)* in ; **~ a row** in fila ; **they come ~ packs of three** vengono venduti in pacchetti da tre.
- 4. *(with time)* : **~ April** ad aprile ; **~ the afternoon** di OR nel pomeriggio ; **at ten o'clock ~ the morning** alle dieci del mattino ; **~ 1994** nel 1994 ; **it'll be ready ~ an hour** sarà pronto fra un'ora ; **they're arriving ~ two weeks** arriveranno fra due settimane.
- 5. *(expressing means)* : **to write ~ ink** scrivere a penna ; **~ writing** per iscritto ; **they were talking ~ English** parlavano in inglese.
- 6. *(wearing)* : **the man ~ the blue jacket** l'uomo con la giacca blu ; **dressed ~ white** vestito di bianco.
- 7. *(expressing state)* : **~ a bad mood** di pessimo umore ; **to be ~ a hurry** essere di fretta ; **to cry ~ pain** gridare di dolore ; **to be ~ pain** soffrire ; **~ ruins** in rovina.
- 8. *(with regard to)* : **a rise ~ prices** un aumento dei prezzi ; **to be 50 metres ~ length** essere lungo 50 metri.
- 9. *(with numbers, ratios)* : **one ~ ten** uno su dieci ; **~ dozens** a dozzine.
- 10. *(expressing age)* : **she's ~ her thirties** è sulla trentina.
- 11. *(with colours)* : **it comes ~ green or blue** è disponibile in verde o in blu.
- 12. *(with superlatives)* di ; **the best ~ the world** il migliore del mondo.
◆ *adv* - 1. *(inside)* dentro ; **you can go ~ now** ora può entrare ; **come ~!** avanti!.
- 2. *(at home, work)* : **she's not ~** non c'è ; **to stay ~** stare a casa.
- 3. *(train, bus, plane)* : **the train's not**

~ **yet** il treno non è ancora arrivato.
- 4. *(tide)* : **the tide is ~** c'è alta marea ; *inf (fashionable)* alla moda.

inability [ˌɪnəˈbɪlətɪ] *n* : ~ **(to do sthg)** incapacità *f* (di fare qc).
inaccessible [ˌɪnəkˈsesəbl] *adj* inaccessibile.
inaccurate [ɪnˈækjʊrət] *adj* inesatto(a), impreciso(a).
inadequate [ɪnˈædɪkwət] *adj* inadeguato(a).
inappropriate [ɪnəˈprəʊprɪət] *adj* non adatto(a).
inauguration [ɪˌnɔːgjʊˈreɪʃn] *n* inaugurazione *f*; *(of president etc)* insediamento *m* in carica.
incapable [ɪnˈkeɪpəbl] *adj* : **to be ~ of doing sthg** essere incapace di fare qc.
incense [ˈɪnsens] *n* incenso *m*.
incentive [ɪnˈsentɪv] *n* incentivo *m*.
inch [ɪntʃ] *n* = 2,5 cm, pollice *m*.
incident [ˈɪnsɪdənt] *n* episodio *m*, caso *m*.
incidentally [ˌɪnsɪˈdentəlɪ] *adv* a proposito.
incline [ˈɪnklaɪn] *n* pendio *m*.
inclined [ɪnˈklaɪnd] *adj (sloping)* inclinato(a) ; **to be ~ to do sthg** essere propenso a fare qc.
include [ɪnˈkluːd] *vt* includere, comprendere.
included [ɪnˈkluːdɪd] *adj (in price)* compreso(a) ; **to be ~ in sthg** essere compreso in qc.
including [ɪnˈkluːdɪŋ] *prep* compreso(a).
inclusive [ɪnˈkluːsɪv] *adj* : **from the 8th to the 16th ~** dall'8 al 16 compreso ; ~ **of VAT** IVA compresa.
income [ˈɪŋkʌm] *n* reddito *m*.
income support *n Br* ≃ sussidio *m* di indigenza.
income tax *n* imposta *f* sul reddito.
incoming [ˈɪnˌkʌmɪŋ] *adj* in arrivo.
incompetent [ɪnˈkɒmpɪtənt] *adj* incompetente.
incomplete [ˌɪnkəmˈpliːt] *adj* incompleto(a).
inconsiderate [ˌɪnkənˈsɪdərət] *adj* sconsiderato(a).
inconsistent [ˌɪnkənˈsɪstənt] *adj* incoerente.
incontinent [ɪnˈkɒntɪnənt] *adj* incontinente.
inconvenient [ˌɪnkənˈviːnjənt] *adj* scomodo(a).
incorporate [ɪnˈkɔːpəreɪt] *vt* incorporare.
incorrect [ˌɪnkəˈrekt] *adj (answer, number)* sbagliato(a) ; *(information)* inesatto(a).
increase [*n* ˈɪnkriːs, *vb* ɪnˈkriːs] *n* aumento *m*. ◆ *vt & vi* aumentare ; **an ~ in sthg** un aumento di qc.
increasingly [ɪnˈkriːsɪŋlɪ] *adv* sempre più.
incredible [ɪnˈkredəbl] *adj* incredibile.
incredibly [ɪnˈkredəblɪ] *adv (very)* incredibilmente.
incur [ɪnˈkɜːʳ] *vt* incorrere in.
indecisive [ˌɪndɪˈsaɪsɪv] *adj* indeciso(a).
indeed [ɪnˈdiːd] *adv (for emphasis)*

davvero ; *(certainly)* certamente.

indefinite [ɪn'defɪnɪt] *adj (time, number)* indefinito(a), indeterminato(a) ; *(an swer, opinion)* vago(a).

indefinitely [ɪn'defɪnətlɪ] *adv (closed, delayed)* indefinitamente.

independence [ˌɪndɪ'pendəns] *n* indipendenza *f*.

independent [ˌɪndɪ'pendənt] *adj* indipendente.

independently [ˌɪndɪ'pendəntlɪ] *adv* indipendentemente.

independent school *n Br* scuola *f* privata.

index ['ɪndeks] *n (of book)* indice *m* ; *(in library)* catalogo *m*.

index finger *n* dito *m* indice.

Indian ['ɪndjən] *adj* indiano(a). ◆ *n* indiano *m*, -a *f* ; **an ~ restaurant** un ristorante indiano.

indicate ['ɪndɪkeɪt] *vi AUT* mettere la freccia. ◆ *vt* indicare.

indicator ['ɪndɪkeɪtə^r] *n AUT* indicatore *m* di direzione, freccia *f*.

indifferent [ɪn'dɪfrənt] *adj (uninterested)* indifferente ; *(not very good)* mediocre.

indigestion [ˌɪndɪ'dʒestʃn] *n* indigestione *f*.

indigo ['ɪndɪgəʊ] *adj* indaco *(inv)*.

indirect [ˌɪndɪ'rekt] *adj* non diretto(a).

individual [ˌɪndɪ'vɪdʒʊəl] *adj* individuale. ◆ *n* individuo *m*.

individually [ˌɪndɪ'vɪdʒʊəlɪ] *adv* individualmente.

indoor ['ɪndɔː^r] *adj (swimming pool)* coperto(a) ; *(sports)* praticato(a) al coperto.

indoors [ˌɪn'dɔːz] *adv* dentro.

indulge [ɪn'dʌldʒ] *vi* : **to ~ in sthg** concedersi qc.

industrial [ɪn'dʌstrɪəl] *adj* industriale.

industrial estate *n Br* zona *f* industriale.

industry ['ɪndəstrɪ] *n* industria *f*.

inedible [ɪn'edɪbl] *adj (unpleasant)* immangiabile ; *(unsafe)* non commestibile.

inefficient [ˌɪnɪ'fɪʃnt] *adj* inefficiente.

inequality [ˌɪnɪ'kwɒlətɪ] *n* disuguaglianza *f*.

inevitable [ɪn'evɪtəbl] *adj* inevitabile.

inevitably [ɪn'evɪtəblɪ] *adv* inevitabilmente.

inexpensive [ˌɪnɪk'spensɪv] *adj* poco costoso(a).

infamous ['ɪnfəməs] *adj* infame.

infant ['ɪnfənt] *n* bambino *m*, -a *f*.

infant school *n Br* scuola *f* elementare *(per bambini da 5 a 7 anni)*.

infatuated [ɪn'fætjʊeɪtɪd] *adj* : **to be ~ with** essere infatuato(a) di.

infected [ɪn'fektɪd] *adj* infetto(a).

infectious [ɪn'fekʃəs] *adj* contagioso(a).

inferior [ɪn'fɪərɪə^r] *adj (person)* inferiore ; *(goods, quality)* scadente.

infinite ['ɪnfɪnət] *adj* infinito(a).

infinitely ['ɪnfɪnətlɪ] *adv* infinitamente.

infinitive [ɪn'fɪnɪtɪv] *n* infinito *m*.

infinity [ɪn'fɪnətɪ] *n (in space, MATH)* infinito *m*.
infirmary [ɪn'fɜːmərɪ] *n* ospedale *m*.
inflamed [ɪn'fleɪmd] *adj MED* infiammato(a).
inflammation [ˌɪnflə'meɪʃn] *n MED* infiammazione *f*.
inflatable [ɪn'fleɪtəbl] *adj* gonfiabile.
inflate [ɪn'fleɪt] *vt* gonfiare.
inflation [ɪn'fleɪʃn] *n (of prices)* inflazione *f*.
inflict [ɪn'flɪkt] *vt* infliggere.
in-flight *adj* durante il volo.
influence ['ɪnfluəns] *vt* influenzare. ◆ *n* : ~ **(on)** influenza *f* (su).
inform [ɪn'fɔːm] *vt* informare.
informal [ɪn'fɔːml] *adj (occasion, dress)* informale.
information [ˌɪnfə'meɪʃn] *n* informazioni *fpl* ; **a piece of ~** un'informazione.
information desk *n* sportello *m* informazioni.
information office *n* ufficio *m* informazioni.
informative [ɪn'fɔːmətɪv] *adj* istruttivo(a).
infuriating [ɪn'fjuərɪeɪtɪŋ] *adj* molto irritante.
ingenious [ɪn'dʒiːnjəs] *adj* ingegnoso(a).
ingredient [ɪn'griːdjənt] *n* ingrediente *m*.
inhabit [ɪn'hæbɪt] *vt* abitare.
inhabitant [ɪn'hæbɪtənt] *n* abitante *mf*.
inhale [ɪn'heɪl] *vi* aspirare.
inhaler [ɪn'heɪləʳ] *n* inalatore *m*.
inherit [ɪn'herɪt] *vt* ereditare.
inhibition [ˌɪnhɪ'bɪʃn] *n* inibizione *f*.
initial [ɪ'nɪʃl] *adj* iniziale. ◆ *vt* siglare. ❑ **initials** *npl* iniziali *fpl*.
initially [ɪ'nɪʃəlɪ] *adv* inizialmente.
initiative [ɪ'nɪʃətɪv] *n* iniziativa *f*.
injection [ɪn'dʒekʃn] *n* iniezione *f*.
injure ['ɪndʒəʳ] *vt (physically)* ferire ; **to ~ o.s.** ferirsi ; **to ~ one's arm** ferirsi al braccio.
injured ['ɪndʒəd] *adj (physically)* ferito(a).
injury ['ɪndʒərɪ] *n (physical)* ferita *f*.
ink [ɪŋk] *n* inchiostro *m*.
inland [*adj* 'ɪnlənd, *adv* ɪn'lænd] *adj* interno(a). ◆ *adv* nell'interno.
Inland Revenue *n Br* ≃ Fisco *m*.
inner ['ɪnəʳ] *adj* interno(a), interiore.
inner city *n quartieri vicino al centro di una città,.*
inner tube *n* camera *f* d'aria.
innocence ['ɪnəsəns] *n* innocenza *f*.
innocent ['ɪnəsənt] *adj* innocente.
inoculate [ɪ'nɒkjuleɪt] *vt* : **to ~ sb (against sthg)** vaccinare qn (contro qc).
inoculation [ɪˌnɒkju'leɪʃn] *n* vaccinazione *f*.
input ['ɪnput] (*pt* & *pp* **input** OR **-ted**) *vt COMPUT* immettere.
inquire [ɪn'kwaɪəʳ] = **enquire**.
inquiry [ɪn'kwaɪərɪ] = **enquiry**.

insane [ɪn'seɪn] *adj* pazzo(a), matto(a).

insect ['ɪnsekt] *n* insetto *m*.

insect repellent [-rə'pelənt] *n* insettifugo *m*.

insensitive [ɪn'sensətɪv] *adj* insensibile.

insert [ɪn'sɜːt] *vt* inserire, introdurre.

inside [ɪn'saɪd] *prep* dentro, all'interno di. ◆ *adv* dentro. ◆ *adj (internal)* interno(a). ◆ *n* : **the ~** *(interior)* l'interno *m* ; AUT *(in UK)* la sinistra ; AUT *(in Europe, US)* la destra ; **~ out** *(clothes)* a rovescio.

inside lane *n* [AUT] *(in UK)* corsia *f* di sinistra ; *(in Europe, US)* corsia di destra.

inside leg *n* cavallo *m* .

insight ['ɪnsaɪt] *n (glimpse)* idea *f*.

insignificant [ˌɪnsɪg'nɪfɪkənt] *adj* insignificante.

insinuate [ɪn'sɪnjʊeɪt] *vt* insinuare.

insist [ɪn'sɪst] *vi* insistere ; **to ~ on doing sthg** insistere nel fare qc.

insole ['ɪnsəʊl] *n* soletta *f*.

insolent ['ɪnsələnt] *adj* insolente.

insomnia [ɪn'sɒmnɪə] *n* insonnia *f*.

inspect [ɪn'spekt] *vt (object)* ispezionare ; *(ticket, passport)* controllare.

inspection [ɪn'spekʃn] *n (of object)* ispezione *f*; *(of ticket, passport)* controllo *m*.

inspector [ɪn'spektəʳ] *n (on bus, train)* controllore *m* ; *(in police force)* ispettore *m*, -trice *f*.

inspiration [ˌɪnspə'reɪʃn] *n* ispirazione *f*.

instal [ɪn'stɔːl] *Am* = **install**.

install [ɪn'stɔːl] *vt Br* installare.

installment [ɪn'stɔːlmənt] *Am* = **instalment**.

instalment [ɪn'stɔːlmənt] *n (payment)* rata *f* ; *(episode)* puntata *f*, parte *f*.

instance ['ɪnstəns] *n (example, case)* esempio *m*, caso *m*.

instant ['ɪnstənt] *adj (results, success)* immediato(a) ; *(coffee)* solubile. ◆ *n (moment)* istante *m*.

instant coffee *n* caffè *m inv* solubile.

instead [ɪn'sted] *adv* invece ; **~ of** invece di.

instep ['ɪnstep] *n* collo *m* del piede.

instinct ['ɪnstɪŋkt] *n* istinto *m*.

institute ['ɪnstɪtjuːt] *n* istituto *m*.

institution [ˌɪnstɪ'tjuːʃn] *n* istituzione *f*.

instructions [ɪn'strʌkʃnz] *npl* istruzioni *fpl*.

instructor [ɪn'strʌktəʳ] *n* istruttore *m*, -trice *f*.

instrument ['ɪnstrʊmənt] *n* strumento *m*.

insufficient [ˌɪnsə'fɪʃnt] *adj* insufficiente.

insulating tape ['ɪnsjʊleɪtɪŋ-] *n* nastro *m* isolante.

insulation [ˌɪnsjʊ'leɪʃn] *n (material)* isolante *m*.

insulin ['ɪnsjʊlɪn] *n* insulina *f*.

insult [*n* 'ɪnsʌlt, *vb* ɪn'sʌlt] *n* insulto *m*. ◆ *v t* insultare.

insurance [ɪnˈʃʊərəns] *n* assicurazione *f*.
insurance certificate *n* certificato *m* di assicurazione.
insurance company *n* compagnia *f* di assicurazione.
insurance policy *n* polizza *f* di assicurazione.
insure [ɪnˈʃʊəʳ] *vt* assicurare.
insured [ɪnˈʃʊəd] *adj* : **to be ~** essere assicurato(a).
intact [ɪnˈtækt] *adj* intatto(a).
intellectual [ˌɪntəˈlektjʊəl] *adj* intellettuale. ◆ *n* intellettuale *mf*.
intelligence [ɪnˈtelɪdʒəns] *n (cleverness)* intelligenza *f*.
intelligent [ɪnˈtelɪdʒənt] *adj* intelligente.
intend [ɪnˈtend] *vt (mean)* : **to ~ to do sthg** avere intenzione di fare qc ; **you weren't ~ed to know** non dovevi saperlo.
intense [ɪnˈtens] *adj* intenso(a).
intensity [ɪnˈtensətɪ] *n* intensità *f*.
intensive [ɪnˈtensɪv] *adj* intensivo(a).
intensive care *n* terapia *f* intensiva.
intent [ɪnˈtent] *adj* : **to be ~ on doing sthg** essere deciso(a) a fare qc.
intention [ɪnˈtenʃn] *n* intenzione *f*.
intentional [ɪnˈtenʃənl] *adj* intenzionale.
intentionally [ɪnˈtenʃənəlɪ] *adv* intenzionalmente, apposta.
interchange [ˈɪntətʃeɪndʒ] *n (on motorway)* svincolo *m*.
Intercity® [ˌɪntəˈsɪtɪ] *n Br* intercity *m inv*.
intercom [ˈɪntəkɒm] *n* interfono *m*.
interest [ˈɪntrəst] *n* interesse *m*. ◆ *v t* interessare ; **to take an ~ in sthg** interessarsi di OR a qc.
interested [ˈɪntrəstɪd] *adj* interessato(a) ; **to be ~ in sthg** interessarsi di qc.
interesting [ˈɪntrəstɪŋ] *adj* interessante.
interest rate *n* tasso *m* d'interesse.
interfere [ˌɪntəˈfɪəʳ] *vi (meddle)* immischiarsi ; **to ~ with sthg** *(damage)* interferire con qc.
interference [ˌɪntəˈfɪərəns] *n (on TV, radio)* interferenza *f*.
interior [ɪnˈtɪərɪəʳ] *adj* interno(a). ◆ *n* interno *m*.
intermediate [ˌɪntəˈmiːdjət] *adj* intermedio(a).
intermission [ˌɪntəˈmɪʃn] *n (at cinema, theatre)* intervallo *m*.
internal [ɪnˈtɜːnl] *adj* interno(a).
internal flight *n* volo *m* interno.
international [ˌɪntəˈnæʃənl] *adj* internazionale.
international flight *n* volo *m* internazionale.
interpret [ɪnˈtɜːprɪt] *vi* fare da interprete.
interpreter [ɪnˈtɜːprɪtəʳ] *n* interprete *mf*.
interrogate [ɪnˈterəgeɪt] *vt* interrogare.
interrupt [ˌɪntəˈrʌpt] *vt* interrompere.
intersection [ˌɪntəˈsekʃn] *n (of roads)* incrocio *m*.
interval [ˈɪntəvl] *n* intervallo *m*.

intervene [ˌɪntəˈviːn] *vi (person, event)* intervenire.

interview [ˈɪntəvjuː] *n (on TV, in magazine)* intervista *f* ; *(for job)* colloquio *m.* ◆ *v t (on TV, in magazine)* intervistare ; *(for job)* fare un colloquio a.

interviewer [ˈɪntəvjuːəʳ] *n (on TV, in magazine)* intervistatore *m*, -trice *f*.

intestine [ɪnˈtestɪn] *n* intestino *m*.

intimate [ˈɪntɪmət] *adj* intimo(a).

intimidate [ɪnˈtɪmɪdeɪt] *vt* intimidire.

into [ˈɪntʊ] *prep (inside)* in, dentro ; *(against)* contro, in ; *(concerning)* su ; **4 ~ 20 goes 5 (times)** il 4 nel 20 sta 5 volte ; **to translate ~ Italian** tradurre in italiano ; **to change ~ sthg** trasformarsi in qc ; **to be ~ sthg** *inf (like)* essere appassionato di qc.

intolerable [ɪnˈtɒlrəbl] *adj* intollerabile.

intransitive [ɪnˈtrænzətɪv] *adj* intransitivo(a).

intricate [ˈɪntrɪkət] *adj* intricato(a).

intriguing [ɪnˈtriːgɪŋ] *adj* affascinante.

introduce [ˌɪntrəˈdjuːs] *vt* presentare ; **I'd like to ~ you to Fred** ti presento Fred.

introduction [ˌɪntrəˈdʌkʃn] *n (to book, programme)* introduzione *f* ; *(to person)* presentazione *f*.

introverted [ˈɪntrəˌvɜːtɪd] *adj* introverso(a).

intruder [ɪnˈtruːdəʳ] *n* intruso *m*, -a *f*.

intuition [ˌɪntjuːˈɪʃn] *n (feeling)* intuizione *f* ; *(faculty)* intuito *m*.

invade [ɪnˈveɪd] *vt* invadere.

invalid [*adj* ɪnˈvælɪd, *n* ˈɪnvəlɪd] *adj (ticket, cheque)* non valido(a). ◆ *n* invalido *m*, -a *f*.

invaluable [ɪnˈvæljʊəbl] *adj* inestimabile.

invariably [ɪnˈveərɪəblɪ] *adv* sempre, invariabilmente.

invasion [ɪnˈveɪʒn] *n* invasione *f*.

invent [ɪnˈvent] *vt* inventare.

invention [ɪnˈvenʃn] *n* invenzione *f*.

inventory [ˈɪnventrɪ] *n* inventario *m*.

inverted commas [ɪnˈvɜːtɪd-] *npl* virgolette *fpl*.

invest [ɪnˈvest] *vt* investire. ◆ *vi* : **to ~ in sthg** investire in qc.

investigate [ɪnˈvestɪgeɪt] *vt* indagare.

investigation [ɪnˌvestɪˈgeɪʃn] *n* indagine *f*.

investment [ɪnˈvestmənt] *n* investimento *m*.

invisible [ɪnˈvɪzɪbl] *adj* invisibile.

invitation [ˌɪnvɪˈteɪʃn] *n* invito *m*.

invite [ɪnˈvaɪt] *vt* invitare ; **to ~ sb to do sthg** *(ask)* invitare qn a fare qc ; **to ~ sb round** invitare qn.

invoice [ˈɪnvɔɪs] *n* fattura *f*.

involve [ɪnˈvɒlv] *vt (entail)* richiedere, comportare ; **what does it ~?** che cosa comporta? ; **to be ~d in sthg** essere coinvolto in qc.

involved [ɪn'vɒlvd] *adj (entailed)* richiesto(a), necessario(a).

inwards ['ɪnwədz] *adv* verso l'interno.

IOU *n* pagherà *m inv*.

IQ *n* Q.I. *m*.

Ireland ['aɪələnd] *n* l'Irlanda *f*.

iris ['aɪərɪs] (*pl* **-es**) ['aɪərɪs] *n (flower)* giaggiolo *m*, iris *f inv*.

Irish ['aɪrɪʃ] *adj* irlandese. ◆ *n (language)* irlandese *m*. ◆ *npl*: **the ~** gli irlandesi.

Irish coffee *n* Irish coffee *m inv (caffè con whisky e panna)*.

Irishman ['aɪrɪʃmən] (*pl* **-men** [-mən]) *n* irlandese *m*.

Irishwoman ['aɪrɪʃˌwʊmən] (*pl* **-women** [-ˌwɪmɪn]) *n* irlandese *f*.

iron ['aɪən] *n (metal)* ferro *m* ; *(for clothes)* ferro da stiro ; *(golf club)* mazza *f* da golf. ◆ *vt* stirare.

ironic [aɪ'rɒnɪk] *adj* ironico(a).

ironing board ['aɪənɪŋ-] *n* asse *f* da stiro.

ironmonger's ['aɪənˌmʌŋgəz] *n Br* ferramenta *f inv*.

irrelevant [ɪ'reləvənt] *adj* non pertinente, irrilevante.

irresistible [ˌɪrɪ'zɪstəbl] *adj* irresistibile.

irrespective [ˌɪrɪ'spektɪv] ◆**irrespective of** *prep* a prescindere da.

irresponsible [ˌɪrɪ'spɒnsəbl] *adj* irresponsabile.

irrigation [ˌɪrɪ'geɪʃn] *n* irrigazione *f*.

irritable ['ɪrɪtəbl] *adj* irritabile.

irritate ['ɪrɪteɪt] *vt* irritare.

irritating ['ɪrɪteɪtɪŋ] *adj* irritante.

IRS *n Am* ≃ Fisco *m*.

is [ɪz] → **be**.

island ['aɪlənd] *n* isola *f*.

isle [aɪl] *n* isola *f*.

isolated ['aɪsəleɪtɪd] *adj* isolato(a).

issue ['ɪʃuː] *n (problem, subject)* questione *f*, problema *m* ; *(of newspaper, magazine)* numero *m*. ◆ *v t (statement, passport, document)* rilasciare ; *(stamps, bank notes)* emettere.

☞

---

it [ɪt] *pron* - 1. *(referring to specific thing : subject, afterprep)* esso(a) ; *(direct object)* lo (la) ; *(indirect object)* gli (le) ; **~'s big** è grande ; **she hit ~** l'ha colpito ; **give ~ to me** dammelo ; **tell me about ~** parlamene ; **we went to ~** ci siamo andati.

- 2. *(nonspecific)* : **~'s nice here** si sta bene qui ; **~'s me** sono io ; **who is ~?** chi è?

- 3. *(used impersonally)* : **~'s hot** fa caldo ; **~'s six o'clock** sono le sei ; **~'s Sunday** è domenica.

Italian [ɪ'tæljən] *adj* italiano(a). ◆ *n (person)* italiano *m*, -a *f* ; *(language)* italiano *m* ; **an ~ restaurant** un ristorante italiano.

Italian Riviera *n* : **the ~** la Riviera Ligure.

Italy ['ɪtəlɪ] *n* l'Italia *f*.

itch [ɪtʃ] *vi (arm, leg)* prudere ; *(person)* avere prurito.

item ['aɪtəm] *n (object)* articolo *m* ; *(on agenda)* punto *m* ; **news ~** notizia *f*.

itemized bill ['aɪtəmaɪzd-] *n* bolletta *f* con lettura dettagliata.

its [ɪts] *adj* il suo (la sua), i suoi, (le sue) *(pl)*.

it's [ɪts] = it is, it has.

itself [ɪt'self] *pron (reflexive)* si ; *(after prep)* se stesso(a), sé ; **the house ~ is fine** la casa in sé va bene.

I've [aɪv] = I have.

ivory ['aɪvərɪ] *n* avorio *m*.

ivy ['aɪvɪ] *n* edera *f*.

IVY LEAGUE

Negli Stati Uniti il termine *Ivy League* è utilizzato per indicare un gruppo di otto università (Dartmouth College, Brown, Columbia, Cornell, Harvard, Pennsylvania, Princeton e Yale) fra le più antiche e prestigiose degli Stati Uniti. Il nome allude all'edera *(ivy)* che ricopre le mura dei vecchi edifici che le ospitano. Un diploma conseguito presso una di queste istituzioni è sicura garanzia di successo in ambito professionale.

J

jab [dʒæb] *n Br inf (injection)* puntura *f*.

jack [dʒæk] *n (for car)* cric *m inv* ; *(playing card)* fante *m*.

jacket ['dʒækɪt] *n (garment)* giacca *f* ; *(of book)* sopraccoperta *f* ; *Am (of record)* copertina *f* ; *(of potato)* buccia *f*.

jacket potato *n patata cotta al forno con la buccia.*

jack-knife *vi* piegarsi su se stesso *(camion)*.

Jacuzzi® [dʒə'ku:zɪ] *n* vasca *f* con idromassaggio.

jade [dʒeɪd] *n* giada *f*.

jail [dʒeɪl] *n* prigione *f*.

jam [dʒæm] *n (food)* marmellata *f* ; *(of traffic)* ingorgo *m* ; *inf (difficult situation)* pasticcio *m*. ◆ *vt (pack tightly)* stipare. ◆ *vi (get stuck)* bloccarsi ; **the roads are jammed** le strade sono intasate.

jam-packed [-'pækt] *adj inf* stipato(a).

Jan. [dʒæn] (*abbr of January*) gen.

January ['dʒænjʊərɪ] *n* gennaio *m* → **September**.

jar [dʒa:ʳ] *n* barattolo *m*, vasetto *m*.

javelin ['dʒævlɪn] *n* giavellotto *m*.

jaw [dʒɔ:] *n* mascella *f*.

jazz [dʒæz] *n* jazz *m*.

jealous ['dʒeləs] *adj* geloso(a).

jeans [dʒi:nz] *npl* jeans *mpl*.

Jeep® [dʒi:p] *n* jeep® *f inv*.

Jello® ['dʒeləʊ] *n Am* gelatina *f*.

jelly ['dʒelɪ] *n (dessert)* gelatina *f* ; *Am (jam)* marmellata *f*.

jellyfish ['dʒelɪfɪʃ] (*pl inv*) *n* medusa *f*.

jeopardize ['dʒepədaɪz] *vt* mettere a repentaglio.

jerk [dʒɜ:k] *n (movement)* strattone *m*, scossa *f* ; *inf (idiot)* imbecille *mf*.

jersey ['dʒɜ:zɪ] (*pl* **-s**) *n (garment)* maglia *f*.

jet [dʒet] *n (aircraft)* jet *m inv* ; *(of liquid, gas)* getto *m* ; *(outlet)* ugello *m*.

jet lag *n* jetlag *m*.

jet-ski *n* acqua-scooter *m inv*.

jetty ['dʒetɪ] *n* molo *m*.

Jew [dʒuː] *n* ebreo *m*, -a *f*.

jewel ['dʒuːəl] *n* gioiello *m*. ❑ **jewels** *npl (jewellery)* gioielli *mpl*.

jeweler's ['dʒuːələz] *Am* = **jeweller's**.

jeweller's ['dʒuːələz] *n Br* gioielleria *f*.

jewellery ['dʒuːəlrɪ] *n Br* gioielli *mpl*.

jewelry ['dʒuːəlrɪ] *Am* = **jewellery**.

Jewish ['dʒuːɪʃ] *adj* ebreo(a).

jigsaw (puzzle) ['dʒɪgsɔː-] *n* puzzle *m inv*.

jingle ['dʒɪŋgl] *n (of advert)* motivo *m* musicale di pubblicità.

job [dʒɒb] *n* lavoro *m* ; **to lose one's ~** perdere il lavoro.

job centre *n Br* ufficio *m* di collocamento.

jockey ['dʒɒkɪ] (*pl* **-s**) *n* fantino *m*, -a *f*.

jog [dʒɒg] *vt (bump)* urtare lievemente. ◆ *vi* fare footing. ◆ *n* : **to go for a ~** andare a fare del footing.

jogging ['dʒɒgɪŋ] *n* footing *m* ; **to go ~** fare del footing.

join [dʒɔɪn] *vt (club, organization)* iscriversi a ; *(fasten together)* unire ; *(other people, celebrations)* unirsi a ; *(road, river)* congiungersi con ; *(connect)* collegare ; **to ~ a queue** mettersi in fila. ❑ **join in** *vt fus* prendere parte a. ◆ *vi* partecipare.

joint [dʒɔɪnt] *adj* comune. ◆ *n (of body)* articolazione *f* ; *Br (of meat)* taglio *m* di carne per arrosto ; *(in structure)* giuntura *f*.

joke [dʒəʊk] *n* scherzo *m* ; *(story)* barzelletta *f*. ◆ *vi* scherzare.

joker ['dʒəʊkəʳ] *n (playing card)* jolly *m inv*, matta *f*.

jolly ['dʒɒlɪ] *adj (cheerful)* allegro(a). ◆ *adv Br inf (very)* molto.

jolt [dʒəʊlt] *n* scossa *f*, sobbalzo *m*.

jot [dʒɒt] ◆**jot down** *vt sep* annotare in fretta.

journal ['dʒɜːnl] *n (professional magazine)* rivista *f* ; *(diary)* diario *m*.

journalist ['dʒɜːnəlɪst] *n* giornalista *mf*.

journey ['dʒɜːnɪ] (*pl* **-s**) *n* viaggio *m*.

joy [dʒɔɪ] *n* gioia *f*.

joypad ['dʒɔɪpæd] *n (of video game)* comandi *mpl*.

joyrider ['dʒɔɪraɪdəʳ] *n chi ruba un'auto per farci un giro e poi l'abbandona*.

joystick ['dʒɔɪstɪk] *n (of video game)* joystick *m inv*.

judge [dʒʌdʒ] *n* giudice *mf*. ◆ *vt* giudicare.

judg(e)ment ['dʒʌdʒmənt] *n* giudizio *m*.

judo ['dʒuːdəʊ] *n* judo *m*.

jug [dʒʌg] *n* brocca *f*, caraffa *f*.

juggernaut ['dʒʌgənɔːt] *n Br* grosso autotreno *m*, bestione *m*.

juggle ['dʒʌgl] *vi* fare giochi di destrezza *(con palle, birilli, ecc.)*.

juice [dʒuːs] *n* succo *m* ; *(from meat)* sugo *m*.

juicy ['dʒu:sɪ] *adj (food)* succoso(a).

jukebox ['dʒu:kbɒks] *n* juke-box *m inv*.

Jul. (*abbr of July*) lug.

July [dʒu:'laɪ] *n* luglio *m* → **September.**

jumble sale ['dʒʌmbl-] *n Br* vendita *f* di cose usate *(a scopo di beneficenza)*.

jumbo ['dʒʌmbəu] *adj inf (big)* gigante.

jumbo jet *n* jumbo-jet *m inv*.

jump [dʒʌmp] *n* salto *m*, balzo *m*. ◆ *vi* saltare, balzare ; *(with fright)* sussultare ; *(increase)* salire. ◆ *vt Am* : **to ~ the train/bus** viaggiare sul treno/sull'autobus senza pagare ; **to ~ the queue** *Br* saltare la fila.

jumper ['dʒʌmpəʳ] *n Br (pullover)* maglione *m*, pullover *m inv* ; *Am (dress)* scamiciato *m*.

jump leads *npl* cavi *mpl* per batteria.

Jun. (*abbr of June*) giu.

junction ['dʒʌŋkʃn] *n (of roads)* incrocio *m* ; *(of railway lines)* nodo *m* ferroviario ; *(on motorways)* uscita *f*.

June [dʒu:n] *n* giugno *m* → **September.**

jungle ['dʒʌŋgl] *n* giungla *f*.

junior ['dʒu:njəʳ] *adj (of lower rank)* di grado inferiore, subalterno(a) ; *Am (after name)* junior. ◆ *n (younger person)* : **to be sb's ~** essere più giovane di qn.

junior school *n Br* scuola *f* elementare *(per bambini da 7 a 11 anni)*.

junk [dʒʌŋk] *n inf (unwanted things)* cianfrusaglie *fpl*.

junk food *n inf* porcherie *fpl*.

junkie ['dʒʌŋkɪ] *n inf* drogato *m*, -a *f*.

junk shop *n* negozio *m* di rigattiere.

jury ['dʒuərɪ] *n* giuria *f*.

just [dʒʌst] *adv (recently, slightly)* appena ; *(in the next moment)* giusto ; *(exactly)* proprio ; *(only)* solo. ◆ *adj* giusto(a) ; **to be ~ about to do sthg** stare per fare qc ; **to have ~ done sthg** avere appena fatto qc ; **~ about** *(almost)* praticamente, quasi ; **(only) ~** per un pelo ; **I've (only) ~ arrived** sono arrivato (appena) adesso ; **I'm ~ coming** vengo (subito) ; **~ a minute!** (solo) un minuto!

justice ['dʒʌstɪs] *n* giustizia *f*.

justify ['dʒʌstɪfaɪ] *vt* giustificare.

jut [dʒʌt] ◆**jut out** *vi* sporgersi.

juvenile ['dʒu:vənaɪl] *adj (young)* giovanile ; *(childish)* puerile ; *(crime)* minorile.

K

kangaroo [ˌkæŋgə'ru:] *n* canguro *m*.

karate [kə'ra:tɪ] *n* karate *m*.

kebab [kɪ'bæb] *n* : **(shish) ~** spiedino *m* di carne ; **(doner) ~** *pane azzimo imbottito con carne di agnello, insalata e salsa piccante*.

keel [ki:l] *n* chiglia *f*.

keen [kiːn] *adj (enthusiastic)* entusiasta ; *(eyesight, hearing)* acuto(a) ; **to be ~ on sthg** essere appassionato(a) di qc ; **to be ~ to do sthg** avere voglia di fare qc.

keep [kiːp] *(pt & pp* **kept**) *vt* tenere ; *(promise)* mantenere ; *(appointment)* rispettare ; *(delay)* trattenere. ◆ *vi (food)* mantenersi ; *(remain)* restare ; **to ~ (on) doing sthg** *(continuously)* continuare a fare qc ; *(repeatedly)* fare qc di continuo ; **to ~ sb from doing sthg** impedire a qn di fare qc ; **~ back!** state indietro! ; **'~ in lane!'** 'restare in corsia' ; **'~ left'** 'tenere la sinistra' ; **'~ off the grass!'** 'vietato calpestare l'erba' ; **'~ out!'** 'vietato l'accesso' ; **'~ your distance!'** 'mantenere la distanza (di sicurezza)' ; **to ~ clear (of)** stare lontano (da). ❑ **keep up** ◆ *vt sep* mantenere, continuare. ◆ *vi* : **to ~ up (with)** tenersi al passo (con).

keep-fit *n Br* ginnastica *f*.

kennel ['kenl] *n* canile *m*.

kept [kept] *pt & pp* → **keep**.

kerb [kɜːb] *n Br* bordo *m* del marciapiede.

kerosene ['kerəsiːn] *n Am* cherosene *m*.

ketchup ['ketʃəp] *n* ketchup *m*.

kettle ['ketl] *n* bollitore *m* ; **to put the ~ on** mettere l'acqua a bollire.

key [kiː] *n* chiave *f*; *(of piano, typewriter)* tasto *m* ; *(of map)* leggenda *f*. ◆ *adj* chiave *(inv)*).

keyboard ['kiːbɔːd] *n* tastiera *f*.

keyhole ['kiːhəʊl] *n* buco *m* della serratura.

keypad ['kiːpæd] *n* tastiera *f*.

key ring *n* portachiavi *m inv*.

kg *(abbr of kilogram)* kg.

kick [kɪk] *n (of foot)* calcio *m*. ◆ *vt* dare calci a, prendere a calci.

kickoff ['kɪkɒf] *n* calcio *m* d'inizio.

kid [kɪd] *n inf (child)* bimbo *m*, -a *f*, bambino *m*, -a *f* ; *(young person)* ragazzo *m*, -a *f*. ◆ *vi (joke)* scherzare.

kidnap ['kɪdnæp] *vt* rapire.

kidnaper ['kɪdnæpər] *Am* = **kidnapper**.

kidnapper ['kɪdnæpə^r] *n Br* rapitore *m*, -trice *f*.

kidney ['kɪdnɪ] *(pl* **-s**) *n (organ)* rene *m* ; *(food)* rognone *m*.

kidney bean *n* fagiolo *m* comune.

kill [kɪl] *vt (person)* uccidere, ammazzare ; *(time)* ammazzare ; **my feet are ~ing me!** i piedi mi fanno un male!

killer ['kɪlə^r] *n* assassino *m*, -a *f*.

kilo ['kiːləʊ] *(pl* **-s**) *n* chilo *m*.

kilogram ['kɪləˌgræm] *n* chilogrammo *m*.

kilometre ['kɪləˌmiːtə^r] *n* chilometro *m*.

kilt [kɪlt] *n* kilt *m inv*.

kind [kaɪnd] *adj* gentile, buono(a). ◆ *n (sort, type)* genere *m*, tipo *m* ; **~ of** *Am inf* un po'.

kindergarten ['kɪndəˌgaːtn] *n* asilo *m* infantile.

kindly ['kaɪndlɪ] *adv* : **would you ~ ...?** potrebbe ..., per favore?

kindness ['kaɪndnɪs] *n* gentilezza *f*, cortesia *f*.

king [kɪŋ] *n* re *m inv*.

kingfisher ['kɪŋˌfɪʃəʳ] *n* martin *m* pescatore, *-i pl.*

king prawn *n* gambero *m.*

king-size bed *n letto largo 160 cm.*

kiosk ['kiːɒsk] *n (for newspapers etc)* chiosco *m*, edicola *f* ; *Br (phone box)* cabina *f* (telefonica).

kipper ['kɪpəʳ] *n* aringa *f* affumicata.

kiss [kɪs] *n* bacio *m.* ◆ *v t* baciare.

kiss of life *n* respirazione *f* bocca a bocca.

kit [kɪt] *n (set)* attrezzatura *f* ; *(clothes)* completo *m* ; *(for assembly)* scatola *f* di montaggio.

kitchen ['kɪtʃɪn] *n* cucina *f.*

kitchen unit *n* mobile *m* componibile (da cucina).

kite [kaɪt] *n (toy)* aquilone *m.*

kitten ['kɪtn] *n* gattino *m*, -a *f.*

kitty ['kɪtɪ] *n (of money)* cassa *f* comune.

kiwi fruit ['kiːwiː-] *n* kiwi *m inv.*

Kleenex® ['kliːneks] *n* fazzoletto *m* di carta.

km (*abbr of kilometre*) km.

km/h (*abbr of kilometres per hour*) km/h.

knack [næk] *n* : **to have the ~ of doing sthg** avere l'abilità di fare qc.

knackered ['nækəd] *adj Br inf* stanco morto (stanca morta).

knapsack ['næpsæk] *n* zaino *m.*

knee [niː] *n* ginocchio *m.*

kneecap ['niːkæp] *n* rotula *f.*

kneel [niːl] (*pt* & *pp* **knelt** [nelt]) *vi* inginocchiarsi.

knew [njuː] *pt* → **know.**

knickers ['nɪkəz] *npl Br (underwear)* mutandine *fpl.*

knife [naɪf] (*pl* **knives**) *n* coltello *m.*

knight [naɪt] *n (in history)* cavaliere *m* ; *(in chess)* cavallo *m.*

knit [nɪt] *vt* fare a maglia.

knitted ['nɪtɪd] *adj* fatto(a) a maglia.

knitting ['nɪtɪŋ] *n* lavoro *m* a maglia.

knitting needle *n* ferro *m* (da calza).

knitwear ['nɪtweəʳ] *n* maglieria *f.*

knives [naɪvz] *pl* → **knife.**

knob [nɒb] *n (on door etc)* pomello *m* ; *(on machine)* manopola *f.*

knock [nɒk] *n (at door)* colpo *m.* ◆ *v t (head, elbow)* battere ; *(chair, table)* sbattere contro. ◆ *vi (at door etc)* bussare. ❑ **knock down** *vt sep (pedestrian)* investire ; *(building)* demolire ; *(price)* ribassare. ❑ **knock out** *vt sep (make unconscious)* tramortire ; *(of competition)* eliminare. ❑ **knock over** *vt sep (glass, vase)* rovesciare ; *(pedestrian)* investire.

knocker ['nɒkəʳ] *n (on door)* battente *m.*

knot [nɒt] *n* nodo *m.*

know [nəʊ] (*pt* **knew**, *pp* **known**) *vt* sapere ; *(person, place)* conoscere ; **to get to ~ sb** imparare a conoscere qc ; **to ~ about sthg** *(understand)* saperne di qc ; *(have heard)* sapere di qc ; **to ~ how to do sthg** saper fare qc ; **to ~ of** sapere di ; **to be ~n as** essere noto come ; **to let**

sb ~ sthg far sapere qc a qn ; you ~ *(for emphasis)* sai.

knowledge ['nɒlɪdʒ] *n* conoscenza *f* ; to my ~ che io sappia.

known [nəʊn] *pp* → know.

knuckle ['nʌkl] *n (of hand)* nocca *f* ; *(of pork)* garretto *m*.

L

l *(abbr of litre)* l.

L *(abbr of learner)* ≃ P.

lab [læb] *n inf* laboratorio *m*.

label ['leɪbl] *n* cartellino *m*, etichetta *f*.

labor ['leɪbər] *Am* = labour.

laboratory [*Br* lə'bɒrətrɪ, *Am* 'læbrəˌtɔːrɪ] *n* laboratorio *m*.

labour ['leɪbəʳ] *n (work)* lavoro *m* ; to be in ~ *MED* avere le doglie.

labourer ['leɪbərəʳ] *n* manovale *m*.

Labour Party *n Br* partito *m* laburista.

labour-saving *adj* che fa risparmiare fatica.

lace [leɪs] *n (material)* merletto *m* ; *(for shoe)* laccio *m*.

lace-ups *npl* scarpe *fpl* con i lacci.

lack [læk] *n* carenza *f*. ◆ *vt* non avere. ◆ *vi* : to be ~ing mancare.

lacquer ['lækəʳ] *n (for hair)* lacca *f* ; *(paint)* vernice *f*.

lad [læd] *n inf* ragazzo *m*.

ladder ['lædəʳ] *n (for climbing)* scala *f* ; *Br (in tights)* smagliatura *f*.

ladies ['leɪdɪz] *n Br (toilet)* toilette *f inv* per signore.

ladies room *Am* = ladies.

ladieswear ['leɪdɪzˌweəʳ] *n* abbigliamento *m* da donna.

ladle ['leɪdl] *n* mestolo *m*.

lady ['leɪdɪ] *n* signora *f*.

ladybird ['leɪdɪbɜːd] *n* coccinella *f*.

ladybug ['leɪdɪbʌg] *n Am* = ladybird.

lag [læg] *vi (trade)* ristagnare ; to ~ behind *(move more slowly)* restare indietro.

lager ['lɑːgəʳ] *n* birra *f* (chiara).

lagoon [lə'guːn] *n* laguna *f*.

laid [leɪd] *pt* & *pp* → lay.

lain [leɪn] *pp* → lie.

lake [leɪk] *n* lago *m*.

lamb [læm] *n* agnello *m*.

lamb chop *n* braciola *f* OR costoletta d'agnello.

lame [leɪm] *adj* zoppo(a).

lamp [læmp] *n* lampada *f* ; *(bicycle lamp)* fanale *m* ; *(in street)* lampione *m*.

lamppost ['læmppəʊst] *n* lampione *m*.

lampshade ['læmpʃeɪd] *n* paralume *m*.

land [lænd] *n* terra *f*. ◆ *vi (plane)* atterrare ; *(passengers)* sbarcare ; *(fall)* cadere.

landing ['lændɪŋ] *n (of plane)* atterraggio *m* ; *(on stairs)* pianerottolo *m*.

landlady ['lændˌleɪdɪ] *n (of house)* padrona *f* di casa ; *(of pub)* proprietaria *f*.

landlord ['lændlɔːd] *n (of house)*

padrone *m* di casa ; *(of pub)* proprietario *m*.

landmark ['lændma:k] *n* punto *m* di riferimento.

landscape ['lændskeɪp] *n* paesaggio *m*.

landslide ['lændslaɪd] *n (of earth, rocks)* frana *f*.

lane [leɪn] *n (narrow road)* stradina *f* ; *(on road, motorway)* corsia *f* ; **'get in ~'** 'disporsi su più file'.

language ['læŋgwɪdʒ] *n (of a people, country)* lingua *f* ; *(system, words)* linguaggio *m*.

lap [læp] *n (of person)* grembo *m* ; *(of race)* giro *m*.

lapel [lə'pel] *n* risvolto *m*.

lapse [læps] *vi (passport, membership)* scadere.

lard [la:d] *n* strutto *m*.

larder ['la:dəʳ] *n* dispensa *f*.

large [la:dʒ] *adj* grande ; *(person, dog, sum)* grosso(a).

largely ['la:dʒlɪ] *adv* in gran parte.

large-scale *adj* su vasta scala.

lark [la:k] *n* allodola *f*.

laryngitis [ˌlærɪn'dʒaɪtɪs] *n* laringite *f*.

lasagne [lə'zænjə] *n* lasagne *fpl*.

laser ['leɪzəʳ] *n* laser *m inv*.

lass [læs] *n inf* ragazza *f*.

last [la:st] *adj* ultimo(a) ; *(week, year, month)* scorso(a). ◆ *adv (most recently)* l'ultima volta ; *(after everything else)* per ultimo. ◆ *vi (continue)* durare. ◆ *pron* : **the ~ to come** l'ultimo ad arrivare ; **the ~ but one** il penultimo (la penultima) ; **the day before ~** l'altro ieri ; **~ year** l'anno scorso ; **at ~** finalmente ; **to arrive ~** arrivare (per) ultimo ; **it won't ~ till tomorrow** *(food)* non va fino a domani.

lastly ['la:stlɪ] *adv* infine.

last-minute *adj* dell'ultimo momento.

latch [lætʃ] *n* serratura *f* a scatto ; **the door is on the ~** la porta non è chiusa a chiave.

late [leɪt] *adj (not on time)* in ritardo ; *(after usual time)* tardi *(inv)* ; *(dead)* defunto(a) ; *(morning, afternoon)* tardo(a). ◆ *adv (not on time)* in ritardo ; *(after usual time)* tardi ; **in ~ June, ~ in June** verso la fine di giugno ; **the train is running two hours ~** il treno viaggia con due ore di ritardo.

lately ['leɪtlɪ] *adv* ultimamente.

late-night *adj* aperto(a) fino a tardi ; **~ opening** apertura prolungata *(di negozi)*.

later ['leɪtəʳ] *adj (train)* successivo(a). ◆ *adv* : **~ (on)** più tardi ; **at a ~ date** in futuro.

latest ['leɪtɪst] *adj* : **the ~ fashion** l'ultima moda ; **the ~** l'ultimo(a) ; **at the ~** al più tardi.

lather ['la:ðəʳ] *n* schiuma *f*.

Latin ['lætɪn] *n* latino *m*.

Latin America *n* l'America *f* Latina.

Latin American *adj* latinoamericano *m*, -a *f*. ◆ *n* latinoamericano *m*, -a *f*.

latitude ['lætɪtju:d] *n (distance from Equator)* latitudine *f*.

latter ['lætəʳ] *n* : **the ~** quest'ultimo(a).

laugh [la:f] *n* risata *f*. ◆ *v i* ridere ; **to have a ~** *Br inf* farsi quattro risate. ❑ **laugh at** *vt fus (mock)* ridere di.

laughter ['lɑːftəʳ] *n* riso *m.*

launch [lɔːntʃ] *vt (boat)* varare ; *(new product)* lanciare.

laund(e)rette [lɔːn'dret] *n* lavanderia *f* (automatica).

laundry ['lɔːndrɪ] *n (washing)* bucato *m* ; *(place)* lavanderia *f.*

lavatory ['lævətrɪ] *n* gabinetto *m.*

lavender ['lævəndəʳ] *n* lavanda *f.*

lavish ['lævɪʃ] *adj (meal,decoration)* sontuoso(a).

law [lɔː] *n* legge *f*; **to be against the ~** essere contro la legge.

lawn [lɔːn] *n* prato *m.*

lawnmower ['lɔːn,məʊəʳ] *n* tagliaerba *m inv.*

lawyer ['lɔːjəʳ] *n (in court)* avvocato *m* ; *(solicitor)* notaio *m.*

laxative ['læksətɪv] *n* lassativo *m.*

lay [leɪ] (*pt* & *pp* **laid**) *pt* → **lie.** ◆ *vt (place)* poggiare ; *(egg)* fare ; **to ~ the table** apparecchiare la tavola. ❑ **lay off** *vt sep (worker)* licenziare. ❑ **lay on** *vt sep (food, transport)* fornire ; *(entertainment)* organizzare. ❑ **lay out** *vt sep (display)* disporre.

lay-by (*pl* **lay-bys**) *n* piazzola *f* di sosta.

layer ['leɪəʳ] *n* strato *m.*

layman ['leɪmən] (*pl* **-men** [-mən]) *n* profano *m*, -a *f.*

layout ['leɪaʊt] *n (of building)* struttura *f*; *(of streets)* tracciato *m.*

lazy ['leɪzɪ] *adj* pigro(a).

lb *abbr* = **pound.**

lead¹ [liːd] (*pt* & *pp* **led**) *vt (take)* condurre ; *(team, party, march)* guidare ; *(procession)* aprire. ◆ *vi (be winning)* condurre. ◆ *n (for dog)* guinzaglio *m* ; *(cable)* cavo *m* ; **to ~ sb to do sthg** indurre qn a fare qc ; **to ~ to** portare a ; **to ~ the way** fare strada ; **to be in the ~** essere in testa.

lead² [led] *n* piombo *m* ; *(for pencil)* mina *f.* ◆ *adj* di piombo.

leaded petrol ['ledɪd-] *n* benzina *f* con piombo.

leader ['liːdəʳ] *n (of group)* capo *m* ; *(of union, party)* leader *mf inv* ; *(in race)* chi è in testa.

leadership ['liːdəʃɪp] *n (position)* direzione *f.*

lead-free [led-] *adj* senza piombo.

leading ['liːdɪŋ] *adj (most important)* principale.

lead singer [liːd-] *n* cantante *mf (solista).*

leaf [liːf] (*pl* **leaves**) *n (of tree)* foglia *f.*

leaflet ['liːflɪt] *n* depliant *m inv.*

league [liːg] *n* SPORT campionato *m* ; *(association)* lega *f.*

leak [liːk] *n (hole)* buco *m* ; *(of gas, water)* perdita *f.* ◆ *vi (tank)* perdere ; *(roof)* gocciolare.

lean [liːn] (*pt* & *pp* **leant** [lent], **-ed**) *adj (meat)* magro(a) ; *(person, animal)* asciutto(a). ◆ *vi (bend)* piegarsi ; *(building)* pendere. ◆ *vt* : **to ~ sthg against sthg** appoggiare qc a qc ; **to ~ on** appoggiarsi a. ❑ **lean forward** *vi* sporgersi (in avanti). ❑ **lean over** *vi* sporgersi.

leap [liːp] (*pt* & *pp* **leapt** [lept], **-ed**) *vi (jump)* balzare.

leap year *n* anno *m* bisestile.

learn [lɜːn] (*pt* & *pp* **learnt** OR **-ed**) *vt* imparare ; **to ~ (how) to do sthg** imparare a fare qc ; **to ~ about sthg** *(hear about)* venire a sapere (di) qc ; *(study)* studiare qc.

learner (driver) ['lɜːnəʳ-] *n* guidatore *m*, -trice *f* principiante.

learnt [lɜːnt] *pt & pp* → **learn**.

lease [liːs] *n* contratto *m* d'affitto. ◆ *vt* affittare ; **to ~ sthg from sb** affittare qc da qn ; **to ~ sthg to sb** affittare qc a qn.

leash [liːʃ] *n* guinzaglio *m*.

least [liːst] *adv* meno (di tutti). ◆ *adj* meno ... di tutti. ◆ *pron* : **(the) ~** meno di tutti ; **at ~** almeno ; **the ~ he could do** il minimo che potesse fare.

leather ['leðəʳ] *n* cuoio *m*, pelle *f*. ❑ **leathers** *npl (of motorcyclist)* tuta *f* di pelle da motociclista.

leave [liːv] (*pt* & *pp* **left**) *vt* lasciare ; *(school)* finire. ◆ *vi (go away)* andarsene ; *(train, bus)* partire. ◆ *n (time off work)* permesso *m* ; **to ~ a message** lasciare un messaggio, left. ❑ **leave behind** *vt sep (not take away)* lasciare. ❑ **leave out** *vt sep* tralasciare.

leaves [liːvz] *pl* → **leaf**.

lecture ['lektʃəʳ] *n (at university)* lezione *f* ; *(at conference)* conferenza *f*.

lecturer ['lektʃərəʳ] *n* docente *mf* (universitario).

lecture theatre *n* aula *f (ad anfiteatro)*.

led [led] *pt & pp* → **lead** ¹.

ledge [ledʒ] *n (of window)* davanzale *m*.

leek [liːk] *n* porro *m*.

left [left] *pt & pp* → **leave**. ◆ *adj (not right)* sinistro(a). ◆ *adv* a sinistra. ◆ *n* sinistra *f* ; **on the ~** a sinistra ; **there are none ~** sono finiti.

left-hand *adj (side)* sinistro(a) ; *(lane)* di sinistra.

left-hand drive *n* guida *f* a sinistra.

left-handed [-'hændɪd] *adj (person)* mancino(a) ; *(implement)* per mancini.

left-luggage locker *n Br* armadietto *m* per deposito bagagli.

left-luggage office *n Br* deposito *m* bagagli.

left-wing *adj* di sinistra.

leg [leg] *n* gamba *f* ; *(of animal)* zampa *f* ; **~ of lamb** cosciotto *f* d'agnello.

legal ['liːgl] *adj* legale.

legal aid *n* assistenza *f* legale gratuita.

legalize ['liːgəlaɪz] *vt* legalizzare.

legal system *n* sistema *f* legale.

legend ['ledʒənd] *n* leggenda *f*.

leggings ['legɪŋz] *npl* fuseaux *mpl*, pantacollant *mpl*.

legible ['ledʒɪbl] *adj* leggibile.

legislation [ˌledʒɪs'leɪʃn] *n* legislazione *f*.

legitimate [lɪ'dʒɪtɪmət] *adj* legittimo(a).

leisure [*Br* 'leʒəʳ, *Am* 'liːʒər] *n* tempo *m* libero.

leisure centre *n* centro *m* sportivo.

leisure pool *n* piscina *f*.

lemon ['lemən] *n* limone *m*.

lemonade [ˌleməˈneɪd] *n* limonata *f*.
lemon curd [-kɜːd] *n Br sorta di marmellata a base di succo e scorza di limone, uova, burro e zucchero.*
lemon juice *n* succo *m* di limone.
lemon sole *n* limanda *f (varietà di sogliola)*.
lemon tea *n* tè *m* al limone.
lend [lend] (*pt* & *pp* **lent**) *vt* prestare ; **to ~ sb sthg** prestare qc a qn.
length [leŋθ] *n (in distance)* lunghezza *f*; *(in time)* durata *f*; *(of swimming pool)* vasca *f*.
lengthen [ˈleŋθən] *vt* allungare.
lens [lenz] *n* lente *f*.
lent [lent] *pt & pp* → **lend**.
Lent [lent] *n* Quaresima *f*.
lentils [ˈlentlz] *npl* lenticchie *fpl*.
Leo (*pl* -s) *n* Leone *m*.
leopard [ˈlepəd] *n* leopardo *m*.
leopard-skin *adj* a pelle di leopardo.
leotard [ˈliːətaːd] *n* calzamaglia *f*.
leper [ˈlepəʳ] *n* lebbroso *m*, -a *f*.
lesbian [ˈlezbɪən] *adj* lesbico(a). ◆ *n* lesbica *f*.
less [les] *adj,adv* & *pron* meno ; **~ than20** meno di 20.
lesson [ˈlesn] *n (class)* lezione *f*.
let [let] (*pt* & *pp* **let**) *vt (allow)* lasciare ; *(rent out)* affittare ; **to ~ sb do sthg** lasciar fare qc a qn ; **to ~ go of sthg** mollare qc ; **to ~ sb have sthg** *(give)* dare qc a qn ; **to ~ sb know sthg** far sapere qc a qn ; **~'s go!** andiamo! ; **'to ~'** 'affittasi'. ❑ **let in** *vt sep (allow to enter)* far entrare. ❑ **let off** *vt sep (excuse)* : **to ~ sb off doing sthg** dispensare qn dal fare qc ; **can you ~ me off at the station?** mi fa scendere alla stazione? ❑ **let out** *vt sep (allow to go out)* far uscire.
letdown [ˈletdaʊn] *n inf* delusione *f*.
lethargic [ləˈθaːdʒɪk] *adj* apatico(a).
letter [ˈletəʳ] *n* lettera *f*.
letterbox [ˈletəbɒks] *n Br* buca *f* delle lettere.
lettuce [ˈletɪs] *n* lattuga *f*.
leuk(a)emia [luːˈkiːmɪə] *n* leucemia *f*.
level [ˈlevl] *adj (flat)* piano(a) ; *(horizontal)* orizzontale. ◆ *n* livello *m* ; *(storey)* piano *m* ; **to be ~ with** essere allo stesso livello di.
level crossing *n Br* passaggio *m* a livello.
lever [*Br* ˈliːvəʳ, *Am* ˈlevər] *n* leva *f*.
liability [ˌlaɪəˈbɪlətɪ] *n (responsibility)* responsabilità *f*.
liable [ˈlaɪəbl] *adj* : **to be ~ to do sthg** avere la tendenza a fare qc ; **to be ~ for sthg** rispondere di qc.
liaise [lɪˈeɪz] *vi* : **to ~ with** mantenere i contatti con.
liar [ˈlaɪəʳ] *n* bugiardo *m*, -a *f*.
liberal [ˈlɪbərəl] *adj (tolerant)* liberale ; *(generous)* generoso(a).
liberate [ˈlɪbəreɪt] *vt* liberare.
liberty [ˈlɪbətɪ] *n* libertà *f inv*.
Libra *n* Bilancia *f*.
librarian [laɪˈbreərɪən] *n* bibliotecario *m*, -a *f*.
library [ˈlaɪbrərɪ] *n* biblioteca *f*.
lice [laɪs] *npl* pidocchi.
licence [ˈlaɪsəns] *n Br (official document)* licenza *f*. ◆ *vt Am* =

license ; driving ~ patente *f (di guida)* ; TV ~ abbonamento *m* alla televisione.
license ['laɪsəns] *vt Br* autorizzare. ◆ *n Am* = licence.
licensed ['laɪsənst] *adj (restaurant, bar) munito di licenza per la vendita di alcolici.*
licensing hours ['laɪsənsɪŋ-] *npl Br orario in cui è consentita la vendita di alcolici.*
lick [lɪk] *vt* leccare.
lid [lɪd] *n (cover)* coperchio *m*.
lie [laɪ] (*pt* lay, *pp* lain, *cont* lying) *n* bugia *f*. ◆ *vi (tell lie : pt & pp lied)* mentire ; *(be horizontal)* essere disteso ; *(lie down)* sdraiarsi ; *(be situated)* trovarsi ; to tell ~s dire bugie ; to ~ about sthg mentire su qc. ❑ **lie down** *vi* sdraiarsi.
lieutenant [*Br* lef'tenənt, *Am* luː'tenənt] *n* tenente *m*.
life [laɪf] (*pl* lives) *n* vita *f*.
life assurance *n* assicurazione *f* sulla vita.
life belt *n* salvagente *m*.
lifeboat ['laɪfbəʊt] *n* scialuppa *f* di salvataggio.
lifeguard ['laɪfgaːd] *n* bagnino *m*, -a *f*.
life jacket *n* giubbotto *m* di salvataggio.
lifelike ['laɪflaɪk] *adj* fedele.
life preserver [-prɪ'zɜːvər] *n [Am] (life belt)* salvagente *m* ; *(life jacket)* giubbotto *m* di salvataggio.
life-size *adj* a grandezza naturale.
lifespan ['laɪfspæn] *n* vita *f*.
lifestyle ['laɪfstaɪl] *n* stile *m* di vita.
lift [lɪft] *n Br (elevator)* ascensore *m*. ◆ *vt (raise)* sollevare, alzare. ◆ *vi (fog)* alzarsi ; to give sb a ~ dare un passaggio a qn. ❑ **lift up** *vt sep* sollevare, alzare.
light [laɪt] (*pt* & *pp* lit OR -ed) *adj* leggero(a) ; *(not dark)* chiaro(a) ; *(traffic)* scorrevole. ◆ *n* luce *f* ; *(of car, bike)* faro *m*. ◆ *vt (fire, cigarette)* accendere ; *(room, stage)* illuminare ; have you got a ~? hai da accendere? ; to set ~ to sthg dar fuoco a qc. ❑ **lights** *npl (traffic lights)* semaforo *m*. ❑ **light up** ◆ *vt sep (house, road)* illuminare. ◆ *vi inf (light a cigarette)* accendersi una sigaretta.
light bulb *n* lampadina *f*.
lighter ['laɪtə'] *n* accendino *m*.
light-hearted [-'haːtɪd] *adj* gioviale.
lighthouse ['laɪthaʊs, *pl* -haʊzɪz] *n* faro *m*.
lighting ['laɪtɪŋ] *n* illuminazione *f*.
light meter *n* contatore *m* della luce.
lightning ['laɪtnɪŋ] *n* lampi *mpl*, fulmini *mpl*.
lightweight ['laɪtweɪt] *adj (clothes, object)* leggero(a).
like [laɪk] *prep* come ; *(typical of)* tipico di. ◆ *vt (want)* volere ; I ~ it mi piace ; I ~ them mi piacciono ; I ~ going out mi piace uscire ; I'd ~ to sit down vorrei sedermi ; I'd ~ a drink vorrei bere qualcosa ; what's it ~? com'è? ; to look ~ sb assomigliare a qn ; do it ~ this fallo così ; it's not ~ him non è da lui.
likelihood ['laɪklɪhʊd] *n* probabilità *f*.

likely ['laɪklɪ] *adj* probabile.

likeness ['laɪknɪs] *n* somiglianza *f*.

likewise ['laɪkwaɪz] *adv* allo stesso modo ; **to do ~** fare lo stesso.

lilac ['laɪlək] *adj* lilla *(inv)*.

Lilo® ['laɪləʊ] (*pl* **-s**) *n Br* materassino *m* (pneumatico).

lily ['lɪlɪ] *n* giglio *m*.

lily of the valley *n* mughetto *m*.

limb [lɪm] *n* arto *m*.

lime [laɪm] *n (fruit)* limetta *f* ; **~ (juice)** succo *m* di limetta.

limestone ['laɪmstəʊn] *n* calcare *m*.

limit ['lɪmɪt] *n* limite *m*. ◆ *vt* limitare ; **the city ~s** i confini della città.

limited ['lɪmɪtɪd] *adj (restricted)* limitato(a) ; *(in company name)* a responsabilità limitata.

limp [lɪmp] *adj* floscio(a). ◆ *vi* zoppicare.

line [laɪn] *n* linea *f* ; *(row)* fila *f* ; *Am (queue)* coda *f*, fila ; *(of words on page)* riga *f* ; *(of poem, song)* verso *m* ; *(for fishing)* lenza *f* ; *(rope, washing line)* corda *f* ; *(of business, work)* settore *m*, ramo *m*. ◆ *vt (coat, drawers)* foderare ; **in ~** *(aligned)* allineato ; **it's a bad ~** la linea è disturbata ; **the ~ is engaged** la linea è occupata ; **to drop sb a ~** *inf* mandare due righe a qn ; **to stand in ~** *Am* stare in fila. ❑ **line up** ◆ *vt sep (arrange)* organizzare. ◆ *vi* allinearsi.

lined [laɪnd] *adj (paper)* rigato(a), a righe.

linen ['lɪnɪn] *n (cloth)* lino *m* ; *(tablecloths, sheets)* biancheria *f*.

liner ['laɪnə^r] *n (ship)* nave *f* di linea.

linesman ['laɪnzmən] (*pl* **-men** [-mən]) *n* guardalinee *m inv*.

linger ['lɪŋgə^r] *vi (in place)* attardarsi.

lingerie ['lænʒərɪ] *n* biancheria *f* intima *(femminile)*.

lining ['laɪnɪŋ] *n (of coat, jacket)* fodera *f* ; *(of brake)* guarnizione *f*.

link [lɪŋk] *n (connection)* collegamento *m* ; *(between countries, companies)* relazione *f*. ◆ *vt (connect)* collegare ; **rail ~** collegamento ferroviario ; **road ~** collegamento stradale.

lino ['laɪnəʊ] *n Br* linoleum *m*.

lion ['laɪən] *n* leone *m*.

lioness ['laɪənes] *n* leonessa *f*.

lip [lɪp] *n (of person)* labbro *m*.

lip salve [-sælv] *n* burro *m* di cacao.

lipstick ['lɪpstɪk] *n* rossetto *m*.

liqueur [lɪ'kjʊə^r] *n* liquore *m* (dolce).

liquid ['lɪkwɪd] *n* liquido *m*.

liquor ['lɪkər] *n Am* superalcolico *m*.

liquorice ['lɪkərɪs] *n* liquirizia *f*.

lisp [lɪsp] *n* difetto *f* di pronuncia *(relativo alla lettera s)*.

list [lɪst] *n* lista *f*, elenco *m*. ◆ *vt* elencare.

listen ['lɪsn] *vi* : **to ~ (to)** ascoltare.

listener ['lɪsnə^r] *n (on radio)* ascoltatore *m*, -trice *f*.

lit [lɪt] *pt & pp* → **light**.

liter ['li:tər] *Am* = litre.

literally ['lɪtərəlɪ] *adv* letteralmente.

literary ['lɪtərərɪ] *adj* letterario(a).

literature ['lɪtrətʃəʳ] *n* letteratura *f* ; *(printed information)* materiale *m* illustrativo.

litre ['li:təʳ] *n Br* litro *m*.

litter ['lɪtəʳ] *n (rubbish)* rifiuti *mpl*.

litterbin ['lɪtəbɪn] *n Br* cestino *m* dei rifiuti.

little ['lɪtl] *adj* piccolo(a) ; *(not much)* poco(a). ◆ *pron & adv* poco ; **as ~ as possible** il meno possibile ; **~ by ~** poco a poco. ❑ **a little** ◆ *pron & adv* un po'. ◆ *adj* un po' di.

little finger *n* mignolo *m*.

live¹ [lɪv] *vi* vivere ; *(have home)* vivere, abitare ; **to ~ with sb** vivere con qn. ❑ **live together** *vi* vivere insieme.

live² [laɪv] *adj (alive)* vivo(a) ; *(programme, performance)* dal vivo ; *(wire)* sotto tensione. ◆ *adv* in diretta.

lively ['laɪvlɪ] *adj (person)* vivace ; *(place, atmosphere)* animato(a).

liver ['lɪvəʳ] *n* fegato *m*.

lives [laɪvz] *pl* → **life**.

living ['lɪvɪŋ] *adj* vivente. ◆ *n* : **to earn a ~** guadagnarsi da vivere ; **what do you do for a ~?** che lavoro fa?

living room *n* soggiorno *m*.

lizard ['lɪzəd] *n* lucertola *f*.

load [ləud] *n (thing carried)* carico *m*. ◆ *vt* caricare ; **~s of** *inf* un sacco di.

loaf [ləuf] (*pl* **loaves**) *n* : **a ~ (of bread)** una pagnotta.

loan [ləun] *n* prestito *m*. ◆ *vt* prestare.

loathe [ləuð] *vt* detestare.

loaves [ləuvz] *pl* → **loaf**.

lobby ['lɒbɪ] *n (hall)* atrio *m*.

lobster ['lɒbstəʳ] *n* aragosta *f*.

local ['ləukl] *adj* locale ; *(train)* regionale. ◆ *n inf (local person)* abitante *mf* del posto ; *Br (pub)* bar *m* vicino ; *Am (train)* regionale *m* ; *Am (bus)* autobus *m inv*.

local anaesthetic *n* anestesia *f* locale.

local call *n* chiamata *f* urbana.

local government *n* amministrazione *f* locale.

locate [*Br* ləu'keɪt, *Am* 'ləukeɪt] *vt (find)* localizzare ; **to be ~d** essere situato.

location [ləu'keɪʃn] *n (place)* posizione *f*.

loch [lɒk] *n Scot* lago *m*.

lock [lɒk] *n (on door, drawer)* serratura *f* ; *(for bike)* lucchetto *m* ; *(on canal)* chiusa *f*. ◆ *v t (door, drawer, car)* chiudere a chiave ; *(keep safely)* chiudere. ◆ *vi (become stuck)* bloccarsi. ❑ **lock in** *vt sep* chiudere dentro. ❑ **lock out** *vt sep* chiudere fuori. ❑ **lock up** ◆ *vt sep (imprison)* mettere dentro. ◆ *vi* chiudere porte e finestre.

locker ['lɒkəʳ] *n* armadietto *m*.

locker room *n Am* spogliatoio *m*.

locket ['lɒkɪt] *n* medaglione *m*.

locum ['ləukəm] *n (doctor)* medico *m* sostituto.

lodge [lɒdʒ] *n (for skiers)* rifugio *m* ; *(for hunters)* casino *m* di caccia. ◆ *vi (stay)* alloggiare ; *(get stuck)* conficcarsi.
lodger ['lɒdʒəʳ] *n* pensionante *mf*.
lodgings ['lɒdʒɪŋz] *npl* camera *f* ammobiliata.
loft [lɒft] *n* soffitta *f*.
log [lɒg] *n (piece of wood)* ceppo *m*.
logic ['lɒdʒɪk] *n* logica *f*.
logical ['lɒdʒɪkl] *adj* logico(a).
logo ['ləʊgəʊ] (*pl* -s) *n* logo *m inv*.
loin [lɔɪn] *n* lombata *f*.
loiter ['lɔɪtəʳ] *vi (remain)* attardarsi ; *(walk around)* bighellonare.
lollipop ['lɒlɪpɒp] *n* lecca lecca *m inv*.
lolly ['lɒlɪ] *n inf (lollipop)* lecca lecca *m inv* ; *Br (ice lolly)* ghiacciolo *m*.
Lombardy *n* la Lombardia.
London ['lʌndən] *n* Londra *f*.
Londoner ['lʌndənəʳ] *n* londinese *mf*.
lonely ['ləʊnlɪ] *adj (person)* solo(a) ; *(place)* isolato(a).
long [lɒŋ] *adj* lungo(a). ◆ *adv* molto ; **it's 2 metres ~** è lungo 2 metri ; **it's two hours ~** dura due ore ; **how ~ is it?** *(in length)* quanto è lungo? ; *(in time)* quanto dura? ; **a ~ time** molto tempo ; **all day ~** tutto il giorno ; **as ~ as** *(provided that)* purché ; **no ~er** non più ; **so ~!** *inf* ciao! ❑ **long for** *vt fus* desiderare ardentemente.
long-distance *adj (phone call)* interurbano(a).
long drink *n* long drink *m inv*.
long-haul *adj* su lunga distanza.
longitude ['lɒndʒɪtju:d] *n* longitudine *f*.
long jump *n* salto *m* in lungo.
long-life *adj (milk, fruit juice)* a lunga conservazione ; *(battery)* a lunga durata.
longsighted [ˌlɒŋ'saɪtɪd] *adj* presbite.
long-term *adj* a lungo termine.
longwearing [ˌlɒŋ'weərɪŋ] *adj Am* resistente.
loo [lu:] (*pl* -s) *n Br inf* gabinetto *m*.
look [lʊk] *n (glance)* sguardo *m*, occhiata *f* ; *(appearance)* aspetto *m*. ◆ *v i* guardare ; *(seem)* sembrare ; **you don't ~ well** non hai una gran bella cera ; **to ~ onto** *(building, room)* dare su ; **to have a ~** dare un'occhiata ; **(good) ~s** bellezza *f* ; **I'm just ~ing** *(in shop)* sto solo guardando ; **~ out!** attento!. ❑ **look after** *vt fus* occuparsi di. ❑ **look at** *vt fus (observe)* guardare ; *(examine)* vedere. ❑ **look for** *vt fus* cercare. ❑ **look forward to** *vt fus* non veder l'ora di. ❑ **look out for** *vt fus* cercare. ❑ **look round** ◆ *vt fus (city, museum)* visitare ; *(shop)* fare un giro da. ◆ *vi* girarsi. ❑ **look up** *vt sep (in dictionary, phone book)* cercare.
loony ['lu:nɪ] *n inf* pazzo *m*, -a *f*.
loop [lu:p] *n* cappio *m*.
loose [lu:s] *adj (not fixed firmly)* allentato(a) ; *(sweets, sheets of paper)* sciolto(a) ; *(clothes)* largo(a) ; **to let sb/sthg ~** lasciar libero qn/qc.
loosen ['lu:sn] *vt* allentare.
lop-sided [-'saɪdɪd] *adj* storto(a).
lord [lɔ:d] *n* lord *m inv*.

lorry ['lɒrɪ] *n Br* camion *m inv*.

lorry driver *n Br* camionista *mf*.

lose [lu:z] (*pt* & *pp* **lost**) *vt* & *vi* perdere ; **to ~ weight** dimagrire.

loser ['lu:zəʳ] *n (incontest)* perdente *mf*.

loss [lɒs] *n* perdita *f*.

lost [lɒst] *pt & pp* → **lose**. ◆ *adj (person)* perso(a) ; **to get ~** *(lose way)* perdersi.

lost-and-found office *n Am* ufficio *m* oggetti smarriti.

lost property office *n Br* ufficio *m* oggetti smarriti.

lot [lɒt] *n (group of people)* gruppo *m* ; *(at auction)* lotto *m* ; *Am (car park)* parcheggio *m* ; **a ~** *(large amount)* molto(a), molti(e) *(pl)* ; *(to a great extent, often)* molto ; **a ~ of time** molto tempo ; **a ~ of problems** molti problemi ; **~s (of)** molto(a), molti(e) *(pl)*, un sacco (di) ; **the ~** *(everything)* tutto quanto (tutta quanta).

lotion ['ləʊʃn] *n* lozione *f*.

lottery ['lɒtərɪ] *n* lotteria *f*.

loud [laʊd] *adj (music, noise)* forte ; *(voice)* alto ; *(colour, clothes)* sgargiante.

loudspeaker [ˌlaʊd'spi:kəʳ] *n* altoparlante *m*.

lounge [laʊndʒ] *n (in house)* salotto *m*, soggiorno *m* ; *(at airport)* sala *f* partenze.

lounge bar *n Br sala di un pub più confortevole e più cara del'public bar' m*.

lousy ['laʊzɪ] *adj inf (poor-quality)* schifoso(a).

lout [laʊt] *n* teppista *mf*.

love [lʌv] *n* amore *m* ; *(in tennis)* zero *m*. ◆ *vt* amare ; **I ~ reading** mi piace molto leggere ; **I'd ~ a coffee** mi andrebbe un caffè ; **I'd ~ to help** vorrei tanto aiutare ; **to be in ~ (with)** essere innamorato (di) ; **(with) ~ from** *(inletter)* con affetto.

love affair *n* relazione *f*.

lovely ['lʌvlɪ] *adj (very beautiful)* bello(a) ; *(very nice)* delizioso(a).

lover ['lʌvəʳ] *n (sexual partner)* amante *mf* ; *(enthusiast)* appassionato *m*, -a *f*.

loving ['lʌvɪŋ] *adj* affettuoso(a).

low [ləʊ] *adj* basso(a) ; *(quantity)* piccolo(a) ; *(supply)* scarso(a) ; *(standard, quality, opinion)* scadente ; *(depressed)* depresso(a). ◆ *n (area of low pressure)* area *f* di bassa pressione ; **we're ~ on petrol** abbiamo poca benzina.

low-alcohol *adj* a basso contenuto alcolico.

low-calorie *adj* ipocalorico(a).

low-cut *adj* scollato(a).

lower ['ləʊəʳ] *adj* inferiore. ◆ *vt* abbassare.

lower sixth *n Br primo anno di studi superiori per studenti di 17 anni che prepareranno gli 'A levels'*.

low-fat *adj* magro(a).

low tide *n* bassa marea *f*.

loyal ['lɔɪəl] *adj* fedele.

loyalty ['lɔɪəltɪ] *n* fedeltà *f*.

lozenge ['lɒzɪndʒ] *n (sweet)* pasticca *f*, pastiglia *f*.

L-plate *n Br targa indicante che chi guida la vettura non ha ancora preso la patente*.

Ltd *(abbr of limited)* ≃ Srl.

lubricate ['lu:brɪkeɪt] *vt* lubrificare.

luck [lʌk] *n* fortuna *f*; **bad ~** sfortuna *f*; **good ~!** buona fortuna!; **with ~** con un po' di fortuna.
luckily ['lʌkɪlɪ] *adv* fortunatamente.
lucky ['lʌkɪ] *adj* fortunato(a); **to be ~** essere fortunato.
ludicrous ['lu:dɪkrəs] *adj* ridicolo(a).
lug [lʌg] *vt inf* trascinare.
luggage ['lʌgɪdʒ] *n* bagagli *mpl*.
luggage compartment *n* bagagliaio *m*.
luggage locker *n* armadietto *m* per deposito bagagli.
luggage rack *n (on train)* portabagagli *m*.
lukewarm ['lu:kwɔ:m] *adj* tiepido(a).
lull [lʌl] *n* pausa *f*.
lullaby ['lʌləbaɪ] *n* ninnananna *f*.
luminous ['lu:mɪnəs] *adj* fosforescente.
lump [lʌmp] *n (of coal, mud, butter)* pezzo *m*; *(of sugar)* zolletta *f*; *(on body)* nodulo *m*.
lump sum *n* compenso *m* forfettario.
lumpy ['lʌmpɪ] *adj (sauce)* grumoso(a); *(mattress)* pieno(a) di bozzi.
lunatic ['lu:nətɪk] *n* pazzo *m*, -a *f*.
lunch [lʌntʃ] *n* pranzo *m*; **to have ~** pranzare.
lunch hour *n* pausa *f* pranzo.
lunchtime ['lʌntʃtaɪm] *n* ora *f* di pranzo.
lung [lʌŋ] *n* polmone *m*.
lunge [lʌndʒ] *vi*: **to ~ at** gettarsi su.
lure [ljʊəʳ] *vt* attirare.
lurk [lɜ:k] *vi (person)* stare in agguato.
lush [lʌʃ] *adj (grass, field)* rigoglioso(a).
lust [lʌst] *n (sexual desire)* libidine *f*.
luxurious [lʌg'ʒʊərɪəs] *adj* di lusso.
luxury ['lʌkʃərɪ] *adj* di lusso. ◆ *n* lusso *m*.
lying ['laɪɪŋ] *cont* → **lie**.
lyrics ['lɪrɪks] *npl* parole *fpl*.

M

m (*abbr of metre*) m. ◆ *abbr* = **mile**.
M *Br* (*abbr of motorway*) A; (*abbr of medium*) M.
MA *n* (*abbr of Master of Arts*) *titolare di master in materie umanistiche*.
mac [mæk] *n Br inf (coat)* impermeabile *m*.
macaroni [ˌmækə'rəʊnɪ] *n* maccheroni *mpl*.
macaroni cheese *n* maccheroni *mpl* gratinati.
machine [mə'ʃi:n] *n* macchina *f*.
machinegun [mə'ʃi:ngʌn] *n* mitragliatrice *f*.
machinery [mə'ʃi:nərɪ] *n* macchine *fpl*.
machine-washable *adj* lavabile in lavatrice.
mackerel ['mækrəl] (*pl inv*) *n* sgombro *m*.
mackintosh ['mækɪntɒʃ] *n Br* impermeabile *m*.

mad [mæd] *adj* pazzo(a), matto(a) ; *(angry)* arrabbiato(a) ; *(uncontrolled)* furioso(a) ; **to be ~ about** *inf (like a lot)* andare pazzo per ; **like ~** come un matto.

Madam ['mædəm] *n (form of address)* signora *f*.

made [meɪd] *pt* & *pp* → **make**.

made-to-measure *adj* fatto(a) su misura.

madness ['mædnɪs] *n* pazzia *f*.

magazine [ˌmægə'ziːn] *n (journal)* rivista *f*.

maggot ['mægət] *n* verme *m*.

magic ['mædʒɪk] *n* magia *f*.

magician [mə'dʒɪʃn] *n (conjurer)* mago *m*, -a *f*.

magistrate ['mædʒɪstreɪt] *n* magistrato *m*.

magnet ['mægnɪt] *n* calamita *f*.

magnetic [mæg'netɪk] *adj* magnetico(a).

magnificent [mæg'nɪfɪsənt] *adj* magnifico(a).

magnifying glass ['mægnɪfaɪɪŋ-] *n* lente *f* d'ingrandimento.

mahogany [mə'hɒgənɪ] *n* mogano *m*.

maid [meɪd] *n* cameriera *f*.

maiden name ['meɪdn-] *n* cognome *m* da nubile.

mail [meɪl] *n* posta *f*. ◆ *vt Am* spedire.

mailbox ['meɪlbɒks] *n Am* cassetta *f* delle lettere.

mailman ['meɪlmən] (*pl* **-men** [-mən]) *n Am* postino *m*.

mail order *n* vendita *f* per corrispondenza.

main [meɪn] *adj* principale.

main course *n* portata *f* principale.

mainland ['meɪnlənd] *n* : **the ~** il continente.

main line *n* linea *f* principale.

mainly ['meɪnlɪ] *adv* principalmente.

main road *n* strada *f* principale.

mains [meɪnz] *npl* : **the ~** le condutture.

main street *n Am* corso *m*.

maintain [meɪn'teɪn] *vt (keep)* mantenere ; *(in good condition)* provvedere alla manutenzione di.

maintenance ['meɪntənəns] *n (of car,machine)* manutenzione *f* ; *(money)* alimenti *mpl*.

maisonette [ˌmeɪzə'net] *n Br* appartamento *m* su due piani.

maize [meɪz] *n* granoturco *m*, mais *m*.

major ['meɪdʒə^r] *adj (important)* importante ; *(most important)* principale. ◆ *n* MIL maggiore *m*. ◆ *vi Am* : **to ~ in** laurearsi in.

majority [mə'dʒɒrətɪ] *n* maggioranza *f*.

major road *n* strada *f* principale.

☞ ———

make [meɪk] (*pt* & *pp* **made**) *vt*
- 1. *(produce, manufacture)* fare ; **to be made of** essere (fatto) di ; **to ~ lunch/supper** preparare il pranzo/la cena ; **made in Japan** fabbricato in Giappone.
- 2. *(perform, do)* fare ; *(decision)* prendere ; **to ~ a mistake** fare un errore ; **to ~ a phone call** fare una telefonata.
- 3. *(cause to be)* rendere ; **to ~ sthg**

better migliorare qc ; **to ~ sb happy** rendere felice qn.
- 4. *(cause to do, force)* fare ; **to ~ sb do sthg** far fare qc a qn, costringere qn a fareqc ; **it made her laugh** l'ha fatta ridere.
- 5. *(amount to, total)* fare ; **that ~s £5** fanno 5 sterline.
- 6. *(calculate)* : **I ~ it £4** mi viene 4 sterline ; **I ~ it seven o'clock** io faccio le sette.
- 7. *(earn)* fare ; **to ~ a loss** registrare una perdita.
- 8. *inf (arrive in time for)* : **I don't think we'll ~ the 10o'clock train** non credo che ce la faremo per il treno delle 10.
- 9. *(friend, enemy)* farsi.
- 10. *(have qualities for)* : **this would ~ a lovely bedroom** sarebbe una camera (da letto) molto carina.
- 11. *(bed)* fare, rifare.
- 12. *(in phrases)* : **to ~ do (with)** arrangiarsi (con) ; **to ~ good** *(damage)* risarcire ; **to ~ it** *(arrive on time, beable to go)* farcela.
◆ *n (of product)* marca *f*.
❑ **make out** *vt sep (cheque, receipt)* fare ; *(form)* compilare ; *(see, hear)* distinguere, capire.
❑ **make up** *vt sep (invent)* inventare ; *(comprise)* costituire, comporre ; *(difference)* coprire.
❑ **make up for** *vt fus* compensare.

makeshift ['meɪkʃɪft] *adj* di fortuna.

make-up *n (cosmetics)* trucco *m*.

malaria [mə'leərɪə] *n* malaria *f*.

male [meɪl] *adj* maschile ; *(child, animal)* maschio. ◆ *n (animal)* maschio *m*.

malfunction [mæl'fʌŋkʃn] *vi fml* funzionare male.

malignant [mə'lɪgnənt] *adj (tumour)* maligno(a).

mall [mɔːl] *n (shopping centre)* centro *m* commerciale.

MALL

Lunga distesa di verde nel cuore di Washington DC, il Mall si estende dal Campidoglio al Lincoln Memorial. Lungo il Mall si trovano i musei della Smithsonian Institution, gallerie d'arte, la Casa Bianca, il Washington Memorial e il Jefferson Memorial. Il muro (*the Wall*), sul quale sono incisi i nomi dei soldati morti o dispersi nella guerra del Vietnam, si trova all'estremità occidentale del Mall. Nel Regno Unito il Mall è il nome del lungo viale alberato nel centro di Londra, che porta da Buckingham Palace a Trafalgar Square.

mallet ['mælɪt] *n* maglio *m*.

maltreat [ˌmæl'triːt] *vt* maltrattare.

malt whisky *n* whisky *m inv* di malto.

mammal ['mæml] *n* mammifero *m*.

man [mæn] (*pl* **men**) *n* uomo *m*. ◆ *vt (office)* dotare di personale ; *(phones)* rispondere a.

manage ['mænɪdʒ] *vt (company, business)* dirigere ; *(suitcase)* farcela a portare ; *(job)* riuscire a fare ; *(food)* farcela a mangiare. ◆ *vi (cope)* farcela ; **can you ~ Friday?**

venerdì ti andrebbe bene? ; **to ~ to do sthg** riuscire a fare qc.

management ['mænɪdʒmənt] *n* direzione *f*.

manager ['mænɪdʒəʳ] *n (of business, bank, shop)* direttore *m* ; *(of sports team)* allenatore *m*.

manageress [ˌmænɪdʒə'res] *n (of business, bank, shop)* direttrice *f*.

managing director ['mænɪdʒɪŋ-] *n* amministratore *m* delegato.

mandarin ['mændərɪn] *n* mandarino *m*.

mane [meɪn] *n* criniera *f*.

maneuver [mə'nuːvər] *Am* = **manoeuvre**.

mangetout [ˌmɒnʒ'tuː] *n* pisello *m* mangiatutto.

mangle ['mæŋgl] *vt (body)* straziare.

mango ['mæŋgəʊ] (*pl* **-es** OR **-s**) *n* mango *m*.

Manhattan [mæn'hætən] *n* Manhattan *f*.

MANHATTAN

Quartiere centrale di New York, è diviso in tre zone principali : Downtown, Midtown e Upper Manhattan. Vi si trovano alcuni fra i grattacieli più famosi del mondo, quali l'Empire State Building, e luoghi celbri quali Central Park, la Quinta Strada (Fifth Avenue), Broadway e il Greenwich Village.

---

manhole ['mænhəʊl] *n* pozzo *m* d'ispezione.

maniac ['meɪnɪæk] *n inf* pazzo *m*, -a *f*.

manicure ['mænɪkjʊəʳ] *n* manicure *f inv*.

manifold ['mænɪfəʊld] *n AUT* collettore *m*.

manipulate [mə'nɪpjʊleɪt] *vt (person)* manipolare ; *(machine, controls)* manovrare.

mankind [ˌmæn'kaɪnd] *n* l'umanità *f*.

manly ['mænlɪ] *adj* virile.

man-made *adj* artificiale.

manner ['mænəʳ] *n (way)* modo *m*. ❑ **manners** *npl* maniere *fpl*.

manoeuvre [mə'nuːvəʳ] *n Br* manovra *f*. ◆ *vt Br* manovrare.

manor ['mænəʳ] *n* grande casa *f* di campagna.

mansion ['mænʃn] *n* casa *f* signorile.

manslaughter ['mænˌslɔːtəʳ] *n* omicidio *m* colposo.

mantelpiece ['mæntlpiːs] *n* mensola *f* del caminetto.

manual ['mænjʊəl] *adj* manuale. ◆ *n* manuale *m*.

manufacture [ˌmænjʊ'fæktʃəʳ] *n* fabbricazione *f*. ◆ *vt (produce)* fabbricare.

manufacturer [ˌmænjʊ'fæktʃərəʳ] *n* fabbricante *m*.

manure [mə'njʊəʳ] *n* concime *m*.

many ['menɪ] (*compar* **more**, *superl* **most**) *adj* molti(e). ◆ *pron* molti *mpl*, -e *fpl* ; **how ~?** quanti(e) ; **so ~** così tanti(e) ; **too ~** troppi(e) ; **take as ~ as you like** prendine quanti ne vuoi ; **twice as ~ as** il doppio di.

map [mæp] *n (of country)* carta *f* geografica ; *(of town)* pianta *f*.
Mar. *(abbr of March)* mar.
marathon ['mærəθn] *n* maratona *f*.
marble ['mɑːbl] *n (stone)* marmo *m* ; *(glass ball)* biglia *f*, pallina *f* di vetro.
march [mɑːtʃ] *n (demonstration)* marcia *f*. ◆ *vi (walk quickly)* avanzare con passo deciso.
March [mɑːtʃ] *n* marzo *m* → September.
mare [meəʳ] *n* giumenta *f*.
margarine [ˌmɑːdʒə'riːn] *n* margarina *f*.
margin ['mɑːdʒɪn] *n* margine *m*.
marina [mə'riːnə] *n* porto *m* turistico.
marinated ['mærɪneɪtɪd] *adj* marinato(a).
marital status ['mærɪtl-] *n* stato *m* civile.
mark [mɑːk] *n (spot)* macchia *f* ; *(cut, symbol)* segno *m* ; SCH voto *m* ; *(of gas oven) numero corrispondente a una certa temperatura.* ◆ *vt (blemish)* macchiare ; *(put symbol on)* segnare ; *(correct)* correggere ; *(show position of)* indicare.
marker pen ['mɑːkə-] *n* (grosso) pennarello *m*.
market ['mɑːkɪt] *n* mercato *m*.
marketing ['mɑːkɪtɪŋ] *n* marketing *m*.
marketplace ['mɑːkɪtpleɪs] *n (place)* piazza *f* del mercato.
markings ['mɑːkɪŋz] *npl (on road)* segnaletica *f* orizzontale.
marmalade ['mɑːməleɪd] *n* marmellata *f* di agrumi.
marquee [mɑː'kiː] *n* padiglione *m*.
marriage ['mærɪdʒ] *n* matrimonio *m*.
married ['mærɪd] *adj* sposato(a) ; **to get ~** sposarsi.
marrow ['mærəʊ] *n (vegetable)* zucca *f*.
marry ['mærɪ] *vt* sposare. ◆ *vi* sposarsi.
marsh [mɑːʃ] *n* palude *f*.
martial arts [ˌmɑːʃl-] *npl* arti *fpl* marziali.
marvellous ['mɑːvələs] *adj Br* meraviglioso(a).
marvelous ['mɑːvələs] *Am* = **marvellous**.
marzipan ['mɑːzɪpæn] *n* marzapane *m*.
mascara [mæs'kɑːrə] *n* mascara *m inv*.
masculine ['mæskjʊlɪn] *adj* maschile ; *(woman)* mascolino(a).
mashed potatoes [mæʃt-] *npl* purè *m inv* di patate.
mask [mɑːsk] *n* maschera *f*.
masonry ['meɪsnrɪ] *n* muratura *f*.
mass [mæs] *n (large amount)* massa *f* ; RELIG messa *f* ; **~es (of)** *inf (lots)* un sacco (di).
massacre ['mæsəkəʳ] *n* massacro *m*.
massage [*Br* 'mæsɑːʒ, *Am* mə'sɑːʒ] *n* massaggio *m*. ◆ *vt* massaggiare.
masseur [mæ'sɜːʳ] *n* massaggiatore *m*.
masseuse [mæ'sɜːz] *n* massaggiatrice *f*.
massive ['mæsɪv] *adj* enorme.
mast [mɑːst] *n (on boat)* albero *m*.

master ['maːstəʳ] *n (at school)* insegnante *m* ; *(of servant, dog)* padrone *m*. ◆ *vt (learn)* imparare a fondo.

masterpiece ['maːstəpiːs] *n* capolavoro *m*.

mat [mæt] *n (small rug)* tappetino *m* ; *(on table)* sottopiatto *m*.

match [mætʃ] *n (for lighting)* fiammifero *m* ; *(game)* partita *f*, incontro *m*. ◆ *vt (in colour, design)* intonarsi a OR con ; *(be the same as)* corrispondere a ; *(be as good as)* uguagliare. ◆ *vi (in colour, design)* intonarsi.

matchbox ['mætʃbɒks] *n* scatola *f* di fiammiferi.

matching ['mætʃɪŋ] *adj* intonato(a).

mate [meɪt] *n inf (friend)* amico *m*, -a *f*. ◆ *vi* accoppiarsi.

material [mə'tɪərɪəl] *n* materiale *m* ; *(cloth)* stoffa *f*. ❑ **materials** *npl (equipment)* occorrente *m*.

maternity leave [mə'tɜːnətɪ-] *n* congedo *m* di maternità.

maternity ward [mə'tɜːnətɪ-] *n* reparto *m* maternità.

math [mæθ] *Am* = **maths**.

mathematics [ˌmæθə'mætɪks] *n* matematica *f*.

maths [mæθs] *n Br* matematica *f*.

matinée ['mætɪneɪ] *n* matinée *f inv*.

matt [mæt] *adj* opaco(a).

matter ['mætəʳ] *n (issue, situation)* questione *f* ; *(physical material)* materia *f*. ◆ *vi* importare ; **it doesn't ~** non importa ; **no ~ what happens** qualsiasi cosa accada ; **there's something the ~ with my car** c'è qualcosa che non va con la mia macchina ; **what's the ~?** che cosa c'è (che non va)? ; **as a ~ of course** come è naturale ; **as a ~ of fact** in realtà.

mattress ['mætrɪs] *n* materasso *m*.

mature [mə'tjʊəʳ] *adj (person, behaviour)* maturo(a) ; *(cheese, wine)* stagionato(a).

mauve [məʊv] *adj* (color) malva *(inv)*.

max. [mæks] *(abbr of maximum)* max.

maximum ['mæksɪməm] *adj* massimo(a). ◆ *n* massimo *m*.

May [meɪ] *n* maggio *m* → **September**.

---

may [meɪ] *aux vb* - **1.** *(expressing possibility)* : **it ~ be done as follows** si può procedere come segue ; **it ~ rain** può darsi che piova ; **they ~ have got lost** può darsi che si siano persi.

- **2.** *(expressing permission)* : **~ I smoke?** posso fumare? ; **you ~ sit, if you wish** può sedersi, se vuole.

- **3.** *(when conceding a point)* : **it ~ be a long walk, but it's worth it** sarà anche lontano a piedi, ma ne vale la pena.

---

maybe ['meɪbiː] *adv* forse.

mayonnaise [ˌmeɪə'neɪz] *n* maionese *f*.

mayor [meəʳ] *n* sindaco *m*.

mayoress ['meərɪs] *n* sindaco *m (donna)*.

maze [meɪz] *n* labirinto *m*.

me [miː] *pron* mi ; *(after prep, stressed)* me ; **she knows ~** (lei) mi conosce ; **it's ~** sono io ; **send it to ~** mandalo a me ; **tell ~** dimmi ; **he's worse than ~** lui è peggio di me.
meadow ['medəʊ] *n* prato *m*.
meal [miːl] *n* pasto *m*.
mealtime ['miːltaɪm] *n* ora *f* di mangiare.
mean [miːn] *(pt & pp* **meant**) *adj (miserly)* avaro(a), gretto(a) ; *(unkind)* scortese, villano(a). ◆ *vt (signify, matter)* significare, voler dire ; *(intend, be serious about)* intendere ; *(be a sign of)* significare ; **I didn't ~ it** non dicevo sul serio ; **to ~ to do sthg** avere l'intenzione di fare qc ; **the bus was meant to leave at 8.30** l'autobus sarebbe dovuto partire alle 8.30 ; **it's meant to be good** dovrebbe essere buono.
meaning ['miːnɪŋ] *n* significato *m*, senso *m*.
meaningless ['miːnɪŋlɪs] *adj (irrelevant)* insignificante.
means [miːnz] *(pl inv) n (method)* mezzo *m*. ◆ *npl (money)* mezzi *mpl* ; **by all ~!** ma certo! ; **by ~ of** per mezzo di.
meant [ment] *pt & pp* → **mean**.
meantime ['miːn ordf·taɪm] ◆**in the meantime** *adv* nel frattempo.
meanwhile ['miːn,waɪl] *adv* nel frattempo.
measles ['miːzlz] *n* morbillo *m*.
measure ['meʒəʳ] *vt* misurare. ◆ *n (step, action)* misura *f*, provvedimento *m* ; *(of alcohol)* dose *f* ; **the room ~s 10 mý** la stanza misura 10 mý.
measurement ['meʒəmənt] *n* misura *f*.
meat [miːt] *n* carne *f* ; **red ~** carne rossa ; **white ~** carne bianca.
meatball ['miːtbɔːl] *n* polpetta *f* (di carne).
mechanic [mɪ'kænɪk] *n* meccanico *m*.
mechanical [mɪ'kænɪkl] *adj (device)* meccanico(a).
mechanism ['mekənɪzm] *n* meccanismo *m*.
medal ['medl] *n* medaglia *f*.
media ['miːdjə] *n or npl* : **the ~** i (mass) media.
Medicaid ['medɪkeɪd] *n Am assistenza f sanitaria*.

MEDICAID, MEDICARE

Poiché gli Stati Uniti non avevano un servizio sanitario nazionale, nel 1965 vennero introdotti i programmi *Medicaid* e *Medicare* allo scopo di offrire un'assicurazione medica ai poveri, agli anziani e ai disabili. *Medicaid* si rivolge ai minori di 65 anni con reddito basso, mentre *Medicare* è per gli ultrasessantacinquenni. Poiché entrambi i programmi necessitano di forti contributi da parte del governo centrale, essi sono spesso al centro di aspre polemiche.

---

medical ['medɪkl] *adj* medico(a). ◆ *n* visita *f* medica.
medication [,medɪ'keɪʃn] *n* medicine *fpl*.
medicine ['medsɪn] *n* medicina *f*.
medicine cabinet *n* armadietto *m* dei medicinali.

medieval [ˌmedɪ'i:vl] *adj* medievale.

mediocre [ˌmi:dɪ'əʊkəʳ] *adj* mediocre.

Mediterranean [ˌmedɪtə'reɪnjən] *n* : the ~ *(region)* la regione del Mediterraneo.

medium ['mi:djəm] *adj* medio(a) ; *(sherry)* semisecco(a).

medium-dry *adj* semisecco(a).

medium-sized [-saɪzd] *adj* di misura media.

medley ['medlɪ] *n* : a ~ of cold meats affettati *mpl* misti.

meet [mi:t] (*pt* & *pp* met) *vt* incontrare ; *(get to know)* fare la conoscenza di, conoscere ; *(go to collect)* andare a prendere ; *(need, requirement)* soddisfare ; *(cost, expenses)* far fronte a. ◆ *vi* incontrarsi ; *(get to know each other)* conoscersi. ❑ **meet up** *vi* incontrarsi. ❑ **meet with** *vt fus* incontrare.

meeting ['mi:tɪŋ] *n (for business)* incontro *m*.

meeting point *n (at airport, station)* punto *m* d'incontro.

melody ['melədɪ] *n* melodia *f*.

melon ['melən] *n* melone *m*.

melt [melt] *vi* sciogliersi ; *(metal)* fondersi.

member ['membəʳ] *n* membro *m*.

Member of Congress [-'kɒŋgres] *n* membro *m* del Congresso (Americano).

Member of Parliament *n* ≃ deputato *m*, -a *f*.

membership ['membəʃɪp] *n (state of being a member)* appartenenza *f* ; *(members)* (numero dei) membri *mpl*.

memorial [mɪ'mɔ:rɪəl] *n* monumento *m*.

memorize ['meməraɪz] *vt* memorizzare.

memory ['memərɪ] *n* memoria *f* ; *(thing remembered)* ricordo *m*.

men [men] *pl* → man.

menacing ['menəsɪŋ] *adj* minaccioso(a).

mend [mend] *vt* accomodare, aggiustare ; *(clothes)* rammendare.

menopause ['menəpɔ:z] *n* menopausa *f*.

men's room *n Am* gabinetto *m* degli uomini.

menstruate ['menstrʊeɪt] *vi* avere le mestruazioni.

menswear ['menzweəʳ] *n* abbigliamento *m* da uomo.

mental ['mentl] *adj* mentale.

mentally handicapped ['mentəlɪ-] *adj* mentalmente handicappato(a). ◆ *npl* : the ~ i portatori di handicap mentale.

mentally ill ['mentəlɪ-] *adj* malato(a) di mente.

mention ['menʃn] *vt* accennare a ; don't ~ it! non c'è di che!

menu ['menju:] *n* menu *m inv* ; children's ~ menu per bambini.

merchandise ['mɜ:tʃəndaɪz] *n* mercanzia *f*, merce *f*.

merchant marine [ˌmɜ:tʃəntmə'ri:n] *Am* = merchant navy.

merchant navy [ˌmɜ:tʃənt-] *n Br* marina *f* mercantile.

mercy ['mɜ:sɪ] *n* pietà *f*.

mere [mɪəʳ] *adj* semplice ; a ~ £5 solo 5 sterline.

merely ['mɪəlɪ] *adv* soltanto.

merge [mɜ:dʒ] *vi (combine)* fondersi, unirsi ; **'merge'** *Am* AUT *segnale che indica agli automobilisti che si immettono su un'autostrada di disporsi sulla corsia di destra.*

merger ['mɜ:dʒəʳ] *n* fusione *f*.

meringue [mə'ræŋ] *n (egg white)* meringa *f*; *(cake)* meringa alla panna.

merit ['merɪt] *n* merito *m*.

merry ['merɪ] *adj* allegro(a) ; Merry Christmas! Buon Natale!

merry-go-round *n* giostra *f*.

mess [mes] *n (untidiness)* disordine *m*, confusione *f*; *(difficult situation)* pasticcio *m* ; in a ~ *(untidy)* in disordine. ❑ **mess about** *vi inf (have fun)* divertirsi ; *(behave foolishly)* fare lo scemo ; to ~ about with sthg *(interfere)* intromettersi in qc. ❑ **mess up** *vt sep inf (ruin, spoil)* mandare a monte.

message ['mesɪdʒ] *n* messaggio *m*.

messenger ['mesɪndʒəʳ] *n* messaggero *m*, -a *f*.

messy ['mesɪ] *adj* disordinato(a).

met [met] *pt & pp* → meet.

metal ['metl] *adj* metallico(a), di metallo. ◆ *n* metallo *m*.

metalwork ['metəlwɜ:k] *n (craft)* lavorazione *f* dei metalli.

meter ['mi:təʳ] *n (device)* contatore *m* ; *Am* = metre.

method ['meθəd] *n* metodo *m*.

methodical [mɪ'θɒdɪkl] *adj* metodico(a).

meticulous [mɪ'tɪkjʊləs] *adj* meticoloso(a).

metre ['mi:təʳ] *n Br* metro *m*.

metric ['metrɪk] *adj* metrico(a).

Mexican ['meksɪkn] *adj* messicano(a). ◆ *n* messicano *m*, -a *f*.

Mexico ['meksɪkəʊ] *n* il Messico.

mg *(abbr of milligram)* mg.

miaow [mi:'aʊ] *vi Br* miagolare.

mice [maɪs] *pl* → mouse.

microchip ['maɪkrəʊtʃɪp] *n* microcircuito *m* integrato, microchip *m inv*.

microphone ['mɪkrəfəʊn] *n* microfono *m*.

microscope ['maɪkrəskəʊp] *n* microscopio *m*.

microwave (oven) ['maɪkrəweɪv-] *n* forno *m* a microonde.

midday [,mɪd'deɪ] *n* mezzogiorno *m*.

middle ['mɪdl] *n* mezzo *m*, parte *f* centrale. ◆ *adj (central)* di mezzo ; in the ~ of the road in mezzo alla strada ; in the ~ of April a metà aprile ; to be in the ~ of doing sthg stare facendo qc.

middle-aged *adj* di mezza età.

middle-class *adj* borghese.

Middle East *n* : the ~ il Medio Oriente.

middle name *n* secondo nome *m*.

midge [mɪdʒ] *n* pappataci *m inv*.

midget ['mɪdʒɪt] *n* nano *m*, -a *f*.

midnight ['mɪdnaɪt] *n* mezzanotte *f*.

midsummer ['mɪd'sʌməʳ] *n* piena estate *f*.

midway [ˌmɪdˈweɪ] *adv (in space)* a metà strada ; *(in time)* a metà.

midweek [*adj* ˈmɪdwiːk, *adv* mɪdˈwiːk] *adj* di metà settimana. ◆ *adv* a metà settimana.

midwife [ˈmɪdwaɪf] (*pl* **-wives** [-waɪvz]) *n* levatrice *f*.

midwinter [ˈmɪdˈwɪntəʳ] *n* pieno inverno *m*.

☞

might [maɪt] *aux vb* - 1. *(expressing possibility)* : **we ~ go to Wales this year** forse andremo in Galles quest'anno ; **I suppose they ~ still come** può ancora darsi che arrivino ; **they ~ have been killed** avrebbero potuto rimanere uccisi.
- 2. *fml (expressing permission)* : **~ I have a few words?** posso parlarle un attimo?
- 3. *(when conceding a point)* : **it ~ be expensive, but it's good quality** sarà anche caro, ma è di buona qualità.
- 4. *(would)* : **I'd hoped you ~ come too** speravo che venissi anche tu.
◆ *n (physical strength)* forza *f*.

migraine [ˈmiːgreɪn, ˈmaɪgreɪn] *n* emicrania *f*.

Milan [mɪˈlæn] *n* Milano *f*.

mild [maɪld] *adj (cheese, person)* dolce ; *(detergent, taste)* delicato(a) ; *(effect, flu)* leggero(a) ; *(weather, climate)* mite ; *(curiosity, surprise)* lieve. ◆ *n Br (beer)* birra *f* leggera.

mile [maɪl] *n* miglio *m* ; **it's ~s away** è lontanissimo.

mileage [ˈmaɪlɪdʒ] *n* distanza *f* in miglia, ≃ chilometraggio *m*.

mileometer [maɪˈlɒmɪtəʳ] *n* ≃ contachilometri *m inv*.

military [ˈmɪlɪtrɪ] *adj* militare.

milk [mɪlk] *n* latte *m*. ◆ *vt (cow)* mungere.

milk chocolate *n* cioccolato *m* al latte.

milkman [ˈmɪlkmən] (*pl* **-men** [-mən]) *n* lattaio *m*.

milk shake *n* frappé *m inv*.

milky [ˈmɪlkɪ] *adj (drink)* con tanto latte.

mill [mɪl] *n (flour-mill)* mulino *m* ; *(for pepper, coffee)* macinino *m* ; *(factory)* fabbrica *f*.

milligram [ˈmɪlɪgræm] *n* milligrammo *m*.

millilitre [ˈmɪlɪˌliːtəʳ] *n* millilitro *m*.

millimetre [ˈmɪlɪˌmiːtəʳ] *n* millimetro *m*.

million [ˈmɪljən] *n* milione *m* ; **~s of** *fig* milioni di.

millionaire [ˌmɪljəˈneəʳ] *n* ≃ miliardario *m*, -a *f*.

mime [maɪm] *vi* mimare.

min. [mɪn] (*abbr of minute, minimum*) min.

mince [mɪns] *n Br* carne *f* macinata.

mincemeat [ˈmɪnsmiːt] *n (sweet filling) miscuglio a base di uvetta e spezie* ; *Am (mince)* carne *f* macinata.

mince pie *n pasticcino con ripieno a base di uvetta e spezie che si mangia durante il periodo natalizio.*

mind [maɪnd] *n* mente *f*. ◆ *vt (be careful of)* fare attenzione a ; *(look after)* badare a. ◆ *vi* : **I don't ~** non m'importa ; **do you ~ if ...?** le dispiace se ...? ; **never ~!** *(don't worry)* non preoccuparti!, non importa! ;

it slipped my ~ mi è sfuggito di mente ; **to my ~** secondo me, a mio parere ; **to bear sthg in ~** tenere presente qc ; **to change one's ~** cambiare idea ; **to have sthg in ~** avere in mente qc ; **to have sthg on one's ~** essere preoccupato per qc ; **to make one's ~ up** decidersi ; **do you ~ the noise?** le dà fastidio il rumore? ; **I wouldn't ~ a drink** non mi dispiacerebbe bere qualcosa ; **'~ the gap!'** *(on underground) annuncio che avverte i viaggiatori sulla metropolitana di fare attenzione allo spazio vuoto tra le carozze e il marciapiede.*

mine[1] [maɪn] *pron* il mio (la mia), i miei (le mie) *(pl)* ; **a friend of ~** un mio amico.

mine[2] [maɪn] *n (for coal etc)* miniera *f* ; *(bomb)* mina *f*.

miner ['maɪnəʳ] *n* minatore *m*.

mineral ['mɪnərəl] *n* minerale *m*.

mineral water *n* acqua *f* minerale.

minestrone [ˌmɪnɪ'strəʊnɪ] *n* minestrone *m*.

miniature ['mɪnətʃəʳ] *adj* in miniatura. ◆ *n (bottle)* bottiglia *f* mignon.

minibar ['mɪnɪbɑːʳ] *n* minibar *m inv*.

minibus ['mɪnɪbʌs] *(pl* **-es***)* *n* minibus *m inv*.

minicab ['mɪnɪkæb] *n Br* radiotaxi *m inv*.

minimal ['mɪnɪml] *adj* minimo(a).

minimum ['mɪnɪməm] *adj* minimo(a). ◆ *n* minimo *m*.

miniskirt ['mɪnɪskɜːt] *n* minigonna *f*.

minister ['mɪnɪstəʳ] *n (in government)* ministro *m* ; *(in church)* pastore *m*.

ministry ['mɪnɪstrɪ] *n (of government)* ministero *m*.

minor ['maɪnəʳ] *adj* minore, di secondaria importanza. ◆ *n fml* minorenne *mf*.

minority [maɪ'nɒrətɪ] *n* minoranza *f*.

minor road *n* strada *f* secondaria.

mint [mɪnt] *n (sweet)* caramella *f* alla menta ; *(plant)* menta *f*.

minus ['maɪnəs] *prep (in subtraction)* meno ; **it's ~ 10 (degrees C)** è meno 10 (gradi).

minuscule ['mɪnəskjuːl] *adj* minuscolo(a).

minute[1] ['mɪnɪt] *n* minuto *m* ; **any ~** da un momento all'altro ; **just a ~!** (solo) un minuto!

minute[2] [maɪ'njuːt] *adj* minuscolo(a).

minute steak [ˌmɪnɪt-] *n* fettina *f (di carne)*.

miracle ['mɪrəkl] *n* miracolo *m*.

miraculous [mɪ'rækjʊləs] *adj* miracoloso(a).

mirror ['mɪrəʳ] *n* specchio *m* ; *(on car)* specchietto *m*.

misbehave [ˌmɪsbɪ'heɪv] *vi* comportarsi male.

miscarriage [ˌmɪs'kærɪdʒ] *n* aborto *m* spontaneo.

miscellaneous [ˌmɪsə'leɪnjəs] *adj (things)* vario(a) ; *(collection)* misto(a).

mischievous ['mɪstʃɪvəs] *adj* birichino(a).
misconduct [ˌmɪs'kɒndʌkt] *n* condotta *f* scorretta.
miser ['maɪzəʳ] *n* avaro *m*, -a *f*.
miserable ['mɪzrəbl] *adj (unhappy)* infelice ; *(place, news, weather)* deprimente ; *(amount)* misero(a).
misery ['mɪzərɪ] *n (unhappiness)* tristezza *f* ; *(poor conditions)* miseria *f*.
misfire [ˌmɪs'faɪəʳ] *vi (car)* perdere colpi.
misfortune [mɪs'fɔːtʃuːn] *n (bad luck)* sfortuna *f*.
mishap ['mɪshæp] *n* disavventura *f*.
misjudge [ˌmɪs'dʒʌdʒ] *vt* giudicare male.
mislay [ˌmɪs'leɪ] (*pt* & *pp* **-laid**) *vt* smarrire.
mislead [ˌmɪs'liːd] (*pt* & *pp* **-led**) *vt* trarre in inganno.
miss [mɪs] *vt* perdere ; *(not notice)* non vedere ; *(fail to hit)* mancare. ◆ *vi* sbagliare ; **I ~ you** mi manchi. ❑ **miss out** ◆ *vt sep* saltare, omettere. ◆ *vi* : **to ~ out on sthg** perdersi qc.
Miss [mɪs] *n* signorina *f*.
missile [*Br* 'mɪsaɪl, *Am* 'mɪsl] *n (weapon)* missile *m* ; *(thing thrown)* oggetto *m (scagliato)*.
missing ['mɪsɪŋ] *adj (lost)* scomparso(a) ; *(after accident)* disperso(a) ; **to be ~** *(not there)* mancare.
missing person *n* persona *f* scomparsa.
mission ['mɪʃn] *n* missione *f*.
missionary ['mɪʃənrɪ] *n* missionario *m*, -a *f*.
mist [mɪst] *n* foschia *f*.
mistake [mɪ'steɪk] (*pt* **-took**, *pp* **-taken**) *n* sbaglio *m*, errore *m*. ◆ *vt (misunderstand)* fraintendere ; **by ~** per sbaglio ; **to make a ~** fare uno sbaglio ; **to ~ sb/sthg for** scambiare qn/qc per.
Mister ['mɪstəʳ] *n* **~ Smith** signor *m* Smith.
mistook [mɪ'stʊk] *pt* → **mistake**.
mistress ['mɪstrɪs] *n (lover)* amante *f* ; *Br (teacher)* insegnante *f*.
mistrust [ˌmɪs'trʌst] *vt* diffidare di.
misty ['mɪstɪ] *adj* nebbioso(a).
misunderstanding [ˌmɪsʌndə'stændɪŋ] *n* malinteso *m*.
misuse [ˌmɪs'juːs] *n* cattivo uso *m*.
mitten ['mɪtn] *n* muffola *f*, manopola *f*.
mix [mɪks] *vt* mescolare. ◆ *n (for cake, sauce)* (miscuglio) preparato *m*. ◆ *vi (socially)* : **to ~ with people** veder gente ; **to ~ sthg with sthg** mescolare qc a OR con qc. ❑ **mix up** *vt sep (confuse)* confondere ; *(put into disorder)* mescolare.
mixed [mɪkst] *adj (school)* misto(a).
mixed grill *n* grigliata *f* mista.
mixed salad *n* insalata *f* mista.
mixed vegetables *npl* verdure *fpl* miste.
mixer ['mɪksəʳ] *n (for food)* frullatore *m* ; *(drink) bevanda analcolica usata nella preparazione di cocktail*.
mixture ['mɪkstʃəʳ] *n (combination)* mescolanza *f*.
mix-up *n inf* confusione *f*.
ml (*abbr of millilitre*) ml.

mm (*abbr of millimetre*) mm.
moan [məʊn] *vi (in pain, grief)* gemere ; *inf (complain)* lamentarsi.
mobile ['məʊbaɪl] *adj* mobile.
mobile phone *n* (telefono) *m* cellulare, telefonino *m*.
mock [mɒk] *adj* finto(a). ◆ *vt* deridere, prendersi gioco di. ◆ *n Br (exam)* esercitazione *f* d'esame.
mode [məʊd] *n* modo *m*.
model ['mɒdl] *n* modello *m* ; *(fashion model)* modello *m*, -a *f*.
moderate ['mɒdərət] *adj* moderato(a).
modern ['mɒdən] *adj* moderno(a).
modernized ['mɒdənaɪzd] *adj* rimodernato(a).
modern languages *npl* lingue *fpl* moderne.
modest ['mɒdɪst] *adj* modesto(a).
modify ['mɒdɪfaɪ] *vt* modificare.
mohair ['məʊheəʳ] *n* mohair *m*.
moist [mɔɪst] *adj* umido(a).
moisture ['mɔɪstʃəʳ] *n* umidità *f*.
moisturizer ['mɔɪstʃəraɪzəʳ] *n* idratante *m*.
molar ['məʊləʳ] *n* molare *m*.
mold [məʊld] *Am* = **mould**.
mole [məʊl] *n (animal)* talpa *f* ; *(spot)* neo *m*.
molest [mə'lest] *vt* molestare.
mom [mɒm] *n Am inf* mamma *f*.
moment ['məʊmənt] *n* momento *m* ; **at the ~** al momento ; **for the ~** per il momento.
Mon. (*abbr of Monday*) lun.
monarchy ['mɒnəkɪ] *n* : **the ~** la monarchia.
monastery ['mɒnəstrɪ] *n* monastero *m*.
Monday ['mʌndɪ] *n* lunedì *m inv* → **Saturday**.
money ['mʌnɪ] *n* denaro *m*, soldi *mpl*.
money belt *n* marsupio *m*.
money order *n* vaglia *m inv* (postale).
mongrel ['mʌŋgrəl] *n* cane *m* bastardo.
monitor ['mɒnɪtəʳ] *n (computer screen)* monitor *m inv*. ◆ *vt (check, observe)* controllare.
monk [mʌŋk] *n* monaco *m*.
monkey ['mʌŋkɪ] (*pl* **monkeys**) *n* scimmia *f*.
monkfish ['mʌŋkfɪʃ] *n* bottatrice *f*.
monopoly [mə'nɒpəlɪ] *n* monopolio *m*.
monorail ['mɒnəʊreɪl] *n* monorotaia *f*.
monotonous [mə'nɒtənəs] *adj* monotono(a).
monsoon [mɒn'suːn] *n* monsone *m*.
monster ['mɒnstəʳ] *n* mostro *m*.
month [mʌnθ] *n* mese *m* ; **every ~** ogni mese ; **in a ~'s time** fra un mese.
monthly ['mʌnθlɪ] *adj* mensile. ◆ *adv* mensilmente, ogni mese.
monument ['mɒnjʊmənt] *n* monumento *m*.
mood [muːd] *n* umore *m* ; **to be in a (bad) ~** essere di cattivo umore ; **to be in a good ~** essere di buon umore.
moody ['muːdɪ] *adj (in a bad*

mood) di malumore ; *(changeable)* lunatico(a), volubile.

moon [muːn] *n* luna *f.*

moonlight ['muːnlaɪt] *n* chiaro *m* di luna.

moor [mɔːʳ] *n* brughiera *f.* ◆ *vt* ormeggiare.

mop [mɒp] *n (for floor)* lavapavimenti *m inv.* ◆ *vt (floor)* lavare con lo straccio. ❑ **mop up** *vt sep (clean up)* asciugare con uno straccio.

moped ['məʊped] *n* ciclomotore *m.*

moral ['mɒrəl] *adj* morale. ◆ *n (lesson)* morale *f.*

morality [mə'rælɪtɪ] *n* moralità *f.*

☞

more [mɔːʳ] *adj* - 1. *(a larger amount of)* più ; **there are ~ tourists than usual** ci sono più turisti del solito.
- 2. *(additional)* altro(a) OR ancora ; **are there any ~ cakes?** ci sono altri pasticcini? ; **I'd like two ~ bottles** vorrei altre due bottiglie ; **there's no ~ wine** non c'è più vino.
- 3. *(in phrases)* : **~ and more** sempre più.
◆ *adv* - 1. *(in comparatives)* più ; **it's ~ difficult than before** è più difficile di prima ; **speak ~ clearly** parla più chiaramente.
- 2. *(to a greater degree)* di più ; **we ought to go to the cinema ~** dovremmo andare più spesso al cinema.
- 3. *(in phrases)* : **not ... any ~** non ... più ; **I don't go there any ~** non ci vado più ; **once ~** ancora una volta, un'altra volta ; **~ or less** più o meno ; **we'd be ~ than happy to help** saremmo più che lieti di dare una mano.
◆ *pron* - 1. *(a larger amount)* più ; **I've got ~ than you** ne ho più di te ; **~ than 20 types of pizza** oltre 20 tipi di pizza.
- 2. *(an additional amount)* ancora ; **is there any ~?** ce n'è ancora? ; **there's no ~** non ce n'è più.

---

moreover [mɔː'rəʊvəʳ] *adv fml* inoltre.

morning ['mɔːnɪŋ] *n* mattina *f,* mattino *m* ; **two o'clock in the ~** le due di notte ; **good ~!** buon giorno! ; **in the ~** *(early in the day)* di mattina ; *(tomorrow morning)* domattina.

morning-after pill *n* pillola *f* del giorno dopo.

morning sickness *n* nausea *f* mattutina.

moron ['mɔːrɒn] *n inf* deficiente *mf.*

mortgage ['mɔːgɪdʒ] *n* mutuo *m* (ipotecario).

mosaic [mə'zeɪɪk] *n* mosaico *m.*

Moslem ['mɒzləm] = **Muslim.**

mosque [mɒsk] *n* moschea *f.*

mosquito [mə'skiːtəʊ] (*pl* **-es**) *n* zanzara *f.*

mosquito net *n* zanzariera *f.*

moss [mɒs] *n* muschio *m.*

☞

most [məʊst] *adj* - 1. *(the majority of)* la maggior parte di ; **~ people agree** la maggior parte della gente è d'accordo.
- 2. *(the largest amount of)* : **I drank (the) ~ beer** sono quello che ha bevuto più birra.

◆ *adv* - 1. *(in superlatives)* più ; **the ~ expensive hotel in town** l'albergo più caro della città.
- 2. *(to the greatest degree)* di più, maggiormente ; **I like this one ~** questo è quello che mi piace di più.
- 3. *fml (very)* molto, estremamente ; **they were ~ welcoming** sono stati estremamente accoglienti.
◆ *pron* - 1. *(the majority)* la maggior parte ; **~ of the villages** la maggior parte dei paesi ; **~ of the time** la maggior parte del tempo.
- 2. *(the largest amount)* : **she earns (the) ~** è quella che guadagna di più.
- 3. *(in phrases)* : **at ~** al massimo ; **to make the ~ of sthg** sfruttare al massimo qc.

---

mostly ['məʊstlɪ] *adv* per lo più.
MOT *n Br (test) revisione annuale obbligatoria degli autoveicoli di più di tre anni.*
moth [mɒθ] *n* farfalla *f* notturna.
mother ['mʌðəʳ] *n* madre *f*.
mother-in-law *n* suocera *f*.
mother-of-pearl *n* madreperla *f*.
motif [məʊ'ti:f] *n* motivo *m*.
motion ['məʊʃn] *n (movement)* movimento *m*, moto *m*. ◆ *vi* : **to ~ to sb** fare cenno a qn.
motionless ['məʊʃənlɪs] *adj* immobile.
motivate ['məʊtɪveɪt] *vt (encourage)* motivare, stimolare.
motive ['məʊtɪv] *n* motivo *m*.
motor ['məʊtəʳ] *n (engine)* motore *m*.
motorbike ['məʊtəbaɪk] *n* moto *f inv*.
motorboat ['məʊtəbəʊt] *n* motoscafo *m*.
motorcar ['məʊtəka:ʳ] *n* automobile *f*.
motorcycle ['məʊtə,saɪkl] *n* motocicletta *f*.
motorcyclist ['məʊtə,saɪklɪst] *n* motociclista *mf*.
motorist ['məʊtərɪst] *n* automobilista *mf*.
motor racing *n* corse *fpl* automobilistiche.
motorway ['məʊtəweɪ] *n Br* autostrada *f*.
motto ['mɒtəʊ] (*pl* **-s**) *n* motto *m*.
mould [məʊld] *n [Br] (shape)* forma *f*, stampo *m* ; *(substance)* muffa *f*. ◆ *vt Br* formare, modellare.
mouldy ['məʊldɪ] *adj (Br)* ammuffito(a).
mound [maʊnd] *n (hill)* monticello *m*, collinetta *f*; *(pile)* mucchio *m*.
mount [maʊnt] *n (for photo)* supporto *m*; *(mountain)* monte *m*. ◆ *vt (horse)* montare a OR su ; *(photo)* sistemare. ◆ *vi (increase)* aumentare.
mountain ['maʊntɪn] *n* montagna *f*.
mountain bike *n* mountain bike *f inv*.
mountaineer [,maʊntɪ'nɪəʳ] *n* alpinista *mf*.
mountaineering [,maʊntɪ'nɪərɪŋ] *n* : **to go ~** fare alpinismo.
mountainous ['maʊntɪnəs] *adj* montagnoso(a).

Mount Rushmore [-'rʌʃmɔːʳ] *n* il monte Rushmore *(nel Sud Dakota)*.

MOUNT RUSHMORE

I ritratti giganteschi dei presidenti degli Stati Uniti Washington, Jefferson, Lincoln e Theodore Roosevelt, scolpiti nella roccia granitica, hanno trasformato il Monte Rushmore, nel Sud Dakota, in monumento nazionale e in grande centro di attrazione turistica.

---

mourning ['mɔːnɪŋ] *n* : **to be in ~** essere in lutto.

mouse [maʊs] (*pl* **mice**) *n (animal)* topo *m* ; *COMPUT* mouse *m inv*.

moussaka [muː'saːkə] *n piatto tipico della cucina greca e turca, composto da strati di carne macinata, melanzane e besciamella.*

mousse [muːs] *n* mousse *f inv*.

moustache [mə'staːʃ] *n Br* baffi *mpl*.

mouth [maʊθ] *n* bocca *f* ; *(of cave, tunnel)* entrata *f*, imboccatura *f* ; *(of river)* foce *f*, bocca.

mouthful ['maʊθfʊl] *n (of food)* boccone *m* ; *(of drink)* sorsata *f*.

mouthpiece ['maʊθpiːs] *n (of telephone)* microfono *m* ; *(of musical instrument)* bocchino *m*.

mouthwash ['maʊθwɒʃ] *n* collutorio *m*.

move [muːv] *n* mossa *f* ; *(change of house)* trasloco *m*. ◆ *vt (shift)* muovere, spostare ; *(emotionally)* commuovere. ◆ *vi (shift)* muoversi, spostarsi ; **to ~ (house)** cambiare casa, traslocare ; **to make a ~** *(leave)* andarsene. ❑ **move along** *vi* circolare, andare avanti. ❑ **move in** *vi (to house)* andare/venire ad abitare. ❑ **move off** *vi (train, car)* partire. ❑ **move on** *vi (after stopping)* ripartire. ❑ **move out** *vi (from house)* sgombrare. ❑ **move over** *vi* spostarsi. ❑ **move up** *vi (make room)* spostarsi.

movement ['muːvmənt] *n* movimento *m*.

movie ['muːvɪ] *n* film *m inv*.

movie theater *n Am* cinema *m inv*.

moving ['muːvɪŋ] *adj (emotionally)* commovente.

mow [məʊ] *vt* : **to ~ the lawn** tagliare l'erba *(del prato)*.

mozzarella [ˌmɒtsə'relə] *n* mozzarella *f*.

MP *n* (*abbr of Member of Parliament*) ≃ deputato *m*, -a *f*.

mph (*abbr of miles per hour*) *miglia all'ora.*

Mr ['mɪstəʳ] *abbr* Sig.

Mrs ['mɪsɪz] *abbr* Sig.ra.

Ms [mɪz] *abbr abbreviazione che comprende sia Mrs che Miss.*

MSc *n* (*abbr of Master of Science*) (degree) master *m inv* in materie scientifiche.

☞ ---

much [mʌtʃ] (*compar* **more**, *superl* **most**) *adj* molto(a) ; **I haven't got ~ money** non ho molti soldi ; **as ~ food as you can eat** tanto cibo quanto ne riesci a mangiare ; **how ~ time is left?** quanto tempo resta? ; **they have so ~ money** hanno

tanti di quei soldi ; **we have too ~ work** abbiamo troppo lavoro.
◆ *adv* - 1. *(to a great extent)* molto ; **it's ~ better** è molto meglio ; **I like it very ~** mi piace moltissimo ; **it's not ~ good** *inf* non è un granché ; **thank you very ~** grazie tante.
- 2. *(often)* spesso, molto ; **we don't go there ~** non ci andiamo spesso.
◆ *pron* molto ; **I haven't got ~** non ne ho molto ; **as ~ as you like** quanto ne vuoi ; **how ~ is it?** quant'è?, quanto costa?

---

muck [mʌk] *n (dirt)* sudiciume *m*. ❑ **muck about** *vi [Br] inf (have fun)* divertirsi ; *(waste time)* gingillarsi. ❑ **muck up** *vt sep Br inf* pasticciare.

mud [mʌd] *n* fango *m*.

muddle ['mʌdl] *n* : **to be in a ~** *(confused)* essere confuso ; *(in a mess)* essere in disordine.

muddy ['mʌdɪ] *adj* fangoso(a).

mudguard ['mʌdgaːd] *n* parafango *m*.

muesli ['mjuːzlɪ] *n* muesli *m inv*.

muffin ['mʌfɪn] *n (roll)* panino *m* soffice *(mangiato caldo, con burro)* ; *(cake)* pasticcino *m* soffice.

muffler ['mʌfləʳ] *n Am (silencer)* marmitta *f*.

mug [mʌg] *n (cup)* tazza *f* cilindrica. ◆ *vt* aggredire e derubare.

mugging ['mʌgɪŋ] *n* aggressione *f (a scopo di rapina)*.

muggy ['mʌgɪ] *adj* afoso(a).

mule [mjuːl] *n* mulo *m*.

multicoloured ['mʌltɪˌkʌləd] *adj* multicolore.

multiple ['mʌltɪpl] *adj* multiplo(a).

multiplex cinema ['mʌltɪpleks-] *n* cinema *m inv* multisala.

multiplication [ˌmʌltɪplɪ'keɪʃn] *n* moltiplicazione *f*.

multiply ['mʌltɪplaɪ] *vt* moltiplicare. ◆ *vi* moltiplicarsi.

multistorey (car park) [ˌmʌltɪ'stɔːrɪ-] *n* parcheggio *m* multipiano.

mum [mʌm] *n Br inf* mamma *f*.

mummy ['mʌmɪ] *n Br inf (mother)* mamma *f*.

mumps [mʌmps] *n* orecchioni *mpl*.

munch [mʌntʃ] *vt* sgranocchiare.

municipal [mjuː'nɪsɪpl] *adj* municipale.

mural ['mjuːərəl] *n* dipinto *m* murale.

murder ['mɜːdəʳ] *n* assassinio *m*, omicidio *m*. ◆ *vt* assassinare.

murderer ['mɜːdərəʳ] *n* assassino *m*, -a *f*, omicida *mf*.

muscle ['mʌsl] *n* muscolo *m*.

museum [mjuː'ziːəm] *n* museo *m*.

mushroom ['mʌʃrum] *n* fungo *m*.

music ['mjuːzɪk] *n* musica *f*.

musical ['mjuːzɪkl] *adj* musicale ; *(person)* portato(a) per la musica. ◆ *n* musical *m inv*.

musical instrument *n* strumento *m* musicale.

musician [mjuː'zɪʃn] *n* musicista *mf*.

Muslim ['muzlɪm] *adj* musulmano(a). ◆ *n* musulmano *m*, -a *f*.

mussels ['mʌslz] *npl* cozze *fpl*.

must [mʌst] *aux vb* dovere. ◆ *n inf* : **it's a ~** è d'obbligo ; **I ~ go** devo andare ; **you ~ have seen it** devi averlo visto ; **you ~ see that film** devi vedere quel film ; **you ~ be joking!** stai scherzando!

mustache ['mʌstæʃ] *Am* = **moustache.**

mustard ['mʌstəd] *n* senape *f*, mostarda *f*.

mustn't ['mʌsənt] = **must not.**

mutter ['mʌtəʳ] *vt* borbottare.

mutual ['mjuːtʃʊəl] *adj (feeling)* reciproco(a), mutuo(a) ; *(friend, interest)* comune.

muzzle ['mʌzl] *n (for dog)* museruola *f*.

my [maɪ] *adj* il mio (la mia), i miei (le mie) *(pl)* ; **~ brother** mio fratello.

myself [maɪ'self] *pron (reflexive)* mi ; *(after prep)* me ; **I did it ~** l'ho fatto da solo.

mysterious [mɪ'stɪərɪəs] *adj* misterioso(a).

mystery ['mɪstərɪ] *n* mistero *m*.

myth [mɪθ] *n* mito *m*.

N

N *(abbr of North)* N.

nag [næg] *vt* tormentare.

nail [neɪl] *n (of finger, toe)* unghia *f* ; *(metal)* chiodo *m*. ◆ *vt (fasten)* inchiodare.

nailbrush ['neɪlbrʌʃ] *n* spazzolino *m* da unghie.

nail file *n* limetta *f* per unghie.

nail scissors *npl* forbicine *fpl* da unghie.

nail varnish *n* smalto *m* per unghie.

nail varnish remover [-rə'muːvəʳ] *n* acetone *m*, solvente *m* per unghie.

naive [naɪ'iːv] *adj* ingenuo(a).

naked ['neɪkɪd] *adj (person)* nudo(a).

name [neɪm] *n* nome *m*. ◆ *vt (baby, animal)* chiamare ; *(place)* denominare ; *(identify)* dire il nome di, nominare ; *(date, price)* fissare ; **first ~** nome di battesimo ; **last ~** cognome *m* ; **what's your ~?** come si chiama? ; **my ~ is ...** mi chiamo ...

namely ['neɪmlɪ] *adv* cioè, vale a dire.

nanny ['nænɪ] *n (childminder)* bambinaia *f* ; *inf (grandmother)* nonna *f*.

nap [næp] *n* : **to have a ~** fare un pisolino.

napkin ['næpkɪn] *n* tovagliolo *m*.

Naples ['neɪplz] *n* Napoli *f*.

nappy ['næpɪ] *n* pannolino *m*.

narcotic [nɑː'kɒtik] *n* narcotico *m*.

narrow ['nærəʊ] *adj (road, gap)* stretto(a). ◆ *vi (road, gap)* restringersi.

narrow-minded [-'maɪndɪd] *adj* di idee ristrette.

nasty ['nɑːstɪ] *adj (person, comment, taste)* cattivo(a) ; *(accident, moment, feeling)* brutto(a).

nation ['neɪʃn] *n* nazione *f*.

national ['næʃənl] *adj* nazionale. ◆ *n* cittadino *m*, -a *f*.

national anthem *n* inno *m* nazionale.

National Health Service *n* ≃ Servizio *m* Sanitario Nazionale.

National Insurance *n Br (contributions)* ≃ Previdenza *f* Sociale.

nationality [ˌnæʃəˈnælətɪ] *n* nazionalità *f inv*.

national park *n* parco *m* nazionale.

NATIONAL PARK

Come in Italia, anche in Gran Bretagna e negli Stati Uniti i parchi naturali sono delle vaste zone protette per la loro bellezza naturale. Aperti al pubblico, sono sempre dotati di campeggi attrezzati. Fra i più famosi parchi della Gran Bretagna ricordiamo Snowdonia, il distretto dei Laghi e il Pick District, mentre Yellowstone e Yosemite sono fra i più famosi parchi nazionali americani.

nationwide [ˈneɪʃənwaɪd] *adj* su scala nazionale.

native [ˈneɪtɪv] *adj (customs, population)* indigeno(a) ; *(country)* d'origine. ◆ *n* nativo *m*, -a *f*; a ~ **speaker of English** una persona di madrelingua inglese.

NATIVE AMERICAN

Le tribù di indigeni americani che popolavano gli Stati Uniti prima dell'arrivo degli europei possedevano ciascuno una propria lingua e una propria cultura. Nel corso di due secoli, dal XVII al XIX, essi si videro costretti a difendere le proprie terre dai coloni europei anche con la forza. Molti indiani morirono in combattimento oppure in seguito a malattie portate in America dagli europei, mentre molti altri vennero obbligati a vivere nelle riserve. Nel corso del XX secolo il governo statunitense ha mostrato un crescente interesse per la storia e per le tradizioni dei gruppi etnici nativi degli Stati Uniti e si è adoperato affinché venissero loro riconosciuti maggiori diritti.

Native American *adj* indiano(a) (d'America). ◆ *n* indiano *m*, -a *f* (d'America).

NATO [ˈneɪtəʊ] *n* NATO *f*.

natural [ˈnætʃrəl] *adj (charm)* naturale ; *(ability)* innato(a) ; *(swimmer, actor)* nato(a).

natural gas *n* metano *m*, gas *m* naturale.

naturally [ˈnætʃrəlɪ] *adv (of course)* naturalmente.

natural yoghurt *n* yogurt *m inv* naturale.

nature [ˈneɪtʃəʳ] *n* natura *f*.

nature reserve *n* riserva *f* naturale.

naughty [ˈnɔːtɪ] *adj (child)* birichino(a).

nausea [ˈnɔːzɪə] *n* nausea *f*.

navigate [ˈnævɪgeɪt] *vi (in boat, plane)* calcolare la rotta ; *(in car)* fare da navigatore.

navy [ˈneɪvɪ] *n (ships)* marina *f* (militare). ◆ *adj* : ~ **(blue)** blu scuro *(inv)*.

NB *(abbr of nota bene)* N.B..

near [nɪəʳ] *adv* vicino. ◆ *adj*

(place, object) vicino(a) ; *(relation)* prossimo(a). ◆ *prep* : ~ **(to)** *(edge, object, place)* vicino a, presso ; **in the ~ future** nel prossimo futuro.
nearby [nɪə'baɪ] *adv* vicino. ◆ *adj* vicino(a).
nearly ['nɪəlɪ] *adv* quasi.
near side *n (for right-hand drive)* destra *f*; *(for left-hand drive)* sinistra *f*.
neat [ni:t] *adj (room)* ordinato(a) ; *(writing)* chiaro(a) ; *(work)* preciso(a) ; *(whisky, vodka etc)* liscio(a).
neatly ['ni:tlɪ] *adv (placed, arranged)* in modo ordinato ; *(written)* in modo chiaro.
necessarily [ˌnesə'serɪlɪ, *Br* 'nesəsrəlɪ] *adv* : **not ~** non necessariamente.
necessary ['nesəsrɪ] *adj* necessario(a) ; **it is ~ to do it** è necessario farlo.
necessity [nɪ'sesətɪ] *n* necessità *f inv*. ❑ **necessities** *npl* necessità *fpl*.
neck [nek] *n* collo *m*.
necklace ['neklɪs] *n* collana *f*.
nectarine ['nektərɪn] *n* pescanoce *f*.
need [ni:d] *n* bisogno *m*. ◆ *vt* avere bisogno di ; **to ~ to do sthg** dover fare qc ; **you don't ~ to go** non c'è bisogno che tu ci vada.
needle ['ni:dl] *n* ago *m* ; *(for record player)* puntina *f*.
needlework ['ni:dlwɜ:k] *n* SCH cucito *m*.
needn't ['ni:dənt] = **need not**.
needy ['ni:dɪ] *adj* bisognoso(a).
negative ['negətɪv] *adj* negativo(a). ◆ *n (in photography)* negativo *m* ; GRAMM negazione *f*.
neglect [nɪ'glekt] *vt* trascurare.
negligence ['neglɪdʒəns] *n* negligenza *f*.
negotiations [nɪˌgəʊʃɪ'eɪʃnz] *npl* negoziati *mpl*, trattative *fpl*.
negro ['ni:grəʊ] (*pl* **-es**) *n* negro *m*, -a *f*.
neighbour ['neɪbəʳ] *n* vicino *m*, -a *f*.
neighbourhood ['neɪbəhʊd] *n* quartiere *m*, vicinato *m*.
neighbouring ['neɪbərɪŋ] *adj* vicino(a), confinante.
neither ['naɪðəʳ, ni:ðəʳ] *adj* : **~ bag is big enough** nessuna delle due borse è abbastanza grande. ◆ *pron* :. ◆ *conj* : : **~ do I** neanch'io, nemmeno io ; **~ ... nor ...** né ... né ...
neon light ['ni:ɒn-] *n* luce *f* al neon.
nephew ['nefju:] *n* nipote *m*.
nerve [nɜ:v] *n (in body)* nervo *m* ; *(courage)* coraggio *m* ; **what a ~!** che faccia tosta!
nervous ['nɜ:vəs] *adj* nervoso(a).
nervous breakdown *n* esaurimento *m* nervoso.
nest [nest] *n* nido *m*.
net [net] *n* rete *f*. ◆ *adj* netto(a).
netball ['netbɔ:l] *n specie di pallacanestro femminile*.
Netherlands ['neðələndz] *npl* : **the ~** i Paesi Bassi.
nettle ['netl] *n* ortica *f*.
network ['netwɜ:k] *n* rete *f*.
neurotic [ˌnjʊə'rɒtɪk] *adj* nevrotico(a).

neutral ['nju:trəl] *adj (country, person)* neutrale ; *(in colour)* neutro(a). ◆ *n* AUT : **in ~** in folle.

never ['nevəʳ] *adv* (non ...) mai ; **she's ~ late** non è mai in ritardo ; **I ~ knew he was married** non sapevo che fosse sposato ; **~ mind!** non preoccuparti!

nevertheless [ˌnevəðə'les] *adv* tuttavia, ciononostante.

new [nju:] *adj* nuovo(a).

newly ['nju:lɪ] *adv* di recente.

news [nju:z] *n (information)* notizie *fpl* ; *(on TV)* telegiornale *m* ; *(on radio)* giornale *m* radio ; **a piece of ~** una notizia.

newsagent ['nju:zeɪdʒənt] *n (shop)* giornalaio *m*.

newspaper ['nju:zˌpeɪpəʳ] *n* giornale *m*.

New Year *n* anno *m* nuovo.

New Year's Day *n* Capodanno.

New Year's Eve *n* l'ultimo *m* dell'anno, San Silvestro *m*.

New Zealand [-'zi:lənd] *n* la Nuova Zelanda.

next [nekst] *adj* prossimo(a) ; *(room, house)* accanto. ◆ *adv (afterwards)* dopo ; *(on next occasion)* di nuovo ; **when does the ~ bus leave?** quando parte il prossimo autobus? ; **~ to** *(by the side of)* accanto a ; **the week after ~** la settimana dopo la prossima.

next door *adv* accanto.

next of kin [-kɪn] *n* parente *m* prossimo (parente prossima *f*).

NHS *n (abbr of National Health Service)* ≃ S.S.N. *m*.

nib [nɪb] *n* pennino *m*.

nibble ['nɪbl] *vt (eat)* mangiucchiare ; *(bite)* mordicchiare.

nice [naɪs] *adj (taste, meal)* buono(a) ; *(day, clothes, house)* bello(a) ; *(person, gesture)* simpatico(a), gentile ; *(feeling, job)* piacevole ; **to have a ~ time** divertirsi ; **~ to see you!** piacere di rivederti!

nickel ['nɪkl] *n (metal)* nichel *m* ; *Am (coin) moneta da cinque centesimi di dollaro*.

nickname ['nɪkneɪm] *n* soprannome *m*.

niece [ni:s] *n* nipote *f*.

night [naɪt] *n* notte *f* ; *(evening)* sera *f* ; **at ~** *(not in daytime)* di notte ; *(in evening)* di sera ; **by ~** di notte ; **last ~** *(yesterday evening)* ieri sera ; *(very late)* ieri notte.

nightclub ['naɪtklʌb] *n* locale *m* notturno.

nightdress ['naɪtdres] *n* camicia *f* da notte.

nightie ['naɪtɪ] *n inf* camicia *f* da notte.

nightlife ['naɪtlaɪf] *n* vita *f* notturna.

nightly ['naɪtlɪ] *adv* ogni notte ; *(every evening)* ogni sera.

nightmare ['naɪtmeəʳ] *n* incubo *m*.

night safe *n* cassa *f* continua.

night school *n* scuola *f* serale.

nightshift ['naɪtʃɪft] *n* turno *m* di notte.

nil [nɪl] *n* SPORT zero *m*.

Nile [naɪl] *n* : **the ~** il Nilo.

nine [naɪn] *num* nove → **six**.

nineteen [ˌnaɪn'ti:n] *num* diciannove ; ~ **ninety-five** millenovecentonovantacinque → **six**.

nineteenth [ˌnaɪnˈtiːnθ] *num* diciannovesimo(a) → **sixth**.

ninetieth [ˈnaɪntɪəθ] *num* novantesimo(a) → **sixth**.

ninety [ˈnaɪntɪ] *num* novanta → **six**.

ninth [naɪnθ] *num* nono(a) → **sixth**.

nip [nɪp] *vt (pinch)* pizzicare.

nipple [ˈnɪpl] *n (of breast)* capezzolo *m* ; *(of bottle)* tettarella *f*.

no [nəʊ] *adv* no. ◆ *adj* nessuno(a). ◆ *n* no *m inv* ; **I've got ~ time** non ho tempo ; **I've got ~ money left** non ho più soldi.

noble [ˈnəʊbl] *adj* nobile.

nobody [ˈnəʊbədɪ] *pron* nessuno.

nod [nɒd] *vi (in agreement)* annuire.

noise [nɔɪz] *n* rumore *m*.

noisy [ˈnɔɪzɪ] *adj* rumoroso(a).

nominate [ˈnɒmɪneɪt] *vt (choose)* nominare ; *(suggest)* proporre come candidato.

non-alcoholic *adj* analcolico(a).

none [nʌn] *pron* nessuno *m*, -a *f* ; **there's ~ left** non ce n'è più.

nonetheless [ˌnʌnðəˈles] *adv* tuttavia, nondimeno.

non-fiction *n* opere *fpl* non narrative *(saggistica, ecc.)*.

non-iron *adj* : **'non-iron'** 'lava e indossa', 'non stiro'.

nonsense [ˈnɒnsəns] *n* sciocchezze *fpl*, fesserie *fpl*.

non-smoker *n* non fumatore *m*, -trice *f*.

non-stick *adj* antiaderente.

non-stop *adj (flight)* diretto(a) ; *(talking, arguing)* continuo(a). ◆ *adv (fly)* senza scalo ; *(run, rain)* ininterrottamente, senza sosta.

noodles [ˈnuːdlz] *npl* taglierini *mpl*.

noon [nuːn] *n* mezzogiorno *m*.

no-one = **nobody**.

nor [nɔːʳ] *conj* neanche, nemmeno ; ~ **do I** neanch'io, nemmeno io, neither.

normal [ˈnɔːml] *adj* normale.

normally [ˈnɔːməlɪ] *adv* normalmente.

north [nɔːθ] *n* nord *m*, settentrione *m*. ◆ *adj* del nord. ◆ *adv (fly, walk)* verso nord ; *(be situated)* a nord ; **in the ~ of England** nel nord dell'Inghilterra.

North America *n* l'America *f* del Nord.

northbound [ˈnɔːθbaʊnd] *adj* diretto(a) a nord.

northeast [ˌnɔːθˈiːst] *n* nord-est *m*.

northern [ˈnɔːðən] *adj* settentrionale, del nord.

Northern Ireland *n* l'Irlanda *f* del Nord.

North Pole *n* Polo *m* Nord.

North Sea *n* Mare *m* del Nord.

northwards [ˈnɔːθwədz] *adv* verso nord.

northwest [ˌnɔːθˈwest] *n* nord-ovest *m*.

Norway [ˈnɔːweɪ] *n* la Norvegia.

Norwegian [nɔːˈwiːdʒən] *adj* norvegese. ◆ *n (person)* norvegese *mf* ; *(language)* norvegese *m*.

nose [nəʊz] *n (of person)* naso *m* ;

(of animal, plane) muso *m* ; *(of rocket)* punta *f*.
nosebleed ['nəuzbli:d] *n* emorragia *f* nasale.
no-smoking area *n* zona *f* non fumatori.
nostril ['nɒstrəl] *n* narice *f*.
nosy ['nəuzɪ] *adj* curioso(a).
not [nɒt] *adv* non ; **she's ~ there** non c'è ; **~ yet** non ancora ; **~ at all** *(pleased, interested)* per niente ; *(in reply to thanks)* di niente, prego.
notably ['nəutəblɪ] *adv (in particular)* in particolare.
note [nəut] *n* nota *f* ; *(message, bank note)* biglietto *m*. ◆ *vt (notice)* notare ; *(write down)* annotare ; **to take ~s** prendere appunti.
notebook ['nəutbuk] *n* taccuino *m*.
noted ['nəutɪd] *adj* celebre.
notepaper ['nəutpeɪpəʳ] *n* carta *f* da lettere.
nothing ['nʌθɪŋ] *pron* niente, nulla ; **he did ~** non ha fatto niente ; **~ new/interesting** niente di nuovo/interessante.
notice ['nəutɪs] *vt* notare, accorgersi di. ◆ *n (written announcement)* avviso *m* ; *(warning)* preavviso *m* ; **to take ~ of** fare caso a ; **to hand in one's ~** dare il preavviso, licenziarsi.
noticeable ['nəutɪsəbl] *adj* evidente.
notice board *n* tabellone *m* per avvisi.
notion ['nəuʃn] *n* idea *f*.
notorious [nəu'tɔ:rɪəs] *adj* famigerato(a).
nougat ['nu:ga:] *n* torrone *m*.
nought [nɔ:t] *n* zero *m*.
noun [naun] *n* nome *m*, sostantivo *m*.
nourishment ['nʌrɪʃmənt] *n* nutrimento *m*.
Nov. *(abbr of November)* nov.
novel ['nɒvl] *n* romanzo *m*. ◆ *adj* nuovo(a).
novelist ['nɒvəlɪst] *n* romanziere *m*, -a *f*.
November [nə'vembəʳ] *n* novembre *m* → **September**.
now [nau] *adv* ora, adesso. ◆ *conj* : **~ (that)** adesso che, ora che ; **just ~** proprio ora ; **right ~** *(at the moment)* in questo momento ; *(immediately)* subito ; **by ~** ormai ; **from ~ on** d'ora in poi.
nowadays ['nauədeɪz] *adv* oggigiorno.
nowhere ['nəuweəʳ] *adv* da nessuna parte, in nessun posto.
nozzle ['nɒzl] *n* boccaglio *m*.
nuclear ['nju:klɪəʳ] *adj* nucleare.
nude [nju:d] *adj* nudo(a).
nudge [nʌdʒ] *vt* dare un colpetto di gomito a.
nuisance ['nju:sns] *n* : **it's a real ~!** è una vera seccatura! ; **he's such a ~!** è un tale scocciatore!
numb [nʌm] *adj* intorpidito(a).
number ['nʌmbəʳ] *n* numero *m*. ◆ *vt (give number to)* numerare.
numberplate ['nʌmbəpleɪt] *n* targa *f*.
numeral ['nju:mərəl] *n* numero *m*, cifra *f*.
numerous ['nju:mərəs] *adj* numeroso(a).
nun [nʌn] *n* suora *f*.
nurse [nɜ:s] *n* infermiera *f*. ◆ *vt*

(look after) avere cura di, curare ; **male ~** infermiere *m*.

nursery ['nɜːsərɪ] *n (in house)* stanza *f* dei bambini ; *(for plants)* vivaio *m*.

nursery (school) *n* scuola *f* materna.

nursery slope *n* pista *f* per sciatori principianti.

nursing ['nɜːsɪŋ] *n (profession)* professione *f* d'infermiera.

nut [nʌt] *n (to eat)* frutta *f* secca *(noci, nocciole, ecc.)* ; *(of metal)* dado *m*.

nutcrackers ['nʌtˌkrækəz] *npl* schiaccianoci *m inv*.

nutmeg ['nʌtmeg] *n* noce *f* moscata.

nylon ['naɪlɒn] *n* nailon *m*. ◆ *adj* di nailon.

oak [əʊk] *n* quercia *f*. ◆ *adj* di quercia.

OAP *abbr* = **old age pensioner.**

oar [ɔːʳ] *n* remo *m*.

oatcake ['əʊtkeɪk] *n* biscotto *m* di farina d'avena.

oath [əʊθ] *n (promise)* giuramento *m*.

oatmeal ['əʊtmiːl] *n* farina *f* d'avena.

oats [əʊts] *npl* avena *f*.

obedient [ə'biːdjənt] *adj* ubbidiente.

obey [ə'beɪ] *vt (person, command)* ubbidire a ; *(regulations)* osservare.

object [*n* 'ɒbdʒɪkt, *vb* ɒb'dʒekt] *n (thing)* oggetto *m* ; *(purpose)* scopo *m* ; GRAMM complemento *m* oggetto. ◆ *vi* : **to ~ (to)** *(disapprove of)* disapprovare ; *(oppose)* opporsi (a), protestare (contro).

objection [əb'dʒekʃn] *n* obiezione *f*.

objective [əb'dʒektɪv] *n* obiettivo *m*.

obligation [ˌɒblɪ'geɪʃn] *n* obbligo *m*, dovere *m*.

obligatory [ə'blɪgətrɪ] *adj* obbligatorio(a).

oblige [ə'blaɪdʒ] *vt* : **to ~ sb to do sthg** obbligare qn a fare qc.

oblique [ə'bliːk] *adj* obliquo(a).

oblong ['ɒblɒŋ] *adj* oblungo(a), rettangolare. ◆ *n* rettangolo *m*.

obnoxious [əb'nɒkʃəs] *adj* odioso(a).

obscene [əb'siːn] *adj* osceno(a).

obscure [əb'skjʊəʳ] *adj* oscuro(a).

observant [əb'zɜːvnt] *adj* dotato(a) di spirito d'osservazione.

observation [ˌɒbzə'veɪʃn] *n* osservazione *f*.

observe [əb'zɜːv] *vt (watch, see)* osservare.

obsessed [əb'sest] *adj* ossessionato(a).

obsession [əb'seʃn] *n* ossessione *f*.

obsolete ['ɒbsəliːt] *adj* obsoleto(a).

obstacle ['ɒbstəkl] *n* ostacolo *m*.

obstinate ['ɒbstənət] *adj* ostinato(a).

obstruct [əb'strʌkt] *vt (road, path)* ostruire.
obstruction [əb'strʌkʃn] *n (in road, path)* ostruzione *f*.
obtain [əb'teɪn] *vt* ottenere.
obtainable [əb'teɪnəbl] *adj* ottenibile.
obvious ['ɒbvɪəs] *adj* ovvio(a), evidente.
obviously ['ɒbvɪəslɪ] *adv* ovviamente.
occasion [ə'keɪʒn] *n* occasione *f*; *(important event)* avvenimento *m*.
occasional [ə'keɪʒənl] *adj* saltuario(a), occasionale.
occasionally [ə'keɪʒnəlɪ] *adv* saltuariamente, di tanto in tanto.
occupant ['ɒkjʊpənt] *n* occupante *mf*.
occupation [ˌɒkjʊ'peɪʃn] *n* lavoro *m*; *(on form)* occupazione *f*.
occupied ['ɒkjʊpaɪd] *adj (toilet)* occupato(a).
occupy ['ɒkjʊpaɪ] *vt* occupare.
occur [ə'kɜːʳ] *vi (happen)* accadere, avvenire; *(exist)* trovarsi, essere presente.
occurrence [ə'kʌrəns] *n (event)* evento *m*, caso *m*.
ocean ['əʊʃn] *n* oceano *m*; **the ~** *Am (sea)* il mare.
o'clock [ə'klɒk] *adv*: **it's one ~** è l'una; **it's seven ~** sono le sette; **at one ~** all'una; **at seven ~** alle sette.
Oct. *(abbr of October)* ott.
October [ɒk'təʊbəʳ] *n* ottobre *m* → **September**.
octopus ['ɒktəpəs] *n* polpo *m*, piovra *f*.
odd [ɒd] *adj (strange)* strano(a); *(number)* dispari *(inv)*; *(not matching)* spaiato(a); *(occasional)* saltuario(a), occasionale; **60 ~ miles** una sessantina di miglia; **some ~ bits of paper** vari pezzetti di carta vari; **~ jobs** lavori *mpl* occasionali.
odds [ɒdz] *npl (in betting)* quota *f*; *(chances)* probabilità *fpl*; **~ and ends** un po' di tutto.
odor ['əʊdər] *Am* = **odour**.
odour ['əʊdəʳ] *n Br* odore *m*.

of [ɒv] *prep* - 1. *(gen)* di; **a group ~ schoolchildren** un gruppo di scolari; **a great love ~ art** un grande amore per l'arte.
- 2. *(expressing amount)* di; **a piece ~ cake** una fetta di torta; **a fall ~ 20%** un ribasso del 20%; **a town ~ 50,000 people** una città di 50 000 abitanti.
- 3. *(made from)* di, in; **a house ~ stone** una casa di pietra; **it's made ~ wood** è di OR in legno.
- 4. *(referring to time)* di; **the summer ~ 1969** l'estate del 1969; **the 26th ~ August** il 26 agosto.
- 5. *(indicating cause)* di; **he died ~ cancer** è morto di cancro.
- 6. *(on the part of)* da parte di; **that was very kind ~ you** è stato molto gentile da parte tua.
- 7. *Am (in telling the time)*: **it's ten ~ four** sono le quattro meno dieci.

off [ɒf] *adv* - 1. *(away)*: **to drive ~** partire; **to get ~** *(from bus, train, plane, boat)* scendere; **we're ~ to Austria next week** partiamo per l'Austria la settimana prossima.
- 2. *(expressing removal)*: **to cut**

sthg ~ tagliare qc ; **to take sthg ~** togliere qc.
- 3. *(so as to stop working)* : **to turn sthg ~** *(TV, radio, engine)* spegnere qc ; *(tap)* chiudere qc.
- 4. *(expressing distance or time away)* : **it's 10 miles ~** è a 10 miglia (da qui) ; **it's two months ~** mancano due mesi ; **it's a long way ~** è lontano.
- 5. *(not at work)* : **I'm ~ next Tuesday** martedì prossimo non lavoro ; **I'm taking a week ~** prendo una settimana di ferie.
◆ *prep* - 1. *(away from)* da ; **to get ~ sthg** scendere da qc ; **~ the coast** al largo della costa ; **just ~ the main road** poco lontano dalla strada principale.
- 2. *(indicating removal)* da ; **take the lid ~ the jar** togli il tappo dal barattolo ; **they've taken £20 ~ the price** mi hanno fatto uno sconto di 20 sterline.
- 3. *(absent from)* : **to be ~ work** essere assente dal lavoro.
- 4. *inf (from)* da ; **I bought it ~ her** l'ho comprato da lei.
- 5. *inf (no longer liking)* : **I'm ~ my food** non ho appetito, non mi va di mangiare.
◆ *adj* - 1. *(food)* andato(a) a male.
- 2. *(TV, radio, engine)* spento(a) ; *(tap)* chiuso(a).
- 3. *(cancelled)* annullato(a).
- 4. *(not available)* esaurito(a).

---

offence [ə'fens] *n [Br] (minor crime)* infrazione *f* ; *(serious crime)* reato *m* ; **to take ~ (at)** offendersi (per).

offend [ə'fend] *vt (upset)* offendere.

offender [ə'fendəʳ] *n (criminal)* delinquente *mf*.

offense [ə'fens] *Am* = **offence**.

offensive [ə'fensɪv] *adj (insulting)* offensivo(a).

offer ['ɒfəʳ] *n* offerta *f*. ◆ *vt* offrire ; **on ~** *(at reduced price)* in offerta ; **to ~ to do sthg** offrirsi di fare qc ; **to ~ sb sthg** offrire qc a qn.

office ['ɒfɪs] *n (room)* ufficio *m*.

office block *n* palazzo *m* di uffici.

officer ['ɒfɪsəʳ] *n (MIL)* ufficiale *m* ; *(policeman)* agente *m* (di polizia).

official [ə'fɪʃl] *adj* ufficiale. ◆ *n* funzionario *m*, -a *f*.

officially [ə'fɪʃəlɪ] *adv* ufficialmente.

off-licence *n Br* negozio *m* di bevande alcoliche.

off-peak *adj (train)* delle ore non di punta ; *(ticket)* a tariffa ridotta.

off-season *n* bassa stagione *f*.

offshore ['ɒfʃɔːʳ] *adj (breeze)* di terra.

off side *n (for right-hand drive)* lato *m* destro ; *(for left-hand drive)* lato sinistro.

off-the-peg *adj* confezionato(a).

often ['ɒfn, 'ɒftn] *adv* spesso ; **how ~ do the buses run?** ogni quanto passano gli autobus? ; **every so ~** ogni tanto.

oh [əʊ] *excl* oh!

oil [ɔɪl] *n* olio *m* ; *(fuel)* petrolio *m*.

oil rig *n* piattaforma *f* petrolifera.

oily ['ɔɪlɪ] *adj* unto(a).

ointment ['ɔɪntmənt] *n* unguento *m*, pomata *f*.
OK [,əʊ'keɪ] *adv inf (expressing agreement)* va bene, d'accordo ; *(satisfactorily, well)* bene. ◆ *adj (of average quality)* non male ; **is that ~?** va bene? ; **are you ~?** tutto bene?
okay [,əʊ'keɪ] = **OK**.
old [əʊld] *adj* vecchio(a) ; *(person)* vecchio, anziano(a) ; **how ~ are you?** quanti anni hai? ; **I'm 36 years ~** ho 36 anni ; **to get ~** invecchiare.
old age *n* vecchiaia *f*.
old age pensioner *n* pensionato *m*, -a *f*.
O level *n esame oggi sostituito dal 'GCSE'*.
olive ['ɒlɪv] *n* oliva *f*.
olive oil *n* olio *m* d'oliva.
omelette ['ɒmlɪt] *n* frittata *f*, omelette *f inv* ; **mushroom ~** frittata ai funghi.
ominous ['ɒmɪnəs] *adj* sinistro(a).
omit [ə'mɪt] *vt* omettere.

☞

on [ɒn] *prep* - 1. *(expressing position, location)* su ; **it's ~ the table** è sul tavolo ; **a picture ~ the wall** un quadro alla parete ; **the exhaust ~ the car** il tubo di scappamento dell'automobile ; **~ my right** alla mia destra ; **~ the right** a OR sulla destra ; **we stayed ~ a farm** ci siamo fermati in una fattoria ; **a hotel ~ George Street** un albergo in George Street.
- 2. *(with forms of transport)* : **~ the train/plane** in treno/aereo ; **to get ~ a bus** salire su un autobus.
- 3. *(expressing means, method)* : **~ foot** a piedi ; **~ the radio** alla radio ; **~ TV** in TV, alla televisione ; **~ the piano** al piano.
- 4. *(using)* : **it runs ~ unleaded petrol** va a benzina verde ; **to be ~ medication** prendere medicine.
- 5. *(about)* su ; **a book ~ Germany** un libro sulla Germania.
- 6. *(expressing time)* : **~ arrival** all'arrivo ; **~ Tuesday** martedì ; **~ 25th August** il 25 agosto.
- 7. *(with regard to)* su ; **a tax ~ imports** una tassa sulle importazioni ; **the effect ~ Britain** l'effetto sulla Gran Bretagna.
- 8. *(describing activity, state)* in ; **~ holiday** in vacanza ; **~ offer** in offerta ; **~ sale** in vendita.
- 9. *(in phrases)* : **do you have any money ~ you?** *inf* hai un po' di soldi con te? ; **the drinks are ~ me** offro io da bere.
◆ *adv* - 1. *(in place, covering)* : **to have sthg ~** *(clothes)* indossare qc ; **put the lid ~** mettici il coperchio ; **to put one's clothes ~** vestirsi.
- 2. *(film, play, programme)* : **the news is ~** c'è il telegiornale ; **what's ~ at the cinema?** cosa danno al cinema?
- 3. *(with transport)* : **to get ~** salire.
- 4. *(functioning)* : **to turn sthg ~** *(TV, radio, engine)* accendere qc ; *(tap)* aprire qc.
- 5. *(taking place)* : **how long is the festival ~?** quanto (tempo) dura il festival?
- 6. *(further forward)* : **to drive ~** continuare a guidare.
- 7. *(in phrases)* : **do you have anything ~ tonight?** fai qualcosa stasera?

◆ *adj (TV, engine, light)* acceso(a) ; *(tap)* aperto(a).

once [wʌns] *adv* una volta. ◆ *conj* una volta che, non appena ; **at ~** *(immediately)* subito ; *(at the same time)* insieme, contemporaneamente ; **for ~** per una volta ; **~ more** ancora una volta.

oncoming ['ɒnˌkʌmɪŋ] *adj (traffic)* che procede in senso opposto.

one [wʌn] *num* uno(a). ◆ *adj (only)* unico(a). ◆ *pron* uno *m*, -a *f* ; **thirty- ~** trentuno ; **~ fifth** un quinto ; **that ~** quello *m*, -a *f* ; **which ~?** quale? ; **this ~** questo *m*, -a *f* ; **I want ~** ne voglio uno ; **the ~ I told you about** quello di cui ti ho detto ; **~ of my friends** uno dei miei amici ; **~ day** un giorno.

oneself [wʌn'self] *pron (reflexive)* si ; *(after prep)* sé, se stesso *m*, -a *f*.

one-way *adj (street)* a senso unico ; *(ticket)* di sola andata.

onion ['ʌnjən] *n* cipolla *f*.

only ['əunlɪ] *adj* solo(a), unico(a). ◆ *adv* solo, soltanto ; **he's an ~ child** è figlio unico ; **I ~ want one** ne voglio solo uno ; **we've ~ just arrived** siamo appena arrivati ; **there's ~ just enough** ce n'è appena a sufficienza ; **'members ~'** 'riservato ai soci' ; **not ~** non solo.

onto ['ɒntu:] *prep (with verbs of movement)* su.

onward ['ɒnwəd] *adv* = **onwards**. ◆ *adj* : **the ~ journey** il proseguimento.

onwards ['ɒnwədz] *adv (forwards)* in avanti ; **from now ~** da ora in poi ; **from October ~** da ottobre in poi.

opal ['əupl] *n* opale *m o f*.

opaque [əu'peɪk] *adj (not transparent)* opaco(a).

open ['əupn] *adj* aperto(a). ◆ *vt* aprire. ◆ *vi (door, lock, meeting)* aprirsi ; *(shop, office, bank)* aprire ; *(play, film)* cominciare ; **are you ~ at the weekend?** siete aperti il fine settimana? ; **wide ~** spalancato(a) ; **in the ~ (air)** all'aperto.
❑ **open onto** *vt fus* dare su.
❑ **open up** *vi* aprire.

OPEN UNIVERSITY

La *Open University (OU)* è un'università inglese che offre corsi a distanza per studenti adulti che vogliano laurearsi studiando da casa. L'insegnamento viene impartito attraverso programmi televisivi e radiofonici, corsi per corrispondenza e corsi estivi che gli studenti possono frequentare di persona.

open-air *adj* all'aperto.

opening ['əupnɪŋ] *n* apertura *f* ; *(opportunity)* opportunità *f inv*.

opening hours *npl* orario *m* di apertura.

open-minded [-'maɪndɪd] *adj* aperto(a).

open-plan *adj* senza pareti divisorie.

opera ['ɒpərə] *n* opera *f*.

opera house *n* teatro *m* dell'opera.

operate ['ɒpəreɪt] *vt (machine)* azionare, far funzionare. ◆ *vi* *(work)* funzionare, agire ; **to ~ on sb** operare qn.

operating room ['ɒpəreɪtɪŋ-] *n Am* = **operating theatre.**

operating theatre ['ɒpəreɪtɪŋ-] *n Br* sala *f* operatoria.

operation [ˌɒpə'reɪʃn] *n* operazione *f* ; **to be in ~** *(law, system)* essere in vigore ; **to have an ~** farsi operare.

operator ['ɒpəreɪtəʳ] *n (on phone)* centralinista *mf.*

opinion [ə'pɪnjən] *n* opinione *f,* parere *m* ; **in my ~** a mio parere, secondo me.

opponent [ə'pəunənt] *n* avversario *m,* -a *f.*

opportunity [ˌɒpə'tju:nətɪ] *n* opportunità *f inv,* occasione *f.*

oppose [ə'pəuz] *vt* opporsi a.

opposed [ə'pəuzd] *adj* **: to be ~ to** essere contrario(a) a.

opposite ['ɒpəzɪt] *adj (facing)* di fronte ; *(totally different)* opposto(a), contrario(a). ◆ *prep* di fronte a. ◆ *n* **: the ~ (of)** il contrario (di).

opposition [ˌɒpə'zɪʃn] *n* opposizione *f* ; *SPORT* avversari *mpl.*

opt [ɒpt] *vt* **: to ~ to do sthg** scegliere di fare qc.

optician's [ɒp'tɪʃns] *n (shop)* ottico *m.*

optimist ['ɒptɪmɪst] *n* ottimista *mf.*

optimistic [ˌɒptɪ'mɪstɪk] *adj* ottimistico(a).

option ['ɒpʃn] *n (alternative)* scelta *f,* alternativa *f* ; *(optional extra)* optional *m inv.*

optional ['ɒpʃənl] *adj* facoltativo(a).

or [ɔ:ʳ] *conj* o, oppure ; *(otherwise)* se no, altrimenti ; *(after negative)* **: I can't read ~ write** non so (né) leggere né scrivere.

oral ['ɔ:rəl] *adj* orale. ◆ *n* orale *m.*

orange ['ɒrɪndʒ] *adj* arancione. ◆ *n (fruit)* arancia *f* ; *(colour)* arancione *m.*

orange juice *n* succo *m* d'arancia.

orange squash *n Br* aranciata *f* non gassata.

orbit ['ɔ:bɪt] *n* orbita *f.*

orchard ['ɔ:tʃəd] *n* frutteto *m.*

orchestra ['ɔ:kɪstrə] *n* orchestra *f.*

ordeal [ɔ:'di:l] *n* (durissima) esperienza *f,* travaglio *m.*

order ['ɔ:dəʳ] *n* ordine *m* ; *(in restaurant, for goods)* ordinazione *f.* ◆ *vt & vi* ordinare ; **in ~ to** allo scopo di, per ; **out of ~** *(not working)* guasto ; **in working ~** funzionante ; **to ~ sb to do sthg** ordinare a qn di fare qc.

order form *n* modulo *m* d'ordinazione.

ordinary ['ɔ:dənrɪ] *adj* ordinario(a), comune.

oregano [ˌɒrɪ'gɑ:nəu] *n* origano *m.*

organ ['ɔ:gən] *n* organo *m.*

organic [ɔ:'gænɪk] *adj (food)* biologico(a).

organization [ˌɔ:gənaɪ'zeɪʃn] *n* organizzazione *f.*

organize ['ɔ:gənaɪz] *vt* organizzare.

organizer ['ɔ:gənaɪzəʳ] *n (person)*

organizzatore *m*, -trice *f*; *(diary)* agenda *f*.

oriental [ˌɔːrɪ'entl] *adj* orientale.

orientate ['ɔːrɪenteɪt] *vt*: **to ~ o.s.** orientarsi.

origin ['ɒrɪdʒɪn] *n* origine *f*.

original [ə'rɪdʒənl] *adj (first)* originario(a) ; *(novel)* originale.

originally [ə'rɪdʒənəlɪ] *adv (formerly)* originariamente.

originate [ə'rɪdʒəneɪt] *vi*: **to ~ (from)** avere origine (da).

ornament ['ɔːnəmənt] *n (object)* soprammobile *m*.

ornamental [ˌɔːnə'mentl] *adj* ornamentale.

orphan ['ɔːfn] *n* orfano *m*, -a *f*.

orthodox ['ɔːθədɒks] *adj* ortodosso(a).

ostentatious [ˌɒstən'teɪʃəs] *adj* pretenzioso(a) ; *(action, behaviour)* ostentato(a).

ostrich ['ɒstrɪtʃ] *n* struzzo *m*.

other ['ʌðə^r] *adj* altro(a). ◆ *pron* altro(a). ◆ *adv* : **~ than** a parte ; **the ~ (one)** l'altro ; **the ~ day** l'altro giorno ; **one after the ~** uno dopo l'altro.

otherwise ['ʌðəwaɪz] *adv* altrimenti.

otter ['ɒtə^r] *n* lontra *f*.

ought [ɔːt] *aux vb* dovere ; **you ~ to have gone** avresti dovuto andarci ; **you ~ to see a doctor** dovresti andare dal dottore ; **the car ~ to be ready by Friday** la macchina dovrebbe essere pronta per venerdì.

ounce [auns] *n (unit of measurement)* = 28,35 g, oncia *f*.

our ['auə^r] *adj* il nostro (la nostra), i nostri (le nostre) *(pl)* ; **~ mother** nostra madre.

ours ['auəz] *pron* il nostro (la nostra), i nostri (le nostre) *(pl)* ; **a friend of ~** un nostro amico.

ourselves [auə'selvz] *pron (reflexive)* ci ; *(after prep)* noi, noi stessi *mpl*, -e *fpl* ; **we did it ~** l'abbiamo fatto da soli.

---

out [aut] *adj* - **1.** *(light, cigarette)* spento(a).

- **2.** *(wrong)* inesatto(a) ; **the bill's £10 ~** c'è un errore di 10 sterline nel conto.

◆ *adv* - **1.** *(outside)* fuori ; **to get ~ (of)** *(car)* scendere (da) ; **to go ~ (of)** uscire (da) ; **it's cold ~** fa freddo fuori.

- **2.** *(not at home, work)* fuori ; **to go ~** uscire, andare fuori.

- **3.** *(so as to be extinguished)* : **to turn sthg ~** spegnere qc ; **put your cigarette ~** spegni la sigaretta.

- **4.** *(expressing removal)* : **to pour sthg ~** versare qc ; **to take sthg ~ (of)** tirar fuori qc (da) ; *(from bank)* ritirare qc (da).

- **5.** *(outwards)* : **to stick ~** sporgere.

- **6.** *(expressing distribution)* : **to hand sthg ~** distribuire qc.

- **7.** *(in phrases)* : **to stay ~ of the sun** evitare il sole ; **made ~ of wood** in OR di legno ; **five ~ of ten women** cinque donne su dieci ; **I'm ~ of cigarettes** ho finito le sigarette.

---

outbreak ['autbreɪk] *n (of fighting)* scoppio *m* ; *(of disease)* epidemia *f*.

outburst ['autbɜːst] *n* scoppio *m*.

outcome ['aʊtkʌm] *n* esito *m*, risultato *m*.
outdated [ˌaʊt'deɪtɪd] *adj* antiquato(a).
outdo [ˌaʊt'du:] (*pt* **-did**, *pp* **-done**) *vt* fare meglio di, superare.
outdoor ['aʊtdɔ:ʳ] *adj* all'aperto.
outdoors [aʊt'dɔ:z] *adv* all'aperto, fuori.
outer ['aʊtəʳ] *adj* esterno(a).
outer space *n* spazio *m* cosmico.
outfit ['aʊtfɪt] *n (clothes)* completo *m*.
outing ['aʊtɪŋ] *n* gita *f*.
outlet ['aʊtlet] *n (pipe)* scarico *m*, sbocco *m* ; **'no ~'** *Am* 'strada senza uscita'.
outline ['aʊtlaɪn] *n* profilo *m*.
outlook ['aʊtlʊk] *n (for future)* prospettiva *f*; *(of weather)* previsioni *fpl* ; *(attitude)* modo *m* di vedere.
out-of-date *adj (old-fashioned)* superato(a) ; *(passport, licence)* scaduto(a).
outpatients' (department) ['aʊtˌpeɪʃnts-] *n* reparto *m* pazienti esterni.
output ['aʊtpʊt] *n (of factory)* produzione *f*; COMPUT *(printout)* output *m inv*, tabulato *m*.
outrage ['aʊtreɪdʒ] *n (cruel act)* atrocità *f inv*.
outrageous [aʊt'reɪdʒəs] *adj (shocking)* scandaloso(a).
outright [ˌaʊt'raɪt] *adv (tell, deny)* apertamente ; *(own)* completamente.
outside [*adv* ˌaʊt'saɪd, *adj, prep & n* 'aʊtsaɪd] *adv* fuori, all'esterno. ◆ *prep* fuori di. ◆ *adj* esterno(a). ◆ *n* : **the ~** *(of building, car, container)* l'esterno *m* ; AUT *(in UK)* la destra ; AUT *(in Europe, US)* la sinistra ; **an ~ line** una linea esterna ; **~ of** *[Am] (on the outside of)* fuori di ; *(apart from)* all'infuori di.
outside lane *n* corsia *f* di sorpasso.
outsize ['aʊtsaɪz] *adj (clothes)* di taglia forte.
outskirts ['aʊtskɜ:ts] *npl* periferia *f*.
outstanding [ˌaʊt'stændɪŋ] *adj (remarkable)* eccellente ; *(problem)* rilevante ; *(debt)* da pagare, in sospeso.
outward ['aʊtwəd] *adj (journey)* di andata ; *(external)* esteriore.
outwards ['aʊtwədz] *adv* verso l'esterno, in fuori.
oval ['əʊvl] *adj* ovale.
ovation [əʊ'veɪʃn] *n* ovazione *f*.
oven ['ʌvn] *n* forno *m*.
oven glove *n* guanto *m* da forno.
ovenproof ['ʌvnpru:f] *adj* da forno.
oven-ready *adj* pronto(a) da mettere in forno.

☞

over ['əʊvəʳ] *prep* - **1.** *(above)* sopra, su ; **a bridge ~ the river** un ponte sul fiume.
- **2.** *(across)* oltre, al di là di ; **with a view ~ the park** con vista sul parco ; **to walk ~ sthg** attraversare qc a piedi ; **it's just ~ the road** è proprio qui di fronte.
- **3.** *(covering)* su ; **put a plaster ~ the**

wound mettere un cerotto sulla ferita.
- 4. *(more than)* più di ; **it cost ~ £1,000** è costato più di 1 000 sterline.
- 5. *(during)* durante ; **~ the past two years** negli ultimi due anni.
- 6. *(with regard to)* su ; **an argument ~ the price** una discussione sul prezzo.
- 7. *(in phrases)* : **all ~ the world/country** in tutto il mondo/paese.
◆ *adv* - 1. *(downwards)* : **to fall ~** cadere ; **to bend ~** piegarsi (in avanti).
- 2. *(referring to position, movement)* : **to fly ~ to Canada** andare in Canada in aereo ; **~ here** qui ; **~ there** là.
- 3. *(round to other side)* : **to turn sthg ~** rigirare qc.
- 4. *(more)* : **children aged 12 and ~** ragazzi dai 12 anni in su.
- 5. *(remaining)* : **to be (left) ~** restare.
- 6. *(to one's house)* : **to invite sb ~ for dinner** invitare qn a cena ; **we have some friends coming ~** verranno da noi OR a trovarci degli amici.
◆ *adj (finished)* : **to be ~** essere finito(a).

---

overall [*adv* ˌəuvər'ɔːl, *n* 'əuvərɔːl] *adv (in general)* complessivamente, nell'insieme. ◆ *n Br (coat)* grembiule *m* ; *Am (boiler suit)* tuta *f* (da lavoro) ; **how much does it cost ~?** quanto costa in tutto? ❑ **overalls** *npl Br (boiler suit)* tuta *f* (da lavoro) ; *Am (dungarees)* salopette *f inv*.

overboard ['əuvəbɔːd] *adv (from ship)* in mare.

overbooked [ˌəuvə'bukt] *adj* : **to be ~** avere più prenotazioni dei posti disponibili.

overcame [ˌəuvə'keɪm] *pt* → **overcome**.

overcast [ˌəuvə'kaːst] *adj* coperto(a).

overcharge [ˌəuvə'tʃaːdʒ] *vt* far pagare un prezzo eccessivo(a).

overcoat ['əuvəkəut] *n* cappotto *m*.

overcome [ˌəuvə'kʌm] (*pt* **-came**, *pp* **-come**) *vt (defeat)* sopraffare ; *(problem)* superare.

overcooked [ˌəuvə'kukt] *adj* troppo cotto(a).

overcrowded [ˌəuvə'kraudɪd] *adj* sovraffollato(a).

overdo [ˌəuvə'duː] (*pt* **-did**, *pp* **-done**) *vt (exaggerate)* esagerare con ; **to ~ it** esagerare.

overdone [ˌəuvə'dʌn] *pp* → **overdo**. ◆ *adj (food)* troppo cotto(a).

overdose ['əuvədəus] *n* overdose *f inv*.

overdraft ['əuvədraːft] *n* scoperto *m (di conto)*.

overdue [ˌəuvə'djuː] *adj (bus, flight)* in ritardo ; *(rent, payment)* in arretrato.

over easy *adj Am (egg)* : **eggs ~** *uova al tegamino fritte da entrambe le parti*.

overexposed [ˌəuvərɪk'spəuzd] *adj (photograph)* sovraesposto(a).

overflow [*vb* ˌəuvə'fləu, *n* 'əuvəfləu] *vi (container, bath)* traboccare ; *(river)* straripare. ◆ *n (pipe)* troppopieno *m*.

overgrown [ˌəuvəˈgrəun] *adj (garden, path)* ricoperto(a) di erbacce.
overhaul [ˌəuvəˈhɔːl] *n (of machine, car)* revisione *f*.
overhead [*adj* ˈəuvəhed, *adv* ˌəuvəˈhed] *adj* aereo(a). ◆ *adv* in alto, al di sopra.
overhear [ˌəuvəˈhɪəʳ] (*pt* & *pp* **-heard**) *vt* sentire (per caso).
overheat [ˌəuvəˈhiːt] *vi* surriscaldarsi.
overland [ˈəuvəlænd] *adv* via terra.
overlap [ˌəuvəˈlæp] *vi* sovrapporsi.
overleaf [ˌəuvəˈliːf] *adv* a tergo.
overload [ˌəuvəˈləud] *vt* sovraccaricare.
overlook [*vb* ˌəuvəˈluk, *n* ˈəuvəluk] *vt (subj : building, room)* dare su ; *(miss)* lasciarsi sfuggire, trascurare. ◆ *n* : **(scenic) ~** *Am* punto *m* panoramico.
overnight [adv ˌəuvəˈnaɪt adj ˈəuvənaɪt] *adv (during the night)* durante la notte ; *(until next day)* per la notte. ◆ *adj (train, journey)* di notte.
overnight bag *n* piccola borsa *f* da viaggio.
overpass [ˈəuvəpaːs] *n* cavalcavia *m inv*.
overpowering [ˌəuvəˈpauərɪŋ] *adj (heat, smell)* opprimente, soffocante.
oversaw [ˌəuvəˈsɔː] *pt* → **oversee**.
overseas [*adv* ˌəuvəˈsiːz, *adj* ˈəuvəsiːz] *adv* all'estero *(oltremare)*. ◆ *adj* straniero(a) ; *(trade)* estero(a).
oversee [ˌəuvəˈsiː] (*pt* **-saw**, *pp* **-seen**) *vt* sovrintendere a.
overshoot [ˌəuvəˈʃuːt] (*pt* & *pp* **-shot**) *vt (turning, motorway exit)* oltrepassare.
oversight [ˈəuvəsaɪt] *n* svista *f*.
oversleep [ˌəuvəˈsliːp] (*pt* & *pp* **-slept**) *vi* non svegliarsi *(all'ora prevista)*.
overtake [ˌəuvəˈteɪk] (*pt* **-took**, *pp* **-taken**) *vt* & *vi* sorpassare ; **'no overtaking'** 'divieto di sorpasso'.
overtime [ˈəuvətaɪm] *n* straordinario *m*.
overtook [ˌəuvəˈtuk] *pt* → **overtake**.
overture [ˈəuvəˌtjuəʳ] *n* MUS ouverture *f inv*.
overturn [ˌəuvəˈtɜːn] *vi* rovesciarsi.
overweight [ˌəuvəˈweɪt] *adj* sovrappeso *(inv)*.
overwhelm [ˌəuvəˈwelm] *vt* sopraffare.
owe [əu] *vt* dovere ; **to ~ sb sthg** dovere qc a qn ; **owing to** a causa di.
owl [aul] *n* gufo *m*.
own [əun] *adj* proprio(a). ◆ *vt* possedere. ◆ *pron* : **my ~** il mio (la mia), i miei (le mie) *(pl)* ; **a room of my ~** una stanza (solo) per me ; **on my ~** da solo ; **to get one's ~ back** prendersi la rivincita. ❑ **own up** *vi* : **to ~ up to sthg** ammettere qc.
owner [ˈəunəʳ] *n* proprietario *m*, -a *f*.
ownership [ˈəunəʃɪp] *n* proprietà *f*, possesso *m*.
ox [ɒks] (*pl* **oxen** [ˈɒksən]) *n* bue *m*.

oxtail soup ['ɒksteɪl-] *n* minestra *f* di coda di bue.

oxygen ['ɒksɪdʒən] *n* ossigeno *m*.

oyster ['ɔɪstəʳ] *n* ostrica *f*.

oz *abbr* = ounce.

ozone-friendly ['əʊzəʊn-] *adj* che non danneggia l'ozono.

P

p (*abbr of page*) p., pag.. ◆ *abbr* = penny, pence.

pace [peɪs] *n* passo *m*.

pacemaker ['peɪs,meɪkəʳ] *n* (*for heart*) pacemaker *m inv*.

Pacific [pə'sɪfɪk] *n* : the ~ (Ocean) il Pacifico, l'Oceano *m* Pacifico.

pacifier ['pæsɪfaɪəʳ] *n Am* (*for baby*) succhiotto *m*.

pacifist ['pæsɪfɪst] *n* pacifista *mf*.

pack [pæk] *n* (*of washing powder*) pacco *m* ; (*of cigarettes, crisps*) pacchetto *m* ; *Br* (*of cards*) mazzo *m* ; (*rucksack*) zaino *m*. ◆ *vt* (*suitcase, bag*) preparare, fare ; (*clothes, camera etc*) mettere in valigia ; (*to package*) impacchettare, imballare. ◆ *vi* (*for journey*) fare i bagagli OR le valigie ; a ~ of lies un mucchio di bugie ; to ~ sthg into sthg stipare qc in qc ; to ~ one's bags fare i bagagli OR le valigie. ❑ **pack up** *vi* (*pack suitcase*) fare la valigia ; (*tidy up*) riordinare ; *Br inf* (*machine, car*) guastarsi.

package ['pækɪdʒ] *n* pacchetto *m*. ◆ *vt* imballare.

package holiday *n* vacanza *f* organizzata.

packaging ['pækɪdʒɪŋ] *n* (*material*) imballaggio *m*, confezione *f*.

packed [pækt] *adj* (*crowded*) stipato(a).

packed lunch *n* pranzo *m* al sacco.

packet ['pækɪt] *n* pacchetto *m* ; it cost a ~ *Br inf* è costato un mucchio di soldi.

packing ['pækɪŋ] *n* (*material*) imballaggio *m* ; to do one's ~ fare i bagagli OR le valigie.

pad [pæd] *n* (*of paper*) blocco *m* ; (*of cloth, cotton wool*) tampone *m* ; (*for protection*) imbottitura *f*.

padded ['pædɪd] *adj* (*jacket, seat*) imbottito(a).

padded envelope *n* busta *f* imbottita.

paddle ['pædl] *n* (*pole*) pagaia *f*. ◆ *vi* (*wade*) sguazzare ; (*in canoe*) remare (*con la pagaia*).

paddling pool ['pædlɪŋ-] *n* piscina *f* per bambini.

padlock ['pædlɒk] *n* lucchetto *m*.

page [peɪdʒ] *n* (*of book, newspaper*) pagina *f*. ◆ *vt* chiamare.

paid [peɪd] *pt* & *pp* → pay. ◆ *adj* (*holiday, work*) pagato(a).

pain [peɪn] *n* dolore *m* ; to be in ~ avere dolore, soffrire ; he's such a ~! *inf* è un tale rompiscatole! ❑ **pains** *npl* (*trouble*) disturbo *m*.

painful ['peɪnfʊl] *adj* doloroso(a).

painkiller ['peɪn,kɪləʳ] *n* analgesico *m*, antidolorifico *m*.

paint [peɪnt] *n* vernice *f*, colore *m*. ◆ *vt* & *vi* dipingere ; to ~ one's nails dipingersi le unghie. ❑ **paints** *npl (tubes, pots etc)* colori *mpl.*

paintbrush ['peɪntbrʌʃ] *n* pennello *m.*

painter ['peɪntəʳ] *n (artist)* pittore *m*, -trice *f* ; *(decorator)* imbianchino *m.*

painting ['peɪntɪŋ] *n (picture)* dipinto *m*, quadro *m* ; *(artistic activity)* pittura *f* ; *(by decorator)* tinteggiatura *f.*

pair [peəʳ] *n (of two things)* paio *m* ; **in ~s** a coppie, a due a due ; **a ~ of pliers** un paio di pinze ; **a ~ of scissors** un paio di forbici ; **a ~ of shorts** un paio di calzoncini ; **a ~ of tights** un paio di collant ; **a ~ of trousers** un paio di pantaloni.

pajamas [pə'dʒɑːməz] *Am* = **pyjamas**.

Pakistan [*Br* ˌpɑːkɪ'stɑːn, *Am* ˌpækɪ'stæn] *n* il Pakistan.

Pakistani [*Br* ˌpɑːkɪ'stɑːnɪ, *Am* ˌpækɪ'stænɪ] *adj* pakistano(a). ◆ *n* pakistano *m*, -a *f.*

pakora [pə'kɔːrə] *npl frittelle piccanti a base di verdura e spezie varie servite come antipasto nella cucina indiana.*

pal [pæl] *n inf* amico *m*, -a *f.*

palace ['pælɪs] *n* palazzo *m.*

palatable ['pælətəbl] *adj (food, drink)* gustoso(a).

palate ['pælət] *n* palato *m.*

pale [peɪl] *adj* pallido(a).

pale ale *n* birra *f* chiara.

palm [pɑːm] *n (of hand)* palmo *m* ; **~ (tree)** palma *f.*

palpitations [ˌpælpɪ'teɪʃnz] *npl* palpitazioni *fpl.*

pamphlet ['pæmflɪt] *n* opuscolo *m.*

pan [pæn] *n (saucepan)* pentola *f* ; *(frying pan)* padella *f.*

pancake ['pænkeɪk] *n* crêpe *f inv.*

pancake roll *n* involtino *m* primavera.

panda ['pændə] *n* panda *m inv.*

panda car *n Br* auto *f inv* della polizia.

pane [peɪn] *n* vetro *m.*

panel ['pænl] *n (of wood)* pannello *m* ; *(group of experts)* gruppo *m* di esperti ; *(on TV, radio)* giuria *f.*

paneling ['pænəlɪŋ] *Am* = **panelling**.

panelling ['pænəlɪŋ] *n Br* rivestimento *m* a pannelli.

panic ['pænɪk] (*pt & pp* **-ked**, *cont* **-king**) *n* panico *m.* ◆ *vi* farsi prendere dal panico.

panniers ['pænɪəz] *npl (for bicycle)* borse *fpl* da bicicletta.

panoramic [ˌpænə'ræmɪk] *adj* panoramico(a).

pant [pænt] *vi* ansare.

panties ['pæntɪz] *npl inf* mutandine *fpl.*

pantomime ['pæntəmaɪm] *n Br spettacolo natalizio per bambini.*

PANTOMIME

Spettacolo teatrale comico per bambini, in cui si alternano parti recitate e parti cantate. Si ispira generalmente a favole famose e viene rappresentato nel periodo natalizio. Di solito il ruolo dell'eroe viene recitato da una giovane attrice, mentre un attore comico interpreta la parte della vecchia signora, la *dame*.

---

pantry ['pæntrɪ] *n* dispensa *f*.

pants [pænts] *npl Br (underwear)* mutande *fpl* ; *Am (trousers)* pantaloni *mpl*.

panty hose ['pæntɪ-] *npl Am* collant *m inv*.

papadum ['pæpədəm] *n* = **poppadom**.

paper ['peɪpəʳ] *n (material)* carta *f* ; *(newspaper)* giornale *m* ; *(exam)* esame *m* (scritto). ◆ *adj* di carta. ◆ *vt* tappezzare (con carta da parati) ; **a piece of ~** un pezzo di carta. ❑ **papers** *npl (documents)* documenti *mpl*.

paperback ['peɪpəbæk] *n* libro *m* in brossura.

paper bag *n* sacchetto *m* di carta.

paperboy ['peɪpəbɔɪ] *n ragazzo che recapita i giornali a domicilio*.

paper clip *n* graffetta *f*.

papergirl ['peɪpəgɜːl] *n ragazza che recapita i giornali a domicilio*.

paper shop *n* giornalaio *m*.

paperweight ['peɪpəweɪt] *n* fermacarte *m inv*.

paprika ['pæprɪkə] *n* paprica *f*.

paracetamol [ˌpærə'siːtəmɒl] *n* paracetamolo *m*.

parachute ['pærəʃuːt] *n* paracadute *m inv*.

parade [pə'reɪd] *n (procession)* parata *f* ; *(of shops)* fila *f* di negozi.

paradise ['pærədaɪs] *n* paradiso *m*.

paraffin ['pærəfɪn] *n* cherosene *m*.

paragraph ['pærəgrɑːf] *n* paragrafo *m*.

parallel ['pærəlel] *adj* : **~ (to)** parallelo(a) (a).

paralysed ['pærəlaɪzd] *adj Br* paralizzato(a).

paralyzed ['pærəlaɪzd] *Am* = **paralysed**.

paramedic [ˌpærə'medɪk] *n* paramedico *m*.

paranoid ['pærənɔɪd] *adj* paranoico(a).

parasite ['pærəsaɪt] *n* parassita *m*.

parasol ['pærəsɒl] *n* parasole *m inv*.

parcel ['pɑːsl] *n* pacco *m*, pacchetto *m*.

parcel post *n* servizio *m* pacchi postali.

pardon ['pɑːdn] *excl* : **pardon?** prego? ; **~ (me)!** mi scusi! ; **I beg your ~!** *(apologizing)* scusi! ; **I beg your ~?** *(asking for repetition)* prego?

parent ['peərənt] *n* genitore *m*.

parish ['pærɪʃ] *n (of church)* parrocchia *f* ; *(village area)* ≃ comune *m*.

park [pɑːk] *n* parco *m*. ◆ *vt* & *vi* parcheggiare.

park and ride *n parcheggio decentrato presso una stazione di mezzi pubblici locali*.

parking ['pɑːkɪŋ] *n* parcheggio *m* ; **'no ~'** 'sosta vietata'.

parking brake *n Am* freno *m* a mano.

parking lot *n Am* parcheggio *m*, posteggio *m*.

parking meter *n* parchimetro *m*.

parking space *n* posto *m* per parcheggiare.

parking ticket *n* multa *f* per sosta vietata.

parkway ['pa:kweɪ] *n Am viale con alberi* OR *piante nella banchina spartitraffico.*

parliament ['pa:ləmənt] *n* parlamento *m*.

Parmesan (cheese) [pa:mɪ-'zæn-] *n* parmigiano *m*, grana *m*.

parrot ['pærət] *n* pappagallo *m*.

parsley ['pa:slɪ] *n* prezzemolo *m*.

parsnip ['pa:snɪp] *n* pastinaca *f*.

parson ['pa:sn] *n* curato *m*, parroco *m*.

part [pa:t] *n* parte *f*; *(of machine, car)* pezzo *m*; *(of serial)* puntata *f*; *Am (in hair)* scriminatura *f*. ◆ *adv* in parte. ◆ *vi (couple)* separarsi; **in this ~ of Italy** in questa zona dell'Italia; **to form ~ of** costituire parte di; **to play a ~ in** avere un ruolo in; **to take ~ in** prendere parte a; **for my ~** da parte mia; **for the most ~** per lo più, in generale; **in these ~s** da queste parti.

partial ['pa:ʃl] *adj (not whole)* parziale; **to be ~ to sthg** avere un debole per qc.

participant [pa:'tɪsɪpənt] *n* partecipante *mf*.

participate [pa:'tɪsɪpeɪt] *vi*: **to ~ (in)** partecipare (a).

particular [pə'tɪkjʊlə^r] *adj* particolare; *(fussy)* esigente; **in ~** in particolare, specialmente; **nothing in ~** niente di particolare. ❑ **particulars** *npl (details)* particolari *mpl*.

particularly [pə'tɪkjʊləlɪ] *adv* particolarmente, soprattutto.

parting ['pa:tɪŋ] *n Br (in hair)* scriminatura *f*.

partition [pa:'tɪʃn] *n (wall)* tramezzo *m*.

partly ['pa:tlɪ] *adv* parzialmente, in parte.

partner ['pa:tnə^r] *n (husband)* marito *m*; *(wife)* moglie *f*; *(lover, in game, dance)* compagno *m*, -a *f*; COMM socio *m*, -a *f*.

partnership ['pa:tnəʃɪp] *n* associazione *f*; COMM società *f inv*.

partridge ['pa:trɪdʒ] *n* pernice *f*.

part-time *adj* & *adv* part time.

party ['pa:tɪ] *n (for fun)* festa *f*; POL partito *m*; *(group of people)* gruppo *m*; **to have a ~** fare una festa.

pass [pa:s] *vt* passare; *(move past)* oltrepassare, passare davanti a; *(test, exam)* passare, superare; *(overtake)* sorpassare; *(law)* approvare. ◆ *vi* passare. ◆ *n (document)* lasciapassare *m inv*, permesso *m*; *(in mountain)* passo *m*; *(in exam)* sufficienza *f*; SPORT passaggio *m*; **to ~ sb sthg** passare qc a qn. ❑ **pass by** ◆ *vt fus (building, window etc)* passare davanti a. ◆ *vi* passare. ❑ **pass on** *vt sep (message)* passare. ❑ **pass out** *vi (faint)* svenire. ❑ **pass up** *vt sep (opportunity)* lasciarsi sfuggire.

passable ['pa:səbl] *adj (road)* transitabile; *(satisfactory)* passabile.

passage ['pæsɪdʒ] *n (corridor)* passaggio *m*, corridoio *m*; *(in* *book)* brano *m*, passo *m* ; *(sea journey)* traversata *f*.

passageway ['pæsɪdʒweɪ] *n* corridoio *m*.

passenger ['pæsɪndʒəʳ] *n* passeggero *m*, -a *f*.

passerby [ˌpaːsə'baɪ] *n* passante *mf*.

passion ['pæʃn] *n* passione *f*.

passionate ['pæʃənət] *adj (showing strong feeling)* appassionato(a) ; *(sexually)* passionale.

passive ['pæsɪv] *n* passivo *m*.

passport ['paːspɔːt] *n* passaporto *m*.

passport control *n* controllo *m* passaporti.

passport photo *n* fototessera *f*.

password ['paːswɜːd] *n (for computer)* password *f inv*, parola *f* d'accesso.

past [paːst] *adj* passato(a) ; *(last)* ultimo(a) ; *(former)* ex *(inv)*. ◆ *prep (in times)* dopo ; *(further than)* oltre, al di là di ; *(in front of)* davanti a. ◆ *adv* oltre. ◆ *n (former time)* passato *m* ; ~ **(tense)** GRAMM passato *m* ; **the ~ month** il mese scorso ; **twenty ~ four** le quattro e venti ; **to run ~** passare di corsa ; **in the ~** in passato.

pasta ['pæstə] *n* pasta *f*.

paste [peɪst] *n (spread)* pasta *f*, crema *f* (da spalmare) ; *(glue)* colla *f*.

pastel ['pæstl] *n (for drawing)* pastello *m* ; *(colour)* colore *m* pastello.

pasteurized ['paːstʃəraɪzd] *adj* pastorizzato(a).

pastille ['pæstɪl] *n* pastiglia *f*.

pastime ['paːstaɪm] *n* passatempo *m*.

pastry ['peɪstrɪ] *n* pasta *f*.

pasture ['paːstʃəʳ] *n* pascolo *m*.

pat [pæt] *vt* dare un colpetto (affettuoso) a.

patch [pætʃ] *n (for clothes)* toppa *f* ; *(of colour, cloud, damp)* macchia *f* ; *(for skin)* cerotto *m* ; *(for eye)* benda *f* ; **a bad ~** *fig* un brutto periodo.

pâté ['pæteɪ] *n* paté *m inv*.

patent [*Br* 'peɪtənt, *Am* 'pætənt] *n* brevetto *m*.

path [paːθ] *n (in park, country)* sentiero *m*, viottolo *m* ; *(in garden)* vialetto *m*.

pathetic [pə'θetɪk] *adj pej (useless)* penoso(a).

patience ['peɪʃns] *n (quality)* pazienza *f* ; *Br (card game)* solitario *m*.

patient ['peɪʃnt] *adj* paziente. ◆ *n* paziente *mf*, malato *m*, -a *f*.

patio ['pætɪəʊ] *n* terrazza *f*.

patriotic [*Br* ˌpætrɪ'ɒtɪk, *Am* ˌpeɪtrɪ'ɒtɪk] *adj* patriottico(a).

patrol [pə'trəʊl] *vt* pattugliare. ◆ *n (group)* pattuglia *f*.

patrol car *n* auto *f inv* di pattuglia.

patron ['peɪtrən] *n fml (customer)* cliente *mf* ; **'~s only'** 'riservato ai clienti'.

patronizing ['pætrənaɪzɪŋ] *adj (person)* che tratta con aria di superiorità.

pattern ['pætn] *n (of shapes, colours)* disegno *m*, motivo *m* ; *(for sewing)* modello *m*.

patterned ['pætənd] *adj* fantasia *(inv)*.
pause [pɔ:z] *n* pausa *f*. ◆ *vi* fare una pausa, soffermarsi.
pavement ['peɪvmənt] *n Br (beside road)* marciapiede *m* ; *Am (roadway)* pavimentazione *f*.
pavilion [pə'vɪljən] *n edificio annesso a campo sportivo, adibito a spogliatoio.*
paving stone ['peɪvɪŋ-] *n* lastra *f* di pietra.
pavlova *n dolce composto da due strati di meringa farciti di panna montata e frutta.*
paw [pɔ:] *n* zampa *f*.
pawn [pɔ:n] *vt* impegnare, dare in pegno. ◆ *n (in chess)* pedone *m*.
pay [peɪ] *(pt & pp* **paid**) *vt* pagare. ◆ *vi (give money)* pagare ; *(be profitable)* rendere. ◆ *n* paga *f*, stipendio *m* ; **to ~ sb for sthg** pagare qn per qc ; **to ~ money into an account** versare dei soldi su un conto ; **to ~ attention (to)** fare attenzione (a) ; **to ~ sb a visit** fare visita a qn ; **to ~ by credit card** pagare con la carta di credito. ❑ **pay back** *vt sep (money)* restituire ; *(person)* rimborsare. ❑ **pay for** *vt fus (purchase)* pagare. ❑ **pay in** *vt sep (cheque, money)* versare. ❑ **pay out** *vt sep (money)* sborsare. ❑ **pay up** *vi* saldare il debito.
payable ['peɪəbl] *adj (bill)* pagabile ; **~ to** *(cheque)* pagabile a, intestato(a) a.
payment ['peɪmənt] *n (of money, bill)* pagamento *m* ; *(amount)* pagamento, versamento *m*.
payphone ['peɪfəun] *n* telefono *m* pubblico.
PC *n (abbr of personal computer)* PC *m inv*. ◆ *abbr Br* = **police constable.**
PE *abbr* = **physical education.**
pea [pi:] *n* pisello *m*.
peace [pi:s] *n* pace *f* ; **to leave sb in ~** lasciare qn in pace ; **~ and quiet** pace e tranquillità.
peaceful ['pi:sful] *adj (place, day, feeling)* tranquillo(a), calmo(a) ; *(demonstration)* pacifico(a).
peach [pi:tʃ] *n* pesca *f*.
peacock ['pi:kɒk] *n* pavone *m*.
peak [pi:k] *n (of mountain)* cima *f*, vetta *f* ; *(of hat)* visiera *f* ; *fig (highest point)* apice *m*, culmine *m*.
peak hours *npl* ore *fpl* di punta.
peak rate *n* tariffa *f* ore di punta.
peanut ['pi:nʌt] *n* arachide *f*, nocciolina *f* (americana).
peanut butter *n* burro *m* di arachidi.
pear [peə'] *n* pera *f*.
pearl [pɜ:l] *n* perla *f*.
peasant ['peznt] *n* contadino *m*, -a *f*.
pebble ['pebl] *n* ciottolo *m*.
pecan pie ['pi:kæn-] *n torta di noci pecan.*
peck [pek] *vi (bird)* beccare.
peculiar [pɪ'kju:ljə'] *adj (strange)* strano(a), singolare ; **to be ~ to** *(exclusive)* essere peculiare di.
peculiarity [pɪˌkju:lɪ'ærətɪ] *n (special feature)* particolarità *f inv*.
pedal ['pedl] *n* pedale *m*. ◆ *vi* pedalare.
pedalo ['pedələu] *(pl* **-s**) *n* moscone *m* a pedali, pedalò® *m inv*.
pedestrian [pɪ'destrɪən] *n* pedone *m*, -a *f*.

pedestrian crossing *n* passaggio *m* pedonale.

pedestrianized [pɪ'destrɪənaɪzd] *adj* riservato(a) ai pedoni.

pedestrian precinct *n Br* zona *f* pedonale.

pedestrian zone *Am* = **pedestrian precinct**.

pee [piː] *vi inf* fare la pipì. ◆ *n* : **to have a ~** *inf* fare la pipì.

peel [piːl] *n* buccia *f* ; *(of orange, lemon)* scorza *f*. ◆ *vt (fruit, vegetables)* sbucciare. ◆ *vi (paint)* staccarsi ; *(skin)* spellarsi.

peep [piːp] *n* : **to have a ~** dare una sbirciatina.

peer [pɪə'] *vi* : **to ~ at** fissare, scrutare.

peg [peg] *n (for tent)* picchetto *m* ; *(hook)* attaccapanni *m inv* ; *(for washing)* molletta *f*.

pelican crossing ['pelɪkən-] *n Br passaggio pedonale con semaforo a comando manuale.*

pelvis ['pelvɪs] *n* bacino *m*.

pen [pen] *n (for writing)* penna *f* ; *(for animals)* recinto *m*.

penalty ['penltɪ] *n (fine)* multa *f*, sanzione *f* ; *(in football)* rigore *m*.

pence [pens] *npl* penny *m inv* ; **it costs 20 ~** costa 20 penny.

pencil ['pensl] *n* matita *f*.

pencil case *n* portamatite *m inv*.

pencil sharpener *n* temperamatite *m inv*.

pendant ['pendənt] *n* pèndente *m*, ciondolo *m*.

pending ['pendɪŋ] *prep fml* in attesa di.

penetrate ['penɪtreɪt] *vt* penetrare.

penfriend ['penfrend] *n* amico *m*, -a *f* per corrispondenza.

penguin ['peŋgwɪn] *n* pinguino *m*.

penicillin [ˌpenɪ'sɪlɪn] *n* penicillina *f*.

peninsula [pə'nɪnsjʊlə] *n* penisola *f*.

penis ['piːnɪs] *n* pene *m*.

penknife ['pennaɪf] (*pl* **-knives**) *n* temperino *m*.

penny ['penɪ] (*pl* **pennies**) *n (in UK)* penny *m inv* ; *(in US)* centesimo *m*.

pension ['penʃn] *n* pensione *f*.

pensioner ['penʃənə'] *n* pensionato *m*, -a *f*.

penthouse ['penthaʊs, *pl* -haʊzɪz] *n* superattico *m*.

penultimate [pe'nʌltɪmət] *adj* penultimo(a).

people ['piːpl] *npl (persons)* persone *fpl* ; *(in general)* gente *f*. ◆ *n (nation)* popolo *m* ; **the ~** *(citizens)* il popolo.

pepper ['pepə'] *n (spice)* pepe *m* ; *(vegetable)* peperone *m*.

peppermint ['pepəmɪnt] *adj* alla menta (piperita). ◆ *n (sweet)* caramella *f* di menta.

pepper pot *n* pepiera *f*.

per [pɜː'] *prep* per, a ; **~ person** a persona ; **~ week** alla settimana ; **£20 ~ night** 20 sterline a notte.

perceive [pə'siːv] *vt* percepire.

per cent *adv* per cento.

percentage [pə'sentɪdʒ] *n* percentuale *f*.

perch [pɜːtʃ] *n (for bird)* posatoio *m*, asticella *f*.

percolator ['pɜːkəleɪtəʳ] *n* caffettiera *f* a filtro.

perfect [*adj & n* 'pɜːfɪkt, *vb* pə'fekt] *adj* perfetto(a). ◆ *vt* perfezionare. ◆ *n* : **the ~ (tense)** il passato prossimo.

perfection [pə'fekʃn] *n* : **to do sthg to ~** fare qc alla perfezione.

perfectly ['pɜːfɪktlɪ] *adv (very well)* perfettamente, alla perfezione.

perform [pə'fɔːm] *vt (task, operation)* eseguire, fare ; *(play)* rappresentare ; *(concert)* eseguire. ◆ *vi (actor)* recitare ; *(singer)* cantare.

performance [pə'fɔːməns] *n (of play, concert, film)* spettacolo *m* ; *(by actor)* interpretazione *f* ; *(musician)* esecuzione *f* ; *(of car)* prestazioni *fpl*.

performer [pə'fɔːməʳ] *n* artista *mf*.

perfume ['pɜːfjuːm] *n* profumo *m*.

perhaps [pə'hæps] *adv* forse.

perimeter [pərɪmɪtəʳ] *n* perimetro *m*.

period ['pɪərɪəd] *n* periodo *m* ; *SCH* lezione *f* ; *(menstruation)* mestruazioni *fpl* ; *Am (full stop)* punto *m*. ◆ *adj (costume, furniture)* d'epoca.

periodic [ˌpɪərɪ'ɒdɪk] *adj* periodico(a).

period pains *npl* dolori *mpl* mestruali.

periphery [pə'rɪfərɪ] *n* periferia *f*.

perishable ['perɪʃəbl] *adj* deperibile.

perk [pɜːk] *n* vantaggio *m*.

perm [pɜːm] *n* permanente *f*. ◆ *vt* : **to have one's hair ~ed** farsi la permanente.

permanent ['pɜːmənənt] *adj* permanente.

permanent address *n* residenza *f*.

permanently ['pɜːmənəntlɪ] *adv* permanentemente.

permissible [pə'mɪsəbl] *adj fml* permissibile, ammissibile.

permission [pə'mɪʃn] *n* permesso *m*.

permit [*vb* pə'mɪt, *n* 'pɜːmɪt] *vt* permettere. ◆ *n* permesso *m* ; **to ~ sb to do sthg** permettere a qn di fare qc ; **'~ holders only'** 'solo autorizzati'.

perpendicular [ˌpɜːpən'dɪkjʊləʳ] *adj* perpendicolare.

persevere [ˌpɜːsɪ'vɪəʳ] *vi* perseverare.

persist [pə'sɪst] *vi* persistere ; **to ~ in doing sthg** ostinarsi a fare qc.

persistent [pə'sɪstənt] *adj* persistente ; *(person)* ostinato(a).

person ['pɜːsn] (*pl* **people**) *n* persona *f* ; **in ~** di persona.

personal ['pɜːsənl] *adj* personale.

personal assistant *n* segretario *m*, -a *f* personale.

personal belongings *npl* effetti *mpl* personali.

personal computer *n* personal computer *m inv*.

personality [ˌpɜːsə'nælətɪ] *n* personalità *f inv*.

personally ['pɜːsnəlɪ] *adv* personalmente.

personal property *n* beni *mpl* mobili.

personal stereo *n* walkman® *m inv*.

personnel [ˌpɜːsə'nel] *npl* personale *m*.

perspective [pə'spektɪv] *n* prospettiva *f*.

perspiration [ˌpɜːspə'reɪʃn] *n* traspirazione *f*, sudore *m*.

persuade [pə'sweɪd] *vt* : **to ~ sb (to do sthg)** persuadere qn (a fare qc) ; **to ~ sb that ...** persuadere qn che ...

persuasive [pə'sweɪsɪv] *adj* persuasivo(a), convincente.

pervert ['pɜːvɜːt] *n* pervertito *m*, -a *f*.

pessimist ['pesɪmɪst] *n* pessimista *mf*.

pessimistic [ˌpesɪ'mɪstɪk] *adj* pessimistico(a).

pest [pest] *n (insect)* insetto *m* nocivo ; *(animal)* animale *m* nocivo ; *inf (person)* peste *f*.

pester ['pestəʳ] *vt* tormentare.

pesticide ['pestɪsaɪd] *n* pesticida *m*.

pet [pet] *n* animale *m* domestico ; **the teacher's ~** il favorito (la favorita) dell'insegnante.

petal ['petl] *n* petalo *m*.

pet food *n* cibo *m* per animali (domestici).

petition [pɪ'tɪʃn] *n (letter)* petizione *f*.

petrified ['petrɪfaɪd] *adj (frightened)* impietrito(a) (dalla paura).

petrol ['petrəl] *n Br* benzina *f*.

petrol gauge *n Br* indicatore *m* di livello della benzina.

petrol pump *n Br* pompa *f* di benzina.

petrol station *n Br* stazione *f* di rifornimento.

petrol tank *n Br* serbatoio *m* della benzina.

pet shop *n* negozio *m* di animali.

petticoat ['petɪkəʊt] *n* sottoveste *f*.

petty ['petɪ] *adj pej (person, rule)* meschino(a).

petty cash *n* piccola cassa *f*.

pew [pjuː] *n* panca *f* (di chiesa).

pewter ['pjuːtəʳ] *adj* di peltro.

PG *(abbr of parental guidance) sigla che contraddistingue i film non vietati ai minori, per i quali è però consigliato l'accompagnamento dei genitori.*

pharmacist ['fɑːməsɪst] *n* farmacista *mf*.

pharmacy ['fɑːməsɪ] *n (shop)* farmacia *f*.

phase [feɪz] *n* fase *f*.

PhD *n (degree)* ≃ dottorato *m* di ricerca.

pheasant ['feznt] *n* fagiano *m*.

phenomena [fɪ'nɒmɪnə] *pl* → phenomenon.

phenomenal [fɪ'nɒmɪnl] *adj* fenomenale.

phenomenon [fɪ'nɒmɪnən] (*pl* **-mena**) *n* fenomeno *m*.

Philippines ['fɪlɪpiːnz] *npl* : **the ~** le Filippine.

philosophy [fɪ'lɒsəfɪ] *n* filosofia *f*.

phlegm [flem] *n (in throat)* catarro *m*.

phone [fəʊn] *n* telefono *m.* ◆ *vt Br* telefonare a. ◆ *vi Br* telefonare ; **to be on the ~** *(talking)* essere al telefono ; *(connected)* avere il telefono. ❑ **phone up** ◆ *vt sep* telefonare a, chiamare. ◆ *vi* telefonare.

phone book *n* elenco *m* telefonico.

phone booth *n* cabina *f* telefonica.

phone box *n Br* cabina *f* telefonica.

phone call *n* telefonata *f.*

phonecard ['fəʊnkɑːd] *n* scheda *f* telefonica.

phone number *n* numero *m* di telefono.

photo ['fəʊtəʊ] (*pl* -s) *n* foto *f inv* ; **to take a ~ of** fare una foto a.

photo album *n* album *m inv* portafotografie.

photocopier [ˌfəʊtəʊ'kɒpɪəʳ] *n* fotocopiatrice *f.*

photocopy ['fəʊtəʊˌkɒpɪ] *n* fotocopia *f.* ◆ *vt* fotocopiare.

photograph ['fəʊtəgrɑːf] *n* fotografia *f.* ◆ *vt* fotografare.

photographer [fə'tɒgrəfəʳ] *n* fotografo *m*, -a *f.*

photography [fə'tɒgrəfɪ] *n* fotografia *f.*

phrase [freɪz] *n* espressione *f.*

phrasebook ['freɪzbʊk] *n* vocabolarietto *m* con frasi tipiche.

physical ['fɪzɪkl] *adj* fisico(a). ◆ *n* visita *f* medica.

physical education *n* educazione *f* fisica.

physics ['fɪzɪks] *n* fisica *f.*

physiotherapy [ˌfɪzɪəʊ'θerəpɪ] *n* fisioterapia *f.*

pianist ['pɪənɪst] *n* pianista *mf.*

piano [pɪ'ænəʊ] (*pl* -s) *n* pianoforte *m.*

pick [pɪk] *vt (select)* scegliere ; *(fruit, flowers)* cogliere. ◆ *n (pickaxe)* piccone *m* ; **to ~ a fight** attaccar briga ; **to ~ one's nose** mettersi le dita nel naso ; **to take one's ~** scegliere. ❑ **pick on** *vt fus* prendersela con, prendere di mira. ❑ **pick out** *vt sep (select)* scegliere ; *(see)* individuare, riconoscere. ❑ **pick up** ◆ *vt sep (lift up)* raccogliere ; *(collect)* passare a prendere ; *(learn)* imparare ; *(habit)* prendere ; *(bargain)* trovare ; *(hitchhiker)* far salire ; *inf (woman, man)* rimorchiare. ◆ *vi (improve)* riprendersi ; **to ~ up the phone** *(answer)* rispondere al telefono.

pickaxe ['pɪkæks] *n* piccone *m.*

pickle ['pɪkl] *n Br (food)* sottaceti *mpl* ; *Am (pickled cucumber)* cetriolo *m* sottaceto.

pickled onion ['pɪkld-] *n* cipollina *f* sottaceto.

pickpocket ['pɪkˌpɒkɪt] *n* borsaiolo *m.*

pick-up (truck) *n* camioncino *m.*

picnic ['pɪknɪk] *n* picnic *m inv.*

picnic area *n* area *f* per picnic.

picture ['pɪktʃəʳ] *n (painting)* quadro *m* ; *(drawing)* disegno *m* ; *(photograph)* fotografia *f* ; *(on TV)* immagine *f* ; *(film)* film *m inv.* ❑ **pictures** *npl* : **the ~s** *Br* il cinema.

picture frame *n* cornice *f.*

picturesque [ˌpɪktʃə'resk] *adj* pittoresco(a).

pie [paɪ] *n (savoury)* pasticcio *m* ; *(sweet)* torta *f*.

piece [pi:s] *n* pezzo *m* ; **a 20p ~** una moneta da 20 penny ; **a ~ of advice** un consiglio ; **a ~ of clothing** un capo di vestiario ; **a ~ of furniture** un mobile ; **to fall to ~s** andare in pezzi ; **in one ~** tutto intero.

pier [pɪəʳ] *n* molo *m*.

pierce [pɪəs] *vt* forare, perforare ; **to have one's ears ~d** farsi i buchi alle orecchie.

pig [pɪg] *n* maiale *m*, porco *m*.

pigeon ['pɪdʒɪn] *n* piccione *m*.

pigeonhole ['pɪdʒɪnhəʊl] *n* casella *f*.

pigtails ['pigteɪlz] *npl* trecce *fpl*.

pike [paɪk] *n (fish)* luccio *m*.

pilau rice ['pɪlaʊ-] *n* riso *m* pilaf.

pilchard ['pɪltʃəd] *n* sardina *f*.

pile [paɪl] *n (heap)* mucchio *m* ; *(neat stack)* pila *f*. ◆ *vt* ammucchiare ; **~s of** *inf (a lot)* mucchi di.
❑ **pile up** ◆ *vt sep* ammucchiare. ◆ *vi (accumulate)* ammucchiarsi.

piles [paɪlz] *npl* MED emorroidi *fpl*.

pileup ['paɪlʌp] *n* tamponamento *m* a catena.

pill [pɪl] *n* pillola *f*.

pillar ['pɪləʳ] *n* colonna *f*.

pillar box *n Br* cassetta *f* delle lettere.

pillion ['pɪljən] *n* : **to ride ~** viaggiare sul sellino posteriore.

pillow ['pɪləʊ] *n* cuscino *m*.

pillowcase ['pɪləʊkeɪs] *n* federa *f*.

pilot ['paɪlət] *n* pilota *mf*.

pilot light *n* fiamma *f* pilota.

pimple ['pɪmpl] *n* foruncolo *m*.

pin [pɪn] *n (for sewing, safety pin)* spillo *m* ; *(drawing pin)* puntina *f* ; *Am (brooch, badge)* spilla *f*. ◆ *vt (fasten)* attaccare con uno spillo ; **a two-~ plug** una spina bipolare ; **~s and needles** formicolio *m*.

pinafore ['pɪnəfɔːʳ] *n (apron)* grembiule *m* ; *Br (dress)* scamiciato *m*.

pinball ['pɪnbɔːl] *n* flipper *m inv*.

pincers ['pɪnsəz] *npl (tool)* tenaglie *fpl*.

pinch [pɪntʃ] *vt (squeeze)* pizzicare, dare un pizzicotto a ; *Br inf (steal)* fregare. ◆ *n (of salt)* pizzico *m*.

pine [paɪn] *n* pino *m*. ◆ *adj* di pino.

pineapple ['paɪnæpl] *n* ananas *m inv*.

pink [pɪŋk] *adj* rosa *(inv)*. ◆ *n (colour)* rosa *m inv*.

pinkie ['pɪŋkɪ] *n Am* mignolo *m*.

PIN (number) *n* numero *m* di codice segreto.

pint [paɪnt] *n (in UK)* = 0,568 l, pinta *f* ; *(in US)* = 0,473 l, pinta ; **a ~ (of beer)** *Br* ≃ una birra grande.

pip [pɪp] *n (of fruit)* seme *m*.

pipe [paɪp] *n (for smoking)* pipa *f* ; *(for gas, water)* tubo *m*.

pipe cleaner *n* scovolino *m*.

pipeline ['paɪplaɪn] *n* conduttura *f* ; *(for oil)* oleodotto *m*.

pipe tobacco *n* tabacco *m* da pipa.

pirate ['paɪrət] *n* pirata *m*.

piss [pɪs] *vi vulg* pisciare. ◆ *n* : **to have a ~** *vulg* pisciare ; **it's ~ing down** *vulg* piove a dirotto.

pissed [pɪst] *adj Br vulg (drunk)*

sbronzo(a) ; *Am vulg (angry)* incazzato(a).

pissed off *adj vulg* incazzato(a).

pistachio [pɪ'stɑːʃɪəʊ] (*pl* -s) *n* pistacchio *m*. ◆ *adj* al pistacchio.

pistol ['pɪstl] *n* pistola *f*.

piston ['pɪstən] *n* pistone *m*.

pit [pɪt] *n (hole)* buca *f*, fossa *f* ; *(coalmine)* miniera *f* (di carbone) ; *(for orchestra)* fossa dell'orchestra ; *Am (in fruit)* nocciolo *m*.

pitch [pɪtʃ] *n Br* SPORT campo *m*. ◆ *vt (throw)* lanciare ; **to ~ a tent** piantare una tenda.

pitcher ['pɪtʃə'] *n* brocca *f*.

pitfall ['pɪtfɔːl] *n* insidia *f*, pericolo *m*.

pith [pɪθ] *n (of orange)* parte *f* interna della scorza.

pitta (bread) ['pɪtə-] *n tipo di schiacciatina di origine mediorientale*.

pitted ['pɪtɪd] *adj (olives)* snocciolato(a).

pity ['pɪtɪ] *n (compassion)* pietà *f* ; **to have ~ on sb** avere pietà di qn ; **it's a ~ that ...** è un peccato che ... ; **what a ~!** che peccato!

pivot ['pɪvət] *n* perno *m*.

pizza ['piːtsə] *n* pizza *f*.

pizzeria [ˌpiːtsə'riːə] *n* pizzeria *f*.

Pl. *(abbr of Place) abbreviazione di strada in alcuni indirizzi*.

placard ['plækɑːd] *n* cartello *m*.

place [pleɪs] *n (location)* posto *m*, luogo *m* ; *(house, flat)* casa *f* ; *(seat, proper position, in race, list)* posto. ◆ *vt (put)* collocare, mettere ; *(an order, bet)* fare ; **in the first ~** *(firstly)* in primo luogo ; **to take ~** avere luogo, avvenire ; **to take sb's ~** *(replace)* prendere il posto di qn ; **all over the ~** dappertutto ; **in ~ of** al posto di.

place mat *n (heat-resistant)* sottopiatto *m* ; *(linen)* tovaglietta *f*.

placement ['pleɪsmənt] *n (work experience)* stage *m inv*.

place of birth *n* luogo *m* di nascita.

plague [pleɪg] *n* peste *f*.

plaice [pleɪs] (*pl inv*) *n* platessa *f*.

plain [pleɪn] *adj (simple)* semplice ; *(in one colour)* in tinta unita ; *(clear)* chiaro(a) ; *(paper)* non rigato(a) ; *pej (not attractive)* scialbo(a). ◆ *n* pianura *f*.

plain chocolate *n* cioccolato *m* fondente.

plainly ['pleɪnlɪ] *adv* chiaramente.

plait [plæt] *n* treccia *f*. ◆ *vt* intrecciare.

plan [plæn] *n (scheme, project)* piano *m*, progetto *m* ; *(drawing)* pianta *f*. ◆ *vt (organize)* programmare, progettare ; **have you any ~s for tonight?** hai qualche programma per stasera? ; **according to ~** secondo i piani ; **to ~ to do sthg, to ~ on doing sthg** progettare di fare qc.

plane [pleɪn] *n (aeroplane)* aereo *m* ; *(tool)* pialla *f*.

planet ['plænɪt] *n* pianeta *m*.

plank [plæŋk] *n* asse *f*, tavola *f*.

plant [plɑːnt] *n* pianta *f* ; *(factory)* stabilimento *m*, fabbrica *f*. ◆ *vt* piantare ; **'heavy ~ crossing'** 'uscita mezzi pesanti'.

plaque [plɑːk] *n* placca *f*.

plaster ['plɑːstə'] *n Br (for cut)*

cerotto *m* ; *(for walls)* intonaco *m* ; in ~ *(arm, leg)* ingessato.

plaster cast *n (for broken bones)* ingessatura *f*.

plastic ['plæstɪk] *n* plastica *f*. ◆ *adj* di plastica.

plastic bag *n* sacchetto *m* di plastica.

Plasticine® ['plæstɪsiːn] *n Br* plastilina® *f*.

plate [pleɪt] *n (for food)* piatto *m* ; *(of metal, glass)* piastra *f*.

plateau ['plætəʊ] *n* altopiano *m*.

plate-glass *adj* di vetro piano.

platform ['plætfɔːm] *n (at railway station)* marciapiede *m* (di binario) ; *(raised structure)* piattaforma *f* ; *(stage)* palco *m* ; ~ **12** binario 12.

platinum ['plætɪnəm] *n* platino *m*.

platter ['plætə^r] *n* CULIN *piatto di affettati o di frutti di mare assortiti.*

play [pleɪ] *vt (sport, game)* giocare a ; *(musical instrument, music)* suonare ; *(opponent)* giocare contro ; *(CD, tape, record)* mettere (su) ; *(role, character)* interpretare. ◆ *vi* giocare ; *(musician)* suonare. ◆ *n (in theatre, on TV)* dramma *m*, commedia *f* ; *(button on CD, tape recorder)* play *m inv*. ❑ **play back** *vt sep (tape)* riascoltare ; *(video)* rivedere. ❑ **play up** *vi (machine, car)* fare i capricci.

player ['pleɪə^r] *n (of sport, game)* giocatore *m*, -trice *f* ; *(of musical instrument)* suonatore *m*, -trice *f*.

playful ['pleɪfʊl] *adj* scherzoso(a), giocoso(a).

playground ['pleɪgraʊnd] *n (in school)* cortile *m* per la ricreazione ; *(in park etc)* parco *m* giochi.

playing card ['pleɪɪŋ-] *n* carta *f* da gioco.

playing field ['pleɪɪŋ-] *n* campo *m* sportivo.

playroom ['pleɪrʊm] *n* stanza *f* dei giochi.

playschool ['pleɪskuːl] = **playgroup**.

playtime ['pleɪtaɪm] *n* ricreazione *f*.

playwright ['pleɪraɪt] *n* drammaturgo *m*, -a *f*.

plc *Br* (*abbr of public limited company*) ≃ S.r.l. *(quotata in borsa)*.

pleasant ['pleznt] *adj* piacevole, gradevole ; *(person)* simpatico(a).

please [pliːz] *adv* per favore, per piacere. ◆ *vt* far piacere a ; ~ **take a seat** prego, si sieda ; **yes ~!** sì, grazie! ; **whatever you ~** quello che ti pare.

pleased [pliːzd] *adj* contento(a) ; **to be ~ with** essere contento di ; ~ **to meet you!** piacere!

pleasure ['pleʒə^r] *n* piacere *m* ; **with ~** con piacere ; **it's a ~!** non c'è di che!, prego!

pleat [pliːt] *n* piega *f*.

pleated ['pliːtɪd] *adj* pieghettato(a).

plentiful ['plentɪfʊl] *adj* abbondante.

plenty ['plentɪ] *pron* : **there's ~** ce n'è in abbondanza ; ~ **of** un sacco di.

pliers ['plaɪəz] *npl* pinze *fpl*.

plonk [plɒŋk] *n Br inf (wine)* vino *m* da poco.

plot [plɒt] *n (scheme)* complotto

m ; *(of story, film, play)* trama *f* ; *(of land)* appezzamento *m*.

plough [plaʊ] *n Br* aratro *m*. ◆ *vt Br* arare.

ploughman's (lunch) ['plaʊmənz-] *n Br piatto a base di formaggi, sottaceti e pane, spesso servito nei pub.*

plow [plaʊ] *Am* = **plough**.

ploy [plɔɪ] *n* tattica *f*.

pluck [plʌk] *vt (eyebrows)* depilare ; *(chicken)* spennare.

plug [plʌg] *n (electrical)* spina *f* ; *(for bath, sink)* tappo *m*. ❑ **plug in** *vt sep* attaccare (a una presa).

plughole ['plʌghəʊl] *n* buco *m (della vasca, ecc.)*.

plum [plʌm] *n* susina *f*, prugna *f*.

plumber ['plʌmə^r] *n* idraulico *m*.

plumbing ['plʌmɪŋ] *n (pipes)* tubature *fpl*.

plump [plʌmp] *adj* grassoccio(a).

plunge [plʌndʒ] *vi (fall)* precipitare, cadere ; *(dive)* tuffarsi ; *(decrease)* precipitare.

plunger ['plʌndʒə^r] *n (for unblocking pipe)* sturalavandini *m inv*.

pluperfect (tense) [ˌpluː'pɜːfɪkt-] *n* : **the ~** il piuccheperfetto.

plural ['plʊərəl] *n* plurale *m* ; **in the ~** al plurale.

plus [plʌs] *prep* più. ◆ *adj* : **30 ~** più di 30.

plush [plʌʃ] *adj* lussuoso(a).

plywood ['plaɪwʊd] *n* compensato *m*.

p.m. *(abbr of post meridiem)* : **at 3 ~** alle 3 del pomeriggio ; **at 10 ~** alle 10 di sera.

PMT *n (abbr of premenstrual tension)* sindrome *f* premestruale.

pneumatic drill [njuː'mætɪk-] *n* martello *m* pneumatico.

pneumonia [njuː'məʊnjə] *n* polmonite *f*.

poached egg [pəʊtʃt-] *n* uovo *m* in camicia.

poached salmon [pəʊtʃt-] *n* salmone *m* bollito.

poacher ['pəʊtʃə^r] *n* bracconiere *m*.

PO Box *n (abbr of Post Office Box)* C.P.

pocket ['pɒkɪt] *n* tasca *f*. ◆ *adj* tascabile.

pocketbook ['pɒkɪtbʊk] *n (notebook)* taccuino *m* ; *Am (handbag)* borsetta *f*.

pocket money *n Br* paghetta *f*, settimana *f*.

podiatrist [pə'daɪətrɪst] *n Am* pedicure *mf*, callista *mf*.

poem ['pəʊɪm] *n* poesia *f*.

poet ['pəʊɪt] *n* poeta *m*, -essa *f*.

poetry ['pəʊɪtrɪ] *n* poesia *f*.

point [pɔɪnt] *n* punto *m* ; *(tip)* punta *f* ; *Br (electric socket)* presa *f*. ◆ *vi* : **to ~ to** indicare ; **five ~ seven** cinque virgola sette ; **what's the ~?** a che serve? ; **there's no ~** è inutile ; **to be on the ~ of doing sthg** essere sul punto di fare qc. ❑ **points** *npl Br (on railway)* scambio *m*. ❑ **point out** *vt sep (object, person)* indicare ; *(fact, mistake)* far notare.

pointed ['pɔɪntɪd] *adj (in shape)* appuntito(a).

pointless ['pɔɪntlɪs] *adj* inutile.

point of view *n* punto *m* di vista.

poison ['pɔɪzn] *n* veleno *m.* ◆ *vt* avvelenare.
poisoning ['pɔɪznɪŋ] *n* avvelenamento *m*, intossicazione *f.*
poisonous ['pɔɪznəs] *adj* velenoso(a).
poke [pəʊk] *vt (with finger, stick, elbow)* dare un colpetto a.
poker ['pəʊkəʳ] *n (card game)* poker *m.*
Poland ['pəʊlənd] *n* la Polonia.
polar bear ['pəʊlə-] *n* orso *m* bianco.
pole [pəʊl] *n (of wood)* palo *m.*
police [pə'li:s] *npl* : the ~ la polizia.
police car *n* auto *f inv* della polizia.
police force *n* forze *fpl* di polizia OR dell'ordine.
policeman [pə'li:smən] (*pl* **-men** [-mən]) *n* poliziotto *m.*
police officer *n* agente *m* di polizia.
police station *n* posto *m* di polizia.
policewoman [pə'li:sˌwʊmən] (*pl* **-women** [-ˌwɪmɪn]) *n* donna *f* poliziotto.
policy ['pɒləsɪ] *n (approach, attitude)* politica *f* ; *(for insurance)* polizza *f.*
policy-holder *n* assicurato *m*, -a *f.*
polio ['pəʊlɪəʊ] *n* polio *f.*
polish ['pɒlɪʃ] *n (for cleaning)* lucido *m*, cera *f.* ◆ *vt* lucidare.
Polish ['pəʊlɪʃ] *adj* polacco(a). ◆ *n (language)* polacco *m.* ◆ *npl* : the ~ i polacchi.
polite [pə'laɪt] *adj* cortese, gentile.
political [pə'lɪtɪkl] *adj* politico(a).
politician [ˌpɒlɪ'tɪʃn] *n* politico *m.*
politics ['pɒlətɪks] *n* politica *f.*
poll [pəʊl] *n (survey)* sondaggio *m* (d'opinioni) ; the ~s *(election)* le elezioni.
pollen ['pɒlən] *n* polline *m.*
pollute [pə'lu:t] *vt* inquinare.
pollution [pə'lu:ʃn] *n* inquinamento *m.*
polo neck ['pəʊləʊ-] *n Br (jumper)* maglione *m* a collo alto.
polyester [ˌpɒlɪ'estəʳ] *n* poliestere *m.*
polystyrene [ˌpɒlɪ'staɪri:n] *n* polistirolo *m.*
polytechnic [ˌpɒlɪ'teknɪk] *n* ≃ politecnico *m.*
polythene bag ['pɒlɪθi:n-] *n* sacchetto *m* di plastica.
pomegranate ['pɒmɪˌgrænɪt] *n* melagrana *f.*
pompous ['pɒmpəs] *adj* pomposo(a).
pond [pɒnd] *n* stagno *m.*
pony ['pəʊnɪ] *n* pony *m inv.*
ponytail ['pəʊnɪteɪl] *n* coda *f* di cavallo.
pony-trekking [-ˌtrekɪŋ] *n Br* escursione *f* a dorso di pony.
poodle ['pu:dl] *n* barboncino *m.*
pool [pu:l] *n* pozza *f* ; *(for swimming)* piscina *f* ; *(game)* biliardo *m* a buca. ❑ **pools** *npl Br* : the ~s ≃ il totocalcio.
poor [pɔ:ʳ] *adj* povero(a) ; *(bad)*

mediocre, scadente. ◆ *npl* : the ~ i poveri.
poorly ['pɔːlɪ] *adv* malamente, male. ◆ *adj Br (ill)* : to be ~ stare poco bene.
pop [pɒp] *n (music)* musica *f* pop. ◆ *vt inf (put)* mettere. ◆ *vi (balloon)* scoppiare ; my ears popped mi si sono stappate le orecchie. ❑ **pop in** *vi Br (visit)* fare un salto.
popcorn ['pɒpkɔːn] *n* popcorn *m*.
Pope [pəʊp] *n* : the ~ il papa.
pop group *n* gruppo *m* pop.
poplar (tree) ['pɒpləʳ-] *n* pioppo *m*.
pop music *n* musica *f* pop.
popper ['pɒpəʳ] *n Br* bottone *m* a pressione.
poppy ['pɒpɪ] *n* papavero *m*.
Popsicle® ['pɒpsɪkl] *n Am* ghiacciolo *m*.
pop socks *npl* gambaletti *mpl*.
pop star *n* pop star *f inv*.
popular ['pɒpjʊləʳ] *adj* popolare ; *(fashionable)* in voga.
popularity [ˌpɒpjʊ'lærətɪ] *n* popolarità *f*.
populated ['pɒpjʊleɪtɪd] *adj* popolato(a).
population [ˌpɒpjʊ'leɪʃn] *n* popolazione *f*.
porcelain ['pɔːsəlɪn] *n* porcellana *f*.
porch [pɔːtʃ] *n (entrance)* portico *m* ; *Am (outside house)* veranda *f*.
pork [pɔːk] *n* carne *f* di maiale.
pork chop *n* braciola *f* di maiale, costoletta *f* di maiale.
pornographic [ˌpɔːnə'græfɪk] *adj* pornografico(a).
porridge ['pɒrɪdʒ] *n* porridge *m*, farinata *f* d'avena.
port [pɔːt] *n* porto *m*.
portable ['pɔːtəbl] *adj* portatile.
porter ['pɔːtəʳ] *n (at hotel, museum)* portiere *m* ; *(at station, airport)* facchino *m*.
portion ['pɔːʃn] *n* porzione *f*.
portrait ['pɔːtreɪt] *n* ritratto *m*.
Portugal ['pɔːtʃʊgl] *n* il Portogallo.
Portuguese [ˌpɔːtʃʊ'giːz] *adj* portoghese. ◆ *n (language)* portoghese *m*. ◆ *npl* : the ~ i portoghesi.
pose [pəʊz] *vt (problem, threat)* porre. ◆ *vi (for photo)* posare.
posh [pɒʃ] *adj inf (person, accent)* snob *inv*, raffinato(a) ; *(hotel, restaurant)* elegante, di lusso.
position [pə'zɪʃn] *n* posizione *f* ; *fml (job)* posto *m* ; '~ closed' *(in bank, post office etc)* 'sportello chiuso'.
positive ['pɒzətɪv] *adj* positivo(a) ; *(certain, sure)* sicuro(a), certo(a).
possess [pə'zes] *vt* possedere.
possession [pə'zeʃn] *n (thing owned)* bene *m*.
possessive [pə'zesɪv] *adj* possessivo(a).
possibility [ˌpɒsə'bɪlətɪ] *n* possibilità *f inv*.
possible ['pɒsəbl] *adj* possibile ; it's ~ that we may be late può darsi che facciamo tardi ; would it be ~ ...? sarebbe possibile ...? ; as much as ~ il più possibile ; if ~ se possibile.
possibly ['pɒsəblɪ] *adv (perhaps)* forse.

post [pəʊst] *n (system, letters, delivery)* posta *f*; *(pole)* palo *m*; *fml (job)* posto *m*. ◆ *vt (letter, parcel)* spedire (per posta); **by ~** per posta.

postage ['pəʊstɪdʒ] *n* affrancatura *f*, spese *fpl* postali; **~ and packing** spese di spedizione (postale); **~ paid** franco di porto, affrancatura pagata.

postage stamp *n fml* francobollo *m*.

postal order ['pəʊstl-] *n* vaglia *m inv* postale.

postbox ['pəʊstbɒks] *n Br* cassetta *f* delle lettere.

postcard ['pəʊstkɑːd] *n* cartolina *f*.

postcode ['pəʊstkəʊd] *n Br* codice *m* (di avviamento) postale.

poster ['pəʊstəʳ] *n* manifesto *m*, poster *m inv*.

post-free *adv* in franchigia postale, con affrancatura pagata.

postgraduate [ˌpəʊst'grædʒʊət] *n laureato(a) che frequenta un corso di specializzazione*.

postman ['pəʊstmən] (*pl* **-men** [-mən]) *n* postino *m*.

postmark ['pəʊstmɑːk] *n* timbro *m* postale.

postmen *pl* → **postman**.

post office *n (building)* ufficio *m* postale; **the Post Office** ≃ le Poste e Telecomunicazioni.

postpone [ˌpəʊst'pəʊn] *vt* rinviare, rimandare.

posture ['pɒstʃəʳ] *n* postura *f*.

postwoman ['pəʊstˌwʊmən] (*pl* **-women** [-ˌwɪmɪn]) *n* postina *f*.

pot [pɒt] *n (for cooking)* pentola *f*; *(for jam, paint)* vasetto *m*, barattolo *m*; *(for coffee)* caffettiera *f*; *(for tea)* teiera *f*; *inf (cannabis)* erba *f*; **a ~ of tea** un tè *(servito in una teiera)*.

potato [pə'teɪtəʊ] (*pl* **-es**) *n* patata *f*.

potato salad *n* patate *fpl* in insalata.

potential [pə'tenʃl] *adj* potenziale. ◆ *n* potenziale *m*.

pothole ['pɒthəʊl] *n (in road)* buca *f*.

pot plant *n* pianta *f* in vaso.

potted ['pɒtɪd] *adj (meat, fish)* in vasetto, in scatola; *(plant)* in vaso.

pottery ['pɒtərɪ] *n (clay objects)* ceramiche *fpl*; *(craft)* ceramica *f*.

potty ['pɒtɪ] *n inf* vasino *m*.

pouch [paʊtʃ] *n (for money, tobacco)* borsellino *f*.

poultry ['pəʊltrɪ] *n* & *npl* pollame *m*.

pound [paʊnd] *n (unit of money)* sterlina *f*; *(unit of weight)* = 453,6 g, libbra *f*. ◆ *vi (heart)* battere forte; *(head)* martellare.

pour [pɔːʳ] *vt* versare. ◆ *vi (flow)* riversarsi; **it's ~ing (with rain)** sta piovendo a dirotto. ❑ **pour out** *vt sep (drink)* versare.

poverty ['pɒvətɪ] *n* povertà *f*, miseria *f*.

powder ['paʊdəʳ] *n* polvere *f*; *(cosmetic)* cipria *f*.

power ['paʊəʳ] *n (control, authority)* potere *m*; *(ability)* capacità *f inv*; *(strength, force)* potenza *f*; *(energy)* energia *f*; *(electricity)* corrente *f*. ◆ *vt* azionare ; **to be in ~** essere al potere.

power cut *n* interruzione *f* di corrente.

power failure *n* interruzione *f* di corrente.

powerful ['paʊəful] *adj* potente.

power point *n Br* presa *f* di corrente.

power station *n* centrale *f* elettrica.

power steering *n* servosterzo *m*.

practical ['præktɪkl] *adj* pratico(a).

practically ['præktɪklɪ] *adv (almost)* praticamente.

practice ['præktɪs] *n (training)* pratica *f*; *(training session)* allenamento *m*, esercizio *m* ; *(of doctor, lawyer)* studio *m* ; *(regular activity, custom)* consuetudine *f*. ◆ *vt Am* **= practise** ; **out of ~** fuori allenamento.

practise ['præktɪs] *vt (sport, music, technique)* allenarsi a, esercitarsi a OR in. ◆ *vi (train)* allenarsi, esercitarsi ; *(doctor, lawyer)* esercitare. ◆ *n Am* **= practice**.

praise [preɪz] *n* elogio *m*, lode *f*. ◆ *vt* elogiare, lodare.

pram [præm] *n Br* carrozzina *f*.

prank [præŋk] *n* burla *f*.

prawn [prɔːn] *n* gamberetto *m*.

prawn cocktail *n* cocktail *m inv* di gamberetti.

prawn crackers *npl* nuvolette *fpl* di drago.

pray [preɪ] *vi* pregare ; **to ~ for sthg** *fig* pregare per qc, invocare qc.

prayer [preəʳ] *n* preghiera *f*.

precarious [prɪ'keərɪəs] *adj* precario(a).

precaution [prɪ'kɔːʃn] *n* precauzione *f*.

precede [prɪ'siːd] *vt fml* precedere.

preceding [prɪ'siːdɪŋ] *adj* precedente.

precinct ['priːsɪŋkt] *n Br (for shopping)* centro *m* commerciale *(chiuso al traffico)* ; *Am (area of town)* circoscrizione *f*.

precious ['preʃəs] *adj* prezioso(a).

precious stone *n* pietra *f* preziosa.

precipice ['presɪpɪs] *n* precipizio *m*.

precise [prɪ'saɪs] *adj* preciso(a).

precisely [prɪ'saɪslɪ] *adv* precisamente.

predecessor ['priːdɪsesəʳ] *n* predecessore *m*.

predicament [prɪ'dɪkəmənt] *n* situazione *f* difficile.

predict [prɪ'dɪkt] *vt* predire.

predictable [prɪ'dɪktəbl] *adj* prevedibile.

prediction [prɪ'dɪkʃn] *n* predizione *f*.

preface ['prefɪs] *n* prefazione *f*.

prefect ['priːfekt] *n Br (at school)* studente *m*, -essa *f* con funzioni disciplinari.

prefer [prɪ'fɜːʳ] *vt* : **to ~ sthg (to)** preferire qc (a) ; **to ~ to do sthg** preferire fare qc.

preferable ['prefrəbl] *adj* preferibile.

preferably ['prefrəblı] *adv* preferibilmente.
preference ['prefərəns] *n* preferenza *f*.
prefix ['pri:fıks] *n* prefisso *m*.
pregnancy ['pregnənsı] *n* gravidanza *f*.
pregnant ['pregnənt] *adj* incinta.
prejudice ['predʒʊdıs] *n* pregiudizio *m*.
prejudiced ['predʒʊdıst] *adj* : ~ **(against)** prevenuto(a) (contro) ; ~ **(in favour of)** ben disposto(a) (verso).
preliminary [prı'lımınərı] *adj* preliminare.
premature ['premə,tjʊəʳ] *adj* prematuro(a).
premier ['premjəʳ] *adj* primo(a). ◆ *n* primo ministro *m*.
premiere ['premıeəʳ] *n* prima *f*.
premises ['premısız] *npl* locali *mpl* ; **on the ~** sul posto.
premium ['pri:mjəm] *n (for insurance)* premio *m*.
premium-quality *adj (meat)* di prima qualità.
preoccupied [pri:'ɒkjʊpaıd] *adj* preoccupato(a).
prepacked [,pri:'pækt] *adj* preconfezionato(a).
prepaid ['pri:peıd] *adj (envelope)* con affrancatura pagata.
preparation [,prepə'reıʃn] *n* preparazione *f*. ❑ **preparations** *npl (arrangements)* preparativi *mpl*.
preparatory school [prı'pærətrı-] *n (in UK)* scuola *f* elementare privata ; *(in US)* scuola *f* secondaria privata *(che prepara agli studi universitari)*.
prepare [prı'peəʳ] *vt* preparare. ◆ *vi* prepararsi.
prepared [prı'peəd] *adj (ready)* preparato(a), pronto(a) ; **to be ~ to do sthg** essere disposto(a) a fare qc.
preposition [,prepə'zıʃn] *n* preposizione *f*.
prep school [prep-] = **preparatory school**.
prescribe [prı'skraıb] *vt* prescrivere.
prescription [prı'skrıpʃn] *n (paper)* ricetta *f* ; *(medicine)* medicine *fpl*.
presence ['prezns] *n* presenza *f* ; **in sb's ~** in presenza di qn.
present [*adj & n* 'preznt, *vb* prı'zent] *adj (in attendance)* presente ; *(current)* attuale. ◆ *n (gift)* regalo *m*. ◆ *vt* presentare ; *(offer)* offrire ; **the ~ (tense)** il (tempo) presente ; **at ~** al momento, attualmente ; **the ~** il presente ; **to ~ sb to sb** presentare qn a qn.
presentable [prı'zentəbl] *adj* presentabile.
presentation [,prezn'teıʃn] *n (way of presenting)* presentazione *f* ; *(ceremony)* consegna *f* (ufficiale).
presenter [prı'zentəʳ] *n (of TV, radio programme)* presentatore *m*, -trice *f*.
presently ['prezəntlı] *adv (soon)* fra poco, a momenti ; *(now)* attualmente.
preservation [,prezə'veıʃn] *n* tutela *f*, protezione *f*.

preservative [prɪ'zɜːvətɪv] *n* conservante *m*.

preserve [prɪ'zɜːv] *n (jam)* marmellata *f*. ◆ *vt (conserve)* mantenere ; *(keep)* preservare, proteggere ; *(food)* conservare.

president ['prezɪdənt] *n* presidente *mf*.

press [pres] *vt (push)* premere, pigiare ; *(iron)* stirare. ◆ *n* : the ~ la stampa ; to ~ sb to do sthg insistere perché qn faccia qc.

press conference *n* conferenza *f* stampa.

press-stud *n* bottone *m* a pressione, automatico *m*.

press-ups *npl* flessioni *fpl* sulle braccia.

pressure ['preʃə'] *n* pressione *f*.

pressure cooker *n* pentola *f* a pressione.

prestigious [pre'stɪdʒəs] *adj* prestigioso(a).

presumably [prɪ'zjuːməblɪ] *adv* presumibilmente.

presume [prɪ'zjuːm] *vt (assume)* presumere, supporre.

pretend [prɪ'tend] *vt* : to ~ to do sthg far finta di fare qc.

pretentious [prɪ'tenʃəs] *adj* pretenzioso(a).

pretty ['prɪtɪ] *adj* grazioso(a), carino(a). ◆ *adv inf (quite)* piuttosto, abbastanza ; *(very)* assai.

prevent [prɪ'vent] *vt* evitare ; to ~ sb/sthg from doing sthg impedire a qn/qc di fare qc.

prevention [prɪ'venʃn] *n* prevenzione *f*.

preview ['priːvjuː] *n* anteprima *f*.

previous ['priːvjəs] *adj* precedente.

previously ['priːvjəslɪ] *adv (formerly)* precedentemente, in precedenza ; *(earlier, before)* prima.

price [praɪs] *n* prezzo *m*. ◆ *vt* fissare il prezzo di.

priceless ['praɪslɪs] *adj* inestimabile, senza prezzo.

price list *n* listino *m* prezzi.

pricey ['praɪsɪ] *adj inf* costoso(a).

prick [prɪk] *vt* pungere.

prickly ['prɪklɪ] *adj (plant, bush)* spinoso(a).

prickly heat *n* sudamina *f*.

pride [praɪd] *n (satisfaction, self-respect)* orgoglio *m* ; *(arrogance)* superbia *f*. ◆ *vt* : to ~ o.s. on sthg vantarsi di qc.

priest [priːst] *n* prete *m*, sacerdote *m*.

primarily ['praɪmərɪlɪ] *adv* principalmente.

primary school ['praɪmərɪ-] *n* scuola *f* elementare.

prime [praɪm] *adj (chief)* fondamentale ; *(beef, cut)* di prima qualità.

prime minister *n* primo ministro *m*.

primitive ['prɪmɪtɪv] *adj* primitivo(a).

primrose ['prɪmrəuz] *n* primula *f*.

prince [prɪns] *n* principe *m*.

princess [prɪn'ses] *n* principessa *f*.

principal ['prɪnsəpl] *adj* principale. ◆ *n (of school)* direttore *m*, -trice *f* ; *(of university)* rettore *m*, -trice *f*.

principle ['prɪnsəpl] *n* principio *m* ; **in ~** in linea di principio.

print [prɪnt] *n (words)* caratteri *mpl* ; *(photo, of painting)* stampa *f* ; *(mark)* impronta *f*. ◆ *vt (book, newspaper, photo)* stampare ; *(publish)* pubblicare ; *(write)* scrivere a stampatello ; **out of ~** esaurito. ❑ **print out** *vt sep* stampare.

printed matter ['prɪntɪd-] *n* stampe *fpl*.

printer ['prɪntəʳ] *n (machine)* stampante *f* ; *(person)* tipografo *m*, -a *f*.

printout ['prɪntaʊt] *n* stampato *m*.

prior ['praɪəʳ] *adj (previous)* precedente ; **~ to** *fml* precedente.

priority [praɪ'ɒrətɪ] *n (important thing)* elemento *m* prioritario ; **to have ~ over** avere la priorità rispetto a.

prison ['prɪzn] *n* prigione *f*.

prisoner ['prɪznəʳ] *n* prigioniero *m*, -a *f*.

prisoner of war *n* prigioniero *m*, -a *f* di guerra.

prison officer *n* guardia *f* carceraria.

privacy ['prɪvəsɪ] *n* privacy *f*.

private ['praɪvɪt] *adj* privato(a) ; *(confidential)* confidenziale ; *(place)* appartato(a) ; *(bathroom)* in camera. ◆ *n MIL* soldato *m* semplice ; **in ~** in privato.

private health care *n* assistenza *f* medica privata.

private property *n* proprietà *f* privata.

private school *n* scuola *f* privata.

privilege ['prɪvɪlɪdʒ] *n* privilegio *m* ; **it's a ~!** è un onore!

prize [praɪz] *n* premio *m*.

prize-giving [-ˌgɪvɪŋ] *n* premiazione *f*.

pro [prəʊ] (*pl* **-s**) *n inf (professional)* professionista *mf*. ❑ **pros** *npl* : **the ~s and cons** i pro e i contro.

probability [ˌprɒbə'bɪlətɪ] *n* probabilità *f*.

probable ['prɒbəbl] *adj* probabile.

probably ['prɒbəblɪ] *adv* probabilmente.

probation officer [prə'beɪʃn-] *n persona incaricata di seguire i criminali in libertà vigilata.*

problem ['prɒbləm] *n* problema *m* ; **no ~!** *inf* non c'è problema!

procedure [prə'siːdʒəʳ] *n* procedura *f*.

proceed [prə'siːd] *vi fml* procedere ; **'~ with caution'** 'procedere con cautela'.

proceeds ['prəʊsiːdz] *npl* ricavato *m*.

process ['prəʊses] *n* processo *m* ; **to be in the ~ of doing sthg** star facendo qc.

processed cheese ['prəʊsest-] *n* formaggio *m* fuso.

procession [prə'seʃn] *n* processione *f*.

prod [prɒd] *vt (poke)* pungolare.

produce [*vb* prə'djuːs, *n* 'prɒdjuːs] *vt* produrre ; *(cause)* creare. ◆ *n* prodotti *mpl* agricoli.

producer [prə'djuːsəʳ] *n* produttore *m*, -trice *f*.

product ['prɒdʌkt] *n* prodotto *m*.

production [prə'dʌkʃn] *n* produzione *f*.

productivity [ˌprɒdʌk'tɪvətɪ] *n* produttività *f*.

profession [prə'feʃn] *n* professione *f*.

professional [prə'feʃənl] *adj (relating to work)* professionale ; *(not amateur)* professionista. ◆ *n* professionista *mf*.

professor [prə'fesəʳ] *n* professore *m*, -essa *f*.

profile ['prəufaɪl] *n* profilo *m*.

profit ['prɒfɪt] *n* profitto *m*. ◆ *vi* : **to ~ (from)** trarre profitto (da).

profitable ['prɒfɪtəbl] *adj (financially)* rimunerativo(a) ; *(useful)* vantaggioso(a).

profiteroles [prə'fɪtərəulz] *npl* profiterole *m inv*.

profound [prə'faund] *adj* profondo(a).

program ['prəugræm] *n* COMPUT programma *m* ; *Am* = **programme**. ◆ *vt* COMPUT programmare.

programme ['prəugræm] *n Br* programma *m*.

progress [*n* 'prəugres, *vb* prə'gres] *n (improvement)* progresso *m* ; *(forward movement)* moto *m*. ◆ *vi (work, talks, student)* progredire ; *(day, meeting)* andare avanti ; **to make ~** *(improve)* fare progressi ; *(in journey)* avanzare ; **in ~** in corso.

progressive [prə'gresɪv] *adj (forward-looking)* progressista.

prohibit [prə'hɪbɪt] *vt* proibire ; **'smoking strictly ~ed'** ' è severamente vietato fumare'.

project ['prɒdʒekt] *n* progetto *m* ; *(at school)* ricerca *f*.

projector [prə'dʒektəʳ] *n* proiettore *m*.

prolong [prə'lɒŋ] *vt* prolungare.

prom [prɒm] *n Am (dance)* ballo *m (per studenti)*.

promenade [ˌprɒmə'nɑːd] *n Br (by the sea)* lungomare *m inv*.

prominent ['prɒmɪnənt] *adj (person)* importante ; *(noticeable)* evidente.

promise ['prɒmɪs] *n* promessa *f*. ◆ *vt & vi* promettere ; **to show ~** promettere (bene) ; **I ~!** te lo prometto ; **I ~ (that) I'll come** prometto che verrò ; **to ~ sb sthg** promettere qc a qn ; **to ~ to do sthg** promettere di fare qc.

promising ['prɒmɪsɪŋ] *adj* promettente.

promote [prə'məut] *vt (in job)* promuovere.

promotion [prə'məuʃn] *n* promozione *f*.

prompt [prɒmpt] *adj (quick)* pronto(a). ◆ *adv* : **at six o'clock ~** alle sei in punto.

prone [prəun] *adj* : **to be ~ to sthg** essere incline a qc ; **to be ~ to do sthg** essere incline a fare qc.

prong [prɒŋ] *n (of fork)* dente *m*.

pronoun ['prəunaun] *n* pronome *m*.

pronounce [prə'nauns] *vt (word)* pronunciare.

pronunciation [prəˌnʌnsɪ'eɪʃn] *n* pronuncia *f*.

proof [pruːf] *n (evidence)* prova *f* ; **to be 12% ~** *(alcohol)* avere 12 gradi.

prop [prɒp] ◆**prop up** *vt sep (support)* sostenere.
propeller [prə'peləʳ] *n* elica *f*.
proper ['prɒpəʳ] *adj (suitable)* adatto(a) ; *(correct)* giusto(a) ; *(socially acceptable)* decoroso(a).
properly ['prɒpəlɪ] *adv (suitably)* adeguatamente ; *(correctly)* correttamente.
property ['prɒpətɪ] *n* proprietà *f inv*.
proportion [prə'pɔːʃn] *n* proporzione *f*; *(in art)* proporzioni *fpl*.
proposal [prə'pəuzl] *n (suggestion)* proposta *f*.
propose [prə'pəuz] *vt (suggest)* proporre. ◆ *vi* : **to ~ (to sb)** fare una proposta di matrimonio (a qn).
proposition [ˌprɒpə'zɪʃn] *n (offer)* proposta *f*.
proprietor [prə'praɪətəʳ] *n fml* proprietario *m*, -a *f*.
prose [prəuz] *n (not poetry)* prosa *f* ; SCH traduzione *f (dalla madrelingua)*.
prosecution [ˌprɒsɪ'kjuːʃn] *n* JUR *(charge)* azione *f* giudiziaria.
prospect ['prɒspekt] *n (possibility)* prospettiva *f*; **I don't relish the ~** non mi attira la prospettiva. ❑ **prospects** *npl (for the future)* prospettive *fpl*.
prospectus [prə'spektəs] (*pl* **-es**) *n* prospetto *m*.
prosperous ['prɒspərəs] *adj* prospero(a).
prostitute ['prɒstɪtjuːt] *n* prostituta *f*.
protect [prə'tekt] *vt* proteggere ; **to ~ sb/sthg from** proteggere qn/qc da ; **to ~ sb/sthg against** proteggere qn/qc da.
protection [prə'tekʃn] *n* protezione *f*.
protection factor *n* fattore *m* di protezione.
protective [prə'tektɪv] *adj (person)* protettivo(a) ; *(clothes)* di protezione.
protein ['prəutiːn] *n* proteina *f*.
protest [*n* 'prəutest, *vb* prə'test] *n* protesta *f*. ◆ *vt Am (protest against)* protestare contro. ◆ *vi* : **to ~ (against)** protestare (contro).
Protestant ['prɒtɪstənt] *n* protestante *mf*.
protester [prə'testəʳ] *n* dimostrante *mf*.
protrude [prə'truːd] *vi* sporgere.
proud [praud] *adj (pleased)* orgoglioso(a) ; *pej (arrogant)* superbo(a) ; **to be ~ of** essere orgoglioso di.
prove [pruːv] (*pp* **-d** OR **proven**) *vt (show to be true)* dimostrare ; *(turn out to be)* dimostrarsi.
proverb ['prɒvɜːb] *n* proverbio *m*.
provide [prə'vaɪd] *vt* fornire ; **to ~ sb with sthg** fornire qc a qn. ❑ **provide for** *vt fus (person)* provvedere a.
provided (that) [prə'vaɪdɪd-] *conj* purché.
providing (that) [prə'vaɪdɪŋ-] = **provided (that)**.
province ['prɒvɪns] *n* regione *f*.
provisional [prə'vɪʒənl] *adj* provvisorio(a).
provisions [prə'vɪʒnz] *npl* provviste *fpl*.

provocative [prəˈvɒkətɪv] *adj* provocatorio(a).
provoke [prəˈvəuk] *vt* provocare.
prowl [praul] *vi* muoversi furtivamente.
prune [pru:n] *n* prugna *f* secca. ◆ *vt (tree, bush)* potare.
PS (*abbr of postscript*) P.S.
psychiatrist [saɪˈkaɪətrɪst] *n* psichiatra *mf*.
psychic [ˈsaɪkɪk] *adj* dotato(a) di poteri paranormali.
psychological [ˌsaɪkəˈlɒdʒɪkl] *adj* psicologico(a).
psychologist [saɪˈkɒlədʒɪst] *n* psicologo *m*, -a *f*.
psychology [saɪˈkɒlədʒɪ] *n* psicologia *f*.
psychotherapist [ˌsaɪkəuˈθerəpɪst] *n* psicoterapeuta *mf*.
pt (*abbr of pint*) pt.
PTO (*abbr of please turn over*) v.r.
pub [pʌb] *n* pub *m inv*.

PUB

Vera e propria istituzione, i pub sono al centro della vita sociale in Gran Bretagna. Soggetti fino a poco tempo fa a rigide restrizioni d'orario, oggi possono generalmente restare aperti dalle 11 alle 23 (e fino a più tardi in Scozia). Le restrizioni relative all'ingresso dei minori di sedici anni variano da regione a regione e da pub a pub mentre rimane il divieto di vendere alcolici ai minorenni. Oltre a una grande varietà di birre e altre bevande alcoliche e non, i pub offrono una discreta scelta di piatti tipici.

puberty [ˈpju:bətɪ] *n* pubertà *f*.
public [ˈpʌblɪk] *adj* pubblico(a). ◆ *n* : **the ~** il pubblico ; **in ~** in pubblico.
publican [ˈpʌblɪkən] *n Br* gestore *m*, -trice *f* di un pub.
publication [ˌpʌblɪˈkeɪʃn] *n* pubblicazione *f*.
public bar *n Br sala di un pub, in cui le bevande costano meno.*
public convenience *n Br* gabinetti *mpl* pubblici.
public footpath *n Br* sentiero *m*.
public holiday *n* giorno *m* festivo.
public house *n Br fml* pub *m inv*.
publicity [pʌbˈlɪsɪtɪ] *n* pubblicità *f*.
public school *n (in UK)* scuola *f* privata ; *(in US)* scuola statale.
public telephone *n* telefono *m* pubblico.
public transport *n* trasporti *mpl* pubblici.
publish [ˈpʌblɪʃ] *vt* pubblicare.
publisher [ˈpʌblɪʃəʳ] *n (person)* editore *m*, -trice *f* ; *(company)* casa *f* editrice.
publishing [ˈpʌblɪʃɪŋ] *n (industry)* editoria *f*.
pub lunch *n pranzo semplice e a basso costo servito in un pub.*
pudding [ˈpudɪŋ] *n (sweet dish)* budino *m* ; *Br (course)* dessert *m inv*.
puddle [ˈpʌdl] *n* pozzanghera *f*.

puff [pʌf] *vi (breathe heavily)* ansare. ◆ *n (of air, smoke)* sbuffo *m* ; **to ~ at** tirare una boccata di.

puff pastry *n* pasta *f* sfoglia.

pull [pʊl] *vt* tirare ; *(trigger)* premere. ◆ *vi* tirare. ◆ *n* : **to give sthg a ~** dare una tirata a qc ; **to ~ a face** fare una smorfia ; **to ~ a muscle** farsi uno strappo muscolare ; **'pull'** *(on door)* 'tirare'. ❑ **pull apart** *vt sep (machine, book)* fare a pezzi. ❑ **pull down** *vt sep (lower)* abbassare ; *(demolish)* demolire. ❑ **pull in** *vi (train)* arrivare ; *(car)* accostare. ❑ **pull out** ◆ *vt sep (tooth, cork, plug)* estrarre. ◆ *vi (train)* partire ; *(car)* entrare in corsia ; *(withdraw)* ritirarsi. ❑ **pull over** *vi (car)* accostare. ❑ **pull up** ◆ *vt sep (socks, trousers, sleeve)* tirare su. ◆ *vi (stop)* fermarsi.

pulley ['pʊlɪ] (*pl* **pulleys**) *n* carrucola *f*.

pull-out *n Am (beside road)* piazzola *f* (di sosta).

pullover ['pʊl,əʊvəʳ] *n* pullover *m inv*.

pulpit ['pʊlpɪt] *n* pulpito *m*.

pulse [pʌls] *n MED* polso *m*.

pump [pʌmp] *n* pompa *f*. ❑ **pumps** *npl (sports shoes)* scarpe *fpl* da ginnastica. ❑ **pump up** *vt sep* gonfiare.

pumpkin ['pʌmpkɪn] *n* zucca *f*.

pun [pʌn] *n* gioco *m* di parole.

punch [pʌntʃ] *n (blow)* pugno *m* ; *(drink)* punch *m inv*. ◆ *vt (hit)* sferrare un pugno a ; *(ticket)* forare.

punctual ['pʌŋktʃʊəl] *adj* puntuale.

punctuation [,pʌŋktʃʊ'eɪʃn] *n* punteggiatura *f*.

puncture ['pʌŋktʃəʳ] *vt* forare. ◆ *n* : **to get a ~** forare (una gomma).

punish ['pʌnɪʃ] *vt* : **to ~ sb (for sthg)** punire qn (per qc).

punishment ['pʌnɪʃmənt] *n* punizione *f*.

punk [pʌŋk] *n (person)* punk *mf inv* ; *(music)* musica *f* punk.

punnet ['pʌnɪt] *n Br* cestino *m*.

pupil ['pju:pl] *n (student)* alunno *m*, -a *f* ; *(of eye)* pupilla *f*.

puppet ['pʌpɪt] *n* burattino *m*.

puppy ['pʌpɪ] *n* cucciolo *m*.

purchase ['pɜ:tʃəs] *vt fml* acquistare. ◆ *n fml* acquisto *m*.

pure [pjʊəʳ] *adj* puro(a).

puree ['pjʊəreɪ] *n* puré *m inv*.

purely ['pjʊəlɪ] *adv (only)* soltanto.

purity ['pjʊərətɪ] *n* purezza *f*.

purple ['pɜ:pl] *adj* viola *(inv)*.

purpose ['pɜ:pəs] *n* scopo *m* ; **on ~** apposta.

purr [pɜ:ʳ] *vi (cat)* fare le fusa.

purse [pɜ:s] *n Br (for money)* portamonete *m inv* ; *Am (handbag)* borsa *f*.

pursue [pə'sju:] *vt (follow)* inseguire ; *(study)* continuare ; *(matter, inquiry)* approfondire.

pus [pʌs] *n* pus *m inv*.

push [pʊʃ] *vt* spingere ; *(button, doorbell)* premere ; *(product)* pubblicizzare. ◆ *vi* spingere. ◆ *n* : **to give sb/sthg a ~** dare una spinta a qn/qc ; **to ~ sb into doing sthg** spingere qn a fare qc ; **'push'** *(on door)* 'spingere'. ❑ **push in** *vi (in queue)* passare avanti. ❑ **push off** *vi inf (go away)* andarsene.

push-button telephone *n* telefono *m* a tastiera.

pushchair ['pʊʃtʃeəʳ] *n Br* passeggino *m*.

pushed [pʊʃt] *adj inf*: **to be ~ (for time)** essere a corto di tempo.

push-ups *npl* flessioni *fpl* (sulle braccia).

put [pʊt] (*pt* & *pp* **put**) *vt* mettere ; *(responsibility)* dare ; *(pressure)* esercitare ; *(express)* esprimere ; *(a question)* porre ; *(estimate)* stimare ; **to ~ a child to bed** mettere a letto un bambino ; **to ~ money into sthg** investire soldi in qc. ❑ **put aside** *vt sep (money)* mettere da parte. ❑ **put away** *vt sep (tidy up)* mettere via. ❑ **put back** *vt sep (replace)* mettere a posto ; *(postpone)* posporre ; *(clock, watch)* mettere indietro. ❑ **put down** *vt sep (on floor, table)* posare ; *(passenger)* far scendere ; *Br (animal)* abbattere ; *(deposit)* dare in acconto. ❑ **put forward** *vt sep (clock, watch)* mettere avanti ; *(suggest)* suggerire. ❑ **put in** *vt sep (insert)* inserire ; *(install)* installare. ❑ **put off** *vt sep (postpone)* rimandare ; *(distract)* distrarre ; *(repel)* disgustare ; *(passenger)* far scendere. ❑ **put on** *vt sep (clothes, glasses, make-up)* mettersi ; *(weight)* mettere su ; *(television, light, radio)* accendere ; *(CD, tape, record)* mettere ; *(play, show)* mettere in scena. ❑ **put out** *vt sep (cigarette, fire, light)* spegnere ; *(publish)* pubblicare ; *(hand, arm, leg)* stendere ; *(inconvenience)* disturbare ; **to ~ one's back out** farsi male alla schiena. ❑ **put together** *vt sep (assemble)* montare ; *(combine)* mettere insieme. ❑ **put up** *vt sep (tent, statue, building)* erigere ; *(umbrella)* aprire ; *(a notice, sign)* mettere ; *(price, rate)* aumentare ; *(provide with accommodation)* ospitare. ◆ *vi Br (in hotel)* alloggiare. ❑ **put up with** *vt fus* sopportare.

putting green ['pʌtɪŋ-] *n* campo *m* da minigolf.

putty ['pʌtɪ] *n* stucco *m*.

puzzle ['pʌzl] *n (game)* rompicapo *m* ; *(jigsaw)* puzzle *m inv* ; *(mystery)* enigma *m*. ◆ *vt* confondere.

puzzling ['pʌzlɪŋ] *adj* sconcertante.

pyjamas [pə'dʒɑːməz] *npl Br* pigiama *m*.

pylon ['paɪlən] *n* traliccio *m*.

pyramid ['pɪrəmɪd] *n* piramide *f*.

Pyrenees [ˌpɪrə'niːz] *npl*: **the ~** i Pirenei.

Pyrex® ['paɪreks] *n* pyrex® *m*.

Q

quail [kweɪl] *n* quaglia *f*.

quail's eggs *npl* uova *fpl* di quaglia.

quaint [kweɪnt] *adj* pittoresco(a).

qualification [ˌkwɒlɪfɪ'keɪʃn] *n (diploma)* qualifica *f* ; *(ability)* qualità *f inv*.

qualified ['kwɒlɪfaɪd] *adj (having qualifications)* qualificato(a).

qualify ['kwɒlɪfaɪ] *vi (for competition)* qualificarsi ; *(pass exam)* abilitarsi.

quality ['kwɒlətɪ] *n* qualità *f inv.* ◆ *adj* di qualità.

quarantine ['kwɒrəntiːn] *n* quarantena *f.*

quarrel ['kwɒrəl] *n* lite *f.* ◆ *vi* litigare.

quarry ['kwɒrɪ] *n (for stone, sand)* cava *f.*

quart [kwɔːt] *n (in UK)* = 1,136 l, ≃ litro *m* ; *(in US)* = 0,946 l, ≃ litro.

quarter ['kwɔːtəʳ] *n (fraction)* quarto *m* ; *Am (coin)* quarto di dollaro ; *(4 ounces)* quarto di libbra ; *(three months)* trimestre *m* ; *(part of town)* quartiere *m* ; **(a) ~ to five** *Br* le cinque meno un quarto ; **(a) ~ of five** *Am* le cinque meno un quarto ; **(a) ~ past five** *Br* le cinque e un quarto ; **(a) ~ after five** *Am* le cinque e un quarto ; **(a) ~ of an hour** un quarto d'ora.

quarterpounder [ˌkwɔːtə'paundəʳ] *n* grosso hamburger *m inv.*

quartet [kwɔː'tet] *n* quartetto *m.*

quartz [kwɔːts] *adj (watch)* al quarzo.

quay [kiː] *n* banchina *f.*

queasy ['kwiːzɪ] *adj inf* : **to feel ~** avere la nausea.

queen [kwiːn] *n* regina *f.*

queer [kwɪəʳ] *adj (strange)* strano(a) ; *inf (homosexual)* omosessuale ; **to feel ~** *(ill)* sentirsi male.

quench [kwentʃ] *vt* : **to ~ one's thirst** dissetarsi.

query ['kwɪərɪ] *n* quesito *m.*

question ['kwestʃn] *n (query, in exam, on questionnaire)* domanda *f* ; *(issue)* questione *f.* ◆ *vt (person)* interrogare ; **it's out of the ~** è fuori discussione.

question mark *n* punto *m* interrogativo.

questionnaire [ˌkwestʃə'neəʳ] *n* questionario *m.*

queue [kjuː] *n Br* coda *f.* ◆ *vi Br* fare la coda. ❑ **queue up** *vi Br* fare la coda.

quiche [kiːʃ] *n* torta *f* salata.

quick [kwɪk] *adj* rapido(a). ◆ *adv* rapidamente.

quickly ['kwɪklɪ] *adv* rapidamente.

quid [kwɪd] (*pl inv*) *n Br inf* sterlina *f.*

quiet ['kwaɪət] *adj* silenzioso(a) ; *(calm, peaceful)* tranquillo(a). ◆ *n* quiete *f* ; **in a ~ voice** a bassa voce ; **keep ~!** silenzio! ; **to keep ~** *(not say anything)* tacere ; **to keep ~ about sthg** tenere segreto qc.

quieten ['kwaɪətn] ◆**quieten down** *vi* calmarsi.

quietly ['kwaɪətlɪ] *adv* silenziosamente ; *(calmly)* tranquillamente.

quilt [kwɪlt] *n (duvet)* piumino *m* ; *(eiderdown)* trapunta *f.*

quince [kwɪns] *n* mela *f* cotogna.

quirk [kwɜːk] *n* stranezza *f.*

quit [kwɪt] (*pt* & *pp* **quit**) *vi (resign)* dimettersi ; *(give up)* smettere. ◆ *vt Am (school, job)* lasciare ; **to ~ doing sthg** smettere di fare qc.

quite [kwaɪt] *adv (fairly)* abbastanza ; *(completely)* proprio ; **not ~** non proprio ; **~ a lot (of)** un bel po' (di).

quiz [kwɪz] (*pl* **-zes**) *n* quiz *m inv.*

quota ['kwəʊtə] *n* quota *f.*

quotation [kwəʊ'teɪʃn] *n (phrase)* citazione *f*; *(estimate)* preventivo *m*.
quotation marks *npl* virgolette *fpl*.
quote [kwəʊt] *vt (phrase, writer)* citare. ◆ *n (phrase)* citazione *f*; *(estimate)* preventivo *m*; **he ~d me a price of £50** mi ha dato un prezzo indicativo di 50 sterline.

R

rabbit ['ræbɪt] *n* coniglio *m*.
rabies ['reɪbiːz] *n* rabbia *f*.
RAC *n* ≃ ACI *(m)*.
race [reɪs] *n (competition)* gara *f*; *(ethnic group)* razza *f*. ◆ *vi (compete)* gareggiare; *(go fast)* correre; *(engine)* imballarsi. ◆ *vt (compete against)* gareggiare con.
racecourse ['reɪskɔːs] *n* ippodromo *m*.
racehorse ['reɪshɔːs] *n* cavallo *m* da corsa.
racetrack ['reɪstræk] *n (for horses)* ippodromo *m*.
racial ['reɪʃl] *adj* razziale.
racing ['reɪsɪŋ] *n*: **(horse) ~** corse *fpl* (di cavalli).
racing car *n* automobile *f* da corsa.
racism ['reɪsɪzm] *n* razzismo *m*.
racist ['reɪsɪst] *n* razzista *mf*.
rack [ræk] *n (for coats)* attaccapanni *m inv*; *(for plates)* scolapiatti *m inv*; *(for bottles)* portabottiglie *m inv*; **(luggage) ~** portabagagli *m inv*; **~ of lamb** carrè *m inv* di agnello.
racket ['rækɪt] *n (for tennis, badminton, squash)* racchetta *f*; *(noise)* baccano *m*.
racquet ['rækɪt] *n* racchetta *f*.
radar ['reɪdɑːʳ] *n* radar *m inv*.
radiation [ˌreɪdɪ'eɪʃn] *n (nuclear)* radiazione *f*.
radiator ['reɪdɪeɪtəʳ] *n* radiatore *m*.
radical ['rædɪkl] *adj* radicale.
radii ['reɪdɪaɪ] *pl* → **radius**.
radio ['reɪdɪəʊ] (*pl* **-s**) *n* radio *f inv*. ◆ *vt (person)* chiamare via radio; **on the ~** alla radio.
radioactive [ˌreɪdɪəʊ'æktɪv] *adj* radioattivo(a).
radio alarm *n* radiosveglia *f*.
radish ['rædɪʃ] *n* ravanello *m*.
radius ['reɪdɪəs] (*pl* **radii**) *n* raggio *m*.
raffle ['ræfl] *n* lotteria *f*.
raft [rɑːft] *n (of wood)* zattera *f*; *(inflatable)* materassino *m* (gonfiabile).
rafter ['rɑːftəʳ] *n* travicello *m*.
rag [ræg] *n (old cloth)* straccio *m*.
rage [reɪdʒ] *n* rabbia *f*.
raid [reɪd] *n* raid *m inv*; *(robbery)* scorreria *f*. ◆ *vt (subj: police)* fare irruzione in; *(subj: thieves)* fare razzia in.
rail [reɪl] *n (bar)* sbarra *f*; *(for curtain)* asta *f*; *(on stairs)* corrimano *m inv*; *(for train, tram)* rotaia *f*. ◆ *adj* ferroviario(a); **by ~** in treno.
railcard ['reɪlkɑːd] *n [Br] (for young people)* tessera per riduzione ferroviaria *f*; *(for pensioners)* ≃ carta d'argento.

railings ['reɪlɪŋz] *npl* ringhiera *f*.
railroad ['reɪlrəud] *Am* = **railway**.
railway ['reɪlweɪ] *n* ferrovia *f*.
railway line *n (route)* linea *f* ferroviaria ; *(track)* binario *m*.
railway station *n* stazione *f* ferroviaria.
rain [reɪn] *n* pioggia *f*. ◆ *v impers* piovere ; **it's ~ing** sta piovendo.
rainbow ['reɪnbəu] *n* arcobaleno *m*.
raincoat ['reɪnkəut] *n* impermeabile *m*.
raindrop ['reɪndrɒp] *n* goccia *f* di pioggia.
rainfall ['reɪnfɔːl] *n* precipitazione *f*.
rainy ['reɪnɪ] *adj* piovoso(a).
raise [reɪz] *vt* sollevare ; *(increase)* aumentare ; *(money)* raccogliere ; *(child, animals)* allevare. ◆ *n Am (pay increase)* aumento *m*.
raisin ['reɪzn] *n* uva *f* passa.
rake [reɪk] *n (gardening tool)* rastrello *m*.
rally ['rælɪ] *n (public meeting)* comizio *m* ; *(motor race)* rally *m inv* ; *(in tennis, badminton, squash)* serie di scambi della palla.
ram [ræm] *n* montone *m*. ◆ *vt (bang into)* speronare.
ramble ['ræmbl] *n* camminata *f*.
ramp [ræmp] *n (slope)* rampa *f* ; *(in roadworks)* dislivello *m* ; *Am (to freeway)* rampa *f* d'accesso ; **'ramp'** *Br (bump)* 'fondo dissestato'.
ramparts ['ræmpaːts] *npl* bastioni *mpl*.
ran [ræn] *pt* → **run**.
ranch [raːntʃ] *n* ranch *m inv*.
rancid ['rænsɪd] *adj* rancido(a).
random ['rændəm] *adj* a caso. ◆ *n* : **at ~** a caso.
rang [ræŋ] *pt* → **ring**.
range [reɪndʒ] *n (of radio, telescope)* portata *f* ; *(of aircraft)* raggio *m* ; *(for shooting)* campo *m* di tiro ; *(of prices, temperatures, goods)* gamma *f* ; *(of hills, mountains)* catena *f* ; *(cooker)* cucina *f* economica. ◆ *vi (vary)* variare.
ranger ['reɪndʒəʳ] *n (of park, forest)* guardia *f* forestale.
rank [ræŋk] *n (in armed forces, police)* rango *m*. ◆ *adj (smell, taste)* rancido(a).
ransom ['rænsəm] *n* riscatto *m*.
rap [ræp] *n (music)* rap *m inv*.
rape [reɪp] *n* stupro *m*. ◆ *vt* stuprare.
rapid ['ræpɪd] *adj* rapido(a). ❑ **rapids** *npl* rapide *fpl*.
rapidly ['ræpɪdlɪ] *adv* rapidamente.
rapist ['reɪpɪst] *n* stupratore *m*.
rare [reəʳ] *adj (not common)* raro(a) ; *(meat)* al sangue.
rarely ['reəlɪ] *adv* raramente.
rash [ræʃ] *n* eruzione *f* cutanea. ◆ *adj* impulsivo(a).
raspberry ['raːzbərɪ] *n* lampone *m*.
rat [ræt] *n* ratto *m*.
ratatouille [rætə'tuːɪ] *n* ratatouille *f inv*.
rate [reɪt] *n (level)* tasso *m* ; *(charge)* tariffa *f* ; *(speed)* ritmo *m*. ◆ *vt (consider)* reputare ; *(deserve)* meritare ; **~ of exchange** tasso di cambio ; **at any ~** in ogni caso ; **at this ~** di questo passo.

rather ['rɑːðəʳ] *adv (quite)* piuttosto ; **I'd ~ not** preferirei di no ; **would you ~ ...?** preferisci ...? ; **~ than** piuttosto che ; **~ a lot** molto.
ratio ['reɪʃɪəʊ] (*pl* -**s**) *n* rapporto *m*.
ration ['ræʃn] *n (share)* razione *f*. ❑ **rations** *npl (food)* razioni *fpl*.
rational ['ræʃnl] *adj* razionale.
rattle ['rætl] *n (of baby)* sonaglio *m*. ◆ *vi* sbatacchiare.
rave [reɪv] *n (party)* rave *m inv*.
raven ['reɪvn] *n* corvo *m*.
ravioli [ˌrævɪ'əʊlɪ] *n* ravioli *mpl*.
raw [rɔː] *adj (uncooked)* crudo(a) ; *(unprocessed)* grezzo(a).
raw material *n* materia *f* prima.
ray [reɪ] *n* raggio *m*.
razor ['reɪzəʳ] *n* rasoio *m*.
razor blade *n* lametta *f* (da barba).
Rd *abbr* = **Road**.
re [riː] *prep* in merito a.
RE *n (abbr of religious education)* religione *f (materia)*.
reach [riːtʃ] *vt* raggiungere. ◆ *n* : **out of ~** lontano ; **within ~ of the beach** a poca distanza dalla spiaggia. ❑ **reach out** *vi* : **to ~ out (for)** allungarsi (per raggiungere).
react [rɪ'ækt] *vi* reagire.
reaction [rɪ'ækʃn] *n* reazione *f*.
read [riːd] (*pt* & *pp* **read** [red]) *vt* leggere ; *(subj : sign, note)* dire ; *(subj : meter, gauge)* segnare. ◆ *vi* leggere ; **to ~ about sthg** leggere di qc. ❑ **read out** *vt sep* leggere ad alta voce.
reader ['riːdəʳ] *n (of newspaper, book)* lettore *m*, -trice *f*.
readily ['redɪlɪ] *adv (willingly)* prontamente ; *(easily)* facilmente.
reading ['riːdɪŋ] *n (of books, papers)* lettura *f* ; *(of meter, gauge)* valore *m* indicato.
reading matter *n* qualcosa da leggere.
ready ['redɪ] *adj* pronto(a) ; **to be ~ for sthg** *(prepared)* essere preparato(a) per qc ; **to be ~ to do sthg** *(willing)* essere pronto a fare qc ; *(likely)* essere sul punto di fare qc ; **to get ~** prepararsi ; **to get sthg ~** preparare qc.
ready cash *n* contante *m*.
ready-cooked [-kʊkt] *adj* precotto(a).
ready-to-wear *adj* confezionato(a).
real ['rɪəl] *adj* vero(a) ; *(world)* reale. ◆ *adv Am* davvero.
real ale *n Br birra rossa prodotta secondo metodi tradizionali.*
real estate *n* proprietà *fpl* immobiliari.
realistic [ˌrɪə'lɪstɪk] *adj* realistico(a).
reality [rɪ'ælətɪ] *n* realtà *f inv* ; **in ~** in realtà.
realize ['rɪəlaɪz] *vt* rendersi conto di ; *(ambition, goal)* realizzare ; **to ~ (that) ...** rendersi conto che OR di ...
really ['rɪəlɪ] *adv* veramente ; *(in reality)* realmente ; **do you like it? - no, not ~** ti piace? - veramente, no ; **~?** *(expressing surprise)* davvero?
realtor ['rɪəltər] *n Am* agente *mf* immobiliare.
rear [rɪəʳ] *adj* posteriore. ◆ *n (back)* retro *m inv*.

rearrange [ˌriːəˈreɪndʒ] *vt* spostare.
rearview mirror [ˈrɪəvjuː-] *n* specchietto *m* retrovisore.
rear-wheel drive *n* trazione *f* posteriore.
reason [ˈriːzn] *n* motivo *m* ; **for some ~** per qualche motivo.
reasonable [ˈriːznəbl] *adj* ragionevole ; *(quite big)* buono(a).
reasonably [ˈriːznəblɪ] *adv* *(quite)* piuttosto.
reasoning [ˈriːznɪŋ] *n* ragionamento *m*.
reassure [ˌriːəˈʃɔːʳ] *vt* rassicurare.
reassuring [ˌriːəˈʃɔːrɪŋ] *adj* rassicurante.
rebate [ˈriːbeɪt] *n* rimborso *m*.
rebel [*n* ˈrebl, *vb* rɪˈbel] *n* ribelle *mf*. ◆ *vi* ribellarsi.
rebound [rɪˈbaʊnd] *vi* *(ball)* rimbalzare.
rebuild [ˌriːˈbɪld] (*pt* & *pp* **rebuilt** [ˌriːˈbɪlt]) *vt* ricostruire.
rebuke [rɪˈbjuːk] *vt* rimproverare.
recall [rɪˈkɔːl] *vt* *(remember)* ricordare.
receipt [rɪˈsiːt] *n* *(for goods, money)* ricevuta *f* ; **on ~ of** al ricevimento di.
receive [rɪˈsiːv] *vt* ricevere.
receiver [rɪˈsiːvəʳ] *n* *(of phone)* ricevitore *m*.
recent [ˈriːsnt] *adj* recente.
recently [ˈriːsntlɪ] *adv* recentemente.
receptacle [rɪˈseptəkl] *n* *fml* ricettacolo *m*.
reception [rɪˈsepʃn] *n* *(in hotel)* reception *f inv* ; *(at hospital)* accettazione *f* ; *(party)* ricevimento *m* ; *(welcome)* accoglienza *f* ; *(of TV, radio)* ricezione *f*.
reception desk *n* banco *m* della reception.
receptionist [rɪˈsepʃənɪst] *n* receptionist *mf inv*.
recess [ˈriːses] *n* *(in wall)* nicchia *f* ; *Am* SCH intervallo *m*.
recession [rɪˈseʃn] *n* recessione *f*.
recipe [ˈresɪpɪ] *n* ricetta *f*.
recite [rɪˈsaɪt] *vt* *(poem)* recitare ; *(list)* elencare.
reckless [ˈreklɪs] *adj* avventato(a).
reckon [ˈrekn] *vt* *inf* *(think)* pensare. ❑ **reckon on** *vt fus* aspettarsi. ❑ **reckon with** *vt fus* *(expect)* aspettarsi.
reclaim [rɪˈkleɪm] *vt* *(baggage)* ritirare.
reclining seat [rɪˈklaɪnɪŋ-] *n* sedile *m* reclinabile.
recognition [ˌrekəgˈnɪʃn] *n* riconoscimento *m*.
recognize [ˈrekəgnaɪz] *vt* riconoscere.
recollect [ˌrekəˈlekt] *vt* ricordare.
recommend [ˌrekəˈmend] *vt* raccomandare ; **to ~ sb to do sthg** consigliare a qn di fare qc.
recommendation [ˌrekəmenˈdeɪʃn] *n* *(suggestion)* indicazione *f*.
reconsider [ˌriːkənˈsɪdəʳ] *vt* riconsiderare.
reconstruct [ˌriːkənˈstrʌkt] *vt* ricostruire.

record [*n* 'rekɔːd, *vb* rɪ'kɔːd] *n* MUS disco *m* ; *(best performance, highest level)* record *m inv* ; *(account)* nota *f*. ◆ *vt (keep account of)* annotare ; *(on tape)* registrare.
recorded delivery [rɪ'kɔːdɪd-] *n Br* ≃ raccomandata *f*.
recorder [rɪ'kɔːdəʳ] *n (tape recorder)* registratore *m* ; *(instrument)* flauto *m* dolce.
recording [rɪ'kɔːdɪŋ] *n* registrazione *f*.
record player *n* giradischi *m inv*.
record shop *n* negozio *m* di dischi.
recover [rɪ'kʌvəʳ] *vt (stolen goods, lost property)* recuperare. ◆ *vi* riprendersi.
recovery [rɪ'kʌvərɪ] *n (from illness)* guarigione *f*.
recovery vehicle *n Br* carro *m* attrezzi.
recreation [ˌrekrɪ'eɪʃn] *n* divertimento *m*.
recreation ground *n* parco *m* (giochi).
recruit [rɪ'kruːt] *n* recluta *mf*. ◆ *vt (staff)* assumere.
rectangle ['rekˌtæŋgl] *n* rettangolo *m*.
rectangular [rek'tæŋgjʊləʳ] *adj* rettangolare.
recycle [ˌriː'saɪkl] *vt* riciclare.
red [red] *adj* rosso(a). ◆ *n (colour)* rosso *m* ; **in the ~** in rosso.
red cabbage *n* cavolo *m* rosso.
Red Cross *n* Croce *f* Rossa.
redcurrant ['redkʌrənt] *n* ribes *m inv*.
redecorate [ˌriː'dekəreɪt] *vt* rimbiancare.
redhead ['redhed] *n* rosso *m*, -a *f*.
red-hot *adj (metal)* rovente.
redial [riː'daɪəl] *vi* rifare il numero.
redirect [ˌriːdɪ'rekt] *vt (letter)* spedire a un nuovo indirizzo ; *(traffic, plane)* dirottare.
red pepper *n* peperone *m* rosso.
reduce [rɪ'djuːs] *vt* ridurre. ◆ *vi Am (slim)* dimagrire.
reduced price [rɪ'djuːst-] *n* prezzo *m* ridotto.
reduction [rɪ'dʌkʃn] *n* riduzione *f*.
redundancy [rɪ'dʌndənsɪ] *n Br* licenziamento *m (per esubero)*.
redundant [rɪ'dʌndənt] *adj Br* : **to be made ~** essere licenziato(a).
red wine *n* vino *m* rosso.
reed [riːd] *n* canna *f*.
reef [riːf] *n* scogliera *f*.
reek [riːk] *vi* puzzare.
reel [riːl] *n (of thread)* rocchetto *m* ; *(on fishing rod)* mulinello *m*.
refectory [rɪ'fektərɪ] *n* refettorio *m*.
refer [rɪ'fɜːʳ] : **refer to** *vt fus (speak about)* fare riferimento a ; *(relate to)* riferirsi a ; *(consult)* consultare.
referee [ˌrefə'riː] *n* SPORT arbitro *m*, -a *f*.
reference ['refrəns] *n (mention)* riferimento *m* ; *(letter for job)* lettera *f* di referenze. ◆ *adj (book, library)* di consultazione ; **with ~ to** con riferimento a.

referendum [ˌrefəˈrendəm] *n* referendum *m inv*.

refill [*n* ˈriːfɪl, *vb* ˌriːˈfɪl] *n (for pen)* ricambio *m*; *inf (drink)* rifornimento *m*. ◆ *vt* riempire.

refinery [rɪˈfaɪnərɪ] *n* raffineria *f*.

reflect [rɪˈflekt] *vt* & *vi* riflettere.

reflection [rɪˈflekʃn] *n (image)* riflesso *m*.

reflector [rɪˈflektəʳ] *n* catarifrangente *m*.

reflex [ˈriːfleks] *n* riflesso *m*.

reflexive [rɪˈfleksɪv] *adj* riflessivo(a).

reform [rɪˈfɔːm] *n* riforma *f*. ◆ *vt* riformare.

refresh [rɪˈfreʃ] *vt* rinfrescare.

refreshing [rɪˈfreʃɪŋ] *adj (drink, breeze, sleep)* rinfrescante; *(change)* piacevole.

refreshments [rɪˈfreʃmənts] *npl* rinfreschi *mpl*.

refrigerator [rɪˈfrɪdʒəreɪtəʳ] *n* frigorifero *m*.

refugee [ˌrefjʊˈdʒiː] *n* rifugiato *m*, -a *f*.

refund [*n* ˈriːfʌnd, *vb* rɪˈfʌnd] *n* rimborso *m*. ◆ *vt* rimborsare.

refundable [rɪˈfʌndəbl] *adj* rimborsabile.

refusal [rɪˈfjuːzl] *n* rifiuto *m*.

refuse[1] [rɪˈfjuːz] *vt (not accept)* rifiutare; *(not allow)* negare. ◆ *vi* rifiutare; **to ~ to do sthg** rifiutare di fare qc.

refuse[2] [ˈrefjuːs] *n fml* rifiuti *mpl*.

refuse collection [ˈrefjuːs-] *n fml* raccolta *f* dei rifiuti.

regard [rɪˈgaːd] *vt (consider)* considerare. ◆ *n*: **with ~ to** riguardo a; **as ~s** per quanto riguarda. ❑ **regards** *npl (in greetings)* saluti *mpl*; **give them my ~s** li saluti da parte mia.

regarding [rɪˈgaːdɪŋ] *prep* riguardo a.

regardless [rɪˈgaːdlɪs] *adv* lo stesso; **~ of** senza tener conto di.

reggae [ˈregeɪ] *n* reggae *m inv*.

regiment [ˈredʒɪmənt] *n* reggimento *m*.

region [ˈriːdʒən] *n* regione *f*; **in the ~ of** circa.

regional [ˈriːdʒənl] *adj* regionale.

register [ˈredʒɪstəʳ] *n* registro *m*. ◆ *vt* registrare; *(subj: machine, gauge)* segnare. ◆ *vi (put one's name down)* iscriversi; *(at hotel)* firmare il registro.

registered [ˈredʒɪstəd] *adj (letter, parcel)* assicurato(a).

registration [ˌredʒɪˈstreɪʃn] *n (for course, at conference)* iscrizione *f*.

registration (number) *n (of car)* numero *m* di targa.

registry office [ˈredʒɪstrɪ-] *n* anagrafe *f*.

regret [rɪˈgret] *n (thing regretted)* rimpianto *m*. ◆ *vt* rimpiangere; **I ~ telling her** mi dispiace (di) averglielo detto; **we ~ any inconvenience caused** ci scusiamo per il disagio causato.

regrettable [rɪˈgretəbl] *adj* spiacevole.

regular [ˈregjʊləʳ] *adj* regolare; *(normal, in size)* normale; *(customer, reader)* abituale. ◆ *n (customer)* cliente *mf* abituale.

regularly ['regjʊləlɪ] *adv* regolarmente.
regulate ['regjʊleɪt] *vt* regolare.
regulation [ˌregjʊ'leɪʃn] *n (rule)* norma *f*.
rehearsal [rɪ'hɜːsl] *n* prova *f*.
rehearse [rɪ'hɜːs] *vt* provare.
reign [reɪn] *n* regno *m*. ◆ *vi* regnare.
reimburse [ˌriːɪm'bɜːs] *vt fml* rimborsare.
reindeer ['reɪnˌdɪəʳ] *(pl inv) n* renna *f*.
reinforce [ˌriːɪn'fɔːs] *vt (wall, handle)* rinforzare ; *(argument, opinion)* rafforzare.
reinforcements [ˌriːɪn'fɔːsmənts] *npl* rinforzi *mpl*.
reins [reɪnz] *npl* briglie *fpl*.
reject [rɪ'dʒekt] *vt (proposal, request, coin)* respingere ; *(applicant, plan)* scartare.
rejection [rɪ'dʒekʃn] *n* rifiuto *m*.
rejoin [ˌriː'dʒɔɪn] *vt (motorway)* riprendere.
relapse [rɪ'læps] *n* ricaduta *f*.
relate [rɪ'leɪt] *vt (connect)* collegare. ◆ *vi* : **to ~ to** *(be connected with)* essere collegato a ; *(concern)* riguardare.
related [rɪ'leɪtɪd] *adj (of same family)* imparentato(a) ; *(connected)* collegato(a).
relation [rɪ'leɪʃn] *n (member of family)* parente *mf* ; *(connection)* rapporto *m* ; **in ~ to** in rapporto a. ❑ **relations** *npl* parenti *mpl*.
relationship [rɪ'leɪʃnʃɪp] *n* rapporto *m*, relazione *f*.
relative ['relətɪv] *adj* relativo(a). ◆ *n* parente *mf*.
relatively ['relətɪvlɪ] *adv* relativamente.
relax [rɪ'læks] *vi (person)* rilassarsi.
relaxation [ˌriːlæk'seɪʃn] *n (of person)* relax *m*.
relaxed [rɪ'lækst] *adj* rilassato(a).
relaxing [rɪ'læksɪŋ] *adj* rilassante.
relay ['riːleɪ] *n (race)* staffetta *f*.
release [rɪ'liːs] *vt (set free)* liberare ; *(let go of)* mollare ; *(record, film)* far uscire ; *(handbrake, catch)* togliere. ◆ *n (record, film)* uscita *f*.
relegate ['relɪgeɪt] *vt* : **to be ~d** *SPORT* essere retrocesso.
relevant ['reləvənt] *adj (connected)* pertinente ; *(important)* importante ; *(appropriate)* appropriato(a).
reliable [rɪ'laɪəbl] *adj (person, machine)* affidabile.
relic ['relɪk] *n (object)* reperto *m* (archeologico).
relief [rɪ'liːf] *n (gladness)* sollievo *m* ; *(aid)* aiuto *m*.
relief road *n* strada *f* di smaltimento.
relieve [rɪ'liːv] *vt (pain, headache)* alleviare.
relieved [rɪ'liːvd] *adj* sollevato(a).
religion [rɪ'lɪdʒn] *n* religione *f*.
religious [rɪ'lɪdʒəs] *adj* religioso(a).
relish ['relɪʃ] *n (sauce)* salsa *f*.
reluctant [rɪ'lʌktənt] *adj* riluttante.

rely [rɪ'laɪ] ◆**rely on** *vt fus (trust)* contare su ; *(depend on)* dipendere da.

remain [rɪ'meɪn] *vi* rimanere. ❑ **remains** *npl* resti *mpl*.

remainder [rɪ'meɪndəʳ] *n* resto *m*.

remaining [rɪ'meɪnɪŋ] *adj* restante.

remark [rɪ'mɑːk] *n* commento *m*. ◆ *vt* commentare.

remarkable [rɪ'mɑːkəbl] *adj* notevole.

remedy ['remədɪ] *n* rimedio *m*.

remember [rɪ'membəʳ] *vt (recall)* ricordare ; *(not forget)* ricordarsi (di). ◆ *vi (recall)* ricordarsi ; **to ~ doing sthg** ricordarsi di aver fatto qc ; **to ~ to do sthg** ricordarsi (di) fare qc.

remind [rɪ'maɪnd] *vt* : **to ~ sb of sthg** ricordare qc a qn ; **to ~ sb to do sthg** ricordare a qn di fare qc.

reminder [rɪ'maɪndəʳ] *n (for bill, library book)* sollecito *m*.

remittance [rɪ'mɪtns] *n* rimessa *f*.

remote [rɪ'məʊt] *adj* remoto(a).

remote control *n* telecomando *m*.

removal [rɪ'muːvl] *n (taking away)* rimozione *f*.

removal van *n* camion *m inv* dei traslochi.

remove [rɪ'muːv] *vt* togliere ; *(clothes)* togliersi.

renew [rɪ'njuː] *vt* rinnovare.

renovate ['renəveɪt] *vt* rinnovare.

renowned [rɪ'naʊnd] *adj* rinomato(a).

rent [rent] *n* affitto *m*. ◆ *vt (flat)* affittare ; *(car, TV)* noleggiare.

rental ['rentl] *n (fee)* affitto *m*.

repaid [riː'peɪd] *pt* & *pp* → **repay**.

repair [rɪ'peəʳ] *vt* riparare. ◆ *n* : **in good ~** in buone condizioni. ❑ **repairs** *npl* riparazioni *fpl*.

repay [riː'peɪ] (*pt* & *pp* **repaid**) *vt* restituire.

repayment [riː'peɪmənt] *n (of loan)* rimborso *m*.

repeat [rɪ'piːt] *vt* ripetere ; *(gossip, news)* riferire. ◆ *n (on TV, radio)* replica *f*.

repetition [ˌrepɪ'tɪʃn] *n* ripetizione *f*.

repetitive [rɪ'petɪtɪv] *adj* ripetitivo(a).

replace [rɪ'pleɪs] *vt* rimpiazzare ; *(put back)* mettere a posto.

replacement [rɪ'pleɪsmənt] *n (substitute)* sostituto *m*, -a *f*.

replay ['riːpleɪ] *n (rematch)* partita *f* ripetuta ; *(on TV)* replay *m inv*.

reply [rɪ'plaɪ] *n* risposta *f*. ◆ *vt* & *vi* rispondere.

report [rɪ'pɔːt] *n (account)* relazione *f* ; *(in newspaper, on TV, radio)* servizio *m* ; *Br* SCH ≃ scheda *f*. ◆ *vt (announce)* riportare ; *(theft, disappearance, person)* denunciare. ◆ *vi (give account)* riferire ; *(for newspaper, TV, radio)* fare un servizio ; **to ~ to sb** *(go to)* presentarsi a qn.

reporter [rɪ'pɔːtəʳ] *n* reporter *mf inv*.

represent [ˌreprɪ'zent] *vt* rappresentare.

representative [ˌreprɪ'zentətɪv] *n* rappresentante *mf*.

repress [rɪ'pres] *vt (feelings)* reprimere ; *(people)* opprimere.
reprieve [rɪ'pri:v] *n (delay)* sospensione *f*.
reprimand ['reprɪma:nd] *vt* rimproverare.
reproach [rɪ'prəʊtʃ] *vt* rimproverare.
reproduction [ˌri:prə'dʌkʃn] *n* riproduzione *f*.
reptile ['reptaɪl] *n* rettile *m*.
republic [rɪ'pʌblɪk] *n* repubblica *f*.
Republican [rɪ'pʌblɪkən] *n* repubblicano *m*, -a *f*. ◆ *adj* repubblicano(a).
repulsive [rɪ'pʌlsɪv] *adj* repellente.
reputable ['repjʊtəbl] *adj* di buona reputazione.
reputation [ˌrepjʊ'teɪʃn] *n* reputazione *f*.
request [rɪ'kwest] *n* richiesta *f*. ◆ *vt* chiedere ; **to ~ sb to do sthg** chiedere a qn di fare qc ; **available on ~** (disponibile) su richiesta.
require [rɪ'kwaɪə'] *vt (subj : person)* avere bisogno di ; *(subj : situation)* richiedere ; **passengers are ~d to show their tickets** i passeggeri sono pregati di presentare i biglietti.
requirement [rɪ'kwaɪəmənt] *n (condition)* requisito *m* ; *(need)* esigenza *f*.
rescue ['reskju:] *vt* salvare.
research [ˌrɪ'sɜ:tʃ] *n* ricerca *f*.
resemblance [rɪ'zembləns] *n* somiglianza *f*.
resemble [rɪ'zembl] *vt* somigliare a.
resent [rɪ'zent] *vt* risentirsi per.
reservation [ˌrezə'veɪʃn] *n (booking)* prenotazione *f* ; *(doubt)* riserva *f* ; **to make a ~** fare una prenotazione.
reserve [rɪ'zɜ:v] *n* riserva *f*. ◆ *vt (book)* prenotare ; *(save)* riservare.
reserved [rɪ'zɜ:vd] *adj* riservato(a).
reservoir ['rezəvwa:'] *n* bacino *m* (idrico).
reset [ˌri:'set] (*pt & pp* **reset**) *vt (watch, device)* rimettere ; *(meter)* azzerare.
residence ['rezɪdəns] *n fml* residenza *f* ; **place of ~** *fml* luogo *m* di residenza.
residence permit *n* permesso *m* di soggiorno.
resident ['rezɪdənt] *n (of country)* residente *mf* ; *(of hotel)* cliente *mf* ; *(of area, house)* abitante *mf* ; **'~s only'** *(for parking)* 'parcheggio riservato ai residenti'.
residential [ˌrezɪ'denʃl] *adj (area)* residenziale.
residue ['rezɪdju:] *n* residuo *m*.
resign [rɪ'zaɪn] *vi* dare le dimissioni. ◆ *vt* : **to ~ o.s. to sthg** rassegnarsi a qc.
resignation [ˌrezɪg'neɪʃn] *n (from job)* dimissioni *fpl*.
resilient [rɪ'zɪlɪənt] *adj (person)* che ha buone capacità di ripresa.
resist [rɪ'zɪst] *vt (fight against)* opporre resistenza a ; *(temptation)* resistere a ; **I can't ~ chocolate** non so resistere al cioccolato ; **to ~ doing sthg** trattenersi dal fare qc.
resistance [rɪ'zɪstəns] *n (refusal to accept)* opposizione *f* ; *(fighting)* resistenza *f*.

resit [ˌriːˈsɪt] (*pt* & *pp* **resat**) *vt* ridare.

resolution [ˌrezəˈluːʃn] *n (promise)* proposito *m*.

resolve [rɪˈzɒlv] *vt (solve)* risolvere.

resort [rɪˈzɔːt] *n (for holidays)* luogo *m* di villeggiatura ; **as a last ~** come ultima risorsa. ❑ **resort to** *vt fus* ricorrere a ; **to ~ to doing sthg** ricorrere a fare qc.

resource [rɪˈsɔːs] *n* risorsa *f*.

resourceful [rɪˈsɔːsfʊl] *adj* pieno(a) di risorse.

respect [rɪˈspekt] *n* rispetto *m*. ◆ *vt* rispettare ; **in some ~s** sotto certi aspetti ; **with ~ to** per quanto riguarda.

respectable [rɪˈspektəbl] *adj (person, job etc)* rispettabile ; *(acceptable)* decente.

respective [rɪˈspektɪv] *adj* rispettivo(a).

respond [rɪˈspɒnd] *vi* rispondere.

response [rɪˈspɒns] *n* risposta *f*.

responsibility [rɪˌspɒnsəˈbɪlətɪ] *n* responsabilità *f inv*.

responsible [rɪˈspɒnsəbl] *adj* responsabile ; **to be ~ (for)** *(accountable)* essere responsabile (di).

rest [rest] *n (relaxation)* riposo *m* ; *(support)* sostegno *m*. ◆ *vi (relax)* riposarsi ; **the ~** *(remainder)* il resto ; **to have a ~** riposarsi ; **to ~ against** appoggiarsi contro.

restaurant [ˈrestərɒnt] *n* ristorante *m*.

restaurant car *n Br* carrozza *f* ristorante.

restful [ˈrestfʊl] *adj* riposante.

restless [ˈrestlɪs] *adj (bored, impatient)* insofferente ; *(fidgety)* agitato(a).

restore [rɪˈstɔːʳ] *vt (building, painting)* restaurare ; *(order)* ripristinare.

restrain [rɪˈstreɪn] *vt* controllare.

restrict [rɪˈstrɪkt] *vt* limitare.

restricted [rɪˈstrɪktɪd] *adj* limitato(a).

restriction [rɪˈstrɪkʃn] *n* restrizione *f*.

rest room *n Am* toilette *f inv*.

result [rɪˈzʌlt] *n* risultato *m*. ◆ *vi* : **to ~ in** avere come conseguenza ; **as a ~ of** in seguito a.

resume [rɪˈzjuːm] *vi* riprendere.

résumé [ˈrezjuːmeɪ] *n (summary)* riassunto *m* ; *Am (curriculum vitae)* curriculum vitae *m inv*.

retail [ˈriːteɪl] *n* vendita *f* al dettaglio. ◆ *vt (sell)* vendere al dettaglio. ◆ *vi* : **to ~ at** essere venduto a.

retailer [ˈriːteɪləʳ] *n* dettagliante *mf*.

retail price *n* prezzo *m* al dettaglio.

retain [rɪˈteɪn] *vt fml* conservare.

retaliate [rɪˈtælɪeɪt] *vi* fare rappresaglie.

retire [rɪˈtaɪəʳ] *vi (stop working)* andare in pensione.

retired [rɪˈtaɪəd] *adj* in pensione.

retirement [rɪˈtaɪəmənt] *n (leaving job)* pensionamento *m* ; *(period after retiring)* periodo *m* dopo il pensionamento.

retreat [rɪˈtriːt] *vi (move away)* indietreggiare. ◆ *n (place)* rifugio *m*.

retrieve [rɪ'tri:v] *vt (get back)* recuperare.

return [rɪ'tɜ:n] *n* ritorno *m* ; *Br (ticket)* biglietto *m* (di) andata e ritorno. ◆ *vt (put back)* rimettere ; *(give back)* restituire ; *(ball, serve)* rimandare. ◆ *vi* ritornare ; *(happen again)* ricomparire. ◆ *adj (journey)* di ritorno ; **to ~ sthg (to sb)** *(give back)* restituire qc a qn ; **by ~ of post** *Br* a giro di posta ; **many happy ~s!** cento di questi giorni! ; **in ~ (for)** in cambio (di).

return flight *n (journey back)* volo *m* di ritorno.

return ticket *n Br* biglietto *m* (di) andata e ritorno.

reunite [ˌri:ju:'naɪt] *vt* riunire.

reveal [rɪ'vi:l] *vt* rivelare.

revelation [ˌrevə'leɪʃn] *n* rivelazione *f*.

revenge [rɪ'vendʒ] *n* vendetta *f*.

reverse [rɪ'vɜ:s] *adj* inverso(a). ◆ *n* AUT retromarcia *f* ; *(of coin)* rovescio *m* ; *(of document)* retro *m*. ◆ *vt (decision)* ribaltare. ◆ *vi (car, driver)* fare marcia indietro ; **in ~ order** in ordine inverso ; **the ~** *(opposite)* l'inverso ; **to ~ the car** fare marcia indietro ; **to ~ the charges** *Br* fare una telefonata a carico del destinatario.

reverse-charge call *n Br* telefonata *f* a carico del destinatario.

review [rɪ'vju:] *n (of book, record, film)* recensione *f*; *(examination)* esame *m*. ◆ *vt Am (for exam)* ripassare.

revise [rɪ'vaɪz] *vt* rivedere. ◆ *vi Br (for exam)* ripassare.

revision [rɪ'vɪʒn] *n Br (for exam)* ripasso *m*.

revive [rɪ'vaɪv] *vt (person)* rianimare ; *(economy)* far riprendere ; *(custom)* riportare in uso.

revolt [rɪ'vəʊlt] *n* rivolta *f*.

revolting [rɪ'vəʊltɪŋ] *adj* disgustoso(a).

revolution [ˌrevə'lu:ʃn] *n* rivoluzione *f*.

revolutionary [ˌrevə'lu:ʃnərɪ] *adj* rivoluzionario(a).

revolver [rɪ'vɒlvə^r] *n* revolver *m inv*.

revolving door [rɪ'vɒlvɪŋ-] *n* porta *f* girevole.

revue [rɪ'vju:] *n* rivista *f (spettacolo)*.

reward [rɪ'wɔ:d] *n* ricompensa *f*. ◆ *vt* ricompensare.

rewind [ˌri:'waɪnd] (*pt* & *pp* **rewound** [ˌri:'waʊnd]) *vt* riavvolgere.

rheumatism ['ru:mətɪzm] *n* reumatismo *m*.

rhinoceros [raɪ'nɒsərəs] (*pl inv* OR **-es**) *n* rinoceronte *m*.

rhubarb ['ru:ba:b] *n* rabarbaro *m*.

rhyme [raɪm] *n (poem)* rima *f*. ◆ *vi* rimafare.

rhythm ['rɪðm] *n* ritmo *m*.

rib [rɪb] *n (of body)* costola *f*.

ribbon ['rɪbən] *n* nastro *m*.

rice [raɪs] *n* riso *m*.

rice pudding *n* budino *m* di riso *(dolce)*.

rich [rɪtʃ] *adj* ricco(a). ◆ *npl* : **the ~** i ricchi ; **to be ~ in sthg** essere ricco di qc.

ricotta cheese [rɪ'kɒtə-] *n* ricotta *f*.

rid [rɪd] *vt* : **to get ~ of** sbarazzarsi di.

ridden ['rɪdn] *pp* → **ride**.

riddle ['rɪdl] *n* indovinello *m*.

ride [raɪd] (*pt* **rode**, *pp* **ridden**) *n* *(on horse)* cavalcata *f* ; *(in vehicle, on bike)* giro *m*. ◆ *vi (on horse)* andare a cavallo ; *(on bike)* andare in bicicletta ; *(in vehicle)* viaggiare. ◆ *vt* : **to ~ a horse** andare a cavallo ; **to go for a ~** *(in car)* andare a fare un giro.

rider ['raɪdə^r] *n (on horse)* persona *f* a cavallo ; *(on bike)* ciclista *mf*.

ridge [rɪdʒ] *n (of mountain)* cresta *f* ; *(raised surface)* increspatura *f*.

ridiculous [rɪ'dɪkjʊləs] *adj* ridicolo(a).

riding ['raɪdɪŋ] *n* equitazione *f*.

riding school *n* scuola *f* d'equitazione.

rifle ['raɪfl] *n* fucile *m*.

rig [rɪg] *n (oilrig at sea)* piattaforma *f* ; *(on land)* pozzo *m* petrolifero. ◆ *vt (fix)* manipolare.

---

right [raɪt] *adj* - 1. *(correct)* giusto(a), corretto(a) ; **to be ~** *(person)* avere ragione ; **to be ~ to do sthg** fare bene a fare qc ; **have you got the ~ time?** ha l'ora esatta? ; **that's ~!** esatto! ; **is this the ~ way?** è la strada giusta?
- 2. *(fair)* giusto(a) ; **that's not ~!** non è giusto!
- 3. *(on the right)* destro(a) ; **the ~ side of the road** il lato destro della strada.
◆ *n* - 1. *(side)* : **the ~** la destra.
- 2. *(entitlement)* diritto *m* ; **to have the ~ to do sthg** avere il diritto di fare qc.
◆ *adv* - 1. *(towards the right)* a destra ; **turn ~ at the post office** all'ufficio postale giri a destra.
- 2. *(correctly)* bene, correttamente ; **am I pronouncing it ~?** lo pronuncio bene?
- 3. *(for emphasis)* proprio ; **~ here** proprio qui ; **I'll be ~ back** torno subito ; **~ away** subito.

---

right angle *n* angolo *m* retto.

right-hand *adj* di destra.

right-hand drive *n* guida *f* a destra.

right-handed [-'hændɪd] *adj* *(person)* destrimane *mf* ; *(implement)* per destrimani.

rightly ['raɪtlɪ] *adv (correctly)* correttamente ; *(justly)* giustamente.

right of way *n* AUT diritto *m* di precedenza ; *(path)* sentiero *m*.

right-wing *adj* di destra.

rigid ['rɪdʒɪd] *adj* rigido(a).

rim [rɪm] *n (of cup)* bordo *m* ; *(of glasses)* montatura *f* ; *(of wheel)* cerchione *m*.

rind [raɪnd] *n (of fruit)* buccia *f* ; *(of bacon)* cotenna *f* ; *(of cheese)* crosta *f*.

ring [rɪŋ] (*pt* **rang**, *pp* **rung**) *n* anello *m* ; *(of people)* cerchio *m* ; *(sound)* trillo *m* ; *(on cooker)* fornello *m* ; *(for boxing)* ring *m inv* ; *(in circus)* pista *f*. ◆ *vt Br (on phone)* telefonare a ; *(bell)* suonare. ◆ *vi (bell, telephone)* suonare ; *Br (make phone call)* telefonare ; **to give sb a ~** fare una telefonata a qn ; **to ~ the bell** suonare il campanello. ❑ **ring back** ◆ *vt sep Br* ritelefonare a. ◆ *vi Br* ritelefonare. ❑ **ring off** *vi Br* mettere giù (il telefono). ❑ **ring**

up ◆ *vt sep Br* telefonare a. ◆ *vi Br* telefonare.
ringing tone ['rɪŋɪŋ-] *n* segnale *m* di libero.
ring road *n* circonvallazione *f*.
rink [rɪŋk] *n* pista *f* di pattinaggio.
rinse [rɪns] *vt* sciacquare. ❑ **rinse out** *vt sep* sciacquare.
riot ['raɪət] *n* sommossa *f*.
rip [rɪp] *n* strappo *m*. ◆ *vt* strappare. ◆ *vi* strapparsi. ❑ **rip up** *vt sep* strappare.
ripe [raɪp] *adj (fruit, vegetable)* maturo(a) ; *(cheese)* stagionato(a).
ripen ['raɪpn] *vi* maturare.
rip-off *n inf* fregatura *f*.
rise [raɪz] (*pt* **rose**, *pp* **risen** ['rɪzn]) *vi* alzarsi ; *(sun, moon)* sorgere ; *(increase)* aumentare. ◆ *n* aumento *m* ; *(slope)* salita *f*.
risk [rɪsk] *n* rischio *m*. ◆ *vt* rischiare ; **to take a ~** correre un rischio ; **at your own ~** a suo rischio (e pericolo) ; **to ~ doing sthg** rischiare di fare qc ; **to ~ it** arrischiarsi.
risky ['rɪskɪ] *adj* rischioso(a).
risotto [rɪ'zɒtəʊ] (*pl* **-s**) *n* risotto *m*.
ritual ['rɪtʃʊəl] *n* rituale *m*.
rival ['raɪvl] *adj* rivale. ◆ *n* rivale *mf*.
river ['rɪvəʳ] *n* fiume *m*.
river bank *n* sponda *f* del fiume.
riverside ['rɪvəsaɪd] *n* riva *f* del fiume.
roach [rəʊtʃ] *n Am (cockroach)* scarafaggio *m*.
road [rəʊd] *n* strada *f* ; **by ~** in macchina.
road book *n* atlante *m* stradale.
road map *n* carta *f* stradale.
road safety *n* sicurezza *f* sulle strade.
roadside ['rəʊdsaɪd] *n* : **the ~** il bordo della strada.
road sign *n* segnale *m* stradale.
road tax *n* tassa *f* di circolazione.
roadway ['rəʊdweɪ] *n* carreggiata *f*.
road works *npl* lavori *mpl* stradali.
roam [rəʊm] *vi* vagabondare.
roar [rɔːʳ] *n (of crowd)* strepito *m* ; *(of plane)* rombo *m*. ◆ *vi (lion)* ruggire ; *(crowd)* strepitare ; *(traffic)* rombare.
roast [rəʊst] *n* arrosto *m*. ◆ *vt* arrostire. ◆ *adj* arrosto *(inv)* ; **~ beef** roast beef *m* ; **~ chicken** pollo *m* arrosto ; **~ lamb** arrosto di agnello ; **~ pork** arrosto di maiale ; **~ potatoes** patate *fpl* arrosto.
rob [rɒb] *vt (house, bank)* svaligiare ; *(person)* derubare ; **to ~ sb of sthg** derubare qn di qc.
robber ['rɒbəʳ] *n* rapinatore *m*, -trice *f*.
robbery ['rɒbərɪ] *n* rapina *f*.
robe [rəʊb] *n Am (bathrobe)* accappatoio *m*.
robin ['rɒbɪn] *n* pettirosso *m*.
robot ['rəʊbɒt] *n* robot *m inv*.
rock [rɒk] *n* roccia *f* ; *Am (stone)* pietra *f* ; *(music)* rock *m* ; *Br (sweet)* bastoncini *mpl* di zucchero. ◆ *vt (baby)* cullare ; *(boat)* far rollare ; **on the ~s** *(drink)* con ghiaccio.
rock climbing *n* roccia *f (sport)* ; **to go ~** fare scalate.

rocket ['rɒkɪt] *n (missile)* missile *m* ; *(space rocket, firework)* razzo *m*.
rocking chair ['rɒkɪŋ-] *n* sedia *f* a dondolo.
rock 'n' roll [ˌrɒkən'rəʊl] *n* rock and roll *m*.
rocky ['rɒkɪ] *adj* roccioso(a).
rod [rɒd] *n (pole)* asta *f* ; *(for fishing)* canna *f* (da pesca).
rode [rəʊd] *pt* → **ride**.
role [rəʊl] *n* ruolo *m*.
roll [rəʊl] *n (of bread)* panino *m* ; *(of film)* rullino *m* ; *(of paper)* rotolo *m*. ◆ *vi (ball, rock)* rotolare ; *(ship)* rollare. ◆ *vt (ball, rock)* far rotolare ; *(cigarette)* arrotolare ; *(dice)* tirare. ❑ **roll over** *vi (person, animal)* rivoltarsi ; *(car)* ribaltarsi. ❑ **roll up** *vt sep* arrotolare.
roller coaster ['rəʊləˌkəʊstə[r]] *n* ottovolante *m*.
roller skate ['rəʊlə-] *n* pattino *m* a rotelle.
roller-skating ['rəʊlə-] *n* pattinaggio *m* a rotelle.
rolling pin ['rəʊlɪŋ-] *n* matterello *m*.
Roman Catholic *n* cattolico *m* romano, cattolica romana *f*.
romance [rəʊ'mæns] *n (love)* amore *m* ; *(love affair)* avventura *f* ; *(novel)* romanzo *m* sentimentale.
Romania [ruː'meɪnjə] *n* la Romania.
romantic [rəʊ'mæntɪk] *adj* romantico(a).
Rome [rəʊm] *n* Roma *f*.
romper suit ['rɒmpə-] *n* pagliaccetto *m*.
roof [ruːf] *n* tetto *m* ; *(of cave)* volta *f*.
roof rack *n* portapacchi *m inv*.
room [ruːm, rʊm] *n* stanza *f*, camera *f* ; *(space)* spazio *m*.
room number *n* numero *m* di stanza.
room service *n* servizio *m* in camera.
room temperature *n* temperatura *f* ambiente.
roomy ['ruːmɪ] *adj* spazioso(a).
root [ruːt] *n* radice *f*.
rope [rəʊp] *n* corda *f*. ◆ *vt* legare.
rose [rəʊz] *pt* → **rise**. ◆ *n (flower)* rosa *f*.
rosé ['rəʊzeɪ] *n* vino *m* rosé.
rosemary ['rəʊzmərɪ] *n* rosmarino *m*.
rot [rɒt] *vi* marcire.
rota ['rəʊtə] *n* turni *mpl*.
rotate [rəʊ'teɪt] *vi* ruotare.
rotten ['rɒtn] *adj (food, wood)* marcio(a) ; *inf (not good)* schifoso(a) ; **I feel ~** *(ill)* mi sento uno schifo.
rough [rʌf] *adj (surface, skin, cloth)* ruvido(a) ; *(sea)* burrascoso(a) ; *(person)* rude ; *(approximate)* approssimativo(a) ; *(conditions)* disagiato(a) ; *(area, town)* brutto(a) ; *(wine)* scadente. ◆ *n (on golf course)* rough *m* ; **to have a ~ time** passarsela male.
roughly ['rʌflɪ] *adv (approximately)* approssimativamente ; *(push, handle)* sgarbatamente.

round [raʊnd] *adj* rotondo(a) ; *(cheeks)* paffuto(a).
◆ *n* - 1. *(of drinks)* giro *m* ; **it's my ~** tocca a me offrire (questo giro).

- 2. *(of sandwiches)* tramezzini *mpl.*
- 3. *(of toast)* fetta *f.*
- 4. *(of competition)* turno *m.*
- 5. *(in golf)* partita *f*; *(in boxing)* round *m inv*, ripresa *f.*
- 6. *(of policeman, postman, milkman)* giro *m.*
◆ *adv* - 1. *(in a circle)* : **to go ~** girare ; **to spin ~** ruotare.
- 2. *(surrounding)* : **all (the way) ~** tutt'intorno.
- 3. *(near)* : **~ about** nei dintorni.
- 4. *(to one's house)* : **to ask some friends ~** invitare (a casa propria) degli amici ; **we went ~ to her place** siamo andati da lei OR a casa sua.
- 5. *(continuously)* : **all year ~** tutto l'anno.
◆ *prep* - 1. *(surrounding, circling)* intorno a ; **to go ~ the corner** girare l'angolo ; **we walked ~ the lake** abbiamo fatto il giro del lago a piedi.
- 2. *(visiting)* : **to go ~ a museum** visitare un museo ; **to show sb ~ sthg** far fare il giro di qc a qn.
- 3. *(approximately)* circa, pressappoco ; **~ (about) 100** circa 100 ; **~ ten o'clock** verso le dieci.
- 4. *(near)* : **~ here** da queste parti.
- 5. *(in phrases)* : **it's just ~ the corner** *(nearby)* è qui vicino ; **~ the clock** 24 ore su 24.
❑ **round off** *vt sep (meal, day)* terminare.

---

roundabout ['raʊndəbaʊt] *n [Br] (in road)* isola *f* rotazionale ; *(in playground, at fairground)* giostra *f.*
rounders ['raʊndəz] *n Br gioco a squadre simile al baseball.*
round trip *n* viaggio *m* di andata e ritorno.
route [ru:t] *n (way)* strada *f*; *(of bus, train)* percorso *m* ; *(of plane)* rotta *f.* ◆ *vt (change course of)* dirottare.
routine [ru:'ti:n] *n* routine *f inv.* ◆ *adj* di routine.
row[1] [rəʊ] *n (line)* fila *f.* ◆ *vt* & *vi* remare ; **in a ~** *(in succession)* di fila.
row[2] [raʊ] *n (argument)* lite *f*; *inf (noise)* baccano *m* ; **to have a ~** litigare.
rowboat ['rəʊbəʊt] *Am* = **rowing boat**.
rowdy ['raʊdɪ] *adj* turbolento(a).
rowing ['rəʊɪŋ] *n* canottaggio *m.*
rowing boat *n Br* barca *f* a remi.
royal ['rɔɪəl] *adj* reale.
royal family *n* famiglia *f* reale.
royalty ['rɔɪəltɪ] *n (royal family)* reali *mpl.*
RRP *(abbr of recommended retail price)* prezzo *m* consigliato.
rub [rʌb] *vt* & *vi* strofinare ; **to ~ sb's back** massaggiare la schiena a qn ; **my shoes are rubbing** mi fanno male le scarpe. ❑ **rub in** *vt sep (lotion, oil)* far penetrare sfregando. ❑ **rub out** *vt sep* cancellare.
rubber ['rʌbəʳ] *adj* di gomma. ◆ *n* gomma *f*; *Am inf (condom)* preservativo *m.*
rubber band *n* elastico *m.*
rubber gloves *npl* guanti *mpl* di gomma.
rubber ring *n* ciambella *f.*
rubbish ['rʌbɪʃ] *n* spazzatura *f*; *inf (nonsense)* cretinate *fpl.*
rubbish bin *n Br* pattumiera *f.*
rubbish dump *n Br* discarica *f.*
rubble ['rʌbl] *n* macerie *fpl.*
ruby ['ru:bɪ] *n* rubino *m.*

rucksack ['rʌksæk] *n* zaino *m*.

rudder ['rʌdəʳ] *n* timone *m*.

rude [ruːd] *adj (person)* sgarbato(a) ; *(behaviour, joke, picture)* volgare.

rug [rʌg] *n (for floor)* tappeto *m* ; *Br (blanket)* coperta *f*.

rugby ['rʌgbɪ] *n* rugby *m*.

ruin ['ruːɪn] *vt* rovinare. ❑ **ruins** *npl* rovine *fpl*.

ruined ['ruːɪnd] *adj (building)* in rovina ; *(clothes, meal, holiday)* rovinato(a).

rule [ruːl] *n (law)* regola *f*. ◆ *vt (country)* governare ; **to be the ~** *(normal)* essere la regola ; **against the ~s** contro le regole ; **as a ~** di regola. ❑ **rule out** *vt sep* escludere.

ruler ['ruːləʳ] *n (of country)* capo *m* di Stato ; *(for measuring)* righello *m*.

rum [rʌm] *n* rum *m inv*.

rumor ['ruːmər] *Am* = **rumour**.

rumour ['ruːməʳ] *n Br* voce *f*.

rump steak [ˌrʌmp-] *n* bistecca *f* di girello.

---

run [rʌn] (*pt* **ran**, *pp* **run**) *vi* - 1. *(on foot)* correre ; **we had to ~ for the bus** abbiamo dovuto fare una corsa per prendere l'autobus.

- 2. *(train, bus)* fare servizio ; **the bus ~s every hour** c'è un autobus ogni ora ; **the train is running an hour late** il treno ha un'ora di ritardo.

- 3. *(operate)* funzionare ; **to ~ on sthg** andare a qc.

- 4. *(tears, liquid, river)* scorrere ; **to ~ through** *(river, road)* passare per ; **the path ~s along the coast** il sentiero corre lungo la costa ; **she left the tap running** ha lasciato il rubinetto aperto.

- 5. *(play, event)* durare ; **'now running at the Palladium'** 'in cartellone al Palladium'.

- 6. *(nose)* gocciolare, colare ; *(eyes)* lacrimare.

- 7. *(colour, dye, clothes)* stingere.

◆ *vt* - 1. *(on foot)* correre.

- 2. *(compete in)* : **to ~ a race** partecipare a una corsa.

- 3. *(business, hotel)* dirigere.

- 4. *(bus, train)* : **we're running a special bus to the airport** mettiamo a disposizione una navetta per andare all'aeroporto.

- 5. *(take in car)* dare un passaggio a ; **I'll ~ you home** ti do un passaggio (fino) a casa.

- 6. *(water)* far correre.

◆ *n* - 1. *(on foot)* corsa *f* ; **to go for a ~** andare a fare una corsa.

- 2. *(in car)* giro *m* ; **to go for a ~** andare a fare un giro (in macchina).

- 3. *(for skiing)* pista *f*.

- 4. *Am (in tights)* smagliatura *f*.

- 5. *(in phrases)* : **in the long ~** alla lunga.

❑ **run away** *vi* scappare.

❑ **run down**

◆ *vt sep (run over)* investire ; *(criticize)* criticare.

◆ *vi (battery)* scaricarsi.

❑ **run into** *vt fus (meet)* incontrare per caso ; *(hit)* sbattere contro ; *(problem, difficulty)* incontrare.

❑ **run out** *vi (be used up)* esaurirsi.

❑ **run out of** *vt fus* finire, esaurire.

❑ **run over** *vt sep (hit)* investire.

runaway ['rʌnəweɪ] *n* fuggiasco *m*, -a *f*.
rung [rʌŋ] *pp* → **ring.** ◆ *n (of ladder)* piolo *m*.
runner ['rʌnə^r] *n (person)* corridore *m* ; *(for door, drawer)* guida *f* ; *(for sledge)* pattino *m*.
runner bean *n* fagiolo *m* rampicante.
runner-up (*pl* **runners-up**) *n* secondo *m* classificato, seconda classificata *f*.
running ['rʌnɪŋ] *n* SPORT corsa *f* ; *(management)* amministrazione *f*. ◆ *adj* : **three days ~** tre giorni di fila ; **to go ~** andare a correre.
running water *n* acqua *f* corrente.
runny ['rʌnɪ] *adj (sauce, egg, omelette)* troppo liquido(a) ; *(nose)* che cola ; *(eye)* che lacrima.
runway ['rʌnweɪ] *n* pista *f* (di volo).
rural ['rʊərəl] *adj* rurale.
rush [rʌʃ] *n (hurry)* fretta *f* ; *(of crowd)* grosso afflusso *m*. ◆ *vi (move quickly)* precipitarsi ; *(hurry)* affrettarsi. ◆ *vt (work)* fare in fretta ; *(food)* mangiare in fretta ; *(transport quickly)* portare d'urgenza ; **to be in a ~** avere fretta ; **there's no ~!** non c'è fretta! ; **don't ~ me!** non mettermi fretta!
rush hour *n* ora *f* di punta.
Russia ['rʌʃə] *n* la Russia.
Russian ['rʌʃn] *adj* russo(a). ◆ *n (person)* russo *m*, -a *f* ; *(language)* russo *m*.
rust [rʌst] *n* ruggine *f*. ◆ *vi* arrugginirsi.
rustic ['rʌstɪk] *adj* rustico(a).
rustle ['rʌsl] *vi* frusciare.
rustproof ['rʌstpru:f] *adj* inossidabile.
rusty ['rʌstɪ] *adj* arrugginito(a).
RV *n Am* (*abbr of recreational vehicle*) camper *m inv*.
rye [raɪ] *n* segale *f*.
rye bread *n* pane *m* di segale.

S

S (*abbr of south, small*) S.
saccharin ['sækərɪn] *n* saccarina *f*.
sachet ['sæʃeɪ] *n* bustina *f*.
sack [sæk] *n (bag)* sacco *m*. ◆ *vt* licenziare ; **to get the ~** essere licenziato.
sacrifice ['sækrɪfaɪs] *n fig* sacrificio *m*.
sad [sæd] *adj* triste.
saddle ['sædl] *n* sella *f*.
saddlebag ['sædlbæg] *n* bisaccia *f*.
sadly ['sædlɪ] *adv (unfortunately)* sfortunatamente ; *(unhappily)* tristemente.
sadness ['sædnɪs] *n* tristezza *f*.
s.a.e. *n Br* (*abbr of stamped addressed envelope*) *busta affrancata e completa d'indirizzo*.
safari park [sə'fa:rɪ-] *n* zoosafari *m inv*.
safe [seɪf] *adj* sicuro(a) ; *(out of harm)* salvo(a) ; *(valuables)* al sicuro. ◆ *n* cassaforte *f* ; **a ~ place** un posto sicuro ; **(have a) ~ journey!**

buon viaggio! ; **~ and sound** sano e salvo.

safe-deposit box *n* cassetta *f* di sicurezza.

safely ['seɪflɪ] *adv (not dangerously)* senza pericolo ; *(arrive)* senza problemi ; *(out of harm)* al sicuro.

safety ['seɪftɪ] *n* sicurezza *f*.

safety belt *n* cintura *f* di sicurezza.

safety pin *n* spilla *f* da balia.

sag [sæg] *vi* avvallarsi.

sage [seɪdʒ] *n (herb)* salvia *f*.

said [sed] *pt & pp* → **say**.

sail [seɪl] *n* vela *f*. ◆ *vi (boat, ship)* navigare ; *(person)* andare in barca ; *(depart)* salpare. ◆ *vt* : **to ~ a boat** condurre una barca ; **to set ~** salpare.

sailboat ['seɪlbəʊt] *Am* = **sailing boat**.

sailing ['seɪlɪŋ] *n (activity)* vela *f* ; *(departure)* partenza *f* ; **to go ~** fare della vela.

sailing boat *n* barca *f* a vela.

sailor ['seɪləʳ] *n* marinaio *m*.

saint [seɪnt] *n* santo *m*, -a *f*.

sake [seɪk] *n* : **for my/their ~** per il mio/il loro bene ; **for God's ~!** per l'amor di Dio!

salad ['sæləd] *n* insalata *f*.

salad bar *n Br (area in restaurant)* tavolo *m* delle insalate ; *(restaurant) locale specializzato in insalate*.

salad bowl *n* insalatiera *f*.

salad cream *n Br salsa per l'insalata, simile alla maionese*.

salad dressing *n* condimento *m* per l'insalata.

salami [sə'lɑːmɪ] *n* salame *m*.

salary ['sælərɪ] *n* stipendio *m*.

sale [seɪl] *n (selling)* vendita *f* ; *(at reduced prices)* svendita *f* ; **'for ~'** 'vendesi' ; **on ~** in vendita. ❑ **sales** *npl* COMM vendite *fpl* ; **the ~s** *(at reduced prices)* i saldi.

sales assistant ['seɪlz-] *n* commesso *m*, -a *f*.

salesclerk ['seɪlzklɜːrk] *Am* = **sales assistant**.

salesman ['seɪlzmən] (*pl* **-men** [-mən]) *n (in shop)* commesso *m* ; *(rep)* rappresentante *m*.

sales rep(resentative) *n* rappresentante *mf*.

saleswoman ['seɪlz,wʊmən] (*pl* **-women** [-,wɪmɪn]) *n (in shop)* commessa *f*.

saliva [sə'laɪvə] *n* saliva *f*.

salmon ['sæmən] (*pl inv*) *n* salmone *m*.

salon ['sælɒn] *n (hairdresser's)* salone *m*.

saloon [sə'luːn] *n Br (car)* berlina *f* ; *Am (bar)* saloon *m inv*.

salopettes [,sælə'pets] *npl* salopette *f inv*.

salt [sɔːlt, sɒlt] *n* sale *m*.

saltcellar ['sɔːlt,seləʳ] *n Br* saliera *f*.

salted peanuts ['sɔːltɪd-] *npl* noccioline *fpl* salate.

salt shaker [-,ʃeɪkəʳ] *Am* = **saltcellar**.

salty ['sɔːltɪ] *adj* salato(a).

salute [sə'luːt] *n* saluto *m*. ◆ *vi* fare il saluto.

same [seɪm] *adj* stesso(a). ◆ *pron* : **the ~** lo stesso ; **they look the ~** sembrano uguali ; **I'll have the ~ as her** prendo lo stesso che ha preso lei ; **you've got the ~ book**

as me hai lo stesso libro che ho io ; **it's all the ~ to me** per me è tutto uguale.
samosa [sə'məʊsə] *n fagottino fritto triangolare, ripieno di carne o verdure, tipico della cucina indiana.*
sample ['sa:mpl] *n* campione *m*. ◆ *vt* assaggiare.
sanctions ['sæŋkʃnz] *npl* sanzioni *fpl*.
sanctuary ['sæŋktʃʊərɪ] *n (for birds, animals)* riserva *f*.
sand [sænd] *n* sabbia *f*. ◆ *vt (wood)* smerigliare.
sandal ['sændl] *n* sandalo *m*.
sandcastle ['sænd,ka:sl] *n* castello *m* di sabbia.
sandpaper ['sænd,peɪpəʳ] *n* carta *f* vetrata.
sandwich ['sænwɪdʒ] *n* tramezzino *m*.
sandwich bar *n* paninoteca *f*.
sandy ['sændɪ] *adj (beach)* sabbioso(a) ; *(hair)* color sabbia *(inv)*.
sang [sæŋ] *pt* → **sing**.
sanitary ['sænɪtrɪ] *adj (conditions, measures)* sanitario(a) ; *(hygienic)* igienico(a).
sanitary napkin *Am* = **sanitary towel**.
sanitary towel *n Br* assorbente *m* igienico.
sank [sæŋk] *pt* → **sink**.
sapphire ['sæfaɪəʳ] *n* zaffiro *m*.
sarcastic [sa:'kæstɪk] *adj* sarcastico(a).
sardine [sa:'di:n] *n* sardina *f*.
Sardinia [sa:'dɪnjə] *n* la Sardegna.
SASE *n Am (abbr of self-addressed stamped envelope) busta affrancata e completa del proprio indirizzo.*
sat [sæt] *pt* & *pp* → **sit**.
Sat. *(abbr of Saturday)* sab.
satchel ['sætʃəl] *n* cartella *f*.
satellite ['sætəlaɪt] *n (in space)* satellite *m* ; *(at airport)* zona *f* satellite.
satellite dish *n* antenna *f* parabolica.
satellite TV *n* televisione *f* via satellite.
satin ['sætɪn] *n* raso *m*.
satisfaction [,sætɪs'fækʃn] *n* soddisfazione *f*.
satisfactory [,sætɪs'fæktərɪ] *adj* soddisfacente.
satisfied ['sætɪsfaɪd] *adj* soddisfatto(a).
satisfy ['sætɪsfaɪ] *vt* soddisfare.
satsuma [,sæt'su:mə] *n Br* mandarino *m*.
saturate ['sætʃəreɪt] *vt (with liquid)* impregnare.
Saturday ['sætədɪ] *n* sabato *m* ; **it's ~** è sabato ; **~ morning** sabato mattina ; **on ~** sabato ; **on ~s** il OR di sabato ; **last ~** sabato scorso ; **this ~** questo sabato ; **next ~** sabato prossimo ; **~ week, a week on ~** sabato a otto.
sauce [sɔ:s] *n* salsa *f*.
saucepan ['sɔ:spən] *n* casseruola *f*.
saucer ['sɔ:səʳ] *n* piattino *m*.
sauna ['sɔ:nə] *n* sauna *f*.
sausage ['sɒsɪdʒ] *n* salsiccia *f*.
sausage roll *n* rustico *m* con salsiccia.
sauté [*Br* 'səʊteɪ, *Am* səʊ'teɪ] *adj* saltato(a).

savage ['sævɪdʒ] *adj* selvaggio(a).

save [seɪv] *vt (rescue, COMPUT)* salvare ; *(money, time)* risparmiare ; *(reserve)* tenere ; *SPORT* parare. ◆ *n* parata *f*. ❑ **save up** *vi* risparmiare ; **to ~ up (for sthg)** mettere da parte i soldi (per qc).

savings ['seɪvɪŋz] *npl* risparmi *mpl*.

savings bank *n* cassa *f* di risparmio.

savory ['seɪvərɪ] *Am* = **savoury**.

savoury ['seɪvərɪ] *adj Br (not sweet)* salato(a).

saw [sɔː] *(Br pt* **-ed**, *pp* **sawn**, *Am & pt & pp* **-ed**) *pt* → **see**. ◆ *n (tool)* sega *f*. ◆ *vt* segare.

sawdust ['sɔːdʌst] *n* segatura *f*.

sawn [sɔːn] *pp* → **saw**.

saxophone ['sæksəfəʊn] *n* sassofono *m*.

say [seɪ] *(pt & pp* **said**) *vt* dire ; *(subj : clock, meter)* segnare. ◆ *n* : **to have a ~ in sthg** avere voce in capitolo riguardo a qc ; **could you ~ that again?** può ripetere, per favore? ; **~ we met at nine?** diciamo che ci vediamo alle nove? ; **what did you ~?** che cosa hai detto?

saying ['seɪɪŋ] *n* detto *m*.

scab [skæb] *n (on skin)* crosta *f*.

scaffolding ['skæfəldɪŋ] *n* impalcatura *f*.

scald [skɔːld] *vt* scottare.

scale [skeɪl] *n* scala *f*; *(of fish, snake)* squama *f* ; *(in kettle)* incrostazione *f*. ❑ **scales** *npl (for weighing)* bilancia *f*.

scallion ['skæljən] *n Am* cipollina *f*.

scallop ['skɒləp] *n* pettine *m (mollusco)*.

scalp [skælp] *n* cuoio *m* capelluto.

scampi ['skæmpɪ] *n* gamberoni *mpl* impanati e fritti.

scan [skæn] *vt (consult quickly)* scorrere. ◆ *n MED* TAC *f*.

scandal ['skændl] *n* scandalo *m*.

scar [skaːʳ] *n* cicatrice *f*.

scarce ['skeəs] *adj* scarso(a).

scarcely ['skeəslɪ] *adv (hardly)* a malapena.

scare [skeəʳ] *vt* spaventare.

scarecrow ['skeəkrəʊ] *n* spaventapasseri *m inv*.

scared ['skeəd] *adj* spaventato(a).

scarf ['skaːf] *(pl* **scarves**) *n (woollen)* sciarpa *f* ; *(for women)* foulard *m inv*.

scarlet ['skaːlət] *adj* scarlatto(a).

scarves [skaːvz] *pl* → **scarf**.

scary ['skeərɪ] *adj inf* terrificante.

scatter ['skætəʳ] *vt* spargere. ◆ *vi* sparpagliarsi.

scene [siːn] *n* scena *f* ; *(view)* vista *f* ; **the music ~** il mondo della musica ; **to make a ~** fare una scenata.

scenery ['siːnərɪ] *n (countryside)* paesaggio *m* ; *(in theatre)* scenario *m*.

scenic ['siːnɪk] *adj* pittoresco(a).

scent [sent] *n* odore *m* ; *(perfume)* profumo *m*.

sceptical ['skeptɪkl] *adj Br* scettico(a).

schedule [*Br* 'ʃedjuːl, *Am* 'skedʒʊl] *n (of work, things to do)* tabella *f* di marcia ; *(timetable)* orario *m* ; *(list)* tabella. ◆ *vt* programmare ;

according to ~ secondo la tabella di marcia ; **behind ~** in ritardo sulla tabella di marcia ; **on ~** puntualmente.

scheduled flight [*Br* 'ʃedju:ld-, *Am* 'skedʒʊld-] *n* volo *m* di linea.

scheme [ski:m] *n (plan)* piano *m* ; *pej (dishonest plan)* intrigo *m*.

scholarship ['skɒləʃɪp] *n (award)* borsa *f* di studio.

school [sku:l] *n* scuola *f* ; *(university department)* facoltà *f inv* ; *Am (university)* università *f inv*. ◆ *adj* scolastico(a) ; **at ~** a scuola.

schoolbag ['sku:lbæg] *n* cartella *f*.

schoolbook ['sku:lbʊk] *n* libro *m* di testo.

schoolboy ['sku:lbɔɪ] *n* scolaro *m*.

school bus *n* scuolabus *m inv*.

schoolchild ['sku:ltʃaɪld] (*pl* **-children** [-tʃɪldrən]) *n* scolaro *m*, -a *f*.

schoolgirl ['sku:lgɜ:l] *n* scolara *f*.

schoolmaster ['sku:lˌma:stəʳ] *n Br* maestro *m*.

schoolmistress ['sku:lˌmɪstrɪs] *n Br* maestra *f*.

schoolteacher ['sku:lˌti:tʃəʳ] *n* insegnante *mf*.

school uniform *n* divisa *f*.

science ['saɪəns] *n* scienza *f* ; *SCH* scienze *fpl*.

science fiction *n* fantascienza *f*.

scientific [ˌsaɪən'tɪfɪk] *adj* scientifico(a).

scientist ['saɪəntɪst] *n* scienziato *m*, -a *f*.

scissors ['sɪzəz] *npl* : **(a pair of) ~** (un paio di) forbici *fpl*.

scone [skɒn] *n pasta rotonda con uvette che si mangia con burro e marmellata durante il tè.*

scoop [sku:p] *n (for ice cream, flour)* paletta *f* ; *(of ice cream)* pallina *f* ; *(in media)* scoop *m inv*.

scooter ['sku:təʳ] *n (motor vehicle)* scooter *m inv*.

scope [skəʊp] *n (possibility)* opportunità *fpl* ; *(range)* portata *f*.

scorch [skɔ:tʃ] *vt* bruciare.

score [skɔ:ʳ] *n (total, final result)* punteggio *m* ; *(current position)* situazione *f*. ◆ *vt SPORT* segnare ; *(in test)* totalizzare. ◆ *vi SPORT* segnare.

scorn [skɔ:n] *n* disprezzo *m*.

Scorpio ['skɔ:pɪəʊ] *n* Scorpione *m*.

scorpion ['skɔ:pjən] *n* scorpione *m*.

Scot [skɒt] *n* scozzese *mf*.

scotch [skɒtʃ] *n* scotch *m inv (whisky)*.

Scotch broth *n minestra a base di brodo di carne, verdure e orzo perlato.*

Scotch tape® *n Am* scotch® *m*.

Scotland ['skɒtlənd] *n* la Scozia.

Scotsman ['skɒtsmən] (*pl* **-men** [-mən]) *n* scozzese *m*.

Scotswoman ['skɒtsˌwʊmən] (*pl* **-women** [-ˌwɪmɪn]) *n* scozzese *f*.

Scottish ['skɒtɪʃ] *adj* scozzese.

scout [skaʊt] *n (child)* scout *mf inv*.

SCOUTS

Gli *scouts* sono membri della Scouting Association, fondata in Gran Bretagna nel 1908 da Lord Baden-Powell, allo scopo di promuovere lo spirito di avventura e il senso di responsabilità e disciplina fra i più giovani. I ragazzi fra gli 11 e i 16 anni sono organizzati in piccoli gruppi che, sotto la guida di un adulto, imparano tecniche di sopravvivenza all'aperto e di pronto soccorso. I ragazzi sotto gli 11 anni possono iscriversi ai *Cub Scouts* (Lupetti). Organizzazioni equivalenti per le ragazze sono le *Guides* e le *Brownies* (Coccinelle).

---

scowl [skaul] *vi* aggrottare le sopracciglia.

scrambled eggs [ˌskræmbld-] *npl* uova *fpl* strapazzate.

scrap [skræp] *n (of paper, cloth)* pezzo *m* ; *(old metal)* rottami *mpl* (di metallo).

scrapbook ['skræpbuk] *n* album *m inv*.

scrape [skreɪp] *vt (rub)* raschiare ; *(scratch)* graffiare.

scrap paper *n Br* carta *f* da brutta copia.

scratch [skrætʃ] *n* graffio *m*. ◆ *vt (cut, mark)* graffiare ; *(rub)* grattare ; **to be up to ~** essere all'altezza della situazione ; **to start from ~** cominciare da zero.

scratch paper *Am* = **scrap paper**.

scream [skriːm] *n* strillo *m*. ◆ *vi* strillare.

screen [skriːn] *n* schermo *m* ; *(hall in cinema)* sala *f* ; *(panel)* paravento *m*. ◆ *vt (film)* proiettare ; *(TV programme)* trasmettere.

screening ['skriːnɪŋ] *n (of film)* proiezione *f*.

screen wash *n* detergente *m* per il parabrezza.

screw [skruː] *n* vite *f*. ◆ *vt (fasten)* avvitare ; *(twist)* torcere.

screwdriver ['skruːˌdraɪvəʳ] *n* cacciavite *m inv*.

scribble ['skrɪbl] *vi* scarabocchiare.

script [skrɪpt] *n (of play, film)* copione *m*.

scrub [skrʌb] *vt* strofinare.

scruffy ['skrʌfɪ] *adj* trasandato(a).

scuba diving ['skuːbə-] *n* immersioni *fpl* (con autorespiratore).

sculptor ['skʌlptəʳ] *n* scultore *m*.

sculpture ['skʌlptʃəʳ] *n* scultura *f*.

sea [siː] *n* mare *m* ; **by ~** via mare ; **by the ~** sul mare.

seafood ['siːfuːd] *n* frutti *mpl* di mare.

seafront ['siːfrʌnt] *n* lungomare *m*.

seagull ['siːgʌl] *n* gabbiano *m*.

seal [siːl] *n (animal)* foca *f* ; *(on bottle, container, official mark)* sigillo *m*. ◆ *vt (envelope, container)* sigillare.

seam [siːm] *n (in clothes)* cucitura *f*.

search [sɜːtʃ] *n* ricerca *f*. ◆ *vt* perquisire. ◆ *vi* : **to ~ for** cercare.
seashell [ˈsiːʃel] *n* conchiglia *f*.
seashore [ˈsiːʃɔːʳ] *n* riva *f* del mare.
seasick [ˈsiːsɪk] *adj* : **to be ~** avere il mal di mare.
seaside [ˈsiːsaɪd] *n* : **the ~** il mare.
seaside resort *n* località *f inv* balneare.
season [ˈsiːzn] *n* stagione *f*. ◆ *vt* condire ; **in ~** *(fruit, vegetables)* di stagione ; *(holiday)* in alta stagione ; **out of ~** *(fruit, vegetables)* fuori stagione ; *(holiday)* in bassa stagione.
seasoning [ˈsiːznɪŋ] *n* condimento *m*.
season ticket *n* abbonamento *m*.
seat [siːt] *n (place, chair)* posto *m* ; *(in parliament)* seggio *m*. ◆ *vt* : **the minibus ~s 12** il minibus ha 12 posti a sedere ; **'please wait to be ~ed'** *cartello che avvisa i clienti di un ristorante di attendere il cameriere per essere condotti al tavolo*.
seat belt *n* cintura *f* di sicurezza.
seaweed [ˈsiːwiːd] *n* alghe *fpl*.
secluded [sɪˈkluːdɪd] *adj* appartato(a).
second [ˈsekənd] *n* secondo *m*. ◆ *num* secondo(a) ; **~ gear** seconda *f* → **sixth**. ❑ **seconds** *npl (goods)* merce *f* di seconda scelta ; *inf (of food)* bis *m inv*.
secondary school [ˈsekəndrɪ-] *n* ≃ scuola *f* media inferiore e superiore.
second-class *adj (ticket)* di seconda classe ; *(stamp) per posta ordinaria sul territorio nazionale* ; *(inferior)* di seconda categoria.
second-hand *adj* di seconda mano.
Second World War *n* : **the ~** la seconda guerra mondiale.
secret [ˈsiːkrɪt] *adj* segreto(a). ◆ *n* segreto *m*.
secretary [*Br* ˈsekrətrɪ, *Am* ˈsekrəˌterɪ] *n* segretario *m*, -a *f*.
Secretary of State *n Am (foreign minister)* segretario *m* di Stato, ≃ ministro *m* degli Esteri ; *Br (government minister)* ministro *m*.
section [ˈsekʃn] *n* sezione *f*.
sector [ˈsektəʳ] *n* settore *m*.
secure [sɪˈkjʊəʳ] *adj (safe, protected)* sicuro(a) ; *(firmly fixed)* saldamente assicurato(a) ; *(free from worry)* tranquillo(a). ◆ *vt (fix)* assicurare ; *fml (obtain)* assicurarsi.
security [sɪˈkjʊərətɪ] *n (protection)* sicurezza *f* ; *(freedom from worry)* tranquillità *f*.
security guard *n* guardia *f* giurata.
sedative [ˈsedətɪv] *n* sedativo *m*.
seduce [sɪˈdjuːs] *vt* sedurre.
see [siː] (*pt* **saw**, *pp* **seen**) *vt* vedere ; *(accompany)* accompagnare. ◆ *vi* vedere ; **I ~** *(understand)* capisco ; **to ~ if one can do sthg** vedere se si può fare qc ; **to ~ to sthg** *(deal with)* occuparsi di qc ; *(repair)* riparare qc ; **~ you!** arrivederci! ; **~ you later!** a più tardi! ; **~ you soon!** a presto! ; **~ p 14** vedi pag. 14. ❑ **see off** *vt sep (say goodbye to)* (andare a) salutare.
seed [siːd] *n* seme *m*.

seeing (as) ['siːɪŋ-] *conj* visto che.

seek [siːk] (*pt & pp* **sought**) *vt fml (look for)* cercare ; *(request)* chiedere.

seem [siːm] *vi* sembrare. ◆ *v impers* : **it ~s (that)** ... sembra (che) ...

seen [siːn] *pp* → **see.**

seesaw ['siːsɔː] *n* altalena *f*.

segment ['segmənt] *n (of fruit)* spicchio *m*.

seize [siːz] *vt (grab)* afferrare ; *(drugs, arms)* sequestrare. ❑ **seize up** *vi* bloccarsi.

seldom ['seldəm] *adv* raramente.

select [sɪ'lekt] *vt* scegliere. ◆ *adj* selezionato(a).

selection [sɪ'lekʃn] *n* selezione *f*.

self-assured [ˌselfə'ʃʊəd] *adj* sicuro(a) di sé.

self-catering [ˌself'keɪtərɪŋ] *adj (flat)* con uso di cucina.

self-confident [ˌself-] *adj* sicuro(a) di sé.

self-conscious [ˌself-] *adj* timido(a).

self-contained [ˌselfkən'teɪnd] *adj (flat)* autosufficiente.

self-defence [ˌself-] *n* autodifesa *f*.

self-employed [ˌself-] *adj* che lavora in proprio.

selfish ['selfɪʃ] *adj* egoista.

self-raising flour [ˌself'reɪzɪŋ-] *n Br* farina *f* con lievito.

self-rising flour [ˌself'raɪzɪŋ-] *Am* = **self-raising flour.**

self-service [ˌself-] *adj* self-service *(inv)*.

sell [sel] (*pt & pp* **sold**) *vt & vi* vendere ; **to ~ for** essere venduto per ; **to ~ sb sthg** vendere qc a qn.

sell-by date *n* data *f* di scadenza.

seller ['selə^r] *n (person)* venditore *m*, -trice *f*.

Sellotape® ['selәteɪp] *n Br* nastro *m* adesivo.

semester [sɪ'mestə^r] *n* semestre *m*.

semicircle ['semɪˌsɜːkl] *n* semicerchio *m*.

semicolon [ˌsemɪ'kəʊlən] *n* punto *m* e virgola.

semidetached [ˌsemɪdɪ'tætʃt] *adj* bifamiliare.

semifinal [ˌsemɪ'faɪnl] *n* semifinale *f*.

seminar ['semɪnɑː^r] *n* seminario *m*.

semolina [ˌsemə'liːnə] *n* semolino *m*.

send [send] (*pt & pp* **sent**) *vt (letter, parcel, goods)* spedire, mandare ; *(person)* mandare ; *(TV or radio signal)* trasmettere ; **to ~ sthg to sb** mandare qc a qn. ❑ **send back** *vt sep (faulty goods)* rimandare. ❑ **send off** *vt sep (letter, parcel)* spedire ; SPORT espellere. ◆ *vi* : **to ~ off (for sthg)** ordinare (qc) per corrispondenza.

sender ['sendə^r] *n* mittente *mf*.

senile ['siːnaɪl] *adj* senile.

senior ['siːnjə^r] *adj* di grado superiore. ◆ *n Br* SCH studente *m* più anziano ; *Am SCH studente dell'ultimo anno di scuola superiore o università.*

senior citizen *n* anziano *m*, -a *f*.

sensation [sen'seɪʃn] *n* sensazione *f* ; to cause a ~ fare colpo.

sensational [sen'seɪʃənl] *adj (very good)* fantastico(a).

sense [sens] *n* senso *m* ; *(common sense)* buonsenso *m* ; *(of word, expression)* senso, significato *m*. ◆ *vt* sentire, percepire ; to make ~ avere senso ; ~ of direction senso dell'orientamento ; ~ of humour senso dell'umorismo.

sensible ['sensəbl] *adj (person)* ragionevole, assennato(a) ; *(clothes, shoes)* pratico(a).

sensitive ['sensɪtɪv] *adj* sensibile ; *(subject, issue)* delicato(a).

sent [sent] *pt & pp* → send.

sentence ['sentəns] *n* GRAMM proposizione *f* ; *(for crime)* sentenza *f*, condanna *f*. ◆ *vt* condannare.

sentimental [ˌsentɪ'mentl] *adj pej* sentimentale.

Sep. *(abbr of September)* set..

separate [*adj* 'seprət, *vb* 'sepəreɪt] *adj* separato(a) ; *(different)* diverso(a). ◆ *vt* separare. ◆ *vi* separarsi. ❑ **separates** *npl Br* coordinati *mpl*.

separately ['seprətlɪ] *adv* separatamente.

separation [ˌsepə'reɪʃn] *n* separazione *f*.

September [sep'tembə^r] *n* settembre *m* ; at the beginning of ~ all'inizio di settembre ; at the end of ~ alla fine di settembre ; during ~ durante il mese di settembre ; every ~ ogni anno a settembre ; in ~ a settembre ; last ~ lo scorso settembre ; next ~ il prossimo settembre ; this ~ a settembre (di quest'anno) ; 2 ~ 1995 *(in letters etc)* 2 settembre 1995.

septic ['septɪk] *adj* infetto(a).

septic tank *n* fossa *f* settica.

sequel ['si:kwəl] *n (to book, film)* seguito *m*.

sequence ['si:kwəns] *n (series)* serie *f inv* ; *(order)* ordine *m*.

sequin ['si:kwɪn] *n* lustrino *m*, paillette *f inv*.

sergeant ['sa:dʒənt] *n (in police force)* ≃ brigadiere *m* ; *(in army)* sergente *m*.

serial ['sɪərɪəl] *n (on TV, radio)* sceneggiato *m*, serial *m inv* ; *(in magazine)* romanzo *m* a puntate.

series ['sɪəri:z] *(pl inv) n* serie *f inv*.

serious ['sɪərɪəs] *adj* serio ; *(illness, problem)* grave, serio ; are you ~? dici sul serio?

seriously ['sɪərɪəslɪ] *adv (really)* seriamente ; *(badly)* gravemente.

sermon ['sɜ:mən] *n* sermone *m*.

servant ['sɜ:vənt] *n* domestico *m*, -a *f*.

serve [sɜ:v] *vt* servire. ◆ *vi* SPORT servire ; *(work)* prestare servizio. ◆ *n* SPORT servizio *m* ; to ~ as *(be used for)* servire da ; the town is ~d by two airports la città è servita da due aeroporti ; '~s two' *(on packaging, menu)* 'per due persone' ; it ~s you right! ben ti sta!

service ['sɜ:vɪs] *n* servizio *m* ; *(at church)* rito *m* ; *(of car)* revisione *f*. ◆ *vt (car)* revisionare ; '~ included' 'servizio incluso' ; '~ not included' 'servizio escluso' ; to be of ~ to sb *fml* essere d'aiuto a qn. ❑ **services**

npl (on motorway) stazione *f* di servizio ; *(of person)* servigi *mpl.*

service area *n* area *f* di servizio.

service charge *n* servizio *m.*

service department *n* servizio *m* clienti.

service station *n* stazione *f* di servizio.

serviette [ˌsɜːvɪ'et] *n* tovagliolo *m.*

serving ['sɜːvɪŋ] *n (helping)* porzione *f.*

serving spoon *n* cucchiaio *m* da portata.

sesame seeds ['sesəmɪ-] *npl* semi *mpl* di sesamo.

session ['seʃn] *n* seduta *f*; a drinking ~ una bevuta.

---

set [set] (*pt* & *pp* set) *adj* - 1. *(price, time)* fisso(a) ; a ~ lunch un menu fisso.
- 2. *(text, book)* assegnato(a).
- 3. *(situated)* situato(a).
◆ *n* - 1. *(of tools etc)* serie *f inv* ; *(of cutlery, dishes)* servizio *m* ; chess ~ gioco *m* degli scacchi.
- 2. *(TV)* : a (TV) ~ un apparecchio televisivo, un televisore.
- 3. *(in tennis)* set *m inv.*
- 4. *(of play)* scenario *m.*
- 5. *(at hairdresser's)* : a shampoo and ~ uno shampoo e messa in piega.
◆ *vt* - 1. *(put)* mettere, posare ; to ~ the table apparecchiare.
- 2. *(cause to be)* : to ~ a machine going avviare una macchina ; to ~ fire to sthg dar fuoco a qc.
- 3. *(clock, alarm, controls)* regolare ; ~ the alarm for 7 a.m. metti la sveglia alle 7.
- 4. *(price, time)* fissare.
- 5. *(a record)* stabilire.
- 6. *(homework, essay)* dare.
- 7. *(play, film, story)* : to be ~ essere ambientato(a).
◆ *vi* - 1. *(sun)* tramontare.
- 2. *(glue)* fare presa ; *(jelly)* rapprendersi.
❑ **set down** *vt sep Br (passengers)* far scendere.
❑ **set off**
◆ *vt sep (alarm)* far scattare.
◆ *vi (on journey)* mettersi in viaggio.
❑ **set out**
◆ *vt sep (arrange)* disporre.
◆ *vi (on journey)* mettersi in viaggio.
❑ **set up** *vt sep (barrier)* erigere ; *(equipment)* installare.

---

set meal *n* menu *m inv* fisso.

set menu *n* menu *m inv* fisso.

settee [se'tiː] *n* divano *m.*

setting ['setɪŋ] *n (on machine)* posizione *f*; *(physical surroundings)* scenario *m* ; *(atmosphere)* ambiente *m.*

settle ['setl] *vt (argument)* sistemare, appianare ; *(bill)* saldare, regolare ; *(stomach, nerves)* calmare ; *(arrange, decide on)* stabilire, decidere. ◆ *vi (start to live)* stabilirsi ; *(come to rest)* posarsi ; *(sediment, dust)* depositarsi. ❑ **settle down** *vi (calm down)* calmarsi ; *(sit comfortably)* accomodarsi. ❑ **settle up** *vi (pay bill)* saldare il conto.

settlement ['setlmənt] *n (agreement)* accordo *m* ; *(place)* insediamento *m.*

seven ['sevn] *num* sette → **six**.

seventeen [ˌsevn'tiːn] *num* diciassette → **six**.

seventeenth [ˌsevn'tiːnθ] *num* diciassettesimo(a) → **sixth**.

seventh ['sevnθ] *num* settimo(a) → **sixth**.

seventieth ['sevntjəθ] *num* settantesimo(a) → **sixth**.

seventy ['sevntɪ] *num* settanta → **six**.

several ['sevrəl] *adj* & *pron* parecchi(chie), diversi(e).

severe [sɪ'vɪəʳ] *adj (conditions, damage, illness)* grave ; *(criticism, person, punishment)* severo(a) ; *(pain)* violento(a), forte.

sew [səʊ] (*pp* **sewn**) *vt* & *vi* cucire.

sewage ['suːɪdʒ] *n* acque *fpl* di scarico.

sewing ['səʊɪŋ] *n (activity)* cucito *m* ; *(things sewn)* lavoro *m*.

sewing machine *n* macchina *f* da cucire.

sewn [səʊn] *pp* → **sew**.

sex [seks] *n (gender)* sesso *m* ; *(sexual intercourse)* rapporto *m* sessuale ; **to have ~ (with)** avere rapporti sessuali (con).

sexist ['seksɪst] *n* sessista *mf*.

sexual ['sekʃʊəl] *adj* sessuale.

sexy ['seksɪ] *adj* sexy *(inv)*.

shabby ['ʃæbɪ] *adj* trasandato(a).

shade [ʃeɪd] *n (shadow)* ombra *f* ; *(lampshade)* paralume *m* ; *(of colour)* sfumatura *f*, tonalità *f inv*. ◆ *vt (protect)* fare ombra a. ❑ **shades** *npl inf (sunglasses)* occhiali *mpl* da sole.

shadow ['ʃædəʊ] *n* ombra *f*.

shady ['ʃeɪdɪ] *adj (place)* ombroso(a) ; *inf (person, deal)* losco(a).

shaft [ʃaːft] *n (of machine)* albero *m* ; *(of lift)* pozzo *m*.

shake [ʃeɪk] (*pt* **shook**, *pp* **shaken** ['ʃeɪkn]) *vt (tree, rug, person)* scuotere ; *(bottle, dice)* agitare ; *(shock)* scuotere, turbare. ◆ *vi* tremare ; **to ~ hands (with sb)** dare OR stringere la mano (a qn) ; **to ~ one's head** *(saying no)* scuotere la testa.

---

shall [*weak form* ʃəl, *strong form* ʃæl] *aux vb* - 1. *(expressing future)* : **I ~ be ready soon** sarò pronto tra poco.

- 2. *(in questions)* : **~ I buy some wine?** devo comprare del vino? ; **~ we listen to the radio?** vogliamo ascoltare la radio? ; **where ~ we go?** dove andiamo?, dove vogliamo andare?

- 3. *fml (expressing order)* : **payment ~ be made within a week** il pagamento dovrà essere effettuato entro una settimana.

---

shallot [ʃə'lɒt] *n* scalogno *m*.

shallow ['ʃæləʊ] *adj* poco profondo(a).

shallow end *n (of swimming pool)* lato *m* meno profondo.

shambles ['ʃæmblz] *n* macello *m*, casino *m*.

shame [ʃeɪm] *n* vergogna *f* ; **it's a ~** è un peccato ; **what a ~!** che peccato!

shampoo [ʃæm'puː] (*pl* **-s**) *n* shampoo *m inv*.

shandy ['ʃændɪ] *n bevanda a base di birra e limonata.*

shape [ʃeɪp] *n* forma *f*; **to be in good/bad ~** essere in/fuori forma.
share [ʃeəʳ] *n (part)* parte *f*; *(in company)* azione *f*. ◆ *vt* dividere. ❑ **share out** *vt sep* dividere.
shark [ʃa:k] *n* squalo *m*, pescecane *m*.
sharp [ʃa:p] *adj (knife, razor)* affilato(a) ; *(pin, nails)* appuntito(a) ; *(teeth)* aguzzo(a) ; *(clear)* nitido(a) ; *(quick, intelligent)* acuto(a), scaltro *m*, -a *f*; *(rise, change, bend)* brusco(a) ; *(painful)* acuto(a), lancinante ; *(food, taste)* aspro(a). ◆ *adv (exactly)* in punto.
sharpen ['ʃa:pn] *vt (pencil)* temperare ; *(knife)* affilare.
shatter ['ʃætəʳ] *vt (break)* frantumare. ◆ *vi* frantumarsi.
shattered ['ʃætəd] *adj Br inf (tired)* distrutto(a).
shave [ʃeɪv] *vt* radere, rasare. ◆ *vi* radersi, rasarsi. ◆ *n* : **to have a ~** farsi la barba.
shaver ['ʃeɪvəʳ] *n* rasoio *m* elettrico.
shaving brush ['ʃeɪvɪŋ-] *n* pennello *m* da barba.
shaving foam ['ʃeɪvɪŋ-] *n* schiuma *f* da barba.
shawl [ʃɔ:l] *n* scialle *m*.
she [ʃi:] *pron* lei ; **~'s tall** è alta.
sheaf [ʃi:f] (*pl* **sheaves**) *n (of paper, notes)* fascio *m*.
shears [ʃɪəz] *npl* cesoie *fpl*.
sheaves [ʃi:vz] *pl* → **sheaf**.
shed [ʃed] (*pt* & *pp* **shed**) *n* capanno *m*. ◆ *vt (tears, blood)* versare.
she'd [*weak form* ʃɪd, *strong form* ʃi:d] = **she had, she would**.
sheep [ʃi:p] (*pl inv*) *n* pecora *f*.
sheepdog ['ʃi:pdɒg] *n* cane *m* da pastore.
sheepskin ['ʃi:pskɪn] *adj* di pelle di pecora.
sheer [ʃɪəʳ] *adj (pure, utter)* puro(a) ; *(cliff)* a picco, a strapiombo ; *(stockings)* velato(a).
sheet [ʃi:t] *n (for bed)* lenzuolo *m* ; *(of paper)* foglio *m* ; *(of glass, metal)* lastra *f* ; *(of wood)* pannello *m*.
shelf [ʃelf] (*pl* **shelves**) *n* scaffale *m*.
shell [ʃel] *n (of egg, nut, animal)* guscio *m* ; *(on beach)* conchiglia *f* ; *(bomb)* granata *f*.
she'll [ʃi:l] = **she will, she shall**.
shellfish ['ʃelfɪʃ] *n (food)* frutti *mpl* di mare.
shelter ['ʃeltəʳ] *n* riparo *m*, rifugio *m* ; *(at bus stop)* pensilina *f*. ◆ *vt (protect)* proteggere, riparare. ◆ *vi* proteggersi, ripararsi ; **to take ~** mettersi al riparo.
sheltered ['ʃeltəd] *adj (place)* riparato(a).
shelves [ʃelvz] *pl* → **shelf**.
shepherd ['ʃepəd] *n* pastore *m*.
shepherd's pie ['ʃepədz-] *n tortino a base di carne macinata coperta da uno spesso strato di purè di patate*.
sheriff ['ʃerɪf] *n (in US)* sceriffo *m*.
sherry ['ʃerɪ] *n* sherry *m inv*.
she's [ʃi:z] = **she is, she has**.
shield [ʃi:ld] *n* scudo *m*. ◆ *vt* proteggere.
shift [ʃɪft] *n (change)* cambiamento *m* ; *(period of work)* turno *m*.

◆ *vt* spostare. ◆ *vi (move)* spostarsi ; *(change)* mutare, cambiare.

shin [ʃɪn] *n* stinco *m*.

shine [ʃaɪn] (*pt* & *pp* **shone**) *vi* brillare, splendere. ◆ *vt (shoes)* lucidare, lustrare ; *(torch)* puntare.

shiny ['ʃaɪnɪ] *adj* scintillante, lucido(a).

ship [ʃɪp] *n* nave *f* ; **by ~** *(travel)* con la nave ; *(send, transport)* via mare.

shipwreck ['ʃɪprek] *n (accident)* naufragio *m* ; *(wrecked ship)* relitto *m*.

shirt [ʃɜːt] *n* camicia *f*.

shit [ʃɪt] *n vulg* merda *f*. ◆ *excl vulg* merda!

shiver ['ʃɪvəʳ] *vi* rabbrividire.

shock [ʃɒk] *n (surprise)* shock *m inv* ; *(force)* urto *m*, scossa *f*. ◆ *vt (surprise)* colpire, scioccare ; *(horrify)* scioccare ; **to be in ~** *MED* essere sotto shock.

shocking ['ʃɒkɪŋ] *adj (very bad)* terribile.

shoe [ʃuː] *n* scarpa *f*.

shoelace ['ʃuːleɪs] *n* stringa *f*.

shoe polish *n* lucido *m* scarpe.

shoe repairer's [-rɪˌpeərəz] *n* calzolaio *m*.

shoe shop *n* calzoleria *f* calzaturificio *m*.

shone [ʃɒn] *pt* & *pp* → **shine**.

shook [ʃʊk] *pt* → **shake**.

shoot [ʃuːt] (*pt* & *pp* **shot**) *vt (kill, injure)* sparare a ; *(gun)* sparare ; *(arrow)* tirare, scoccare ; *(film)* girare. ◆ *vi (with gun)* sparare ; *(move quickly)* sfrecciare ; *SPORT* tirare. ◆ *n (of plant)* germoglio *m*.

shop [ʃɒp] *n* negozio *m*. ◆ *vi* fare acquisti.

shop assistant *n Br* commesso *m*, -a *f*.

shop floor *n (place) area di una fabbrica dove lavorano gli operai.*

shopkeeper ['ʃɒpˌkiːpəʳ] *n* negoziante *mf*.

shoplifter ['ʃɒpˌlɪftəʳ] *n* taccheggiatore *m*, -trice *f*.

shopper ['ʃɒpəʳ] *n* cliente *mf*, acquirente *mf*.

shopping ['ʃɒpɪŋ] *n* spesa *f* ; **to do the ~** fare la spesa ; **to go ~** andare a fare spese.

shopping bag *n* borsa *f* per la spesa.

shopping basket *n* sporta *f* per la spesa.

shopping centre *n* centro *m* commerciale.

shopping list *n* lista *f* della spesa.

shopping mall *n* centro *m* commerciale.

shop steward *n* rappresentante *mf* sindacale.

shop window *n* vetrina *f*.

shore [ʃɔːʳ] *n* riva *f* ; **on ~** a terra.

short [ʃɔːt] *adj (not tall)* basso(a) ; *(letter, speech)* corto(a), breve ; *(hair, skirt)* corto ; *(in time, distance)* breve. ◆ *adv (cut hair)* corti. ◆ *n Br (drink)* bicchierino *m* ; *(film)* cortometraggio *m* ; **to be ~ of sthg** *(time, money)* essere a corto di qc ; **to be ~ for sthg** *(be abbreviation of)* essere l'abbreviazione di qc ; **to be ~ of breath** essere senza fiato ; **in ~** in breve. ❑ **shorts** *npl (short trousers)* calzoncini *mpl*, pantaloncini *mpl*; *Am (underpants)* boxer *mpl*.

shortage ['ʃɔːtɪdʒ] *n* carenza *f*.

shortbread ['ʃɔːtbred] *n* biscotto *m* di pasta frolla.

short-circuit *vi* fare cortocircuito.

shortcrust pastry ['ʃɔːtkrʌst-] *n* pasta *f* frolla.

short cut *n* scorciatoia *f*.

shorten ['ʃɔːtn] *vt* accorciare.

shortly ['ʃɔːtlɪ] *adv (soon)* presto, fra poco ; ~ **before** poco prima di.

shortsighted [ˌʃɔːt'saɪtɪd] *adj* miope.

short-sleeved [-ˌsliːvd] *adj* a maniche corte.

short story *n* racconto *m*, novella *f*.

shot [ʃɒt] *pt* & *pp* → **shoot**. ◆ *n (of gun)* sparo *m*; *(in football, tennis, golf etc)* tiro *m*; *(photo)* foto *f inv*; *(in film)* ripresa *f*; *inf (attempt)* prova *f*, tentativo *m*; *(drink)* bicchierino *m*.

shotgun ['ʃɒtgʌn] *n* fucile *m* da caccia.

☞

should [ʃʊd] *aux vb* - 1. *(expressing desirability)* : **we ~ leave now** ora dovremmo OR sarebbe meglio andare.
- 2. *(asking for advice)* : **~ I go too?** devo andarci anch'io?
- 3. *(expressing probability)* : **she ~ be home soon** dovrebbe arrivare a momenti.
- 4. *(ought to)* : **they ~ have won the match** avrebbero dovuto vincere la partita.
- 5. *fml (in conditionals)* : **~ you need anything, call reception** se dovesse aver bisogno di qualcosa, chiami la reception.
- 6. *fml (expressing wish)* : **I ~ like to come with you** mi piacerebbe venire con voi.

---

shoulder ['ʃəʊldəʳ] *n* spalla *f*; *Am (of road)* corsia *f* d'emergenza.

shoulder pad *n* spallina *f*.

shouldn't ['ʃʊdnt] = **should not**.

should've ['ʃʊdəv] = **should have**.

shout [ʃaʊt] *n* grido *m*, urlo *m*. ◆ *vt* & *vi* gridare, urlare. ❑ **shout out** *vt sep* gridare.

shove [ʃʌv] *vt (push)* spingere; *(put carelessly)* ficcare, cacciare.

shovel ['ʃʌvl] *n* pala *f*.

show [ʃəʊ] (*pp* **-ed** OR **shown**) *n (at theatre, on TV)* spettacolo *m*; *(on radio)* programma *m*; *(exhibition)* mostra *f*. ◆ *vt* mostrare; *(represent, depict)* raffigurare; *(accompany)* accompagnare; *(film, TV programme)* dare. ◆ *vi (be visible)* vedersi, essere visibile; *(film)* essere in programmazione; **to ~ sthg to sb** mostrare qc a qn; **to ~ sb how to do sthg** mostrare a qn come fare qc. ❑ **show off** *vi* mettersi in mostra. ❑ **show up** *vi (come along)* farsi vivo, arrivare; *(be visible)* risaltare.

shower ['ʃaʊəʳ] *n (for washing)* doccia *f*; *(of rain)* acquazzone *m*. ◆ *vi* fare la doccia; **to have a ~** fare la doccia.

shower gel *n* gel *m inv* per la doccia.
shower unit *n* blocco *m* doccia.
showing ['ʃəuɪŋ] *n (of film)* proiezione *f*.
shown [ʃəun] *pp* → **show**.
showroom ['ʃəurum] *n* salone *m* d'esposizione.
shrank [ʃræŋk] *pt* → **shrink**.
shrimp [ʃrɪmp] *n* gamberetto *m*.
shrine [ʃraɪn] *n* santuario *m*.
shrink [ʃrɪŋk] (*pt* **shrank**, *pp* **shrunk**) *n inf (psychoanalyst)* strizzacervelli *mf inv*. ◆ *vi (clothes)* restringersi ; *(number, amount)* ridursi, diminuire.
shrub [ʃrʌb] *n* arbusto *m*.
shrug [ʃrʌg] *n* scrollata *f* di spalle. ◆ *vi* scrollare le spalle.
shrunk [ʃrʌŋk] *pp* → **shrink**.
shuffle ['ʃʌfl] *vt (cards)* mischiare. ◆ *vi (walk)* camminare strascicando i piedi.
shut [ʃʌt] (*pt* & *pp* **shut**) *adj* chiuso(a). ◆ *vt* chiudere. ◆ *vi (door, mouth, eyes)* chiudersi ; *(shop, restaurant)* chiudere. ❑ **shut down** *vt sep* chiudere i battenti. ❑ **shut up** *vi inf (stop talking)* tacere, stare zitto ; ~ **up**! chiudi il becco!
shutter ['ʃʌtə^r] *n (on window)* imposta *f* ; *(on camera)* otturatore *m*.
shuttle ['ʃʌtl] *n (plane, bus etc)* navetta *f*.
shuttlecock ['ʃʌtlkɒk] *n* volano *m*.
shy [ʃaɪ] *adj* timido(a).
Sicily ['sɪsɪlɪ] *n* la Sicilia.
sick [sɪk] *adj (ill)* malato(a) ; **to be** ~ *(vomit)* vomitare ; **to feel** ~ *(nauseous)* avere la nausea ; **to be** ~ **of** *(fed up with)* essere stufo(a) di.
sick bag *n sacchetto di emergenza per viaggiatori che soffrono di nausea e vomito.*
sickness ['sɪknɪs] *n (illness)* malattia *f*.
sick pay *n* indennità *f* per malattia.
side [saɪd] *n* lato *m* ; *(of road, pitch)* margine *m* ; *(of river)* sponda *f* ; *(team)* squadra *f* ; *(in argument)* parte *f* ; *Br (TV channel)* canale *m*. ◆ *adj (door, pocket)* laterale ; **at the** ~ **of** a fianco di ; *(road)* al margine di ; *(river)* sulla riva di ; **on the other** ~ dall'altra parte ; **on this** ~ da questo lato ; ~ **by** ~ fianco a fianco.
sideboard ['saɪdbɔːd] *n* credenza *f*.
side dish *n* contorno *m*.
side effect *n* effetto *m* collaterale.
side order *n* contorno *m*.
side salad *n* insalata *f* di contorno.
side street *n* traversa *f*.
sidewalk ['saɪdwɔːk] *n Am* marciapiede *m*.
sideways ['saɪdweɪz] *adv (move)* di lato, di fianco ; *(look)* di traverso.
sieve [sɪv] *n* setaccio *m*.
sigh [saɪ] *n* sospiro *m*. ◆ *vi* sospirare.
sight [saɪt] *n (eyesight)* vista *f* ; *(thing seen)* spettacolo *m* ; **at first** ~ a prima vista ; **to catch** ~ **of** intravedere ; **in** ~ in vista ; **to lose** ~ **of** perdere di vista. ❑ **sights** *npl (of*

city, country) luoghi *mpl* di maggiore interesse.

sightseeing ['saɪt,siːɪŋ] *n*: **to go ~** fare un giro turistico.

sign [saɪn] *n (in shop, station)* insegna *f*; *(next to road)* segnale *m*, cartello *m*; *(symbol, indication)* segno *m*; *(signal)* segnale. ◆ *vt* & *vi* firmare; **there's no ~ of her** non c'è traccia di lei. ❑ **sign in** *vi (at hotel, club)* firmare il registro (all'arrivo).

signal ['sɪgnl] *n* segnale *m*; *Am (traffic lights)* semaforo *m*. ◆ *vi (in car, on bike)* segnalare.

signature ['sɪgnətʃəʳ] *n* firma *f*.

significant [sɪg'nɪfɪkənt] *adj (large)* considerevole; *(important)* importante.

signpost ['saɪnpəʊst] *n* cartello *m* stradale.

sikh [siːk] *n* Sikh *mf inv*.

silence ['saɪləns] *n* silenzio *m*.

silencer ['saɪlənsəʳ] *n Br* AUT marmitta *f*.

silent ['saɪlənt] *adj* silenzioso(a).

Silicon Valley *n* Silicon Valley *f*.

SILICON VALLEY

Silicon Valley è il nome che è stato dato a quella parte della California settentrionale dove sono concentrate numerosissime società informatiche e che è considerata la culla dell'industria dei computer.

---

silk [sɪlk] *n* seta *f*.

sill [sɪl] *n* davanzale *m*.

silly ['sɪlɪ] *adj* sciocco(a), stupido(a).

silver ['sɪlvəʳ] *n (substance)* argento *m*; *(coins)* monete *fpl* d'argento. ◆ *adj* d'argento.

silver foil *n* stagnola *f*, carta *f* argentata.

silver-plated [-'pleɪtɪd] *adj* placcato(a) d'argento.

similar ['sɪmɪləʳ] *adj* simile; **to be ~ to** essere simile a.

similarity [,sɪmɪ'lærətɪ] *n (resemblance)* somiglianza *f*; *(similar point)* affinità *f inv*.

simmer ['sɪməʳ] *vi* cuocere a fuoco lento.

simple ['sɪmpl] *adj* semplice.

simplify ['sɪmplɪfaɪ] *vt* semplificare.

simply ['sɪmplɪ] *adv* semplicemente.

simulate ['sɪmjʊleɪt] *vt* simulare.

simultaneous [*Br* ,sɪməl'teɪnjəs, *Am* ,saɪməl'teɪnjəs] *adj* simultaneo(a).

simultaneously [*Br* ,sɪməl'teɪnjəslɪ, *Am* ,saɪməl'teɪnjəslɪ] *adv* simultaneamente.

sin [sɪn] *n* peccato *m*. ◆ *vi* peccare.

since [sɪns] *adv* da allora. ◆ *prep* da. ◆ *conj (in time)* da quando, da che; *(as)* dato che, poiché; **ever ~** fin da, da che, fin da quando.

sincere [sɪn'sɪəʳ] *adj* sincero(a).

sincerely [sɪn'sɪəlɪ] *adv* sinceramente; **Yours ~** Distinti saluti.

sing [sɪŋ] (*pt* **sang**, *pp* **sung**) *vt* & *vi* cantare.

singer ['sɪŋəʳ] *n* cantante *mf*.

single ['sɪŋgl] *adj* solo(a); *(man)*

celibe ; *(woman)* nubile. ◆ *n Br (ticket)* biglietto *m* di sola andata ; *(record)* 45 giri *m inv* ; **every ~** ogni. ❑ **singles** ◆ *n* SPORT singolo *m*. ◆ *adj (bar, club)* per single.

single bed *n* letto *m* a una piazza.

single cream *n Br* panna *f* liquida.

single parent *n* genitore *m* single.

single room *n* camera *f* singola.

singular ['sɪŋgjʊlə^r] *n* singolare *m* ; **in the ~** al singolare.

sinister ['sɪnɪstə^r] *adj* sinistro(a).

sink [sɪŋk] (*pt* **sank**, *pp* **sunk**) *n* lavandino *m*. ◆ *vi (in water, mud)* affondare ; *(decrease)* calare, diminuire.

sink unit *n* blocco *m* lavello.

sinuses ['saɪnəsɪz] *npl* seni *mpl* paranasali.

sip [sɪp] *n* sorso *m*. ◆ *vt* sorseggiare.

siphon ['saɪfn] *n* sifone *m*. ◆ *vt* travasare.

sir [sɜː^r] *n* signore *m* ; **Dear Sir** Egregio Signore.

siren ['saɪərən] *n* sirena *f*.

sirloin steak [ˌsɜːlɔɪn-] *n* bistecca *f* di lombo.

sister ['sɪstə^r] *n* sorella *f*; *Br (nurse)* caposala *f*.

sister-in-law *n* cognata *f*.

sit [sɪt] (*pt* & *pp* **sat**) *vi* sedere ; *(be situated)* trovarsi. ◆ *vt (to place)* far sedere ; *Br (exam)* sostenere, dare ; **to be sitting** essere seduto. ❑ **sit down** *vi* sedersi ; **to be sitting down** essere seduto. ❑ **sit up** *vi (after lying down)* tirarsi su a sedere ; *(stay up late)* stare in piedi fino a tardi.

site [saɪt] *n* luogo *m* ; *(building site)* cantiere *m*.

sitting room ['sɪtɪŋ-] *n* salotto *m*.

situated ['sɪtjʊeɪtɪd] *adj* : **to be ~** essere situato(a).

situation [ˌsɪtjʊ'eɪʃn] *n (state of affairs)* situazione *f*; *fml (location)* ubicazione *f*; **' ~s vacant'** 'offerte di lavoro'.

six [sɪks] *num adj* & *n* sei ; **to be ~ (years old)** avere sei anni ; **it's ~ (o'clock)** sono le sei ; **a hundred and ~** centosei ; **~ Hill Street** Hill Street (numero) sei ; **it's minus ~ (degrees)** è meno sei.

sixteen [sɪks'tiːn] *num* sedici → **six**.

sixteenth [sɪks'tiːnθ] *num* sedicesimo(a) → **sixth**.

sixth [sɪksθ] *num adj, adv* & *pron* sesto(a). ◆ *num n* sesto *m* ; **the ~ (of September)** il sei (di settembre).

sixth form *n Br ultimi due anni facoltativi della scuola superiore.*

sixth-form college *n Br istituto che prepara agli esami dell'ultimo anno di scuola superiore.*

sixtieth ['sɪkstɪəθ] *num* sessantesimo(a) → **sixth**.

sixty ['sɪkstɪ] *num* sessanta → **six**.

size [saɪz] *n* dimensioni *fpl* ; *(of clothes, hats)* taglia *f*, misura *f*; *(of shoes)* numero *m* ; **what ~ do you take?** che taglia porta? ; **what ~ is this?** che taglia è?

sizeable ['saɪzəbl] *adj* notevole.

skate [skeɪt] *n (ice skate, roller*

skate) pattino *m* ; *(fish : pl inv)* razza *f.* ◆ *vi* pattinare.

skateboard ['skeɪtbɔːd] *n* skateboard *m inv*.

skater ['skeɪtəʳ] *n* pattinatore *m*, -trice *f*.

skating ['skeɪtɪŋ] *n* : **to go ~** andare a pattinare.

skeleton ['skelɪtn] *n* scheletro *m*.

skeptical ['skeptɪkl] *Am* = **sceptical**.

sketch [sketʃ] *n (drawing)* schizzo *m* ; *(humorous)* sketch *m inv*, scenetta *f.* ◆ *vt* schizzare.

skewer ['skjʊəʳ] *n* spiedo *m*.

ski [skiː] *(pt & pp* **skied**, *cont* **skiing**) *n* sci *m inv*. ◆ *vi* sciare.

ski boots *npl* scarponi *mpl* da sci.

skid [skɪd] *n* slittamento *m*, sbandamento *m.* ◆ *vi* slittare, sbandare.

skier ['skiːəʳ] *n* sciatore *m*, -trice *f*.

skiing ['skiːɪŋ] *n* sci *m* ; **to go ~** andare a sciare ; **a ~ holiday** una vacanza sulla neve.

skilful ['skɪlfʊl] *adj Br* abile.

ski lift *n* sciovia *f*.

skill [skɪl] *n (ability)* abilità *f inv* ; *(technique)* tecnica *f*.

skilled [skɪld] *adj (worker, job)* qualificato(a) ; *(driver, chef)* provetto(a).

skillful ['skɪlfʊl] *Am* = **skilful**.

skimmed milk ['skɪmd-] *n* latte *m* scremato.

skin [skɪn] *n* pelle *f* ; *(on fruit, vegetable)* buccia *f* ; *(on milk)* pellicola *f*.

skin freshener [-ˌfreʃnəʳ] *n* tonico *m*.

skinny ['skɪnɪ] *adj* magrissimo(a).

skip [skɪp] *vi (with rope)* saltare la corda ; *(jump)* saltellare. ◆ *vt (omit)* saltare. ◆ *n (container)* cassonetto *m*.

ski pants *npl* pantaloni *mpl* da sci.

ski pass *n* ski-pass *m inv*.

ski pole *n* racchetta *f* da sci.

skipping rope ['skɪpɪŋ-] *n* corda *f* per saltare.

skirt [skɜːt] *n* gonna *f*.

ski slope *n* pista *f* da sci.

ski tow *n* ski-lift *m inv*.

skittles ['skɪtlz] *n* birilli *mpl*.

skull [skʌl] *n* cranio *m*.

sky [skaɪ] *n* cielo *m*.

skylight ['skaɪlaɪt] *n* lucernario *m*.

skyscraper ['skaɪˌskreɪpəʳ] *n* grattacielo *m*.

slab [slæb] *n (of stone, concrete)* lastra *f*.

slack [slæk] *adj (rope)* non tirato(a) ; *(careless)* negligente ; *(not busy)* calmo(a) ; *(period)* morto(a).

slacks [slæks] *npl* pantaloni *mpl*.

slam [slæm] *vt & vi* sbattere.

slander ['slaːndəʳ] *n* calunnia *f* ; *(in law)* diffamazione *f*.

slang [slæŋ] *n* slang *m*, gergo *m*.

slant [slaːnt] *n (slope)* pendenza *f.* ◆ *vi* pendere.

slap [slæp] *n (smack)* schiaffo *m.* ◆ *vt* schiaffeggiare.

slash [slæʃ] *vt (cut)* tagliare ; *(face)*

sfregiare ; *fig (prices)* ridurre. ◆ *n (written symbol)* barra *f*.

slate [sleɪt] *n (rock)* ardesia *f* ; *(on roof)* tegola *f* di ardesia.

slaughter ['slɔːtəʳ] *vt (people, team)* massacrare ; *(animal)* macellare.

slave [sleɪv] *n* schiavo *m*, -a *f*.

sled [sled] = **sledge**.

sledge [sledʒ] *n* slitta *f*.

sleep [sliːp] (*pt* & *pp* **slept**) *n* sonno *m*. ◆ *vi* dormire. ◆ *vt* : **the house ~s six** la casa ha sei posti letto ; **did you ~ well?** hai dormito bene? ; **I couldn't get to ~** non riuscivo a prender sonno ; **to go to ~** addormentarsi ; **to ~ with sb** andare a letto con qn.

sleeper ['sliːpəʳ] *n (train)* treno *m* con vagoni letto ; *(sleeping car)* vagone *m* letto ; *Br (on railway track)* traversina *f* ; *Br (earring)* campanella *f*.

sleeping bag ['sliːpɪŋ-] *n* sacco *m* a pelo.

sleeping car ['sliːpɪŋ-] *n* vagone *m* letto.

sleeping pill ['sliːpɪŋ-] *n* sonnifero *m*.

sleepy ['sliːpɪ] *adj* insonnolito(a) ; **I'm ~** ho sonno.

sleet [sliːt] *n* nevischio *m*. ◆ *v impers* : **it's ~ing** sta nevischiando.

sleeve [sliːv] *n (of garment)* manica *f* ; *(of record)* copertina *f*.

sleeveless ['sliːvlɪs] *adj* senza maniche.

slept [slept] *pt* & *pp* → **sleep**.

slice [slaɪs] *n* fetta *f*. ◆ *vt* affettare, tagliare a fette.

sliced bread [ˌslaɪst-] *n* pane *m* a cassetta.

slide [slaɪd] (*pt* & *pp* **slid** [slɪd]) *n (in playground)* scivolo *m* ; *(of photograph)* diapositiva *f* ; *Br (hair slide)* fermacapelli *m inv*. ◆ *vi (slip)* scivolare.

sliding door [ˌslaɪdɪŋ-] *n* porta *f* scorrevole.

slight [slaɪt] *adj (minor)* lieve ; **the ~est** il minimo (la minima) ; **not in the ~est** affatto.

slightly ['slaɪtlɪ] *adv (a bit)* leggermente ; **I know him ~** lo conosco appena.

slim [slɪm] *adj (person, waist)* snello(a). ◆ *vi* dimagrire.

slimming ['slɪmɪŋ] *n* dimagrimento *m*.

sling [slɪŋ] (*pt* & *pp* **slung**) *vt inf (throw)* buttare. ◆ *n* : **to have one's arm in a ~** portare il braccio al collo.

slip [slɪp] *vi* scivolare. ◆ *n (mistake)* errore *m* ; *(of paper)* foglietto *m* ; *(petticoat)* sottoveste *f*. ❑ **slip up** *vi (make a mistake)* fare un errore.

slipper ['slɪpəʳ] *n* pantofola *f*.

slippery ['slɪpərɪ] *adj* scivoloso(a).

slip road *n Br* raccordo *m* autostradale.

slit [slɪt] *n* fessura *f*.

slob [slɒb] *n inf* sciattone *m*, -a *f*.

slogan ['sləʊgən] *n* slogan *m inv*.

slope [sləʊp] *n (incline)* pendio *m* ; *(hill)* fianco *m* ; *(for skiing)* pista *f* da sci. ◆ *vi (hill, path)* scendere ; *(floor, roof, shelf)* essere inclinato.

sloping ['sləʊpɪŋ] *adj (floor, roof,*

shelf) inclinato(a) ; *(hill)* degradante.

slot [slɒt] *n (for coin)* fessura *f* ; *(groove)* scanalatura *f*.

slot machine *n (vending machine)* distributore *m* automatico ; *(for gambling)* slot-machine *f inv*.

Slovakia [slə'vækɪə] *n* la Slovacchia.

slow [sləʊ] *adj* lento(a) ; *(business)* fiacco(a). ◆ *adv* lentamente ; **'slow'** *(sign on road)* 'rallentare' ; **a ~ train** un accelerato ; **to be ~** *(clock)* essere indietro. ❑ **slow down** *vt sep* & *vi* rallentare.

slowly ['sləʊlɪ] *adv* lentamente.

slug [slʌg] *n (animal)* lumaca *f*.

slum [slʌm] *n (building)* baracca *f*. ❑ **slums** *npl (district)* bassifondi *mpl*.

slung [slʌŋ] *pt* & *pp* → **sling**.

slush [slʌʃ] *n* neve *f* in parte sciolta.

sly [slaɪ] *adj (cunning)* astuto(a) ; *(deceitful)* scaltro(a).

smack [smæk] *n (slap)* schiaffo *m*. ◆ *vt* schiaffeggiare.

small [smɔːl] *adj* piccolo(a) ; *(in height)* basso(a).

small change *n* spiccioli *mpl*.

smallpox ['smɔːlpɒks] *n* vaiolo *m*.

smart [smaːt] *adj (elegant, posh)* elegante ; *(clever)* intelligente.

smart card *n* carta *f* intelligente.

smash [smæʃ] *n* SPORT smash *m inv*, schiacciata *f* ; *inf (car crash)* scontro *m*. ◆ *vt (plate, window)* frantumare. ◆ *vi (plate, vase etc)* frantumarsi.

smashing ['smæʃɪŋ] *adj Br inf* fantastico(a).

smear test ['smɪə-] *n* striscio *m*, pap-test *m inv*.

smell [smel] (*pt* & *pp* **-ed** OR **smelt**) *n* odore *m* ; *(bad odour)* puzza *f*. ◆ *vt (sniff at)* annusare ; *(detect)* sentire odore di. ◆ *vi* avere un odore ; *(have bad odour)* puzzare ; **to ~ of sthg** *(pleasant)* profumare di qc ; *(unpleasant)* puzzare di qc.

smelly ['smelɪ] *adj* puzzolente.

smelt [smelt] *pt* & *pp* → **smell**.

smile [smaɪl] *n* sorriso *m*. ◆ *vi* sorridere.

smoke [sməʊk] *n* fumo *m*. ◆ *vt* & *vi* fumare ; **to have a ~** fumare una sigaretta.

smoked [sməʊkt] *adj* affumicato(a).

smoked salmon *n* salmone *m* affumicato.

smoker ['sməʊkə^r] *n (person)* fumatore *m*, -trice *f*.

smoking ['sməʊkɪŋ] *n* fumo *m* ; **'no ~'** 'vietato fumare'.

smoking area *n* area *f* per fumatori.

smoking compartment *n* scompartimento *m* per fumatori.

smoky ['sməʊkɪ] *adj (room)* fumoso(a).

smooth [smuːð] *adj (surface, skin, road)* liscio(a) ; *(takeoff, landing)* dolce, morbido(a) ; *(flight, journey, life)* tranquillo(a) ; *(mixture, liquid)* vellutato(a), omogeneo(a) ; *(wine, beer)* amabile ; *pej (suave)* mellifluo(a). ❑ **smooth down** *vt sep* lisciare.

smother ['smʌðəʳ] *vt (cover)* coprire.
smudge [smʌdʒ] *n* sbavatura *f*.
smuggle ['smʌgl] *vt* contrabbandare.
snack [snæk] *n* spuntino *m*, snack *m inv*.
snack bar *n* snack-bar *m inv*, tavola *f* calda.
snail [sneɪl] *n* chiocciola *f*.
snake [sneɪk] *n (animal)* serpente *m*.
snap [snæp] *vt (break)* spezzare. ◆ *vi (break)* spezzarsi. ◆ *n inf (photo)* foto *f inv* ; *Br (card game)* rubamazzo *m*.
snatch [snætʃ] *vt* strappare.
sneakers ['sni:kəz] *npl Am* scarpe *fpl* da ginnastica.
sneeze [sni:z] *n* starnuto *m*. ◆ *vi* starnutire.
sniff [snɪf] *vi* tirar su col naso. ◆ *vt (smell)* annusare.
snip [snɪp] *vt* tagliare.
snob [snɒb] *n* snob *mf inv*.
snog [snɒg] *vi Br inf* pomiciare.
snooker ['snu:kəʳ] *n* snooker *m (specie di biliardo giocato con 22 palle)*.
snooze [snu:z] *n* pisolino *m*.
snore [snɔ:ʳ] *vi* russare.
snorkel ['snɔ:kl] *n* respiratore *m* (subacqueo).
snout [snaʊt] *n* muso *m*, grugno *m*.
snow [snəʊ] *n* neve *f*. ◆ *v impers* : **it's ~ing** sta nevicando.
snowball ['snəʊbɔ:l] *n* palla *f* di neve.
snowdrift ['snəʊdrɪft] *n* cumulo *m* di neve.
snowflake ['snəʊfleɪk] *n* fiocco *m* di neve.
snowman ['snəʊmæn] (*pl* **-men** [-men]) *n* pupazzo *m* di neve.
snowplough ['snəʊplaʊ] *n* spazzaneve *m inv*.
snowstorm ['snəʊstɔ:m] *n* bufera *f* di neve.
snug [snʌg] *adj (person)* comodo(a) ; *(place)* accogliente.

☞

so [səʊ] *adv* - 1. *(emphasizing degree)* così, talmente ; **it's ~ difficult (that ...)** è così difficile (che ...).
- 2. *(referring back)* : **I don't think ~** credo di no ; **I'm afraid ~** temo proprio di sì ; **if ~** se è così, in tal caso.
- 3. *(also)* : **~ do I** anch'io.
- 4. *(in this way)* così, in questo modo.
- 5. *(expressing agreement)* : **~ there is** proprio così, già.
- 6. *(in phrases)* : **or ~** all'incirca ; **~ as** per, così da ; **~ that** affinché, perché.
◆ *conj* - 1. *(therefore)* quindi, perciò ; **nobody answered ~ we went away** non rispondeva nessuno perciò ce ne siamo andati.
- 2. *(summarizing)* allora ; **~ what have you been up to?** allora come vanno le cose?
- 3. *(in phrases)* : **~ what?** *inf* e allora? ; **~ there!** *inf* ecco!

soak [səʊk] *vt (leave in water)* mettere a bagno OR a mollo ; *(make very wet)* impregnare, infradiciare. ◆ *vi* : **to ~ through sthg** infiltrarsi in qc. ❑ **soak up** *vt sep* assorbire.

soaked [səukt] *adj* fradicio(a).
soaking ['səukıŋ] *adj* fradicio(a).
soap [səup] *n* sapone *m*.
soap opera *n* soap opera *f inv*, telenovela *f*.
soap powder *n* detersivo *m* in polvere.
sob [sɒb] *n* singhiozzo *m*. ◆ *vi* singhiozzare.
sober ['səubəʳ] *adj (not drunk)* sobrio(a).
soccer ['sɒkəʳ] *n* calcio *m*.
sociable ['səuʃəbl] *adj* socievole.
social ['səuʃl] *adj (problem, conditions, class)* sociale.
social club *n* circolo *m* sociale.
socialist ['səuʃəlıst] *adj* socialista. ◆ *n* socialista *mf*.
social life *n* vita *f* sociale.
social security *n* previdenza *f* sociale.
social worker *n* assistente *mf* sociale.
society [sə'saıətı] *n* società *f inv* ; *(organization, club)* associazione *f*, società.
sociology [ˌsəusı'ɒlədʒı] *n* sociologia *f*.
sock [sɒk] *n* calzino *m*.
socket ['sɒkıt] *n (for plug)* presa *f* ; *(for light bulb)* portalampada *m inv*.
sod [sɒd] *n Br vulg (nasty person)* stronzo *m*, -a *f*.
soda ['səudə] *n (soda water)* seltz *m inv* ; *Am (fizzy drink)* spuma *f*.
soda water *n* acqua *f* di seltz.
sofa ['səufə] *n* divano *m*, sofà *m inv*.
sofa bed *n* divano *m* letto.
soft [sɒft] *adj (bed, ground, skin)* soffice, morbido(a) ; *(breeze, tap, sound)* leggero(a).
soft cheese *n* formaggio *m* molle.
soft drink *n* analcolico *m*.
software ['sɒftweəʳ] *n* software *m inv*.
soil [sɔıl] *n (earth)* suolo *m*.
solarium [sə'leərıəm] *n* solarium *m inv*.
solar panel ['səulə-] *n* pannello *m* solare.
sold [səuld] *pt* & *pp* → **sell**.
soldier ['səuldʒəʳ] *n* soldato *m*, militare *m*.
sold out *adj* esaurito(a).
sole [səul] *adj (only)* solo(a), unico(a) ; *(exclusive)* esclusivo(a). ◆ *n (of shoe)* suola *f* ; *(of foot)* pianta *f* ; *(fish : pl inv)* sogliola *f*.
solemn ['sɒləm] *adj (person)* serio(a) ; *(occasion)* solenne.
solicitor [sə'lısıtəʳ] *n Br* ≃ notaio *m*.
solid ['sɒlıd] *adj* solido(a) ; *(not hollow)* pieno(a) ; *(gold, silver, oak)* massiccio(a) ; *(uninterrupted)* ininterrotto(a) ; **three hours ~** tre ore intere.
solo ['səuləu] *(pl* **-s***)* *n* assolo *m*.
soluble ['sɒljubl] *adj* solubile.
solution [sə'lu:ʃn] *n* soluzione *f*.
solve [sɒlv] *vt* risolvere.

☞

some [sʌm] *adj* - 1. *(certain amount of)* : **~ meat** della carne ; **~ money** del denaro ; **I had ~ difficulty getting here** ho avuto qualche difficoltà ad arrivare qui. - 2. *(cer-*

tain number of) : ~ **sweets** delle caramelle ; ~ **boys** dei ragazzi ; ~ **people** della gente ; **I've known him for ~ years** lo conosco da anni. - 3. *(not all)* certi(e) ; ~ **jobs are better paid than others** certi lavori sono pagati meglio di altri. - 4. *(in imprecise statements)* : **she married ~ writer (or other)** ha sposato un certo scrittore ; **they're staying in ~ posh hotel** stanno in un albergo di lusso. ◆ *pron* - 1. *(certain amount)* un po' ; **can I have ~?** me ne dai un po'? ; ~ **of the money** una parte dei soldi. - 2. *(certain number)* alcuni(e), certi(e) ; **can I have ~?** me ne dai qualcuno? ; ~ **(of them) left early** alcuni (di loro) sono andati via presto. ◆ *adv (approximately)* circa ; **there were ~ 7,000 people there** c'erano circa 7.000 persone.

somebody ['sʌmbədɪ] = **someone.**

somehow ['sʌmhaʊ] *adv (some way or other)* in qualche modo, in un modo o nell'altro ; *(for some reason)* per qualche motivo.

someone ['sʌmwʌn] *pron* qualcuno.

someplace ['sʌmpleɪs] *Am* = **somewhere.**

somersault ['sʌməsɔːlt] *n* capriola *f*, salto *m* mortale.

something ['sʌmθɪŋ] *pron* qualcosa ; **it's really ~** è veramente eccezionale ; **or ~** *inf* o qualcosa del genere ; ~ **like** all'incirca, pressappoco.

sometime ['sʌmtaɪm] *adv* : ~ **in May** in maggio.

sometimes ['sʌmtaɪmz] *adv* a volte.

somewhere ['sʌmweəʳ] *adv (in or to unspecified place)* da qualche parte, in qualche posto ; *(approximately)* all'incirca.

son [sʌn] *n* figlio *m*.

song [sɒŋ] *n* canzone *f*.

son-in-law *n* genero *m*.

soon [suːn] *adv* presto ; **how ~ can you do it?** fra quanto può farlo? ; **as ~ as** (non) appena ; **as ~ as possible** al più presto possibile ; ~ **after** poco dopo ; **~er or later** prima o poi.

soot [sʊt] *n* fuliggine *f*.

soothe [suːð] *vt* calmare ; *(pain)* alleviare.

sophisticated [sə'fɪstɪkeɪtɪd] *adj (refined, chic)* sofisticato(a), raffinato(a) ; *(complex)* sofisticato, complesso(a).

sorbet ['sɔːbeɪ] *n* sorbetto *m*.

sore [sɔːʳ] *adj (painful)* dolorante ; *Am inf (angry)* incavolato(a). ◆ *n* piaga *f* ; **to have a ~ throat** avere mal di gola.

sorry ['sɒrɪ] *adj* : **I'm ~!** scusa! ; **I'm ~ I'm late** scusa il ritardo ; **~?** *(asking for repetition)* scusa? ; **to feel ~ for sb** dispiacersi per qn ; **I'm ~ you can't come** mi dispiace che tu non venga ; **I'm ~ about the mess** scusa il disordine.

sort [sɔːt] *n* tipo *m*. ◆ *vt* ordinare ; ~ **of** *(more or less)* più o meno ; **it's ~ of difficult** è piuttosto difficile. ❑ **sort out** *vt sep (classify)* ordinare ; *(resolve)* chiarire.

so-so *adj* & *adv inf* così così.

soufflé ['suːfleɪ] *n* soufflé *m inv*.

sought [sɔːt] *pt* & *pp* → **seek.**

soul [səʊl] *n (spirit)* anima *f* ; *(soul music)* musica *f* soul.

sound [saʊnd] *n* suono *m* ; *(noise)* rumore *m* ; *(volume)* volume *m*. ◆ *vt (horn, bell)* suonare. ◆ *vi (alarm, bell, voice)* suonare ; *(seem to be)* sembrare. ◆ *adj (building, structure)* solido(a) ; *(heart)* sano(a) ; *(advice, idea)* valido(a) ; **to ~ like** sembrare ; *(seem to be)* sembrare, avere l'aria di.

soundproof ['saʊndpru:f] *adj* insonorizzato(a).

soup [su:p] *n* zuppa *f*, minestra *f*.

soup spoon *n* cucchiaio *m* da minestra.

sour ['saʊəʳ] *adj (taste)* aspro(a) ; *(milk)* acido(a) ; **to go ~** inacidire.

source [sɔ:s] *n (supply, origin)* fonte *f* ; *(cause)* causa *f* ; *(of river)* sorgente *f*.

sour cream *n* panna *f* acida.

south [saʊθ] *n* sud *m*, meridione *m*. ◆ *adj* del sud. ◆ *adv (fly, walk)* verso sud ; *(be situated)* a sud ; **in the ~ of England** a sud dell'Inghilterra.

South America *n* l'America *f* del sud, il Sudamerica.

southbound ['saʊθbaʊnd] *adj* diretto(a) a sud.

southeast [ˌsaʊθ'i:st] *n* sud-est *m*.

southern ['sʌðən] *adj* meridionale, del sud.

South Pole *n* Polo *m* Sud.

southwards ['saʊθwədz] *adv* verso sud.

southwest [ˌsaʊθ'west] *n* sud-ovest *m*.

souvenir [ˌsu:və'nɪəʳ] *n* souvenir *m inv*, ricordo *m*.

sow[1] [səʊ] (*pp* **sown** [səʊn]) *vt (seeds)* seminare.

sow[2] [saʊ] *n (pig)* scrofa *f*.

soya ['sɔɪə] *n* soia *f*.

soya bean *n* seme *m* di soia.

soy sauce [ˌsɔɪ-] *n* salsa *f* di soia.

spa [spa:] *n* terme *fpl*.

space [speɪs] *n* spazio *m* ; *(empty place)* posto *m* ; *(room)* spazio, posto ; *(period)* periodo *m*. ◆ *vt* distanziare.

spaceship ['speɪsʃɪp] *n* astronave *f*.

space shuttle *n* shuttle *m inv*.

spacious ['speɪʃəs] *adj* spazioso(a).

spade [speɪd] *n (tool)* vanga *f*, badile *m*. ❑ **spades** *npl (in cards)* picche *fpl*.

spaghetti [spə'getɪ] *n* spaghetti *mpl*.

Spain [speɪn] *n* la Spagna.

span [spæn] *pt* → **spin**. ◆ *n (of time)* periodo *m*, arco *m* di tempo.

Spaniard ['spænjəd] *n* spagnolo *m*, -a *f*.

spaniel ['spænjəl] *n* spaniel *m inv*.

Spanish ['spænɪʃ] *adj* spagnolo. ◆ *n (language)* spagnolo *m*.

spank [spæŋk] *vt* sculacciare.

spanner ['spænəʳ] *n* chiave *f (arnese)*.

spare [speəʳ] *adj (kept in reserve)* di riserva ; *(not in use)* in più. ◆ *n (spare part)* ricambio *m* ; *(spare wheel)* ruota *f* di scorta. ◆ *vt* : **to ~ sb sthg** *(money)* dare qc a qn ; **can**

you ~ me ten minutes? hai dieci minuti? ; with ten minutes to ~ con dieci minuti di anticipo.

spare part *n* pezzo *m* di ricambio.

spare ribs *npl* costine *fpl* di maiale.

spare room *n* camera *f* degli ospiti.

spare time *n* tempo *m* libero.

spark [spaːk] *n* scintilla *f*.

sparkling ['spaːklɪŋ-] *adj (mineral water, soft drink)* frizzante.

sparkling wine *n* vino *m* frizzante.

sparrow ['spærəʊ] *n* passero *m*.

spat [spæt] *pt* & *pp* → spit.

speak [spiːk] (*pt* spoke, *pp* spoken) *vt (language)* parlare ; *(say)* dire. ◆ *vi* parlare ; who's ~ing? *(on phone)* chi parla? ; can I ~ to Sarah? - ~ing! *(on phone)* posso parlare con Sarah? - sono io! ; to ~ to sb about sthg parlare a qn di qc. ❑ **speak up** *vi (more loudly)* parlare più forte.

speaker ['spiːkəʳ] *n (at conference)* oratore *m*, -trice *f* ; *(loudspeaker, of stereo)* altoparlante *m* ; an English ~ una persona che parla inglese.

spear [spɪəʳ] *n* lancia *f*.

special ['speʃl] *adj* speciale. ◆ *n* : today's ~ piatto del giorno.

special delivery *n Br* ≃ espresso *m*.

special effects *npl* effetti *mpl* speciali.

specialist ['speʃəlɪst] *n (doctor)* specialista *mf*.

speciality [ˌspeʃɪ'ælətɪ] *n* specialità *f inv*.

specialize ['speʃəlaɪz] *vi* : to ~ (in) specializzarsi (in).

specially ['speʃəlɪ] *adv (specifically)* specialmente ; *(on purpose)* appositamente ; *(particularly)* particolarmente.

special offer *n* offerta *f* speciale.

special school *n Br* ≃ scuola *f* speciale.

specialty ['speʃltɪ] *Am* = speciality.

species ['spiːʃiːz] *n* specie *f inv*.

specific [spə'sɪfɪk] *adj (particular)* specifico(a).

specification [ˌspesɪfɪ'keɪʃn] *n (of machine, car)* caratteristiche *fpl* tecniche.

specimen ['spesɪmən] *n* MED campione *m* ; *(example)* esemplare *m*.

specs [speks] *npl inf* occhiali *mpl*.

spectacle ['spektəkl] *n (sight)* scena *f*.

spectacles ['spektəklz] *npl* occhiali *mpl*.

spectacular [spek'tækjʊləʳ] *adj* spettacolare.

spectator [spek'teɪtəʳ] *n* spettatore *m*, -trice *f*.

sped [sped] *pt* & *pp* → speed.

speech [spiːtʃ] *n (ability to speak)* parola *f* ; *(manner of speaking)* modo *m* di parlare ; *(talk)* discorso *m*.

speech impediment [-ɪmˌpedɪmənt] *n* difetto *m* di pronuncia.

speed [spiːd] (*pt* & *pp* -ed OR sped) *n* velocità *f inv* ; *(fast rate)* alta velocità ; *(of film)* sensibilità *f inv* ; *(bicycle gear)* marcia *f*. ◆ *vi (move quickly)* andare velocemente ; *(drive too fast)* andare a velocità eccessiva. ❑ **speed up** *vi* accelerare.

speedboat ['spi:dbəut] *n* fuoribordo *m inv*.

speeding ['spi:dɪŋ] *n* eccesso *m* di velocità.

speed limit *n* limite *m* di velocità.

speedometer [spɪ'dɒmɪtəʳ] *n* tachimetro *m*.

spell [spel] (*Br pt* & *pp* **-ed** OR **spelt**, *Am pt* & *pp* **-ed**) *vt (word, name)* scrivere ; *(subj : letters)* formare la parola. ◆ *n (period)* periodo *m* ; *(magic)* incantesimo *m*.

spelling ['spelɪŋ] *n (correct order)* ortografia *f*.

spelt [spelt] *pt* & *pp Br* → **spell**.

spend [spend] (*pt* & *pp* **spent** [spent]) *vt (money)* spendere ; *(time)* passare.

sphere [sfɪəʳ] *n* sfera *f*.

spice [spaɪs] *n* spezia *f*. ◆ *vt* condire con delle spezie.

spicy ['spaɪsɪ] *adj* piccante.

spider ['spaɪdəʳ] *n* ragno *m*.

spider's web *n* ragnatela *f*.

spike [spaɪk] *n (metal)* punta *f*.

spill [spɪl] (*Br pt* & *pp* **-ed** OR **spilt**, *Am pt* & *pp* **-ed**) *vt* versare. ◆ *vi* versarsi.

spin [spɪn] (*pt* **span** OR **spun**, *pp* **spun**) *vt (wheel)* far girare ; *(washing)* centrifugare. ◆ *n (on ball)* effetto *m* ; **to go for a ~** *inf* andare a fare un giro in macchina.

spinach ['spɪnɪdʒ] *n* spinaci *mpl*.

spine [spaɪn] *n* spina *f* dorsale ; *(of book)* costa *f*.

spinster ['spɪnstəʳ] *n* zitella *f*.

spiral ['spaɪərəl] *n* spirale *f*.

spiral staircase *n* scala *f* a chiocciola.

spire ['spaɪəʳ] *n* guglia *f*.

spirit ['spɪrɪt] *n* spirito *m* ; *(mood)* umore *m*. ❑ **spirits** *npl Br (alcohol)* superalcolici *mpl*.

spit [spɪt] (*Br pt* & *pp* **spat**, *Am pt* & *pp* **spit**) *vi (person)* sputare ; *(fire, food)* scoppiettare. ◆ *n (saliva)* saliva *f* ; *(for cooking)* spiedo *m*. ◆ *v impers* : **it's spitting** pioviggina.

spite [spaɪt] ◆**in spite of** *prep* nonostante.

spiteful ['spaɪtful] *adj* malevolo(a).

splash [splæʃ] *n (sound)* tonfo *m*. ◆ *vt* schizzare.

splendid ['splendɪd] *adj* splendido(a).

splint [splɪnt] *n* stecca *f*.

splinter ['splɪntəʳ] *n* scheggia *f*.

split [splɪt] (*pt* & *pp* **split**) *n (tear)* strappo *m* ; *(crack, in skirt)* spacco *m*. ◆ *vt (wood, stone)* spaccare ; *(tear)* strappare ; *(bill, cost, profits, work)* dividere. ◆ *vi (wood, stone)* spaccarsi ; *(tear)* strapparsi. ❑ **split up** *vi (couple)* lasciarsi ; *(group)* dividersi.

spoil [spɔɪl] (*pt* & *pp* **-ed** OR **spoilt**) *vt (ruin)* rovinare ; *(child)* viziare.

spoke [spəuk] *pt* → **speak**. ◆ *n* raggio *m*.

spoken ['spəukn] *pp* → **speak**.

spokesman ['spəuksmən] (*pl* **-men** [-mən]) *n* portavoce *m inv*.

spokeswoman ['spəuks,wumən] (*pl* **-women** [-,wɪmɪn]) *n* portavoce *f inv*.

sponge [spʌndʒ] *n (for cleaning, washing)* spugna *f.*
sponge bag *n Br* nécessaire *m inv* (da viaggio).
sponge cake *n* pan *m* di Spagna.
sponsor ['spɒnsəʳ] *n (of event, TV programme)* sponsor *m inv.*
sponsored walk [ˌspɒnsəd-] *n* marcia *f* di beneficenza.
spontaneous [spɒn'teɪnjəs] *adj* spontaneo(a).
spoon [spuːn] *n* cucchiaio *m.*
spoonful ['spuːnfʊl] *n* cucchiaiata *f.*
sport [spɔːt] *n* sport *m inv.*
sports car [spɔːts-] *n* automobile *f* sportiva.
sports centre [spɔːts-] *n* centro *m* sportivo.
sports jacket [spɔːts-] *n* giacca *f* sportiva.
sportsman ['spɔːtsmən] (*pl* **-men** [-mən]) *n* sportivo *m.*
sports shop [spɔːts-] *n* negozio *m* di articoli sportivi.
sportswoman ['spɔːtsˌwʊmən] (*pl* **-women** [-ˌwɪmɪn]) *n* sportiva *f.*
spot [spɒt] *n (of paint, rain)* goccia *f* ; *(on clothes)* macchia *f* ; *(on skin)* brufolo *m* ; *(place)* posto *m.* ◆ *vt* notare ; **on the ~** *(at once)* immediatamente ; *(at the scene)* sul posto.
spotless ['spɒtlɪs] *adj* pulitissimo(a).
spotlight ['spɒtlaɪt] *n* riflettore *m.*
spotty ['spɒtɪ] *adj* brufoloso(a).
spouse [spaʊs] *n fml* coniuge *mf.*
spout [spaʊt] *n* beccuccio *m.*
sprain [spreɪn] *vt (ankle, wrist)* slogarsi.
sprang [spræŋ] *pt* → **spring**.
spray [spreɪ] *n (aerosol)* spray *m inv* ; *(for perfume)* vaporizzatore *m* ; *(droplets)* spruzzi *mpl.* ◆ *vt* spruzzare.
spread [spred] (*pt & pp* **spread**) *vt (butter, jam, glue)* spalmare ; *(map, tablecloth, blanket)* stendere ; *(legs, fingers, arms)* distendere ; *(disease, news, rumour)* diffondere. ◆ *vi* diffondersi. ◆ *n (food)* crema *f* da spalmare. ❑ **spread out** *vi (disperse)* disperdersi.
spring [sprɪŋ] (*pt* **sprang**, *pp* **sprung**) *n (season)* primavera *f* ; *(coil)* molla *f* ; *(in ground)* sorgente *f.* ◆ *vi (leap)* balzare ; **in (the) ~** in primavera.
springboard ['sprɪŋbɔːd] *n* trampolino *m.*
spring-cleaning [-'kliːnɪŋ] *n* pulizie *fpl* di Pasqua.
spring onion *n* cipollina *f.*
spring roll *n* involtino *m* primavera.
sprinkle ['sprɪŋkl] *vt* : **to ~ sthg with sugar** spolverizzare qc di zucchero ; **to ~ sthg with water** spruzzare dell'acqua su qc.
sprinkler ['sprɪŋkləʳ] *n (for fire)* sprinkler *m inv* ; *(for grass)* irrigatore *m.*
sprint [sprɪnt] *vi (run fast)* scattare. ◆ *n (race)* : **the 100-metres ~** i 100 metri piani.
sprout [spraʊt] *n (vegetable)* cavoletto *m* di Bruxelles.
spruce [spruːs] *n* abete *m.*

sprung [sprʌŋ] *pp* → spring. ◆ *adj (mattress)* a molle.
spud [spʌd] *n inf* patata *f.*
spun [spʌn] *pt* & *pp* → spin.
spur [spɜːʳ] *n (for horse rider)* sperone *m* ; on the ~ of the moment d'impulso.
spurt [spɜːt] *vi* sprizzare.
spy [spaɪ] *n* spia *f.*
squalor [ˈskwɒləʳ] *n* squallore *m.*
square [skweəʳ] *adj (in shape)* quadrato(a). ◆ *n (shape)* quadrato *m* ; *(in town)* piazza *f* ; *(on chessboard)* scacco *m* ; it's 2 metres ~ misura 2 metri per 2 ; we're (all) ~ now *(not owing money)* adesso siamo pari.
squash [skwɒʃ] *n (game)* squash *m* ; *Am (vegetable)* zucca *f* ; *Br (drink)* : orange/lemon ~ sciroppo *m* di arancia/limone, schiacciare.
squat [skwɒt] *adj* tozzo(a). ◆ *vi (crouch)* accovacciarsi.
squeak [skwiːk] *vi (door, wheel)* cigolare ; *(mouse)* squittire.
squeeze [skwiːz] *vt (tube, orange)* spremere ; *(hand)* stringere. ◆ *vi* : to ~ in infilarsi.
squid [skwɪd] *n* calamaro *m.*
squint [skwɪnt] *n* strabismo *m.* ◆ *vi* : to ~ at guardare con gli occhi socchiusi.
squirrel [*Br* ˈskwɪrəl, *Am* ˈskwɜːrəl] *n* scoiattolo *m.*
squirt [skwɜːt] *vi* schizzare.
St *(abbr of Street)* V. ; *(abbr of Saint)* S.
stab [stæb] *vt (with knife)* pugnalare.
stable [ˈsteɪbl] *adj* stabile. ◆ *n* stalla *f.*
stack [stæk] *n (pile)* pila *f* ; ~s of *inf (lots)* un mucchio di.
stadium [ˈsteɪdjəm] *n* stadio *m.*
staff [stɑːf] *n (workers)* personale *m.*
stage [steɪdʒ] *n (phase)* stadio *m* ; *(in theatre)* palcoscenico *m.*
stagger [ˈstægəʳ] *vt (arrange in stages)* scaglionare. ◆ *vi* barcollare.
stagnant [ˈstægnənt] *adj* stagnante.
stain [steɪn] *n* macchia *f.* ◆ *vt* macchiare.
stained glass [ˌsteɪnd-] *n* vetro *m* colorato.
stainless steel [ˈsteɪnlɪs-] *n* acciaio *m* inossidabile.
staircase [ˈsteəkeɪs] *n* scala *f.*
stairs [steəz] *npl* scale *fpl.*
stairwell [ˈsteəwel] *n* tromba *f* delle scale.
stake [steɪk] *n (share)* quota *f* ; *(in gambling)* posta *f* ; *(post)* palo *m* ; at ~ in gioco.
stale [steɪl] *adj (food)* stantio(a).
stalk [stɔːk] *n* gambo *m.*
stall [stɔːl] *n (in market, at exhibition)* banco *m.* ◆ *vi (car, engine)* spegnersi. ❑ **stalls** *npl Br (in theatre)* platea *f.*
stamina [ˈstæmɪnə] *n* resistenza *f.*
stammer [ˈstæməʳ] *vi* balbettare.
stamp [stæmp] *n (for letter)* francobollo *m* ; *(in passport, on document)* timbro *m.* ◆ *vt (passport,*

document) timbrare. ◆ *vi* : **to ~ on sthg** pestare qc.
stamp-collecting [-kəˌlektɪŋ] *n* filatelia *f.*
stamp machine *n* distributore *m* di francobolli.
stand [stænd] (*pt* & *pp* **stood**) *vi* *(be on feet)* stare in piedi ; *(be situated)* trovarsi ; *(get to one's feet)* alzarsi. ◆ *vt (place)* mettere ; *(bear)* sopportare ; *(withstand)* tollerare. ◆ *n (stall)* banco *m* ; *(for umbrellas)* portaombrelli *m inv* ; *(for coats)* attaccapanni *m inv* ; *(on bike, motorbike)* cavalletto *m* ; *(at sports stadium)* tribuna *f* ; **newspaper ~** edicola *f* ; **to be ~ing** stare in piedi ; **to ~ sb a drink** offrire da bere a qn ; **no ~ing** *Am* AUT divieto di sosta. ❑ **stand back** *vi* tirarsi indietro. ❑ **stand for** *vt fus (mean)* stare per ; *(tolerate)* tollerare. ❑ **stand in** *vi* : **to ~ in for sb** sostituire qn. ❑ **stand out** *vi* spiccare. ❑ **stand up** ◆ *vi (be on feet)* stare in piedi ; *(get to one's feet)* alzarsi. ◆ *vt sep inf (boyfriend, girlfriend etc)* tirare un bidone a. ❑ **stand up for** *vt fus* difendere.
standard ['stændəd] *adj (normal)* standard *(inv).* ◆ *n (level)* livello *m* ; *(norm)* standard *m inv* ; **up to ~** (di livello) soddisfacente. ❑ **standards** *npl (principles)* principi *mpl.*
standard-class *adj Br (on train)* di seconda classe.
standby ['stændbaɪ] *adj (ticket)* stand-by *(inv).*
stank [stæŋk] *pt* → **stink.**
staple ['steɪpl] *n (for paper)* punto *m* metallico.
stapler ['steɪplə'] *n* cucitrice *f.*
star [stɑː'] *n* stella *f.* ◆ *vt (subj : film, play etc)* avere come protagonista. ❑ **stars** *npl (horoscope)* oroscopo *m.*
starch ['stɑːtʃ] *n* amido *m.*
stare [steə'] *vi* : **to ~ at** fissare.
starfish ['stɑːfɪʃ] *(pl inv) n* stella *f* marina.
starling ['stɑːlɪŋ] *n* storno *m.*
Stars and Stripes *n* : **the ~** la bandiera a stelle e strisce.

STARS AND STRIPES

È uno dei tanti nomi con i quali viene comunemente indicata la bandiera americana, oltre a *Old Glory*, *Star-Spangled Banner* e *Stars and Bars*. Le 50 stelle (*stars*) rappresentano i 50 Stati che attualmente fanno parte degli Stati Uniti, mentre le 13 strisce (*stripes*) rosse e bianche rappresentano i 13 stati che formavano originariamente l'Unione. Gli americani sono molto orgogliosi della loro bandiera e non è perciò raro vederla sventolare dalle case di molti privati cittadini.

start [stɑːt] *n (beginning)* inizio *m* ; *(starting place)* partenza *f.* ◆ *vt* cominciare, iniziare ; *(car, engine)* mettere in moto ; *(company, club)* fondare. ◆ *vi* cominciare ; *(car, engine, on journey)* partire ; **prices ~ at** OR **from £5** i prezzi partono da 5 sterline ; **to ~ doing sthg** OR **to do sthg** cominciare a fare qc ; **to ~ with ...** per cominciare ... ❑ **start out** *vi (on journey)* partire ; *(be originally)* cominciare. ❑ **start up** *vt* *sep (car, engine)* mettere in moto ; *(business)* intraprendere ; *(shop)* aprire.

starter ['sta:tə^r] *n Br (of meal)* antipasto *m* ; *(of car)* starter *m inv* ; **for ~s** *(in meal)* per antipasto.

starter motor *n* motorino *m* di avviamento.

starting point ['sta:tɪŋ-] *n* punto *m* di partenza.

startle ['sta:tl] *vt* far trasalire.

starvation [sta:'veɪʃn] *n* fame *f*.

starve [sta:v] *vi (have no food)* morire di fame ; **I'm starving!** muoio di fame!

state [steɪt] *n* stato *m*. ◆ *vt (declare)* dichiarare ; *(specify)* specificare ; **the State** lo Stato ; **the States** gli Stati Uniti.

statement ['steɪtmənt] *n (declaration)* dichiarazione *f* ; *(from bank)* estratto *m* conto.

state school *n* scuola *f* statale.

statesman ['steɪtsmən] (*pl* **-men** [-mən]) *n* statista *m*.

static ['stætɪk] *n (on radio, TV)* scarica *f* (elettrostatica).

station ['steɪʃn] *n* stazione *f*.

stationary ['steɪʃnərɪ] *adj* stazionario(a).

stationer's ['steɪʃnəz] *n (shop)* cartoleria *f*.

stationery ['steɪʃnərɪ] *n* cancelleria *f*.

station wagon *n Am* station wagon *f inv*.

statistics [stə'tɪstɪks] *npl (facts)* statistiche *fpl*.

statue ['stætʃu:] *n* statua *f*.

Statue of Liberty *n* : **the ~** la Statua della Libertà.

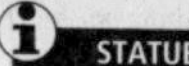

STATUE OF LIBERTY

Su un'isoletta al largo del porto di New York si erge la Statua della Libertà, scultura gigante di una donna che regge nella mano destra una fiaccola. Fu donata agli Stati Uniti dalla Francia nel 1884 ed è aperta al pubblico.

status ['steɪtəs] *n (legal position)* stato *m* ; *(social position)* condizione *f* sociale ; *(prestige)* prestigio *m*.

stay [steɪ] *n (time spent)* soggiorno *m*. ◆ *vi (remain)* rimanere ; *(as guest)* alloggiare ; *Scot (reside)* abitare ; **to ~ the night** passare la notte. ❑ **stay away** *vi* : **to ~ away (from)** *(not attend)* non andare (a) ; *(not go near)* stare lontano (da). ❑ **stay in** *vi* rimanere a casa. ❑ **stay out** *vi (from home)* rimanere fuori. ❑ **stay up** *vi* rimanere alzato.

STD code *n* prefisso *m*.

steady ['stedɪ] *adj (not shaking, firm)* stabile ; *(gradual, stable)* costante ; *(job)* fisso(a). ◆ *vt (stop from shaking)* tenere fermo.

steak [steɪk] *n (type of meat)* carne *f* di manzo ; *(piece of meat)* bistecca *f* ; *(piece of fish)* trancia *f*.

steak and kidney pie *n pasticcio di carne di manzo e rognone*.

steakhouse ['steɪkhaus, *pl* -hauzɪz] *n* ristorante *m* specializzato in bistecche.

steal [sti:l] (*pt* **stole**, *pp* **stolen**) *vt*

rubare ; **to ~ sthg from sb** rubare qc a qn.

steam [sti:m] *n* vapore *m*. ◆ *vt (food)* cuocere a vapore.

steam engine *n* locomotiva *f* a vapore.

steam iron *n* ferro *m* a vapore.

steel [sti:l] *n* acciaio *m*. ◆ *adj* di acciaio.

steep [sti:p] *adj (hill, path)* ripido(a) ; *(increase, drop)* notevole.

steeple ['sti:pl] *n* campanile *m*.

steer ['stɪəʳ] *vt (car, boat, plane)* condurre.

steering ['stɪərɪŋ] *n* sterzo *m*.

steering wheel *n* volante *m*.

stem [stem] *n* stelo *m*.

step [step] *n (stair)* gradino *m* ; *(rung)* piolo *m* ; *(pace)* passo *m* ; *(measure)* misura *f* ; *(stage)* mossa *f*. ◆ *vi* : **to ~ on sthg** calpestare qc ; **mind the ~** attenti al gradino. ❑ **steps** *npl (stairs)* scala *f*. ❑ **step aside** *vi (move aside)* farsi da parte. ❑ **step back** *vi (move back)* tirarsi indietro.

step aerobics *n* step *m*.

stepbrother ['step,brʌðəʳ] *n* fratellastro *m*.

stepdaughter ['step,dɔ:təʳ] *n* figliastra *f*.

stepfather ['step,fa:ðəʳ] *n* patrigno *m*.

stepladder ['step,lædəʳ] *n* scala *f* (a pioli).

stepmother ['step,mʌðəʳ] *n* matrigna *f*.

stepsister ['step,sɪstəʳ] *n* sorellastra *f*.

stepson ['stepsʌn] *n* figliastro *m*.

stereo ['sterɪəʊ] (*pl* **-s**) *adj* stereofonico(a). ◆ *n (hi-fi)* stereo *m inv* ; *(stereo sound)* stereofonia *f*.

sterile ['steraɪl] *adj* sterile.

sterilize ['sterəlaɪz] *vt* sterilizzare.

sterling ['stɜ:lɪŋ] *adj (pound)* sterlina. ◆ *n* sterlina *f*.

sterling silver *n* argento *m* di buona lega.

stern [stɜ:n] *adj* severo(a). ◆ *n* poppa *f*.

stew [stju:] *n* stufato *m*.

steward ['stjʊəd] *n (on plane, ship)* steward *m inv* ; *(at public event)* membro *m* del servizio d'ordine.

stewardess ['stjʊədɪs] *n* hostess *f inv*.

stewed [stju:d] *adj (fruit)* cotto(a).

stick [stɪk] (*pt* & *pp* **stuck**) *n (of wood)* bastone *m* ; *(of chalk)* pezzetto *m* ; *(of celery)* bastoncino *m*. ◆ *vt (glue)* attaccare ; *(push, insert)* ficcare ; *inf (put)* ficcare. ◆ *vi (become attached)* attaccarsi ; *(jam)* incastrarsi. ❑ **stick out** *vi (protrude)* sporgere ; *(be noticeable)* saltare agli occhi. ❑ **stick to** *vt fus (decision, promise)* mantenere ; *(principles)* tener fede a. ❑ **stick up** ◆ *vt sep (poster, notice)* attaccare. ◆ *vi* sporgere. ❑ **stick up for** *vt fus* difendere.

sticker ['stɪkəʳ] *n* adesivo *m*.

stick shift *n Am (car)* auto *f* con cambio manuale.

sticky ['stɪkɪ] *adj (substance, hands, weather)* appiccicoso(a) ; *(label, tape)* adesivo(a).

stiff [stɪf] *adj* duro(a) ; *(back, neck, person)* rigido(a). ◆ *adv* : **to be bored ~** *inf* essere annoiato a morte.

stiletto heels [stɪ'letəʊ-] *npl* tacchi *mpl* a spillo.

still [stɪl] *adv* ancora ; *(despite that)* comunque. ◆ *adj (motionless)* immobile ; *(quiet, calm)* calmo(a) ; *(not fizzy)* non gassato(a) ; **we've ~ got ten minutes** abbiamo ancora dieci minuti ; **~ more** ancora di più ; **to stand ~** stare fermo.

stimulate ['stɪmjʊleɪt] *vt (encourage)* stimolare.

sting [stɪŋ] (*pt* & *pp* **stung**) *vt* pungere. ◆ *vi (skin, eyes)* pizzicare.

stingy ['stɪndʒɪ] *adj inf* tirchio(a).

stink [stɪŋk] (*pt* **stank** OR **stunk**, *pp* **stunk**) *vi (smell bad)* puzzare.

stipulate ['stɪpjʊleɪt] *vt* stipulare.

stir [stɜːʳ] *vt* mescolare.

stir-fry *n* piatto *m* saltato. ◆ *vt* saltare *(in padella)*.

stirrup ['stɪrəp] *n* staffa *f*.

stitch [stɪtʃ] *n (in sewing, knitting)* punto *m* ; **to have a ~** *(stomach pain)* avere una fitta. ❑ **stitches** *npl (for wound)* punti *mpl*.

stock [stɒk] *n (of shop, business)* stock *m inv* ; *(supply)* scorta *f* ; FIN azioni *fpl* ; *(in cooking)* brodo *m*. ◆ *vt (have in stock)* avere in magazzino ; **in ~** in magazzino ; **out of ~** esaurito.

stock cube *n* dado *m* (per il brodo).

Stock Exchange *n* Borsa *f* valori.

stocking ['stɒkɪŋ] *n* calza *f*.

stock market *n* borsa *f* valori.

stodgy ['stɒdʒɪ] *adj (food)* pesante.

stole [stəʊl] *pt* → **steal**.

stolen ['stəʊln] *pp* → **steal**.

stomach ['stʌmək] *n (organ)* stomaco *m* ; *(belly)* pancia *f*.

stomachache ['stʌməkeɪk] *n* mal *m* di stomaco.

stomach upset [-'ʌpset] *n* disturbo *m* di stomaco.

stone [stəʊn] *n (substance)* pietra *f* ; *(in fruit)* nocciolo *m* ; *(measurement : pl inv)* = 6,35 kg ; *(gem)* pietra preziosa. ◆ *adj* di pietra.

stonewashed ['stəʊnwɒʃt] *adj* délavé *(inv)*.

stood [stʊd] *pt* & *pp* → **stand**.

stool [stuːl] *n (for sitting on)* sgabello *m*.

stop [stɒp] *n (for bus, train)* fermata *f* ; *(in journey)* tappa *f*. ◆ *vt (cause to cease)* porre fine a ; *(car, machine)* fermare ; *(prevent)* impedire. ◆ *vi* fermarsi ; **to ~ sb/sthg from doing sthg** impedire a qn/qc di fare qc ; **to ~ doing sthg** smettere di fare qc ; **to put a ~ to sthg** porre fine a qc ; **Stop** *(road sign)* stop. ❑ **stop off** *vi* fare una sosta.

stopover ['stɒp,əʊvəʳ] *n* sosta *f*.

stopper ['stɒpəʳ] *n* tappo *m*.

stopwatch ['stɒpwɒtʃ] *n* cronografo *m*.

storage ['stɔːrɪdʒ] *n* immagazzinamento *m*.

store [stɔːʳ] *n (shop)* negozio *m* ; *(supply)* scorta *f*. ◆ *vt* immagazzinare.

storehouse ['stɔːhaʊs, *pl* -haʊzɪz] *n* magazzino *m*.

storeroom ['stɔːrum] *n* stanzino *m*.

storey ['stɔːrɪ] (*pl* -s) *n Br* piano *m*.

stork [stɔːk] *n* cicogna *f*.

storm [stɔːm] *n* tempesta *f*.

stormy ['stɔːmɪ] *adj (weather)* burrascoso(a).

story ['stɔːrɪ] *n (account, tale)* storia *f*; *(news item)* notizia *f*; *Am* = **storey**.

stout [staut] *adj (fat)* corpulento(a). ◆ *n (drink)* birra *f* scura.

stove [stəuv] *n (for cooking)* cucina *f*; *(for heating)* stufa *f*.

straight [streɪt] *adj (not curved)* diritto(a) ; *(hair, drink)* liscio(a) ; *(consecutive)* di seguito. ◆ *adv (in a straight line)* dritto ; *(upright)* in posizione eretta ; *(directly, without delay)* direttamente ; ~ **ahead** sempre diritto ; ~ **away** subito.

straightforward [ˌstreɪt'fɔːwəd] *adj (easy)* semplice.

strain [streɪn] *n (force)* sforzo *m* ; *(tension, nervous stress)* tensione *f*; *(injury)* distorsione *f*. ◆ *vt (muscle, eyes)* sforzare ; *(food)* scolare ; *(tea)* filtrare.

strainer ['streɪnəʳ] *n* colino *m*.

strait [streɪt] *n* stretto *m*.

strange [streɪndʒ] *adj (unusual)* strano(a) ; *(unfamiliar)* sconosciuto(a).

stranger ['streɪndʒəʳ] *n (unfamiliar person)* sconosciuto *m*, -a *f*; *(person from different place)* forestiero *m*, -a *f*.

strangle ['stræŋgl] *vt* strangolare.

strap [stræp] *n (of bag, camera)* tracolla *f*; *(of watch, shoe)* cinturino *m* ; *(of dress)* bretella *f*.

strapless ['stræplɪs] *adj* senza spalline.

strategy ['strætɪdʒɪ] *n (plan)* strategia *f*.

Stratford-upon-Avon [ˌstrætfədəpɒn'eɪvn] *n* Stratford-upon-Avon.

straw [strɔː] *n* paglia *f*; *(for drinking)* cannuccia *f*.

strawberry ['strɔːbərɪ] *n* fragola *f*.

stray [streɪ] *adj (animal)* randagio(a). ◆ *vi* vagare.

streak [striːk] *n (stripe, mark)* striscia *f*; *(period)* periodo *m*.

stream [striːm] *n (river)* ruscello *m* ; *(of traffic, people, blood)* flusso *m*.

street [striːt] *n* via *f*, strada *f*.

streetcar ['striːtkaːʳ] *n Am* tram *m inv*.

street light *n* lampione *m*.

street plan *n* piantina *f*.

strength [streŋθ] *n* forza *f* ; *(of structure)* robustezza *f* ; *(influence)* potere *m* ; *(strong point)* punto *m* di forza ; *(of feeling, smell)* intensità *f*; *(of drink)* gradazione *f* alcolica.

strengthen ['streŋθn] *vt (structure)* rafforzare.

stress [stres] *n (tension)* stress *m inv* ; *(on word, syllable)* accento *m*. ◆ *vt (emphasize)* sottolineare ; *(word, syllable)* accentare.

stretch [stretʃ] *n (of land, water)* distesa *f*; *(of time)* periodo *m*. ◆ *vt* tendere ; *(body)* stirare. ◆ *vi (land, sea)* estendersi ; *(person, animal)* stirarsi ; **to ~ one's legs** *fig* sgranchirsi le gambe. ❑ **stretch out** ◆ *vt sep (hand)* tendere. ◆ *vi (lie down)* distendersi.

stretcher ['stretʃə'] *n* barella *f*.

strict [strɪkt] *adj (person)* severo(a) ; *(rule, instructions)* rigido(a) ; *(exact)* stretto(a).

strictly ['strɪktlɪ] *adv* strettamente ; ~ **speaking** per essere precisi.

stride [straɪd] *n* falcata *f*.

strike [straɪk] (*pt* & *pp* **struck**) *n (of employees)* sciopero *m*. ◆ *vt fml (hit)* colpire ; *fml (collide with)* urtare ; *(a match)* accendere. ◆ *vi (refuse to work)* scioperare ; *(happen suddenly)* colpire ; **the clock struck eight** l'orologio ha battuto le otto.

striking ['straɪkɪŋ] *adj (noticeable)* impressionante ; *(attractive)* appariscente.

string [strɪŋ] *n* spago *m* ; *(of pearls, beads)* filo *m* ; *(of musical instrument, tennis racket)* corda *f* ; *(series)* serie *f inv* ; **a piece of ~** un pezzo di spago.

strip [strɪp] *n* striscia *f*. ◆ *vt (paint, wallpaper)* togliere. ◆ *vi (undress)* spogliarsi.

stripe [straɪp] *n* striscia *f*.

striped [straɪpt] *adj* a strisce.

strip-search *vt* perquisire (facendo spogliare).

stroke [strəuk] *n* MED colpo *m* ; *(in tennis)* battuta *f* ; *(in golf)* tiro *m* ; *(swimming style)* stile *m*. ◆ *vt* accarezzare ; **a ~ of luck** un colpo di fortuna.

stroll [strəul] *n* passeggiata *f*.

stroller ['strəulər] *n Am (pushchair)* passeggino *m*.

strong [strɒŋ] *adj* forte ; *(structure, bridge, chair)* robusto(a) ; *(feeling, smell)* intenso(a).

struck [strʌk] *pt* & *pp* → **strike**.

structure ['strʌktʃə'] *n* struttura *f*.

struggle ['strʌgl] *n (great effort)* sforzo *m*. ◆ *vi (fight)* lottare ; *(in order to get free)* divincolarsi ; **to ~ to do sthg** sforzarsi di fare qc.

stub [stʌb] *n (of cigarette)* mozzicone *m* ; *(of cheque, ticket)* matrice *f*.

stubble ['stʌbl] *n (on face)* barba *f* ispida.

stubborn ['stʌbən] *adj (person)* ostinato(a).

stuck [stʌk] *pt* & *pp* → **stick**. ◆ *adj (jammed)* incastrato(a) ; *(unable to continue, stranded)* bloccato(a).

stud [stʌd] *n (on boots)* borchia *f* ; *(fastener)* bottone *m* automatico ; *(earring)* mini orecchino *m*.

student ['stju:dnt] *n* studente *m*, -essa *f*.

student card *n* carta *f* dello studente.

students' union [ˌstju:dnts-] *n (place)* circolo *m* studentesco.

studio ['stju:dɪəu] (*pl* **-s**) *n* studio *m*.

studio apartment *Am* = **studio flat**.

studio flat *n Br* miniappartamento *m*.

study ['stʌdɪ] *n (learning)* studio *m*. ◆ *vt* & *vi* studiare.

stuff [stʌf] *n inf* roba *f*. ◆ *vt (put roughly)* ficcare ; *(fill)* riempire.

stuffed [stʌft] *adj (food)* ripieno(a) ; *inf (full up)* pieno(a) ; *(dead animal)* imbalsamato(a).

stuffing ['stʌfɪŋ] *n (food)* ripieno *m* ; *(of pillow, cushion)* imbottitura *f*.

stuffy ['stʌfɪ] *adj (room, atmosphere)* che sa di chiuso.

stumble ['stʌmbl] *vi (when walking)* inciampare.

stump [stʌmp] *n (of tree)* ceppo *m*.

stun [stʌn] *vt (shock)* sbalordire.

stung [stʌŋ] *pt* & *pp* → **sting**.

stunk [stʌŋk] *pt* & *pp* → **stink**.

stunning ['stʌnɪŋ] *adj (very beautiful)* favoloso(a) ; *(very surprising)* sbalorditivo(a).

stupid ['stju:pɪd] *adj* stupido(a).

sturdy ['stɜ:dɪ] *adj* robusto(a).

stutter ['stʌtəʳ] *vi* balbettare.

sty [staɪ] *n (pigsty)* porcile *m* ; *(on eye)* orzaiolo *m*.

style [staɪl] *n* stile *m*. ◆ *vt (hair)* acconciare.

stylish ['staɪlɪʃ] *adj* elegante.

stylist ['staɪlɪst] *n (hairdresser)* acconciatore *m*, -trice *f*.

sub [sʌb] *n inf (substitute)* riserva *f*; *Br (subscription)* quota *f* (d'iscrizione).

subdued [səb'dju:d] *adj (person)* abbacchiato(a) ; *(lighting, colour)* smorzato(a).

subject [*n* 'sʌbdʒekt, *vb* səb-'dʒekt] *n (topic)* argomento *m* ; *(at school, university)* materia *f* ; GRAMM soggetto *m* ; *fml (of country)* cittadino *m*, -a *f*. ◆ *vt* : **to ~ sb to sthg** sottoporre qn a qc ; '**~ to availability**' 'fino ad esaurimento' ; **they are ~ to an additional charge** sono suscettibili di sovrapprezzo.

subjunctive [səb'dʒʌŋktɪv] *n* congiuntivo *m*.

submarine [ˌsʌbmə'ri:n] *n* sottomarino *m*.

submit [səb'mɪt] *vt* presentare. ◆ *vi* sottomettersi.

subordinate [sə'bɔ:dɪnət] *adj* subordinato(a).

subscribe [səb'skraɪb] *vi (to magazine, newspaper)* abbonarsi.

subscription [səb'skrɪpʃn] *n* abbonamento *m*.

subsequent ['sʌbsɪkwənt] *adj* successivo(a).

subside [səb'saɪd] *vi (ground)* cedere ; *(noise, feeling)* smorzarsi.

substance ['sʌbstəns] *n* sostanza *f*.

substantial [səb'stænʃl] *adj (large)* sostanziale.

substitute ['sʌbstɪtju:t] *n (person)* sostituto *m*, -a *f* ; *(thing)* surrogato *m* ; SPORT riserva *f*.

subtitles ['sʌbˌtaɪtlz] *npl* sottotitoli *mpl*.

subtle ['sʌtl] *adj (difference, change)* sottile ; *(person, plan)* astuto(a).

subtract [səb'trækt] *vt* sottrarre.

subtraction [səb'trækʃn] *n* sottrazione *f*.

suburb ['sʌbɜ:b] *n* sobborgo *m* ; **the ~s** la periferia.

subway ['sʌbweɪ] *n Br (for pedestrians)* sottopassaggio *m* ; *Am (underground railway)* metropolitana *f*.

succeed [sək'si:d] *vi (be success-*

ful) avere successo. ◆ *vt fml (follow)* succedere a ; **to ~ in doing sthg** riuscire a fare qc.

success [sək'ses] *n* successo *m.*

successful [sək'sesfʊl] *adj (plan, attempt)* riuscito(a) ; *(film, book, politician)* di successo ; **to be ~** *(person)* riuscire.

succulent ['sʌkjʊlənt] *adj* succulento(a).

such [sʌtʃ] *adj* tale. ◆ *adv* : **~ a lot** così tanto ; **it's ~ a lovely day** è una giornata così bella ; **~ good luck** una tale fortuna ; **~ a thing should never have happened** una cosa simile non sarebbe mai dovuta accadere ; **~ as** come.

suck [sʌk] *vt* succhiare.

sudden ['sʌdn] *adj* improvviso(a) ; **all of a ~** all'improvviso.

suddenly ['sʌdnlɪ] *adv* improvvisamente.

sue [su:] *vt* citare (in giudizio).

suede [sweɪd] *n* pelle *f* scamosciata.

suffer ['sʌfəʳ] *vt (defeat, injury)* subire. ◆ *vi* soffrire ; **to ~ from** *(illness)* soffrire di.

suffering ['sʌfrɪŋ] *n* sofferenza *f.*

sufficient [sə'fɪʃnt] *adj fml* sufficiente.

sufficiently [sə'fɪʃntlɪ] *adv fml* sufficientemente.

suffix ['sʌfɪks] *n* suffisso *m.*

suffocate ['sʌfəkeɪt] *vi* soffocare.

sugar ['ʃʊgəʳ] *n* zucchero *m.*

suggest [sə'dʒest] *vt* suggerire ; **to ~ doing sthg** suggerire di fare qc.

suggestion [sə'dʒestʃn] *n (proposal)* suggerimento *m* ; *(hint)* accenno *m.*

suicide ['sʊɪsaɪd] *n* suicidio *m* ; **to commit ~** suicidarsi.

suit [su:t] *n (clothes)* completo *m* ; *(in cards)* seme *m* ; JUR causa *f.* ◆ *vt (subj : clothes, colour, shoes)* star bene a ; *(be convenient for)* andare bene a ; *(be appropriate for)* addirsi a ; **to be ~ed to** essere adatto a.

suitable ['su:təbl] *adj* adatto(a) ; **to be ~ for** essere adatto a.

suitcase ['su:tkeɪs] *n* valigia *f.*

suite [swi:t] *n (set of rooms)* suite *f inv* ; *(furniture)* : **a three-piece ~** un divano e due poltrone (coordinati).

sulk [sʌlk] *vi* mettere il broncio.

sultana [səl'ta:nə] *n Br* uva *f* sultanina.

sum [sʌm] *n* somma *f.* ❑ **sum up** *vt sep* riassumere.

summarize ['sʌməraɪz] *vt* riassumere.

summary ['sʌmərɪ] *n* riassunto *m.*

summer ['sʌməʳ] *n* estate *f*; **in (the) ~** d'estate ; **~ holidays** vacanze *fpl* estive.

summertime ['sʌmətaɪm] *n* estate *f.*

summit ['sʌmɪt] *n (of mountain)* cima *f* ; *(meeting)* summit *m inv.*

summon ['sʌmən] *vt (send for)* convocare ; JUR citare.

sun [sʌn] *n* sole *m.* ◆ *vt* : **to ~ o.s.** prendere il sole ; **to catch the ~** prendere il sole ; **in the ~** al sole ; **out of the ~** al riparo dal sole.

Sun. *(abbr of Sunday)* dom.

sunbathe ['sʌnbeɪð] *vi* prendere il sole.
sunbed ['sʌnbed] *n* lettino *m.*
sun block *n* crema *f* solare a protezione totale.
sunburn ['sʌnbɜːn] *n* scottatura *f.*
sunburnt ['sʌnbɜːnt] *adj* scottato(a).
Sunday ['sʌndɪ] *n* domenica *f* → Saturday.
Sunday school *n* ≃ scuola *f* di catechismo.
sundress ['sʌndres] *n* prendisole *m inv.*
sundries ['sʌndrɪz] *npl (on bill)* varie *fpl.*
sunflower ['sʌnˌflaʊəʳ] *n* girasole *m.*
sunflower oil *n* olio *m* di semi di girasole.
sung [sʌŋ] *pt* → sing.
sunglasses ['sʌnˌglaːsɪz] *npl* occhiali *mpl* da sole.
sunhat ['sʌnhæt] *n* cappello *m (per il sole).*
sunk [sʌŋk] *pp* → sink.
sunlight ['sʌnlaɪt] *n* luce *f* del sole.
sun lounger [-ˌlaʊndʒəʳ] *n (chair)* lettino *m.*
sunny ['sʌnɪ] *adj (day)* di sole ; *(weather)* bello(a) ; *(room, place)* soleggiato(a) ; **it's ~** c'è il sole.
sunrise ['sʌnraɪz] *n* alba *f.*
sunroof ['sʌnruːf] *n* tettuccio *m* apribile.
sunset ['sʌnset] *n* tramonto *m.*
sunshine ['sʌnʃaɪn] *n* luce *f* del sole ; **in the ~** al sole.
sunstroke ['sʌnstrəʊk] *n* insolazione *f.*
suntan ['sʌntæn] *n* abbronzatura *f.*
suntan cream *n* crema *f* abbronzante.
suntan lotion *n* lozione *f* abbronzante.
super ['suːpəʳ] *adj* fantastico(a). ◆ *n (petrol)* super *f inv.*
superb [suː'pɜːb] *adj* splendido(a).
Super Bowl *n Am* : **the ~** il Super Bowl.

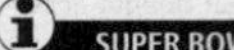
SUPER BOWL

Il *Super Bowl* è la partita conclusiva del campionato di football americano durante la quale si affrontano le squadre vincitrici delle due divisioni o *conferences* più importanti. Si gioca a fine gennaio ed è seguita alla televisione da migliaia e migliaia di persone dentro e fuori gli Stati Uniti.

superficial [ˌsuːpə'fɪʃl] *adj* superficiale.
superfluous [suː'pɜːfluəs] *adj* superfluo(a).
Superglue® ['suːpəgluː] *n* colla *f* a presa rapida.
superior [suː'pɪərɪəʳ] *adj* superiore. ◆ *n* superiore *mf.*
supermarket ['suːpəˌmaːkɪt] *n* supermercato *m.*
superstitious [ˌsuːpə'stɪʃəs] *adj* superstizioso(a).

superstore ['su:pəstɔ:ʳ] *n* grande supermercato *m*.

supervise ['su:pəvaɪz] *vt* sorvegliare.

supervisor ['su:pəvaɪzəʳ] *n (of workers)* sovrintendente *mf*.

supper ['sʌpəʳ] *n (evening meal)* cena *f*; *(before bed)* spuntino *m*.

supple ['sʌpl] *adj* agile.

supplement [*n* 'sʌplɪmənt, *vb* 'sʌplɪment] *n* supplemento *m* ; *(of diet)* integratore *m* alimentare. ◆ *vt* integrare.

supplementary [,sʌplɪ'mentərɪ] *adj* supplementare.

supply [sə'plaɪ] *n (store)* scorta *f* ; *(providing)* approvvigionamento *m* ; *(of electricity, gas etc)* erogazione *f*. ◆ *vt* fornire ; **to ~ sb with sthg** fornire qc a qn. ❑ **supplies** *npl* scorte *fpl*.

support [sə'pɔ:t] *n (for cause, candidate)* appoggio *m* ; *(object, encouragement)* sostegno *m*. ◆ *vt (cause, campaign, person)* appoggiare ; SPORT tifare per ; *(hold up)* sostenere ; *(financially)* mantenere.

supporter [sə'pɔ:təʳ] *n* SPORT tifoso *m*, -a *f*; *(of cause, political party)* sostenitore *m*, -trice *f*.

suppose [sə'pəuz] *vt (assume)* immaginare ; *(think)* credere. ◆ *conj* = **supposing** ; **I ~ so** penso di sì ; **you were ~d to be home at six o'clock** dovevate essere a casa alle sei ; **it's ~d to be the best** è ritenuto il migliore.

supposing [sə'pəuzɪŋ] *conj* supponendo che.

surcharge ['sɜ:tʃa:dʒ] *n* sovrapprezzo *m*.

sure [ʃuəʳ] *adj* sicuro(a). ◆ *adv inf (yes)* certo! ; *Am inf (certainly)* certamente ; **to be ~ of o.s.** essere sicuro di sé ; **to make ~ that ...** assicurarsi che.

surely ['ʃuəlɪ] *adv* sicuramente.

surf [sɜ:f] *n (foam)* spuma *f*. ◆ *vi* fare surf.

surface ['sɜ:fɪs] *n* superficie *f*.

surface mail *n* posta *f* ordinaria.

surfboard ['sɜ:fbɔ:d] *n* tavola *f* da surf.

surfing ['sɜ:fɪŋ] *n* surf *m* ; **to go ~** andare a fare surf.

surgeon ['sɜ:dʒən] *n* chirurgo *m*.

surgery ['sɜ:dʒərɪ] *n (treatment)* chirurgia *f* ; *Br (building)* ambulatorio *m* ; *Br (period)* orario *m* d'ambulatorio.

surname ['sɜ:neɪm] *n* cognome *m*.

surprise [sə'praɪz] *n* sorpresa *f*. ◆ *vt* sorprendere.

surprised [sə'praɪzd] *adj* sorpreso(a).

surprising [sə'praɪzɪŋ] *adj* sorprendente.

surrender [sə'rendəʳ] *vi* arrendersi. ◆ *vt fml (hand over)* consegnare.

surround [sə'raund] *vt* circondare.

surrounding [sə'raundɪŋ] *adj* circostante. ❑ **surroundings** *npl* dintorni *mpl*.

survey ['sɜ:veɪ] *n (investigation)* studio *m* ; *(poll)* sondaggio *m* ; *(of* *land)* rilevamento *m* (topografico) ; *Br (of house)* sopralluogo *m*.

surveyor [sə'veɪəʳ] *n Br (of houses)* perito *m* ; *(of land)* agrimensore *m*.

survival [sə'vaɪvl] *n* sopravvivenza *f*.

survive [sə'vaɪv] *vi* sopravvivere. ◆ *vt* sopravvivere a.

survivor [sə'vaɪvəʳ] *n* sopravvissuto *m*, -a *f*.

suspect [*vb* sə'spekt, *n & adj* 'sʌspekt] *vt* sospettare. ◆ *n* sospetto *m*. ◆ *adj* sospetto(a) ; **to ~ sb of sthg** sospettare qn di qc.

suspend [sə'spend] *vt* sospendere.

suspender belt [sə'spendə-] *n* reggicalze *m inv*.

suspenders [sə'spendəz] *npl Br (for stockings)* giarrettiere *fpl* ; *Am (for trousers)* bretelle *fpl*.

suspense [sə'spens] *n* suspense *f*.

suspension [sə'spenʃn] *n* sospensione *f*.

suspicion [sə'spɪʃn] *n (mistrust, idea)* sospetto *m* ; *(trace)* accenno *m*.

suspicious [sə'spɪʃəs] *adj (behaviour, situation)* sospetto(a) ; **to be ~ of** *(distrustful)* sospettare (di).

swallow ['swɒləʊ] *n (bird)* rondine *f*. ◆ *vt & vi* ingoiare.

swam [swæm] *pt* → **swim**.

swamp [swɒmp] *n* palude *f*.

swan [swɒn] *n* cigno *m*.

swap [swɒp] *vt (possessions, places)* scambiare ; *(ideas, stories)* scambiarsi ; **to ~ sthg for sthg** scambiare qc con qc.

swarm [swɔːm] *n (of bees)* sciame *m*.

swear [sweəʳ] (*pt* **swore**, *pp* **sworn**) *vi (use rude language)* imprecare ; *(promise)* giurare. ◆ *vt* : **to ~ to do sthg** promettere di fare qc.

swearword ['sweəwɜːd] *n* parolaccia *f*.

sweat [swet] *n* sudore *m*. ◆ *vi* sudare.

sweater ['swetəʳ] *n* maglione *m*.

sweatshirt ['swetʃɜːt] *n* felpa *f*.

swede [swiːd] *n Br* rapa *f* svedese.

Sweden ['swiːdn] *n* la Svezia.

Swedish ['swiːdɪʃ] *adj* svedese. ◆ *n (language)* svedese *m*. ◆ *npl* : **the ~** gli svedesi.

sweep [swiːp] (*pt & pp* **swept**) *vt (with brush, broom)* scopare.

sweet [swiːt] *adj* dolce ; *(kind)* gentile, carino(a). ◆ *n [Br] (candy)* caramella *f* ; *(dessert)* dolce *m*.

sweet-and-sour *adj (pork)* in agrodolce ; *(sauce)* agrodolce.

sweet corn *n* granturco *m* dolce.

sweetener ['swiːtnəʳ] *n (for drink)* dolcificante *m*.

sweet potato *n* patata *f* americana.

sweet shop *n Br* negozio *m* di dolciumi.

swell [swel] (*pp* **swollen**) *vi (ankle, arm etc)* gonfiarsi.

swelling ['swelɪŋ] *n* gonfiore *m*.

swept [swept] *pt & pp* → **sweep**.

swerve [swɜːv] *vi (vehicle)* sterzare.
swig [swɪg] *n inf* sorsata *f*.
swim [swɪm] (*pt* **swam**, *pp* **swum**) *n* nuotata *f*, bagno *m*. ◆ *vi (in water)* nuotare ; **to go for a ~** andare a fare il bagno.
swimmer ['swɪmə'] *n* nuotatore *m*, -trice *f*.
swimming ['swɪmɪŋ] *n* nuoto *m* ; **to go ~** andare in piscina.
swimming baths *npl Br* piscina *f* coperta.
swimming cap *n* cuffia *f*.
swimming costume *n Br* costume *m* da bagno.
swimming pool *n* piscina *f*.
swimming trunks *npl* costume *m* da bagno *(da uomo)*.
swimsuit ['swɪmsuːt] *n* costume *m* da bagno.
swindle ['swɪndl] *n* truffa *f*.
swing [swɪŋ] (*pt* & *pp* **swung**) *n (for children)* altalena *f*. ◆ *vt* & *vi (from side to side)* dondolare.
swipe [swaɪp] *vt (credit card etc)* far passare nel lettore magnetico.
Swiss [swɪs] *adj* svizzero(a). ◆ *n (person)* svizzero *m*, -a *f*. ◆ *npl* : **the ~** gli svizzeri.
swiss roll *n rotolo di pan di Spagna farcito di marmellata.*
switch [swɪtʃ] *n (for light, power, television set)* interruttore *m*. ◆ *vt (change)* cambiare ; *(exchange)* scambiare. ◆ *vi* cambiare. ❑ **switch off** *vt sep* spegnere. ❑ **switch on** *vt sep* accendere.
switchboard ['swɪtʃbɔːd] *n* centralino *m*.
Switzerland ['swɪtsələnd] *n* la Svizzera.
swivel ['swɪvl] *vi* girarsi.
swollen ['swəʊln] *pp* → **swell**. ◆ *adj (ankle, arm etc)* gonfio(a).
swop [swɒp] = **swap**.
sword [sɔːd] *n* spada *f*.
swordfish ['sɔːdfɪʃ] (*pl inv*) *n* pesce *m* spada.
swore [swɔː'] *pt* → **swear**.
sworn [swɔːn] *pp* → **swear**.
swum [swʌm] *pp* → **swim**.
swung [swʌŋ] *pt* & *pp* → **swing**.
syllable ['sɪləbl] *n* sillaba *f*.
syllabus ['sɪləbəs] *n* programma *m*.
symbol ['sɪmbl] *n* simbolo *m*.
sympathetic [ˌsɪmpə'θetɪk] *adj (understanding)* comprensivo(a).
sympathize ['sɪmpəθaɪz] *vi* : **to ~ (with)** *(feel sorry)* provare compassione (per) ; *(understand)* capire.
sympathy ['sɪmpəθɪ] *n (understanding)* comprensione *f*.
symphony ['sɪmfənɪ] *n* sinfonia *f*.
symptom ['sɪmptəm] *n* sintomo *m*.
synagogue ['sɪnəgɒg] *n* sinagoga *f*.
synthesizer ['sɪnθəsaɪzə'] *n* sintetizzatore *m*.
synthetic [sɪn'θetɪk] *adj* sintetico(a).
syringe [sɪ'rɪndʒ] *n* siringa *f*.
syrup ['sɪrəp] *n (for fruit etc)* sciroppo *m*.
system ['sɪstəm] *n* sistema *m* ; *(hi-fi, computer, for heating etc)* impianto *m*.

T

ta [taː] *excl Br inf* grazie!

tab [tæb] *n (of cloth, paper etc)* etichetta *f* ; *(bill)* conto *m* ; **put it on my ~** lo metta sul mio conto.

table ['teɪbl] *n (piece of furniture)* tavolo *m* ; *(of figures etc)* tavola *f*.

tablecloth ['teɪblklɒθ] *n* tovaglia *f*.

tablemat ['teɪblmæt] *n* sottopiatto *m*.

tablespoon ['teɪblspuːn] *n* cucchiaio *m* da tavola.

tablet ['tæblɪt] *n (pill)* compressa *f* ; *(of chocolate)* tavoletta *f* ; **~ of soap** saponetta *f*.

table tennis *n* ping-pong® *m*.

table wine *n* vino *m* da tavola.

tabloid ['tæblɔɪd] *n* tabloid *m inv*.

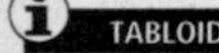

TABLOID

Tabloid è il termine generico con il quale vengono indicati i quotidiani di formato ridotto rispetto a quello dei *broadsheet*, dai quali si differenziano anche per il contenuto. Gli articoli che vi compaiono, infatti, sono piuttosto superficiali, accompagnati da molto materiale fotografico, e sono scritti con stile semplice e toni spesso sensazionalistici. I tabloid a maggior tiratura sono pieni di articoli fondati su pettegolezzi, con un enfasi sul sesso e sulla vita privata di personaggi famosi, e sono considerati con disprezzo da certi settori del pubblico. Il termine *tabloid press* viene usato con riferimento ad un tipo di giornalismo che si serve di metodi poco ortodossi per ottenere le informazioni desiderate e che spesso spingono le persone colpite ad intentare azioni legali per diffamazione nei confronti dei quotidiani.

---

tack [tæk] *n (nail)* puntina *f*.

tackle ['tækl] *n (in football)* tackle *m* ; *(in rugby)* placcaggio *m* ; *(for fishing)* attrezzatura *f*. ◆ *vt (in football)* contrastare ; *(in rugby)* placcare ; *(deal with)* affrontare.

tacky ['tækɪ] *adj inf (jewellery, design etc)* pacchiano(a).

taco ['tækəʊ] (*pl* **-s**) *n* taco *m (schiacciatina a base di farina di granturco farcita di carne o fagioli, tipica della cucina messicana)*.

tact [tækt] *n* tatto *m*.

tactful ['tæktful] *adj* discreto(a).

tactics ['tæktɪks] *npl* tattica *f*.

tag [tæg] *n (label)* etichetta *f*.

tagliatelle [ˌtægljə'telɪ] *n* tagliatelle *fpl*.

tail [teɪl] *n* coda *f*. ❑ **tails** *n (of coin)* croce *f*. ◆ *npl (formal dress)* frac *m inv*.

tailgate ['teɪlgeɪt] *n (of car)* portellone *m*.

tailor ['teɪləʳ] *n* sarto *m*.

take [teɪk] (*pt* **took**, *pp* **taken**) *vt* - 1. *gen* prendere.

- 2. *(carry, drive)* portare.
- 3. *(do, make)* fare ; **to ~ a bath/shower** fare un bagno/una doccia ; **to ~ an exam** fare OR dare un esame ; **to ~ a decision** prendere una decisione.
- 4. *(time, effort)* volerci, richiedere ; **how long will it ~?** quanto ci vorrà? ; **it won't ~ long** non ci vorrà molto tempo.
- 5. *(size in clothes, shoes)* portare, avere ; **what size do you ~?** *(clothes)* che taglia porta? ; *(shoes)* che misura porta?
- 6. *(subtract)* sottrarre, togliere.
- 7. *(accept)* accettare ; **do you ~ traveller's cheques?** accettate traveller's cheques? ; **to ~ sb's advice** seguire il consiglio di qn.
- 8. *(contain)* contenere.
- 9. *(control, power)* assumere ; **to ~ charge of** assumere la direzione di.
- 10. *(tolerate)* sopportare.
- 11. *(assume)* : **I ~ it that ...** suppongo che ...
- 12. *(rent)* prendere in affitto.
❑ **take apart** *vt sep (dismantle)* smontare.
❑ **take away** *vt sep (remove)* portare via ; *(subtract)* togliere.
❑ **take back** *vt sep (return)* riportare ; *(statement)* ritrattare.
❑ **take down** *vt sep (picture, decorations)* togliere.
❑ **take in** *vt sep (include)* includere ; *(understand)* capire ; *(deceive)* abbindolare ; *(clothes)* restringere.
❑ **take off** *vi (plane)* decollare. ◆ *vt sep (remove)* togliere ; *(as holiday)* : **to ~ a week off** prendere una settimana di ferie.
❑ **take out** *vt sep (from container, pocket)* tirare fuori ; *(loan, insurance policy)* ottenere ; *(go out with)* portare fuori.
❑ **take over** *vi* assumere il comando ; **to ~ over from sb** prendere le consegne da qn.
❑ **take up** *vt sep (begin)* dedicarsi a ; *(use up)* prendere ; *(trousers, dress)* accorciare.

---

takeaway ['teɪkəˌweɪ] *n [Br] (shop) locale che prepara piatti pronti da asporto* ; *(food)* cibo *m* da asporto.
taken ['teɪkn] *pp* → **take.**
takeoff ['teɪkɒf] *n (of plane)* decollo *m.*
takeout ['teɪkaut] *Am* = **takeaway.**
takings ['teɪkɪŋz] *npl* incasso *m.*
talcum powder ['tælkəm-] *n* borotalco® *m.*
tale [teɪl] *n (story)* storia *f*; *(account)* racconto *m.*
talent ['tælənt] *n* talento *m.*
talk [tɔːk] *n (conversation)* conversazione *f*; *(speech)* discorso *m.* ◆ *vi* parlare ; **to ~ to sb (about sthg)** parlare con qn (di qc) ; **to ~ with sb** parlare con qn. ❑ **talks** *npl* negoziati *mpl.*
talkative ['tɔːkətɪv] *adj* loquace.
tall [tɔːl] *adj* alto(a) ; **how ~ are you?** quanto sei alto? ; **I'm five and a half feet ~** sono alto un metro e 65.
tame [teɪm] *adj (animal)* addomesticato(a).
tampon ['tæmpɒn] *n* tampone *m.*
tan [tæn] *n (suntan)* abbronzatura *f.* ◆ *vi* abbronzarsi. ◆ *adj (colour)* marrone chiaro *(inv).*

tangerine [ˌtændʒəˈriːn] *n (fruit)* mandarino *m*.
tank [tæŋk] *n (container)* serbatoio *m* ; *(vehicle)* carro *m* armato.
tanker [ˈtæŋkəʳ] *n (truck)* autocisterna *f*.
tanned [tænd] *adj (suntanned)* abbronzato(a).
tap [tæp] *n (for water)* rubinetto *m*. ◆ *vt (hit)* dare un colpetto a.
tape [teɪp] *n (cassette, video)* cassetta *f* ; *(in cassette)* nastro *m* ; *(adhesive material)* nastro *m* adesivo ; *(strip of material)* fettuccia *f*. ◆ *vt (record)* registrare ; *(stick)* attaccare con nastro adesivo.
tape measure *n* metro *m*.
tape recorder *n* registratore *m*.
tapestry [ˈtæpɪstrɪ] *n* arazzo *m*.
tap water *n* acqua *f* di rubinetto.
tar [tɑːʳ] *n (for roads)* catrame *m* ; *(in cigarettes)* condensato *m*.
target [ˈtɑːgɪt] *n* bersaglio *m*.
tariff [ˈtærɪf] *n (price list)* tariffario *m* ; *Br (menu)* listino *m* prezzi ; *(at customs)* tariffa *f* doganale.
tarmac [ˈtɑːmæk] *n (at airport)* pista *f*. ❑ **Tarmac®** *n (on road)* asfalto *m*.
tarpaulin [tɑːˈpɔːlɪn] *n* telone *m*.
tart [tɑːt] *n (sweet)* crostata *f*.
tartan [ˈtɑːtn] *n (design)* scozzese *m* ; *(cloth)* tartan *m*.
tartare sauce [ˌtɑːtə-] *n* salsa *f* tartara.
task [tɑːsk] *n* compito *m*.
taste [teɪst] *n* gusto *m* ; *(flavour)* gusto, sapore *m*. ◆ *vt (sample)* assaggiare ; *(detect)* sentire il gusto di. ◆ *vi* : **to ~ of sthg** sapere di qc ; **it ~s bad** ha un cattivo sapore ; **it ~s good** ha un buon sapore ; **to have a ~ of sthg** *(food, drink)* assaggiare qc ; *fig (experience)* provare qc ; **bad ~** cattivo gusto ; **good ~** buon gusto.
tasteful [ˈteɪstfʊl] *adj* di buon gusto.
tasteless [ˈteɪstlɪs] *adj (food)* insipido(a) ; *(comment, decoration)* di cattivo gusto.
tasty [ˈteɪstɪ] *adj* gustoso(a).
tattoo [təˈtuː] (*pl* **-s**) *n (on skin)* tatuaggio *m* ; *(military display)* parata *f*.
taught [tɔːt] *pt* & *pp* → **teach**.
taut [tɔːt] *adj* teso(a).
tax [tæks] *n (on income)* imposta *f*, tasse *fpl* ; *(on import, goods)* tassa *f*. ◆ *vt (goods, person)* tassare.
tax disc *n Br* ≃ bollo *m*.
tax-free *adj* esentasse *(inv)*.
taxi [ˈtæksɪ] *n* taxi *m inv*. ◆ *vi (plane)* rullare.
taxi driver *n* tassista *mf*.
taxi rank *n Br* posteggio *m* dei taxi.
taxi stand *Am* = **taxi rank**.
T-bone steak *n* costata *f* alla fiorentina.
tea [tiː] *n* tè *m inv* ; *(evening meal)* cena *f*.
tea bag *n* bustina *f* di tè.
teacake [ˈtiːkeɪk] *n panino dolce all'uvetta*.
teach [tiːtʃ] (*pt* & *pp* **taught**) *vt (subject)* insegnare ; *(person)* insegnare a. ◆ *vi* insegnare ; **to ~ sb sthg, to ~ sthg to sb** insegnare qc a qn ; **to ~ sb (how) to do sthg** insegnare a qn a fare qc.

teacher ['ti:tʃəʳ] *n* insegnante *mf*; *(in primary school)* maestro *m*, -a *f*; *(in secondary school)* professore *m*, -essa *f*.
teaching ['ti:tʃɪŋ] *n* insegnamento *m*.
tea cloth = **tea towel**.
teacup ['ti:kʌp] *n* tazza *f* da tè.
team [ti:m] *n* squadra *f*.
teapot ['ti:pɒt] *n* teiera *f*.
tear[1] [teəʳ] (*pt* **tore**, *pp* **torn**) *vt* *(rip)* strappare. ◆ *vi* *(rip)* strapparsi; *(move quickly)* precipitarsi. ◆ *n* *(rip)* strappo *m*. ❑ **tear up** *vt sep* strappare.
tear[2] [tɪəʳ] *n* lacrima *f*.
tearoom ['ti:rʊm] *n* sala *f* da tè.
tease [ti:z] *vt* prendere in giro.
tea set *n* servizio *m* da tè.
teaspoon ['ti:spu:n] *n* cucchiaino *m*.
teaspoonful ['ti:spu:nˌfʊl] *n* cucchiaino *m*.
teat [ti:t] *n* *(of animal)* capezzolo *m*; *Br (of bottle)* tettarella *f*.
teatime ['ti:taɪm] *n* ora *f* del tè.
tea towel *n* strofinaccio *m*.
technical ['teknɪkl] *adj* tecnico(a).
technician [tek'nɪʃn] *n* tecnico *m*, -a *f*.
technique [tek'ni:k] *n* tecnica *f*.
technological [ˌteknə'lɒdʒɪkl] *adj* tecnologico(a).
technology [tek'nɒlədʒɪ] *n* tecnologia *f*.
teddy (bear) ['tedɪ-] *n* orsacchiotto *m*.
tedious ['ti:djəs] *adj* noioso(a).
teenager ['ti:nˌeɪdʒəʳ] *n* adolescente *mf*.
teeth [ti:θ] *pl* → **tooth**.
teethe [ti:ð] *vi*: **to be teething** mettere i denti.
teetotal [ti:'təʊtl] *adj* astemio(a).
telegram ['telɪgræm] *n* telegramma *m*.
telegraph pole *n* palo *m* del telegrafo.
telephone ['telɪfəʊn] *n* telefono *m*. ◆ *vt* *(person)* telefonare a. ◆ *vi* telefonare; **to be on the ~** *(talking)* essere al telefono; *(connected)* avere il telefono.
telephone booth *n* cabina *f* telefonica.
telephone box *n* cabina *f* telefonica.
telephone call *n* telefonata *f*.
telephone directory *n* elenco *m* telefonico.
telephone number *n* numero *m* di telefono.
telephonist [tɪ'lefənɪst] *n* *Br* centralinista *mf*.
telephoto lens [ˌtelɪ'fəʊtəʊ-] *n* teleobiettivo *m*.
telescope ['telɪskəʊp] *n* telescopio *m*.
television ['telɪˌvɪʒn] *n* televisione *f*; *(set)* televisore *m*; **on (the) ~** *(broadcast)* alla televisione.
telex ['teleks] *n* telex *m inv*.
tell [tel] (*pt & pp* **told**) *vt* dire; *(story, joke)* raccontare; *(distinguish)* distinguere. ◆ *vi*: **I can ~** si vede; **can you ~ me the time?** sa dirmi l'ora?; **to ~ sb sthg** dire qc a qn; **to ~ sb about sthg** raccontare

qc a qn ; **to ~ sb how to do sthg** dire a qn come fare qc ; **to ~ sb to do sthg** dire a qn di fare qc. ❑ **tell off** *vt sep* rimproverare.

teller ['teləʳ] *n (in bank)* cassiere *m*, -a *f*.

telly ['telɪ] *n Br inf* tele *f*.

temp [temp] *n* impiegato *m* straordinario, (impiegata *f* straordinaria). ◆ *vi* avere un impiego temporaneo.

temper ['tempəʳ] *n (character)* carattere *m* ; **to be in a ~** essere in collera ; **to lose one's ~** andare in collera.

temperature ['temprətʃəʳ] *n* temperatura *f* ; **to have a ~** avere la febbre.

temple ['templ] *n (building)* tempio *m* ; *(of forehead)* tempia *f*.

temporary ['tempərərɪ] *adj* temporaneo(a).

tempt [tempt] *vt* tentare ; **to be ~ed to do sthg** essere tentato di fare qc.

temptation [temp'teɪʃn] *n* tentazione *f*.

tempting ['temptɪŋ] *adj* allettante.

ten [ten] *num* dieci → **six**.

tenant ['tenənt] *n* inquilino *m*, -a *f*.

tend [tend] *vi* : **to ~ to do sthg** tendere a fare qc.

tendency ['tendənsɪ] *n* tendenza *f*.

tender ['tendəʳ] *adj* tenero(a) ; *(sore)* dolorante. ◆ *vt fml (pay)* presentare.

tendon ['tendən] *n* tendine *m*.

tenement ['tenəmənt] *n* caseggiato *m*.

tennis ['tenɪs] *n* tennis *m*.

tennis ball *n* palla *f* da tennis.

tennis court *n* campo *m* da tennis.

tennis racket *n* racchetta *f* da tennis.

tenpin bowling ['tenpɪn-] *n Br* bowling *m*.

tenpins ['tenpɪnz] *Am* = **tenpin bowling**.

tense [tens] *adj* teso(a). ◆ *n* GRAMM tempo *m*.

tension ['tenʃn] *n* tensione *f*.

tent [tent] *n* tenda *f*.

tenth [tenθ] *num* decimo(a) → **sixth**.

tent peg *n* picchetto *m* da tenda.

tepid ['tepɪd] *adj (water)* tiepido(a).

tequila [tɪ'ki:lə] *n* tequila *f*.

term [tɜ:m] *n (word, expression)* termine *m* ; *(at school, university)* trimestre *m* ; **in the long ~** a lungo andare ; **in the short ~** a breve scadenza ; **in ~s of** per quanto riguarda ; **in business ~s** dal punto di vista commerciale. ❑ **terms** *npl (price, of contract)* condizioni *fpl*.

terminal ['tɜ:mɪnl] *adj (illness)* terminale. ◆ *n (for buses)* capolinea *m* ; *(at airport)* terminal *m inv* ; COMPUT terminale *m*.

terminate ['tɜ:mɪneɪt] *vi (train, bus)* fare capolinea.

terminus ['tɜ:mɪnəs] *n (of buses)* capolinea *m* ; *(of trains)* stazione *f* terminale.

terrace ['terəs] *n (patio)* terrazza

f ; **the ~s** *(at football ground)* le gradinate.

terraced house ['terəst-] *n Br* casa *f* a schiera.

terrible ['terəbl] *adj* terribile ; *(very ill)* : **to feel ~** stare malissimo.

terribly ['terəblı] *adv (extremely)* terribilmente ; *(very badly)* malissimo.

terrific [tə'rıfık] *adj inf (very good)* fantastico(a) ; *(very great)* grande.

terrified ['terıfaıd] *adj* terrorizzato(a).

territory ['terətrı] *n (political area)* territorio *m* ; *(terrain)* terreno *m*.

terror ['terə[r]] *n* terrore *m*.

terrorism ['terərızm] *n* terrorismo *m*.

terrorist ['terərıst] *n* terrorista *mf*.

terrorize ['terəraız] *vt* terrorizzare.

test [test] *n (at school)* prova *f*; *(check)* controllo *m* ; *MED* esame *m*. ◆ *vt (check)* controllare ; *(give exam to)* esaminare ; *(try)* provare ; **driving ~** esame di guida.

testicles ['testıklz] *npl* testicoli *mpl*.

tetanus ['tetənəs] *n* tetano *m*.

text [tekst] *n* testo *m*.

textbook ['tekstbuk] *n* libro *m* di testo.

textile ['tekstaıl] *n* tessuto *m*.

texture ['tekstʃə[r]] *n* consistenza *f*; *(of fabric)* trama *f*.

Thames [temz] *n* : **the ~** il Tamigi.

than [*weak form* ðən, *strong form* ðæn] *prep* di. ◆ *conj* che ; **you're better ~ me** sei più bravo di me ; **I'd rather stay in ~ go out** preferisco restare a casa piuttosto che uscire ; **more ~ six** più di sei.

thank [θæŋk] *vt* : **to ~ sb (for sthg)** ringraziare qn (per qc). ❑ **thanks** *npl* ringraziamenti *mpl*. ◆ *excl* grazie! ; **~s to** grazie a ; **many ~s** grazie infinite.

Thanksgiving ['θæŋks,gıvıŋ] *n* festa *f* del Ringraziamento *(festa nazionale americana)*.

THANKSGIVING

Le origini di questa festa nazionale, celebrata ogni anno negli Stati Uniti il quarto giovedì di novembre, risalgono al 1621, anno in cui i Padri Pellegrini resero grazie al Signore per il primo raccolto dal loro arrivo dall'Inghilterra. Il tacchino arrosto e la torta di zucca sono i due piatti tipici serviti durante il pranzo della festa del Ringraziamento.

---

thank you *excl* grazie! ; **~ very much!** tante OR mille grazie! ; **no ~!** no, grazie!.

that [ðæt, *weak form of pron senses 3, 4, 5 & conj* ðət] (*pl* **those**) *adj* - 1. *(referring to thing, person mentioned)* quel/quello (quella/quell'), quegli/quei (quelle) *(pl)* ; **~ book** quel libro ; **who's ~ man?** chi è quell'uomo? ; **those chocolates are delicious** quei cioccolatini sono buonissimi.

- 2. *(referring to thing, person further away)* quello(a) là ; **I prefer ~ book** preferisco quel libro ; **I'll have ~ one** prendo quello là.
◆ *pron* - 1. *(referring to thing mentioned)* ciò ; **what's ~?** che cos'è (quello)? ; **I can't do ~** non posso farlo ; **who's ~?** chi è quello? ; **is ~ Lucy?** è Lucy?
- 2. *(referring to thing, person further away)* quello, quelli(e) *(pl)*.
- 3. *(introducing relative clause)* che ; **a shop ~ sells antiques** un negozio che vende oggetti d'antiquariato ; **the film ~ I saw** il film che ho visto.
- 4. *(introducing relative clause : after prep)* cui ; **the person ~ I was telling you about** la persona di cui ti stavo parlando ; **the place ~ I'm looking for** il posto che sto cercando.
◆ *adv* tanto, così ; **it wasn't ~ bad/good** non era così cattivo/buono.
◆ *conj* che ; **tell him ~ I'm going to be late** digli che farò tardi.

---

thatched [θætʃt] *adj (roof)* di paglia.

that's [ðæts] = **that is**.

thaw [θɔ:] *vi (snow, ice)* sciogliersi. ◆ *vt (frozen food)* scongelare.

---

the [*weak form* ðə, *before vowel* ðɪ, *strong form* ði:] *definite article*
- 1. *(gen)* il/lo (la), i/gli (le) ; **~ book** il libro ; **~ man** l'uomo ; **~ mirror** lo specchio ; **~ woman** la donna ; **~ island** l'isola ; **~ men** gli uomini ; **~ girls** le ragazze ; **~ Wilsons** i Wilsons.
- 2. *(with an adjective to form a noun)* : **~ British** i britannici ; **~ young** i giovani.
- 3. *(in dates)* : **Friday ~ nineteenth of May** venerdì diciannove maggio ; **~ twelfth** il dodici ; **~ forties** gli anni quaranta.
- 4. *(in titles)* : **Elizabeth ~ Second** Elisabetta Seconda.

---

theater ['θɪətəʳ] *n Am (for plays, drama)* = **theatre** ; *(for films)* cinema *m inv*.

theatre ['θɪətəʳ] *n Br (for plays)* teatro *m*.

theft [θeft] *n* furto *m*.

their [ðeəʳ] *adj* il loro (la loro), i loro (le loro) *(pl)*.

theirs [ðeəz] *pron* il loro (la loro), i loro (le loro) *(pl)* ; **a friend of ~** un loro amico.

them [*weak form* ðəm, *strong form* ðem] *pron (direct)* li (le) ; *(indirect)* gli ; *(after prep with people)* loro ; *(after prep with things)* essi(e) ; **I know ~** li conosco ; **it's ~** sono loro ; **send it to ~** mandaglielo ; **tell ~** diglielo ; **he's worse than ~** è peggio di loro.

theme [θi:m] *n* tema *m*.

theme park *n* parco *m* di divertimenti.

themselves [ðəm'selvz] *pron (reflexive)* si ; *(after prep)* se stessi, (se stesse), sé ; **they did it ~** l'hanno fatto da soli.

then [ðen] *adv* allora ; *(next, afterwards)* dopo, poi ; **from ~ on** da allora in poi ; **until ~** fino ad allora.

theory ['θɪərɪ] *n* teoria *f* ; **in ~** in teoria.

therapist ['θerəpɪst] *n* terapeuta *mf*.

therapy ['θerəpɪ] *n* terapia *f*.

there [ðeəʳ] *adv (at, in, to that*

place) lì, là. ◆ *pron* : ~ **is** c'è ; ~ **are** ci sono ; **is anyone ~?** c'è nessuno? ; **is Bob ~, please?** *(on phone)* c'è Bob, per cortesia? ; **we're going ~ tomorrow** ci andiamo domani ; **over ~** laggiù ; ~ **you are** *(when giving)* ecco a lei.

thereabouts [ˌðeərə'bauts] *adv* : **or ~** o giù di lì.

therefore ['ðeəfɔːʳ] *adv* perciò.

there's [ðeəz] = **there is.**

thermal underwear [ˌθɜːml-] *n* biancheria *f* termica.

thermometer [θə'mɒmɪtəʳ] *n* termometro *m*.

Thermos (flask)® ['θɜːməs-] *n* thermos® *m inv*.

thermostat ['θɜːməstæt] *n* termostato *m*.

these [ðiːz] *pl* → **this.**

they [ðeɪ] *pron* essi (esse) ; *(referring to people)* loro ; **~'re tall** sono alti.

thick [θɪk] *adj (in size)* spesso(a) ; *(hair)* folto(a) ; *(sauce, smoke)* denso(a) ; *(fog)* fitto(a) ; *inf (stupid)* tonto(a) ; **it's one metre ~** ha uno spessore di un metro.

thicken ['θɪkn] *vt (sauce, soup)* rendere più denso. ◆ *vi (mist, fog)* infittirsi.

thickness ['θɪknɪs] *n* spessore *m*.

thief [θiːf] (*pl* **thieves** [θiːvz]) *n* ladro *m*, -a *f*.

thigh [θaɪ] *n* coscia *f*.

thimble ['θɪmbl] *n* ditale *m*.

thin [θɪn] *adj* sottile ; *(person, animal)* magro(a) ; *(soup, sauce)* liquido(a).

thing [θɪŋ] *n* cosa *f* ; **the ~ is** il fatto è. ❑ **things** *npl (clothes, possessions)* cose *fpl* ; **how are ~s?** *inf* come vanno le cose.

thingummyjig ['θɪŋəmɪdʒɪg] *n inf* coso *m*, -a *f*.

think [θɪŋk] (*pt* & *pp* **thought**) *vt* pensare. ◆ *vi* pensare ; **to ~ that** pensare che ; **to ~ about** pensare a ; **to ~ of** pensare a ; **to ~ of doing sthg** pensare di fare qc ; **I ~ so** penso di sì ; **I don't ~ so** penso di no ; **do you ~ you could...?** potrebbe...? ; **I'll think about it** ci penserò ; **I can't ~ of his address** non mi viene in mente il suo indirizzo ; **to ~ highly of sb** avere una buona opinione di qn. ❑ **think over** *vt sep* riflettere su. ❑ **think up** *vt sep* escogitare.

third [θɜːd] *num* terzo(a) → **sixth.**

third party insurance *n* assicurazione *f* contro terzi.

Third World *n* : **the ~** il Terzo Mondo.

thirst [θɜːst] *n* sete *f*.

thirsty ['θɜːstɪ] *adj* : **to be ~** avere sete.

thirteen [ˌθɜː'tiːn] *num* tredici → **six.**

thirteenth [ˌθɜː'tiːnθ] *num* tredicesimo(a) → **sixth.**

thirtieth ['θɜːtɪəθ] *num* trentesimo(a) → **sixth.**

thirty ['θɜːtɪ] *num* trenta → **six.**

☞

this [ðɪs] (*pl* **these**) *adj* - **1.** *(referring to thing, person mentioned)* questo ; **these chocolates are delicious** questi cioccolatini sono buonissimi ; ~ **morning** stamattina ; ~ **week** questa settimana.

- **2.** *(referring to thing, person nearer)* questo ; **I prefer ~ book** preferisco

questo libro ; **I'll have ~ one** prendo questo.
- 3. *inf (when telling a story)* : **there was ~ man ...** c'era un tizio ...
◆ *pron* - 1. *(referring to thing, person mentioned)* questo(a) ; **~ is for you** questo è per te ; **what are these?** che cosa sono questi? ; **~ is David Gregory** *(introducing someone)* questo è David Gregory ; *(on telephone)* sono David Gregory.
- 2. *(referring to thing, person nearer)* questo(a).
◆ *adv* : **it was ~ big** era grande così.
◆ *adv* : **it was ~ big.**

---

thistle ['θɪsl] *n* cardo *m.*
thorn [θɔːn] *n* spina *f.*
thorough ['θʌrə] *adj (check, search)* accurato(a) ; *(person)* preciso(a).
thoroughly ['θʌrəlɪ] *adv (completely)* a fondo.
those [ðəuz] *pl* → **that.**
though [ðəu] *conj* benché, sebbene. ◆ *adv* tuttavia ; **even ~** anche se.
thought [θɔːt] *pt* & *pp* → **think.** ◆ *n* pensiero *m* ; *(idea)* idea *f.*
thoughtful ['θɔːtful] *adj (quiet and serious)* pensieroso(a) ; *(considerate)* premuroso(a).
thoughtless ['θɔːtlɪs] *adj* sconsiderato(a).
thousand ['θauznd] *num* mille ; **a** OR **one ~** mille ; **~s of** migliaia di, six.
thrash [θræʃ] *vt inf (defeat heavily)* battere.
thread [θred] *n (of cotton etc)* filo *m.* ◆ *vt (needle)* infilare.
threadbare ['θredbeəʳ] *adj* logoro(a).
threat [θret] *n* minaccia *f.*
threaten ['θretn] *vt* minacciare ; **to ~ to do sthg** minacciare di fare qc.
threatening ['θretnɪŋ] *adj* minaccioso(a).
three [θriː] *num* tre → **six.**
three-D *n* : **in ~** tridimensionale.
three-piece suite *n* divano *m* e due poltrone coordinati.
three-quarters ['↓kwɔːtəz] *n* tre quarti *mpl* ; **~ of an hour** tre quarti d'ora.
threshold ['θreʃhəuld] *n fml* soglia *f.*
threw [θruː] *pt* → **throw.**
thrifty ['θrɪftɪ] *adj* parsimonioso(a).
thrilled [θrɪld] *adj* contentissimo(a).
thriller ['θrɪləʳ] *n* thriller *m inv.*
thrive [θraɪv] *vi (plant, animal, person)* crescere bene ; *(business, tourism, place)* prosperare.
throat [θrəut] *n* gola *f.*
throb [θrɒb] *vi (noise, engine)* vibrare ; **my head is throbbing** ho un mal di testa lancinante.
throne [θrəun] *n* trono *m.*
through [θruː] *prep* attraverso ; *(because of)* grazie a ; *(from beginning to end of)* per tutta la durata di ; *(across all of)* per tutto(a). ◆ *adv (to other side)* attraverso ; *(from beginning to end)* dall'inizio alla fine. ◆ *adj* : **to be ~ (with sthg)** *(finished)* avere finito (con qc) ; **you're ~** *(on phone)* è in linea ; **Monday ~ Thursday** *Am* dal lunedì al

giovedì ; **to go ~** *(to somewhere else)* passare ; **to let sb ~** far passare qn ; **I slept ~ the entire film** ho dormito per tutto il film ; **~ traffic** traffico *m* di attraversamento ; **a ~ train** un treno diretto ; **no ~ road** *Br* strada senza uscita.

throughout [θru:'aʊt] *prep (day, morning, year)* per tutto(a) ; *(place, country, building)* in tutto(a). ◆ *adv (all the time)* per tutto il tempo ; *(everywhere)* dappertutto.

throw [θrəʊ] (*pt* **threw**, *pp* **thrown** [θrəʊn]) *vt* gettare ; *(ball, javelin)* lanciare ; *(dice)* tirare ; **to ~ sthg in the bin** gettare qc nel cestino. ❑ **throw away** *vt sep (get rid of)* buttare OR gettare via. ❑ **throw out** *vt sep (get rid of)* buttare OR gettare via ; *(person)* buttare fuori. ❑ **throw up** *vi inf (vomit)* rimettere.

thru [θru:] *Am* = **through**.

thrush [θrʌʃ] *n (bird)* tordo *m*.

thud [θʌd] *n* tonfo *m*.

thug [θʌg] *n* delinquente *mf*.

thumb [θʌm] *n* pollice *m*. ◆ *vt* : **to ~ a lift** fare l'autostop.

thumbtack ['θʌmtæk] *n Am* puntina *f* da disegno.

thump [θʌmp] *n (punch)* pugno *m* ; *(sound)* tonfo *m*. ◆ *vt* picchiare.

thunder ['θʌndə'] *n* tuono *m*.

thunderstorm ['θʌndəstɔ:m] *n* temporale *m*.

Thurs. (*abbr of Thursday*) gio..

Thursday ['θɜ:zdɪ] *n* giovedì *m inv* → **Saturday**.

thyme [taɪm] *n* timo *m*.

Tiber ['taɪbə'] *n* : **the ~** il Tevere.

tick [tɪk] *n (written mark)* segno *m* ; *(insect)* zecca *f*. ◆ *vt* spuntare. ◆ *vi (clock, watch)* fare tic tac. ❑ **tick off** *vt sep (mark off)* spuntare.

ticket ['tɪkɪt] *n (for travel, cinema, theatre, match)* biglietto *m* ; *(label)* etichetta *f* ; *(speeding ticket, parking ticket)* multa *f*.

ticket collector *n* controllore *m*.

ticket inspector *n* controllore *m*.

ticket machine *n* distributore *m* automatico di biglietti.

ticket office *n* biglietteria *f*.

tickle ['tɪkl] *vt* fare il solletico a.

ticklish ['tɪklɪʃ] *adj* : **to be ~** soffrire il solletico.

tick-tack-toe *n Am* tris *m (gioco)*.

tide [taɪd] *n (of sea)* marea *f*.

tidy ['taɪdɪ] *adj (room, desk, person)* ordinato(a) ; *(hair, clothes)* in ordine. ❑ **tidy up** *vt sep* riordinare, mettere in ordine.

tie [taɪ] (*pt* & *pp* **tied**, *cont* **tying**) *n (around neck)* cravatta *f* ; *(draw)* pareggio *m* ; *Am (on railway track)* traversa *f*. ◆ *vt (fasten)* legare ; *(laces)* allacciare ; *(knot)* fare. ◆ *vi (draw)* pareggiare. ❑ **tie up** *vt sep (fasten)* legare ; *(laces)* annodare.

tied up ['taɪd-] *adj* occupato(a).

tier [tɪə'] *n (of seats)* fila *f*.

tiger ['taɪgə'] *n* tigre *f*.

tight [taɪt] *adj* stretto(a) ; *(rope)* teso(a) ; *(chest)* chiuso(a) ; *inf (drunk)* sbronzo(a). ◆ *adv (hold)* stretto(a).

tighten ['taɪtn] *vt* stringere.

tightrope ['taɪtrəʊp] *n* corda *f*

(sulla quale si esibiscono i funamboli).

tights [taɪts] *npl* collant *m inv* ; **a pair of ~** un paio di collant.

tile ['taɪl] *n (for roof)* tegola *f*; *(for floor, wall)* mattonella *f*, piastrella *f*.

till [tɪl] *n (for money)* cassa *f*. ◆ *prep* fino a. ◆ *conj* finché non.

tilt [tɪlt] *vt* inclinare. ◆ *vi* inclinarsi.

timber ['tɪmbəʳ] *n (wood)* legname *m* ; *(of roof)* trave *f*.

time [taɪm] *n* tempo *m* ; *(measured by clock)* ora *f* ; *(of train, flight, bus)* orario *m* ; *(moment)* momento *m* ; *(occasion)* volta *f*. ◆ *vt (measure)* cronometrare ; *(arrange)* programmare ; **to ~ sthg well** fare qc al momento giusto ; **I haven't got the ~** non ho tempo ; **it's ~ to go** è ora di andare ; **what's the ~?** che ore sono? ; **two ~s two** due per due ; **two at a ~** due per volta ; **five ~s as much** cinque volte tanto ; **in a month's ~** fra un mese ; **to have a good ~** divertirsi ; **all the ~** sempre ; **every ~** ogni volta ; **from ~ to ~** di tanto in tanto ; **for the ~ being** per il momento ; **in ~** *(arrive)* in tempo ; **in good ~** per tempo ; **last ~** l'ultima volta ; **most of the ~** la maggior parte del tempo ; **on ~** puntuale ; **some of the ~** parte del tempo ; **this ~** questa volta.

time difference *n* differenza *f* di fuso orario.

time limit *n* termine *m* massimo.

timer ['taɪməʳ] *n* timer *m inv*.

time share *n* multiproprietà *f inv*.

timetable ['taɪm,teɪbl] *n* orario *m* ; *(of events)* calendario *m*.

time zone *n* fuso *m* orario.

timid ['tɪmɪd] *adj (shy)* timido(a) ; *(easily frightened)* pauroso(a).

tin [tɪn] *n (metal)* stagno *m* ; *(container)* scatola *f*. ◆ *adj* di latta.

tinfoil ['tɪnfɔɪl] *n* stagnola *f*.

tinned food [tɪnd-] *n Br* cibo *m* in scatola.

tin opener [-,əʊpnəʳ] *n Br* apriscatole *m inv*.

tinsel ['tɪnsl] *n* fili *mpl* argentati *(per decorare l'albero di Natale)*.

tint [tɪnt] *n* tinta *f*.

tinted glass [,tɪntɪd-] *n* vetro *m* colorato.

tiny ['taɪnɪ] *adj* molto piccolo(a).

tip [tɪp] *n (point, end)* punta *f* ; *(to waiter, taxi driver etc)* mancia *f* ; *(piece of advice)* suggerimento *m* ; *(rubbish dump)* discarica *f*. ◆ *vt (waiter, taxi driver etc)* dare la mancia a ; *(tilt)* inclinare ; *(pour)* versare. ❑ **tip over** ◆ *vt sep* rovesciare. ◆ *vi* rovesciarsi.

i TIPPING

Sia negli Stati Uniti che in Gran Bretagna si usa dare la mancia a chiunque offra un servizio. Al bar e al ristorante si lascia di solito una mancia che può andare dal 12 al 20% del conto. Ai tassisti generalmente si lascia il 10 o il 15% in più rispetto al costo della corsa. La mancia per i portabagagli è di una sterlina in Gran Bretagna, mentre negli Stati Uniti è di un dollaro a valigia.

tire ['taɪəʳ] *vi* stancarsi. ◆ *n Am* = **tyre**.

tired ['taɪəd] *adj* stanco(a) ; **to be ~ of** *(fed up with)* essere stanco di.

tired out *adj* esausto(a).

tiring ['taɪərɪŋ] *adj* faticoso(a).

tissue ['tɪʃu:] *n (handkerchief)* fazzolettino *m* di carta.

tissue paper *n* carta *f* velina.

tit [tɪt] *n vulg (breast)* tetta *f*.

title ['taɪtl] *n* titolo *m*.

T-junction *n* incrocio *m* a T.

---

to [*unstressed before consonant* tə, *unstressed before vowel* tʊ, *stressed* tu:] *prep* - 1. *(indicating direction)* a ; **to go ~ Milan** andare a Milano ; **to go ~ France** andare in Francia ; **to go ~ school** andare a scuola ; **to go ~ the office** andare in ufficio.
- 2. *(indicating position)* a ; **~ the left/right** a sinistra/destra.
- 3. *(expressing indirect object)* a ; **to give sthg ~ sb** dare qc a qn ; **to listen ~ the radio** ascoltare la radio.
- 4. *(indicating reaction, effect)* a ; **to be favourable ~ sthg** essere favorevole a qc ; **~ my surprise** con mia grande sorpresa.
- 5. *(until)* fino a ; **to count ~ ten** contare fino a dieci ; **we work from nine ~ five** lavoriamo dalle nove alle cinque.
- 6. *(indicating change of state)* : **to turn ~ sthg** trasformarsi in qc ; **it could lead ~ trouble** potrebbe causare problemi.
- 7. *Br (in expressions of time)* : **it's ten ~ three** sono le tre meno dieci ; **at quarter ~ seven** alle sette meno un quarto.
- 8. *(in ratios, rates)* : **40 miles ~ the gallon** ≃ 100 chilometri con 7 litri ; **there are sixteen ounces ~ the pound** sedici once fanno una libbra.
- 9. *(of, for)* : **the keys ~ the car** le chiavi dell'automobile ; **a letter ~ my daughter** una lettera a mia figlia.
- 10. *(indicating attitude)* con, verso ; **to be rude ~ sb** essere scortese con qn.
◆ *with infinitive* - 1. *(forming simple infinitive)* : **~ walk** camminare ; **~ laugh** ridere.
- 2. *(following another verb)* : **to begin ~ do sthg** cominciare a fare qc ; **to try ~ do sthg** cercare di fare qc.
- 3. *(following an adjective)* : **difficult ~ do** difficile da fare ; **ready ~ go** pronto a partire.
- 4. *(indicating purpose)* per ; **we came here ~ look at the castle** siamo venuti qui per visitare il castello.

---

toad [təʊd] *n* rospo *m*.

toadstool ['təʊdstu:l] *n* fungo *m* velenoso.

toast [təʊst] *n (bread)* pane *m* tostato ; *(when drinking)* brindisi *m inv*. ◆ *vt (bread)* tostare ; **a piece** OR **slice of ~** una fetta di pane tostato.

toasted sandwich ['təʊstɪd-] *n* toast *m inv*.

toaster ['təʊstəʳ] *n* tostapane *m inv*.

toastie ['təʊstɪ] = **toasted sandwich**.

tobacco [tə'bækəʊ] *n* tabacco *m*.

tobacconist's [tə'bækənɪsts] *n (shop)* tabaccaio *m*.

toboggan [tə'bɒgən] *n* toboga *m inv*.

today [tə'deɪ] *n* oggi *m*. ◆ *adv* oggi.

toddler ['tɒdlə^r] *n* bambino *m*, -a *f (che muove i primi passi)*.

toe [təʊ] *n (of person)* dito *m* del piede.

toenail ['təʊneɪl] *n* unghia *f* del piede.

toffee ['tɒfɪ] *n (sweet)* caramella *f* mou *(inv)*.

together [tə'geðə^r] *adv* insieme ; ~ with insieme a.

toilet ['tɔɪlɪt] *n (room)* gabinetto *m* ; *(bowl)* water *m (inv)* ; to go to the ~ andare al gabinetto ; where's the ~? dov'è il gabinetto?

toilet bag *n* nécessaire *m inv* da toilette.

toilet paper *n* carta *f* igienica.

toiletries ['tɔɪlɪtrɪz] *npl* prodotti *mpl* cosmetici.

toilet roll *n* rotolo *m* di carta igienica.

toilet water *n* acqua *f* di colonia.

token ['təʊkn] *n (metal disc)* gettone *m*.

told [təʊld] *pt* & *pp* → tell.

tolerable ['tɒlərəbl] *adj (fairly good)* passabile ; *(bearable)* sopportabile.

tolerant ['tɒlərənt] *adj* tollerante.

tolerate ['tɒləreɪt] *vt* tollerare.

toll [təʊl] *n (for road, bridge)* pedaggio *m*.

toll-free *adj Am* : ~ number ≃ numero *m* verde.

tomato [*Br* tə'mɑːtəʊ, *Am* tə'meɪtəʊ] (*pl* -es) *n* pomodoro *m*.

tomato juice *n* succo *m* di pomodoro.

tomato ketchup *n* ketchup *m*.

tomato puree *n* conserva *f* di pomodoro.

tomato sauce *n* sugo *m* di pomodoro.

tomb [tuːm] *n* tomba *f*.

tomorrow [tə'mɒrəʊ] *n* domani *m*. ◆ *adv* domani ; the day after ~ dopodomani ; ~ afternoon domani pomeriggio ; ~ morning domani mattina ; ~ night domani sera.

ton [tʌn] *n (in Britain)* = 1016 kg ; *(in U.S.)* = 907 kg ; *(metric tonne)* tonnellata *f* ; ~s of *inf* un sacco di.

tone [təʊn] *n (of voice)* tono *m* ; *(on phone)* segnale *m* ; *(of colour)* tonalità *f inv*.

tongs [tɒŋz] *npl (for hair)* arricciacapelli *m inv* ; *(for sugar)* mollette *fpl*.

tongue [tʌŋ] *n* lingua *f*.

tonic ['tɒnɪk] *n (tonic water)* acqua *f* tonica ; *(medicine)* ricostituente *m*.

tonic water *n* acqua *f* tonica.

tonight [tə'naɪt] *n (night)* questa notte *f* ; *(evening)* questa sera *f*. ◆ *adv (night)* stanotte, questa notte ; *(evening)* stasera, questa sera.

tonne [tʌn] *n* tonnellata *f*.

tonsillitis [ˌtɒnsɪ'laɪtɪs] *n* tonsillite *f*.

too [tuː] *adv (excessively)* troppo ; *(also)* anche ; it's ~ late to go out è troppo tardi per uscire ; ~ many troppi(e) ; ~ much troppo(a).

took [tʊk] *pt* → take.

tool [tu:l] *n* attrezzo *m*.
tool kit *n* attrezzi *mpl*.
tooth [tu:θ] (*pl* **teeth**) *n* dente *m*.
toothache ['tu:θeɪk] *n* mal *m* di denti.
toothbrush ['tu:θbrʌʃ] *n* spazzolino *m* da denti.
toothpaste ['tu:θpeɪst] *n* dentifricio *m*.
toothpick ['tu:θpɪk] *n* stuzzicadenti *m*.
top [tɒp] *adj (highest)* più alto(a) ; *(step, stair)* ultimo(a) ; *(best)* migliore ; *(most important)* più importante. ◆ *n (of stairs, hill, page)* cima *f* ; *(of table)* piano *m* ; *(of class, league)* primo *m*, -a *f* ; *(for bottle, tube)* tappo *m* ; *(for jar, box)* coperchio *m* ; *(of pyjamas, bikini)* sopra *m inv* ; *(blouse)* camicetta *f* ; *(T-shirt)* maglietta *f* ; **at the ~ (of)** *(stairs, list, mountain)* in cima (a) ; **on ~ of** *(table etc)* sopra , su ; *(in addition to)* oltre a ; **at ~ speed** a tutta velocità ; **~ gear** ≃ quinta *f*. ❑ **top up** ◆ *vt sep (glass, drink)* riempire. ◆ *vi (with petrol)* fare il pieno.
top floor *n* ultimo piano *m*.
topic ['tɒpɪk] *n* argomento *m*.
topical ['tɒpɪkl] *adj* d'attualità.
topless ['tɒplɪs] *adj* : **to go ~** mettersi in topless.
topped [tɒpt] *adj* : **~ with** *(cream etc)* ricoperto di.
topping ['tɒpɪŋ] *n* guarnizione *f (su pizza ecc.)*.
torch [tɔ:tʃ] *n Br (electric light)* torcia *f* elettrica.
tore [tɔ:ʳ] *pt* → **tear** [1].
torn [tɔ:n] *pp* → **tear** [1]. ◆ *adj (ripped)* strappato(a).
tortoise ['tɔ:təs] *n* tartaruga *f*.
tortoiseshell ['tɔ:təʃel] *n* tartaruga *f*.
torture ['tɔ:tʃəʳ] *n* tortura *f*. ◆ *vt* torturare.
Tory ['tɔ:rɪ] *n membro del partito conservatore britannico*.
toss [tɒs] *vt (throw)* lanciare ; *(salad, vegetables)* mescolare ; **to ~ a coin** fare testa o croce.
total ['təʊtl] *adj* totale. ◆ *n* totale *m* ; **in ~** in totale.
touch [tʌtʃ] *n (sense)* tatto *m* ; *(small amount)* tantino *m* ; *(detail)* tocco *m*. ◆ *vt* toccare. ◆ *vi* toccarsi ; **to get in ~ (with sb)** mettersi in contatto (con qn) ; **to keep in ~ (with sb)** tenersi in contatto (con qn). ❑ **touch down** *vi (plane)* atterrare.
touching ['tʌtʃɪŋ] *adj* toccante.
tough [tʌf] *adj* duro(a) ; *(resilient)* tenace ; *(hard, strong)* resistente.
tour [tʊəʳ] *n (journey)* viaggio *m* ; *(of city, castle etc)* visita *f* ; *(of pop group, theatre company)* tournée *f inv*. ◆ *vt* visitare ; **on ~** in tournée.
tourism ['tʊərɪzm] *n* turismo *m*.
tourist ['tʊərɪst] *n* turista *mf*.
tourist class *n* classe *f* turistica.
tourist information office *n* ufficio *m* d'informazione turistica.
tournament ['tɔ:nəmənt] *n* torneo *m*.
tour operator *n* operatore *m* turistico, (operatrice turistica *f*).
tout [taʊt] *n* bagarino *m*.
tow [təʊ] *vt* rimorchiare.
toward [tə'wɔ:d] *Am* = **towards**.

towards [tə'wɔːdz] *prep [Br]* verso ; *(with regard to)* nei confronti di ; *(to help pay for)* per.
towel ['tauəl] *n* asciugamano *m*.
toweling ['tauəlɪŋ] *Am* = **towelling**.
towelling ['tauəlɪŋ] *n Br* spugna *f*.
towel rail *n* portasciugamano *m*.
tower ['tauə^r] *n* torre *f*.
tower block *n Br* grattacielo *m*.
Tower Bridge *n* Tower Bridge *(famoso ponte levatoio di Londra)*.

TOWER BRIDGE

Costruito in stile gotico nel diciannovesimo secolo, questo ponte sul Tamigi è costituito da due caratteristici ponti levatoi gemelli che si alzano per permettere il passaggio delle navi più grandi.

Tower of London *n* : the ~ la Torre di Londra.

TOWER OF LONDON

Situata sulla riva nord del Tamigi, la Torre di Londra è una fortezza che risale all'undicesimo secolo e fu residenza reale fino al diciassettesimo secolo. Oggi è un'attrazione turistica aperta al pubblico e ospita al suo interno un museo.

town [taun] *n* città *f* ; *(town centre)* centro *m* (città).
town centre *n* centro *m* (città).
town hall *n* comune *m*.
towpath ['təupaːθ, *pl* -paːðz] *n* alzaia *f*.
towrope ['təurəup] *n* cavo *m* di rimorchio.
tow truck *n Am* carro *m* attrezzi.
toxic ['tɒksɪk] *adj* tossico(a).
toy [tɔɪ] *n* giocattolo *m*.
toy shop *n* negozio *m* di giocattoli.
trace [treɪs] *n* traccia *f*. ◆ *vt (find)* rintracciare.
tracing paper ['treɪsɪŋ-] *n* carta *f* da ricalco.
track [træk] *n (path)* sentiero *m* ; *(of railway)* binario *m*, rotaie *fpl* ; SPORT pista *f* ; *(song)* pezzo *m*. ❑ **track down** *vt sep* trovare.
tracksuit ['træksuːt] *n* tuta *f* da ginnastica.
tractor ['træktə^r] *n* trattore *m*.
trade [treɪd] *n* COMM commercio *m* ; *(job)* mestiere *m*. ◆ *vt* scambiare. ◆ *vi* commerciare.
trademark ['treɪdmaːk] *n* marchio *m* di fabbrica.
trader ['treɪdə^r] *n* commerciante *mf*.
tradesman ['treɪdzmən] (*pl* **-men** [-mən]) *n (deliveryman)* addetto *m* alle consegne ; *(shopkeeper)* commerciante *mf*.
trade union *n* sindacato *m*.
tradition [trə'dɪʃn] *n* tradizione *f*.
traditional [trə'dɪʃənl] *adj* tradizionale.
traffic ['træfɪk] (*pt* & *pp* **-ked**) *n (cars etc)* traffico *m*. ◆ *vi* : **to ~ in** trafficare in.
traffic circle *n Am* rotatoria *f*.

traffic island *n* salvagente *m*.
traffic jam *n* ingorgo *m*.
traffic lights *npl* semaforo *m*.
traffic warden *n Br* ≃ vigile *m* urbano *(addetto al controllo dei divieti e limiti di sosta)*.
tragedy ['trædʒədɪ] *n* tragedia *f*.
tragic ['trædʒɪk] *adj* tragico(a).
trail [treɪl] *n (path)* sentiero *m* ; *(marks)* tracce *fpl*. ◆ *vi (be losing)* essere in svantaggio.
trailer ['treɪlə^r] *n (for boat, luggage)* rimorchio *m* ; *Am (caravan)* roulotte *f inv* ; *(for film, programme)* trailer *m inv*.
train [treɪn] *n (on railway)* treno *m*. ◆ *vt (teach)* formare ; *(animal)* addestrare. ◆ *vi* SPORT allenarsi ; by ~ in treno.
train driver *n* macchinista *m*.
trainee [treɪ'ni:] *n (for profession)* tirocinante *mf* ; *(for trade)* apprendista *mf*.
trainer ['treɪnə^r] *n (of athlete etc)* allenatore *m*, -trice *f*. ❑ **trainers** *npl Br (shoes)* scarpe *fpl* da ginnastica.
training ['treɪnɪŋ] *n (instruction)* formazione *f*, addestramento *m* ; *(exercises)* allenamento *m*.
training shoes *npl Br* scarpe *fpl* da ginnastica.
tram [træm] *n Br* tram *m inv*.
tramp [træmp] *n* vagabondo *m*, -a *f*.
trampoline ['træmpəli:n] *n* trampolino *m*.
trance [trɑ:ns] *n* trance *f*.
tranquilizer ['træŋkwɪlaɪzər] *Am* = **tranquillizer**.
tranquillizer ['træŋkwɪlaɪzə^r] *n Br* tranquillante *m*.
transaction [træn'zækʃn] *n* transazione *f*.
transatlantic [ˌtrænzət'læntɪk] *adj* transatlantico(a).
transfer [*n* 'trænsfɜ:^r, *vb* træns'fɜ:^r] *n* trasferimento *m* ; *(of power, property)* passaggio *m* ; *(picture)* decalcomania *f* ; *Am (ticket) biglietto che dà la possibilità di cambiare autobus, treno ecc. senza pagare alcun supplemento*. ◆ *vt* trasferire. ◆ *vi (change bus, plane etc)* cambiare ; '~s' *(in airport)* 'transiti'.
transform [træns'fɔ:m] *vt* trasformare.
transfusion [træns'fju:ʒn] *n* trasfusione *f*.
transit ['trænzɪt] ◆**in transit** *adv* in transito.
transitive ['trænzɪtɪv] *adj* transitivo(a).
transit lounge *n* sala *f* transiti.
translate [træns'leɪt] *vt* tradurre.
translation [træns'leɪʃn] *n* traduzione *f*.
translator [træns'leɪtə^r] *n* traduttore *m*, -trice *f*.
transmission [trænz'mɪʃn] *n* trasmissione *f*.
transmit [trænz'mɪt] *vt* trasmettere.
transparent [træns'pærənt] *adj* trasparente.
transplant ['trænsplɑ:nt] *n* trapianto *m*.
transport [*n* 'trænspɔ:t, *vb* træn'spɔ:t] *n (cars, trains, planes etc)* tra-

sporti *mpl* ; *(moving)* trasporto *m*. ◆ *vt* trasportare.

transportation [ˌtrænspɔːˈteɪʃn] *n Am (cars, trains, planes etc)* trasporti *mpl* ; *(moving)* trasporto *m*.

trap [træp] *n* trappola *f*. ◆ *vt* : **to be trapped** *(stuck)* essere intrappolato.

trash [træʃ] *n Am (waste material)* spazzatura *f*.

trashcan [ˈtræʃkæn] *n Am* pattumiera *f*.

trauma [ˈtrɔːmə] *n (bad experience)* trauma *m*.

traumatic [trɔːˈmætɪk] *adj* traumatico(a).

travel [ˈtrævl] *n* viaggi *mpl*. ◆ *vt (distance)* percorrere. ◆ *vi* viaggiare.

travel agency *n* agenzia *f* di viaggi.

travel agent *n* agente *mf* di viaggi ; **~'s** *(shop)* agenzia *f* di viaggi.

travel centre *n (in railway, bus station) ufficio informazioni e biglietteria.*

traveler [ˈtrævlər] *Am* = **traveller**.

travel insurance *n* assicurazione *f* viaggio.

traveller [ˈtrævləʳ] *n Br* viaggiatore *m*, -trice *f*.

traveller's cheque *n* traveller's cheque *m inv*.

travelsick [ˈtrævəlsɪk] *adj* : **to be ~** *(in car)* soffrire il mal d'auto ; *(on boat)* soffrire il mal di mare ; *(on plane)* soffrire il mal d'aria.

tray [treɪ] *n* vassoio *m*.

treacherous [ˈtretʃərəs] *adj (person)* infido(a) ; *(roads, conditions)* insidioso(a).

treacle [ˈtriːkl] *n Br* melassa *f*.

tread [tred] (*pt* **trod**, *pp* **trodden**) *n (of tyre)* battistrada *m inv*. ◆ *vi* : **to ~ on sthg** calpestare qc.

treasure [ˈtreʒəʳ] *n* tesoro *m*.

treat [triːt] *vt* trattare ; *(patient, illness)* curare. ◆ *n* regalo *m* ; **to ~ sb to sthg** offrire qc a qn.

treatment [ˈtriːtmənt] *n MED* cure *fpl* ; *(of person)* trattamento *m* ; *(of subject)* trattazione *f*.

treble [ˈtrebl] *adj* triplo(a).

tree [triː] *n* albero *m*.

trek [trek] *n* escursione *f*.

tremble [ˈtrembl] *vi* tremare.

tremendous [trɪˈmendəs] *adj (very large)* enorme ; *inf (very good)* formidabile.

trench [trentʃ] *n* fosso *m*.

trend [trend] *n (tendency)* tendenza *f* ; *(fashion)* moda *f*.

trendy [ˈtrendɪ] *adj inf* alla moda.

trespasser [ˈtrespəsəʳ] *n* : **'~s will be prosecuted'** 'vietato l'accesso. I trasgressori saranno puniti ai termini di legge'.

trial [ˈtraɪəl] *n JUR* processo *m* ; *(test)* prova *f* ; **a ~ period** un periodo di prova.

triangle [ˈtraɪæŋgl] *n* triangolo *m*.

triangular [traɪˈæŋgjuləʳ] *adj* triangolare.

tribe [traɪb] *n* tribù *f inv*.

trick [trɪk] *n* trucco *m* ; *(conjuring trick)* gioco *m* di prestigio. ◆ *vt* imbrogliare, ingannare ; **to play a ~ on sb** giocare un brutto tiro a qn.

trickle ['trɪkl] *vi (liquid)* gocciolare, colare.
tricky ['trɪkɪ] *adj* difficile.
tricycle ['traɪsɪkl] *n* triciclo *m*.
trifle ['traɪfl] *n (dessert)* zuppa *f* inglese.
trigger ['trɪgə'] *n* grilletto *m*.
trim [trɪm] *n (haircut)* spuntata *f*. ◆ *vt (hair, beard)* spuntare ; *(hedge)* regolare.
trio ['tri:əʊ] *(pl -s) n* trio *m*.
trip [trɪp] *n (journey)* viaggio *m* ; *(short)* gita *f*, escursione *f*. ◆ *vi* inciampare. ❑ **trip up** *vi* inciampare.
triple ['trɪpl] *adj* triplo(a).
tripod ['traɪpɒd] *n* treppiedi *m inv*.
triumph ['traɪəmf] *n* trionfo *m*.
trivial ['trɪvɪəl] *adj pej* insignificante, banale.
trod [trɒd] *pt* → **tread**.
trodden ['trɒdn] *pp* → **tread**.
trolley ['trɒlɪ] *(pl -s) n Br (in supermarket, at airport, for food)* carrello *m* ; *Am (tram)* tram *m inv*.
trombone [trɒm'bəʊn] *n* trombone *m*.
troops [tru:ps] *npl* truppe *fpl*.
trophy ['trəʊfɪ] *n* trofeo *m*.
tropical ['trɒpɪkl] *adj* tropicale.
trot [trɒt] *vi (horse)* trottare. ◆ *n* : **on the ~** *inf* di fila.
trouble ['trʌbl] *n* problemi *mpl*. ◆ *vt (worry)* preoccupare ; *(bother)* disturbare ; **to be in ~** essere nei guai ; **to get into ~** mettersi nei guai ; **to take the ~ to do sthg** darsi la pena di fare qc ; **it's no ~** non si preoccupi ; *(in reply to thanks)* di niente.
trousers ['traʊzəz] *npl* pantaloni *mpl* ; **a pair of ~** un paio di pantaloni.
trout [traʊt] *(pl inv) n* trota *f*.
trowel ['traʊəl] *n (for gardening)* paletta *f*.
truant ['tru:ənt] *n* : **to play ~** marinare la scuola.
truce [tru:s] *n* tregua *f*.
truck [trʌk] *n (lorry)* camion *m inv*, autocarro *m*.
true [tru:] *adj* vero(a).
truly ['tru:lɪ] *adv* : **yours ~** distinti saluti.
trumpet ['trʌmpɪt] *n* tromba *f*.
trumps [trʌmps] *npl* atout *m inv*.
truncheon ['trʌntʃən] *n* sfollagente *m inv*.
trunk [trʌŋk] *n (of tree)* tronco *m* ; *Am (of car)* bagagliaio *m* ; *(case, box)* baule *m* ; *(of elephant)* proboscide *f*.
trunk call *n Br* interurbana *f*.
trunk road *n Br* strada *f* statale.
trunks [trʌŋks] *npl* costume *m* da bagno da uomo.
trust [trʌst] *n (confidence)* fiducia *f*. ◆ *vt (believe, have confidence in)* fidarsi di, aver fiducia in ; *fml (hope)* sperare.
trustworthy ['trʌst,wɜ:ðɪ] *adj* degno di fiducia.
truth [tru:θ] *n (true facts)* verità *f* ; *(quality of being true)* veridicità *f*.
truthful ['tru:θfʊl] *adj (statement, account)* veritiero(a) ; *(person)* sincero(a).
try [traɪ] *n (attempt)* tentativo *m*, prova *f*. ◆ *vt* provare ; JUR giudicare. ◆ *vi* provare ; **to ~ to do sthg** provare a fare qc. ❑ **try on** *vt sep*

(clothes) provare, provarsi. ❑ **try out** *vt sep* provare.
T-shirt *n* maglietta *f.*
tub [tʌb] *n (of margarine etc)* vaschetta *f*; *inf (bath)* vasca *f* (da bagno).
tube [tju:b] *n (container)* tubetto *m*; *Br inf (underground)* metropolitana *f*; *(pipe)* tubo *m*; **by ~** in metropolitana.
tube station *n Br inf* stazione *f* della metropolitana.
tuck [tʌk] ◆**tuck in** *vt sep (shirt)* mettersi dentro; *(child, person)* rimboccare le coperte a. ◆ *vi inf* mangiare di buon appetito.
tuck shop *n Br piccolo negozio di merendine, caramelle ecc., presso una scuola.*
Tues. *(abbr of Tuesday)* mar.
Tuesday ['tju:zdɪ] *n* martedì *m inv* → **Saturday**.
tuft [tʌft] *n* ciuffo *m.*
tug [tʌg] *vt* tirare. ◆ *n (boat)* rimorchiatore *m.*
tuition [tju:'ɪʃn] *n* lezioni *fpl.*
tulip ['tju:lɪp] *n* tulipano *m.*
tumble-dryer ['tʌmbldraɪəʳ] *n* asciugabiancheria *m inv.*
tumbler ['tʌmbləʳ] *n (glass)* bicchiere *m (senza stelo).*
tummy ['tʌmɪ] *n inf* pancia *f.*
tummy upset *n inf* disturbi *mpl* di pancia.
tumor ['tu:mər] *Am* = **tumour**.
tumour ['tju:məʳ] *n Br* tumore *m.*
tuna (fish) [*Br* 'tju:nə, *Am* 'tu:nə-] *n (food)* tonno *m.*
tune [tju:n] *n (melody)* melodia *f.* ◆ *vt (radio, TV)* sintonizzare; *(engine)* mettere a punto; *(instrument)* accordare; **in ~** *(person)* intonato; *(instrument)* accordato; **out of ~** *(person)* stonato; *(instrument)* scordato.
tunic ['tju:nɪk] *n* tunica *f.*
tunnel ['tʌnl] *n* tunnel *m inv*, galleria *f.*
turban ['tɜ:bən] *n* turbante *m.*
turbulence ['tɜ:bjʊləns] *n (when flying)* turbolenza *f.*
turf [tɜ:f] *n (grass)* tappeto *m* erboso.
Turin [tjʊ'rɪn] *n* Torino *f.*
turkey ['tɜ:kɪ] (*pl* **-s**) *n* tacchino *m.*
turn [tɜ:n] *n (in road)* curva *f*; *(of knob, key, switch)* giro *m*; *(go, chance)* turno *m.* ◆ *vt* girare; *(a bend)* prendere; *(become)* diventare; *(cause to become)* far diventare. ◆ *vi* girare; *(person)* girarsi; *(milk)* andare a male; **to ~ into sthg** *(become)* diventare qc; **to ~ sthg into sthg** trasformare qc in qc; **to ~ left/right** girare a sinistra/a destra; **it's your ~** tocca a te; **at the ~ of the century** all'inizio del secolo; **to take it in ~s to do sthg** fare qc a turno; **to ~ sthg inside out** rigirare qc. ❑ **turn back** ◆ *vt sep (person, car)* mandare indietro. ◆ *vi* tornare indietro. ❑ **turn down** *vt sep (radio, volume, heating)* abbassare; *(offer, request)* rifiutare. ❑ **turn off** ◆ *vt sep (light, TV, engine)* spegnere; *(water, gas, tap)* chiudere. ◆ *vi (leave road)* girare, svoltare. ❑ **turn on** *vt sep (light, TV, engine)* accendere; *(water, gas, tap)* aprire. ❑ **turn out** ◆ *vt fus (be in the end)* rivelarsi. ◆ *vt sep (light, fire)* spegnere. ◆ *vi (come, attend)* af-

fluire ; **to ~ out to be sthg** risultare essere qc. ❑ **turn over** ◆ *vi (in bed)* girarsi, rigirarsi ; *Br (change channels)* cambiare canale. ◆ *vt sep* girare. ❑ **turn round** ◆ *vt sep (car, table etc)* girare. ◆ *vi (person)* girarsi, voltarsi. ❑ **turn up** ◆ *vt sep (radio, volume, heating)* alzare. ◆ *vi (come)* venire.

turning ['tɜːnɪŋ] *n (off road)* svolta *f*.

turnip ['tɜːnɪp] *n* rapa *f*.

turn-up *n Br (on trousers)* risvolto *m*.

turquoise ['tɜːkwɔɪz] *adj* turchese.

turtle ['tɜːtl] *n* tartaruga *f* (acquatica).

turtleneck ['tɜːtlnek] *n* maglione *m* a collo alto.

Tuscany ['tʌskənɪ] *n* la Toscana.

tutor ['tjuːtəʳ] *n (private teacher)* insegnante *m* privato, insegnante privata *f*.

tuxedo [tʌk'siːdəʊ] (*pl* **-s**) *n Am* smoking *m inv*.

TV *n* tivù *f inv*, TV *f inv* ; **on ~** alla tivù.

tweed [twiːd] *n* tweed *m inv*.

tweezers ['twiːzəz] *npl* pinzette *fpl*.

twelfth [twelfθ] *num* dodicesimo(a) → **sixth**.

twelve [twelv] *num* dodici → **six**.

twentieth ['twentɪəθ] *num* ventesimo(a) ; **the ~ century** il ventesimo secolo, sixth.

twenty ['twentɪ] *num* venti → **six**.

twice [twaɪs] *adv* due volte ; **it's ~ as good** è due volte meglio ; **~ as much** il doppio.

twig [twɪg] *n* ramoscello *m*.

twilight ['twaɪlaɪt] *n* crepuscolo *m*.

twin [twɪn] *n* gemello *m*, -a *f*.

twin beds *npl* letti *mpl* gemelli.

twist [twɪst] *vt (wire)* torcere, piegare ; *(rope, hair)* attorcigliare ; *(bottle top, lid, knob)* girare ; **to ~ one's ankle** slogarsi la caviglia.

twisting ['twɪstɪŋ] *adj (road, river)* tortuoso *m*, -a *f*.

two [tuː] *num* due → **six**.

two-piece *adj (swimsuit, suit)* a due pezzi *(inv)*.

type [taɪp] *n (kind)* tipo *m*. ◆ *vt* battere a macchina. ◆ *vi* battere a macchina.

typewriter ['taɪpˌraɪtəʳ] *n* macchina *f* da scrivere.

typhoid ['taɪfɔɪd] *n* febbre *f* tifoide.

typical ['tɪpɪkl] *adj* tipico(a).

typist ['taɪpɪst] *n* dattilografo *m*, -a *f*.

tyre ['taɪəʳ] *n Br* gomma *f*, pneumatico *m*.

U

U *adj Br (film)* per tutti.

UFO *n* (*abbr of unidentified flying object*) UFO *m inv*.

ugly ['ʌglɪ] *adj* brutto(a).

UHT *adj* (*abbr of ultra heat treated*) UHT.

UK *n* : **the ~** il Regno Unito.

ulcer ['ʌlsəʳ] *n* ulcera *f*.

Ulster ['ʌlstəʳ] *n* l'Ulster *m*.
ultimate ['ʌltɪmət] *adj (final)* finale ; *(best, greatest)* ideale.
ultraviolet [ˌʌltrə'vaɪələt] *adj* ultravioletto(a).
umbrella [ʌm'brelə] *n* ombrello *m*.
umpire ['ʌmpaɪəʳ] *n* arbitro *m*.
UN *n (abbr of United Nations)*: the ~ l'ONU *f*.
unable [ʌn'eɪbl] *adj* : to be ~ to do sthg non poter fare qc.
unacceptable [ˌʌnək'septəbl] *adj* inaccettabile.
unaccustomed [ˌʌnə'kʌstəmd] *adj* : to be ~ to sthg non essere abituato(a) a qc.
unanimous [juː'nænɪməs] *adj* unanime.
unattended [ˌʌnə'tendɪd] *adj (baggage)* incustodito(a).
unattractive [ˌʌnə'træktɪv] *adj (person, idea)* poco attraente ; *(place)* privo(a) di attrattiva.
unauthorized [ˌʌn'ɔːθəraɪzd] *adj* non autorizzato(a).
unavailable [ˌʌnə'veɪləbl] *adj* non disponibile.
unavoidable [ˌʌnə'vɔɪdəbl] *adj* inevitabile.
unaware [ˌʌnə'weəʳ] *adj* : to be ~ of sthg/that ignorare qc/che.
unbearable [ʌn'beərəbl] *adj* insopportabile.
unbelievable [ˌʌnbɪ'liːvəbl] *adj* incredibile.
unbutton [ˌʌn'bʌtn] *vt* sbottonare.
uncertain [ʌn'sɜːtn] *adj* incerto(a).
uncertainty [ˌʌn'sɜːtntɪ] *n* incertezza *f*.
uncle ['ʌŋkl] *n* zio *m*.
unclean [ˌʌn'kliːn] *adj* sporco(a).
unclear [ˌʌn'klɪəʳ] *adj* non chiaro(a).
uncomfortable [ˌʌn'kʌmftəbl] *adj (person, chair)* scomodo(a) ; *fig (awkward)* a disagio.
uncommon [ʌn'kɒmən] *adj (rare)* raro(a).
unconscious [ʌn'kɒnʃəs] *adj (after accident)* privo(a) di sensi ; *(unaware)* inconsapevole.
unconvincing [ˌʌnkən'vɪnsɪŋ] *adj* poco convincente.
uncooperative [ˌʌnkəʊ'ɒpərətɪv] *adj* poco disposto(a) a collaborare.
uncork [ˌʌn'kɔːk] *vt* stappare.
uncouth [ʌn'kuːθ] *adj* villano(a), grossolano(a).
uncover [ʌn'kʌvəʳ] *vt* scoprire.
under ['ʌndəʳ] *prep* sotto ; *(less than)* meno di, al di sotto di ; *(according to)* secondo ; children ~ ten bambini sotto i dieci anni ; ~ the circumstances date le circostanze ; to be ~ pressure essere sotto pressione.
underage [ʌndər'eɪdʒ] *adj* minorenne.
undercarriage ['ʌndəˌkærɪdʒ] *n* carrello *m*.
underdone [ˌʌndə'dʌn] *adj* poco cotto(a).
underestimate [ˌʌndər'estɪmeɪt] *vt* sottovalutare.
underexposed [ˌʌndərɪk'spəʊzd] *adj (photograph)* sottoesposto(a).

undergo [ˌʌndəˈgəʊ] (*pt* **-went**, *pp* **-gone**) *vt* subire.

undergraduate [ˌʌndəˈgrædjʊət] *n* studente *m* universitario, studentessa universitaria *f*.

underground [ˈʌndəgraʊnd] *adj* *(below earth's surface)* sotterraneo(a) ; *(secret)* clandestino(a). ◆ *n Br (railway)* metropolitana *f*.

undergrowth [ˈʌndəgrəʊθ] *n* sottobosco *m*.

underline [ˌʌndəˈlaɪn] *vt* sottolineare.

underneath [ˌʌndəˈniːθ] *prep* & *adv* sotto. ◆ *n* sotto *m*.

underpants [ˈʌndəpænts] *npl* mutande *fpl*, slip *m inv*.

underpass [ˈʌndəpaːs] *n* sottopassaggio *m*.

undershirt [ˈʌndəʃɜːt] *n Am* maglietta *f*.

underskirt [ˈʌndəskɜːt] *n* sottoveste *f*.

understand [ˌʌndəˈstænd] (*pt* & *pp* **-stood**) *vt* capire ; *(believe)* credere. ◆ *vi* capire ; **I don't ~** non capisco ; **to make o.s. understood** farsi capire.

understanding [ˌʌndəˈstændɪŋ] *adj* comprensivo(a). ◆ *n (agreement)* accordo *m* ; *(knowledge)* conoscenza *f* ; *(interpretation)* interpretazione *f* ; *(sympathy)* comprensione *f*.

understatement [ˌʌndəˈsteɪtmənt] *n* : **that's an ~!** a dir poco!

understood [ˌʌndəˈstʊd] *pt* & *pp* → **understand**.

undertake [ˌʌndəˈteɪk] (*pt* **-took**, *pp* **-taken**) *vt* intraprendere ; **to ~ to do sthg** impegnarsi a fare qc.

undertaker [ˈʌndəˌteɪkə^r] *n* impresario di pompe funebri.

undertaking [ˌʌndəˈteɪkɪŋ] *n* *(promise)* promessa *f* ; *(task)* impresa *f*.

undertook [ˌʌndəˈtʊk] *pt* → **undertake**.

underwater [ˌʌndəˈwɔːtə^r] *adj* subacqueo(a). ◆ *adv* sott'acqua.

underwear [ˈʌndəweə^r] *n* biancheria *f* intima.

underwent [ˌʌndəˈwent] *pt* → **undergo**.

undo [ˌʌnˈduː] (*pt* **-did**, *pp* **-done**) *vt* *(coat, shirt)* sbottonare ; *(shoelaces)* slacciare ; *(tie)* sciogliere il nodo di ; *(parcel)* sfare.

undone [ˌʌnˈdʌn] *adj* *(coat, shirt)* sbottonato(a) ; *(shoelaces)* slacciato(a).

undress [ˌʌnˈdres] *vi* spogliarsi. ◆ *vt* spogliare.

undressed [ˌʌnˈdrest] *adj* spogliato(a) ; **to get ~** spogliarsi.

uneasy [ʌnˈiːzɪ] *adj* a disagio.

uneducated [ˌʌnˈedjʊkeɪtɪd] *adj* non istruito(a).

unemployed [ˌʌnɪmˈplɔɪd] *adj* disoccupato(a). ◆ *npl* : **the ~** i disoccupati.

unemployment [ˌʌnɪmˈplɔɪmənt] *n* disoccupazione *f*.

unemployment benefit *n* sussidio *m* di disoccupazione.

unequal [ˌʌnˈiːkwəl] *adj* *(not the same)* disuguale ; *(not fair)* iniquo(a).

uneven [ˌʌnˈiːvn] *adj* *(surface,*

speed, beat) irregolare ; *(share, distribution)* ineguale.

uneventful [ˌʌnɪ'ventful] *adj* tranquillo(a).

unexpected [ˌʌnɪk'spektɪd] *adj* inaspettato(a).

unexpectedly [ˌʌnɪk'spektɪdlɪ] *adv* inaspettatamente.

unfair [ˌʌn'feəʳ] *adj* ingiusto(a).

unfairly [ˌʌn'feəlɪ] *adv* ingiustamente.

unfaithful [ˌʌn'feɪθful] *adj* infedele.

unfamiliar [ˌʌnfə'mɪljəʳ] *adj* sconosciuto(a) ; **to be ~ with** non conoscere bene.

unfashionable [ˌʌn'fæʃnəbl] *adj* fuori moda.

unfasten [ˌʌn'fɑːsn] *vt (seatbelt, belt, laces)* slacciare ; *(knot)* disfare, sciogliere.

unfavourable [ˌʌn'feɪvrəbl] *adj* sfavorevole.

unfinished [ˌʌn'fɪnɪʃt] *adj* incompiuto(a).

unfit [ˌʌn'fɪt] *adj (not healthy)* non in forma ; **to be ~ for sthg** *(not suitable)* essere inadatto(a) a qc.

unfold [ʌn'fəuld] *vt* spiegare ; *(tovaglia)* cartina.

unforgettable [ˌʌnfə'getəbl] *adj* indimenticabile.

unforgivable [ˌʌnfə'gɪvəbl] *adj* imperdonabile.

unfortunate [ʌn'fɔːtʃnət] *adj (unlucky)* sfortunato(a) ; *(regrettable)* infelice ; **it is ~ that** è un peccato che.

unfortunately [ʌn'fɔːtʃnətlɪ] *adv* sfortunatamente.

unfriendly [ˌʌn'frendlɪ] *adj* poco amichevole.

unfurnished [ˌʌn'fɜːnɪʃt] *adj* non ammobiliato(a).

ungrateful [ʌn'greɪtful] *adj* ingrato(a).

unhappy [ʌn'hæpɪ] *adj (sad)* infelice ; *(not pleased)* insoddisfatto(a) ; **to be ~ about sthg** essere insoddisfatto di qc.

unharmed [ˌʌn'hɑːmd] *adj* indenne.

unhealthy [ʌn'helθɪ] *adj (person)* malaticcio(a) ; *(food, smoking)* dannoso(a) per la salute ; *(place)* malsano(a).

unhelpful [ˌʌn'helpful] *adj (person)* poco disponibile ; *(advice, instructions)* inutile.

unhurt [ˌʌn'hɜːt] *adj* indenne.

unhygienic [ˌʌnhaɪ'dʒiːnɪk] *adj* non igienico(a).

unification [ˌjuːnɪfɪ'keɪʃn] *n* unificazione *f*.

uniform ['junɪfɔːm] *n* uniforme *f*.

unimportant [ˌʌnɪm'pɔːtənt] *adj* senza importanza.

unintelligent [ˌʌnɪn'telɪdʒənt] *adj* poco intelligente.

unintentional [ˌʌnɪn'tenʃənl] *adj* involontario(a).

uninterested [ˌʌn'ɪntrəstɪd] *adj* indifferente.

uninteresting [ˌʌn'ɪntrestɪŋ] *adj* poco interessante, noioso(a).

union ['juːnjən] *n (of workers)* sindacato *m*.

Union Jack *n* : **the ~** *la bandiera nazionale del Regno Unito*.

unique [ju:'ni:k] *adj* unico(a) ; to be ~ to essere proprio(a) di.

unisex ['ju:nıseks] *adj* unisex *(inv)*.

unit ['ju:nıt] *n* unità *f inv* ; *(department, building)* reparto *m* ; *(piece of furniture)* elemento *m* ; *(machine)* apparecchio *m*.

unite [ju:'naıt] *vt* unire. ◆ *vi* unirsi.

United Kingdom [ju:'naıtıd-] *n* : the ~ il Regno Unito.

United Nations [ju:'naıtıd-] *npl* : the ~ le Nazioni Unite.

United States (of America) [ju:'naıtıd-] *npl* : the ~ gli Stati Uniti (d'America).

unity ['ju:nətı] *n* unità *f*.

universal [,ju:nı'vɜ:sl] *adj* universale.

universe ['ju:nıvɜ:s] *n* universo *m*.

university [,ju:nı'vɜ:sətı] *n* università *f inv*.

unjust [,ʌn'dʒʌst] *adj* ingiusto(a).

unkind [ʌn'kaınd] *adj* scortese.

unknown [,ʌn'nəʊn] *adj* sconosciuto(a).

unleaded (petrol) [,ʌn'ledıd-] *n* benzina *f* senza piombo.

unless [ən'les] *conj* a meno che non ; ~ it rains a meno che non piova.

unlike [,ʌn'laık] *prep* a differenza di ; that's ~ her non è da lei.

unlikely [ʌn'laıklı] *adj* improbabile ; he is ~ to arrive before six è improbabile che arrivi prima delle sei.

unlimited [ʌn'lımıtıd] *adj* illimitato(a).

unlisted [ʌn'lıstıd] *adj Am (phone number)* : to be ~ non essere sull'elenco telefonico.

unload [,ʌn'ləʊd] *vt* scaricare.

unlock [,ʌn'lɒk] *vt* aprire.

unlucky [ʌn'lʌkı] *adj (unfortunate)* sfortunato(a) ; *(bringing bad luck)* che porta sfortuna.

unmarried [,ʌn'mærıd] *adj* non sposato(a).

unnatural [ʌn'nætʃrəl] *adj (unusual)* inconsueto(a) ; *(behaviour, person)* poco naturale.

unnecessary [ʌn'nesəsərı] *adj* inutile.

unobtainable [,ʌnəb'teınəbl] *adj (product)* non disponibile ; *(phone number)* non ottenibile.

unoccupied [,ʌn'ɒkjʊpaıd] *adj (place, seat)* libero(a).

unofficial [,ʌnə'fıʃl] *adj* non ufficiale ; *(strike)* non autorizzato *m*.

unpack [,ʌn'pæk] *vt (bags, suitcase)* disfare. ◆ *vi* disfare le valigie.

unpleasant [ʌn'pleznt] *adj (smell, weather, etc)* sgradevole ; *(person)* spiacevole, antipatico(a).

unplug [ʌn'plʌg] *vt* staccare.

unpopular [,ʌn'pɒpjʊlə^r] *adj* impopolare.

unpredictable [,ʌnprı'dıktəbl] *adj* imprevedibile.

unprepared [,ʌnprı'peəd] *adj* impreparato(a).

unprotected [,ʌnprə'tektıd] *adj* senza protezione.

unqualified [ˌʌn'kwɒlɪfaɪd] *adj (person)* non qualificato(a).
unreal [ˌʌn'rɪəl] *adj* irreale.
unreasonable [ʌn'ri:znəbl] *adj* irragionevole.
unrecognizable [ˌʌnrekəg-'naɪzəbl] *adj* irriconoscibile.
unreliable [ˌʌnrɪ'laɪəbl] *adj* inaffidabile.
unrest [ˌʌn'rest] *n* agitazione *f*.
unroll [ˌʌn'rəʊl] *vt* srotolare.
unsafe [ˌʌn'seɪf] *adj (dangerous)* pericoloso(a) ; *(in danger)* in pericolo.
unsatisfactory [ˌʌnsætɪs-'fæktərɪ] *adj* insoddisfacente.
unscrew [ˌʌn'skru:] *vt (lid, top)* svitare.
unsightly [ʌn'saɪtlɪ] *adj* brutto(a).
unskilled [ˌʌn'skɪld] *adj (worker)* non qualificato(a).
unsociable [ʌn'səʊʃəbl] *adj* poco socievole.
unsound [ˌʌn'saʊnd] *adj (building, structure)* poco saldo(a) ; *(argument)* che non regge.
unspoiled [ˌʌn'spɔɪlt] *adj (place, beach)* incontaminato(a).
unsteady [ˌʌn'stedɪ] *adj* instabile ; *(hand)* malfermo(a).
unstuck [ˌʌn'stʌk] *adj* : **to come ~** *(label, poster etc)* staccarsi.
unsuccessful [ˌʌnsək'sesful] *adj* che non ha successo.
unsuitable [ˌʌn'su:təbl] *adj* inadatto(a), inadeguato(a) ; *(moment)* inopportuno(a).
unsure [ˌʌn'ʃɔ:ʳ] *adj* : **to be ~ (about)** non essere sicuro(a) (di).
unsweetened [ˌʌn'swi:tnd] *adj* senza zucchero.
untidy [ʌn'taɪdɪ] *adj (person)* disordinato(a) ; *(room, desk)* in disordine.
untie [ˌʌn'taɪ] (*cont* **untying** [ˌʌn-'taɪɪŋ]) *vt (person)* slegare ; *(knot)* sciogliere, sfare.
until [ən'tɪl] *prep* fino a. ◆ *conj* finché ; *(after negative, in past)* prima che, prima di ; **it won't be ready ~ Thursday** non sarà pronto prima di giovedì.
untrue [ˌʌn'tru:] *adj* falso(a).
untrustworthy [ˌʌn'trʌst-ˌwɜ:ðɪ] *adj* che non è degno(a) di fiducia.
untying [ˌʌn'taɪɪŋ] *cont* → **untie**.
unusual [ʌn'ju:ʒl] *adj* insolito(a).
unusually [ʌn'ju:ʒəlɪ] *adv (more than usual)* insolitamente.
unwell [ˌʌn'wel] *adj* indisposto(a) ; **to feel ~** non sentirsi bene.
unwilling [ˌʌn'wɪlɪŋ] *adj* : **to be ~ to do sthg** non voler fare qc.
unwind [ˌʌn'waɪnd] (*pt & pp* **unwound** [ˌʌnwaʊnd]) *vt* svolgere. ◆ *vi (relax)* rilassarsi, distendersi.
unwrap [ˌʌn'ræp] *vt* aprire.
unzip [ˌʌn'zɪp] *vt* aprire (la cerniera di).

up [ʌp] *adv* - 1. *(towards higher position)* su, in alto ; **to go ~** salire ; **we walked ~ to the top** siamo saliti fino in cima ; **to pick sthg ~** raccogliere qc.
- 2. *(in higher position)* su, in alto ;

she's ~ in her bedroom è su nella sua stanza ; **~ there** lassù.
- 3. *(into upright position)* : **to stand ~** alzarsi ; **to sit ~** *(from lying position)* tirarsi su a sedere ; *(sit straight)* stare seduto diritto.
- 4. *(to increased level)* : **prices are going ~** i prezzi stanno salendo.
- 5. *(northwards)* : **~ in Scotland** in Scozia.
- 6. *(in phrases)* : **to walk ~ and down** andare su e giù ; **~ to ten people** fino a dieci persone ; **are you ~ to travelling?** te la senti di viaggiare? ; **what are you ~ to?** cosa stai combinando? ; **it's ~ to you** sta a te decidere ; **~ until ten o'clock** fino alle dieci.
◆ *prep* - 1. *(towards higher position)* : **to walk ~ a hill** salire su per una collina ; **I went ~ the stairs** sono salito per le scale.
- 2. *(in higher position)* in cima a ; **~ a hill** in cima ad una collina ; **~ a ladder** in cima ad una scala.
- 3. *(at end of)* : **they live ~ the road from us** abitano un po' più su di noi.
◆ *adj* - 1. *(out of bed)* alzato(a) ; **I was ~ at six today** mi sono alzato alle sei oggi.
- 2. *(at an end)* : **time's ~** tempo scaduto.
- 3. *(rising)* : **the ~ escalator** la scala mobile per salire.
◆ *n* : **~s and downs** alti e bassi *mpl.*

---

update [ˌʌp'deɪt] *vt* aggiornare.
uphill [ˌʌp'hɪl] *adv* in salita.
upholstery [ʌp'həʊlstərɪ] *n* tappezzeria *f.*
upkeep ['ʌpkiːp] *n* manutenzione *f.*
up-market *adj* rivolto(a) alla fascia alta del mercato.
upon [ə'pɒn] *prep fml (on)* su.
upper ['ʌpəʳ] *adj* superiore. ◆ *n (of shoe)* tomaia *f.*
upper class *n* : **the ~** i ceti alti.
uppermost ['ʌpəməʊst] *adj (highest)* il più alto (la più alta).
upper sixth *n Br* SCH *secondo anno del corso biennale che prepara agli 'A levels'.*
upright ['ʌpraɪt] *adj (person)* diritto(a) ; *(object)* verticale. ◆ *adv* diritto.
upset [ʌp'set] (*pt & pp* **upset**) *adj (distressed)* addolorato(a). ◆ *vt (distress)* addolorare, sconvolgere ; *(cause to go wrong)* scombussolare ; *(knock over)* rovesciare ; **to have an ~ stomach** avere disturbi intestinali.
upside down [ˌʌpsaɪd-] *adj* capovolto(a) ; *(person)* a testa in giù. ◆ *adv* sottosopra.
upstairs [ˌʌp'steəz] *adj* di sopra. ◆ *adv (on a higher floor)* di sopra, al piano superiore ; **to go ~** andare di sopra.
up-to-date *adj (modern)* moderno(a) ; *(well-informed)* aggiornato(a).
upwards ['ʌpwədz] *adv (to a higher place)* verso l'alto, in su ; *(to a higher level)* verso l'alto ; **~ of 100 people** più di 100 persone.
urban ['ɜːbən] *adj* urbano(a).
urge [ɜːdʒ] *vt* : **to ~ sb to do sthg** esortare qn a fare qc.
urgent ['ɜːdʒənt] *adj* urgente.
urgently ['ɜːdʒəntlɪ] *adv (immediately)* d'urgenza, urgentemente.

urinal [juə'raɪnl] *n [fml] (bowl)* orinale *m* ; *(place)* vespasiano *m*.
urinate ['juərɪneɪt] *vi fml* urinare.
urine ['juərɪn] *n* urina *f*.
us [ʌs] *pron* ci ; *(after prep)* noi ; **they know ~** ci conoscono ; **it's ~** siamo noi ; **send it to ~** mandacelo ; **tell ~** dicci ; **they're worse than ~** sono peggio di noi.
US *n (abbr of United States)* : **the ~** gli USA.
USA *n (abbr of United States of America)* : **the ~** gli USA.
usable ['ju:zəbl] *adj* utilizzabile.
use [*n* ju:s, *vb* ju:z] *n* uso *m*. ◆ *vt* usare ; *(run on)* andare a ; **to be of ~** essere utile, servire ; **to have the ~ of sthg** avere accesso a qc ; **to make ~ of sthg** sfruttare qc ; **to be in ~** essere in uso ; **it's no ~** non serve a niente ; **what's the ~?** a che scopo? ; **to ~ sthg as sthg** usare qc come qc ; **'~ before ...'** *(food, drink)* 'da consumarsi preferibilmente entro ...'. ❑ **use up** *vt sep* consumare.
used [*adj* ju:zd, *aux vb* ju:st] *adj (towel, glass etc)* sporco(a) ; *(car)* usato(a). ◆ *aux vb* : **I ~ to live near here** una volta abitavo qui vicino ; **I ~ to go there every day** una volta ci andavo tutti i giorni ; **to be ~ to sthg** essere abituato(a) a qc ; **to get ~ to sthg** abituarsi a qc.
useful ['ju:sful] *adj* utile.
useless ['ju:slɪs] *adj* inutile ; *inf (very bad)* : **he's ~** non è buono a nulla.
user ['ju:zə^r] *n* utente *mf*.
usher ['ʌʃə^r] *n (at cinema, theatre)* maschera *f*.
usherette [,ʌʃə'ret] *n* maschera *f*.
usual ['ju:ʒəl] *adj* solito(a) ; **as ~** *(in the normal way)* come al solito.
usually ['ju:ʒəlɪ] *adv* di solito.
utensil [ju:'tensl] *n* utensile *m*.
utilize ['ju:təlaɪz] *vt fml* utilizzare.
utmost ['ʌtməust] *adj* estremo(a). ◆ *n* : **to do one's ~** fare tutto il possibile.
utter ['ʌtə^r] *adj* totale. ◆ *vt (word)* proferire, pronunciare ; *(cry)* emettere.
utterly ['ʌtəlɪ] *adv* completamente, del tutto.
U-turn *n (in vehicle)* inversione *f* a U.

V

vacancy ['veɪkənsɪ] *n (job)* posto *m* vacante ; **'vacancies'** 'si affittano camere' ; **'no vacancies'** 'completo'.
vacant ['veɪkənt] *adj* libero(a).
vacate [və'keɪt] *vt fml (room, house)* lasciare libero.
vacation [və'keɪʃn] *n (Am) (period of time)* vacanze *fpl* ; *(time off work)* ferie *fpl*. ◆ *vi Am* passare le vacanze ; **to go on ~** andare in vacanza.
vaccination [,væksɪ'neɪʃn] *n* vaccinazione *f*.
vaccine [*Br* 'væksi:n, *Am* væk'si:n] *n* vaccino *m*.
vacuum ['vækjuəm] *vt* pulire con l'aspirapolvere.

vacuum cleaner *n* aspirapolvere *m inv*.
vague [veɪg] *adj* vago(a) ; *(shape, outline)* indistinto(a).
vain [veɪn] *adj pej (conceited)* vanitoso(a) ; **in ~** invano.
Valentine card ['væləntaɪn-] *n biglietto che si manda per San Valentino alla persona che si ama o di cui si è innamorati.*
Valentine's Day ['væləntaɪnz-] *n* San Valentino.
valid ['vælɪd] *adj (ticket, passport)* valido(a).
validate ['vælɪdeɪt] *vt (ticket)* convalidare.
valley ['vælɪ] *n* valle *f*.
valuable ['væljʊəbl] *adj (jewellery, object)* di valore ; *(advice, help)* prezioso(a). ❑ **valuables** *npl* oggetti *mpl* di valore.
value ['vælju:] *n (financial)* valore *m* ; *(usefulness)* utilità *f* ; **a ~ pack** una confezione ; **to be good ~ (for money)** essere conveniente. ❑ **values** *npl (principles)* valori *mpl*.
valve [vælv] *n* valvola *f*.
van [væn] *n* furgone *m*.
vandal ['vændl] *n* vandalo *m*, -a *f*.
vandalize ['vændəlaɪz] *vt* vandalizzare.
vanilla [və'nɪlə] *n* vaniglia *f*.
vanish ['vænɪʃ] *vi* svanire, scomparire.
vapor ['veɪpər] *Am* = **vapour**.
vapour ['veɪpə^r] *n Br* vapore *m*.
variable ['veərɪəbl] *adj* variabile.
varicose veins ['værɪkəʊs-] *npl* vene *fpl* varicose.
varied ['veərɪd] *adj* vario(a).
variety [və'raɪətɪ] *n* varietà *f inv*.
various ['veərɪəs] *adj* vari(e).
varnish ['vɑ:nɪʃ] *n* vernice *f*. ◆ *vt* verniciare.
vary ['veərɪ] *vi* & *vt* variare.
vase [*Br* vɑ:z, *Am* veɪz] *n* vaso *m*.
vast [vɑ:st] *adj* vasto(a).
VAT [væt, vi:eɪ'ti:] *n (abbr of value added tax)* IVA *f*.

Negli Stati Uniti l'IVA non si usa, pertanto l'imposta è già inclusa nel prezzo indicato sull'etichetta In Gran Bretagna il VAT, che equivale all'IVA, è del 17,5% mentre negli Stati Uniti la tassa varia da stato a stato e va dallo 0% all'8,5%. I generi alimentari non sono tassati, se non nei ristoranti, né in Gran Bretagna né negli Stati Uniti dove in qualche stato non vengono tassate nemmeno le calzature e l'abbigliamento. Sia in Gran Bretagna che in alcuni stati americani i turisti possono richiedere il rimborso dell'imposta pagata sugli articoli acquistati

vault [vɔ:lt] *n (in bank)* camera *f* blindata ; *(in church)* cripta *f*.
VCR *n (abbr of video cassette recorder)* videoregistratore *m*.
VDU *n (abbr of visual display unit)* monitor *m inv*.
veal [vi:l] *n* vitello *m*.
veg [vedʒ] *abbr* = **vegetable**.
vegan ['vi:gən] *adj* vegetaliano(a). ◆ *n* vegetaliano *m*, -a *f*.
vegetable ['vedʒtəbl] *n* verdura *f*.

vegetable oil *n* olio *m* vegetale.
vegetarian [ˌvedʒɪ'teərɪən] *adj* vegetariano(a). ◆ *n* vegetariano *m*, -a *f*.
vegetation [ˌvedʒɪ'teɪʃn] *n* vegetazione *f*.
vehicle ['viːəkl] *n* veicolo *m*.
veil [veɪl] *n* velo *m*.
vein [veɪn] *n* vena *f*.
Velcro® ['velkrəʊ] *n* velcro® *m*.
velvet ['velvɪt] *n* velluto *m*.
vending machine ['vendɪŋ-] *n* distributore *m* automatico.
venetian blind [vɪˌniːʃn-] *n* veneziana *f*.
Venice ['venɪs] *n* Venezia *f*.
venison ['venɪzn] *n* carne *m* di cervo.
vent [vent] *n (for air, smoke etc)* presa *f* d'aria.
ventilation [ˌventɪ'leɪʃn] *n* ventilazione *f*.
ventilator ['ventɪleɪtəʳ] *n* ventilatore *m*.
venture ['ventʃəʳ] *n* impresa *f*. ◆ *vi (go)* avventurarsi.
venue ['venjuː] *n* luogo *m (di partita, concerto ecc.)*.
veranda [və'rændə] *n* veranda *f*.
verb [vɜːb] *n* verbo *m*.
verdict ['vɜːdɪkt] *n* verdetto *m*.
verge [vɜːdʒ] *n (of road, lawn, path)* bordo *m*.
verify ['verɪfaɪ] *vt* verificare.
vermin ['vɜːmɪn] *n roditori che portano malattie e distruggono raccolti*.
vermouth ['vɜːməθ] *n* vermut *m inv*.
versa → **vice versa**.
versatile ['vɜːsətaɪl] *adj* versatile.
verse [vɜːs] *n (of song, poem)* strofa *f* ; *(poetry)* versi *mpl*.
version ['vɜːʃn] *n* versione *f*.
versus ['vɜːsəs] *prep* contro.
vertical ['vɜːtɪkl] *adj* verticale.
vertigo ['vɜːtɪgəʊ] *n* : **to suffer from ~** soffrire di vertigini.
very ['verɪ] *adv* molto. ◆ *adj* : **at the ~ bottom** proprio in fondo ; **~ much** molto ; **not ~ big** non molto grande ; **my ~ own room** una stanza tutta per me ; **~ rich** ricchissimo, molto ricco ; **it's the ~ thing I need** è proprio quello di cui avevo bisogno.
vessel ['vesl] *n fml (ship)* vascello *m*.
vest [vest] *n Br (underwear)* maglietta *f*; *(sleeveless)* canottiera *f*; *Am (waistcoat)* gilè *m inv*.
Vesuvius [vɪ'suːvjəs] *n* Vesuvio *m*.
vet [vet] *n Br* veterinario *m*, -a *f*.
veteran ['vetrən] *n (of war)* vecchio combattente *m*.
veterinarian [ˌvetərɪ'neərɪən] *Am* = **vet**.
veterinary surgeon ['vetərɪnrɪ-] *Br fml* = **vet**.
VHS *n (abbr of video home system)* VHS *m*.
via ['vaɪə] *prep (place)* via ; *(by means of)* tramite.
viaduct ['vaɪədʌkt] *n* viadotto *m*.
vibrate [vaɪ'breɪt] *vi* vibrare.

vibration [vaɪ'breɪʃn] *n* vibrazione *f*.

vicar ['vɪkəʳ] *n* pastore *m*.

vicarage ['vɪkərɪdʒ] *n* presbiterio *m*.

vice [vaɪs] *n (moral fault)* vizio *m* ; *(crime)* crimine *m* ; *Br (tool)* morsa *f*.

vice-president *n* vice-presidente *mf*.

vice versa [ˌvaɪsɪ'vɜːsə] *adv* viceversa.

vicinity [vɪ'sɪnətɪ] *n* : **in the ~** nelle vicinanze.

vicious ['vɪʃəs] *adj (attack)* violento(a) ; *(animal)* feroce ; *(comment)* cattivo(a), maligno(a).

victim ['vɪktɪm] *n* vittima *f*.

Victorian [vɪk'tɔːrɪən] *adj* vittoriano(a).

victory ['vɪktərɪ] *n* vittoria *f*.

video ['vɪdɪəʊ] (*pl* **-s**) *n (video recording)* video *m inv* ; *(videotape)* videocassetta *f* ; *(video recorder)* videoregistratore *m*. ◆ *vt (using video recorder)* videoregistrare ; *(using camera)* filmare ; **on ~** su videocassetta.

video camera *n* videocamera *f*.

video game *n* videogioco *m*.

video recorder *n* videoregistratore *m*.

video shop *n* videoteca *f*.

videotape ['vɪdɪəʊteɪp] *n* videocassetta *f*.

view [vjuː] *n* vista *f* ; *(opinion)* opinione *f*. ◆ *vt (house)* vedere ; *(situation)* considerare ; **in my ~** secondo me ; **in ~ of** *(considering)* considerato.

viewer ['vjuːəʳ] *n (of TV)* telespettatore *m*, -trice *f*.

viewfinder ['vjuːˌfaɪndəʳ] *n* mirino *m*.

viewpoint ['vjuːpɔɪnt] *n (opinion)* punto *m* di vista ; *(place)* punto d'osservazione.

vigilant ['vɪdʒɪlənt] *adj fml* vigile.

villa ['vɪlə] *n* villa *f*.

village ['vɪlɪdʒ] *n* paese *m*.

villager ['vɪlɪdʒəʳ] *n* abitante *mf* di paese.

villain ['vɪlən] *n (of book, film)* cattivo *m* ; *(criminal)* malvivente *mf*.

vinaigrette [ˌvɪnɪ'gret] *n condimento per insalata a base di olio, aceto, sale, pepe ed erbe aromatiche.*

vine [vaɪn] *n (grapevine)* vite *f* ; *(climbing plant)* rampicante *m*.

vinegar ['vɪnɪgəʳ] *n* aceto *m*.

vineyard ['vɪnjəd] *n* vigna *f*.

vintage ['vɪntɪdʒ] *adj (wine)* d'annata. ◆ *n (year)* annata *f*.

vinyl ['vaɪnɪl] *n* vinile *m*.

viola [vɪ'əʊlə] *n* viola *f*.

violence ['vaɪələns] *n* violenza *f*.

violent ['vaɪələnt] *adj* violento(a).

violet ['vaɪələt] *adj* viola *(inv)*. ◆ *n (flower)* viola *f*.

violin [ˌvaɪə'lɪn] *n* violino *m*.

VIP *n* (*abbr of very important person*) vip *mf inv*.

virgin ['vɜːdʒɪn] *n* vergine *f*.

virtually ['vɜːtʃʊəlɪ] *adv* praticamente.

virtual reality ['vɜːtʃʊəl-] *n* realtà *f* virtuale.

virus ['vaɪrəs] *n* virus *m inv*.
visa ['vi:zə] *n* visto *m*.
viscose ['vɪskəʊs] *n* viscosa *f*.
visibility [,vɪzɪ'bɪlətɪ] *n* visibilità *f*.
visible ['vɪzəbl] *adj* visibile.
visit ['vɪzɪt] *vt (person)* andare a trovare ; *(place)* visitare. ◆ *n* visita *f*.
visiting hours ['vɪzɪtɪŋ-] *npl* orario *m* delle visite.
visitor ['vɪzɪtə^r] *n (to person)* visita *f* ; *(to place)* visitatore *m*, -trice *f*.
visitors' book *n* registro *m* dei visitatori.
visor ['vaɪzə^r] *n* visiera *f*.
vital ['vaɪtl] *adj* vitale.
vitamin [*Br* 'vɪtəmɪn, *Am* 'vaɪtəmɪn] *n* vitamina *f*.
vivid ['vɪvɪd] *adj* vivido(a).
V-neck *n (design)* scollo *m* a V.
vocabulary [və'kæbjʊlərɪ] *n* vocabolario *m*.
vodka ['vɒdkə] *n* vodka *f*.
voice [vɔɪs] *n* voce *f*.
volcano [vɒl'keɪnəʊ] (*pl* **-es** OR **-s**) *n* vulcano *m*.
volleyball ['vɒlɪbɔ:l] *n* pallavolo *f*.
volt [vəʊlt] *n* volt *m inv*.
voltage ['vəʊltɪdʒ] *n* voltaggio *m*.
volume ['vɒlju:m] *n* volume *m*.
voluntary ['vɒləntrɪ] *adj* volontario(a).
volunteer [,vɒlən'tɪə^r] *n* volontario *m*, -a *f*. ◆ *vt* : **to ~ to do sthg** offrirsi di fare qc.
vomit ['vɒmɪt] *n* vomito *m*. ◆ *vi* vomitare.
vote [vəʊt] *n* voto *m* ; *(number of votes)* voti *mpl*. ◆ *vi* : **to ~ (for)** votare (per).
voter ['vəʊtə^r] *n* elettore(trice).
voucher ['vaʊtʃə^r] *n* buono *m*.
vowel ['vaʊəl] *n* vocale *f*.
voyage ['vɔɪɪdʒ] *n* viaggio *m (per mare)*.
vulgar ['vʌlgə^r] *adj* volgare.
vulture ['vʌltʃə^r] *n* avvoltoio *m*.

W

W *(abbr of west)* O.
wad [wɒd] *n (of paper, banknotes)* fascio *m* ; *(of cotton)* batuffolo *m*.
wade [weɪd] *vi* camminare *(a fatica)*.
wading pool ['weɪdɪŋ-] *n Am* piscina *f* per bambini.
wafer ['weɪfə^r] *n (biscuit)* cialda *f*.
waffle ['wɒfl] *n (pancake) cialda dalla caratteristica superficie a quadretti che si mangia con sciroppo d'acero, panna o frutta.* ◆ *vi inf* parlare molto e dire poco.
wag [wæg] *vt* agitare.
wage [weɪdʒ] *n* salario *m*. ❑ **wages** *npl* salario *m*.
wagon ['wægən] *n (vehicle)* carro *m* ; *Br (of train)* vagone *m*.
waist [weɪst] *n* vita *f*.
waistcoat ['weɪskəʊt] *n* gilè *m inv*.
wait [weɪt] *n* attesa *f*. ◆ *vi* aspettare ; **to ~ for sb to do sthg** aspettare che qn faccia qc ; **I can't ~!** non vedo l'ora! ❑ **wait for** *vt fus* aspettare.

waiter ['weɪtəʳ] *n* cameriere *m*.

waiting room ['weɪtɪŋ-] *n* sala *f* d'attesa OR d'aspetto.

waitress ['weɪtrɪs] *n* cameriera *f*.

wake [weɪk] (*pt* **woke**, *pp* **woken**) *vt* svegliare. ◆ *vi* svegliarsi. ❑ **wake up** ◆ *vt sep* svegliare. ◆ *vi* svegliarsi.

Wales [weɪlz] *n* il Galles.

walk [wɔ:k] *n (journey, path)* passeggiata *f*. ◆ *vi* camminare. ◆ *vt (distance)* percorrere a piedi ; *(dog)* portare a spasso ; **to go for a ~** andare a fare una passeggiata ; **it's a short ~** a piedi è vicino ; **to take the dog for a ~** portare a spasso il cane ; **'walk'** *Am* 'avanti'. ❑ **walk away** *vi* andarsene. ❑ **walk in** *vi* entrare. ❑ **walk out** *vi (leave angrily)* andarsene.

walker ['wɔ:kəʳ] *n* camminatore *m*, -trice *f*.

walking boots ['wɔ:kɪŋ-] *npl* scarponcini *mpl*.

walking stick ['wɔ:kɪŋ-] *n* bastone *m*.

Walkman® ['wɔ:kmən] *n* walkman® *m*.

wall [wɔ:l] *n* muro *m* ; *(internal)* parete *f*, muro.

wallet ['wɒlɪt] *n (for money)* portafoglio *m*.

wallpaper ['wɔ:l,peɪpəʳ] *n* carta *f* da parati.

WALL STREET *n* Wall Street.

WALL STREET

A Wall Street, una stradina nel cuore di Manhattan, a New York, troviamo la Borsa degli Stati Uniti e numerosissime banche ed è per questo motivo che 'Wall Street' viene usato, per estensione, per riferirsi in generale al mondo della finanza americana.

---

wally ['wɒlɪ] *n Br inf* cretino *m*, -a *f*.

walnut ['wɔ:lnʌt] *n (nut)* noce *f*.

waltz [wɔ:ls] *n* valzer *m inv*.

wander ['wɒndəʳ] *vi* vagare.

want [wɒnt] *vt* volere ; *(need)* aver bisogno di ; **to ~ to do sthg** voler fare qc ; **to ~ sb to do sthg** volere che qn faccia qc.

war [wɔ:ʳ] *n* guerra *f*.

ward [wɔ:d] *n (in hospital)* reparto *m*.

warden ['wɔ:dn] *n (of park)* guardiano *m* ; *(of youth hostel)* custode *mf*.

wardrobe ['wɔ:drəʊb] *n (cupboard)* armadio *m* ; *(clothes)* guardaroba *m inv*.

warehouse ['weəhaʊs, *pl* -haʊzɪz] *n* magazzino *m*.

warm [wɔ:m] *adj* caldo(a) ; *(person, smile)* cordiale ; *(welcome)* caloroso(a). ◆ *vt* scaldare, riscaldare ; **to be ~** *(person)* avere caldo ; **it's ~** *(weather)* è OR fa caldo. ❑ **warm up** ◆ *vt sep* scaldare, riscaldare. ◆ *vi (get warmer)* scaldarsi, riscaldarsi ; *(do exercises)* riscaldarsi ; *(machine, engine)* scaldare.

warmth [wɔ:mθ] *n* calore *m*.

warn [wɔ:n] *vt* avvertire, avvisare ; **to ~ sb about sthg** avvisare qn di qc ; **to ~ sb not to do sthg** avvertire qn di non fare qc.

warning ['wɔ:nɪŋ] *n (of danger)*

avvertimento *m*; *(advance notice)* preavviso *m*.
warranty ['wɒrəntɪ] *n fml* garanzia *f*.
warship ['wɔːʃɪp] *n* nave *f* da guerra.
wart [wɔːt] *n* verruca *f*.
was [wɒz] *pt* → be.
wash [wɒʃ] *vt* lavare. ◆ *vi* lavarsi. ◆ *n* : to give sthg a ~ dare una lavata a qc; to have a ~ lavarsi; to ~ one's hands/face lavarsi le mani/il viso. ❑ **wash up** *vi Br (do washing-up)* lavare i piatti ; *Am (clean o.s.)* lavarsi.
washable ['wɒʃəbl] *adj* lavabile.
washbasin ['wɒʃˌbeɪsn] *n* lavabo *m*.
washbowl ['wɒʃbəʊl] *n Am* lavabo *m*.
washer ['wɒʃəʳ] *n (ring)* rondella *f*.
washing ['wɒʃɪŋ] *n* bucato *m*.
washing line *n* corda *f* del bucato.
washing machine *n* lavatrice *f*.
washing powder *n* detersivo *m* (in polvere).
washing-up *n Br* : to do the ~ fare i piatti.
washing-up bowl *n Br* bacinella *f*.
washing-up liquid *n Br* detersivo *m* liquido per piatti.
washroom ['wɒʃrʊm] *n Am* gabinetto *m*, bagno *m*.
wasn't [wɒznt] = was not.
wasp [wɒsp] *n* vespa *f*.
waste [weɪst] *n (rubbish)* rifiuti *mpl*. ◆ *vt* sprecare ; a ~ of money uno spreco di denaro ; a ~ of time una perdita di tempo.
wastebin ['weɪstbɪn] *n* cestino *m* (dei rifiuti).
wastepaper basket [ˌweɪst'peɪpə-] *n* cestino *m* (per la carta straccia).
watch [wɒtʃ] *n (wristwatch)* orologio *m*. ◆ *vt (observe)* guardare ; *(spy on)* sorvegliare ; *(be careful with)* fare attenzione a. ❑ **watch out** *vi (be careful)* stare attento, fare attenzione ; to ~ out for *(look for)* cercare.
watchstrap ['wɒtʃstræp] *n* cinturino *m* dell'orologio.
water ['wɔːtəʳ] *n* acqua *f*. ◆ *vt (plants, garden)* annaffiare. ◆ *vi (eyes)* lacrimare ; it makes my mouth ~ mi fa venire l'acquolina in bocca.
water bottle *n* borraccia *f*.
watercolour ['wɔːtəˌkʌləʳ] *n* acquerello *m*.
watercress ['wɔːtəkres] *n* crescione *m*.
waterfall ['wɔːtəfɔːl] *n* cascata *f*.
watering can ['wɔːtərɪŋ-] *n* annaffiatoio *m*.
watermelon ['wɔːtəˌmelən] *n* cocomero *m*, anguria *f*.
waterproof ['wɔːtəpruːf] *adj* impermeabile.
water purification tablets [-pjʊərɪfɪ'keɪʃn-] *npl* compresse *fpl* per la disinfezione dell'acqua.
water skiing *n* sci *m* nautico.
watersports ['wɔːtəspɔːts] *npl* sport *mpl* acquatici.
water tank *n* cisterna *f*.

watertight ['wɔːtətaɪt] *adj* stagno(a).

watt [wɒt] *n* watt *m inv* ; a 60-~ **bulb** una lampadina da 60 watt.

wave [weɪv] *n* onda *f* ; *(of crime, violence)* ondata *f.* ◆ *vt (hand)* agitare ; *(flag)* sventolare. ◆ *vi (to attract attention)* fare un cenno (con la mano) ; *(when greeting, saying goodbye)* salutare con la mano.

wavelength ['weɪvleŋθ] *n* lunghezza *f* d'onda.

wavy ['weɪvɪ] *adj (hair)* ondulato(a).

wax [wæks] *n (for candles)* cera *f* ; *(in ears)* cerume *m*.

way [weɪ] *n (manner, means)* modo *m* ; *(route)* strada *f* ; *(direction)* parte *f*, direzione *f* ; *(distance travelled)* tragitto *m* ; **which ~ is the station?** da che parte è la stazione? ; **the town is out of our ~** la città non è sulla nostra strada ; **to be in the ~** essere d'intralcio ; **to be on the ~** *(person)* stare arrivando ; *(meal)* essere in arrivo ; **to get out of sb's ~** lasciar passare qn ; **to get under ~** cominciare ; **a long ~ away** lontano ; **to lose one's ~** smarrirsi ; **on the ~ back** al ritorno ; **on the ~ there** all'andata ; **that ~** *(like that)* in quel modo ; *(in that direction)* da quella parte ; **this ~** *(like this)* in questo modo ; *(in this direction)* da questa parte ; **' ~ in'** 'entrata' ; **' ~ out'** 'uscita' ; **no ~!** *inf* neanche per sogno!

WC *n* (*abbr of water closet*) W.C. *m inv*.

we [wiː] *pron* noi ; **~'re fine** stiamo bene.

weak [wiːk] *adj* debole ; *(drink)* leggero(a) ; *(soup)* liquido(a).

weaken ['wiːkn] *vt* indebolire.

weakness ['wiːknɪs] *n* debolezza *f*.

wealth [welθ] *n* ricchezza *f*.

wealthy ['welθɪ] *adj* ricco(a).

weapon ['wepən] *n* arma *f*.

wear [weəʳ] (*pt* **wore**, *pp* **worn**) *vt* portare, indossare. ◆ *n (clothes)* abbigliamento *m* ; **~ and tear** usura *f*. ❑ **wear off** *vi* passare. ❑ **wear out** *vi* consumarsi.

weary ['wɪərɪ] *adj* stanco(a).

weather ['weðəʳ] *n* tempo *m* ; **what's the ~ like?** che tempo fa? ; **to be under the ~** *inf* sentirsi poco bene.

weather forecast *n* previsioni *fpl* del tempo.

weather forecaster [-fɔːkaːstəʳ] *n* meteorologo *m*, -a *f*.

weather report *n* bollettino *m* meteorologico.

weather vane [-veɪn] *n* banderuola *f*.

weave [wiːv] (*pt* **wove**, *pp* **woven**) *vt* tessere.

web [web] *n (of spider)* ragnatela *f*.

Wed. (*abbr of Wednesday*) mer.

wedding ['wedɪŋ] *n* matrimonio *m*.

wedding anniversary *n* anniversario *m* di matrimonio.

wedding dress *n* abito *m* da sposa.

wedding ring *n* fede *f*.

wedge [wedʒ] *n (of cake)* fetta *f* ; *(of wood etc)* cuneo *m*.

Wednesday ['wenzdɪ] *n* mercoledì *m inv* → **Saturday**.

wee [wi:] *adj Scot* piccolo(a). ◆ *n inf* pipì *f*.

weed [wi:d] *n* erbaccia *f*.

week [wi:k] *n* settimana *f*; **a ~ today** oggi a otto ; **in a ~'s time** fra una settimana.

weekday ['wi:kdeɪ] *n* giorno *m* feriale.

weekend [ˌwi:k'end] *n* fine settimana *m inv*.

weekly ['wi:klɪ] *adj* settimanale. ◆ *adv* ogni settimana. ◆ *n* settimanale *m*.

weep [wi:p] (*pt* & *pp* **wept**) *vi* piangere.

weigh [weɪ] *vt* pesare ; **how much does it ~?** quanto pesa?

weight [weɪt] *n* peso *m* ; **to lose ~** dimagrire ; **to put on ~** ingrassare. ❑ **weights** *npl (for weight training)* pesi *mpl*.

weightlifting ['weɪtˌlɪftɪŋ] *n* sollevamento *m* pesi.

weight training *n* allenamento *m* ai pesi.

weird [wɪəd] *adj* strano(a).

welcome ['welkəm] *adj (guest)* benvenuto(a)! ; *(appreciated)* gradito(a). ◆ *n* accoglienza *f*. ◆ *vt (greet)* dare il benvenuto a ; *(be grateful for)* gradire. ◆ *excl* benvenuto(a!) ; **you're ~ to help yourself** si serva pure ; **to make sb feel ~** far sentire qn benaccetto ; **you're ~!** prego!.

weld [weld] *vt* saldare.

welfare ['welfeəʳ] *n (happiness, comfort)* benessere *m* ; *Am (money)* sussidio *m*.

well [wel] (*compar* **better**, *superl* **best**) *adj* bene. ◆ *adv* bene ; *(a lot)* molto. ◆ *n* pozzo *m* ; **to get ~** guarire ; **to go ~** andar bene ; **~ done!** bravo! ; **it may ~ happen** è assai probabile che accada ; **it's ~ worth** it ne vale ben la pena ; **as ~** *(in addition)* anche ; **as ~ as** *(in addition to)* oltre a.

we'll [wi:l] = **we shall, we will**.

well-behaved [-bɪ'heɪvd] *adj* educato(a).

well-built *adj* aitante.

well-done *adj (meat)* ben cotto(a).

well-dressed [-'drest] *adj* vestito(a) bene.

wellington (boot) ['welɪŋtən-] *n* stivale *m* di gomma.

well-known *adj* noto(a).

well-off *adj (rich)* ricco(a).

well-paid *adj* ben pagato(a).

welly ['welɪ] *n Br inf* stivale *m* di gomma.

Welsh [welʃ] *adj* gallese. ◆ *n (language)* gallese *m*. ◆ *npl* : **the ~** i gallesi.

Welshman ['welʃmən] (*pl* **-men** [-mən]) *n* gallese *m*.

Welshwoman ['welʃˌwʊmən] (*pl* **-women** [-ˌwɪmɪn]) *n* gallese *f*.

went [went] *pt* → **go**.

wept [wept] *pt* & *pp* → **weep**.

were [wɜ:ʳ] *pt* → **be**.

we're [wɪəʳ] = **we are**.

weren't [wɜ:nt] = **were not**.

west [west] *n* ovest *m*, occidente *m*. ◆ *adj* dell'ovest. ◆ *adv (fly, walk)* verso ovest ; *(be situated)* a ovest ; **in the ~ of England** nell'Inghilterra occidentale.

westbound ['westbaund] *adj* diretto(a) a ovest.

West Country *n* : **the ~** l'Inghilterra *f* sud-occidentale.

western ['westən] *adj* occidentale. ◆ *n (film)* western *m inv*.

Westminster ['westmɪnstəʳ] *n* *quartiere nel centro di Londra.*

WESTMINSTER

In questo quartiere di Londra, situato lungo il Tamigi, si trovano sia il Palazzo del Parlamento che l'Abbazia di Westminster. Il termine *Westminster* designa, per estensione, il Parlamento stesso.

Westminster Abbey *n* l'abbazia *f* di Westminster.

WESTMINSTER ABBEY

Situata nel quartiere londinese di Westminster, questa è la chiesa dove ha luogo l'incoronazione dei sovrani britannici. Vi sono sepolti molti personaggi famosi e una parte della chiesa, il *Poet's Corner* (*l'Angolo dei Poeti*), ospita le tombe di poeti e scrittori di chiara fama, tra i quali Chaucer, Dickens e Hardy.

westwards ['westwədz] *adv* verso ovest.

wet [wet] (*pt* & *pp* **wet** OR **-ted**) *adj (soaked, damp)* bagnato(a) ; *(rainy)* piovoso(a). ◆ *vt* bagnare ; **to get ~** bagnarsi ; **'~ paint'** 'vernice fresca'.

wet suit *n* muta *f*.

we've [wiːv] = **we have**.

whale [weɪl] *n* balena *f*.

wharf [wɔːf] (*pl* **-s** OR **wharves**) *n* banchina *f*.

what [wɒt] *adj* - **1.** *(in questions)* che, quale ; **~ colour is it?** di che colore è? ; **he asked me ~ colour it was** mi ha chiesto di che colore era.
- **2.** *(in exclamations)* : **~ a surprise!** che sorpresa! ; **~ a beautiful day!** che bella giornata!
◆ *pron* - **1.** *(in direct questions)* (che) cosa ; **~ is going on?** (che) cosa succede? ; **~ are they doing?** (che) cosa fanno? ; **~ is that?** (che) cos'è? ; **~ is it called?** come si chiama? ; **~ are they talking about?** di (che) cosa parlano? ; **~ is it for?** a (che) cosa serve?
- **2.** *(in indirect questions, relative clauses)* cosa ; **she asked me ~ had happened** mi ha chiesto cos'era successo ; **she asked me ~ I had seen** mi ha chiesto cosa avevo visto ; **she asked me ~ I was thinking about** mi ha chiesto a cosa pensavo ; **~ worries me is ...** ciò che OR quello che mi preoccupa ... ; **I didn't see ~ happened** non ho visto cos'è successo ; **you can't have ~ you want** non puoi avere quello che vuoi.
- **3.** *(in phrases)* : **~ for?** a che scopo?, perché? ; **~ about going out for a meal?** cosa ne diresti di mangiare fuori?
◆ *excl* come?

whatever [wɒt'evəʳ] *pron* : **take ~ you want** prendi quello che vuoi ; **~ I do, I'll lose** qualsiasi cosa faccia, perderò ; ~ **that may be** quale che sia.

wheat [wi:t] *n* grano *m*, frumento *m*.

wheel [wi:l] *n* ruota *f* ; *(steering wheel)* volante *m*.

wheelbarrow ['wi:l,bærəʊ] *n* carriola *f*.

wheelchair ['wi:l,tʃeəʳ] *n* sedia *f* a rotelle.

wheelclamp [,wi:l'klæmp] *n* bloccaruota *m inv*.

wheezy ['wi:zɪ] *adj* ansante.

when [wen] *adv* quando. ◆ *conj* quando ; *(although, seeing as)* sebbene, mentre ; ~ **it's ready** quando è pronto ; ~ **I've finished** quando avrò finito.

whenever [wen'evəʳ] *conj* ogni volta che ; ~ **you like** quando vuoi.

where [weəʳ] *adv* & *conj* dove ; **this is ~ you'll be sleeping** è qui che dormirà.

whereabouts ['weərəbaʊts] *adv* dove. ◆ *npl* : **his ~ are unknown** nessuno sa dove si trovi.

whereas [weər'æz] *conj* mentre.

wherever [weər'evəʳ] *conj* dovunque ; ~ **you like** dove vuoi ; ~ **that may be** dove che sia.

whether ['weðəʳ] *conj* se ; ~ **you like it or not** ti piaccia o no.

☞

which [wɪtʃ] *adj (in questions)* quale ; ~ **room do you want?** quale stanza vuole? ; ~ **one?** quale? ; **she asked me ~ room I wanted** mi ha chiesto quale stanza volevo.
◆ *pron* - 1. *(in questions)* quale ; ~ **is the cheapest?** qual è il più economico? ; ~ **do you prefer?** quale preferisci? ; **he asked me ~ was the best** mi ha chiesto qual era il migliore ; **he asked me ~ I preferred** mi ha chiesto quale preferivo.
- 2. *(introducing relative clause)* che ; **the house ~ is on the corner** la casa che è all'angolo ; **the television ~ I bought** il televisore che ho comprato.
- 3. *(introducing relative clause : after prep)* il quale (la quale) ; **the settee on ~ I'm sitting** il divano su cui siedo ; **the book about ~ we were talking** il libro di cui stavamo parlando.
- 4. *(referring back)* il che, cosa che ; **he's late, ~ annoys me** è in ritardo, il che mi secca molto.

---

whichever [wɪtʃ'evəʳ] *pron* quello, quelli(e) *(pl)*, che. ◆ *adj* : ~ **chocolate you take** qualsiasi cioccolatino tu prenda.

while [waɪl] *conj* mentre ; *(although)* sebbene. ◆ *n* : **a ~** un po' (di tempo) ; **for a ~** per un po' ; **in a ~** fra un po'.

whim [wɪm] *n* capriccio *m*.

whine [waɪn] *vi* gemere ; *(complain)* frignare.

whip [wɪp] *n* frusta *f*. ◆ *vt (with whip)* frustare.

whipped cream [wɪpt-] *n* panna *f* montata.

whisk [wɪsk] *n (utensil)* frusta *f*, frullino *m*. ◆ *vt (eggs, cream)* sbattere.

whiskers ['wɪskəz] *npl (of person)* favoriti *m* ; *(of animal)* baffi *m*.

whiskey ['wɪskɪ] (*pl* **-s**) *n* whisky *m inv (irlandese o americano)*.

whisky ['wɪskɪ] *n* whisky *m inv (scozzese).*

whisper ['wɪspəʳ] *vt & vi* sussurrare.

whistle ['wɪsl] *n (instrument)* fischietto *m* ; *(sound)* fischio *m.* ◆ *vi* fischiare.

white [waɪt] *adj* bianco(a) ; *(tea)* con latte. ◆ *n* bianco *m* ; *(person)* bianco *m*, -a *f* ; ~ **coffee** caffè *m inv* con latte.

white bread *n* pane *m* bianco.

White House *n* : **the** ~ la Casa Bianca.

WHITE HOUSE

La casa Bianca è la residenza ufficiale e il luogo di lavoro del presidente degli Stati Uniti. Si trova a Washington D.C., capitale e sede del governo federale, ed è il simbolo della presidenza e del potere esecutivo del governo americano.

---

white sauce *n* besciamella *f.*

white spirit *n* acquaragia *f.*

whitewash ['waɪtwɒʃ] *vt* imbiancare.

white wine *n* vino *m* bianco.

whiting ['waɪtɪŋ] *(pl inv) n* merlango *m.*

Whitsun ['wɪtsn] *n* Pentecoste *f.*

who [hu:] *pron (in questions)* chi ; *(in relative clauses)* che.

whoever [hu:'evəʳ] *pron* chiunque ; ~ **it is** chiunque sia.

whole [həʊl] *adj* intero(a). ◆ *n* : **the** ~ **of the journey** tutto il viaggio ; **on the** ~ nel complesso ; **the** ~ **time** tutto il tempo.

wholefoods ['həʊlfu:dz] *npl* prodotti *mpl* integrali.

wholemeal bread ['həʊlmi:l-] *n Br* pane *m* integrale.

wholesale ['həʊlseɪl] *adv (COMM)* all'ingrosso.

wholewheat bread ['həʊl-wi:t-] *n Am* = **wholemeal bread.**

whom [hu:m] *pron fml (in questions)* chi ; *(in relative clauses)* che ; **to** ~**?** a chi? ; **the person to** ~ **I wrote** la persona alla quale ho scritto.

whooping cough ['hu:pɪŋ-] *n* pertosse *f.*

whose [hu:z] *adj & pron* : ~ **jumper is this?** di chi è questo maglione? ; **she asked** ~ **jumper it was** ha chiesto di chi era il maglione ; **this is the woman** ~ **son is a priest** questa è la donna il cui figlio è un prete ; ~ **is this?** di chi è questo?

why [waɪ] *adv & conj* perché ; ~ **not?** perché no? ; ~ **not do it tomorrow?** perché non farlo domani?

wick [wɪk] *n (of candle, lighter)* stoppino *m.*

wicked ['wɪkɪd] *adj (evil)* malvagio(a) ; *(mischievous)* malizioso(a).

wicker ['wɪkəʳ] *adj* di vimini.

wide [waɪd] *adj* largo(a) ; *(opening)* ampio(a) ; *(range, variety)* vasto(a) ; *(difference, gap)* grande. ◆ *adv* : **to open sthg** ~ spalancare qc ; **how** ~ **is the road?** quanto è larga la strada? ; **it's 12 metres** ~ è largo 12 metri ; ~ **open** spalancato.

widely ['waɪdlɪ] *adv (known)* generalmente ; *(travel)* molto.

widen ['waɪdn] *vt (make broader)* allargare. ◆ *vi (gap, difference)* aumentare.

widespread ['waɪdspred] *adj* molto diffuso(a).

widow ['wɪdəʊ] *n* vedova *f*.

widower ['wɪdəʊəʳ] *n* vedovo *m*.

width [wɪdθ] *n* larghezza *f*.

wife [waɪf] (*pl* **wives**) *n* moglie *f*.

wig [wɪg] *n* parrucca *f*.

wild [waɪld] *adj (animal, plant)* selvatico(a) ; *(land, area)* selvaggio(a) ; *(uncontrolled)* sfrenato(a) ; *(crazy)* folle ; **to be ~ about** *inf* andare pazzo(a) per.

wild flower *n* fiore *m* di campo.

wildlife ['waɪldlaɪf] *n* flora e fauna *f*.

☞

will¹ [wɪl] *aux vb* - 1. *(expressing future tense)* : **I ~ see you next week** ci vediamo la settimana prossima ; **~ you be here next Friday?** sarai qui venerdì prossimo? ; **yes I ~** sì ; **no I won't** no.

- 2. *(expressing willingness)* : **I won't do it** mi rifiuto di farlo.

- 3. *(expressing polite question)* : **~ you have some more tea?** vuole ancora un po' di tè?

- 4. *(in commands, requests)* : **~ you please be quiet!** volete tacere! ; **close that window, ~ you?** chiudi la finestra, per favore.

will² [wɪl] *n (document)* testamento *m* ; **against one's ~** contro la propria volontà.

willing ['wɪlɪŋ] *adj* : **to be ~ to do sthg** essere disposto(a) a fare qc.

willingly ['wɪlɪŋlɪ] *adv* volentieri.

willow ['wɪləʊ] *n* salice *m*.

win [wɪn] (*pt* & *pp* **won**) *n* vittoria *f*. ◆ *vt* vincere ; *(support, approval, friends)* guadagnarsi. ◆ *vi* vincere.

wind¹ [wɪnd] *n* vento *m* ; *(in stomach)* aria *f*.

wind² [waɪnd] (*pt* & *pp* **wound**) *vi (road, river)* snodarsi. ◆ *vt* : **to ~ sthg round sthg** avvolgere qc intorno a qc. ❑ **wind up** *vt sep Br inf (annoy)* dare sui nervi a ; *(car window)* tirare su, chiudere ; *(clock, watch)* caricare.

windbreak ['wɪndbreɪk] *n* frangivento *m*.

windmill ['wɪndmɪl] *n* mulino *m* a vento.

window ['wɪndəʊ] *n (of house)* finestra *f* ; *(of shop)* vetrina *f* ; *(of car)* finestrino *m*.

window box *n* cassetta *f* per fiori.

window cleaner *n* lavavetri *mf*.

windowpane ['wɪndəʊˌpeɪn] *n* vetro *m*.

window seat *n (on plane)* posto *m* finestrino.

window-shopping *n* : **to go ~** andare a guardare le vetrine.

windowsill ['wɪndəʊsɪl] *n* davanzale *m*.

windscreen ['wɪndskriːn] *n Br* parabrezza *m inv*.

windscreen wipers *npl Br* tergicristalli *mpl*.

windshield ['wɪndʃiːld] *n Am* parabrezza *m inv*.

windsurfing ['wɪnd,sɜːfɪŋ] *n* windsurf *m* ; **to go ~** fare del windsurf.
windy ['wɪndɪ] *adj* ventoso(a) ; **it's ~** c'è vento.
wine [waɪn] *n* vino *m*.
wine bar *n Br* ≃ enoteca *f*.
wineglass ['waɪnglaːs] *n* bicchiere *m* da vino.
wine list *n* lista *f* dei vini.
wine tasting [-'teɪstɪŋ] *n* degustazione *f* dei vini.
wine waiter *n* sommelier *mf inv*.
wing [wɪŋ] *n* ala *f* ; *Br (of car)* fiancata *f*. ❑ **wings** *npl* : **the ~s** *(in theatre)* le quinte.
wink [wɪŋk] *vi* strizzare l'occhio.
winner ['wɪnəʳ] *n* vincitore *m*, -trice *f*.
winning ['wɪnɪŋ] *adj* vincente.
winter ['wɪntəʳ] *n* inverno ; **in (the) ~** d'inverno.
wintertime ['wɪntətaɪm] *n* inverno *m*.
wipe [waɪp] *vt* pulire ; **to ~ one's hands/feet** pulirsi le mani/le scarpe. ❑ **wipe up** *vt sep (liquid)* asciugare ; *(dirt)* pulire. ◆ *vi (dry the dishes)* asciugare i piatti.
wiper ['waɪpəʳ] *n (windscreen wiper)* tergicristallo *m*.
wire ['waɪəʳ] *n* filo *m* di ferro ; *(electrical)* filo (elettrico). ◆ *vt (plug)* collegare.
wireless ['waɪəlɪs] *n* radio *f inv*.
wiring ['waɪərɪŋ] *n* impianto *m* elettrico.
wisdom tooth ['wɪzdəm-] *n* dente *m* del giudizio.
wise [waɪz] *adj* saggio(a).
wish [wɪʃ] *n (desire)* desiderio *m*. ◆ *vt (desire)* desiderare ; **best ~es** *(for birthday, recovery)* auguri ; *(at end of letter)* cordiali saluti ; **I ~ you'd told me earlier!** perché non me l'hai detto prima! ; **I ~ I was younger** vorrei tanto essere più giovane ; **to ~ to do sthg** *fml* desiderare fare qc ; **to ~ sb luck/happy birthday** augurare buona fortuna/buon compleanno a qn ; **if you ~** *fml* se vuole.
witch [wɪtʃ] *n* strega *f*.

---

with [wɪð] *prep* - 1. *(gen)* con ; **come ~ me** vieni con me ; **a man ~ a beard** un uomo con la barba.
- 2. *(at house of)* da, a casa di ; **we stayed ~ friends** siamo stati da amici.
- 3. *(indicating emotion)* di, per ; **to tremble ~ fear** tremare di paura.
- 4. *(indicating opposition)* : **to argue ~ sb** litigare con qn ; **to fight ~ sb** combattere contro qn.
- 5. *(indicating covering, contents)* di ; **to fill sthg ~ sthg** riempire qc di qc ; **topped ~ cream** ricoperto di panna.

---

withdraw [wɪð'drɔː] (*pt* **-drew**, *pp* **-drawn**) *vt (take out)* ritirare ; *(money)* prelevare. ◆ *vi (from race, contest)* ritirarsi.
withdrawal [wɪð'drɔːəl] *n (from bank account)* prelievo *m*.
withdrawn [wɪð'drɔːn] *pp* → **withdraw**.
withdrew [wɪð'druː] *pt* → **withdraw**.
wither ['wɪðəʳ] *vi* appassire.

within [wɪ'ðɪn] *prep (inside)* all'interno di ; *(not exceeding)* entro. ◆ *adv* all'interno, dentro ; ~ **walking distance** raggiungibile a piedi ; ~ **10 miles of ...** a non più di 10 miglia da ... ; **it arrived ~ a week** è arrivato nel giro di una settimana ; ~ **the next week** entro la prossima settimana.

without [wɪð'aʊt] *prep* senza ; ~ **doing sthg** senza fare qc.

withstand [wɪð'stænd] (*pt* & *pp* **-stood**) *vt* resistere a.

witness ['wɪtnɪs] *n* testimone *mf*. ◆ *vt (see)* assistere a.

witty ['wɪtɪ] *adj* arguto(a).

wives [waɪvz] *pl* → **wife**.

wobbly ['wɒblɪ] *adj (table, chair)* traballante.

wok [wɒk] *n padella larga e profonda usata nella cucina cinese.*

woke [wəʊk] *pt* → **wake**.

woken ['wəʊkn] *pp* → **wake**.

wolf [wʊlf] (*pl* **wolves** [wʊlvz]) *n* lupo *m*.

woman ['wʊmən] (*pl* **women**) *n* donna *f*.

womb [wu:m] *n* utero *m*.

women ['wɪmɪn] *pl* → **woman**.

won [wʌn] *pt* & *pp* → **win**.

wonder ['wʌndəʳ] *vi (ask o.s.)* chiedersi, domandarsi. ◆ *n (amazement)* meraviglia *f* ; **to ~ if** domandarsi se ; **I ~ if I could ask you a favour?** potrei chiederle un favore?

wonderful ['wʌndəfʊl] *adj* meraviglioso(a).

won't [wəʊnt] = **will not**.

wood [wʊd] *n (substance)* legno *m* ; *(small forest)* bosco *m* ; *(golf club)* mazza *f* di legno.

wooden ['wʊdn] *adj* di legno.

woodland ['wʊdlənd] *n* terreno *m* boschivo.

woodpecker ['wʊd,pekəʳ] *n* picchio *m*.

woodwork ['wʊdwɜ:k] *n SCH* falegnameria *f*.

wool [wʊl] *n* lana *f*.

woolen ['wʊlən] *Am* = **woollen**.

woollen ['wʊlən] *adj Br* di lana.

woolly ['wʊlɪ] *adj* di lana.

wooly ['wʊlɪ] *Am* = **woolly**.

word [wɜ:d] *n* parola *f* ; **in other ~s** in altre parole ; **to have a ~ with sb** parlare con qn.

wording ['wɜ:dɪŋ] *n* formulazione *f*.

word processing [-'prəʊsesɪŋ] *n* videoscrittura *f*.

word processor [-'prəʊsesəʳ] *n* sistema *m* di videoscrittura.

wore [wɔ:ʳ] *pt* → **wear**.

work [wɜ:k] *n* lavoro *m* ; *(painting, novel etc)* opera *f*. ◆ *vi* lavorare ; *(operate, have desired effect)* funzionare ; *(take effect)* fare effetto. ◆ *vt (machine, controls)* far funzionare ; **out of ~** senza lavoro ; **to be at ~** *(at workplace)* essere al lavoro ; *(working)* lavorare ; **to be off ~** *(on holiday)* essere in ferie ; *(ill)* essere in malattia ; **the ~s** *inf (everything)* tutto quanto ; **how does it ~?** come funziona? ; **it's not ~ing** non funziona. ❑ **work out** ◆ *vt sep (price, total)* calcolare ; *(understand)* capire ; *(solution)* trovare ; *(method, plan)* mettere a punto.

◆ *vi (result, be successful)* funzionare ; *(do exercise)* fare ginnastica ; **it ~s out at £20 each** *(bill, total)* fa 20 sterline a testa.

worker ['wɜːkəʳ] *n* lavoratore *m*, -trice *f*.

working class ['wɜːkɪŋ↓] *n* : **the ~** la classe operaia.

working hours ['wɜːkɪŋ↓] *npl* orario *m* di lavoro.

workman ['wɜːkmən] (*pl* **-men** [↓mən]) *n* operaio *m*.

work of art *n* opera *f* d'arte.

workout ['wɜːkaʊt] *n* allenamento *m*.

work permit *n* permesso *m* di lavoro.

workplace ['wɜːkpleɪs] *n* posto *m* di lavoro.

workshop ['wɜːkʃɒp] *n (for repairs)* officina *f*.

work surface *n* piano *m* di lavoro.

world [ˌwɜːld] *n* mondo *m*.◆ *adj* mondiale ; *the best in the~* le migliore del mondo.

World Series *n Am* : **the ~** *il campionato di baseball degli Stati Uniti.*

WORLD SERIES

Con il termine *World Series* si descrive il ciclo di sette partite con il quale si conclude il campionato di baseball negli Stati Uniti. Si incontrano le squadre campione delle due divisioni più importanti, la *National League* e l' *American League*, e vince la squadra che per prima riporta quattro vittorie. È uno degli avvenimenti sportivi più importanti degli Stati Uniti, al punto tale che la tradizione vuole che sia il Presidente a lanciare la prima palla.

worldwide [ˌwɜːld'waɪd] *adv* in tutto il mondo.

worm [wɜːm] *n* verme *m*.

worn [wɔːn] *pp* → **wear**. ◆ *adj (clothes, carpet)* consumato(a).

worn-out *adj (clothes, shoes etc)* consumato(a) ; *(tired)* esausto(a).

worried ['wʌrɪd] *adj* preoccupato(a).

worry ['wʌrɪ] *n* preoccupazione *f*. ◆ *vt* preoccupare. ◆ *vi* : **to ~ (about)** preoccuparsi (per).

worrying ['wʌrɪɪŋ] *adj* preoccupante.

worse [wɜːs] *adj* peggiore. ◆ *adv* peggio ; **to get ~** peggiorare ; **~ off** *(in worse position)* in una situazione peggiore ; *(poorer)* più povero.

worsen ['wɜːsn] *vi* peggiorare.

worship ['wɜːʃɪp] *n* culto *m*. ◆ *vt* adorare.

worst [wɜːst] *adj* peggiore. ◆ *adv* peggio. ◆ *n* : **the ~** il peggiore (la peggiore).

worth [wɜːθ] *prep* : **how much is it ~?** quanto vale? ; **it's ~ £50** vale 50 sterline ; **it's ~ seeing** vale la pena vederlo ; **it's not ~ it** non ne vale la pena ; **£50 ~ of traveller's cheques** traveller's cheques per un valore di 50 sterline.

worthless ['wɜːθlɪs] *adj* di nessun valore.

worthwhile [ˌwɜːθ'waɪl] *adj* : **to be ~** valere la pena.

worthy ['wɜːðɪ] *adj (winner, cause)* degno(a) ; **to be ~ of sthg** essere degno di qc.

☞

would [wʊd] *aux vb* - 1. *(in reported speech)* : **she said she ~ come** ha detto che sarebbe venuta.
- 2. *(indicating condition)* : **what ~ you do?** tu cosa faresti? ; **what ~ you have done?** tu cosa avresti fatto? ; **I ~ be most grateful** le sarei molto grato.
- 3. *(indicating willingness)* : **she ~n't go** non ci è voluta andare ; **he ~ do anything for her** farebbe qualsiasi cosa per lei.
- 4. *(in polite questions)* : **~ you like a drink?** vuole qualcosa da bere? ; **~ you mind closing the window?** le spiacerebbe chiudere la finestra?
- 5. *(indicating inevitability)* : **he ~ say that** era ovvio che dicesse così.
- 6. *(giving advice)* : **I ~ report it if I were you** se fossi in voi lo riferirei.
- 7. *(expressing opinions)* : **I ~ prefer ...** preferirei ... ; **I ~ have thought (that) ...** avrei pensato che ...

---

wound[1] [wu:nd] *n* ferita *f*. ◆ *vt* ferire.

wound[2] [waʊnd] *pt* & *pp* → **wind**[2].

wove [wəʊv] *pt* → **weave**.

woven ['wəʊvn] *pp* → **weave**.

wrap [ræp] *vt (package)* incartare ; **to ~ sthg round sthg** avvolgere qc intorno a qc. ❑ **wrap up** *vt sep (package)* incartare. ◆ *vi (dress warmly)* coprirsi bene.

wrapper ['ræpə^r] *n (for sweets)* carta *f*.

wrapping ['ræpɪŋ] *n* involucro *m*.

wrapping paper *n (for present)* carta *f* da regalo ; *(for parcel)* carta da pacchi.

wreath [ri:θ] *n* corona *f*.

wreck [rek] *n (of plane, car)* rottame *m* ; *(of ship)* relitto *m*. ◆ *vt (destroy)* distruggere ; *(spoil)* rovinare ; **to be ~ed** *(ship)* fare naufragio.

wreckage ['rekɪdʒ] *n (of plane, car)* rottami *mpl* ; *(of building)* macerie *fpl*.

wrench [rentʃ] *n Br (monkey wrench)* chiave *f* inglese ; *Am (spanner)* chiave.

wrestler ['reslə^r] *n* lottatore *m*, -trice *f*.

wrestling ['reslɪŋ] *n* lotta *f* libera.

wretched ['retʃɪd] *adj (miserable)* infelice ; *(very bad)* orribile.

wring [rɪŋ] (*pt* & *pp* **wrung**) *vt (clothes, cloth)* strizzare.

wrinkle ['rɪŋkl] *n* ruga *f*.

wrist [rɪst] *n* polso *m*.

wristwatch ['rɪstwɒtʃ] *n* orologio *m* da polso.

write [raɪt] (*pt* **wrote**, *pp* **written**) *vt* scrivere ; *(cheque, prescription)* fare ; *Am (send letter to)* scrivere a. ◆ *vi* scrivere ; **to ~ to sb** *Br* scrivere a qn. ❑ **write back** *vi* rispondere. ❑ **write down** *vt sep* scrivere. ❑ **write off** ◆ *vt sep Br inf (car)* distruggere. ◆ *vi* : **to ~ off for sthg** richiedere qc per posta. ❑ **write out** *vt sep (list, essay)* scrivere ; *(cheque, receipt)* fare.

write-off *n (vehicle)* rottame *m*.

writer ['raɪtə^r] *n (author)* scrittore *m*, -trice *f*.

writing ['raɪtɪŋ] *n (handwriting)* scrittura *f* ; *(written words)* scritto *m* ; *(activity)* scrivere *m*.

writing desk *n* scrivania *f*.

writing pad *n* blocchetto *m* per appunti.

writing paper *n* carta *f* da lettere.

written ['rɪtn] *pp* → **write.** ◆ *adj (exam, notice, confirmation)* scritto(a).

wrong [rɒŋ] *adv* male. ◆ *adj (incorrect, unsuitable)* sbagliato(a) ; *(bad, immoral)* : **it's ~ to steal** non si deve rubare ; **what's ~?** cosa c'è che non va? ; **what's ~ with her?** cos'ha? ; **something's ~ with the car** la macchina ha qualcosa che non va ; **to be ~** *(person)* sbagliarsi ; **to be in the ~** essere in torto ; **to get sthg ~** sbagliare qc ; **to go ~** *(machine)* non funzionare più ; **' ~ way'** *Am cartello che segnala agli automobilisti il senso vietato.*

wrongly ['rɒŋlɪ] *adv (accused)* ingiustamente ; *(informed)* male.

wrong number *n* : **to get the ~** sbagliare numero.

wrote [rəʊt] *pt* → **write.**

wrought iron [rɔːt-] *n* ferro *m* battuto.

wrung [rʌŋ] *pt* & *pp* → **wring.**

XL (*abbr of extra-large*) XL.

Xmas ['eksməs] *n inf* Natale *m*.

X-ray *n (picture)* radiografia *f*. ◆ *vt* fare una radiografia ; **to have an ~** fare una radiografia.

yacht [jɒt] *n* yacht *m inv*.

Yankee ['jæŋkɪ] *n Am (citizen)* Yankee *mf*.

YANKEE

Originariamente il termine *Yankee* veniva usato per indicare gli immigrati olandesi che si erano stabiliti nel nord-est degli Stati Uniti. In seguito, venne ad indicare un qualsiasi abitante del nord-est, cosicché durante la Guerra di Secessione *Yankee* divenne il soprannome dato dai Sudisti ai Nordisti. Ancor oggi c'è chi negli stati del sud usa il termine in tono dispregiativo per riferirsi agli abitanti del nord.

---

yard [jaːd] *n (unit of measurement)* = 91,44 cm, iarda *f* ; *(enclosed area)* cortile *m* ; *Am (behind house)* giardino *m*.

yard sale *n Am vendita di oggetti di seconda mano organizzata da un privato nel giardino di casa.*

yarn [jaːn] *n (thread)* filato *m*.

yawn [jɔːn] *vi (person)* sbadigliare.

yd abbr = yard.

yeah [jeə] *adv inf* sì.

year [jɪəʳ] *n* anno *m* ; **next ~** l'anno prossimo ; **this ~** quest'anno ; **I'm 15 ~s old** ho 15 anni ; **I haven't seen her for ~s** *inf* sono anni che non la vedo.

yearly ['jɪəlɪ] *adj* annuale, annuo(a).

yeast [ji:st] *n* lievito *m*.

yell [jel] *vi* urlare.

yellow ['jeləu] *adj* giallo(a). ◆ *n* giallo *m*.

yellow lines *npl* strisce *fpl* gialle *(che regolano la sosta dei veicoli)*.

YELLOW LINES

In Gran Bretagna le linee gialle, singole o doppie, sul bordo della strada indicano restrizioni relative alla sosta dei veicoli. Un'unica linea gialla indica il divieto di sosta dalle 8 alle 18.30 dei giorni feriali, mentre una linea doppia indica il divieto di sosta permanente. La sosta è quindi consentita solo sulle linee gialle singole dopo le 18.30, oppure tutta la domenica.

---

yes [jes] *adv* sì ; **to say ~** dire di sì.

yesterday ['jestədɪ] *n* ieri *m*. ◆ *adv* ieri ; **the day before ~** l'altro ieri ; **~ afternoon** ieri pomeriggio ; **~ morning** ieri mattina.

yet [jet] *adv* ancora. ◆ *conj* ma ; **have they arrived ~?** sono già arrivati? ; **the best one ~** il migliore fino a questo momento ; **not ~** non ancora ; **I've ~ to do it** devo ancora farlo ; **~ again** ancora una volta ; **~ another delay** ancora un altro ritardo.

yew [ju:] *n* tasso *m (pianta)*.

yield [ji:ld] *vt* dare, rendere. ◆ *vi (break, give way)* cedere.

YMCA *n associazione cristiana dei giovani che offre alloggi a buon prezzo.*

yob [jɒb] *n Br inf* teppista *mf*.

yoga ['jəugə] *n* yoga *m*.

yoghurt ['jɒgət] *n* yogurt *m inv*.

yolk [jəuk] *n* tuorlo *m*, rosso *m* d'uovo.

☞

you [ju:] *pron* - **1.** *(subject : singular)* tu ; *(subject : polite form)* lei ; *(subject : plural)* voi ; **~ Italians** voi italiani.

- **2.** *(direct object : singular)* ti ; *(direct object : polite form)* la ; *(direct object : plural)* vi ; **I called ~, not him** ho chiamato te, non lui.

- **3.** *(indirect object : singular)* ti ; *(indirect object : polite form)* le ; *(indirect object : plural)* vi.

- **4.** *(after prep : singular)* te ; *(after prep : polite form)* lei ; *(after prep : plural)* voi ; **I'm shorter than ~** sono più basso di te/lei/voi.

- **5.** *(indefinite use)* si ; **~ never know** non si sa mai ; **swimming is good for ~** nuotare fa bene.

---

young [jʌŋ] *adj* giovane. ◆ *npl* : **the ~** i giovani.

younger ['jʌŋgəʳ] *adj (brother, sister)* minore, più giovane.

youngest ['jʌŋgəst] *adj (brother, sister)* minore, il più giovane.

youngster ['jʌŋstəʳ] *n* giovane *mf*.

your [jɔ:ʳ] *adj* - **1.** *(singular subject)* il tuo (la tua), i tuoi (le tue) *(pl)* ; *singular subject (polite form)* il suo (la sua), i suoi (le sue) *(pl)* ; *(plural subject)* il vostro (la vostra), i vostri

(le vostre) *(pl)* ; ~ **dog** il tuo/suo/vostro cane ; ~ **house** la tua/sua/vostra casa ; ~ **children** i tuoi/suoi/vostri bambini ; ~ **mother** tua/sua/vostra madre.
- 2. *(indefinite subject)* : **it's good for ~ health** fa bene alla salute.

yours [jɔːz] *pron (referring to singular subject)* il tuo (la tua), i tuoi (le tue) *(pl)* ; *(polite form)* il suo (la sua), i suoi (le sue) *(pl)* ; *(referring to plural subject)* il vostro (la vostra), i vostri (le vostre) *(pl)* ; **a friend of ~** un tuo/suo/vostro amico ; **are these shoes ~?** queste scarpe sono tue/sue/vostre?

☞

yourself [jɔː'self] *(pl* **-selves**) *pron* - 1. *(reflexive : singular)* ti ; *(reflexive : polite form)* si ; *(reflexive : plural)* vi.
- 2. *(after prep : singular)* te ; *(after prep : polite form)* sé ; *(after prep : plural)* voi.
- 3. *(emphatic use : singular)* tu stesso(a) ; *(emphatic use : polite form)* lei stesso(a) ; *(emphatic use : plural)* voi stessi(e) ; **did you do it ~?** *(singular)* l'hai fatto da solo?

youth [juːθ] *n (period of life)* gioventù *f* ; *(quality)* giovinezza *f* ; *(young man)* giovane *m*.

youth club *n* circolo *m* giovanile.

youth hostel *n* ostello *m* della gioventù.

yuppie ['jʌpɪ] *n* yuppie *mf inv*.

YWCA *n associazione cristiana delle giovani che offre alloggi a buon prezzo.*

Z

zebra [*Br* 'zebrə, *Am* 'ziːbrə] *n* zebra *f*.

zebra crossing *n Br* strisce *fpl* pedonali.

zero ['zɪərəʊ] *(pl* **-es**) *n* zero *m* ; **five degrees below ~** cinque gradi sotto zero.

zest [zest] *n (of lemon, orange)* scorza *f*.

zigzag ['zɪgzæg] *vi* procedere a zigzag.

zinc [zɪŋk] *n* zinco *m*.

zip [zɪp] *n (of clothes) Br* cerniera *f* OR chiusura *f* lampo *(inv)* ; INFOR zip *m*. ◆ *vt* chiudere la cerniera di. ❑ **zip up** *vt sep* chiudere la cerniera di.

zip code *n Am* codice *m* di avviamento postale.

zipper ['zɪpə^r] *n Am* cerniera *f* OR chiusura lampo *(inv)*.

zit [zɪt] *n inf* brufolo *m*.

zodiac ['zəʊdɪæk] *n* zodiaco *m*.

zone [zəʊn] *n* zona *f*.

zoo [zuː] *(pl* **-s**) *n* zoo *m inv*.

zoom (lens) [zuːm-] *n* zoom *m inv*.

zucchini [zuː'kiːnɪ] *(pl inv) n Am* zucchine *fpl*.

CONVERSATION GUIDE

GUIDA DI CONVERSAZIONE

CONTENTS	SOMMARIO	P

CONTENTS	SOMMARIO	P
At the garage	Dal meccanico	10
Taking a taxi *(Br)* O cab *(Am)*	Prendere un taxi	11
Taking the bus	Prendere l'autobus	11
Taking the train	Prendere il treno	12
At the airport	All'aeroporto	13
Asking the way	Chiedere la strada	14
At the hotel	In albergo	15
At the shops	Per negozi	16
Out and about	In città	17
Sports	Sport	18
Getting around town	In giro per la città	18
At the restaurant	Al ristorante	19
At the café	Al bar	20
At the bank	In banca	20
At the post office	All'ufficio postale	21
At the doctor's	Dal medico	22
At the chemist's *(Br)* O drugstore *(Am)*	In farmacia	22
At the dentist's	Dal dentista	23
Emergencies	Emergenze	23

GREETING SOMEONE	SALUTARE QUALCUNO
Good morning.	Buongiorno.
Good afternoon.	Buon pomeriggio.
Good evening.	Buonasera.
Hello!	Ciao !
Hi!	Ciao !
How are you?	Come sta ? [polite form]/ Come stai ? [to a friend]
Very well, thank you.	Benissimo, grazie.
Fine, thank you.	Bene, grazie.
And you?	E lei ? [polite form]/E tu ? [to a friend]

INTRODUCING YOURSELF	PRESENTARSI
My name is Paul.	Mi chiamo Paul.
I am British.	Sono inglese.
I come from London.	Sono di Londra.

MAKING INTRODUCTIONS	FARE LE PRESENTAZIONI
This is Mr. Raymond.	Questo è il signor Raymond.
I'd like to introduce Mr. Raymond.	Le presento il signor Raymond.
Pleased to meet you.	Piacere.
How are you?	Come sta ?
Welcome.	Benvenuto/benvenuta.

SAYING GOODBYE	CONGEDARSI
▸ Goodbye, bye [informal]	▸ Arrivederci.
▸ See you later.	▸ A più tardi.
▸ See you soon.	▸ A presto.
▸ Good night.	▸ Buonanotte.
▸ Enjoy your trip.	▸ Buon viaggio.
▸ It was nice to meet you.	▸ Piacere di averla conosciuta. [polite form]

SAYING THANK YOU	RINGRAZIARE
▸ Thank you (very much).	▸ Grazie (mille).
▸ Thank you. The same to you.	▸ Grazie. Altrettanto.
▸ Thank you for your help.	▸ Grazie dell'aiuto.

REPLYING TO THANKS	RISPONDERE AI RINGRAZIAMENTI
▸ Don't mention it.	▸ Non c'è di che.
▸ Not at all.	▸ Di niente.
▸ You're welcome.	▸ Prego.

ACCEPTING AN APOLOGY	ACCETTARE DELLE SCUSE
▸ It doesn't matter.	▸ Non fa niente.
▸ That's all right.	▸ Non importa.
▸ No harm done.	▸ Non importa.
▸ These things happen.	▸ Sono cose che succedono.

APOLOGIZING	SCUSARSI
Excuse me.	Scusi.
I'm sorry.	Mi dispiace
Sorry.	Scusi. [polite form]/Scusa. [to a friend]
Forgive me.	Scusi.
I'm sorry I'm late/ to bother you.	Scusi il ritardo/se la disturbo. [polite form]/ Scusa il ritardo/se ti disturbo. [to a friend]

WISHES AND GREETINGS	AUGURI E SALUTI
Good luck!	Buona fortuna !
Have fun!/Enjoy yourself!	Si diverta. [polite form]
	Divertiti ! [to a friend]
Enjoy your meal!	Buon appetito !
Happy Birthday!	Buon compleanno !
Happy Easter!	Buona Pasqua !
Merry Christmas!	Buon Natale !
Happy New Year!	Buon anno !
Have a good weekend!	Buon fine settimana !
Enjoy your holiday *(Br)* O vacation *(Am)*!	Buone vacanze !
Have a nice day!	Buona giornata !

WHAT'S THE WEATHER LIKE?	CHE TEMPO FA ?
It's a beautiful day.	E' una bella giornata.
It's nice/It's sunny.	Fa bello/C'è il sole.
It's raining.	Piove.
It's cloudy.	E' nuvoloso.
It's supposed to rain tomorrow.	Per domani si prevede pioggia.
What horrible (or awful) weather!	Che brutto tempo !
It's (very) hot/cold.	Fa (molto) caldo/freddo.

EXPRESSING LIKES AND DISLIKES	GUSTI E RICHIESTE
I like it.	Mi piace.
I don't like it.	Non mi piace.
Would you like something to drink/eat?	Vuole qualcosa da bere/ mangiare ? [polite form]/ Vuoi qualcosa da bere/ mangiare ? [to a friend]
Yes, please.	Sì, grazie.
No, thanks.	No, grazie.
Would you like to come to the park with us?	Vuole venire al parco con noi ? [polite form]/Vuoi venire al parco con noi ? [to a friend]
Yes, I'd love to.	Sì, volentieri.

PHONING	AL TELEFONO
▸ Hello.	▸ Pronto?
▸ Jennifer Martin speaking.	▸ Sono Jennifer Martin.
▸ I'd like to speak to Mr. Gladstone.	▸ Vorrei parlare con il signor Gladstone.
▸ I'll call back in ten minutes.	▸ Richiamo tra dieci minuti.
▸ Can I leave him a message?	▸ Posso lasciare un messaggio?
▸ Sorry, I must have dialed the wrong number.	▸ Scusi, ho sbagliato numero.
▸ Who's calling?	▸ Chi parla?

BUSINESS	LAVORO
▸ Hello. I'm from Biotech Ltd.	▸ Buongiorno. Sono della Biotech.
▸ I have an appointment with Mr. Martin at 2.30 pm.	▸ Ho un appuntamento con il signor Martin alle 2.30.
▸ Here's my business card.	▸ Questo è il mio biglietto da visita.
▸ I'd like to see the managing director.	▸ Vorrei vedere il direttore.
▸ My e-mail address is paul@easyconnect.com.	▸ Il mio indirizzo e-mail è paul@easyconnect.com.
▸ Could you fax me some information please?	▸ Potrebbe faxarmi alcune informazioni, per favore?

HIRING *(BR)* O RENTING *(AM)* A CAR	NOLEGGIARE UNA MACCHINA
I'd like to hire *(Br)* O rent *(Am)* a car with air-conditioning.	Vorrei noleggiare una macchina con l'aria condizionata.
What's the cost for one day?	Quanto costa per un giorno ?
Is the mileage unlimited?	Il chilometraggio è illimitato ?
How much does it cost for comprehensive insurance?	Quanto costa la polizza casco ?
Can I leave the car at the airport?	Posso lasciare la macchina all'aeroporto ?

IN THE CAR	IN MACCHINA
How do we get to the city centre/motorway?	Come arrivo in centro/all'autostrada ?
Is there a car park nearby?	C'è un parcheggio qui vicino ?
Can I park here?	Posso parcheggiare qui ?
I'm looking for a petrol *(Br)*/gas *(Am)* station.	Sto cercando un benzinaio.
Where's the nearest garage?	Dov'è il garage più vicino ?

AT THE PETROL *(BR)* O GAS *(AM)* STATION	DAL BENZINAIO
I've run out of petrol *(Br)*/gas *(Am)*.	Ho finito la benzina.
Fill it up, please.	Il pieno, per favore.
I'd like to check the tyre pressure.	Vorrei controllare la pressione delle gomme.
Pump number three.	Pompa numero tre.

AT THE GARAGE	DAL MECCANICO
I've broken down.	Mi si è fermata la macchina.
The exhaust pipe has fallen off.	Ho perso il tubo di scappamento.
My car has an oil leak.	La macchina perde olio.
The engine is overheating.	Il motore si surriscalda.
Could you check the breaks?	Potrebbe controllare i freni ?
The battery is flat *(Br)*/dead *(Am)*.	La batteria è scarica.
The air-conditioning doesn't work.	L'aria condizionata non funziona.
I've got a puncture *(Br)*/a flat tire *(Am)*. The tyre needs to be repaired.	Ho una gomma a terra. Bisogna cambiarla.
How much will the repairs cost?	Quanto costano le riparazioni ?

TAKING A TAXI *(BR)* O CAB *(AM)*	PRENDERE UN TAXI
Could you call me a taxi *(Br)* O cab *(Am)*?	Potrebbe chiamarmi un taxi ?
To the bus station/train station/airport, please.	Alla stazione degli autobus/alla stazione ferroviaria/all'aeroporto, per favore.
Stop here/at the lights/at the corner, please.	Si fermi qui/al semaforo/all'angolo, per favore.
Can you wait for me?	Può aspettarmi ?
How much is it?	Quant'è ?
Can I have a receipt, please?	Mi può fare una ricevuta, per favore ?
Keep the change.	Tenga il resto.

TAKING THE BUS	PRENDERE L'AUTOBUS
What time is the next bus to Oxford?	A che ora è il prossimo autobus per Oxford ?
Which platform does the bus leave?	Da che marciapiede parte l'autobus ?
How much is a return *(Br)* O round-trip *(Am)* ticket to Chicago?	Quanto costa un biglietto di andata e ritorno per Chicago ?
Excuse me, is this seat taken?	Scusi, è occupato questo posto ?

TAKING THE TRAIN	PRENDERE IL TRENO
• Where is the ticket office?	• Dov'è la biglietteria ?
• When does the next train to London leave?	• Quando parte il prossimo treno per Londra?
• Which platform does it leave fom?	• Da che binario parte ?
• How much is a return to Boston?	• Quanto costa un'andata e ritorno per Boston ?
• Is there a left-luggage office?	• C'è un deposito bagagli ?
• A window seat in a non-smoking coach please.	• Un posto accanto al finestrino in una carrozza non fumatori, per favore.
• I'd like to reserve a sleeper on the 21:00 train to Rome.	• Vorrei riservare una cuccetta sul treno delle 21:00 per Roma.
• Where do I validate my ticket?	• Dove si convalida il biglietto ?
• Excuse me, is this seat free?	• Scusi, è libero questo posto ?
• Where is the restaurant car?	• Dov'è il vagone ristorante ?
• Tickets, please.	• Biglietti, prego.

AT THE AIRPORT	ALL'AEROPORTO
Where is terminal 1/gate number 2?	Dov'è il terminal 1/l'uscita numero 2 ?
Where is the check-in desk?	Dov'è il check-in ?
Where is the Alitalia desk?	Dov'è lo sportello dell'Alitalia ?
I'd like an aisle/window seat.	Vorrei un posto accanto al corridoio/finestrino.
What time is boarding?	A che ora è l'imbarco ?
I've missed my connection.	Ho perso la coincidenza.
When is the next flight to Seattle?	Quando parte il prossimo volo per Seattle ?
I've lost my boarding card.	Ho perso la carta d'imbarco.
Where is the baggage reclaim?	Dove si ritirano i bagagli ?
Where's the shuttle bus to the city centre?	Dov'è la navetta per andare in centro ?
Do you sell duty-free articles during the fly?	Vendete degli articoli in duty-free durante il volo ?

ASKING THE WAY	CHIEDERE LA STRADA
Could you show me where we are on the map?	Mi può indicare sulla piantina dove siamo?
Where is the closest underground station?	Dov'è la stazione della metropolitana più vicina?
Is there a bus stop nearby?	C'è una fermata dell' autobus nei dintorni?
Where is the bus station/post office?	Dov'è la stazione degli autobus/l'ufficio postale?
Excuse me, how do I get to Bond Street?	Scusi, come si arriva a Bond Street?
Keep going straight then take the first street on the right.	Continui sempre dritto poi prenda la prima (strada) a destra.
Is it far?	E' lontano?
Is it within walking distance?	Ci posso arrivare a piedi?
Will I/we have to take a bus/the métro?	Devo/Dobbiamo prendere l'autobus/ la metropolitana?
How far is it to the city center?	Quant'è lontano il centro (della città)?
Half an hour on foot, ten minutes on the bus.	Mezz'ora a piedi, dieci minuti in autobus.

AT THE HOTEL	IN ALBERGO
We'd like a double room/two single rooms.	Vorremmo una camera doppia/due camere singole.
I'd like a room for two nights, please.	Vorrei una camera per due notti.
I have a reservation in the name of Berger.	Ho una prenotazione a nome Berger.
I reserved a room with a shower/bathroom.	Ho prenotato una camera con doccia/bagno.
Is there a car park for hotel guests?	C'è un parcheggio per i clienti dell'albergo?
Could I have the key for room 121 please?	Posso avere la chiave della (camera) 121?
Are there any messages for me?	Ci sono messaggi per me?
What time is breakfast served?	A che ora servite la prima colazione?
I'd like breakfast in my room.	Vorrei la colazione in camera.
I'd like a wake-up call at 7 a.m., please.	Vorrei essere svegliato alle 7, per favore.
I'd like to check out now.	Vorrei saldare il conto adesso.

AT THE SHOPS	PER NEGOZI
Can I help you?	Posso esserle d'aiuto?
No thanks, I'm just looking.	No, grazie, sto solo dando un'occhiata.
How much is this?	Quanto costa questo?
I'd like to buy sunglasses/ a swimsuit *(Br)* O bathing suit *(Am)*.	Vorrei degli occhiali da sole/un costume.
What size are you?	Che taglia/numero di scarpe porta?
I'm a size 10.	Porto la taglia 42.
I take a size 7. [di scarpe]	Porto il 40. [shoe]
Can I try this on?	Posso provarlo?
Can I exchange it?	Me lo cambia?
Where are the fitting rooms?	Dove sono i camerini?
Do you have this in a bigger/smaller size?	Avete una taglia più grande/più piccola?
Do you have this in blue?	C'è in blu?
Do you sell envelopes/ street maps?	Avete delle buste/cartine stradali?
I'd like to buy a film for my camera please.	Vorrei un rullino fotografico, per favore.
What time do you close?	A che ora chiudete?

OUT AND ABOUT	IN CITTÀ
What time does the museum close?	A che ora chiude il museo ?
Have you got a city map?	Ha una piantina della città ?
I'm looking for an hotel that's not too expensive.	Sto cercando un albergo non troppo caro.
Have you got a town restaurant guide?	Ha una guida ai ristoranti della città ?
Where is the nearest public swimming pool?	Dov'è la piscina più vicina ?
Could you tell me where the nearest (Catholic/ Baptist) church is?	Mi sa dire dov'è la chiesa (cattolica/battista) più vicina ?
Do you know what time mass/the next service is?	Mi sa dire a che ora c'è la prossima messa/ funzione ?
Is there a cinema *(Br)* O movie theater *(Am)* nearby?	C'è un cinema qui vicino ?
How far is it to the beach?	Quanto dista la spiaggia ?
Have you got a town restaurant guide?	Ha una guida ai ristoranti della città ?
Where are the campingsites?	Dove si trovano i campeggi/camping ?

SPORTS

- We'd like to see a football match *(Br)*/game *(Am)*. Is there one on tonight?
- Where's the stadium?
- Where can we hire *(Br)*/ rent *(Am)* bicycles?
- I'd like to book a tennis court for 7.00 pm.
- Where can we change?
- Is there a ski resort nearby?
- Can we hire *(Br)*/rent *(Am)* equipment?

SPORT

- Vorremmo assistere a una partita di calcio. Ce n'è una stasera ?
- Dov'è lo stadio ?
- Dove si possono noleggiare delle biciclette ?
- Vorrei prenotare un campo da tennis per le 7:00 del pomeriggio.
- Dove possiamo cambiarci ?
- C'è una località sciistica vicina ?
- Possiamo noleggiare l'attrezzatura ?

GETTING AROUND TOWN

- Which bus goes to the airport?
- I would like a one day ticket
- Where do I catch the bus for the station railway?
- Could you tell me when we get there?
- Bus Stop.

IN GIRO PER LA CITTÀ

- Qual è l'autobus per l'aeroporto ?
- Vorrei un biglietto giornaliero.
- Dove prendo l'autobus per la stazione ?
- Mi avverte quando ci arriviamo, per favore ?
- Fermata d'autobus.

AT THE RESTAURANT	AL RISTORANTE
▸ I'd like to reserve a table for 8 pm.	▸ Vorrei prenotare un tavolo per le 8.
▸ A table for two, please.	▸ Un tavolo per due, grazie.
▸ Can we have a table in the non-smoking section?	▸ C'è un tavolo nella zona non-fumatori ?
▸ Can we see the menu/wine list?	▸ Possiamo vedere il menù/la carta dei vini ?
▸ Do you have a vegetarian/children's menu?	▸ Avete un menù vegetariano/per bambini ?
▸ We'd like an aperitif.	▸ Vorremmo un aperitivo.
▸ What would you like to drink?	▸ Cosa desiderate bere ?
▸ A bottle of house white/red, please.	▸ Una bottiglia di vino rosso/bianco della casa, per favore.
▸ What is the house speciality?	▸ Qual è la specialità della casa ?
▸ What desserts do you have?	▸ Cosa avete come dessert ?
▸ Can I have the bill *(Br)* O check *(Am)*, please?	▸ Il conto, per favore.

AT THE CAFÉ	AL BAR
Is this table/seat free?	E' libero questo tavolo?/ E' libera questa sedia?
Excuse me!	Scusi!
Two cups of black coffee/ white coffee *(Br)* O coffee with cream *(Am)*, please.	Due caffè/caffè macchiati.
An orange juice/a mineral water.	Un succo d'arancia/ un bicchiere d'acqua minerale.
Can I have another beer, please?	Un'altra birra, per favore.
Where is the toilet *(Br)* O restroom *(Am)*?	Dov'è il gabinetto?

AT THE BANK	IN BANCA
I'd like to change 100 euros into dollars please.	Vorrei cambiare 100 euro in dollari.
In small denominations, please.	In banconote di piccolo taglio, per favore.
What is the exchange rate for dollars?	Quant'è il cambio del dollaro?
I'd like to cash some traveler's checks.	Vorrei cambiare dei traveller's cheque.
Where is the cash point *(Br)* O ATM *(Am)*?	Dov'è il Bancomat®?

AT THE POST OFFICE	ALL'UFFICIO POSTALE
▸ How much is it to send a letter/postcard to Rome?	▸ Quant'è un francobollo per una lettera/cartolina per Roma ?
▸ I'd like ten stamps for Italy.	▸ Vorrei dieci francobolli per l'Italia.
▸ I'd like to send this parcel by registered post *(Br)* O mail *(Am)*.	▸ Vorrei spedire questo pacco per raccomandata.
▸ How much is it to send an urgent letter?	▸ Quando costa una lettera per posta prioritaria/ celere ?
▸ How long will it take to get there?	▸ Quanto ci mette per arrivare ?
▸ I'd like to have the directory of Brighton.	▸ Vorrei l'elenco (telefonico) di Brighton.
▸ I'd like a 50 unit phone card.	▸ Vorrei una scheda telefonica da 7 euro e 50.
▸ Can I send a fax?	▸ Posso spedire un fax ?
▸ I'd like to send an e-mail. Can you tell me where I can find an Internet cafe?	▸ Vorrei mandare un'e-mail. Mi sa dire dov'è un Internet café?
▸ I'd like to buy collection stamps, please.	▸ Vorrei comprare dei francobolli da collezione.

AT THE DOCTOR'S	DAL MEDICO
I've been vomiting and I have diarrhoea.	Ho vomitato e ho la diarrea.
My stomach hurts.	Mi fa male la pancia.
My son has a cough and a fever.	Mio figlio ha la tosse e la febbre.
I'm allergic to penicillin.	Sono allergico/allergica alla penicillina.
I've got high blood pressure.	Ho la pressione alta.
I'm diabetic.	Ho il diabete.
How long should I follow the treatment for?	Fino a quando devo seguire la cura ?

AT THE CHEMIST'S *(BR)* O DRUGSTORE *(AM)*	IN FARMACIA
Can you give me something for a headache/ sore throat/diarrhoea?	Vorrei qualcosa contro il mal di testa/il mal di gola/la diarrea.
Can I have some aspirin/ Band-Aids®, please?	Vorrei dell'aspirina/dei cerotti.
I need some high protection suntan lotion.	Vorrei una lozione solare con fattore di protezione alto.
Do you have any insect repellant?	Ha dell' Autan® ?
Could you recommend a doctor?	Mi sa indicare un buon medico ?

AT THE DENTIST'S	DAL DENTISTA
▸ I have a toothache.	▸ Ho mal di denti.
▸ One of my molars hurts.	▸ Mi fa male un molare.
▸ I've lost a filling.	▸ Ho perso un'otturazione.
▸ Could you give me a local anaesthetic?	▸ Può farmi un'anestesia locale?

EMERGENCIES	EMERGENZE
▸ Call a doctor/the fire brigade/the fire department/the police!	▸ Chiamate un medico/i pompieri/la polizia!
▸ Where's the nearest hospital?	▸ Dov'è l'ospedale più vicino?
▸ My son's blood group is O positive *(Br)*/blood type O *(Am)*.	▸ Il gruppo sanguigno di mio figlio è zero positivo.
▸ I've been robbed/attacked.	▸ Mi hanno derubato/aggredito.
▸ There's been an accident.	▸ C'è stato un incidente.
▸ My car's been stolen.	▸ Mi hanno rubato la macchina.
▸ Someone stole my papers.	▸ Mi hanno rubato i documenti.

Achevé d'imprimer en Août 2002
sur les presses de «La Tipografica Varese S.p.A.» à Varese (Italie)